Springer Series in Statistics

Advisors:
P. Bickel, P. Diggle, S. Feinberg, U. Gather,
I. Olkin, S. Zeger

For other titles published in this series, go to
http://www.springer.com/series/692

Dear MyCopy Customer,

This Springer book is a monochrome print version of the eBook to which your library gives you access via SpringerLink. It is available to you as a subsidized price since your library subscribes to at least one Springer eBook subject collection.

Please note that MyCopy books are only offered to library patrons with access to at least one Springer eBook subject collection. MyCopy books are strictly for individual use only.

You may cite this book by referencing the bibliographic data and/or the DOI (Digital Object Identifier) found in the front matter. This book is an exact but monochrome copy of the print version of the eBook on SpringerLink.

Albert W. Marshall · Ingram Olkin
Barry C. Arnold

Inequalities: Theory of Majorization and Its Applications

Second Edition

Springer

Albert W. Marshall
Department of Statistics
University of British Columbia
Vancouver, BC V6T 1Z2
Canada
and mailing address
2781 W. Shore Drive
Lummi Island, WA 98262
almarshall@earthlink.net

Barry C. Arnold
Department of Statistics
University of California
Riverside, CA 92521
USA
barry.arnold@ucr.edu

Ingram Olkin
Department of Statistics
Stanford University
Stanford, CA 94305
USA
iolkin@stat.stanford.edu

ISSN 0172-7397
DOI 10.1007/978-0-387-68276-1
Springer New York Dordrecht Heidelberg London

© Springer Science+Business Media, LLC 2011
All rights reserved. This work may not be translated or copied in whole or in part without the written permission of the publisher (Springer Science+Business Media, LLC, 233 Spring Street, New York, NY 10013, USA), except for brief excerpts in connection with reviews or scholarly analysis. Use in connection with any form of information storage and retrieval, electronic adaptation, computer software, or by similar or dissimilar methodology now known or hereafter developed is forbidden.
The use in this publication of trade names, trademarks, service marks, and similar terms, even if they are not identified as such, is not to be taken as an expression of opinion as to whether or not they are subject to proprietary rights.

Printed on acid-free paper

Springer is part of Springer Science+Business Media (www.springer.com/mycopy)

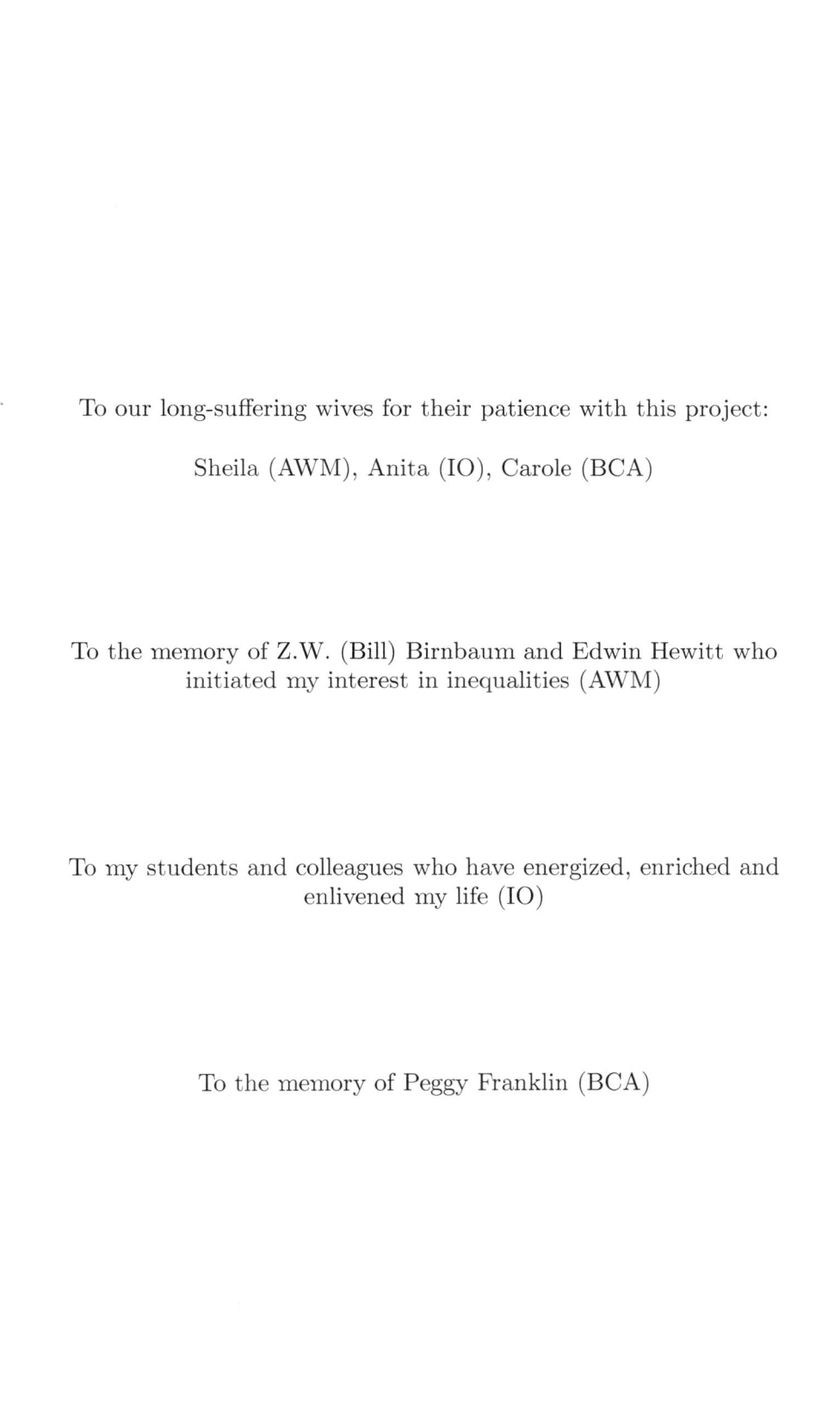

To our long-suffering wives for their patience with this project:

Sheila (AWM), Anita (IO), Carole (BCA)

To the memory of Z.W. (Bill) Birnbaum and Edwin Hewitt who initiated my interest in inequalities (AWM)

To my students and colleagues who have energized, enriched and enlivened my life (IO)

To the memory of Peggy Franklin (BCA)

Preface and Acknowledgments from the First Edition

Preface

Although they play a fundamental role in nearly all branches of mathematics, inequalities are usually obtained by ad hoc methods rather than as consequences of some underlying "theory of inequalities." For certain kinds of inequalities, the notion of majorization leads to such a theory that is sometimes extremely useful and powerful for deriving inequalities. Moreover, the derivation of an inequality by methods of majorization is often very helpful both for providing a deeper understanding and for suggesting natural generalizations.

As the 1960s progressed, we became more and more aware of these facts. Our awareness was reinforced by a series of seminars we gave while visiting the University of Cambridge in 1967–1968. Because the ideas associated with majorization deserve to be better known, we decided by 1970 to write a little monograph on the subject—one that might have as many as 100 pages—and that was the genesis of this book.

The idea of majorization is a special case of several more general notions, but these generalizations are mentioned in this book only for the perspective they provide. We have limited ourselves to various aspects of majorization partly because we want to emphasize its importance and partly because its simplicity appeals to us. However, to make the book reasonably self-contained, five chapters at the end of the book are included which contain complementary material.

Because the basic ideas of majorization are elementary, we originally intended to write a book accessible at least to advanced undergraduate or beginning graduate students. Perhaps to some degree we have succeeded in this aim with the first 10 chapters of the book. Most of the second 10 chapters involve more sophistication, and there the level and required background are quite uneven. However, anyone wishing to employ majorization as a tool in applications can make use of the theorems without studying their proofs; for the most part, their statements are easily understood.

The book is organized so that it can be used in a variety of ways for a variety of purposes. Sequential reading is not necessary. Extensive cross referencing has been attempted so that related material can easily be found; we hope this will enhance the book's value as a reference. For the same purpose, a detailed table of contents and an extensive index are also provided.

Basic background of interest to all readers is found in Chapters 1 and 4, with Chapter 5 as a reference. See also the Basic Notation and Terminology immediately following the Acknowledgments.

Technical details concerning majorization are given in Chapters 2 and 3 (especially important are Sections 2.A, 2.B, and 3.A). Added perspective is given in Chapters 14 and 15.

Analytic inequalities are discussed in Chapter 3 and in Sections 16.A–16.D, with Chapter 6 also of some relevance.

Elementary geometric inequalities are found in Chapter 8.

Combinatorics are discussed primarily in Chapter 7, but Chapters 2, 6, and Section 5.D are also pertinent.

Matrix theory is found especially in Chapters 9 and 10, but also in Chapters 2, 19, 20, and Sections 16.E and 16.F.

Numerical analysis is found in Chapter 10; Chapters 2 and 9 and Sections 16.E and 16.F may also be of interest.

Probability and statistics are discussed primarily in Chapters 11–13, and also in Chapters 15, 17, and 18.

Partly for historical interest, we have tried to give credit to original authors and to cite their original writings. This policy resulted in a bibliography of approximately 450 items. Nevertheless, it is surely far from being complete. As Hardy, Littlewood, and Pólya (1934, 1952) say in the preface to the first edition of their book on inequalities:

> Historical and bibliographical questions are particularly troublesome in a subject like this, which has application in

every part of mathematics but has never been developed systematically.

It is often really difficult to trace the origin of a familiar inequality. It is quite likely to occur first as an auxiliary proposition, often without explicit statement, in a memoir on geometry or astronomy; it may have been rediscovered, many years later, by half a dozen different authors,...

We apologize for the inevitable errors of omission or commission that have been made in giving credits for various results.

Occasionally the proofs provided by original authors have been reproduced. More often, new proofs are given that follow the central theme of majorization and build upon earlier results in the book.

Acknowledgments

The photographs in this book were collected only through the generosity of a number of people. G. Pólya provided the photos of himself and of I. Schur. A. Gillespie was instrumental in tracing members of the family of R. F. Muirhead; photos of him were loaned to us by W. A. Henderson, and they were expertly restored by John Coury. Trinity College provided a photo of J. E. Littlewood and a photo of G. H. Hardy and J. E. Littlewood together. The photos of G. H. Hardy and H. Dalton were obtained from the *Radio Times* Hulton Picture Library, London.

We have been heavily influenced by the books of Hardy, Littlewood, and Pólya (1934, 1952), Beckenbach and Bellman (1961), and Mitrinović (1970); to these authors we owe a debt of gratitude. We are also indebted to numerous colleagues for comments on various versions of the manuscript. In addition to many errors that were called to our attention, very significant substantive comments were made, enabling us to considerably improve the manuscript. In particular, we acknowledge such help from Kumar Jogdeo, Frank Proschan, Robert C. Thompson, Yung Liang Tong, and Robert A. Wijsman. Koon-Wing Cheng was especially helpful with Chapters 2 and 3, and Michael D. Perlman gave us insightful comments about Chapters 11 and 12. Moshe Shaked read a number of drafts and contributed both critical comments and bibliographic material over a period of several years. Perceptive comments about several chapters were made by Tom Snijders; in particular, Chapter 17 would not have been written in its present form without his comments. Friedrich Pukelsheim read nearly all of the manuscript; his meticulously detailed comments were invaluable to us.

As visitors to Western Washington State University and Imperial College, we were generously granted the same use of facilities and services as were regular members of the faculty. Much work on the manuscript was accomplished at these institutions.

The National Science Foundation has contributed essential financial support throughout the duration of this project, and support has also been provided for the past two years by the National Research Council of Canada.

Typing of the manuscript has been especially difficult because of our many revisions and corrections. The dependability, enduring patience, and accurate and efficient services of Carolyn Knutsen and Nancy Steege through the duration of this project are most gratefully acknowledged.

Albert W. Marshall
Ingram Olkin

History and Preface of the Second Edition

History

Preparation of the first edition of this book, published in 1979, began in 1967–1968 while AWM and IO were visiting the Statistical Laboratory in Cambridge, England. From 1968 to 1979, we were fortunate to have many opportunities to visit each other: the summer of 1977 at Imperial College, London; three months at ETH in Zurich; and a number of times at Stanford University. With this background of commitment for the first edition, it was clear to both of us that an appropriate revision would be a major commitment that we were reluctant to consider undertaking alone. Fortunately, we had the wisdom to invite Barry Arnold to join us. Without his diligence, knowledge, and sustained efforts, this revision would not exist. We suspect that he was duped (probably by us) into thinking that the revision would move along quickly. This has not been the case, and we can only thank him for persevering until the end.

Albert W. Marshall
Ingram Olkin
December 2009

Preface

The large number of appearances of majorization in so many different fields of application over the last 25 years has been a pleasant surprise. One of the early origins of majorization is in comparisons of income inequality. Because inequality appears in many guises in physics, chemistry, political science, engineering, economics and so on, perhaps the plethora of applications should not be surprising. In any case, since 1979 when the first edition appeared, many new applications of the majorization ordering have appeared. This revision attempts to bring these uses to the fore so that the reader can see the extent and variation in its use, thereby perhaps finding it helpful in his or her own research.

A key feature of the first edition was the use of majorization to obtain new proofs and generalizations of known results. Since the appearance of the first edition, many new results have been obtained that already use a majorization argument. In general, such results are included in this edition without proof. Consequently, the reader may need to check the referenced sources for proofs.

The chapters of the original version remain intact; additions appear within the text and as supplements at the end of chapters. The bibliography has increased by over 50%. A new, large addition is the discussion of Lorenz curves.

The authors are grateful to numerous readers of the first edition for their concern and help in uncovering and correcting errors. Readers are urged to bring to our attention any errors found in the current version.

We are especially grateful to James Bondar (1994) for his article "Comments and complements to Inequalities". This paper, written 15 years after the appearance of the first edition, provides a retrospective view of majorization, and a clarification of some of the concepts. His section on complements adds some new material. An Errata Appendix helped the authors to prepare this new edition. Finally, we thank him for his help in the discussion of converse theorems in Section 9.G.

To enhance the usefulness of the book, we have taken special care to make it easy to find particular results. Definitions have been provided. Numerous headings have been included, as well as a detailed table of contents and listing of the basic notation used. The subject index is expanded with permuted entries, which should help in a search. At times the author index can also help in locating facts.

We are indebted to Slobodanka Janković for supplying the photograph of Jovan Karamata, and to Martin Jacobsen for uncovering a photo of J. W. V. Jensen. Thanks to Bo Lindgren for his help with the biography of Jensen.

We thank Peggy Franklin for her heroic transcription of some notoriously illegible handwriting into a clear typescript, and for patiently dealing with a semi-infinite number of revisions. Thanks to Carole Arnold for editorial advice and assistance, especially with many of the references. Thanks to Linda Yamamota for her library help, in particular with the many searches.

We thank the anonymous reviewers who made helpful comments and helped us correct errors in the final drafts of this second edition. Pietro Cerone also provided helpful suggestions for improvement.

A special thanks to our Springer editor, John Kimmel, who has gone to great lengths to help this revision come to fruition.

Barry C. Arnold
Albert W. Marshall
Ingram Olkin
December 2009

Overview and Roadmap

There are several ways to characterize the ordering of majorization, each one of which leads to a variety of results. Inevitably, there are loops or repetitions in this monograph; the material does not lend itself naturally to the linear organization forced upon it by the structure of a book. There are several ways that the material could be organized, and there are several routes to a study of the subject.

Chapter 1 offers an overview of basic results. Chapter 2 discusses the connection with doubly stochastic matrices and offers important insight into the geometry of majorization. Chapter 3 discusses Schur-convex functions; these are the functions that preserve the ordering of majorization, and it is through them that many inequalities emerge. Chapters 4, 5, and 6 offer equivalent conditions for majorization and show some ways that the ordering can arise. These six chapters constitute Part I of the book.

Beyond Part I, the reader should feel free to jump in almost anywhere. We have taken care to include references to various parts of the book that may be relevant to a specific topic; these references may ask the reader to jump ahead as well as back in the book.

George Pólya, who was not only a great mathematician, but also a great expositor, made the point that one who only can generalize is like a monkey who can only climb up a tree, and one who can only specialize is like a monkey who can only climb down. Pólya urged mathematicians to look for generality behind the particular case, to look for significant particular cases in the general statement. With this in mind and the recognition that different fields of application need different special cases and different generalizations, this book contains what one reviewer called a "blizzard of results". (It was not a tsunami, but only a blizzard.) The inclusion of so many special cases was by design to help the researcher find both particular results and generalizations.

The application chapters of Part II relate to mathematics (Combinatorial Analysis, Geometric Inequalities, Matrix Theory, and Numerical Analysis). Stochastic applications are given in Part III. Various generalizations of majorization are discussed in Part IV (Chapters 14 and 15).

To make the book as complete as possible and to avoid sending the reader to other sources, the complementary topics of convex functions and classical inequalities (Chapter 16), stochastic ordering (Chapter 17), total positivity (Chapter 18), matrix factorization, compounds, direct products and M-matrices (Chapter 19), and extremal representations of matrix functions (Chapter 20) together are included. These together constitute Part V of the book.

Contents

I Theory of Majorization

1 Introduction   3
    A   Motivation and Basic Definitions   3
    B   Majorization as a Partial Ordering   18
    C   Order-Preserving Functions   19
    D   Various Generalizations of Majorization   21

2 Doubly Stochastic Matrices   29
    A   Doubly Stochastic Matrices and Permutation Matrices   29
    B   Characterization of Majorization Using Doubly Stochastic Matrices   32
    C   Doubly Substochastic Matrices and Weak Majorization   36
    D   Doubly Superstochastic Matrices and Weak Majorization   42
    E   Orderings on $\mathscr{D}$ 45
    F   Proofs of Birkhoff's Theorem and Refinements . . .   47
    G   Classes of Doubly Stochastic Matrices   52

xviii   Contents

	H	More Examples of Doubly Stochastic and Doubly Substochastic Matrices	61
	I	Properties of Doubly Stochastic Matrices	67
	J	Diagonal Equivalence of Nonnegative Matrices	76

3 Schur-Convex Functions 79

	A	Characterization of Schur-Convex Functions	80
	B	Compositions Involving Schur-Convex Functions	88
	C	Some General Classes of Schur-Convex Functions	91
	D	Examples I. Sums of Convex Functions	101
	E	Examples II. Products of Logarithmically Concave (Convex) Functions	105
	F	Examples III. Elementary Symmetric Functions	114
	G	Muirhead's Theorem	120
	H	Schur-Convex Functions on $\mathscr{D}$ and Their Extension to $\mathscr{R}^n$	132
	I	Miscellaneous Specific Examples	138
	J	Integral Transformations Preserving Schur-Convexity	145
	K	Physical Interpretations of Inequalities	153

4 Equivalent Conditions for Majorization 155

	A	Characterization by Linear Transformations	155
	B	Characterization in Terms of Order-Preserving Functions	156
	C	A Geometric Characterization	162
	D	A Characterization Involving Top Wage Earners	163

5 Preservation and Generation of Majorization 165

	A	Operations Preserving Majorization	165
	B	Generation of Majorization	185
	C	Maximal and Minimal Vectors Under Constraints	192
	D	Majorization in Integers	194
	E	Partitions	199
	F	Linear Transformations That Preserve Majorization	202

6 Rearrangements and Majorization 203

	A	Majorizations from Additions of Vectors	204
	B	Majorizations from Functions of Vectors	210
	C	Weak Majorizations from Rearrangements	213
	D	L-Superadditive Functions—Properties and Examples	217

E	Inequalities Without Majorization	225
F	A Relative Arrangement Partial Order	228

II Mathematical Applications

7 Combinatorial Analysis   243
A	Some Preliminaries on Graphs, Incidence Matrices, and Networks	243
B	Conjugate Sequences	245
C	The Theorem of Gale and Ryser	249
D	Some Applications of the Gale–Ryser Theorem . . .	254
E	s-Graphs and a Generalization of the Gale–Ryser Theorem	258
F	Tournaments	260
G	Edge Coloring in Graphs	265
H	Some Graph Theory Settings in Which Majorization Plays a Role	267

8 Geometric Inequalities   269
A	Inequalities for the Angles of a Triangle	271
B	Inequalities for the Sides of a Triangle	276
C	Inequalities for the Exradii and Altitudes	282
D	Inequalities for the Sides, Exradii, and Medians . .	284
E	Isoperimetric-Type Inequalities for Plane Figures .	287
F	Duality Between Triangle Inequalities and Inequalities Involving Positive Numbers	294
G	Inequalities for Polygons and Simplexes	295

9 Matrix Theory   297
A	Notation and Preliminaries	298
B	Diagonal Elements and Eigenvalues of a Hermitian Matrix	300
C	Eigenvalues of a Hermitian Matrix and Its Principal Submatrices	308
D	Diagonal Elements and Singular Values	313
E	Absolute Value of Eigenvalues and Singular Values	317
F	Eigenvalues and Singular Values	324
G	Eigenvalues and Singular Values of A, B, and $A+B$	329
H	Eigenvalues and Singular Values of A, B, and AB .	338
I	Absolute Values of Eigenvalues and Row Sums . . .	347

xx   Contents

J	Schur or Hadamard Products of Matrices	352
K	A Totally Positive Matrix and an M-Matrix	357
L	Loewner Ordering and Majorization	360
M	Nonnegative Matrix-Valued Functions	361
N	Zeros of Polynomials	362
O	Other Settings in Matrix Theory Where Majorization Has Proved Useful	363

10 Numerical Analysis   367
A	Unitarily Invariant Norms and Symmetric Gauge Functions	367
B	Matrices Closest to a Given Matrix	370
C	Condition Numbers and Linear Equations	376
D	Condition Numbers of Submatrices and Augmented Matrices	380
E	Condition Numbers and Norms	380

III Stochastic Applications

11 Stochastic Majorizations   387
A	Introduction	387
B	Convex Functions and Exchangeable Random Variables	392
C	Families of Distributions Parameterized to Preserve Symmetry and Convexity	397
D	Some Consequences of the Stochastic Majorization $E_1(P_1)$	401
E	Parameterization to Preserve Schur-Convexity	403
F	Additional Stochastic Majorizations and Properties	420
G	Weak Stochastic Majorizations	427
H	Additional Stochastic Weak Majorizations and Properties	435
I	Stochastic Schur-Convexity	440

12 Probabilistic, Statistical, and Other Applications   441
A	Sampling from a Finite Population	442
B	Majorization Using Jensen's Inequality	456
C	Probabilities of Realizing at Least k of n Events	457
D	Expected Values of Ordered Random Variables	461
E	Eigenvalues of a Random Matrix	469
F	Special Results for Bernoulli and Geometric Random Variables	474

G	Weighted Sums of Symmetric Random Variables	476
H	Stochastic Ordering from Ordered Random Variables	481
I	Another Stochastic Majorization Based on Stochastic Ordering	487
J	Peakedness of Distributions of Linear Combinations	490
K	Tail Probabilities for Linear Combinations	494
L	Schur-Concave Distribution Functions and Survival Functions	500
M	Bivariate Probability Distributions with Fixed Marginals	505
N	Combining Random Variables	507
O	Concentration Inequalities for Multivariate Distributions	510
P	Miscellaneous Cameo Appearances of Majorization	511
Q	Some Other Settings in Which Majorization Plays a Role	525

13 Additional Statistical Applications 527

A	Unbiasedness of Tests and Monotonicity of Power Functions	528
B	Linear Combinations of Observations	535
C	Ranking and Selection	541
D	Majorization in Reliability Theory	549
E	Entropy	556
F	Measuring Inequality and Diversity	559
G	Schur-Convex Likelihood Functions	566
H	Probability Content of Geometric Regions for Schur-Concave Densities	567
I	Optimal Experimental Design	568
J	Comparison of Experiments	570

IV Generalizations

14 Orderings Extending Majorization 577

A	Majorization with Weights	578
B	Majorization Relative to d	585
C	Semigroup and Group Majorization	587
D	Partial Orderings Induced by Convex Cones	595
E	Orderings Derived from Function Sets	598
F	Other Relatives of Majorization	603

	G	Majorization with Respect to a Partial Order . . .	605
	H	Rearrangements and Majorizations for Functions	606

15 Multivariate Majorization — 611
	A	Some Basic Orders	611
	B	The Order-Preserving Functions	621
	C	Majorization for Matrices of Differing Dimensions .	623
	D	Additional Extensions	628
	E	Probability Inequalities	630

V Complementary Topics

16 Convex Functions and Some Classical Inequalities — 637
	A	Monotone Functions	637
	B	Convex Functions	641
	C	Jensen's Inequality	654
	D	Some Additional Fundamental Inequalities	657
	E	Matrix-Monotone and Matrix-Convex Functions . .	670
	F	Real-Valued Functions of Matrices	684

17 Stochastic Ordering — 693
	A	Some Basic Stochastic Orders	694
	B	Stochastic Orders from Convex Cones	700
	C	The Lorenz Order	712
	D	Lorenz Order: Applications and Related Results . .	734
	E	An Uncertainty Order	748

18 Total Positivity — 757
	A	Totally Positive Functions	757
	B	Pólya Frequency Functions	762
	C	Pólya Frequency Sequences	767
	D	Total Positivity of Matrices	767

19 Matrix Factorizations, Compounds, Direct Products, and M-Matrices — 769
	A	Eigenvalue Decompositions	769
	B	Singular Value Decomposition	771
	C	Square Roots and the Polar Decomposition	772
	D	A Duality Between Positive Semidefinite Hermitian Matrices	774
	E	Simultaneous Reduction of Two Hermitian Matrices	775

F	Compound Matrices	775
G	Kronecker Product and Sum	780
H	M-Matrices	782

20 Extremal Representations of Matrix Functions   783
A	Eigenvalues of a Hermitian Matrix	783
B	Singular Values	789
C	Other Extremal Representations	794

Biographies   797

References   813

Author Index   879

Subject Index 893

Basic Notation and Terminology

Interchapter cross references include the chapter number as a prefix. Cross references within a chapter do not have this prefix.

The following notation is used throughout this book. It is given here in tabular form for easy reference.

$$\mathscr{R} = (-\infty, \infty),$$
$$\mathscr{R}_+ = [0, \infty),$$
$$\mathscr{R}_{++} = (0, \infty),$$

$$\mathscr{R}^n = \{(x_1, \ldots, x_n) : x_i \in \mathscr{R} \text{ for all } i\},$$
$$\mathscr{R}_+^n = \{(x_1, \ldots, x_n) : x_i \geq 0 \text{ for all } i\},$$
$$\mathscr{R}_{++}^n = \{(x_1, \ldots, x_n) : x_i > 0 \text{ for all } i\},$$

$$\mathscr{D} = \{(x_1, \ldots, x_n) : x_i \geq \cdots \geq x_n\},$$
$$\mathscr{D}_+ = \{(x_1, \ldots, x_n) : x_i \geq \cdots \geq x_n \geq 0\},$$
$$\mathscr{D}_{++} = \{(x_1, \ldots, x_n) : x_i \geq \cdots \geq x_n > 0\}.$$

$$u^+ = \max(u, 0).$$

Throughout this book, *increasing* means nondecreasing and *decreasing* means nonincreasing. Thus if $f : \mathscr{R} \to \mathscr{R}$, f is

$$\begin{aligned}
&\textit{increasing} && \text{if } x \leq y \Rightarrow f(x) \leq f(y), \\
&\textit{strictly increasing} && \text{if } x < y \Rightarrow f(x) < f(y), \\
\\
&\textit{decreasing} && \text{if } x \leq y \Rightarrow f(x) \geq f(y), \\
&\textit{strictly decreasing} && \text{if } x < y \Rightarrow f(x) > f(y).
\end{aligned}$$

For typographic simplicity, any vector x is a row vector, and x' is its transpose.

For any $x = (x_1, \ldots, x_n) \in \mathscr{R}^n$, let

$$x_{[1]} \geq \cdots \geq x_{[n]}$$

denote the components of x in decreasing order, and let

$$x_\downarrow = (x_{[1]}, \ldots, x_{[n]})$$

denote the *decreasing rearrangement* of x.

Similarly, let

$$x_{(1)} \leq \cdots \leq x_{(n)}$$

denote the components of x in increasing order, and let

$$x_\uparrow = (x_{(1)}, \ldots, x_{(n)})$$

denote the *increasing rearrangement* of x.

The vector with ith component 1 and all other components 0 is denoted by e_i, and the vector with all components 1 is denoted by e.

The elementwise vector ordering $x_i \leq y_i, i = 1, \ldots, n$, is denoted by

$$x \leq y.$$

For matrices A and B, the direct sum is denoted by

$$A \oplus B = \begin{bmatrix} A & 0 \\ 0 & B \end{bmatrix}.$$

For matrices A and B conformable for multiplication, write

$$\langle A, B \rangle = \Sigma a_{ij} b_{ij} = \operatorname{tr} AB'.$$

$A > 0$ $(A \geq 0)$ denotes that A is positive definite (semidefinite).

$A > B$ $(A \geq B)$ means that $A - B > 0$ $(A - B \geq 0)$.

For $A = (a_{ij})$, $B = (b_{ij})$, $A \circ B = (a_{ij} b_{ij})$.

Eigenvalues are generally denoted by λ, and are ordered $\lambda_1 \geq \cdots \geq \lambda_n$, unless otherwise noted.

Behind every theorem lies an inequality.

Attributed to A.N. Kolmogorov

Inequalities play a role in most branches of mathematics and have widely different applications.

George Pólya

Part I
Theory of Majorization

1
Introduction

A Motivation and Basic Definitions

There is a certain intuitive appeal to the vague notion that the components of a vector x are "less spread out" or "more nearly equal" than are the components of a vector y. Not surprisingly, the notion arises in a variety of contexts, and it can be made precise in a number of ways. But in remarkably many cases, the appropriate precise statement is that "x is majorized by y" (written $x \prec y$ and defined ahead in Definition A.1). Some of these cases are reviewed here.

This chapter provides some historical origins of majorization. The key contributors are Muirhead (1903), Lorenz (1905), Dalton (1920), Schur (1923), and Hardy, Littlewood, and Pólya (1929). Many important contributions were made by other authors. In particular, the comprehensive survey by Ando (1989) provides alternative derivations, generalizations, and a different viewpoint. For an elementary discussion of majorization, see Marshall and Olkin (1983).

Extension of Inequalities

Many well-known elementary inequalities can be put in the form

$$\phi(\overline{y}, \ldots, \overline{y}) \leq \phi(y_1, \ldots, y_n),$$

where $\overline{y} = (1/n)\sum y_i$ and $y_1, \ldots, y_n$ lie in a specified set. Such inequalities suggest the possibility of more general comparisons

$$\phi(x_1, \ldots, x_n) \leq \phi(y_1, \ldots, y_n),$$

where $x_1, \ldots, x_n$ need not be all equal, but only "less spread out" than $y_1, \ldots, y_n$.

For example, the inequality

$$\sum_1^n g(\overline{y}) \leq \sum_1^n g(y_i)$$

holds for all convex functions $g: \mathscr{R} \to \mathscr{R}$. So it is natural to ask for conditions on $x_1, \ldots, x_n$ and $y_1, \ldots, y_n$ in order that

$$\sum_1^n g(x_i) \leq \sum_1^n g(y_i) \tag{1}$$

for all convex functions g. This question was posed by Hardy, Littlewood, and Pólya (1929), and they provided this answer: A necessary and sufficient condition for (1) to hold for all convex functions g is that x be majorized by y.

Mathematical Origins

A second origin of majorization is illustrated by the work of Schur (1923) on Hadamard's determinant inequality. As a preliminary to proving this inequality, Schur proved that the diagonal elements $a_1, \ldots, a_n$ of a positive semidefinite Hermitian matrix are majorized by the eigenvalues $\lambda_1, \ldots, \lambda_n$, i.e.,

$$(a_1, \ldots, a_n) \prec (\lambda_1, \ldots, \lambda_n). \tag{2}$$

Later, Horn (1954a) showed that (2) actually characterizes those numbers $a_1, \ldots, a_n$ and $\lambda_1, \ldots, \lambda_n$ that can arise together as, respectively, the diagonal elements and eigenvalues of the same Hermitian matrix.

By identifying all functions ϕ that satisfy

$$x \prec y \quad \text{implies} \quad \phi(x) \leq \phi(y)$$

whenever $x, y \in \mathscr{R}_+^n$, Schur in essence identified all possible inequalities which, for a positive semidefinite Hermitian matrix, compare a function of the diagonal elements with the same function of the eigenvalues. Hadamard's determinant inequality is but one example.

Several other mathematical characterization problems are known to have solutions that involve majorization. In each case, Schur's results or minor extensions lead to a variety of inequalities.

Measurement of Income Inequality

Early in the 20th century, economists became interested in measuring inequality of incomes or of wealth. In order to evaluate proposed measures, it became desirable to determine how income or wealth distributions might be compared in order to say that one distribution was "more equal" than another. The first discussion of this kind of which we are aware was provided by Lorenz (1905) in introducing what has become known as the *Lorenz curve*. Later, Dalton (1920) took a different viewpoint, leading to his *principle of transfers*. Both ideas are of considerable interest.

The Lorenz Curve

Consider a population of n individuals, and let x_i be the wealth of individual i, $i = 1, \ldots, n$. Order the individuals from poorest to richest to obtain $x_{(1)}, \ldots, x_{(n)}$. Now plot the points $(k/n, S_k/S_n)$, $k = 0, \ldots, n$, where $S_0 = 0$ and $S_k = \sum_{i=1}^{k} x_{(i)}$ is the total wealth of the poorest k individuals in the population. Join these points by line segments to obtain a curve connecting the origin with the point $(1,1)$. [Actually, Lorenz (1905) used a continuous approximation, so this last step was unnecessary.] Notice that if total wealth is uniformly distributed in the population, then the Lorenz curve is a straight line (Fig. 1, curve A). Otherwise, the curve is convex and lies under this straight line. Lorenz (1905, p. 217) writes that "With an unequal distribution, the curves will always begin and end in the same points as with an equal distribution, but they will be bent in the middle; and the rule of interpretation will be, as the bow is bent, concentration increases." Thus curve B of Fig. 1 represents a more even distribution of wealth than does C.

Let $x_1, \ldots, x_n$ represent the wealth of individuals for the distribution of total wealth T that leads to curve B of Fig. 1. Similarly, let $y_1, \ldots, y_n$ lead to curve C. Then, according to the idea of Lorenz, $(x_1, \ldots, x_n)$ represents a more even distribution of wealth than does $(y_1, \ldots, y_n)$ if and only if

$$\sum_{1}^{k} x_{(i)} \geq \sum_{1}^{k} y_{(i)}, \qquad k = 1, \ldots, n-1. \tag{3}$$

Of course,

$$\sum_{1}^{n} x_{(i)} = \sum_{1}^{n} y_{(i)} = T. \tag{4}$$

The relations (3) and (4) are a way of saying that x is majorized by y.

6   1. Introduction

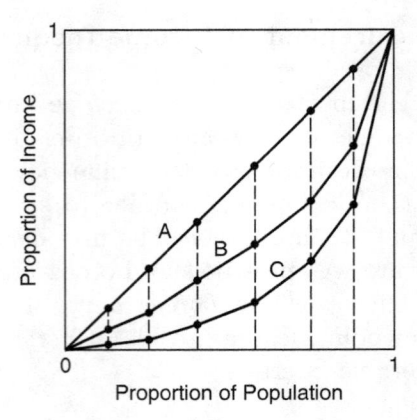

Figure 1. Lorenz curves.

The Principle of Transfers

The "principle of transfers" was already hinted at by Pigou (1912, p. 24), but in the context of income distribution, it was first clearly described by Dalton (1920, p. 351) as follows:

> If there are only two income-receivers and a transfer of income takes place from the richer to the poorer, inequality is diminished. There is, indeed, an obvious limiting condition. The transfer must not be so large as to more than reverse the relative positions of the two income receivers, and it will produce its maximum result, that is to say, create equality, when it is equal to half the difference between the two incomes. And, we may safely go further and say that, however great the number of income receivers and whatever the amount of their incomes, any transfer between any two of them, or, in general, any series of such transfers, subject to the above condition, will diminish inequality. It is possible that, in comparing two distributions, in which both the total income and the number of income-receivers are the same, we may see that one might be able to be evolved from the other by means of a series of transfers of this kind. In such a case we could say with certainty that the inequality of one was less than that of the other.

A. Motivation and Basic Definitions

If y_k is the income of individual k, $k = 1, \ldots, n$, if $y_i < y_j$, and if an amount Δ of income is transferred from individual j to i, then Dalton's observation is that income inequality is diminished provided $\Delta < y_j - y_i$:

$$\begin{array}{cccc} \underset{y_i}{+} & \underset{y_i + \Delta}{+} & \underset{y_j - \Delta}{+} & \underset{y_j}{+} \end{array} \quad \text{or} \quad \begin{array}{cccc} \underset{y_i}{+} & \underset{y_j - \Delta}{+} & \underset{y_i + \Delta}{+} & \underset{y_j}{+} \end{array}$$

Note that if the amount Δ transferred is less than $(y_j - y_i)/2$, then the relative order of individuals i and j is unchanged and the left-hand figure illustrates this case. If Δ is larger than $(y_j - y_i)/2$, then the relative order of individuals i and j is reversed by the transfer and the right-hand figure is descriptive of the situation. Note that in both diagrams the difference between the incomes of the two individuals has been reduced by the transfer and inequality in the population has been lessened.

Such an operation, involving the shifting of some income or wealth from one individual to a relatively poorer individual, may be evocatively labeled as a *Robin Hood transfer* (Arnold, 1987) since it mirrors precisely an operation by that "worthy" outlaw in Sherwood Forest. That Robin Hood's activities tend to reduce inequality seems to be very generally accepted, and perhaps for this reason, Dalton's principle has received considerable support. Such a transfer has also been called a *pinch*.

In a paper generalizing the arithmetic–geometric mean inequality, Muirhead (1903) had already discussed what Dalton calls a transfer. Muirhead proved that if the components of x and y are nonnegative integers, then the following conditions are equivalent:

(i) x can be derived from y by a finite number of transfers (each satisfying Dalton's restriction);

(ii) the sum of the k largest components of x is less than or equal to the sum of the k largest components of y, $k = 1, 2, \ldots, n$, with equality when $k = n$;

(iii) $\sum_\pi \alpha_{\pi(1)}^{x_1} \alpha_{\pi(2)}^{x_2} \cdots \alpha_{\pi(n)}^{x_n} \leq \sum_\pi \alpha_{\pi(1)}^{y_1} \alpha_{\pi(2)}^{y_2} \cdots \alpha_{\pi(n)}^{y_n}$ whenever each $\alpha_i > 0$. Here $\sum_\pi$ denotes summation over all permutations.

Condition (ii) is easily seen to be equivalent to conditions (3) and (4) of Lorenz (1905); it is particularly useful as a definition because it is easy to check.

A.1. Definition. For $x, y \in \mathscr{R}^n$,

$$x \prec y \quad \text{if} \quad \begin{cases} \sum_{i=1}^{k} x_{[i]} \leq \sum_{i=1}^{k} y_{[i]}, & k = 1, \ldots, n-1, \\ \sum_{i=1}^{n} x_{[i]} = \sum_{i=1}^{n} y_{[i]}. \end{cases} \tag{5}$$

When $x \prec y$, x is said to be *majorized* by y (y majorizes x). This notation and terminology was introduced by Hardy, Littlewood, and Pólya (1934, 1952).

Note that the conditions (5) are equivalent to the conditions

$$\begin{aligned} \sum_{1}^{k} x_{(i)} &\geq \sum_{1}^{k} y_{(i)}, \quad k = 1, \ldots, n-1, \\ \sum_{1}^{n} x_{(i)} &= \sum_{1}^{n} y_{(i)}. \end{aligned} \tag{5a}$$

The term *strict majorization* is used when $\sum_1^k x_{[i]} < \sum_1^k y_{[i]}$, for $k = 1, \ldots, n-1$.

A.1.a. Definition. For a set $\mathscr{A} \subset \mathscr{R}^n$,

$$x \prec y \quad \text{on} \quad \mathscr{A}$$

means $x, y \in \mathscr{A}$ and $x \prec y$.

A.1.b. Remark. In order to verify that $x \prec y$, it is sometimes convenient to use the fact that $x \prec y$ if and only if, for some $m \in \{1, 2, \ldots, n\}$,

$$\sum_{i=1}^{k} x_{[i]} \leq \sum_{i=1}^{k} y_{[i]}, \quad k = 1, \ldots, m,$$

$$\sum_{i=1}^{k} x_{(i)} \leq \sum_{i=1}^{k} y_{(i)}, \quad k = 1, \ldots, n-m,$$

and

$$\sum_{i=1}^{n} x_i = \sum_{i=1}^{n} y_i.$$

In particular, when $m = 0$, the sums in the first inequality are empty and the conditions for majorization reduce to (5a).

A.1.c. Remark (Malamud, 2005). The convex hull of a set A of real numbers (denoted by conv A) is the line segment joining the minimal and maximal elements of A. With this in mind, along with (5) and (5a), it can be seen that $x \prec y$ if and only if, for $j = 1, \ldots, n$,

$$\operatorname{conv} \{x_{i_1} + \cdots + x_{i_j} : 1 \leq i_1 \leq \cdots \leq i_j \leq n\}$$
$$\subset \operatorname{conv} \{y_{i_1} + \cdots + y_{i_j} : 1 \leq i_1 \leq \cdots \leq i_j \leq n\}. \tag{5b}$$

Some Basic Examples

The following are important though trivial examples of majorization. Further examples are given in Chapter 5.

$$\left(\frac{1}{n}, \ldots, \frac{1}{n}\right) \prec \left(\frac{1}{n-1}, \ldots, \frac{1}{n-1}, 0\right) \prec \cdots$$
$$\prec (\tfrac{1}{2}, \tfrac{1}{2}, 0, \ldots, 0) \prec (1, 0, \ldots, 0). \tag{6}$$

More generally, if $m \geq l$ and $lc = mac$ (i.e., $\alpha = l/m \leq 1$), then

$$(\underbrace{\alpha c, \ldots, \alpha c}_{m}, 0, \ldots, 0) \prec (\underbrace{c, \ldots, c}_{l}, 0, \ldots, 0), \tag{7}$$

$$\left(\frac{1}{n}, \ldots, \frac{1}{n}\right) \prec (a_1, \ldots, a_n) \prec (1, 0, \ldots, 0) \tag{8}$$

whenever $a_i \geq 0$, $\sum a_i = 1$.

$$(x_1 + c, \ldots, x_n + c)/(\sum x_i + nc) \prec x/(\sum x_i), \quad c \geq 0, \tag{9}$$

provided that $x_i > 0$.

Notice that in the above discussion of incomes, if $\Delta \leq y_j - y_i$, the replacement of y_i and y_j by $y_i + \Delta$ and $y_j - \Delta$ amounts to the replacement of y_i and y_j by averages. If $0 \leq \alpha = \Delta/(y_j - y_i) \leq 1$ and $\overline{\alpha} = 1 - \alpha$, then

$$y_i + \Delta = \overline{\alpha} y_i + \alpha y_j \quad \text{and} \quad y_j - \Delta = \alpha y_i + \overline{\alpha} y_j.$$

In many respects, averages like this are more convenient to work with than are transfers.

According to Lemma 2.B.1 of Hardy, Littlewood, and Pólya (1934, 1952), repeated averages of two incomes at a time can produce the same result as the replacement of y_j by an arbitrary average of the form

$$x_j = y_1 p_{1j} + \cdots + y_n p_{nj}, \qquad j = 1, \ldots, n,$$

where $p_{ij} \geq 0$ for all i, j,

$$\sum_{i=1}^n p_{ij} = 1 \text{ for all } j, \quad \text{and} \quad \sum_{j=1}^n p_{ij} = 1 \text{ for all } i.$$

Of course $\sum_{i=1}^n p_{ij} = 1$ as a consequence of x_j being an average of $y_1, \ldots, y_n$. Notice that the equality $\sum_{j=1}^n p_{ij} = 1$ is just a reflection of the fact that all of the original income y_i of individual i is either retained by i or transferred to some other individual. The above properties mean that (5) holds if and only if

$$x = yP, \tag{10}$$

where the matrix $P = (p_{ij})$ is *doubly stochastic* (i.e., P has nonnegative entries and each row and each column sums to unity). This characterization of majorization is not surprising; indeed, the fact that averaging is a smoothing operation has been recognized for a long time.

The relationship (10) was apparently first discussed by Schur (1923), who encountered it in his work on Hadamard's inequality.

Geometry of Majorization

Some geometrical insight into majorization can be obtained from (10) with the aid of Birkhoff's Theorem 2.A.2. This theorem says that the doubly stochastic matrices constitute the convex hull of the permutation matrices. Consequently, if $x \prec y$, so that $x = yP$ for some doubly stochastic matrix P, then there exist constants $a_i \geq 0$, $\sum a_i = 1$, such that

$$x = y(\sum a_i \Pi_i) = \sum a_i (y \Pi_i),$$

where the Π_i are permutation matrices. This means, as was noted by Rado (1952), that x lies in the convex hull of the orbit of y under the group of permutation matrices (see Figs. 2 and 3).

Weak Majorization

As already noted, in the presence of $\sum_{i=1}^n x_i = \sum_{i=1}^n y_i$, the inequalities

$$\sum_{i=1}^k x_{[i]} \leq \sum_{i=1}^k y_{[i]}$$

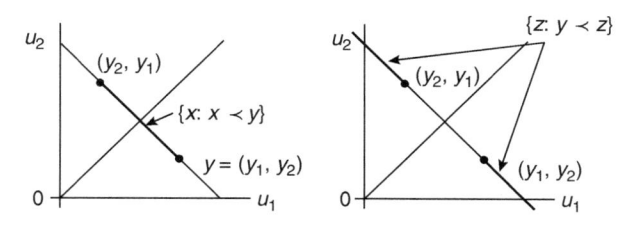

Figure 2. Orbits of y under permutations and the sets $\{x : x \prec y\}$, $\{z : y \prec z\}$ for the case $n = 2$.

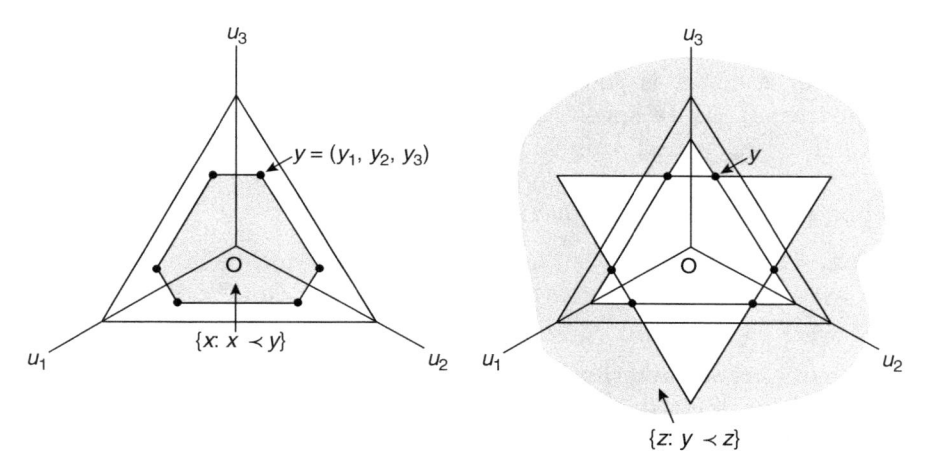

Figure 3. Orbits of y under permutations and the sets $\{x : x \prec y\}$, $\{z : y \prec z\}$ for the case $n = 3$.

and

$$\sum_{i=k+1}^{n} x_{[i]} = \sum_{i=1}^{n-k} x_{(i)} \geq \sum_{i=1}^{n-k} y_{(i)} = \sum_{i=k+1}^{n} y_{[i]}$$

are equivalent. Thus condition (5) for majorization can be rewritten as (3) and (4), i.e.,

$$\sum_{i=1}^{k} x_{(i)} \geq \sum_{i=1}^{k} y_{(i)}, \qquad k = 1, \ldots, n-1,$$

$$\sum_{i=1}^{n} x_{(i)} = \sum_{i=1}^{n} y_{(i)}.$$

Replacement of the equality in (4) or (5) by a corresponding inequality leads to the concept of "weak" majorization.

A.2. Definition. For $x, y \in \mathscr{R}^n$,

$$x \prec_{\mathrm{w}} y \quad \text{if} \quad \sum_1^k x_{[i]} \leq \sum_1^k y_{[i]}, \quad k = 1, \ldots, n, \tag{11}$$

and

$$x \prec^{\mathrm{w}} y \quad \text{if} \quad \sum_1^k x_{(i)} \geq \sum_1^k y_{(i)}, \quad k = 1, \ldots, n. \tag{12}$$

In either case, x is said to be *weakly majorized* by y (y *weakly majorizes* x). More specifically, x is said to be *weakly submajorized* by y if $x \prec_{\mathrm{w}} y$ and x is said to be *weakly supermajorized* by y if $x \prec^{\mathrm{w}} y$. Alternatively, we say *weakly majorized from below* or *weakly majorized from above*, respectively.

A.2.a. Definition. $x \prec_{\mathrm{w}} y$ ($x \prec^{\mathrm{w}} y$) on $\mathscr{A}$ means $x, y \in \mathscr{A}$ and $x \prec_{\mathrm{w}} y$ ($x \prec^{\mathrm{w}} y$). Equivalently, we write $y \succ_{\mathrm{w}} x$ ($y \succ^{\mathrm{w}} x$).

The origins of the terms "submajorized" and "supermajorized" lie in the following limited characterizations of weak majorization in terms of linear transformations:

$x \prec_{\mathrm{w}} y$ on $\mathscr{R}_+^n$ if and only if $x = yP$ for some doubly substochastic matrix P,

i.e., for some nonnegative matrix $P = (p_{ij})$ for which there exists a doubly stochastic matrix $D = (d_{ij})$ satisfying $p_{ij} \leq d_{ij}$ for all i, j (see 2.C.1). Similarly,

$x \prec^{\mathrm{w}} y$ on $\mathscr{R}_+^n$ if and only if $x = yP$ for some doubly superstochastic matrix P,

i.e., for some matrix $P = (p_{ij})$ for which there exists a doubly stochastic matrix $D = (d_{ij})$ satisfying $p_{ij} \geq d_{ij}$ for all i, j (see 2.D.1).

Although these characterizations are limited to weak majorization on $\mathscr{R}_+^n$, no such positivity restriction is necessary for characterizations in terms of convex functions:

$x \prec_{\mathrm{w}} y$ if and only if $\sum g(x_i) \leq \sum g(y_i)$ for all continuous increasing convex functions $g \colon \mathscr{R} \to \mathscr{R}$

(see 3.C.1.b and 4.B.2);

$x \prec^{\mathrm{w}} y$ if and only if $\sum g(x_i) \leq \sum g(y_i)$ for all continuous decreasing convex functions $g\colon \mathscr{R} \to \mathscr{R}$
(see 3.C.1.b and 4.B.2).

More general notions of weak majorization can be defined by writing conditions (5) in the form

$$\sum_{i=1}^{k} x_{[i]} \leq \sum_{i=1}^{k} y_{[i]}, \qquad k \in S \subset \{1,\ldots,n\},$$

$$\sum_{i=1}^{n-k} x_{(i)} \geq \sum_{i=1}^{n-k} y_{(i)}, \qquad k \in \{1,\ldots,n\} - S, \qquad (5')$$

$$\sum_{i=1}^{n} x_i = \sum_{i=1}^{n} y_i,$$

and by then dropping the equality constraint. Such weak majorizations are not discussed in this book.

Some Consequences of the Definitions

The following results are often useful:

$$x \prec y \Leftrightarrow -x \prec -y, \qquad (13\mathrm{a})$$

$$x \prec_{\mathrm{w}} y \Leftrightarrow -x \prec^{\mathrm{w}} -y, \qquad (13\mathrm{b})$$

$$x \prec_{\mathrm{w}} y \text{ and } x \prec^{\mathrm{w}} y \Leftrightarrow x \prec y, \qquad (14)$$

$$x \leq y \text{ (that is, } x_i \leq y_i, i = 1,\ldots,n) \Rightarrow x \prec_{\mathrm{w}} y \text{ and } x \prec^{\mathrm{w}} y, \quad (15\mathrm{a})$$

$$x \leq y \text{ and } \Sigma x_i = \Sigma y_i \Rightarrow x = y, \qquad (15\mathrm{b})$$

$$x \prec y \Rightarrow (x_{[1]},\ldots,x_{[n-1]}) \prec_{\mathrm{w}} (y_{[1]},\ldots,y_{[n-1]}), \qquad (16\mathrm{a})$$

and

$$x \prec y \Rightarrow (x_{[2]},\ldots,x_{[n]}) \prec^{\mathrm{w}} (y_{[2]},\ldots,y_{[n]}). \qquad (16\mathrm{b})$$

It is not quite so easy to show also that

$$x \prec_w y \iff \text{for some } u,\ x \leq u \text{ and } u \prec y \qquad \text{(see 5.A.9),} \quad (17)$$

$$x \prec^w y \iff \text{for some } v,\ x \prec v \text{ and } v \geq y \qquad \text{(see 5.A.9.a).} \quad (18)$$

Summary of Some Majorization Equivalents

A.3. Majorization. The following conditions are equivalent:

(i) $x \prec y$, that is,

$$\sum_1^k x_{[i]} \leq \sum_1^k y_{[i]}, \qquad k = 1,\ldots,n, \qquad \sum_1^n x_{[i]} = \sum_1^n y_{[i]};$$

(ii) $x = yP$ for some doubly stochastic matrix P (see 2.B.2);

(iii) x can be derived from y by successive applications of a finite number of T-transforms (see 2.B.1).

(iv) $\sum \phi(x_i) \leq \sum \phi(y_i)$ for all continuous convex functions ϕ (see 4.B.1);

(v) $\sum x_i = \sum y_i$ and $\sum (x_i - a)^+ \leq \sum (y_i - a)^+$ for all $a \in \mathscr{R}$ (see 4.B.3);

(vi) $\Sigma |x_i - a| \leq \Sigma |y_i - a|$ for all $a \in \mathscr{R}$ (see 4.B.3.a);

(vii) x is in the convex hull of the $n!$ permutations of y (see 4.C.1);

(viii) $\sum_\pi \alpha_{\pi(1)}^{x_1} \alpha_{\pi(2)}^{x_2} \cdots \alpha_{\pi(n)}^{x_n} \leq \sum_\pi \alpha_{\pi(1)}^{y_1} \alpha_{\pi(2)}^{y_2} \cdots \alpha_{\pi(n)}^{y_n}$ for all $\alpha_1,\ldots,\alpha_n > 0$ (see 4.B.5).

A.4. Weak submajorization. The following conditions are equivalent:

(i) $x \prec_w y$, i.e., $\sum_1^k x_{[i]} \leq \sum_1^k y_{[i]}$, $k = 1,\ldots,n$;

(ii) $x = yP$ for some doubly substochastic matrix P (in case; $x, y \in \mathscr{R}_+^n$) (see 2.C.4);

A. Motivation and Basic Definitions   15

(iii) $\sum \phi(x_i) \leq \sum \phi(y_i)$ for all continuous increasing convex functions ϕ (see 4.B.2);

(iv) $\sum (x_i - z)^+ \leq \sum (y_i - z)^+$ for all $z \in \mathscr{R}$ (see 4.B.4);

(v) there exist a finite number $T_1, \ldots, T_k$ of T-transforms such that

$$x \leq y T_1 \cdots T_k$$

(see 2.C.6);

(vi) for $x, y \in \mathscr{R}_+^n$, x can be derived from y by successive applications of a finite number of T-transforms followed by a finite number of transformations of the form

$$T(z) = (z_1, \ldots, z_{i-1}, \alpha z_i, z_{i+1}, \ldots, z_n), \qquad 0 \leq \alpha \leq 1$$

(see 2.C.6.a).

A.5. Weak supermajorization. The following conditions are equivalent:

(i) $x \prec^w y$, i.e., $\sum_1^k x_{(i)} \geq \sum_1^k y_{(i)}$, $k = 1, \ldots, n$;

(ii) $x = yP$ for some doubly superstochastic matrix P (in case $x, y \in \mathscr{R}_+^n$) (see 2.D.2.b);

(iii) $\sum \phi(x_i) \leq \sum \phi(y_i)$ for all continuous decreasing convex functions ϕ (see 4.B.2);

(iv) $\sum (z - x_i)^+ \leq \sum (z - y_i)^+$ for all $z \in \mathscr{R}$ (see 4.B.4);

(v) there exist a finite number $T_1, \ldots, T_k$ of T-transforms such that $x \geq y T_1 \cdots T_k$ (see 2.D.2);

(vi) for $x, y \in \mathscr{R}_{++}^n$, x can be derived from y by successive application of a finite number of T-transforms followed by a finite number of transformations of the form

$$T(z) = (z_1, \ldots, z_{i-1}, \alpha z_i, z_{i+1}, \ldots, z_n), \qquad \alpha > 1$$

(see 2.D.2.a).

Sufficient Conditions for Majorization

Pečarić and Zwick (1989) provide the following sufficient conditions for $x \prec y$ which may sometimes be useful. Note that these sufficient conditions for majorization are stated in terms of the unordered coordinates of x and y.

A.6. Lemma. (Pečarić and Zwick, 1989). Let $x, y \in \mathscr{R}^n$. Then $x \prec y$ if the following conditions hold:

(i) $\sum_{i=1}^{n} x_i = \sum_{i=1}^{n} y_i$;

(ii) $\sum_{i=1}^{k} x_i \geq \sum_{i=1}^{k} y_i$; $k = 1, 2, \ldots, n-1$;

(iii) $x_i \geq y_{i-1}$, $i = 2, 3, \ldots, n$.

Logarithmic Majorization

Majorization as defined in Definition A.1 is based on partial sums. Motivated by matrix inequalities, Weyl (1949) defined a multiplicative version.

A.7. Definition. For $x, y \in \mathscr{R}_+^n$, x is said to be *weakly log-majorized* by y, denoted by $x \prec_{\text{w} \atop \log} y$, if

$$\prod_1^k x_{[i]} \leq \prod_1^k x_{[i]}, \quad k = 1, \ldots, n; \tag{19}$$

x is said to be *log-majorized* by y, denoted by $x \prec_{\log} y$, if (19) holds with equality for $k = n$.

If $x, y \in \mathscr{R}_{++}^n$, then (19) is equivalent to $\log x \prec_{\text{w}} \log y$.

The ordering introduced in A.7, called *log-majorization*, was studied by Ando and Hiai (1994), who delved deeply into applications in matrix theory. See also Chapter 9.

Note that weak log-majorization implies weak majorization. See 5.A.2.b.

Notes on Terminology

A.8. Majorization in an economics context. Because majorization arises in different contexts, terminology in the literature is not well standardized. To better understand terminology, consider two individuals, the first receiving the income $a + \Delta$, and the second receiving the income a. Income inequality is reduced if the first individual transfers to the second any amount up to Δ. This kind of transfer is called a *Dalton transfer* (see p. 6 for Dalton's discussion). If the amount transferred is limited to $\Delta/2$, the transfer is sometimes called an *altruistic transfer* or an *altruistic Dalton transfer*. With an altruistic transfer, the individual starting with the highest income does not end up with less income than the individual receiving the transfer. The altruistic transfer is said to be *extreme* if the two individuals end up sharing their joint income equally.

Denote by Q a permutation matrix that interchanges two coordinates. A transfer replaces the vector x of incomes by xT, where

$$T = \lambda I + (1 - \lambda)Q. \qquad (20)$$

For a Dalton transfer, $0 \leq \lambda \leq 1$; for an altruistic transfer, $1/2 \leq \lambda \leq 1$.

With the restriction $0 \leq \lambda \leq 1$, matrices of the form (20) are called *T-transforms* (2.B). The term "T-transform" is often used in the place of "Dalton transfer." A Dalton transfer is sometimes called a *pinch*, in which case the matrix (20) is called a *pinching matrix*. Dalton transfers are also called *Robin Hood transfers*.

Altruistic transfers are discussed by Kolm (1969, 1996). Regrettably, they are called Dalton transfers in those publications.

Even more restrictive transfers are introduced by Hoffman (1969), who allows only those transfers that leave the entire population ordering unchanged. With this restriction, for example, the highest-income individual cannot transfer so much income to the lowest-income individual that he or she receives more income than the person with the next-to-lowest income. Relatives of the majorization partial order induced by these different transfer principles are discussed in Thon and Wallace (2004).

A.9. Majorization in physics and chemistry: Mixing. Majorization is also useful in certain physical science contexts. In chemistry and physics, the terms "x is more *mixed* than y," "x is more *chaotic* than y," and "x is more *disordered* than y" are directly related to the majorization and inequality ordering, $x \prec y$. To clarify the term "mixing," consider several identical cylindrical beakers containing different amounts of liquid. As some liquid from a beaker containing a large amount of liquid is "mixed" with the liquid from a beaker containing a lesser amount, the result is that of majorization. The use of the term "chaotic" stems from physical laws. Thus, one vector is said to be more chaotic than another to mean that one vector majorizes the other. This term has its origin in terms of entropy. In a similar vein, one vector is said to be *more random* than another to mean that one vector majorizes the other. See Section 3.K for further discussion of this nexus.

A.10. Weak majorization in group theory. Weak majorization arises naturally in a variety of contexts in group theory. In the representation theory of the symmetric groups, James (1978, p. 8) uses the term *dominance* for weak majorization. Hazewinkel and Martin (1983) note that the *natural order* and *Snapper order* have also been used to mean weak majorization. Further discussion is contained in 5.D.

B   Majorization as a Partial Ordering

Because $x_1, \ldots, x_n$ and $y_1, \ldots, y_n$ are reordered decreasingly in the definition of majorization, their original order plays no role. Thus, the fact that these numbers are viewed as components of vectors is not important to the concept of majorization. But it is convenient to regard $x = (x_1, \ldots, x_n)$ and $y = (y_1, \ldots, y_n)$ as vectors so that the relationship $x = yP$ can be written with standard notation.

With x viewed as a vector, it is easy to see that

$$x \prec x\Pi \quad \text{for all permutation matrices } \Pi. \tag{1}$$

A kind of converse is also true:

$$x \prec y \text{ and } y \prec x \quad \text{together imply that } x = y\Pi \text{ for some}$$
$$\text{permutation matrix } \Pi; \tag{2}$$

this follows from the fact that the partial sum conditions (5) of Section A imply $x_\downarrow = y_\downarrow$ when $x \prec y$ and $y \prec x$. The same statements can be made with $\prec_w$ or $\prec^w$ in place of $\prec$.

A *preordering* of a set $\mathscr{A}$ is a binary relation $\leq$ on $\mathscr{A}$ satisfying

$$x \leq x \quad \text{for all} \quad x \in \mathscr{A}; \tag{3}$$

$$x \leq y \text{ and } y \leq z \quad \text{implies} \quad x \leq z \quad \text{when } x, y, z \in \mathscr{A}. \tag{4}$$

If also

$$x \leq y \text{ and } y \leq x \quad \text{implies} \quad x = y, \tag{5}$$

then $\leq$ is called a *partial ordering*. Because conditions (3) and (4) are easily verified from the definitions, it follows that the orderings $\prec$, $\prec_w$, and $\prec^w$ defined on $\mathscr{R}^n$ are all preorderings. But, strictly speaking, they are not partial orderings because, in place of (5), only the weaker condition (2) holds. Restricted to $\mathscr{D} = \{z : z_1 \geq \cdots \geq z_n\}$, the orderings are proper partial orderings. They are also proper partial orderings if they are regarded as orderings of sets of numbers rather than as orderings of vectors. In fact, $\mathscr{D}$ is a *complete lattice* (a partially ordered set in which all subsets have both an infimum and a supremum) under these weak orderings [see Bapat (1991) for details].

For a given $x \in \mathscr{R}^n$, the set of all antecedents of x in the majorization preordering is denoted by $\gamma(x)$. Thus

$$\gamma(x) = \{y : y \prec x\} \tag{6}$$

is the convex hull of the set of permutations of x (2.B.3). Viewing γ as a mapping from $\mathscr{R}^n$ into the set of all subsets of $\mathscr{R}^n$, Nachman (2005) observes that γ, called *antecedent mapping*, is a compact convex-valued continuous correspondence. The transitivity of majorization guarantees that if $y \in \gamma(x)$, then $\gamma(y) \subset \gamma(x)$.

For future reference (in 11.D.2), the graph of the relation γ will be denoted by K. Thus

$$K = \{(y, x) \in \mathscr{R}^n \times \mathscr{R}^n : y \in \gamma(x)\}. \tag{7}$$

K is a closed set in $\mathscr{R}^{2n}$.

C Order-Preserving Functions

A variety of inequalities is obtainable for any partial ordering once the order-preserving functions are identified. If $\leq$ is a preordering or a partial ordering defined on some set $\mathscr{A} \subset \mathscr{R}^n$, a function $\phi : \mathscr{A} \to \mathscr{R}$ is said to be *order-preserving* or *isotonic* if

$$x \leq y \quad \text{implies} \quad \phi(x) \leq \phi(y), \quad x, y \in \mathscr{A}.$$

For the ordering of majorization, the theorem of Muirhead (1903) (see 3.G.2.e) identifies a class of order-preserving functions. Additional such functions were identified by Dalton (1920). Dalton's motivation was to evaluate certain proposed measures of income inequality, including

$$\phi^{(1)}(x) = \sum_1^n |x_i - \overline{x}|,$$

where

$$\overline{x} = (1/n) \sum_1^n x_i,$$

$$\phi^{(2)}(x) = [(1/n) \sum (x_i - \overline{x})^2]^{1/2},$$

and

$$\phi^{(3)}(x) = \sum_{i,j} |x_i - x_j|.$$

Dalton also noted that $\phi^{(2)}$ and $\phi^{(3)}$ satisfy the strict inequality property

$$x \prec y \text{ and } x \not\sim y \quad \text{implies} \quad \phi(x) < \phi(y).$$

The first comprehensive study of the functions preserving the ordering of majorization was made by Schur (1923). Schur confined himself to majorization on $\mathscr{R}_+^n$, and he showed that if $\phi \colon \mathscr{R}_+^n \to \mathscr{R}$ has continuous first partial derivatives $\phi_{(i)} = \partial \phi / \partial x_i$, then

$$x \prec y \text{ on } \mathscr{R}_+^n \quad \text{implies} \quad \phi(x) \leq \phi(y)$$

if and only if

(i) ϕ is permutation symmetric [i.e., $\phi(x) = \phi(x\Pi)$ for all $x \in \mathscr{R}_+^n$ and all permutations Π], and

(ii) $(x_1 - x_2)[\phi_{(1)}(x) - \phi_{(2)}(x)] \geq 0$ for all $x \in \mathscr{R}_+^n$.

Schur called such functions "convex" as opposed to "convex in the sense of Jensen." In modern terminology, "convex in the sense of Jensen" is simply "convex." Consequently, when Ostrowski (1952) showed that Schur's conditions (i) and (ii) are also appropriate for identifying the order-preserving functions for majorization on $\mathscr{R}^n$ (as opposed to $\mathscr{R}_+^n$), he called the order-preserving functions "convex in the sense of Schur." Subsequent writers have adopted this terminology or modifications of it. We feel that it would be more appropriate to call these functions "Schur-increasing," but we adhere to the historically accepted term "Schur-convex."

Because $(\bar{y}, \ldots, \bar{y}) \prec (y_1, \ldots, y_n)$, where $\bar{y} = (1/n) \sum_1^n y_i$, it follows that for any Schur-convex function ϕ,

$$\phi(\bar{y}, \ldots, \bar{y}) \leq \phi(y_1, \ldots, y_n) \qquad \text{for all} \quad y \in \mathscr{R}^n.$$

The fact that the minimum is achieved if $y_1 = \cdots = y_n$ is suggested by the symmetry in $y_1, \ldots, y_n$ of $\phi(y_1, \ldots, y_n)$. Indeed, this is an example of what Pólya (1967), following Leibniz, calls the "principle of nonsufficient reason." Briefly, Leibniz's principle can be stated as: "Where there is no sufficient reason to distinguish, there can be no distinction."

D Various Generalizations of Majorization

Majorization can be characterized in various ways, each of which may suggest generalizations. Here, several such generalizations are mentioned. Except as noted, they are not further discussed in this book.

Partial Orderings Induced by Convex Cones

A subset $\mathscr{C}$ of a real linear space (for us, $\mathscr{R}^n$) is a *convex cone* if

$$x, y \in \mathscr{C} \text{ implies } \lambda_1 x + \lambda_2 y \in \mathscr{C} \qquad \text{for all} \quad \lambda_1, \lambda_2 \geq 0.$$

The *cone ordering* (or *vector ordering*) on a set $\mathscr{A} \subset \mathscr{R}^n$ induced by the convex cone $\mathscr{C}$ is the relation $\leq$ on $\mathscr{A}$ defined by

$$x \leq y \qquad \text{if and only if} \quad y - x \in \mathscr{C}.$$

On $\mathscr{D}$, majorization $\prec$ and the weak majorizations $\prec_{\mathrm{w}}$, $\prec^{\mathrm{w}}$ are all cone orderings. Some results for the orderings $\prec$, $\prec_{\mathrm{w}}$, and $\prec^{\mathrm{w}}$ can be generalized to cone orderings, which are discussed in Section 14.D.

Partial Orderings Generated by Groups of Transformations

As noted in discussing the geometry of majorization in Section A, $x \prec y$ if and only if x lies in the convex hull of the orbit of y under the group of permutation matrices. It is possible to generalize the idea of majorization by replacing the group of permutations by an arbitrary group of linear transformations. Such extensions are discussed in Section 14.C.

Continuous Majorization

Suppose that f and g are integrable functions defined in $[0,1]$ with the property that

$$\int_0^1 \phi(f(u))\,du \leq \int_0^1 \phi(g(u))\,du \tag{1}$$

for all continuous convex functions ϕ. Because

$$\sum \phi(x_i) \leq \sum \phi(y_i) \qquad \text{for all continuous convex functions } \phi$$

is equivalent to $x \prec y$, it is natural to write $f \prec g$ when (1) holds. Ruch, Schranner, and Seligman (1978) note that (1) holds if it holds for a certain subclass of the convex functions.

There is an analog of the partial sums definition that is equivalent to $f \prec g$, but this requires the notion of a decreasing rearrangement of a function. This notion has been discussed by various authors [see, e.g., Hardy, Littlewood, and Pólya (1929, 1934, 1952, Chapter X), Ryff (1963), Burkill (1964)].

D.1. Definition. For an integrable function f defined on the interval $[0,1]$, let $m(y) = \lambda\{u : f(u) > y\}$, where λ is Lebesgue measure. The function

$$f_\downarrow(x) = \sup\{y : m(y) > x\}, \quad 0 \leq x \leq 1,$$

is called the (right continuous) *decreasing rearrangement* of f.

D.2. Theorem (Hardy, Littlewood, and Pólya, 1929). Let f and g be integrable functions defined on $[0,1]$. Then (1) holds for all continuous convex functions ϕ if and only if

$$\int_0^x f_\downarrow(u)\,du \leq \int_0^x g_\downarrow(u)\,du, \qquad 0 \leq x \leq 1, \tag{2}$$

$$\int_0^1 f_\downarrow(u)\,du = \int_0^1 g_\downarrow(u)\,du. \tag{3}$$

The proof of this theorem is essentially the same as the proof of Proposition 17.E.4.

Because $x \prec y$ if and only if $x = yP$ for some doubly stochastic matrix P, it is natural to ask for a characterization of the linear transformations T such that $Tf \prec f$. Such a characterization is given by

Ryff (1963). Ryff shows that $f \prec g$ if and only if $f = Tg$ for some such operator [see also Ryff (1965, 1967)].

D.3. Example. If X and Y are random variables such that

$$E\phi(X) \leq E\phi(Y)$$

for all convex functions ϕ such that the expectations exist, then X is said to be less than Y in the convex order written $X \leq_{cx} Y$ (Definition 17.B.15). Suppose that the respective distributions F and G of X and Y are continuous and strictly increasing, so that they have well-defined inverses F^{-1} and G^{-1}. Then

$$E\phi(X) = \int_{-\infty}^{\infty} \phi(x) dF(x) = \int_0^1 \phi(F^{-1}(z)) dz$$

and

$$E\phi(Y) = \int_0^1 \phi(G^{-1}(z)) dz.$$

Thus

$$F^{-1} \prec G^{-1} \quad \text{if and only if} \quad X \leq_{cx} Y.$$

These inverse distributions are increasing; their decreasing rearrangements are defined by $F^{-1}(1-z) = \overline{F}^{-1}(z)$ and $G^{-1}(1-z) = \overline{G}^{-1}(z)$, where $\overline{F} = 1 - F$ and $\overline{G} = 1 - G$.

The conditions of continuity and monotonicity can be dispensed with if a more general definition of F^{-1} is used [see 17.C.1 and Marshall and Olkin (2007, p. 639)].

Continuous majorization has also been called a *generalized averaging operation*. In the context of densities, $g \prec f$ has been referred to as "g has at least as much randomness as f" (14.H).

Generalized Continuous Majorization

It is natural to extend (1) to allow consideration of functions defined on a quite arbitrary measure space instead of the interval $[0, 1]$ [see, e.g., Joe (1992)]. Further discussion of this concept is given in Section 14.H. Order-preserving functionals are characterized by Chan, Proschan, and Sethuraman (1987) and by Ruch, Schranner, and Seligman (1978).

Majorization for Vectors of Unequal Length

When vectors are of unequal length, the usual definitions of majorization do not apply. However, an indirect definition permits a majorization comparison.

Let $x = (x_1, \ldots, x_n)$ and $y = (y_1, \ldots, y_m)$ be vectors such that $\Sigma x_i/n = \Sigma y_i/m$. Consider the following two conditions:

Condition 1. For all convex $\phi : \mathscr{R} \to \mathscr{R}$,

$$\frac{1}{n} \sum_1^n \phi(x_i) \leq \frac{1}{m} \sum_1^m \phi(y_i).$$

Condition 2. $\qquad L_x(u) \geq L_y(u), \qquad 0 \leq u \leq 1,$

where $L_x(u)$ is the Lorenz curve generated by the vector x.

D.4. Proposition. Conditions 1 and 2 are equivalent.

Proof. For $x = (x_1, \ldots, x_n)$ and $y = (y_1, \ldots, y_m)$, define the mn-dimensional vectors

$$\widetilde{x} = \underbrace{(x, \ldots, x)}_{m}, \qquad \widetilde{y} = \underbrace{(y, \ldots, y)}_{n}.$$

Condition 1 holds if and only if $\widetilde{x} \prec \widetilde{y}$. Condition 2 (with $\Sigma_1^n x_i/n = \Sigma_1^m y_i/m$) holds if and only if $\widetilde{x} \prec \widetilde{y}$, because $L_x(u) = L_{\widetilde{x}}(u) \geq L_{\widetilde{y}}(u) = L_y(u)$. ||

Remark. When $n = m$, $\widetilde{x} \prec \widetilde{y}$ is equivalent to $x \prec y$, as can be shown by using the partial sum Definition A.1.

Note. To show that $L_{\widetilde{x}} = L_x$, for $x \in \mathscr{R}^n$, write $L_x(k/n) = S_k/S_n$, $k = 1, \ldots, n$, where $S_k = \Sigma_1^k x_{(i)}$. For $u \in ((k-1)/n, k/n)$, $L_x(u)$ is a straight-line segment with slope

$$\frac{(S_k/S_n) - (S_{k-1}/S_n)}{1/n} = \frac{nx_{(k)}}{S_n},$$

where $S_0 = 0$. Thus if $x_{(k+1)} = x_{(k)}$, then the slope of $L_x(u)$ is constant on the interval $((k-1)/n, (k+1)/n)$. Now apply this argument to the vector

$$\widetilde{x} = (\underbrace{x_1, \ldots, x_1}_{m}, \ldots, \underbrace{x_n, \ldots, x_n}_{m}).$$

The slope of $L_{\tilde{x}}$ between the points
$$\frac{k-1}{n} = \frac{(k-1)m}{mn} \quad \text{and} \quad \frac{k}{n} = \frac{km}{mn}$$
does not change. Moreover,
$$L_{\tilde{x}}(k/n) = \frac{mS_k}{mS_n} = L_x(k/n), \quad k = 0, 1, \ldots, n.$$
Thus $L_{\tilde{x}}(u) = L_x(u)$, $0 \leq u \leq 1$.

Majorization for Infinite Sequences

The extension of majorization to infinite sequences $x = (x_1, x_2, \ldots)$ and $y = (y_1, y_2, \ldots)$ has been discussed by various authors [see particularly Markus (1964)].

Here appropriate definitions are

$$x \prec_w y \quad \text{if} \quad \sup_\pi \sum_{i=1}^k x_{\pi_j} \leq \sup_\pi \sum_{j=1}^k y_{\pi_j}, \quad k = 1, 2, \ldots,$$

$$x \prec^w y \quad \text{if} \quad -x \prec_w -y.$$

If $\sum_1^\infty |x_i| \leq \infty$ and $\sum_1^\infty |y_i| < \infty$, then

$$x \prec y \quad \text{if} \quad x \prec_w y, \quad x \prec^w y, \quad \text{and} \quad \sum_1^\infty x_i = \sum_1^\infty y_i.$$

Now suppose $x_1 \geq x_2 \geq \cdots \geq 0$ and $y_1 \geq y_2 \geq \cdots \geq 0$. Then Lemma 3.1 of Markus (1964) states that $x \prec_w y$ if and only if there exist numbers $p_{ij} \geq 0$, $i, j = 1, 2, \ldots$, such that

$$\sum_{j=1}^\infty p_{ij} \leq 1 \quad \text{for all} \quad i, \tag{4}$$

$$\sum_{i=1}^\infty p_{ij} \leq 1 \quad \text{for all} \quad j, \tag{5}$$

and $x_i = \sum_{j=1}^\infty p_{ij} y_j$. From this lemma it is not difficult to conclude that $x \prec y$ if and only if there exist numbers $p_{ij} \geq 0$ as above with equality in (4) and (5).

The extreme points of the class of infinite doubly stochastic matrices must be permutation matrices, as has been proved by Kendall and Kiefer [see Kendall (1960)]. For an alternative proof see Mauldon (1969). Various other results for infinite sequences that parallel results in the finite-dimensional case are known, but they are not further discussed here.

Majorization for Matrices

Instead of discussing a partial order on vectors in $\mathscr{R}^n$, it is natural to consider ordering matrices. Majorization in its usual sense applies to vectors with fixed element totals. For $m \times n$ matrices, several avenues of generalization are open. Two matrices can be considered as being ordered if one is obtainable from the other by postmultiplication by a doubly stochastic matrix [a natural generalizations of (10) in Section A]. This relates $m \times n$ matrices with fixed row totals. There are, however, several variations on this approach that merit attention. There is also the possibility [suggested by Joe (1985)] of relating matrices with fixed row and column totals. Discussion of various matrix partial orders is found in Chapter 15, Multivariate Majorization.

Lorenz Ordering

The Lorenz curve (see Fig. 1 in Section A) was introduced as a graphical summary of the inequality displayed by a set of n non-negative numbers (described as wealths of individuals). The curve can also be viewed as being related to a discrete random variable representing a randomly chosen individual in the population of n individuals. In order to compare inequality in populations of different sizes, an extended definition of the Lorenz curve proves to be convenient. A Lorenz curve can be associated with any nonnegative random variable with finite expectation in a manner consistent with the association of Lorenz's original curve with the random variable corresponding to the random selection of an individual in a finite population. This more general Lorenz curve is simply a scaled partial integral of the quantile function (or inverse distribution function) of the random variable in question. Further discussion of this more general Lorenz ordering is found in Chapter 17.

Majorization and Dilations

Let μ and ν be probability measures on a locally convex topological vector space $\mathscr{X}$. If

$$\int \phi \, d\mu \leq \int \phi \, d\nu$$

for all continuous convex functions ϕ defined on $\mathscr{X}$, then ν is said to be a *dilation* (or *dilatation*) of μ. Notice that if $\mathscr{X} = \mathscr{R}$, μ is the measure with mass $1/n$ at x_i and ν is the measure with mass $1/n$ at

D. Various Generalizations of Majorization   27

y_i, $i = 1, \ldots, n$, then ν is a dilation of μ if and only if $x \prec y$. This follows because

$$(1/n) \sum \phi(x_i) = \int \phi \, d\mu \leq \int \phi \, d\nu = (1/n) \sum \phi(y_i)$$

for all continuous convex ϕ is equivalent to $x \prec y$ (see 4.B.1).

The notion of a dilation is a generalization of majorization that has been studied or used by a number of authors. But it is beyond the scope of this book. See Phelps (1966) or Meyer (1966) for basic results and additional references.

It should be noted that there are a number of other possible generalizations of majorization that are defined similarly to dilations. Suppose $\mathscr{C}$ is a class of real functions on $\mathscr{R}^n$ with the property that

$$\phi(x) \leq \phi(y) \quad \text{for all } \phi \in \mathscr{C} \quad \text{if and only if} \quad x \prec y.$$

For probability measures μ and ν on $\mathscr{R}^n$, write $\mu \prec_{\mathscr{C}} \nu$ if

$$\int \phi \, d\mu \leq \int \phi \, d\nu \quad \text{for all} \quad \phi \in \mathscr{C}.$$

This condition generalizes majorization because if μ is degenerate at x and ν is degenerate at y, then $\mu \prec_{\mathscr{C}} \nu$ if and only if $x \prec y$. This kind of extension of majorization is discussed in Chapter 11. See in particular 11.F.2.

Complex Majorization

It is intriguing to speculate on the possibility of extending the majorization partial order to deal with complex rather than real vectors. Any definition of majorization which requires ordering the elements of the vectors (as does the basic definition A.1) serves poorly in the complex setting because it requires a selection of an ordering of the complex numbers. However, the definition, alluded to in Equation A(10), involving multiplication by a doubly stochastic matrix P continues to make sense in the complex setting. Goldberg and Straus (1977/1978) introduce this partial order in $\mathscr{C}^n$ in their discussion of generalized numerical ranges of matrices. For two vectors $z^{(1)}$ and $z^{(2)}$ in $\mathscr{C}^n$, write $z^{(1)} \prec z^{(2)}$ if there exists a doubly stochastic matrix P such that $z^{(1)} = z^{(2)} P$. It is plausible to call this ordering majorization because, when restricted to $\mathscr{R}^n$, it coincides with a version of the usual definition of majorization. In $\mathscr{R}^n$, it is possible (see Lemma 2.B.1) to characterize majorization in terms of successive applications of a finite number of matrices of the form $\lambda I + (1-\lambda)Q$, where $0 \leq \lambda \leq 1$, and Q is a permutation matrix which interchanges two coordinates. Goldberg and Straus say that $z^{(1)}$ is obtained from $z^{(2)}$ by *pinching* if $z^{(1)} = z^{(2)}(\lambda I + (1-\lambda)Q)$. If $z^{(1)}$ can be obtained from $z^{(2)}$ by a finite number of pinchings, write $z^{(1)} \prec\prec z^{(2)}$. In $\mathscr{R}^n$, the two partial orders $\prec$ and $\prec\prec$ coincide. In $\mathscr{C}^n$, Goldberg and Straus (1977/1978) show that $z^{(1)} \prec\prec z^{(2)}$ implies $z^{(1)} \prec z^{(2)}$ but not conversely. They give the example P_1 of 2.G.1 to show that the orderings $\prec$ and $\prec\prec$ are distinct.

Complex majorization can be viewed as a special form of matrix majorization, as discussed in 15.A.4.

2
Doubly Stochastic Matrices

An important tool in the study of majorization is a theorem due to Hardy, Littlewood, and Pólya (1929) which states that for $x, y \in \mathscr{R}^n$, $x \prec y$ if and only if

$$x = yP \qquad \text{for some doubly stochastic matrix } P. \qquad (*)$$

For many purposes, the condition $(*)$ is more convenient than the partial sums conditions defining majorization. In fact, $(*)$ is used by Schur (1923) as a definition. The theorem of Hardy, Littlewood, and Pólya and some related results are discussed in this chapter after a review of some important properties of doubly stochastic matrices.

Much of the material in this chapter can be found in an excellent paper by Mirsky (1962/1963). For further discussion of doubly stochastic matrices, see Ando (1989), Bhatia (1997) and Seneta (2006).

A Doubly Stochastic Matrices and Permutation Matrices

A square matrix P is said to be *stochastic* if its elements are all nonnegative and all row sums are one. If, in addition to being stochastic, all column sums are one, the matrix is said to be *doubly stochastic*. This definition can be stated formally as follows:

A.1. Definition. An $n \times n$ matrix $P = (p_{ij})$ is *doubly stochastic* if

$$p_{ij} \geq 0 \qquad \text{for} \quad i, j = 1, \ldots, n, \qquad (1)$$

and
$$\sum_i p_{ij} = 1, \quad j = 1, \ldots, n; \qquad \sum_j p_{ij} = 1, \quad i = 1, \ldots, n. \qquad (2)$$

In terms of the vector $e = (1, \ldots, 1)$, conditions (2) have the more compact form
$$eP = e; \qquad Pe' = e'. \qquad (3)$$
Thus, 1 is a eigenvalue of P corresponding to the eigenvector e.

The term "stochastic matrix" goes back at least to Romanovsky (1931, p. 267), in which he writes: "Matrices with these properties play a large role in the theory of discrete Markov chains. That is why we call these matrices stochastic." Shortly thereafter, Romanovsky (1935) provided a detailed discussion of stochastic matrices. Doubly stochastic matrices are also called *Schur transformations* (Beckenbach and Bellman, 1965, p. 31), or they are said to be *bistochastic* (Berge, 1963, p. 180). The term "doubly stochastic" appears to have been first introduced by Feller (1950, 1968).

An obvious example of a doubly stochastic matrix is the $n \times n$ matrix in which each entry is $1/n$. This is the unique irreducible (idempotent) $n \times n$ doubly stochastic matrix (Schwarz, 1967). See Section I for further discussion of idempotent doubly stochastic matrices.

Particularly interesting examples are provided by the permutation matrices. A square matrix Π is said to be a permutation matrix if each row and column has a single unit entry, and all other entries are zero. There are $n!$ such matrices of size $n \times n$, each of which is obtained by interchanging rows (or columns) of the identity matrix.

It is straightforward to verify that the set of $n \times n$ doubly stochastic matrices is convex. It can also be verified that the permutation matrices are extreme points of this set. A striking and useful fact is that the convex hull of the permutation matrices coincides with the set of doubly stochastic matrices.

A.2. Theorem (Birkhoff, 1946). The permutation matrices constitute the extreme points of the set of doubly stochastic matrices. Moreover, the set of doubly stochastic matrices is the convex hull of the permutation matrices.

A proof of this theorem and various refinements of it are given in Section F.

Much has been written about the Birkhoff theorem. For a general discussion including its historical origins, see Ando (1989) and Bapat and Raghavan (1997).

A.3. If P_1 and P_2 are doubly stochastic, then the product $P = P_1 P_2$ is doubly stochastic.

Proof. Because P_1 and P_2 have nonnegative elements, one sees directly from the definition of a matrix product that P also has nonnegative elements. Also,

$$eP = eP_1 P_2 = eP_2 = e, \qquad Pe' = P_1 P_2 e' = P_1 e' = e'. \quad \|$$

Characterization of Doubly Stochastic Matrices via Majorization

A.4. Theorem. An $n \times n$ matrix $P = (p_{ij})$ is doubly stochastic if and only if $yP \prec y$ for all $y \in \mathscr{R}^n$.

Proof. Suppose first that $yP \prec y$ for all $y \in \mathscr{R}^n$. In particular, $eP \prec e$, where $e \equiv (1, \ldots, 1)$. But if for some vector z, $z \prec e$, then $z = e$, hence $eP = e$. Next, take $y = e_i$ (i.e., $y_i = 1$, $y_j = 0$ if $j \neq i$), to obtain $e_i P = (p_{i1}, p_{i2}, \ldots, p_{in}) \prec e_i$. This means that $\sum_j p_{ij} = 1$, i.e., $Pe' = e'$; it also means that $p_{ij} \geq 0$, because $a \prec b$ implies $\min_i a_i \geq \min_i b_i$. Consequently, P is doubly stochastic.

Now, suppose P is doubly stochastic. Also, suppose that $x = yP$ and that $x_1 \geq \cdots \geq x_n$, $y_1 \geq \cdots \geq y_n$ (otherwise replace P by $Q^{-1}PR$, y by yQ, and x by xR, where Q and R are permutation matrices chosen so that yQ and xR have decreasing components). Then

$$\sum_{j=1}^{k} x_j = \sum_{j=1}^{k} \sum_{i=1}^{n} y_i p_{ij} = \sum_{i=1}^{n} y_i t_i,$$

where

$$0 \leq t_i = \sum_{j=1}^{k} p_{ij} \leq 1 \quad \text{and} \quad \sum_{i=1}^{n} t_i = k.$$

Thus

$$\sum_{j=1}^{k} x_j - \sum_{j=1}^{k} y_j = \sum_{i=1}^{n} y_i t_i - \sum_{i=1}^{k} y_i = \sum_{i=1}^{n} y_i t_i - \sum_{i=1}^{k} y_i + y_k \left(k - \sum_{i=1}^{n} t_i \right)$$

$$= \sum_{i=1}^{k} (y_i - y_k)(t_i - 1) + \sum_{i=k+1}^{n} t_i (y_i - y_k) \leq 0.$$

Clearly, $\sum_{i=1}^{n} x_i = yPe' = ye' = \sum_{i=1}^{n} y_i$. $\|$

The second half of the above proof follows Ostrowski (1952). In view of the fact that the convex hull of the permutation matrices is just the class of doubly stochastic matrices, this part of the theorem can also be obtained as a special case of Proposition 6.A.1.

Notice that since the ordering of majorization is transitive, A.3 is an easy consequence of A.4.

A.4.a. Remark If $yP \prec y$ for $y = e_i$, $i = 1, \ldots, n$, then P is doubly stochastic.

B Characterization of Majorization Using Doubly Stochastic Matrices

We turn here to the theorem of Hardy, Littlewood, and Pólya (1929) which introduced this chapter, namely, that $x \prec y$ if and only if $x = yP$ for some doubly stochastic matrix P. (In general, the matrix P is not unique, and this fact leads to some interesting related theorems.) To this end, a preliminary lemma is proved that is perhaps of greater importance than the theorem. This lemma shows that it is often sufficient to consider only the case $n = 2$ in proving theorems about majorization on $\mathscr{R}^n$.

The lemma involves a special kind of linear transformation called a *T-transformation*, or more briefly a *T-transform*. The matrix of a T-transform has the form

$$T = \lambda I + (1 - \lambda)Q,$$

where $0 \leq \lambda \leq 1$ and Q is a permutation matrix that just interchanges two coordinates. Thus xT has the form

$$xT = (x_1, \ldots, x_{j-1}, \lambda x_j + (1-\lambda)x_k, x_{j+1}, \ldots, x_{k-1},$$
$$\lambda x_k + (1-\lambda)x_j, x_{k+1}, \ldots, x_n).$$

B.1. Lemma (Muirhead, 1903; Hardy, Littlewood, and Pólya, 1934, 1952, p. 47). If $x \prec y$, then x can be derived from y by successive applications of a finite number of T-transforms.

Proof. Because permutation matrices Q that just interchange two coordinates are T-transforms, and because any permutation matrix is the product of such simple permutation matrices, we assume that x is not obtainable from y by permuting arguments. Moreover, assume without loss of generality that $x_1 \geq \cdots \geq x_n$, $y_1 \geq \cdots \geq y_n$.

Let j be the largest index such that $x_j < y_j$, and let k be the smallest index greater than j such that $x_k > y_k$. Such a pair j, k must exist, because the largest index i for which $x_i \neq y_i$ must satisfy $x_i > y_i$. By the choice of j and k,

$$y_j > x_j \geq x_k > y_k. \tag{1}$$

B. Characterization of Majorization Using Doubly Stochastic Matrices

Let $\delta = \min(y_j - x_j, x_k - y_k)$, $1 - \lambda = \delta/(y_j - y_k)$, and

$$y^* = (y_1, \ldots, y_{j-1}, y_j - \delta, y_{j+1}, \ldots, y_{k-1}, y_k + \delta, y_{k+1}, \ldots, y_n).$$

It follows from (1) that $0 < \lambda < 1$, and it is easy to verify that

$$y^* = \lambda y + (1-\lambda)(y_1, \ldots, y_{j-1}, y_k, y_{j+1}, \ldots, y_{k-1}, y_j, y_{k+1}, \ldots, y_n).$$

Thus, $y^* = yT$ for $T = \lambda I + (1-\lambda)Q$, where Q interchanges the jth and kth coordinates. Consequently, $y^* \prec y$; this can also be seen directly. It is also true that $x \prec y^*$. To see this, note that

$$\sum_1^\nu y_i^* = \sum_1^\nu y_i \geq \sum_1^\nu x_i, \qquad \nu = 1, \ldots, j-1,$$

$$y_j^* \geq x_j, \quad y_i^* = y_i, \qquad i = j+1, \ldots, k-1,$$

$$\sum_1^\nu y_i^* = \sum_1^\nu y_i \geq \sum_1^\nu x_i, \qquad \nu = k+1, \ldots, n,$$

$$\sum_1^n y_i^* = \sum_1^n y_i = \sum_1^n x_i.$$

For any two vectors u, v let $d(u,v)$ be the number of nonzero differences $u_i - v_i$. Because $y_j^* = x_j$ if $\delta = y_j - x_j$ and $y_k^* = x_k$ if $\delta = x_k - y_k$, it follows that $d(x, y^*) \leq d(x,y) - 1$. Hence, y can be derived from x by a finite number of T-transformations. ∥

Muirhead (1903) obtained B.1 for the case that x and y have integer components; the result was given in the above form by Hardy, Littlewood, and Pólya (1934, 1952).

B.1.a. If $x \prec y$, then x can be derived from y by successive applications of at most $n-1$ T-transforms. This follows from the above proof because $d(u,v) \leq n$ and $d(u,v) \neq 1$ (otherwise, $\sum u_i \neq \sum v_i$).

B.2. Theorem (Hardy, Littlewood, and Pólya, 1929). A necessary and sufficient condition that $x \prec y$ is that there exist a doubly stochastic matrix P such that $x = yP$.

Proof. Suppose first that for some doubly stochastic matrix P, $x = yP$. Then by A.4, $x \prec y$. Next, suppose $x \prec y$. Because T-transforms are doubly stochastic, the product of T-transformations is doubly stochastic. Thus, the existence of a doubly stochastic matrix such that $x = yP$ follows from B.1. ∥

As noted by Horn (1954a), B.2 can be combined with Birkhoff's theorem A.2 to yield an important corollary on the geometry of majorization (see also 4.C.1).

B.3. Corollary (Rado, 1952). The set $\{x : x \prec y\}$ is the convex hull of points obtained by permuting the components of y.

Corollary B.3 was obtained by Rado (1952) as a direct consequence of the fact that $u \in \mathscr{R}^n$ lies in the convex hull of vectors $u^{(1)}, \ldots, u^{(m)}$ if and only if

$$ua' \leq \max_{1 \leq i \leq m} u^{(i)} a' \quad \text{for all} \quad a \in \mathscr{R}^n.$$

Mirsky (1958a) has made use of B.3 to obtain a simple proof of B.2. A proof and historical remarks are also given by Markus (1964).

If $x \prec y$, then according to B.2, $x = yP$ for some doubly stochastic matrix P. The matrix P is not necessarily unique, as seen from the following example.

B.4. Example. If $x = (4, 3, 2)$ and $y = (5, 3, 1)$, then P can be either

$$P_1 = \begin{bmatrix} \frac{1}{2} & \frac{1}{2} & 0 \\ \frac{1}{2} & 0 & \frac{1}{2} \\ 0 & \frac{1}{2} & \frac{1}{2} \end{bmatrix}, \quad P_2 = \begin{bmatrix} \frac{3}{4} & 0 & \frac{1}{4} \\ 0 & 1 & 0 \\ \frac{1}{4} & 0 & \frac{3}{4} \end{bmatrix},$$

or any convex combination of P_1 and P_2. The matrix P_2 is a T-transform, but P_1 is not; in fact, P_1 is not even a product of T-transforms (or any other pair of doubly stochastic matrices, apart from permutation matrices). The class of doubly stochastic matrices that maps $y = (5, 3, 1)$ to $x = (4, 3, 2)$ is discussed more thoroughly in Example G.2.

When $x \prec y$, then according to B.1, it is possible to choose P to be a product of T-transforms. It is also possible to choose P from certain other subclasses of doubly stochastic matrices. To state these results, some definitions are required.

B.5. Definitions. A matrix $Q = (q_{ij})$ is said to be *orthostochastic* if there exists an orthogonal matrix $\Gamma = (\gamma_{ij})$ such that $q_{ij} = \gamma_{ij}^2$. A matrix $Q = (q_{ij})$ is said to be *unitary-stochastic* if there exists a unitary matrix $U = (u_{ij})$ such that $q_{ij} = |u_{ij}|^2$. (Of course, orthostochastic matrices are unitary-stochastic and unitary-stochastic matrices are doubly stochastic.) A doubly stochastic matrix $R = (r_{ij})$ is said to be *uniformly tapered* if

$$r_{11} \geq r_{12} \geq \cdots \geq r_{1n}, \tag{2}$$

B. Characterization of Majorization Using Doubly Stochastic Matrices

$$r_{nn} \geq r_{n-1,n} \geq \cdots \geq r_{1n}, \qquad (3)$$
$$r_{ij} + r_{i-1,j+1} \geq r_{i-1,j} + r_{i,j+1} \quad \text{if } 2 \leq i \leq j \leq n-1. \qquad (4)$$

Some explicit examples are given G.1. There, P_5, P_6, P_7, and P_9 are orthostochastic; P_4, P_6, P_8, and P_9 are uniformly tapered.

B.6. Theorem. If $x, y \in \mathscr{R}^n$, the following conditions are equivalent:

(i) $x \prec y$;

(ii) $x = yP$ for some doubly stochastic matrix P;

(iii) $x = yP$, where P is a product of at most $n-1$ T-transformations;

(iv) $x = yQ$ for some orthostochastic matrix Q;

(v) $x = y\Pi_1 R\Pi_2$ for some uniformly tapered matrix R and permutation matrices Π_1, Π_2.

Because (ii) implies (i) as shown in A.4 or B.2, it is also true that (iii), (iv), and (v) each implies (i). That (i) implies (ii) is given in B.2. That (i) implies (iii) is the content of B.1.a. A proof that (i) implies (iv) is not given in this book. That (i) implies (v) is proved in G.3.

An alternative proof of B.2 that (i) and (ii) are equivalent is given by Levow (1972); his proof is similar to the proof of Hardy, Littlewood, and Pólya and also yields B.1. Various proofs that (i) implies (ii) have been given by Fan (1957, 1966, 1975) and by Ryff (1965). A particularly simple proof that (i) implies (ii) is given by Smiley (1966); this proof also yields B.1. The fact that (i) implies (iv) is due to Horn (1954a) and is also proved by Mirsky (1958a). That (i) implies (v) is due to Hoffman (1969).

Hessenberg matrices constitute another important class of doubly stochastic matrices. These and other classes of matrices are discussed in Section G.

Remark. If $x \prec y$, then necessarily there exists a doubly stochastic matrix P such that $x = yP$. Even though x can be obtained from y by applications of successive T-transforms, not every choice of P satisfying $x = yP$ can be written as a product (finite or infinite) of T-transforms. Refer back to the matrix P_1 in Example B.4. In fact, Marcus, Kidman, and Sandy (1984) showed that any $n \times n$ doubly stochastic matrix, $n \geq 3$, with a single diagonal of zeros and all $n^2 - n$ other entries strictly positive cannot be written as a product of T-transforms. This is particularly easy to verify in the case $n = 3$.

They also prove that for $n \geq 4$, there exists an $n \times n$ orthostochastic matrix which cannot be written as a product (finite or infinite) of T-transforms. The following 3×3 doubly stochastic matrix, in which the notation $\bar{x} = 1 - x$ is used, provides an example of this phenomenon:

$$\begin{pmatrix} 0 & a & \bar{a} \\ \bar{a} & 0 & a \\ a & \bar{a} & 0 \end{pmatrix},$$

where $0 < a < 1$. The equation

$$\begin{pmatrix} 0 & a & \bar{a} \\ \bar{a} & 0 & a \\ a & \bar{a} & 0 \end{pmatrix} = \begin{pmatrix} u & \bar{u} & 0 \\ \bar{u} & u & 0 \\ 0 & 0 & 1 \end{pmatrix} \begin{pmatrix} v & 0 & \bar{v} \\ 0 & 1 & 0 \\ \bar{v} & 0 & v \end{pmatrix} \begin{pmatrix} 1 & 0 & 0 \\ 0 & w & \bar{w} \\ 0 & \bar{w} & w \end{pmatrix}$$

has no solution for u, v, w for any permutation of the three matrices on the right-hand side of the equation.

C Doubly Substochastic Matrices and Weak Majorization

In the study of the ordering $\prec_w$ of lower weak majorization, doubly substochastic matrices play much the same role that doubly stochastic matrices play with respect to majorization.

A square matrix P is said to be *doubly substochastic* if its elements are all nonnegative and if all row and column sums are at most one. Thus the $n \times n$ matrix $P = (p_{ij})$ is doubly substochastic if

$$p_{ij} \geq 0 \quad \text{for} \quad i, j = 1, \ldots, n, \tag{1}$$

$$\sum_i p_{ij} \leq 1, \quad j = 1, \ldots, n, \qquad \sum_j p_{ij} \leq 1, \quad i = 1, \ldots, n. \tag{2}$$

With the notation $(x_1, \ldots, x_n) \leq (y_1, \ldots, y_n)$ to mean $x_i \leq y_i$, $i = 1, \ldots, n$, (2) can be rewritten as

$$eP \leq e, \qquad Pe' \leq e'. \tag{3}$$

Such matrices P are sometimes called *sub-Markovian matrices*.

It is clear that the $n \times n$ doubly substochastic matrices form a convex set and that they can be viewed as points of a convex polytope in $\mathscr{R}^{n^2}$.

C. Doubly Substochastic Matrices and Weak Majorization

If each entry in a doubly stochastic matrix is diminished (while maintaining nonnegativity), then a doubly substochastic matrix is obtained. There is a converse to this:

C.1. Theorem (von Neumann, 1953). If $P = (p_{ij})$ is doubly substochastic, then there exists a doubly stochastic matrix $D = (d_{ij})$ such that
$$p_{ij} \leq d_{ij} \qquad \text{for all} \quad i, j.$$

Proof. If P is an $n \times n$ doubly substochastic matrix that is not doubly stochastic, then some row or column sum is less than one. If a row sum is less than one, then the sum of all elements of P is less than n, so some column sum is less than one. Similarly, if a column sum is less than one, then also a row sum is less than one. Thus $\sum_k p_{kj} < 1$ for some j and $\sum_m p_{im} < 1$ for some i. Let $\varepsilon = 1 - \max(\sum_k p_{kj}, \sum_m p_{im})$. Then obtain P_1 from P by adding ε to the element in the (i, j)th position and keeping the remaining elements fixed. This reduces by at least 1 the number of row sums plus the number of column sums that are strictly less than one. Clearly, a continuation of this process leads to a doubly stochastic matrix D satisfying the conditions of the lemma. ||

Augmentation of Doubly Substochastic Matrices

If an equal number of rows and columns in a doubly stochastic matrix are deleted, a doubly substochastic matrix is obtained. Conversely, a doubly substochastic matrix can be augmented to yield a doubly stochastic matrix. Thus, if P is an $n \times n$ doubly substochastic matrix and has row sums $r_1, \ldots, r_n$ and column sums $c_1, \ldots, c_n$, then the matrix

$$\widetilde{P} = \begin{bmatrix} P & I - D_r \\ I - D_c & P' \end{bmatrix}, \qquad (4)$$

where $D_r = \mathrm{diag}(r_1, \ldots, r_n)$, $D_c = \mathrm{diag}(c_1, \ldots, c_n)$, is doubly stochastic. It is not necessarily possible to augment P to obtain a doubly stochastic matrix of size less than $2n \times 2n$, as can be seen by taking $P = (p_{ij})$, where $p_{ij} = 0$ for all i, j. Here the matrix must be augmented with additional rows to make the n column sums each 1, and it must be augmented with additional columns to make the n row sums each 1. This means that the augmented matrix must have entries adding to at least $2n$. Because it is to be doubly stochastic, it must therefore be at least $2n \times 2n$.

A nonsquare matrix with nonnegative entries and with row and column sums less than or equal to 1 can also be augmented to yield doubly stochastic matrices (first, augment with zeros so the matrix is square). A particularly interesting case is an $n \times k$ matrix P_1, $k < n$, with column sums 1. The addition of $n - k$ columns of zeros yields the doubly substochastic matrix $P = (P_1, 0)$. A doubly stochastic matrix $D = d_{ij}$ satisfying $d_{ij} > p_{ij}$ must be of the form (P_1, P_2) because the column sums of P_1 are already 1.

There is a counterpart to Birkhoff's theorem for doubly substochastic matrices that can be obtained using augmentation.

C.2. Theorem (Mirsky, 1959a). The set of $n \times n$ doubly substochastic matrices is the convex hull of the set of $n \times n$ matrices that have at most one unit in each row and each column, and all other entries are zero.

Proof. Let P be a doubly substochastic matrix, and let $\widetilde{P}$ be defined as in (4). Then by A.2, $\widetilde{P} = \sum_{i=1}^{k} \alpha_i \widetilde{P}_i$, where the $\widetilde{P}_i$ are $2n \times 2n$ permutation matrices and $\alpha_i \geq 0$, $i = 1, 2, \ldots, k$, $\sum_i \alpha_i = 1$. Let P_i be obtained from $\widetilde{P}_i$ by deleting the last n rows and columns. Then $P = \sum_{i=1}^{k} \alpha_i P_i$; each P_i has at most one unit in each row and each column, and all other entries are zero. ||

A more direct proof of C.2 can be obtained by modifying the first proof of A.2 given in Section F.

Notice that C.1 can be proved easily with the aid of C.2. For suppose $P = (p_{ij})$ is a convex combination of matrices, each of which is obtainable by possibly decreasing entries in some permutation matrix. Then in this convex combination, the replacement of each matrix by the permutation matrix from which it was obtained yields a doubly stochastic matrix $D = (d_{ij})$ such that $d_{ij} \geq p_{ij}$ for all i, j.

By Carathéodory's theorem [see, e.g., Rockafellar (1970, p. 153) or Roberts and Varberg (1973, p. 76)], one can represent the $n \times n$ doubly substochastic matrices as a convex combination of at most $n^2 + 1$ zero–one doubly substochastic matrices. This is a much better estimate than $(n-1)^2 + 1$ obtainable via F.2 and the above proof.

Consider now the possibility of obtaining results analogous to A.4 and B.2 with the ordering $\prec$ of majorization replaced by the ordering $\prec_w$ of weak majorization.

Theorem A.4 characterizes the doubly stochastic matrices as those matrices P for which $yP \prec y$ for all $y \in \mathscr{R}^n$. If we try to obtain a similar result for weak majorization, we are confronted with the

C. Doubly Substochastic Matrices and Weak Majorization

fact that if $yP \prec_w y$ for all $y \in \mathcal{R}^n$, then also $(-y)P \prec_w (-y)$. Consequently, $yP \prec y$, and no interesting new results are obtainable. On the other hand, a requirement that y and yP have nonnegative components presents a framework in which results analogous to A.4 and B.2 are obtainable.

C.3. An $n \times n$ matrix $P = (p_{ij})$ is doubly substochastic if and only if $y \in \mathcal{R}_+^n$ implies $yP \in \mathcal{R}_+^n$ and $yP \prec_w y$.

Proof. Suppose first that P satisfies $yP \prec_w y$ for all $y \in \mathcal{R}_+^n$. With $y = e$, it follows that

$$\left(\sum_{i=1}^n p_{i1}, \sum_{i=1}^n p_{i2}, \ldots, \sum_{i=1}^n p_{in}\right) \prec_w (1, 1, \ldots, 1).$$

This means that $\max_j \sum_{i=1}^n p_{ij} \leq 1$, and hence $eP \leq e$. With $y = e_i$, where e_i has its ith component equal to 1, and all other components equal to 0, it follows that

$$(p_{i1}, p_{i2}, \ldots, p_{in}) \prec_w e_i,$$

so that $\sum_{j=1}^n p_{ij} \leq 1$, $i = 1, \ldots, n$; i.e., $Pe' \leq e'$. The choice $y = e_i$ in the condition $yP \in \mathcal{R}_+^n$ yields $p_{ij} \geq 0$.

Next, suppose that P is doubly substochastic, and let $x = yP$. Clearly, $x \in \mathcal{R}_+^n$. As in the proof of A.4, the orderings $y_1 \geq \cdots \geq y_n$ and $x_1 \geq \cdots \geq x_n$ can be achieved through the use of permutation matrices. Then

$$\sum_{j=1}^k x_j = \sum_{j=1}^k \sum_{i=1}^n y_i p_{ij} = \sum_{i=1}^n y_i t_i,$$

where

$$0 \leq t_i = \sum_{j=1}^k p_{ij} \leq 1 \quad \text{and} \quad \sum_{i=1}^n t_i \leq k.$$

Thus

$$\sum_{j=1}^k x_j - \sum_{j=1}^k y_j = \sum_{i=1}^n y_i t_i - \sum_{i=1}^k y_i \leq \sum_{i=1}^n y_i t_i - \sum_{i=1}^k y_i + y_k\left(k - \sum_{i=1}^n t_i\right)$$

$$= \sum_{i=1}^k (y_i - y_k)(t_i - 1) + \sum_{i=k+1}^n t_i(y_i - y_k) \leq 0. \quad \|$$

Theorem C.3 characterizes doubly substochastic matrices in terms of the weak majorization $\prec_w$ on $\mathscr{R}_+^n$. In a manner analogous to B.2, weak majorization can also be characterized in terms of doubly substochastic matrices.

C.4. Theorem. A necessary and sufficient condition that $x \prec_w y$ on $\mathscr{R}_+^n$ is that there exists a doubly substochastic matrix P such that $x = yP$.

Proof. Suppose first that $x \prec_w y$; then $\delta = \sum_1^n y_i - \sum_1^n x_i \geq 0$. If $\delta = 0$, then $x \prec y$ and the result follows from B.6. Next consider the case that $\delta > 0$. If $x = 0$, take P to have all components zero. If $x \neq 0$, suppose that $x_{[m]}$ ($m \leq n$) is the smallest nonzero component of x, and let ℓ be the smallest integer such that $\ell x_{[m]} \geq \delta$. Then if $\tilde{x} = (x_1, \ldots, x_n, \delta/\ell, \ldots, \delta/\ell)$ and $\tilde{y} = (y_1, \ldots, y_n, 0, \ldots, 0)$ have ℓ more components than x and y, it follows that $\tilde{x} \prec \tilde{y}$ (note that, because $\delta/\ell \leq x_{[m]}$, the δ/ℓ's are the smallest nonzero elements of $\tilde{x}$). Consequently, by B.2 there exists a doubly stochastic matrix $\tilde{P}$ such that $\tilde{x} = \tilde{y}\tilde{P}$. But then $x = yP$, where P is the upper left $n \times n$ submatrix of $\tilde{P}$. Clearly, P is doubly substochastic.

Finally, suppose that $x = yP$, where P is doubly substochastic. Then $x \prec_w y$ by C.1. ||

Theorems C.2 and C.4 together yield the following analog of Rado's theorem (B.3):

C.5. Corollary (Mirsky, 1959a). For $y \in \mathscr{R}_+^n$, the set $\{x : x \in \mathscr{R}_+^n$ and $x \prec_w y\}$ is the convex hull of points of the form $(\eta_1 y_{\pi_1}, \ldots, \eta_n y_{\pi_n})$, where π is a permutation and each η_i is 0 or 1.

Although the above proof of C.4 depends upon B.2, C.4 also follows from a weak majorization analog of B.1.

For any vector $z \in \mathscr{R}^n$, let $|z| = (|z_1|, \ldots, |z_n|)$.

C.5.a. Corollary (Markus, 1964). For $y \in \mathscr{R}^n$, the set $\{x : |x| \prec |y|\}$ is the convex hull of points of the form $(\varepsilon_1 y_{\pi_1}, \ldots, \varepsilon_n y_{\pi_n})$, where π is a permutation and each ε_i is -1 or 1.

Proof. Let $\mathscr{C}$ denote the convex hull of points of the form $(\eta_1 y_{\pi_1}, \ldots, \eta_n y_{\pi_n})$, where π is a permutation and each η_i is 0 or 1. Similarly, let $\widetilde{\mathscr{C}}$ denote the convex hull of points of the form $(\varepsilon_1 y_{\pi_1}, \ldots, \varepsilon_n y_{\pi_n})$, where each ε_i is -1 or 1. Then C.5.a follows from C.5 because $\widetilde{\mathscr{C}} = \{x : |x| \in \mathscr{C}\}$. ||

C. Doubly Substochastic Matrices and Weak Majorization 41

Another proof of C.5.a is given by Mitjagin (1964). A related result is given by Thompson and Ishaq (1977/1978).

C.6. Proposition (Mirsky, 1959a; Chong, 1976a). For $x, y \in \mathscr{R}_+^n$, $x \prec_w y$ if and only if there exist a finite number $T_1, \ldots, T_k$ of T-transforms such that
$$x \leq yT_1 \cdots T_k.$$

The proof of this result is not given here, but it easily follows from B.1 and 5.A.9. Notice that C.6 does not require $x, y \in \mathscr{R}_+^n$.

Mirsky (1959a) proves only that $x \leq yD$ for some doubly stochastic matrix D; this result must be combined with B.1 to obtain C.6. Chong (1976a) obtains the above form of C.6.

C.6.a. For $x, y \in \mathscr{R}_+^n$, $x \prec_w y$ if and only if x can be derived from y by successive applications of a finite number of T-transforms followed by a finite number of transformations of the form
$$T(z) = (z_1, \ldots, z_{i-1}, \alpha z_i, z_{i+1}, \ldots, z_n), \qquad 0 \leq \alpha \leq 1.$$

This result follows from C.6 and the definition of weak majorization.

Weak Majorization and Complex Vectors

For any vector $z = (z_1, \ldots, z_n)$ of complex numbers, let $|z| = (|z_1|, \ldots, |z_n|)$.

C.7. Theorem (Thompson, 1977). Let x and y be complex vectors. Then $|x| \prec_w |y|$ if and only if there exists a square complex matrix $W = (w_{ij})$ such that $x = yW$ and $(|w_{ij}|)$ is doubly substochastic.

Proof. Suppose first that $x = yW$, where $(|w_{ij}|)$ is doubly substochastic. Assume $|x_1| \geq \cdots \geq |x_n|$, $|y_1| \geq \cdots \geq |y_n|$ (or make use of permutation matrices to achieve this). Then $|x_j| = |\sum_{i=1}^n y_i w_{ij}| \leq \sum_i |y_i||w_{ij}|$ and $\sum_{j=1}^k |x_j| \leq \sum_{j=1}^k \sum_{i=1}^n |y_i||w_{ij}| = \sum_{i=1}^n |y_i| \sum_{j=1}^k |w_{ij}| = \sum_{i=1}^n |y_i| t_i$, where $t_i = \sum_{j=1}^k |w_{ij}|$. As in the proof of C.3, $0 \leq t_i \leq 1$ and $\sum_{i=1}^n t_i \leq k$, so by the argument used there, $\sum_1^k |x_j| - \sum_1^k |y_j| \leq 0$, $k = 1, \ldots, n$.

Next, suppose $|x| \prec_w |y|$. Then by C.4, $|x| = |y|P$, where P is doubly substochastic. Let $D_1 = \mathrm{diag}(a_1, \ldots, a_n)$, where $\arg a_i = \arg x_i$ and $|a_i| = 1$, $i = 1, \ldots, n$. Similarly, let $D_2 = \mathrm{diag}(b_1, \ldots, b_n)$, where $\arg b_i = \arg y_i$ and $|b_i| = 1$, $i = 1, \ldots, n$. Then $|x| = xD_1$, $|y| = yD_2$, so $x = yD_2 P D_1^{-1}$. Clearly, $W = D_2 P D_1^{-1}$ has the required properties. ‖

The following is an analog of Birkhoff's theorem A.2 or, more properly, of Mirsky's theorem C.2 concerning the extreme points of the set of complex matrices W such that $(|w_{ij}|)$ is doubly substochastic.

C.8. Theorem (Thompson, 1977). The set $\mathscr{W}$ of complex $n \times n$ matrices W such that $(|w_{ij}|)$ is doubly substochastic is the convex hull of the matrices with a single nonzero entry in each row and each column, the nonzero entries being complex numbers of modulus 1.

The proof of this result is not given here.

D Doubly Superstochastic Matrices and Weak Majorization

In Section C the role played by the doubly substochastic matrices with respect to the ordering $\prec_w$ of lower weak majorization is studied. A similar role is played by doubly superstochastic matrices with respect to the ordering $\prec^w$ of upper weak majorization. Although there are some analogies, there are surprisingly many differences, and the theory is not yet complete.

For a nonnegative square matrix $P = (p_{ij})$, it is easy to see with the aid of C.1 that the following conditions are equivalent:

(i) all row and column sums are at most one;

(ii) there exists a doubly stochastic matrix $D = (d_{ij})$ such that $p_{ij} \leq d_{ij}$ for all i, j.

Either of the conditions (i) or (ii) can be used to define "doubly substochastic." But consider the companion conditions:

(iii) all row and all column sums are at least one;

(iv) there exists a doubly stochastic matrix $D = (d_{ij})$ such that $p_{ij} \geq d_{ij}$ for all i, j.

If (iv) holds, then $eP \geq eD = e$ and $Pe' \geq De' = e'$, so that (iii) holds. On the other hand,

$$\begin{bmatrix} 0 & \frac{3}{4} & \frac{3}{4} \\ \frac{3}{4} & \frac{1}{4} & 0 \\ \frac{3}{4} & 0 & \frac{1}{4} \end{bmatrix}$$

satisfies (iii) but not (iv).

D. Doubly Superstochastic Matrices and Weak Majorization

Because (iii) and (iv) are not equivalent, care must be taken in defining "doubly superstochastic."

D.1. Definition. A square matrix $P = (p_{ij})$ is said to be *doubly superstochastic* if there exists a doubly stochastic matrix D such that $p_{ij} \geq d_{ij}$ for all i, j.

The class of all doubly superstochastic matrices is convex. However, the only extreme points are permutation matrices, so the class is not the convex hull of its extreme points. It can be shown, however, that the class of doubly superstochastic matrices is the convex hull of its extreme points and extreme rays (Rockafellar, 1970, Theorem 18.5).

D.2. Proposition. $x \prec^w y$ if and only if there exist a finite number $T_1, \ldots, T_k$ of T-transforms such that $x \geq y T_1 \cdots T_k$.

Proof. According to 5.A.9.a, $x \prec^w y$ implies that there exists $u \in \mathscr{R}^n$ such that $x \geq u$ and $u \prec y$. By B.1, u can be written in the form $u = y T_1 \cdots T_k$. Conversely, if $x \geq y T_1 \cdots T_k$, then it is easily seen that $x \prec^w y$. ‖

D.2.a. Proposition. Let $x, y \in \mathscr{R}^n_{++}$. Then, $x \prec^w y$ if and only if x can be derived from y by successive application of a finite number of T-transforms followed by a finite number of transformations of the form

$$T(z) = (z_1, \ldots, z_{i-1}, \alpha z_i, z_{i+1}, \ldots, z_n), \qquad \alpha > 1. \tag{1}$$

Proof. This result is just a restatement of D.2. Here, $\mathscr{R}^n_{++}$ cannot be replaced by $\mathscr{R}^n_+$, as can be seen by taking $y = (0, \ldots, 0)$. ‖

D.2.b. Proposition. Let $x, y \in \mathscr{R}^n_{++}$. Then $x \prec^w y$ if and only if there exists a doubly superstochastic matrix P such that $x = yP$.

Proof. Suppose first that $x = yP$ and $P = D + Q$, where D is doubly stochastic and Q has nonnegative entries. If $z = yD$, then $z \prec y$ and

$$\sum_{1}^{k} x_{[n-i+1]} \geq \sum_{1}^{k} z_{[n-i+1]} \geq \sum_{1}^{k} y_{[n-i+1]}, \qquad k = 1, \ldots, n,$$

so $x \prec^w y$.

Next, suppose that $x \prec^w y$. Then by D.2.a, $x = yP$ where P is a product of T-transforms and transformations of the form (1). Because products of doubly superstochastic matrices are doubly superstochastic, P is doubly superstochastic. ‖

D.3. Proposition. If P is a doubly superstochastic matrix, then for $k, l = 1, \ldots, n$,

(the sum of elements in any k columns) $- k$
$\geq$ (the sum of elements in the intersection of the k columns and any l rows) $- l$; (2)

(the sum of elements in any l rows) $- l$
$\geq$ (the sum of elements in the intersection of the l rows and any k columns) $- k$. (3)

Proof. Let $P = D + Q$, where D is doubly stochastic and Q is nonnegative. To verify (2) for the first k columns and first l rows, let $\delta_j = (1, \ldots, 1, 0, \ldots, 0)$ be the vector with first j components 1 and remaining components 0, $j = 1, \ldots, n$. Then

$$eP\delta'_k - k = eQ\delta'_k \geq \delta_l Q \delta'_k \geq \delta_l Q \delta'_k + \delta_l D \delta'_k - l = \delta_l P \delta'_k - l.$$

The remaining conditions of (2) can be obtained by suitable interchanges of rows and columns of P and repeating the above argument. Similarly, (3) follows by applying (2) to P'. ||

To describe necessary and sufficient conditions for a matrix P to be doubly superstochastic, it is convenient to introduce the following notation.

For any subsets I and J of the set of integers $\{1, 2, \ldots, n\}$, write

$$P(I, J) = \sum_{i \in I} \sum_{j \in J} p_{ij}.$$

In addition, write $|I|$ to indicate the cardinality of I.

D.4. Theorem (Ando, 1989). The following conditions for an $n \times n$ matrix P are equivalent:

(i) P is doubly superstochastic;

(ii) $yP \prec^w y$ for all $y \in \mathscr{R}^n_+$;

(iii) $P(I, J) \geq (|I| + |J| - n)^+$ for every I and J.

Bhandari and Das Gupta (1985) independently proved the equivalence of conditions (i) and (ii) in Theorem D.4.

The proof of D.4 provided by Ando uses the following "interpolation" result. It can be used to characterize both doubly superstochastic and doubly substochastic matrices.

D.5. Theorem (Ando, 1989). If two $n \times n$ matrices $B = (b_{ij})$ and $C = (c_{ij})$ satisfy $b_{ij} \geq c_{ij} \geq 0$ for all i and j, then there exists a doubly stochastic matrix $A = (a_{ij})$ such that

$$b_{ij} \geq a_{ij} \geq c_{ij} \geq 0 \text{ for all } i \text{ and } j$$

if and only if

$$B(I, J) \geq C(I^c, J^c) + |I| + |J| - n \text{ for all } I \text{ and } J,$$

where $I^c = \{1, 2, \ldots, n\} - I$.

Observe that having row and column sums of P at least 1 does not guarantee that P is superstochastic nor that $yP \prec^{\mathrm{w}} P$ for all $y \in \mathcal{R}_+^n$. For example,

$$\left(\tfrac{15}{4}, \tfrac{5}{4}, \tfrac{6}{4}\right) = (1, 2, 3) \begin{bmatrix} 0 & \tfrac{3}{4} & \tfrac{3}{4} \\ \tfrac{3}{4} & \tfrac{1}{4} & 0 \\ \tfrac{3}{4} & 0 & \tfrac{1}{4} \end{bmatrix},$$

but $\left(\tfrac{15}{4}, \tfrac{5}{4}, \tfrac{6}{4}\right) \not\prec^{\mathrm{w}} (1, 2, 3)$.

E Orderings on $\mathscr{D}$

To obtain results analogous to those of preceding sections for orderings of vectors in $\mathscr{D} = \{x : x_1 \geq x_2 \geq \cdots \geq x_n\}$, use can be made of the fact that $\mathscr{D}$ is a convex cone with a very simple structure. Let $\delta_k = (1, \ldots, 1, 0, \ldots, 0)$ have its first k components equal to 1, and remaining components 0, $k = 1, \ldots, n$. For each k, $\delta_k \in \mathscr{D}$, and also $-\delta_n = -e \in \mathscr{D}$. Moreover, $\mathscr{D}$ is a finitely generated convex cone (Rockafellar, 1970, p. 170) *spanned positively* by

$$\mathscr{T} = \{\delta_1, \delta_2, \ldots, \delta_n, -\delta_n\}$$

in the sense that if $x \in \mathscr{D}$, then x can be written in the form $x = \sum \alpha_i \delta_i + \beta(-\delta_n)$, where $\alpha_i \geq 0$, $i = 1, \ldots, n, \beta \geq 0$.

As a preliminary result, conditions are obtained on matrices P that ensure that $y \in \mathscr{D}$ implies $yP \in \mathscr{D}$.

E.1. Proposition. $yP \in \mathscr{D}$ for all $y \in \mathscr{D}$ if and only if

$$\sum_{i=1}^{k} p_{ij} \text{ is decreasing in } j, \qquad k = 1, \ldots, n-1, \tag{1}$$

46   2. Doubly Stochastic Matrices

and
$$\sum_{i=1}^{n} p_{i1} = \cdots = \sum_{i=1}^{n} p_{in}. \tag{2}$$

Proof. Notice that $yP \in \mathscr{D}$ for all $y \in \mathscr{D}$ if and only if $tP \in \mathscr{D}$ for all $t \in \mathscr{T}$. But (1) is equivalent to $\delta_k P \in \mathscr{D}$, $k = 1, \ldots, n-1$, and (2) is equivalent to $\delta_n P$ and $-\delta_n P \in \mathscr{D}$. ||

Observe that even though conditions (1) and (2) of E.1 look very much like $p^{(1)} \succ p^{(2)} \succ \cdots \succ p^{(n)}$, where $p^{(i)}$ is the ith column of P, condition (1) does not require that the components of $p^{(i)}$ be ordered decreasingly.

E.2. Proposition.   An $n \times n$ matrix P satisfies
$$yP \in \mathscr{D} \text{ and } yP \prec_{\text{w}} y \quad \text{ for all } \quad y \in \mathscr{D}$$
if and only if
$$1 \geq \sum_{i=1}^{k} p_{i1} \geq \sum_{i=1}^{k} p_{i2} \geq \cdots \geq \sum_{i=1}^{k} p_{in}, \quad k = 1, \ldots, n-1, \tag{3}$$
$$\sum_{i=1}^{n} p_{ij} = 1, \quad j = 1, \ldots, n, \tag{4}$$
and
$$k \geq \sum_{j=1}^{l} \sum_{i=1}^{k} p_{ij} \quad \text{for all} \quad k < l, \quad l = 2, \ldots, n. \tag{5}$$

Proof. Suppose first that $yP \in \mathscr{D}$ and $yP \prec_{\text{w}} y$ whenever $y \in \mathscr{D}$. Then (1) and (2) follow by E.1. Because $\delta_k P \prec_{\text{w}} \delta_k$, $k = 1, \ldots, n-1$,

(i) $\sum_{j=1}^{l} \sum_{i=1}^{k} p_{ij} \leq \min(k, l)$ whenever $1 \leq k \leq n-1$ and $1 \leq l \leq n$.

Because $\delta_n P \prec_{\text{w}} \delta_n$ and $-\delta_n P \prec_{\text{w}} -\delta_n$,

(ii) $\sum_{j=1}^{l} \sum_{i=1}^{n} p_{ij} = l$, $\quad l = 1, \ldots, n$.

Condition (3) follows from (1) and (i) with $l = 1$. Condition (4) follows from (ii) upon taking differences with adjacent values of l, and (5) is a special case of (i).

Next, suppose that (3), (4), and (5) hold. Then (3) implies (1), and (4) implies (2) so that $yP \in \mathscr{D}$ for all $y \in \mathscr{D}$. From (3) it follows that
$$\sum_{j=1}^{l} \sum_{i=1}^{k} p_{ij} \leq l,$$

which combines with (5) to yield (i). From (4), it follows that (ii) holds. Consequently, $yP \prec_w y$ for all $y \in \mathscr{D}$, and this implies $yP \prec_w y$ for all $y \in \mathscr{D}$. ||

E.3. Proposition. An $n \times n$ matrix P satisfies
$$yP \in \mathscr{D} \text{ and } yP \prec^w y \qquad \text{for all} \quad y \in \mathscr{D}$$
if and only if
$$\sum_{i=1}^{k} p_{i1} \geq \sum_{i=1}^{k} p_{i2} \geq \cdots \geq \sum_{i=1}^{k} p_{in} \geq 0, \qquad k = 1, \ldots, n-1, \tag{3'}$$

$$\sum_{i=1}^{n} p_{ij} = 1, \qquad j = 1, \ldots, n, \tag{4}$$

$$\sum_{j=l}^{n} \sum_{i=1}^{k} p_{ij} \geq k - l + 1 \qquad \text{for all} \quad l \leq k, \quad l = 2, \ldots, n. \tag{5'}$$

The proof of this result follows that of E.2 and is omitted.

E.4. Proposition. An $n \times n$ matrix P satisfies
$$yP \in \mathscr{D} \text{ and } yP \prec y \qquad \text{for all} \quad y \in \mathscr{D}$$
if and only if (3), (4), and (5) hold and
$$\sum_{j=1}^{n} p_{ij} = 1, \qquad i = 1, \ldots, n. \tag{6}$$

Proof. Suppose that $yP \in \mathscr{D}$ and $yP \prec y$ for all $y \in \mathscr{D}$. Then by E.2, (3), (4), and (5) hold. With $y = e_k$, the condition $yPe' = ye'$ becomes $\sum_{i=1}^{k} \sum_{j=1}^{n} p_{ij} = k$, $k = 1, \ldots, n$, which is equivalent to (6). This result can also be obtained by combining (5) with $l = n$ and (5') with $l = 1$.

Conversely, if (3), (4), (5), and (6) hold, then by E.2, $yP \prec_w y$ for all $y \in \mathscr{D}$. But (6) also yields $yPe' = ye'$, so that $yP \prec y$. ||

F Proofs of Birkhoff's Theorem and Refinements

A number of proofs of Birkhoff's theorem (Theorem A.2) have been offered; see, e.g., Berge (1958, 1959, 1971), Dulmage and Halperin (1955), Hammersley and Mauldon (1956), Hoffman and Wielandt

48   2. Doubly Stochastic Matrices

(1953), von Neumann (1953), Mirsky (1958c), Révész (1962), Ryser (1963), and Vogel (1963). Dantzig (1951) gives an algorithm for solving a transportation problem, the solution of which leads to Birkhoff's theorem. Most of these proofs either have a combinatorial nature or are geometrically oriented. Here one proof of each kind is given. The geometric proof makes use of some elementary properties of convex sets. General discussions of doubly stochastic matrices and Birkhoff's theorem are given by Ando (1989) and Seneta (2006).

Geometric Preliminaries

The convex hull of a finite nonempty set of points in $\mathscr{R}^k$ is called a *convex polytope*. Every bounded nonempty intersection of a finite number of closed half-spaces (i.e., sets of the form $\{x : ax' \leq q\}$, where $a \in \mathscr{R}^k$ and $q \in \mathscr{R}$) is a convex polytope (Grünbaum, 1967, p. 32).

The $n \times n$ doubly stochastic matrices can be viewed as a convex polytope in $\mathscr{R}^k$ with $k = n^2$. To see this, rewrite conditions (1) and (2) of Section A as

$$p_{ij} \geq 0, \quad i,j = 1,\ldots,n, \tag{1}$$

$$\sum_i p_{ij} \leq 1, \quad \sum_i p_{ij} \geq 1, \quad j = 1,\ldots,n,$$
$$\sum_j p_{ij} \leq 1, \quad \sum_j p_{ij} \geq 1, \quad i = 1,\ldots,n-1. \tag{2}$$

Here the index i is allowed to run only up to $n - 1$ to eliminate an obvious redundancy in the conditions. Each of the $n^2 + 4n - 2$ conditions of (1) and (2) defines a closed half-space in $\mathscr{R}^{n^2}$, and the doubly stochastic matrices constitute their intersection. By exhibiting examples it is easy to see that the intersection is not empty. It is also clear that the intersection is bounded because it lies in the positive orthant and on the hyperplane $\sum_{i,j} p_{ij} = n$.

Each extreme point of the convex polytope

$$\bigcap_{l=1}^{N} \{x : a^{(l)} x' \leq q_l\} \subset \mathscr{R}^k$$

must lie on at least k distinct hyperplanes $\{x : a^{(l)} x' = q_l\}$, where $a^{(l)} = (a_1^{(l)}, \ldots, a_k^{(l)})$. This is just a consequence of the familiar algebraic fact that a point in $\mathscr{R}^k$ is not determined by less than k linear equations.

For the convex polytope in $\mathscr{R}^{n^2}$ that is formed by the doubly stochastic matrices, an extreme point must satisfy $p_{ij} = 0$ for at least

F. Proofs of Birkhoff's Theorem and Refinements

$n^2 - (2n - 1) = (n - 1)^2$ pairs (i, j) because there are at most $2n - 1$ distinct hyperplanes among the faces of the half-spaces (2).

First proof of A.2. Suppose that $P = (p_{ij})$ is an extreme point in the convex set of doubly stochastic $n \times n$ matrices. Then, as was just observed, it must be that $p_{ij} = 0$ for at least $(n-1)^2$ pairs (i, j). At least one row must have $n - 1$ zero entries and the remaining entry one [by putting only $n - 2$ zero entries in each row, only $n(n-2) = (n-1)^2 - 1$ zeros would be distributed]. In the column containing this unit entry, all other entries must be zero. If this row and column are deleted from P, then an $(n - 1) \times (n - 1)$ doubly stochastic matrix P^* is obtained.

To see that P^* must be an extreme point in the set of $(n-1) \times (n-1)$ doubly stochastic matrices, suppose for notational convenience that P^* is obtained from P by deleting the last row and column. Then if P^* has a representation as $\lambda P_1^* + (1 - \lambda) P_2^*$, $0 < \lambda < 1$, where P_1^* and P_2^* are doubly stochastic, it follows that

$$P = \lambda \begin{bmatrix} P_1^* & 0 \\ 0 & 1 \end{bmatrix} + (1 - \lambda) \begin{bmatrix} P_2^* & 0 \\ 0 & 1 \end{bmatrix}.$$

But this shows that $P_1^* = P_2^*$ (because P is extreme); hence, P^* is extreme.

A repetition of the preceding argument shows that P^* must have at least one row with a unit entry and all other entries zero. By using an induction on n, it follows that P is a permutation matrix.

To show that each $n \times n$ permutation matrix is extreme, suppose that P is a permutation matrix and $P = \lambda P_1 + (1 - \lambda) P_2$, $0 < \lambda < 1$, where P_1 and P_2 are doubly stochastic. Because P_1 and P_2 have entries in the interval $[0, 1]$, P cannot have entries consisting of zeros and units unless $P_1 = P_2$.

To complete the proof, it must be shown that the class of doubly stochastic matrices is the convex hull of its extreme points. This follows from the fact that the class of doubly stochastic matrices is closed and bounded (Rockafellar, 1970, Corollary 18.5.1). ∥

The theorem of Philip Hall on systems of distinct representatives or the equivalent theorem of Dénes König [see, e.g., Mirsky (1971, pp. 27 and 188), or Brualdi and Ryser (1991)] can be used to provide combinatorial proofs of A.2 (Berge, 1962, p. 106; Birkhoff, 1946; Dulmage and Halperin, 1955; Hall, 1967, p. 52; Mirsky, 1971, p. 192). One way of doing this is to use the Hall–König result to first prove the following lemma.

F.1. Lemma. If the $n \times n$ matrix $P = (p_{ij})$ is doubly stochastic, then for some permutation $(i_1, \ldots, i_n)$ of $(1, 2, \ldots, n)$,
$$p_{1i_1} p_{2i_2} \cdots p_{ni_n} > 0.$$

Proofs of F.1 are given by Mirsky (1971, p. 185) and Berge (1962, p. 105).

Before applying the lemma to prove Birkhoff's theorem, notice that it is equivalent to the fact that the permanent of a doubly stochastic matrix is strictly positive. The *permanent*, per P, of the $n \times n$ matrix $P = (p_{ij})$ is given by
$$\text{per } P = \sum_\pi p_{1\pi(1)} p_{2\pi(2)} \cdots p_{n\pi(n)},$$
where the summation extends over all $n!$ permutations π of $(1, \ldots, n)$. Detailed discussions of permanents are given by Minc (1978) and Brualdi and Ryser (1991).

Remark. A much stronger claim was made by the *conjecture of van der Waerden* (1926) which says that if P is doubly stochastic and $n \times n$, then the permanent per $(P) \geq n!/n^n$. The lower bound here is just the permanent of the matrix with all entries equal to $1/n$. This conjecture received considerable attention and spawned a spectrum of generalizations, variations, and partial resolutions. By 1969, the conjecture had been proved for $n \leq 5$. In 1981, two independent proofs of the conjecture for every n were announced [Egorychev (1981) and Falikman (1981)]. A third proof was provided by Gyires (1980). The result is now associated with the name Egorychev, or sometimes Egorychev–Falikman. To obtain some insight into the priority conflict, and more importantly into the methods of proof used by these researchers, the reader will profit by perusing Egorychev (1996) and Gyires (1996). See also Gyires (2001), which suggests that key ideas for the proof were already available in 1977. An excellent brief survey of the life and times of the van der Waerden conjecture can be found in Minc's (1982) review of a 1980 preprint of Egorychev's proof. A self-contained discussion of Egorychev's method can also be found in the excellent survey article by Ando (1989). See also Minc (1978).

Second proof of A.2. The idea of the following proof seems to have originated with Dulmage and Halperin (1955).

Let $(i_1, \ldots, i_n)$ be a permutation of $(1, 2, \ldots, n)$ such that the product $p_{1i_1} p_{2i_2} \cdots p_{ni_n} \neq 0$, the existence of which is ensured by F.1. Denote the permutation matrix corresponding to $(i_1, \ldots, i_n)$ by P_1; let $c_1 = \min\{p_{1i_1}, \ldots, p_{ni_n}\}$, and define R by
$$P = c_1 P_1 + R.$$

Because $c_1 P_1$ has element c_1 in positions $1i_1, 2i_2, \ldots, ni_n$ and P has elements $p_{1i_1}, \ldots, p_{ni_n}$ in the corresponding positions, the choice of c_1 ensures $p_{k i_k} - c_1 \geq 0$ with equality for some k. Consequently, R has nonnegative elements and contains at least one more zero element than P. Now observe that
$$e = eP = ec_1 P_1 + eR = c_1 e + eR,$$
$$e' = Pe' = c_1 P_1 e' + Re' = c_1 e' + Re'. \tag{3}$$
If $c_1 = 1$, then $R = 0$ and P is already a permutation matrix so the desired decomposition is trivial. Otherwise, $c_1 < 1$ and from (3) it follows that $R/(1 - c_1)$ is doubly stochastic. In this case, R can be decomposed so as to reduce again the number of nonzero entries in the remainder. Consequently, for some k,
$$P = c_1 P_1 + \cdots + c_k P_k,$$
where each P_i is a permutation matrix.

It remains to observe that
$$e = eP = c_1 e P_1 + \cdots + c_k e P_k = (c_1 + \cdots + c_k) e,$$
so that $\sum c_i = 1$. ||

Note. Zhu (2004) provides a variational proof of Birkhoff's theorem A.2 that the extreme points of the convex set of doubly stochastic matrices are the permutation matrices.

Refinements of Birkhoff's Theorem

In giving the second proof of A.2 above, Dulmage and Halperin (1955) show that after at most $n^2 - n$ steps of the decomposition, one arrives at a matrix of nonnegative elements with exactly n positive elements. Consequently, they conclude that every doubly stochastic matrix can be written as a convex combination of at most $n^2 - n + 1$ permutation matrices.

This result was improved independently by Marcus and Ree (1959) and by Farahat and Mirsky (1960), who show that the bound $n^2 - n + 1$ can be reduced to $n^2 - 2n + 2$. Additionally, Farahat and Mirsky (1960) show that $n^2 - 2n + 2$ is the best possible bound. These results are stated formally in the following theorem.

F.2. Theorem. Every $n \times n$ doubly stochastic matrix can be represented as a convex combination of at most $n^2 - 2n + 2$ permutation matrices. The number $n^2 - 2n + 2$ cannot be replaced by a smaller number.

Farahat and Mirsky (1960) obtain that the bound $n^2 - 2n + 2$ cannot be improved via a series of lemmas, and the proof of this result is omitted. We give the geometric proof of Marcus and Ree (1959) that shows that representation in terms of $n^2 - 2n + 2$ permutation matrices is possible. A similar proof was given by Hammersley (1961).

Proof. Because an $n \times n$ doubly stochastic matrix is determined by the elements in its first $n - 1$ rows and columns, the class of all $n \times n$ doubly stochastic matrices can be regarded as a convex polytope in $(n-1)^2$ dimensions. Now we apply the basic theorem of Carathéodory [see, e.g., Grünbaum (1967)] which says that if A is a convex subset of $\mathscr{R}^d$, then each point in A is expressible as a convex combination of at most $d + 1$ extreme points. In our case, $d = (n-1)^2$, so $d + 1 = (n-1)^2 + 1 = n^2 - 2n + 2$. ||

A refinement of the bound $n^2 - 2n + 2$ based on additional conditions has been obtained by Johnson, Dulmage, and Mendelsohn (1960). See G.8 for another bound.

Extensions of Birkhoff's theorem

Caron, Li, Mikusiński, Sherwood, and Taylor (1996) discuss the problem of characterizing the extreme points of the set of all $n \times m$ matrices with unit row averages and unit column averages (i.e., matrices P such that $p_{ij} \geq 0$ and $\sum_{i=1}^{m} p_{ij} = m$, $j = 1, 2, \ldots, n$, and $\sum_{j=1}^{n} p_{ij} = n$, $i = 1, 2, \ldots, m$). (In their paper, they call such matrices $n \times m$ doubly stochastic matrices. Some potential for confusion exists because the definition does not reduce to the usual definition of a doubly stochastic matrix when $m = n$.)

Li, Mikusiński, Sherwood, and Taylor (1996) discuss the extreme points of the convex polygon of all nonnegative functions on the product $\{1, 2, \ldots, m_1\} \times \cdots \times \{1, 2, \ldots, m_k\}$ with fixed marginals, which can be viewed as an extension of doubly stochastic matrices to the k-dimensional case. A complete characterization is provided in the $3 \times 3 \times 3$ case.

G Classes of Doubly Stochastic Matrices

Three special classes of $n \times n$ doubly stochastic matrices are introduced in Section B: products of a finite number (or at most $n - 1$) T-transforms; orthostochastic matrices; and uniformly tapered matrices. If $x \prec y$, then according to B.6, x is the image of y under at least one doubly stochastic matrix from each of these classes. In this section, some additional properties of these classes are obtained.

G. Classes of Doubly Stochastic Matrices   53

All 2×2 doubly stochastic matrices are orthostochastic. They are all T-transforms and they can all be written as a product of a uniformly tapered matrix and a permutation matrix. But in higher dimensions, these classes of matrices are distinct.

G.1. Examples. Let

$$P_1 = \frac{1}{2}\begin{bmatrix} 1 & 1 & 0 \\ 1 & 0 & 1 \\ 0 & 1 & 1 \end{bmatrix}, \qquad P_2 = \frac{1}{6}\begin{bmatrix} 0 & 3 & 3 \\ 3 & 1 & 2 \\ 3 & 2 & 1 \end{bmatrix},$$

$$P_3 = \begin{bmatrix} 1 & 0 & 0 \\ 0 & \frac{1}{4} & \frac{3}{4} \\ 0 & \frac{3}{4} & \frac{1}{4} \end{bmatrix} \begin{bmatrix} \frac{1}{2} & 0 & \frac{1}{2} \\ 0 & 1 & 0 \\ \frac{1}{2} & 0 & \frac{1}{2} \end{bmatrix} \begin{bmatrix} \frac{1}{2} & \frac{1}{2} & 0 \\ \frac{1}{2} & \frac{1}{2} & 0 \\ 0 & 0 & 1 \end{bmatrix} = \frac{1}{16}\begin{bmatrix} 4 & 4 & 8 \\ 5 & 5 & 6 \\ 7 & 7 & 2 \end{bmatrix},$$

$$P_4 = \frac{1}{4}\begin{bmatrix} 3 & 1 & 0 \\ 1 & 2 & 1 \\ 0 & 1 & 3 \end{bmatrix}, \qquad P_5 = \frac{1}{16}\begin{bmatrix} 9 & 6 & 1 \\ 6 & 4 & 6 \\ 1 & 6 & 9 \end{bmatrix},$$

$$P_6 = \frac{1}{64}\begin{bmatrix} 49 & 14 & 1 \\ 14 & 36 & 14 \\ 1 & 14 & 49 \end{bmatrix}, \quad P_7 = \begin{bmatrix} 1 & 0 & 0 \\ 0 & \frac{1}{4} & \frac{3}{4} \\ 0 & \frac{3}{4} & \frac{1}{4} \end{bmatrix} \begin{bmatrix} \frac{1}{2} & 0 & \frac{1}{2} \\ 0 & 1 & 0 \\ \frac{1}{2} & 0 & \frac{1}{2} \end{bmatrix} = \begin{bmatrix} \frac{1}{2} & 0 & \frac{1}{2} \\ \frac{3}{8} & \frac{1}{4} & \frac{3}{8} \\ \frac{1}{8} & \frac{3}{4} & \frac{1}{8} \end{bmatrix},$$

$$P_8 = \begin{bmatrix} 1 & 0 & 0 \\ 0 & \frac{1}{2} & \frac{1}{2} \\ 0 & \frac{1}{2} & \frac{1}{2} \end{bmatrix} \begin{bmatrix} \frac{1}{2} & 0 & \frac{1}{2} \\ 0 & 1 & 0 \\ \frac{1}{2} & 0 & \frac{1}{2} \end{bmatrix} \begin{bmatrix} 1 & 0 & 0 \\ 0 & \frac{1}{2} & \frac{1}{2} \\ 0 & \frac{1}{2} & \frac{1}{2} \end{bmatrix} = \begin{bmatrix} \frac{1}{2} & \frac{1}{4} & \frac{1}{4} \\ \frac{1}{4} & \frac{3}{8} & \frac{3}{8} \\ \frac{1}{4} & \frac{3}{8} & \frac{3}{8} \end{bmatrix},$$

$$P_9 = \begin{bmatrix} 1 & 0 & 0 \\ 0 & \frac{1}{2} & \frac{1}{2} \\ 0 & \frac{1}{2} & \frac{1}{2} \end{bmatrix}.$$

The properties of these matrices are exhibited in Table 1.

TABLE 1

	P_1	P_2	P_3	P_4	P_5	P_6	P_7	P_8	P_9
Product of T-transforms	No	(No)	Yes	No	(No)	(No)	Yes	Yes	Yes
Permuted uniformly tapered	No	No	No	Yes	No	Yes	No	Yes	Yes
Orthostochastic	No	No	No	No	Yes	Yes	Yes	No	Yes
Hessenberg	Yes	No	No	Yes	No	No	No	No	Yes
Positive Semiddefinite	No	No	No	Yes	No	Yes	No	Yes	Yes

Explanation of Table 1

In Table 1, the entries (No) indicate that the corresponding matrices are not products of at most $n-1 = 2$ T-transforms; whether or not they are products of more than 2 T-transforms has not been determined. In the labeling of the first row, "Product of T-transforms" means a product of finitely many T-transforms. "Permuted uniformly tapered" means that the matrix is of the form $\Pi_1 R \Pi_2$, where Π_1 and Π_2 are permutation matrices and R is uniformly tapered.

Example P_1 was given by Alan Hoffman (Horn, 1954a) to show that there are doubly stochastic matrices that are not orthostochastic, and P_2 was given by Schur (1923) for the same purpose.

Most of the entries in Table 1 are easily verified. That P_1 and P_4 are not products of T-transforms follows from the fact that, in the 3×3 case, finite products of T-transforms can never have 2 or 3 zero entries (only 6, 4, 1, or 0). The orthostochastic matrices P_5 and P_6 derive from the orthogonal matrices Γ_5 and Γ_6, where

$$\Gamma_5 = \frac{1}{4} \begin{bmatrix} 3 & \sqrt{6} & 1 \\ -\sqrt{6} & 2 & \sqrt{6} \\ 1 & -\sqrt{6} & 3 \end{bmatrix}, \quad \Gamma_6 = \frac{1}{8} \begin{bmatrix} 7 & \sqrt{14} & 1 \\ -\sqrt{14} & 6 & \sqrt{14} \\ 1 & \sqrt{14} & 7 \end{bmatrix}.$$

The example P_3 is a product of three T-transforms that is not orthostochastic. But products of two T-transforms, like P_7, are always orthostochastic. To see this, it is sufficient to consider the product of two 3×3 T-transforms:

$$\begin{bmatrix} \alpha & \overline{\alpha} & 0 \\ \overline{\alpha} & \alpha & 0 \\ 0 & 0 & 1 \end{bmatrix} \begin{bmatrix} \beta & 0 & \overline{\beta} \\ 0 & 1 & 0 \\ \overline{\beta} & 0 & \beta \end{bmatrix} = \begin{bmatrix} \alpha\beta & \overline{\alpha} & \alpha\overline{\beta} \\ \overline{\alpha}\beta & \alpha & \overline{\alpha}\overline{\beta} \\ \overline{\beta} & 0 & \beta \end{bmatrix},$$

where $0 \leq \alpha \leq 1$, $\overline{\alpha} = 1 - \alpha$, $0 \leq \beta \leq 1$, $\overline{\beta} = 1 - \beta$. Then the choice of signs as in

$$\begin{bmatrix} -\sqrt{\alpha\beta} & +\sqrt{\overline{\alpha}} & -\sqrt{\alpha\overline{\beta}} \\ +\sqrt{\overline{\alpha}\beta} & +\sqrt{\alpha} & +\sqrt{\overline{\alpha}\overline{\beta}} \\ +\sqrt{\overline{\beta}} & 0 & -\sqrt{\beta} \end{bmatrix}$$

yields an orthogonal matrix.

The Doubly Stochastic Matrices of a Given Majorization

For given vectors x and y such that $x \prec y$, the set of doubly stochastic matrices P such that $x = yP$ is clearly convex. Very little is known

G. Classes of Doubly Stochastic Matrices 55

about this set beyond the fact that it includes a product of at most $n-1$ T-transforms, an orthostochastic matrix, and a product $\Pi_1 R \Pi_2$ of a uniformly tapered matrix R and permutation matrices Π_1, Π_2.

The set of all doubly stochastic matrices P such that $x = yP$ can contain but one matrix, as is the case, e.g., when y has distinct components and P is a permutation. Lemma G.6 provides necessary and sufficient conditions for uniqueness. The following example may be of interest.

G.2. Example. If $x = (4, 3, 2)$ and $y = (5, 3, 1)$, then $x \prec y$. For any doubly stochastic matrix $P = (p_{ij})$ such that $x = yP$,

$$x_j = \sum_{i=1}^{3} y_i p_{ij}, \qquad j = 1, 2, 3.$$

It follows from the first two equations (the third is redundant) and the fact that the columns add to 1 that

$$3 = 4p_{11} + 2p_{21},$$
$$2 = 4p_{12} + 2p_{22}.$$

If $u = p_{12}$ and $v = p_{21}$, then $P = P(u, v)$ has the form

$$P(u,v) = \begin{bmatrix} \dfrac{3-2v}{4} & u & \dfrac{1}{4} + \dfrac{v}{2} - u \\ v & 1 - 2u & 2u - v \\ \dfrac{1-2v}{4} & u & \dfrac{3}{4} + \dfrac{v}{2} - u \end{bmatrix}.$$

Since all the elements are nonnegative, the feasible region for u and v is shaded in Fig. 1. The extreme points are the matrices $P(u, v)$:

$$P(0,0) = \begin{bmatrix} \tfrac{3}{4} & 0 & \tfrac{1}{4} \\ 0 & 1 & 0 \\ \tfrac{1}{4} & 0 & \tfrac{3}{4} \end{bmatrix}, \qquad P(\tfrac{1}{2}, \tfrac{1}{2}) = \begin{bmatrix} \tfrac{1}{2} & \tfrac{1}{2} & 0 \\ \tfrac{1}{2} & 0 & \tfrac{1}{2} \\ 0 & \tfrac{1}{2} & \tfrac{1}{2} \end{bmatrix},$$

$$P(\tfrac{1}{4}, 0) = \begin{bmatrix} \tfrac{3}{4} & \tfrac{1}{4} & 0 \\ 0 & \tfrac{1}{2} & \tfrac{1}{2} \\ \tfrac{1}{4} & \tfrac{1}{4} & \tfrac{1}{2} \end{bmatrix}, \qquad P(\tfrac{1}{4}, \tfrac{1}{2}) = \begin{bmatrix} \tfrac{1}{2} & \tfrac{1}{4} & \tfrac{1}{4} \\ \tfrac{1}{2} & \tfrac{1}{2} & 0 \\ 0 & \tfrac{1}{4} & \tfrac{3}{4} \end{bmatrix}.$$

T-Transform

The matrix $P(0, 0)$ is itself a T-transform and satisfies $x = yP$.

56   2. Doubly Stochastic Matrices

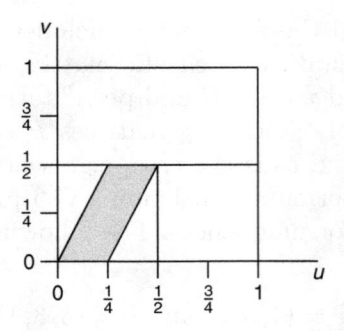

Figure 1. Feasible regions for (u, v).

Uniformly Tapered

The conditions for $P(u, v)$ to be uniformly tapered require symmetry, so that $u = v$. This yields

$$P(u, u) = \begin{bmatrix} \frac{3}{4} - \frac{u}{2} & u & \frac{1}{4} - \frac{u}{2} \\ u & 1 - 2u & u \\ \frac{1}{4} - \frac{u}{2} & u & \frac{3}{4} - \frac{u}{2} \end{bmatrix},$$

and the condition that $P(u, u)$ be uniformly tapered imposes the constraint $\frac{1}{6} \leq u \leq \frac{1}{3}$.

Symmetric Orthostochastic

The conditions of orthogonality require

$$\epsilon_1 \sqrt{\left(\frac{3}{4} - \frac{u}{2}\right)u} + \epsilon_2 \sqrt{u(1 - 2u)} + \epsilon_3 \sqrt{\left(\frac{1}{4} - \frac{u}{2}\right)(4)} = 0,$$

$$\delta_1 \sqrt{\left(\frac{3 - 2u}{4}\right)\left(\frac{1 - 2u}{4}\right)} + \delta_2 u + \delta_3 \sqrt{\left(\frac{3 - 2u}{4}\right)\left(\frac{1 - 2u}{4}\right)} = 0,$$

where the ϵ_i and δ_i are ± 1. The choice $\delta_1 = -\delta_3$ yields $u = 0$ and the condition $\delta_1 = \delta_3$ yields $u = \frac{3}{8}$. Consequently,

$$P(\tfrac{3}{8}, \tfrac{3}{8}) = \begin{bmatrix} \frac{9}{16} & \frac{3}{8} & \frac{1}{16} \\ \frac{3}{8} & \frac{2}{8} & \frac{3}{8} \\ \frac{1}{16} & \frac{3}{8} & \frac{9}{16} \end{bmatrix}$$

is symmetric orthostochastic, and the orthogonal matrix generating this matrix is

$$\begin{bmatrix} +\sqrt{\frac{9}{16}} & +\sqrt{\frac{3}{8}} & +\sqrt{\frac{1}{16}} \\ -\sqrt{\frac{3}{8}} & +\sqrt{\frac{2}{8}} & +\sqrt{\frac{3}{8}} \\ +\sqrt{\frac{1}{16}} & -\sqrt{\frac{3}{8}} & +\sqrt{\frac{9}{16}} \end{bmatrix}.$$

In the above example, the set of doubly stochastic matrices P such that $x = yP$ has four extreme points. Even in the case $n = 3$, the number of extreme points is not known.

Uniformly Tapered Matrices

G.3. Proposition (Hoffman, 1969). $x \prec y$ if and only if there exists a uniformly tapered matrix R such that $x_\downarrow = y_\downarrow R$.

Of course, $x_\downarrow = y_\downarrow R$ means that there exist permutation matrices Π_1, Π_2 such that $x = y\Pi_1 R \Pi_2$.

Hoffman (1969) gives three proofs of this result. A proof due to Dragomir Djoković is the simplest of the three, though perhaps the least illuminating.

Proof. For notational convenience, assume that $x, y \in \mathcal{D}$; that is, $x = x_\downarrow$, $y = y_\downarrow$.

The result is trivial for $n = 1$. For $n > 1$, two cases are considered.

Case 1. Suppose there is a coincidence at k; i.e., $\sum_1^k x_i = \sum_1^k y_i$ for some $k < n$. Write $x = (\dot{x}, \ddot{x})$, $y = (\dot{y}, \ddot{y})$, with $\dot{x} : 1 \times k$, $\dot{y} : 1 \times k$, $\dot{x} \prec \dot{y}$, $\ddot{x} \prec \ddot{y}$ so that, by induction, there exist uniformly tapered matrices $R^{(1)}$ and $R^{(2)}$ such that

$$\dot{x} = \dot{y} R^{(1)}, \qquad \ddot{x} = \ddot{y} R^{(2)}.$$

But then

$$(\dot{x}, \ddot{x}) = (\dot{y}, \ddot{y}) \begin{bmatrix} R^{(1)} & 0 \\ 0 & R^{(2)} \end{bmatrix}.$$

The proof for this case will be completed by showing that $R = \mathrm{diag}(R^{(1)}, R^{(2)})$ is uniformly tapered. The first row and last column of R are $r_{11}^{(1)}, \ldots, r_{1k}^{(1)}, 0, \ldots, 0$ and $r_{nn}^{(2)}, \ldots, r_{n,n-k+1}^{(2)}, 0, \ldots, 0$, which satisfy (2) and (3) of B.5, respectively. Condition (4) of B.5 is satisfied if $2 \leq i \leq j \leq k-1$ or $k+2 \leq i \leq j \leq n-1$. Thus it is necessary only to check the case that $i \leq k$ and $j \geq k$. The only nontrivial choice of i and j is when $i \leq k$ and $j = k$. But then

$$\begin{bmatrix} r_{i-1,k} & r_{i-1,k+1} \\ r_{i,k} & r_{i,k+1} \end{bmatrix} = \begin{bmatrix} r_{i-1,k}^{(1)} & 0 \\ r_{i,k}^{(1)} & 0 \end{bmatrix},$$

in which case condition (4) of B.5 reduces to $r_{i,k}^{(1)} \geq r_{i-1,k}^{(1)}$, which was guaranteed by the hypothesis.

Case 2. Suppose that for all $k = 1, \ldots, n-1$, $\sum_1^k x_i < \sum_1^k y_i$. By 5.A.7.b there exists a unique α, $0 < \alpha \leq 1$, such that $x \prec \alpha(\overline{y}, \ldots, \overline{y}) + (1-\alpha)y \equiv z$ has a coincidence for at least one point k. By case 1, there exists a doubly stochastic uniformly tapered matrix R such that

$$x = zR = [\alpha(\overline{y}, \ldots, \overline{y}) + (1-\alpha)y]R.$$

Note that $(\overline{y}, \ldots, \overline{y}) = ye'e/n \equiv yR_0$, where R_0 is uniformly tapered. Consequently,

$$x = [\alpha y R_0 + (1-\alpha)y]R = y[\alpha R_0 + (1-\alpha)R].$$

But the set of uniformly tapered matrices is convex, which completes the proof. ||

We have used the fact that the set of doubly stochastic uniformly tapered matrices is convex, and it is of interest to identify the extreme points.

G.3.a. Proposition (Hoffman, 1969). The extreme points of the set of uniformly tapered matrices have the form

$$R = E_{r_1} \oplus \cdots \oplus E_{r_k}, \qquad (1)$$

where $E_r = (1/r)e'e$ is the $r \times r$ matrix with all entries equal to $1/r$.

Of course, the set of uniformly tapered matrices is the convex hull of these extreme points, because the class of uniformly tapered matrices is closed and bounded (Rockafellar, 1970, Corollary 18.5.1).

For further discussion of uniformly tapered matrices and a generalization, see Kästner and Zylka (1993).

Nonsingular Doubly Stochastic Matrices

Doubly stochastic matrices may or may not be singular. For what pairs of vectors x, y such that $x \prec y$ does there exist a nonsingular doubly stochastic matrix P such that $x = yP$?

The answer to this question involves the notion of a coincidence. If $x, y \in \mathscr{D}$ and $\sum_1^k x_i = \sum_1^k y_i$ for some $k < n$, then we say there is a *coincidence at* k.

G.4. Lemma (Levow, 1972). If $n > 1$, $x \prec y$ on $\mathscr{D}$, $x_1 > x_n$, and there are no coincidences, then there is a nonsingular doubly stochastic matrix P such that $x = yP$.

The proof of this result is not given here.

G.4.a. Suppose that $x \prec y$ on $\mathscr{D}$ and coincidences occur only at $k_1 < k_2 < \cdots < k_{l+1} = n$. If $x_1 > x_{k_1}$ and x_{k_i+1}, $i = 1, \ldots, l$, then there is a nonsingular doubly stochastic matrix P such that $x = yP$.

To prove this result, it is necessary to observe only that P can be obtained as a direct sum of nonsingular doubly stochastic matrices obtained from G.4.

Positive Doubly Stochastic Matrices

For what pairs of vectors x, y such that $x \prec y$ does there exist a strictly positive doubly stochastic matrix P (i.e., with $p_{ij} > 0$ for every i, j) such that $x = yP$?

G.5. Lemma (Brualdi, 1984). If $x, y \in \mathscr{D}$ are such that $x \prec y$, then there exists a doubly stochastic matrix P with all elements strictly positive such that $x = yP$ if and only if one of the following holds:

(i) $x = c(1, \ldots, 1)$, for some $c \in \mathscr{R}$;

(ii) there are no coincidences between x and y.

Uniqueness of the Doubly Stochastic Matrix of a Given Majorization

Brualdi (1984) identifies a simple necessary and sufficient condition to ensure that a unique doubly stochastic matrix is associated with a given majorization.

G.6. Lemma (Brualdi, 1984). Let $x, y \in \mathscr{D}$ be such that $x \prec y$. There exists a unique doubly stochastic matrix P with $x = yP$ if and only if the following two conditions hold:

(i) y has distinct components;

(ii) for some integer $q \leq n$, x and y have coincidences at positions $1 \leq k_1 < k_2 < \ldots < k_{q-1} \leq n-1$, where $k_j - k_{j-1} \leq 2$ for each $j = 1, 2, \ldots, q-2$.

Dahl (2004) provides a characterization of situations in which the unique doubly stochastic matrix in G.6 is of tridiagonal form.

Hessenberg Matrices

Instead of characterizing majorization in terms of uniformly tapered matrices, Brualdi and Hwang (1996) provide an alternative description in terms of Hessenberg matrices.

An $n \times n$ matrix $H = (h_{ij})$ is called a *lower Hessenberg matrix* or, more simply, a *Hessenberg matrix* if it is of the form

$$H = \begin{bmatrix} h_{11} & h_{12} & 0 & \cdots & 0 \\ h_{21} & h_{22} & h_{23} & 0 & \cdots \\ & & \cdots & & \\ & & \cdots & & \\ h_{n1} & h_{n2} & \cdots & & h_{nn} \end{bmatrix};$$

that is, $h_{ij} = 0$ for $j > i+1$. The transpose of a Hessenberg matrix is an upper Hessenberg matrix with elements satisfying $h_{ij} = 0$ if $j < i - 1$. Note that identity matrices and lower triangular matrices are simple examples of Hessenberg matrices.

A suitable doubly stochastic matrix for the majorization $x \prec y$ can be constructed using Hessenberg matrices as follows.

G.7. Proposition (Brualdi and Hwang, 1996). A necessary and sufficient condition for $x \prec y$ is that for some $r \leq n$ there exist doubly stochastic Hessenberg matrices $H_i, i = 1, 2, \ldots, r$, such that

$$x_\downarrow = y_\downarrow (H_1 \oplus H_2 \oplus \ldots \oplus H_r)',$$

where the sum of the orders of the H_i is n.

G.7.a. Proposition (Brualdi and Hwang, 1996). If $x \prec y$, then $x_\downarrow = y_\downarrow PHQ$, where P and Q are permutation matrices and H is a doubly stochastic Hessenberg matrix.

Note. Proposition G.7 contains both necessary and sufficient conditions, whereas the result G.7.a is only in one direction.

Proposition G.7 is used in the proof of the following:

G.8. Corollary (Brualdi and Hwang, 1996). The majorization $x \prec y$ holds if and only if x is expressible as a convex combination of at most $(n^2 - n + 2)/2$ permutations of y.

Notes. Hwang (1999) supplies an alternative proof of G.8 using a more complicated version of Hessenberg matrices. A significant improvement of the bound in G.8 is obtained by Zhan (2003) by reducing the bound from $(n^2 - n + 2)/2$ to n.

G.9. Proposition (Chao and Wong, 1992). For $x, y \in \mathscr{R}^n$, $x \prec y$ if and only if $x_{\downarrow} = y_{\downarrow} A$ for some positive semidefinite doubly stochastic matrix A.

The proof provided by Chao and Wong (1992) uses the theory of M-matrices (see 9.I) and is too detailed to reproduce here.

H More Examples of Doubly Stochastic and Doubly Substochastic Matrices

In the following, some general examples of doubly stochastic matrices are generated.

H.1. Example. A *Latin square* of order n is an $n \times n$ matrix in which for some $a_1, \ldots, a_n$, every row and every column is a permutation of $\{a_1, a_2, \ldots, a_n\}$. Examples of Latin squares of order 3, 4, and 5 are

$$\begin{bmatrix} 1 & 2 & 3 \\ 3 & 1 & 2 \\ 2 & 3 & 1 \end{bmatrix}, \quad \begin{bmatrix} 1 & 2 & 3 & 4 \\ 4 & 3 & 2 & 1 \\ 2 & 1 & 4 & 3 \\ 3 & 4 & 1 & 2 \end{bmatrix}, \quad \begin{bmatrix} 5 & 1 & 4 & 2 & 3 \\ 1 & 2 & 5 & 3 & 4 \\ 4 & 5 & 3 & 1 & 2 \\ 2 & 3 & 1 & 4 & 5 \\ 3 & 4 & 2 & 5 & 1 \end{bmatrix}.$$

Define an $n \times n$ matrix $A = (a_{ij})$ by

$$a_{ij} = \left\{ (-1)^i \left[\frac{i}{2}\right] + (-1)^j \left[\frac{j}{2}\right] \right\} \pmod{n},$$

where $[x]$ is the least integer $\geq x$. The matrix of order 5 above is of this form. Such a matrix has the property that each integer $1, 2, \ldots, n$ appears exactly once in every row and every column and is consequently a Latin square. This class of matrices and its relation to graphs is discussed by Beineke and Harary (1965) and Brualdi and Ryser (1991). By making the correspondence i with p_i, where $p_i \geq 0$, $\sum p_i = 1$, a doubly stochastic matrix is obtained. Because some doubly stochastic matrices have rows (or columns) that are not permutations of each other, it is clear that not all doubly stochastic matrices arise in this way.

Circulant Matrices

H.2. Example. A matrix of the form

$$C = \begin{bmatrix} a_0 & a_1 & a_2 & \cdots & a_{n-1} \\ a_{n-1} & a_0 & a_1 & \cdots & a_{n-2} \\ a_{n-2} & a_{n-1} & a_0 & \cdots & a_{n-3} \\ \vdots & \vdots & \vdots & \vdots & \vdots \\ a_1 & a_2 & a_3 & \cdots & a_0 \end{bmatrix}$$

is called a *circular matrix*, or a *circulant*. (The literature is unclear on this name; in some instances the term "circulant" refers to the determinant of such a matrix.) Note that the matrix C is also a Latin square; not every Latin square can be permuted to become a circulant. For a more detailed discussion of circulant matrices beyond that given here, see Davis (1979).

Because the first row of C determines all the elements of the matrix, the notation $C(a_0, a_1, \ldots, a_{n-1})$ or $C(a)$, where $a = (a_0, a_1, \ldots, a_{n-1})$, provides a convenient representation of the matrix.

The particular matrix $Q = C(0, 1, 0, \ldots, 0)$ plays a singular role because

$$Q^k = C(0, , \ldots, 0, 1, 0, \ldots, 0),$$

where the 1 is in the $(k+1)$st position. Consequently,

$$C(a) = a_0 I + a_1 Q + a_2 Q^2 + \cdots + a_{n-1} Q^{n-1}. \tag{1}$$

Note that $Q^0 = Q^n = I$.

If $C(a)$ is nonsingular, then its inverse is a circulant:

$$C^{-1}(a) = C(b) = b_0 I + b_1 Q + b_2 Q^2 + \cdots + b_{n-1} Q^{n-1}.$$

In general, there is no simple formula for the inverse, but the coefficients $b_0, b_1, \ldots, b_{n-1}$ can be obtained by solving

$$C(a)C(b) = \Sigma_{i,j=0}^{n-1} a_i b_j Q^{i+j} = I,$$

where $i + j$ is taken $(\mathrm{mod}\ n)$.

If each $a_i \geq 0$ and $\sum_0^{n-1} a_i = 1$, then $C(a)$ is doubly stochastic. An important example is that of a circular moving average.

Circular Moving Average

H.3. Definition. The vector of *k*th order circular moving averages of a set of elements $x_1, x_2, \ldots, x_n$ is $x^{(k)} = (x_1^{(k)}, \ldots, x_n^{(k)})$, in which

$$x_i^{(k)} = (x_i + x_{i+1} + \cdots + x_{i+k-1})/k, \tag{2}$$

where $i+k-1$ is taken (mod n).

Equivalently, for $k = 1, \ldots, n$,
$$x^{(k)} = (x_1, x_2, \ldots, x_n) C(1/k, 0, \ldots, 0, \underbrace{1/k, \ldots, 1/k}). \tag{3}$$

For example, for $n = 4, k = 3$,
$$x^{(3)} = \left(\frac{x_1 + x_2 + x_3}{3}, \frac{x_2 + x_3 + x_4}{3}, \frac{x_3 + x_4 + x_1}{3}, \frac{x_4 + x_1 + x_2}{3} \right).$$

Clearly, a vector of moving averages has elements that are "more equal" than the elements of the original vector. In statistical time series analysis, moving averages are used to smooth data.

H.3.a. Proposition For all $k = 1, \ldots, n$, $x \succ x^{(k)}$.

Proof. This follows from (3) and the fact that $C(1/k, 0, \ldots, 0, \underbrace{1/k, \ldots, 1/k})$ is doubly stochastic. ||

H.3.b. Remark. It seems intuitive that $x^{(k)} \succ x^{(k+1)}$, because at each stage the vector of elements becomes more equal until ultimately $x^{(n)} = (\bar{x}, \ldots, \bar{x})$, where $\bar{x} = \Sigma x_i / n$. However, a proof that $x^{(k)} \succ x^{(k+1)}$ remains elusive. Note that the assumption that $x_1 \geq \cdots \geq x_n$ is necessary, as can be seen from the example $x = (6, 0, 6, 0)$, in which case $x^{(2)} = (3, 3, 3, 3)$ and $x^{(3)} = (4, 2, 4, 2)$, so that $x^{(3)} \succ x^{(2)}$. But if the same elements of x are arranged in decreasing order as $x = (6, 6, 0, 0)$, then $x^{(2)} = (6, 3, 0, 3)$ and $x^{(3)} = (4, 2, 2, 4)$, so that $x^{(2)} \succ x^{(3)}$.

Other Patterned Matrices

H.4. g-Circulants. The classical circulant, as above, shifts by one column. When the shift is by g columns, the matrix is called a *g-circulant*. From the fact that if A is a g-circulant and B is an h-circulant, then AB is a gh-circulant, a variety of doubly stochastic matrices can be generated from a single doubly stochastic matrix.

H.4.a. The following is an $(n-1)$-circulant

$$\widetilde{C} = \begin{bmatrix} a_0 & a_1 & \cdots & a_{n-2} & a_{n-1} \\ a_1 & a_2 & \cdots & a_{n-1} & a_0 \\ a_2 & a_3 & \cdots & a_0 & a_1 \\ \vdots & \vdots & & \vdots & \vdots \\ a_{n-1} & a_0 & \cdots & & a_{n-2} \end{bmatrix},$$

which is doubly stochastic whenever each $a_i \geq 0$ and $\sum_0^{n-1} a_i = 1$. Here,
$$\widetilde{C} = W_2 C = C W_2,$$
where W_2 is equal to $\widetilde{C}$ in which $a_0 = 1$ and $a_j = 0$ for $j \neq 0$.

Particularly simple special cases of C and $\widetilde{C}$ arise when $a_i = b$ if $i \neq k$ and $a_k = 1 - (n-1)b \equiv a$, $k = 0, 1, \ldots, n-1$. In order that C and $\widetilde{C}$ have nonnegative entries, b is restricted to $0 \leq b \leq 1/(n-1)$. Define W_1 equal to $\widetilde{C}$ in which $a_1 = 1$ and $a_j = 0$ for $j \neq 1$. It can be verified that

$$C^{-1} = W_1^{n-1} \left(\frac{1-b}{1-nb} I - \frac{b}{1-nb} \sum_{j=1}^{n} W_1^j \right), \quad \widetilde{C}^{-1} = W_2 C^{-1}.$$

In case $k = 0$,
$$C = \begin{bmatrix} a & b & b & \cdots & b \\ b & a & b & \cdots & b \\ \vdots & \vdots & \vdots & & \vdots \\ b & b & b & \cdots & a \end{bmatrix}, \quad \widetilde{C} = \begin{bmatrix} b & b & \cdots & b & b & a \\ b & b & \cdots & b & a & b \\ \vdots & \vdots & & \vdots & \vdots & \vdots \\ a & b & \cdots & b & b & b \end{bmatrix},$$

and
$$C^{-1} = \frac{1}{1-nb} \begin{bmatrix} 1-b & -b & -b & \cdots & -b \\ -b & 1-b & -b & \cdots & -b \\ \vdots & \vdots & \vdots & & \vdots \\ -b & -b & -b & \cdots & 1-b \end{bmatrix},$$

$$\widetilde{C}^{-1} = \frac{1}{1-nb} \begin{bmatrix} -b & -b & \cdots & -b & -b & 1-b \\ -b & -b & \cdots & -b & 1-b & -b \\ \vdots & \vdots & & \vdots & \vdots & \vdots \\ 1-b & -b & \cdots & -b & -b & -b \end{bmatrix}.$$

H.5. Symmetric tridiagonal matrix. For $0 < \alpha_i$, $i = 1, \ldots, n-1$, $\alpha_i + \alpha_{i+1} = 1$, $i = 1, \ldots, n-2$, the matrix $A_\alpha =$

$$\begin{bmatrix} 1-\alpha_1 & \alpha_1 & 0 & 0 & \cdots & 0 \\ \alpha_1 & 1-\alpha_1-\alpha_2 & \alpha_2 & 0 & \cdots & 0 \\ 0 & \alpha_2 & 1-\alpha_2-\alpha_3 & \alpha_3 & \cdots & 0 \\ \vdots & \vdots & \vdots & \vdots & & \vdots \\ 0 & 0 & \cdots & \alpha_{n-2} & 1-\alpha_{n-2}-\alpha_{n-1} & \alpha_{n-1} \\ 0 & 0 & \cdots & \cdots & \alpha_{n-1} & 1-\alpha_{n-1} \end{bmatrix}$$

H. Examples of Doubly Stochastic Matrices

is a doubly stochastic symmetric tridiagonal matrix. If $\alpha_i + \alpha_{i+1} < 1$ for some i, then A_α is doubly substochastic.

H.6. Examples. The following are examples of orthogonal matrices having $e/\sqrt{n}$ as a first row, and which yield orthostochastic matrices with first row e/n.

H.6.a. $\Gamma = (\gamma_{ij})$, where

$$\gamma_{ij} = \frac{1}{\sqrt{n}}\left[\sin\frac{2\pi(i-1)(j-1)}{n} + \cos\frac{2\pi(i-1)(j-1)}{n}\right].$$

This matrix is symmetric. The case $n = 3$ yields

$$\begin{bmatrix} \frac{1}{\sqrt{3}} & \frac{1}{\sqrt{3}} & \frac{1}{\sqrt{3}} \\ \frac{1}{\sqrt{3}} & \frac{\sqrt{3}-1}{2\sqrt{3}} & \frac{\sqrt{3}-1}{2\sqrt{3}} \\ \frac{1}{\sqrt{3}} & \frac{\sqrt{3}-1}{2\sqrt{3}} & \frac{+\sqrt{3}-1}{2\sqrt{3}} \end{bmatrix}, \quad \begin{bmatrix} \frac{1}{3} & \frac{1}{3} & \frac{1}{3} \\ \frac{1}{3} & \frac{4-2\sqrt{3}}{12} & \frac{4+2\sqrt{3}}{12} \\ \frac{1}{3} & \frac{4+2\sqrt{3}}{12} & \frac{4-2\sqrt{3}}{12} \end{bmatrix}$$

as the orthogonal matrix and the orthostochastic matrix generated from it.

H.6.b. To obtain the generalized Helmert matrix, let $w_1, \ldots, w_n$ be positive with $\sum w_i^2 = 1$, and define $s_j = (w_1^2 + \cdots + w_j^2)^{1/2}$. Then

$$H = \begin{bmatrix} w_1 & w_2 & w_3 & w_4 & \cdots & w_n \\ \frac{w_1 w_2}{s_1 s_2} & -\frac{s_1}{s_2} & 0 & 0 & \cdots & 0 \\ \frac{w_1 w_3}{s_1 s_3} & \frac{w_2 w_3}{s_2 s_3} & -\frac{s_2}{s_3} & 0 & \cdots & 0 \\ \vdots & \vdots & \vdots & \vdots & & \vdots \\ \frac{w_1 w_n}{s_1 s_n} & \frac{w_2 w_n}{s_2 s_n} & \frac{w_3 w_n}{s_3 s_n} & \cdots & & -\frac{s_{n-1}}{s_n} \end{bmatrix}$$

is orthogonal. The case $w_i = 1/n$ is a well-known special Helmert matrix.

H.7. If $P = (p_{ij})$ and $Q = (q_{ij})$ are doubly substochastic, then the Hadamard – Schur product (see 9.J)

$$R = P \circ Q = (p_{ij} q_{ij})$$

is doubly substochastic. This result follows from the observations that each $p_{ij}q_{ij} \geq 0$ and

$$\sum_i p_{ij}q_{ij} \leq \sum_i q_{ij} \leq 1, \qquad \sum_j p_{ij}q_{ij} \leq \sum_j q_{ij} \leq 1.$$

H.7.a. If U and V are unitary matrices, then the matrices

$$(|u_{ij}v_{ij}|), \qquad (|\mathscr{R}(u_{ij})|), \qquad (|\mathscr{R}(u_{ij}v_{ij})|)$$

are all doubly substochastic, where $\mathscr{R}(u_{ij})$ denotes the real part of u_{ij}.

These observations follow from the facts that the matrices $(|u_{ij}|)$ and $(|v_{ij}|)$ are doubly stochastic and $|\mathscr{R}(u_{ij})| \leq |u_{ij}|$.

H.7.b. Proposition. If P and Q are $m \times m$ and $n \times n$ doubly stochastic matrices, respectively, then the Kronecker product (see 19.G) $P \otimes Q$ is an $mn \times mn$ doubly stochastic matrix.

If either P or Q is doubly substochastic (superstochastic), then $P \otimes Q$ is doubly substochastic (superstochastic),

Proof. From 19.G.1,

$$(e \otimes e)(P \otimes Q) = (eP \otimes eQ) = (e \otimes e),$$

with a similar argument for columns. The proofs for substochastic and superstochastic cases are similar. ||

H.7.c. Proposition. If P and Q are $m \times m$ and $n \times n$ doubly stochastic matrices, respectively, then the Kronecker sum (see 19.G) $P \oplus Q$ is an $mn \times mn$ doubly stochastic matrix.

If either P or Q is doubly substochastic (superstochastic), then $P \oplus Q$ is doubly substochastic (superstochastic).

Proof. From the definition in 19.G,

$$\begin{aligned} e(P \oplus Q) &= ((p_{11} + \cdots + p_{n1})\,eQ, \ldots, (p_{1n} + \cdots + p_{nn})\,eQ) \\ &= (e, \ldots, e) = e. \qquad || \end{aligned}$$

H.8. Proposition (Martignon, 1984). Let $1 = \lambda_1 \geq \lambda_j \geq \ldots \geq \lambda_n \geq 0$. There exists an $n \times n$ doubly stochastic matrix P whose eigenvalues are $\{\lambda_1, \ldots, \lambda_n\}$, with elements

$$p_{ii} = \sum_{k=1}^{i} \frac{\alpha_k}{n-k+1} + \sum_{k=i+1}^{n} \alpha_k, \quad i = 1, 2, \ldots, n,$$

and

$$p_{ij} = p_{ji} = \frac{\alpha_1}{n} + \frac{\alpha_2}{n-1} + \cdots + \frac{\alpha_i}{n-i+1}, \quad 1 \leq i < j \leq n,$$

where $\alpha_j = \lambda_j - \lambda_{j+1}, j = 2, \ldots, n$, and $\lambda_{n+1} = 0$.

Proof. A direct argument shows that $\sum_{j=1}^{n} p_{ij} = \sum_{1}^{n} \alpha_j = \lambda_1$, so that P is stochastic. But P is a symmetric matrix, so it is doubly stochastic. The determination of the eigenvalues is obtained by showing that $\det(P - \lambda_j I) = 0, j = 1, ..., n$. ||

I Properties of Doubly Stochastic Matrices

Properties of doubly stochastic matrices are considered here that deal with inverses, idempotents, products, square roots, and some special classes of matrices.

Inverse of a Doubly Stochastic Matrix

I.1. If P is doubly stochastic and nonsingular, then $Q = P^{-1}$ satisfies
$$eQ = e \quad \text{and} \quad Qe' = e'.$$

Proof. The result follows immediately by noting that $eP = e$ implies $e = eP^{-1} = eQ$, and $Pe' = e'$ implies $e' = P^{-1}e' = Qe'$. ||

Note that Q need not have nonnegative elements, so that Q need not be doubly stochastic. However, if P is a permutation matrix, then $P^{-1} = P'$ so Q is doubly stochastic.

I.1.a. If P and $P^{-1} = Q$ are both doubly stochastic, then P is a permutation matrix.

Proof (Snijders, 1976). Because P is doubly stochastic, $xP \prec x$ for all $x \in \mathscr{R}^n$. Because P^{-1} is doubly stochastic and $x = (xP)P^{-1}$, $x \prec xP$ for all $x \in \mathscr{R}^n$. But $x \prec xP \prec x$ for all x implies that P is a permutation matrix. ||

A simple elementary proof of I.1.a is given by Berge (1963) which makes use of the Cauchy–Schwarz inequality. Farahat (1965/1966) gives a proof based on the fact that the eigenvalues of a doubly stochastic matrix lie in the closed unit disk.

I.1.b. If P is a doubly stochastic matrix such that $P^{-1} = P'$, then P is a permutation matrix.

This is an immediate consequence of I.1.a.

The Moore–Penrose inverse A^G is the unique matrix satisfying $A = AA^G A$, $A^G = A^G A A^G$, (AA^G) and $(A^G A)$ Hermitian. Plemmons and Cline (1972) show that A and A^G are both doubly stochastic if and only if $A = AXA$ has a solution, X, that is doubly stochastic. In this case, $A^{\mathrm{G}} = A'$.

Because a doubly stochastic matrix can be singular, one might ask, if P and P^{G} are both doubly stochastic, does this imply that P is a permutation matrix? That this is not the case may be seen by choosing $P = (1/n)e'e$, in which case $P^{\mathrm{G}} = (1/n)e'e$. A more general discussion of such questions is considered by Montague and Plemmons (1973). They define a doubly stochastic matrix P to be *regular* provided the matrix equation $PXP = P$ has a solution X that is doubly stochastic, and prove the result: Every regular doubly stochastic matrix is orthostochastic. The converse of this result is not true, as can be seen from the example

$$A = \frac{1}{3}\begin{bmatrix} 1 & 2 \\ 2 & 1 \end{bmatrix},$$

which is orthostochastic, but not regular.

Idempotent Doubly Stochastic Matrices

Note that the doubly stochastic matrices $E = (1/m)e'e$ are idempotent of rank 1. Doob (1942, Theorem 2) characterized the class of stochastic idempotent matrices. His result, when applied to doubly stochastic matrices, yields the following simple theorem.

I.2. Theorem (Doob, 1942). An $n \times n$ doubly stochastic matrix E of rank k is idempotent if and only if

$$E = PRP',$$

where P is a permutation matrix and R has the form (1) of G.3.a with $r_1 \geq \cdots \geq r_k \geq 1$.

For example, the idempotents of order 4 are

(i) one idempotent of rank 1:

$$\begin{bmatrix} \frac{1}{4} & \frac{1}{4} & \frac{1}{4} & \frac{1}{4} \\ \frac{1}{4} & \frac{1}{4} & \frac{1}{4} & \frac{1}{4} \\ \frac{1}{4} & \frac{1}{4} & \frac{1}{4} & \frac{1}{4} \\ \frac{1}{4} & \frac{1}{4} & \frac{1}{4} & \frac{1}{4} \end{bmatrix};$$

(ii) six idempotents of rank 2, which are permutations of

$$\begin{bmatrix} \frac{1}{2} & \frac{1}{2} & 0 & 0 \\ \frac{1}{2} & \frac{1}{2} & 0 & 0 \\ 0 & 0 & \frac{1}{2} & \frac{1}{2} \\ 0 & 0 & \frac{1}{2} & \frac{1}{2} \end{bmatrix};$$

and four additional idempotents of rank 2 which are permutations of

$$\begin{bmatrix} \frac{1}{3} & \frac{1}{3} & \frac{1}{3} & 0 \\ \frac{1}{3} & \frac{1}{3} & \frac{1}{3} & 0 \\ \frac{1}{3} & \frac{1}{3} & \frac{1}{3} & 0 \\ 0 & 0 & 0 & 1 \end{bmatrix};$$

(iii) one idempotent of rank 4:

$$\begin{bmatrix} 1 & 0 & 0 & 0 \\ 0 & 1 & 0 & 0 \\ 0 & 0 & 1 & 0 \\ 0 & 0 & 0 & 1 \end{bmatrix}.$$

Alternative proofs of I.2 and more detailed discussions of idempotents are given by Farahat (1965/1966) and Schwarz (1967). Achilles and Sinkhorn (1995) characterize all doubly stochastic matrices whose squares are idempotent.

Positive Semidefinite Doubly Stochastic Matrices

For what positive semidefinite doubly stochastic matrices are the positive semidefinite square roots doubly stochastic? This question is considered by Marcus and Minc (1962).

I.3. Theorem. If P is positive semidefinite and doubly stochastic and if $p_{ii} \leq 1/(n-1)$, then the positive semidefinite square root $P^{1/2}$ is doubly stochastic.

Proof. We can write $P = \Gamma D_\lambda \Gamma'$, where Γ is orthogonal and $D_\lambda = \text{diag}(\lambda_1, \ldots, \lambda_n)$, and the eigenvalues $\lambda \equiv \lambda(P)$ are nonnegative. Then, by hypothesis,

$$eP = e\Gamma D_\lambda \Gamma' = e,$$

so that $e\Gamma D_\lambda = e\Gamma$. Let $x = e\Gamma$, so that $x_i \lambda_i = x_i$. Then $x_i = 0$ or $\lambda_i = 1$. But in either case, $x_i \lambda_i^{1/2} = x_i$, so that $e\Gamma D_\lambda^{1/2} = e\Gamma$. But then $e(\Gamma D_\lambda^{1/2} \Gamma') \equiv eP^{1/2} = e$. Thus, the row (and column) sums are one.

Now suppose that some element, say t_{1n}, of $P^{1/2} \equiv T$ is negative. Because $t_{11} + t_{12} + \cdots + t_{1n} = 1$, it follows that $t_{11} + t_{12} + \cdots + t_{1,n-1} = 1 - t_{1n} > 1$. By the Cauchy–Schwarz inequality,

$$1 < (t_{11} + \cdots + t_{1,n-1})^2$$
$$\leq (t_{11}^2 + \cdots + t_{1,n-1}^2)(n-1)$$
$$\leq (t_{11}^2 + \cdots + t_{1n}^2)(n-1) = p_{11}(n-1),$$

which contradicts the hypothesis. ∥

The example

$$P = \begin{bmatrix} \frac{3}{4} & 0 & \frac{1}{4} \\ 0 & \frac{3}{4} & \frac{1}{4} \\ \frac{1}{4} & \frac{1}{4} & \frac{1}{2} \end{bmatrix}, \quad P^{1/2} = \frac{1}{12}\begin{bmatrix} 5+3\sqrt{3} & 5-3\sqrt{3} & 2 \\ 5-3\sqrt{3} & 5+3\sqrt{3} & 2 \\ 2 & 2 & 8 \end{bmatrix}$$

shows that the condition $p_{ii} \leq 1/(n-1)$ cannot be dropped. Note that the rows (and columns) of $P^{1/2}$ sum to one.

I.3.a. If $A > 0$, then the Hadamard–Schur product $A \circ A^{-1}$ is doubly stochastic and is positive definite.

Ordering Doubly Stochastic Matrices

Sherman (1952) has introduced a partial ordering of the $n \times n$ doubly stochastic matrices by defining

$$P_1 \triangleleft P_2$$

to mean that there exists a doubly stochastic matrix P_3 such that

$$P_1 = P_2 P_3.$$

By A.3, we conclude that

$$P_1 \triangleleft P_2 \quad \text{implies} \quad yP_1 \prec yP_2$$

for all $y \in \mathscr{R}^n$. Shizuo Kakutani posed the conjecture that the converse is true: If $yP_1 \prec yP_2$ for all $y \in \mathscr{R}^n$, then $P_1 \triangleleft P_2$. However, a counterexample to this conjecture was provided by Alfred Horn (see Sherman, 1954). To find a counterexample, one must go as high

I. Properties of Doubly Stochastic Matrices 71

as $n = 4$ dimensions. It has been shown by Schreiber (1958) that Kakutani's conjecture is true if P_2 is nonsingular.

Convergence of Deterministic and Random Sequences Ordered by Majorization

Let $D_1, D_2, \ldots$ be a sequence of $n \times n$ doubly stochastic matrices. With an initial vector $x^{(0)} = (x_1, x_2, \ldots, x_n)$, the equations

$$x^{(j)} = x^{(j-1)} D_j = x^{(0)} D_1 D_2 \cdots D_j, \quad j = 1, 2, \ldots, \quad (1)$$

define a sequence of vectors ordered by majorization. That is,

$$x^{(0)} \succ x^{(1)} \succ x^{(2)} \succ \cdots .$$

Each term in this sequence majorizes $\bar{x}e$, where $\bar{x} = \frac{1}{n}\sum_1^n x_i$ and $e = (1, \ldots, 1)$. The corresponding sequence of ordered vectors $\{x_\downarrow^{(j)}\}_{j=0}^\infty$ must converge. Some questions about the convergence of the sequence $\{x^{(j)}\}_{j=0}^\infty$ are considered in this section. Cases where the D_j are all equal are readily dealt with. In some respects, cases where the D_j are not necessarily equal and where they are allowed to be random are more interesting.

Note that when $x^{(0)}$ is a probability vector, i.e., $x_i \geq 0$, $i = 1, 2, \ldots, n$, and $\sum x_i = 1$, then $x^{(j)}$ can be thought of as the state probabilities in a Markov chain with n states. In this context with D_j independent of j, issues of convergence in stationary Markov chains are well understood. If the D_j are not all the same, there are results available for convergence in such nonstationary Markov chains, usually involving consideration of ergodic coefficients.

I.4. Example. The matrix

$$D = \begin{bmatrix} 0 & \frac{1}{2} & 0 & \frac{1}{2} \\ \frac{1}{2} & 0 & \frac{1}{2} & 0 \\ 0 & \frac{1}{2} & 0 & \frac{1}{2} \\ \frac{1}{2} & 0 & \frac{1}{2} & 0 \end{bmatrix}$$

is *periodic*;

$$D^2 = \begin{bmatrix} \frac{1}{2} & 0 & \frac{1}{2} & 0 \\ 0 & \frac{1}{2} & 0 & \frac{1}{2} \\ \frac{1}{2} & 0 & \frac{1}{2} & 0 \\ 0 & \frac{1}{2} & 0 & \frac{1}{2} \end{bmatrix}$$

72   2. Doubly Stochastic Matrices

and $D^3 = D$. So, in general, $D^{2k+1} = D$ and $D^{2k} = D^2$, $k = 1, 2, \ldots$. Consequently, if $D_j = D$, $j = 1, 2, \ldots$, in (1), then

$$x^{(2k+1)} = x^{(1)} = \left(\frac{x_2 + x_4}{2}, \frac{x_1 + x_3}{2}, \frac{x_2 + x_4}{2}, \frac{x_1 + x_3}{2} \right),$$

and

$$x^{(2k)} = x^{(2)} = \left(\frac{x_1 + x_3}{2}, \frac{x_2 + x_4}{2}, \frac{x_1 + x_3}{2}, \frac{x_2 + x_4}{2} \right).$$

Thus the sequence $\{x^{(j)}\}_{j=0}^{\infty}$ does not converge, but alternates between two orderings of $x_{\downarrow}^{(1)}$. However, $\{x_{\downarrow}^{(j)}\}_{j=0}^{\infty}$ does converge (rapidly) to (y_1, y_1, y_2, y_2), where

$$y_1 = \max \left\{ \frac{x_1 + x_3}{2}, \frac{x_2 + x_4}{2} \right\} \quad \text{and} \quad y_2 = \min \left\{ \frac{x_1 + x_3}{2}, \frac{x_2 + x_4}{2} \right\}.$$

Notice that in this example, D^2 is idempotent. If in (1), $D_j = D^2$, $j = 1, 2, \ldots$, then

$$x^{(j)} = \left(\frac{x_1 + x_3}{2}, \frac{x_2 + x_4}{2}, \frac{x_1 + x_3}{2}, \frac{x_2 + x_4}{2} \right),$$

so the sequence $\{x^{(j)}\}_{j=0}^{\infty}$ converges, but not to $\bar{x}e$. The matrix D^2 is said to be *reducible*; with D^2 as the transition matrix of a Markov chain, states 1 and 3 form a *closed class*, as do states 2 and 4. No transitions occur between states in different closed classes.

In Example I.4, (1) holds with all matrices D_j equal. When D_j is allowed to vary with j, the sequence $\{x^{(j)}\}_{j=0}^{\infty}$ can converge to a variety of limits.

I.5. Example. Suppose that $n = 2$ and $x^{(0)} = (x_1^{(0)}, x_2^{(0)}) \succ (y_1, y_2)$, where $x_1^{(0)} > x_2^{(0)}$, $y_1 \geq y_2$, and $x_1^{(0)} > y_1$. The aim of this example is to define a sequence $D_1, D_2, \ldots$ of strictly positive doubly stochastic matrices such that with $x^{(j)}$ defined by (1), $\lim_{j \to \infty} x^{(j)} = y$.

Let

$$D_1 = \begin{bmatrix} \alpha_1 & \bar{\alpha}_1 \\ \bar{\alpha}_1 & \alpha_1 \end{bmatrix}, \quad \text{where } \bar{\alpha}_1 = 1 - \alpha_1 \text{ and } \alpha_1 = \frac{x_1^{(0)} + y_1 - 2x_2^{(0)}}{2(x_1^{(0)} - x_2^{(0)})}.$$

Recursively define

$$D_j = \begin{bmatrix} \alpha_j & \bar{\alpha}_j \\ \bar{\alpha}_j & \alpha_j \end{bmatrix}, \quad \text{where } \alpha_j = \frac{x_1^{(j-1)} + y_1 - 2x_2^{(j-1)}}{2(x_1^{(j-1)} - x_2^{(j-1)})}.$$

This sequence of matrices is chosen so that $x_1^{(1)}$ moves half the way from $x_1^{(0)}$ to y_1, $x_1^{(2)}$ moves half the way from $x_1^{(1)}$ to y_1, and the process proceeds by always moving half of the remaining distance to y_1. In this process, $x_2^{(j)}$ moves up half the remaining distance to y_2. Thus $\lim_{j\to\infty} x^{(j)} = y$. This requires $\lim_{j\to\infty} \alpha_j = 1$, and $\lim_{j\to\infty} D_j$ is the 2×2 identity matrix.

I.6. Lemma. For $x \in \mathscr{R}^n$, let $d(x) = \max_i x_i - \min_i x_i = x_{[1]} - x_{[n]}$. If $D = (d_{ij})$ is an $n \times n$ doubly stochastic matrix with all elements $\geq \varepsilon$, then $d(xD) \leq (1 - 2\varepsilon) d(x)$.

Proof. Let $y = xD$, so that $y_j = \sum x_i d_{ij}$. Then

$$\varepsilon x_{[1]} + (1-\varepsilon)x_{[n]} \leq y_j \leq (1-\varepsilon)x_{[1]} + \varepsilon x_{[n]}, \quad j = 1, 2, \ldots, n.$$

If $y_i > y_j$, then

$$y_i - y_j \leq (1-\varepsilon)x_{[1]} + \varepsilon x_{[n]} - [\varepsilon x_{[1]} + (1-\varepsilon)x_{[n]}]$$
$$= (1-2\varepsilon)x_{[1]} - (1-2\varepsilon)x_{[n]} = (1-2\varepsilon)d(x). \quad \|$$

I.7. Proposition. Let D_j, $j = 1, 2, \ldots$, be a sequence of doubly stochastic matrices, let $x^{(0)} \in \mathscr{R}^n$, and let $x^{(1)}, x^{(2)}, \ldots$ be defined by (1). If

(i) all elements of every D_j are $\geq \varepsilon$,

or more generally, if

(ii) there exists a pair of interlacing sequences $\{k_j\}$ and $\{\ell_j\}$, for which $k_j \leq \ell_j < k_{j+1}$, $j = 1, 2, \ldots$ such that for each j, $\prod_{i=k_j}^{\ell_j} D_i$ has all elements $\geq \varepsilon$,

then

$$\lim_{j\to\infty} x^{(j)} = \bar{x}e. \qquad (2)$$

Proof. Suppose first that (i) holds. Then by Lemma I.6,

$$d(x^{(j)}) \leq (1 - 2\varepsilon) d(x^{(j-1)}), \quad j+1, 2, \ldots,$$

and consequently $d(x^{(j)}) \leq (1 - 2\varepsilon)^j d(x^0)$. Thus $\lim_{j\to\infty} d(x^{(j)}) = 0$.

Next suppose that (ii) holds. Then the subsequence $\{x^{(\ell_j)}\}$ satisfies (i), so $\lim_{j \to \infty} d(x^{(\ell_j)}) = 0$. Because all of the D_j are doubly stochastic, $d(x^{(j)})$ is decreasing in j, and (2) follows. ||

Remark. If the matrices D_j are random, but the conditions of Proposition I.7 hold with probability 1, then the conclusion also holds with probability 1.

Denote by $Q(r,s)$ the permutation matrix that interchanges the coordinates r and s. Recall from Section B that a matrix of the form
$$T(r,s) = \lambda I + (1-\lambda)Q(r,s), \quad 0 \le \lambda < 1, \tag{3}$$
is called a *T-transform*.

I.8. Proposition (Proschan and Shaked, 1984). Let D_1 be a T-transform of the form (3) with r and s chosen at random from a distribution that places positive probability on all of the $\binom{n}{2}$ pairs. Assume further that $\lambda \in [0,1)$ is chosen at random from a distribution with no mass at 0. Repeat this process [using the same distribution for the new pair (r,s) and the same distribution for λ] to obtain $D_2, D_3, \ldots$. If $x^{(0)} \in \mathscr{R}^n$, and $x^{(1)}, x^{(2)}, \ldots$ are obtained from (1), then
$$\lim_{j \to \infty} x^{(j)} = \bar{x}e \text{ with probability 1.}$$

Proof. This result follows from Proposition I.7 once it is verified that a doubly stochastic matrix with positive elements can be obtained as product of finitely many T-transforms. This is a consequence of Lemma B.1. Such a product will arise infinitely often with probability 1 if the D_j are chosen according to the process described in the statement of this proposition. ||

I.9. Proposition. Let P be a doubly stochastic matrix that is not a permutation matrix and let Q_j, $j = 1, 2, \ldots$, be a sequence of independent identically distributed random permutations with a distribution that places positive probability on each of the $n!$ permutation matrices of order n. If $x^{(0)} \in \mathscr{R}^n$ and $x^{(j)} = x^{(j-1)} P Q_j$, $j = 1, 2, \ldots$, then $\lim_{j \to \infty} x^{(j)} = \bar{x}e$ with probability 1.

Proof. If P has all entries positive, this result follows from Proposition I.7. Suppose that some elements of P are 0 and use Theorem A.2 to write P in the form $P = \sum_1^k \alpha_i \Pi_i$, where each Π_i is a permutation matrix, $\alpha_i > 0$, $i = 1, 2, \ldots, k$, and $\sum_1^k \alpha_i = 1$.

I. Properties of Doubly Stochastic Matrices 75

Assume that $\Pi_1 = I$ is the identity matrix; otherwise, replace Q_j by $\Pi_1^{-1} Q_j$, $j = 1, 2, \ldots$. This ensures that P has a positive main diagonal so that P is not periodic.

If P is reducible, then $\{1, 2, \ldots, n\}$ can be written as a union of disjoint closed classes $C_1, \ldots, C_q$. With probability 1 there will be a finite value j such that the product $R = PQ_1 PQ_2 \cdots PQ_j$ involves a permutation Q_i that interchanges elements of C_r and C_s for all pairs r, s. A basic theorem of Markov chain theory is that for every irreducible aperiodic transition matrix R, there is an integer m such that R^m has all positive elements (see Feller, 1950, 1968). Because in the sequence $PQ_1 PQ_2 PQ_3 \cdots$ there is positive probability that R will appear m times consecutively, and in fact this will occur infinitely often with probability 1, the proposition follows from Proposition I.7. ∥

Alternate proof of Proposition I.9. Using Theorem A.2, write P in the form $P = \sum_1^k \alpha_i \Pi_i$, and as in the first proof, assume that $\Pi_1 = I$. Let $S = \{I, \Pi_2, \ldots, \Pi_k\}$ and define D by

$$D = \begin{bmatrix} 0 & 1 & 0 & \cdots & 0 & 0 \\ 0 & 0 & 1 & \cdots & 0 & 0 \\ \vdots & \vdots & \vdots & & \vdots & \vdots \\ 0 & 0 & 0 & \cdots & 0 & 1 \\ 1 & 0 & 0 & \cdots & 0 & 0 \end{bmatrix}.$$

Because $\sum_1^n D^i$ has all elements equal to 1, $D \in S$ implies that all elements of P^n are positive. If $D \notin S$, consider the product

$$PDP = \sum_{i,j} \alpha_i \alpha_j \Pi_i D \Pi_j.$$

Because $\Pi_1 = I$, this sum includes the term $\alpha_1^2 D$ and consequently $(PDP)^n$ has all elements positive. Since the string $PDPI$ will appear n consecutive times in the sequence $PQ_1 PQ_2 PQ_3 \cdots$ infinitely often with probability 1, the result follows from Proposition I.7. ∥

Note According to this proof, the distribution of the Q_j does not need to place positive probability on all the $n!$ permutations. It is necessary to put positive probability only on D and on Π_1^{-1} (so as to get $I \in S$).

J Diagonal Equivalence of Nonnegative Matrices and Doubly Stochastic Matrices

Given an $n \times n$ matrix $A = (a_{ij})$ of nonnegative elements, when do there exist diagonal matrices D_1 and D_2 with positive diagonals such that $D_1 A D_2$ is doubly stochastic? This problem has arisen in several different contexts, and there is now a considerable literature on the subject. Only a brief resume of results is given here. For a more comprehensive discussion, see Brualdi and Ryser (1991).

The origins of these studies stem mainly from the statistical analyses of contingency tables, from the scaling of matrices in numerical analysis, and from the problem of estimating the transition matrix of a Markov chain known to be doubly stochastic.

The first paper in this area appears to be that of Deming and Stephan (1940). The problem considered was to estimate theoretical cell probabilities $p_{ij}(i = 1, \ldots, r; \; j = 1, \ldots, c)$, where the row and column totals

$$\sum_{j=1}^{c} p_{ij} \equiv p_{i.}, \qquad \sum_{i=1}^{r} p_{ij} \equiv p_{.j}$$

are known and fixed. The available data are cell frequencies n_{ij} (assumed to be strictly positive). The criterion of fit is to

$$\text{minimize} \sum_{j} \sum_{i} (n_{ij} - n p_{ij})^2 / n_{ij}$$

subject to the condition on row and column totals. Deming and Stephan (1940) proposed a solution which has been called the *iterative proportional fitting procedure*. One paper providing a proof of convergence is that of Ireland and Kullback (1968). There are a number of papers extending the models and discussing convergence [for further reference, see Fienberg (1970)].

Sinkhorn (1964) showed that if A is a positive square matrix, there exist positive diagonal matrices D_1 and D_2 such that $D_1 A D_2$ is doubly stochastic. The method of proof is based on an iterative procedure of alternately normalizing the rows and columns of A. Subsequently, using a similar iterative procedure, Sinkhorn (1967) extended this result by showing that a positive rectangular matrix A is diagonally equivalent to a positive matrix with prescribed row and column sums. The iterative procedure of Sinkhorn is equivalent to that of Deming and Stephan.

The condition that A be strictly positive was later relaxed to the condition that A be fully indecomposable. With this hypothesis, the result was proved by Brualdi, Parter, and Schneider (1966), by Sinkhorn and Knopp (1967), and by Marshall and Olkin (1968). In the latter paper, it is shown that the diagonal elements of D_1 and D_2 can be obtained as a solution of the extremal problem:

$$\min_{x,y} xAy' \quad \text{subject to} \quad \prod_1^n x_j^{r_j} = 1, \quad \prod_1^m y_j^{c_j} = 1, \quad x_i > 0, \quad y_i > 0.$$

A variety of alternative proofs now exist; e.g., see Borobia and Cantó (1998). Rothblum (1989) uses the above extremal model to obtain scalings for a multidimensional matrix.

The connection with estimating the transition matrix of a Markov chain that is known to be doubly stochastic is discussed by Hobby and Pyke (1965). See also Seneta (2006). A connection with graph theory is described in Brualdi and Ryser (1991). Bacharach (1970) finds use for this material in the context of input–output analysis.

Another motivation for this area of study is its possible use in the scaling of matrices, because the doubly stochastic matrix $D_1 A D_2$ may be more amenable to numerical computations than A itself. For a discussion of matrix scaling, see, e.g., Householder (1964) or Seneta (2006). A comprehensive exposition of matrix scaling that includes an exhaustive set of references is provided by Bapat and Raghavan (1997). See also Chapter 10.

3
Schur-Convex Functions

For any given partial ordering $\precsim$ of a set $\mathscr{X}$, real-valued functions ϕ defined on $\mathscr{X}$ which satisfy $\phi(x) \leq \phi(y)$ whenever $x \precsim y$ are variously referred to as "monotonic," "isotonic," or "order-preserving." For the ordering of majorization, the order-preserving functions were first systematically studied by Schur (1923). In Schur's honor, such functions are said to be "convex in the sense of Schur," "Schur-convex," or "S-convex." The historical origin of these terms is described in Section 1.C.

Specifically, Schur characterized the differentiable functions that preserve the ordering $\prec$ on the positive orthant $\mathscr{R}^n_{++}$. Ostrowski (1952) observed that the restriction to $\mathscr{R}^n_{++}$ is unnecessary.

The orderings $\prec_w$ and $\prec^w$ have received less attention, although special cases of functions that preserve these orderings have been exhibited by various authors; see, e.g., Fan (1951). General characterizations of the functions that preserve the orderings $\prec_w$ or $\prec^w$ can be obtained without difficulty from the characterizations of functions preserving the ordering $\prec$.

The problem of identifying order-preserving functions for orderings generated by a convex cone has been studied by Marshall, Walkup, and Wets (1967). This work and its application to majorization are discussed in Section 14.D.

Many of the inequalities that arise from a majorization can be obtained simply by identifying an appropriate order-preserving function. Historically, such inequalities have often been proved by direct methods without an awareness that a majorization underlies the validity of the inequality. The classic example of this is the Hadamard determinant inequality, where the underlying majorization was discovered by Schur (1923). Following Schur, our approach is to identify (in this chapter) the functions that preserve the ordering of majorization. Inequalities of the form $\phi(x) \leq \phi(y)$ can then be obtained using any order-preserving function ϕ for any vectors x and y such that $x \prec y$.

A Characterization of Schur-Convex Functions

Functions that preserve the ordering of majorization are said to be Schur-convex. Perhaps "Schur-increasing" would be more appropriate, but the term "Schur-convex" is by now well entrenched in the literature.

A.1. Definition. A real-valued function ϕ defined on a set $\mathscr{A} \subset \mathscr{R}^n$ is said to be *Schur-convex on* $\mathscr{A}$ if

$$x \prec y \quad \text{on} \quad \mathscr{A} \Rightarrow \phi(x) \leq \phi(y).$$

If, in addition, $\phi(x) < \phi(y)$ whenever $x \prec y$ but x is not a permutation of y, then ϕ is said to be *strictly Schur-convex on* $\mathscr{A}$. If $\mathscr{A} = \mathscr{R}^n$, then ϕ is simply said to be *Schur-convex* or *strictly Schur-convex*. Similarly, ϕ is said to be *Schur-concave on* $\mathscr{A}$ if

$$x \prec y \quad \text{on} \quad \mathscr{A} \Rightarrow \phi(x) \geq \phi(y),$$

and ϕ is *strictly Schur-concave on* $\mathscr{A}$ if strict inequality $\phi(x) > \phi(y)$ holds when x is not a permutation of y.

Of course, ϕ is Schur-concave if and only if $-\phi$ is Schur-convex.

Remark. Because the ordering $\prec$ on $\mathscr{R}^n$ has the property that $x \prec x\Pi \prec x$ for all permutation matrices Π, it follows that if ϕ is Schur-convex or Schur-concave on a symmetric set $\mathscr{A}$ (that is, a set $\mathscr{A}$ such that $x \in \mathscr{A}$ implies $x\Pi \in \mathscr{A}$ for every permutation Π), then ϕ is symmetric on $\mathscr{A}$ [i.e., $\phi(x) = \phi(x\Pi)$ for every permutation Π]. Thus, if ϕ is symmetric on a symmetric set $\mathscr{A}$ and Schur-convex on $\mathscr{D} \cap \mathscr{A}$, where

$$\mathscr{D} = \{x : x_1 \geq \cdots \geq x_n\},$$

then ϕ is Schur-convex on $\mathscr{A}$.

A. Characterization of Schur-Convex Functions

With the above remark in mind, consider first the characterization of Schur-convex functions defined on $\mathscr{D}$. There are several derivations, but the simplest one is via a useful interplay between majorization and componentwise ordering. With the change of variables

$$\widetilde{z}_k = \sum_{i=1}^{k} z_i, \qquad k = 1, \ldots, n,$$

it follows directly from the definition that on $\mathscr{D}$, $x \prec y$ if and only if

$$\widetilde{x}_k \leq \widetilde{y}_k, \qquad k = 1, \ldots, n-1, \tag{1}$$

and

$$\widetilde{x}_n = \widetilde{y}_n. \tag{2}$$

For the componentwise ordering $u \leq v$, it is immediate that $u \leq v$ implies $\psi(u) \leq \psi(v)$ if and only if ψ is increasing in each argument. From this and from (1) and (2), it follows that $x \prec y$ on $\mathscr{D}$ implies $\phi(x) \leq \phi(y)$ if and only if

$$\phi(z_1, \ldots, z_n) = \phi(\widetilde{z}_1, \widetilde{z}_2 - \widetilde{z}_1, \ldots, \widetilde{z}_n - \widetilde{z}_{n-1}) \tag{3}$$

is increasing in $\widetilde{z}_k$, $k = 1, \ldots, n-1$, over the region where $z \in \mathscr{D}$. This leads to:

A.2. Lemma. Let ϕ be a continuous real-valued function defined on $\mathscr{D}$. Then

$$x \prec y \text{ on } \mathscr{D} \qquad \text{implies} \qquad \phi(x) \leq \phi(y) \tag{4}$$

if and only if, for all $z \in \mathscr{D}$ and $k = 1, \ldots, n-1$,

$$\phi(z_1, \ldots, z_{k-1}, z_k + \varepsilon, z_{k+1} - \varepsilon, z_{k+2}, \ldots, z_n) \tag{5}$$

is increasing in ε over the region

$$0 \leq \varepsilon \leq \min[z_{k-1} - z_k, z_{k+1} - z_{k+2}], \qquad k = 1, \ldots, n-2,$$
$$0 \leq \varepsilon \leq z_{n-2} - z_{n-1}, \qquad k = n-1.$$

Note. Hwang and Rothblum (1993) pointed out the necessity of assuming continuity in Lemma A.2. Consider with $n = 3$ the function

$$\phi^*(x) = 1 \quad \text{if } x = (2, 2, 2),$$
$$= 0 \quad \text{otherwise.}$$

This discontinuous function satisfies condition (5), but clearly $(2,2,2) \prec (1,2,3)$ and $\phi^*(2,2,2) > \phi^*(1,2,3)$.

To clarify this point, it is helpful to introduce the concept of an elementary T-transform. Recall the definition of a T-transform given in Section 2.B which involves a transfer of mass from one coordinate of x to another coordinate. An *elementary T-transform* is of the form

$$T^* = \lambda I + (1-\lambda)Q^*,$$

where now Q^* is a permutation matrix that interchanges two neighboring coordinates. If an elementary T^*-transform is applied to a vector in $\mathscr{D}$, it transfers money (in income terms) to an individual from the person whose income is immediately above in the income ranking. Lemma 2.B.1 assures us that if $x \prec y$ then x can be obtained from y by the successive application of a finite number of T-transforms. However, a countable number of elementary T-transforms may be required in some cases [e.g., consider $(2,2,2)$ and $(1,2,3)$]. Condition (5) effectively deals with monotonicity of ϕ under elementary T-transforms. This is not enough to guarantee monotonicity with respect to T-transforms without continuity.

A.2.a. The arguments leading to A.2 also yield conditions for strict inequality in (4). These arguments show that for ϕ continuous

$$\phi(x) < \phi(y) \qquad \text{for all} \quad x \prec y \text{ on } \mathscr{D}, \quad x \neq y$$

if and only if (5) is strictly increasing in ε over the indicated region.

With the aid of the remark following A.1, A.2 yields the following:

A.2.b. Let $\mathscr{A}$ be a set with the property

$$y \in \mathscr{A} \text{ and } x \prec y \qquad \text{implies} \quad x \in \mathscr{A}.$$

A continuous function ϕ defined on $\mathscr{A}$ is Schur-convex on $\mathscr{A}$ if and only if ϕ is symmetric and

$$\phi(x_1, s - x_1, x_3, \ldots, x_n) \qquad \text{is increasing in} \quad x_1 \geq s/2$$

for each fixed $s, x_3, \ldots, x_n$.

To see this, note that the monotonicity in ε of (5) can easily be obtained from A.2.a using the symmetry of ϕ.

The conditions of A.2 can be expressed in terms of derivatives when ϕ is differentiable. In this case, denote the partial derivative of ϕ with respect to its kth argument by $\phi_{(k)}$:

$$\phi_{(k)}(z) = \partial \phi(z)/\partial z_k.$$

A. Characterization of Schur-Convex Functions

A.3. Theorem. Let ϕ be a real-valued function, defined and continuous on $\mathscr{D}$ and continuously differentiable on the interior of $\mathscr{D}$. Then

$$x \prec y \text{ on } \mathscr{D} \quad \text{implies} \quad \phi(x) \leq \phi(y) \qquad (6)$$

if and only if

$$\phi_{(k)}(z) \quad \text{is decreasing in} \quad k = 1, \ldots, n,$$

i.e., the gradient $\nabla \phi(z) \in \mathscr{D}$, for all z in the interior of $\mathscr{D}$.

Proof. Because ϕ is continuous on the boundary of $\mathscr{D}$, attention can be confined to the interior of $\mathscr{D}$. Thus, the condition of A.2 can be replaced by the condition that for all z in the interior of $\mathscr{D}$,

$$\phi(z_1, \ldots, z_{k-1}, z_k + \varepsilon, z_{k+1} - \varepsilon, z_{k+2}, \ldots, z_n)$$

is increasing in ε when

$$0 < \varepsilon < \min[z_{k-1} - z_k, z_{k+1} - z_{k+2}], \quad k = 1, \ldots, n-2,$$
$$0 < \varepsilon < z_{n-2} - z_{n-1}, \quad k = n-1.$$

Since ϕ is differentiable, this condition is equivalent to

$$\frac{d}{d\varepsilon} \phi(z_1, \ldots, z_{k-1}, z_k + \varepsilon, z_{k+1} - \varepsilon, z_{k+2}, \ldots, z_n) \geq 0,$$

that is,

$$\phi_{(k)}(z_1, \ldots, z_{k-1}, z_k + \varepsilon, z_{k+1} - \varepsilon, z_{k+2}, \ldots, z_n)$$
$$- \phi_{(k+1)}(z_1, \ldots, z_{k-1}, z_k + \varepsilon, z_{k+1} - \varepsilon, z_{k+2}, \ldots, z_n) \geq 0,$$

where $(z_1, \ldots, z_{k+1}, z_k + \varepsilon, z_{k+1} - \varepsilon, z_{k+2}, \ldots, z_n)$ is in the interior of $\mathscr{D}$. This, together with A.2, completes the proof. ||

Let

$$\phi_{(i,j)}(z) = \frac{\partial^2 \phi(z)}{\partial z_i \, \partial z_j}.$$

A.3.a. Theorem (Schur, 1923). Let ϕ be a real-valued function defined on $\mathscr{D}$ and twice differentiable on the interior of $\mathscr{D}$. Suppose ϕ is Schur-convex on $\mathscr{D}$. If $\phi_{(k)}(z) = \phi_{(k+1)}(z)$ implies

$$\phi_{(k,k)}(z) - \phi_{(k,k+1)}(z) - \phi_{(k+1,k)}(z) + \phi_{(k+1,k+1)}(z) > 0, \qquad (7)$$

then

$$x \prec y \text{ on } \mathscr{D} \text{ and } x \neq y \quad \text{implies} \quad \phi(x) < \phi(y).$$

Proof. Suppose that f is a real-valued function defined on a closed interval $[a,b] \subset \mathscr{R}$ and is twice differentiable on (a,b). If $f'(x) \geq 0$ for all $x \in (a,b)$ and $f''(x) > 0$ for all x such that $f'(x) = 0$, then f is strictly increasing on $[a,b]$. Application of this to the function of ε defined in (5) yields the theorem. ||

Further comments about strict inequality are given in A.4.b and A.9.

The following very basic theorem follows from A.3 with the aid of the remark following A.1.

A.4. Theorem (Schur, 1923; Ostrowski, 1952). Let $I \subset \mathscr{R}$ be an open interval and let $\phi : I^n \to \mathscr{R}$ be continuously differentiable. Necessary and sufficient conditions for ϕ to be Schur-convex on I^n are

$$\phi \text{ is symmetric on } I^n, \tag{8}$$

and

$$\phi_{(i)}(z) \text{ is decreasing in } i = 1, \ldots, n \quad \text{for all} \quad z \in \mathscr{D} \cap I^n. \tag{9}$$

Alternatively, ϕ is Schur-convex on I^n if and only if (8) holds and, for all $i \neq j$,

$$(z_i - z_j)[\phi_{(i)}(z) - \phi_{(j)}(z)] \geq 0 \quad \text{for all} \quad z \in I^n. \tag{10}$$

The above theorem can be reformulated; for Schur-concave functions "decreasing" is replaced by "increasing" in (9) and inequality (10) is reversed.

Schur (1923) obtained A.4 for the case $I = (0, \infty)$ and Ostrowski (1952) obtained the result for an arbitrary open interval. Condition (10) is often called *Schur's condition*.

With the aid of (8), condition (10) can be replaced by the condition

$$(z_1 - z_2)[\phi_{(1)}(z) - \phi_{(2)}(z)] \geq 0 \quad \text{for all} \quad z \in I^n. \tag{10'}$$

This simplified condition is sometimes more convenient to verify.

Theorem A.4 is not sufficiently general for all applications because the domain of ϕ may not be a Cartesian product.

A.4.a. Let $\mathscr{A} \subset \mathscr{R}^n$ be a set with the following properties:

(i) $\mathscr{A}$ is symmetric in the sense that $x \in \mathscr{A} \Rightarrow x\Pi \in \mathscr{A}$ for all permutations Π;

(ii) $\mathscr{A}$ is convex and has a nonempty interior.

If ϕ is continuously differentiable on the interior of $\mathscr{A}$ and continuous on $\mathscr{A}$, then I^n can be replaced by $\mathscr{A}$ in A.4.

It is difficult to overemphasize the usefulness of the conditions of A.4 for determining whether or not a given function is Schur-convex or Schur-concave. On the other hand, it is usually possible to find a more elegant and simpler proof of special cases. The reader should not be misled by the fact that the usefulness of A.4 is obscured in this book, but should understand that many or even most of the theorems giving Schur-convexity were first discovered by checking (8) and (9) or (8) and (10).

A.4.b. Theorem. If $\phi: \mathscr{R}^n \to \mathscr{R}$ is twice differentiable, if conditions (8) and (9) are satisfied, and if $\phi_{(k)}(z) = \phi_{(k+1)}(z)$ implies (7), then ϕ is strictly Schur-convex on $\mathscr{R}^n$.

This result follows from A.2.a and is essentially due to Schur (1923).

A.5. In proving that a function ϕ is Schur-convex, it is often helpful to realize that, in effect, one can take $n = 2$ without loss of generality. This fact is a consequence of 2.B.1, which says that if $x \prec y$, then x can be derived from y by a finite number of T-transforms. Consequently, it is sufficient to prove that $\phi(x) \leq \phi(y)$ when $x \prec y$ and x differs from y in only two components, so that all but two arguments of ϕ are fixed. Because ϕ is necessarily symmetric, it is sufficient to prove that $\phi(z_1, z_2, \overset{\bullet}{z}k)$ is Schur-convex in z_1 and z_2.

Weak Majorization

The argument leading to A.1 requires only slight modification for the characterization of functions that preserve the orderings $\prec_w$ or $\prec^w$. With the notation $\tilde{z}_k = \sum_1^k z_i$ and $\tilde{\tilde{z}}_k = \sum_k^n z_i$, $k = 1, \ldots, n$, the conditions for weak majorization on $\mathscr{D}$ can be rewritten as follows: If $x, y \in \mathscr{D}$, then

$$x \prec_w y \Leftrightarrow \tilde{x}_k \leq \tilde{y}_k, \quad k = 1, \ldots, n,$$
$$x \prec^w y \Leftrightarrow \tilde{\tilde{x}}_k \geq \tilde{\tilde{y}}_k, \quad k = 1, \ldots, n.$$

This means that for $x, y \in \mathscr{D}$:

(i) $x \prec_w y \Rightarrow \phi(x) \leq \phi(y)$ if and only if

$$\phi(z_1, \ldots, z_n) = \phi(\tilde{z}_1, \tilde{z}_2 - \tilde{z}_1, \ldots, \tilde{z}_n - \tilde{z}_{n-1})$$

is increasing in $\tilde{z}_i$, $i = 1, \ldots, n$, over the set $z \in \mathscr{D}$;

(ii) $x \prec^{\mathrm{w}} y \Rightarrow \phi(x) \leq \phi(y)$ if and only if

$$\phi(z_1, \ldots, z_n) = \phi(\widetilde{\widetilde{z}}_1 - \widetilde{\widetilde{z}}_2, \ldots, \widetilde{\widetilde{z}}_{n-1} - \widetilde{\widetilde{z}}_n, \widetilde{\widetilde{z}}_n)$$

is decreasing in $\widetilde{\widetilde{z}}_i$, $i = 1, \ldots, n$.

These facts can be combined with A.1 and rewritten as follows.

A.6. Lemma. Let ϕ be continuous and real valued on $\mathscr{D}$. Then

$$\phi(x) \leq \phi(y) \qquad \text{whenever} \quad x \prec_{\mathrm{w}} y \text{ on } \mathscr{D}$$

if and only if $x \prec y$ on $\mathscr{D}$ implies $\phi(x) \leq \phi(y)$, and in addition

$$\phi(z_1, \ldots, z_{n-1}, z_n + \varepsilon)$$

is increasing in ε over the region $0 \leq \varepsilon \leq z_{n-1} - z_n$ for all $z \in \mathscr{D}$. Similarly,

$$\phi(x) \leq \phi(y) \qquad \text{whenever} \quad x \prec^{\mathrm{w}} y \text{ on } \mathscr{D}$$

if and only if $x \prec y$ on $\mathscr{D}$ implies $\phi(x) \leq \phi(y)$, and in addition

$$\phi(z_1 + \varepsilon, z_2, \ldots, z_n)$$

is decreasing in ε over the region $0 \geq \varepsilon \geq z_2 - z_1$ for all $z \in \mathscr{D}$.

A.6.a. The arguments leading to A.6 also show that

$$\phi(x) < \phi(y) \qquad \text{for all} \quad x \prec_{\mathrm{w}} y \text{ on } \mathscr{D}, \quad x \neq y,$$

if and only if ϕ satisfies the conditions of A.2.a, and in addition $\phi(z_1, \ldots, z_{n-1}, z_n + \varepsilon)$ is strictly increasing in ε, $0 \leq \varepsilon \leq z_{n-1} - z_n$, for all $z \in \mathscr{D}$. Similarly,

$$\phi(x) < \phi(y) \qquad \text{for all} \quad x \prec^{\mathrm{w}} y \text{ on } \mathscr{D}, \quad x \neq y,$$

if and only if ϕ satisfies the conditions of A.2.a, and in addition

$$\phi(z_1 + \varepsilon, z_2, \ldots, z_n)$$

is strictly decreasing in ε, $0 \geq \varepsilon \geq z_2 - z_1$, for all $z \in \mathscr{D}$.

The conditions of A.6 for a function to preserve the ordering of weak majorization can be put into a more convenient form provided ϕ is differentiable.

A.7. Theorem (Ostrowski, 1952). Let ϕ be a real-valued function, defined and continuous on $\mathscr{D}$, and continuously differentiable on the interior of $\mathscr{D}$. Then

$$\phi(x) \leq \phi(y) \qquad \text{whenever} \quad x \prec_{\mathrm{w}} y \text{ on } \mathscr{D}$$

if and only if
$$\phi_{(1)}(z) \geq \phi_{(2)}(z) \geq \cdots \geq \phi_{(n)}(z) \geq 0,$$
i.e., the gradient $\nabla \phi(z) \in \mathscr{D}_+$ for all z in the interior of $\mathscr{D}$.
Similarly,
$$\phi(x) \leq \phi(y) \quad \text{whenever} \quad x \prec^{\mathrm{w}} y \text{ on } \mathscr{D}$$
if and only if
$$0 \geq \phi_{(1)}(z) \geq \phi_{(2)}(z) \geq \cdots \geq \phi_{(n)}(z)$$
for all z in the interior of $\mathscr{D}$.

The proof of A.7 is similar to the proof of A.3.

A.8. Theorem. A real-valued function ϕ defined on a set $\mathscr{A} \subset \mathscr{R}^n$ satisfies
$$x \prec_{\mathrm{w}} y \text{ on } \mathscr{A} \Rightarrow \phi(x) \leq \phi(y)$$
if and only if ϕ is increasing and Schur-convex on $\mathscr{A}$. Similarly, ϕ satisfies
$$x \prec^{\mathrm{w}} y \text{ on } \mathscr{A} \Rightarrow \phi(x) \leq \phi(y)$$
if and only if ϕ is decreasing and Schur-convex on $\mathscr{A}$.

This theorem can be obtained by comparing A.2 and A.6 and by observing that for all permutation matrices Π,
$$x \prec_{\mathrm{w}} x\Pi \prec_{\mathrm{w}} x, \qquad x \prec^{\mathrm{w}} x\Pi \prec^{\mathrm{w}} x.$$

A.8.a. Let ϕ be a real-valued function defined on the set $\mathscr{A} \subset \mathscr{R}^n$. Then
$$x \prec_{\mathrm{w}} y \text{ on } \mathscr{A} \text{ and } x \text{ is not a permutation of } y \Rightarrow \phi(x) < \phi(y)$$
if and only if ϕ is strictly increasing and strictly Schur-convex on $\mathscr{A}$. Similarly,
$$x \prec^{\mathrm{w}} y \text{ on } \mathscr{A} \text{ and } x \text{ is not a permutation of } y \Rightarrow \phi(x) < \phi(y)$$
if and only if ϕ is strictly decreasing and strictly Schur-convex on $\mathscr{A}$.

A.8.b. (Chong, 1976c). Let $\mathscr{A} \subset \mathscr{R}^n$ have a Schur-concave indicator function and let ϕ be a strictly increasing Schur-convex function defined on $\mathscr{A}$. If $x \prec_{\mathrm{w}} y$ on $\mathscr{A}$ and $\phi(x) = \phi(y)$, then $x \prec y$. Similarly, if ϕ is strictly decreasing and Schur-concave, $x \prec^{\mathrm{w}} y$ and $\phi(x) = \phi(y)$, then $x \prec y$.

Proof. If $x \prec_w y$, then by 5.A.9 there exists a vector u such that $x \leq u \prec y$. Because $\mathscr{A}$ has a Schur-concave indicator function, $u \in \mathscr{A}$ and $\phi(x) \leq \phi(u) \leq \phi(y)$. But $\phi(x) = \phi(y)$; hence $\phi(x) = \phi(u)$. Since ϕ is strictly increasing, this means $x = u$. If $x \prec^w y$, the proof makes use of 5.A.9.a. ||

A.9. Condition for equality. One use of order-preserving functions is in deriving inequalities. A common procedure is to fix x or y, say $x = x^0$ is fixed, to obtain an inequality of the form $\phi(x^0) \leq \phi(y)$ for all y in an appropriate set. Conditions for equality or for strict inequality are often of considerable interest. It should be observed that the conditions of A.2.a, A.3.a, A.4.b, and A.8.a provide sufficient conditions for strict inequality, but the conditions may not be necessary. The reason for this is that the requirement (i) $\phi(x^0) < \phi(y)$ for appropriate y is weaker than the requirement (ii) for all x, $\phi(x) < \phi(y)$ for appropriate y. Fortunately, most functions ϕ of practical interest satisfy the sufficient conditions and one knows equality holds if and only if y is a permutation of x^0.

B Compositions Involving Schur-Convex Functions

There are a number of simple but useful facts relating to compositions that involve Schur-convex or Schur-concave functions. Some of these results have been given by Berge (1963, pp. 219–220) and by Ostrowski (1952).

Since there are several closely related results, it may be helpful to present them informally in tabular form rather than as formal propositions.

B.1. Consider compositions of the form

$$\psi(x) = h(\phi_1(x), \ldots, \phi_k(x)),$$

where h is a real-valued function defined on $\mathscr{R}^k$, and the real functions $\phi_1, \ldots, \phi_k$ have common domain $\mathscr{A} \subset \mathscr{R}^n$. Of course, this is then the domain of ψ.

In Table 1 each ϕ_i is a symmetric function of $x_1, \ldots, x_n$ and is defined on $\mathscr{A}$. Each row of the table gives a separate result: If h and each ϕ_i satisfy the indicated condition, then so does ψ. In the table, "increasing" means increasing in each argument.

B. Compositions Involving Schur-Convex Functions 89

Table 1
Composition of Functions of the Form
$\psi(x_1, \ldots, x_n) = h(\phi_1(x), \ldots, \phi_k(x))$

	h on $\mathscr{R}^k$	Each ϕ_i on $\mathscr{A}$	$h(\phi_1(x), \ldots, \phi_k(x))$ on $\mathscr{A}$
(i)	Increasing	Schur-convex	Schur-convex
(ii)	Decreasing	Schur-convex	Schur-concave
(iii)	Increasing	Schur-concave	Schur-concave
(iv)	Decreasing	Schur-concave	Schur-convex
(v)	Increasing	Increasing and Schur-convex	Increasing and Schur-convex
(vi)	Decreasing	Increasing and Schur-convex	Decreasing and Schur-concave
(vii)	Increasing	Decreasing and Schur-concave	Decreasing and Schur-concave
(viii)	Decreasing	Decreasing and Schur-concave	Increasing and Schur-convex
(ix)	Increasing	Decreasing and Schur-convex	Decreasing and Schur-convex
(x)	Decreasing	Increasing and Schur-concave	Decreasing and Schur-convex
(xi)	Increasing	Increasing and Schur-concave	Increasing and Schur-concave
(xii)	Decreasing	Decreasing and Schur-convex	Increasing and Schur-concave

All of the propositions summarized in Table 1 can be proved in a straightforward way, and all have similar proofs. For example, consider (i). If $x \prec y$ on $\mathscr{D}$, then because each ϕ_i is Schur-convex, $\phi_i(x) \leq \phi_i(y)$, $i = 1, \ldots, k$. Combining this with the fact that h is increasing in each argument yields

$$h(\phi_1(x), \ldots, \phi_k(x)) \leq h(\phi_1(y), \ldots, \phi_k(y)).$$

The following are some special cases of interest.

B.1.a. The class of Schur-convex functions forms a convex cone. This is a trivial consequence of the order-preserving property these functions represent, but it also follows from (i) with $h(z_1, \ldots, z_k) = \sum_{i=1}^{k} a_i z_i$, where $a_1 \geq 0, \ldots, a_k \geq 0$.

B.1.b. An increasing function of a Schur-convex function is Schur-convex. Again, this is immediate from the order-preserving viewpoint, and it follows from (i) with $k = 1$. A case of particular interest is given in B.1.e below.

B.1.c. If $\phi_1, \ldots, \phi_k$ are Schur-convex, then

$$\min(\phi_1, \ldots, \phi_k) \quad \text{and} \quad \max(\phi_1, \ldots, \phi_k)$$

are Schur-convex.

B.1.d. If ϕ_i is Schur-convex (concave), $i = 1, \ldots, k$, and $\phi_i(x) \geq 0$ for all i and x, then

$$\psi(x) = \prod_1^k \phi_i(x)$$

is Schur-convex (concave).

Proof. Because $h(u) = \prod_1^k u_i$ is increasing on $\mathscr{R}_+^k = \{z : z_i \geq 0$ for all $i\}$, the result follows from (i) and (iii) of Table 1. ∥

B.1.e. If ϕ is Schur-convex on $\mathscr{A} \subset \mathscr{R}^n$ and for all $x \in \mathscr{A}$,

$$\psi_t(x) = \begin{cases} 1 & \text{if } \phi(x) \geq t, \\ 0 & \text{otherwise}, \end{cases}$$

then ψ_t is Schur-convex on $\mathscr{A}$. Similarly, if ϕ is Schur-concave on $\mathscr{A}$ and for all $x \in \mathscr{A}$

$$\psi_t(x) = \begin{cases} 1 & \text{if } \phi(x) \geq t, \\ 0 & \text{otherwise}, \end{cases}$$

then ψ_t is Schur-concave on $\mathscr{A}$.

This means that indicator (characteristic) functions of "level sets"

$$\{x : \phi(x) \geq t\}$$

are Schur-convex when ϕ is Schur-convex, and they are Schur-concave when ϕ is Schur-concave. Of course, the same statements are true if "$\geq$" is replaced by "$>$" above.

B.2. Another class of compositions yielding Schur-convex functions has the form

$$\psi(x) = \phi(g(x_1), \ldots, g(x_n)),$$

where $\phi : \mathscr{R}^n \to \mathscr{R}$ and $g : \mathscr{R} \to \mathscr{R}$.

Results of this kind are tabulated in Table 2.

Proof of (i)–(vi) *in Table 2.* By A.5, it is sufficient to prove these results for $n = 2$. First consider (i). If $x \prec y$, then it follows from 2.B.2 that for some α, $0 \leq \alpha \leq 1$, $\overline{\alpha} = 1 - \alpha$,

$$x_1 = \alpha y_1 + \overline{\alpha} y_2, \qquad x_2 = \overline{\alpha} y_1 + \alpha y_2.$$

C. Some General Classes of Schur-Convex Functions

Table 2
Composition of Functions of the Form
$\psi(x_1, \ldots, x_n) = \phi(g(x_1), \ldots, g(x_n))$

	ϕ	g	ψ
(i)	Increasing and Schur-convex	Convex	Schur-convex
(ii)	Decreasing and Schur-convex	Concave	Schur-convex
(iii)	Increasing and Schur-convex	Increasing and convex	Increasing and Schur-convex
(iv)	Decreasing and Schur-convex	Decreasing and concave	Increasing and Schur-convex
(v)	Increasing and Schur-convex	Decreasing and convex	Decreasing and Schur-convex
(vi)	Decreasing and Schur-convex	Increasing and concave	Decreasing and Schur-convex

By using the convexity of g and monotonicity of ϕ, it follows that

$$\phi(g(x_1), g(x_2)) = \phi(g(\alpha y_1 + \overline{\alpha} y_2), g(\overline{\alpha} y_1 + \alpha y_2))$$
$$\leq \phi(\alpha g(y_1) + \overline{\alpha} g(y_2), \overline{\alpha} g(y_1) + \alpha g(y_2))$$
$$= \phi(\alpha[g(y_1), g(y_2)] + \overline{\alpha}[g(y_2), g(y_1)]).$$

Because

$$(\alpha[g(y_1), g(y_2)] + \overline{\alpha}[g(y_2), g(y_1)]) \prec (g(y_1), g(y_2))$$

(again from 2.B.2) and because ϕ is Schur-convex,

$$\phi(\alpha[g(y_1), g(y_2)] + \overline{\alpha}[g(y_2), g(y_1)]) \leq \phi(g(y_1), g(y_2)).$$

By combining these inequalities, it follows that

$$x \prec y \Rightarrow \phi(g(x_1), g(x_2)) \leq \phi(g(y_1), g(y_2)).$$

The proof of (ii) is similar. It is easy to obtain (iii) and (v) from (i), and to obtain (iv) and (vi) from (ii). ∥

C Some General Classes of Schur-Convex Functions

The classes of Schur-convex functions identified in this section are illustrated with more specific examples in Sections D–I.

Symmetric Convex Functions—Variables Separate

As a motivation for the definition of majorization it is suggested in Chapter 1 that $\sum g(x_i) \leq \sum g(y_i)$ whenever $x \prec y$ and g is convex. This is the content of the following proposition.

C.1. Proposition (Schur, 1923; Hardy, Littlewood, and Pólya, 1929). If $I \subset \mathscr{R}$ is an interval and $g : I \to \mathscr{R}$ is convex, then

$$\phi(x) = \sum_1^n g(x_i)$$

is Schur-convex on I^n. Consequently, $x \prec y$ on I^n implies $\phi(x) \leq \phi(y)$.

Proof. By A.5, it is sufficient to prove this result for $n = 2$. Then if $x \prec y$, x has the form $x_1 = \alpha y_1 + \overline{\alpha} y_2$, $x_2 = \overline{\alpha} y_1 + \alpha y_2$ for some $\alpha \in [0, 1]$, $\overline{\alpha} = 1 - \alpha$. Because g is convex,

$$\begin{aligned}
g(x_1) + g(x_2) &= g(\alpha y_1 + \overline{\alpha} y_2) + g(\overline{\alpha} y_1 + \alpha y_2) \\
&\leq [\alpha g(y_1) + \overline{\alpha} g(y_2)] + [\overline{\alpha} g(y_1) + \alpha g(y_2)] \\
&= g(y_1) + g(y_2). \quad \|
\end{aligned}$$

Various other proofs can be given. In particular, if g is differentiable, the conditions of A.4 can be verified. Notice also that C.1 follows from (i) of Table 2 with $\phi(z) = \sum z_i$.

C.1.a. Let $I \subset \mathscr{R}$ be an interval and let $\phi(x) = \sum_1^n g(x_i)$, where $g : I \to \mathscr{R}$.

(i) (Schur, 1923) If g is strictly convex on I, then ϕ is strictly Schur-convex on I^n.

(ii) If ϕ is strictly Schur-convex on I^n, then g is strictly convex on I.

Proof. In the proof of C.1, if g is strictly convex, $\alpha \in (0, 1)$, and $y_1 \neq y_2$, then the inequality in that proof becomes strict, which proves (i). The result (ii) follows from A.2.a. $\|$

C.1.b. (Tomić, 1949; Weyl, 1949). If $g : \mathscr{R} \to \mathscr{R}$ is convex and increasing (decreasing), then $\phi(x) = \sum_1^n g(x_i)$ is increasing (decreasing) and Schur-convex. Consequently, $x \prec_w y (x \prec^w y)$ implies $\phi(x) \leq \phi(y)$. This result is an immediate consequence of C.1 and A.8.

C. Some General Classes of Schur-Convex Functions

Historical Remarks

A result very close to C.1 was first proved by Schur. Schur did not have the definition of majorization in terms of partial sums (Definition 1.A.1), but instead he proved that if $x = yP$ for some doubly stochastic matrix P, then

$$\sum_1^n g(x_i) \leq \sum_1^n g(y_i) \tag{1}$$

for all continuous convex functions g. Schur's beautifully simple proof is as follows: Since $x_j = \sum y_i p_{ij}$, where $\sum_i p_{ij} = 1$, it follows from Jensen's inequality or directly from the definition of convexity that

$$g(x_j) \leq \sum_{i=1}^n p_{ij} g(y_i).$$

Because $\sum_j p_{ij} = 1$,

$$\sum_{j=1}^n g(x_j) \leq \sum_{j=1}^n \sum_{i=1}^n p_{ij} g(y_i) = \sum_{i=1}^n \sum_{j=1}^n p_{ij} g(y_i) = \sum_{i=1}^n g(y_i).$$

Although this proof holds quite generally, Schur's paper is unclear as to whether or not he had in mind the restriction $x_i \geq 0$, $y_i \geq 0$ for all i.

Proposition C.1 together with its converse 4.B.1 were first given by Hardy, Littlewood, and Pólya (1929), who explicitly prove only a continuous analog.

Apparently quite independently, Karamata (1932) proved a substantial generalization of C.1 and 4.B.1. Karamata begins by asking for necessary and sufficient conditions on $x_1, \ldots, x_n, y_1, \ldots, y_n \in (a, b)$ in order that (1) holds for all functions g continuous and convex on (a, b). By defining

$$x(t) = \text{number of } x_i \leq t, \qquad y(t) = \text{number of } y_i \leq t,$$

and noting that (1) can be rewritten in terms of Stieltjes integrals as

$$\int_a^b g(t)\, dx(t) \leq \int_a^b g(t)\, dy(t), \tag{2}$$

Karamata arrived at a more general question: What conditions are necessary and sufficient in order that functions x and y, nondecreasing on (a, b), satisfy (2) for all functions g convex on (a, b)? Karamata's elegant answer is discussed in 16.B.4.a.

94   3. Schur-Convex Functions

A quite different approach to C.1 was taken by Tomić (1949). Tomić obtains C.1 from C.1.b with the aid of 5.A.11. He shows that for C.1.b it is enough to prove the case $x \prec^w y$ because the case $x \prec_w y$ then follows by a change of variables. To obtain C.1.b with $x \prec^w y$, Tomić argues as follows: Since $x \prec^w y$, $x_{[n]} \geq y_{[n]}$ and because g is decreasing, $g(x_{[n]}) \leq g(y_{[n]})$. If $x_{[n-1]} \geq y_{[n-1]}$, a similar argument shows that $g(x_{[n]}) + g(x_{[n-1]}) \leq g(y_{[n]}) + g(y_{[n-1]})$. On the other hand, if $x_{[n-1]} < y_{[n-1]}$, then because of the ordering $y_{[n]} \leq x_{[n]} \leq x_{[n-1]} < y_{[n-1]}$ and because g is convex, the chord joining $M_1 = (y_{[n]}, g(y_{[n]}))$ with $M_2 = (y_{[n-1]}, g(y_{[n-1]}))$ lies entirely above the chord joining $m_1 = (x_{[n]}, g(x_{[n]}))$ with $m_2 = (x_{[n-1]}, g(x_{[n-2]}))$. Because $x_{[n]} + x_{[n-1]} \geq y_{[n]} + y_{[n-1]}$, the point $T_1 = \frac{1}{2}[M_1 + M_2]$ lies to the left of the point $t_1 = \frac{1}{2}(m_1 + m_2)$. These facts and the fact that the chords have negative slope together imply that $g(x_{[n]}) + g(x_{[n-1]}) \leq g(y_{[n]}) + g(y_{[n-1]})$ (see Fig. 1).

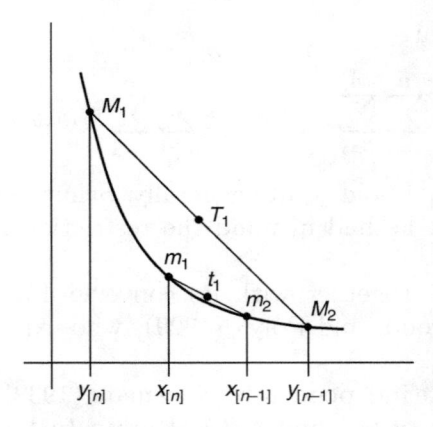

Figure 1. A graphical explanation.

The argument now repeats with minor modifications. If $x_{[n-2]} \geq y_{[n-2]}$, then, because g is decreasing, it is easy to see from the foregoing that

$$g(x_{[n]}) + g(x_{[n-1]}) + g(x_{[n-2]}) \leq g(y_{[n]}) + g(y_{[n-1]}) + g(y_{[n-2]}). \quad (3)$$

If $x_{[n-2]} < y_{[n-2]}$, then the chord joining T_1 with $M_3 = (y_{[n-2]}, g(y_{[n-2]}))$ lies above the chord joining t_1 with $m_3 = (x_{[n-2]}, g(x_{[n-2]}))$. Because $x_{[n]} + x_{[n-1]} + x_{[n-2]} \geq y_{[n]} + y_{[n-1]} + y_{[n-2]}$, it follows that the point $T_2 = (2T_1 + M_3)/3$ lies to the left of the point $t_2 = (2t_1 + m_3)/3$. These facts, together with the fact that the chords have negative slope, imply that (3) again holds (see Fig. 2). It is clear that the above ideas lead to an inductive proof.

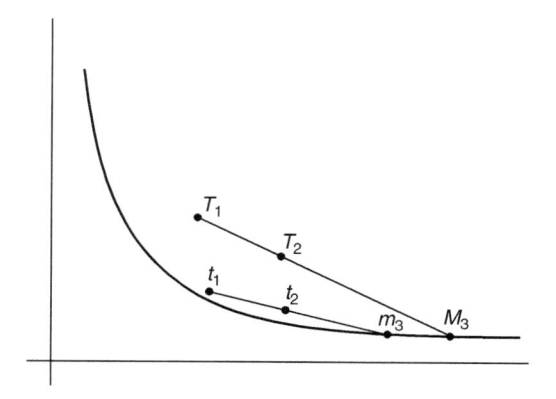

C. Some General Classes of Schur-Convex Functions

Figure 2. A graphical explanation.

Pólya (1950) shows that C.1.b is a consequence of C.1. His proof makes use of 5.A.8.

Converses of C.1 and C.1.b are given in 4.B.1 and 4.B.2. Another kind of converse is given here.

C.1.c. Let $I \subset \mathscr{R}$ be an interval, and let g be continuous on I. If $\phi(x) = \sum g(x_i)$ is Schur-convex on I^n, then g is convex on I. If ϕ is strictly Schur-convex on I^n, then g is strictly convex on I.

Proof. Take $x_1 = x_2 = (y_1 + y_2)/2$, $x_i = y_i$, $i = 3, 4, \ldots, n$. Then $x \prec y$, so that $\sum g(x_i) \leq \sum g(y_i)$; i.e.,

$$2g\left(\frac{y_1 + y_2}{2}\right) \leq g(y_1) + g(y_2).$$

In the same way, g is strictly convex when ϕ is strictly Schur-convex. ||

Note: If the continuity condition is deleted from C.1.c, the conclusion must be modified slightly. Ng (1987) proves the equivalence of the following four conditions:

(i) $\sum_{i=1}^{n} g(x_i)$ is Schur-convex on I^n for some $n \geq 2$;

(ii) $\sum_{i=1}^{n} g(x_i)$ is Schur-convex on I^n for every $n \geq 2$;

(iii) g satisfies the inequality

$$g(\alpha x + (1-\alpha)y) + g(\alpha y + (1-\alpha)x) \leq g(x) + g(y)$$

for every $x, y \in I$ and every $\alpha \in [0,1]$;

(iv) g admits the representation

$$g(x) = c(x) + a(x),$$

where $c(x)$ is convex on I and $a(x)$ is additive [i.e., $a(x+y) = a(x) + a(y)$, for every $x, y \in I$].

Condition (iv) confirms the suspicion that $g(x)$ must be "almost" convex to ensure the Schur-convexity of $\sum_{i=1}^{n} g(x_i)$. Condition (iii) is slightly weaker than the analogous sufficient condition for convexity found in 16.B.3 which reduces to condition (iii) when $\alpha = \beta$.

C.1.d. Let $I \subset \mathscr{R}$ be an interval. If $\phi(x) = \sum g(x_i)$ is Schur-convex and increasing (decreasing) on I^n, and if g is continuous on I, then g is convex and increasing (decreasing) on I.

Proof. Convexity follows from C.1.c and monotonicity is trivial.   ‖

Various specific applications of C.1 are given in Sections D and E.

C.1.e. Technical remark. That $g(z) = \log[(1/z) - 1]$ is convex on $I = (0, \frac{1}{2}]$, but not convex on $[\frac{1}{2}, 1)$ is easily checked. On the other hand, the conditions of A.4 can be used to show that $\phi(x) = g(x_1) + g(x_2)$ is Schur-convex on $\{x : x_i > 0,\ x_2 > 0,\ x_1 + x_2 \leq 1\}$, a somewhat larger set than I^2. The proof of C.1.c shows more than the convexity of g on $(0, \frac{1}{2}]$, because it yields inequalities such as $g(\frac{1}{2}) \leq g(\varepsilon) + g(1-\varepsilon)$, $0 < \varepsilon < 1$, that involve the behavior of g outside the interval $I = (0, \frac{1}{2}]$. But, of course, such comparisons stop short of showing that g is convex on $(0, 1)$.

C.1.f. Proposition (Guan and Shen, 2006). If $g : I \to \mathscr{R}$ is convex, and for $k = 1, \ldots, n$, $\phi_k : I^n \to \mathscr{R}$ is defined by

$$\phi_k(x) = \sum_S g\left(\frac{1}{k} \sum_{j=1}^{k} x_{i_j}\right) \bigg/ \binom{n}{k},$$

where $S = \{(i_1, \ldots, i_k) : 1 \leq i_1 < \ldots < i_k \leq n\}$, then ϕ_k is Schur-convex.

Proposition C.1 corresponds to the case $k = 1$. As a consequence of C.1.f, Guan and Shen present several extensions of results presented below in Sections D and E.

C. Some General Classes of Schur-Convex Functions   97

Schur-convexity of ϕ_1 ensures that $\phi_1(x) \geq \phi_n(x) = \phi_1(\bar{x}, \ldots, \bar{x})$, where $\bar{x} = \Sigma x_i/n$, a result that can be viewed as a version of Jensen's inequality (discussed further in Section 16.C). Pečarić and Svrtan (1998) observe that a more general ordering result is true for the ϕ_k's. Specifically, they show that

$$\phi_1(x) \geq \phi_2(x) \geq \cdots \geq \phi_n(x)$$

for every $x \in I^n$, which can be viewed as a further extension of Jensen's inequality.

Symmetric Convex Functions—General Case

The following proposition is a generalization of C.1 that was also essentially proved by Schur (1923), but Schur restricted the domain of ϕ to $\mathscr{R}_{++}^n$. [See also Berge (1955)].

C.2. Proposition. If ϕ is symmetric and convex, then ϕ is Schur-convex. Consequently, $x \prec y$ implies $\phi(x) \leq \phi(y)$.

Proof. By A.5 it is sufficient to prove this for $n = 2$. Then if $x \prec y$, x has the form $x_1 = \alpha y_1 + \bar{\alpha} y_2$, $x_2 = \bar{\alpha} y_1 + \alpha y_2$ for some $\alpha \in [0, 1]$, $\bar{\alpha} = 1 - \alpha$. Because ϕ is convex,

$$\phi(x_1, x_2) = \phi(\alpha y_1 + \bar{\alpha} y_2, \bar{\alpha} y_1 + \alpha y_2) = \phi(\alpha(y_1, y_2) + \bar{\alpha}(y_2, y_1))$$
$$\leq \alpha \phi(y_1, y_2) + \bar{\alpha} \phi(y_2, y_1) = \phi(y_1, y_2). \quad ||$$

C.2.a. If ϕ is symmetric and convex in each pair of arguments, the other arguments being fixed, then ϕ is Schur-convex.

C.2.b. If ϕ is symmetric and if $\phi(x_1, s - x_1, x_3, \ldots, x_n)$ is convex in x_1 for each fixed $s, x_3, \ldots, x_n$, then ϕ is Schur-convex.

These two results successively weaken the hypothesis of C.2 on ϕ. Careful examination of the proof of C.2 shows that C.2.b is actually proved.

C.2.c. If ϕ is symmetric and strictly convex on sets of the form $\{z: \sum z_i = c\}$, then ϕ is strictly Schur-convex.

Proof. If ϕ is strictly convex, $\alpha \in (0, 1)$, and $y_1 \neq y_2$, then the inequality in the proof of C.2 is strict. $||$

C.2.d. If ϕ is symmetric, convex, and increasing (decreasing), then ϕ is Schur-convex and increasing (decreasing). Consequently, $x \prec_w y$ ($x \prec^w y$) implies $\phi(x) \leq \phi(y)$.

This result is immediate from C.2.

C.2.e. If ϕ is Schur-convex on $\mathscr{A}$, then $\phi_{-}(x) = \phi(-x)$ defines a Schur-convex function on $-\mathscr{A}$.

This follows from 1.A(13a).

C.2.f. If ϕ is symmetric and log concave, then ϕ is Schur-concave.

Quasi-Convex Functions

In various contexts, especially in optimization theory, it has been found that convexity can often be replaced by quasi-convexity or pseudo-convexity.

A function $\phi: \mathscr{R}^n \to \mathscr{R}$ is said to be *quasi-convex* if

$$\phi(\alpha u + (1-\alpha)v) \leq \max[\phi(u), \phi(v)] \qquad (4)$$

for all $\alpha \in [0,1]$ and $u, v \in \mathscr{R}^n$ (or the domain of ϕ may be some other convex set). A condition equivalent to (4) is that the "level sets"

$$L_a = \{x : \phi(x) \leq a\} \qquad (5)$$

be convex. Still another statement equivalent to (4) is that

$$\phi(u) \leq \phi(v) \text{ and } z = \alpha u + (1-\alpha)v (0 \leq \alpha \leq 1) \quad \text{implies} \quad \phi(z) \leq \phi(v).$$

In this form, condition (4) can be more easily compared with the condition of pseudo-convexity: A function $\phi: \mathscr{R}^n \to \mathscr{R}$ is called *pseudo-convex* if

$$\phi(u) < \phi(v) \text{ and } z = \alpha u + (1-\alpha)v (0 < \alpha < 1) \quad \text{implies} \quad \phi(z) < \phi(v).$$

Symmetric quasi-convex functions are Schur-convex (C.3), but pseudo-convex functions need not be Schur-convex (C.3.a).

C.3. If ϕ is symmetric and quasi-convex, then ϕ is Schur-convex.

Proof. Denote by $\langle K_y \rangle$ the convex hull of the set $K_y = \{yP : P \text{ is a permutation matrix}\}$. By 2.B.3, $\langle K_y \rangle = \{x : x \prec y\}$. But $L_{\phi(y)} = \{z : \phi(z) \leq \phi(y)\}$ is convex. Moreover, $K_y \subset L_{\phi(y)}$ because ϕ is symmetric. Consequently, $\langle K_y \rangle \subset L_{\phi(y)}$; i.e., $x \prec y$ implies $\phi(x) \leq \phi(y)$. ||

An alternate proof of C.3 can be obtained using A.2.b.

Now, consider some examples.

C.3.a. Example. Let ϕ be a real function defined on $\{x : x \in \mathscr{R}^2 \text{ and } |x_1| + |x_2| \leq 2\}$ by

$$\phi(x) = \begin{cases} 1 & \text{if } |x_1| = |x_2| = 1, \\ 0 & \text{otherwise.} \end{cases}$$

This function is symmetric and pseudo-convex, but not quasi-convex or Schur-convex.

C.3.b. Example. Let $\phi : \mathscr{R}^2 \to \mathscr{R}$ be defined by $\phi(x_1, x_2) = -x_1 x_2$. It is easily verified that ϕ is Schur-convex.

Let $x = (1,1)$ and $y = (-\frac{1}{2}, -\frac{1}{2})$. Then $\phi(x) = -1 < -\frac{1}{4} = \phi(y)$. If $z = \frac{1}{3}x + \frac{2}{3}y = 0$, then $\phi(z) = 0 > \phi(y) = -\frac{1}{4}$ so ϕ is not pseudo-convex. Also, ϕ is not quasi-convex because $\phi(z) > \max(\phi(x), \phi(y))$.

C.3.c. Example. Let $\phi : \mathscr{R} \to \mathscr{R}$ be defined by

$$\phi(x) = \begin{cases} 1 & \text{if } x \geq 0, \\ 0 & \text{if } x < 0. \end{cases}$$

Then ϕ is quasi-convex, but consideration of the points 1 and -1 shows that ϕ is not pseudo-convex.

The Structure of the Class of Schur-Convex Functions

Because the class $\mathscr{C}$ of Schur-convex functions defined on a set $\mathscr{A}$ is a class of order-preserving functions, it forms a convex cone that is closed under pointwise convergence and contains the constant functions. That is,

if $\phi_1 \in \mathscr{C}$, $\phi_2 \in \mathscr{C}$ and $a \geq 0$, $b \geq 0$, then $a\phi_1 + b\phi_2 \in \mathscr{C}$; (6)

if $\phi_1, \phi_2, \ldots$ is a sequence of functions in $\mathscr{C}$ and

$$\phi(x) = \lim_{n \to \infty} \phi_n(x) \text{ for all } x \in \mathscr{A}, \quad \text{then } \phi \in \mathscr{C};$$ (7)

if $c \in \mathscr{R}$ and $\phi(x) = c$ for all $x \in \mathscr{A}$, then ϕ is Schur-convex. (8)

As a convex cone, the structure of the extreme rays is of interest. Here, proper interpretation of the notion of an "extreme ray" is complicated by the presence of (8), which essentially requires that functions differing by a constant be regarded as equivalent. Otherwise, the relationship

$$\tfrac{1}{2}[\phi(x) + c] + \tfrac{1}{2}[\phi(x) - c] = \phi(x)$$

would say that there are no extreme rays at all.

Now let ϕ be a Schur-convex function defined on $\mathscr{A}$ and let $\mathscr{S} \subset \mathscr{R}$. Let

$$\phi_1(x) = \begin{cases} \phi(x) & \text{if } \sum x_i \in \mathscr{S}, \\ 0 & \text{if } \sum x_i \notin \mathscr{S}, \end{cases} \qquad \phi_2(x) = \begin{cases} \phi(x) & \text{if } \sum x_i \notin \mathscr{S}, \\ 0 & \text{if } \sum x_i \in \mathscr{S}. \end{cases}$$

Then ϕ_1 and ϕ_2 are Schur-convex and $\phi_1 + \phi_2 = \phi$. This means that if ϕ lies on an extreme ray of the convex cone of Schur-convex functions, then there exists $a \in \mathcal{R}$ such that $\sum x_i \neq a$ implies $\phi(x) = 0$. If $A_a \subset \mathcal{R}^n$ is any set satisfying

(i) $x \in A_a \Rightarrow \sum x_i = a$,

(ii) $x \in A_a$ and $x \prec y \Rightarrow y \in A_a$,

then the indicator function of the set A_a does in fact lie on an extreme ray of the convex cone. Moreover, any function that lies on an extreme ray must be of this form (apart from addition of a constant or multiplication by a positive number).

C.4. Let $\{\phi_a : -\infty < a < \infty\}$ be a family of Schur-convex functions and let

$$\phi(x) = \phi_a(x) \quad \text{if} \quad \sum x_i = a, \quad -\infty < a < \infty.$$

Then ϕ is Schur-convex.

Proof. The comparison $\phi(x) \leq \phi(y)$ whenever $x \prec y$ is equivalent to the comparison $\phi_a(x) \leq \phi_a(y)$, where $a = \sum x = \sum y$. ‖

Of course, ϕ_a need not be defined for all $a \in (-\infty, \infty)$, but only on $\{a : \sum x_i = a \text{ for some } x \text{ in the domain of } \phi\}$.

A consequence of C.4 is that Schur-convex functions need not be measurable; their behavior on the various hyperplanes $\sum x_i = a$ can be completely unrelated.

Integral Mixtures of Schur-Convex Functions

The following generalization of (6) is often useful.

C.5. Proposition. Suppose that $\phi(x, t)$ is Schur-convex in $x \in \mathcal{R}^n$ for all $t \in T$; then

$$\int_T \phi(x, t) \, d\mu(t)$$

is Schur-convex in x whenever the integral exists.

Proof. If $x \prec y$, then $\phi(x, t) \leq \phi(y, t)$ for all t. Consequently, $\int_T \phi(x, t) \, d\mu(t) \leq \int_T \phi(y, t) \, d\mu(t)$. ‖

For a more general result, see Proposition 15.E.4.

D Examples I. Sums of Convex Functions

According to C.1, $\phi(x) = \sum_1^n g(x_i)$ is Schur-convex whenever g is convex. Here some special cases are listed.

Entropy

D.1. If $p_i \geq 0$, $i = 1, \ldots, n$, and $\sum p_i = 1$, the function

$$H(p_1, \ldots, p_n) = -\sum p_i \log p_i$$

is called the *entropy* of p, or the *Shannon information entropy* of p. (Here $x \log x = 0$ for $x = 0$.) With $g(x) = x \log x$ in C.1.a, it follows that $H(p)$ is strictly Schur-concave. Consequently, $H(p) \geq H(q)$ whenever $p \prec q$, and in particular,

$$H(1, 0, \ldots, 0) \leq H(p) \leq H(1/n, \ldots, 1/n).$$

D.1.a. A more general entropy function, known as *Kapur's entropy of order 1 and type t* (Kapur, 1967) is defined for $t > 0$ by

$$H_t(p_1, \ldots, p_n) = -\sum_{i=1}^n p_i^t \log p_i^t \Big/ \sum_{i=1}^n p_i^t.$$

When $t = 1$, this reduces to the usual entropy function.

Consider the inequality

$$H_t(p) \leq \log n \text{ for every probability vector } p.$$

This inequality holds for $t = 1$ as remarked in D.1. It does not hold for every $t > 0$. Stolarsky (1980) shows that it holds only for $t \geq t_0(n)$, where $t_0(n)$ is a constant depending on n. Subsequently, Clausing (1983) verified that if $n > 3$ and $t = t_0(n)$, then equality holds in (1) for a probability vector $p \neq (\frac{1}{n}, \ldots, \frac{1}{n})$. Thus for this value of t, H_t is not strictly Schur-convex.

D.2. Let $\bar{x} = (1/n) \sum x_i$. The function $\phi(x) = [(1/n) \sum (x_i - \bar{x})^2]^{1/2}$ is called the *standard deviation* of numbers $x_1, \ldots, x_n$. With $g(x) = (x - \bar{x})^2$ in C.1.a, it follows that $\sum (x_i - \bar{x})^2$ is strictly Schur-convex and consequently ϕ is strictly Schur-convex. As already mentioned in Section 1.C, this fact was first proved by Dalton (1920), who considered ϕ as a measure of income inequality.

D.3. The function
$$\phi(x) = \sum (1/x_i)$$
is strictly Schur-convex and decreasing on $\mathscr{R}_{++}^n$. This is another consequence of C.1.a.

A Kantorovich Inequality

D.3.a. (Schweitzer, 1914). If $0 < m \le a_i \le M$, $i = 1, \ldots, n$, then
$$\left(\frac{1}{n}\sum a_i\right)\left(\frac{1}{n}\sum \frac{1}{a_i}\right) \le \frac{(M+m)^2}{4mM} = \left(\frac{M+m}{2}\right)\left(\frac{M^{-1}+m^{-1}}{2}\right).$$

Proof. From 5.C.1, it follows that there exist unique integers s, t such that
$$a \prec (\underbrace{m, \ldots, m}_{s}, \mu, \underbrace{M, \ldots, M}_{t}) = b,$$
where $m \le \mu < M$. With $\phi(x) = \sum(1/x_i)$, this yields the inequality
$$\left(\sum a_i\right)\phi(a) \le \left(\sum a_i\right)\phi(b),$$
which can be rewritten as
$$\sum a_i \sum \frac{1}{a_i} \le (sm + \mu + tM)\left(\frac{s}{m} + \frac{1}{\mu} + \frac{t}{M}\right).$$

The right-hand side is a convex function of μ, so that the maximum occurs at $\mu = m$ or M. Consequently, with an appropriate choice of $\alpha = s/n$ or $\alpha = (s+1)/n$ and $\overline{\alpha} = 1 - \alpha$, it follows that
$$\frac{1}{n^2}(sm + \mu + tM)\left(\frac{s}{m} + \frac{1}{\mu} + \frac{t}{M}\right) \le (\alpha m + \overline{\alpha}M)\left(\frac{\alpha}{m} + \frac{\overline{\alpha}}{M}\right)$$
$$\le \frac{(M+m)^2}{4mM},$$
which yields D.3.a. ‖

Inequality D.3.a has been called a *Kantorovich-type inequality*. Other names are *reversal* or *complementary inequalities*. The name "reversal" arises from the fact that
$$1 \le \left(\frac{1}{n}\sum a_i\right)\left(\frac{1}{n}\sum \frac{1}{a_i}\right),$$

but no upper bound exists without further assumptions. The assumption that $0 < m \leq a_i \leq M$, $i = 1, \ldots, n$, permits an upper bound. Indeed, with such constraints, new bounds could be obtained for some of the examples in this section. There are now many generalizations and variations of Kantorovich-type inequalities. For an extensive bibliography, see Alpargu and Styan (1996, 2000). See also Mitrinović (1970, p. 59) and Liu and Neudecker (1996).

D.3.b. Just and Schaumberger (1964) posed the following problem: If $x_i > 0$, $i = 1, \ldots, n$, and $s = \sum_1^n x_i$, show that

$$\sum_{j=1}^n \frac{s - x_j}{x_j} \geq n(n-1). \tag{1}$$

Inequality (1) can be written as $\sum_1^n (1/x_j) \geq (n^2/s)$. Because $x \succ (s, \ldots, s)/n$, the inequality immediately follows from D.3.

D.3.c. Walker (1971) posed the problem: If a, b, c are positive numbers and if $x = b + c - a$, $y = c + a - b$, $z = a + b - c$, then $abc(yz + zx + xy) \geq xyz(bc + ca + ab)$. To see this, notice that $(a, b, c) = (x, y, z)P$, where

$$P = \begin{pmatrix} 0 & \frac{1}{2} & \frac{1}{2} \\ \frac{1}{2} & 0 & \frac{1}{2} \\ \frac{1}{2} & \frac{1}{2} & 0 \end{pmatrix}$$

is doubly stochastic, so that $(a, b, c) \prec (x, y, z)$. Consequently, it follows from D.3 that

$$\frac{1}{a} + \frac{1}{b} + \frac{1}{c} \leq \frac{1}{x} + \frac{1}{y} + \frac{1}{z},$$

which is the inequality of Walker.

D.4. For all $a > 0$, the function

$$\phi(x) = \sum_{i=1}^n \left(x_i + \frac{1}{x_i}\right)^a$$

is strictly Schur-convex on $(0, 1]^n$. This follows from C.1.a, because $g(z) = [z + (1/z)]^a$ is strictly convex on $(0, 1]$. [For $a \geq 1$, g is strictly convex on $(0, \infty)$.]

If $x_i > 0$, $\sum x_i = 1$, then $x \succ (1/n, \ldots, 1/n)$ so that $\phi(x) \geq \phi(1/n, \ldots, 1/n)$; that is,

$$\sum_{i=1}^{n} \left(x_i + \frac{1}{x_i} \right)^a \geq \frac{(n^2+1)^a}{n^{a-1}}. \tag{2}$$

Inequality (2) is given by Mitrinović (1970, p. 282).

D.5. The function

$$\phi(x) = \sum \log x_i$$

is strictly Schur-concave on $\mathscr{R}_{++}^n$. This is an immediate consequence of C.1.a.

If $y_i \geq 0$, $i = 1, \ldots, n$, $\bar{y} = (1/n) \sum_1^n y_i$, and $\tilde{y} = (\prod y_i)^{1/n}$, then it follows from D.5 and the arithmetic–geometric mean inequality that

$$\sum \log(1+y_i) \geq n \log(1+\bar{y}) \geq n \log(1+\tilde{y});$$

that is,

$$\prod_1^n (1+y_i) \geq (1+\tilde{y})^n = \left[1 + \prod_1^n y_i^{1/n} \right]^n. \tag{3}$$

Inequality (3) is given by Mitrinović (1970, p. 208).

D.6. The functions

$$\phi_1(x) = \frac{x_1}{x_2 \cdots x_n} + \frac{x_2}{x_1 x_3 \cdots x_n} + \cdots + \frac{x_n}{x_1 \cdots x_{n-1}},$$

$$\phi_2(x) = \frac{x_1}{x_2 + \cdots + x_n} + \frac{x_2}{x_1 + x_3 + \cdots + x_n} + \cdots + \frac{x_n}{x_1 + \cdots + x_{n-1}}$$

are strictly Schur-convex on $\mathscr{R}_{++}^n$.

Proof. Notice that $\phi_1(x) = (\sum_1^n x_i^2)/(\prod_1^n x_i)$. Because $\sum_1^n x_i^2$ is strictly Schur-convex (C.1.a) and because $\prod_1^n x_i$ is Schur-concave on $\mathscr{R}_+^n$ (as is easily verified using A.4, but see F.1), it follows that ϕ_1 is strictly Schur-convex on $\mathscr{R}_{++}^n$.

Let $s = x_1 + \cdots + x_n$. Because $\phi_2(x) = \sum_{i=1}^n [x_i/(s-x_i)]$ and because $g(z) = z/(s-z)$ is strictly convex in z, $0 \leq z \leq s$, it follows from C.1.a that ϕ_2 is strictly Schur-convex. ∥

If $x_i > 0$ and $\sum_1^n x_i = 1$, then $x \succ (1/n, \ldots, 1/n)$, so that because ϕ_1 and ϕ_2 are strictly Schur-convex on $\mathscr{R}_{++}^n$,

$$\sum_1^n \frac{x_i}{\prod_{j \neq i} x_j} \geq n^{n-1},$$

$$\sum_{1}^{n} \frac{x_i}{1-x_i} \geq \frac{n}{n-1},$$

with equality only if $x_i = 1/n$, $i = 1,\ldots,n$. The first of these inequalities is given by Mitrinović (1970, p. 209).

D.6.a. Bagdasar (2008) posed the following problem. For a positive vector $(x_1, x_2, \ldots, x_n)$ with sum $s = x_1 + \ldots + x_n$, if $y_i = s - x_i$ and $s' = y_1 + \ldots + y_n$, then

$$\prod_{i=1}^{n} \left(\frac{x_i}{s - x_i} \right) \leq \prod_{i=1}^{n} \left(\frac{y_i}{s' - y_i} \right). \qquad (4)$$

To see this, define $z_i = y_i/(n-1)$ so that $z_1 + z_2 + \ldots + z_n = s$. Inequality (4) is equivalent to

$$\prod_{i=1}^{n} \left(\frac{x_i}{s - x_i} \right) \leq \prod_{i=1}^{n} \left(\frac{z_i}{s - z_i} \right),$$

i.e., $\phi_1(x) \leq \phi_1(z)$, where ϕ_1 is as defined in D.6. Because $z_i = \sum_{j \neq i} x_j/(n-1)$, it can be verified that $z = xP$, where P is the doubly stochastic matrix with $p_{ii} = 0$ and $p_{ij} = 1/(n-1)$, $i \neq j$. Thus $z \prec x$, and the desired result is a consequence of the Schur-convexity of ϕ_1 on $\mathscr{R}_{++}^n$.

E Examples II. Products of Logarithmically Concave (Convex) Functions

Further discussion of logarithmically concave functions is given in 18.B.2.c and especially 16.D.

E.1. Proposition. Let g be a continuous nonnegative function defined on an interval $I \subset \mathscr{R}$. Then

$$\phi(x) = \prod_{i=1}^{n} g(x_i), \qquad x \in I^n,$$

is Schur-convex on I^n if and only if $\log g$ is convex on I. Moreover, ϕ is strictly Schur-convex on I^n if and only if $\log g$ is strictly convex on I.

Proof. The function ϕ is Schur-convex if and only if $\log \phi$ is Schur-convex, that is, $\sum \log g(x_i)$ is Schur-convex. By C.1 and C.1.c, this holds if and only if $\log g$ is convex. The strictness part follows using C.1.a and C.1.c. ||

106   3. Schur-Convex Functions

Of course, it follows from E.1 that $\phi(x) = \prod_{i=1}^{n} g(x_i)$ is Schur-concave if and only if $\log g$ is concave. Interesting examples can be found in both the concave and convex cases by the identification of logarithmically convex or concave functions g.

E.1.a. Examples. The functions

$$\phi_1(x) = \prod_{i=1}^{n} \frac{1+x_i}{x_i}, \qquad \phi_2(x) = \prod_{i=1}^{n} \frac{1-x_i}{x_i}, \qquad \phi_3(x) = \prod_{i=1}^{n} \frac{1+x_i}{1-x_i}$$

are strictly Schur-convex on their domains $\mathscr{R}_{++}^n$, $(0, 1/2)^n$, and $(0, 1)^n$, respectively.

Proof. A direct verification shows that $\log[(1+z)/z]$, $\log[(1-z)/z]$, and $\log[(1+z)/(1-z)]$ are all strictly convex on their domains $\mathscr{R}_{++}$, $(0, 1/2)$, and $(0, 1)$, respectively, so the result is immediate from E.1. ||

With $x_i > 0$, $\sum x_i = 1$, it follows that $(1/n, \ldots, 1/n) \prec x$. By combining this with the strict Schur-convexity of ϕ_1, ϕ_2, and ϕ_3, it follows that:

If $x_i > 0$, $i = 1, \ldots, n$, and $\sum x_i = 1$, then

$$\prod_{i=1}^{n} \frac{1+x_i}{x_i} \geq (n+1)^n, \qquad \prod_{i=1}^{n} \frac{1-x_i}{x_i} \geq (n-1)^n,$$

and

$$\prod_{i=1}^{n} \frac{1+x_i}{1-x_i} \geq \left(\frac{n+1}{n-1}\right)^n,$$

where equality holds if and only if $x_i = 1/n$, $i = 1, \ldots, n$. The first two of these inequalities are due to Klamkin and Newman (1970), and the third is due to Klamkin (1975).

Let F be a probability distribution function such that $F(0) = 0$, and let $\overline{F} = 1 - F$. If $\log \overline{F}$ is concave, then F is said to have an *increasing hazard rate* (IHR). Similarly, if $\log \overline{F}$ is convex on $[0, \infty)$, F is said to have a *decreasing hazard rate* (DHR). Such distributions arise in reliability theory. For further discussion of logarithmic concavity and its application in reliability, see Marshall and Olkin (2007).

E.1.b. The function $\Pi \overline{F}(x_i)$ is Schur-concave (or Schur-convex) on $\mathscr{R}_+^n$; consequently,

$$\phi(x) = \Pi \overline{F}(x_i) - \overline{F}(\Pi x_i)$$

is Schur-concave or Schur-convex on $\mathcal{R}_+^n$ according to whether F is IHR or DHR. In case F is IHR, $\phi(x) \geq \phi(\sum x_i, 0, \ldots, 0) = 0$ on $\mathcal{R}_+^n$. For the special case $n = 2$ and $F(x) = (2/\sqrt{\pi}) \int_0^x e^{-t^2}\,dt$, the inequality $\phi(x) \geq 0$ was given as a problem by Mitrinović (1968). This choice of F is IHR because it has a logarithmically concave density (18.B.2.b).

E.2. Proposition. If ν is a measure on $[0, \infty)$ such that $g(x) = \int_0^\infty z^x\,d\nu(z)$ exists for all x in an interval I, then $\log g$ is convex on I. Unless ν concentrates its mass on a set of the form $\{0, z_0\}$, $\log g$ is strictly convex on I.

When ν is a probability measure [$g(0) = 1$], then the notation $g(x) \equiv \mu_x$ is often used. With this notation, the logarithmic convexity of μ is equivalent to *Lyapunov's inequality*,

$$\mu_s^{r-t} \leq \mu_t^{r-s}\mu_r^{s-t}, \qquad r \geq s \geq t.$$

For a proof of E.2, see 16.D.1.d.

Just as the log convexity of g leads to Lyapunov's inequality, log convexity and log concavity for other functions lead to what might be called Lyapunov-type inequalities. This kind of inequality is discussed in Section 16.D.

E.3. (Tong, 1977). Let μ_r be the rth moment of a nonnegative random variable, i.e., $\mu_r = \int_0^\infty x^r\,d\nu(x)$ for some probability measure ν, and suppose that μ_r exists for all r in the interval $I \subset \mathcal{R}$. Then

$$\phi(r) = \prod_{i=1}^n \mu_{r_i}$$

is Schur-convex in $r = (r_1, \ldots, r_n) \in I^n$. Unless ν concentrates its mass on a set of the form $\{0, x_0\}$, ϕ is strictly Schur-convex on I^n.

Proof. This is immediate from E.1 and E.2. ||

A generalization of E.3 is given in G.2.h.

E.3.a. If g is a Laplace transform, i.e., $g(s) = \int_0^\infty e^{-sz}\,d\nu(z)$, then $\phi(x) = \Pi g(x_i)$ is Schur-convex on $\mathcal{R}_+^n$.

Proof. This follows from E.1 and E.2 with an obvious change of variables. ||

Proposition E.1 has applications in probability theory and statistics because many important probability densities are logarithmically concave (18.B.2.c).

A variant of Lyapunov's inequality (and other extensions) is obtained by Simić (2007).

E.3.b. Using the notation introduced following E.2, define

$$\theta_t = \frac{2(\mu_t - \mu_1^t)}{t(t-1)}, \quad t \neq 1.$$

Then

$$\theta_s^{r-t} \leq \theta_t^{r-s} \theta_r^{s-t}, \quad r \geq s \geq t \geq 0, \ r,s,t \neq 1.$$

A probability density f is *completely monotone* if it is a mixture of exponential densities (18.B.5).

E.4. Proposition. Let f be a probability density with distribution function F such that $F(0) = 0$. Let $\mu_r = \int_0^\infty x^r \, dF(x)$, and let $\lambda_r = \mu_r / \Gamma(r+1)$ (these quantities are taken to be ∞ if the integral does not converge). Then

$$\begin{aligned}
f \text{ is completely monotone} &\implies \log \lambda_r \text{ is convex in } r > -1, \\
\log f \text{ is concave on } [0, \infty) &\implies \log \lambda_r \text{ is concave in } r \geq 0, \\
\log f \text{ is convex on } [0, \infty) &\implies \log \lambda_r \text{ is convex in } r \geq 0, \\
\log \overline{F} \text{ is concave on } [0, \infty) &\implies \log \lambda_r \text{ is concave in } r \geq 1, \\
\log \overline{F} \text{ is convex on } [0, \infty) &\implies \log \lambda_r \text{ is convex in } r \geq 1.
\end{aligned}$$

A proof of these results is given in 18.B.3, 18.B.4, and 18.B.6.

E.4.a. Remark. A statement that $\log \lambda_r$ is convex is stronger than the statement that $\log \mu_r$ is convex because

$$\log \lambda_r = \log \mu_r - \log \Gamma(r+1),$$

and because $\log \Gamma(r+1)$ is convex, $r > -1$ (E.6.a). However, the convexity of $\log \mu_r$ may hold for a broader range of r than the convexity of $\log \lambda_r$.

Examples Involving the Gamma Function

The gamma function appears in many contexts and is discussed in great detail in Artin (1931, 1964). For a history and general discussion, see Davis (1959) and Srinivasan (2007). A brief description that suffices for general use is given by Marshall and Olkin (2007, Chapter 23). Many of the results in this section are given by Marshall and Olkin (2007).

E. Products of Logarithmically Concave (Convex) Functions

Here Schur-convexity properties are obtained. As usual, let Γ denote the gamma function. The key to proving Schur-convexity is to show that each function arises as a moment of some distribution, and then to invoke E.3.

E.5. The function
$$\phi(x) = \prod_1^n \Gamma(x_i)$$
is strictly Schur-convex on $\mathscr{R}_{++}^n$.

Proof. In E.3, take ν to be the probability measure with density $f(z) = e^{-z}$, $0 \leq z < \infty$. Then $\mu_r = \Gamma(r+1), r > -1$. ||
See also 16.B.8.a.

By taking ν to be the probability measure with density $f(z) = e^{-z}/(1 - e^{-x})$, $0 \leq z \leq x$, the gamma function in E.5 is replaced by an incomplete gamma function.

Mitrinović (1970, p. 285) has used the fact that $\log \Gamma(z)$ is convex in $z > 0$ to obtain that
$$\prod_1^n \Gamma(x_i) \geq \left[\Gamma\left(\sum x_i/n\right)\right]^n.$$
This inequality follows from Jensen's inequality or from E.5 and the fact that $(\sum x_i/n)(1, \ldots, 1) \prec (x_1, \ldots, x_n)$. But, of course, much more general comparisons are obtainable from E.5.

It also follows from E.5 that the *generalized beta function*
$$B(x_1, \ldots, x_n) = \prod_1^n \Gamma(x_i)/\Gamma(\Sigma x_i), \quad x_i > 0,$$
is Schur-convex. The beta function $B(x_1, \ldots, x_n)$ is decreasing in each argument with the others held fixed. This follows by taking derivatives in the integral representation
$$B(x_1, \ldots, x_n) = \int_\Omega \Pi_1^n t_i^{x_i-1} \Pi_1^n dt_i,$$
where $\Omega = \{t : t_i \geq 0, \Sigma t_i = 1\}$.
See also Dedić, Matić, and Pečarić (2000).

E.6.a. Let ν be the gamma distribution with density
$$f(z|a) = z^{a-1}e^{-z}/\Gamma(a)), \quad 0 \leq z < \infty, \ a > 0.$$

It follows from E.2 that
$$\mu_r = \Gamma(r+a), \quad r \geq -a,$$
is logarithmically convex, and consequently (E.3) the function
$$\phi(x) = \prod_1^n \Gamma(x_i + a), \quad a > 0,$$
is strictly Schur-convex in $(-a, \infty)^n$.

E.6.b. For $0 < a \leq 1$, the gamma density can be written in the form
$$f(z|a) = \int_0^\infty \theta e^{-\theta z} g(\theta|a) d\theta, \text{ where } g(\theta|a) = \theta^{-1}(\theta-1)^{-\alpha}/B(\alpha, 1-\alpha)$$
[see Marshall and Olkin (2007, p. 312)]. Consequently, f is completely monotone for $0 < a < 1$, and it follows from E.4 that
$$\lambda_r = \Gamma(r+a)/\Gamma(r+1), \quad r \geq -a$$
is logarithmically convex in $r \geq -a$ when $0 < a \leq 1$. Thus
$$\phi(x) = \prod_{i=1}^n \Gamma(x_i + a)/\Gamma(x_i + 1), \quad x_i > -a,$$
is Schur-convex for $0 < a \leq 1$. Because $\log \lambda_r = \log \mu_r - \log \Gamma(r+1)$ and $\log \Gamma(r+1)$ are convex in $r > -1$ (E.6.a), the convexity of $\log \lambda_r$ implies the convexity of $\log \mu_r$, but only for $0 < a < 1$.

It can be verified that the gamma density is log concave when $a \geq 1$. From this and E.4, it follows that $\log \lambda_r$ is concave in $r \geq 0$. This means that ϕ is Schur-concave on $\mathscr{R}_+^n$ when $a \geq 1$.

E.7.a. If, in E.2, ν has the beta density
$$f(z|a, b) = \frac{x^{a-1}(1-x)^{b-1}}{B(a,b)}, \quad 0 \leq x \leq 1, \ a, b > 0,$$
then it follows that
$$\mu_r = B(a+r, b)/B(a, b), \quad r > -a,$$
is strictly log convex. Because multiplicative constants do not affect log convexity, it follows that
$$g(r) = \Gamma(r+a)/\Gamma(r+a+b)$$
is strictly log convex in $r > -a$. From E.3 it follows that the function
$$\phi(x) = \prod_1^n \frac{\Gamma(x_i+a)}{\Gamma(x_i+a+b)}, \quad a, b > 0,$$
is strictly Schur-convex on $(-a, \infty)^n$.

E. Products of Logarithmically Concave (Convex) Functions

E.7.b. It can be verified that the density of the beta distribution is log convex for $a, b \leq 1$ and log concave for $a, b \geq 1$. It follows from E.4 that $\log \lambda_r$ is convex in $r \geq 0$ when $a, b \leq 1$, and $\log \lambda_r$ is concave in $r \geq 0$ when $a, b \leq 1$. This means that

$$g(r) = \frac{\Gamma(r+a)}{\Gamma(r+a+b)\Gamma(r+1)}$$

is log convex in $r \geq 0$ when $a, b \leq 1$, and log concave in $r \geq 0$ when $a, b \geq 1$. It follows that for $x \in \mathscr{R}_+^n$, the function

$$\phi(x) = \prod_1^n \frac{\Gamma(x_i+a)}{\Gamma(x_i+a+b)\Gamma(x_i+1)}$$

is Schur-convex when $a, b \leq 1$ and Schur-concave when $a, b \geq 1$.

E.8.a. The function

$$g(x) = \prod_{i=1}^n \frac{x_i^{x_i+1}}{\Gamma(x_i+1)}$$

is Schur-concave on $\mathscr{R}_{++}^n$.

Proof. From the integral representation of the gamma function,

$$\frac{\Gamma(x+1)}{x^{x+1}} = \int_0^\infty (te^{-t})^x \, dt = \int_0^\infty z^x \, d\nu(z),$$

where

$$\nu(-\infty, z] = \int_{\{te^{-t} \leq z, t \geq 0\}} te^{-t} dt.$$

It follows from E.2 that $\log[\Gamma(x+1)/x^{x+1}]$ is convex in $x > 0$; i.e., $\log[x^{x+1}/\Gamma(x+1)]$ is concave in $x > 0$. According to E.3, this means that

$$\phi(x) = \prod_1^n \frac{x_i^{x_i+1}}{\Gamma(x_i+1)}, \quad x \in \mathscr{R}^n,$$

is Schur-concave. ∥

The fact that $\log[\Gamma(x+1)/x^{x+1}]$ is convex in $x > 0$ is the content of a problem posed by Eliezer (1971). This convexity can be written in the form

$$\left[\frac{\Gamma(x+1)}{x^{x+1}} \cdot \frac{\Gamma(y+1)}{y^{y+1}}\right]^{1/2} \geq \frac{\Gamma[\frac{1}{2}(x+y)+1]}{[\frac{1}{2}(x+y)]^{\frac{1}{2}(x+y)+1}}.$$

3. Schur-Convex Functions

An application of the arithmetic–geometric mean inequality yields

$$\frac{1}{2}\left[\frac{\Gamma(x+1)}{x^{x+1}} + \frac{\Gamma(y+1)}{y^{y+1}}\right] \geq \frac{\Gamma[\frac{1}{2}(x+y)]+1}{[\frac{1}{2}(x+y)]^{\frac{1}{2}(x+y)+1}},$$

which is another inequality posed by Eliezer (1971).

E.8.b. The function

$$\phi(x) = \prod_{i=1}^{n}[x_i^{x_i}/\Gamma(x_i+1)]$$

is Schur-convex on $\mathscr{R}_+^n$.

Proof. Marshall, Olkin, and Proschan (1967) give a proof due to Herman Rubin that for $r > 0$, $\mu_r = r^r$ is the rth moment of a density of the form

$$f(x) = \int_0^\infty e^{\lambda x} d\nu(\lambda).$$

Thus, f is completely monotone and the result follows from E.1 and E.4. ||

This result is to be contrasted with E.8.a, which is obtained above using an entirely different probability measure.

E.9. The function

$$\phi(x) = \prod_{i=1}^{n} \frac{\Gamma(mx_i+a)}{\Gamma^k(x_i+a)}, \quad m = 1, 2, \ldots, \ k = 1, \ldots, m,$$

is Schur-convex on $(-a/m, \infty)^n$, provided that $a \geq (m-1)/(k-1)$ (for $k > 1$). The Schur-convexity is strict for $m > 1$.

Proof. The Gauss-Legendre multiplication formula 16.B.8.b permits the expansion

$$\Gamma(mz+a) = \frac{m^{mz+a-1/2}}{(2\pi)^{(m-1)/2}} \prod_{j=1}^{m} \Gamma\left(z + \frac{a+j-1}{m}\right).$$

Thus

$$\prod_{i=1}^{n} \frac{\Gamma(mx_i+a)}{\Gamma^k(x_i+a)} = c(m,a) \ m^{\sum x_i} \prod_{j=1}^{m} \phi_j(x),$$

where $c(m,a)$ depends only on m and a, and

$$\phi_j(x) = \prod_{i=1}^{n} \frac{\Gamma(x_i + \frac{a+j-1}{m})}{\Gamma(x_i+a)} \quad \text{for} \ j = 1, \ldots, k,$$

E. Products of Logarithmically Concave (Convex) Functions 113

$$\phi_j(x) = \prod_{i=1}^{n} \Gamma\left(x_i + \frac{a+j-1}{m}\right) \quad \text{for } j = k+1, \ldots, m.$$

For $j = 1, \ldots, k$, ϕ_j is strictly Schur-convex on $(-a/m, \infty)^n$ by E.7.a. For $j = k+1, \ldots, m$, ϕ_j is strictly Schur-convex on $(-a/m, \infty)^n$ by E.6.a. Consequently, ϕ is a product of nonnegative Schur-convex functions, all but one of which is strictly Schur-convex. Consequently, ϕ is strictly Schur-convex. ‖

The above result was obtained by Li, Zhao, and Chen (2006). For $m = 2$, Merkle (1997) shows that $g(x) = \Gamma(2x)/\Gamma^2(x)$ is log-convex. Further results are obtained by Chen (2005) and by Li, Zhao, and Chen (2006).

If $m_1, \ldots, m_n$ are nonnegative integers such that $m_1 + \cdots + m_n = s$, then $(m_1, \ldots, m_n, 0, \ldots, 0) \succ (1, \ldots, 1)$. It then follows from E.9 with $k = 1, m = 2$, and $a = 1$ that

$$\prod_{i=1}^{n} \frac{(2m_i)!}{m_i!} = \prod_{1}^{n} \frac{\Gamma(2m_i + 1)}{\Gamma(m_i + 1)} \geq 2^s.$$

This inequality is due to Khintchine (1923); see also Mitrinović (1970, p. 194).

E.9.a. The function

$$\phi(x) = \binom{n}{x_1, \ldots, x_k} \bigg/ \binom{mn}{mx_1, \ldots, mx_k}, \quad m = 2, 3, \ldots,$$

of multinomial coefficients is strictly Schur-convex in $x_1, \ldots, x_k$, where each x_i is a nonnegative integer and $\sum_{1}^{n} x_i = n$.

Proof. Because $j! = \Gamma(j+1)$ for nonnegative integers j,

$$\phi(x) = \frac{\Gamma(n+1)}{\Gamma(mn+1)} \prod_{i=1}^{n} \frac{\Gamma(mx_i + 1)}{\Gamma(x_i + 1)},$$

so the result follows from E.9 with $a = 1$. ‖

E.10. If f is a twice-differentiable nonnegative increasing concave function defined on $\mathscr{R}_{++}$, then $g(z) = z \log f(s-z)$ is concave (i.e., $[f(s-z)]^z$ is log concave).

Proof. This result can be verified by computing the second derivative of g. ‖

E.10.a. (Kwong, 2007). If f satisfies the conditions of E.10 and $s = x_1 + \ldots + x_n$, then

$$\max_x \prod_{i=1}^n [f(s - x_i)]^{x_i/s} \leq f\left(\frac{n-1}{n}s\right).$$

Equality holds if the x_i's are equal.

Proof. By E.10 and E.1, the function $\prod_{i=1}^n [f(s - x_i)]^{x_i/s}$ is Schur-concave. The result follows from $(\overline{x}, \ldots, \overline{x}) \prec (x_1, \ldots, x_n)$. ||

E.10.b. Proposition. (Merkle, 1998). The function

$$\phi(x, y) = \frac{\log \Gamma(x) - \log \Gamma(y)}{x - y}, \quad x \neq y,$$
$$= \psi(x) = \Gamma'(x)/\Gamma(x), \quad x = y,$$

is strictly Schur-concave on $x > 0, y > 0$.

Proof. The condition for Schur-concavity is equivalent to the condition

$$\frac{\psi(x) + \psi(y)}{2} < \frac{\log \Gamma(y) - \log \Gamma(x)}{y - x}, \quad 0 < x < y.$$

The mean-value theorem is then used to prove the inequality. ||

For $x > 0, a > 0$, a bound for the ratio $\Gamma(x+a)/\Gamma(x)$ is obtained from the majorization $(x+a, x) \succ (x + a/2, x + a/2)$:

$$\exp \frac{a[\psi(x+a) + \psi(x)]}{2} \frac{\Gamma(x+a)}{\Gamma(x)} < \exp a\psi(x + a/2).$$

Other inequalities for the gamma function are obtained by Merkle (1998). A generalization of E.10.b is given by Elezović and Pečarić (2000).

F Examples III. Elementary Symmetric Functions

Denote by $S_k(x)$ the kth elementary symmetric function of $x_1, \ldots, x_n$. That is,

$$S_0(x) \equiv 1, \quad S_1(x) = \sum_{i=1}^n x_i, \quad S_2(x) = \sum_{i<j} x_i x_j,$$

$$S_3(x) = \sum_{i<j<k} x_i x_j x_k, \quad \ldots, \quad S_n(x) = \prod_1^n x_i.$$

F. Examples III. Elementary Symmetric Functions

F.1. Proposition (Schur, 1923). The function S_k is increasing and Schur-concave on $\mathscr{R}_+^n$. If $k > 1$, S_k is strictly Schur-concave on $\mathscr{R}_{++}^n$.

Proof. Let $\phi(x) = S_k(x)$ and verify (10) of A.4:

$$[\phi_{(i)}(x) - \phi_{(j)}(x)](x_i - x_j)$$
$$= [S_{k-1}(x_1, \ldots, x_{i-1}, x_{i+1}, \ldots, x_n)$$
$$\quad - S_{k-1}(x_1, \ldots, x_{j-1}, x_{j+1}, \ldots, x_n)](x_i - x_j) \leq 0.$$

Strict Schur-concavity on $\mathscr{R}_{++}^n$ follows from A.4.b. ||

Remark. S_2 is actually Schur-concave on $\mathscr{R}^n$, not just on $\mathscr{R}_+^n$. The restriction to $\mathscr{R}_+^n$ is needed for Schur-convexity of S_k when $k > 2$.

F.1.a. If $x, y \in \mathscr{R}_+^n$, then

$$x \prec y \Rightarrow \prod_1^n x_i \geq \prod_1^n y_i,$$

with strict inequality unless x is a permutation of y.

Proof. This follows from F.1 with $k = n$. ||

This result has numerous applications, and for many well-known inequalities of the form $\prod_1^n x_i \geq \prod_1^n y_i$, there is an underlying majorization. For example, if $x_i = \sum_1^n y_i/n$ for each i in F.1.a, the arithmetic–geometric mean inequality G.2.f is obtained.

F.1.b. Daykin (1969) posed the following problem: If $y_i > 0$, $i = 1, \ldots, n$, $y_{n+j} = y_j$, $j = 1, \ldots, n$, and if $x_j = (y_{j+1} + \cdots + y_{j+m})/m$, then $\prod_1^n y_i \leq \prod_1^n x_i$, with equality if and only if $y_1 = \cdots = y_n$ or $m = 1$. This result follows from F.1.a because $x = yP$, where P is the doubly stochastic matrix $\widetilde{C}$ of 2.H.4.a with $a_1 = \cdots = a_m = 1/m$, $a_0 = a_{m+1} = \cdots = a_n = 0$.

F.1.c. (Oppenheim, 1965a, 1968; Mitrinović, 1970, p. 339). If $0 < \min(a_1, a_2, a_3) \leq c_k \leq \max(a_1, a_2, a_3)$ for $k = 1, 2, 3$, and $c_1 + c_2 + c_3 \geq a_1 + a_2 + a_3$, then

$$c_1 c_2 c_3 \geq a_1 a_2 a_3,$$
$$c_2 c_3 + c_3 c_1 + c_1 c_2 \geq a_2 a_3 + a_3 a_1 + a_1 a_2.$$

Proof. For convenience, suppose that $a_1 \geq a_2 \geq a_3$ and $c_1 \geq c_2 \geq c_3$. Then the conditions give directly that $c_3 \geq a_3$. Addition of the inequalities $c_1 + c_2 + c_3 \geq a_1 + a_2 + a_3$ and $a_1 \geq c_1$ yields $c_2 + c_3 \geq a_2 + a_3$. Consequently, $c \prec^w a$. Thus the above inequalities follow from F.1 and A.8 with $\phi = -S_2$ and $\phi = -S_3$. ||

F.2. The function $\phi(x) = [S_k(x)]^{1/k}$ is concave and increasing (in fact, strictly concave if $k \neq 1$) in $x \in \mathscr{R}_+^n$; hence, ϕ is Schur-concave (strictly Schur-concave if $k \neq 1$) and increasing, $k = 1, \ldots, n$, in $x \in \mathscr{R}_+^n$.

Proof. The concavity of $S_k^{1/k}$ follows from F.1. It is also a consequence of the inequality

$$[S_k(x+y)]^{1/k} \geq [S_k(x)]^{1/k} + [S_k(y)]^{1/k},$$

which is due to Marcus and Lopes (1957) and to Henri Frédéric Bohnenblust as reported by Marcus and Lopes (1957). See also Beckenbach and Bellman (1961, p. 35). ||

F.2.a. If $\widetilde{x} = (1 - x_1, 1 - x_2, \ldots, 1 - x_n)$, then

$$[S_k(x)]^{1/k} + [S_k(\widetilde{x})]^{1/k}$$

is Schur-concave on $\{z : 0 \leq z_i \leq 1 \text{ for all } i\}$. In particular,

$$\left(\prod x_i\right)^{1/n} + \left[\prod (1 - x_i)\right]^{1/n}$$

is Schur-concave.

Proof. This follows directly from F.2. ||

One can very easily verify that $[S_k(x)]^{1/k} + [S_k(\widetilde{x})]^{1/k}$ is Schur-concave on $\{z : 0 \leq z_i \leq 1 \text{ for all } i\}$ directly from the condition of A.4.

F.3. (Schur, 1923; Marcus and Lopes, 1957). The ratio S_k/S_{k-1} is concave (in fact, strictly concave unless $k = 1$) in $x \in \mathscr{R}_{++}^n$; hence, S_k/S_{k-1} is Schur-concave, $k = 1, \ldots, n$, in $x \in \mathscr{R}_{++}^n$.

F. Examples III. Elementary Symmetric Functions   117

Proof. The concavity of S_k/S_{k-1} is an immediate consequence of the inequality

$$\frac{S_k(x+y)}{S_{k-1}(x+y)} \geq \frac{S_k(x)}{S_{k-1}(x)} + \frac{S_k(y)}{s_{k-1}(y)},$$

which is due to Marcus and Lopes (1957). See also Beckenbach and Bellman (1961, p. 33) ||

That S_k/S_{k-1} is Schur-concave was proved by Schur (1923).

F.3.a. (Bullen and Marcus, 1961).   If $1 \leq p \leq k \leq n$, then

$$F_{k,p}(x) = [S_k(x)/S_{k-p}(x)]^{1/p}$$

is a concave function of $x \in \mathcal{R}_{++}^n$. Hence, $F_{k,p}$ is Schur-concave on $\mathcal{R}_{++}^n$, $1 \leq p \leq k \leq n$.

Proof. The concavity of $F_{k,p}$ is equivalent to the inequality

$$F_{k,p}(x+y) \geq F_{k,p}(x) + F_{k,p}(y), \qquad x, y \in \mathcal{R}_{++}^n,$$

which is proved by Bullen and Marcus (1961). ||

Notice that the case $p = 1$ in F.3.a is just F.3.

F.4. (Schur, 1923).   If $S_k(x)$ is the kth elementary symmetric function of $x_1, \ldots, x_n$, then

$$\phi(x) = S_1^{n-\nu}(x) S_\nu(x) - (n-2)^{n-\nu} \binom{n-2}{\nu-2} S_n(x)$$

is Schur-concave in x on $\mathcal{R}_{++}^n$, $\nu = 2, 3, \ldots, n-1$.

Proof. Because of symmetry, it is sufficient to verify condition (10′) of A.4. As in the proof of F.1,

$$\frac{\partial S_k(x_1, \ldots, x_n)}{\partial x_1} - \frac{\partial S_k(x_1, \ldots, x_n)}{\partial x_2} = -(x_1 - x_2) S_{k-2}(x_3, \ldots, x_n).$$

3. Schur-Convex Functions

Using this, it follows directly that

$$[\phi_{(1)}(x) - \phi_{(2)}(x)](x_1 - x_2)$$
$$= -(x_1 - x_2)^2 S_1^{n-\nu}(x_1, \ldots, x_n) S_{\nu-2}(x_3, \ldots, x_n)$$
$$+ (n-2)^{n-\nu} \binom{n-2}{n-\nu} (x_1 - x_2)^2 S_{n-2}(x_3, \ldots, x_n)$$
$$\leq (x_1 - x_2)^2 \Bigl[-S_1^{n-\nu}(x_3, \ldots, x_n) S_{\nu-2}(x_3, \ldots, x_n)$$
$$+ (n-2)^{n-\nu} \binom{n-2}{n-\nu} S_{n-2}(x_3, \ldots, x_n) \Bigr]$$
$$= (x_1 - x_2)^2 \binom{n-2}{n-\nu} (n-2)^{n-\nu} \Bigl\{ S_{n-2}(x_3, \ldots, x_n)$$
$$- \Bigl[S_{\nu-2}(x_3, \ldots, x_n) \Big/ \binom{n-2}{\nu-2} \Bigr]$$
$$\times \Bigl[S_1(x_3, \ldots, x_n) \Big/ \binom{n-2}{1} \Bigr]^{n-\nu} \Bigr\}.$$

But this is nonpositive by virtue of the fact that

$$\Bigl[S_{k+1}(x_3, \ldots, x_n) \Big/ \binom{n-2}{k+1-2} \Bigr] \Big/ \Bigl[S_k(x_3, \ldots, x_n) \Big/ \binom{n-2}{k-2} \Bigr]$$

is decreasing in $k = 1, \ldots, n-1$. ||

F.4.a. (Schur, 1923). If $x, y \in \mathscr{R}_+^n$ and $x \prec y$, then

$$0 \leq \prod_1^n x_i - \prod_1^n y_i \leq \frac{(\sum x_i)^{n-2}}{n-2} \frac{(\sum y_i^2 - \sum x_i^2)}{2}. \tag{1}$$

Proof. To obtain the right-hand inequality, for $\nu = 2$ in F.4,

$$[S_1(x)]^{n-2} S_2(x) - (n-2)^{n-2} S_n(x)$$
$$\geq [S_1(y)]^{n-2} S_2(y) - (n-2)^{n-2} S_n(y). \tag{2}$$

Because $S_1(x) = S_1(y)$,

$$\prod_1^n x_i - \prod_1^n y_i = S_n(x) - S_n(y) \leq \left(\frac{\sum x_i}{n-2}\right)^{n-2} [S_2(x) - S_2(y)].$$

Inequality (1) follows by noting that

$$2[S_2(x) - S_2(y)] = \Bigl[\Bigl(\sum x_i\Bigr)^2 - \Bigl(\sum x_i^2\Bigr) \Bigr] - \Bigl[\Bigl(\sum y_i\Bigr)^2 - \Bigl(\sum y_i^2\Bigr) \Bigr]$$
$$= \sum y_i^2 - \sum x_i^2. ||$$

Complete Symmetric Functions

The elementary symmetric function S_k can be defined by

$$S_k(x) = \sum_{\substack{i_1+\cdots+i_n=k \\ i_j = 0 \text{ or } 1}} x_1^{i_1} \cdots x_n^{i_n}.$$

Corresponding to this is the *complete symmetric function*

$$C_k(x) = \sum_{\substack{i_1+\cdots+i_n=k \\ i_j \geq 0}} x_1^{i_1} \cdots x_n^{i_n}.$$

As stated in F.2, $[S_k(x)]^{1/k}$ is a concave function of $x \in \mathscr{R}_+^n$; in contrast to this, $[C_k(x)]^{1/k}$ is convex. These results are included as special cases of the following:

F.5. Proposition (Whiteley, 1958). For $l \neq 0$ and $k = 1, \ldots, n$, let

$$T_k^{(l)}(x) = \sum_{\substack{i_1+\cdots+i_n=k \\ i_j \geq 0}} \lambda_{i_1} \cdots \lambda_{i_n} x_1^{i_1} \cdots x_n^{i_n},$$

where $\lambda_i = \binom{l}{i}$ if $l > 0$, $\lambda_i = (-1)^i \binom{l}{i}$ if $l < 0$.
If $l < 0$, then

$$[T_k^{(l)}(x+y)]^{1/k} \leq [T_k^{(l)}(x)]^{1/k} + [T_k^{(l)}(y)]^{1/k}. \quad (3)$$

If $l > 0$ and $k < l+1$, unless l is an integer, the inequality (3) is reversed.

The proof of this result is not given here.

Because $[T_k^{(l)}(x)]^{1/k}$ is homogeneous of degree 1 in x, inequality (3) says that this function is convex and the reversal of (3) says this function is concave. Because $T_k^{(l)}$ is symmetric, the functions ϕ_1, ϕ_2 defined by

$$\phi_1(x) = [T_k^{(l)}(x)]^{1/k}, \qquad \phi_2(x) = T_k^{(l)}(x)$$

are Schur-convex if $l < 0$, and are Schur-concave if $l > 0$ and $k < l+1$, unless k is an integer.

The case of S_k is obtained with $l = 1$; the case of C_k is obtained with $l = -1$.

The fact that S_k is Schur-concave and C_k is Schur-convex has been generalized by Daykin (1971) and Baston (1976/1977, 1978). There are misprints in these papers; some of the inequalities are reversed. The Schur-convexity of $C_k(x)$ and $C_k(x)/C_{k-1}(x)$ for $k = 1, \ldots, n$ is shown by Guan (2006).

G Symmetrization of Convex and Schur-Convex Functions: Muirhead's Theorem

According to C.2, a function ϕ is Schur-convex if it is symmetric and convex. As was pointed out in the remark following A.1, all Schur-convex functions are symmetric, so that the symmetry condition here is essential. If ϕ is convex but not symmetric, then there are various ways to symmetrize ϕ while preserving convexity so as to generate a Schur-convex function. The early result of Muirhead (1903) can be viewed in this way.

All of the propositions of this section that identify Schur-convex functions can be easily modified to yield monotone Schur-convex functions with trivial additions to the proofs. Because these modifications are obvious, they are omitted in many cases.

Let $S_n = \{\pi_1, \ldots, \pi_{n!}\}$ be the group of all permutations of $\{1, 2, \ldots, n\}$, and let

$$\pi_i(x) = (x_{\pi_i(1)}, \ldots, x_{\pi_i(n)}).$$

G.1. Proposition. If $\phi : \mathscr{R}^n \to \mathscr{R}$ is convex and $h : \mathscr{R}^{n!} \to \mathscr{R}$ is symmetric, increasing, and convex, then

$$\psi(x) = h(\phi(\pi_1 x), \ldots, \phi(\pi_{n!} x))$$

is symmetric and convex.

Proof. That ψ is symmetric is trivial. Convexity of ψ follows from 16.B.7. ‖

G.1.a. If $\phi : \mathscr{R}^n \to \mathscr{R}$ is convex, $h : \mathscr{R}^{n!} \to \mathscr{R}$ is symmetric, increasing, and convex, and if $t_1, \ldots, t_n$ are real numbers, then

$$\psi(x) = h(\phi(t_1 x_{\pi_1(1)}, \ldots, t_n x_{\pi_1(n)}), \ldots, \phi(t_1 x_{\pi_{n!}(1)}, \ldots, t_n x_{\pi_{n!}(n)}))$$

is a symmetric convex function. If ϕ is increasing (decreasing) as well as convex, and if $t_1, \ldots, t_n$ are nonnegative, then ψ is symmetric, increasing (decreasing), and convex.

Proof. If ϕ is convex, then

$$\widetilde{\phi}(x) = \phi(t_1 x_1, \ldots, t_n x_n)$$

is convex. With $\widetilde{\phi}$ in place of ϕ, G.1 becomes G.1.a. ‖

Notation. The notation $\sum_{k,\pi} \phi(t_1 x_{\pi(1)}, \ldots, t_n x_{\pi(n)})$ denotes summation over the k largest values assumed by $\phi(t_1 x_{\pi(1)}, \ldots, t_n x_{\pi(n)})$ as π ranges over the $n!$ permutations of $1, \ldots, n$.

A specific choice of h in G.1.a yields G.1.b:

G.1.b. If $\phi: \mathscr{R}^n \to \mathscr{R}$ is convex and $t_1, \ldots, t_n$ are real numbers, then

$$\psi_k(x) = \sum_{k,\pi} \phi(t_1 x_{\pi(1)}, \ldots, t_n x_{\pi(n)}), \quad k = 1, \ldots, n!,$$

is symmetric and convex.

With particular choices of k in G.1.b, both G.1.c and G.1.d are obtained.

G.1.c. If $\phi: \mathscr{R}^n \to \mathscr{R}$ is convex and $t_1, \ldots, t_n$ are real numbers, then

$$\psi(x) = \sum_{\pi} \phi(t_1 x_{\pi(1)}, \ldots, t_n x_{\pi(n)})$$

is symmetric and convex.

G.1.d. If $\phi: \mathscr{R}^n \to \mathscr{R}$ is convex and $t_1, \ldots, t_n$ are real numbers, then

$$\psi(x) = \max_{\pi} \phi(t_1 x_{\pi(1)}, \ldots, t_n x_{\pi(n)})$$

is symmetric and convex. If $t_1, \ldots, t_n \geq 0$ ($t_1, \ldots, t_n \leq 0$), then ψ is also increasing (decreasing).

Another consequence of G.1.b is

G.1.e. If $t_1, \ldots, t_n$ are real numbers, then

$$\psi_k(x) = \sum_{k,\pi} (t_1 x_{\pi(1)} + \cdots + t_n x_{\pi(n)})$$

is symmetric and convex, $k = 1, 2, \ldots, n!$.

Note that in case $k = n!$,

$$\psi_{n!}(x) = (n-1)! \left(\sum t_i\right) \left(\sum x_i\right)$$

is a function of $\sum x_i$. If $k = 1$,

$$\psi_1(x) = \max_{\pi} (t_1 x_{\pi(1)} + \cdots + t_n x_{\pi(n)})$$

is a special case of G.1.d. That ψ_1 is Schur-convex is due to Mirsky (1957a).

G.1.f. If $g_j : \mathscr{R} \to \mathscr{R}$ is convex, $j = 1, \ldots, n$, and $h : \mathscr{R}^n \to \mathscr{R}$ is symmetric increasing and convex, then

$$\psi(x) = h\left(\sum_{j=1}^n g_j(x_{\pi_1(j)}), \ldots, \sum_{j=1}^n g_j(x_{\pi_{n!}(j)})\right)$$

is symmetric and convex.

Proof. Because $\phi(x) = \sum_{j=1}^n g_j(x_j)$ is convex, this follows from G.1. ∥

G.1.g. If $g : \mathscr{R} \to \mathscr{R}$ is convex, then

$$\psi_k(x) = \sum_{k,\pi} \sum_{i=1}^n g(t_i x_{\pi(i)}), \quad k = 1, \ldots, n!,$$

is symmetric and convex.

G.1.h. If $g_j : \mathscr{R} \to (0, \infty)$ and $\log g_j$ is convex, $j = 1, \ldots, n$, and if $h : \mathscr{R}^{n!} \to \mathscr{R}$ is symmetric, increasing, and convex, then

$$\psi(x) = h\left(\prod_{j=1}^n g_j(x_{\pi_1(j)}), \ldots, \prod_{j=1}^n g_j(x_{\pi_{n!}(j)})\right)$$

is symmetric and convex.

Proof. Because $\sum_{j=1}^n \log g_j(x_j) = \log \prod_{j=1}^n g_j(x_j)$ is convex in x, it follows from 16.B.7.b that $\phi(x) = \prod_{j=1}^n g_j(x_j)$ is convex, so the result follows from G.1. ∥

G.1.i. If $g_j : \mathscr{R} \to (0, \infty)$ and $\log g_j$ is convex, $j = 1, \ldots, n$, then

$$\psi_k(x) = \sum_{k,\pi} \prod_{j=1}^n g_j(x_{\pi(j)})$$

is symmetric and convex, $1 \leq k \leq n!$.

The choices $k = 1$ and $k = n!$ in G.1.i yield the following:

G.1.j. If $g_j : \mathscr{R} \to (0, \infty)$ and $\log g_j$ is convex, $j = 1, \ldots, n$, then

$$\psi_{n!}(x) = \sum_\pi \prod_{j=1}^n g_j(x_{\pi(j)}) \quad \text{and} \quad \psi_1(x) = \max_\pi \prod_{j=1}^n g_j(x_{\pi(j)})$$

are symmetric and convex.

That $\psi_{n!}$ is symmetric and convex is due to Proschan and Sethuraman (1973).

G.1.k. If $a_j > 0$, $j = 1, \ldots, n$, the function

$$\psi(x) = \sum_\pi \prod_{j=1}^n x_{\pi(j)}^{-a_j}$$

is symmetric and convex on $\mathscr{R}_{++}^n$.

G.1.l. If $g: \mathscr{R} \to (0, \infty)$ and $\log g$ is convex, and if h is symmetric, increasing, and convex, then

$$h\left(\prod_1^n g(t_j x_{\pi_1(j)}), \ldots, \prod_1^n g(t_j x_{\pi_{n!}(j)})\right)$$

is symmetric and convex.

G.1.m. If $a > 0$,

$$\psi_k(x) = \sum_{i_1 < \cdots < i_k} \prod_{j=1}^k \left(\frac{1}{x_{i_j}}\right)^a, \quad k = 1, \ldots, n!, \tag{1}$$

is symmetric decreasing and convex on

$$\mathscr{R}_{++} = \{z : z_i > 0, i = 1, 2, \ldots, n\}.$$

Proof. In G.1.h take $g_j(x) = x^{-a}$, $j = 1, \ldots, k$, $g_j(x) \equiv 1$ for $j = k+1, \ldots, n$, and $h(z_1, \ldots, z_{n!}) = [(n-k)!/(n!k!)] \sum_1^{n!} z_i$. Thus ψ is symmetric and convex. The monotonicity is trivial. ∥

If each $x_i > 0$ and $\sum_1^n x_i \leq 1$, then from G.1.m and the fact that $x \succ^w (1/n, \ldots, 1/n)$, it follows that

$$\sum_{i_1 < \cdots < i_k} \prod_{j=1}^k \left(\frac{1}{x_{i_j}}\right)^a \geq \binom{n}{k} n^{ka}. \tag{2}$$

If $x_i < 1$, $i = 1, \ldots, n$, then x_i can be replaced by $1 - x_i$ in (1) to obtain an increasing convex function. An argument similar to that for (2) shows that if each $x_i \leq 1$ and $\sum_1^n x_i \geq 1$, then

$$\sum_{i_1 < \cdots < i_k} \prod_{j=1}^k \left(\frac{1}{1-x_{i_j}}\right)^a \geq \binom{n}{k}\left(\frac{n}{n-1}\right)^{ka}. \tag{3}$$

G.1.n. The function

$$\psi_k(x) = \prod_{i_1 < \cdots < i_k} \sum_{j=1}^k x_{i_j}, \quad k = 1, \ldots, n, \tag{4}$$

is increasing and Schur-concave on $\mathscr{R}_+$.

Proof. Since $\log \psi$ is increasing concave and symmetric, $\log \psi$ is increasing and Schur-concave, and hence ψ is increasing and Schur-concave. ∥

With the fact that $x \succ^w (1/n, \ldots, 1/n)$ when $\sum_1^n x_i \leq 1$, it follows that if $\sum_1^n x_i \leq 1$ and $x_i \geq 0$, $i = 1, \ldots, n$, then

$$\prod_{i_1 < \cdots < i_k} \sum_{j=1}^k x_{i_j} \leq \left(\frac{k}{n}\right)^{\binom{n}{k}}. \tag{5}$$

If $x_i \leq 1$, $i = 1, \ldots, n$, then x_i can be replaced by $1 - x_i$ in (4) to obtain a decreasing Schur-concave function. An argument similar to that for (5) shows that if $\sum_1^n x_i \geq 1$ and $x_i \leq 1$, $i = 1, \ldots, n$, then

$$\prod_{i_1 < \cdots < i_k} \sum_{j=1}^k (1 - x_{i_j}) \leq \left(\frac{(n-1)k}{n}\right)^{\binom{n}{k}}. \tag{6}$$

Inequalities (2), (3), (5), and (6) have been given by Mitrinović (1970, p. 343) for the case that $\sum_1^n x_i = 1$.

G.1.o. The function

$$\psi_k(x) = \frac{\prod_{1 \leq i_1 < \cdots < i_n \leq n} \sum_{j=1}^k (1 - x_{i_j})}{\prod_{1 \leq i_1 < \cdots < i_n \leq n} \sum_{j=1}^k (x_{i_j})}, \quad k = 1, \ldots, n,$$

is Schur-convex on $(0, 1/2]^n$.

This inequality is one of many inequalities called *Ky Fan-inequalities*. For other inequalities on similar symmetric functions, see Guan and Shen (2006).

G.2. Proposition. If $\phi : \mathscr{R}^n \to \mathscr{R}$ is symmetric and convex, $h : \mathscr{R}^{n!} \to \mathscr{R}$ is symmetric, increasing, and convex, and if $t_1, \ldots, t_n$ are real numbers, then

$$\psi(x) = h(\phi(t_{\pi_1(1)} x_1, \ldots, t_{\pi_1(n)} x_n), \ldots, \phi(t_{\pi_{n!}(1)} x_1, \ldots, t_{\pi_{n!}(n)} x_n))$$

is a symmetric convex function.

Proof. This follows from G.1.a since for any permutation π,

$$\phi(t_1 x_{\pi(1)}, \ldots, t_n x_{\pi(n)}) = \phi(t_{\pi^{-1}(1)} x_1, \ldots, t_{\pi^{-1}(n)} x_n). \quad \|$$

Of course, the symmetry of ϕ is essential here.

Particular cases of G.2 are the following:

G.2.a. If ϕ is symmetric and convex and $t_1, \ldots, t_n$ are real numbers,
$$\psi_k(x) = \sum_{k,\pi} \phi(t_{\pi(1)}x_1, \ldots, t_{\pi(n)}x_n)$$
is symmetric and convex, $k = 1, \ldots, n!$ (as follows from G.1.b). The case $k = n!$ was given by Marshall and Proschan (1965).

G.2.b. If $t_1, \ldots, t_n$ are real numbers,
$$\psi_k(x) = \sum_{k,\pi}(t_{\pi(1)}x_1 + \cdots + t_{\pi(n)}x_n), \quad k = 1, \ldots, n!,$$
is symmetric and convex. This is a restatement of G.1.e.

G.2.c. If $g : \mathscr{R} \to \mathscr{R}$ is convex, then
$$\psi_k(x) = \sum_{k,\pi} \sum_{i=1}^{n} g(t_{\pi(i)}x_i), \quad k = 1, \ldots, n!,$$
is symmetric and convex. This special case of G.2.a is a restatement of G.1.g.

G.2.d. If $g : \mathscr{R} \to (0, \infty)$ and $\log g$ is convex, then
$$\psi_k(x) = \sum_{k,\pi} \prod_{j=1}^{n} g(t_{\pi(j)}x_j)$$
is symmetric and convex. This is a restatement of special cases of G.1.i and G.1.l.

G.2.e. (Muirhead, 1903; Hardy, Littlewood, and Pólya, 1934, 1952, p. 44). If $y_i > 0$, $i = 1, \ldots, n$, and $a \prec b$, then
$$\sum_\pi y_{\pi(1)}^{a_1} y_{\pi(2)}^{a_2} \cdots y_{\pi(n)}^{a_n} \leq \sum_\pi y_{\pi(1)}^{b_1} y_{\pi(2)}^{b_2} \cdots y_{\pi(n)}^{b_n}. \tag{7}$$

Proof. In G.2.a take $k = n!$, $\phi(z) = \exp(\sum z_i)$, $t_i = \log y_i$. Or alternatively, in G.2.d using $\psi_{n!}$, take $g(x) = e^x$, $t_i = \log y_i$. ∥

A converse and a more direct proof of G.2.e are given in 4.B.5. A generalization of Muirhead's theorem involving partitions rather than permutations in the context of inductive logic is provided by Paris and Venkovská (2008).

G.2.f. Arithmetic–geometric mean inequality. If $y_i > 0$ for $i = 1, \ldots, n$, then
$$\left(\prod y_i\right)^{1/n} \leq \sum y_i/n.$$

Proof. In G.2.e, take $a = (1/n, \ldots, 1/n)$ and $b = (1, 0, \ldots, 0)$. ||

G.2.g. If $y_i \geq 1$, $i = 1, \ldots, n$, then (7) holds whenever $a \prec_w b$; if $0 < y_i \leq 1$, $i = 1, \ldots, n$, then (7) holds whenever $a \prec^w b$.

Proof. It is easy to see that $\psi(a) = \sum_\pi y_{\pi(1)}^{a_1} \cdots y_{\pi(n)}^{a_n}$ is increasing (decreasing) if $y_i \geq 1$, $i = 1, \ldots, n$ ($0 < y_i \leq 1, i = 1, \ldots, n$). The results follow from these observations and G.2.e. ||

G.2.h. (Proschan, private communication, 1965; Tong, 1977). If $X_1, \ldots, X_n$ are exchangeable nonnegative random variables, then

$$\phi(a_1, \ldots, a_n) = E \prod_{j=1}^n X_j^{a_j}$$

is Schur-convex in $a_1, \ldots, a_n$ over that region where the expectation exists.

Proof. Because $X_1, \ldots, X_n$ are exchangeable random variables,

$$\phi(a_1, \ldots, a_n) = \frac{1}{n!} \sum_\pi E \prod_{j=1}^n X_{\pi(j)}^{a_j}.$$

If $a \prec b$, it follows from Muirhead's theorem that with probability 1,

$$\frac{1}{n!} \sum_\pi \prod_{j=1}^n X_{\pi(j)}^{a_j} \leq \frac{1}{n!} \sum_\pi \prod_{j=1}^n X_{\pi(j)}^{b_j},$$

and, upon taking expectations, it follows that $\phi(a) \leq \phi(b)$. ||

Notice that if $X_1, \ldots, X_n$ are independent and identically distributed, then they are exchangeable. In this case, G.2.h reduces to E.3.

G.2.i. (Fink and Jodeit, 1990). Let μ be a nonnegative Borel measure and

$$g(x) = \int_0^x (x-t)^m \, d\mu(t).$$

Denote the rth derivative of g by $g^{(r)}$, and let

$$\phi(k_1, \ldots, k_n) = \prod_1^n \Gamma(n - k_i + 1) g^{(k_i)}(x).$$

Then ϕ is Schur-convex on the set of integers $k_1, \ldots, k_n$ satisfying $0 \leq k_i \leq m$, $i = 1, \ldots, n$.

Proof. Note that

$\phi(k_1, \ldots, k_n)$
$= \left[\prod_{i=1}^{n} \frac{\Gamma(n+1)}{\Gamma(n-k_i+1)}\right] \int_0^x \cdots \int_0^x \prod_{i=1}^{n} [(x-t_i)^{m-k_i} d\mu(t_i)]$
$= \left[\prod_{i=1}^{n} \frac{\Gamma(n+1)}{\Gamma(n-k_i+1)}\right] \int_0^x \cdots \int_0^x \frac{1}{n!} \sum_\pi \left[\prod_{i=1}^{n} (x-t_{\pi(i)})^{m-k_i} d\mu(t_{\pi(i)})\right].$

The Schur-convexity is now immediate from Muirhead's theorem after noting that $a \prec b$ implies $(p - a_1, \ldots, p - a_n) \prec (p - b_1, \ldots, p - b_n)$. This follows directly from the definition of majorization, from 5.A.1.f, or as a consequence of 6.A.1.b. ∥

The restriction of the k_i to integer values can be removed using fractional derivatives [see; e.g., Courant (1936, p. 339)].

The same argument yields a similar result for

$$g(x) = \int_x^\infty (t-x)^m d\mu(t).$$

G.2.j. (Chong, 1974d). If $y_i > 0$, $i = 1, \ldots, n$ and $a \prec b$, then

$$\prod_\pi (1 + y_{\pi(1)}^{a_1} y_{\pi(2)}^{a_2} \cdots y_{\pi(n)}^{a_n}) \leq \prod_\pi (1 + y_{\pi(1)}^{b_1} y_{\pi(2)}^{b_2} \cdots y_{\pi(n)}^{b_n}),$$

with equality if and only if a is a permutation of b or $y_1 = \cdots = y_n$.

Proof. Let $t_i = \log y_i$. It is equivalent to show that

$$\sum_\pi \log[1 + \exp(a_1 t_{\pi(1)} + \cdots + a_n t_{\pi(n)})]$$
$$\leq \sum_\pi \log[1 + \exp(b_1 t_{\pi(1)} + \cdots + b_n t_{\pi(n)})].$$

This inequality follows from G.2.a with $k = n!$ once it is determined that $\phi(x) = \log[1 + \exp(x_1 + \cdots + x_n)]$ is symmetric and convex. This convexity is a consequence of the easily verified fact that $g(z) = \log(1 + e^z)$ is convex. The condition $y_1 = \cdots = y_n$ for equality is just the condition that $\psi(x) = \sum_\pi \log[1 + \exp(\sum x_i t_{\pi(i)})]$ is not strictly convex on sets of the form $\{x: \sum x_i = c\}$ (see C.2.c). ∥

G.3. Proposition. Let $\mathscr{A}$ be a symmetric convex subset of $\mathscr{R}^l$ and let ϕ be a Schur-convex function defined on $\mathscr{A}$ with the property that for each fixed $x_2, \ldots, x_l$,

$\phi(z, x_2, \ldots, x_l)$ is convex in z on $\{z: (z, x_2, \ldots, x_l) \in \mathscr{A}\}$.

128   3. Schur-Convex Functions

Then for any $n > l$,
$$\psi(x_1, \ldots, x_n) = \sum_\pi \phi(x_{\pi(1)}, \ldots, x_{\pi(l)})$$
is Schur-convex on
$$\mathscr{B} = \{(x_1, \ldots, x_n) : (x_{\pi(1)}, \ldots, x_{\pi(l)}) \in \mathscr{A} \text{ for all permutations } \pi\}.$$

In most applications, $\mathscr{A}$ has the form I^l for some interval $I \subset \mathscr{R}$ and in this case $\mathscr{B} = I^n$. Notice that the convexity of ϕ in its first argument also implies that ϕ is convex in each argument, the other arguments being fixed, because ϕ is symmetric.

Proof of G.3. To verify condition (10) of A.4, denote by $\sum_{\pi(i,j)}$ the summation over all permutations π such that $\pi(i) = 1$, $\pi(j) = 2$. Because ϕ is symmetric,

$$\psi(x_1, \ldots, x_n)$$
$$= \sum_{\substack{i,j \leq l \\ i \neq j}} \sum_{\pi(i,j)} \phi(x_1, x_2, x_{\pi(1)}, \ldots, x_{\pi(i-1)}, x_{\pi(i+1)}, \ldots,$$
$$x_{\pi(j-1)}, x_{\pi(j+1)}, \ldots, x_{\pi(l)})$$
$$+ \sum_{i \leq l < j} \sum_{\pi(i,j)} \phi(x_1, x_{\pi(1)}, \ldots, x_{\pi(i-1)}, x_{\pi(i+1)}, \ldots, x_{\pi(l)})$$
$$+ \sum_{j \leq l < i} \sum_{\pi(i,j)} \phi(x_2, x_{\pi(1)}, \ldots, x_{\pi(j-1)}, x_{\pi(j+1)}, \ldots, x_{\pi(l)})$$
$$+ \sum_{\substack{l < i,j \\ i \neq j}} \sum_{\pi(i,j)} \phi(x_{\pi(1)}, \ldots, x_{\pi(l)}).$$

Then
$$\left(\frac{\partial \psi}{\partial x_1} - \frac{\partial \psi}{\partial x_2}\right)(x_1 - x_2)$$
$$= \sum_{\substack{i,j \leq l \\ i \neq j}} \sum_{\pi(i,j)} (\phi_{(1)} - \phi_{(2)})(x_1, x_2, x_{\pi(1)}, \ldots, x_{\pi(i-1)}, x_{\pi(i+1)}, \ldots,$$
$$x_{\pi(j-1)}, x_{\pi(j+1)}, \ldots, x_{\pi(l)})(x_1 - x_2)$$
$$+ \sum_{i \leq l < j} \sum_{\pi(i,j)} [\phi_{(1)}(x_1, x_{\pi(1)}, \ldots, x_{\pi(i-1)}, x_{\pi(i+1)}, \ldots, x_{\pi(l)})$$
$$- \phi_{(1)}(x_2, x_{\pi(1)}, \ldots, x_{\pi(i-1)}, x_{\pi(i+1)}, \ldots, x_{\pi(l)})](x_1 - x_2).$$

Here, $(\phi_{(1)} - \phi_{(2)})(x_1 - x_2) \geq 0$ because ϕ is Schur-convex, and $[\phi_{(1)}(x_1, z) - \phi_{(1)}(x_2, z)](x_1 - x_2) \geq 0$ because ϕ is convex in its first argument. ||

G.3.a. Notice that if
$$\widetilde{\psi}(x) = \psi(x)/l!(n-l)!,$$
where ψ is the function defined in G.3, then
$$\widetilde{\psi}(x_1, \ldots, x_n) = \sum_{C(n,l)} \phi(x_1, \ldots, x_l),$$
where $(x_1, \ldots, x_l)$ is generic notation for an arbitrary selection of l of the variables $x_1, \ldots, x_n$ and $\sum_{C(n,l)}$ denotes summation over all $\binom{n}{l}$ such selections. Of course, $\widetilde{\psi}$ is Schur-convex whenever ψ is Schur-convex.

Notice that G.3 is a generalization of F.1 which says that the lth elementary symmetric function is Schur-concave on $\mathscr{R}_+^n$. In fact, it is easy to check that $\phi(z_1, \ldots, z_n) = -\prod_{j=1}^l z_j$ satisfies the conditions of G.3 and in this case, $-\widetilde{\psi}$ is the lth symmetric function.

G.3.b. The function
$$\widetilde{\psi}(x) = \sum_{C(n,l)} \frac{x_1 + \cdots + x_l}{x_1 \cdots x_l}$$
is Schur-convex on $\mathscr{R}_{++}^n$.

This follows from G.3.a because $\phi(y) = \sum_1^l y_i / \prod_1^l y_i$ is Schur-convex on $\mathscr{R}_{++}^l$ ($\prod_1^l y_i$ is Schur-concave on $\mathscr{R}_{++}^l$). If $x_i > 0$, $i = 1, \ldots, n$, and $\sum_1^n x_i = 1$, then $x \succ (1/n, \ldots, 1/n)$ and it follows that
$$\sum_{C(n,l)} \frac{x_1 + \cdots + x_l}{x_1 \cdots x_l} \geq l\binom{n}{l}n^{l-1}.$$

This inequality is given by Mitrinović (1970, p. 209).

G.3.c. The function
$$\psi(x) = \sum_{C(n,l)} \frac{x_1 \cdots x_l}{x_1 + \cdots + x_l}$$
is Schur-concave on $\mathscr{R}_{++}^n$.

This follows from G.3.a since on $\mathscr{R}_{++}^2$, $\phi(y) = \prod_1^l y_i / (\sum_1^l y_i)$ is Schur-concave and concave in each argument separately (F.1.a).

If $x_i > 0$, $i = 1, \ldots, n$, and $\sum_1^n x_i = 1$, then $x \succ (1/n, \ldots, 1/n)$ and it follows that

$$\sum_{i \neq j} \frac{x_i x_j}{x_i + x_j} \leq \frac{n-1}{2}.$$

This inequality is given by Mitrinović (1970, p. 209).

Because $x \succ (\bar{x}, \ldots, \bar{x})$, where $\bar{x} = (1/n) \sum_1^n x_i$, it follows from G.3.a that

$$l \sum_{C(n,l)} \frac{x_1 \cdots x_l}{x_1 + \cdots + x_l} \leq \binom{n}{l} \bar{x}^{l-1}.$$

This inequality was posed as a problem by Klamkin (1976).

G.3.d. There are many variations of Schur-concave functions similar to that in G.3.c, such as

$$\psi(x) = \sum_1^n \left(\frac{x_i}{\sum_{j \neq i} x_j}\right)^m = \sum_1^n \left(\frac{x_i}{T - x_i}\right), \quad T = \sum_1^n x_i.$$

This function suggests further generalization. Define

$$\pi(x_1, \ldots, x_l) = x_1 x_2 \cdots x_l,$$

$$\bar{\pi}(x_1, \ldots, x_l) = \left(\prod_1^n x_i\right) / \pi(x_1, \ldots, x_l),$$

and similarly,

$$s(x_1, \ldots, x_l) = x_1 + x_2 + \cdots + x_l,$$

$$\bar{s}(x_1, \ldots, x_l) = \left(\sum_1^n x_i\right) - s(x_1, \ldots, x_l).$$

This construction generates a variety of symmetric functions, such as

$$\sum_{C(n,l)} \frac{\pi(x_1, \ldots, x_l)}{\bar{s}(x_1, \ldots, x_l)}.$$

See Satnoianu and Zhou (2005).

G.3.e. If $a > 0$, the function

$$\psi(x) = \sum_{C(n,l)} \prod_{i=1}^l \left(\frac{1-x_i}{x_i}\right)^a$$

is Schur-convex on $\mathscr{B} = \{x : x \in \mathscr{R}_{++}^n \text{ and } x_i + x_j \leq 1 \text{ for all } i \neq j\}$, and is Schur-concave on $\widetilde{\mathscr{B}} = \{x : x \in \mathscr{R}_{++}^n \text{ and } x_i + x_j \geq 1 \text{ for all } i \neq j\}$.

Proof. It is easy to verify that $\phi(z) = \prod_{i=1}^{l}[(1-z_i)/z_i]$ is Schur-convex on $\mathscr{A} = \{z \in \mathscr{R}_{++}^l : z_i + z_j \leq 1 \text{ for all } i \neq j\}$, say by verifying (10) of A.4 and using A.4.a. Consequently, $[\phi(z)]^a$ is Schur-convex on the same set for all $a > 0$. From G.3.a it follows that ψ is Schur-convex on $\mathscr{B}$. A similar argument shows that ψ is Schur-concave on $\widetilde{\mathscr{B}}$. ||

If $x_i > 0$, $i = 1, \ldots, n$, and $x \succ (1/n, \ldots, 1/n)$, it follows from G.3.e that

$$\sum_{j_1 < \cdots < j_l} \prod_{i=1}^{l} \left(\frac{1-x_{j_i}}{x_{j_i}}\right)^a \geq \binom{n}{l}(n-1)^{la}.$$

This inequality is given by Mitrinović (1970, p. 343).

G.3.f. (Bondar, 1994). For given $a \in \mathscr{R}^n$, the symmetrized sum $\psi(y) = \Sigma_\pi y_{\pi(1)}^{a_1} \cdots y_{\pi(n)}^{a_n}$ is Schur-convex as a function of $(\log y_1, \ldots, \log y_n)$, where $(y_1, \ldots, y_n) \in \mathscr{D}_{++}$; i.e., if

$$x_1 \geq \cdots \geq x_n > 0, \ y_1 \geq \cdots \geq y_n > 0,$$

and

$$\prod_{i=1}^{k} x_i \leq \prod_{i=1}^{k} y_i \quad \text{for } k = 1, \ldots, n, \tag{8}$$

with equality for $k = n$, then $\psi(x) \leq \psi(y)$.

Proof. Let $u_i = \log y_i$. Then

$$\psi(y) = \sum_\pi \prod_{i=1}^n \exp\{a_i u_{\pi(i)}\}$$
$$= \sum_\pi (e^{a_{\pi(1)}})^{u_1} \cdots (e^{a_{\pi(n)}})^{u_n}.$$

Now, by Muirhead's theorem (G.2.e), this last expression is Schur-convex as a function of $(u_1, \ldots, u_n)$; hence, $\sum_1^k \log x_i \leq \sum_1^k \log y_i$ and $\sum_1^n \log x_i = \sum_1^n \log y_i$ [which is equivalent to (8)] implies $\psi(x) \leq \psi(y)$. ||

H Schur-Convex Functions on $\mathscr{D}$ and Their Extension to $\mathscr{R}^n$

If ϕ is defined on $\mathscr{D}$ and is Schur-convex, then ϕ can be easily extended to $\mathscr{R}^n$ in such a way as to preserve Schur-convexity.

H.1. Proposition. Let ϕ be a real function defined on $\mathscr{D}$ and suppose that ϕ is Schur-convex. If

$$\widetilde{\phi}(x) = \phi(x_\downarrow), \qquad x \in \mathscr{R}^n,$$

where $x_\downarrow = (x_{[1]}, \ldots, x_{[n]})$ is obtained from x by writing the components in decreasing order, then $\widetilde{\phi}$ is Schur-convex on $\mathscr{R}^n$. Moreover, $\widetilde{\phi}$ is the unique Schur-convex extension of ϕ to $\mathscr{R}^n$.

This proposition is a simple consequence of the fact that $x \prec x\Pi \prec x$ for all permutations Π, or it follows from the fact that Schur-convex functions on $\mathscr{R}^n$ are necessarily symmetric (invariant under permutations of the arguments). However, H.1 is of some interest because the extension of ϕ to $\widetilde{\phi}$ is not always the most obvious extension to $\mathscr{R}^n$. Without the observation of H.1, a number of examples of Schur-convex functions can be easily overlooked.

The following examples are mostly defined on $\mathscr{D}$ or $\mathscr{D}_+$, with the understanding that they can be extended to $\mathscr{R}^n$ or $\mathscr{R}_+^n$ using H.1.

H.2. Proposition. Let $\phi(x) = \sum g_i(x_i)$, $x \in \mathscr{D}$, where $g_i : \mathscr{R} \to \mathscr{R}$ is differentiable, $i = 1, \ldots, n$. Then ϕ is Schur-convex on $\mathscr{D}$ if and only if

$$g_i'(a) \geq g_{i+1}'(b) \qquad \text{whenever} \quad a \geq b, \quad i = 1, \ldots, n-1. \qquad (1)$$

Proof. Since $\phi_{(i)}(x_i) = g_i'(x_i)$, this result follows directly from A.3. ‖

H.2.a. According to H.2, $\phi(x) \leq \phi(y)$ whenever $x \prec y$ on $\mathscr{D}$ and ϕ satisfies the stated conditions. However, it is unnecessary that $x \in \mathscr{D}$.

Proof. It is sufficient to show that

$$z \in \mathscr{D} \text{ implies } \phi(z\Pi) \leq \phi(z) \qquad \text{for all permutations } \Pi,$$

or, alternatively, that

$$u_i \geq u_{i+1} \qquad \text{implies} \quad \phi(u_1, \ldots, u_{i-1}, u_{i+1}, u_i, u_{i+2}, \ldots, u_n) \geq \phi(u).$$

This inequality is equivalent to

$$g_i(u_i) - g_{i+1}(u_i) \geq g_i(u_{i+1}) - g_{i+1}(u_{i+1}), \qquad u_i \geq u_{i+1},$$

H. Schur-Convex Functions on $\mathscr{D}$ and Their Extension to $\mathscr{R}^n$ 133

which follows from condition (1) that $g'_i(a) \geq g'_{i+1}(a)$ for all a. ||

H.2.b. Let $\phi(x) = \sum u_i g(x_i)$, where g is increasing (decreasing) and convex. If $u \in \mathscr{D}_+$, then ϕ is Schur-convex (Schur-concave) on $\mathscr{D}$. Thus

$$u \in \mathscr{D}_+ \text{ and } x \prec y \text{ on } \mathscr{D} \Rightarrow \sum u_i g(x_i) \leq \sum u_i g(y_i).$$

This result follows from H.2 with $g_i(z) = u_i g(z)$ or directly from A.4.

H.2.c. If $x \prec y$ on $\mathscr{D}$, then

$$\sum x_i u_i \leq \sum y_i u_i \qquad \text{for all} \quad u \in \mathscr{D}.$$

This is a consequence of H.2 or A.4. A converse is given in 4.B.7.

H.2.d. Fix $a, b \in \mathscr{R}_+^n$ and let $A_k = \sum_k^n a_j$, $B_k = \sum_k^n b_j$, $k = 1, \ldots, n$. Then

(i) $\sum a_k \phi(k) \leq \sum b_k \phi(k)$ for all convex functions ϕ on $\{1, \ldots, n\}$ if and only if

(ii) $A_1 = B_1$ and $(A_2, \ldots, A_n) \succ (B_2, \ldots, B_n)$.

Proof. Suppose (ii) and rewrite (i) in the form

(iii) $-A_1 \phi(1) + \sum_2^n A_k[\phi(k-1) - \phi(k)]$

$$\geq -B_1 \phi(1) + \sum_2^n B_k[\phi(k-1) - \phi(k)].$$

Because $a, b \in \mathscr{R}_+^n$, $(A_2, \ldots, A_n)$, $(B_2, \ldots, B_n) \in \mathscr{D}$. Because ϕ is convex, $u \equiv (\phi(1) - \phi(2), \ldots, \phi(n-1) - \phi(n)) \in \mathscr{D}$. Thus (iii) follows from H.2.c. The converse follows from 4.B.6. ||

Remark. The restriction of H.2.d that $a_i \geq 0$, $b_i \geq 0$, $i = 1, \ldots, n$, guarantees $(A_2, \ldots, A_n)$ and $(B_2, \ldots, B_n)$ are in $\mathscr{D}$ so that the partial sums conditions $\sum_2^k A_j \geq \sum_2^k B_j$, $k = 2, \ldots, n$, can be written as majorization. That the restriction is not essential can be seen by observing that (i) holds if and only if $\sum (a_k + M)\phi(k) \leq \sum (b_k + M)\phi(k)$ for all convex functions ϕ and all $M \in \mathscr{R}$. H.2.d has been given, for example, by Karlin and Novikoff (1963). It is a special case of 16.B.4.a.

H.2.e. If $x_0, \ldots, x_n$ are positive numbers, then

$$\phi(a) = \prod_{j=0}^{n} x_j^{a_j - a_{j+1}} \qquad (a_0 = a_{n+1} = 0)$$

is Schur-convex on $\mathscr{D}$ if and only if

$$x_1/x_0 \geq x_2/x_1 \geq \cdots \geq x_n/x_{n-1}. \tag{2}$$

Thus, if (2) is satisfied, $a \prec b$ on $\mathscr{D}$, and $a_0 = a_{n+1} = b_0 = b_{n+1} = 0$, then

$$\prod_{j=0}^{n} x_j^{a_j - a_{j+1}} \leq \prod_{j=0}^{n} x_j^{b_j - b_{j+1}}. \tag{3a}$$

H.2.f. If $x_j = S_j / \binom{n}{j}$, where S_j is the jth elementary symmetric function of n positive numbers, then (2) is satisfied (Hardy, Littlewood, and Pólya, 1952, p. 52). Since $x_0 = 1$, (3a) can be written here as

$$\prod_{j=1}^{n} x_j^{a_j - a_{j+1}} \leq \prod_{j=1}^{n} x_j^{b_j - b_{j+1}}. \tag{3b}$$

This result is discussed by Hardy, Littlewood, and Pólya (1952, p. 64), where the condition $a \prec b$ has been written in terms of the differences $\alpha'_j = a_j - a_{j+1}$, $\alpha_j = b_j - b_{j+1}$.

Recall the kth elementary symmetric function of z is denoted by $S_k(z) = \Sigma z_{i_1} \cdots z_{i_k}$.

H.2.g. Corollary. With $E_k = S_k(z)/\binom{n}{k}$, $z_i > 0$, $i = 1, \ldots, n$,

$$E_k^2 \geq E_{k-1} E_{k+1}, \quad 1 \leq k \leq n-1; \tag{3c}$$

more generally, if $\alpha k + \overline{\alpha} k'$ is an integer, then

$$E_{\alpha k + \overline{\alpha} k'} \geq E_k^\alpha E_{k'}^{\overline{\alpha}}, \quad 0 \leq \alpha \leq 1. \tag{3d}$$

That E_k is a log concave function of k follows from (3c) or (3d).

Proof. To obtain (3c), choose $a = (\underbrace{1, \ldots, 1}_{k-1}, 1/2, 1/2, 0, \ldots, 0)$ and $b = (\underbrace{1, \ldots, 1}_{k}, 0, \ldots, 0)$. For (3d) with $k' \leq k$, choose

$$a = (\underbrace{1, \ldots, 1}_{k}, \underbrace{\overline{\alpha}, \ldots, \overline{\alpha}}_{(k-k')\overline{\alpha}}, 0, \ldots, 0), \quad b = (\underbrace{1, \ldots, 1}_{\alpha k + \overline{\alpha} k'}, 0, \ldots, 0). \quad \|$$

Inequalities (3c) and (3d) are obtained by Niculescu (2000), who notes that inequality (3c) is due to Isaac Newton and also provides some historical comments.

A probabilistic interpretation is also illuminating. Let Z_k be a random variable that takes values $z_{i_1} \cdots z_{i_k}$ with probability $1/\binom{n}{k}$, $1 \leq i_1 < \cdots < i_k \leq n$. Then for $z_i > 0$, $i = 1, \ldots, n$,

$$EZ_k^t = \sum z_{i_1}^t \cdots z_{i_k}^t \Big/ \binom{n}{k}$$

is a moment. Hence, for fixed k, the Lyapunov inequality (16.D.1.d) yields

$$(EZ_k^s)^{r-t} \leq (EZ_k^t)^{r-s}(EZ_k^r)^{s-t}, \quad r \geq s \geq t.$$

H.2.h. If $a, b \in \mathscr{D}$, then one easily verifies that

$$x \equiv \frac{\sum a_j}{|\sum a_j|}\left(\frac{1}{n}, \ldots, \frac{1}{n}\right) \prec \frac{1}{|\sum a_j|}(a_1, \ldots, a_n) \equiv y \quad \text{on} \quad \mathscr{D}.$$

Since $u = b/|\sum b_j| \in \mathscr{D}$, H.2.c can be applied to obtain

$$\frac{1}{n}\frac{\sum a_j}{|\sum a_j|} \cdot \frac{\sum b_j}{|\sum b_j|} \leq \sum \frac{a_i}{|\sum a_j|} \cdot \frac{b_i}{|\sum b_j|}.$$

Thus

$$\left(\frac{1}{n}\sum a_i\right)\left(\frac{1}{n}\sum b_i\right) \leq \frac{1}{n}\sum a_i b_i. \tag{4}$$

Inequality (4) is usually attributed to Chebyshev [see; e.g., Hardy, Littlewood, and Pólya, 1952, p. 43). A definitive history of the inequality is given by Mitrinović and Vasić (1974). Actually, much more general versions of (4) are easily proved directly, but majorization can lead to other forms by different choices of x and y.

H.2.i. If $g_i : \mathscr{R} \to \mathscr{R}$ is differentiable, $i = 1, \ldots, n$, then $\prod g_i(x_i)$ is Schur-convex in $(x_1, \ldots, x_n)$ on $\mathscr{D}$ if and only if

$$\frac{g_i'(a)}{g_i(a)} \geq \frac{g_{i+1}'(b)}{g_{i+1}(b)} \quad \text{whenever} \quad a \geq b, \quad i = 1, \ldots, n-1.$$

Conditions for this in terms of total positivity are given implicitly by Karlin (1968, p. 126, Lemma 5.2).

H.3. Let $\phi(x) = \sum g_i(x_i)$, $x \in \mathscr{D}$, where each $g_i : \mathscr{R} \to \mathscr{R}$ is differentiable. Then ϕ is increasing and Schur-convex on $\mathscr{D}$ if and only if

$$g_i'(a) \geq g_{i+1}'(b) \geq 0 \quad \text{whenever} \quad a \geq b, i = 1, \ldots, n-1; \tag{5}$$

ϕ is decreasing and Schur-convex on $\mathscr{D}$ if and only if

$$0 \geq g_i'(a) \geq g_{i+1}'(b) \quad \text{whenever} \quad a \geq b, i = 1, \ldots, n-1. \tag{6}$$

Proof. This amounts to little more than a restatement of H.2. ∥

H.3.a. If (5) is satisfied, then

$$x \prec_w y \text{ on } \mathscr{D} \quad \text{implies} \quad \sum_1^k g_i(x_i) \leq \sum_1^k g_i(y_i), \quad k = 1, \ldots, n; \tag{7}$$

if (6), then

$$x \prec^w y \text{ on } \mathscr{D} \quad \text{implies} \quad \sum_k^n g_i(x_i) \leq \sum_k^n g_i(y_i), \quad k = 1, \ldots, n. \tag{8}$$

Proof. In H.3, take $g_i(a) \equiv 0$, $i = k+1, \ldots, n$. Then (5) is still satisfied so (7) follows from H.3. The proof of (8) is similar. ‖

H.3.b. If $x \prec_w y$ on $\mathscr{D}$, then

$$\sum x_i u_i \leq \sum y_i u_i \quad \text{for all } u \in \mathscr{D}_+.$$

This is a consequence of H.3.a or A.7. A converse is given in 4.B.7.

H.3.c. (Pledger and Proschan, 1971). If $x \prec_w y$ on $\mathscr{D}_+$ and $a \prec_w b$ on $\mathscr{D}_+$, then on $\mathscr{D}_+$

$$(x_1 a_1, \ldots, x_n a_n) \prec_w (y_1 b_1, \ldots, y_n b_n).$$

Proof. In H.3.b, take $u = (a_1, \ldots, a_k, 0, \ldots, 0)$ to obtain $\sum_1^k x_i a_i \leq \sum_1^k y_i a_i$. Again apply H.3.b with $u = (y_1, \ldots, y_k, 0, \ldots, 0)$ to obtain $\sum_1^k y_i a_i \leq \sum_1^k y_i b_i$. Both $(x_1 a_1, \ldots, x_n a_n)$ and $(y_1 b_1, \ldots, y_n b_n) \in \mathscr{D}$, which completes the proof. ‖

H.4. Let $A = (a_{ij})$ be a real symmetric $n \times n$ matrix. Then

$$\phi(x) = xAx'$$

is Schur-convex on $\mathscr{D}_+ = \{z : z_1 \geq \cdots \geq z_n \geq 0\}$ if and only if

$$\sum_{j=1}^i (a_{k,j} - a_{k+1,j}) \geq 0, \quad i = 1, \ldots, n, \quad k = 1, \ldots, n-1. \tag{9}$$

Thus, if (9) is satisfied,

$$x \prec y \quad \text{on} \quad \mathscr{D}_+ \Rightarrow xAx' \leq yAy'.$$

Proof. To verify this (with the use of A.3), assume that $x \in \mathscr{D}_+$ and compute

$$\phi_{(k)}(x) = 2(a_{k,1}, \ldots, a_{k,n})x',$$

so that

$$\phi_{(k)}(x) - \phi_{(k+1)}(x) = 2\sum_{j=1}^{n}(a_{k,j} - a_{k+1,j})x_j$$

$$= 2\sum_{i=1}^{n}(x_i - x_{i+1})\sum_{j=1}^{i}(a_{k,j} - a_{k+1,j}).$$

It is now apparent that $\phi_{(k)}(x) - \phi_{(k+1)}(x) \geq 0$ for all x in the interior of $\mathscr{D}$ if and only if A satisfies (9). ‖

A result closely related to H.4 is given in 4.B.9.

H.4.a. If $c_0 \geq c_1 \geq \cdots \geq c_{2n-2}$, $a_{ij} = c_{i+j-2}$, and $A = (a_{ij})$, then the conditions of H.4 are satisfied. In particular, the conditions are satisfied if $c_j = EX^j$ is the jth moment of a random variable X for which $P\{0 \leq X \leq 1\} = 1$.

H.4.b. Let $A = (a_{ij})$ be a real symmetric $n \times n$ matrix. Then $\phi(x) = xAx'$ is increasing (decreasing) and Schur-convex on $\mathscr{D}_+$ if and only if (9) is satisfied and, in addition,

$$\sum_{j=1}^{i} a_{n,j} \geq 0 \left(\sum_{j=1}^{i} a_{1j} \leq 0\right), \qquad i = 1, \ldots, n. \tag{10}$$

Thus, if (9) and (10) are satisfied,

$$x \prec_w y \qquad \text{on} \qquad \mathscr{D}_+ \Rightarrow xAx' \leq yAy'.$$

Proof. By A.7, the conditions of H.4 need only be augmented by the condition that $\phi_{(n)}(x) \geq 0 (\phi_{(1)}(x) \leq 0)$. ‖

H.5. If $\phi(x, y) = x^\alpha - \alpha xy^{\alpha-1} + (\alpha - 1)y^\alpha$, then with A.3 it is easily verified that ϕ is Schur-convex on $\mathscr{D}_+$ if $\alpha > 1$ or $\alpha < 0$, and ϕ is Schur-concave on $\mathscr{D}_+$ if $0 \leq \alpha \leq 1$. Since $(x, y) \succ (c, c)$, where $c = (x + y)/2$, and since $\phi(c, c) = 0$, it follows that

$$x^\alpha - \alpha xy^{\alpha-1} + (\alpha - 1)y^\alpha \geq 0 \qquad \text{if} \quad x \geq y > 0 \text{ and } \alpha > 1 \text{ or } \alpha < 0,$$

$$x^\alpha - \alpha xy^{\alpha-1} + (\alpha - 1)y^\alpha \leq 0 \qquad \text{if} \quad x \geq y > 0 \text{ and } 0 \leq \alpha \leq 1.$$

These inequalities have been given, e.g., by Beckenbach and Bellman (1961, p. 12), who discuss their utility. See also Tchakaloff (1963).

I Miscellaneous Specific Examples

I.1. A function $\phi: \mathscr{R}^n \to \mathscr{R}$ is called a *symmetric gauge function* if

(i) $\phi(u) > 0$ when $u \neq 0$,

(ii) $\phi(\gamma u) = |\gamma| \phi(u)$ for all real γ,

(iii) $\phi(u+v) \leq \phi(u) + \phi(v)$,

(iv) $\phi(u_1, \ldots, u_n) = \phi(\varepsilon_1 u_{i_1}, \ldots, \varepsilon_n u_{i_n})$ whenever each $\varepsilon_i = \pm 1$ and $(i_1, \ldots, i_n)$ is a permutation of $(1, \ldots, n)$.

If ϕ is a symmetric gauge function, then ϕ is symmetric and convex [see, e.g., Rockafellar (1970) or Schatten (1950)]. Hence ϕ is Schur-convex. As special cases, it follows that the following are Schur-convex:

$$\phi(x) = \max |x_i|;$$
$$\phi(x) = \left(\sum |x_i|^r\right)^{1/r}, \qquad r \geq 1;$$
$$\phi(x) = \max_{i_1 < i_2 < \cdots < i_k} (|x_{i_1}| + \cdots + |x_{i_k}|).$$

I.1.a. (Fan, 1951). A symmetric gauge function is known to be increasing on $\mathscr{R}_+^n = \{x : x \in \mathscr{R}^n \text{ and } x_i \geq 0 \text{ for all } i\}$ (Schatten, 1950, p. 85). Consequently, it is Schur-convex and increasing on $\mathscr{R}_+^n$.

By using (v) of Table 2 in Section B, with $g(z) = z^{-1}$, it follows that for any symmetric gauge function ϕ, $\phi(x_1^{-1}, \ldots, x_n^{-1})$ is decreasing and Schur-convex in $x \in \mathscr{R}_+^n$. This result was proved by Marshall and Olkin (1965).

Bhatia (1997) includes considerable discussion of symmetric gauge functions, including the fact that all such functions are continuous. See also Horn and Johnson (1991) and Stewart and Sun (1990).

I.1.b. As indicated in the examples above, the power sums

$$\phi(x) = \left(\sum x_i^r\right)^{1/r}, \qquad x \in \mathscr{R}_{++}^n,$$

are Schur-convex in x if $r \geq 1$. In fact, the Schur-convexity is strict if $r > 1$. If $r < 1$, $r \neq 0$, then ϕ is strictly Schur-concave.

To see this, note that $g(z) = z^r$ is convex in $z \geq 0$ if $r \geq 1$ or $r \leq 0$ (strictly convex if $r > 1$ or $r < 0$), and g is strictly concave in $z \geq 0$ if $0 < r < 1$. It follows from C.1 and C.1.a that

$$\psi(x) = \sum x_i^r$$

I. Miscellaneous Specific Examples   139

is Schur-convex on $\mathscr{R}_{++}^n$ if $r \geq 1$ or $r \leq 0$ (strictly if $r > 1$ or $r < 0$), and ψ is strictly Schur-concave on $\mathscr{R}_+^n$ if $0 < r < 1$. Because $h(z) = z^{1/r}$ is strictly increasing in $z \geq 0$ for $r > 0$ and h is strictly decreasing in $z \geq 0$ for $r < 0$, it follows that $\phi(x) = h(\psi(x))$ is Schur-convex for $r \geq 1$ (strictly, if $r > 1$) and strictly Schur-concave if $r < 1$.

Notice that also the power mean

$$\widehat{\phi}(x) = \left(\frac{1}{n}\sum x_i^r\right)^{1/r}$$

is Schur-convex in $x \in \mathscr{R}_{++}^n$ for $r \geq 1$ and Schur-concave for $0 < r \leq 1$.

Because ψ is Schur-convex on $\mathscr{R}_{++}^n$ for $r \geq 1$ or $r \leq 0$ (strictly Schur-convex if $r > 1$ or $r < 0$), it follows that if $y_1, \ldots, y_n$ are nonnegative numbers (not all zero), then $y/\sum y_i \succ (1/n, \ldots, 1/n)$ and

$$\sum_1^n \left(\frac{y_i}{\sum_1^n y_j}\right)^r \geq \frac{1}{n^{r-1}}, \qquad r \geq 1 \text{ or } r \leq 0,$$

with equality if and only if $y_1 = \cdots = y_n$ in case $r > 1$ or $r < 0$. In case $z_1, \ldots, z_n$ are complex numbers not all zero, this inequality together with the triangle inequality gives

$$\sum_{i=1}^n |z_i|^r \geq \frac{1}{n^{r-1}}\left(\sum_{i=1}^n |z_i|\right)^r \geq \frac{1}{n^{r-1}}\left|\sum_{i=1}^n z_i\right|^r, \qquad r \geq 1 \text{ or } r \leq 0.$$

For $n = 2$ and $r \geq 1$, this inequality is given by Mitrinović (1970, p. 338).

I.1.c. An extremal problem (Melman, 2009). For $x \in \mathscr{R}_+^n$ with $\Sigma_1^n x_i = 1$, $0 < c < 1$, $p \geq 1$, and $q \geq 1$,

$$\frac{n}{(n^{1/r} - c)^q} \leq \sum_1^n \frac{x_i^{q/p}}{(1 - cx_i^{1/p})^q} \leq \frac{1}{(1 - c)^q}$$

with equality in the extreme cases in which $x = (1/n, \ldots, 1/n)$ and $x = e_i$ for some $i = 1, \ldots, n$. This result follows because the function in between the two inequalities is Schur-concave.

I.2. (Fan, 1951). On the set $\{x : 0 < x_i \leq \frac{1}{2}, i = 1, \ldots, n\}$,

$$\phi(x) = \frac{[\prod_1^n (1 - x_i)]^{1/n}}{\sum_1^n (1 - x_i)} \cdot \frac{\sum_1^n x_i}{(\prod_1^n x_i)^{1/n}}$$

is symmetric and Schur-convex.

Proof. The equivalent fact that $\psi(x) = \log \phi(x)$ is Schur-convex can be verified using A.4. Direct computation shows that

$$\psi_{(1)}(x) - \psi_{(2)}(x) = \frac{1}{n}\left\{\frac{1}{x_2(1-x_2)} - \frac{1}{x_1(1-x_1)}\right\} \geq 0$$

because $1/[z(1-z)]$ is decreasing in $z \in [0, \frac{1}{2}]$. ||

From $x \succ [(\sum x_i)/n](1,\ldots,1) \equiv y$, it follows that $\phi(x) \geq \phi(y)$. More explicitly,

$$\frac{\prod_1^n x_i}{(\sum_1^n x_i)^n} \leq \frac{\prod_1^n (1-x_i)}{(\sum_1^n (1-x_i))^n} \quad \text{whenever} \quad 0 < x_i \leq \frac{1}{2}, \quad i = 1,\ldots,n.$$

This is an inequality due to Ky Fan [see, e.g., Beckenbach and Bellman (1961, p. 5) or Mitrinović (1970, p. 363)]. For extensions of this inequality see, e.g., Bullen (1998, p. 150) and Rooin (2008). A probabilistic proof is given by Olkin and Shepp (2006).

I.3. Szegö (1950) shows that if $a_1 \geq a_2 \geq \cdots \geq a_{2m-1} \geq 0$ and g is convex on $[0, a_1]$, then

$$\sum_1^{2m-1} (-1)^{j-1} g(a_j) \geq g\left(\sum_1^{2m-1} (-1)^{j-1} a_j\right).$$

Bellman (1953b) shows that if $a_1 \geq a_2 \geq \cdots \geq a_m > 0$, if g is convex on $[0, a_1]$, and if $g(0) \leq 0$, then

$$\sum_1^m (-1)^{j-1} g(a_j) \geq g\left(\sum_1^m (-1)^{j-1} a_j\right).$$

Wright (1954) and Olkin (1959) observe that these results follow from Proposition C.1 because of the majorizations

$$(a_1, a_3, \ldots, a_{2m-1}, 0) \succ \left(\sum_1^{2m} (-1)^{j-1} a_j, a_2, a_4, \ldots, a_{2m}\right),$$

$$(a_1, a_3, \ldots, a_{2m-1}) \succ \left(\sum_1^{2m-1} (-1)^{j-1} a_j, a_2, a_4, \ldots, a_{2m-2}\right).$$

Generalizations of the above inequalities and further references are given by Barlow, Marshall, and Proschan (1969).

Bounds for Means

A *mean* is a function $M(x) = M(x_1, \ldots, x_n)$ that maps $\mathscr{R}_+^n \to \mathscr{R}_+$ and satisfies the conditions (a) $M(1, \ldots, 1) = 1$, (b) $M(\lambda x_1, \ldots, \lambda x_n) = \lambda M(x_1, \ldots, x_n)$ for all $\lambda > 0$, (c) $M(\Pi x) = M(x)$ for all permutation matrices Π, (d) $x_i \leq y_i$, $i = 1, \ldots, n$ implies that $M(x) \leq M(y)$. It follows that

$$\min x_i \leq M(x) \leq \max x_i.$$

There are many classes of means, the most notable being the *power means* $(\Sigma x_i^r/n)^{1/r}$, sometimes called *binomial means*. A compendium of means is given by Bullen (2003).

When $M(x)$ is Schur-concave, as is the case for many choices of means, then

$$M(\Sigma x_i, 0, \ldots, 0) \leq M(x) \leq M(\bar{x}, \ldots, \bar{x}),$$

where $\bar{x} = \Sigma x_i/n$. The inequalities are reversed for Schur-convexity. In the following, several classes of means are shown to be Schur-concave. The listing is illustrative and not exhaustive.

Logarithmic Mean

I.4. Definition. For $x, y \in \mathscr{R}_{++}$, the *logarithmic mean* of x and y is

$$L(x, y) = \begin{cases} \dfrac{x - y}{\log x - \log y} & \text{if } x \neq y, \\ x & \text{if } x = y. \end{cases}$$

The logarithmic mean was introduced by Ostle and Terwilliger (1957), who noted that engineers use the arithmetic mean to approximate $L(x, y)$. They proved that $L(x, y) \leq (x + y)/2$. A stronger result by Carlson (1972) is

$$\sqrt{xy} \leq (xy)^{1/4} \left(\frac{\sqrt{x} + \sqrt{y}}{2}\right) \leq L(x, y) \leq \left(\frac{\sqrt{x} + \sqrt{y}}{2}\right)^2 \leq \frac{x + y}{2}. \quad (1)$$

I.4.a. Proposition. $L(x, y)$ is Schur-concave in $(x, y) \in \mathscr{R}_{++}^2$.

Proof. Condition (10′) of A.4 reduces to the inequality

$$g(z) = z - \frac{1}{z} - 2 \log z \geq 0, \qquad z \geq 1,$$

which follows from the fact $g(1) = 0$ and g is increasing in $z > 0$. ∥

The Schur-convexity of $L(x,y)/\sqrt{xy}$ can similarly be verified. Condition (10′) of A.4 reduces to the inequality

$$h(z) = \log z - \frac{z^2 - 1}{z^2 + 1} \geq 0, \qquad z \geq 1,$$

and this follows from the fact that $h(z)$ is increasing in z and $h(1) = 0$.

As a consequence of the Schur-concavity (convexity),

$$L(x,y) \leq L\left(\frac{x+y}{2}, \frac{x+y}{2}\right) = \frac{x+y}{2},$$

and

$$\frac{L(x,y)}{\sqrt{xy}} \geq L\left(\frac{x+y}{2}, \frac{x+y}{2}\right) \bigg/ \frac{x+y}{2} = 1.$$

Two integral representations of $L(x,y)$ are

$$L(x,y) = \int_0^1 x^{1-t} y^t \, dt = \int_0^{1/2} (x^{1-t} y^t + x^t y^{1-t}) dt, \qquad (2a)$$

$$L^{-1}(x,y) = \int_0^\infty \frac{dt}{(t+x)(t+y)}. \qquad (2b)$$

An alternative proof of I.4.a can be obtained from the integral representations (2a) or (2b) using C.5.

Stolarsky (1975) introduced the class of means

$$S(x,y|r) = \begin{cases} \left[\dfrac{(x^r - y^r)}{r(x-y)}\right]^{1/(r-1)}, & \text{if } x \neq y, \ r \neq 0, 1, \\ x, & \text{if } x = y. \end{cases} \qquad (3)$$

A corresponding integral representation is given by

$$S(x,y|r) = \left[\int_0^1 [tx + (1-t)y]^r dt\right]^{1/r}.$$

This class does not include $L(x,y)$, but the following extension rectifies this.

I. Miscellaneous Specific Examples 143

I.4.b. Definition. For $(x, y) \in \mathcal{R}_{++}^2$, the *extended logarithmic mean* of x and y ($x \neq y$) is

$$L(x,y|r,s) = \begin{cases} \left(\dfrac{(x^s - y^s)/s}{(x^r - y^r)/r}\right)^{1/(s-r)}, & \text{if } x \neq y, \ r, s \neq 0, \ r \neq s, \\ \left(\dfrac{(x^r - y^r)/r}{\log x - \log y}\right)^{1/r}, & \text{if } x \neq y, \ s = 0, \ r \neq 0, \\ x, & \text{if } x = y. \end{cases}$$

The case $r = 1, s = 0$ is the logarithmic mean.

I.4.c. Proposition (Shi, Wu, and Qi, 2006). The function $L(x, y|r, s)$ is Schur-concave in $(x, y) \in \mathcal{R}_{++}^2$ for fixed r and s.

Multivariate versions of $L(x, y)$, $S(x, y|r)$, or $L(x, y|r, s)$ are not immediate except with integral representations, and a variety of proposals have appeared. One class of means similar to the extended logarithmic means that has an immediate extension to any number of variables is

$$G(x,y|r,s) = \left(\frac{\Sigma x_i^s}{\Sigma y_i^r}\right)^{1/(s-r)}, \quad r \neq s. \tag{4}$$

I.4.d. Proposition. The function $G(x, y|r, s)$ is Schur-concave in $(x, y) \in \mathcal{R}_{++}^2$ for fixed r and s, $r \neq s$.

Remark. Shi, Jiang, and Jiang (2009) study Schur-convexity properties of the Gini mean (Gini, 1938) defined for $x, y > 0$ and $r \neq s$ by

$$\widetilde{G}(x,y|r,s) = \left(\frac{(x^s + y^s)/s}{(x^r + y^r)/r}\right)^{1/(s-r)}.$$

I.4.e. Proposition (Zheng, Zhang, and Zhang, 2007). For $x \in \mathcal{R}_{++}^n$, the means

$$M(x|r) = (n-1)! \left[\int_{\Omega_n} (\sum_{i=1}^n \alpha_i x_i)^r \prod_1^{n-1} d\alpha_i\right]^{1/r}, \quad r \neq 0,$$

$$\mathscr{M}(x|r) = (n-1)! \left[\int_{\Omega_n} (\sum_{i=1}^n \alpha_i x_i^r)^{1/r} \prod_1^{n-1} d\alpha_i\right], \quad r \neq 0,$$

where
$$\Omega_n = \{(\alpha_1, \ldots, \alpha_{n-1}) : \alpha_i \geq 0, \sum_{i=1}^{n-1} \alpha_i \leq 1\}$$
and
$$\alpha_n = 1 - \sum_1^{n-1} \alpha_i$$
are Schur-convex for $r \geq 1$ and Schur-concave for $r \leq 1$, $r \neq 0$.

I.4.f. Remark That $M(1, \ldots, 1|r) = 1$ and $\mathcal{M}(1, \ldots, 1|r)$ follows from the Dirichlet distribution 11.E.12. With $x_i = 1$, $i = 1, \ldots, n$, the integrals in $M(1, \ldots, 1|r) = 1$ and $\mathcal{M}(1, \ldots, 1|r)$ become

$$\int_{\Omega_n} \prod_1^{n-1} d\alpha_i = [\Gamma(1)]^n / \Gamma(n) = 1/(n-1)!.$$

I.4.g. Proposition. For $(x_1, \ldots, x_n) \in \mathcal{R}_+^n$, the *Heinz mean*
$$H(x_1, \ldots, x_n | \alpha_1, \ldots, \alpha_n) = \sum_\pi (x_{\pi(1)}^{\alpha_1} \cdots x_{\pi(n)}^{\alpha_n})/n!,$$
where $0 \leq \alpha_i \leq 1/n$, $\Sigma \alpha_i = 1$, is Schur-concave in $x \in \mathcal{R}_+^n$.

Note that
$$\prod x_i^{1/n} \leq H(x) \leq \sum x_i/n.$$

I.4.h. Proposition. For $(x, y) \in \mathcal{R}_+^2$, the *Heronian mean*
$$H(x, y) = (x + \sqrt{xy} + y)/3$$
is Schur-concave.

Note that
$$\sqrt{xy} \leq H(x, y) \leq (x+y)/2.$$

I.5. Motivated by some inequalities for sides of triangles (discussed in 8.B), consider the following functions on $\mathcal{R}_{++}^n$:
$$\psi_1^{(k)}(x) = \left(\prod_{i_1 < \cdots < i_k} \sum_{j=1}^k x_{i_j} \right) \Big/ \left(\sum_{i=1}^n x_i \right)^{\binom{n}{k}}$$

and
$$\psi_2^{(k)}(x) = \left(\prod_{i_1<\cdots<i_k}\sum_{j=1}^k x_{i_j}\right)\bigg/\left(\sum_{i=1}^n x_i^{\binom{n}{k}}\right).$$

The numerators in $\psi_1^{(k)}$ and $\psi_2^{(k)}$ are Schur-concave (G.1.n) and the denominators are clearly Schur-convex. Thus $\psi_1^{(k)}(x)$ and $\psi_2^{(k)}(x)$ are Schur-concave; consequently,

$$0 < \psi_1^{(k)}(x) \leq \left(\frac{k}{n}\right)^{\binom{n}{k}}$$

and

$$0 < \psi_2^{(k)}(x) \leq \left(\frac{k\binom{n}{k}}{n}\right).$$

I.6. In the context of multicarrier multiple-input multiple-output channels, Palomar, Cioffi, and Lagunas (2003) use majorization to obtain extrema of the objective functions

$$\varphi_1(x) = \prod_1^n x_i^{w_i},$$

$$\varphi_2(x) = \sum w_i x_i^{-1},$$

$$\varphi_3(x) = -\prod_1^n (x_i^{-1} - 1)^{w_i}.$$

Here if $x \in \mathscr{D}$ and $0 < w_1 \leq w_2 \leq \cdots \leq w_n$, then φ_1 and φ_2 are Schur-concave on $\mathscr{D}$; if, in addition, $0 < x_i < 1/2$, then φ_3 is Schur-concave.

J Integral Transformations Preserving Schur-Convexity

Let K be defined on $\mathscr{R}^n \times \mathscr{R}^n$, let ϕ be defined on $\mathscr{R}^n$, and let

$$\psi(\theta) = \int K(\theta, x)\phi(x)\, d\mu(x).$$

What conditions must the function K and measure μ satisfy in order that ψ be Schur-convex whenever ϕ is Schur-convex? The answer to this question is unknown, but some sufficient conditions can be given.

Consider first a convolution transform, in which $K(\theta, x) = g(\theta - x)$.

J.1. Theorem (Marshall and Olkin, 1974). If ϕ and g are Schur-concave functions defined on $\mathscr{R}^n$, then the function ψ defined on $\mathscr{R}^n$ by

$$\psi(\theta) = \int_{\mathscr{R}^n} g(\theta - x)\phi(x)\,dx$$

is Schur-concave (whenever the integral exists).

Proof. By virtue of A.5, it is sufficient to prove the theorem for $n = 2$. Let $\theta \prec \xi$, and write

$\psi(\theta) - \psi(\xi)$
$$= \iint [g(x_1, \theta_2 - \xi_2 + x_2) - g(x_1 + \xi_1 - \theta_1, x_2)]$$
$$\times \phi(\theta_1 - x_1, \xi_2 - x_2)\,dx_1\,dx_2.$$

Notice that by first interchanging x_1 and x_2, and then using the symmetry of g together with $\xi_1 - \theta_1 = \theta_2 - \xi_2$, it follows that

$$\iint_{x_1 \leq x_2} [g(x_1, \theta_2 - \xi_2 + x_2) - g(x_1 + \xi_1 - \theta_1, x_2)]$$
$$\times \phi(\theta_1 - x_1, \xi_2 - x_2)\,dx_1\,dx_2$$

$$= \iint_{x_1 \geq x_2} [g(x_2, \theta_2 - \xi_2 + x_1) - g(x_2 + \xi_1 - \theta_1, x_1)]$$
$$\times \phi(\theta_1 - x_2, \xi_2 - x_1)\,dx_1\,dx_2$$

$$= \iint_{x_1 \geq x_2} [g(x_1 + \xi_1 - \theta_1, x_2) - g(x_1, x_2 + \theta_2 - \xi_2)]$$
$$\times \phi(\theta_1 - x_2, \xi_2 - x_1)\,dx_1\,dx_2.$$

Thus

$$\psi(\theta) - \psi(\xi) = \iint_{x_1 \geq x_2} [g(x_1, \xi_1 - \theta_1 + x_2) - g(x_1 + \xi_1 - \theta_1, x_2)]$$
$$\times [\phi(\theta_1 - x_1, \xi_2 - x_2) - \phi(\theta_1 - x_2, \xi_2 - x_1)]\,dx_1\,dx_2.$$

Since $\theta \prec \xi$, $\xi_1 \geq \theta_1 \geq \theta_2 \geq \xi_2$; this together with $x_1 \geq x_2$ implies

$$(x_1, \xi_1 - \theta_1 + x_2) \prec (x_1 + \xi_1 - \theta_1, x_2)$$

and

$$(\theta_1 - x_1, \xi_2 - x_2) \prec (\theta_1 - x_2, \xi_2 - x_1).$$

Because g and ϕ are Schur-concave, the above integrand is nonnegative, and hence $\psi(\theta) \geq \psi(\xi)$. Thus ψ is Schur-concave. ‖

The above proof is due to Frank Proschan (private communication); essentially the same proof was also communicated to us privately by Koon Wing Cheng. Theorem J.1 is also obtained in 6.F.12.a as a consequence of 6.F.12.

Karlin and Rinott (1988) discuss a generalized Binet–Cauchy formula and a corresponding concept of generalized total positivity with respect to $\mathscr{H}$, a subgroup of the symmetric group ζ_n. Schur-convexity fits into this scheme as generalized total positivity with respect to the subgroup of permutations involving only two elements and the kernel $k(x,y) = \varphi(x+y)$. Generalized total positivity of this kernel is equivalent to Schur-convexity of $\varphi(x)$. It is possible to view Theorem J.1 as a special case of a more general theorem dealing with the preservation of generalized total positivity under convolutions.

J.1.a. Corollary. If ϕ is a Schur-concave function defined on $\mathscr{R}^n$ and $A \subset \mathscr{R}^n$ is a permutation-symmetric Lebesgue-measurable set which satisfies

$$y \in A \quad \text{and} \quad x \prec y \Rightarrow x \in A, \tag{1}$$

then

$$\psi(\theta) = \int_{A+\theta} \phi(x)\, dx$$

is a Schur-concave function of θ.

Proof. Condition (1) is a way of saying that the indicator function I_A of A is Schur-concave. This means that $g(z) = I_A(-z)$ is also Schur-concave. From J.1, it follows that

$$\int g(\theta - x)\phi(x)\, dx = \int I_A(x-\theta)\phi(x)\, dx = \int_{A+\theta} \phi(x)\, dx$$

is Schur-concave. ‖

Corollary J.1.a is closely related to Theorem 14.C.17, which generalizes a theorem of Anderson (1955). The conclusion of J.1.a is obtained as a special case of Theorems 14.C.16.a and 14.C.17 but with the additional hypothesis that A is convex.

A direct proof of J.1.a can be given and J.1 then follows. This was the original approach of Marshall and Olkin (1974).

J.1.b. Corollary. If g and ϕ are Schur-concave on $\mathscr{R}^n$, ϕ is nonnegative, and g is increasing (decreasing), then the convolution ψ of ϕ and g is increasing (decreasing) and Schur-concave.

This immediate consequence of J.1 can be useful for identifying functions that preserve weak majorization.

Another important class of integral transforms that preserve Schur-convexity was found by Proschan and Sethuraman (1977). This transformation involves a function α that is totally positive of order 2 (see Definition 18.A.1).

J.2. Theorem (Proschan and Sethuraman, 1977). Suppose that

(i) $\mathscr{X} = \mathscr{R}$, $\Theta \subset \mathscr{R}$ is an interval and μ is Lebesgue measure, or

(ii) $\mathscr{X} = \{\ldots, -1, 0, 1, 2, \ldots\}$, Θ is an interval (or an interval of integers) and μ is counting measure.

If α is a function defined on $\Theta \times \mathscr{X}$ such that

$$\alpha(\theta, x) = 0 \quad \text{if} \quad x < 0, \tag{2}$$

$$\alpha \text{ is totally positive of order 2}, \tag{3}$$

$$\alpha \text{ satisfies the following semigroup property:} \tag{4}$$

$$\alpha(\theta_1 + \theta_2, y) = \int_{\mathscr{X}} \alpha(\theta_1, x) \alpha(\theta_2, y - x) \, d\nu(x)$$

for some measure ν on $\mathscr{X}$, then the function ψ defined for $\theta_i \in \Theta$, $i = 1, \ldots, n$, by

$$\psi(\theta) = \int \prod \alpha(x_i, \theta_i) \phi(x) \prod d\mu(x_i)$$

is Schur-convex whenever ϕ is Schur-convex.

Similarly, if ϕ is Schur-concave, then ψ is Schur-concave.

Proof. We prove the theorem in the case that ϕ is Schur-convex. To show that $\psi(\theta) \leq \psi(\xi)$ when $\theta \prec \xi$ it is sufficient (by A.5) to consider only the case that θ and ξ differ in but two components, say the first two. Then

$$\psi(\xi) - \psi(\theta)$$
$$= \int \prod_{2}^{n} \alpha(\theta_i, x_i)$$
$$\times \left\{ \iint [\alpha(\xi_1, x_1)\alpha(\xi_2, x_2) - \alpha(\theta_1, x_1)\alpha(\theta_2, x_2)]\phi(x)\, d\mu(x_1)\, d\mu(x_2) \right\}$$
$$\times \prod_{3}^{n} d\mu(x_i).$$

Consequently, it is sufficient to show that the inner integral is nonnegative and this amounts to proving the theorem in case $n = 2$. For convenience suppose that $\theta_1 \geq \theta_2$ and $\xi_1 \geq \xi_2$. Then
$$\psi(\xi_1, \xi_2) - \psi(\theta_1, \theta_2)$$
$$= \iint [\alpha(\xi_1, x_1)\alpha(\xi_2, x_2) - \alpha(\theta_1, x_1)\alpha(\theta_2, x_2)]\phi(x_1, x_2)\, d\mu(x_1)\, d\mu(x_2).$$

Now, make use of the semigroup property and the fact $\xi_1 - \theta_1 = \theta_2 - \xi_2$ to write (with an interchange in order of integration)
$$\psi(\xi_1, \xi_2) - \psi(\theta_1, \theta_2)$$
$$= \int \alpha(\xi_1 - \theta_1, y) \iint [\alpha(\theta_1, x_1 - y)\alpha(\xi_2, x_2) - \alpha(\theta_1, x_1)\alpha(\xi_2, x_2 - y)]$$
$$\times \phi(x_1, x_2)\, d\mu(x_1)\, d\mu(x_2)\, d\nu(y).$$

To show that the inner integral here is nonnegative when $y \geq 0$, write
$$\iint \alpha(\theta_1, x_1 - y)\alpha(\xi_2, x_2)\phi(x_1, x_2)\, d\mu(x_1)\, d\mu(x_2)$$
$$- \iint \alpha(\theta_1, x_1)\alpha(\xi_2, x_2 - y)\phi(x_1, x_2)\, d\mu(x_1)\, d\mu(x_2)$$
$$= \iint \alpha(\theta_1, u_1)\alpha(\xi_2, x_2)\phi(u_1 + y, x_2)\, d\mu(u_1)\, d\mu(x_2)$$
$$- \iint \alpha(\theta_1, x_1)\alpha(\xi_2, u_2)\phi(x_1, u_2 + y)\, d\mu(x_1)\, d\mu(u_2)$$
$$= \iint \alpha(\theta_1, x_1)\alpha(\xi_2, x_2)[\phi(x_1 + y, x_2) - \phi(x_1, x_2 + y)]\, d\mu(x_1)\, d\mu(x_2)$$
$$= \iint_{x_1 \geq x_2} [\alpha(\theta_1, x_1)\alpha(\xi_2, x_2) - \alpha(\theta_1, x_2)\alpha(\xi_2, x_1)]$$
$$\times [\phi(x_1 + y, x_2) - \phi(x_1, x_2 + y)]\, d\mu(x_1)\, d\mu(x_2).$$

The last equality here utilizes the symmetry $\phi(u,v) = \phi(v,u)$ of ϕ.

Because ϕ is Schur-convex, $[\phi(x_1+y, x_2) - \phi(x_1, x_2+y)] \geq 0$ whenever $x_1 \geq x_2$. Because α is totally positive of order 2 and $\theta_1 \geq \xi_2$, $x_1 \geq x_2$, $\alpha(\theta_1, x_1)\alpha(\xi_2, x_2) - \alpha(\theta_1, x_2)\alpha(\xi_2, x_1) \geq 0$. Thus $\psi(\xi) - \psi(\theta) \geq 0$. ||

J.2.a. Corollary. If B is a nonnegative function of two real variables, then under the conditions of J.2,

$$h(\theta) = \int B\left(\sum \theta_i, \sum x_i\right) \prod \alpha(\theta_i, x_i) \phi(x) \prod d\mu(x_i)$$

is Schur-convex whenever ϕ is Schur-convex.

Proof. In any comparison $\psi(\xi) - \psi(\theta)$ where $\theta \prec \xi$, the equality $\Sigma \theta_i = \Sigma \xi_i$ must hold. But the Schur-convexity of ϕ implies the Schur-convexity of $B(\Sigma \theta_i, \Sigma x_i)\phi(x)$ for each fixed $\Sigma \theta_i$, so the result follows from J.2. ||

Some Examples

J.2.b. For $0 \leq \theta \leq 1$, let

$$\alpha(\theta, x) = \begin{cases} \dfrac{\theta^x}{x!}, & x = 0, 1, \ldots, \\ 0, & x = -1, -2, \ldots. \end{cases}$$

Then α satisfies the conditions of J.2 with ν being counting measure.

Proof. The total positivity of $\alpha(\theta, x)$ is well known and easily checked directly from the definition. The semigroup property is a consequence of the binomial theorem. ||

J.2.c. For $M = 1, 2, \ldots$, and nonnegative integer x, let

$$\alpha(M, x) = \binom{M}{x}.$$

Then α satisfies the conditions of J.2 with ν being counting measure.

Proof. The required total positivity of α can be checked directly by verifying the conditions of the definition [see Karlin (1968, p. 137)]. The semigroup property

$$\sum_{x=0}^{y} \binom{M}{x}\binom{K}{y-x} = \binom{M+K}{y}$$

is a well-known property of binomial coefficients [see Feller (1968, p. 64)]. ||

J.2.d. For $\theta > 0$, let

$$\alpha(\theta, x) = \begin{cases} \dfrac{\Gamma(\theta + x)}{x!\Gamma(\theta)} & x = 0, 1, \dots, \\ 0, & \text{otherwise}. \end{cases}$$

Then α satisfies the conditions of J.2, with ν being counting measure.

Proof. The total positivity of α follows from the log convexity of Γ (see 16.B.8.a). The semigroup property is obtained from the identity

$$B(\theta_1, \theta_2) = \sum_{x=0}^{y} \binom{y}{x} B(\theta_1 + x, \theta_2 + y - x),$$

where B is the usual beta function. To verify this identity, note that

$$\sum_{x=0}^{y} \binom{y}{x} B(\theta_1 + x, \theta_2 + y - x)$$

$$= \sum_{x=0}^{y} \binom{y}{x} \int_0^1 z^{\theta_1 + x - 1}(1-z)^{\theta_2 + y - x - 1} \, dz$$

$$= \int_0^1 z^{\theta_1 - 1}(1-z)^{\theta_2 - 1} \sum \binom{y}{x} z^x (1-z)^{y-x} \, dz$$

$$= \int_0^1 z^{\theta_1 - 1}(1-z)^{\theta_2 - 1} \, dz = B(\theta_1, \theta_2). \quad \|$$

J.2.e. For $\theta > 0$, let

$$\alpha(\theta, x) = \begin{cases} \dfrac{x^{\theta - 1}}{\Gamma(\theta)}, & x \geq 0, \\ 0, & x < 0. \end{cases}$$

Then α satisfies the conditions of J.2 with ν being Lebesgue measure.

Proof. The total positivity here is essentially the same as in J.2.a. The semigroup property is well known because it is equivalent to the fact that the beta density on $[0, y]$ integrates to 1. $\|$

J.3. Theorem (Cheng, 1977). Let $\mathscr{X}$, Θ, and μ be as in J.2. Let $K : \mathscr{R}^{2n} \to \mathscr{R}$ be a function of the form

$$K(\theta, x) = B\left(\sum_1^n \theta_i, \sum_1^n x_i\right) \prod_{i=1}^n \alpha(\theta_i, x_i),$$

where α is a nonnegative function satisfying (2) and (4) of J.2 and B is a nonnegative function on $\mathscr{R}^n \times \mathscr{R}^n$ satisfying the condition

$$B(\theta, x) = \int B(\lambda + \theta, x + y)\alpha(\lambda, y)\,d\mu(y) \tag{5}$$

whenever $\theta, \lambda \in \Theta$ and $\lambda > 0$. Then

$$\psi(\theta) = \int \phi(x) K(\theta, x) \prod d\mu(x_i)$$

is increasing in $\theta \in \Theta$ whenever ϕ is increasing in $x \in \mathscr{X}$.

Proof. To show that ψ is increasing in θ_k, let $\lambda, \theta_i \in \Theta$, $\lambda > 0$. Then

$\psi(\theta_1, \ldots, \theta_{k-1}, \theta_k + \lambda, \theta_{k+1}, \ldots, \theta_n)$

$= \int \phi(x) B\left(\sum \theta_i + \lambda, \sum x_i\right) \prod_{i \neq k} \alpha(\theta_i, x_i) \alpha(\theta_k + \lambda, x_k) \prod d\mu(x_i)$

$= \int \phi(x) B\left(\sum \theta_i + \lambda, \sum x_i\right) \prod_{i \neq k} \alpha(\theta_i, x_i) \alpha(\theta_k, x_k - y) \alpha(\lambda, y)$
$\quad \times \prod d\mu(x_i)\,d\nu(y)$

$= \int \phi(x_1, \ldots, x_{k-1}, x_k + y, x_{k+1}, \ldots, x_n) B\left(\sum \theta_i + \lambda, \sum x_i + y\right)$
$\quad \times \prod \alpha(\theta_i, x_i) \alpha(\lambda, y) \prod d\mu(x_i)\,d\nu(y)$

$\geq \int \phi(x) B\left(\sum \theta_i + \lambda, \sum x_i + y\right) \prod \alpha(\theta_i, x_i) \alpha(\lambda, y) \prod d\mu(x_i)\,d\nu(y)$

$= \int \phi(x) B\left(\sum \theta_i, \sum x_i\right) \prod \alpha(\theta_i, x_i) \prod d\mu(x_i) = \psi(\theta). \quad \|$

The condition (5) imposed on B has a simple interpretation when K is a probability density in x for each θ. If K is the density of the random variables $X_1, \ldots, X_n$, then (5) says that a marginal density, say of $X_1, \ldots, X_{n-1}$, has the same form with $n-1$ in place of n.

Theorem J.3 can be combined with J.2 to give conditions for preservation of monotonicity and Schur-convexity; this preservation is of interest in the context of weak majorization.

K Physical Interpretations of Inequalities

Zylka and Vojta (1991), developing ideas suggested by Sommerfield (1965), point out that some of the inequalities in this chapter can be obtained using thermodynamic arguments. For example, consider a closed thermodynamic system consisting of n subsystems characterized by their temperatures $T_1, T_2, \ldots, T_n$ and equal heat capacities C. After temperature equalization, the common temperature in the subsystem is $\overline{T} = \frac{1}{n}\sum_{i=1}^{n} T_i$. Assuming that the subsystems are ideal gases, the entropy change of the total system, ΔS, is given by

$$\Delta S = C \log(\overline{T}/T_1) + \cdots + C \log(\overline{T}/T_n). \tag{1}$$

However, $\Delta S \geq 0$, so it follows from (1) that

$$\frac{1}{n}\sum_{i=1}^{n} T_i \geq \prod_{i=1}^{n} T_i^{1/n}, \tag{2}$$

thus providing a "physical" derivation of the arithmetic–geometric mean inequality.

It is also possible to obtain (2) by considering, under suitable assumptions, the entropy and internal energy of ideal gas systems. By applying these ideas to other systems, such as ideal degenerate Bose gases, black-body radiators, and spin-systems in high-temperature approximation, other inequalities are obtained with physical derivations. Ideal degenerate Bose gas systems yield the inequality

$$n^2 \left(\sum_{i=1}^{n} T_i^{5/2}\right)^3 \geq \left(\sum_{i=1}^{n} T_i^{3/2}\right)^5. \tag{3}$$

With $x_i = T_i^{5/2}$, inequality (3) takes the form

$$\left(\frac{1}{n}\sum_{i=1}^{n} x_i\right)^{3/5} \geq \frac{1}{n}\sum_{i=1}^{n} x_i^{3/5},$$

which is a physical justification of a result that follows from I.1.b by noting that the function $(\sum x_i^{3/5})^{5/3}$ is Schur-concave on $\mathscr{R}_+^n$. Alternatively, it can be obtained from the Lyapunov inequality (16.D.1.d). Black-body radiator systems yield the inequality

$$n \left(\sum_{i=1}^{n} T_i^4\right)^3 \geq \left(\sum_{i=1}^{n} T_i^3\right)^4, \tag{4}$$

which is also obtainable using I.1.b, setting $x_i = T_i^4$. Analogously, the spin-system in high-temperature approximation provides a physical justification of the inequality

$$\left(\sum_{i=1}^n \frac{1}{T_i}\right)^2 \leq n \sum_{i=1}^n \left(\frac{1}{T_i}\right)^2, \tag{5}$$

also obtainable from I.1.b by setting $x_i = 1/T_i$. Note that (5) is valid for T_i's that can be positive or negative (which is appropriate for spin systems). Of course, this is the well-known statement that the variance of a discrete random variable is positive.

4
Equivalent Conditions for Majorization

In order to verify that x is majorized by y, the conditions of the definition might be directly checked, but it is sometimes more convenient to check alternative conditions. The purpose of this chapter is to collect some such alternatives.

A Characterization by Linear Transformations

The following results have already been established in Section 2.B:

A.1. Proposition (Hardy, Littlewood, and Pólya, 1929; 1934, 1952). For $x, y \in \mathscr{R}^n$, the following conditions are equivalent:

(i) $x \prec y$;

(ii) $x = yP$ for some doubly stochastic matrix P;

(iii) x can be derived from y by successive applications of a finite number of T-transformations, that is, transformations T having for some $1 \leq i < j \leq n$ and some $\alpha \in [0,1]$, $\overline{\alpha} = 1 - \alpha$, the form

$$T(z) = (z_1, \ldots, z_{i-1}, \alpha z_i + \overline{\alpha} z_j, z_{i+1}, \ldots, z_{j-1}, \overline{\alpha} z_i + \alpha z_j, z_{j+1}, \ldots, z_n).$$

This result follows from 2.B.1, 2.B.2, and the fact that products of matrices of T-transformations are doubly stochastic.

The equivalence of (i) and (iii) was essentially proved already by Muirhead (1903) in the case that the components of x and y are nonnegative integers.

A.2. Proposition. For $x, y \in \mathscr{R}_+^n$, the following conditions are equivalent:

(i) $x \prec_w y$ $(x \prec^w y)$;

(ii) $x = yP$ for some doubly substochastic (superstochastic) matrix P;

(iii) x can be derived from y by successive applications of a finite number of T-transformations, or transformations T of the form

$$T(z) = (z_1, \ldots, z_{i-1}, \alpha z_i, z_{i+1}, \ldots, z_n), \quad \text{where} \quad 0 \leq \alpha < 1 (\alpha > 1).$$

This result follows from 2.C.4, 2.C.6.a, 2.D.2.a, and 2.D.2.b.

B Characterization in Terms of Order-Preserving Functions

It is easy to prove that if $\phi(x) \leq \phi(y)$ for all Schur-convex functions ϕ, then $x \prec y$. But it is not necessary to check $\phi(x) \leq \phi(y)$ for all Schur-convex functions ϕ; certain subclasses of functions suffice. The purpose of this section is to give some such examples.

For $u \in \mathscr{R}$, let $u^+ = \max(u, 0)$.

B.1. Proposition (Hardy, Littlewood, and Pólya, 1929; 1934, 1952). The inequality

$$\sum g(x_i) \leq \sum g(y_i) \tag{1}$$

holds for all continuous convex functions $g : \mathscr{R} \to \mathscr{R}$ if and only if $x \prec y$.

Proof. If $x \prec y$, then (1) holds by 3.C.1. Suppose then that (1) holds. If for fixed k, $g(z) = (z - y_{[k]})^+$, then g is increasing so that

$$\sum_{i=1}^k g(y_{[i]}) = \sum_{i=1}^k y_{[i]} - k y_{[k]} \quad \text{and} \quad \sum_{i=k+1}^n g(y_{[i]}) = 0.$$

B. Characterization in Terms of Order-Preserving Functions   157

Addition of these equalities yields

$$\sum_{i=1}^{n} g(y_{[i]}) = \sum_{i=1}^{k} y_{[i]} - k y_{[k]}.$$

Because g is continuous and convex, $\sum_{1}^{n} g(y_{[i]}) \geq \sum_{1}^{n} g(x_{[i]})$. Moreover, $g(z) \geq 0$ and $g(z) \geq z - y_{[k]}$. Successive use of these facts yields

$$\sum_{i=1}^{k} y_{[i]} - k y_{[k]} \geq \sum_{1}^{n} g(x_{[i]}) \geq \sum_{1}^{k} g(x_{[i]}) \geq \sum_{1}^{k} x_{[i]} - k y_{[k]};$$

that is,

$$\sum_{1}^{k} x_{[i]} \leq \sum_{1}^{k} y_{[i]}.$$

This shows that $x \prec_w y$. To complete the proof, take $g(z) = -z$ in (1) to obtain $\sum_{1}^{n} x_i \geq \sum_{1}^{n} y_i$. ∥

Credit for Proposition B.1 has sometimes gone to Karamata (1932), who discovered it independently.

B.2. Proposition (Tomić, 1949).   The inequality

$$\sum g(x_i) \leq \sum g(y_i) \qquad (2)$$

holds for all continuous increasing convex functions g if and only if $x \prec_w y$. Similarly, (2) holds for all continuous decreasing convex functions g if and only if $x \prec^w y$.

Proof. If $x \prec_w y$, then according to 3.C.1.b, (2) holds for all continuous increasing convex functions g. Likewise, if $x \prec^w y$, then by 3.C.1.b, (2) holds for all continuous decreasing convex functions g.

Suppose that (2) holds for all continuous increasing convex functions g. Since $g(z) = \max[z - y_{[k]}, 0]$ is continuous, increasing, and convex, it follows as in the proof of B.1 that $x \prec_w y$.

If (2) holds for all continuous decreasing convex functions g, it follows in a similar manner that $x \prec^w y$. In this case, the argument makes use of $g(z) = \max[-z + y_{(k)}, 0]$. ∥

That (2) holds when $x \prec_w y$ and g is increasing and convex was also proved by Weyl (1949). Pólya (1950) showed that this fact can be obtained from B.1.

Remark. Fink (1994) discusses the relation between x and y when (2) holds for all g whose k-th derivative is increasing and convex.

B.3. Proposition (Hardy, Littlewood, and Pólya, 1929; 1934, 1952).

$$\sum x_i = \sum y_i \text{ and } \sum (x_i - a)^+ \leq \sum (y_i - a)^+ \quad \text{for all} \quad a \in \mathscr{R} \tag{3}$$

if and only if $x \prec y$.

Proof. Suppose first that $x \prec y$. Because $g(z) = (z-a)^+$ is convex, it follows from B.1 or 3.C.1 that (3) holds. Conversely, if (3) holds, then the proof of B.1 shows $x \prec y$. ∥

B.3.a. Corollary (Ando, 1989). The inequality $\Sigma |x_i - a| \leq \Sigma |y_i - a|$ holds for every $a \in \mathscr{R}$ if and only if $x \prec y$.

Proof. The inequality is immediate from $x \prec y$. To prove the converse, consider large and small values of a in the inequality to conclude that $\Sigma x_i = \Sigma y_i$. Next use the fact that $x_i + |x_i| = 2x_i^+$ to conclude that (3) also holds. ∥

B.4. Proposition.

$$\sum (x_i - a)^+ \leq \sum (y_i - a)^+ \quad \text{for all} \quad a \in \mathscr{R} \tag{4}$$

if and only if $x \prec_w y$. Similarly,

$$\sum (a - x_i)^+ \leq \sum (a - y_i)^+ \quad \text{for all} \quad a \in \mathscr{R} \tag{5}$$

if and only if $x \prec^w y$.

Proof. If $x \prec_w y$ or $x \prec^w y$, then the corresponding inequality follows from B.2 or from 3.C.1.b.

If (4) holds, then the proof of B.2 shows $x \prec_w y$; if (5) holds, it similarly follows that $x \prec^w y$. ∥

It is a triviality that if $\mathscr{C}$ and $\widetilde{\mathscr{C}}$ are classes of functions having the property

(i) $\phi(x) \leq \phi(y)$ for all $\phi \in \mathscr{C} \Rightarrow x \prec y$, and

(ii) $\mathscr{C} \subset \widetilde{\mathscr{C}}$,

then

(iii) $\phi(x) \leq \phi(y)$ for all $\phi \in \widetilde{\mathscr{C}} \Rightarrow x \prec y$.

From this and B.1 or B.3, it follows that

(iv) $\phi(x) \leq \phi(y)$ for all Schur-convex functions $\phi \Rightarrow x \prec y$,

B. Characterization in Terms of Order-Preserving Functions   159

(v) $\phi(x) \leq \phi(y)$ for all symmetric quasi-convex functions $\phi \Rightarrow x \prec y$,

(vi) $\phi(x) \leq \phi(y)$ for all symmetric convex functions $\phi \Rightarrow x \prec y$.

Note that (v) is a converse of 3.C.3 and (vi) is a converse of 3.C.2. By imposing a monotonicity condition on ϕ, similar results hold for weak majorization.

A number of other equivalences of majorization can be obtained using various families of Schur-convex functions. Some of these are given below.

B.5. Proposition (Muirhead, 1903; Hardy, Littlewood, and Pólya, 1934, 1952, p. 44).

$$\sum_{\pi} \alpha_{\pi(1)}^{x_1} \alpha_{\pi(2)}^{x_2} \cdots \alpha_{\pi(n)}^{x_n} \leq \sum_{\pi} \alpha_{\pi(1)}^{y_1} \alpha_{\pi(2)}^{y_2} \cdots \alpha_{\pi(n)}^{y_n} \qquad (6)$$

for all $\alpha = (\alpha_1, \ldots, \alpha_n) \in \mathscr{R}_{++}^n$ if and only if $x \prec y$. Similarly,

(6) holds for all $\alpha \in [1, \infty]^n$ if and only if $x \prec_w y$,
(6) holds for all $\alpha \in (0, 1]^n$ if and only if $x \prec^w y$.

Proof. If $x \prec y$, then (6) holds for all $\alpha \in \mathscr{R}_{++}^n$ by 3.G.2.e. If $x \prec_w y$ or $x \prec^w y$, (6) holds for the indicated α by 3.G.2.g.

Suppose (6) holds for all $\alpha \in [1, \infty)^n$. With $\alpha_1 = \cdots = \alpha_n > 1$, it follows that $\alpha_1^{\Sigma x_i} \leq \alpha_1^{\Sigma y_i}$; because $\alpha_1 > 1$, this means $\sum x_i \leq \sum y_i$. Next denote by $\mathscr{S}$ the set of all subsets of $\{1, \ldots, n\}$ of size k and take $\alpha_1 = \cdots = \alpha_k > 1$, $\alpha_{k+1} = \cdots = \alpha_n = 1$. Then from (6) it follows that

$$\sum_{S \in \mathscr{S}} \alpha_1^{\Sigma_{i \in S} x_i} \leq \sum_{S \in \mathscr{S}} \alpha_1^{\Sigma_{i \in S} y_i}. \qquad (7)$$

If $\sum_1^k x_{[i]} > \sum_1^k y_{[i]}$, this leads to a contradiction for large α_1. Thus $x \prec_w y$.

If (6) holds for all $x \in (0,1]^n$, then similar arguments apply: If $\sum_1^k x_{(i)} < \sum_1^k y_{(i)}$, then (7) leads to a contradiction for α_1 near zero. Thus $x \prec^w y$.

Finally, if (6) holds for all $\alpha \in \mathscr{R}_{++}^n$, then $x \prec_w y$ and $x \prec^w y$, so $x \prec y$. ||

Because of its historical importance, an alternative proof that $x \prec y$ implies (6) for all $\alpha \in \mathscr{R}_{++}^n$ is given. This proof is essentially the original proof of Muirhead (1903); see also Hardy, Littlewood, and Pólya (1934, 1952, p. 46).

Alternative proof of (6). Suppose that $x \prec y$ and $\alpha \in \mathscr{R}_{++}^n$. By 2.B.1, it is sufficient to prove (6) in case x and y differ in but two components, say $x_i = y_i$, $i = 3, \ldots, n$. Possibly relabel so that $x_1 > x_2$, $y_1 > y_2$. Then there exists δ, $0 < \delta < y_1 - y_2$, such that $x_1 = y_1 - \delta$, $x_2 = y_2 + \delta$.

$$\sum_\pi \alpha_{\pi(1)}^{y_1} \cdots \alpha_{\pi(n)}^{y_n} - \sum_\pi \alpha_{\pi(1)}^{x_1} \cdots \alpha_{\pi(n)}^{x_n}$$

$$= \frac{1}{2} \sum_\pi [\alpha_{\pi(1)}^{y_1} \alpha_{\pi(2)}^{y_2} - \alpha_{\pi(1)}^{y_1-\delta} \alpha_{\pi(2)}^{y_2+\delta} + \alpha_{\pi(2)}^{y_1} \alpha_{\pi(1)}^{y_2} - \alpha_{\pi(2)}^{y_1-\delta} \alpha_{\pi(1)}^{y_2+\delta}] \prod_3^n \alpha_{\pi(i)}^{y_i}$$

$$= \frac{1}{2} \sum_\pi (\alpha_{\pi(1)} \alpha_{\pi(2)})^{y_2} (\alpha_{\pi(1)}^{y_1-y_2-\delta} - \alpha_{\pi(2)}^{y_1-y_2-\delta})(\alpha_{\pi(1)}^{\delta} - \alpha_{\pi(2)}^{\delta}) \prod_3^n \alpha_{\pi(i)}^{y_i}$$

≥ 0. ||

B.6. Proposition (Fan, 1951; Mirsky, 1960a). If $x, y \in \mathscr{R}_+^n$, then

$$\Phi(x) \leq \Phi(y) \qquad (8)$$

for all symmetric gauge functions if and only if $x \prec_w y$.

Proof. If $x \prec_w y$ on $\mathscr{R}_+^n$, then (8) holds for all symmetric gauge functions by 3.I.1.a. Conversely, if (8) holds for all symmetric gauge functions, then $x \prec_w y$ because $\Phi(x) = |x_{[i]}| + \cdots + |x_{[k]}|$ is a symmetric gauge function, $k = 1, \ldots, n$. ||

B.7. Proposition. The inequality

$$\sum x_i u_i \leq \sum y_i u_i \qquad (9)$$

holds for all $u \in \mathscr{D}$ if and only if $x \prec y$ on $\mathscr{D}$.

Similarly, (9) holds for all $u \in \mathscr{D}_+$ if and only if $x \prec_w y$.

Proof. Suppose (9) holds for all $u \in \mathscr{D}_+$. Then the choice $u = (1, \ldots, 1, 0, \ldots, 0)$ yields $\sum_1^k x_i \leq \sum_1^k y_i$. For $x, y \in \mathscr{D}$, this shows that $x \prec_w y$. If (9) holds for all $u \in \mathscr{D}$, then the particular choice $u = (-1, \ldots, -1)$ yields additionally $\sum_1^n x_i \geq \sum_1^n y_i$, so $x \prec y$. The remainder of the proposition follows from 3.H.2.c and 3.H.3.b. ||

B.8. Proposition.

$$\max_\pi \sum t_i x_{\pi(i)} \leq \max_\pi \sum t_i y_{\pi(i)} \qquad (10)$$

for all $t \in \mathscr{R}^n$ if and only if $x \prec y$. Similarly,

(10) holds for all $t \in \mathscr{R}_+^n$ if and only if $x \prec_w y$,

(10) holds for all t such that $-t \in \mathscr{R}_+^n$ if and only if $x \prec^w y$.

B. Characterization in Terms of Order-Preserving Functions

Proof. If $x \prec y$, then (10) holds by 3.G.1.d or 3.G.1.e. If $x \prec_w y$ or $x \prec^w y$, then (10) follows from 3.G.1.d. The converses follow with $t = (1, \ldots, 1, 0, \ldots, 0)$ or $t = (-1, \ldots, -1, 0, \ldots, 0)$. ∥

B.8.a. Proposition.

$$\sum t_i x_i \leq \max_\pi \sum t_i y_{\pi(i)} \text{ for all } t \in \mathscr{R}^n \tag{10a}$$

if and only if $x \prec y$.

Proof. If $x \prec y$, then (10a) follows from (10). If (10a) holds, assume without loss of generality that $x_1 \geq x_2 \geq \cdots \geq x_n$, and then choose $t = (1, \ldots, 1, 0, \ldots, 0)$ to conclude that $\sum_1^k x_i \leq \sum_1^k y_{[i]}$, $k = 1, \ldots, n$. Choose $t = (-1, \ldots, -1)$ to obtain $\sum_1^n x_i \geq \sum_1^n y_i$. Thus $x \prec y$. ∥

B.9. Proposition. The inequality

$$xAx' \leq yAy' \tag{11}$$

holds for all real symmetric matrices $A = (a_{ij})$ satisfying

$$\sum_{j=1}^{i}(a_{k,j} - a_{k+1,j}) \geq 0, \quad i = 1, \ldots, n, \quad k = 1, \ldots, n-1, \tag{12}$$

if and only if $x \prec y$ on $\mathscr{D}_+$. Similarly,

(11) holds whenever (12) and $\sum_{j=1}^{i} a_{n,j} \geq 0$, $i = 1, \ldots, n$,

if and only if $x \prec_w y$ on $\mathscr{D}_+$,

(11) holds whenever (12) and $\sum_{j=1}^{i} a_{ij} \leq 0$, $i = 1, \ldots, n$,

if and only if $x \prec^w y$ on $\mathscr{D}_+$.

Proof. If $x \prec y$, then (11) holds whenever A satisfies (12) by 3.H.4. If $x \prec_w y$ or $x \prec^w y$, then (11) holds when A satisfies the corresponding conditions by 3.H.4.b.

By successively taking

$$A = \begin{pmatrix} 1 & 0 & \cdots & 0 \\ 0 & 0 & \cdots & 0 \\ \vdots & \vdots & & \vdots \\ 0 & 0 & \cdots & 0 \end{pmatrix}, \begin{pmatrix} 1 & 1 & 0 & \cdots & 0 \\ 1 & 1 & 0 & \cdots & 0 \\ 0 & 0 & 0 & \cdots & 0 \\ \vdots & \vdots & \vdots & & \vdots \\ 0 & 0 & 0 & \cdots & 0 \end{pmatrix}, \ldots, \begin{pmatrix} 1 & \cdots & 1 \\ \vdots & & \vdots \\ 1 & \cdots & 1 \end{pmatrix},$$

it follows from (11) that $(\sum_{i=1}^{k} x_i)^2 \leq (\sum_{i=1}^{k} y_i)^2$, $k = 1, \ldots, n$, so that if $x, y \in \mathscr{D}_+$, then $x \prec_w y$.

By successively taking

$$A = \begin{pmatrix} 0 & \cdots & 0 & 0 \\ \vdots & & \vdots & \vdots \\ 0 & \cdots & 0 & 0 \\ 0 & \cdots & 0 & -1 \end{pmatrix}, \begin{pmatrix} 0 & \cdots & 0 & 0 & 0 \\ \vdots & & \vdots & \vdots & \vdots \\ 0 & \cdots & 0 & 0 & 0 \\ 0 & \cdots & 0 & -1 & -1 \\ 0 & \cdots & 0 & -1 & -1 \end{pmatrix}, \ldots, \begin{pmatrix} -1 & \cdots & -1 \\ \vdots & & \vdots \\ -1 & \cdots & -1 \end{pmatrix},$$

it follows that $x \prec^w y$ on $\mathscr{D}_+$. Of course, if $x \prec_w y$ and $x \prec^w y$, then $x \prec y$. ||

C A Geometric Characterization

The following result relates to Chapter 1, Figs. 2 and 3.

C.1. Proposition (Rado, 1952). $x \prec y$ if and only if x lies in the convex hull of the $n!$ permutations of y.

Proof. Because the doubly stochastic matrices constitute the convex hull of the permutation matrices (see Birkhoff's theorem 2.A.2), a matrix P is doubly stochastic if and only if it can be written in the form

$$P = \sum_{i=1}^{n!} a_i \Pi_i,$$

where $\Pi_1, \ldots, \Pi_{n!}$ are the permutation matrices, $a_i \geq 0$, $i = 1, \ldots, n!$, and $\sum_{1}^{n!} a_i = 1$. Thus $x = yP$ for some doubly stochastic matrix if and only if

$$x = \sum_{1}^{n!} a_i(y\Pi_i),$$

i.e., if and only if x lies in the convex hull of the permutations of y. By A.1, $x = yP$ for some doubly stochastic matrix is equivalent to $x \prec y$. ||

It was noted by Horn (1954a) that C.1 is a direct consequence of 2.A.2. Rado's proof is somewhat more complicated because it does not depend upon A.1 or upon Birkhoff's theorem. Rather, it makes use of a separating hyperplane theorem.

C.2. Proposition. For $x, y \in \mathscr{R}_+^n$, $x \prec_w y$ if and only if x lies in the convex hull of the set of all vectors z which have the form

$$z = (\varepsilon_1 y_{\pi(1)}, \ldots, \varepsilon_n y_{\pi(n)}),$$

where π is a permutation and each $\varepsilon_1, \ldots, \varepsilon_n = 0$ or 1.

Proof. The proof is similar to that of C.1 but uses the fact 2.C.2 that the doubly substochastic matrices constitute the convex hull of the set of all matrices with at most one unit in each row and each column and all other entries equal to zero. ||

There is no counterpart to C.1 for the weak majorization $\prec^w$ because the doubly superstochastic matrices form an unbounded convex set that is not the convex hull of its extreme points.

D A Characterization Involving Top Wage Earners

When income inequality within a specific population is addressed, figures such as "the top 1% of wage earners receive 21% of the total income" are often quoted. To address this kind of inequality reporting, suppose that $x_1 \geq x_2 \geq \cdots \geq x_n \geq 0$ are the incomes of individuals in a population of size n, and let $T = \Sigma_1^n x_i$. For a specified proportion α of T, define $s = s(x; \alpha)$ by the conditions $\Sigma_1^{s-1} x_i < \alpha T$, $\Sigma_1^s x_i \geq \alpha T$. Thus individuals $1, 2, \ldots, s$ receive at least $100\alpha\%$ of the total income T, but all smaller groups receive a lesser proportion.

D.1. Proposition. For allocations $x_1 \geq x_2 \geq \cdots \geq x_n \geq 0$ and $y_1 \geq y_2 \geq \cdots \geq y_n \geq 0$ of the total income T,

$$s(x; \alpha) \geq s(y; \alpha) \quad \text{for all } \alpha \in (0, 1)$$

if and only if $x \prec y$.

Proof. Suppose first that $s(x; \alpha) \geq s(y; \alpha)$ for all $\alpha \in (0, 1)$. Choose $\alpha = \Sigma_1^k x_i / T$, so that $s(x; \alpha) = k$. Because $s(x; \alpha) \geq s(y; \alpha)$, it follows that $k \geq s(y; \alpha)$, that is, $\Sigma_1^k y_i \geq \alpha T = \Sigma_1^k x_i$. Next, suppose that $x \prec y$. Then $\Sigma_1^{s-1} y_i < \alpha T$ implies $\Sigma_1^{s-1} x_i < \alpha T$. But $\Sigma_1^s y_i \geq \alpha T$ does not imply $\Sigma_1^s x_i \geq \alpha T$, and consequently $s(x; \alpha) \geq s(y; \alpha)$. ||

5
Preservation and Generation of Majorization

There are a number of conditions on vectors u and v that imply a majorization of some kind. Many of these conditions involve the generation of u and v from other vectors where majorization is already present. Such results are summarized in Section A. In other cases, u and v are generated from vectors having various properties besides majorization, or v is derived from u in a specified manner. These kinds of origins of majorization are summarized in Section B. In Section C, extreme vectors (in the ordering of majorization) under constraints are identified, and Section D gives some special results for vectors with integer components.

Majorizations that arise from rearrangements can be found in Chapter 6 and are not repeated here.

A Operations Preserving Majorization

A.1. Theorem. For all convex functions g,

$$x \prec y \Rightarrow (g(x_1),\ldots,g(x_n)) \prec_{\mathrm{w}} (g(y_1),\ldots,g(y_n)); \qquad (1)$$

and for all concave functions g,

$$x \prec y \Rightarrow (g(x_1),\ldots,g(x_n)) \prec^{\mathrm{w}} (g(y_1),\ldots,g(y_n)). \qquad (2)$$

Proof. These results can be proved in various ways. For example, if 3.G.1.g is applied with $t_1 = \cdots = t_n = 1$, then (1) is immediate. Because $u \prec_w v$ if and only if $-u \prec^w -v$, (2) is equivalent to (1). ||

A.1.a.
$$x \prec y \Rightarrow (|x_1|, \ldots, |x_n|) \prec_w (|y_1|, \ldots, |y_n|).$$

A.1.b.
$$x \prec y \Rightarrow (x_1^2, \ldots, x_n^2) \prec_w (y_1^2, \ldots, y_n^2).$$

A.1.c. For $a \in \mathscr{R}$,
$$x \prec y \Rightarrow (x_1(a - x_1), \ldots, x_n(a - x_n)) \prec^w (y_1(a - y_1), \ldots, y_n(a - y_n)).$$

A.1.d.
$$x \prec y \text{ on } \mathscr{R}_{++}^n \Rightarrow (\log x_1, \ldots, \log x_n) \prec^w (\log y_1, \ldots, \log y_n);$$
that is,
$$x \prec y \text{ on } \mathscr{R}_{++}^n \Rightarrow \prod_{i=k}^n x_{[i]} \geq \prod_{i=k}^n y_{[i]}, \qquad k = 1, \ldots, n.$$

This conclusion with a weaker hypothesis is given in A.2.c.

A.1.e. Suppose that $g : \mathscr{R} \to \mathscr{R}$ is continuous at some point or is bounded above by a measurable function on some set of positive Lebesgue measure. Then
$$x \prec y \Rightarrow (g(x_1), \ldots, g(x_n)) \prec (g(y_1), \ldots, g(y_n))$$
if and only if g is linear.

Proof. The implied majorization is trivial when g is linear. To see that linearity is essentially a necessary condition, note first that $a \prec b$ is equivalent to $a \prec_w b$ and $a \prec^w b$. Thus, from the proof of 3.C.1.c, it follows that $2g((u+v)/2) = g(u) + g(v)$. This functional equation together with the hypotheses on g implies that g is linear (Aczél, 1966, p. 43 or Castillo and Ruiz-Cobo, 1992, p. 108). ||

A.1.f. If $x \prec y$, then for any $a, b \in \mathscr{R}$,
$$(ax_1 + b, \ldots, ax_n + b) \prec (ay_1 + b, \ldots, ay_n + b).$$

Proof. This is a direct consequence of A.1.e. Alternatively, one may argue as follows. Because $x \prec y$, there exists a doubly stochastic matrix

P such that $x = yP$ and $ax = ayP$. Because $be = beP$, it follows that $(ax + be) = (ay + be)P$; thus,
$$(ax_1 + b, \ldots, ax_n + b) \prec (ay_1 + b, \ldots, ay_n + b). \qquad \|$$

A.1.g. For $m = 1, 2, \ldots$,
$$(\underbrace{x_1, \ldots, x_1}_{m}, \underbrace{x_2, \ldots, x_2}_{m}, \ldots, \underbrace{x_n, \ldots, x_n}_{m})$$
$$\prec (\underbrace{y_1, \ldots, y_1}_{m}, \underbrace{y_2, \ldots, y_2}_{m}, \ldots, \underbrace{y_n, \ldots, y_n}_{m})$$
if and only if $(x_1, \ldots, x_n) \prec (y_1, \ldots, y_n)$.

This result can be verified directly using Definition 1.A.1. Note that in the first majorization, each x_i and y_i must be duplicated the same number m of times.

As a consequence of A.1.g, if $\phi : \mathscr{R}^{mn} \to \mathscr{R}$ is Schur-convex, then $\psi : \mathscr{R}^n \to \mathscr{R}$ is Schur-convex, where
$$\psi(x_1, \ldots, x_n) = \phi(\underbrace{x_1, \ldots, x_1}_{m}, \underbrace{x_2, \ldots, x_2}_{m}, \ldots, \underbrace{x_n, \ldots, x_n}_{m}).$$

A.2. Theorem. (i) For all increasing convex functions g,
$$x \prec_w y \Rightarrow (g(x_1), \ldots, g(x_n)) \prec_w (g(y_1), \ldots, g(y_n)).$$
(ii) For all increasing concave functions g,
$$x \prec^w y \Rightarrow (g(x_1), \ldots, g(x_n)) \prec^w (g(y_1), \ldots, g(y_n)).$$
(iii) For all decreasing convex functions g,
$$x \prec^w y \Rightarrow (g(x_1), \ldots, g(x_n)) \prec_w (g(y_1), \ldots, g(y_n)).$$
(iv) For all decreasing concave functions g,
$$x \prec_w y \Rightarrow (g(x_1), \ldots, g(x_n)) \prec^w (g(y_1), \ldots, g(y_n)).$$

Proof. First consider (i). If $x \prec_w y$, then for $k = 1, \ldots, n$, $(x_{[1]}, \ldots, x_{[k]}) \prec_w (y_{[1]}, \ldots, y_{[k]})$. Thus it follows from 3.C.1.b that $\sum_1^k g(x_{[i]}) \leq \sum_1^k g(y_{[i]})$, $k = 1, \ldots, n$. On account of the fact that $g(x_{[1]}) \geq \cdots \geq g(x_{[n]})$, this is just the statement that $(g(x_1), \ldots, g(x_n)) \prec_w (g(y_1), \ldots, g(y_n))$. Upon replacing g by $-g$, (iv) is obtained from (i). If x is replaced by $-x$ and y is replaced by $-y$, (iii) follows from (i) and (ii) follows from (iv). $\|$

A.2.a. (Weyl, 1949). If $x, y \in \mathscr{R}_{++}^n$, and $g(e^z)$ is convex and increasing, then

$$(\log x_1, \ldots, \log x_n) \prec_w (\log y_1, \ldots, \log y_n)$$
$$\Rightarrow (g(x_1), \ldots, g(x_n)) \prec_w (g(y_1), \ldots, g(y_n)).$$

Proof. This result is essentially the same as (i) of A.2. ||

A.2.b. If $x, y \in \mathscr{R}_{++}^n$,

$$(\log x_1, \ldots, \log x_n) \prec_w (\log y_1, \ldots, \log y_n) \Rightarrow x \prec_w y.$$

This is the special case $g(x) = x$ in A.2.a. It can be rewritten using a continuity argument as follows: If $x, y \in \mathscr{R}_+$, then

$$\prod_1^k x_{[i]} \leq \prod_1^k y_{[i]}, \quad k = 1, \ldots, n \Rightarrow \sum_1^k x_{[i]} \leq \sum_1^k y_{[i]}, \quad k = 1, \ldots, n.$$

A.2.c.

$$x \prec^w y \text{ on } \mathscr{R}_{++}^n \Rightarrow (\log x_1, \ldots, \log x_n) \prec^w (\log y_1, \ldots, \log y_n).$$

If $x, y \in \mathscr{R}_{++}$, this result, with the aid of a continuity argument, can be rewritten as

$$\sum_k^n x_{[i]} \geq \sum_k^n y_{[i]}, \quad k = 1, \ldots, n \Rightarrow \prod_k^n x_{[i]} \geq \prod_k^n y_{[i]}, \quad k = 1, \ldots, n.$$

A.2.d.

$$x \prec_w y \Rightarrow (x_1^+, \ldots, x_n^+) \prec_w (y_1^+, \ldots, y_n^+), \text{ where } \alpha^+ = \max(\alpha, 0).$$

A.2.e.

$$x \prec^w y \Rightarrow (\tilde{x}_1, \ldots, \tilde{x}_n) \prec^w (\tilde{y}_1, \ldots, \tilde{y}_n), \text{ where } \tilde{\alpha} = \min(\alpha, 1).$$

A.2.f.

$$x \prec^w y \Rightarrow (1 - e^{-x_1}, \ldots, 1 - e^{-x_n}) \prec^w (1 - e^{-y_1}, \ldots, 1 - e^{-y_n}).$$

A.2.g.

$$x \prec^w y \Rightarrow (e^{-x_1}, \ldots, e^{-x_n}) \prec_w (e^{-y_1}, \ldots, e^{-y_n}),$$

$$x \prec_w y \Rightarrow (e^{x_1}, \ldots, e^{x_n}) \prec_w (e^{y_1}, \ldots, e^{y_n}).$$

A.2.h.

$$x \prec^w y \text{ on } \mathscr{R}^n_{++} \Rightarrow (x_1^r, \ldots, x_n^r) \prec_w (y_1^r, \ldots, y_n^r), \quad r < 0,$$

$$x \prec^w y \text{ on } \mathscr{R}^n_{++} \Rightarrow (x_1^r, \ldots, x_n^r) \prec^w (y_1^r, \ldots, y_n^r), \quad 0 < r < 1,$$

$$x \prec_w y \text{ on } \mathscr{R}^n_{++} \Rightarrow (x_1^r, \ldots, x_n^r) \prec_w (y_1^r, \ldots, y_n^r), \quad r > 1.$$

A.3. Theorem. Suppose that $g_i : \mathscr{R} \to \mathscr{R}$ is differentiable for $i = 1, \ldots, n$. If $g_1, \ldots, g_n$ satisfy the conditions

$$g_i'(a) \geq g_{i+1}'(b) \geq 0 \qquad \text{whenever} \quad a \geq b, \quad i = 1, \ldots, n-1, \quad (3)$$

$$g_1(z) \geq g_2(z) \geq \cdots \geq g_n(z) \qquad \text{for all} \quad z, \quad (4)$$

then

$$x \prec_w y \text{ on } \mathscr{D} \Rightarrow (g_1(x_1), \ldots, g_n(x_n)) \prec_w (g_1(y_1), \ldots, g_n(y_n)) \text{ on } \mathscr{D}.$$

If $g_1, \ldots, g_n$ satisfy the conditions

$$0 \geq g_i'(a) \geq g_{i+1}'(b) \qquad \text{whenever} \quad a \geq b, \quad i = 1, \ldots, n-1, \quad (5)$$

$$g_1(z) \leq \cdots \leq g_n(z) \qquad \text{for all} \quad z, \quad (6)$$

then

$$x \prec^w y \text{ on } \mathscr{D} \Rightarrow (g_n(x_n), \ldots, g_1(x_1)) \prec_w (g_n(y_n), \ldots, g_1(y_1)) \text{ on } \mathscr{D}.$$

Proof. According to 3.H.3.a(3), together with the majorization $x \prec_w y$ on $\mathscr{D}$, implies that

$$\sum_1^k g_i(x_i) \leq \sum_1^k g_i(y_i), \qquad k = 1, \ldots, n.$$

Because of (4), $g_1(x_1) \geq \cdots \geq g_n(x_n)$ and $g_1(y_1) \geq \cdots \geq g_n(y_n)$. Thus these inequalities are equivalent to

$$(g_1(x_1), \ldots, g_n(x_n)) \prec_w (g_1(y_1), \ldots, g_n(y_n)).$$

The proof for the case $x \prec^w y$ on $\mathscr{D}$ is similar and makes use of 3.H.3.a (8). ∥

A.4. Theorem. Let $\phi : \mathscr{R}^m \to \mathscr{R}$ satisfy the conditions

(i) ϕ is increasing and convex in each argument, the other arguments being fixed,

(ii) the derivative $\phi_{(i)}$ of ϕ with respect to its ith argument satisfies $\phi_{(i)}(x_1, \ldots, x_m)$ is increasing in x_j for all $j \neq i$, x_i being fixed for $i = 1, \ldots, m$.

Then
$$x^{(i)} \prec_w y^{(i)} \text{ on } \mathscr{D}, \quad i = 1, \ldots, m,$$
$$\Rightarrow (\phi(x_1^{(1)}, \ldots, x_1^{(m)}), \ldots, \phi(x_n^{(1)}, \ldots, x_n^{(m)}))$$
$$\prec_w (\phi(y_1^{(1)}, \ldots, y_1^{(m)}), \ldots, \phi(y_n^{(1)}, \ldots, y_n^{(m)})) \text{ on } \mathscr{D}.$$

Remark. Condition (ii) is encountered in Chapter 6, where it is called *L-superadditivity*. See particularly Section 6.D. Theorem A.4 is related to an inequality of Fan and Lorentz (1954), which appears as 6.E.2.

Proof of A.4. By showing that
$$(\phi(x_1^{(1)}, \ldots, x_1^{(m)}), \ldots, \phi(x_n^{(1)}, \ldots, x_n^{(m)}))$$
$$\prec_w (\phi(y_1^{(1)}, x_1^{(2)}, \ldots, x_1^{(m)}), \ldots, \phi(y_n^{(1)}, x_n^{(2)}, \ldots, x_n^{(m)}))$$

and then continuing to successively substitute the $y^{(i)}$ for $x^{(i)}$ one at a time, the theorem is proved. Because conditions (i) and (ii) are symmetric in the arguments of ϕ, it is consequently sufficient to prove the theorem with $m = 2$ and $x^{(2)} = y^{(2)}$. To repeat in simplified notation, it is necessary to prove that

(iii) $\quad x \prec_w y \text{ on } \mathscr{D} \quad \text{and} \quad a \in \mathscr{D}$
$$\Rightarrow (\phi(x_1, a_1), \ldots, \phi(x_n, a_n)) \prec_w (\phi(y_1, a_1), \ldots, \phi(y_n, a_n)).$$

Let $\phi_i(x) = \phi(x, a_i)$, $i = 1, \ldots, n$. By 4.B.2, the conclusion of (iii) holds provided that

$$\sum_{i=1}^n g(\phi_i(x_i)) \leq \sum_{i=1}^n g(\phi_i(y_i)) \qquad \text{for all increasing convex functions } g.$$

With the supposition that each ϕ_i is differentiable, this holds (by 3.H.3) provided only that the composed functions $g \circ \phi_i$ satisfy

$$(g \circ \phi_i)'(u) \geq (g \circ \phi_{i+1})'(v) \qquad \text{for all} \quad u \geq v, \quad i = 1, \ldots, n-1;$$

that is,

(iv) $\quad g'(\phi_i(u))\phi_i'(u) \geq g'(\phi_{i+1}(v))\phi_{i+1}'(v), \quad u \geq v, \, i = 1, \ldots, n-1.$

Because ϕ is increasing in each argument and $a \in \mathscr{D}$, it follows that

$$\phi_i(u) \geq \phi_{i+1}(u) \geq \phi_{i+1}(v), \qquad u \geq v.$$

But g is convex and increasing, so

(v) $$g'(\phi_i(u)) \geq g'(\phi_{i+1}(v)) \geq 0.$$

Because ϕ is convex in each argument separately, ϕ_i' is increasing, so $\phi_i'(u) \geq \phi_i'(v)$; by (ii) and $a \in \mathscr{D}$, $\phi_i'(v) \geq \phi_{i+1}'(v)$. Putting these together with the fact that ϕ_{i+1} is increasing yields

(vi) $$\phi_i'(u) \geq \phi_{i+1}'(v) \geq 0.$$

Now, multiplication of (v) and (vi) yields (iv). ||

A.4.a. If ϕ satisfies conditions (i) and (ii) of A.4, if $x^{(i)} \prec_{\mathrm{w}} y^{(i)}$, $i = 1, \ldots, m$, and if the vectors $y^{(1)}, \ldots, y^{(m)}$ are similarly ordered [i.e., $(y_i^{(k)} - y_j^{(k)})(y_i^{(l)} - y_j^{(l)}) \geq 0$ for all i, j, k, l], then

$$(\phi(x_1^{(1)}, \ldots, x_1^{(m)}), \ldots, \phi(x_n^{(1)}, \ldots, x_n^{(m)}))$$
$$\prec_{\mathrm{w}} (\phi(y_1^{(1)}, \ldots, y_1^{(m)}), \ldots, \phi(y_n^{(1)}, \ldots, y_n^{(m)})).$$

The conclusion is weaker than that of A.4 in that here these vectors need not be in $\mathscr{D}$.

Proof. The proof is essentially the same as the proof of A.4, but makes use of 3.H.3.a rather than 3.H.3. ||

A.4.b. (i) If $x^{(i)} \prec_{\mathrm{w}} y^{(i)}$ on $\mathscr{D}$, $i = 1, \ldots, m$, then

$$\sum_{i=1}^{m} x^{(i)} \prec_{\mathrm{w}} \sum_{i=1}^{m} y^{(i)} \text{ on } \mathscr{D}.$$

(ii) If $x^{(i)} \prec_{\mathrm{w}} y^{(i)}$, $i = 1, \ldots, m$, and the $y^{(i)}$'s are similarly ordered (see definition following 6.A.1.a), then

$$\sum_{i=1}^{m} x^{(i)} \prec_{\mathrm{w}} \sum_{i=1}^{m} y^{(i)}.$$

(iii) If $x^{(i)} \prec^{\mathrm{w}} y^{(i)}$ on $\mathscr{D}$, $i = 1, \ldots, m$, then $\sum_{i=1}^{m} x^{(i)} \prec^{\mathrm{w}} \sum_{i=1}^{m} y^{(i)}$ on $\mathscr{D}$.

(iv) If $x^{(i)} \prec^{\mathrm{w}} y^{(i)}$, $i = 1, \ldots, m$, and the $y^{(i)}$'s are similarly ordered, then

$$\sum_{i=1}^{m} x^{(i)} \prec^{\mathrm{w}} \sum_{i=1}^{m} y^{(i)}.$$

A generalization of A.4.b is given in A.12, A.12.a, and A.12.b.

A.4.c. Let $\alpha^+ = \max(\alpha, 0)$ and let $S_k^+(\alpha_1, \ldots, \alpha_m) = S_k(\alpha_1^+, \ldots, \alpha_m^+)$, $1 \leq k \leq m$, where S_k is the kth elementary symmetric function. Then

$$x^{(i)} \prec_w y^{(i)} \text{ on } \mathscr{D}, \quad i = 1, \ldots, m,$$
$$\Rightarrow (S_k^+(x_1^{(1)}, \ldots, x_1^{(m)}), \ldots, S_k^+(x_n^{(1)}, \ldots, x_n^{(m)}))$$
$$\prec_w (S_k^+(y_1^{(1)}, \ldots, y_1^{(m)}), \ldots, S_k^+(y_n^{(1)}, \ldots, y_n^{(m)})) \text{ on } \mathscr{D}_+.$$

This can be obtained directly from A.4, but questions of differentiability are avoided by using A.2.d and proving the result for $x^{(i)}$ and $y^{(i)}$ in $\mathscr{D}_+$ with S_k in place of S_k^+.

A.4.d. If $x^{(i)} \prec_w y^{(i)}$ on $\mathscr{D}_+$, $i = 1, \ldots, m$, then

$$\left(\prod_{i=1}^m x_1^{(i)}, \ldots, \prod_{i=1}^m x_n^{(i)}\right) \prec_w \left(\prod_{i=1}^m y_1^{(i)}, \ldots, \prod_{i=1}^m y_n^{(i)}\right)$$

on $\mathscr{D}_+$. In particular, $x \prec_w y$ on $\mathscr{D}_+$ and $a \in \mathscr{D}_+$ implies

$$(a_1 x_1, \ldots, a_n x_n) \prec_w (a_1 y_1, \ldots, a_n y_n).$$

This is a special case of A.4.c. For $m = 2$, it is due to Pledger and Proschan (1971) and is given in 3.H.2.c. Of course, successive reapplication of the result for $m = 2$ yields the result for arbitrary m.

A.4.e. If $\phi(u, v) = (u+1)^{v+1}$, then ϕ satisfies conditions (i) and (ii) of A.4 with $m = 2$ provided that $u, v \geq 0$. Thus

$$x \prec_w y \text{ and } a \prec_w b \text{ on } \mathscr{D}_+$$
$$\Rightarrow ((x_1+1)^{a_1+1}, \ldots, (x_n+1)^{a_n+1})$$
$$\prec_w ((y_1+1)^{b_1+1}, \ldots, (y_n+1)^{b_n+1}).$$

A.4.f. If $\phi(u, v) = uv$, then ϕ satisfies conditions (i) and (ii) of A.4 with $m = 2$ provided that $u, v \geq 0$. Thus, if $x \prec_w y$ and $a \prec_w b$ on $\mathscr{D}_+$, then $(x_1 a_1, \ldots x_n a_n) \prec_w (y_1 b_1, \ldots y_n b_n)$.

A.5. Theorem. Let $\phi : \mathscr{R}^m \to \mathscr{R}$ satisfy the conditions:

(i) ϕ is concave and increasing in each argument, the other arguments being fixed;

(ii) the derivative ϕ_i of ϕ with respect to its ith argument satisfies $\phi_{(i)}(x_1, \ldots, x_n)$ is decreasing in x_j for all $j \neq i$, x_i being fixed for $i = 1, 2, \ldots, m$.

Then
$$x^{(i)} \prec^{\mathrm{w}} y^{(i)} \text{ on } \mathscr{D}, \quad i = 1, \ldots, m,$$
$$\Rightarrow (\phi(x_1^{(1)}, \ldots, x_1^{(m)}), \ldots, \phi(x_n^{(1)}, \ldots, x_n^{(m)}))$$
$$\prec^{\mathrm{w}} (\phi(y_1^{(1)}, \ldots, y_1^{(m)}), \ldots, \phi(y_n^{(1)}, \ldots, y_n^{(m)})) \text{ on } \mathscr{D}.$$

This result is equivalent to A.4.

A.6. If $x^{(i)} \prec y^{(i)}$, $i = 1, \ldots, m$, and $y^{(1)}, \ldots, y^{(m)}$ are similarly ordered, then
$$\sum x^{(i)} \prec \sum y^{(i)}.$$
In particular, if $x^{(i)} \prec y^{(i)}$ on $\mathscr{D}$, $i = 1, \ldots, m$, then $\sum x^{(i)} \prec \sum y^{(i)}$.

Proof. This follows from 6.A.1.b. ‖

Theorems A.3–A.6 involve generation of a majorization from several given majorizations by taking functions of corresponding arguments. Another way to combine majorizations is the following:

A.7. Proposition (Richard Rado; see Hardy, Littlewood, and Pólya, 1934, 1952, p. 63).

(i) $x \prec y$ on $\mathscr{R}^n$ and $a \prec b$ on $\mathscr{R}^m \Rightarrow (x, a) \prec (y, b)$ on $\mathscr{R}^{n+m}$;
(ii) $x \prec_{\mathrm{w}} y$ on $\mathscr{R}^n$ and $a \prec_{\mathrm{w}} b$ on $\mathscr{R}^m \Rightarrow (x, a) \prec_{\mathrm{w}} (y, b)$ on $\mathscr{R}^{n+m}$;
(iii) $x \prec^{\mathrm{w}} y$ on $\mathscr{R}^n$ and $a \prec^{\mathrm{w}} b$ on $\mathscr{R}^m \Rightarrow (x, a) \prec^{\mathrm{w}} (y, b)$ on $\mathscr{R}^{n+m}$.

Proof. For any convex function $\phi: \mathscr{R} \to \mathscr{R}$, it follows from 3.C.1 that $\sum_{i=1}^n \phi(x_i) \leq \sum_{i=1}^n \phi(y_i)$ and $\sum_{i=1}^m \phi(a_i) \leq \sum_{i=1}^m \phi(b_i)$. Add these inequalities and apply 4.B.1 to obtain (i). Similarly, (ii) is obtained using 3.C.1.b and 4.B.2. Of course, (ii) and (iii) are equivalent. Alternatively, notice that if P_1 and P_2 are doubly stochastic (doubly substochastic), then
$$P = \begin{bmatrix} P_1 & 0 \\ 0 & P_2 \end{bmatrix}$$
is doubly stochastic (doubly substochastic). So (i) follows from 2.B.2. ‖

A.7.a. If $x_l = y_l$ for all $l \neq j, k$, then

(i) $(x_j, x_k) \prec (y_j, y_k) \Rightarrow x \prec y$,

(ii) $(x_j, x_k) \prec_{\mathrm{w}} (y_j, y_k) \Rightarrow x \prec_{\mathrm{w}} y$,

(iii) $(x_j, x_k) \prec^{\mathrm{w}} (y_j, y_k) \Rightarrow x \prec^{\mathrm{w}} y$.

174   5. Preservation and Generation of Majorization

A.7.b. If $x \prec y$ and the components of y are not all equal, then there exists a unique $\alpha_0 \in [0, 1)$ such that

(i) $x \prec z = \alpha_0(\overline{y}, \ldots, \overline{y}) + (1 - \alpha_0)y$, where $\overline{y} = \sum y_i/n$,

(ii) in the inequalities $\sum_1^k x_{[i]} \leq \sum_1^k z_{[i]}$, $k = 1, \ldots, n - 1$, there is equality for at least one value of k,

(iii) for all $\alpha \in [0, \alpha_0]$,

$$x \prec z = \alpha(\overline{y}, \ldots, \overline{y}) + (1 - \alpha)y \prec y.$$

Notice that if equality holds for $k = l$, then the majorization $x \prec z$ "splits" into the two majorizations $\dot{x} \prec \dot{z}$, $\ddot{x} \prec \ddot{z}$, where $\dot{x} = (x_{[1]}, \ldots, x_{[l]})$, $\ddot{x} = (x_{[l+1]}, \ldots, x_{[n]})$, and $\dot{z}, \ddot{z}$ are similarly ordered (see definition following 6.A.1.a). By A.7, $\dot{x} \prec \dot{z}$ and $\ddot{x} \prec \ddot{z}$ imply $(\dot{x}, \ddot{x}) \prec (\dot{z}, \ddot{z})$, i.e., $x \prec z$.

Proof of A.7.b. For $1 \leq k \leq n$, the functions

$$g_k(\alpha) = \sum_1^k z_{[i]} - \sum_1^k x_{[i]} = k\alpha\overline{y} + (1 - \alpha)\sum_1^k y_{[i]} - \sum_1^k x_{[i]}$$

are continuous and decreasing in $\alpha \in [0, 1]$, and $g_k(0) \geq 0$, $g_k(1) \leq 0$. Thus there exists α_0 such that $\min_{1 \leq k \leq n} g_k(\alpha_0) = 0$. This α_0 satisfies the required conditions. Unless $y = ce$, the g_k's are strictly decreasing, so that α_0 is unique. ||

A.7.c.   Under the conditions of A.7.b,

$$\alpha_0 = \min_{1 \leq k \leq n-1} \frac{\sum_1^k y_{[i]} - \sum_1^k x_{[i]}}{\sum_1^k (y_{[i]} - \overline{y})}$$

$$= \min_{1 \leq k \leq n-1} \frac{\sum_1^k x_{(i)} - \sum_1^k y_{(i)}}{\sum_1^k (\overline{y} - y_{(i)})}.$$

Proof. Suppose that $x \prec y$ and $y \neq ce$, and suppose further that

$$x \prec (1 - \alpha)y + \alpha\overline{y}e \prec y.$$

Only the left-hand majorization is a concern; the right-hand majorization holds for all $\alpha \in [0, 1]$. From the left-hand majorization, it follows that

$$\sum_1^k y_{[i]} - \sum_1^k x_{[i]} \geq \alpha\left[\sum_1^k y_{[i]} - k\overline{y}\right], \quad k = 1, \ldots, n - 1.$$

For $k=n$, both sides are zero. Note that $\sum_1^k y_{[i]} - k\overline{y} > 0$ for $k < n$, and hence

$$\alpha \leq \min_{1 \leq k \leq n-1} \frac{\sum_1^k y_{[i]} - \sum_1^k x_{[i]}}{\sum_1^k (y_{[i]} - \overline{y})}. \quad \|$$

A.7.d. Remark. By 4.B.1,

$$x \prec \alpha_0(\overline{y}, \ldots, \overline{y}) + (1 - \alpha_0)y$$

is equivalent to the condition that

$$\sum \phi(x_i) \leq \sum \phi(\alpha_0 \overline{y} + (1 - \alpha_0)y_i) \leq \sum \phi(y_i)$$

for all convex $\phi : \mathscr{R} \to \mathscr{R}$. Because ϕ is convex and because

$$n\phi(\overline{y}) \leq \sum \phi(y_i),$$

it follows that

$$\sum \phi(x_i) \leq \sum \phi(\alpha_0 \overline{y} + (1-\alpha_0)y_i)$$
$$\leq \alpha_0 n\phi(\overline{y}) + (1 - \alpha_0) \sum \phi(y_i) \leq \sum \phi(y_i).$$

Recall from A.7.b that α_0 is unique, but in the inequalities

$$\sum \phi(x_i) \leq \alpha n \phi(\overline{y}) + (1 - \alpha) \sum \phi(y_i) \leq \sum \phi(y_i),$$

$\alpha \in [0, \alpha_0]$ is not unique.

The following proposition singles out a specific choice of α in the last set of inequalities.

A.7.e. Proposition (Cohen, Derriennic, and Zbăganu, 1993). Suppose $y \in \mathscr{R}_{++}^n$ with $\Sigma y_i = 1$, and $x = yA$ for some doubly stochastic matrix A. Then for all convex functions $\phi : \mathscr{R} \to \mathscr{R}$,

$$\sum_1^n \phi(x_i) \leq \alpha(A) n \phi\left(\frac{1}{n}\right) + (1 - \alpha(A)) \sum_1^n \phi(y_i) \leq \sum_1^n \phi(y_i),$$

where

$$\alpha(A) = \min_{j,k} \sum_{i=1}^n \min(a_{ji}, a_{ki}),$$
$$= 1 - \frac{1}{2} \max_{j,k} \sum_{i=1}^n |a_{ji} - a_{ki}|.$$

A.7.f. Remark. The coefficient $\alpha(A)$ is called the *coefficient of ergodicity* of A and satisfies

$$\alpha(A) = 1 - \sup \frac{\|(u-v)A\|}{\|u-v\|},$$

for $u, v \in \mathscr{R}_{++}^n$, $\|u\| = \|v\|$, where $\|z\| = \sum |z_i|$. For further discussion see Seneta (2006).

A.7.g. Remark. The development of A.7.b, A.7.d, and A.7.e raises the question of the possible relation between α_0 and the coefficient of ergodicity $\alpha(A)$. Examples can be constructed in which $\alpha(A) < \alpha_0$ and other examples in which $\alpha(A) > \alpha_0$.

Let $y = (1/20)(1, 3, 6, 10)$ and

$$A = \frac{1}{4}\begin{bmatrix} 4 & 0 & 0 & 0 \\ 0 & 4 & 0 & 0 \\ 0 & 0 & 3 & 1 \\ 0 & 0 & 1 & 3 \end{bmatrix}.$$

In this case, $x = yA = (1/20)(1, 3, 7, 9)$, the ergodic coefficient of A is $\alpha(A) = 1/2$ and $\alpha_0 = 0$, so that $\alpha(A) > \alpha_0$.

On the other hand, if $y = (1/10)(1, 3, 6)$ and

$$A = \frac{1}{6}\begin{bmatrix} 3 & 2 & 1 \\ 1 & 3 & 2 \\ 2 & 1 & 3 \end{bmatrix},$$

then $x = yA = (0.300, 0.267, 0.433)$, $\alpha(A) = 4/6$ whereas $\alpha_0 = 0.714$. Consequently, in this case, $\alpha_0 > \alpha(A)$.

It is interesting to observe that, in this last example, if one retains the same doubly stochastic matrix A but replaces $y = (1/10)(1, 3, 6)$ by $\widetilde{y} = (1/10)(6, 3, 1)$, one finds $\alpha_0 = 0.641 < \alpha(A)$.

A.8. Proposition (Pólya, 1950). If $x \prec_w y$, there exist $x_{n+1}, y_{n+1} \in \mathscr{R}$ such that

$$(x, x_{n+1}) \prec (y, y_{n+1}).$$

Proof. Let $x_{n+1} = \min(x_1, \ldots, x_n, y_1, \ldots, y_n)$ and let $y_{n+1} = \sum_1^{n+1} x_i - \sum_1^n y_i$. Since $\sum_1^n y_i - \sum_1^n x_i = x_{n+1} - y_{n+1} \geq 0$, it follows that $x_i \geq x_{n+1}$, $y_i \geq y_{n+1}$, $i = 1, \ldots, n$. ∥

Pólya uses this result to deduce 3.C.1.b from 3.C.1.

A.8.a. If $x \prec^w y$, there exist $x_0, y_0 \in \mathscr{R}$ such that

$$(x_0, x) \prec (y_0, y).$$

Proof. Let $x_0 = \max(x_1, \ldots, x_n, y_1, \ldots, y_n)$, $y_0 = \sum_0^n x_i - \sum_1^n y_i$. Then, as in A.8, $y_0 \geq x_0$, so $x_0 \geq x_i$, $y_0 \geq y_i$, $i = 1, \ldots, n$. ||

A.8.b. If $x \prec_w y$, where $x \in \mathscr{R}_+^n$, $y \in \mathscr{R}$, and $\delta = \sum_{i=1}^n (y_i - x_i)$, then for any integer k

$$(x, \underbrace{\frac{\delta}{k}, \frac{\delta}{k}, \ldots, \frac{\delta}{k}}_{k}) \prec (y, \underbrace{0, 0, \ldots, 0}_{k}).$$

Shi (2006) includes this result for the case $k = n$.

A.9. If $x \prec_w y$, then there exist vectors u and v such that

$$x \leq u \quad \text{and} \quad u \prec y, \qquad x \prec v \quad \text{and} \quad v \leq y.$$

Proof. To obtain v, it is necessary only to diminish $y_{[n]}$. Consider now the existence of u. For $n = 1$, the result is trivial. Suppose it is true for vectors of any length up to n, and for notational convenience, assume that $x_1 \geq \cdots \geq x_n$, $y_1 \geq \cdots \geq y_n$. Let $\alpha_1 = \min_{1 \leq k \leq n}(\sum_1^k y_i - \sum_1^k x_i)$ and let $\widetilde{x} = x + \alpha_1 e_1$ (e_i has a 1 in the ith place and zeros elsewhere). Then $\widetilde{x}_1 \geq \cdots \geq \widetilde{x}_n$, and for some k, $\sum_1^k \widetilde{x}_i = \sum_1^k \widetilde{y}_i$. Thus $(\widetilde{x}_1, \ldots, \widetilde{x}_k) \prec (\widetilde{y}_1, \ldots, \widetilde{y}_k)$ and $(\widetilde{x}_{k+1}, \ldots, \widetilde{x}_n) \prec_w (y_{k+1}, \ldots, y_n)$. Now apply the induction hypothesis to $(\widetilde{x}_{k+1}, \ldots, \widetilde{x}_n)$ and $(y_{k+1}, \ldots, y_n)$ to obtain $(\widetilde{\widetilde{x}}_{k+1}, \ldots, \widetilde{\widetilde{x}}_n)$, satisfying $(\widetilde{x}_{k+1}, \ldots, \widetilde{x}_n) \leq (\widetilde{\widetilde{x}}_{k+1}, \ldots, \widetilde{\widetilde{x}}_n) \prec (y_{k+1}, \ldots, y_n)$. Then by A.7(i), $x \leq (\widetilde{x}_1, \ldots, \widetilde{x}_k, \widetilde{\widetilde{x}}_{k+1}, \ldots, \widetilde{\widetilde{x}}_n) \prec y$. ||

The existence of the vector v was noted by Mirsky (1960a). The existence of the vector u is due to Fan (1951); it is equivalent to 2.C.6, which is due to Mirsky (1959a) and Chong (1976a).

A.9.a. If $x \prec^w y$, then there exist vectors u and v such that

$$x \geq u \quad \text{and} \quad u \prec y, \qquad v \geq y \quad \text{and} \quad x \prec v.$$

The following results are two of several that involve interlaced numbers (see B.4).

A.9.b. If $u \prec_w y$ and $v \prec^w y$ with $u_i \leq v_i$, $i = 1, \ldots, n$, then there exists an x such that $u_i \leq x_i \leq v_i$ and $x \prec y$.

A.10.a. Proposition (Mirsky, 1958a). If $x \prec y$ on $\mathscr{D}$, there exist $c_1, \ldots, c_{n-1}$ such that $y_1 \geq c_1 \geq y_2 \geq \cdots \geq c_{n-1} \geq y_n$ and

$$(x_1, \ldots, x_{n-1}) \prec (c_1, \ldots, c_{n-1}).$$

178   5. Preservation and Generation of Majorization

Proof. Because the result is trivial for $n = 2$, assume that $n \geq 3$ and denote by Δ the bounded closed convex set of points z in $\mathscr{R}^{n-1}$ specified by the inequalities

$$y_1 \geq z_1 \geq y_2 \geq \cdots \geq z_{n-1} \geq y_n,$$

$$\sum_1^k x_i \leq \sum_1^k z_i, \quad k = 1, \ldots, n-2.$$

Let $m^* = \max_\Delta \sum_1^{n-1} z_i$, $m_* = \min_\Delta \sum_1^{n-1} z_i$. Because Δ is convex and because

$$m^* = y_1 + \cdots + y_{n-1} \geq x_1 + \cdots + x_{n-1},$$

it is sufficient to prove that $m_* \leq x_1 + \cdots + x_{n-1}$. Let $(d_1, \ldots, d_{n-1}) \in \Delta$ satisfy $\sum_1^{n-1} d_i = m_*$ and note that

$$d_{n-1} \geq y_n, \quad d_k \geq y_{k+1}, \quad k = 1, \ldots, n-2, \tag{7}$$

and

$$\sum_1^k x_i \leq \sum_1^k d_i, \quad k = 1, \ldots, n-2. \tag{8}$$

Case 1. If all the inequalities in (8) are strict, then $d_k = y_{k+1}$, $k = 1, \ldots, n-2$, for otherwise some d_k could be diminished, contradicting $\sum_1^n d_i = m_*$. Thus, in this case,

$$m_* = \sum_2^n y_i \leq \sum_2^n x_i \leq \sum_1^n x_i,$$

as was to be proved.

Case 2. If equality holds in (8) for at least one value of k, denote the largest such k by r. Then $\sum_1^r x_i = \sum_1^r d_i$, but $\sum_1^k x_i < \sum_1^k d_i$, $r < k < n - 2$. Then by the reasoning used in Case 1, $d_k = y_{k+1}$, $k = r+1, \ldots, n-2$. Hence,

$$\begin{aligned}
m_* &= (d_1 + \cdots + d_r) + (d_{r+1} + \cdots + d_{n-1}) \\
&= (x_1 + \cdots + x_r) + y_{r+2} + \cdots + y_n \\
&\leq x_1 + \cdots + x_r + x_{r+2} + \cdots + x_n \\
&\leq x_1 + \cdots + x_{n-1}. \quad \|
\end{aligned}$$

Of course, $x \prec y$ on $\mathscr{D}$ implies $(x_1, \ldots, x_{n-1}) \prec_w (y_1, \ldots, y_{n-1})$, so that by A.9, there exists $v \leq (y_1, \ldots, y_{n-1})$ such that $x \prec v$. But this does not give the interlacing property obtained by Mirsky.

A.10.b. Proposition (Chong, 1976b). If $x \prec y$ on $\mathscr{D}$, then there exist a least integer k, $1 \leq k \leq n$, and a vector

$$z = (y_1, \ldots, y_{k-2}, y_{k-1} + y_k - x_1, x_1, y_{k+1}, \ldots, y_n)$$

such that

$$x \prec z \prec y.$$

A.11. Proposition (Tomić, 1949). Suppose that $x \prec y$ on $\mathscr{D}$, a is a fixed constant, and l, m are determined by

$$x_1 \geq \cdots \geq x_l \geq a > x_{l+1} \geq \cdots \geq x_n,$$
$$y_1 \geq \cdots \geq y_m \geq a > y_{m+1} \geq \cdots \geq y_n.$$

If $l \geq m$, then

$$(x_1, \ldots, x_l) \prec_w (y_1, \ldots, y_m, \underbrace{a, \ldots, a}_{l-m}), \tag{9}$$

$$(\underbrace{a, \ldots, a}_{l-m}, x_{l+1}, \ldots, x_n) \prec^w (y_{m+1}, \ldots, y_n). \tag{10}$$

If $l < m$, then

$$(x_1, \ldots, x_l, \underbrace{a, \ldots, a}_{m-l}) \prec_w (y_1, \ldots, y_m), \tag{11}$$

$$(x_{l+1}, \ldots, x_n) \prec^w (\underbrace{a, \ldots, a}_{m-l}, y_{m+1}, \ldots, y_n). \tag{12}$$

Proof. To verify (9), note that because $x \prec y$, $\sum_1^k x_i \leq \sum_1^k y_i$, $k = 1, \ldots, m$, and $\sum_1^k x_i \leq \sum_1^k y_i \leq \sum_1^m y_i + (k-m)a$, $k = m+1, \ldots, l$. The proofs of (10), (11), and (12) are similar. ∥

A.12. If $x \prec y$ on $\mathscr{D}$ and if $0 \leq \alpha \leq \beta \leq 1$, then

$$\beta x + (1 - \beta)y \prec \alpha x + (1 - \alpha)y.$$

More generally, if $x^{(1)} \prec x^{(2)} \prec \cdots \prec x^{(m)}$ on $\mathscr{D}$ and if

(i) $\sum_1^k \alpha_i \leq \sum_1^k \beta_i$, $k = 1, \ldots, m-1$,

(ii) $\sum_1^m \alpha_i = \sum_1^m \beta_i$,

then

$$\sum_{i=1}^m \beta_i x^{(i)} \prec \sum_{i=1}^m \alpha_i x^{(i)} \qquad \text{on } \mathscr{D}.$$

Proof. For fixed k, $1 \leq k \leq n$, let $S_i = \sum_{j=1}^k x_j^{(i)}$. Then, the required inequality

$$\sum_{i=1}^m \beta_i \sum_{j=1}^k x_j^{(i)} \leq \sum_{i=1}^m \alpha_i \sum_{j=1}^k x_j^{(i)}$$

can be written more compactly as

(iii) $\sum_{i=1}^m \beta_i S_i \leq \sum_{i=1}^m \alpha_i S_i$.

Because of the assumed majorization, $S_1 \leq \cdots \leq S_m$, and thus one can write $S_i = \sum_{l=1}^i t_l$, where $t_l \geq 0$, $l > 1$. The sufficiency of (i) and (ii) can be seen clearly by making this substitution and interchanging the order of summation. Alternatively, (i) and (ii) are sufficient for (iii) by 16.A.2.a. ||

A.12.a. If $x^{(1)} \prec_w x^{(2)} \prec_w \cdots \prec_w x^{(m)}$ on $\mathscr{D}$ and if α and β satisfy (i) and (ii) of A.12, then

$$\sum_{i=1}^m \beta_i x^{(i)} \prec_w \sum_{i=1}^m \alpha_i x^{(i)} \qquad \text{on } \mathscr{D}.$$

A.12.b. If $x^{(1)} \prec^w x^{(2)} \prec^w \cdots \prec^w x^{(m)}$ on $\mathscr{D}$ and if α and β satisfy (i) and (ii) of A.12, then

$$\sum_{i=1}^m \beta_i x^{(i)} \prec^w \sum_{i=1}^m \alpha_i x^{(i)} \qquad \text{on } \mathscr{D}.$$

Remark. Note that conditions (i) and (ii) in A.12 do not say $\alpha \prec \beta$ because there is no prescribed ordering of the components of α and β. On the other hand, there is a way to generate majorization from vectors α and β that satisfy (i) and (ii).

A.13. For any vector $z \in \mathscr{R}^n$, let

$$z_i^* = \max_{k \geq i} \min_{j \leq i} \sum_{l=j}^{k} z_l/(k-j+1).$$

If $\sum_1^k x_i \leq \sum_1^k y_i$, $k = 1, \ldots, n-1$, $\sum_1^n x_i = \sum_1^n y_i$, then $x^* \prec y^*$ on $\mathscr{D}$. If $\sum_1^k x_i \leq \sum_1^k y_i$, $k = 1, \ldots, n$, then $x^* \prec_{\mathrm{w}} y^*$ on $\mathscr{D}$.

Proof. Let $S_i(z) = \sum_{l=1}^{i} z_l$, $i = 1, \ldots, n$. Call a vector $(u_1, \ldots, u_n)$ *concave* if $u_i - u_{i-1}$ is decreasing in $i = 2, \ldots, n$. Because $z_1^* \geq \cdots \geq z_n^*$, the vector $(S_1(z^*), \ldots, S_n(z^*))$ is concave; in fact, it is the least concave majorant of $(S_1(z), \ldots, S_n(z))$. Graphically one can think of placing a pin at each of the points $(i, S(z_i))$ in the plane and then placing a taut string above these pins. Such a string will pass through the points $(i, S(z_i^*))$.

Because $S_k(x) \leq S_k(y)$, $k = 1, \ldots, n$, it follows that $S_k(x^*) \leq S_k(y^*)$, $k = 1, \ldots, n$. Moreover, $\sum_1^n x_i = \sum_1^n x_i^*$ and $\sum_1^n y_i = \sum_1^n y_i^*$. Because x^* and $y^* \in \mathscr{D}$, the proof is complete. ||

The ideas touched upon in the above proof are discussed in detail by Barlow, Bartholomew, Bremner, and Brunk (1972).

Vector Functions Preserving Majorization

Propositions A.1–A.6 are concerned with results which have the general form

$$x^{(i)} \prec y^{(i)}, \quad i = 1, \ldots, m \Rightarrow (\phi(x_1^{(1)}, \ldots, x_1^{(m)}), \ldots, \phi(x_n^{(1)}, \ldots, x_n^{(m)}))$$
$$\prec (\phi(y_1^{(1)}, \ldots, y_1^{(m)}), \ldots, \phi(y_n^{(1)}, \ldots, y_n^{(m)})),$$

where the majorizations may be weak or strong. The arguments of ϕ all consist of 1st components or ... or nth components of the vectors $x^{(i)}$ and $y^{(i)}$. The following proposition does not have this characteristic.

A.14. Proposition. (i) If $\phi_1, \ldots, \phi_m$ are Schur-convex functions, then

$$x \prec y \Rightarrow (\phi_1(x), \ldots, \phi_m(x)) \prec_{\mathrm{w}} (\phi_1(y), \ldots, \phi_m(y)).$$

(ii) If $\phi_1, \ldots, \phi_m$ are increasing Schur-convex functions, then

$$x \prec_{\mathrm{w}} y \Rightarrow (\phi_1(x), \ldots, \phi_m(x)) \prec_{\mathrm{w}} (\phi_1(y), \ldots, \phi_m(y)).$$

(iii) If $\phi_1, \ldots, \phi_m$ are decreasing Schur-convex functions, then

$$x \prec^{\mathrm{w}} y \Rightarrow (\phi_1(x), \ldots, \phi_m(x)) \prec_{\mathrm{w}} (\phi_1(y), \ldots, \phi_m(y)).$$

If in (i), (ii), and (iii) the ϕ_i are, respectively, Schur-concave, decreasing and Schur-concave, or increasing and Schur-concave, then in the conclusions $\prec_w$ is replaced by $\prec^w$.

Proof. The results follow from (i), (v), and (ix) of Table 1 of Section 3.B, taking $h(z_1, \ldots, z_m)$ to be the sum of the k largest of $z_1, \ldots, z_m$, $k = 1, \ldots, m$. ||

Parts (i) and (ii) of A.14 were obtained by Chong (1976c) under the condition that each ϕ_i is symmetric and convex.

A.15. Let D be an $n \times m$ matrix. If $x \prec y$ on $\mathscr{D} \equiv \mathscr{D}_n$, then $xD \in \mathscr{D} \equiv \mathscr{D}_m$, $yD \in \mathscr{D} \equiv \mathscr{D}_m$, and $xD \prec yD$ if and only if for some real number α,

(a) $e_{(n)}D = n\alpha e_{(m)}$, where $e_{(\ell)} = (1, \ldots, 1) \in \mathscr{R}^\ell$,

(b) $De'_{(m)} = m\alpha e'_{(n)}$,

(c) $\sum_{j=1}^{k} d_{ij}$ is decreasing in $i = 1, \ldots, n$ for $k = 1, \ldots, m-1$,

(d) $\sum_{i=1}^{k} d_{ij}$ is decreasing in $j = 1, \ldots, m$ for $k = 1, \ldots, n-1$.

Proof. First, suppose (a)–(d) hold. By 2.E.1, it follows from (a) and (d) that $xD \in \mathscr{D}$ and $yD \in \mathscr{D}$. Thus $xD \prec yD$ if

$$\sigma_k(x) \equiv \sum_{j=1}^{k} \sum_{i=1}^{n} x_i d_{ij} \leq \sigma_k(y), \qquad k = 1, \ldots, m-1, \qquad (13)$$

and $\sigma_m(x) = \sigma_m(y)$ whenever $x \prec y$ on $\mathscr{D} \equiv \mathscr{D}_n$. Since $x, y \in \mathscr{D} \equiv \mathscr{D}_n$, (13) follows from (c) by 16.A.2.a.

From (b) and $\sum x_i = \sum y_i$, it follows that $xDe' = yDe'$; that is, $\sigma_m(x) = \sigma_m(y)$. Alternatively, one can observe that (c) is the condition that σ_k is Schur-convex on $\mathscr{D}$ and (b) is the condition that σ_m and $-\sigma_m$ are Schur-convex on $\mathscr{D}$.

Next, suppose that $xD \prec yD$ on $\mathscr{D} \equiv \mathscr{D}_m$ whenever $x \prec y$ on $\mathscr{D} \equiv \mathscr{D}_n$. Then (a) and (d) hold by 2.E.1. Because the majorization implies that σ_k, $k = 1, \ldots, m$, and $-\sigma_m$ are Schur-convex on $\mathscr{D}$, (b) and (c) are obtained from 3.A.3 and 3.H.2. Of course, α in (a) must be the same as in (b) because $e_{(m)}De'_{(n)} = nm\alpha$ is the sum of all elements in D. ||

A.16. Let D be an $n \times m$ matrix. If $x \prec_w y$ on $\mathscr{D} \equiv \mathscr{D}_n$, then $xD \in \mathscr{D} \equiv \mathscr{D}_m$, $yD \in \mathscr{D} \equiv \mathscr{D}_m$, and $xD \prec_w yD$ if and only if

(a) $\sum_{i=1}^{k} d_{ij}$ is decreasing in $j = 1, \ldots, m$ for $k = 1, \ldots, n-1$,

(b) $\sum_{i=1}^{n} d_{ij}$ is independent of j [that is, $e_{(n)}D = n\alpha e_{(m)}$, for some α, where $e_{(\ell)} = (1, \ldots, 1) \in \mathscr{R}^{\ell}$],

(c) $\sum_{j=1}^{k} d_{ij}$ is decreasing in $i = 1, \ldots, n$ for $k = 1, \ldots, m$,

(d) $\sum_{j=1}^{k} d_{nj} \geq 0$, $k = 1, \ldots, m$.

Proof. Suppose (a)–(d) hold. By 2.E.1, it follows from (a) and (b) that $xD \in \mathscr{D}_m$ and $yD \in \mathscr{D}_m$. Thus $xD \prec_w yD$ if

$$\sigma_k(x) \equiv \sum_{j=1}^{k} \sum_{i=1}^{n} x_i d_{ij} \leq \sigma_k(y), \qquad k = 1, \ldots, m,$$

whenever $x \prec_w y$ on $\mathscr{D}$. But this follows from 3.A.7 because, according to 3.H.3, conditions (c) and (d) imply that σ_k is Schur-convex and increasing.

Next, suppose that $xD \prec_w yD$ on $\mathscr{D} \equiv \mathscr{D}_m$ whenever $x \prec_w y$ on $\mathscr{D} \equiv \mathscr{D}_n$. Then (a) and (b) follow by 2.E.1. Because the majorization implies that the σ_k are increasing and Schur-convex on $\mathscr{D}$, it must be that (c) and (d) hold. ∥

A.17. Proposition (Chong, 1974d). Let D be an $n \times m$ matrix with the property that for every $n \times n$ permutation matrix Π, there exists an $m \times m$ permutation matrix $\widetilde{\Pi}$ such that $\Pi D = D\widetilde{\Pi}$. If $x, y \in \mathscr{R}^n$ and $x \prec y$, then $xD \prec yD$ (on $\mathscr{R}^m$).

Proof. If $x \prec y$, then by 2.A.2 and 2.B.2, $x = y(\sum \alpha_i \Pi_i)$ where $\alpha_i \geq 0$, $\sum \alpha_i = 1$, and the Π_i are permutation matrices. Thus

$$xD = y(\sum \alpha_i \Pi_i)D = y(\sum \alpha_i D\widetilde{\Pi}_i) = yD(\sum \alpha_i \widetilde{\Pi}_i).$$

But $\sum \alpha_i \widetilde{\Pi}_i$ is doubly stochastic, so by 2.B.2, $xD \prec yD$. ∥

Examples of matrices satisfying the condition of A.17 are easily found with the aid of the following:

A.17.a. (Chong, 1974d). A matrix D satisfies the condition of A.17 if and only if all permutations of any column of D are also columns of D.

With the aid of A.17.a, A.17 can also be proved using 3.G.2.b.

A.17.b. (Chong, 1974d). If D has nonnegative elements and satisfies the condition of A.17, then

$$x \prec_w y \quad \text{implies} \quad xD \prec_w yD,$$

and

$$x \prec^w y \quad \text{implies} \quad xD \prec^w yD.$$

Proof. If $x \prec_w y$, then by A.9 there exists a vector u such that $x \leq u \prec y$. Thus, by A.17 and because D is nonnegative, $xD \leq uD \prec yD$ and this means $xD \prec_w yD$. The proof for $\prec^w$ follows similarly from A.9.a or from the case $\prec_w$ using $a \prec_w b \Leftrightarrow -a \prec^w -b$. ||

A.17 has been generalized by Ando (1989) to nonlinear functions mapping $\mathscr{R}^n \to \mathscr{R}^m$.

A.18. Definition. $\Phi : \mathscr{R}^n \to \mathscr{R}^m$ is said to be *increasing* if

$$\Phi(x) \leq \Phi(y) \quad \text{whenever} \quad x_i \leq y_i, \quad i = 1, \ldots, n,$$

and Φ is said to be convex if

$$\Phi(\alpha x + \overline{\alpha} y) \leq \alpha \Phi(x) + \overline{\alpha} \Phi(y), \quad 0 \leq \alpha \leq 1, \ \overline{\alpha} = 1 - \alpha.$$

Here $\leq$ denotes componentwise ordering.

A.19. Proposition (Ando, 1989). If $\Phi : \mathscr{R}^n \to \mathscr{R}^m$ is convex and if for any $n \times n$ permutation matrix Π there exists an $m \times m$ permutation matrix Π^* such that

$$\Phi(x)\Pi^* = \Phi(x\Pi) \quad \text{for all } x,$$

then

$$x \prec y \quad \text{implies} \quad \Phi(x) \prec_w \Phi(y).$$

If, in addition, Φ is increasing, then

$$x \prec_w y \quad \text{implies} \quad \Phi(x) \prec_w \Phi(y).$$

A.20. Majorization for sums and products. A large class of sum and product inequalities are of the following form: If

$$\alpha_1 \geq \cdots \geq \alpha_n, \quad \beta_1 \geq \cdots \geq \beta_n, \quad \gamma_1 \geq \cdots \geq \gamma_n,$$

then

$$\sum_{s=1}^{k} \gamma_{i_s + j_s - s} \leq \sum_{s=1}^{k} \alpha_{i_s} + \sum_{s=1}^{k} \beta_{j_s}, \quad k = 1, \ldots, n, \tag{14}$$

where $1 \leq i_1 < \cdots < i_k \leq n$, $1 \leq j_1 < \cdots < j_k \leq n$. The set of inequalities (14) is stronger than the majorization $\gamma \prec_w \alpha + \beta$. To see this, choose $j_s = s$, in which case inequality (14) becomes

$$\sum_{s=1}^k \gamma_{i_s} \leq \sum_{s=1}^k \alpha_{i_s} + \sum_{s=1}^k \beta_s, \quad k = 1, \ldots, n,$$

which is equivalent to

$$(\gamma - \alpha) \prec_w \beta. \tag{15}$$

From (14) with $i_s = j_s = s$, or from (15) with the aid of A.4.b, it follows that

$$\gamma \prec_w \alpha + \beta. \tag{16}$$

The majorization in (15) is strong if equality holds in (14) for $k = n$.

Analogous to (14), multiplicative inequalities of the following form sometimes arise: If $\alpha_n \geq 0$, $\beta_n \geq 0$, $\gamma_n \geq 0$,

$$\prod_{s=1}^k \gamma_{i_s + j_s - s} \leq \prod_{s=1}^k \alpha_{i_s} \beta_{j_s}, \quad k = 1, \ldots, n. \tag{17}$$

In particular, (17) implies

$$\prod_1^k \gamma_{i_s} \leq \prod_1^k \alpha_{i_s} \beta_s, \quad k = 1, \ldots, n. \tag{18}$$

If $\alpha_n > 0$, $\beta_n > 0$, $\gamma_n > 0$, then (18) is equivalent to

$$(\log \gamma - \log \alpha) \prec_w \log \beta. \tag{19}$$

In turn, (17) or (19) implies that

$$(\log \gamma) \prec_w (\log \alpha + \log \beta). \tag{20}$$

Several papers provide general surveys of results such as (14) and (17). In particular, see Markus (1964) and Thompson (1974), who discuss the relation between additive and multiplicative versions. For a survey of some of the results in the following sections, see Mirsky (1964). See also Chapter 9.

B Generation of Majorization

In this section, some conditions on pairs of vectors are given which are stronger than majorization. These conditions are sometimes more easily checked than the conditions of majorization. In addition, one of these conditions suggests an answer to the following question: What functions ψ have the property that

$$(x_1,\ldots,x_n) \Big/ \sum x_i \prec (\psi(x_1),\ldots,\psi(x_n)) \Big/ \sum \psi(x_i)$$

for all vectors x?

Consider the following conditions:

(a) $y_i - x_i$ is decreasing in $i = 1,\ldots,n$;

(a') $x_i > 0$ for all i and y_i/x_i is decreasing in $i = 1,\ldots,n$;

(b) for some k, $1 \leq k < n$, $x_i \leq y_i$, $i = 1,\ldots,k$, $x_i \geq y_i$ for $i = k+1,\ldots,n$;

(b') for some k, $1 \leq k \leq n$, $x_i \leq y_i$, $i = 1,\ldots,k$, $x_i \geq y_i$ for $i = k+1,\ldots,n$.

B.1. Proposition. If $x \in \mathscr{D}$ and $\sum x_i = \sum y_i$, then

$$\text{(a)} \implies \text{(b)} \implies x \prec y.$$

If $x \in \mathscr{D}_{++}$ and $\sum x_i = \sum y_i$, then

$$\text{(a')} \implies \text{(b)} \implies x \prec y.$$

Proof. Suppose (a). Since $\sum x_i = \sum y_i$, i.e., $\sum(y_i - x_i) = 0$, and because $y_i - x_i$ is decreasing in i, there exists k, $1 \leq k \leq n$, such that

$$y_i - x_i \geq 0, \quad i = 1,\ldots,k, \qquad y_i - x_i \leq 0, \quad i = k+1,\ldots,n.$$

This is (b).

Suppose (b). Then $\sum_1^j x_i \leq \sum_1^j y_i$, $j = 1,\ldots,k$, and $\sum_j^n x_i \geq \sum_j^n y_i$, $j = k+1,\ldots,n$. Because $\sum x_i = \sum y_i$, these last $n-k$ inequalities can be rewritten as $\sum_1^{j-1} x_i \leq \sum_1^{j-1} y_i$, $j = k+1,\ldots,n$. Thus for each k, the sum of the k largest of the x_i is dominated by $\sum_1^k y_i$. Hence, $x \prec y$.

The proof that (a') $\implies$ (b) is essentially the same as the proof that (a) $\implies$ (b). ‖

The fact that (a') $\Rightarrow x \prec y$ when $x \in \mathscr{D}_{++}$ is due to Marshall, Olkin, and Proschan (1967).

B. Generation of Majorization

For small values of n, some of the implications of Proposition B.1 reverse. Suppose that $x \in \mathscr{D}$ and $x \prec y$.

$$\text{For } n = 2, \quad (a) \iff (b) \iff x \prec y;$$

$$\text{for } n = 3, \quad (a) \not\Leftarrow (b) \iff x \prec y;$$

$$\text{for } n = 4, \quad (a) \not\Leftarrow (b) \not\Leftarrow x \prec y.$$

To verify this, note that for $n = 2$, $x \prec y$ implies $y_1 \geq x_1$ and $y_2 \leq x_2$, so that (a) and (b) hold. For $n = 3$, $y_1 - x_1 \geq 0$ and $y_3 - x_3 \leq 0$, so (b) holds regardless of the sign of $y_2 - x_2$. However, if $x = (2, 1, 0)$ and $y = (3, 0, 0)$, then $x \prec y$ but $y - x = (1, -1, 0)$, so (a) fails. For $n = 4$, take $x = (5, 4, 1, 1)$ and $y = (6, 3, 2, 0)$; here, $x \prec y$ but $y - x = (1, -1, 1, -1)$, so (b) fails.

Note. Zheng (2007) defines *utility gap dominance* between x and y as follows. For a strictly increasing function u, write $x \prec_u y$ if

$$u(y_i) - u(x_i) \text{ is decreasing in } \quad i = 1, 2, \ldots, n.$$

Furthermore if $x \prec_u y$ and $\Sigma x_i = \Sigma y_i$, then condition (b) holds, and hence $x \prec y$. Observe that conditions (a) and (a') correspond to the choices $u(x) = x$ and $u(x) = \log x$, respectively.

Note that Zheng (2007) uses a definition of the Lorenz order that is reversed from that of Definition 17.C.6; this is a possible source of confusion.

B.1.a. If $x \in \mathscr{D}$ and $\sum x_i \leq \sum y_i$, then

$$(a) \Rightarrow (b') \Rightarrow x \prec_w y.$$

If $x \in \mathscr{D}_{++}$ and $\sum x_i \leq \sum y_i$, then

$$(a') \Rightarrow (b') \Rightarrow x \prec_w y.$$

The proofs of these results parallel those of B.1.

Notice that in condition (a'), x_i can be replaced by x_i/c and y_i can be replaced by y_i/d, provided that $c > 0, d > 0$. This leads to the following version of B.1, which again avoids the condition $\sum x_j = \sum y_j$, and which substitutes for (b) the condition

(b″) for some k, $1 \leq k < n$, $x_i/\Sigma x_j \leq y_i/\Sigma y_j$, $i = 1, \ldots, k$,

$$\frac{x_i}{\sum x_j} \geq \frac{y_i}{\sum y_j}, \quad i = k+1, \ldots, n.$$

B.1.b. If $x \in \mathscr{D}_{++}$, and if $\sum_{j=1}^{n} y_j > 0$, then

$$(a') \Rightarrow (b'') \Rightarrow \left(\frac{x_1}{\sum x_j}, \ldots, \frac{x_n}{\sum x_j}\right) \prec \left(\frac{y_1}{\sum y_j}, \ldots, \frac{y_n}{\sum y_j}\right).$$

B.1.c. Proposition B.1 can be used to prove the following results.

(i) If $a > 0$, then using (a),

$$(0, \ldots, 0) \prec (\underbrace{a, \ldots, a}_{n-1}, -(n-1)a).$$

(ii) If $a > 1$, then using (a'),

$$(1, \ldots, 1) \prec (\underbrace{a, \ldots, a}_{n-1}, n - (n-1)a).$$

B.1.d. (Alberti and Uhlmann, 1982). Suppose that $x, y \in \mathscr{D}$ and (a) holds. Then

$$(e^{x_1}, \ldots, e^{x_n}) \Big/ \sum_{j=1}^{n} e^{x_j} \prec (e^{y_1}, \ldots, e^{y_n}) \Big/ \sum_{j=1}^{n} e^{y_j}. \tag{1}$$

Proof. From (a), it follows that $e^{y_i - x_i}$ is decreasing in $i = 1, \ldots, n$. Consequently,

$$\frac{e^{y_i}/\sum_1^n e^{y_j}}{e^{x_i}/\sum_1^n e^{x_j}}$$

is decreasing in $i = 1, \ldots, n$. It follows from Proposition B.1 that (1) holds. ||

For an application of B.1.d in physics, see, 12.P.

B.2. Proposition (Marshall, Olkin, and Proschan, 1967). If ψ is a star-shaped function see 16.B defined on $[0, \infty)$, if $x_i > 0$, $i = 1, \ldots,$ and if $\sum_{j=1}^{n} \psi(x_j) > 0$, then

$$\frac{(x_1, \ldots, x_n)}{\sum x_j} \prec \frac{(\psi(x_1), \ldots, \psi(x_n))}{\sum \psi(x_j)}.$$

Proof. Suppose for convenience that $x_1 \geq \cdots \geq x_n \geq 0$. Because $\psi(z)/z$ is increasing in $z > 0$, $\psi(x_i)/x_i$ is decreasing in $i = 1, \ldots, n$. Thus the conclusion follows from B.1.b. ||

B.2.a. If $x_i > 0$, $i = 1, \ldots, n$, then for all nonnegative constants c satisfying $0 \leq c < \Sigma x_i/n$,

$$\frac{(x_1, \ldots, x_n)}{\sum x_j} \prec \frac{(x_1 - c, \ldots, x_n - c)}{\sum (x_j - c)}$$

or, equivalently, for $c \geq 0$,

$$\frac{(x_1 + c, \ldots, x_n + c)}{\sum (x_j + c)} \prec \frac{(x_1, \ldots, x_n)}{\sum x_j}.$$

This result follows from B.2 by using $\psi(z) = \max(z - c, 0)$.

B.2.b. Proposition (Marshall and Olkin, 1965). If $x_i > 0$ for $i = 1, \ldots, n$, and $0 < r \leq s$, then

$$\frac{(x_1^r, \ldots, x_n^r)}{\sum x_i^r} \prec \frac{(x_1^s, \ldots, x_n^s)}{\sum x_i^s}.$$

Proof. Let $t = s/r$ and take $\psi(z) = z^t$. Then apply B.2 with x_i replaced by x_i^r. ||

Monotonicity of Ratio of Means

The results in this subsection have been given by Marshall, Olkin, and Proschan (1967).

B.3. Proposition. Suppose that x, y satisfy (a′) and $x \in \mathscr{D}_{++}$; i.e., $x \in \mathscr{D}_{++}$ and y_i/x_i is decreasing in $i = 1, \ldots, n$. Let

$$g(r) = \begin{cases} [\sum x_i^r / \sum y_i^r]^{1/r} & \text{if } r \neq 0, \\ \prod x_i / \prod y_i & \text{if } r = 0. \end{cases}$$

Then $g(r)$ is decreasing in r.

Proof. If (a′) and $x \in \mathscr{D}_{++}$, it follows from B.1 that

$$\frac{(x_1^r, \ldots, x_n^r)}{\sum x_j^r} \prec \frac{(y_1^r, \ldots, y_n^r)}{\sum y_j^r}$$

for all real r. Because $\phi(x) = \sum x_i^t$ is Schur-convex for $t \geq 1$, it follows that

$$\frac{\sum x_i^{rt}}{\left(\sum x_j^r\right)^t} \leq \frac{\sum y_i^{rt}}{\left(\sum y_j^r\right)^t}, \qquad t \geq 1. \tag{2}$$

Now fix r and s such that $|s| \geq |r|$ and $rs > 0$, and let $t = s/r$. It follows from (2) that $g(r) \geq g(s)$ if $s \geq r > 0$ and $g(s) \geq g(r)$ if $s \leq r < 0$. Because g is continuous at 0, this completes the proof. ∥

The special comparison $g(1) \geq g(2)$ is used by Cleveland (1979) in the analysis of weighted regression.

B.3.a. If x and y satisfy the conditions of B.3 and $p_i \geq 0$, $i = 1, \ldots, n$, $\sum p_i = 1$, then

$$g_p(r) = \begin{cases} [\sum p_i x_i^r / \sum p_i y_i^r]^{1/r} & \text{if } r \neq 0, \\ \prod x_i^{p_i} / \prod y_i^{p_i} & \text{if } r = 0, \end{cases}$$

is increasing in r. This fact can be obtained for rational p_i directly from B.3. If $p_i = l_i/m$, $i = 1, \ldots, n$, then apply B.3 to the vectors x^* and $y^* \in \mathscr{R}^m$, where x_i and y_i appear l_i times, $i = 1, \ldots, n$. The general case follows by limiting arguments.

A still more general version of B.3 can be obtained with an additional limiting argument. For any probability distribution function H such that $H(0) = 0$, let $\overline{H}(x) = 1 - H(x)$ and let

$$\overline{H}^{-1}(p) = \inf\{x \geq 0 : \overline{H}(x) \leq p\}.$$

B.3.b. If F and G are probability distribution functions such that $F(0) = 0 = G(0)$ and $\overline{F}^{-1}(p)/\overline{G}^{-1}(p)$ is increasing in p, then

$$\left[\int x^r \, dG(x) \bigg/ \int x^r \, dF(x) \right]^{1/r}$$

is increasing in r.

Another type of ratio of means appears in an inequality due to Alzer (1993).

B.3.c. For $r > 0$,

$$\frac{n}{n+1} \leq \left[\frac{\sum_1^n i^r / n}{\sum_1^{n+1} i^r / (n+1)} \right]^{1/r} \leq \frac{(n!)^{1/n}}{((n+1)!)^{1/(n+1)}}.$$

The two bounds in B.3.c correspond to the cases $r = 0$ and $r = \infty$, which suggests that the ratio is monotone in r. This monotonicity result and various extensions are discussed in Abramovich, Barić, Matić, and Pečarić (2007).

Interlaced Numbers

The numbers $b_1 \geq \cdots \geq b_{n-1}$ are said to *interlace* or *separate* the numbers $a_1 \geq \cdots \geq a_n$ if

$$a_1 \geq b_1 \geq a_2 \geq \cdots \geq b_{n-1} \geq a_n.$$

See also A.10.a and Section 9.B.

B.4. If $b_1 \geq \cdots \geq b_{n-1}$ interlace $a_1 \geq \cdots \geq a_n$, then

$$(a_1, \ldots, a_{n-1}) \succ_w (b_1, \ldots, b_{n-1}) \succ_w (a_2, \ldots, a_n) \qquad (3)$$

and

$$(a_1, \ldots, a_n) \succ (b_1, \ldots, b_{n-1}, b^*), \qquad (4)$$

where $b^* = \sum_1^n a_i - \sum_1^{n-1} b_i$.

Proof. Since (3) is trivial, consider only (4). By the definition of b^*, $a_1 \geq b^* \geq a_n$. Consequently, there is an integer l, $1 \leq l \leq n-1$, such that one of the following orderings holds:

(i) $a_1 \geq b_1 \geq a_2 \geq \cdots \geq a_l \geq b^* \geq b_l \geq a_{l+1} \geq \cdots \geq a_n$;

(ii) $a_1 \geq b_1 \geq a_2 \geq \cdots \geq a_l \geq b_l \geq b^* \geq a_{l+1} \geq \cdots \geq a_n$.

If (i), then from elementwise comparisons,

$$\sum_1^k a_i \geq \sum_1^k b_i, \qquad k = 1, \ldots, l-1,$$

$$\sum_1^l a_i \geq \sum_1^{l-1} b_i + b^*; \qquad \sum_k^n a_i \leq \sum_{k-1}^{n-1} b_i, \qquad k = l+1, \ldots, n.$$

These inequalities are precisely (4). If (ii), the proof is similar. ∥

Notice that (3) together with Pólya's theorem A.8 implies that for some u, v, $(a_1, \ldots, a_{n-1}, u) \succ (b_1, \ldots, b_{n-1}, v)$, but the u and v provided in the proof of A.8 are not the same as a_n and b^*.

192   5. Preservation and Generation of Majorization

C   Maximal and Minimal Vectors Under Constraints

Let $A \subset \mathscr{R}^n$ be a nonempty set with a Schur-concave indicator function. Then $x \in A$ implies $x\Pi \in A$ for all permutation matrices Π and, moreover, $(\sum x_i, \ldots, \sum x_i)/n \in A$. This means that if $B = \{x : x \in A$ and $\sum x_i = s\}$ is not empty, then B contains the minimal element $u = (s, \ldots, s)/n$; i.e., $x \in B$ implies $u \prec x$. On the other hand, there need not exist $v \in B$ such that $x \prec v$ even if B is a closed set. Such a maximal vector v does exist in important special cases.

C.1. Proposition (Kemperman, 1973).   Suppose that $m \leq x_i \leq M$, $i = 1, \ldots, n$. Then there exist a unique $\theta \in [m, M)$ and a unique integer $l \in [0, 1, \ldots, n]$ such that

$$\sum x_i = (n - l - 1)m + \theta + lM.$$

With l and θ so determined,

$$x \prec (\underbrace{M, \ldots, M}_{l}, \theta, \underbrace{m, \ldots, m}_{n-l-1}) \equiv v. \qquad (1)$$

Proof.   Because $m \leq x_i \leq M$, $i = 1, \ldots, n$,

$$\sum_{1}^{k} x_{[i]} \leq \sum_{1}^{k} v_{[i]} = kM, \qquad k = 1, \ldots, l,$$

and

$$\sum_{k+1}^{n} x_{[i]} \geq \sum_{k+1}^{n} v_{[i]} = (n-k)m, \qquad k = l+1, \ldots, n.$$

Since $\sum_{k+1}^{n} x_{[i]} \geq \sum_{k+1}^{n} v_{[i]}$ if and only if $\sum_{1}^{k} x_{[i]} \leq \sum_{1}^{k} v_{[i]}$, this completes the proof. $\|$

Notice that because $\theta = \sum x_i - (n - l - 1)m - lM \in [m, M)$,

$$\frac{\sum x_i - nm}{M - m} - 1 \leq l < \frac{\sum x_i - nm}{M - m},$$

and this determines l.

C.1.a.   If $c \geq 1$ and $x_{[1]} \geq cx_{[2]}$, $x_{[n]} \geq 0$, then

$$x \prec (x_{[1]}, \underbrace{x_{[1]}/c, \ldots, x_{[1]}/c}_{l}, \theta, 0, \ldots, 0), \qquad (2)$$

where $0 \leq \theta < x_{[1]}/c$ and $\sum x_i = x_{[1]} + l[x_{[1]}/c] + \theta$.

C. Maximal and Minimal Vectors Under Constraints

Proof. Because $0 \leq x_{[i]} \leq x_{[1]}/c$, $i = 2, \ldots, n$, it follows from C.1 that

$$(x_{[2]}, \ldots, x_{[n]}) \prec (\underbrace{x_{[1]}/c, \ldots, x_{[1]}/c}_{l}, \theta, \underbrace{0, \ldots, 0}_{n-l-2}),$$

and (2) follows. ||

C.1.b. If $b \geq 0$ and $x_{[1]} \geq x_{[2]} + b$, $x_{[n]} \geq 0$, then

$$x \prec (x_{[1]}, \underbrace{x_{[1]} - b, \ldots, x_{[1]} - b}_{l}, \theta, \underbrace{0, \ldots, 0}_{n-l-2}), \tag{3}$$

where $0 \leq \theta < x_{[1]} - b$ and $\sum_1^n x_i = x_{[1]} + l(x_{[1]} - b) + \theta$.

The proof of (3) is similar to the proof of C.1.a.

C.1.c. If $b \geq 0$, $c \geq 1$ and $x_{[1]} \geq cx_{[2]}$, $x_{[1]} \geq x_{[2]} + b$, $x_{[n]} \geq 0$, then

$$x \prec (x_{[1]}, z, \ldots, z, \theta, 0, \ldots, 0),$$

where $z = \min(x_{[1]}/c, x_{[1]} - b)$ and $0 \leq \theta \leq z$.

This result follows from C.1.a and C.1.b.

C.2. Proposition (Parker and Ram, 1997). If $0 \leq x_i \leq c_i$ for $i = 1, \ldots, n$, $c_1 \geq \cdots \geq c_n$, and $\Sigma x_i = s$, then

$$x \prec \left(c_1, \ldots, c_r, s - \sum_1^r c_i, 0, \ldots, 0 \right),$$

where $r \in \{1, \ldots, n-1\}$ is such that $\Sigma_1^r c_i < s$ and $\Sigma_1^{r+1} c_i \geq s$. If no such integer exists, then $r = n$.

C.2.a. If $0 \leq a_i \leq x_i$, $i = 1, \ldots, n$, $a_1 \geq \cdots \geq a_n$, and $\Sigma x_i = s$, then

$$x \succ \left(a_1, \ldots, a_r, s - \sum_1^r a_i, 0, \ldots, 0 \right),$$

where $r \in \{1, \ldots, n-1\}$ is such that $\Sigma_1^r a_i < s$ and $\Sigma_1^{r+1} a_i \geq s$. If no such integer exists, then $r = n$.

C.2.b. If $x_{[n]} \leq cx_{[n-1]}$, then

$$x \prec (x_{[n]}, x_{[n]}/c, \ldots, x_{[n]}/c, M), \tag{4}$$

where $\sum x_i = x_{[n]} + (n-2)x_{[n]}/c + M$ determines M.

C.2.c. If $x_{[n]} \leq x_{[n-1]} - d$, then

$$x \prec (x_{[n]}, x_{[n]} + d, \ldots, x_{[n]} + d, M),$$

where $\sum x_i = x_{[n]} + (n-2)(x_{[n]} + d) + M$ determines M.

There is a variation of C.1 that admits an improved lower bound.

C.3. Suppose that $m = \min_i x_i$, $M = \max_i x_i$. Then
$$\left(m, \frac{\sum x_i - m - M}{n-2}, \ldots, \frac{\sum x_i - m - M}{n-2}, M\right) \prec x.$$

This is a consequence of the fact that $\sum_2^{n-1} x_{[i]} = \sum_1^n x_i - m - M$, so that
$$(x_{[2]}, \ldots, x_{[n-1]}) \succ \left(\sum x_i - m - M, \ldots, \sum x_i - m - M\right)/(n-2).$$

C.4.a. For $x \in \mathcal{D}_+$, $c > \Sigma x_i = 1$,
$$\left(\frac{c - x_1}{nc - 1}, \ldots, \frac{c - x_n}{nc - 1}\right) \prec (x_1, \ldots, x_n).$$

C.4.b. For $x \in \mathcal{D}_+$, $\Sigma x_i = 1$, $c \geq 0$,
$$\left(\frac{c + x_1}{nc + 1}, \ldots, \frac{c + x_n}{nc + 1}\right) \prec (x_1, \ldots, x_n).$$

Proofs. The results in C.4.a and C.4.b follow from Definition 1.A.1. ||

D Majorization in Integers

There are several majorization results that apply only to vectors with integer-valued components. Such results have applications, for example, in combinatorics (Chapter 7).

Consider the basic Lemma 2.B.1, which states that if $x \prec y$, then x can be derived from y by successive applications of a finite number of "T-transforms." Recall that a T-transform leaves all but two components of a vector unchanged, and replaces these two components by averages. If $a_1, \ldots, a_n$ and $b_1, \ldots, b_n$ are integers and $a \prec b$, can a be derived from b by successive applications of a finite number of T-transforms in such a way that after the application of each T-transform a vector with integer components is obtained? An affirmative answer was given by Muirhead (1903) and by Folkman and Fulkerson (1969). Using the same term as Dalton (1920), Folkman and

Fulkerson (1969) define an operation called a *transfer*. If $b_1 \geq \cdots \geq b_n$ are integers and $b_i > b_j$, then the transformation

$$b'_i = b_i - 1,$$
$$b'_j = b_j + 1,$$
$$b'_k = b_k, \qquad k \neq i, j,$$

is called a *transfer from i to j*. This transfer is a T-transform, because

$$b'_i = \alpha b_i + (1-\alpha)b_j, \qquad b'_j = (1-\alpha)b_i + \alpha b_j,$$

where $\alpha = (b_i - b_j - 1)/(b_i - b_j)$.

D.1. Lemma (Muirhead, 1903). If $a_1, \ldots, a_n, b_1, \ldots, b_n$ are integers and $a \prec b$, then a can be derived from b by successive applications of a finite number of transfers.

Proof. Suppose for convenience that $a_1 \geq \cdots \geq a_n$ and $b_1 \geq \cdots \geq b_n$, and assume that $a \neq b$. Let l be the largest integer for which

$$\sum_1^l a_i < \sum_1^l b_i.$$

Then $a_{l+1} > b_{l+1}$, and there is a largest integer $k < l$ for which $a_k < b_k$. Thus

$$b_k > a_k > a_{l+1} > b_{l+1}.$$

Let b' be obtained from b by a transfer from k to $l+1$. Then $a \prec b' \prec b$, and repetition of this process a finite number of times brings us to the vector a. ‖

D.1.a. Definition. Suppose that a and b are vectors with nonnegative integer components such that $a \prec b$. The vector b is said to *cover* the vector a if there does not exist a vector c with integer components distinct from a and b such that $a \prec c \prec b$.

D.1.b. Proposition (Wan, 1984, 1986). Let $a, b \in \mathscr{D}$ be vectors of nonnegative integers such that $a \prec b$. Then b covers a if and only if there exist indices $i < j$ such that $a = b - e_i + e_j$ and either $j = i+1$ or $a_i = a_{i+1} = \cdots = a_{j-1} > a_j$.

See Fig. 1 (Section E) for illustrations of Proposition D.1.b, which shows that when b covers a, then a is obtained from b by a simple transfer.

Note that with integer components, there are a finite number of vectors a with $a \prec b$. This means that there is a finite chain of vectors with integer components c_i, $i = 1, \ldots, m$, such that

$$a \prec c_1 \prec c_2 \prec \cdots \prec c_m \prec b,$$

and b covers c_m, c_{i+1} covers c_i, $i = 1, \ldots, m-1$, and c_1 covers a. Thus Lemma D.1 is a consequence of Proposition D.1.b. An algorithm for constructing a maximal length chain $c_1, \ldots, c_m$ from a to b is provided by Wan and Wootton (2000, Section 4.4).

The following striking lemma of Fulkerson and Ryser (1962) states that under certain conditions a majorization $a \prec b$ is preserved if 1 is subtracted from a component of each vector. This subtraction may alter the ordering of the components of the vectors, so the result is not entirely trivial. The preservation of majorization need not hold without the condition that the vectors involved have integer components.

D.2. Lemma (Fulkerson and Ryser, 1962). Let $a_1 \geq \cdots \geq a_n$ and $b_1 \geq \cdots \geq b_n$ be integers. If $a \prec b$ and $i \leq j$, then

$$a - e_i \prec b - e_j.$$

Proof. The vectors $a - e_i$ and $b - e_j$ may not have components in decreasing magnitude, but if $i' \geq i$ is chosen so that

$$a_i = a_{i+1} = \cdots = a_{i'} \quad \text{and} \quad \text{either } a_{i'} > a_{i'+1} \quad \text{or } i' = n, \quad (1)$$

then $a - e_{i'}$ has the components of $a - e_i$ reordered decreasingly. Similarly, if $j' \geq j$ satisfies

$$b_j = b_{j+1} = \cdots = b_{j'} \quad \text{and} \quad \text{either } b_{j'} > b_{j'+1} \quad \text{or } j' = n, \quad (2)$$

then $b - e_{j'}$ has the components of $b - e_j$ reordered decreasingly. Rather than show $a - e_i \prec b - e_j$, it is more convenient to show the equivalent fact that

$$u \equiv a - e_{i'} \prec b - e_{j'} \equiv v.$$

For $k < \min(i', j')$,

$$\sum_1^k u_\alpha = \sum_1^k a_\alpha \leq \sum_1^k b_\alpha = \sum_1^k v_\alpha;$$

for $k \geq \max(i', j')$,

$$\sum_1^k u_\alpha = \sum_1^k a_\alpha - 1 \leq \sum_1^k b_\alpha - 1 = \sum_1^k v_\alpha;$$

and for $k = n$,

$$\sum_1^n u_\alpha = \sum_1^n a_\alpha - 1 = \sum_1^n b_\alpha - 1 = \sum_1^n v_\alpha.$$

If $i' \leq j'$, then immediately for $i' \leq k < j'$,
$$\sum_1^k u_\alpha = \sum_1^k a_\alpha - 1 < \sum_1^k b_\alpha = \sum_1^k v_\alpha.$$
It remains to show, for the case that $i' > j'$ and $j' \leq k < i'$, that $\sum_1^k u_\alpha \leq \sum_1^k v_\alpha$.

Notice that $\sum_1^k u_\alpha \leq \sum_1^k v_\alpha$ is equivalent to $\sum_1^k a_\alpha < \sum_1^k b_\alpha$. If $a_{k+1} > b_{k+1}$, then $\sum_1^k (b_\alpha - a_\alpha) > \sum_1^{k+1}(b_\alpha - a_\alpha) \geq 0$, the last inequality holding because $a \prec b$. The remaining case is $a_{k+1} \leq b_{k+1}$. Because $i \leq j \leq j' \leq k < i'$,
$$a_{j'} = \cdots = a_{k+1} \leq b_{k+1} \leq b_k \leq \cdots \leq b_{j'+1} < b_j;$$
this yields
$$0 < \sum_{j'}^k (b_\alpha - a_\alpha) \leq \sum_{j'}^k (b_\alpha - a_\alpha) - \sum_{j'}^n (b_\alpha - a_\alpha) = -\sum_{k+1}^n (b_\alpha - a_\alpha)$$
$$= \sum_1^k (b_\alpha - a_\alpha). \quad \|$$

The above proof is essentially due to Tom Snijders.

Repeated application of D.2 yields the following extension:

D.3. Lemma (Fulkerson and Ryser, 1962). Let $a_1 \geq \cdots \geq a_n$, $b_1 \geq \cdots \geq b_n$ be integers. Let u be obtained from a by reducing components in positions $i_1, i_2, \ldots, i_k$ by 1. Similarly, let v be obtained from b by reducing components in positions $j_1, j_2, \ldots, j_k$ by 1. If $i_1 \leq j_1$, $i_2 \leq j_2, \ldots, i_k \leq j_k$, and $a \prec b$, then $u \prec v$.

An important special case of D.3 was obtained by Gale (1957). This is the case that $i_l = j_l = l$, $l = 1, 2, \ldots, k$. We make use of this special case (as did Gale) to give a proof of the Gale–Ryser theorem discussed in Section 7.C.

The final result of this section involves the notion of a conjugate sequence: If $a_1, \ldots, a_n$ are nonnegative integers and a_j^* is the number of these a_i that are greater than or equal to j, then $a_1^*, a_2^*, \ldots$ is *conjugate* to $a_1, \ldots, a_n, 0, 0, \ldots$. Conjugate sequences are discussed in greater detail in Section 7.B.

D.4. If $x^* = (x_1^*, \ldots, x_{\max(y_i)}^*)$ and $y^* = (y_1^*, \ldots, y_{\max(y_i)}^*)$, then
$$x \prec y \Rightarrow x^* \succ y^*.$$
This is a restatement of 7.B.5.

D.5. Example (Shi, 2006). For positive integers $n < m$, define
$$n^* = n - \frac{1}{2}(m+1)(n+1)(m-n).$$

With this notation,
$$(\underbrace{n,\ldots,n}_{n+1},\underbrace{n+1,\ldots,n+1}_{n+1},\underbrace{n+2,\ldots,n+2}_{n+1},\ldots,\underbrace{n+m,\ldots,n+m}_{n+1})$$
$$\prec_w (\underbrace{m,m,\ldots,m}_{m+1},\underbrace{m+1,\ldots,m+1}_{m+1},\ldots,\underbrace{m+n,\ldots,m+n}_{m+1});$$
consequently,
$$(n,\underbrace{n,\ldots,n}_{n+1},\underbrace{n+1,\ldots,n+1}_{n+1},\ldots,\underbrace{n+m,\ldots,n+m}_{n+1})$$
$$\prec (\underbrace{m,\ldots,m}_{m+1},\underbrace{m+1,\ldots,m+1}_{m+1},\ldots,\underbrace{m+n,\ldots,m+n}_{m+1},n^*).$$

Note that each vector has $1+(n+1)(m+1)$ elements. Similarly,
$$(\underbrace{0,0,\ldots,0}_{m+1},\underbrace{1,\ldots,1}_{m+1},\ldots,\underbrace{n,\ldots,n}_{m+1})$$
$$\prec (\underbrace{0,\ldots,0}_{n+1},\underbrace{1,\ldots,1}_{n+1},\ldots,\underbrace{m,\ldots,m}_{n+1},n^*).$$

Sequences of 0's and 1's

In computer science, majorization concepts are related to sequences of 0's and 1's, i.e., for vectors $x, y \in \{0,1\}^n$. For ordering vectors in $\{0,1\}^n$, four partial orders are of potential interest: majorization, unordered majorization (14.E.6), submajorization, and unordered submajorization.

The partial order of majorization on $\{0,1\}^n$ is vacuous because for $x, y \in \{0,1\}^n$, $x \prec y$ if and only if $x = y$. The submajorization ordering on $\{0,1\}^n$ is slightly more interesting: $x \prec_w y$ if and only if $\sum_1^n x_i \leq \sum_1^n y_i$.

It is the unordered versions of majorization and submajorization that are of potential interest in computer science. Knuth (2010, Exercise 109) obtains some majorizations in this context. However, note that the partial order that Knuth calls *majorization* denoted by $\prec_k$ is, in the nomenclature of this book, unordered submajorization. It is defined by

$$x \prec_k y \quad \text{if and only if} \quad \sum_1^j x_i \leq \sum_1^j y_i, \; j=1,\ldots,n.$$

Unordered majorization is discussed in 14.E.

E Partitions

Majorization provides a natural partial order in the analysis of partitions of a positive integer n into a sum of n integers. James (1978) states that "The dominance order (i.e., majorization) is certainly the 'correct' order to use for partitions ... ." Figure 1 illustrates the complete lattice of partitions of 7.

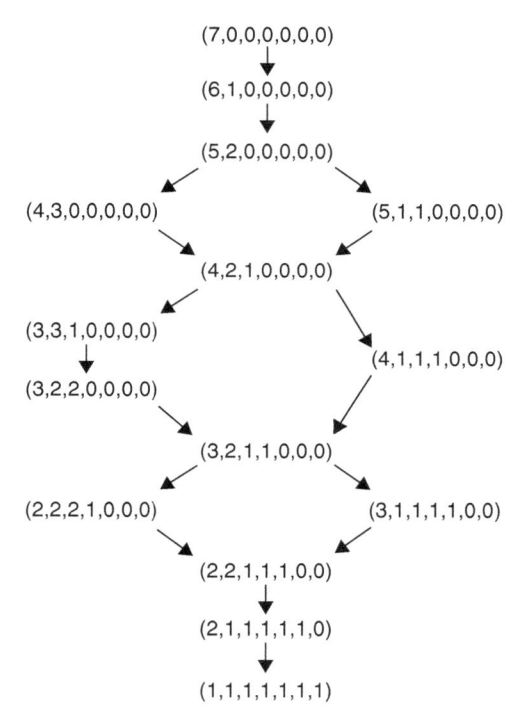

Figure 1. Partitions of 7 as a lattice

A partition such as $(3, 3, 1, 0, 0, 0, 0)$ can be symbolically diagrammed as

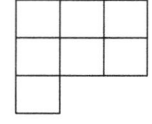

Such diagrams are known as *Young diagrams*. A lattice such as that of Fig. 1 can compactly be represented using Young diagrams. In this way, the lattice of partitions of $n = 1, \ldots, 8$ are represented in Fig. 2.

For applications in computer science, see Knuth (2010, Exercises 54–58).

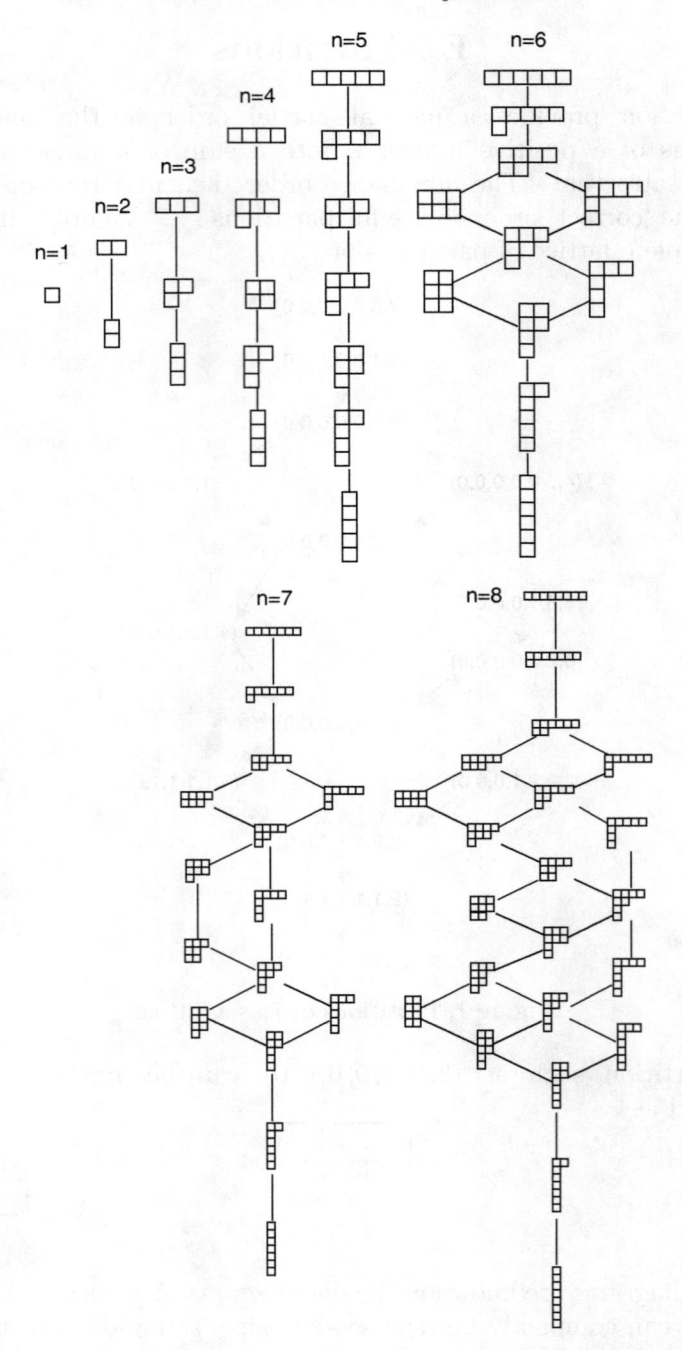

200   5. Preservation and Generation of Majorization

Figure 2. Partitions of $n = 1, \ldots, 8$ using Young diagrams.

Majorization in Group Theory

As noted in Section 1.A, majorization arises in a variety of contexts in group theory.

As already noted by Young (1901), there exists a one-to-one correspondence between diagrams with n boxes and the irreducible representation of the symmetric group on n letters. See, e.g., Ruch (1975). An extensive discussion of group representations in probability and statistics is provided by Diaconis (1988, pp. 40, 131). In particular, if one partition $(\lambda_1, \ldots, \lambda_n)$ of n majorizes (in integers) another partition $(\mu_1, \ldots, \mu_n)$, then a certain function $r(\cdot)$ of the group characters is Schur-convex, and hence $r(\lambda) \geq r(\mu)$.

A discussion of other applications in group theory would take us far afield, but see Hazewinkel and Martin (1983).

Partitions of n into k Parts

In various applications (e.g., chemistry and biology), partitions of n into $k < n$ parts are of interest. The lattice of such partitions is a sublattice of the partitions of n into n parts that includes only those vectors with no more than k nonzero entries. Such partitions can be represented by vectors of length k.

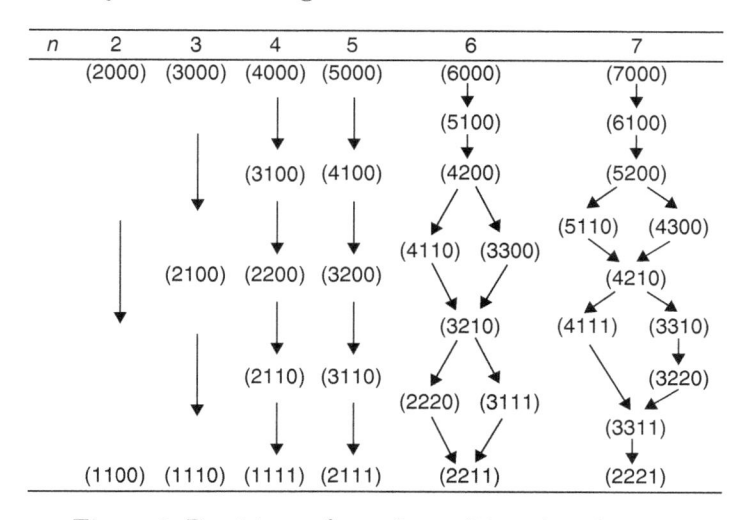

n	2	3	4	5	6	7
	(2000)	(3000)	(4000)	(5000)	(6000)	(7000)
					↓	↓
					(5100)	(6100)
					↓	↓
			(3100)	(4100)	(4200)	(5200)
						(5110) (4300)
					(4110) (3300)	
	↓	(2100)	(2200)	(3200)		(4210)
					(3210)	(4111) (3310)
			(2110)	(3110)		(3220)
					(2220) (3111)	
						(3311)
	(1100)	(1110)	(1111)	(2111)	(2211)	(2221)

Figure 3. Partitions of $n = 2, \ldots, 7$ into $k = 4$ parts.

DNA Sequences

Partitions into $k = 4$ parts arise in the study of DNA sequences and are discussed in detail by Wan and Wootton (2000).

F Linear Transformations That Preserve Majorization

A linear transformation $A: \mathscr{R}^m \to \mathscr{R}^n$ is said to preserve majorization if $xA \prec yA$ whenever $x \prec y$. Dean and Verducci (1990) characterize such transformations. The following preliminary result is useful.

F.1. Lemma. The linear transformation $A: \mathscr{R}^m \to \mathscr{R}^n$ preserves majorization if and only if, for every $m \times m$ permutation matrix P there is an $n \times n$ permutation matrix Q such that $PA = AQ$.

The structure of a matrix A that satisfies the condition of F.1 can be explicitly described.

F.2. Theorem (Dean and Verducci, 1990). A linear transformation $A: \mathscr{R}^m \to \mathscr{R}^n$ preserves majorization if and only if A can be represented in the form

$$A = (A_1, \ldots, A_t)Q,$$

where Q is an $n \times n$ permutation matrix and for each $i = 1, 2, \ldots, t$, A_i is an $m \times n_i$ matrix satisfying the following conditions:

If the first column of A_i contains the distinct elements $d_1, d_2, \ldots, d_k$ with multiplicities $p_1, p_2, \ldots, p_k$ ($\sum p_i = m$), then the n_i columns of A_i consist of the $n_i = m!/\prod(p_j!)$ distinct permutations of the first column of A_i.

Some simplification is possible when $m = n$.

F.3. Corollary. A nonsingular linear transformation $A: \mathscr{R}^n \to \mathscr{R}^n$ preserves majorization if and only if it can be represented in the form

$$A = aQ + bJ,$$

where Q is a permutation matrix, $J = e'e$ is the $n \times n$ matrix with all entries 1, and $a, b \in \mathscr{R}$.

Dean and Verducci (1990) also show that if A is nonsingular and preserves majorization, then A^{-1} preserves Schur-concavity in the sense that if a random vector X has a Schur-concave density, then $Y = XA^{-1}$ has a Schur-concave density.

6
Rearrangements and Majorization

Many inequalities are known that involve real vectors and vectors with the components rearranged. Such inequalities are discussed in Chapter X of Hardy, Littlewood, and Pólya (1934, 1952), but a number of new results have been obtained since that book was written. Particularly noteworthy is the early work of Lorentz (1953) and Day (1972).

The purpose of this chapter is to discuss some majorizations that arise from rearrangements and to show how these majorizations yield various inequalities. Consequently, inequalities involving rearrangements of functions are not discussed here; for such inequalities, see Lorentz (1953), Ryff (1965), Day (1972, 1973), and Chong (1974a,b,c). Most of the basic results in Sections A and C are given by Day (1972) but from a different approach. Day proves a general theorem from which all his results follow as special cases. Here, simple initial results are used to simplify the proofs of more general results. Unlike Day, we confine our considerations to vectors with real components.

Rearrangement inequalities typically compare the value of a function of vector arguments with the value of the same function after the components of the vectors have been similarly ordered, or, if there are only two vectors, after the components have been oppositely ordered. For functions of two vector arguments, such inequalities are extended in Section F using an ordering of pairs of vectors implicit in the work of Hollander, Proschan, and Sethuraman (1977) and of Tchen (1980).

204   6. Rearrangements and Majorization

The partial ordering allows many additional comparisons and provides significant clarifications of the theory.

Recall that $a_\downarrow = (a_{[1]}, \ldots, a_{[n]})$ is the decreasing rearrangement of $(a_1, \ldots, a_n)$ and $a_\uparrow = (a_{(1)}, \ldots, a_{(n)})$ is the increasing rearrangement of $(a_1, \ldots, a_n)$.

A Majorizations from Additions of Vectors

Let $x^{(i)} = (x_1^{(i)}, \ldots, x_n^{(i)})$, $i = 1, \ldots, m$, be m real n-dimensional vectors and let

$$s_j = \sum_{i=1}^{m} x_j^{(i)}, \qquad \sigma_j = \sum_{i=1}^{m} x_{[j]}^{(i)},$$

$j = 1, \ldots, n$. To obtain $s_{[1]}, s_{[2]}, \ldots, s_{[n]}$, the vectors $x^{(i)}$ are added and then the components of the sum are reordered decreasingly. To obtain $\sigma_{[1]}, \sigma_{[2]}, \ldots, \sigma_{[n]}$, the vectors $x^{(i)}$ are first reordered to have decreasing components and then the reordered vectors are added. Of course, $\sigma_1 = \sigma_{[1]}$, $\sigma_2 = \sigma_{[2]}, \ldots, \sigma_n = \sigma_{[n]}$.

A.1. Proposition (Day, 1972). $(s_1, \ldots, s_n) \prec (\sigma_1, \ldots, \sigma_n)$; that is, $\sum_1^m x^{(i)} \prec \sum_1^m x_\downarrow^{(i)}$.

Proof. Let π be a permutation for which $s_{[j]} = s_{\pi(j)}$, $j = 1, \ldots, n$. If $1 \leq k \leq n$,

$$\sum_{j=1}^{k} s_{[j]} = \sum_{j=1}^{k} \sum_{i=1}^{m} x_{\pi(j)}^{(i)} \leq \sum_{j=1}^{k} \sum_{i=1}^{m} x_{[j]}^{(i)} = \sum_{j=1}^{k} \sigma_{[j]}.$$

Furthermore, $\sum_{j=1}^{n} s_{[j]} = \sum_{i=1}^{m} \sum_{j=1}^{n} x_j^{(i)} = \sum_{j=1}^{n} \sigma_{[j]}$. ||

Alternatively, A.1 may be viewed as a special case of a result obtained earlier by Fan (1949) in a matrix context. See 9.G.1 in the case in which the matrices involved are diagonal.

Proposition A.1 involves sums of a finite number of vectors, but the same result holds for weighted sums of an arbitrary number of vectors.

A.1.a. Proposition. Let $(\mathscr{X}, \mathscr{A}, \mu)$ be a measure space and let $x^{(\alpha)}$, $\alpha \in \mathscr{X}$, be a vector-valued μ-integrable function of α. Then

$$\int_{\mathscr{X}} x^{(\alpha)} \mu(d\alpha) \prec \int_{\mathscr{X}} x_\downarrow^{(\alpha)} \mu(d\alpha),$$

provided all integrals are finite.

A. Majorizations from Additions of Vectors   205

Proof. Let π be a permutation-valued function of α (to avoid complex formulae, write this as π and not π_α) such that for each α, $x^{(\alpha)}_{\pi(j)}$ is decreasing in $j = 1, \ldots, n$. Then

$$\sum_{j=1}^{k} \int_{\mathscr{X}} x^{(\alpha)}_{\pi(j)} \mu(d\alpha) \leq \sum_{j=1}^{k} \int_{\mathscr{X}} x^{(\alpha)}_{[j]} \mu(d\alpha) = \sum_{j=1}^{k} \sigma_j.$$

Furthermore, equality holds when $k = n$. ||

Because the majorization $s \prec \sigma$ does not depend upon the components of σ being in a particular order, the truth of A.1 and A.1.a. does not depend upon the fact that $\sigma = x^{(1)}_{\downarrow} + \cdots + x^{(m)}_{\downarrow}$: It is essential only that the vectors $x^{(i)}$ be reordered similarly before adding. Vectors x and y are said to be *similarly ordered* if there is a permutation π such that $x_{[i]} = x_{\pi(i)}$, $y_{[i]} = y_{\pi(i)}$, $i = 1, \ldots, n$. Equivalently, x and y are similarly ordered if $(x_i - x_j)(y_i - y_j) \geq 0$ for all i, j.

There is a useful consequence of A.1 that involves similar ordering.

A.1.b. Proposition. If $a \prec b$, $u \prec v$ and if b and v are similarly ordered, then $a + u \prec b + v$.

Proof. Clearly, $\sum_{i=1}^{n}(b+v)_i = \sum_{i=1}^{n}(a+u)_i$. Moreover,

$$\sum_{i=1}^{k}(b+v)_{[i]} = \sum_{i=1}^{k}(b_{[i]} + v_{[i]}) \geq \sum_{i=1}^{k}(a_{[i]} + u_{[i]}) \geq \sum_{i=1}^{k}(a+u)_{[i]},$$

$k = 1, \ldots, n-1$. The equality holds because b and v are similarly ordered. The first inequality is a consequence of $b \succ a$, $v \succ u$. The last inequality is an application of A.1 with $m = 2$. ||

It is possible to give a simple proof of A.1 using induction on m, and using A.1.b.

An extension of A.1.b is given in 5.A.6.

A.1.c. Proposition. For $x, y \in \mathscr{R}^n$,

$$x + y \prec x_\downarrow + y_\downarrow, \qquad x - y \prec x_\downarrow - y_\uparrow.$$

Proof. In Proposition A.1.b, take $a = x$, $b = x_\downarrow$, $u = y$, $v = y_\downarrow$. This gives the first majorization. For the second majorization, replace y by $-y$ and note that $(-y)_\downarrow = -y_\uparrow$. ||

There is a converse to A.1 that says that all majorizations can be obtained by means of rearrangements.

A.1.d. Proposition. Let σ and s be vectors in $\mathscr{R}^n$ such that $s \prec \sigma$. Then there exist an $m < \infty$ and vectors $x^{(1)}, \ldots, x^{(m)}$ such that $s_j = \sum_{i=1}^{m} x_j^{(i)}$, $\sigma_{[j]} = \sum_{i=1}^{m} x_{[j]}^{(i)}$.

Proof. This proposition is an immediate consequence of 4.C.1, which says that $s \prec \sigma$ implies s lies in the convex hull of points obtained by permuting components of σ. (It is immediate that m can be taken to be $\leq n!$; in fact, it is possible to take $m \leq n^2 - 2n + 2$. See 2.F.2.) ∥

Proposition A.1 involves the similar ordering of vectors $x^{(1)}, \ldots, x^{(m)}$. In case $m = 2$, it is possible to consider what happens when the vectors are oppositely ordered.

A.2. Proposition (Day, 1972). $x_{\downarrow}^{(1)} + x_{\uparrow}^{(2)} \prec x^{(1)} + x^{(2)}$ on $\mathscr{R}^n$.

Proof. For notational convenience, suppose $x_1^{(1)} \geq \cdots \geq x_n^{(1)}$ and suppose first that $n = 2$. Let $s = x^{(1)} + x^{(2)}$ and let $\tau = x_{\downarrow}^{(1)} + x_{\uparrow}^{(2)}$. If $x_1^{(2)} \leq x_2^{(2)}$, then $\tau = s$. If $x_1^{(2)} > x_2^{(2)}$, then $s = \sigma$ and the result follows from A.1 with $x^{(2)}$ replaced by $(x_2^{(2)}, x_1^{(2)})$.

Now consider the case that $n > 2$. If $x_1^{(2)} \leq \cdots \leq x_n^{(2)}$, then $\tau = s$. Otherwise, there exist j and k, $1 \leq j < k \leq n$, such that $x_j^{(2)} > x_k^{(2)}$. Interchange $x_j^{(2)}$ and $x_k^{(2)}$ before adding, to get s^*:

$$s_i^* = s_i, \quad i \neq j, k; \qquad s_j^* = x_j^{(1)} + x_k^{(2)}; \qquad s_k^* = x_k^{(1)} + x_j^{(2)}.$$

Then $s_i^* = s_i$ except for two values of i and it follows from the case $n = 2$ that $s^* \prec s$. If $s^* = \tau$, the proof is complete. Otherwise, start with s^* in place of s and follow the above procedure to obtain $s^{**} \prec s^*$. Since a finite number of steps leads to τ, it follows that $\tau \prec s$. ∥

A.2.a. If $a_{[1]} \geq \cdots \geq a_{[n]}, b_{[1]} \geq \cdots \geq b_{[n]}$, then

$$(|b_{[1]} - a_{[1]}|, \ldots, |b_{[n]} - a_{[n]}|) \prec_w (|b_1 - a_1|, \ldots, |b_n - a_n|).$$

Proof. This majorization follows from two steps. The first is that

$$(b_{[1]} - a_{[1]}, \ldots, b_{[n]} - a_{[n]}) \prec (b_1 - a_1, \ldots, b_n - a_n),$$

which follows from A.2. Weak majorization in the absolute values then follows from 5.A.1.a.

A. Majorizations from Additions of Vectors

Perhaps the best-known inequality for rearrangements is the classical result of Hardy, Littlewood, and Pólya, which involves sums of products:

A.3. Proposition (Hardy, Littlewood, and Pólya, 1934, 1952, p. 261). If a_i, b_i, $i = 1, \ldots, n$, are two sets of numbers, then

$$\sum_{i=1}^n a_{[i]} b_{[n-i+1]} \leq \sum_{i=1}^n a_i b_i \leq \sum_{i=1}^n a_{[i]} b_{[i]}. \qquad (1)$$

Hardy, Littlewood, and Pólya give the following intuitive interpretation of A.3:

> ... interpret a as distances along a rod to hooks and the b as weights to be suspended from the hooks. To get the maximum statistical moment with respect to an end of the rod, we hang the heaviest weights on the hooks farthest from that end.

For a similar interpretation, see Klamkin (1970).

A simple elementary proof of A.3 can be given [see Hardy, Littlewood, and Pólya (1934, 1952, p. 262)]. The following proof makes use of majorization, but requires $a_i > 0, b_i > 0, i = 1, \ldots, n$.

Proof of A.3. Assume $a_i > 0$, $b_i > 0$, and in A.1 and A.2, let $x_i^{(1)} = \log a_i$, $x_i^{(2)} = \log b_i$, $i = 1, \ldots, n$. Because $\tau \prec s \prec \sigma$, and because $\sum_{i=1}^n e^{x_i}$ is a Schur-convex function (3.C.1), it follows that

$$\sum_{i=1}^n \exp(\log a_{[i]} + \log b_{[n-i+1]}) \leq \sum_{i=1}^n \exp(\log a_i + \log b_i)$$
$$\leq \sum_{i=1}^n \exp(\log a_{[i]} + \log b_{[i]}).$$

But this is exactly the desired inequality. ‖

A.3.a. If $a_i \geq 0$, $b_i \geq 0$, $i = 1, \ldots, n$, then

$$(a_1 b_1, \ldots, a_n b_n) \prec_{\mathrm{w}} (a_{[1]} b_{[1]}, \ldots, a_{[n]} b_{[n]}) \qquad (2\mathrm{a})$$

and

$$(a_{[1]} b_{[n]}, a_{[2]} b_{[n-1]}, \ldots, a_{[n]} b_{[1]}) \prec_{\mathrm{w}} (a_1 b_1, \ldots, a_n b_n). \qquad (2\mathrm{b})$$

Inequality (2a) follows directly from the partial sum definition of majorization, because $\sum_1^k a_i b_i \leq \sum_1^k a_{[i]} b_{[i]}$ for $k = 1, \ldots, n$. Inequality (2b) follows from A.2 and A.1 with the translation $x_i^{(1)} = \log a_i$ and $x_i^{(2)} = \log b_i$, $i = 1, \ldots, n$.

208   6. Rearrangements and Majorization

The hypothesis can be weakened to permit some negative values, in particular, the number of negative a's and b's must be equal, but the result becomes more complex.

A.3.b. If $a_i > 0$, $b_i > 0$, $i = 1, \ldots, n$, the majorizations of (2a) and (2b) are equivalent to

$$\left(\frac{b_{[n]}}{a_{[n]}}, \frac{b_{[n-1]}}{a_{[n-1]}}, \ldots, \frac{b_{[1]}}{a_{[1]}}\right) \prec_w \left(\frac{b_1}{a_1}, \ldots, \frac{b_n}{a_n}\right) \prec_w \left(\frac{b_{[1]}}{a_{[n]}}, \ldots, \frac{b_{[n]}}{a_{[1]}}\right).$$

From these majorizations and 3.C.1.b, it follows that for all increasing convex functions g,

$$\sum_{i=1}^n g\left(\frac{b_{[i]}}{a_{[i]}}\right) \leq \sum_{i=1}^n g\left(\frac{b_i}{a_i}\right) \leq \sum_{i=1}^n g\left(\frac{b_{[i]}}{a_{[n-i+1]}}\right).$$

This result is due to London (1970), and by virtue of 4.B.2, it is equivalent to A.3.b.

Proposition A.3 concerns sums of products; it is in fact true that similar results can be obtained for products of sums.

A.4. Proposition. If $a_i > 0$, $b_i > 0$, $i = 1, \ldots, n$, then

$$\prod_{i=1}^n (a_{[i]} + b_{[i]}) \leq \prod_{i=1}^n (a_i + b_i) \leq \prod_{i=1}^n (a_{[i]} + b_{[n-i+1]}). \qquad (3)$$

Proof. In A.1 and A.2, let $x_i^{(1)} = a_i$, $x_i^{(2)} = b_i$, $i = 1, \ldots, n$. Then $\tau \prec s \prec \sigma$ and by 5.A.1.d, $\prod_1^n \tau_i \geq \prod_1^n s_i \geq \prod_1^n \sigma_i$. ||

The right side of (3) is a special case of a result of Ruderman (1952). See A.5 below. The result as stated here was apparently first published by Oppenheim (1954). It was obtained independently by Minc [1970, 1971; see also London (1970)]. As noted by Minc (1971), A.4 is equivalent to A.3.

Here, 5.A.1.d is much more than what is needed. In fact, if 5.A.1.d is fully utilized, one obtains an analog of A.3.a:

A.4.a. Proposition (Day, 1972). If $a_i > 0$, $b_i > 0$, $i = 1, \ldots, n$, then

$$\begin{aligned}
&(\log(a_{[1]} + b_{[n]}), \ldots, \log(a_{[n]} + b_{[1]}))\\
&\prec^w (\log(a_1 + b_1), \ldots, \log(a_n + b_n))\\
&\prec^w (\log(a_{[1]} + b_{[1]}), \ldots, \log(a_{[n]} + b_{[n]})).
\end{aligned} \qquad (4)$$

A similar ordering is involved in the right-hand inequality of (1) and the left-hand inequality of (3). By using A.1 for an arbitrary number of vectors, extensions of (1) and (3) are immediate:

A.5. Proposition (Ruderman, 1952). If $x^{(i)}$, $i = 1,\ldots,m$, are vectors with positive components, then

$$\sum_{j=1}^{n}\prod_{i=1}^{m} x_j^{(i)} \le \sum_{j=1}^{n}\prod_{i=1}^{m} x_{[j]}^{(i)} \tag{5}$$

and

$$\prod_{j=1}^{n}\sum_{i=1}^{m} x_{[j]}^{(i)} \le \prod_{j=1}^{n}\sum_{i=1}^{m} x_j^{(i)}. \tag{6}$$

The proof of these inequalities is essentially the same as the proofs of A.3 and A.4, but here, A.1 is used with arbitrary m.

Inequalities (5) and (6) can be written more generally as

$$\left(\prod_{i=1}^{m} x_1^{(i)}, \ldots, \prod_{i=1}^{m} x_n^{(i)}\right) \prec_{\mathrm{w}} \left(\prod_{i=1}^{m} x_{[1]}^{(i)}, \ldots, \prod_{i=1}^{m} x_{[n]}^{(i)}\right), \tag{7}$$

$$\left(\log \sum_{i=1}^{m} x_1^{(i)}, \ldots, \log \sum_{i=1}^{m} x_n^{(i)}\right) \prec^{\mathrm{w}} \left(\log \sum_{i=1}^{m} x_{[1]}^{(i)}, \ldots, \log \sum_{i=1}^{m} x_{[n]}^{(i)}\right), \tag{8}$$

and the proofs of these results are similar to the proofs of (2) and (4).

Somewhat more general inequalities are obtainable using A.1.a in place of A.1. These results are as follows:

A.5.a. Let $(\mathscr{X}, \mathscr{A}, \mu)$ be a measure space and let $x^{(\alpha)}$, $\alpha \in \mathscr{X}$, be a μ-integrable function of α taking values in $\mathscr{R}^n$. Then

$$\sum_{j=1}^{n} \exp\left\{\int_{\mathscr{X}} \log x_j^{(\alpha)} \mu(d\alpha)\right\} \le \sum_{j=1}^{n} \exp\left\{\int_{\mathscr{X}} \log x_{[j]}^{(\alpha)} \mu(d\alpha)\right\}, \tag{5'}$$

$$\prod_{j=1}^{n} \int_{\mathscr{X}} x_{[j]}^{(\alpha)} \mu(d\alpha) \le \prod_{j=1}^{n} \int_{\mathscr{X}} x_j^{(\alpha)} \mu(d\alpha), \tag{6'}$$

$$\left(\exp\left\{\int_{\mathscr{X}} \log x_1^{(\alpha)} \mu(d\alpha)\right\}, \ldots, \exp\left\{\int_{\mathscr{X}} \log x_n^{(\alpha)} \mu(d\alpha)\right\}\right)$$
$$\prec_{\mathrm{w}} \left(\exp\left\{\int_{\mathscr{X}} \log x_{[1]}^{(\alpha)} \mu(d\alpha)\right\}, \ldots, \exp\left\{\int_{\mathscr{X}} \log x_{[n]}^{(\alpha)} \mu(d\alpha)\right\}\right), \tag{7'}$$

$$\left(\log \int_{\mathscr{X}} x_1^{(\alpha)}\mu(d\alpha),\ldots,\log\int_{\mathscr{X}} x_n^{(\alpha)}\mu(d\alpha)\right)$$
$$\prec^{\mathrm{w}} \left(\log \int_{\mathscr{X}} x_{[1]}^{(\alpha)}\mu(d\alpha),\ldots,\log\int_{\mathscr{X}} x_{[n]}^{(\alpha)}\mu(d\alpha)\right). \tag{8'}$$

Majorization from Matrix Sums and Products

It may be of some interest to note that Propositions A.1 and A.2 of Day (1972) are very special cases of a much earlier result. It is somewhat surprising that this seems to have gone unnoticed.

A.6. Proposition (Fan, 1949). If G and H are $n \times n$ Hermitian matrices with ordered eigenvalues $\lambda_1 \geq \cdots \geq \lambda_n$, then

$$(\lambda_1(G+H),\ldots,\lambda_n(G+H)) \prec (\lambda_1(G)+\lambda_1(H),\ldots,\lambda_n(G)+\lambda_n(H)).$$

This majorization is discussed in some detail in 9.G.

From A.6, it is immediate that for Hermitian matrices $G_1,\ldots,G_m$ with eigenvalues $\lambda_1(G_i) \geq \cdots \geq \lambda_n(G_i)$, $i=1,\ldots,m$,

$$\left(\lambda_1\left(\sum_1^m G_i\right),\ldots,\lambda_n\left(\sum_1^m G_i\right)\right) \prec \left(\sum_1^m \lambda_1(G_i),\ldots,\sum_1^m \lambda_n(G_i)\right).$$

Now specialize this result to diagonal matrices:

(a) If $G_i = \mathrm{diag}(x_1^{(i)},\ldots,x_n^{(i)})$, $i=1,\ldots,m$, then Proposition A.1 is obtained.

(b) If in A.6, $G = \mathrm{diag}(x_{[1]},\ldots,x_{[n]})$ and $H = \mathrm{diag}(x_{(1)},\ldots,x_{(n)})$, then Proposition A.2 is obtained.

Other specializations of majorizations in matrix theory can be obtained. For example, (2a) follows from 9.H.1(2a) and 5.A.2.b. Other examples also can be given.

B Majorizations from Functions of Vectors

Propositions A.1 and A.2 both involve the addition of corresponding components of vectors. Other ways to combine components may be of

B. Majorizations from Functions of Vectors   211

interest: For any real-valued function ϕ of m real variables, one can form the vectors

$$u = (\phi(x_1^{(1)}, \ldots, x_1^{(m)}), \ldots, \phi(x_n^{(1)}, \ldots, x_n^{(m)})),$$
$$v = (\phi(x_{[1]}^{(1)}, \ldots, x_{[1]}^{(m)}), \ldots, \phi(x_{[n]}^{(1)}, \ldots, x_{[n]}^{(m)})),$$

and ask for conditions on ϕ to ensure that $u \prec v$.

B.1. Proposition. $u \prec v$ for all $n \geq 2$ and all n-vectors $x^{(1)}, \ldots, x^{(m)}$ if and only if ϕ has the form

$$\phi(a_1, \ldots, a_m) = \sum_{i=1}^{m} f_i(a_i),$$

where $f_1, \ldots, f_m$ are all monotone in the same direction.

Proof. Suppose first that ϕ has the required special form. Let

$$\widetilde{x}^{(i)} = (f_i(x_1^{(i)}), \ldots, f_i(x_n^{(i)})), \qquad i = 1, \ldots, m.$$

If the f_i are increasing, then

$$\widetilde{x}_{[j]}^{(i)} = f_i(x_{[j]}^{(i)}), \qquad i = 1, \ldots, m, \quad j = 1, \ldots, n,$$

so $u \prec v$ by A.1.

If the f_i are decreasing, then

$$\widetilde{x}_{[j]}^{(i)} = f_i(x_{[n-j+1]}^{(i)}), \qquad i = 1, \ldots, m, \quad j = 1, \ldots, n.$$

Because $a \prec b$ if and only if $(a_n, \ldots, a_1) \prec (b_n, \ldots, b_1)$, it again follows from A.1 that $u \prec v$.

Now, suppose that $u \prec v$ for all vectors $x^{(1)}, \ldots, x^{(m)}$. To show that $\phi(a_1, \ldots, a_m)$ has the form $\sum_{i=1}^{m} f_i(a_i)$, suppose first that $m = 2$. With $n = 2$ and using $\sum u_i = \sum v_i$ it follows that for any $\delta_1 \geq 0$, $\delta_2 \geq 0$,

$$\phi(\alpha_1 + \delta_1, \alpha_2 + \delta_2) + \phi(\alpha_1 - \delta_1, \alpha_2 - \delta_2)$$
$$= \phi(\alpha_1 + \delta_1, \alpha_2 - \delta_2) + \phi(\alpha_1 - \delta_1, \alpha_2 + \delta_2).$$

With $\delta_1 = |\alpha_1|$ and $\delta_2 = |\alpha_2|$, this equation reduces (independently of the signs of α_1 and α_2) to

$$\phi(2\alpha_1, 2\alpha_2) + \phi(0, 0) = \phi(2\alpha_1, 0) + \phi(0, 2\alpha_2);$$

that is,

$$\phi(r, s) = \phi(r, 0) + \phi(0, s) - \phi(0, 0).$$

If, for example, $f_1(r) = \phi(r, 0)$ and $f_2(s) = \phi(0, s) - \phi(0, 0)$, then ϕ has the form $\phi(r, s) = f_1(r) + f_2(s)$.

Because $u \prec v$, it must also be true that either

$$\phi(\alpha_1 + \delta_1, \alpha_2 + \delta_2) \geq \max[\phi(\alpha_1 + \delta_1, \alpha_2 - \delta_2), \phi(\alpha_1 - \delta_1, \alpha_2 + \delta_2)]$$

(ϕ is increasing in each argument), or

$$\phi(\alpha_1 - \delta_1, \alpha_2 - \delta_2) \geq \max[\phi(\alpha_1 + \delta_1, \alpha_2 - \delta_2), \phi(\alpha_1 - \delta_1, \alpha_2 - \delta_2)]$$

(ϕ is decreasing in each argument). Thus f_1 and f_2 must be monotone in the same direction. This shows that ϕ must have the required form when $n = 2$. Suppose it is true that ϕ must have the required form when it has $m-1$ arguments (there are $m-1$ vectors). Again with $n = 2$ and using $\sum u_i = \sum v_i$, it follows that for any $\delta_i \geq 0$, $i = 1, \ldots, m$,

$$\phi(\alpha_1 + \delta_1, \ldots, \alpha_m + \delta_m) + \phi(\alpha_1 - \delta_1, \ldots, \alpha_m - \delta_m)$$
$$= \phi(\alpha_1 + \epsilon_1 \delta_1, \ldots, \alpha_m + \epsilon_m \delta_m) + \phi(\alpha_1 - \epsilon_1 \delta_1, \ldots, \alpha_m - \epsilon_m \delta_m)$$

for any choice of signs $\epsilon_1, \epsilon_2, \ldots, \epsilon_m$. This means that

$$\phi(\alpha_1 + \eta_1 \delta_1, \ldots, \alpha_m + \eta_m \delta_m) + \phi(\alpha_1 - \eta_1 \delta_1, \ldots, \alpha_m - \eta_m \delta_m)$$
$$= \phi(\alpha_1 + \epsilon_1 \delta_1, \ldots, \alpha_m + \epsilon_m \delta_m) + \phi(\alpha_1 - \epsilon_1 \delta_1, \ldots, \alpha_m - \epsilon_m \delta_m)$$

for any choice of signs $\epsilon_1, \ldots, \epsilon_m, \eta_1, \ldots, n_m$. Take $\delta_i = |\alpha_i|$, $\eta_i = \text{sign } \alpha_i$, $i = 1, 2, \ldots, m$, and take $\epsilon_1 = \text{sign } \alpha_1$, $\epsilon_j = -\text{sign } \alpha_j$, $j = 2, \ldots, m$. Then this equation reduces to

$$\phi(2\alpha_1, \ldots, 2\alpha_m) = \phi(2\alpha_1, 0, \ldots, 0) + \phi(0, 2\alpha_2, \ldots, 2\alpha_m);$$

that is,

$$\phi(r_1, \ldots, r_m) = \phi(r_1, 0, \ldots, 0) + \phi(0, r_2, \ldots, r_m).$$

The induction hypothesis can be applied to the function $\phi(0, r_2, \ldots, r_m)$ to conclude that

$$\phi(r_1, \ldots, r_m) = \sum_{i=1}^{m} f_i(r_i).$$

By keeping all but two arguments of ϕ fixed, it follows from the case of $m = 2$ that each f_i must be increasing or each f_i must be decreasing. ||

The case of oppositely ordered vectors can again be considered when $m = 2$. Let ϕ be a real-valued function of two real variables and consider the vectors

$$u = (\phi(x_1^{(1)}, x_1^{(2)}), \ldots, \phi(x_n^{(1)}, x_n^{(2)})),$$
$$w = (\phi(x_{[1]}^{(1)}, x_{[n]}^{(2)}), \phi(x_{[2]}^{(1)}, x_{[n-1]}^{(2)}), \ldots, \phi(x_{[n]}^{(1)}, x_{[1]}^{(2)})).$$

B.2. Proposition. The majorization $w \prec u$ for all $n \geq 2$ and all n-vectors $x^{(1)}$, $x^{(2)}$ if and only if $\phi(a_1, a_2) = f_1(a_1) + f_2(a_2)$, where f_1 and f_2 are monotone in the same direction.

The proof of this is virtually identical to the proof of B.1 with $m = 2$.

C Weak Majorizations from Rearrangements

The questions considered in the previous section for strong majorization can also be asked for weak majorization. However, much more general conditions will lead to weak majorization. The results of this section are more interesting than those of the preceding section and they are more useful in proving inequalities.

As before, let $x^{(1)}, x^{(2)}, \ldots, x^{(m)}$ be vectors of n components, let ϕ be a real function of m real variables, and let

$$u = (\phi(x_1^{(1)}, \ldots, x_1^{(m)}), \ldots, \phi(x_n^{(1)}, \ldots, x_n^{(m)})),$$
$$v = (\phi(x_{[1]}^{(1)}, \ldots, x_{[1]}^{(m)}), \ldots, \phi(x_{[n]}^{(1)}, \ldots, x_{[n]}^{(m)})).$$

C.1. Proposition (Day, 1972). If $m = 2$, then $u \prec_w v$ for all $n \geq 2$ and all vectors $x^{(1)}$, $x^{(2)}$ in $\mathscr{R}^n$ if and only if

$$\phi(\alpha_1 + \delta_1, \alpha_2 + \delta_2) + \phi(\alpha_1 - \delta_1, \alpha_2 - \delta_2)$$
$$\geq \phi(\alpha_1 + \delta_1, \alpha_2 - \delta_2) + \phi(\alpha_1 - \delta_1, \alpha_2 + \delta_2) \quad (1)$$

whenever $\delta_1, \delta_2 \geq 0$, and

> either ϕ is increasing in each argument or ϕ is decreasing in each argument. (2)

A proof of C.1 is given ahead. But first note that property (1) is sufficiently important to be given a name.

C.2. Definition. A real-valued function ϕ defined on $\mathscr{R}^2$ is said to be *L-superadditive* (lattice-superadditive) if it satisfies (1). More generally, a real-valued function ϕ defined on $\mathscr{R}^m$ is called *L-superadditive* if

> ϕ satisfies (1) in any pair of arguments, the others being fixed. (3)

In the literature such functions are sometimes said to be *supermodular*. If, in addition,

> ϕ is either increasing in each argument or decreasing in each argument, (4)

then ϕ is said to be a *monotone L-superadditive* function.

214   6. Rearrangements and Majorization

L-superadditive functions are discussed in Section D, where examples are given, and the name is explained.

Proof of C.1. Suppose first that for all $n \geq 2$ and all $x^{(1)}, x^{(2)} \in \mathscr{R}^n$, $u \prec_w v$. With $n = 2$, $x_1^{(1)} = \alpha_1 + \delta_1$, $x_2^{(1)} = \alpha_1 - \delta_1$, $x_1^{(2)} = \alpha_2 - \delta_2$, $x_2^{(2)} = \alpha_2 + \delta_2 (\delta_1, \delta_2 \geq 0)$, the requirement that $u_1 + u_2 \leq v_1 + v_2$ yields (1). Because also $\max(u_1, u_2) \leq \max(v_1, v_2)$, it follows that either

(i) $\phi(\alpha_1 + \delta_1, \alpha_2 + \delta_2) \geq \phi(\alpha_1 - \delta_1, \alpha_2 + \delta_2)$, and
$\phi(\alpha_1 + \delta_1, \alpha_2 + \delta_2) \geq \phi(\alpha_1 + \delta_1, \alpha_2 - \delta_2)$

or

(ii) $\phi(\alpha_1 - \delta_1, \alpha_2 - \delta_2) \geq \phi(\alpha_1 - \delta_1, \alpha_2 + \delta_2)$, and
$\phi(\alpha_1 - \delta_1, \alpha_2 - \delta_2) \geq \phi(\alpha_1 + \delta_1, \alpha_2 - \delta_2)$.

But (i) says ϕ is increasing in both arguments and (ii) says ϕ is decreasing in both arguments. Consequently, conditions (1) and (2) are necessary for $u \prec_w v$.

Next, suppose that (1) and (2) hold. For notational convenience, suppose that $x_1^{(1)} \geq \cdots \geq x_n^{(1)}$. If also $x_1^{(2)} \geq \cdots \geq x_n^{(2)}$, then $u = v$. Otherwise, there exists $i < j$ such that $x_i^{(2)} < x_j^{(2)}$. Let

$$\widetilde{u} = (u_1, \ldots, u_{i-1}, \phi(x_i^{(1)}, x_j^{(2)}), u_{i+1}, \ldots, u_{j-1}, \phi(x_j^{(1)}, x_i^{(2)}), u_{j+1}, \ldots, u_n).$$

Then, as a direct consequence of (1) and (2),

$$(\phi(x_i^{(1)}, x_i^{(2)}), \phi(x_j^{(1)}, x_j^{(2)})) \prec_w (\phi(x_i^{(1)}, x_j^{(2)}), \phi(x_j^{(1)}, x_i^{(2)})).$$

It follows from 5.A.7 that $u \prec_w \widetilde{u}$. Repeat this argument with $\widetilde{u}$ in place of u. After a finite number of steps, a $\widetilde{u} = v$ is obtained. Thus

$$u \prec_w \widetilde{u} \prec_w \widetilde{\widetilde{u}} \prec_w \cdots \prec_w v. \quad \|$$

C.3. Proposition (Day, 1972). $u \prec_w v$ for all $n \geq 2$ and all $x^{(1)}, \ldots, x^{(m)}$ in $\mathscr{R}^n$ if and only if φ is a monotone L-superadditive function.

Proof. Suppose first that $u \prec_w v$ for all $n \geq 2$ and all $x^{(1)}, \ldots, x^{(m)} \in \mathscr{R}^n$. In particular, let $n = 2$ and for fixed i, j, let $x_1^{(l)} = x_2^{(l)}$ for all $l \neq i$, $l \neq j$. Then $u_1 + u_2 \leq v_1 + v_2$ implies that ϕ is L-superadditive. In addition, $\max(u_1, u_2) \leq \max(v_1, v_2)$ implies that either ϕ is increasing in the ith and jth arguments or decreasing in these arguments. By keeping i fixed and letting j assume all values $\neq i$, (4) is obtained.

Next suppose that ϕ is monotone and L-superadditive. If $m = 2$, it follows from C.1 that $u \prec_w v$; with $n = 2$, suppose that $u \prec_w v$ for

C. Weak Majorizations from Rearrangements   215

any number less than m of vectors $x^{(i)}$. Assume also, without loss of generality, that for some integer l, $0 \leq l \leq m$,

$$x^{(i)} = (\alpha_i + \delta_i, \alpha_i - \delta_i), \quad i = 1, \ldots, l,$$
$$x^{(i)} = (\alpha_i - \delta_i, \alpha_i + \delta_i), \quad i = l+1, \ldots, m,$$

where $\delta_i \geq 0$, $i = 1, \ldots, m$. It is convenient now to consider separately the cases $l = m$, $0 \leq l \leq m-2$, and $l = m-1$.

Case 1. $l = m$. In this case, $u = v$ and there is nothing to prove.

Case 2. $0 \leq l \leq m-2$. By the induction hypothesis applied to the function $\phi^*(x_1, \ldots, x_{m-1}) = \phi(x_1, \ldots, x_{m-1}, \alpha_m + \delta_m)$, i.e., with the mth argument fixed,

$$\phi(\alpha_1 + \delta_1, \ldots, \alpha_{m-1} + \delta_{m-1}, \alpha_m + \delta_m)$$
$$+ \phi(\alpha_1 - \delta_1, \ldots, \alpha_{m-1} - \delta_{m-1}, \alpha_m + \delta_m)$$
$$\geq \phi(\alpha_1 + \delta_1, \ldots, \alpha_l + \delta_l, \alpha_{l+1} - \delta_{l+1}, \ldots, \alpha_{m-1} - \delta_{m-1}, \alpha_m + \delta_m)$$
$$+ \phi(\alpha_1 - \delta_1, \ldots, \alpha_l - \delta_l, \alpha_{l+1} + \delta_{l+1}, \ldots, \alpha_{m-1} + \delta_{m-1}, \alpha_m + \delta_m). \quad (5)$$

Similarly, with the $(l+1)$th through the $(m-1)$th arguments fixed, the induction hypothesis applied with $l+1$ vectors yields

$$\phi(\alpha_1 + \delta_1, \ldots, \alpha_l + \delta_l, \alpha_{l+1} - \delta_{l+1}, \ldots, \alpha_{m-1} - \delta_{m-1}, \alpha_m + \delta_m)$$
$$+ \phi(\alpha_1 - \delta_1, \ldots, \alpha_l - \delta_l, \alpha_{l+1} - \delta_{l+1}, \ldots, \alpha_{m-1} - \delta_{m-1}, \alpha_m - \delta_m)$$
$$\geq \phi(\alpha_1 + \delta_1, \ldots, \alpha_l + \delta_l, \alpha_{l+1} - \delta_{l+1}, \ldots, \alpha_{m-1} - \delta_{m-1}, \alpha_m - \delta_m)$$
$$+ \phi(\alpha_1 - \delta_1, \ldots, \alpha_l - \delta_l, -\delta_{l+1}, \ldots, \alpha_{m-1} - \delta_{m-1}, \alpha_m + \delta_m). \quad (6)$$

Now, add (5) and (6) to obtain

$$\phi(\alpha_1 + \delta_1, \ldots, \alpha_m + \delta_m) + \phi(\alpha_1 - \delta_1, \ldots, \alpha_m - \delta_m)$$
$$\geq \phi(\alpha_1 + \delta_1, \ldots, \alpha_l + \delta_l, \alpha_{l+1} - \delta_{l+1}, \ldots, \alpha_m - \delta_m)$$
$$+ \phi(\alpha_1 - \delta_1, \ldots, \alpha_l - \delta_l, \alpha_{l+1} + \delta_{l+1}, \ldots, \alpha_m + \delta_m),$$

that is, $u_1 + u_2 \geq v_1 + v_2$. If follows from monotonicity that $\max(u_1, u_2) \leq \max(v_1, v_2)$, so $u \prec_w v$.

216   6. Rearrangements and Majorization

Case 3. $l = k - 1$. Here a similar argument can be used: With the induction hypothesis and first argument fixed,

$$\phi(\alpha_1 + \delta_1, \alpha_2 + \delta_2, \ldots, \alpha_m + \delta_m) + \phi(\alpha_1 + \delta_1, \alpha_2 - \delta_2, \ldots, \alpha_m - \delta_m)$$
$$\geq \phi(\alpha_1 + \delta_1, \alpha_2 + \delta_2, \ldots, \alpha_{m-1} + \delta_{m-1}, \alpha_m - \delta_m)$$
$$+ \phi(\alpha_1 + \delta_1, \alpha_2 - \delta_2, \ldots, \alpha_{m-1} - \delta_{m-1}, \alpha_m + \delta_m).$$

With all but the first and last arguments fixed,

$$\phi(\alpha_1 + \delta_1, \alpha_2 - \delta_2, \ldots, \alpha_{m-1} - \delta_{m-1}, \alpha_m + \delta_m)$$
$$+ \phi(\alpha_1 - \delta_1, \alpha_2 - \delta_2, \ldots, \alpha_{m-1} - \delta_{m-1}, \alpha_m - \delta_m)$$
$$\geq \phi(\alpha_1 - \delta_1, \alpha_2 - \delta_2, \ldots, \alpha_{m-1} - \delta_{m-1}, \alpha_m + \delta_m)$$
$$+ \phi(\alpha_1 + \delta_1, \alpha_2 - \delta_2, \ldots, \alpha_{m-1} - \delta_{m-1}, \alpha_m - \delta_m).$$

Addition of these two inequalities gives $u_1 + u_2 \leq v_1 + v_2$. This shows that if ϕ is a monotone L-superadditive function, then $u \prec_w v$ when $m \geq 2$ is an integer and $n = 2$.

For an arbitrary dimension n, it is convenient to suppose (without loss of generality) that $x_1^{(1)} \geq \cdots \geq x_n^{(1)}$. If $x_1^{(l)} \geq \cdots \geq x_n^{(l)}$ for $l = 2, \ldots, m$, then $u = v$ and there is nothing to prove. Otherwise, there are a pair i, j ($i < j$) and a nonempty set $L \subset \{2, \ldots, m\}$ such that $x_i^{(l)} < x_j^{(l)}$ for all $l \in L$, $x_i^{(l)} \geq x_j^{(l)}$ for all $l \notin L$. For all $l \in L$, interchange $x_i^{(l)}$ and $x_j^{(l)}$ to obtain $\widetilde{x}^{(1)}, \ldots, \widetilde{x}^{(m)}$. From these vectors, form $\widetilde{u}$. Note that $\widetilde{u}_k = u_k$ if $k \neq i$ and $k \neq j$. Apply 5.A.7 together with the above results for $n = 2$ to obtain that $u \prec_w \widetilde{u}$. Continuing in this manner, v is reached after a finite number of steps. Moreover, $u \prec_w \widetilde{u} \prec_w \widetilde{\widetilde{u}} \prec_w \cdots \prec_w v$. ||

As in Section B, it is possible with $m = 2$ to consider comparisons of

$$u = (\phi(x_1^{(1)}, x_1^{(2)}), \ldots, \phi(x_n^{(1)}, x_n^{(2)}))$$

and

$$w = (\phi(x_{[1]}^{(1)}, x_{[n]}^{(2)}), \ldots, \phi(x_{[n]}^{(1)}, x_{[1]}^{(2)})).$$

C.4. Proposition (Day, 1972). $w \prec_w u$ for all $n \geq 2$ and all $x^{(1)}, x^{(2)}$ in $\mathscr{R}^n$ if and only if ϕ is monotone and L-superadditive.

Proof. As in B.1, it is easy to see that with $n = 2$, $w \prec_w u$ implies that ϕ is monotone and L-superadditive.

Suppose that ϕ is monotone and L-superadditive, and for notational convenience, suppose $x_1^{(1)} \geq \cdots \geq x_n^{(1)}$. If $x_1^{(2)} \leq \cdots \leq x_n^{(2)}$, then $w = u$.

Otherwise, there exists $i < j$ such that $x_i^{(2)} > x_j^{(2)}$. Let

$$u_{(1)} = (u_1, .., u_{i-1}, \phi(x_i^{(1)}, x_j^{(2)}), u_{i+1}, .., u_{j-1}, \phi(x_j^{(1)}, x_i^{(2)}), u_{j+1}, .., u_n),$$

or, if $j = i + 1$,

$$u_{(1)} = (u_1, \ldots, u_{i-1}, \phi(x_i^{(1)}, x_j^{(2)}), \phi(x_j^{(1)}, x_i^{(2)}), u_{j+1}, \ldots, u_n).$$

Then

$$(\phi(x_i^{(1)}, x_j^{(2)}), \phi(x_j^{(1)}, x_i^{(2)})) \prec_w (\phi(x_i^{(1)}, x_i^{(2)}), \phi(x_j^{(1)}, x_j^{(2)})),$$

so that by 5.A.7, $u \succ_w u_{(1)}$. Repeat this argument with $u_{(1)}$ in place of u. After a finite number of such repetitions, the vector w is obtained. Thus

$$u \succ_w u_{(1)} \succ_w u_{(2)} \succ_w \cdots \succ_w w. \quad \|$$

C.4.a. Proposition. Let $u = (\phi(x_1^{(1)}, x_1^{(2)}), \ldots, \phi(x_n^{(1)}, x_n^{(2)}))$ and $v = (\phi(x_{[1]}^{(1)}, x_{[1]}^{(2)}), \ldots, \phi(x_{[n]}^{(1)}, x_{[n]}^{(2)}))$. Then $u \prec_w v$ for all $n \geq 2$ and all $x^{(1)}, x^{(2)}$ in $\mathscr{R}^n$ if and only if ϕ is monotone and L-superadditive.

The questions discussed in this section concerning the weak majorization $x \prec_w y$ can also be asked about the alternative weak majorization $x \prec^w y$.

C.5. Proposition. $u \prec^w v$ for all $n \geq 2$ and all $x^{(1)}, \ldots, x^{(m)}$ in $\mathscr{R}^n$ if and only if $-\phi$ is monotone and L-superadditive. For $m = 2$, $w \prec^w u$ for all $n \geq 2$ and all $x^{(1)}, x^{(2)}$ in $\mathscr{R}^n$ if and only if $-\phi$ is monotone and L-superadditive.

Proof. These results follow from C.3 and C.4 because $x \prec^w y$ is equivalent to $-x \prec_w -y$. $\|$

D $\;$ *L*-Superadditive Functions—Properties and Examples

Condition (1) of Section C can be put into various forms that are sometimes useful in verifying L-superadditivity. In particular, the condition

$$\phi(\alpha_1 + \delta_1, \alpha_2 + \delta_2) + \phi(\alpha_1 - \delta_1, \alpha_2 - \delta_2)$$
$$\geq \phi(\alpha_1 + \delta_1, \alpha_2 - \delta_2) + \phi(\alpha_1 - \delta_1, \alpha_2 + \delta_2) \qquad (1)$$

whenever $\delta_1, \delta_2 \geq 0$ can be rewritten as

$$\phi(r+\eta, s) - \phi(r, s) \text{ is increasing in } s \text{ for all } r \text{ and all } \eta > 0, \quad (1a)$$

or as

$$\phi(r, s+\eta) - \phi(r, s) \text{ is increasing in } r \text{ for all } s \text{ and all } \eta > 0. \quad (1b)$$

If ϕ has second partial derivatives, notice that the partial derivative of $\phi(r+\eta, s) - \phi(r, s)$ with respect to s is nonnegative if and only if $\partial\phi(r,s)/\partial s$ is increasing in r. Consequently, (1) is also equivalent to

$$\frac{\partial^2}{\partial r \partial s}\phi(r, s) \geq 0. \quad (1c)$$

This equivalence was noted by Lorentz (1953). See also Day (1972) and Chong (1974b).

In other contexts, L-superadditivity has been encountered by Topkis (1968), Tchen (1975, 1980), Whitt (1976), and Cambanis, Simons, and Stout (1976).

Some Background

The term "superadditive" as used here was apparently first used by Arthur F. Veinott, Jr., in unpublished work as a natural counterpart to "subadditivity" in the sense of Fan (1967). According to Fan's definition, a real-valued function ϕ defined on a lattice L is called *subadditive* if

$$\phi(x) + \phi(y) \geq (\phi(x \wedge y) + \phi(x \vee y)) \qquad \text{for all } x, y \in L.$$

Here, of course, $x \wedge y$ is the greatest lower bound of x and y and $x \vee y$ is the least upper bound of x and y. For this notion, we prefer the term "lattice subadditive" or "L-subadditive" to avoid confusion with the more standard notion of subadditivity, namely,

$$\phi(x+y) \leq \phi(x) + \phi(y).$$

The term "subadditive" is also used by Meyer (1966) in the sense of Fan, where L is a lattice of sets.

If the lattice L is $\mathscr{R}^m$ with componentwise ordering, then ϕ is subadditive in Fan's sense if and only if $-\phi$ is L-superadditive in the sense of Definition C.2. The fact that it is sufficient to consider the arguments of ϕ only in pairs, as in Definition C.2, is due to Lorentz (1953). See also Chong (1974b).

When $m = 2$, the condition of L-superadditivity is just the condition that distribution functions must satisfy to correspond to a *nonnegative*

D. *L*-Superadditive Functions—Properties and Examples

Lebesgue–Stieltjes measure defined on appropriate subsets of $\mathscr{R}^2$. For $m \neq 2$, the property of distribution functions is not the same as *L*-superadditivity. For this reason, the term "positive set function," sometimes used in place of *L*-superadditive, seems inappropriate.

Compositions and *L*-Superadditivity

D.1. If ϕ is *L*-superadditive (monotone and *L*-superadditive) and if $g_i : \mathscr{R} \to \mathscr{R}$, $i = 1, \ldots, m$, are monotone in the same direction, then the composition $\phi(g_1, \ldots, g_m)$ is *L*-superadditive (monotone and *L*-superadditive).

This result is particularly easy to see from (1a) or (1b).

D.2. (Topkis, 1968; Day, 1972). If ϕ is a monotone *L*-superadditive function and $f : \mathscr{R} \to \mathscr{R}$ is convex and increasing, then the composition $f \circ \phi$ is monotone and *L*-superadditive.

This result is easy to verify if differentiability is assumed and (1c) is used.

Some Examples

D.3. Let g and h be real-valued functions defined on $\mathscr{R}^2$ such that for each fixed θ, $g(x, \theta)$ is increasing in x and $h(\theta, y)$ is increasing in y (alternatively, both functions are decreasing). If μ is a nonnegative measure, then

$$\phi(x, y) = \int g(x, \theta) h(\theta, y) \mu(d\theta)$$

is monotone and *L*-superadditive provided the integral exists.

Proof. Because the monotone *L*-superadditive functions form a convex cone, it is sufficient to prove that for each fixed θ, $g(x, \theta) h(\theta, y)$ is monotone and *L*-superadditive. But this is trivial. ‖

D.3 is reminiscent of a standard way to construct bivariate probability distributions as mixtures of bivariate distributions with independent marginals.

D.3.a. If S_k is the kth elementary symmetric function of m variables, then S_k is *L*-superadditive on $\mathscr{R}_+^m$.

D.4. If $\phi(z_1, \ldots, z_n) = \psi(z_1 + \cdots + z_n)$, then ϕ is L-superadditive if and only if ψ is convex (Lorentz, 1953). Also, ϕ is monotone if ψ is monotone. If ψ is monotone and convex, it follows that

$$\left(\psi\left(\sum_1^m x_1^{(i)}\right), \ldots, \psi\left(\sum_1^m x_n^{(i)}\right)\right) \prec_w \left(\psi\left(\sum_1^m x_{[1]}^{(i)}\right), \ldots, \psi\left(\sum_1^m x_{[n]}^{(i)}\right)\right), \quad (2)$$

and

$$(\psi(x_{[1]}^{(1)} + x_{[n]}^{(2)}), \ldots, \psi(x_{[n]}^{(1)} + x_{[1]}^{(2)}))$$
$$\prec_w (\psi(x_1^{(1)} + x_1^{(2)}), \ldots, \psi(x_n^{(1)} + x_n^{(2)})). \quad (3)$$

Of course, this means that for any monotone convex function,

$$\sum_{j=1}^n \psi\left(\sum_{i=1}^m x_j^{(i)}\right) \leq \sum_{j=1}^n \psi\left(\sum_{i=1}^m x_{[j]}^{(i)}\right), \quad (4)$$

and

$$\sum_{j=1}^n \psi(x_{[j]}^{(1)} + x_{[n-j+1]}^{(2)}) \leq \sum_{j=1}^n \psi(x_j^{(1)} + x_j^{(2)}). \quad (5)$$

Inequalities (2), (3), (4), and (5) are also immediate consequences of the majorizations of A.1 or A.2 and 5.A.2. Possible choices of ψ include $\psi_1(z) = e^z$, $\psi_2(z) = \max(0, z)$, $\psi_3(z) = 0$ if $z < 0$, $\psi_3(z) = z^\alpha (\alpha \geq 1)$, $z \geq 0$. In case the vectors have nonnegative components, one can use $\psi_4(z) = -\log z$ or $\psi_5(z) = z^{-1}e^{-z}$. Lorentz (1953) pointed out that with ψ_4, one can obtain the inequality (6) of A.5 that is due to Ruderman (1952).

D.4.a. If ψ is monotone and concave, it follows from C.5 and D.3 that

$$\left(\psi\left(\sum_1^m x_1^{(i)}\right), \ldots, \psi\left(\sum_1^m x_n^{(i)}\right)\right) \prec^w \left(\psi\left(\sum_1^m x_{[1]}^{(i)}\right), \ldots, \psi\left(\sum_1^m x_{[n]}^{(i)}\right)\right), \quad (6)$$

and

$$(\psi(x_{[1]}^{(1)} + x_{[n]}^{(2)}), \ldots, \psi(x_{[n]}^{(1)} + x_{[1]}^{(2)}))$$
$$\prec^w (\psi(x_1^{(1)} + x_1^{(2)}), \ldots, \psi(x_n^{(1)} + x_n^{(2)})). \quad (7)$$

Here, possible choices of ψ include $\psi(z) = \log z$ and $\psi(z) = z^\alpha$ for $0 < \alpha < 1$, $z \geq 0$.

For any vector $z \in \mathscr{R}^n$, let

$$\Delta z = (z_2 - z_1, \ldots, z_n - z_{n-1}),$$

and let $|\Delta z| = (|z_2 - z_1|, \ldots, |z_n - z_{n-1}|)$.

D.4.b. (Chong, 1975). For any vector $a \in \mathscr{R}^n$,
$$|\Delta a_\downarrow| \prec_w |\Delta a|.$$

Proof. Write $x \approx y$ if x is a permutation of y. After possibly interchanging summands in some components of $|\Delta a|$ if necessary,
$$|\Delta a| \approx (|a_{i_1} - a_{[1]}|, \ldots, |a_{i_{n-1}} - a_{[n-1]}|)$$
for some permutation $(i_1, \ldots, i_n)$ of $(1, \ldots, n)$.

Suppose first that $i_n = 1$ so that
$$a_{[1]} \notin \{a_{i_1}, \ldots, a_{i_{n-1}}\} \quad \text{and} \quad (a_{i_1}, \ldots, a_{i_{n-1}}) \approx (a_{[2]}, \ldots, a_{[n]}).$$

With $x = (a_{i_1}, \ldots, a_{i_{n-1}})$, $y = (-a_{[2]}, \ldots, -a_{[n]})$, and with the L-superadditive function $\phi(r, s) = |r + s|$, it follows from C.4 that
$$(\phi(x_{[1]}, y_{[n-1]}), \ldots, \phi(x_{[n-1]}, y_{[1]}))$$
$$\prec_w (\phi(x_1, y_{[n-1]}), \ldots, \phi(x_{n-1}, y_{[1]}));$$
that is, $|\Delta a_\downarrow| \prec_w |\Delta a|$.

Next, suppose that $i_n \neq 1$ so $a_{[1]} = a_{i_j}$ for some $j \leq n-1$. Then
$$|\Delta a| \approx (|a_{i_1} - a_{[1]}|, \ldots, |a_{i_j} - a_{[j]}|, \ldots, |a_{i_{n-1}} - a_{[n-1]}|)$$
$$\geq (|a_{i_1} - a_{[1]}|, \ldots, |a_{i_{j-1}} - a_{[j-1]}|, |a_{i_n} - a_{[j]}|,$$
$$|a_{i_{j+1}} - a_{[j+1]}|, \ldots, |a_{i_{n-1}} - a_{[n-1]}|)$$
$$\succ_w (|a_{[2]} - a_{[n]}|, \ldots, |a_{[n]} - a_{[n-1]}|).$$

Here the first inequality (componentwise ordering) follows because a substitution is made for $a_{[1]}$, the largest component of a. The second inequality (weak majorization) follows from C.4 as in the first case above. ∥

D.4.c. (Duff, 1967). If $a \in \mathscr{R}^n$ and $p \geq 1$, then
$$\sum_{k=1}^{n-1} |\Delta a_{[k]}|^p \leq \sum_{k=1}^{n-1} |\Delta a_k|^p.$$

More generally, $\phi(|\Delta a_\downarrow|) \leq \phi(|\Delta a|)$ for all increasing symmetric convex functions $\phi: \mathscr{R}_+^{n-1} \to \mathscr{R}$. These results follow from D.4.b and 3.C.2.d.

D.5. If $\phi(z_1, \ldots, z_n) = \psi(\Pi_1^n z_i)$, $z_i \geq 0$, and if ψ is twice differentiable, then ϕ is L-superadditive if ψ satisfies
$$\psi'(z) + z\psi''(z) \geq 0.$$

6. Rearrangements and Majorization

Essentially this result was found by Borell (1973). To obtain monotonicity, the domain of ϕ can be restricted by the requirement that each $z_i \geq 0$, in which case ψ must also be monotone. If ψ is monotone and $\psi'(z) + z\psi''(z) \geq 0$, and if $x_j^{(i)} \geq 0$ for all i and j,

$$\left(\psi\left(\prod_1^m x_1^{(i)}\right),\ldots,\psi\left(\prod_1^m x_n^{(i)}\right)\right) \prec_w \left(\psi\left(\prod_1^m x_{[1]}^{(i)}\right),\ldots,\psi\left(\prod_1^m x_{[n]}^{(i)}\right)\right) \tag{8}$$

and

$$(\psi(x_{[1]}^{(1)} x_{[n]}^{(2)}),\ldots,\psi(x_{[n]}^{(1)} x_{[1]}^{(2)})) \prec_w (\psi(x_1^{(1)} x_1^{(2)}),\ldots,\psi(x_n^{(1)} x_n^{(2)})). \tag{9}$$

As a consequence of (8), (9), and 3.C.1.b, it follows that for any increasing convex function g,

$$\sum_{j=1}^n g\left(\psi\left(\prod_{i=1}^m x_j^{(i)}\right)\right) \leq \sum_{j=1}^n g\left(\psi\left(\prod_{i=1}^n x_{[j]}^{(i)}\right)\right) \tag{10}$$

and

$$\sum_{j=1}^n g(\psi(x_{[j]}^{(1)} x_{[n-j+1]}^{(2)})) \leq \sum_{j=1}^n g(\psi(x_j^{(1)} x_j^{(2)})). \tag{11}$$

The choice $\psi(z) = z$ in (8) yields the inequality (5) of A.5 due to Ruderman (1952). The choice $\psi(z) = \log(1+z)$ in (8) and (9) yields

$$\sum_{j=1}^n F(1 + x_{[j]}^{(1)} x_{[n-j+1]}^{(2)}) \leq \sum_{j=1}^n F(1 + x_j^{(1)} x_j^{(2)}) \leq \sum_{j=1}^n F(1 + x_{[j]}^{(1)} x_{[j]}^{(2)}),$$

where $F(z) = g(\log z)$ and g is increasing and convex. This result is due to London (1970).

D.6. If $\phi(z_1,\ldots,z_n) = \psi(\min_i(z_i, c))$, where ψ is increasing, then ϕ is monotone and L-superadditive. This can be verified, e.g., by showing that $\phi(r,s) = \psi(\min(r,s,\tilde{c}))$ satisfies (1a) when ψ is increasing.

For any increasing function ψ, it follows that

$$(\psi(\min_i x_1^{(i)}),\ldots,\psi(\min_i x_n^{(i)})) \prec_w (\psi(\min_i x_{[1]}^{(i)}),\ldots,\psi(\min_i x_{[n]}^{(i)})) \tag{12}$$

and

$$(\psi(\min(x_{[1]}^{(1)}, x_{[n]}^{(2)})),\ldots,\psi(\min(x_{[n]}^{(1)}, x_{[1]}^{(2)})))$$
$$\prec_w (\psi(\min(x_1^{(1)}, x_1^{(2)})),\ldots,\psi(\min(x_n^{(1)}, x_n^{(2)}))). \tag{13}$$

With these results it follows that for any increasing function ψ,

$$\sum_{j=1}^{n} \psi(\min_{i} x_j^{(i)}) \leq \sum_{j=1}^{n} \psi(\min_{i} x_{[j]}^{(i)}) \qquad (14)$$

and

$$\sum_{j=1}^{n} \psi(\min(x_{[j]}^{(1)}, x_{[n-j+1]}^{(2)})) \leq \sum_{j=1}^{n} \psi(\min(x_j^{(1)}, x_j^{(2)})). \qquad (15)$$

D.6.a. With $\psi(z) = \log z$ and the assumption that $x_j^{(i)} > 0$ for all i, j, it follows that

$$\prod_{j=1}^{n} \min_{i} x_j^{(i)} \leq \prod_{j=1}^{n} \min_{i} x_{[j]}^{(i)};$$

with $\psi(z) = z$, it follows that

$$\sum_{j=1}^{n} \min_{i} x_j^{(i)} \leq \sum_{j=1}^{n} \min_{i} x_{[j]}^{(i)}.$$

These inequalities are due to Minc (1971).

D.7. If $\phi(z_1, \ldots, z_n) = \psi(\max_i(z_i, c))$, where ψ is decreasing, then ϕ is monotone and L-superadditive. This fact is closely related to D.6. For any decreasing function ψ, it follows that (12), (13), (14), and (15) hold with min replaced by max.

D.7.a. With $\psi(z) = -z$, and using the equivalence $x \prec_w y$ if and only if $-x \prec^w -y$, it follows that

$$(\max_{i} x_1^{(i)}, \ldots, \max_{i} x_n^{(i)}) \prec^w (\max_{i} x_{[1]}^{(i)}, \ldots, \max_{i} x_{[n]}^{(i)})$$

and

$$(\max(x_{[1]}^{(1)}, x_{[n]}^{(2)}), \ldots, \max(x_{[n]}^{(1)}, x_{[1]}^{(2)}))$$

$$\prec^w (\max(x_1^{(1)}, x_1^{(2)}), \ldots, \max(x_n^{(1)}, x_n^{(2)})).$$

From the first of these inequalities, it follows that

$$\sum_{j=1}^{n} \max_{i} x_j^{(i)} \geq \sum_{j=1}^{n} \max_{i} x_{[j]}^{(i)}.$$

This inequality is due to Minc (1971).

D.7.b. With $\psi(z) = -\log z$, it follows that if $x_j^{(i)} > 0$ for all i, j,

$$(\log \max_i x_1^{(i)}, \ldots, \log \max_i x_n^{(i)}) \prec^w (\log \max_i x_{[1]}^i, \ldots, \log \max_i x_{[n]}^{(i)}),$$

and of course there is a similar result if $m = 2$ and the vectors are oppositely ordered. As a consequence, if $x_j^{(i)} > 0$ for all i, j,

$$\prod_{j=1}^n \max_i x_j^{(i)} \geq \prod_{j=1}^n \max_i x_{[j]}^{(i)},$$

a result due to Minc (1971).

Summary for Rearrangements

D.8.a. Rearrangements for majorization.

(i) $x_\downarrow + y_\uparrow \prec x + y \prec x_\uparrow + y_\uparrow$, $x, y \in \mathscr{R}^n$;

(ii) $x_\downarrow y_\uparrow \prec_w xy \prec x_\uparrow y_\uparrow$, $x, y \in \mathscr{R}_+^n$,

where $u\nu = (u_1\nu_1, \ldots, u_n\nu_n)$;

(iii) $\min(x_\uparrow, y_\downarrow) \prec_w \min(x, y) \prec_w (x_\uparrow, y_\uparrow)$, $x, y \in \mathscr{R}^n$,

where $\min(u, v) = (\min(u_1 v_1), \ldots, \min(u_n, v_n))$;

(iv) $\max(x_\uparrow, y_\downarrow) \prec^w \max(x, y) \prec^w \max(x_\uparrow, y_\uparrow)$, $x, y \in \mathscr{R}^n$.

D.8.b. Rearrangements for log majorization.

Recall the notation $x_{[1]} \geq \cdots \geq x_{[n]}$ and $x_{(1)} \leq \cdots \leq x_{(n)}$. For $x, y \in \mathscr{R}_{++}^n$ and for $k = 1, \ldots, n$,

(i) $\prod_1^k (x_{(i)} + y_{[n-i+1]}) \leq \prod_1^k (x_i + y_i) \leq \prod_1^k (x_{[i]} + y_{[i]})$;

(ii) $\prod_1^k (x_{[i]} y_{(n-i+1)}) \leq \prod_1^k x_i y_i \leq \prod_1^k x_{[i]} y_{[i]}$;

(iii) $\prod_1^k \min(x_{[i]}, y_{(i)}) \leq \prod_1^k \min(x_i, y_i) \leq \prod_1^k \min(x_{[i]}, y_{[i]})$;

(iv) $\prod_1^k \max(x_{(i)}, y_{[n-i+1]}) \leq \prod_1^k \max(x_i, y_i) \leq \prod_1^k \max(x_{[i]}, y_{[i]})$.

Alternatively, (i)–(iv) can be written as majorizations:

(i) $\log(x_\uparrow + y_\downarrow) \prec^w \log(x + y) \prec^w \log(x_\uparrow + y_\uparrow)$;

(ii) $\log(x_\uparrow \circ y_\downarrow) \prec_w \log(x \circ y) \prec_w \log(x_\uparrow \circ y_\uparrow)$,

where $x \circ y = (x_1 y_1, \ldots, x_n y_n)$;

(iii) $\log(x_\uparrow \wedge y_\downarrow) \prec_w \log(x \wedge y) \prec_w \log(x_\uparrow \wedge y_\uparrow)$,

where $s \wedge t = \min(s,t)$;

(iv) $\log(x_\uparrow \vee y_\downarrow) \prec^w \log(x \vee y) \prec^w \log(x_\uparrow \vee y_\uparrow)$,

where $s \vee t = \max(s,t)$.

E Inequalities Without Majorization

The known inequalities that occur as examples in Section D do not, for the most part, take full advantage of the weak majorizations from which they are obtained. In fact, a result $x \prec_w y$ is mostly used simply to yield $\sum x_i \leq \sum y_i$. So there is a natural question: If $u, v,$ and w are defined as in Section B, i.e.,

$$u = (\phi(x_1^{(1)}, \ldots, x_1^{(m)}), \ldots, \phi(x_n^{(1)}, \ldots, x_n^{(m)})),$$
$$v = (\phi(x_{[1]}^{(1)}, \ldots, x_{[1]}^{(m)}), \ldots, \phi(x_{[n]}^{(1)}, \ldots, x_{[n]}^{(m)})),$$
$$w = (\phi(x_{[1]}^{(1)}, x_{[n]}^{(2)}), \ldots, \phi(x_{[n]}^{(1)}, x_{[1]}^{(2)})),$$

then what conditions must ϕ satisfy in order that $\sum u_i \leq \sum v_i$ and (when $m = 2$) $\sum w_i \leq \sum u_i$? A continuous version of this question has been answered by Lorentz (1953). Here, with some simplifications in the problem considered, the condition of Lorentz is given in a discrete setting.

E.1. Proposition (Lorentz, 1953). For all vectors $x^{(1)}, \ldots, x^{(m)}$ in $\mathscr{R}^n$ and all n,

$$\sum_{j=1}^{n} \phi(x_{[j]}^{(1)}, x_{[n-j+1]}^{(2)}) \leq \sum_{j=1}^{n} \phi(x_j^{(1)}, x_j^{(2)}) \tag{1}$$

and

$$\sum_{j=1}^{n} \phi(x_j^{(1)}, \ldots, x_j^{(m)}) \leq \sum_{j=1}^{n} \phi(x_{[j]}^{(1)}, \ldots, x_{[j]}^{(m)}) \tag{2}$$

if and only if ϕ is L-superadditive.

Notice that the difference between this result and C.1 and C.3 is that here no monotonicity condition is imposed on ϕ.

The proof of E.1 is similar to the preceding proofs. With $m = 2$, the condition is shown to be necessary by taking $n = 2$. It is also easily shown to be sufficient when $n = 2$. For general n, start with the pairs

$$(x_{[1]}^{(1)}, x_1^{(2)}), \ldots, (x_{[n]}^{(1)}, x_n^{(2)}).$$

Repeatedly interchange two of the $x_i^{(2)}$ to transform the pairs to

$$(x_{[1]}^{(1)}, x_{[1]}^{(2)}), \ldots, (x_{[n]}^{(1)}, x_{[n]}^{(2)}).$$

Then, at each interchange, $\sum_j \phi(x_{[j]}^{(1)}, x_{\pi(j)}^{(2)})$ increases because of the inequality with $n = 2$. A similar argument proves the left-hand inequality. However, Day (1972) and more explicitly Borell (1973) show that (1) and (2) with $m = 2$ are equivalent. Borell also gives a proof of E.1 and $m = 2$. Inequality (2) is proved by Derman, Lieberman, and Ross (1972).

E.1.a. If ψ is convex, then

$$\sum_{j=1}^{n} \psi(x_{[j]}^{(1)} + x_{[n-j+1]}^{(2)}) \leq \sum_{j=1}^{n} \psi(x_j^{(1)} + x_j^{(2)}) \leq \sum_{j=1}^{n} \psi(x_{[j]}^{(1)} + x_{[j]}^{(2)}),$$

and the inequalities are reversed if ψ is concave.

This results from E.1 and D.4. With $\psi(z) = \log z, z \geq 0$, these inequalities yield inequality (6) of A.5.

E.1.b. If ψ satisfies

$$\psi'(z) + z\psi''(z) \geq 0 \quad \text{for all} \quad z,$$

then

$$\sum_{j=1}^{n} \psi(x_{[j]}^{(1)} x_{[n-j+1]}^{(2)}) \leq \sum_{j=1}^{n} \psi(x_j^{(1)} x_j^{(2)}) \leq \sum_{j=1}^{n} \psi(x_{[j]}^{(1)} x_{[j]}^{(2)}).$$

This follows directly from E.1 and D.5. With $\psi(z) = z$, inequality (5) of A.5 is obtained.

An Inequality of Fan and Lorentz

Companion results to those of Lorentz (1953) were obtained by Fan and Lorentz (1954). These important results can be stated in a discrete setting similar to that of E.1.

E.2. Proposition (Fan and Lorentz, 1954). Let $\phi: \mathscr{R}^m \to \mathscr{R}$ be an L-superadditive function that is convex in each argument separately.

E. Inequalities Without Majorization 227

If $x^{(i)} \prec y^{(i)}$ on $\mathscr{D}$, $i = 1, \ldots, m$, then

$$\sum_{j=1}^{n} \phi(x_j^{(1)}, \ldots, x_j^{(m)}) \leq \sum_{j=1}^{n} \phi(y_j^{(1)}, \ldots, y_j^{(m)}). \tag{3}$$

With the additional assumption that ϕ is increasing in each argument, a stronger conclusion than (3) is obtained in 5.A.4.

Proof of E.2. Exactly as in the proof of 5.A.4, it is sufficient to prove the result for $m = 2$. The remainder of the proof given here is due to Rinott (1973).

Let

$$\Phi(u^{(1)}, u^{(2)}) = \begin{bmatrix} \phi(u_1^{(1)}, u_1^{(2)}) & \cdots & \phi(u_1^{(1)}, u_n^{(2)}) \\ \vdots & & \vdots \\ \phi(u_n^{(1)}, u_1^{(2)}) & \cdots & \phi(u_n^{(1)}, u_n^{(2)}) \end{bmatrix},$$

and observe that (2) of E.1 can be written in the form

$$\operatorname{tr} \Pi \, \Phi(u^{(1)}, u^{(2)}) \leq \operatorname{tr} \Phi(u_{\downarrow}^{(1)}, u_{\downarrow}^{(2)})$$

for all permutation matrices Π, where tr denotes trace. Because the trace is a linear function, it follows with the aid of Birkhoff's theorem 2.A.2 that for all doubly stochastic matrices P,

$$\operatorname{tr} P \, \Phi(u^{(1)}, u^{(2)}) \leq \operatorname{tr} \Phi(u_{\downarrow}^{(1)}, u_{\downarrow}^{(2)}). \tag{4}$$

Because $x^{(1)} \prec y^{(1)}$ and $x^{(2)} \prec y^{(2)}$, it follows that there exist doubly stochastic matrices Q and R such that

$$x^{(1)} = y^{(2)} Q, \qquad x^{(2)} = y^{(2)} R.$$

By first using the convexity of ϕ in each argument and then using (4), it follows that

$$\operatorname{tr} \Phi(x^{(1)}, x^{(2)}) = \operatorname{tr} \Phi(y^{(1)} Q, y^{(2)} R) \leq \operatorname{tr} Q R' \Phi(y^{(1)}, y^{(2)})$$

$$\leq \operatorname{tr} \Phi(y_{\downarrow}^{(1)}, y_{\downarrow}^{(2)}) = \operatorname{tr} \Phi(y^{(1)}, y^{(2)}).$$

But this inequality is (3) with $m = 2$. ||

The various examples of Section D, modified by dropping monotonicity, apply to provide examples here. Thus from D.4 one sees that for any convex function ψ,

$$\sum_{1}^{n} \psi(x_i - y_i) \leq \sum_{1}^{n} \psi(x_{[i]} - y_{(i)}). \tag{5}$$

Inequality (2) was given by Rinott (1973), who noted the interesting special case

$$\sum_{i=1}^{n}|x_i - y_i|^p \leq \sum_{i=1}^{n}|x_{[i]} - y_{(i)}|^p, \qquad p \geq 1. \tag{6}$$

A direct proof of (5) and (6) can be obtained using Proposition 3.C.1 [$\Sigma\psi(z_i)$ is Schur-convex when ψ is convex] together with the second majorization of A.1.c.

Equations (5) and (6) remain valid if, instead of n, the upper limit of the summations is any $k \in \{1,\ldots,n\}$.

E.3. For any convex function ψ and $x, y \in \mathscr{R}^n$,

$$(\psi(x_1-y_1),\ldots,\psi(x_n-y_n)) \prec_w (\psi(x_{[1]}-y_{(1)}),\ldots,\psi(x_{[n]}-y_{(n)})). \tag{7}$$

Proof. Clearly, $x \prec x_\downarrow$ and $-y \prec -(y_\uparrow)$. Because $x_\downarrow$ and $-(y_\uparrow)$ are similarly ordered, it follows from A.1.b that $x - y \prec x_\downarrow - y_\uparrow$. Equation (7) is then a consequence of 5.A.1. ||

F   A Relative Arrangement Partial Order

Where only two vectors are involved, the rearrangement inequalities of preceding sections have the form

$$\phi(x_\uparrow, y_\downarrow) = \phi(x_\downarrow, y_\uparrow) \leq \phi(x,y) \leq \phi(x_\downarrow, y_\downarrow) = \phi(x_\uparrow, y_\uparrow).$$

To extend these inequalities, it is useful to define a partial ordering $\leq^a$ of pairs of vectors which relates only to their relative arrangement and satisfies

$$(x_\uparrow, y_\downarrow) \leq^a (x,y) \leq^a (x_\uparrow, y_\uparrow).$$

Then the identification of the functions of two vector arguments that preserve the ordering $\leq^a$ will lead to a variety of inequalities, and will permit a variety of new comparisons. Such a partial ordering $\leq^a$ is implicit in the work of Hollander, Proschan, and Sethuraman (1977). One way to define this ordering is to make use of a particular partial ordering of permutations, and for this, some notation is convenient.

Following Mirsky (1955a, p. 256), the permutation π of $\lambda_1,\ldots,\lambda_n$ which replaces λ_j by μ_j, $j = 1,\ldots,n$, is denoted by

$$\pi = \begin{pmatrix} \lambda_1,\ldots,\lambda_n \\ \mu_1,\ldots,\mu_n \end{pmatrix}.$$

Notice that
$$\begin{pmatrix} \lambda_{k_1}, \ldots, \lambda_{k_n} \\ \mu_{k_1}, \ldots, \mu_{k_n} \end{pmatrix} = \begin{pmatrix} \lambda_1, \ldots, \lambda_n \\ \mu_1, \ldots, \mu_n \end{pmatrix}.$$

In case $\lambda_1, \ldots, \lambda_n$ are real numbers, it is consequently possible to assume without loss of generality that $\lambda_1 \leq \cdots \leq \lambda_n$. This suggests writing π more compactly as

$$\pi = \pi(\lambda_1, \ldots, \lambda_n) = (\mu_1, \ldots, \mu_n).$$

Of course, the permutation π corresponds to a permutation matrix Π such that $\mu = \lambda\Pi$. Both notations are useful and preference depends upon the context.

For permutations $\pi^{(1)} = (\mu_1^{(1)}, \ldots, \mu_n^{(1)})$ and $\pi^{(2)} = (\mu_1^{(2)}, \ldots, \mu_n^{(2)})$, write $\pi^{(1)} \leq^b \pi^{(2)}$ to mean that $\pi^{(2)}$ can be reached from $\pi^{(1)}$ by successive interchanges, each of which corrects an inversion (of the natural order). In this ordering, $(\mu_1, \ldots, \mu_n)$ is said to *immediately precede* $(v_1, \ldots, v_n)$, written $\mu <^P v$, if for some indices i and j where $1 \leq i < j \leq n$,

$$v_i < v_j, \qquad v_i = \mu_j, \qquad v_j = \mu_i, \qquad \mu_l = v_l, \qquad l \neq i, j.$$

Then $\pi^{(1)} \leq^b \pi^{(2)}$ if $\pi^{(1)} = \pi^{(2)}$ or if there exists a finite chain $\psi^{(1)}, \ldots, \psi^{(k)}$ of permutations such that

$$\pi^{(1)} <^P \psi^{(1)} <^P \cdots <^P \psi^{(k)} <^P \pi^{(2)}.$$

The ordering $\leq^b$ was defined by Sobel (1954), by Savage (1957), and by Lehmann (1966). Lehmann also considered another ordering of permutations. Yet another ordering of permutations is considered by Yanagimoto and Okamoto (1969), who impose the requirement $j = i + 1$ in the above definition. In much of what follows, this more restrictive ordering could replace the ordering $\leq^b$.

As already indicated, the partial ordering $\leq^b$ of permutations has been introduced above as a step toward defining the relative-arrangement partial order $\leq^a$ of pairs of vectors. Because we are interested in relative arrangement only, an appropriate definition must satisfy

$$(x\Pi, y\Pi) \stackrel{a}{=} (x, y)$$

in the sense that $(x, y) \leq^a (x\Pi, y\Pi) \leq^a (x, y)$ for all permutation matrices Π. Consequently, in defining $(x, y) \leq^a (u, v)$, we may as well assume that $x = x_\uparrow$, $u = u_\uparrow$. For purposes of extending rearrangement inequalities, $(x, y) \leq^a (u, v)$ can be meaningful only if u is a permutation of x and v is a permutation of y. In this case and if $x = x_\uparrow$, $u = u_\uparrow (= x_\uparrow)$, then $(x, y) \leq^a (u, v)$ if and only if $y \leq^b v$. More precisely,

$$(x, y) \leq^a (u, v)$$

if u is a permutation of x, v is a permutation of y, and if there exist permutations $\pi^{(1)}$ and $\pi^{(2)}$ such that

$$\pi^{(1)}(x) = x_\uparrow, \qquad \pi^{(2)}(u) = u_\uparrow (= x_\uparrow), \qquad \text{and} \qquad \pi^{(1)}(y) \leq^b \pi^{(2)}(v).$$

In case the components of x (or u) are not unique, the permutations $\pi^{(1)}$ and $\pi^{(2)}$ are not unique. Then, it is possible to have $(x, y) \stackrel{a}{=} (u, v)$ even though, for a particular $\pi^{(1)}$ and $\pi^{(2)}$, $\pi^{(1)}(y) \neq \pi^{(2)}(v)$.

F.1. $(x, y) \stackrel{a}{=} (u, v)$, that is, $(x, y) \leq^a (u, v)$ and $(x, y) \geq^a (u, v)$, if and only if there exists a permutation π such that $x = \pi(u)$, $y = \pi(v)$. This observation is a direct consequence of the definition.

F.2. If $(x, y) \leq^a (u, v)$, then there exists a finite number of vectors $z^{(1)}, \ldots, z^{(k)}$ such that

(i) $(x, y) \stackrel{a}{=} (x_\uparrow, z^{(1)}) \leq^a \cdots \leq^a (x_\uparrow, z^{(k)}) \stackrel{a}{=} (u, v)$,

(ii) $z^{(i-1)}$ can be obtained from $z^{(i)}$ by an interchange of two components of $z^{(i)}$, the first of which is less than the second.

This result follows from F.1 and is the genesis of the ordering $\leq^a$ in the relation $<^p$.

A function g of two vector arguments that preserves the ordering $\leq^a$ is called *arrangement-increasing* (AI). If the components of x and y are fixed apart from order, $g(x; y)$ takes on a maximum value when x and y are similarly ordered and a minimum value when they are oppositely ordered. It is by means of arrangement-increasing functions that extensions of rearrangement inequalities are obtained.

Arrangement-increasing functions are said to be "decreasing in transposition" by Hollander, Proschan, and Sethuraman (1977). We have not used their terminology here because we prefer not to refer to order-preserving functions as "decreasing."

F.3. If g is arrangement-increasing, then g is *permutation invariant* in the sense that

$$g(x; y) = g(x\Pi; y\Pi) \qquad \text{for all permutations matrices } \Pi. \qquad (1)$$

F. A Relative Arrangement Partial Order 231

Any natural domain $\mathscr{L} \subset \mathscr{R}^n \times \mathscr{R}^n$ for an AI function has the property that

$$(x,y) \in \mathscr{L} \text{ implies } (x\Pi^{(1)}, y\Pi^{(2)}) \in \mathscr{L}$$

for all permutation matrices $\Pi^{(1)}$ and $\Pi^{(2)}$. (2)

In particular, g may be defined on $\mathscr{R}^n \times \mathscr{R}^n$ or it may be defined only on a set of the form

$$A(x_\downarrow, y_\downarrow) = \{(u,v) : u_\downarrow = x_\downarrow, v_\downarrow = y_\downarrow\}.$$

F.4. Suppose that $\mathscr{L}$ is a subset of $\mathscr{R}^n \times \mathscr{R}^n$ with property (2). If for each $(x_\downarrow, y_\downarrow) \in \mathscr{L}$, $g_{x_\downarrow, y_\downarrow}$ is an AI function defined on $A(x_\downarrow, y_\downarrow)$, then g, defined on $\mathscr{L}$ by

$$g(x;y) = g_{x_\downarrow, y_\downarrow}(x;y),$$

is an AI function defined on $\mathscr{L}$.

Because the condition of being AI involves no connections between behavior on different sets of the form $A(x_\downarrow, y_\downarrow)$, it follows that such functions can be badly behaved. For example, they need not be measurable.

There are two basic results involving compositions that are useful in the study of arrangement-increasing functions.

F.5. If $g_1, \ldots, g_k$ are AI functions on a set $\mathscr{L}$ satisfying (2), and if $h : \mathscr{R}^k \to \mathscr{R}$ is increasing in each argument, then the composition $h(g_1, \ldots, g_k)$ is an AI function on $\mathscr{L}$.

F.5.a. If g is an AI function defined on a set $\mathscr{L}$ satisfying (2), then the indicator function $\widetilde{g}(x,y)$ of the set

$$\widetilde{g}(x;y) = I_{\{(x,y):g(x,y)>t\}}(x;y)$$

is AI on $\mathscr{L}$.

This fact is obtainable from F.5 with $k = 1$, $h(u) = 1$, $u > t$, $h(u) = 0$, $u \leq t$.

F.6. If g is AI on $\mathscr{R}^n \times \mathscr{R}^n$ and if $\phi : \mathscr{R} \to \mathscr{R}$, $\psi : \mathscr{R} \to \mathscr{R}$ are monotone in the same direction, then g^* defined by

$$g^*(x;y) = g(\phi(x_1), \ldots, \phi(x_n); \psi(y_1), \ldots, \psi(y_n))$$

is AI on $\mathscr{L}^* = \{(u,v) : u = (\phi(x_1), \ldots, \phi(x_n)), v = (\psi(y_1), \ldots, \psi(y_n))$ for some $(x,y) \in \mathscr{L}\}$.

F.6.a. If the hypotheses of F.6 hold with the modification that ϕ and ψ are monotone in opposite directions, then $-g^*$ is AI on $\mathscr{L}^*$.

Of course, analogs of F.5 and F.6 hold for order-preserving functions whatever the partial ordering might be.

The Convex Cone of Arrangement-Increasing Functions

Let the set $\mathscr{L} \in \mathscr{R}^n \times \mathscr{R}^n$ satisfy (2). From particular cases of F.5 it follows that the class of arrangement-increasing functions defined on $\mathscr{L}$ is a convex cone. This convex cone has a reasonably simple structure that can be described by first supposing that the set $\mathscr{L} = A(1, 2, \ldots, n; 1, 2, \ldots, n) \equiv A$. For $(x, y) \in A$, let

$$B(x, y) = \{(u, v) : (x, y) \leq^{\mathrm{a}} (u, v)\}.$$

The indicator function $I_{B(x,y)}$ of $B(x, y)$ is clearly arrangement-increasing. Moreover, for any subset C of A,

$$I_C = \max_{(x,y) \in C} I_{B(x,y)}$$

is arrangement-increasing. Functions of the form $\alpha I_C, \alpha > 0$, constitute the extreme rays of the convex cone of AI functions defined on A. Because there are finitely many functions of the form I_C, the cone is finitely generated. It would be interesting to count the number of distinct functions of the form I_C for $n = 2, 3, \ldots$.

For any (x, y), the AI functions defined on $A(x; y)$ can be obtained from those defined on A by means of F.6 using functions ϕ and ψ such that $\phi(i) = x_{(i)}$ and $\psi(i) = y_{(i)}$, $i = 1, 2, \ldots, n$. The AI functions for more general domains are then obtainable by using F.4.

Functions g that are arrangement-decreasing in the sense that $-g$ is AI also form a convex cone. The common boundary of these convex cones consists of functions g having the property that

$$g(x; y) = g(x\Pi_1; y\Pi_2) \text{ for all permutation matrices } \Pi_1 \text{ and } \Pi_2.$$

Identification of Arrangement-Increasing Functions

The above characterizations are not particularly useful in checking whether or not a given function is arrangement-increasing. Fortunately, there is a way of doing this that is usually convenient.

F.7. Proposition. Let $\mathscr{L} \subset \mathscr{R}^n \times \mathscr{R}^n$ satisfy (2). A function g defined on $\mathscr{L}$ is AI if and only if

(i) g is permutation invariant in the sense of (1) (see F.3), and

(ii) $(x, y) \in \mathscr{Z}$, $x_1 < x_2$, $y_1 < y_2$ implies
$$g(x; y) \geq g(x; y_2, y_1, y_3, \ldots, y_n).$$

This characterization follows from F.1 and F.2 and is used by Hollander, Proschan, and Sethuraman (1977).

Examples of Arrangement-Increasing Functions

The following examples of AI functions are all due to Hollander, Proschan, and Sethuraman (1977).

F.8. If g has the form $g(u; v) = \phi(u + v)$, $u, v \in \mathscr{R}^n$, then g is AI on $\mathscr{R}^n \times \mathscr{R}^n$ if and only if ϕ is Schur-convex on $\mathscr{R}^n$.

Proof. By virtue of 2.B.1 and of F.7, it is sufficient to prove this for $n = 2$. By A.1.c, $x \prec y$ on $\mathscr{R}^2$ if and only if $x_\uparrow$ and $y_\uparrow$ have the form
$$(x_{(1)}, x_{(2)}) = (r_2 + s_1, r_1 + s_2), \qquad (y_{(1)}, y_{(2)}) = (r_1 + s_1, r_2 + s_2),$$
where $r_1 < r_2, s_1 < s_2$.

If g is AI on $\mathscr{R}^n \times \mathscr{R}^n$, it follows that

(i) $g(r_1, r_2; s_2, s_1) = g(r_2, r_1; s_1, s_2)$
$\leq g(r_1, r_2; s_1, s_2) = g(r_2, r_1; s_2, s_1);$

that is,

(ii) $\phi(r_1 + s_2, r_2 + s_1) = \phi(r_2 + s_1, r_1 + s_2)$
$\leq \phi(r_1 + s_1, r_2 + s_2) = \phi(r_2 + s_2, r_1 + s_1).$

Consequently, ϕ is Schur-convex on $\mathscr{R}^2$. Conversely, if ϕ is Schur-convex on $\mathscr{R}^2$, then (ii) holds whenever $r_1 < r_2$, $s_1 < s_2$, i.e., (i) holds, so g is AI on $\mathscr{R}^2$. ||

Extensions of this result are discussed in Karlin and Rinott (1988). Du and Hwang (1990) provide an alternative proof of F.8 (their Theorem 2) and make use of it in the context of reliability.

F.8.a. If g has the form $g(u; v) = \phi(u - v)$ for all $u, v \in \mathscr{R}^n$, then g is AI on $\mathscr{R}^n \times \mathscr{R}^n$ if and only if ϕ is Schur-concave on $\mathscr{R}^n$.

The proof of the result is similar to the proof of F.8. Alternatively, F.8.a follows from F.8 with the aid of F.11 ahead.

F.9. If g has the form $g(u; v) = \sum_1^n \phi(u_i, v_i)$, then g is AI if and only if ϕ is L-superadditive.

234   6. Rearrangements and Majorization

This result is immediate upon writing out the condition that g is AI.

F.9.a. If g has the form $g(u;v) = \prod_1^n \phi(u_i, v_i)$, then g is AI if and only if ϕ is totally positive of order 2.

This result is also immediate upon writing out the condition that g is AI. It is also obtainable from F.9 and F.5.

Additional Operations Preserving the Arrangement-Increasing Property

Propositions F.5 and F.6 provide examples of operations on AI functions that preserve the AI property. Several additional results of this kind are known.

F.10. If g_1 and g_2 are positive AI functions defined on a set $\mathscr{X}$ satisfying (2), then the product $g_1 g_2$ is AI on $\mathscr{X}$.

Proof. If g_1 and g_2 are AI, it follows from F.5 that $\log g_1 + \log g_2 = \log g_1 g_2$ is AI, and again by F.5, this implies $g_1 g_2$ is AI. ||

F.11. If g is an AI function, then the function h defined by

$$h(x;y) = -g(x;-y)$$

is AI.

Proof. This is a special case of F.6.a. ||

The following theorem says that the convolution of AI functions is again AI.

F.12. Theorem (Hollander, Proschan, and Sethuraman, 1977). Let μ be a measure defined on the Borel subsets on $\mathscr{R}^n$ with the property that for all Borel sets $A \subset \mathscr{R}^n$, and all permutation matrices Π, $\mu(A) = \mu(A\Pi)$, where $A\Pi = \{y : y = x\Pi \text{ for some } x \in A\}$. If g_i is AI on $\mathscr{R}^n \times \mathscr{R}^n$, $i = 1, 2$, then the convolution g defined by

$$g(x;z) = \int g_1(x;y) g_2(y;z) \mu(dy)$$

is AI on $\mathscr{R}^n \times \mathscr{R}^n$, provided the integral exists.

Proof. First note that

$$g(x\Pi; z\Pi) = \int g_1(x\Pi; y) \, g_2(y; z\Pi) \, \mu(dy)$$

$$= \int g_1(x\Pi; y\Pi) \, g_2(y\Pi; z\Pi) \, \mu(dy\Pi^{-1})$$

F. A Relative Arrangement Partial Order   235

$$= \int g_1(x;y)\, g_2(y;z)\, \mu(dy)$$
$$= g(x;z)$$

because of the permutation invariance of μ and because g_1 and g_2 are AI.

Let Π^0 be the permutation for which $z\Pi^0 = (z_2, z_1, z_3, \ldots, z_n)$ for all z. By virtue of F.7, it is sufficient to show that

$$0 \leq g(x;z) - g(x;z\Pi^0) = \int \left[g_1(x;y)g_2(y;z) - g_1(x;y)g_2(y;z\Pi^0)\right]\mu(dy).$$

Break the region of integration into the regions $y_1 < y_2$ and $y_1 \geq y_2$ and make a change of variables in the second region to obtain

$$g(x;z) - g(x;z\Pi^0)$$
$$= \int_{y_1 < y_2} \left[g_1(x;y)\, g_2(y;z) - g_1(x;y)\, g_2(y;z\Pi^0)\right.$$
$$\left. + g_1(x;y\Pi^0)\, g_2(y\Pi^0;z) - g_1(x;y\Pi^0)\, g_2(y\Pi^0;z\Pi^0)\right]\, \mu(dy)$$
$$= \int_{y_1 < y_2} \left[g_1(x;y)\, g_2(y;z) - g_1(x;y)\, g_2(y;z\Pi^0)\right.$$
$$\left. + g_1(x;y\Pi^0)\, g_2(y;z\Pi^0) - g_1(x;y\Pi^0)\, g_2(y;z)\right]\, \mu(dy)$$
$$= \int_{y_1 < y_2} \left[g_1(x;y) - g_1(x;y\Pi^0)\right]\left[g_2(y;z) - g_2(y;z\Pi^0)\right]\mu(dy).$$

Because g_1 and g_2 are AI, the integrand is nonnegative, so g is AI. ||

As noted by Hollander, Proschan, and Sethuraman (1977), 3.J.1 can be obtained as a corollary to F.12:

F.12.a. Corollary. If ϕ_i is Schur-concave on $\mathscr{R}^n$, $i = 1, 2$, then the convolution h defined by

$$h(x) = \int \phi_1(x-y)\phi_2(y)\, dy$$

is Schur-concave on $\mathscr{R}^n$, provided the integral exists.

Proof. This is immediate from F.12 and F.8.a. ||

Application to Rank Order Statistics

The rank order corresponding to n distinct numbers $x_1, \ldots, x_n$ is the vector $r = (r_1, \ldots, r_n)$, where r_i is the number of x_j's $\leq x_i$. When the x's are not distinct, the average rank is used. More precisely,

$$r_i = \frac{1}{2} + \sum_{\alpha=1}^{n} I(x_i, x_\alpha),$$

where $I(a,b) = 1$ if $a > b$, $I(a,b) = \frac{1}{2}$ if $a = b$, and $I(a,b) = 0$ if $a < b$.

For random variables $X_1, \ldots, X_n$, the corresponding random rank orders are denoted by $R_1, \ldots, R_n$.

F.12.b. Proposition (Hollander, Proschan, and Sethuraman, 1977). If $X_1, \ldots, X_n$ have an AI joint density function $f(x_1, \ldots, x_n; \lambda_1, \ldots, \lambda_n)$ on $\mathscr{R}^n \times \mathscr{R}^n$, and if $R_1, \ldots, R_n$ are the rank orders, then

$$\psi(r, \lambda) = P_\lambda\{R_1 = r_1, \ldots, R_n = r_n\}$$

is AI on $\mathscr{R}^n \times \mathscr{R}^n$.

Proof. This result follows directly from F.12 after noting that the function

$$\phi(x_1, \ldots, x_n; r_1, \ldots, r_n) = \begin{cases} 1 & \text{if } x_i \text{ has rank } r_i, \quad i = 1, \ldots, n, \\ 0 & \text{otherwise} \end{cases}$$

is an AI function. ||

The special case that $X_1, \ldots, X_n$ are independent and X_i has a density $g_i(x, \lambda_i)$ that is totally positive of order 2 (TP$_2$) in x and $\lambda_i \in \mathscr{R}$ (Definition 18.A.1) is obtained by Savage (1957). He also obtains a stronger result for the exponential class of densities

$$g(x, \lambda_i) = a(\lambda_i) h(x) \exp(\lambda_i x), \qquad i = 1, \ldots, n.$$

This family is TP$_2$, and hence is AI, so that F.12.b applies. Savage (1957) shows that for $\lambda_i = i\lambda$, the weaker hypothesis

$$\sum_{1}^{i} r'_\alpha \geq \sum_{1}^{i} r_\alpha, \qquad i = 1, \ldots, n,$$

with strict inequality for some i, implies that

$$P_\lambda\{R_1 = r_1, \ldots, R_n = r_n\} > P_\lambda\{R_1 = r'_1, \ldots, R_n = r'_n\}.$$

It is interesting to note that without characterizing the order-preserving functions for the ordering $\leq^a$, Savage (1957) provided a catalog of some order-preserving functions used as test statistics in nonparametric analysis. That these are AI functions on $\mathscr{R}^n \times \mathscr{R}^n$ can be verified directly from F.7:

(i) $T_1(1,\ldots,n;r_1,\ldots,r_n) = \sum_1^n i r_i;$

(ii) $T_2(1,\ldots,n;r_1,\ldots,r_n) = \prod_1^n (r_1 + \cdots + r_i)^{-1};$

(iii) $T_3(1,\ldots,n;r_1,\ldots,r_n) = \sum_{i,j=1}^n d(r_i, r_j),$

where $d(a,b) = 1$ if $a < b$, $d(a,b) = 0$ if $a \geq b$;

(iv) $T_4(1,\ldots,n;r_1,\ldots,r_n) = \sum_{n+1}^{2n} d(n, r_i);$

(v) $T(E_1,\ldots,E_n;r_1,\ldots,r_n) = \sum_1^n E_i r_i,$

where E_i is the expected value of the ith smallest observation in a sample of size n from a standard normal distribution.

Hollander, Proschan, and Sethuraman (1977) note that if $B_1,\ldots,B_n$ are real numbers ordered such that $B_1 \leq \cdots \leq B_n$, then

$$T(B_1,\ldots,B_n;r_1,\ldots,r_n) = \sum_1^m B_{r_i}, \quad m = 1,\ldots,n,$$

is AI. The choices $B_j = j$ and $B_j = E_j$ yield (i) and (v).

F.12.c (Savage, 1957; Hollander, Proschan, and Sethuraman, 1977). If $T(x,r)$ is AI and $X_1,\ldots,X_n$ have an AI joint density $f(x,\lambda)$, then

$$h_a(x;\lambda) = P_\lambda\{T(x;R) \geq a\}$$

is an AI function.

This is another direct application of F.12. From F.12.c it follows that if $\pi \leq^b \pi'$, $x_1 \leq \cdots \leq x_n$, and $T(x;r)$ is AI, then $T(x;R)$ is stochastically larger when $X_1,\ldots,X_n$ has an AI distribution with parameter $\lambda_{\pi'(1)},\ldots,\lambda_{\pi'(n)}$ than when the parameter is $\lambda_{\pi(1)},\ldots,\lambda_{\pi(n)}$.

Application to Rearrangement Inequalities

Notice that F.9 and E.1 can be combined as follows: For functions $g: \mathscr{R}^n \times \mathscr{R}^n \to \mathscr{R}$ of the form $g(x,y) = \sum_{j=1}^n \phi(x_j, y_j)$,

$g(x, y) \leq g(x_\downarrow, y_\downarrow)$ for all x, y, implies ϕ is L-superadditive. If ϕ is L-superadditive, then g is AI.

Of course, F.9 leads to a variety of inequalities not obtainable from E.1.

Although F.9 does not directly generalize C.1 or C.4, it is easy to provide such a generalization using the ordering $\leq^{\mathrm{a}}$.

F.13. Theorem. Let ϕ be a monotone L-superadditive function. If $(x, y) \leq^{\mathrm{a}} (u, v)$, then

$$(\phi(x_1, y_1), \ldots, \phi(x_n, y_n)) \prec_{\mathrm{w}} (\phi(u_1, v_1), \ldots \phi(u_n, v_n)).$$

Proof. Define $T_k(x; y)$ to be the sum of the k largest of $\phi(x_i, y_i)$, $i = 1, \ldots, n$. To show that T_k is AI, it is sufficient to show that T_k satisfies conditions (i) and (ii) of F.7. Condition (i) is trivial; to verify (ii), suppose that $x_1 < x_2$, $y_1 < y_2$. Then,

$$(\phi(x_1, y_1) + \phi(x_2, y_2)) \geq \phi(x_1, y_2) + \phi(x_2, y_1)$$

since ϕ is L-superadditive. Consequently, T_k satisfies (ii) of F.7. ||

There is a companion to F.13 which extends B.1 and B.2.

F.14. Theorem. Let $\phi(x_1, x_2) = f_1(x_1) + f_2(x_2)$, where f_1 and f_2 are monotone in the same direction. If $(x, y) \leq^{\mathrm{a}} (u, v)$, then

$$(\phi(x_1, y_1), \ldots, \phi(x_n, y_n)) \prec (\phi(u_1, v_1), \ldots, \phi(u_n, v_n)).$$

Proof. By virtue of F.13, it is necessary only to show that

$$\sum_1^n \phi(x_i, y_i) = \sum_1^n \phi(u_i, v_i).$$

But because u is a permutation of x and v is a permutation of y, this is immediate. ||

Preservation of Schur-Convexity

In Section 3.J, two theorems are given concerning integral transforms that preserve Schur-convexity. One of these, 3.J.1, is generalized by F.12. Here a generalization of 3.J.2 is given after some required definitions.

Let Λ and T be semigroups in $\mathscr{R}$ (with addition as the operation). A σ-finite measure μ which assigns measure 0 to the complement of T is said to be *invariant* if

$$\mu(A \cap T) = \mu((A + x) \cap T)$$

for each Borel set $A \subset \mathscr{R}$ and each $x \in T$. A measurable function $\phi : T^n \times \Lambda^n \to \mathscr{R}$ is said to have the *semigroup property* with respect to μ if the integral

$$\int \phi(x-y, \lambda^{(1)})\phi(y, \lambda^{(2)}) \, d\mu(y_1) \cdots d\mu(y_n)$$

over the region $\{(x,y) : y \in T^n, x - y \in T^n\}$ exists and is equal to $\phi(x, \lambda^{(1)} + \lambda^{(2)})$.

F.15. Theorem (Hollander, Proschan, and Sethuraman, 1977). Let $\phi : T^n \times \Lambda^n \to \mathscr{R}$ be an AI function having the semigroup property with respect to the invariant measure μ. If $f : T^n \to \mathscr{R}$ is Schur-convex, then the function

$$h(\lambda) = \int_{T^n} \phi(x, \lambda) f(x) \, d\mu(x_1) \cdots d\mu(x_n)$$

is Schur-convex on Λ^n.

Proof. Let $\mathscr{T} = \{x, y : x \in T^n, y \in T^n, x - y \in T^n\}$. Then

$$h(\lambda^{(1)} + \lambda^{(2)})$$
$$= \int_{T^n} \phi(x, \lambda^{(1)} + \lambda^{(2)}) f(x) \, d\mu(x_1) \cdots d\mu(x_n)$$
$$= \int_{\mathscr{T}} \phi(x-y, \lambda^{(1)}) \phi(y, \lambda^{(2)}) f(x) \prod_1^n d\mu(y_i) \prod_1^n d\mu(x_i).$$

Now let $z = x - y$, so that by the invariance of μ,

$$h(\lambda^{(1)} + \lambda^{(2)})$$
$$= \int_{T^n} \phi(y, \lambda^{(2)}) \left[\int_{T^n} \phi(z, \lambda^{(1)}) f(y+z) \prod_1^n d\mu(z_i) \right] \prod_1^n d\mu(y_i).$$

Because $\phi(z, \lambda^{(1)})$ is AI in $\lambda^{(1)}$ and z, $f(z+y)$ is AI in z and y (F.8), the inner integral here is AI by F.12. By a second application of F.12, $h(\lambda^{(1)} + \lambda^{(2)})$ is AI in $\lambda^{(1)}$ and $\lambda^{(2)}$. Consequently, h is Schur-convex by F.8. ‖

As remarked in Section 3.J, Karlin and Rinott (1988) provide further extensions of results of this genre in the context of generalized total positivity.

Part II
Mathematical Applications

7
Combinatorial Analysis

Majorization arises in several related topics of a basically combinatorial nature, namely, in graph theory, the theory of network flows, and the study of incidence matrices. As is to be expected, results can often be stated equivalently in the language of each discipline. Some of this language is reviewed in Section A. An excellent discussion of matrix theory and graph theory is given by Brualdi (2006). In combinatorial analysis, majorization is almost always in integers. See 5.D.

A Some Preliminaries on Graphs, Incidence Matrices, and Networks

A *directed graph* $G = (X, U)$ consists of a nonempty set X of points, called *vertices* or *nodes*, and a set U of ordered pairs (x, y) where $x, y \in X$. The pairs (x, y) are called *arcs* or *edges* of the graph. We are concerned only with finite graphs, i.e., graphs with a finite number of vertices, and we often refer to G as a "graph" rather than as a "directed graph."

Corresponding to each finite graph $G = (X, U)$ is an associated incidence matrix. An *incidence matrix* is a matrix in which each entry

7. Combinatorial Analysis

is either 0 or 1. For a given ordering $x_1, x_2, \ldots, x_n$ of the points in X, the matrix $A = (a_{ij})$ with

$$a_{ij} = \begin{cases} 1 & \text{if } (x_i, x_j) \in U, \\ 0 & \text{if } (x_i, x_j) \notin U \end{cases}$$

is called the associated *incidence matrix*. For example, if $n = 4$ and $U = \{(x_1, x_2), (x_1, x_4), (x_4, x_2), (x_4, x_3)\}$ as in Fig. 1, then the associated incidence matrix is given by

$$A = \begin{bmatrix} 0 & 1 & 0 & 1 \\ 0 & 0 & 0 & 0 \\ 0 & 0 & 0 & 0 \\ 0 & 1 & 1 & 0 \end{bmatrix}.$$

Of course, U is completely determined by the matrix A.

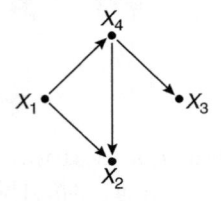

Figure 1. A directed graph of four points.

In network theory, one has a finite directed graph $G = (X, U)$ without loops [i.e., there are no arcs of the form (x, x)]. Associated with each arc (x, y) is a nonnegative number $c(x, y)$ called the *capacity* of the arc. In this context, the graph itself is called a *network*.

A "flow" in the network is represented by a function f defined on the arcs of G; $f(x, y)$ is thought of as the flow from x to y along the arc (x, y). In keeping with the directional nature of the graph, it is required that $f(x, y) \geq 0$. Additionally, the flow $f(x, y)$ may not exceed the capacity $c(x, y)$ of the arc.

For a given flow, a vertex of the graph is classified as a "source," "intermediate vertex," or "sink" depending on whether the total flow issuing from the vertex is greater than, equal to, or less than the flow into the vertex. Often, there is only one source, s, and only one sink, t.

To make this more precise, let $A(x) = \{y : (x, y) \in U\}$ be the set of vertices at which arcs emanating from x terminate, and let $B(x) = \{y : (y, x) \in U\}$ be the set of vertices from which arcs issue to terminate at x. A real-valued function f defined on U is called a *flow from s to t* if

$$0 \leq f(x, y) \leq c(x, y) \quad \text{for all} \quad (x, y) \in U,$$

and

$$\sum_{y\in A(x)} f(x,y) - \sum_{y\in B(x)} f(y,x) = \begin{cases} v & \text{if } x = s, \\ 0 & \text{if } x \neq s, t, \\ -v & \text{if } x = t. \end{cases}$$

The quantity v is called the *value* of the flow. The second condition of the definition is concerned with the total flow emanating from a vertex minus the total flow into the vertex, and reflects the properties of source, intermediate vertex, and sink.

For further discussions of networks, see Ford and Fulkerson (1962) or Berge (1958). See also Brualdi and Ryser (1991) for a discussion of matrices and graphs.

B Conjugate Sequences

In the study of majorization in nonnegative integers, one often encounters a new sequence of integers generated from an old sequence in a particular way. This new sequence is called the *conjugate sequence*.

For any finite set E, denote the number of distinct elements of E by $|E|$.

B.1. Definition. Let $a_1, a_2, \ldots, a_n$ be nonnegative integers, and define

$$a_j^* = |\{a_i; a_i \geq j\}|, \qquad j = 1, 2, \ldots. \tag{1}$$

The sequence $a_1^*, a_2^*, a_3^*, \ldots$ is said to be *conjugate* to the sequence $a_1, a_2, \ldots, a_n, 0, 0, \ldots$.

Note that a_j^* is the number of integers a_i which are greater than or equal to j. For example,

if $a = (2, 1, 1)$, then $\{a_i^*\} = (3, 1, 0, 0, \ldots)$,
if $a = (3, 2, 1)$, then $\{a_i^*\} = (3, 2, 1, 0, 0, \ldots)$,
if $a = (1, 0, 0)$, then $\{a_i^*\} = (1, 0, 0, \ldots)$,
if $a = (1, 1, 1)$, then $\{a_i^*\} = (3, 0, 0, \ldots)$.

Of course, the sequence $\{a_i^*\}$ does not depend upon the order of $a_1, a_2, \ldots, a_n$; it is always a decreasing sequence, with $a_1^* \leq n$ and $a_j^* = 0$ for $j > \max(a_1, a_2, \ldots, a_n)$.

The nonzero elements of the conjugate sequence can be obtained in terms of the corresponding incidence matrix. This matrix is created using a greedy algorithm as follows. Let

$$\delta_i = (1, \ldots, 1, 0, \ldots, 0), \qquad i = 1, \ldots, k,$$

be the k-dimensional vector with first i components equal to 1 and remaining $k - i$ components equal to zero. Ordinarily, k is clear from the context.

Given nonnegative integers $a_1 \geq a_2 \geq \cdots \geq a_n$, take $k = a_1$ and let $\overline{A}$ be the $n \times k$ matrix with ith row δ_{a_i}. Then $\overline{A}$ has row sums a_i; $\overline{A}$ is sometimes called the *maximal matrix* with row sums $a_1, \ldots, a_n$. The vector $(a_1^*, a_2^*, \ldots, a_k^*)$ is just the vector of column sums of $\overline{A}$.

Example. $a = (3, 2, 2, 1, 1)$, $\quad a^* = (5, 3, 1, 0, 0)$,

$$\begin{array}{ccccc|c}
1 & 1 & 1 & 0 & 0 & 3 \\
1 & 1 & 0 & 0 & 0 & 2 \\
1 & 1 & 0 & 0 & 0 & 2 \\
1 & 0 & 0 & 0 & 0 & 1 \\
1 & 0 & 0 & 0 & 0 & 1 \\
\hline
5 & 3 & 1 & 0 & 0 &
\end{array}$$

Alternatively, the vectors a and a^* are often displayed by means of what are called *Ferreri–Sylvester diagrams*.

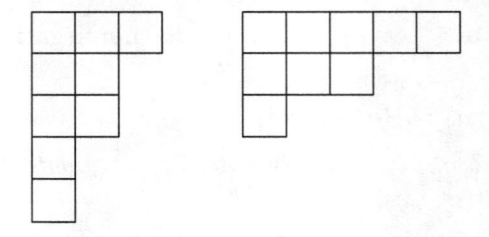

B.2. Apart from their order, the a_i's can be retrieved from the nonzero a_j^*'s, and Gale (1957) gave the following method for doing this: Form the $m \times n$ maximal matrix $\overline{A}^*$ with row sums $a_1^*, \ldots, a_m^*$, where m is the largest index for which ($a_m^* > 0$). Then the column sums of $\overline{A}^*$ are $a_1^{**}, \ldots, a_n^{**}$. To see that

$$a_i^{**} = a_{[i]}, \qquad i = 1, \ldots, n, \tag{2}$$

observe that the transpose of $\overline{A}^*$ is just the matrix $\overline{A}$.

B.3. For later reference we record the fact that

$$\sum_1^n a_i = \sum_1^{a_1} a_i^*,$$

B. Conjugate Sequences   247

where $a_1 \geq \cdots \geq a_n \geq 0$. This can be seen by observing that both $\sum_1^n a_i$ and $\sum_1^{a_1} a_i^*$ give the number of units in the maximal matrix $\overline{A}$ with row sums $a_1, a_2, \ldots, a_n$. More formally,

$$\sum_{j=1}^{a_1} a_j^* = \sum_{i \leq j \leq a_1} \sum_{1 \leq i \leq n,\ a_i \geq j} 1 = \sum_{1 \leq i \leq n} \sum_{1 \leq j \leq a_i} 1 = \sum_1^n a_i.$$

B.4. For $m = 1, 2, \ldots,$

$$\sum_{j=1}^m a_j^* = \sum_{i=1}^n \min(a_i, m).$$

This relation is apparent from consideration of the maximal matrix $\overline{A}$ and the fact that its column sums are the nonzero a_j^*.

Often it is convenient to write

$$a^* = (a_1^*, a_2^*, \ldots, a_k^*)$$

without explicitly indicating the value of k. However, we always take k sufficiently large that $a_{k+1}^* = 0$.

B.5. It is an interesting observation that

$$x \prec y \quad \text{implies} \quad x^* \succ y^*$$

when x^* and $y*$ are of length at least $\max(y_i)$.

To prove this, suppose for convenience that $x_1 \geq \cdots \geq x_n$ and $y_1 \geq \cdots \geq y_n$. From $x \prec y$, it follows that

$$\sum_{k+1}^n x_i \geq \sum_{k+1}^n y_i, \quad k = 0, 1, \ldots, n-1.$$

Denote by l the largest index for which $x_l > m$. Then from B.4 it follows that

$$\sum_1^m x_i^* = \sum_{i=1}^n \min(x_i, m) = lm + \sum_{l+1}^n x_i$$

$$\geq lm + \sum_{l+1}^n y_i \geq \sum_1^n \min(y_i, m) = \sum_1^m y_i^*.$$

By B.3, $\sum_1^n x_i = \sum_1^{y_1} x_i^*$ and $\sum_1^n y_i = \sum_i^{y_1} y_i^*$, so that $\sum_1^{y_1} x_i^* = \sum_1^{y_1} y_i^*$, and this completes the proof. ||

It is possible to give an alternative proof of B.5 by showing that the maximal matrix $\overline{Y}$ can be transformed to $\overline{X}$ by moving units in Y down and left.

The following lemma, implicit in the work of Vogel (1963), has been given by Mirsky (1971, p. 207). It relates to weak majorization, a condition that is encountered in the next section.

Recall that $|E|$ denotes the number of distinct elements in the finite set E.

B.6. Lemma (Mirsky, 1971). Let a_i and b_j, $1 \leq i \leq m$, $1 \leq j \leq n$, be nonnegative integers. Then the inequality

$$|I||J| \geq \sum_{i \in I} a_i - \sum_{j \notin J} b_j \tag{3}$$

holds for all $I \subset \{1, \ldots, m\}$ and $J \subset \{1, \ldots, n\}$ if and only if

$$a \prec_{\mathrm{w}} b^*. \tag{4}$$

Proof. Suppose that (3) holds and choose

$$I \subset \{1, \ldots, m\}, \qquad J = \{j : 1 \leq j \leq n, b_j \geq |I|\}.$$

Then from B.4 it follows that

$$\sum_{i \in I} a_i \leq |I||J| + \sum_{j \notin J} b_j = \sum_{j \in J} I + \sum_{j \notin J} b_j = \sum_{j=1}^n \min(b_j, |I|) = \sum_{i=1}^{|I|} b_i^*;$$

this proves (4). If (4) holds, so that

$$\sum_{i \in I} a_i \leq \sum_{i=1}^{|I|} b_i^*$$

whenever $I \subset \{1, \ldots, m\}$, B.4 can be used again to obtain

$$\sum_{i \in I} a_i \leq \sum_{i=1}^{|I|} b_i^* = \sum_{j=1}^n \min(b_j, |I|)$$

$$= \sum_{j \in J} \min(b_j, |I|) + \sum_{j \notin J} \min(b_j, |I|)$$

$$\leq \sum_{j \in J} |I| + \sum_{j \notin J} b_j = |I||J| + \sum_{j \notin J} b_j. \quad \|$$

Note that if $\sum_1^m a_i = \sum_1^n b_i = S$, say, then (3) can be written as

$$|I||J| \geq \sum_{i \in I} a_i + \sum_{j \in J} b_j - S,$$

with a symmetry not always present in (3). By B.3, $\sum_1^m a_i = \sum_1^n b_i$ also means that $\sum_1^m a_i = \sum_1^{b_1} b_i^*$, and (4) can be written (symmetrically, by B.5) as
$$(a, 0) \prec (b_1^*, \ldots, b_l^*),$$
where $l = \max(b_1, m)$ and $(a, 0)$ has length l.

C The Theorem of Gale and Ryser

We begin by expressing the theorem of Gale and Ryser in terms of incidence matrices. This is the simplest way to state the result. But later on, some equivalent formulations are mentioned that are oriented toward applications.

Ryser (1957) has answered, in terms of majorization, the following question: What are necessary and sufficient conditions in order that the numbers $r_1, \ldots, r_m$ and $c_1, \ldots, c_n$ are the row sums and column sums, respectively, of an $m \times n$ incidence matrix?

In the same year, Gale (1957) answered essentially the same question: What are necessary and sufficient conditions for the existence of an $m \times n$ incidence matrix with jth row sum greater than or equal to b_j and ith column sum less than or equal to a_i for all i and j? In case $\sum a_i = \sum b_j$, such a matrix must have row sums b_j and column sums a_i, so that this question is exactly the question of Ryser.

A more general formulation has been considered by Fulkerson (1959), who obtained necessary and sufficient conditions for the existence of an incidence matrix with row and column sums falling between prescribed upper and lower bounds. This result is given later in C.1. Various other related results have been discussed by Mirsky (1971). For more details on matrices and graphs, see Brualdi and Ryser (1991). Krause (1996) provides an alternative proof of Theorem C.1, and notes that it arises in several other mathematical contexts. See also Brualdi (2006).

C.1. Theorem (Gale, 1957; Ryser, 1957). Let $r_1, \ldots, r_m$ be nonnegative integers not exceeding n, and let $c_1, \ldots, c_n$ be nonnegative integers. A necessary and sufficient condition for the existence of an $m \times n$ incidence matrix with row sums $r_1, \ldots, r_m$ and column sums $c_1, \ldots, c_n$ is that

$$c \equiv (c_1, \ldots, c_n) \prec (r_1^*, \ldots, r_n^*) \equiv r^*. \tag{1}$$

Proof. Suppose that A is an incidence matrix with row sums r_i and column sums c_j. Form a new incidence matrix $\overline{A}$ (the maximal matrix with these row sums) with the same row sums but with 0's and 1's distributed in each row so that all 1's precede the first zero, as below.

$$\begin{bmatrix} 1 & 1 & 1 & \cdots & 1 & 1 & \cdots & 1 & 0 & \cdots & 0 \\ 1 & 1 & 1 & \cdots & 1 & 0 & \cdots & 0 & 0 & \cdots & 0 \\ \vdots & \vdots & \vdots & & & & & & & & \vdots \\ 1 & 1 & 0 & & & \cdots & & & & & 0 \end{bmatrix} \begin{matrix} \text{Row} \\ \text{Sums} \\ r_1 \\ r_2 \\ \vdots \\ r_m \end{matrix}$$

Column Sums r_1^* r_2^* $\qquad \cdots \qquad r_n^*$

In conjunction with the discussion of maximal matrices in Section B, it has already been observed that the new column sums are $r_1^*, \ldots, r_n^*$. It is readily seen that $\sum_1^k c_i \le \sum_1^k r_i^*, k = 1, \ldots, n-1$, and $\sum_1^n c_i = \sum_1^n r_i^*$, so that $c \prec r^*$.

The more difficult part of the theorem is that (1) guarantees the existence of the incidence matrix. An explicit construction for the matrix can be given using 5.D.3 to show that the construction can always be carried out. To describe this construction, suppose without loss of generality that $r_1 \ge r_2 \ge \cdots \ge r_m$ and $c_1 \ge c_2 \ge \cdots \ge c_n$. Then, starting with the first row and proceeding consecutively through the remaining rows, distribute units in the matrix from left to right as follows: With the ith row, place a unit in the first column if fewer than c_1 units have already been placed in the first column and $r_i \ge 1$; place a unit in the second column if fewer than c_2 units have already been placed in the second column and fewer than r_i units have been placed in the ith row. In general, place a unit in the jth column if fewer than c_j units have been placed in the jth column and rows $1, \ldots, i-1$, and if fewer than r_i units have been placed in the ith row and columns $1, \ldots, j-1$.

For illustration, consider the example with $r = (8, 8, 5, 5, 4)$ and $c = (5, 5, 4, 4, 4, 3, 2, 1, 1, 1)$, so that a 5×10 incidence matrix is required. With the first row, no units have yet been distributed, so place 8 units, followed by two zeros.

1	1	1	1	1	1	1	1	0	0	8
1	1	1	1	1	1	1	0	1	0	8
1	1	1	1	1	0	0	0	0	0	5
1	1	1	1	1	0	0	0	0	0	5
1	1	0	0	0	1	0	0	0	1	4
5	5	4	4	4	3	2	1	1	1	

With the second row, place units until reaching column 8, where the required $c_8 = 1$ has already been achieved. But place a unit in column 9, since no units have yet been placed there and since one more unit is required to achieve $r_2 = 8$. In the last row, the phenomenon is again encountered that required column sums have already been achieved (in columns 2, 3, 4 and 7, 8, 9). Consequently, place a unit in the sixth column rather than the third, and in the eighth column rather than the fourth.

To prove that this construction can always be carried out, use induction on the number m of rows. Suppose that the construction can always be carried out with $m - 1$ rows. Form the matrix with first row $(1, \ldots, 1, 0, \ldots, 0)$ consisting of r_1 ones followed by $n - r_1$ zeros. To complete the construction, an $m - 1 \times n$ incidence matrix must be obtained with row sums $r_2, r_3, \ldots, r_m$ and column sums

$$c_1 - 1, c_2 - 1, \ldots, c_{r_1} - 1, c_{r_1+1}, \ldots, c_n.$$

If use is to be made of the induction hypotheses, then it must be that

$$(c_1 - 1, \ldots, c_{r_1} - 1, c_{r_1+1}, \ldots, c_n) \prec (\widetilde{r}_2, \widetilde{r}_3, \ldots, \widetilde{r}_{n+1}),$$

where $\widetilde{r}_i$, the number of the $r_2, r_3, \ldots, r_m$ greater than or equal to $i-1$, is the conjugate sequence of $r_2, \ldots, r_m$. But

$$(\widetilde{r}_2, \widetilde{r}_3, \ldots, \widetilde{r}_{n+1}) = (r_1^* - 1, \ldots, r_{r_1}^* - 1, r_{r_1+1}^*, \ldots, r_n^*),$$

and

$$(c_1 - 1, \ldots, c_{r_1} - 1, c_{r_1+1}, \ldots, c_n) \prec (r_1^* - 1, \ldots, r_{r_1}^* - 1, r_{r_1+1}^*, \ldots, r_n^*)$$

by 5.D.3. ||

Very similar constructions for an incidence matrix to achieve specified row sums $r_1, \ldots, r_m$ and column sums $c_1, \ldots, c_n$ have been given by Gale (1957) and Fulkerson and Ryser (1962). The construction of Fulkerson and Ryser is as follows: Select any column j and insert 1's in the positions corresponding to the c_j largest row sums; delete column j, reduce each of these c_j row sums by 1, and repeat the entire procedure on another column. Essentially, this same construction is given by Ryser (1963) to prove C.1. Another kind of proof is given by Mirsky (1971, p. 76).

The following theorem generalizes a result of Hoffman (1960) and has been given by Kellerer (1961, 1964). Unfortunately, its proof would carry us too far afield, so we simply quote the result, and refer to Mirsky (1971, p. 205) for a proof.

C.2. Theorem. Let $0 \leq \rho'_i \leq \rho_i$, $0 \leq \sigma'_j \leq \sigma_j$, and $a_{ij} \geq 0$ for $1 \leq i \leq m$, $1 \leq j \leq n$, be integers. Then there exists an $m \times n$ matrix $Q = (q_{ij})$ of integral elements with row sums $r_1, \ldots, r_m$ and column sums $c_1, \ldots, c_n$ such that

$$\rho'_i \leq r_i \leq \rho_i, \quad 1 \leq i \leq m,$$
$$\sigma'_j \leq c_j \leq \sigma_j, \quad 1 \leq j \leq n,$$
$$0 \leq q_{ij} \leq a_{ij}, \quad 1 \leq i \leq m, 1 \leq j \leq n,$$

if and only if, for all $I \subset \{1, \ldots, m\}$, $J \subset \{1, \ldots, n\}$,

$$\sum_{\substack{i \in I \\ j \in J}} a_{ij} \geq \max \left\{ \sum_{i \in I} \rho'_i - \sum_{j \notin J} \sigma_j, \sum_{j \in J} \sigma'_j - \sum_{i \notin I} \rho_i \right\}.$$

C.3. Theorem (Fulkerson, 1959). There exists an $m \times n$ incidence matrix Q with row sums $r_1, \ldots, r_m$ and column sums $c_1, \ldots, c_n$ such that

$$\rho'_i \leq r_i \leq \rho_i, \quad 1 \leq i \leq m,$$
$$\sigma'_j \leq c_j \leq \sigma_j, \quad 1 \leq j \leq n,$$

if and only if

$$(\rho'_1, \ldots, \rho'_m) \prec_w (\sigma_1^*, \ldots, \sigma_m^*),$$
$$(\sigma'_1, \ldots, \sigma'_n) \prec_w (\rho_1^*, \ldots, \rho_n^*).$$

Proof. In C.2, take $a_{ij} = 1$ for all i, j to obtain that the required incidence matrix Q exists if and only if, for all $I \subset \{1, \ldots, m\}$ and $J \subset \{1, \ldots, n\}$,

$$|I||J| \geq \sum_{i \in I} \rho'_i - \sum_{j \notin J} \sigma_j \quad \text{and} \quad |I||J| \geq \sum_{j \in J} \sigma'_j - \sum_{i \notin I} \rho_i.$$

The theorem is now immediate from B.6. ||

C.4. Corollary (Gale, 1957). There exists an $m \times n$ incidence matrix Q with row sums $r_1, \ldots, r_m$ and column sums $c_1, \ldots, c_n$ such that

$$r_i \leq \rho_i, \quad 1 \leq i \leq m, \quad \text{and} \quad \sigma'_j \leq c_j, \quad 1 \leq j \leq n,$$

if and only if

$$(\sigma'_1, \ldots, \sigma'_n) \prec_w (\rho_1^*, \ldots, \rho_n^*).$$

Proof. In C.3, take $\rho'_i = 0$, $1 \leq i \leq m$, and $\sigma_j = \infty$, $1 \leq j \leq n$. ∥

Fulkerson (1960) considers a variant of the Gale–Ryser theorem by asking this question: What are necessary and sufficient conditions for the existence of a square incidence matrix with prescribed row and column sums and zero trace? The answer to this question can be stated in terms of a majorization when the prescribed row and column sums are similarly ordered.

Instead of requiring that Q be an incidence matrix with entries that are 0's or 1's, in the context of capacity–constrained supply–demand networks, it is of interest to consider the existence of $m \times n$ matrices with nonnegative entries that are uniformly bounded that have given row and column sums.

C.5. Theorem (Brualdi and Ryser, 1991, Theorem 6.2.4). Let $r_1, \ldots, r_m$ and $c_1, \ldots, c_n$ be nonnegative integers satisfying $\sum_{i=1}^{m} r_i = \sum_{i=1}^{n} c_j$. In addition, assume that $c_1 \geq c_2 \ldots \geq c_n$ and let b be a positive integer. There exists an $m \times n$ nonnegative integral matrix $A = (a_{ij})$ with row sums $r_1, \ldots, r_m$ and column sums $c_1, \ldots, c_n$ satisfying $a_{ij} \leq b$ $(1 \leq i \leq m, 1 \leq j \leq n)$ if and only if

$$\sum_{j=1}^{k} c_j \leq \sum_{i=1}^{m} \min(r_i, bk), \quad k = 1, 2, \ldots, n.$$

The case $b = 1$ in C.5. corresponds to the Gale-Ryser theorem, C.1.

Brualdi and Ryser (1991) also present results parallel to C.5 that provide necessary and sufficient conditions for the existence of a matrix A that is as described in C.5, but in addition is (i) symmetric and (ii) symmetric with zero trace. Specialized to deal with incidence matrices, these results can be stated in terms of majorizations involving conjugate sequences.

C.6. Theorem (Brualdi and Ryser, 1991, Section 6.3). For integers $r_1 \geq \cdots \geq r_n \geq 0$, the following are equivalent:

(i) There exists a symmetric incidence matrix with row sums $r_1, \ldots, r_n$.

(ii) $(r_1, \ldots, r_n) \prec (r_1^*, \ldots, r_n^*)$.

C.7. Theorem (Erdös and Gallai, 1960). Let $r_1 \geq r_2 \geq \ldots \geq r_n$ be nonnegative integers whose sum is an even integer. The following are equivalent:

(i) There exists a symmetric incidence matrix with zero trace with row sums $r_1, \ldots, r_n$.

(ii) $(r_1, \ldots, r_n) \prec (r_1^{**}, \ldots, r_n^{**})$.

Proofs of C.6 and C.7 together with references for algorithms for construction of the matrices described in C.5–C.7 are contained in Brualdi and Ryser (1991, Chapter 6).

D Some Applications of the Gale–Ryser Theorem

In this section, Theorem C.1 of Gale and Ryser is applied to obtain results in several areas. Most of these results are equivalent or essentially equivalent to C.1; the principal difference is one of terminology.

Demidegrees of a Graph

For each fixed vertex x of a (directed) graph $G = (X, U)$, the number

$$d^+(x) = |\{y : (x, y) \in U\}|$$

of arcs emanating from x, and the number

$$d^-(x) = |\{z : (z, x) \in U\}|$$

of arcs terminating at x, are called, respectively, the *outward demidegree* and the *inward demidegree* of the vertex x.

Given integers $r_1, r_2, \ldots, r_n, c_1, c_2, \ldots, c_n$, under what conditions does there exist a graph with vertices $x_1, x_2, \ldots, x_n$ satisfying

$$d^+(x_k) = r_k, \quad d^-(x_k) = c_k, \quad k = 1, \ldots, n?$$

To answer this question, notice that for any graph $G = (X, U)$, the associated incidence matrix A has kth row sum $d^+(x_k)$ and kth column sum $d^-(x_k)$. Thus the question can be rephrased in terms of the existence of an incidence matrix with prescribed row and column sums. Consequently, the following equivalent result is obtained from C.1:

D. Some Applications of the Gale–Ryser Theorem

D.1. Theorem. A necessary and sufficient condition for the integers $r_1, \ldots, r_n$ and $c_1, \ldots, c_n$ to constitute, respectively, the outward and inward demidegrees of a graph is that

$$(c_1, \ldots, c_n) \prec (r_1^*, \ldots, r_n^*).$$

Properties of Elements of a Set and a Majorization of Probabilities

Here C.1 is related to the following result concerning properties of elements of a finite set.

D.2. Theorem. Let $S = \{s_1, \ldots, s_m\}$ be a finite set, and let $N_1, \ldots, N_n, M_1, \ldots, M_n$ be numbers. Then there exists a set of properties $\{\Pi_1, \ldots, \Pi_n\}$ such that N_i is the number of elements in S having property Π_i, and M_i is the number of elements in S having i or more of the properties $\Pi_1, \ldots, \Pi_n$, $i = 1, \ldots, n$, if and only if

$$(N_1, \ldots, N_n) \prec (M_1, \ldots, M_n).$$

This theorem can be translated into slightly different language by letting E_i be the set of all elements in S having property Π_i for $i = 1, \ldots, n$. Then $N_i = |E_i|$ and M_i is the number of elements belonging to at least i of the sets $E_1, \ldots, E_n$.

To prove D.2, construct an $m \times n$ incidence matrix $Q = (q_{ij})$, where

$$q_{ij} = \begin{cases} 1 & \text{if } s_i \in E_j, \\ 0 & \text{if } s_i \notin E_j. \end{cases}$$

Conversely, an $m \times n$ incidence matrix will determine sets $E_1, \ldots, E_n$ and Π_i can be defined as the property of belonging to the set E_i. Clearly, the ith column sum c_i of Q is the number $N_i = |E_i|$ of elements in E_i, and the ith row sum r_i of Q is the number of subsets containing the element s_i of S.

Recall that the conjugate sequence $r_i^*, \ldots, r_n^*$ can be obtained as column sums of the maximal matrix $\overline{Q}$ derived from Q by "sliding units left" so that each row takes the form $(1, \ldots, 1, 0, \ldots, 0)$. The ith row contributes a unit to the sum r_j^* if and only if $r_i \geq j$. Consequently, $r_j^* = M_j$ is the number of elements in S that have at least j of the properties $\Pi_1, \ldots, \Pi_n$.

With the identifications $c_i = N_i$ and $r_j^* = M_j$, it is apparent that D.2 is equivalent to C.1.

Now suppose that an element is chosen at random from the set S, with each element equally likely. Then c_j/n is the probability of the event E_j that the chosen element has property Π_j, $j = 1, \ldots, n$.

Moreover, r_j^*/n is the probability that j or more of the events $E_1, \ldots, E_n$ occur simultaneously. Theorem D.2 yields

$$(c_1/n, \ldots, c_n/n) \prec (r_1^*/n, \ldots, r_n^*/n).$$

Of course, the probabilities here are all multiples of $1/n$. However, the same majorization is proved in Section 12.C without this restriction. There, it is shown that if in some probability space, $E_1, \ldots, E_n$ are arbitrary events with respective probabilities $p_1, \ldots, p_n$, and if

$$q_j = P(\text{at least } j \text{ of the events } E_i \text{ occur}), \qquad j = 1, \ldots, n,$$

then

$$(p_1, \ldots, p_n) \prec (q_1, \ldots, q_n).$$

This result can be regarded as a generalization of D.2, which concludes that the majorization must hold. However, the converse part of the probability theorem, also proved in Proposition 12.C.1, is not a generalization of the converse part of D.2 because the integral character of D.2 is lacking in the probability result.

A Theorem on Partial Transversals

Let $\mathscr{A} = \{A_i : i \in I\}$ be an indexed family of subsets $A_i \subset E$. If for all $i \in I$, one element x_i can be selected from A_i in such a way that the elements x_i, $i \in I$, are distinct, then the set $\{x_i : i \in I\}$ is called a *transversal* of $\mathscr{A}$. Formally, a subset T of E is called a transversal of $\mathscr{A} = \{A_i : i \in I\}$ if there exists a one-to-one map $\psi : T \to I$ such that $x \in A_{\psi(x)}$ for all $x \in T$. A subset X of E is a *partial transversal* of $\mathscr{A}$ if X is a transversal of a subfamily of $\mathscr{A}$.

A *system of distinct representatives* for $\mathscr{A}$ is an indexed family $\mathscr{X} = \{x_j : j \in J\}$ of distinct elements of E for which there exists a one-to-one mapping $\phi : J \to I$ such that $x_j \in A_{\phi(j)}$. A transversal is a set, whereas a system of distinct representatives can be regarded as a function mapping the index set J onto a transversal.

The following theorem is obtained by Mirsky (1971) as a corollary to a theorem of Philip Higgins that extends Marshall Hall's fundamental theorem concerning systems of distinct representatives. Mirsky makes use of D.3 below to prove C.1. But we already have C.1, and we follow a reverse procedure by using it to obtain D.3.

D.3. Theorem (Mirsky, 1971). Let $m \geq 1$ and $n \geq 1$ be integers, let $r_1 \geq \cdots \geq r_m$ be nonnegative integers not exceeding n, and let $\mathscr{A} = (A_1, \ldots, A_n)$ be a family of pairwise disjoint sets containing

D. Some Applications of the Gale–Ryser Theorem 257

$s_1 \geq \cdots \geq s_n$ elements, respectively. Then $\mathscr{A}$ possesses m pairwise disjoint partial transversals of cardinality $r_1, \ldots, r_m \leq n$, respectively, if and only if

$$(s_1, \ldots, s_n) \prec^{\mathrm{w}} (r_1^*, \ldots, r_n^*). \tag{1}$$

Proof. Suppose first that $\mathscr{A}$ possesses m pairwise disjoint partial transversals $T_1, \ldots, T_m$ of cardinality $r_1, \ldots, r_m$, respectively. Let $Q = (q_{ij})$ be the $m \times n$ incidence matrix with

$$q_{ij} = \begin{cases} 1 & \text{if } T_i \cap A_j \text{ is not empty,} \\ 0 & \text{if } T_i \cap A_j \text{ is empty.} \end{cases}$$

Then Q has row sums $r_1, \ldots, r_m$ and column sums $c_1, \ldots, c_n$ satisfying

$$c_j \leq s_j, \quad j = 1, \ldots, n;$$

hence, by C.1,

$$(c_1, \ldots, c_n) \prec (r_1^*, \ldots, r_n^*). \tag{2}$$

Let $(\pi_1, \ldots, \pi_n)$ be a permutation of $(1, \ldots, n)$ such that

$$c_{\pi_1} \geq c_{\pi_2} \geq \cdots \geq c_{\pi_n}.$$

Then from (2),

$$\sum_k^n s_i \geq \sum_k^n c_i \geq \sum_k^n c_{\pi_i} \geq \sum_k^n r_i^*, \quad k = 1, \ldots, n,$$

which yields (1).

Next, suppose that (1) holds. Let

$$\delta = \sum_1^n s_j - \sum_1^n r_j, \quad s_0 = \max(s_1, r_1 - \delta, m), \quad r_0 = s_0 + \delta.$$

Then $s_0 \geq s_1 \geq \cdots \geq s_n, r_0^* \geq r_1^* \geq \cdots \geq r_n^*$, and

$$(s_0, s_1, \ldots, s_n) \prec (r_0^*, r_1^*, \ldots, r_n^*).$$

Let $\tilde{r}_1, \tilde{r}_2, \ldots, \tilde{r}_{s_0}$ be the first s_0 elements of the sequence conjugate to $(r_0^*, r_1^*, \ldots, r_n^*)$. Then $\tilde{r}_1 \leq n+1$, and by C.1, an $s_0 \times (n+1)$ incidence matrix $Q = (q_{ij})$ can be constructed with row sums $\tilde{r}_1, \tilde{r}_2, \ldots, \tilde{r}_{s_0}$ and column sums $s_0, s_1, \ldots, s_n$. Form the set T_i by placing an element from A_j in T_i if and only if $q_{ij} = 1$, $i = 1, \ldots, m$, $j = 1, \ldots, n$. Then $r_1 = \tilde{r}_1 - 1, \ldots, r_m = \tilde{r}_m - 1$ are the cardinalities of the disjoint sets $T_1, \ldots, T_m$, respectively. ∥

E s-Graphs and a Generalization of the Gale–Ryser Theorem

The theorem of Gale and Ryser can be applied to obtain the result of D.1 concerning the inward and outward demidegrees of a graph. A generalization of this result for s-graphs is of interest.

An *s-graph* is a generalized graph in which there can be as many as s arcs in a given direction joining the same pair of vertices. An s-graph with n vertices $x_1, \ldots, x_n$ can be characterized by an $n \times n$ matrix $Q = (q_{ij})$, where q_{ij} is the number of arcs from x_i which terminate at x_j. Of course, the outward demidegree $d^+(x_k)$ of the kth vertex (number of arcs emanating from x_k) is just the kth row sum, r_k, of Q. Similarly, the inward demidegree $d^-(x_k)$ of the kth vertex (number of arcs terminating at x_k) is the kth column sum, c_k, of Q.

In the context of the Gale–Ryser theorem, one can ask for necessary and sufficient conditions on integers $r_1, \ldots, r_m, c_1, \ldots, c_n$ in order that they be, respectively, the row and column sums of a matrix Q with elements taking the values $1, \ldots, s$. Such conditions can be obtained from C.2. Here some conditions are given in terms of majorization. These conditions require a generalization of the notion of a conjugate sequence.

E.1. Definition. Given nonnegative integers $a_1, \ldots, a_n$, define

$$a_j^{s^*} = \sum_{i=1}^{n} \{\min[a_i, js] - \min[a_i, (j-1)s]\}, \qquad j = 1, 2, \ldots. \qquad (1)$$

When $s = 1$, B.4 can be used to see that this becomes the conjugate sequence defined in B.1. Of course,

$$\sum_{j=1}^{m} a_j^{s^*} = \sum_{i=1}^{n} \min[a_i, ms], \qquad m = 1, 2, \ldots. \qquad (2)$$

With $a_1 \geq a_2 \geq \cdots \geq a_n$, take k to satisfy $(k-1)s < a_1 \leq ks$, and let $\overline{A}_s$ be the $n \times k$ matrix with ith row $a^{(i)}$ having the sum a_i and the form

$$a^{(i)} = (s, s, \ldots, s, t, 0, \ldots, 0),$$

where $0 \leq t < s$, $i = 1, \ldots, n$. [Note that $a^{(i)}$ is the largest vector under the ordering of majorization with components in the interval $[0, s]$ that sum to a_i—see 5.C.1.] Then $(a_1^{s^*}, \ldots, a_k^{s^*})$ is just the vector of column sums of $\overline{A}_s$ and $a_i^{s^*} = 0$ for $i > k$.

E. s-Graphs and a Generalization of the Gale–Ryser Theorem

Unlike the case that $s = 1$, the columns of $\overline{A}_s$ need not have the same form as the rows. For example, if $s = 2$, the second column of

$$\overline{A}_2 = \begin{bmatrix} 2 & 1 \\ 2 & 1 \end{bmatrix}$$

does not have the indicated form. For this reason, the a_i cannot in general be retrieved from the a_i^{s*}, and for $s > 1$, it may be that $(a_i^{s*})^{s*} \neq a_{[i]}$ in spite of B.2. However, the following observations of D. Adema (private communication) can be made:

$$((a_i^{s*})^{s*})^{s*} = a_i^{s*}, \qquad i = 1, 2, \ldots; \tag{3}$$

$$(a_1, \ldots, a_n, 0, \ldots, 0) \prec (a_1^{s*}, \ldots, a_m^{s*}), \tag{4}$$

where $m = \max(n, k)$ and k is as above,

$$s < t \quad \text{implies} \quad (a_1^{s*}, \ldots, a_k^{s*}) \prec (a_1^{t*}, \ldots, a_k^{t*}). \tag{5}$$

To obtain (3), form the maximal matrix $\overline{\overline{A}}_s$ from $\overline{A}_s$ by "moving units up" in each column so that column sums are undisturbed but the columns have the maximal form $(s, \ldots, s, t, 0, \ldots, 0)$, $0 \leq t < s$. Then both the rows and columns of $\overline{\overline{A}}_s$ have the maximal form and $\overline{\overline{A}}_s$ has the row sums $(a_i^{s*})^{s*}$ and column sums a_i^{s*}. One obtains (3) using an argument similar to that of 7.B.2.

The majorization (4) is easily obtained by comparing the matrices $\overline{A}_s$ and $\overline{\overline{A}}_s$. Similarly, (5) follows from the fact that $\overline{A}_t$ can be obtained from $\overline{A}_s$ by "moving units left." Formally, it is a trivial consequence of (2).

An extension of B.5 is

$$x \prec y \quad \text{implies} \quad x^{s*} \succ y^{s*} \tag{6}$$

whenever x^{s*} and y^{s*} are of sufficient length to incorporate all nonzero components x_i^{s*}, y_i^{s*}. The proof of this is a simple modification of the proof of B.5 and is based upon (2).

E.2. Lemma. Let a_i and b_j, $1 \leq i \leq m$, $1 \leq j \leq n$, be nonnegative integers. The inequality

$$s|I||J| \geq \sum_{i \in I} a_i - \sum_{j \in J} b_j$$

holds for all $I \subset \{1, \ldots, m\}$, $J \subset \{1, \ldots, n\}$ if and only if

$$a \prec_w b^{s*}.$$

The proof of this is analogous to the proof of B.6. The result was noted by Marshall and Olkin (1973a) and by Mahmoodian (1975).

E.3. Theorem. Let $r_1, \ldots, r_m$ be nonnegative integers not exceeding sn and let $c_1, \ldots, c_n$ be nonnegative integers. A necessary and sufficient condition for the existence of an $m \times n$ matrix with elements $0, 1, \ldots,$ or s, row sums $r_1, \ldots, r_m$, and column sums $c_1, \ldots, c_n$ is that

$$c \equiv (c_1, \ldots, c_n) \prec (r_1^{s^*}, \ldots, r_n^{s^*}) \equiv r^{s^*}.$$

This theorem can be proved quite analogously to the proof given for C.1. Alternatively, it follows from E.2 and C.2 with $\rho_i' = \rho_i = r_i$, $\sigma_j' = \sigma_j = c_j$, $a_{ij} = s$, $1 \leq i \leq m$, $1 \leq j \leq n$.

In terms of s-graphs, the following result can be obtained from E.3.

E.4. Theorem (Berge, 1958). Consider n pairs of nonnegative integers $(r_1, c_1), \ldots, (r_n, c_n)$ which have been indexed so that

$$c_1 \geq \cdots \geq c_n.$$

Then $r_1, \ldots, r_n$ and $c_1, \ldots, c_n$ constitute, respectively, the outward and inward demidegrees of an s-graph if and only if

$$(c_1, \ldots, c_n) \prec (r_1^{s^*}, \ldots, r_n^{s^*}).$$

Various additional results concerning the existence of graphs and directed graphs with given degrees are given by Chen (1971, Chapter 6).

F Tournaments

A tournament is a finite graph $G = (X, U)$ without loops [i.e., $(x, x) \notin U$ for all $x \in X$] such that for each pair of distinct vertices x, y, either $(x, y) \in U$ or $(y, x) \in U$, but not both. For example, the graph of Fig. 2 with 5 vertices represents a tournament.

Tournaments arise in round-robin competitions, in dominance relations in groups of animals, and in preference relations or paired comparisons. For general surveys, see Harary and Moser (1966), Moon (1968), or Ryser (1964). Brualdi (2006) provides an excellent discussion of the connection between tournaments and graphs.

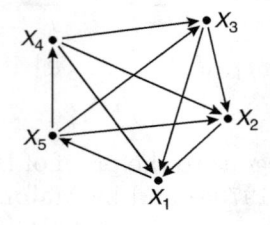

Figure 2. A graph representation of a tournament.

The incidence matrix associated with the tournament of Fig. 2 is

$$Q = \begin{bmatrix} 0 & 0 & 0 & 0 & 1 \\ 1 & 0 & 0 & 0 & 0 \\ 1 & 1 & 0 & 0 & 0 \\ 1 & 1 & 1 & 0 & 0 \\ 0 & 1 & 1 & 1 & 0 \end{bmatrix}.$$

Here, the element q_{ij} in the (i,j)th position is 1 if and only if $(x_i, x_j) \in U$. The main diagonal elements $q_{ii} = 0$ because the graph has no loops. When $i \neq j$, $(x_i, x_j) \in U$ or $(x_j, x_i) \in U$, but not both, so that $q_{ij} = 1 - q_{ji}$. This means that the ith row determines the ith column in a tournament matrix.

The *score* s_i of $x_i \in X$ is the number of distinct pairs $(x_i, x_j) \in U$; i.e., s_i is the outward demidegree of x_i. In terms of the associated incidence matrix, s_i is just the ith row sum. The *score vector* of $G = (X, U)$ is the vector $(s_1, \ldots, s_n)$ of scores. It is customary in the theory of tournaments to index the points in X so that

$$s_1 \leq \cdots \leq s_n.$$

For the example of Fig. 2, the row sums of Q are $(1, 1, 2, 3, 3)$, and this is the score vector. Because the ordering adopted for majorization is decreasing, we write $t_j = s_{n-j+1}$, $j = 1, \ldots, n$. Then

$$t_1 \geq \cdots \geq t_n$$

are the components of the score vector in reverse order. For the tournament of Fig. 2,

$$(t_1, t_2, t_3, t_4, t_5) = (3, 3, 2, 1, 1).$$

A question first considered by Landau (1953) [see also Moon (1968), Ryser (1964), and Brauer, Gentry, and Shaw (1968)] is the following: When can a set of integers be the score vector of some tournament?

F.1. Theorem (Landau, 1953). Let $s_1 \leq \cdots \leq s_n$ be nonnegative integers. A necessary and sufficient condition for $(s_1, \ldots, s_n)$ to be the score vector of some tournament is that

$$(s_1, \ldots, s_n) \prec (n-1, n-2, \ldots, 1, 0). \tag{1}$$

Remark. From the fact that $\binom{k}{2} = 1 + 2 + \cdots + (k-1)$ so that

$$\binom{n}{2} - \binom{n-k}{2} = (n-1) + (n-2) + \cdots + (n-k),$$

(1) can be written as

$$\sum_1^k t_i \leq \binom{k}{2}, \quad k=1,\ldots,n-1, \quad \sum_1^n t_i = \binom{n}{2}, \qquad (2)$$

where $t_j = s_{n-j+1}$, $j = 1,\ldots,n$. This is a more common form for the condition, but we prefer (1) so as not to mask the majorization that is present.

Proof of (1) *when* $(s_1,\ldots,s_n)$ *is a score vector.* Note that $\sum_1^n t_i = \binom{n}{2}$ because the graph $G = (X,U)$ of the tournament satisfies $(x,y) \in U$ or $(y,x) \in U$ when $x \neq y$, but not both. Consider a subgraph $G' = (X',U')$, where $X' \subset X$ has k elements and $(x,y) \in U'$ if and only if $x,y \in X'$ and $(x,y) \in U$. Then G' is again a tournament so that, as already argued, $\sum_1^k t'_i = \binom{k}{2}$. But $t'_i \geq t_i$ for all i, which completes the proof. ||

For an alternative proof, consider the tournament with associated $n \times n$ incidence matrix $T = (t_{ij})$, where $t_{ij} = 1$ if and only if $i < j$; i.e.,

$$T = \begin{bmatrix} 0 & 1 & 1 & \cdots & 1 & 1 \\ 0 & 0 & 1 & \cdots & 1 & 1 \\ 0 & 0 & 0 & \cdots & 1 & 1 \\ \vdots & \vdots & \vdots & & \vdots & \vdots \\ 0 & 0 & 0 & \cdots & 0 & 1 \\ 0 & 0 & 0 & \cdots & 0 & 0 \end{bmatrix}.$$

Here, the row sums are $n-1, n-2, \ldots, 1, 0$, and the column sums are $0, 1, \ldots, n-1$. To see that the row sums (which are components of the score vector) of this tournament are maximal in the sense of majorization, observe that any principal submatrix of a tournament incidence matrix is again a tournament incidence matrix. Thus if T is partitioned as

$$T = \begin{bmatrix} T_1 & T_2 \\ 0 & T_3 \end{bmatrix}, \quad T_1 : k \times k, \quad T_3 : l \times l, \quad k + l = n,$$

then T_1 is a tournament matrix. But the total number of ones in a $k \times k$ tournament matrix is $\binom{k}{2}$. Since T_2 consists of all ones, the first k rows of any tournament matrix can have no more ones than do the first k rows of T. ||

Proof that (1) *implies* $(s_1,\ldots,s_n)$ *is a score vector.* The fact that $(s_1,\ldots,s_n)$ is a score vector under the conditions (1) can be proved by explicitly constructing a tournament incidence matrix with row sums

$s_1, \ldots, s_n$. This construction is as follows: Begin by inserting t_1 ones in the last row starting at the left. This determines the last column. Next, insert t_2 ones in the next-to-last row, starting at the left, but taking into account any ones in the last column. In general, if at the $(k-1)$th stage there are already l ones in row k, place t_{k-l} ones in row k starting at the left, and then complete the kth column.

This construction is illustrated by the example of Fig. 2, where $t = (3, 3, 2, 1, 1)$. The sequence of steps is exhibited in Fig. 3.

$$
\begin{array}{ccccc|c}
0 & \cdot & \cdot & \cdot & 0 & 1 \\
\cdot & 0 & \cdot & \cdot & 0 & 1 \\
\cdot & \cdot & 0 & \cdot & 0 & 2 \\
\cdot & \cdot & \cdot & 0 & 1 & 3 \\
1 & 1 & 1 & 0 & 0 & 3 \\
\hline
3 & 3 & 2 & 1 & 1
\end{array}
\qquad
\begin{array}{ccccc|c}
0 & \cdot & \cdot & 0 & 0 & 1 \\
\cdot & 0 & \cdot & 0 & 0 & 1 \\
\cdot & \cdot & 0 & 1 & 0 & 2 \\
1 & 1 & 0 & 0 & 1 & 3 \\
1 & 1 & 1 & 0 & 0 & 3 \\
\hline
3 & 3 & 2 & 1 & 1
\end{array}
$$
$$\text{Step 1} \qquad\qquad \text{Step 2}$$

$$
\begin{array}{ccccc|c}
0 & \cdot & 0 & 0 & 0 & 1 \\
\cdot & 0 & 1 & 0 & 0 & 1 \\
1 & 0 & 0 & 1 & 0 & 2 \\
1 & 1 & 0 & 0 & 1 & 3 \\
1 & 1 & 1 & 0 & 0 & 3 \\
\hline
3 & 3 & 2 & 1 & 1
\end{array}
\qquad
\begin{array}{ccccc|c}
0 & 1 & 0 & 0 & 0 & 1 \\
0 & 0 & 1 & 0 & 0 & 1 \\
1 & 0 & 0 & 1 & 0 & 2 \\
1 & 1 & 0 & 0 & 1 & 3 \\
1 & 1 & 1 & 0 & 0 & 3 \\
\hline
3 & 3 & 2 & 1 & 1
\end{array}
$$
$$\text{Step 3} \qquad\qquad \text{Step 4}$$

Figure 3. Steps in the construction of a tournament matrix with score $(3, 3, 2, 1, 1)$.

That this construction is always successful can be proved by induction. Given nonnegative integers $u_1 \geq \cdots \geq u_{n-1}$ such that $(u_1, \ldots, u_{n-1}) \prec (n-2, n-3, \ldots, 1, 0)$, assume that there exists a tournament with the score vector $(u_{n-1}, \ldots, u_1)$. Now suppose that $t_1 \geq \cdots \geq t_n$ are nonnegative integers satisfying the majorization $(t_1, \ldots, t_n) \prec (n-1, n-2, \ldots, 1, 0)$, and consider the partitioned incidence matrix as follows:

	1 2 $\quad$ $(n-1)$	n
1	0	0
2	$\quad$ 0	$\vdots$ $\Big\}t_1$
$\vdots$		0
		1
$(n-1)$		$\vdots$ $\Big\}n - t_1$
n	$\underbrace{1, 1, \ldots, 1,}\ \underbrace{0, \ldots, 0}$	1 \\ 0

In reverse order, the row sums (scores)

$$\bar{t} \equiv \underbrace{(t_2 - 1, t_3 - 1, \ldots, t_{n-t_1} - 1}_{n-t_1-1}, \underbrace{t_{n-t_1+1}, \ldots, t_n}_{t_1})$$

are required from the $(n-1) \times (n-1)$ submatrix because there are $n - t_1 - 1$ ones in the nth column. If it can be shown that

$$\bar{t} \prec (n - 2, n - 3, \ldots, 1, 0),$$

then, by the induction hypothesis, the construction can be completed. But $\bar{t} \prec (n - 2, n - 3, \ldots, 1, 0)$ is equivalent to

$$(0, t_2-1, t_3-1, \ldots, t_{n-t_1}-1, t_{n-t_1+1}, \ldots, t_n) \prec (n-2, n-3, \ldots, 1, 0, 0),$$

and this follows from 5.D.3 with $k = n-1$, $i_1 = \cdots = i_{t_1} = 1$, $i_{t_1+1} = 2$, $i_{t_1+2} = 3, \ldots, i_{n-1} = n - t_1$, and $j_1 = 1$, $j_2 = 2, \ldots, j_{n-1} = n - 1$. ||

A Generalized Tournament

If all pairs of teams in a league are to play exactly one game, then the collection of all games played is a tournament. If all pairs of teams play exactly r games, then the collection of all games played might be called an r-tournament. Here each team plays $r(n-1)$ games, where n is the number of teams in the league.

Bloom (1966) proposed the following problem: Show that $a = (a_1, \ldots, a_n)$ is a possible score vector in an r-tournament if

$$(a_1, \ldots, a_n) \prec r(n - 1, n - 2, \ldots, 1, 0). \qquad (3)$$

This is an easy consequence of F.1. For think of an r-tournament as a repetition r times of an ordinary tournament and let $s^{(i)}$ be the score vector of the ith repetition, $i = 1, \ldots, r$. If the vectors $s^{(i)}$ are similarly ordered, say each $s^{(i)} \in \mathscr{D}$, then $(a_1, \ldots, a_n) = \sum_1^r s^{(i)}$. Moreover, it follows from F.1 (with the aid of 5.A.6) that $\sum_1^r s^{(i)} \prec r(n-1, \ldots, 1, 0)$. This argument shows that (3) is a sufficient condition for a to be the score vector of an r-tournament. It would be of some interest to determine necessary and sufficient conditions.

Nondirected Graphs

For a nondirected graph with n vertices, let $d = (d_1, \ldots, d_n)$ be the vector of degrees (a degree sequence). Because the graph is nondirected, each edge is counted twice, so Σd_i must be even. The *corrected conjugate* sequence d' of d is defined by

$$d'_j = |\{i : i < j \text{ and } d_i \geq j-1\}| + |\{i : i > j \text{ and } d_i \geq j\}|.$$

The calculation of the d' sequence is readily accomplished by a translation to the corresponding incidence matrix as follows. Let the elements of d be row sums and create an incidence matrix using a greedy algorithm but omitting the diagonal elements. The column sums are then the elements of d'.

For example, if $d = (3, 2, 2, 2, 1)$:

*	1	1	1	0	3
1	*	1	0	0	2
1	1	*	0	0	2
1	1	0	*	0	2
1	0	0	0	*	1
4	3	2	1	0	

Thus $d' = (4, 3, 2, 1, 0)$.

F.2. Proposition. A sequence $d = (d_1, \ldots, d_n)$ with the order $n - 1 \geq d_1 \geq \cdots \geq d_n \geq 0$ is a degree sequence if and only if $d \prec d'$, with Σd_i an even number.

For further discussion of material in this subsection, see Arikati and Peled (1999).

G   Edge Coloring in Graphs

Although edge-coloring problems for finite graphs are in general quite difficult, some results have been obtained by Folkman and Fulkerson (1969) for bipartite graphs. They have also obtained a result for general graphs involving majorization.

An *edge coloring* of a graph G assigns colors to the edges of G in such a way that any two edges with a common vertex have distinct colors (e.g., see Fig. 4). A sequence $p_1, \ldots, p_l$ of positive integers is said to be *color-feasible* in the graph G if there exists an edge coloring of G in which precisely p_i edges have color $i, i = 1, \ldots, l$. For the edge coloring of the graph of Fig. 4, 3 edges have the color red, 3 edges have the color green, and 1 edge has the color blue. Thus the integers $(3, 3, 1)$ are color-feasible in the graph G.

266   7. Combinatorial Analysis

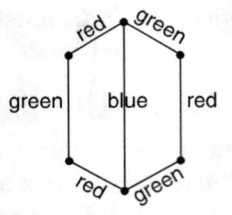

Figure 4. An edge coloring of a graph.

The notions of "circuit" and "chain" are useful. A *circuit* is a sequence of edges $(x_{i_1}, x_{i_2}), (x_{i_2}, x_{i_3}), \ldots, (x_{i_n}, x_{i_1})$, with $x_{i_1}, \ldots x_{i_n}$ all distinct vertices. A *chain* is a sequence of edges $(x_{i_1}, x_{i_2}), \ldots, (x_{i_{n-1}}, x_{i_n})$, again with $x_{i_1}, \ldots, x_{i_n}$ all distinct.

G.1. Theorem (Folkman and Fulkerson, 1969). Let $G = (X, U)$ be an arbitrary graph and suppose that $P = (p_1, \ldots, p_n)$ is color-feasible in G. If

$$P \succ Q = (q_1, \ldots, q_n),$$

then Q is also color-feasible in G.

To exemplify G.1, note that $(3, 3, 1)$ is color-feasible in the graph of Fig. 4. Since $(3, 3, 1) \succ (3, 2, 2)$, it follows from the theorem that $(3, 2, 2)$ is also color-feasible. An edge coloring corresponding to the sequence $(3, 2, 2)$ is given in Fig. 5.

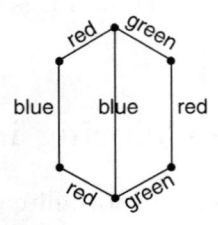

Figure 5. An edge coloring of a graph corresponding to the sequence $(3, 2, 2)$.

Proof. By 5.D.1, it is sufficient to prove that if P' is obtained from P by a transfer from i to j, then P' is color-feasible. Let the graph $U = U_1 \cup \cdots \cup U_n$, where U_k consists of the p_k edges with color k, $k = 1, \ldots, n$. Then $G_k = (X, U_k)$ consists of unconnected edges. Suppose that $p_i > p_j$ and consider $G_i + G_j = (X, U_i \cup U_j)$. Each connected component of this subgraph must be an even circuit or a chain with edges alternating in U_i and U_j. Since $p_i > p_j$, there must be at least one such chain having its first and last edge in U_i. Let U'_i

and U_j' be obtained from U_i and U_j by interchanging the edges in this chain. This produces a coloring of G in which $p_i' = p_i - 1$ edges have color i and $p_j' = p_j + 1$ edges have color j. ||

H Some Graph Theory Settings in Which Majorization Plays a Role

H1. Laplacian spectra of graphs (Grone and Merris, 1990, 1994; Grone, Merris, and Sunder, 1990)

H2. Schur-convex functions on the spectra of graphs (Constantine, 1983)

8
Geometric Inequalities

Although the triangle has a limited number of parameters (sides, angles, altitudes, etc.), the range of inequalities among these entities is surprisingly large. Bottema, Djordjević, Janić, Mitrinović, and Vasić (1969), in their book *Geometric Inequalities*, have collected approximately 400 inequalities for the triangle. It is shown in this chapter that majorization provides a unified approach to obtaining many known geometric inequalities. This unification also has the advantage of suggesting new inequalities.

Because of the repeated references made to it, the book *Geometric Inequalities*, cited above, is referred to as GI. Other inequalities are from the *American Mathematical Monthly*, which is a fertile source of geometric inequalities; this journal is referred to more simply as the *Monthly*.

Mitrinović, Pečarić, and Volenec (1989) provide a sequel to GI in the book *Recent Advances to Geometric Inequalities*(RAGI). These two books, GI and RAGI, constitute an encyclopedia of geometric inequalities. **References where the dates appear without parentheses are taken from GI or RAGI and are not repeated in the bibliography of this book.**

That majorization can play a role in generating inequalities for the triangle was noted by Steinig (1965), who obtained majorizations between the sides of a triangle and the exradii, and between the sides of a triangle and the medians. For the triangle, the sum of the angles is fixed, and majorization arises quite naturally. Many inequalities for the angles of a triangle are obtained as a direct application of a majorization using a Schur-convex function. A paper by Oppenheim (1971), published in 1978, also contains the idea of using majorization to obtain inequalities for triangles. Mitrinović, Pečarić, and Volenec (1989, Chapter VIII, Section F) discuss majorization in the context of geometric inequalities. A perusal of the two books GI and RAGI should suggest examples other than those discussed here that might have a proof using majorization.

In presenting these geometric inequalities, the case of equality (when it can be achieved) is often readily identified. The reason for this is that if ϕ is strictly Schur-convex, then in an inequality of the form

$$\phi(x) \geq \phi(a) \qquad \text{for all} \quad x \succ a,$$

or of the form

$$\phi(x) \leq \phi(a) \qquad \text{for all} \quad x \prec a,$$

equality holds only if x is a permutation of a. The Schur-convex functions used in this chapter are strictly Schur-convex (mostly as a consequence of 3.C.1.a).

Trigonometric inequalities for the triangle comprise Section A and are organized according to whether they relate to the sines, cosines, or tangents of the angles of a triangle. Other inequalities for the cotangents, secants, and cosecants of the angles are obtainable, but are omitted because they follow similar patterns and tend to be repetitive.

A second class of inequalities relates the sides and the semiperimeter minus the sides, or equivalently, the altitudes and the exradii. These are in Sections B, C, and D.

Two plane figures are called *isoperimetric* if their perimeters are equal. Isoperimetric inequalities generally relate some characteristic of two isoperimetric figures. One of the simplest such inequalities is that the equilateral triangle has the maximum area among all isoperimetric triangles. New proofs of some isoperimetric inequalities for plane figures are provided in Section E. A duality between triangle inequalities and inequalities for positive numbers is the subject of Section F.

In all of these sections, the inequalities given as examples have been chosen because they have already appeared in print or because they extend inequalities in print. Other examples are readily obtainable using other Schur-convex functions.

A Inequalities for the Angles of a Triangle

If $\alpha_1, \alpha_2, \alpha_3$ are the angles of a plane triangle, then $\alpha_1 + \alpha_2 + \alpha_3 = \pi$, and

$$\left(\frac{\pi}{3}, \frac{\pi}{3}, \frac{\pi}{3}\right) \prec (\alpha_1, \alpha_2, \alpha_3) \prec (\pi, 0, 0) \quad \text{for all triangles,} \tag{1}$$

$$\left(\frac{\pi}{3}, \frac{\pi}{3}, \frac{\pi}{3}\right) \prec (\alpha_1, \alpha_2, \alpha_3) \prec \left(\frac{\pi}{2}, \frac{\pi}{2}, 0\right) \quad \text{for acute triangles,} \tag{2}$$

$$\left(\frac{\pi}{2}, \frac{\pi}{4}, \frac{\pi}{4}\right) \prec (\alpha_1, \alpha_2, \alpha_3) \prec (\pi, 0, 0) \quad \text{for obtuse triangles.} \tag{3}$$

Consequently, if $\phi : \mathcal{R}^3 \to \mathcal{R}$ is a Schur-convex function, then from 3.C.1 and (1), (2), or (3), we obtain

$$\phi\left(\frac{\pi}{3}, \frac{\pi}{3}, \frac{\pi}{3}\right) \leq \phi(\alpha_1, \alpha_2, \alpha_3) \leq \phi(\pi, 0, 0) \quad \text{for all triangles,} \tag{4}$$

$$\phi\left(\frac{\pi}{3}, \frac{\pi}{3}, \frac{\pi}{3}\right) \leq \phi(\alpha_1, \alpha_2, \alpha_3) \leq \phi\left(\frac{\pi}{2}, \frac{\pi}{2}, 0\right) \quad \text{for acute triangles,} \tag{5}$$

$$\phi\left(\frac{\pi}{2}, \frac{\pi}{4}, \frac{\pi}{4}\right) \leq \phi(\alpha_1, \alpha_2, \alpha_3) \leq \phi(\pi, 0, 0) \quad \text{for obtuse triangles.} \tag{6}$$

The bounds obtained usually will be the best possible. When only one bound is given below, an additional assumption that the triangle is acute or obtuse does not yield an improvement in the inequality. In a statement of strict inequality, degenerate triangles are not allowed.

Most of the choices of Schur-convex functions ϕ are of the form $\sum g(x_i)$, where g is convex. Examples are given for the sine, cosine, and tangent functions.

The Sine Function

A.1. The functions $\sin x$, $\sqrt{\sin x}$, and $\log \sin x$ are strictly concave on $(0, \pi)$; the function $\sin^2(x/2)$ is strictly convex, $0 \leq x \leq \pi/2$; the function $\sin(kx)$ is strictly concave, $0 \leq x \leq \pi/k$. Consequently, it follows from (4), (5), (6) with the aid of 3.C.1 that

$$0 < \sin \alpha_1 + \sin \alpha_2 + \sin \alpha_3 \leq 3\sqrt{3}/2 \quad \text{for all triangles,}$$

$$2 < \sin \alpha_1 + \sin \alpha_2 + \sin \alpha_3 \leq 3\sqrt{3}/2 \quad \text{for acute triangles,}$$

$$0 < \sin \alpha_1 + \sin \alpha_2 + \sin \alpha_3 \leq 1 + \sqrt{2} \quad \text{for obtuse triangles.}$$

These inequalities are GI 2.1 and 2.2 and are attributed to Padoa, 1925, Curry, 1963, Bottema, 1954/1955, and Kooistra, 1957/1958.

A.2.

$$\sqrt{2} < \sin(\alpha_1/2) + \sin(\alpha_2/2) + \sin(\alpha_3/2) \leq \tfrac{3}{2} \quad \text{for acute triangles.}$$

272   8. Geometric Inequalities

The right-hand inequality is GI 2.9 and is attributed to Child, 1939, and Kooistra, 1957/1958. See also Oppenheim (1971). The left-hand inequality is an improvement over GI 2.9.

A.3.

$$0 < \sqrt{\sin \alpha_1} + \sqrt{\sin \alpha_2} + \sqrt{\sin \alpha_3} \leq 3(\tfrac{3}{4})^{1/4} \quad \text{for all triangles,}$$
$$2 < \sqrt{\sin \alpha_1} + \sqrt{\sin \alpha_2} + \sqrt{\sin \alpha_3} \leq 3(\tfrac{3}{4})^{1/4} \quad \text{for acute triangles,}$$
$$0 < \sqrt{\sin \alpha_1} + \sqrt{\sin \alpha_2} + \sqrt{\sin \alpha_3} \leq 1 + 2^{3/4} \quad \text{for obtuse triangles.}$$

The first of these inequalities is GI 2.5 and is attributed to Albu, 1963.

A.4.

$$0 < \sin \alpha_1 \sin \alpha_2 \sin \alpha_3 \leq 3\sqrt{3}/8 \quad \text{for all triangles,}$$
$$0 < \sin \alpha_1 \sin \alpha_2 \sin \alpha_3 \leq 1/2 \quad \text{for obtuse triangles.}$$

The first inequality is GI 2.7 and 2.8 and is attributed to Wilkins, 1939, and Kooistra, 1957/1958. The second bound is an improvement over GI 2.8, which gives the upper bound $\sqrt{3}/3$.

A.5.

$$0 < \sin(\tfrac{1}{2}\alpha_1) \sin(\tfrac{1}{2}\alpha_2) \sin(\tfrac{1}{2}\alpha_3) \leq \tfrac{1}{8} \quad \text{for acute triangles.}$$

This inequality is GI 2.12.

A.6.

$$\tfrac{3}{4} \leq \sin^2(\tfrac{1}{2}\alpha_1) + \sin^2(\tfrac{1}{2}\alpha_2) + \sin^2(\tfrac{1}{2}\alpha_3) < 1 \quad \text{for all triangles.}$$

This is inequality GI 2.14. This follows from a simple majorization argument and is attributed to Kooistra, 1957/1958.

A.7.

$$0 < \sin(\tfrac{1}{2}\alpha_1)\sin(\tfrac{1}{2}\alpha_2) + \sin(\tfrac{1}{2}\alpha_1)\sin(\tfrac{1}{2}\alpha_3) + \sin(\tfrac{1}{2}\alpha_2)\sin(\tfrac{1}{2}\alpha_3) \leq \tfrac{3}{4}$$

for all triangles,

$$\tfrac{1}{2} < \sin(\tfrac{1}{2}\alpha_1)\sin(\tfrac{1}{2}\alpha_2) + \sin(\tfrac{1}{2}\alpha_1)\sin(\tfrac{1}{2}\alpha_3) + \sin(\tfrac{1}{2}\alpha_2)\sin(\tfrac{1}{2}\alpha_3) \leq \tfrac{3}{4}$$

for acute triangles,

$$0 < \sin(\tfrac{1}{2}\alpha_1)\sin(\tfrac{1}{2}\alpha_2) + \sin(\tfrac{1}{2}\alpha_1)\sin(\tfrac{1}{2}\alpha_3) + \sin(\tfrac{1}{2}\alpha_2)\sin(\tfrac{1}{2}\alpha_3)$$
$$\leq (2-\sqrt{2})/4 + \sqrt{(2-\sqrt{2})/2}$$

for obtuse triangles.

These inequalities follow from the fact that the second elementary function in $(\sin(\alpha_1/2), \sin(\alpha_2/2), \sin(\alpha_3/2))$ is Schur-concave (see 3.F.1 and Table 2 in 3.B). The first inequality is GI 2.15 attributed to Child, 1939.

A.8. Definition. The *power means* $M_k(x, y, z)$ are defined as follows:

$$M_k(x, y, z) = [\tfrac{1}{3}(x^k + y^k + z^k)]^{1/k} \quad \text{for} \quad k \neq 0, \pm\infty,$$
$$M_{-\infty}(x, y, z) = \min(x, y, z),$$
$$M_0(x, y, z) = (xyz)^{1/3},$$
$$M_\infty(x, y, z) = \max(x, y, z).$$

A.8.a. If $k \neq 0, -\infty$, $k \leq 1$, then

(i) $0 < M_k(\sin\alpha_1, \sin\alpha_2, \sin\alpha_3) \leq \sqrt{3}/2$ for all triangles,

(ii) $(\tfrac{2}{3})^{1/k} < M_k(\sin\alpha_1, \sin\alpha_2, \sin\alpha_3) \leq \sqrt{3}/2$ for acute triangles,

(iii) $0 < M_k(\sin\alpha_1, \sin\alpha_2, \sin\alpha_3) \leq [(1 + 2^{1-k/2})/3]^{1/k}$ for obtuse triangles.

If $k = 0$, the inequalities are essentially A.4. If $k = -\infty$, the inequalities become

(iv) $0 < \min(\sin\alpha_1, \sin\alpha_2, \sin\alpha_3) \leq \sqrt{3}/2$ for all triangles,

(v) $0 < \min(\sin\alpha_1, \sin\alpha_2, \sin\alpha_3) \leq \sqrt{2}/2$ for obtuse triangles.

These inequalities follow from the fact that $\sin x$ is concave, $0 \leq x \leq \pi$, $M_k(x_1, x_2, x_3)$ is concave and increasing (see 3.I.1.b), so that by Section 3.B.2, Table 2, $M_k(\sin x_1, \sin x_2, \sin x_3)$ is Schur-concave. Inequality (i) is GI 2.6.

Remark. For $x, y, z \in (0, \pi)$, the following inequality is reported in RAGI (p. 637, 6.6).

$$f(x, y, z) = \frac{\sin(\frac{x+y}{2})\,\sin(\frac{x+z}{2})\,\sin(\frac{y+z}{2})}{\sin x\,\sin y\,\sin z} \geq 1$$

with equality if $x = y = z$. The natural question of whether this function $f(x, y, z)$ is Schur-convex remains open.

The Cosine Function

The functions $\cos x$, $\cos^2(x/2)$ are strictly concave in $(0, \pi/2)$; the function $\log \cos(kx)$ is strictly concave in $(0, \pi/2k)$. The following inequalities are consequences of (1), (2), (3) and 3.C.1.

A.9.
$$1 < \cos \alpha_1 + \cos \alpha_2 + \cos \alpha_3 \leq 3/2 \qquad \text{for acute triangles.}$$

This inequality is GI 2.16. It also follows from the identity $\sum_1^3 \cos \alpha_i = 1 + 4 \prod_1^3 \sin(\alpha_i/2)$ and A.5.

A.10.
$$2 < \cos(\alpha_1/2) + \cos(\alpha_2/2) + \cos(\alpha_3/2) \leq 3\sqrt{3}/2 \qquad \text{for all triangles.}$$

This inequality is GI 2.27 and is attributed to Kooistra, 1957/1958.

A.11.
$$2 < \cos^2(\alpha_1/2) + \cos^2(\alpha_2/2) + \cos^2(\alpha_3/2) \leq 9/4 \qquad \text{for all triangles.}$$

This inequality is GI 2.29 and is equivalent to A.6.

A.12.

(i) $\cos \alpha_1 \cos \alpha_2 \cos \alpha_3 \leq 1/8$,

(ii) $0 < \cos(\alpha_1/2) \cos(\alpha_2/2) \cos(\alpha_3/2) \leq 3\sqrt{3}/8$ for all triangles,

(iii) $1/2 < \cos(\alpha_1/2) \cos(\alpha_2/2) \cos(\alpha_3/2) \leq 3\sqrt{3}/8$ for acute triangles,

(iv) $0 < \cos(\alpha_1/2) \cos(\alpha_2/2) \cos(\alpha_3/2) \leq (1 + \sqrt{2})/4$ for obtuse triangles,

(v) $\cos \alpha_1 \cos \alpha_2 + \cos \alpha_1 \cos \alpha_3 + \cos \alpha_2 \cos \alpha_3 \leq 3/4$.

Inequalities (i) to (iv) follow from the concavity of $\log \cos(kx)$. Inequality (v) is a consequence of the Schur-concavity of the elementary symmetric functions (3.F.1 and Table 2 in 3.B). Inequality (i) is GI 2.23 and is attributed to Popovici, 1925, and Child, 1939. The inequalities (ii) and (iii) are GI 2.28 and are attributed to Kooistra, 1957–1958. Inequality (iv) is new and is sharper than that in GI 2.28. Inequality (v) is GI 2.22 and is attributed to Child, 1939.

A.13. Define
$$h(\alpha_1, \alpha_2, \alpha_3) \equiv (1 + \cos\alpha_1 \cos\alpha_2 \cos\alpha_3)/(\sin\alpha_1 \sin\alpha_2 \sin\alpha_3).$$

$$h(\alpha_1, \alpha_2, \alpha_3) \geq \begin{cases} \sqrt{3} & \text{for all triangles,} \\ 2 & \text{for obtuse triangles.} \end{cases}$$

These inequalities follow from the majorizations (1), (2), and (3) and the Schur-convexity of $h(\alpha_1, \alpha_2, \alpha_3)$. This can be verified directly using 3.A.4 to yield

$$\frac{\partial h}{\partial \alpha_1} - \frac{\partial h}{\partial \alpha_2} = \frac{\sin(\alpha_1 - \alpha_2)\sin\alpha_3[1 + \cos\alpha_3 \cos(\alpha_1 + \alpha_2)]}{\prod_1^3 \sin^2 \alpha_i}.$$

The first inequality is GI 2.59 and is due to Guggenheimer, 1967.

A.14. Open problem (*Monthly*, 2007, p. 114, 11176). For a nondegenerate triangle with angles $\alpha_1, \alpha_2, \alpha_3$ is

$$\phi(\alpha_1, \alpha_2, \alpha_3) = \frac{\Sigma \cos^3 \alpha_i}{\Sigma \cos \alpha_i}$$

Schur-convex in $\alpha_1, \alpha_2, \alpha_3 \in (0, \pi)$?

The Tangent Function

The functions $(\tan x)^m$, $m \geq 1$, are strictly convex on $(0, \pi/2)$; the function $\log \tan(kx)$ is strictly concave on $(0, \pi/4k)$, $k > 0$. These facts together with (4)–(6) imply the following inequalities.

A.15. For $m \geq 1$,

(i) $3^{(m+2)/2} \leq \tan^m \alpha_1 + \tan^m \alpha_2 + \tan^m \alpha_3$ for acute triangles,

(ii) $3^{-(m-2)/2} \leq \tan^m(\alpha_2/2) + \tan^m(\alpha_2/2) + \tan^m(\alpha_3/2)$,

(iii) $0 < \tan(\alpha_1/2)\tan(\alpha_2/2)\tan(\alpha_3/2) \leq \sqrt{3}/9$ for acute triangles.

Inequality (i) for $m = 1$ and $m = 2$ are GI 2.30 and 2.31 and are attributed to Kooistra, 1957/1958 (see also GI 11.6). The bound of $3(m+2)/2$ given in GI 11.7 is weaker than (i). The case of general m is GI 11.8 and is attributed to Kritikos, 1934. Inequality (i) holds for $m \geq 0$; however, the function $\sum \tan^m \alpha_i$ is not Schur-convex for $0 < m < 1$.

276   8. Geometric Inequalities

Inequality (ii) for $m = 1$ is GI 2.33 and is attributed to Karamata, 1948, and Kooistra, 1957/1958. The case $m = 2$ is GI 2.35 and is attributed to Durell and Robson, 1948, and Kooistra, 1957/1958. For $m = 6$, inequality (ii) is GI 2.36.

Inequality (iii) is GI 2.34 and is attributed to Kooistra, 1957/1958.

B   Inequalities for the Sides of a Triangle

There are three key majorizations involving the sides a_1, a_2, a_3 of a triangle with semiperimeter $s = \frac{1}{2}(a_1 + a_2 + a_3)$ and average side length $\bar{a} = \frac{1}{3}(a_1 + a_2 + a_3) = 2s/3$,

$$(\bar{a}, \bar{a}, \bar{a}) \prec (a_1, a_2, a_3) \prec (s, s, 0) \quad \text{for all triangles;} \tag{1}$$

$$(\bar{a}, \bar{a}, \bar{a}) \prec (a_1, a_2, a_3) \prec (s, s/2, s/2) \quad \text{for isosceles triangles;} \tag{2}$$

$$\frac{s}{1+\sqrt{2}}(2, \sqrt{2}, \sqrt{2}) \prec (a_1, a_2, a_3) \prec (s, s, 0) \text{ for obtuse triangles.} \tag{3}$$

The left hand majorizations in (1) and (2) hold for any numbers. The remaining majorizations make use of properties of triangles.

It follows that if φ is a continuous Schur-convex function, then

$$\varphi(\bar{a}, \bar{a}, \bar{a}) \leq \varphi(a_1, a_2, a_3) < \varphi(s, s, 0) \quad \text{for all triangles,} \tag{4}$$

$$\varphi(\bar{a}, \bar{a}, \bar{a}) \leq \varphi(a_1, a_2, a_3) < \varphi(s, s/2, s/2) \text{ for isosceles triangles,} \tag{5}$$

$$\varphi\left(\frac{2s}{1+\sqrt{2}}, \frac{\sqrt{2}s}{1+\sqrt{2}}, \frac{\sqrt{2}s}{1+\sqrt{2}}\right) < \varphi(a_1, a_2, a_3) < \varphi(s, s, 0)$$

$$\text{for obtuse triangles,} \tag{6}$$

and these inequalities are the best possible. For Schur-concave functions, the inequalities are reversed. The corresponding majorization for acute triangles is identical to (1), so specializing to acute triangles gives the same inequality (4) as is obtained for all triangles. For right triangles, the relevant majorizations are given by (3), yielding inequalities identical to the ones for obtuse triangles, namely, (6).

If

$$s_1 \equiv 2(s - a_1) = -a_1 + a_2 + a_3,$$
$$s_2 \equiv 2(s - a_2) = a_1 - a_2 + a_3,$$
$$s_3 \equiv 2(s - a_3) = a_1 + a_2 - a_3,$$

then
$$a_1 = \tfrac{1}{2}(s_2 + s_3), \qquad a_2 = \tfrac{1}{2}(s_1 + s_3), \qquad a_3 = \tfrac{1}{2}(s_1 + s_2),$$
and
$$(a_1, a_2, a_3) = (s_1, s_2, s_3) \begin{bmatrix} 0 & \tfrac{1}{2} & \tfrac{1}{2} \\ \tfrac{1}{2} & 0 & \tfrac{1}{2} \\ \tfrac{1}{2} & \tfrac{1}{2} & 0 \end{bmatrix},$$

so that by 2.B.2
$$(a_1, a_2, a_3) \prec (s_1, s_2, s_3). \tag{7}$$

A geometric interpretation of s_1, s_2, s_3 is given in Fig. 1. Note that
$$\tfrac{2}{3}(s, s, s) \prec (s_1, s_2, s_3) \prec (2s, 0, 0). \tag{8}$$

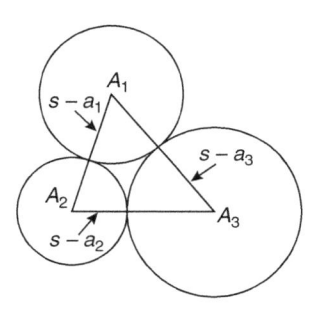

Figure 1.

The majorizations in (8) hold for all triangles. Parallel results are available for specialized classes of triangles as follows:

$$\tfrac{2}{3}(s, s, s) \prec (s_1, s_2, s_3) \prec (s, s, 0) \qquad \text{for isosceles triangles}, \tag{9}$$

$$2s(\sqrt{2} - 1)(1, 1, \sqrt{2}) \prec (s_1, s_2, s_3) \prec (2s, 0, 0) \tag{10}$$
$$\text{for obtuse triangles}.$$

Inequalities for the Sides (a_1, a_2, a_3)

The following inequalities for the sides of a triangle are direct applications of the majorizations (1), (2), and (3) to a Schur-convex function. The inequalities relating the sides (a_1, a_2, a_3) to the quantities (s_1, s_2, s_3) make use of (1) and (7), and the inequalities relating the sides (a_1, a_2, a_3) to the angles $(\alpha_1, \alpha_2, \alpha_3)$ require a further majorization.

B.1. The inequalities

(i) $\quad \dfrac{1}{3} \leq \dfrac{a_1^2 + a_2^2 + a_3^2}{(a_1 + a_2 + a_3)^2} < \dfrac{1}{2} \quad$ for all triangles,

(ii) $\quad \dfrac{1}{3} \leq \dfrac{a_1^2 + a_2^2 + a_3^2}{(a_1 + a_2 + a_3)^2} < \dfrac{3}{8} \quad$ for isosceles triangles,

(iii) $0.343 \approx \dfrac{2}{(1 + \sqrt{2})^2} \leq \dfrac{a_1^2 + a_2^2 + a_3^2}{(a_1 + a_2 + a_3)^2} < \dfrac{1}{2} \quad$ for obtuse triangles

follow from the Schur-convexity of the middle term. Inequality (i) is GI 1.19 and is attributed to Petrović, 1916.

In the remaining inequalities listed in this section, we provide only the inequalities that hold for all triangles [obtained using (1) and (8)]. Analogous inequalities for isosceles and obtuse triangles are obtainable using (2), (3), (9), and (10).

B.2. The inequalities

$$\frac{1}{4} < \frac{a_1 a_2 + a_1 a_3 + a_2 a_3}{(a_1 + a_2 + a_3)^2} \leq \frac{1}{3}$$

follow from the Schur-concavity of the second elementary symmetric function (3.F.1), are GI 1.1, and are attributed to Wood, 1938.

B.3. The inequalities

$$\frac{1}{4} < \frac{(a_1 + a_2)(a_1 + a_3)(a_2 + a_3)}{(a_1 + a_2 + a_3)^3} \leq \frac{8}{27} \qquad (11)$$

are a consequence of the Schur-concavity of the middle term. Similarly,

$$\frac{1}{2} < \frac{(a_1 + a_2)(a_1 + a_3)(a_2 + a_3)}{a_1^3 + a_2^3 + a_3^3} \leq \frac{8}{3} \approx 0.296 \qquad (12)$$

because of the Schur-concavity of the numerator and Schur-convexity of the denominator of the middle term in (12). The right-hand inequality of (12) is GI 1.5 and is attributed to Padoa, 1925. Extension of these results involving more than three a_i's (and thus not being interpretable in terms of sides of triangles) may be found in 3.I.5.

B.4. For $d \geq 0$,

$$\frac{4(9-2d)}{27}s^2 \leq a_1^2 + a_2^2 + a_3^2 - d\frac{a_1 a_2 a_3}{s} < 2s^2. \tag{13}$$

Inequalities (13) follow from the Schur-convexity of the middle term. With $d = 36/35$, the left-hand inequality is GI 1.2 and is attributed to Darling and Moser, 1961.

B.5. For $d \geq 0$,

$$\frac{3(3d+2)}{4} \leq \frac{ds+a_1}{a_2+a_3} + \frac{ds+a_2}{a_1+a_3} + \frac{ds+a_3}{a_1+a_2} < \frac{5d+4}{2}. \tag{14}$$

Inequalities (14) follow from the Schur-convexity of the middle term. The left-hand inequality with $d = 0$ is GI 1.16 and is attributed to Nesbitt 1903, and to Petrović, 1932. For $d = 1$, the left-hand inequality is GI 1.17.

B.6. The inequalities

$$\sqrt{s} < \sqrt{s-a_1} + \sqrt{s-a_2} + \sqrt{s-a_3}$$

$$\equiv \sqrt{s_1/2} + \sqrt{s_2/2} + \sqrt{s_3/2} \leq \sqrt{3s}$$

are consequences of the concavity of $\sqrt{x}$ or $\sqrt{s-x}$.

B.6 is GI 1.20 and is attributed to Santaló, 1943, and Gotman, 1965.

B.7. The inequality

$$\sqrt{a_1(s-a_1)} + \sqrt{a_2(s-a_2)} + \sqrt{a_3(s-a_3)} \leq \sqrt{2}s$$

follows from the concavity of $\sqrt{x(s-x)}$, $0 < x < s$, and is stated in GI 5.47 in terms of the sides and exradii. The upper bound of $3s/2$ given there in place of $\sqrt{2}s$ is not the best possible.

B.8. The inequality

$$\frac{9}{s} \leq \frac{1}{s-a_1} + \frac{1}{s-a_2} + \frac{1}{s-a_3} = \frac{2}{s_1} + \frac{2}{s_2} + \frac{2}{s_3}$$

follows from the convexity of $(s-x)^{-1}$ for $0 < x < s$, or x^{-1} for $0 < x$, and is GI 1.15.

B.9. The inequality

$$s^2 \geq 3\sqrt{3}\Delta,$$

where Δ is the area of the triangle, is GI 4.2 and is attributed to Hadwiger, 1939, and Santaló, 1943. Because $\Delta^2 = s\prod_1^3(s_i/2)$, this inequality is equivalent to

$$\prod_1^3(s_i/2) = \prod_1^3(s-a_i) \leq (s/3)^3,$$

which follows from the Schur-concavity of the product.

B.10. The inequality

$$a_1a_2a_3 \leq \tfrac{1}{8}(a_1+a_2)(a_1+a_3)(a_2+a_3)$$

follows from a related majorization. Let

$$u_1 = \tfrac{1}{2}(a_1+a_2), \qquad u_2 = \tfrac{1}{2}(a_1+a_3), \qquad u_3 = \tfrac{1}{2}(a_2+a_3);$$

then

$$(u_1,u_2,u_3) \prec (a_1,a_2,a_3)$$

for the same reason that (7) holds.

The result then follows from the Schur-concavity of the product. This inequality is GI 1.4 and is attributed to Cesàro, 1880.

Inequalities between (a_1,a_2,a_3) and (s_1,s_2,s_3)

The inequalities relating the sides (a_1,a_2,a_3) and the quantities $s_1 = 2(s-a_1)$, $s_2 = 2(s-a_2)$, $s_3 = 2(s-a_3)$ involve the elementary symmetric functions $S_k(x_1,\ldots,x_n)$ on $\mathscr{R}^3_{++}$.

B.11.

(i) $s_1s_2s_3 \leq a_1a_2a_3$,

(ii) $\dfrac{s_1s_2s_3}{s_1s_2+s_1s_3+s_2s_3} \leq \dfrac{a_1a_2a_3}{a_1a_2+a_1a_3+a_2a_3}$,

(iii) $(s_1s_2s_3)(s_1s_2+s_1s_3+s_2s_3) \leq (a_1a_2a_3)(a_1a_2+a_1a_3+a_2a_3)$.

Inequality (i) follows from the Schur-concavity of $S_3(x_1,x_2,x_3)$ (3.F.1); inequality (ii) follows from the Schur-concavity of the ratio $S_3(x_1,x_2,x_3)/S_2(x_1,x_2,x_3)$ (3.F.3); inequality (iii) similarly uses the product $S_3(x_1,x_2,x_3)S_2(x_1,x_2,x_3)$ (3.B.1.d) of the elementary symmetric functions on $\mathscr{R}^3_{++}$. Inequality (i) is posed by Walker as *Monthly*

Problem E2284 (1971); it is GI 1.3 and is attributed to Padoa, 1925. It appeared earlier in a different form (see C.1) in *Monthly* Problem E1675 (Makowski, 1964).

Inequalities for the Sides and Angles of a Triangle

If a_i is the side opposite angle α_i, and $a_1 \geq a_2 \geq a_3$, then $\alpha_1 \geq \alpha_2 \geq \alpha_3$, so that the sides and angles are similarly ordered. Define

$$\tau_1 = \tfrac{1}{2}(\alpha_1 + \alpha_2), \qquad \tau_2 = \tfrac{1}{2}(\alpha_1 + \alpha_3), \qquad \tau_3 = \tfrac{1}{2}(\alpha_2 + \alpha_3).$$

Then

$$\tau_1 \geq \tau_2 \geq \tau_3,$$

and

$$(\tau_1, \tau_2, \tau_3) \prec (\alpha_1, \alpha_2, \alpha_3)$$

for the same reason that (7) holds. This yields the inequalities

(i) $a_1\alpha_1 + a_2\alpha_2 + a_3\alpha_3 \geq a_1\tau_1 + a_2\tau_2 + a_3\tau_3 \geq a_1\tau_3 + a_2\tau_2 + a_3\tau_1,$

which are consequences of 3.H.2.c and 6.A.3. The left-hand inequality in (i) is new and is stronger than GI 3.2.

(ii) $\dfrac{\pi}{3} \leq \dfrac{a_1\alpha_1 + a_2\alpha_2 + a_3\alpha_3}{a_1 + a_2 + a_3} < \dfrac{\pi}{2}.$

This inequality follows from 3.H.3.c and is GI 3.3.

Again by 3.H.3.c,

$$\dfrac{a_1\alpha_1 + a_2\alpha_2 + a_3\alpha_3}{a_1 + a_2 + a_3} \leq \dfrac{1}{2}(\alpha_1 + \alpha_2) = \dfrac{\pi - \alpha_3}{2},$$

which is GI 3.4.

An Inequality for the Sides of a Polygon

Inequality B.5 can be extended to the case of a polygon.

B.12. If $a_1, \ldots, a_n$ are the sides of a polygon with perimeter $p = a_1 + \cdots + a_n$ and if $a_i \leq t$, $i = 1, \ldots, n$, where for some integer l, $p/(l+1) \leq t \leq p/l$, then from 5.C.1,

(i) $\dfrac{1}{n}(p, \ldots, p) \prec (a_1, \ldots, a_n) \prec (\underbrace{t, \ldots, t}_{l}, \underbrace{p - lt}_{1}, \underbrace{0, \ldots, 0}_{n-l-1}).$

The function $g(x) = (pd + x)/(p - x)$ is convex for $0 \leq x < p$, $d \geq 0$, so that

(ii) $\dfrac{n(nd+1)}{n-1} \leq \dfrac{pd+a_1}{p-a_1} + \dfrac{pd+a_2}{p-a_2} + \cdots + \dfrac{pd+a_n}{p-a_n}$

$\leq \dfrac{l(pd+t)}{p-t} + \dfrac{pd+p-lt}{lt} + d(n-l-1).$

Remark. The left-hand inequality of (ii) holds for all nonnegative numbers as noted by Mitrinović (1964, paragraphs 7.31, 7.32). The right-hand inequality holds for all polygons by virtue of (i).

C Inequalities for the Exradii and Altitudes

For a triangle with vertices A_1, A_2, A_3, sides a_1, a_2, a_3 (with a_i opposite A_i), altitudes h_1, h_2, h_3 (with h_i from A_i), and exradii r_1, r_2, r_3 (with r_i tangent to a_i) as in Fig. 2, there is a fundamental duality between the pairs (a_i, s_i) and (h_i, r_i) that arises from the relations

$$2\Delta = a_1 h_1 = a_2 h_2 = a_3 h_3$$
$$= s_1 r_1 = s_2 r_2 = s_3 r_3. \qquad (1)$$

(As before, Δ is the area of the triangle.)

It follows from (1) that

$$\dfrac{1}{h_1} = \dfrac{1}{2}\left(\dfrac{1}{r_2} + \dfrac{1}{r_3}\right), \quad \dfrac{1}{h_2} = \dfrac{1}{2}\left(\dfrac{1}{r_1} + \dfrac{1}{r_3}\right), \quad \dfrac{1}{h_3} = \dfrac{1}{2}\left(\dfrac{1}{r_1} + \dfrac{1}{r_2}\right). \qquad (2)$$

As in the proof of (7), Section B, this means that

$$\left(\dfrac{1}{h_1}, \dfrac{1}{h_2}, \dfrac{1}{h_3}\right) \prec \left(\dfrac{1}{r_1}, \dfrac{1}{r_2}, \dfrac{1}{r_3}\right). \qquad (3)$$

If r denotes the radius of the incircle, then

$$\dfrac{1}{r} = \dfrac{1}{h_1} + \dfrac{1}{h_2} + \dfrac{1}{h_3}, \qquad (4)$$

so that

$$\left(\dfrac{1}{3r}, \dfrac{1}{3r}, \dfrac{1}{3r}\right) \prec \left(\dfrac{1}{h_1}, \dfrac{1}{h_2}, \dfrac{1}{h_3}\right). \qquad (5)$$

C.1. If d_1, d_2, d_3 are nonnegative numbers, then

$$\sum_\pi h_{\pi(1)}^{d_1} h_{\pi(2)}^{d_2} h_{\pi(3)}^{d_3} \leq \sum_\pi r_{\pi(1)}^{d_1} r_{\pi(2)}^{d_2} r_{\pi(3)}^{d_3},$$

or equivalently,
$$\sum_\pi a_{\pi(1)}^{-d_1} a_{\pi(2)}^{-d_2} a_{\pi(3)}^{-d_3} \leq \sum_\pi s_{\pi(1)}^{-d_1} s_{\pi(2)}^{-d_2} s_{\pi(3)}^{-d_3}.$$

This inequality follows from the majorization (3) and the Schur-convexity in x of
$$\sum_\pi x_{\pi(1)}^{-a_1} x_{\pi(2)}^{-a_2} x_{\pi(3)}^{-a_3}, \qquad a_i > 0, \quad x_j > 0,$$

given in 3.G.1.k.

This inequality is posed by Nasser as *Monthly* Problem E1847 (1966). (Note that the inequality is reversed in the *Monthly*.)

The case $d_1 = d_2 = 1$, $d_3 = 0$ yields
$$h_1 h_2 + h_1 h_3 + h_2 h_3 \leq r_1 r_2 + r_1 r_3 + r_2 r_3,$$

which was posed by Makowski as *Monthly* Problem E1675 (1964). It was noted by Oppenheim (1965b) to be equivalent to B.2.(i).

The case $d_2 = d_3 = 0$ is GI 6.19 and is attributed to Makowski, 1961. By a direct argument based on the convexity of x^{-d}, $x > 0$ for $d > 0$ or $d < -1$ and concavity for $-1 < d < 0$, we obtain
$$\sum h_i^d \leq \sum r_i^d, \qquad d > 0 \text{ or } d < -1,$$
$$\sum h_i^d \geq \sum r_i^d, \qquad -1 < d < 0.$$

C.2. The inequalities

(i) $\prod_1^3 h_i \geq 27 r^3$,

(ii) $\sum_1^3 h_i \geq 9r$,

(iii) $\sum_1^3 1/(h_i - 2r) \geq 3/r$,

(iv) $\sum_1^3 (h_i + r)/(h_i - r) \geq 6$

follow immediately from (5) and the Schur-convexity of the respective functions. Inequalities (i) and (ii) are GI 6.16 and GI 6.8, respectively, and are attributed to Zetel', 1948. Inequality (iii) is GI 6.21 and is attributed to Bokov, 1966. Inequality (iv) is GI 6.22 and is attributed to Cosnita and Turtoiu, 1965.

C.3. For $m \geq 1$,
$$(r_1/h_1)^m + (r_2/h_2)^m + (r_3/h_3)^m \geq 3.$$

For $m = 1$, this inequality was posed by Demir as *Monthly* Problem E1779 (1965). The extension to general m is given by Guggenheimer (1966) and is discussed in GI 6.28.

The inequality of C.3 follows directly from the convexity of $g(x) = x^m$, $m \geq 1$, and the majorization

$$(r_1/h_1, r_2/h_2, r_3/h_3) \succ_w (1, 1, 1). \tag{6}$$

With the aid of (2), (6) can be written in terms of r_1, r_2, and r_3 alone. Then by assuming an ordering, say $r_1 \geq r_2 \geq r_3$, and by using $x + (1/x) \geq 2$, $x \geq 0$, (6) is not difficult to verify.

D Inequalities for the Sides, Exradii, and Medians

Consider a triangle with vertices A_1, A_2, A_3, opposite sides a_1, a_2, a_3, medians m_1, m_2, m_3 (with m_i from A_i), and exradii r_1, r_2, r_3 as in Fig. 2. Steinig (1965) proved two majorizations, one between the sides and exradii, and one between the sides and medians. A number of known inequalities may be obtained as a consequence. The present development is essentially that of Steinig (1965).

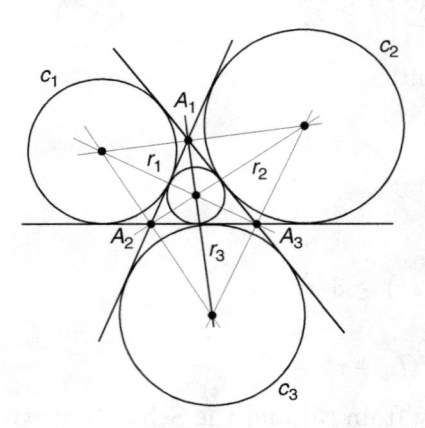

Figure 2.

Sides and Exradii

D.1. For each $t \geq 1$,

$$(\sqrt{3}/2)^t (a_1^t, a_2^t, a_3^t) \prec_w (r_1^t, r_2^t, r_3^t). \tag{1}$$

D. Inequalities for the Sides, Exradii, and Medians

Sketch of proof. The sides and exradii of a triangle are related by

$$a_1 = \frac{r_1(r_2+r_3)}{\sqrt{r_1r_2+r_1r_3+r_3r_3}}, \qquad a_2 = \frac{r_2(r_1+r_3)}{\sqrt{r_1r_2+r_1r_3+r_2r_3}}, \qquad (2)$$

$$a_3 = \frac{r_3(r_1+r_2)}{\sqrt{r_1r_2+r_1r_3+r_2r_3}}.$$

If $a_1 \geq a_2 \geq a_3$, then (2) yields the ordering $r_1 \geq r_2 \geq r_3$. It is known that

$$(\sqrt{3}/2)a_1 \leq r_1, \qquad (\sqrt{3}/2)a_3 \geq r_3. \qquad (3)$$

Suppose that for some σ in $(0, 1)$, the equality

$$(\sqrt{3}/2)^\sigma (a_1^\sigma + a_2^\sigma + a_3^\sigma) = r_1^\sigma + r_2^\sigma + r_3^\sigma \qquad (4)$$

holds. Then by virtue of (3) and (4),

$$(\sqrt{3}/2)^\sigma (a_1^\sigma, a_2^\sigma, a_3^\sigma) \prec (r_1^\sigma, r_2^\sigma, r_3^\sigma). \qquad (5)$$

The proof that such a σ exists is due to Leuenberger, 1961, who shows that if

$$g(u) = \left(\frac{\sum_1^3 (\sqrt{3}a_i/2)^u}{3}\right)^{1/u} - \left(\frac{\sum_1^3 r_i^{-u}}{3}\right)^{1/u},$$

then $g(0) > 0 > g(1)$. Consequently, there is a σ in $(0,1)$ such that $g(\sigma) = 0$, which yields (4). For any $t \geq 1$ (so that $t > \sigma$), (1) follows from (5) and 5.A.1. ||

D.1.a. The inequality

$$(\sqrt{3}/2)^t (a_1^t + a_2^t + a_3^t) \leq r_1^t + r_2^t + r_3^t, \qquad t \geq 1,$$

follows from (1). The case $t = 1$ is GI 5.29 and is attributed to Gerretsen, 1953, and Leuenberger, 1961.

D.1.b. For $t \geq 1$,

$$(\sqrt{3}/2) M_k(a_1^t, a_2^t, a_3^t) \leq M_k(r_1^t, r_2^t, r_3^t), \qquad k \geq 1.$$

This follows from the fact that the power mean M_k is Schur-convex and increasing for $k \geq 1$ (see A.8 and 3.I.1.b).

D.1.c. The inequality

$$r_1 r_2 r_3 \leq (3\sqrt{3}/8) a_1 a_2 a_3$$

follows from the Schur-concavity of $\prod x_i$, $x_i > 0$, together with (1). This inequality is GI 5.35 and is due to Leuenberger, 1961.

Exradii and Medians

D.2. If $a_1 \geq a_2 \geq a_3$, then as noted in D.1, $r_1 \geq r_2 \geq r_3$. Also, $m_1 \leq m_2 \leq m_3$, as can be seen from the relations between the medians and the sides:

$$m_1^2 = \tfrac{1}{4}[2a_2^2 + 2a_3^2 - a_1^2],$$
$$m_2^2 = \tfrac{1}{4}[2a_1^2 + 2a_3^2 - a_2^2], \tag{6}$$
$$m_3^2 = \tfrac{1}{4}[2a_1^2 + 2a_2^2 - a_3^2].$$

Substituting (2) in (6) yields relations between the medians and the exradii:

$$m_1^2 = \frac{2r_3^2(r_1+r_2)^2 + 2r_2^2(r_1+r_3)^2 - r_1^2(r_2+r_3)^2}{4(r_1r_2 + r_1r_3 + r_2r_3)},$$

$$m_2^2 = \frac{2r_1^2(r_2+r_3)^2 + 2r_3^2(r_1+r_2)^2 - r_2^2(r_1+r_3)^2}{4(r_1r_2 + r_1r_3 + r_2r_3)},$$

$$m_3^2 = \frac{2r_1^2(r_2+r_3)^2 + 2r_2^2(r_1+r_3)^2 - r_3^2(r_1+r_2)^2}{4(r_1r_2 + r_1r_3 + r_2r_3)}.$$

By a direct, though tedious, calculation,

$$m_1 \geq r_3, \qquad m_3 \leq r_1. \tag{7}$$

Following the same argument as in D.1, form the function

$$h(v) = \left(\sum m_i^v / n\right)^{1/v} - \left(\sum r_i^v / n\right)^{1/v}.$$

It is shown by Leuenberger, 1961 that $h(0) \geq 0 \geq h(1)$, and hence there exists a $\tau \in [0,1]$ such that $h(\tau) = 0$. Consequently,

$$m_1^\tau + m_2^\tau + m_3^\tau = r_1^\tau + r_2^\tau + r_3^\tau,$$

which, with (7), implies that

$$(m_1^\tau, m_2^\tau, m_3^\tau) \prec (r_1^\tau, r_2^\tau, r_3^\tau). \tag{8}$$

For any $t \geq \tau$ (hence for any $t \geq 1$), it follows from 5.A.1 that

$$(m_1^t, m_2^t, m_3^t) \prec_w (r_1^t, r_1^t, r_1^t).$$

D.2.a. For $t \geq 1$,

$$M_k(m_1^t, m_2^t, m_3^t) \leq M_k(r_1^t, r_2^t, r_3^t), \qquad k \geq 1,$$

where M_k is defined in A.8.

This follows from the monotonicity and Schur-convexity of M_k for $k \geq 1$ or $k \leq 0$ (3.I.1.b).

E Isoperimetric-Type Inequalities for Plane Figures

In the present section are described a number of inequalities, some of which are isoperimetric in that they compare plane figures with a fixed perimeter. In others the perimeter is not held constant, but the inequalities closely resemble the format of isoperimetric inequalities.

The exposition owes much to the discussions given in Kazarinoff (1961) and Guggenheimer (1967), who deal mainly with isoperimetric inequalities for plane figures. A discussion of isoperimetric inequalities in mathematical physics is provided in Pólya and Szegö (1951).

For a class C of plane figures, isoperimetric inequalities are often stated in one of these two forms:

(i) Of all figures in C with perimeter p, the Figure F has the greatest area.

(ii) Of all figures in C with area Δ, the Figure F has the least perimeter.

These are dual theorems; a particularly simple proof of the equivalence is given by Kazarinoff (1961, p. 43).

What is shown in this chapter is that for plane figures possessing certain properties, the area is a Schur-concave function of the parameters (e.g., sides, angles) of the plane figure. Consequently, the area is maximized when these parameters are equal, from which the isoperimetric result follows.

Inequalities for the Triangle and Quadrilateral

Two of the simplest isoperimetric inequalities relate to the triangle:

(a) Of all triangles with a common base and a fixed perimeter, the isosceles triangle has the greatest area.

(b) Of all triangles with the same perimeter, the equilateral triangle has the greatest area.

The majorizations that yield (a) and (b) are as follows.

E.1. Proposition. (i) The area of a triangle with one fixed side is a Schur-concave function of the other sides.

(ii) The area of a triangle is a Schur-concave function of the sides.

Proof. A result of Heron relates the area Δ of a triangle to the sides a_1, a_2, a_3:

$$\Delta^2 = s(s - a_1)(s - a_2)(s - a_3), \tag{1}$$

where $s = \frac{1}{2}(a_1 + a_2 + a_3)$ is the semiperimeter.

By 3.A.4, Δ is Schur-concave in (a_1, a_2, a_3). That (ii) implies (i) follows immediately. ||

There is an isoperimetric inequality for the quadrilateral:

(i) Of all quadrilaterals with a given perimeter, the square has the greatest area.

Two steps are required in the proof. The first is to show that the quadrilateral with greatest area is one that can be inscribed in a circle. There are a variety of proofs of this result. One most suitable to our purposes is that of Kazarinoff (1961), who shows that the area Δ of a quadrilateral is related to the sides a_1, a_2, a_3, a_4 and two opposite angles α and β (included between sides a_1 and a_2 and between sides a_3 and a_4, respectively) by

$$\Delta^2 = \tfrac{1}{16}[4a_1^2 a_2^2 + 4a_3^2 a_4^2 - (a_1^2 + a_2^2 - a_3^2 - a_4^2)^2 - 2a_1 a_2 a_3 a_4 \cos(\alpha + \beta)]. \tag{2}$$

Consequently, Δ^2 is maximized for $\alpha + \beta = \pi$, i.e., when the quadrilateral is inscribed in a circle.

E.2. Proposition. The area of a quadrilateral inscribed in a circle is a Schur-concave function of the sides.

Proof. From (2) with $\cos(\alpha + \beta) = -1$, algebraic simplification yields

$$\Delta^2 = (s - a_1)(s - a_2)(s - a_3)(s - a_4), \tag{3}$$

where $s = \sum a_i / 2$ is the semiperimeter. It is now immediate (see 3.F.1) that Δ is a Schur-concave function of (a_1, a_2, a_3, a_4). ||

An isoperimetric theorem similar to E.1(ii) is: Of all triangles with a given perimeter, the equilateral triangle has the smallest circumcircle; i.e., the radius R of the circumcircle is smallest.

E.3. Proposition. The radius R of the circumcircle of a triangle is a Schur-convex function of the sides.

Proof. The result follows from the representation

$$R = \frac{1}{4\sqrt{s}} \frac{a_1 a_2 a_3}{\sqrt{(s - a_1)(s - a_2)(s - a_3)}},$$

which by 3.A.4 is Schur-convex in (a_1, a_2, a_3). ||

E. Isoperimetric-Type Inequalities for Plane Figures   289

E.4. The volume V and surface S of a box are Schur-concave functions of the side lengths a_1, a_2, a_3.

Proof. Because $V = a_1 a_2 a_3$ and $S = 2(a_1 a_2 + a_1 a_3 + a_2 a_3)$, the result follows from 3.F.1. ||

Polygons Inscribed in a Given Circle

It is shown above that the area of a triangle and that of a quadrilateral inscribed in a circle are Schur-concave functions of the sides. This idea is extended to the case of a polygon of n sides that can be inscribed in a circle.

More precisely, let H be a polygon of n sides $a_1, \ldots, a_n$, with vertices $A_1, \ldots, A_n$, inscribed in a circle of radius r and center O. Suppose that O is contained in H, and let $\theta_1, \ldots, \theta_n$ be the central angles subtended by the arcs $A_1 A_2, A_2 A_3, \ldots, A_n A_1$. Further, let $h_1, \ldots, h_n$ denote the altitudes from O to the corresponding sides (see Fig. 3).

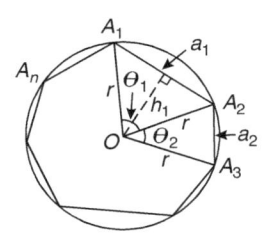

Figure 3.

E.5. Proposition. Let H be a polygon inscribed in a circle of radius r and containing the center O of the circle. The area of H is a Schur-concave function of the angles $\theta_1, \ldots, \theta_n$, of the sides $a_1, \ldots, a_n$, and of the altitudes $h_1, \ldots, h_n$.

Proof. The area of triangle $OA_1 A_2$ is $\frac{1}{2} a_1 h_1 = r^2 \sin \theta_1$. Consequently, the area Δ of the polygon is

$$\Delta = r^2 \sum_1^n \sin \theta_i, \qquad (4)$$

which by 3.C.1 is Schur-concave in $(\theta_1, \ldots, \theta_n)$ for $0 < \theta_i < \pi$. Alternatively, from $r^2 = h_i^2 + a_i^2/4$,

$$\Delta = \tfrac{1}{2} \sum h_i a_i = \tfrac{1}{2} \sum a_i (r^2 - a_i^2/4)^{1/2} = \sum h_i (r^2 - h_i^2)^{1/2}.$$

Since $x(c^2 - x^2)^{1/2}$ is concave in x for $0 < x < c$, the area Δ is a Schur-concave function in $a_1, \ldots, a_n$ and in $h_1, \ldots, h_n$. ‖

As a consequence of E.5, the area of a polygon containing O is maximized when the angles, or the sides, or the altitudes are equal, i.e., when the polygon is regular.

To prove the isoperimetric theorem, it remains to show that the polygon with the greatest area contains the center O of the circle. If this is not the case, as in Fig. 4, then the area of such a polygon is less than $\pi r^2/2$, which is the area of a semicircle. But the area of a regular polygon of n sides containing the center is $r^2 n \sin(2\pi/n)$. From $(\sin x)/x > 2/\pi$ for $x \in (-\pi/2, \pi/2)$, it follows that for $n > 3$, the area is greater than $\pi r^2/2$, and hence the n-gon with the largest area contains the origin.

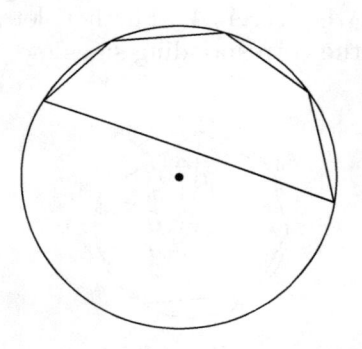

Figure 4.

Not only is Δ, the area of the polygon containing O, a Schur-concave function (4) of $(\theta_1, \ldots, \theta_n)$, but so also is $P = 2r \sum_1^n \sin(\theta_i/2)$, the perimeter of the polygon as a function of $(\theta_1, \ldots, \theta_n)$. Using this observation, Klamkin (1980) provides a proof of the following result [for earlier discussion, see Uspensky (1927)]. If P, Δ and P', Δ' are the perimeters and areas of two polygons containing O inscribed in the same circle and if the greatest side of the second is less than or equal to the smallest side of the first, then $P' \geq P$ and $\Delta' \geq \Delta$ with equality if and only if the polygons are congruent and regular. An analogous result for circumscribed polygons is also presented.

Polygons with Given Perimeter Inscribed in a Circle

The previous proposition deals with the case of a fixed circle with points $A_1, \ldots, A_n$ that generate a polygon of n sides. The points are movable; equal spacings yield the maximum area.

E. Isoperimetric-Type Inequalities for Plane Figures   291

When the perimeter is fixed, alteration of any two sides means that the figure is no longer inscribed in the same circle. Consequently, a more delicate argument is needed.

E.6. Proposition. The area of a polygon of n sides with fixed perimeter inscribed in a circle is a Schur-concave function in the lengths of the sides.

Proof. The proof is based on showing that the area increases by averaging two sides. First note that the area is invariant upon a reordering of the sides, so that we may reorder in ascending order. Now consider three vertices A_1, A_2, B as in Fig. 5. Holding the points A_1, A_2 fixed as pivots, the locus of points with $a + b$ fixed is an ellipse. Thus any averaging of a and b yields a triangle $A_1 B^* A_2$, where B^* lies on the portion BB' of the ellipse. From E.1(i) the area of a triangle with base $A_1 A_2$ fixed is a Schur-concave function of the sides.

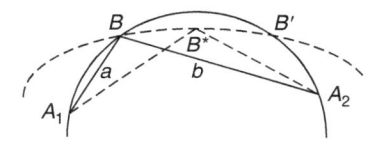

Figure 5.

The resulting polygon will no longer be inscribed in the original circle. However, there is a polygon with the same side lengths that can be inscribed in a circle; this inscribed polygon has a greater area than the original polygon [see, e.g., Kazarinoff (1961, Chapter 2)]. ||

From the fact that for a vector of length $n + 1$,

$$\left(\frac{p}{n}, \ldots, \frac{p}{n}, 0\right) \succ \left(\frac{p}{n+1}, \ldots, \frac{p}{n+1}\right),$$

it follows that with fixed perimeter p, the area of a polygon with $n+1$ sides is greater than the area of a polygon with n sides. Consequently, the area increases as the number of sides increases. By a limiting argument, for a fixed perimeter, the circle is the plane figure with maximum area.

Zhang (1998) identifies some other interesting Schur-convex functions of the lengths of the sides of polygons inscribed in a circle. He considers positive solutions of the differential equation

$$f(\theta) f''(\theta) = a_0 + a_1 f'(\theta) + a_2 [f'(\theta)]^2.$$

In certain cases, he verifies the Schur-concavity of the function

$$F(\theta_1,\ldots,\theta_n) = \left[\sum_{i=1}^{n} f(\theta_i)\right]^2 - \frac{f(\overline{\theta})}{f'(\overline{\theta})} \sum_{i=1}^{n} f(\theta_i) f'(\theta_i)$$
$$- \left[nf(\overline{\theta}) - \sum_{i=1}^{n} f(\theta_i)\right]^2,$$

where $\overline{\theta} = \sum \theta_i/n$.

Using this approach, he shows, for example, that the amount of irregularity of a polygon inscribed in a circle can be expressed in terms of a Schur-convex function.

A Probability Inequality for Polygons Circumscribing a Circle

Let H be a polygon of n sides that circumscribes the *unit* circle with points of tangency $A_1,\ldots,A_n$. These points generate n arc lengths $A_1A_2, A_2A_3, \ldots, A_{n-1}A_n$ labeled $c_1,\ldots,c_n$, and n subtended angles $\theta_1,\ldots,\theta_n$ (see Fig. 6).

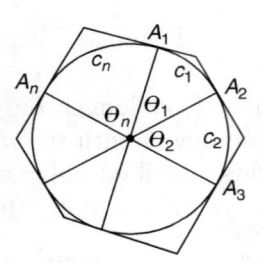

Figure 6.

Write $H(c_1,\ldots,c_n) \equiv H(\theta_1,\ldots,\theta_n)$ to denote the polygon as a function of the arc lengths or subtended angles. Note that

$$\sum c_i = \sum \theta_i = 2\pi.$$

Now consider probability measures μ that are circularly symmetric, i.e., measures that are invariant under rotation about the origin. Write $\mu(H)$ to denote the probability content of the polygon H.

Let $H_1 \equiv H(\alpha_1,\ldots,\alpha_n)$ and $H_2 \equiv H(\beta_1,\ldots,\beta_n)$ be two polygons generated by the angles $\alpha_1,\ldots,\alpha_n$ and $\beta_1,\ldots,\beta_n$, respectively.

E.7. Proposition (Wynn, 1977). A necessary and sufficient condition that

$$\mu(H(\alpha_1,\ldots,\alpha_n)) \geq \mu(H(\beta_1,\ldots,\beta_n))$$

E. Isoperimetric-Type Inequalities for Plane Figures

for every circularly symmetric probability measure μ is that

(i) $\alpha \succ \beta$.

The proof of this theorem makes use of the fact (4.B.3) that (i) is equivalent to

(ii) $\sum_1^n (\alpha_i - \psi)^+ \geq \sum_1^n (\beta_i - \psi)^+$ for all $\psi \in [0, \pi]$,

where $x^+ = x$ if $x \geq 0$ and $x^+ = 0$ otherwise.

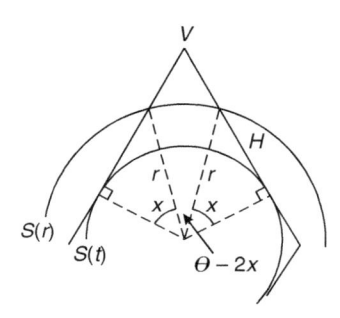

Figure 7.

Proof. Let $S(r)$ denote the circle of radius r with center at the origin, and define $h(r)$ to be the length of that part of the circle lying within the polygon H. The key point in the proof is that for two polygons H_1 and H_2, $\mu(H_1) \geq \mu(H_2)$ for all circularly symmetric measures μ if and only if $h_1(r) \geq h_2(r)$ for all $r \geq 1$.

For any vertex V lying outside the circle $S(r)$, consider a subtended angle θ and the corresponding angle $x < \theta/2$ as indicated in Fig. 7. Then $\cos x = 1/r$ and $\theta - 2x = \theta - 2\cos^{-1}(1/r)$. Let $k_1(r)$ and $k_2(r)$ be the number of vertices of H_1 and H_2 that lie exterior to the circle $S(r)$, i.e., the number of angles α_i and β_i for which $\alpha_i - 2\cos^{-1}(1/r) > 0$, respectively. Then

$$h_1(r) = r\{\sum{}^* \alpha_i - 2k_1(r) \cos^{-1}(1/r)\},$$
$$h_2(r) = r\{\sum{}^* \beta_j - 2k_2(r) \cos^{-1}(1/r)\},$$

where the sum $\sum^*$ is over those i and j counted in $k_1(r)$ and $k_2(r)$, respectively. But now, $h_1(r)$ and $h_2(r)$ can be rewritten

(iii) $h_1(r) = r \sum_1^n (\alpha_i - \psi)^+, h_2(r) = r \sum_1^n (\beta_j - \psi)^+,$

where $\psi = 2\cos^{-1}(1/r)$. Recall that $\mu(H_1) \geq \mu(H_2)$ for all circularly symmetric probability measures μ if and only if $h_1(r) \geq h_2(r)$. But the representations (iii) show that this is equivalent to (ii). ∥

F Duality Between Triangle Inequalities and Inequalities Involving Positive Numbers

Mitrinović, Pečarić, and Volenec (1989) provide a useful link between inequalities for sides of triangles and inequalities involving 3 positive numbers. If a triangle has sides a_1, a_2, a_3 opposite the vertices A_1, A_2, A_3, it is possible to associate 3 positive numbers x_1, x_2, x_3 with the side lengths a by the relations

$$\begin{aligned} a_1 &= x_2 + x_3, \\ a_2 &= x_1 + x_3, \\ a_3 &= x_1 + x_2. \end{aligned} \tag{1}$$

Equations (1) imply the majorization $(a_1, a_2, a_3) \prec (2x_1, 2x_2, 2x_3)$. Consequently, various inequalities follow by associating the a's and x's to parameters of a triangle.

The conditions necessary for a_1, a_2, a_3 to be the sides of a triangle are equivalent to the condition that $x_1, x_2, x_3 > 0$. By using Equations (1), any inequality involving sides of triangles can be transformed into an inequality involving 3 positive numbers, and vice versa. A geometric interpretation of (1) is provided in Fig. 8.

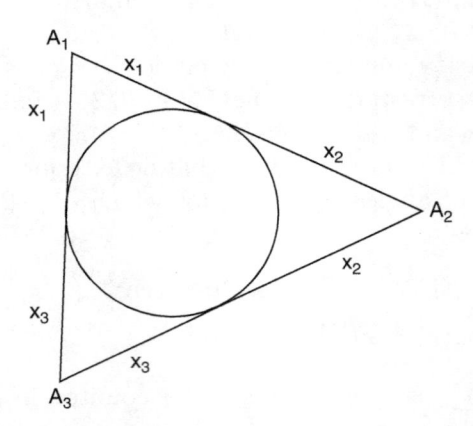

Figure 8. Duality between a and x.

In the figure, a circle is inscribed within an arbitrary triangle and the relation (1) holds because two tangents from an external point to a circle are equal in length.

Of course, inequalities involving sides of triangles lead to inequalities for any 3 positive numbers. Analogous inequalities for more than 3 numbers can often be anticipated, though they may need to be checked on a case-by-case basis.

Observe that the vectors $x = (x_1, x_2, x_3)$ and $a = (a_1, a_2, a_3)$ are related by

$$a = x(J_3 - I_3), \tag{2}$$

$$x = \frac{1}{2} a(J_3 - 2I_3), \tag{3}$$

where J_3 is a 3×3 matrix with all elements equal to 1 and I_3 is the 3×3 identity matrix. Equation (1), extended to k dimensions, becomes $a = xC_k$, where C_k is a $k \times k$ circulant (see 2.H.2) with first row $(0, 1, 1, 0, \ldots, 0)$. It can be thought of as defining the k-sided polygon circumscribing a circle.

Observe that, because of 5.F.3, C_k preserves majorization if and only if $k = 3$. If k is odd and greater than 3, C_k is non-singular, so that any inequality involving k positive numbers can be transformed to yield an inequality involving the sides of a k-sided polygon, and vice versa. If k is even, C_k is singular and the transformation can consequently only be made in one direction.

G Inequalities for Polygons and Simplexes

Chapter XVIII of the book RAGI provides many inequalities for polygons and simplexes. However, only several of these inequalities are examples for which Schur-convexity provides a proof. The reader might consider other examples as a challenge.

The following propositions hold for all numbers, but are applied to polygons and simplexes.

G.1. Let f be a convex function on $\mathscr{R}_{++}$. Define $x_{n+i} = x_i$, $1 \leq i \leq n$. Then for $m = 1, \ldots, n$,

$$\sum_1^m f(x_i + x_{i+1} + \cdots + x_{i+k-1}) \leq \sum_1^m f((n-k)(s - x_i)). \tag{1}$$

Proof. Let $z_i = x_i + x_{i+1} + \cdots + x_{i+k-1}$ and $u_i = (n-k)(s-x_i)$, to show that $(z_1, \ldots, z_n) = (u_1, \ldots, u_n)P$, where P is a doubly stochastic matrix. Consequently, $z \prec u$ and the result follows fron 5.A.1. ||

If $(n-k)s$ is the perimeter of an n-gon with sides x_i such that $x_i < s$, $1 \leq i \leq n$, then (1) holds. This result, with $m = n$, is RAGI, Chapter XV, 10.

G.2. If $f : \mathscr{R}^n \to \mathscr{R}$ is convex, then for every $k \in \{1, 2, \ldots, n+1\}$,

$$\sum f\left(\sum_{j=1}^k \lambda_{i_j}\right) \geq \binom{n+1}{k} f\left(\frac{k}{n+1}\right), \qquad (2)$$

where the summation is over $1 \leq i_1 < \ldots < i_k \leq n+1$. The inequality is reversed if f is concave.

Proof. The Schur-convexity of

$$\sum_{1 \leq i_1 < i_2 < \ldots < i_k \leq n+1} f\left(\sum_{j=1}^k \lambda_{ij}\right)$$

follows from 3.G.3.a and 3.G.3 upon setting $\ell = k$ and $\phi(x_1, \ldots, x_k) = \sum_{i=1}^k f(x_i)$. The result then follows as a consequence of the majorization $\lambda \succ (1/(n+1), \ldots, 1/(n+1))$. ||

If $\lambda_1, \ldots, \lambda_{n+1}$ are the barycentric coordinates of a point in a simplex, so that $\Sigma \lambda_i = 1$, then (2) holds. See RAGI, Chapter VIII, 2.1.

9
Matrix Theory

The pioneering work of Issai Schur (1923) on majorization was motivated by his discovery that the eigenvalues of a positive semidefinite Hermitian matrix majorize the diagonal elements. This discovery provided a new and fundamental understanding of Hadamard's determinant inequality that led Schur to a remarkable variety of related inequalities. Since Schur's discovery, a number of other majorizations have been found in the context of matrix theory. These majorizations primarily involve quantities such as the eigenvalues or singular values of matrix sums or products. An integral part of the development of majorization in matrix theory is the extremal representations of Chapter 20.

Subsequent to the publication of the first edition in 1979, there appeared books and survey papers that include discussion of majorization in matrix theory. Extensive treatments are given by Bhatia (1997, Chapter 2), and Ando (1989, 1994), whose survey provides a short course on this topic. Texts by Horn and Johnson (1985), Zhang (1999), and Bernstein (2005) include material on matrix inequalities and majorization. Many of the results of this chapter have been extended to compact operators in complex Hilbert space. Such results are not discussed here.

A Notation and Preliminaries

A.1. Notation for the eigenvalues and singular values. The vector of eigenvalues of an $n \times n$ matrix A is denoted by

$$\lambda(A) = (\lambda_1(A), \ldots, \lambda_n(A)).$$

When the eigenvalues are real, they are ordered

$$\lambda_1(A) \geq \cdots \geq \lambda_n(A);$$

otherwise, the real parts

$$\mathscr{R}\lambda_1(A) \geq \cdots \geq \mathscr{R}\lambda_n(A)$$

or the moduli

$$|\lambda_1(A)| \geq \cdots \geq |\lambda_n(A)|$$

are ordered. The following is a key fact about eigenvalues that is used repeatedly in this chapter.

A.1.a. If A is an $m \times n$ matrix, and B is an $n \times m$ matrix where $m \leq n$, then the n eigenvalues of BA are the m eigenvalues of AB together with $n - m$ zeros; i.e.,

$$\{\lambda_1(AB), \ldots, \lambda_m(AB), \underbrace{0, \ldots, 0}_{n-m}\} = \{\lambda_1(BA), \ldots, \lambda_n(BA)\}.$$

In particular, the nonzero eigenvalues of AB are the nonzero eigenvalues of BA (see, e.g., Mirsky, 1955a, p. 200)].

The *singular values* $\sigma(B)$ of an $m \times n$ matrix B, arranged in decreasing order and denoted by

$$\sigma(B) = (\sigma_1(B), \ldots, \sigma_m(B)),$$

are the nonnegative square roots of the eigenvalues of the positive semidefinite matrix BB^*, or equivalently, they are the eigenvalues of the positive semidefinite square root $(BB^*)^{1/2}$, so that

$$\sigma_i(B) = [\lambda_i(BB^*)]^{1/2} = \lambda_i[(BB^*)^{1/2}], \qquad i = 1, \ldots, m.$$

The singular values are real and nonnegative.

Because B is an $m \times n$ rectangular matrix, $\sigma(B) \in \mathscr{R}^m$, whereas $\sigma(B^*) \in \mathscr{R}^n$. However, the nonzero elements of $\sigma(B)$ and $\sigma(B^*)$ coincide. Because of this, it is often convenient to assume that $m \leq n$.

If $B = \begin{pmatrix} B_1 \\ 0 \end{pmatrix}$ is an $n \times n$ matrix and B_1 is an $m \times n$ submatrix, then $\sigma(B) = (\sigma(B_1), 0)$, where the zero vector has $n - m$ zero components. Consequently, results for square matrices can be modified to include results for rectangular matrices.

Mirsky (1964) uses the term *associated roots* to denote the eigenvalues of $\frac{1}{2}(A + A^*)$. Amir-Moéz and Horn (1958) call these *real singular values*, and use the term *absolute singular values* for singular values. This conveys the fact that the roots of $\frac{1}{2}(A + A^*)$ are real and can be positive or negative, whereas the roots of $(AA^*)^{1/2}$ are nonnegative. They call the eigenvalues of $(A - A^*)/2i$ the *imaginary singular values*.

A.2. It was noted by Helmut Wielandt [see Fan and Hoffman (1955)] that if A is an $m \times n$ complex matrix, then the nonzero eigenvalues of the Hermitian matrix

$$\widetilde{A} = \begin{bmatrix} 0 & A \\ A^* & 0 \end{bmatrix}$$

are the nonzero singular values of A and their negatives. As a consequence, results for Hermitian matrices can be related to results for arbitrary matrices.

For an $n \times n$ Hermitian matrix H, $\sigma_i(H) = |\lambda_i(H)|$, and for a positive semidefinite Hermitian matrix H, $\sigma_i(H) = \lambda_i(H)$, $i = 1, \ldots, n$.

A.3. The notation

$$D_z \equiv \operatorname{diag}(z_1, \ldots, z_n)$$

is used to denote a diagonal matrix with diagonal elements $z_1, \ldots, z_n$. The elements z_i can be square matrices of different dimensions.

A.4. For any matrix A, denote by

$$A \begin{pmatrix} i_1, i_2, \ldots, i_k \\ j_1, j_2, \ldots, j_k \end{pmatrix}$$

the submatrix A consisting of rows $i_1, \ldots, i_k$ and columns $j_1, \ldots, j_k$. This notation is also used in the literature to denote the determinant of the submatrix.

When no confusion can arise, we adopt the simpler notation

$$A_k \equiv A \begin{pmatrix} 1, 2, \ldots, k \\ 1, 2, \ldots, k \end{pmatrix}$$

to denote the submatrix consisting of rows and columns $1, \ldots, k$. This notation is particularly useful for inductive proofs.

B Diagonal Elements and Eigenvalues of a Hermitian Matrix

Historically, the first example of majorization arising in matrix theory is the comparison between the diagonal elements and the eigenvalues of a Hermitian matrix. In discovering this, Schur (1923) was motivated by a desire to prove and extend Hadamard's determinant inequality, which states that for any $n \times n$ positive semidefinite Hermitian matrix $H = (h_{ij})$, $\prod_1^n \lambda_i(H) = \det H \leq \prod_1^n h_{ii}$. Because this inequality is generally not true for arbitrary matrices, Schur confined his attention to the positive semidefinite case. However, the majorization holds more generally for Hermitian matrices.

B.1. Theorem (Schur, 1923). If H is an $n \times n$ Hermitian matrix with diagonal elements $h_1, \ldots, h_n$ and eigenvalues $\lambda_1, \ldots, \lambda_n$, then

$$h \prec \lambda.$$

This result has aroused considerable interest and a variety of proofs have been given. The first proof by Schur (1923) does not crucially use his assumption that H is positive semidefinite. This proof and the later one by Mirsky (1957a) relate the eigenvalues and the diagonal elements via a doubly stochastic matrix. A second proof by Schneider as reported by Mirsky (1957a) uses an interlacing theorem and induction. A third proof of Fan (1949) is based on an extremal property for the sum of the k largest eigenvalues.

First proof (Schur, 1923; Mirsky, 1957a). By 19.A.4 there exists a unitary matrix U such that $H = UD_\lambda U^*$, where $\lambda_1, \ldots, \lambda_n$ are the roots of H. The diagonal elements $h_1, \ldots, h_n$ of H are

$$h_i = \sum_j u_{ij} \overline{u}_{ij} \lambda_j \equiv \sum_j p_{ij} \lambda_j, \qquad i = 1, \ldots, n,$$

B. Diagonal Elements and Eigenvalues of a Hermitian Matrix 301

where $p_{ij} = u_{ij}\bar{u}_{ij}$. Because U is unitary, by 2.B.5, the matrix $P = (p_{ij})$ is doubly stochastic. Consequently,

$$(h_1, \ldots, h_n) = (\lambda_1, \ldots, \lambda_n)P,$$

so that by 2.B.2, $h \prec \lambda$. ||

Second proof (Hans Schneider, see Mirsky, 1957a). Assume that $h_1 \geq \cdots \geq h_n$; otherwise, permute the rows and corresponding columns of H to achieve this (an operation that does not change the eigenvalues $\lambda_1, \ldots, \lambda_n$). For $k = 1, \ldots, n$, let $H_k = (h_{ij})$, $i, j = 1, \ldots, k$, so that $H_n \equiv H$. Let $\lambda_1^{(k)} \geq \cdots \geq \lambda_k^{(k)}$ be the eigenvalues of H_k. By a well-known interlacing theorem [e.g., see Browne (1930a), Bellman (1972, p. 115), Householder (1964, p. 76), Bhatia (1997, p. 59), Horn and Johnson (1985, p. 185)], the roots of H_k and H_{k+1} satisfy the following inequalities for $k = 1, \ldots, n-1$:

$$\lambda_1^{(k+1)} \geq \lambda_1^{(k)} \geq \lambda_2^{(k+1)} \geq \cdots \geq \lambda_k^{(k)} \geq \lambda_{k+1}^{(k+1)}.$$

Hence,

$$h_1 + \cdots + h_k = \lambda_1^{(k)} + \cdots + \lambda_k^{(k)}$$
$$\leq \lambda_1^{(k+1)} + \cdots + \lambda_k^{(k+1)}$$
$$\vdots$$
$$\leq \lambda_1^{(n)} + \cdots + \lambda_k^{(n)} \equiv \lambda_1 + \cdots + \lambda_k.$$

Equality clearly holds for $k = n$. ||

Remark. The abovementioned interlacing theorem has reappeared in the literature a number of times. It was obtained by Cauchy in 1829; sometimes the names Poincaré or Sturm are attached to it. Browne (1930a) gives an explicit statement and proof.

A third proof of B.1 is based on the extremal representation of 20.A.2: If H is an $n \times n$ Hermitian matrix, then

$$\max_{UU^*=I_k} \operatorname{tr} UHU^* = \lambda_1(H) + \cdots + \lambda_k(H), \tag{1}$$

where the maximum is taken over all $k \times n$ complex matrices U.

Third proof (Fan, 1949). With $h_1 \geq \cdots \geq h_n$, an application of (1) yields

$$\sum_1^k \lambda_i(H) = \max_{UU^*=I_k} \operatorname{tr} UHU^* \geq \operatorname{tr} (I_k 0)H(I_k 0)' = \sum_1^k h_i,$$

for $k = 1, \ldots, n-1$. Clearly, equality holds for $k = n$. ‖

The significance of B.1 is considerably enhanced by the knowledge that no stronger ordering between h and λ is generally true. This means that majorization is somehow intrinsic in the comparison. That h and λ cannot be compared by an ordering stronger than majorization is a consequence of the following converse.

B.2. Theorem (Horn, 1954a; Mirsky, 1958a). If $h_1 \geq \cdots \geq h_n$ and $\lambda_1 \geq \cdots \geq \lambda_n$ are $2n$ numbers satisfying $h \prec \lambda$ on $\mathscr{R}^n$, then there exists a real symmetric matrix H with diagonal elements $h_1, \ldots, h_n$ and eigenvalues $\lambda_1, \ldots, \lambda_n$.

Discussion of B.2. Note that B.2 is stronger than the converse of B.1 in that it guarantees the existence of a real symmetric matrix rather than a Hermitian matrix.

Before proving B.2, we mention a rather curious application. According to 2.B.6,

(i) $x \prec y$ on $\mathscr{R}^n$

implies

(iv) $x = yQ$ for some orthostochastic matrix Q.

To see how this can be easily proved using B.2, suppose $x \prec y$ and use B.2 to guarantee the existence of a real symmetric matrix H with diagonal elements $x_1, \ldots, x_n$ and eigenvalues $y_1, \ldots, y_n$. Then the representation $H = \Gamma' D_y \Gamma$, where $\Gamma = (\gamma_{ij})$ is orthogonal, implies $x = yQ$ where $q_{ij} = \gamma_{ij}^2$, so that Q is orthostochastic.

The argument of Horn (1954a) is in the opposite direction; he uses the fact (i) implies (iv) of 2.B.6 to prove B.2 as follows. If $h \prec \lambda$, then by (iv), there exists an orthostochastic matrix Q such that $h = \lambda Q$. This means that $h_j = \sum_i \lambda_i q_{ij} = \sum \lambda_i \gamma_{ij}^2$, where $\Gamma = (\gamma_{ij})$ is unitary. Hence, $\Gamma^* D_\lambda \Gamma$ has diagonal elements h_j and $\Gamma^* D_\lambda \Gamma$ is the desired real symmetric matrix. The difficulty in Horn's proof lies in proving (i) implies (iv), which we did not do directly.

To avoid a circular argument in proving that (i) implies (iv) from B.2, it is necessary to give an independent proof of B.2. Below is such

B. Diagonal Elements and Eigenvalues of a Hermitian Matrix   303

a proof; it follows the development of Mirsky (1958a), and depends upon the following lemma.

B.3. Lemma (Mirsky, 1958a). Given real numbers $c_1, \ldots, c_{n-1}$ and $\lambda_1, \ldots, \lambda_n$ satisfying the interlacing property

$$\lambda_1 \geq c_1 \geq \lambda_2 \geq \cdots \geq c_{n-1} \geq \lambda_n, \qquad (2)$$

there exists a real symmetric $n \times n$ matrix of the form

$$W = \begin{bmatrix} D_c & v' \\ v & v_n \end{bmatrix}$$

with eigenvalues $\lambda_1, \ldots, \lambda_n$.

Proof. For square matrices A and C with A nonsingular,

$$\det \begin{bmatrix} A & B' \\ B & C \end{bmatrix} = \det(A)\det(C - BA^{-1}B').$$

Consequently, the eigenvalues of W are given by the solution of

$$\det(\lambda I - W) = \det(\lambda I - D_c)[\lambda - v_n - v(\lambda I - D_c)^{-1}v']$$

$$= \left[\prod_1^{n-1}(\lambda - c_i)\right]\left(\lambda - v_n - \sum_1^{n-1} \frac{v_j^2}{\lambda - c_j}\right) = 0. \qquad (3)$$

Because $c_1, \ldots, c_{n-1}$ and $\lambda_1, \ldots, \lambda_n$ are given, the problem is to choose $v = (v_1, \ldots, v_{n-1})$ and v_n judiciously so that $\lambda_1, \ldots, \lambda_n$ are the roots of (3). When $\lambda_1, \ldots, \lambda_n$ are distinct, this can be accomplished as follows. Let

$$f(\lambda) = \prod_1^n (\lambda - \lambda_i), \qquad g(\lambda) = \prod_1^{n-1}(\lambda - c_i).$$

By a direct verification or by Lagrange's interpolation formula (Householder, 1953, Section 5.1),

$$\frac{f(\lambda)}{g(\lambda)} = \lambda - (\lambda_1 + \cdots + \lambda_n - c_1 - \cdots - c_{n-1}) + \sum_1^{n-1} \frac{f(c_k)}{g'(c_k)} \frac{1}{(\lambda - c_k)}.$$

Because of the interlacing property (2),

$$f(c_k) = (-1)^k \prod_{i=1}^n |c_k - \lambda_i|,$$

$$g'(c_k) = (-1)^{k-1} \prod_{\substack{i=1 \\ i \neq k}}^{n-1} |c_k - c_i|,$$

so that $f(c_k)/g'(c_k)$ is nonpositive for $k = 1, \ldots, n-1$. Thus the choice

$$v_k^2 = -f(c_k)/g'(c_k), \qquad k = 1, \ldots, n-1,$$
$$v_n = \sum_1^n \lambda_i - \sum_1^{n-1} c_i, \tag{4}$$

yields $f(\lambda) = \det(\lambda I - w)$, so this provides the desired solution. When the roots are not distinct, some modification of this proof is required. ||

Proof of B.2. The proof is by induction. First observe that the result clearly holds for $n = 1$; assume it holds for $n - 1$. Without loss in generality, let

$$h_1 \geq \cdots \geq h_n, \qquad \lambda_1 \geq \cdots \geq \lambda_n.$$

From $h \prec \lambda$ and by 5.A.10.a, there exist numbers $c_1, \ldots, c_{n-1}$ such that

$$\lambda_1 \geq c_1 \geq \lambda_2 \geq \cdots \geq c_{n-1} \geq \lambda_n$$

and

$$(h_1, \ldots, h_{n-1}) \prec (c_1, \ldots, c_{n-1}).$$

By the inductive hypothesis, there exists an $n - 1 \times n - 1$ real symmetric matrix S_1 with diagonal elements $h_1, \ldots, h_{n-1}$, and eigenvalues $c_1, \ldots, c_{n-1}$. Let Γ be an orthogonal matrix which transforms S_1 to diagonal form; that is,

$$\Gamma' S_1 \Gamma = D_c \equiv \mathrm{diag}(c_1, \ldots, c_{n-1}).$$

By B.3, there exists an $n \times n$ real symmetric matrix

$$W = \begin{bmatrix} D_c & v' \\ v & v_n \end{bmatrix},$$

with eigenvalues $\lambda_1, \ldots, \lambda_n$. Now form the matrix

$$\begin{bmatrix} \Gamma & 0 \\ 0 & 1 \end{bmatrix} \begin{bmatrix} D_c & v' \\ v & v_n \end{bmatrix} \begin{bmatrix} \Gamma' & 0 \\ 0 & 1 \end{bmatrix} = \begin{bmatrix} \Gamma D_c \Gamma' & \Gamma v' \\ v \Gamma' & v_n \end{bmatrix} = \begin{bmatrix} S_1 & \Gamma v' \\ v \Gamma' & v_n \end{bmatrix} \equiv S.$$

Then S has eigenvalues $\lambda_1, \ldots, \lambda_n$ and diagonal elements $h_1, \ldots, h_{n-1}, v_n$. But from (4), $v_n = h_n$, which completes the proof. ||

B.3.a. Remark. Theorem B.2 ensures the existence of a real symmetric matrix H that has given diagonal elements and eigenvalues. Chu (1995) provides an algorithm to obtain the matrix H.

B. Diagonal Elements and Eigenvalues of a Hermitian Matrix   305

B.3.b. Remark. Grone, Johnson, Marques de Sa, and Wolkowicz (1984) study a class of optimization problems in which diagonal elements $a_{11}, \ldots, a_{nn}$ are given. The problem is to find the largest eigenvalue among all Hermitian matrices A with the given diagonal elements, and satisfying the condition $\operatorname{tr} A^2 \leq L$ (given). Clearly, the eigenvalues $\lambda_1, \ldots, \lambda_n$ need to satisfy the majorization

$$(a_{11}, \ldots, a_{nn}) \prec (\lambda_1, \ldots, \lambda_n).$$

A Related Converse Connecting the Diagonal Elements of a Matrix and the Characteristic Polynomial

The converse B.2 of Horn (1954a) shows that majorization is the appropriate condition for the existence of a real symmetric matrix with diagonal elements $h_1, \ldots, h_n$ and eigenvalues $\lambda_1, \ldots, \lambda_n$. Mirsky (1960b) considers a related question, namely, what are the conditions for the existence of a real symmetric matrix given the diagonal elements and characteristic polynomial, rather than eigenvalues? He proves the following.

B.4. Theorem (Mirsky, 1960b). Let $a_1, \ldots, a_n$ be given real numbers, and let

$$\chi(x) = x^n - c_1 x^{n-1} + \cdots + (-1)^{n-1} c_{n-1} x + (-1)^n c_n$$

be a given polynomial with real coefficients. Necessary and sufficient conditions for the existence of a real symmetric matrix A with diagonal elements $a_1, \ldots, a_n$ and characteristic polynomial $\chi(x)$ are (i) all the zeros of $\chi(x)$ are real, (ii) $a_1 + \cdots + a_n = c_1$, and (iii) $\chi^{[k]}(x + a_{[1]} + \cdots + a_{[k]}) \in \mathcal{N}$, $k = 1, \ldots, n-1$, where $\chi^{[k]}(x)$ is the monic polynomial of degree $\binom{n}{k}$ whose zeros are the numbers $\lambda_{i_1} + \cdots + \lambda_{i_k}$, for $1 \leq i_1 < \cdots < i_k \leq n$, and a monic polynomial $\chi(x) \in \mathcal{N}$ if either (a) the last coefficient of $\chi(x)$ vanishes, or (b) some coefficient of $\chi(x)$ is negative, or both (a) and (b) occur.

Implications of the Majorization Between Eigenvalues and Diagonal Elements

From B.1, $(h_{11}, \ldots, h_{nn}) \prec (\lambda_1(H), \ldots, \lambda_n(H))$, where without loss of generality, $h_{11} \geq \cdots \geq h_{nn}$. Hence

$$(h_{11}, \ldots, h_{kk}) \prec_{\mathrm{w}} (\lambda_1(H), \ldots, \lambda_k(H)),$$
$$(h_{kk}, \ldots, h_{nn}) \prec^{\mathrm{w}} (\lambda_k(H), \ldots, \lambda_n(H)), \qquad k = 1, \ldots, n.$$

Consequently, for all Schur-convex functions ϕ on $\mathscr{D}$,

$$\phi(h_{11}, \ldots, h_{nn}) \leq \phi(\lambda_1(H), \ldots, \lambda_n(H)); \tag{5a}$$

for all increasing Schur-convex functions ϕ on $\mathscr{D}$,

$$\phi(h_{11}, \ldots, h_{kk}) \leq \phi(\lambda_1(H), \ldots, \lambda_k(H)), \qquad k = 1, \ldots, n; \tag{5b}$$

for all decreasing Schur-convex functions ϕ on $\mathscr{D}$,

$$\phi(h_{kk}, \ldots, h_{nn}) \leq \phi(\lambda_k(H), \ldots, \lambda_n(H)), \qquad k = 1, \ldots, n. \tag{5c}$$

B.5. If H is an $n \times n$ positive semidefinite Hermitian matrix such that $h_{11} \geq \cdots \geq h_{nn}$, then

$$\prod_k^n h_{ii} \geq \prod_k^n \lambda_i(H), \qquad k = 1, \ldots, n. \tag{6}$$

Proof. This special case of (5c) follows from 3.F.1.a. ||

With $k = 1$, (6) is called *Hadamard's inequality*.

Another proof of this inequality due to Schur (1923) uses 3.C.1 with $g(x) = -\log x$.

B.5.a. If A is an $m \times n$ complex matrix, then

$$\det(AA^*) \leq \prod_{i=1}^m \sum_{j=1}^n |a_{ij}|^2.$$

This is an alternate form of Hadamard's inequality obtained from (6) with $k = 1$ and $H = AA^*$.

The Hadamard inequality can be extended in terms of elementary symmetric functions, $S_k(x_1, \ldots, x_n)$, $k = 1, \ldots, n$.

B.5.b. Theorem (Schur, 1923). If H is an $n \times n$ positive semidefinite Hermitian matrix, then

$$S_k(\lambda_1(H), \ldots, \lambda_n(H)) \leq S_k(h_{11}, \ldots, h_{nn}), \qquad k = 1, \ldots, n. \tag{7}$$

Proof. The result follows from the majorization B.1 and the fact 3.F.1 that S_k is Schur-concave. ||

B. Diagonal Elements and Eigenvalues of a Hermitian Matrix

The case $k = n$ is equivalent to Hadamard's inequality.

B.5.c. Theorem (Schur, 1923). If H is an $n \times n$ positive definite Hermitian matrix, then

$$\frac{S_n(h_{11},\ldots,h_{nn})}{S_n(\lambda_1(H),\ldots,\lambda_n(H))} \geq \frac{S_{n-1}(h_{11},\ldots,h_{nn})}{S_{n-1}(\lambda_1(H),\ldots,\lambda_n(H))} \geq \cdots$$

$$\geq \frac{S_1(h_{11},\ldots,h_{nn})}{S_1(\lambda_1(H),\ldots,\lambda_n(H))} = 1.$$

Proof. This result follows from B.1 and the fact 3.F.3 that $S_{k+1}(x)/S_k(x)$ is Schur-concave on $\mathcal{R}_{++}^n$. ∥

Another direction for refining the Hadamard inequality is to bound the discrepancy: $\prod_1^n \lambda_i(H) - \prod_1^n h_{ii}$.

B.5.d. Theorem (Schur, 1923). If H is an $n \times n$ positive semidefinite Hermitian matrix, then

$$0 \leq \prod_1^n h_{ii} - \prod_1^n \lambda_i(H) \leq \frac{(\sum_1^n h_{ii})^{n-2}}{n-2} \cdot \frac{\sum_1^n \lambda_i^2 - \sum_1^n h_{ii}^2}{2}. \qquad (8)$$

Proof. To obtain the right-hand inequality, apply B.1 to 3.F.4 with $\nu = 2$ to obtain

$$[S_1(h)]^{n-2} S_2(h) - (n-2)^{n-2} S_n(h)$$
$$\geq [S_1(\lambda(H))]^{n-2} S_2(\lambda(H)) - (n-2)^{n-2} S_n(\lambda(H)), \qquad (9)$$

where $S_k(h) \equiv S_k(h_{11},\ldots,h_{nn})$ and $S_k(\lambda(H)) \equiv S_k(\lambda_1(H),\ldots,\lambda_n(H))$, $k = 1,\ldots,n$. Since $S_1(h) = S_1(\lambda(H)) = \sum_1^n h_{ii}$, (10) can be rewritten as

$$\prod_1^n h_{ii} - \prod_1^n \lambda_i(H) = S_n(h) - S_n(\lambda(H))$$

$$\leq \left(\frac{\sum h_{ii}}{n-2}\right)^{n-2} [S_2(h) - S_2(\lambda(H))].$$

Inequality (8) follows by noting that

$$2[S_2(h) - S_2(\lambda(H))] = \left[\left(\sum h_{ii}\right)^2 - \sum h_{ii}^2\right] - \left[\left(\sum \lambda_i\right)^2 - \sum \lambda_i^2\right]$$
$$= \sum \lambda_i^2 - \sum h_{ii}^2. \quad \|$$

Hermitian Matrices with Prescribed Diagonal Elements and Spectrum

B.6. In statistics, multivariate models occasionally require the construction of a correlation matrix (with diagonal elements equal to 1) with prescribed eigenvalues.

In a more general context, Dhillon, Heath, Sustik, and Tropp (2005) generate several numerical algorithms in which majorization plays a central role.

Suppose A is a Hermitian matrix with ordered diagonal elements $a_{(1)} \leq \cdots \leq a_{(n)}$ and corresponding eigenvalues $\lambda_1, \ldots, \lambda_n$. The problem is to construct a matrix B that has specified diagonal elements $b_1, \ldots, b_n$ and eigenvalues $\lambda_1, \ldots, \lambda_n$. Because of Schur's theorem, the given vector $b = (b_1, \ldots, b_n)$ must satisfy $b \prec \lambda$.

C Eigenvalues of a Hermitian Matrix and Its Principal Submatrices

Majorization of the diagonal elements by the eigenvalues of a Hermitian matrix can be viewed as the last step in an iterative comparison between the eigenvalues of diagonal blocks of a Hermitian matrix and the eigenvalues of the matrix. This section deals with such comparisons.

C.1. Theorem (Fan, 1954). If H and $\overline{H}$ are $n \times n$ Hermitian matrices of the form

$$H = \begin{bmatrix} H_{11} & H_{12} \\ H_{21} & H_{22} \end{bmatrix}, \qquad \overline{H} = \begin{bmatrix} H_{11} & 0 \\ 0 & H_{22} \end{bmatrix},$$

where $H_{11} : l \times l$, $H_{22} : m \times m$, $l + m = n$, then

$$(\lambda(H_{11}), \lambda(H_{22})) = \lambda(\overline{H}) \prec \lambda(H). \tag{1}$$

Proof. Let $\alpha_1, \ldots, \alpha_l$ and $\beta_1, \ldots, \beta_m$ be, respectively, the eigenvalues of H_{11} and H_{22}. By 19.A.4, there exist an $l \times l$ unitary matrix U_1 and an $m \times m$ unitary matrix U_2 such that

$$U_1 H_{11} U_1^* = D_\alpha, \qquad U_2 H_{22} U_2^* = D_\beta.$$

Form the $n \times n$ matrix $U = \operatorname{diag}(U_1, U_2)$ and note that

$$U \overline{H} U^* = \begin{bmatrix} D_\alpha & 0 \\ 0 & D_\beta \end{bmatrix}, \qquad U H U^* = \begin{bmatrix} D_\alpha & M \\ M^* & D_\beta \end{bmatrix},$$

C. Eigenvalues of a Hermitian Matrix and Its Principal Submatrices   309

where $M = U_1 H_{12} U_2^*$. Because U is unitary, $\lambda(\overline{H}) = \lambda(U\overline{H}U^*)$ and $\lambda(H) = \lambda(UHU^*)$, so that by B.1,

$$\lambda(\overline{H}) = \lambda(U\overline{H}U^*) = (\lambda(H_{11}), \lambda(H_{22})) \prec \lambda(UHU^*) = \lambda(H). \quad \|$$

C.1.a. Example. That the zeros cannot be placed in arbitrary positions can be seen from the following example. If

$$H = \begin{bmatrix} 1 & a & a \\ a & 1 & a \\ a & a & 1 \end{bmatrix} \quad \text{and} \quad \overline{H} = \begin{bmatrix} 1 & a & 0 \\ a & 1 & a \\ 0 & a & 1 \end{bmatrix},$$

where $|a| < 1/\sqrt{2}$, then

$$\lambda(H) = (1-a, 1-a, 1+2a), \qquad \lambda(\overline{H}) = (1-a\sqrt{2}, 1, 1+a\sqrt{2}),$$

and it is readily verified that no majorization occurs.

C.1.b. If H is a Hermitian matrix partitioned as in C.1,

$$(\lambda_1(H_{11}), \ldots, \lambda_l(H_{11}), 0, \ldots, 0) \prec_w \lambda(H).$$

This follows trivially from the fact that $(\lambda(H_{11}), 0) \prec_w (\lambda(H_{11}), \lambda(H_{22})) \equiv \lambda(\overline{H})$.

C.1.c. If H is a Hermitian matrix partitioned as in C.1 and

$$H_\theta = \begin{bmatrix} H_{11} & \theta H_{12} \\ \theta H_{21} & H_{22} \end{bmatrix},$$

then

$$\lambda(H_{\theta_1}) \prec \lambda(H_{\theta_2}), \qquad 0 \le \theta_1 < \theta_2 \le 1.$$

Proof. It is sufficient to prove the result with $\theta_2 = 1$, for this special case applied to $H = H_{\theta_2}$ is the general case. Write $H_\theta = \theta H_1 + \overline{\theta} H_0$, where $\overline{\theta} = 1 - \theta$. From the convexity of $\sum_1^k \lambda_i(H)$ (see 16.F.3) and $\lambda(H_0) \prec \lambda(H_1)$,

$$\lambda(H_\theta) = \lambda(\theta H_1 + \overline{\theta} H_0) \prec \theta \lambda(H_1) + \overline{\theta} \lambda(H_0)$$
$$\prec \theta \lambda(H_1) + \overline{\theta} \lambda(H_1) = \lambda(H_1). \quad \|$$

Of course, the case $\theta_1 = 0$, $\theta_2 = 1$ in C.1.c is just C.1.

C.1.d. Theorem (Fischer, 1908). If H is an $n \times n$ positive semidefinite Hermitian matrix, then

$$\det H \begin{pmatrix} 1, \ldots, n \\ 1, \ldots, n \end{pmatrix}$$

$$\leq \det H \begin{pmatrix} 1, \ldots, k \\ 1, \ldots, k \end{pmatrix} \det H \begin{pmatrix} k+1, \ldots, n \\ k+1, \ldots, n \end{pmatrix}, \quad k = 1, \ldots, n-1. \quad (2)$$

Proof. Apply 3.F.1.a to the majorization (1). ∥

Inequality (2) is also obtained by Fan (1955a), Krull (1958), and Gantmacher (1959, p. 255).

C.2. (Fan, 1955a). If H is a positive semidefinite Hermitian matrix partitioned as in C.1, then

$$\prod_1^m \lambda_{n-i+1}(H) \leq \prod_1^m \lambda_{l-i+1}(H_{11}), \quad m = 1, \ldots, l. \quad (3)$$

Proof. From 5.A.1.d and C.1,

$$\prod_1^m \lambda_{n-i+1}(H) \leq \prod_1^m \lambda_{n-i+1}(\overline{H}). \quad (4)$$

Further, from the interlacing property of the eigenvalues, the l smallest eigenvalues of $\overline{H}$ are, respectively, less than or equal to the l eigenvalues of H_{11}, so that

$$\prod_1^m \lambda_{n-i+1}(\overline{H}) \leq \prod_1^m \lambda_{l-i+1}(H_{11}). \quad \| \quad (5)$$

C.3. (Fan, 1955a). Let H be an $n \times n$ positive definite Hermitian matrix partitioned as in C.1. Let

$$\eta_j = \det H \begin{pmatrix} j, l+1, \ldots, n \\ j, l+1, \ldots, n \end{pmatrix}, \quad j = 1, \ldots, l,$$

and suppose $\eta_1 \geq \cdots \geq \eta_l$. Then

$$\prod_1^k \eta_{l-i+1} \geq \prod_1^k \lambda_{n-i+1}(H), \quad k = 1, \ldots, l.$$

Note that the ordering $\eta_1 \geq \cdots \geq \eta_l$ can be accomplished by permuting the rows and columns of H_{11} without altering the eigenvalues of H.

C. Eigenvalues of a Hermitian Matrix and Its Principal Submatrices

Additional Inequalities for a Partitioned Hermitian Matrix

For a Hermitian matrix partitioned as in C.1, inequalities in addition to those of C.1 are known that compare the eigenvalues of H and of $\overline{H}$. Some such inequalities arise as a generalized interlacing property. When H_{11} is $(n-1) \times (n-1)$, the $n-1$ eigenvalues of H_{11} interlace the eigenvalues of H. More generally, if H_{11} and H_{22} are $l \times l$ and $m \times m$, respectively, then

$$\begin{aligned} \lambda_j(H) \geq \lambda_j(H_{11}), &\quad \lambda_{l-j+1}(H_{11}) \geq \lambda_{n-j+1}(H), \quad j=1,\ldots,l, \\ \lambda_j(H) \geq \lambda_j(H_{22}), &\quad \lambda_{m-j+1}(H_{22}) \geq \lambda_{n-j+1}(H), \quad j=1,\ldots,m, \end{aligned} \quad (6)$$

[see, e.g., Householder (1964, p. 76)].

Other kinds of inequalities, obtained by Thompson and Therianos (1972), can best be stated under the assumption $l \geq m$ in terms of the $2l \times 2l$ augmented matrix

$$\widehat{H} = \begin{bmatrix} H_{11} & H_{12} & 0 \\ H_{21} & H_{22} & 0 \\ 0 & 0 & 0 \end{bmatrix}.$$

Here, H_{11} and $\text{diag}(H_{22}, 0)$ are $l \times l$ submatrices of $\widehat{H}$.

C.4. Theorem (Thompson and Therianos, 1972). If H is a positive semidefinite Hermitian matrix, and the eigenvalues of H_{11}, $\text{diag}(H_{22}, 0)$, and $\widehat{H}$ are ordered,

$$\alpha_1 \geq \cdots \geq \alpha_m \geq 0, \quad \beta_1 \geq \cdots \geq \beta_m \geq 0, \quad \gamma_1 \geq \cdots \geq \gamma_{2m} \geq 0,$$

respectively, then

$$\sum_{s=1}^k \gamma_{i_s+j_s-s} + \sum_{s=1}^k \gamma_{2l-k+s} \leq \sum_{s=1}^k \alpha_{i_s} + \sum_{s=1}^k \beta_{j_s}, \quad k=1,\ldots,l, \quad (7)$$

$1 \leq i_1 < \cdots < i_k \leq l,\ 1 \leq j_1 < \cdots < j_k \leq l$.

From (7) together with the ordering of α and β,

$$\sum_{s=1}^k (\gamma_s + \gamma_{2l-k+s}) \leq \sum_1^k \alpha_i + \sum_1^k \beta_i, \quad k=1,\ldots,l. \quad (8)$$

The inequalities (8) closely resemble majorization, and yield majorization if $\gamma_1 + \gamma_{2l} \geq \gamma_2 + \gamma_{2l-1} \geq \cdots \geq \gamma_l + \gamma_{l+1}$.

Eigenvalue Inequalities

The following inequalities are majorization generalizations of what have been called Bloomfield–Watson–Knott inequalities. For an exposition and references, see Ando (2001).

Let $A > 0$ (i.e., A is positive definite) be an $n \times n$ matrix partitioned as

$$A = \begin{bmatrix} A_{11} & A_{12} \\ A_{21} & A_{22} \end{bmatrix},$$

with A_{11} an $m \times m$ matrix of rank $m \leq n - m$. Further, let $\lambda_1(\cdot) \geq \cdots \geq \lambda_n(\cdot)$ denote ordered eigenvalues, and let $\alpha_1 \geq \cdots \geq \alpha_n$ denote the ordered eigenvalues of A.

C.5. Proposition (Ando, 2001). For $k = 1, \ldots, m$,

$$\prod_1^k \frac{1}{1 - \lambda_j(|A_{22}^{-1/2} A_{21} A_{11}^{-1/2}|)^2} \leq \prod_1^k \frac{(\alpha_j + \alpha_{n-j+1})^2}{4\alpha_j \alpha_{n-j+1}}, \tag{9}$$

$$\sum_1^k \lambda_j(|A_{22}^{-1/2} A_{21} A_{11}^{-1/2}|)^2 \leq \sum_1^k \frac{(\alpha_j - \alpha_{n-j+1})^2}{4\alpha_j \alpha_{n-j+1}}, \tag{10}$$

$$\prod_1^k [1 + \lambda_j(|A_{21} A_{11}^{-1}|)^2] \leq \prod_1^k \frac{(\alpha_j + \alpha_{n-j+1})^2}{4\alpha_j \alpha_{n-j+1}}, \tag{11}$$

$$\sum_1^k \lambda_j(|A_{21} A_{11}^{-1}|)^2 \leq \sum_1^k \frac{(\alpha_j - \alpha_{n-j+1})^2}{4\alpha_j \alpha_{n-j+1}}, \tag{12}$$

$$\sum_1^k \lambda_j(|A_{21}|) \leq \sum_1^k \frac{\alpha_j - \alpha_{n-j+1}}{2}. \tag{13}$$

Converse Theorems

C.6. Jacobi matrix. A symmetric tridiagonal matrix of the form

$$J = \begin{bmatrix} a_0 & b_1 & 0 & 0 & \cdots & 0 & 0 \\ b_1 & a_1 & b_2 & 0 & \cdots & 0 & 0 \\ 0 & b_2 & a_2 & b_3 & \cdots & 0 & 0 \\ & & & \cdots & & & \\ & & & \cdots & & & \\ 0 & 0 & 0 & 0 & \cdots & b_{n-1} & a_n \end{bmatrix},$$

where all a_i, b_i are real and $b_i > 0$, is called a *Jacobi matrix*. Denote by $J_{(1)}$ the truncated $n \times n$ matrix obtained by deleting the first row and first column of J.

The ordered eigenvalues $\lambda_0 > \lambda_1 > \cdots > \lambda_n$ of J and the ordered eigenvalues $\mu_1 > \mu_2 > \cdots > \mu_n$ of $J_{(1)}$ are real, distinct, and interlace in the form

$$\lambda_0 > \mu_1 > \lambda_1 > \cdots > \mu_n > \lambda_n. \tag{14}$$

The inverse problem is to show how to construct a Jacobi matrix given $2n+1$ numbers satisfying (14). The choice of these numbers cannot be arbitrary, but must be feasible in the sense that there exists a Jacobi matrix with these $2n+1$ associated eigenvalues. Hochstadt (1974) then shows how to construct the unique corresponding Jacobi matrix.

C.7. Normal matrix. A matrix A is a normal matrix if $AA^* = A^*A$. This class includes Hermitian matrices. However, there are two important differences; the eigenvalues need not be real, and principal submatrices need not be normal. Malamud (2005) provides necessary and sufficient conditions for two sequences $\lambda_1, \ldots, \lambda_n$ and $\mu_1, \ldots, \mu_{n-1}$ to be the spectra of a normal matrix A and of its principal submatrix obtained by deleting the last row and column of A (see 10.B.9).

D Diagonal Elements and Singular Values

As is proved in Section B, the diagonal elements a_{ii} and eigenvalues $\lambda_i(A)$, $i = 1, \ldots, n$, of an $n \times n$ Hermitian matrix A are real and satisfy $(a_{11}, \ldots, a_{nn}) \prec (\lambda_1(A), \ldots, \lambda_n(A))$. For an arbitrary complex matrix A, the roots and/or the diagonal elements can be complex, so that similar comparisons require some modifications.

A possible comparison is between the real part of the diagonal elements and that of the eigenvalues. Such a comparison would have to be in the direction $\mathscr{R}(a_{11}, \ldots, a_{nn}) \prec \mathscr{R}(\lambda_1(A), \ldots, \lambda_n(A))$ already established in the Hermitian case. That no such majorization exists can be seen from the example

$$A = \frac{1}{5}\begin{bmatrix} 7+3i & 1+4i \\ -4+4i & 3-3i \end{bmatrix} = \frac{1}{5}\begin{bmatrix} 2 & 1 \\ 1 & -2 \end{bmatrix}\begin{bmatrix} 1+i & 0 \\ 0 & 1-i \end{bmatrix}\begin{bmatrix} 2 & 1 \\ 1 & -2 \end{bmatrix}.$$

Here, $\mathscr{R}(a_{ii}) = (\frac{7}{5}, \frac{3}{5})$, and $\mathscr{R}(\lambda) = (1, 1)$, so that $(\mathscr{R}(a_{ii})) \succ (\mathscr{R}(\lambda))$.

Another alternative is to compare absolute values. Note that $\sum |a_{ii}| \neq \sum |\lambda_i(A)|$ for arbitrary matrices, so that at best weak majorization can be expected. In the above example,

$$(|a_{11}|, |a_{22}|) = (58/25, 18/25), \qquad (|\lambda_1|, |\lambda_2|) = (2, 2),$$

and no majorization in either direction exists.

However, a comparison between the absolute values or the real part of the diagonal elements and the singular values is possible.

D.1. Theorem (Fan, 1951). If A is an arbitrary $n \times n$ matrix with diagonal elements $a_1, \ldots, a_n$, then

$$\begin{aligned}\mathscr{R}(a) &\equiv (\mathscr{R}(a_1), \ldots, \mathscr{R}(a_n)) \prec_w (|a_1|, \ldots, |a_n|) \\ &\prec_w (\sigma_1(A), \ldots, \sigma_n(A)) \equiv \sigma(A) \quad \text{on } \mathscr{R}^n. \end{aligned} \quad (1)$$

Proof. According to 19.B.1, there exist unitary matrices U and V such that

$$A = U D_\sigma V^*,$$

where $\sigma_i \equiv \sigma_i(A)$, $i = 1, \ldots, n$. Then

$$a_j = \sum_l (u_{jl} \bar{v}_{jl}) \sigma_l \quad (2)$$

and

$$|a_j| \leq \sum_l |u_{jl} \bar{v}_{jl}| \sigma_l \equiv \sum_l p_{jl} \sigma_l. \quad (3)$$

By 2.H.7.a, $P = (p_{ij})$ is doubly substochastic. Let $d_j = |a_j|/\sum_l p_{jl}\sigma_l$, $j = 1, \ldots, n$, and $D_d = \text{diag}(d_1, \ldots, d_n)$. Then from (3),

$$(|a_1|, \ldots, |a_n|) = (\sigma_1, \ldots, \sigma_n) P D_d \equiv \sigma Q.$$

Because $0 \leq d_j \leq 1$, $j = 1, \ldots, n$, D_d is doubly substochastic, so that $Q = P D_d$ is doubly substochastic, which proves the right-hand majorization in (1).

The left-hand majorization in (1) follows trivially from $|a_j| \geq \mathscr{R}(a_j)$, $j = 1, \ldots, n$. ||

An alternative proof of $\mathscr{R}(a) \prec_w \sigma(A)$ can be based on the extremal representation of 20.B.1. Rearrange the rows and columns of A so that $a_1 \geq \cdots \geq a_n$. Then

$$\sum_1^k \sigma_i(A) = \max \mathscr{R} \text{ tr } UAV^* \geq \mathscr{R}[\text{tr}(I_k, 0)A(I_k, 0)'] = \sum_1^k \mathscr{R}a_i,$$

where the maximum is over all $k \times n$ matrices U and V such that $UU^* = VV^* = I_k$.

Alternative proof of D.1. Thompson (1977) provides an interesting proof that uses the interlacing property of the eigenvalues of a Hermitian matrix and a principal submatrix (see B.1). Let $D_\epsilon = \text{diag}(\epsilon_1, \ldots, \epsilon_n)$ satisfy $b_{ii} = \epsilon_i a_i = |a_i|$, $i = 1, \ldots, n$, and let $B = D_\epsilon A$. Then $|\epsilon_i| = 1$, $i = 1, \ldots, n$ and $\sigma(B) = \sigma(D_\epsilon A) = \sigma(A)$. Further, let $B_k = (b_{ij})$, $i, j = 1, \ldots, k$. Then

$$\sum_1^k |a_i| = \sum_1^k b_{ii} = \text{tr} B_k = |\text{tr} B_k| = |\sum_1^k \lambda_i(B_k)| \leq \sum_1^k |\lambda_i(B_k)|.$$

By E.1.a, $\sum_1^k |\lambda_i(B_k)| \leq \sum_1^k \sigma_i(B_k)$, and from the interlacing property for submatrices of a Hermitian matrix, $\sigma_i(B_k) \leq \sigma_i(B)$ for $i = 1, \ldots, k$, so that $\sum_1^k \sigma_i(B_k) \leq \sum_1^k \sigma_i(B)$, $k = 1, \ldots, n$, which completes the proof. ||

Recall that there is no majorization between the diagonal elements and the eigenvalues of an arbitrary matrix. However, these quantities are loosely related, as indicated by the following theorem.

D.2. Theorem (Mirsky, 1958a). A necessary and sufficient condition for the existence of a real (complex) matrix A with real (complex) eigenvalues $\lambda_1, \ldots, \lambda_n$ and diagonal elements $a_1, \ldots, a_n$ is

$$a_1 + \cdots + a_n = \lambda_1 + \cdots + \lambda_n.$$

Proof. Necessity follows from the fact that if A has eigenvalues $\lambda_1, \ldots, \lambda_n$ and diagonal elements $a_1, \ldots, a_n$, then $\text{tr} A = \sum_1^n a_i = \sum_1^n \lambda_i$.

The proof of sufficiency is by induction on n and is similar to the proof of B.3. Let $b_1, \ldots, b_{n-1}$ be distinct numbers satisfying $\sum_1^{n-1} a_i = \sum_1^{n-1} b_i$. By the induction hypothesis, there exists an $(n-1) \times (n-1)$ matrix A_1 with diagonal elements $a_1, \ldots, a_{n-1}$ and eigenvalues $b_1, \ldots, b_{n-1}$. It remains to augment the matrix A_1 to obtain an $n \times n$ matrix A which has the desired diagonal elements and eigenvalues.

Let Q be a nonsingular matrix for which

$$Q^{-1}A_1 Q = D_b \equiv \text{diag}(b_1, \ldots, b_{n-1}),$$

316   9. Matrix Theory

and form the matrix

$$A = A(u,v) = \begin{bmatrix} Q & 0 \\ 0 & 1 \end{bmatrix} \begin{bmatrix} D_b & u' \\ v & a_n \end{bmatrix} \begin{bmatrix} Q^{-1} & 0 \\ 0 & 1 \end{bmatrix}$$

$$= \begin{bmatrix} QD_bQ^{-1} & Qu' \\ vQ^{-1} & a_n \end{bmatrix} = \begin{bmatrix} A_1 & Qu' \\ vQ^{-1} & a_n \end{bmatrix}.$$

First note that the diagonal elements of A are $a_1, \ldots, a_n$ as desired. The vectors $u = (u_1, \ldots, u_{n-1})$ and $v = (v_1, \ldots, v_{n-1})$ are yet to be chosen so that the eigenvalues of A are $\lambda_1, \ldots, \lambda_n$.

By using the partitioned form of A, it can be seen that the roots of $\det(\lambda I - A) = 0$ are the roots of

$$\det(\lambda I - A_1)[\lambda - a_n - vQ^{-1}(\lambda I - A_1)^{-1}Qu']$$
$$= \left[\prod_1^{n-1}(\lambda - b_i)\right]\left(\lambda - a_n - \sum_1^{n-1} \frac{v_j u_j}{\lambda - b_j}\right) = 0. \tag{4}$$

The choice of v_j and u_j can be made so that $\lambda_1, \ldots, \lambda_n$ are the roots of (4) as follows. Let

$$f(\lambda) = \prod_1^n (\lambda - \lambda_i), \qquad g(\lambda) = \prod_1^{n-1}(\lambda - b_i).$$

As in the argument of B.3, Lagrange's interpolation formula [see, e.g., Householder (1953, Section 5.1)] yields

$$\frac{f(\lambda)}{g(\lambda)} = \lambda - \left(\sum_1^n \lambda_i - \sum_1^{n-1} b_i\right) + \sum_1^{n-1} \frac{f(b_j)}{g'(b_j)} \frac{1}{\lambda - b_j}. \tag{5}$$

Since $a_n = \sum_1^n \lambda_i - \sum_1^{n-1} b_i$, upon comparing (4) and (5), it is seen that the choice

$$u_j v_j = -\frac{f(b_j)}{g'(b_j)}, \qquad j = 1, \ldots, n-1,$$

satisfies the requirements. ||

D.3. Theorem (Thompson, 1975).   The conditions

(i) $(|d_1|, \ldots, |d_n|) \prec_w (\sigma_1, \ldots, \sigma_n)$,

(ii) $\sum_1^{n-1} |d_i| - |d_n| \leq \sum_1^{n-1} \sigma_i - \sigma_n$

are necessary and sufficient for the existence of an $n \times n$ matrix with (possibly complex) diagonal elements $d_1, \ldots, d_n$ with $|d_1| \geq \cdots \geq |d_n|$ and singular values $\sigma_1, \ldots, \sigma_n$.

The necessity of (i) is given by D.1. The proof of the converse is quite involved and is omitted.

E Absolute Value of Eigenvalues and Singular Values

When A is Hermitian, $|\lambda(A)| = \lambda^{1/2}(AA^*) = \sigma(A)$, so that the absolute values of the eigenvalues are the singular values. When A is not Hermitian, what restrictions are placed on the eigenvalues $\lambda(A)$ by knowledge of the singular values $\sigma(A)$? An answer to this question is provided by a key result of Weyl (1949) that has generated considerable research. In particular, see Ando and Hiai (1994).

E.1. Theorem (Weyl, 1949). For any $n \times n$ complex matrix A with eigenvalues ordered $|\lambda_1(A)| \geq \cdots \geq |\lambda_n(A)|$,

$$\prod_1^k |\lambda_j(A)| \leq \prod_1^k \sigma_j(A), \qquad k = 1, \ldots, n-1,$$
$$\prod_1^n |\lambda_j(A)| = \prod_1^n \sigma_j(A). \tag{1}$$

If $|\lambda_n(A)| > 0$, these conditions are equivalent to

$$(\log|\lambda_1(A)|, \ldots, \log|\lambda_n(A)|) \prec (\log \sigma_1(A), \ldots, \log \sigma_n(A)). \tag{2}$$

Further discussion of log-majorization is given in 1.A. Examples of log-majorization occur throughout this book.

Alternative proofs of E.1 have been provided by Horn (1950) and by Visser and Zaanen (1952). The following proof is essentially the same as that of Marcus and Minc (1964).

Proof. The well-known inequality

$$|\lambda_1(A)| \leq \sigma_1(A)$$

of Browne (1928) applied to the kth compound $A^{(k)}$ (refer to 19.F.1) yields

$$|\lambda_1(A^{(k)})| \leq \sigma_1(A^{(k)}). \tag{3}$$

9. Matrix Theory

By 19.F.2.c, the eigenvalues of $A^{(k)}$ are products $\prod_{j=1}^{k} \lambda_{i_j}(A)$ of the eigenvalues of A, k at a time, so that

$$\lambda_1(A^{(k)}) = \lambda_1(A) \cdots \lambda_k(A), \qquad k = 1, \ldots, n. \tag{4}$$

As a consequence of the Binet–Cauchy theorem 19.F.2,

$$(AB)^{(k)} = A^{(k)} B^{(k)}.$$

Thus

$$[\sigma_1(A^{(k)})]^2 = \lambda_1(A^{(k)} A^{*(k)}) = \lambda_1((AA^*)^{(k)})$$
$$= \prod_1^k \lambda_j(AA^*), \quad k = 1, \ldots, n. \tag{5}$$

Using (4) and (5) in (3) yields (1) after noting that for $k = n$, equality in (3) is achieved. ∥

E.1.a. For any $n \times n$ nonsingular complex matrix A,

$$(|\lambda_1(A)|, \ldots, |\lambda_n(A)|) \prec_w (\sigma_1(A), \ldots, \sigma_n(A)).$$

Proof. This is an application of 5.A.1 to (2). ∥

E.1.b. For any nonsingular complex matrix A,

$$(|\lambda_1(A)|^2, \ldots, |\lambda_n(A)|^2) \prec_w (\sigma_1^2(A), \ldots, \sigma_n^2(A))$$
$$= (\lambda_1(AA^*), \ldots, \lambda_n(AA^*)).$$

Proof. This is a consequence of E.1.a and 5.A.2. ∥

E.1.c. (Schur, 1909). For any nonsingular complex matrix A,

$$\sum_1^n \lambda_i(AA^*) = \operatorname{tr} AA^* = \sum_{i,j} |a_{ij}|^2 \geq \sum_1^n |\lambda_i(A)|^2.$$

Proof. This is immediate from E.1.b. ∥

In the inequality of E.1.c, the judicious choice

$$A = \begin{bmatrix} 0 & \sqrt{x_1} & 0 & \cdots & 0 \\ 0 & 0 & \sqrt{x_2} & \cdots & 0 \\ \vdots & \vdots & \vdots & & \vdots \\ 0 & 0 & 0 & \cdots & \sqrt{x_{n-1}} \\ \sqrt{x_n} & 0 & 0 & \cdots & 0 \end{bmatrix}, \quad x_i > 0,$$

E. Absolute Value of Eigenvalues and Singular Values

yields the inequality

$$\sum_1^n x_i \geq n \prod_1^n x_i^{1/n},$$

which is the arithmetic-geometric mean inequality. The computation is based on the fact that the eigenvalues of A are the nth roots of $\prod_1^n \sqrt{x_i}$. This idea and proof are due to Gaines (1967).

Note. E.1.c can be generalized. In fact, for any $r \in [1, 2]$ we have $\sum_{i,j} |a_{ij}|^r \geq \sum_{i=1}^n |\lambda_i(A)|^r$. Ikramov (1994) proves this by using the Weyl inequalities (E.1),

$$\sum_{i=1}^k |\lambda_i(A)|^r \leq \sum_{i=1}^k [\sigma_i(A)]^r, \qquad 1 \leq k \leq n, \qquad 0 < r < \infty,$$

and the fact that $f(x) = x^{r/2}$ is strictly concave for $x > 0$ when $1 \leq r < 2$.

The inequality

$$\prod_1^k (1 + r|\lambda_i(A)|) \leq \prod_1^k (1 + r|\sigma_i(A)|), \qquad 1 \leq k \leq n,$$

also holds for all complex matrices A and $0 < r < \infty$.

Note. E.1.a, E.1.b, and E.1.c hold even for any singular matrix A. The nonsingularity condition is required for log-majorization. See Kittaneh (1995) for further discussion.

E.2. (Fan, 1949). For any complex matrix A and positive integer s,

$$\sigma^2(A^s) \prec_w \sigma^{2s}(A).$$

To prove this, Fan makes a transformation using the polar decomposition 19.C.3, and then applies an extremal representation.

E.3. (Tung, 1964). If A is an $n \times n$ complex matrix, and U is unitary, then

$$\prod_1^n \frac{1 - \sigma_i(A)}{1 + \sigma_i(A)} \leq \frac{\det(I - AA^*)}{\det(I - AU^*)(I - UA^*)} \leq \prod_1^n \frac{1 + \sigma_i(A)}{1 - \sigma_i(A)}. \qquad (6)$$

Note that

$$\det(I - AA^*) = \prod_1^n (1 - \sigma_i^2(A)), \qquad \det(I - AU^*) = \det(I - UA^*);$$

if $1 > \sigma_i$, $i = 1, \ldots, n$, then inequality (6) can be simplified to

$$\prod_1^n (1 - \sigma_i(A)) \leq |\det(I - AU^*)| \leq \prod_1^n (1 + \sigma_i(A)). \tag{7}$$

Marcus (1965) uses majorization to obtain an extension of (7):

E.3.a. Theorem (Marcus, 1965). Let A be an $n \times n$ complex matrix with eigenvalues ordered $|\lambda_1| \geq \cdots \geq |\lambda_n|$ such that $I - AA^*$ is positive definite. If $1 \geq c_1 \geq \cdots \geq c_n > 0$, then for $k = 1, \ldots, n$,

$$\begin{aligned}
\prod_1^k [1 - c_i \sigma_i(A)] &\leq \prod_1^k [1 - c_i |\lambda_i|] \leq \prod_1^k |1 - c_i \lambda_i| \\
&\leq \prod_1^k [1 + c_i |\lambda_i|] \leq \prod_1^k [1 + c_i \sigma_i(A)].
\end{aligned} \tag{8a}$$

With the notation $\widetilde{\sigma}_i = c_i \sigma_i(A)$, $\widetilde{\lambda}_i = c_i \lambda_i$, $i = 1, \ldots, n$, (8a) can be rewritten equivalently as

(i) $\qquad \log(1 - |\widetilde{\lambda}|) \prec^{\mathrm{w}} \log(1 - \widetilde{\sigma})$,

(ii) $\qquad \log(1 - |\widetilde{\lambda}|) \prec_{\mathrm{w}} \log|1 - \widetilde{\lambda}| \prec_{\mathrm{w}} \log(1 + |\widetilde{\lambda}|)$, $\qquad$ (8b)

(iii) $\qquad \log(1 + |\widetilde{\lambda}|) \prec_{\mathrm{w}} \log(1 + \widetilde{\sigma})$.

Proof. Applying 3.H.3.c to (2) yields $(\log |\widetilde{\lambda}|) \prec (\log \widetilde{\sigma})$, which together with 5.A.1(2) and 5.A.1(1) with the choices $g(x) = \log(1 - e^x)$ and $g(x) = \log(1 + e^x)$, respectively, yields (i) and (iii). The remaining majorizations (ii) follow trivially from a termwise argument after noting that $1 - |x| \leq |1 - x| \leq 1 + |x|$. $\quad ||$

E.4. Theorem (Hua, 1955). If A and B are $n \times n$ complex matrices such that $I - A^*A$ and $I - B^*B$ are positive semidefinite, then

$$|\det(I - A^*B)|^2 = \prod_1^n |\lambda_i(I - A^*B)|^2 \geq \prod_1^n \lambda_i(I - A^*A) \lambda_i(I - B^*B)$$
$$= \det(I - A^*A) \det(I - B^*B).$$

With slightly stronger hypotheses, Hua's inequality can be extended to a majorization result.

E.4.a. Theorem (Marcus, 1958). If $I - A^*A$ and $I - B^*B$ are positive definite and the eigenvalues of $I - A^*B$, $I - A^*A$, and $I - B^*B$ are ordered so that

E. Absolute Value of Eigenvalues and Singular Values 321

$$|\lambda_1(I - A^*B)| \geq \cdots \geq |\lambda_n(I - A^*B)|,$$
$$\lambda_1(I - A^*A) \geq \cdots \geq \lambda_n(I - A^*A),$$
$$\lambda_1(I - B^*B) \geq \cdots \geq \lambda_n(I - B^*B),$$

then, for $k = 1, \ldots, n$,

$$\prod_k^n |\lambda_i(I - A^*B)|^2 \geq \prod_k^n \lambda_i(I - A^*A)\, \lambda_i(I - B^*B), \tag{9a}$$

or equivalently,

$$[\log |\lambda(I - A^*B)|^2] \prec^w [\log \lambda(I - A^*A) + \log \lambda(I - B^*B)]. \tag{9b}$$

Proof. Write $U \leq V$ to mean that $V - U$ is positive semidefinite. Under the hypotheses of E.4.a,

$$I - A^*A \leq (I - A^*B)(I - B^*B)^{-1}(I - B^*A). \tag{10}$$

[Inequality (10) is essentially posed by Redheffer (1964).] For simplicity of notation, let $L = (I - A^*B)$, $G = (I - B^*B)$, $H = (I - A^*A)$. Then from (10) and 20.A.1.b, it follows that

$$\lambda_n(H) \leq \lambda_n(LG^{-1}L^*). \tag{11}$$

By A.1.a and the inequality 20.A.1.a,

$$\lambda_n(LG^{-1}L^*) = \lambda_n(G^{-1}L^*L)$$
$$\leq \lambda_n(L^*L)\lambda_1(G^{-1}) = \lambda_n(LL^*)/\lambda_n(G). \tag{12}$$

From (11) and (12), and by E.1,

$$\lambda_n(G)\lambda_n(H) \leq \lambda_n(LL^*) \leq |\lambda_n(L)|^2. \tag{13}$$

The proof is completed by using the kth compound with (13). ∥

Open problem. Inequalities (9a) suggest the more general problem of characterizing the class of matrix-valued functions F of matrices for which

$$\prod_k^n |\lambda_i(F(A^*B))|^2 \geq \prod_k^n \lambda_i(F(A^*A))\, \lambda_i(F(B^*B)), \qquad k = 1, \ldots, n.$$

The choice $F(X) = I - X$ then yields (9a).

E.4.b. (Xu, Xu, and Zhang, 2009). Let A and B be Hermitian matrices with $A > 0$ and $B \geq 0$, and with respective ordered eigenvalues

$\alpha_1 \geq \cdots \geq \alpha_n$ and $\beta_1 \geq \cdots \geq \beta_n$; let C be a complex matrix with eigenvalues ordered in modulus $|\gamma_1| \geq \cdots \geq |\gamma_n|$. If $C^* A^{-1} C \geq B$, then for $k = 1, \ldots, n$,

$$\prod_{j=1}^{k} |\gamma_{n-j+1}|^2 \geq \prod_{j=1}^{k} \alpha_{n-j+1} \beta_{n-j+1}.$$

Converse Theorems Connecting Eigenvalues and Singular Values of a Matrix

The following basic result of Horn (1954b) shows that the relations (1) provide a characterization of the absolute value of the eigenvalues and the singular values of a complex matrix.

E.5. Theorem (Horn, 1954b). If $x_1 \geq \cdots \geq x_n \geq 0$, $y_1 \geq \cdots \geq y_n \geq 0$, and

$$\prod_{1}^{k} y_i \leq \prod_{1}^{k} x_i, \qquad k = 1, \ldots, n-1, \qquad \prod_{1}^{n} y_i = \prod_{1}^{n} x_i, \qquad (14)$$

then there exists a matrix A such that $y_j = |\lambda_j(A)|$ and $x_j = \sigma_j(A)$, $j = 1, \ldots, n$.

Horn's proof is inductive; he shows that (14) implies the existence of a triangular matrix with eigenvalues $y_1, \ldots, y_n$ and singular values $x_1, \ldots, x_n$. For $n = 2$, (14) and $x_1 \geq x_2$, $y_1 \geq y_2$ imply $x_1 \geq y_1 \geq y_2 \geq x_2 \geq 0$ and also that $x_1^2 + x_2^2 \geq y_1^2 + y_2^2$. The matrix

$$\begin{bmatrix} y_1 & t \\ 0 & y_2 \end{bmatrix}$$

has eigenvalues y_1, y_2; the choice $t = (x_1^2 + x_2^2 - y_1^2 - y_2^2)^{1/2}$ yields singular values x_1, x_2. For $n > 2$, Horn treats the cases $x_n > 0$, $y_n > 0$ and $x_n = 0$ or $y_n = 0$ separately, and completes the induction by making use of the unitary equivalence to a diagonal matrix.

Horn further shows that when $x_n > 0$, $y_n > 0$, E.5 is equivalent to the following:

E.6. Theorem (Horn, 1954b). If (14) holds and $x_1 \geq \cdots \geq x_n > 0$, $y_1 \geq \cdots \geq y_n > 0$, then there exists a positive definite symmetric matrix H with eigenvalues $x_j = \lambda_j(H)$, $j = 1, \ldots, n$, such that

E. Absolute Value of Eigenvalues and Singular Values

$$\prod_1^k y_j = \det H_k, \quad k = 1, \ldots, n, \tag{15}$$

where $H_k = (h_{ij})$, $i, j = 1, 2, \ldots, k$.

Indication of proof. Horn (1954b) shows that (14) implies the existence of a lower triangular matrix T with eigenvalues $t_{ii} = y_i^{1/2}$ and singular values $x_i^{1/2}$. Consequently, if $H = TT^*$, then $\det H_k = \det T_k T_k^* = \prod_1^k y_i$, which is (15).

Conversely, suppose (15) holds. Because each $y_i > 0$, $\det H_k > 0$, $k = 1, \ldots, n$, and hence, H is positive definite. Write $H = TT^*$, where T is lower triangular. Since $\det H_k = \prod_1^k t_{ii} \bar{t}_{ii}$, and the y_i are real, the diagonal elements of T are the eigenvalues $y_1^{1/2}, \ldots, y_n^{1/2}$. But now $\prod_1^k y_i^{1/2} \leq \prod_1^k x_i^{1/2}$, $k = 1, \ldots, n$, so that (14) holds.

Alternative proof of E.6. Mirsky (1959c) gives an alternative inductive proof that makes use of the interlacing property 5.A.10.a.

The result is clearly true for $n = 1$. Assume that it holds for $n - 1$. Let $x_1 \geq \cdots \geq x_n > 0$ and $y_1 \cdots \geq y_n > 0$ be given numbers satisfying

$$(\log y_1, \ldots, \log y_n) \prec (\log x_1, \ldots, \log x_n).$$

From 5.A.10.a, there exist positive numbers $c_1, \ldots, c_{n-1}$ that interlace $\log x_1, \ldots, \log x_n$ and satisfy

$$(\log y_1, \ldots, \log y_{n-1}) \prec (c_1, \ldots, c_{n-1}) \equiv (\log q_1, \ldots, \log q_{n-1}). \tag{16}$$

By the induction hypothesis applied to (16), there exists a real symmetric $(n-1) \times (n-1)$ matrix Q with eigenvalues $q_1, \ldots, q_{n-1}$ and such that

$$\prod_1^k y_i = \det Q_k, \quad k = 1, \ldots, n-1.$$

As in the proof of B.3, there exist a vector $v = (v_1, \ldots, v_{n-1})$ and a scalar w such that

$$S = \begin{bmatrix} Q & v' \\ v & w \end{bmatrix}$$

has eigenvalues $x_1, \ldots, x_n$. ∥

Eigenvalues of a Matrix and Its Unitary Part

From the polar decomposition 19.C.3, a complex matrix A can be written $A = HU$, where H is the positive semidefinite square root of AA^* and U is an $n \times n$ unitary matrix. The matrix U is called the *unitary part* of A. If A is nonsingular, then U is unique.

Earlier in this section the following question is discussed: Given the eigenvalues of H (singular values of A), what restrictions does this place on the eigenvalues of A? Horn and Steinberg (1959) answer a similar question given the eigenvalues of U.

E.7. Theorem (Horn and Steinberg, 1959). If $A = HU$, where H is a positive definite Hermitian matrix and U is a unitary matrix, then

$$(\arg \lambda_1(A), \ldots, \arg \lambda_n(A)) \prec (\arg \lambda_1(U), \ldots, \arg \lambda_n(U)).$$

Furthermore, if $(\lambda_1, \ldots, \lambda_n) \prec (\alpha_1, \ldots, \alpha_n)$, $\lambda_i \neq 0$, $|\alpha_i| = 1$, for $i = 1, \ldots, n$, then there exists a matrix A with $\lambda_i = \lambda_i(A)$, $\alpha_i = \lambda_i(U)$, $i = 1, \ldots, n$, where U is the unitary part of A.

F Eigenvalues and Singular Values

Eigenvalues of A and $\frac{1}{2}(A + A^*)$

The real parts of the eigenvalues of a complex matrix A can be compared with the eigenvalues of the symmetric version $\frac{1}{2}(A + A^*)$ as a consequence of the extremal representation 20.A.2 or by using the additive compound discussed in 19.F.3.

F.1. Theorem (Fan, 1950). For any $n \times n$ complex matrix A,

$$(\mathscr{R}\lambda_1(A), \ldots, \mathscr{R}\lambda_n(A)) \prec \left(\lambda_1\left(\frac{A+A^*}{2}\right), \ldots, \lambda_n\left(\frac{A+A^*}{2}\right)\right).$$

Proof. According to 19.A.3, A can be written in the form $A = \Delta T \Delta^*$, where Δ is an $n \times n$ unitary matrix and T is lower triangular with $t_{ii} = \lambda_i(A)$, $i = 1, \ldots, n$. With the eigenvalues labeled so that

$$\lambda_1\left(\frac{A+A^*}{2}\right) \geq \cdots \geq \lambda_n\left(\frac{A+A^*}{2}\right), \qquad \mathscr{R}\lambda_1(A) \geq \cdots \geq \mathscr{R}\lambda_n(A),$$

F. Eigenvalues and Singular Values   325

it follows from the extremal representation 20.A.2 that

$$\sum_1^k \lambda_i\left(\frac{A+A^*}{2}\right) = \max_{UU^*=I_k} \mathscr{R} \operatorname{tr} U\left(\frac{A+A^*}{2}\right)U^*$$

$$= \max_{UU^*=I_k} \mathscr{R} \operatorname{tr} U\Delta\left(\frac{T+T^*}{2}\right)\Delta^*U^*$$

$$\geq \mathscr{R} \operatorname{tr}(I_k 0)\left(\frac{T+T^*}{2}\right)\binom{I_k}{0}$$

$$= \sum_1^k \mathscr{R}\lambda_i(A), \qquad k=1,\ldots,n. \quad \|$$

If in addition $\mathscr{R}\lambda_i(A) > 0$, $\lambda_i(A+A^*) > 0$, then from 5.A.1.d,

$$\prod_k^n \mathscr{R}\lambda_i(A) \geq \prod_k^n \lambda_i\left(\frac{A+A^*}{2}\right), \quad k+1,\ldots,n.$$

F.1.a. (Bendixson, 1902; Hirsch, 1902). Under the hypotheses of F.1,

$$\mathscr{R}\lambda_1(A) \leq \lambda_1\left(\frac{A+A^*}{2}\right). \tag{1}$$

This case ($k=1$) of F.1 was obtained by Bendixson for real matrices and by Hirsch for complex matrices. An alternative proof is given by Browne (1930b).

That (1) implies F.1 is somewhat surprising. But using (1) with the kth additive compound Δ_k (see 19.F) yields

$$\mathscr{R}\lambda_1(\Delta_k(A)) \leq \lambda_1\left(\frac{\Delta_k(A)+(\Delta_k(A))^*}{2}\right).$$

The left-hand side is $\mathscr{R}\sum_1^k \lambda_i(A) = \sum_1^k \mathscr{R}\lambda_i(A)$. Because $(\Delta_k(A))^* = \Delta_k(A^*)$ and because the additive compound is linear,

$$\lambda_1\left(\Delta_k\left(\frac{A+A^*}{2}\right)\right) = \lambda_1\left(\Delta_k\left(\frac{A}{2}\right) + \Delta_k\left(\frac{A^*}{2}\right)\right)$$

$$= \sum_1^k \lambda_i\left(\frac{A+A^*}{2}\right).$$

The following result provides a converse to F.1.

F.2. Theorem (Amir-Moéz and Horn, 1958; Mirsky, 1958a). If $\omega_1,\ldots,\omega_n$ are complex numbers and $\alpha_1,\ldots,\alpha_n$ are real numbers satisfying

$$(\mathscr{R}\omega_1,\ldots,\mathscr{R}\omega_n) \prec (\alpha_1,\ldots,\alpha_n), \tag{2}$$

then there exists an $n \times n$ complex matrix A with $\omega_i = \lambda_i(A)$ and $\alpha_i = \lambda_i(\frac{1}{2}(A+A^*))$, $i=1,\ldots,n$.

Proof. If the given $2n$ numbers $\alpha_1,\ldots,\alpha_n$ and $\omega_1,\ldots,\omega_n$ satisfy (2), then by B.2 there exists a real symmetric matrix B with eigenvalues $\alpha_1,\ldots,\alpha_n$ and diagonal elements $\mathscr{R}\omega_1,\ldots,\mathscr{R}\omega_n$. By 19.A.3.b there exists an orthogonal matrix Γ such that

$$\Gamma'B\Gamma = D_\alpha = \mathrm{diag}(\alpha_1,\ldots,\alpha_n).$$

To construct the desired matrix A, first form the lower triangular matrix L defined by $l_{ii} = \omega_i$, $l_{ij} = 2b_{ij}(i>j)$, $l_{ij} = 0(i<j)$. Then $\omega_i = \lambda_i(L) = \lambda_i(\Gamma'L\Gamma)$. Let $A = \Gamma'L\Gamma$. Then

$$\frac{A+A^*}{2} = \Gamma'\left(\frac{L+L^*}{2}\right)\Gamma = \Gamma'B\Gamma = D_\alpha,$$

so that the matrix A fulfills the requirements. ||

Eigenvalues of A and $(A-A^*)/(2i)$

It was noted by Fan (1950) that a result similar to F.1 holds for the imaginary singular values [i.e., the eigenvalues of $(A-A^*)/(2i)$]. This is stated explicitly by Amir-Moéz and Horn (1958), who also note the converse.

F.3. Theorem (Fan, 1950; Amir-Moéz and Horn, 1958). Let $\theta_1,\ldots,\theta_n$ and $\beta_1,\ldots,\beta_n$ be real numbers. A necessary and sufficient condition for the existence of an $n \times n$ complex matrix A with imaginary singular values $\lambda_j((A-A^*)/(2i)) = \beta_j$ and with eigenvalues having imaginary parts $\mathscr{I}\lambda_j(A) = \theta_j$, $j = 1,\ldots,n$, is

$$(\theta_1,\ldots,\theta_n) \prec (\beta_1,\ldots,\beta_n). \tag{3}$$

The proof parallels that of F.1 and F.2. Alternatively, the necessity of (3) can be obtained using the kth additive compound in the following result.

F.3.a. (Bromwich, 1906). If A is an $n \times n$ complex matrix with

$$\lambda_1\left(\frac{A-A^*}{2i}\right) \geq \cdots \geq \lambda_n\left(\frac{A-A^*}{2i}\right),$$

then

$$\lambda_n\left(\frac{A-A^*}{2i}\right) \leq \mathscr{I}\lambda_j(A) \leq \lambda_1\left(\frac{A-A^*}{2i}\right), \qquad j=1,\ldots,n. \tag{4}$$

Eigenvalues of $(A+A^*)/2$ and AA^*

Comparisons between the eigenvalues of $\frac{1}{2}(A+A^*)$ and the singular values can be obtained as a consequence of F.4 below.

F.4. Theorem (Fan and Hoffman, 1955). Let A be an $n \times n$ complex matrix. Label the eigenvalues of $\frac{1}{2}(A+A^*)$ so that

$$\lambda_1((A+A^*)/2) \geq \cdots \geq \lambda_n((A+A^*)/2),$$

and similarly order the singular values of A. Then

$$\lambda_i((A+A^*)/2) \leq \sigma_i(A), \quad i = 1, \ldots, n. \tag{5}$$

Alternative proofs of (5) are given by Fan (1974) and by Thompson (1975, 1976).

Since $\sigma_i(-A) = \sigma_i(A)$, $\lambda_i((-A-A^*)/2) = -\lambda_i((A+A^*)/2)$, $i = 1, \ldots, n$, (5) implies that

$$|\lambda_i((A+A^*)/2)| \leq \sigma_i(A), \ i = 1, \ldots, n.$$

F.4.a. (Fan and Hoffman, 1955). For any $n \times n$ complex matrix A,

$$\left(\left|\lambda_1\left(\frac{A+A^*}{2}\right)\right|, \ldots, \left|\lambda_n\left(\frac{A+A^*}{2}\right)\right|\right) \prec_w (\sigma_1(A), \ldots, \sigma_n(A)). \tag{6}$$

Note that the extremal representation 20.A.2 yields a result weaker than (6); namely, for $k = 1, \ldots, n$,

$$\sum_1^k \lambda_i((A+A^*)/2) = \max_{UU^*=I_k} \operatorname{tr} U((A+A^*)/2)U^* \tag{7a}$$

$$\leq \max_{\substack{UU^*=I_k \\ VV^*=I_k}} \mathscr{R} \operatorname{tr} UAV^* = \sum_1^k \sigma_i(A),$$

or equivalently,

$$(\lambda_1((A+A^*)/2), \ldots, \lambda_n((A+A^*)/2)) \prec_w (\sigma_1(A), \ldots, \sigma_n(A)). \tag{7b}$$

F.4.b. Theorem (R. C. Thompson, 1971). If A and B are $n \times n$ complex matrices and $\gamma_i = \lambda_i((AB+B^*A^*)/2)$ are ordered $|\gamma_1| \geq \cdots \geq |\gamma_n|$, then

$$(|\gamma_1|, \ldots, |\gamma_n|) \prec_w (\sigma_1(A)\sigma_1(B), \ldots, \sigma_n(A)\sigma_n(B)). \tag{8}$$

Proof. Replacement of A by AB in (6), and application of H.1 (1a) with 5.A.2.b, yields (8). ∥

Other results of R. C. Thompson (1971) are considerably stronger than F.4.b.

Eigenvalues of the Real Part of a Hermitian Matrix

F.5. If G and H are $n \times n$ Hermitian matrices, then
$$(\mathscr{R}\lambda_1(G+iH),\ldots,\mathscr{R}\lambda_n(G+iH)) \prec (\lambda_1(G),\ldots,\lambda_n(G)).$$

Proof. In F.1 let $A = G + iH$, so that $(A+A^*)/2 = G$. ∥

The following is a partial converse.

F.5.a. (Sherman and Thompson, 1972). If G is a given Hermitian matrix with eigenvalues $\lambda_1 \geq \cdots \geq \lambda_n$, and $\alpha_1 \geq \cdots \geq \alpha_n$ are given real numbers satisfying
$$(\alpha_1,\ldots,\alpha_n) \prec (\lambda_1,\ldots,\lambda_n),$$
then there exists a Hermitian matrix H such that
$$\alpha_j = \mathscr{R}\lambda_j(G+iH), \qquad j = 1,\ldots,n.$$

The proof of this result is a rather involved induction and is omitted.

Singular Values of $A + B$ and $A + iB$

For Hermitian matrices A and B, let $\alpha_1,\ldots,\alpha_n$ and $\beta_1,\ldots,\beta_n$ denote the singular values of $A + B$ and $A + iB$ respectively.

F.6. Proposition (Bhatia and Kittaneh, 2009).
$$(\alpha_1,\ldots,\alpha_n) \prec_w \sqrt{2}(\beta_1,\ldots,\beta_n). \tag{9}$$

If $A \geq 0$, then
$$\prod_1^k \alpha_i \leq 2^{k/2} \prod_1^k \beta_i, \quad k = 1,\ldots,n.$$

If $A, B \geq 0$, then
$$\sum_1^k \alpha_i \leq \sqrt{2} \sum_1^k \beta_i, \quad k = 1,\ldots,n.$$

G Eigenvalues and Singular Values of A, B, and $A + B$

In this section, comparisons between the eigenvalues and/or singular values of matrices and sums of matrices are discussed. All eigenvalues $\lambda_1, \ldots, \lambda_n$ are in descending order; i.e., $\lambda_1 \geq \cdots \geq \lambda_n$.

The first comparison between the eigenvalues of a sum of matrices, due to Ky Fan, is one of the earliest important results.

G.1. Theorem (Fan, 1949). If G and H are $n \times n$ Hermitian matrices, then

$$(\lambda_1(G+H), \ldots, \lambda_n(G+H))$$
$$\prec (\lambda_1(G) + \lambda_1(H), \ldots, \lambda_n(G) + \lambda_n(H)). \tag{1}$$

Proof. This result is a consequence of the extremal representation 20.A.2: If U is a $k \times n$ unitary matrix, then

$$\max_{UU^*=I_k} \operatorname{tr} U(G+H)U^* \leq \max_{UU^*=I_k} \operatorname{tr} UGU^* + \max_{UU^*+I_k} \operatorname{tr} UHU^*,$$

which yields (1).

Equality holds for $k = n$, because the trace is linear. ||

As in the case of F.1.a, (1) somewhat surprisingly follows from the better-known inequality

$$\lambda_1(G+H) \leq \lambda_1(G) + \lambda_1(H). \tag{2}$$

Alternative proof of G.1. Use the kth additive compound in (2) and the fact 19.F.4 that the k-additive compound is linear. Then

$$\lambda_1(\Delta_k(G+H)) = \lambda_1(\Delta_k(G)+\Delta_k(H)) \leq \lambda_1(\Delta_k(G)) + \lambda_1(\Delta_k(H)). \tag{3}$$

Since $\lambda_1(\Delta_k(A)) = \sum_1^k \lambda_i(A)$, inequality (3) yields

$$\sum_1^k \lambda_i(G+H) \leq \sum_1^k \lambda_i(G) + \sum_1^k \lambda_i(H), \qquad k = 1, \ldots, n,$$

which is equivalent to (1). ||

G.1.a. Theorem (Wielandt, 1955). If G and H are $n \times n$ Hermitian matrices and $1 \leq i_1 < \cdots < i_k \leq n$, then

$$\sum_{j=1}^{k} \lambda_{i_j}(G+H) \le \sum_{j=1}^{k} \lambda_{i_j}(G) + \sum_{i=1}^{k} \lambda_i(H), \qquad k=1,\ldots,n; \qquad (4)$$

equality holds for $k = n$.

Thompson (1974) gives a general discussion of both additive and multiplicative versions of inequalities such as (4), and Markus (1964) provides a survey of results.

When G and H are positive semidefinite, then a "reversal" majorization is possible.

G.1.b. Theorem (Rotfel'd, 1969; Thompson, 1977). If G and H are $n \times n$ positive semidefinite Hermitian matrices, then

$$(\lambda(G), \lambda(H)) \prec (\lambda(G+H), 0). \qquad (5)$$

Proof. Since G and H are positive semidefinite and Hermitian, they can be written in the form $G = XX^*$, $H = YY^*$, where X and Y are $n \times n$ matrices. If $A = (X, Y)$, then $G + H = AA^*$. Further, the nonzero eigenvalues of AA^* coincide with the nonzero eigenvalues of

$$A^*A = \begin{bmatrix} X^*X & X^*Y \\ Y^*X & Y^*Y \end{bmatrix};$$

i.e., $\lambda(A^*A) = (\lambda(AA^*), 0)$. It follows from C.1 that

$$(\lambda(G), \lambda(H)) = (\lambda(X^*X), \lambda(Y^*Y)) \prec \lambda(A^*A) = (\lambda(AA^*), 0)$$
$$= (\lambda(G+H), 0). \quad \|$$

G.1.c. If A is an $n \times n$ Hermitian matrix and B is an $n \times r$ complex matrix, $n \ge r$, then

$$\lambda(A) \prec_w \lambda(A + B^*B)$$
$$\prec (\lambda_1(A) + \lambda_1(B^*B), \ldots, \lambda_r(A) + \lambda_r(B^*B), \lambda_{r+1}(A), \ldots, \lambda_n(A)).$$

Proof. Because $B^*B \ge 0$, it follows from 16.F.1 that $\lambda_i(A + B^*B) \ge \lambda_i(A)$, $i = 1, \ldots, n$, thereby implying the left-hand majorization. The right-hand majorization is a consequence of (1) because $\lambda_i(B^*B) = 0$ for $i = r+1, \ldots, n$. $\quad \|$

The case that $r = 1$ occurs in various contexts and is the most common case.

G.1.d. (Fan, 1951). If A and B are $n \times n$ complex matrices, then

$$\sigma(A+B) \prec_w \sigma(A) + \sigma(B). \qquad (6)$$

G. Eigenvalues and Singular Values of A, B, and $A+B$ 331

Proof. Apply G.1 to the symmetrized matrices $\widetilde{A}$ and $\widetilde{B}$ defined in A.2, to obtain
$$(\sigma(A+B), -\sigma(A+B)) \prec_w (\sigma(A)+\sigma(B), -\sigma(A)-\sigma(B)).$$
The result then follows trivially. ||

Alternative proof. From the extremal representation 20.A.2,
$$\sum_1^k \sigma_i(A+B) = \max \mathscr{R} \; \text{tr} \; U(A+B)V^*$$
$$\leq \max \mathscr{R} \; \text{tr} \; UAV^* + \max \mathscr{R} \; \text{tr} \; UBV^*$$
$$= \sum_1^k \sigma_i(A) + \sum_1^k \sigma_i(B), \qquad k=1,\ldots,n,$$
where the maximization is over $k \times n$ complex matrices U and V satisfying $UU^* = I_k$, $VV^* = I_k$. ||

The majorization (6) is discussed by Rotfel'd (1967). It implies
$$\sigma_1(A+B) \leq \sigma_1(A) + \sigma_1(B),$$
which is attributed to Wittmeyer (1936); this inequality is extended by Fan (1951) to
$$\sigma_{r+s+1}(A+B) \leq \sigma_{r+1}(A) + \sigma_{s+1}(B),$$
$r \geq 0$, $s \geq 0$, $r+s+1 \leq n$. When $s=0$, $i=r+1$,
$$\sigma_i(A+B) \leq \sigma_i(A) + \sigma_1(B).$$

The following result is an important generalization of G.1.

G.1.e. Proposition (Ando and Zhan, 1999). If $A \geq 0$, $B \geq 0$, and ϕ a convex matrix function defined on an interval I, then for $k=1,\ldots,n$,
$$\sum_1^k \lambda_j(\phi(A)+\phi(B)) \leq \sum_1^k \lambda_j(\phi(A+B)),$$
or equivalently,
$$\lambda(\phi(A)+\phi(B)) \prec_w \lambda(\phi(A+B)).$$

G.1.f. Proposition (Aujla and Silva, 2003). With A, B and ϕ as defined in G.1.e,
$$\lambda(\phi(\alpha A + \overline{\alpha} B)) \prec_w \lambda(\alpha \phi(A) + \overline{\alpha} \phi(B)).$$

G.1.g. Proposition (Ando and Zhan, 1999). For $A, B \geq 0$,
$$\lambda(A^r + B^r) \prec_w \lambda((A+B)^r), \quad r \geq 1;$$
the inequality is reversed for $0 \leq r \leq 1$.

Proof. This result follows from G.1.e. ||

Averages of Matrices

For a Hermitian matrix $A = (a_{ij})$, define
$$A_i = D_i A D_i, \quad i = 1, \ldots, 2^n,$$
where the D_i's are distinct diagonal matrices of the form $D_i = \mathrm{diag}(\epsilon_1, \ldots, \epsilon_n)$, with $\epsilon_j = \pm 1$, $j = 1, \ldots, n$. Then
$$\frac{1}{2^n} \sum_{i=1}^{2^n} A_i = \frac{1}{2^n} \sum_{i=1}^{2^n} D_i A D_i = \mathrm{diag}(a_{11}, \ldots, a_{nn}).$$
Consequently, by G.1,
$$(a_{11}, \ldots, a_{nn}) \prec (\lambda_1(A), \ldots, \lambda_n(A)), \tag{7}$$
which provides another proof of B.1.

This development by Marshall and Olkin (1982) can be extended in a variety of ways.

G.1.h. If A is $n \times n$ Hermitian and Γ_1 and Γ_2 are orthogonal matrices, then by using G.1, it follows that
$$\lambda \left(\frac{1}{2} \Gamma_1 A \Gamma_1' + \frac{1}{2} \Gamma_2 A \Gamma_2' \right) \prec \lambda \left(\frac{1}{2} \Gamma_1 A \Gamma_1' \right) + \lambda \left(\frac{1}{2} \Gamma_2 A \Gamma_2' \right)$$
$$= \frac{1}{2} \lambda(\Gamma_1 A \Gamma_1') + \frac{1}{2} \lambda(\Gamma_2 A \Gamma_2') = \lambda(A).$$

If Γ_1 has the form $\begin{pmatrix} I_{n_1} & 0 \\ 0 & -I_{n_2} \end{pmatrix}$, where $n_1 + n_2 = n$, and $\Gamma_2 = I_n$, then $\frac{1}{2} \Gamma_1 A \Gamma_1' + \frac{1}{2} \Gamma_2 A \Gamma_2' = \begin{pmatrix} A_{11} & 0 \\ 0 & A_{22} \end{pmatrix}$, where $A = \begin{pmatrix} A_{11} & A_{12} \\ A_{21} & A_{22} \end{pmatrix}$. Consequently, $\lambda(A) \succ \lambda(\begin{pmatrix} A_{11} & 0 \\ 0 & A_{22} \end{pmatrix})$, which provides an alternative proof of C.1.

Repeated use of this argument yields $\lambda(A) \succ (a_{11}, a_{22}, \ldots, a_{nn})$, which is Schur's theorem B.1.

G.1.i. If $R = (r_{ij})$ is an $n \times n$ correlation matrix, that is, $r_{ii} = 1$ and $R > 0$, and $\widetilde{R} = (\widetilde{r}_{ij})$, where $\widetilde{r}_{ii} = 1$, and
$$\widetilde{r}_{ij} = \bar{r} = \Sigma_{i<j} r_{ij}/(n(n-1)/2), \quad i \neq j,$$

then
$$\lambda(R) \succ \lambda(\widetilde{R}).$$

Proof. If Γ_{ij} denotes a permutation matrix that interchanges the ith and jth rows and columns, then
$$\widetilde{R} = \sum_{i<j} \Gamma_{ij} R \Gamma'_{ij} / (n(n-1)/2).$$
The result follows from G.1. ||

For other examples in which the matrices Γ_{ij} are elements of a finite group, see Andersson and Perlman (1988).

Matrices with Real Roots

G.2. If A and B are $n \times n$ complex matrices such that $aA + bB$ has real eigenvalues for all $a, b \in \mathscr{R}$, then
$$(\lambda_1(A+B), \ldots, \lambda_n(A+B)) \prec (\lambda_1(A)+\lambda_1(B), \ldots, \lambda_n(A)+\lambda_n(B)). \quad (8)$$

Proof. From 16.F.7 with $\alpha = \frac{1}{2}$, it follows that $\lambda_1(A+B) \leq \lambda_1(A) + \lambda_1(B)$. Replace A and B in this inequality by their kth additive compounds. By using the linearity 19.F.4 of the kth additive compound, (7) is obtained. ||

G.2.a. If the hypotheses of G.2 are satisfied and $\lambda_n(A) + \lambda_n(B) \geq 0$, then
$$\prod_k^n \lambda_i(A+B) \geq \prod_k^n [\lambda_i(A) + \lambda_i(B)], \qquad k = 1, \ldots, n.$$

Proof. The result is an immediate application of (7) and 5.A.2.c. ||

The case $k = 1$ in G.2.a is
$$\det(A+B) \geq \prod_1^n [\lambda_i(A) + \lambda_i(B)], \qquad (9)$$

which is obtained by Fiedler (1971) under the assumption that A and B are Hermitian.

Related Inequalities

G.3. (Fiedler, 1971). If G and H are $n \times n$ Hermitian matrices, then

$$\det(G+H) = \prod_1^n \lambda_i(G+H) \leq \prod_1^n [\lambda_i(G) + \lambda_{n-i+1}(H)].$$

This "reversal" of (8) suggests an additive version of G.2.a.

G.3.a. If G and H are $n \times n$ Hermitian matrices, then

$$\sum_1^k \lambda_i(G+H) \geq \sum_1^k \lambda_i(G) + \sum_1^k \lambda_{n-i+1}(H), \qquad k=1,\ldots,n. \quad (10)$$

Proof. From the extremal representation 20.A.2,

$$\sum_1^k \lambda_i(G+H) = \max \ \text{tr} \ U(G+H)U^*$$

$$\geq \max[\ \text{tr} \ UGU^* + \min \ \text{tr} \ UHU^*]$$

$$= \max \left[\text{tr} \ UGU^* + \sum_1^k \lambda_{n-i+1}(H) \right]$$

$$= \sum_1^k \lambda_i(G) + \sum_1^k \lambda_{n-i+1}(H), \qquad k=1,\ldots,n,$$

where the extrema are over $k \times n$ matrices U satisfying $UU^* = I_k$. ∥

Notice that (10) is not a majorization result because of the lack of an ordering: The sum $\lambda_i(G) + \lambda_{n-i+1}(H)$ is not monotone in i.

The following is an inequality similar to (10) which complements G.1.a.

G.3.b. If A and B are $n \times n$ complex matrices, then

$$\sum_1^k \sigma_i(A+B) \geq \sum_1^k \sigma_i(A) - \sum_1^k \sigma_{n-i+1}(B), \qquad k=1,\ldots,n. \quad (11)$$

G. Eigenvalues and Singular Values of A, B, and $A + B$ 335

Proof. The proof parallels that of (10):

$$\sum_1^k \sigma_i(A+B) = \max \mathscr{R} \text{ tr } U(A+B)V^*$$

$$\geq \max[\mathscr{R} \text{ tr } UAV^* + \min \mathscr{R} \text{ tr } UBV^*]$$

$$= \sum_1^k \sigma_i(A) - \sum_1^k \sigma_{n-i+1}(B), \quad k = 1, \ldots, n,$$

where the extrema are over $k \times n$ matrices U and V satisfying $UU^* = VV^* = I_k$. ||

Mathias (1993) obtains perturbation bounds in terms of unitarily invariant norms and weak majorization. See Chapter 10.

G.3.c. (Mathias, 1993).   For complex matrices A and B,

$$\sum_1^k [\sigma_{n+1-i}(A) - \sigma_i(B)] \leq \sum_1^k \sigma_{n+1-i}(A+B), \quad k = 1, \ldots, n.$$

G.4. (Zhan, 2000).   For positive semidefinite matrices A and B with ordered singular values $\sigma_1 \geq \cdots \geq \sigma_n$, and for any complex number z,

$$\prod_1^k \sigma_i(A - |z|B) \leq \prod_1^k \sigma_i(A + zB) \leq \prod_1^k \sigma_i(A + |z|B), \quad k = 1, \ldots, n.$$

Converse Theorems Connecting Eigenvalues of A, B, and $A + B$

Denote the eigenvalues of A, B, and $A + B$ by

$$\alpha_1 \geq \cdots \geq \alpha_n, \; \beta_1 \geq \cdots \geq \beta_n, \; \gamma_1 \geq \cdots \geq \gamma_n,$$

respectively. Theorem G.1 states that

$$\sum_1^k \gamma_i \leq \sum_1^k (\alpha_i + \beta_i), \quad k = 1, \ldots, n, \tag{12}$$

with equality for $k = n$. In a fundamental paper, Horn (1962) posed the question, what relations must these three n-tuples of real numbers satisfy in order to be eigenvalues of some Hermitian matrices A, B, and $A + B$?

336   9. Matrix Theory

The solution was obtained in steps, and was ultimately resolved in papers by Klyachko (1998) and Knutson and Tao (1999). The listing of the myriad of inequalities is based on a representation in terms of *honeycombs*. This involves considerably deeper mathematics, and a description is beyond the scope of this book. An excellent lucid survey of the solution is provided by Bhatia (2001). See also Bhatia (1997). The present discussion focuses only on a history of some of the basic results, together with a statement of Horn's conjecture.

Clearly, the majorization result (11) is necessary. Earlier Weyl (1912) obtained the following additional necessary conditions:

$$\gamma_{i+j-1} \leq \alpha_i + \beta_j, \quad i+j-1 \leq n. \tag{13}$$

This result can be obtained from the Courant–Fischer minmax Theorem 20.A.1.

For $n = 2$, majorization requires that

$$\gamma_1 \leq \alpha_1 + \beta_1, \quad \gamma_1 + \gamma_2 = \alpha_1 + \alpha_2 + \beta_1 + \beta_2,$$

whereas (12) contains the conditions

$$\gamma_1 \leq \alpha_1 + \beta_1, \quad \gamma_2 \leq \alpha_2 + \beta_1, \quad \gamma_2 \leq \alpha_1 + \beta_2. \tag{14}$$

The choice $\alpha = (10,3)$, $\beta = (1,1)$, $\gamma = (10,5)$ for which $\gamma \prec \alpha + \beta$ has $\gamma_2 > \alpha_2 + \beta_1$, thus violating (13). Thus, majorization alone does not guarantee the existence of the required matrices A and B.

The case $n = 2$ involves 3 valid inequalities (including the trace equality as a trivial inequality). The case $n = 3$ requires 7 inequalities; three from majorization, three from (12), plus one additional inequality:

$$\gamma_2 + \gamma_3 \leq \alpha_1 + \alpha_3 + \beta_1 + \beta_3. \tag{15}$$

The number of inequalities spectacularly increases as n increases; for $n = 7$, 2,062 inequalities are necessary. Listing these is not straightforward.

Subsequent necessary inequalities in addition to (12) were obtained by Lidskiĭ (1950), Wielandt (1955), Amir-Moéz (1956), and Thompson and Freede (1971). Examples are:

for $1 \leq i_1 < \cdots < i_k \leq n$,

$$\sum_{s=1}^{k} \gamma_{i_s} \leq \sum_{s=1}^{k} \alpha_{i_s} + \sum_{s=1}^{k} \beta_{i_s}, \quad 1 \leq k \leq n; \tag{16}$$

for $1 \leq j_1 < \cdots < j_k \leq n$, with $i_s + j_s - s \leq n$,

$$\sum_{s=1}^{k} \gamma_{i_s+j_s-s} \leq \sum_{s=1}^{k} \alpha_{i_s} + \sum_{s=1}^{k} \beta_{j_s}, \quad 1 \leq k \leq n. \tag{17}$$

These inequalities can be stated in general terms as

$$\sum_{i \in \mathscr{C}} \gamma_i \leq \sum_{i \in \mathscr{A}} \alpha_i + \sum_{i \in \mathscr{B}} \beta_i,$$

over certain sets of indices $\mathscr{A}$, $\mathscr{B}$, and $\mathscr{C}$. A description of the sets $\mathscr{A}$, $\mathscr{B}$, and $\mathscr{C}$ comprises the necessary conditions.

More specifically, Horn (1962) showed that a complete set of necessary conditions is given by $\text{tr}(A+B) = \text{tr} A + \text{tr} B$, i.e.,

$$\sum_{1}^{n} \gamma_i = \sum_{1}^{n} \alpha_i + \sum_{1}^{n} \beta_i,$$

together with a set of linear inequalities of the form

$$\sum_{s=1}^{k} \gamma_{m_s} \leq \sum_{s=1}^{k} \alpha_{i_s} + \sum_{s=1}^{k} \beta_{j_s}, \quad 1 \leq k \leq n,$$

for all triplets of indices

$$1 \leq i_1 < \cdots < i_k \leq n, \quad 1 \leq j_1 < \cdots < j_k \leq n,$$
$$1 \leq m_1 < \cdots < m_k \leq n, \quad 1 \leq k \leq n, \tag{18}$$

in a certain finite set $T(k,n)$.

The second part of the picture was to describe the set $T(k,n)$.

G.5. Conjecture of Horn. The set $T(k,n)$ is the set of triplets (17) that satisfy

$$\sum_{s=1}^{k} i_s + \sum_{s=1}^{k} j_s = \sum_{s=1}^{k} m_s + k(k+1)/2, \quad 1 \leq k \leq n, \tag{19}$$

$$\sum_{s=1}^{k} i_{a_s} + \sum_{s=1}^{k} j_{b_s} \geq \sum_{s=1}^{k} m_{c_s} + k(k+1)/2, \tag{20}$$

for all $1 \leq s < k$, $1 \leq a_1 < \cdots < a_s \leq k$, $1 \leq b_1 < \cdots < b_s \leq k$, $1 \leq c_1 < \cdots < c_s \leq k$ in $T(s,k)$.

The following is a weaker converse of Theorem G.1; here the eigenvalues of B are not fixed in advance.

G.6. (Sherman and Thompson, 1972). Let A be an $n \times n$ Hermitian matrix with eigenvalues $\alpha_i = \lambda_i(A)$, $i = 1, \ldots, n$. If $c_1 \geq \cdots \geq c_n$ are given numbers such that

$$(\alpha_1, \ldots, \alpha_n) \succ (c_1, \ldots, c_n),$$

then there exists a Hermitian matrix B such that $A + B$ has distinct eigenvalues $c_i + \lambda_i(B) = \lambda_i(A + B)$, $i = 1, \ldots, n$.

The inductive proof of Sherman and Thompson (1972) is lengthy and is omitted.

H Eigenvalues and Singular Values of A, B, and AB

One of the earliest comparisons is the well-known result connecting the singular values of the product AB and the product of the singular values of A and B.

H.1. Theorem (Horn, 1950; Visser and Zaanen, 1952; de Bruijn, 1956). If A and B are $n \times n$ complex matrices, then

$$\prod_{1}^{k} \sigma_i(AB) \leq \prod_{1}^{k} \sigma_i(A)\sigma_i(B), \qquad k = 1, \ldots, n-1,$$
$$\prod_{1}^{n} \sigma_i(AB) = \prod_{1}^{n} \sigma_i(A)\sigma_i(B). \tag{1a}$$

If $\sigma_n(AB) > 0$, (1a) is equivalent to

$$(\log \sigma_1(AB), \ldots, \log \sigma_n(AB))$$
$$\prec (\log \sigma_1(A)\sigma_1(B), \ldots, \log \sigma_n(A)\sigma_n(B)). \tag{1b}$$

Because

$$\sigma_i(A) = \lambda_i^{1/2}(AA^*), \qquad \sigma_i(AB) = \lambda_i^{1/2}(ABB^*A^*) = \lambda_i^{1/2}(A^*ABB^*),$$

for $i = 1, \ldots, n$, H.1 can be reformulated.

H.1.a. Theorem. If U and V are $n \times n$ positive semidefinite Hermitian matrices, then

H. Eigenvalues and Singular Values of A, B, and AB 339

$$\prod_1^k \lambda_i(UV) \leq \prod_1^k \lambda_i(U)\lambda_i(V), \qquad k = 1, \ldots, n-1,$$
$$\prod_1^n \lambda_i(UV) = \prod_1^n \lambda_i(U)\lambda_i(V). \tag{2a}$$

If $\lambda_n(UV) > 0$, (2a) is equivalent to

$$(\log \lambda_1(UV), \ldots, \log \lambda_n(UV))$$
$$\prec (\log \lambda_1(U) + \log \lambda_1(V), \ldots, \log \lambda_n(U) + \log \lambda_n(V)). \tag{2b}$$

Proof of H.1 and H.1.a (de Bruijn, 1956). It is well known (Browne, 1928) and easy to establish that for U and V positive semidefinite Hermitian,

$$\lambda_1(UV) \leq \lambda_1(U)\lambda_1(V). \tag{3}$$

By applying (3) to the kth compound and using the Binet–Cauchy theorem 19.F.2, together with 19.F.2.c, it follows that

$$\prod_1^k \lambda_i(UV) = \lambda_1((UV)^{(k)}) = \lambda_1(U^{(k)}V^{(k)})$$
$$\leq \lambda_1(U^{(k)})\lambda_1(V^{(k)}) = \prod_1^k \lambda_i(U)\lambda_i(V). \quad \|$$

H.1.b. If $A_1, \ldots, A_m$ are $n \times n$ complex matrices, then

$$\prod_1^k \sigma_i(A_1 \cdots A_m) \leq \prod_1^k \sigma_i(A_1) \cdots \sigma_i(A_m), \qquad k = 1, \ldots, n-1,$$
$$\prod_1^n \sigma_i(A_1 \cdots A_m) = \prod_1^n \sigma_i(A) \cdots \sigma_i(A_m). \tag{4a}$$

If $\sigma_n(A_1 \cdots A_m) > 0$, then (4a) is equivalent to

$$(\log \sigma_1(A_1 \cdots A_m), \ldots, \log \sigma_n(A_1 \cdots A_m))$$
$$\prec (\log \sigma_1(A_1) \cdots \sigma_1(A_m), \ldots, \log \sigma_n(A_1) \cdots \sigma_n(A_m)). \tag{4b}$$

This result is an obvious extension of H.1.

Extensions

The following two stronger versions of H.1 and H.1.a are stated here without proof. They provide necessary conditions for connecting the singular values of A, B, and AB.

H.1.c. Theorem (Gel'fand and Naimark, 1950). If A and B are $n \times n$ complex matrices, then for $k = 1, \ldots, n$,

$$\prod_1^k \sigma_{i_s}(AB) \leq \prod_1^k \sigma_{i_s}(A)\sigma_s(B), \qquad 1 \leq i_1 < \cdots < i_k \leq n, \qquad (5)$$

with equality for $k = n$.

H.1.d. Theorem (Lidskiĭ, 1950). If U and V are $n \times n$ positive semidefinite Hermitian matrices, then for $k = 1, \ldots, n$,

$$\prod_1^k \lambda_{i_s}(UV) \leq \prod_1^k \lambda_{i_s}(U)\lambda_s(V), \qquad 1 \leq i_1 < \cdots < i_k \leq n, \qquad (6)$$

with equality for $k = n$.

Both H.1.c and H.1.d immediately imply majorizations that are stronger than (1b) and (2b) (see 5.A.20).

H.1.e. If A and B are $n \times n$ complex matrices with $\sigma_n(AB) > 0$, then

$$\log \sigma(AB) - \log \sigma(A) \prec \log \sigma(B).$$

H.1.f. If U and V are $n \times n$ positive semidefinite Hermitian matrices with $\lambda_n(UV) > 0$, then

$$\log \lambda(UV) - \log \lambda(U) \prec \log \lambda(V).$$

Additive Versions for Products

H.1.g. If U and V are $n \times n$ positive semidefinite Hermitian matrices, then

$$\operatorname{tr} UV = \sum_1^n \lambda_i(UV) \leq \sum_1^n \lambda_i(U)\lambda_i(V). \qquad (7)$$

This result is a consequence of (2a) and 5.A.2.b. It is obtained by Richter (1958), Mirsky (1959b), and Theobald (1975), and can be obtained as a consequence of results of Marcus (1956).

In fact, the hypothesis of positive semidefiniteness in (7) is actually not needed, though the proof suggested above uses this hypothesis. Mirsky (personal communication) notes that U and V can be replaced by $U + \tau I$ and $V + \tau I$, respectively, with τ sufficiently large. Because (7) holds for any Hermitian matrix U and V, replace V by $-V$ to obtain the following results

H.1.h. (Ruhe, 1970). If U and V are $n \times n$ positive semidefinite Hermitian matrices, then

$$\operatorname{tr} UV = \sum_1^n \lambda_i(UV) \geq \sum_1^n \lambda_i(U)\lambda_{n-i+1}(V). \tag{8}$$

In (8) also, the assumption of positive semidefiniteness is not needed. Inequality (8) can be extended.

H.1.i. If U and V are $n \times n$ positive semidefinite Hermitian matrices, then

$$\sum_1^k \lambda_i(UV) \geq \sum_1^k \lambda_i(U)\lambda_{n-i+1}(V), \qquad k = 1, \ldots, n. \tag{9}$$

Proof. Without loss in generality, assume that U is diagonal; that is, $U = D_u = \operatorname{diag}(u_1, \ldots, u_n)$, $u_i = \lambda_i(U) \geq 0$, $i = 1, \ldots, n$. Let $\ddot{D}_u = \operatorname{diag}(u_1, \ldots, u_k, 0, \ldots, 0)$. Then

$$\sum_1^k \lambda_i(UV) = \sum_1^k \lambda_i(D_u^{1/2} V D_u^{1/2}) = \max \operatorname{tr} X D_u^{1/2} V D_u^{1/2} X^*$$

$$\geq \operatorname{tr} (I_k\ 0) D_u^{1/2} V D_u^{1/2} \begin{pmatrix} I_k \\ 0 \end{pmatrix}$$

$$= \operatorname{tr} \ddot{D}_u V \geq \sum_1^n \lambda_i(\ddot{D}_u)\lambda_{n-i+1}(V) = \sum_1^k \lambda_i(U)\lambda_{n-i+1}(V),$$

where the maximum is over all $k \times n$ matrices satisfying $XX^* = I_k$. The last inequality is an application of (8). ||

H.1.j. (Lieb and Thirring, 1976). If $A \geq 0$, $B \geq 0$, then

$$\operatorname{tr} (AB)^\alpha \leq \operatorname{tr} (A^\alpha B^\alpha), \qquad \alpha > 1;$$

the inequality is reversed for $0 < \alpha \leq 1$.

This result has been strengthened to a majorization result.

H.1.k. (Audenaert, 2009). If $A \geq 0$, $B \geq 0$, then

$$\sigma((AB)^\alpha) \prec_w \sigma(A^\alpha B^\alpha), \quad \alpha \geq 1;$$

the majorization is reversed for $0 < \alpha \leq 1$.

H.2. If A and B are $n \times n$ complex matrices, then

$$\sum_1^k \sigma_i(AB) \leq \sum_1^k \frac{1}{2}[\lambda_i(AA^*) + \lambda_i(BB^*)], \quad k = 1, \ldots, n.$$

Proof. Use (1a), 5.A.2.b, and the arithmetic–geometric mean inequality 16.C.1.a to obtain

$$\sum_1^k \sigma_i(AB) \leq \sum_1^k \sigma_i(A)\sigma_i(B)$$

$$\leq \sum_1^k \frac{1}{2}[\sigma_i^2(A) + \sigma_i^2(B)], \quad k = 1, \ldots, n. \quad \|$$

By using (4a), this result can be extended trivially to m matrices $A_1, \ldots, A_m$: For $k = 1, \ldots, n$,

$$\sum_1^k \sigma_i(A_1 \cdots A_m) \leq \sum_1^k \sigma_i(A_1) \cdots \sigma_i(A_m)$$
$$\leq \sum_1^k \frac{1}{m}[\sigma_i^m(A_1) + \cdots + \sigma_i^m(A_m)]. \quad \| \quad (10)$$

H.2.a. (Marcus, 1969). If $A_1, \ldots, A_m$ are $n \times n$ complex matrices, and ϕ is a nondecreasing convex function, then

$$\sum_1^k \phi(\sigma_i(A_1 \cdots A_m)) \leq \sum_1^k \frac{1}{m}[\phi(\sigma_i^m(A_1)) + \cdots + \phi(\sigma_i^m(A_m))]. \quad (11)$$

Proof. The result follows from (4a) and 5.A.2. $\|$

The motivation for H.2.a by Marcus is an inequality of Ault (1967), namely,

$$\mathrm{tr}\left(\frac{B + B^*}{2}\right) \leq \frac{1}{m} \mathrm{tr}[(A_1 A_1^*)^{m/2} + \cdots + (A_m A_m^*)^{m/2}], \quad (12)$$

H. Eigenvalues and Singular Values of A, B, and AB 343

where $B = A_1 \cdots A_m$. To obtain (12), take $k = n$ and $\phi(x) \equiv x$; then H.2.a becomes

$$\operatorname{tr}(BB^*)^{1/2} = \operatorname{tr}[(A_1 \cdots A_m)(A_1 \cdots A_m)^*]^{1/2}$$
$$\leq \frac{1}{m}\operatorname{tr}[(A_1 A_1^*)^{m/2} + \cdots + (A_m A_m^*)^{m/2}].$$

Then (12) is a consequence of

$$\operatorname{tr}\left(\frac{B + B^*}{2}\right) \leq \operatorname{tr}(BB^*)^{1/2},$$

which follows directly from F(4).

H.2.b. Proposition (Wang and Zhang, 1995). For $A \geq 0$, $B \geq 0$, and $0 < \alpha < \beta$, then for $k = 1, \ldots, n$,

$$\prod_1^k [\lambda_j(A^\alpha B^\alpha)]^{1/\alpha} \leq \prod_1^k \lambda_j[(A^\beta B^\beta)]^{1/\beta};$$

and for $|\alpha| \leq 1$,

$$\lambda(A^\alpha B^\alpha) \prec_{\mathrm{w}} \lambda^\alpha(AB).$$

Comparisons Involving Unitary Matrices

H.3. (Horn, 1950). If H is an $n \times n$ Hermitian matrix and U is an $m \times n$ matrix satisfying $UU^* = I_m$, $m < n$, then for $k = 1, \ldots, m$,

$$\prod_1^k \lambda_i(UHU^*) \leq \prod_1^k \lambda_i(H), \qquad (13\mathrm{a})$$

$$\prod_1^k \lambda_{m-i+1}(UHU^*) \geq \prod_1^k \lambda_{n-i+1}(H). \qquad (13\mathrm{b})$$

Proof. In H.1 let $A = \binom{U}{0}$, where U is an $m \times n$ matrix satisfying $UU^* = I_m$, and let $H = BB^*$. Then (1a) yields (13a). Similarly, the choice $A = \binom{0}{U}$ yields (13b). ||

H.3.a. Theorem (Fan and Pall, 1957). Let $\omega_1 \geq \cdots \geq \omega_n$ and $\alpha_1 \geq \cdots \geq \alpha_m$, $n \geq m$, be $n + m$ real numbers. There exist an $n \times n$ Hermitian matrix H with eigenvalues $\omega = \lambda(H)$ and an $m \times n$ complex matrix U satisfying $UU^* = I_m$ with eigenvalues $\alpha = \lambda(UHU^*)$ if and only if

$$\omega_i \geq \alpha_i, \qquad \omega_{n-i+1} \leq \alpha_{m-i+1}, \qquad i = 1, \ldots, m.$$

Following the development of H.3, comparisons can be made between the singular values of A and the eigenvalues of UAV^*, where U and V are $k \times n$ matrices satisfying $UU^* = VV^* = I_m$.

H.3.b. If A is an $n \times n$ complex matrix and U and V are $m \times n$ complex matrices satisfying $UU^* = I_m$, $VV^* = I_m$, then

$$\prod_1^k |\lambda_i(UAV^*)| \leq \prod_1^k \sigma_i(A), \qquad k = 1, \ldots, m.$$

Proof. From E.1,

$$\prod_1^k |\lambda_i(AB)| \leq \prod_1^k \sigma_i(AB), \qquad k = 1, \ldots, n, \qquad (14)$$

with equality for $k = n$. With $B = V^*U$, (14) yields

$$\prod_1^k |\lambda_i(AV^*U)| = \prod_1^k |\lambda_i(UAV^*)|$$
$$\leq \prod_1^k \sigma_i(AV^*U) = \prod_1^k \lambda_i^{1/2}(AV^*VA^*)$$
$$= \prod_1^k \lambda_i^{1/2}(VA^*AV^*) \leq \prod_1^k \sigma_i(A), \quad k = 1, \ldots, m. \quad \|$$

For simplicity of notation, write $\widetilde{X} = (XX^*)^{1/2}$ to denote the unique positive semidefinite square root of XX^*. Denote by spec X the collection of eigenvalues of X.

H.4. Theorem (C. J. Thompson, 1971). Let A and B be $n \times n$ complex matrices. There exist unitary matrices U and V such that

$$\text{spec}(\widetilde{A}U\widetilde{A}V) = \text{spec}(B) \qquad (15)$$

if and only if

$$\prod_1^k \lambda(\widetilde{A}) \geq \prod_1^k \lambda(\widetilde{B}), \quad k = 1, \ldots, n-1, \qquad (16a)$$

with equality for $k = n$, or equivalently, if and only if

$$(\log \sigma_1(A), \ldots, \log \sigma_n(A)) \succ (\log \sigma_1(B), \ldots, \log \sigma_n(B)), \qquad (16b)$$

provided $\lambda(\widetilde{A}) > 0$, $\lambda(\widetilde{B}) > 0$.

Moreover, the same conclusion holds if (15) is replaced by

$$\text{spec}(\widetilde{A}U) = \text{spec}(\widetilde{B}). \tag{15a}$$

If (15) holds, then (15a) follows, which implies that $\sigma(A) \succ_w \sigma(B)$, which in turn implies that $\|A\| \geq \|B\|$ for any unitarily invariant norm (see 10.A.2).

Theorem H.4 is used by C. J. Thompson (1971) to prove the following.

H.4.a. Theorem (Lenard, 1971; C. J. Thompson, 1971). If A and B are $n \times n$ Hermitian matrices, then

$$(\lambda_1(e^{A+B}), \ldots, \lambda_n(e^{A+B})) \prec_w (\lambda_1(e^A e^B), \ldots, \lambda_n(e^A e^B)). \tag{17}$$

H.4.b. (Golden, 1965). If A and B are $n \times n$ Hermitian matrices, then

$$\text{tr } e^A e^B \geq \text{tr } e^{A+B}, \tag{18}$$

with equality if and only if A and B commute.

Inequality (18) follows directly from the majorization (17). Thompson (1965) and Lenard (1971) obtain inequalities of the form $g(e^A e^B) \geq g(e^{A+B})$ for certain functions g.

Product of a Matrix and a Unitary Matrix

If U is a unitary matrix and if A and $B = AU$ are positive definite Hermitian matrices such that $\text{spec}(AU) = \text{spec}(B)$, then from E.1 and H.1,

$$\prod_1^k \lambda_i(B) = \prod_1^k |\lambda_i(AU)| \leq \prod_1^k \sigma_i(AU) \leq \prod_1^k \sigma_i(A) = \prod_1^k \lambda_i(A),$$

for $k = 1, \ldots, n$, with equality for $k = n$. The following provides a partial converse.

Note. $\lambda_1 \geq \cdots \geq \lambda_n$; $|\lambda|_1 \geq \cdots \geq |\lambda|_n$; $\sigma_1 \geq \cdots \geq \sigma_n$.

H.5. Theorem (C. J. Thompson, 1971). If A and B are given $n \times n$ positive definite Hermitian matrices satisfying

$$\prod_1^k \lambda_i(A) \geq \prod_1^k \lambda_i(B), \qquad k = 1, \ldots, n-1,$$

$$\prod_1^n \lambda_i(A) = \prod_1^n \lambda_i(B),$$

then there exists a unitary matrix U such that $\operatorname{spec}(B) = \operatorname{spec}(AU)$.

The inductive proof of Thompson is lengthy and is omitted. Theorem H.5 can be extended to the case in which B is an arbitrary complex matrix.

H.5.a. Theorem (Sherman and Thompson, 1972). Let A be an $n \times n$ positive definite Hermitian matrix, and let B be an $n \times n$ complex matrix with $|\lambda_1(B)| \geq \cdots \geq |\lambda_n(B)| > 0$. If

$$\prod_1^k \lambda_i(A) \geq \prod_1^k |\lambda_i(B)|, \qquad k = 1, \ldots, n-1,$$

$$\prod_1^n \lambda_i(A) = \prod_1^n |\lambda_i(B)|,$$

then there exists a unitary matrix U such that

$$\operatorname{spec}(B) = \operatorname{spec}(AU).$$

Comparisons for $A^r B^s A^r$

H.6.a. Proposition (Aujla and Bourin, 2007). For $A \geq 0$, $B \geq 0$,

$$\prod_1^k \lambda_j(ABAB) \leq \prod_1^k \lambda_j(AB^2A), \qquad k = 1, \ldots, n.$$

H.6.b. Proposition (Aujla and Bourin, 2007). For $A \geq 0$, $B \geq 0$,

$$\prod_k^n \lambda_j((AB^2A)^{1/2}) \leq \prod_k^n \lambda_j\left(\frac{A+B}{2}\right), \qquad k = 1, \ldots, n.$$

H.6.c. Proposition (Araki, 1990). For $A \geq 0$, $B \geq 0$, $0 < r \leq s$,

$$\prod_1^k [\lambda_i(A^{r/2} B^r A^{r/2})]^{1/r} \leq \prod_1^k [\lambda_i(A^{s/2} B^s A^{s/2})]^{1/s}, \qquad k = 1, \ldots, n.$$

The following is a product extension of H.6.c. For a complex matrix X, let $|X| = (X^*X)^{1/2}$.

H.6.d. Proposition (Ando and Hiai, 1994). For $A > 0$, $B > 0$,

$$\prod_1^k \lambda_i(|A^{\alpha_1}B^{\beta_1}\cdots A^{\alpha_m}B^{\beta_m}|) \le \prod_1^k \lambda_i(|AB|), \quad k = 1,\ldots,n,$$

where

$$\sum_1^m \alpha_i = \sum_1^m \beta_i = 1, \ 0 \le \sum_1^k \beta_i - \sum_1^k \alpha_i \le \frac{1}{2}, \quad k = 1,\ldots n-1,$$

and

$$0 \le \sum_1^k \alpha_i - \sum_1^{k-1} \beta_i \le \frac{1}{2}, \quad k = 2,\ldots n.$$

See also Ando, Hiai, and Okubo (2000) for extensions of H.6.d.

H.6.e. Proposition (Furuta, 1987; Zhan, 2002). If $A \ge B \ge 0$, then

$$(B^r A^s B^r)^{1/q} \ge B^{(s+2r)/q},$$

$$A^{(s+2r)/q} \ge (A^r B^s A^r)^{1/q},$$

where $r, s \ge 0$, $q \ge \max(1, (s+2r)/(1+2r))$.

I Absolute Values of Eigenvalues, Row Sums, and Variations of Hadamard's Inequality

For a complex matrix A, an extended Hadamard's inequality is given by

$$\prod_k^n |\lambda_i(A)| \le \prod_k^n \left(\sum_{\alpha=1}^n |a_{i\alpha}|^2\right)^{1/2}, \quad k = 1,\ldots,n. \tag{1}$$

The case $k = 1$ includes the basic Hadamard inequality (B.5). A variety of complementary comparisons can be given involving the absolute value of the eigenvalues and the row and column sums of absolute values.

Write

$$R_i \equiv R_i(A) = \sum_{j=1}^n |a_{ij}|, \quad C_j \equiv C_j(A) = \sum_{i=1}^n |a_{ij}|, \quad i,j = 1,\ldots,n.$$

I.1. (Frobenius, 1908; see also Brauer, 1946). If A is an $n \times n$ complex matrix, then

$$|\lambda_1(A)| \leq \min(R_{[1]}, C_{[1]}). \qquad (2)$$

With the assumption $a_{ij} > 0$ for all i, j, inequality (2) dates back to Frobenius. An immediate consequence of (2) is

$$|\lambda_1(A)| \leq \sqrt{R_{[1]} C_{[1]}}.$$

A more delicate version is due to Farnell (1944); see also Ostrowski (1951):

$$|\lambda_1(A)| \leq \max_i (R_i C_i)^{1/2}.$$

These results can be extended to yield comparisons via majorization.

I.2. Theorem (Schneider, 1953; Shi and Wang, 1965). If A is an $n \times n$ complex matrix, then

$$\prod_1^k |\lambda_i(A)| \leq \prod_1^k R_{[i]}, \qquad k = 1, \ldots, n. \qquad (3)$$

Proof. Using the kth compound in (2), we obtain

$$\prod_1^k |\lambda_i(A)| = |\lambda_1(A^{(k)})| \leq R_{[1]}(A^{(k)}).$$

The proof is completed by showing that

$$R_{[1]}(A^{(k)}) \leq \prod_1^k R_{[i]}(A).$$

The elements of $A^{(k)}$ are the kth order minors of the matrix A, so that a typical element of $A^{(k)}$ is

$$\det A \begin{pmatrix} i_1, i_2, \ldots, i_k \\ j_1, j_2, \ldots, j_k \end{pmatrix}, \quad 1 \leq i_1 < \cdots < i_k \leq n, \ 1 \leq j_1 < \cdots < j_k \leq n.$$

Since the elements of $A^{(k)}$ are arranged in lexicographical order, an element of the first row of $A^{(k)}$ is

$$\det A \begin{pmatrix} 1, 2, \ldots, k \\ j_1, j_2, \ldots, j_k \end{pmatrix}, \quad 1 \leq j_1 < \cdots < j_k \leq n.$$

The sum of the absolute values of the elements of the first row of $A^{(k)}$ is bounded by

$$\sum_{1\leq j_1<\cdots<j_k\leq n}\left|\det A\begin{pmatrix}1,2,\ldots,k\\j_1,j_2,\ldots,j_k\end{pmatrix}\right|\leq \sum_{1\leq j_1<\cdots<j_k\leq n}|a_{1j_1}||a_{2j_2}|\cdots|a_{kj_k}|$$

$$\leq \sum_{j_1,\ldots,j_k}|a_{1j_1}||a_{2j_2}|\cdots|a_{kj_k}| = \left(\sum_{j_1=1}^{n}|a_{1j_1}|\right)\cdots\left(\sum_{j_k=1}^{n}|a_{kj_k}|\right),$$

which are kth order products of row sums of A. Thus, the largest row sum of absolute values of elements of $A^{(k)}$, $\mathscr{R}_{(1)}(A^{(k)})$ is less than or equal to the largest kth order product $\prod_1^k R_{(i)}(A)$ of row sums of A, which completes the proof. ∥

I.2.a. Theorem (Schneider, 1953). If A is an $n \times n$ complex matrix, $w_1,\ldots,w_n$ are positive numbers, and

$$R_i^* = \sum_{j=1}^{n}|a_{ij}|\frac{w_j}{w_i}, \qquad i=1,\ldots,n,$$

then

$$\prod_1^k|\lambda_i(A)|\leq \prod_1^k R_{[i]}^*, \qquad k=1,\ldots,n. \tag{4}$$

Although I.2.a appears to be more general than I.2, the two results are equivalent. I.2.a implies I.2 by taking $w_1 = \cdots = w_n$. To obtain I.2.a from I.2, apply I.2 to $D_w A D_w^{-1}$, where $D_w = \operatorname{diag}(w_1,\ldots,w_n)$.

I.2.b. If A is an $n \times n$ complex matrix, then

$$\prod_1^k|\lambda_i(A)|\leq \min\left(\prod_1^k C_{[i]},\prod_1^k R_{[i]}\right), \qquad k=1,\ldots,n.$$

I.2.c. Let A be an $n \times n$ complex matrix, $0\leq \theta\leq 1$, $\bar\theta = 1-\theta$, and $T_j = R_j^\theta C_j^{\bar\theta}$, $j=1,\ldots,k$. Then

$$\prod_1^k|\lambda_i(A)|\leq \prod_1^k T_{[i]}, \qquad k=1,\ldots,n.$$

Proof. From (2), $|\lambda_1(A)|\leq T_{[1]}$, which, when applied to the kth compound, yields the result. ∥

Recall the comparisons (1) and (3). Because $(\sum |a_{ij}|^2)^{1/2} \leq \sum |a_{ij}|$, (3) with $k = n$ does not yield an improvement of (1). However, (1) holds only for the product of all n terms, whereas (3) holds for the product of k terms. A modified version of (1) does lead to a majorization result.

I.3. (Shi and Wang, 1965). If A is a nonsingular $n \times n$ complex matrix and

$$E_i = \left(\sum_{j=1}^n |a_{ij}|^2\right)^{1/2},$$

$$\overline{E}_{[i]} = E_{[i]}\left[\binom{n}{i} \bigg/ \binom{n}{i-1}\right] = E_{[i]} \frac{n-i+1}{i}, \qquad i = 1, \ldots, n,$$

then

$$\prod_1^k |\lambda_i(A)| \leq \binom{n}{k} \prod_1^k E_{[i]} = \prod_1^k \overline{E}_{[i]}, \qquad k = 1, \ldots, n. \tag{5}$$

Proof. Let $A^{(k)} = (a_{ij}^{(k)})$ be the kth compound of A. By (1),

$$|a_{1\alpha}^{(k)}| = \left|\det A\begin{pmatrix} 1, 2, \ldots, k \\ j_1, j_2, \ldots, j_k \end{pmatrix}\right|$$

$$\leq \left(\sum_{j=1}^n |a_{1j}|^2 \cdots \sum_{j=1}^n |a_{kj}|^2\right)^{1/2}$$

$$\leq E_{[1]} \cdots E_{[k]}.$$

There are $\binom{n}{k}$ elements in the first row of $A^{(k)}$, so that

$$R_1(A^{(k)}) = \sum_{\alpha=1}^{\binom{n}{k}} |a_{1\alpha}^{(k)}| \leq \binom{n}{k} E_{[1]} \cdots E_{[k]}, \tag{6}$$

which together with (2) yields the inequality in (5). The equality in (5) holds because the E_i and $\overline{E}_i$, $i = 1, \ldots, n$, are similarly ordered. ||

Further Remarks About Hadamard's Inequality

I.4. If A is an $n \times n$ positive definite Hermitian matrix and

$$B = \begin{bmatrix} B_{11} & B_{12} \\ B_{21} & B_{22} \end{bmatrix} = A^{-1} = \begin{bmatrix} A_{11} & A_{12} \\ A_{21} & A_{22} \end{bmatrix}^{-1},$$

where B_{11} and A_{11} are $p \times p$ matrices, then

$$\inf \det(I_p, Z)A(I_p, Z)^* = \det A / \det A_{22}, \qquad (7)$$

where Z ranges over $p \times (n-p)$ complex matrices.

Proof. With $A_{11 \cdot 2} = A_{11} - A_{12} A_{22}^{-1} A_{21}$,

$$\begin{aligned}(I, Z)A(I, Z)^* &= A_{11 \cdot 2} + (Z + A_{12} A_{22}^{-1}) A_{22} (Z + A_{12} A_{22}^{-1})^* \\ &= B_{11}^{-1} + (Z - B_{11}^{-1} B_{12}) A_{22} (Z - B_{11}^{-1} B_{12})^* \\ &\geq B_{11}^{-1},\end{aligned}$$

with equality when $Z = B_{11}^{-1} B_{12}$. By 20.A.1.b,

$$\lambda_i((I, Z)A(I, Z)^*) \geq \lambda_i(B_{11}^{-1}), \qquad i = 1, \ldots, p,$$

so that

$$\det[(I, Z)A(I, Z)^*] \geq \det B_{11}^{-1} = \det A / \det A_{22}. \quad \|$$

The case $p = 1$ was obtained in a statistical context by Olkin and Pratt (1958) and is discussed by Mirsky (1963). It is contained in the work of Fan (1955b), who obtained a variety of consequences from it.

Alternative forms of I.4 when $p = 1$ can be given [see, e.g., Gantmacher (1959), pp. 248–250)]. In I.4 take $p = 1$, and let $A_{n-1} = A \binom{1, 2, \ldots, n-1}{1, 2, \ldots, n-1}$ to obtain

$$\frac{\det A}{\det A_{n-1}} = \inf_{x_n = 1} xAx' \leq (0, \ldots, 0, 1) A (0, \ldots, 0, 1)'$$

$$= a_{nn}, \qquad -\infty < x_i < \infty, \quad i = 1, \ldots, n-1. \qquad (8)$$

Mirsky (1963) notes that this provides a proof of Hadamard's inequality.

In a similar manner, use of I.4 with $X = (I, 0)$ yields the extended Hadamard inequality

$$\det A \leq (\det A_{11})(\det A_{22}) \equiv \det A \binom{1, 2, \ldots, p}{1, 2, \ldots, p} \det A \binom{p+1, \ldots, n}{p+1, \ldots, n},$$

which is given in C.1.d.

I.4.a. (Mirsky, 1963). If A is an $n \times n$ positive definite Hermitian matrix, then

$$\frac{\det A \binom{1, \ldots, n}{1, \ldots, n}}{\det A \binom{2, \ldots, n}{2, \ldots, n}} \leq \frac{\det A \binom{1, 3, \ldots, n}{1, 3, \ldots, n}}{\det A \binom{3, \ldots, n}{3, \ldots, n}} \leq \cdots \leq \frac{\det A \binom{1, n}{1, n}}{\det A \binom{n}{n}} \leq \frac{\det A \binom{1}{1}}{1}. \qquad (9)$$

Proof. Inequality (9) follows by an iteration of

$$\frac{\det A\binom{1,\ldots,n}{1,\ldots,n}}{\det A\binom{2,\ldots,n}{2,\ldots,n}} = \inf_{x,y}(1,x,y)A(1,x,y)' \leq \inf_{x}(1,0,x)A(1,0,x)'$$

$$= \frac{\det A\binom{1,3,\ldots,n}{1,3,\ldots,n}}{\det A\binom{3,\ldots,n}{3,\ldots,n}}, \qquad (10)$$

where the inf is over $(n-2)$-dimensional vectors x and scalars y. ‖

The first and last terms of (9) yield

$$\det A\binom{1,\ldots,n}{1,\ldots,n} \leq A\binom{1}{1}\det A\binom{2,\ldots,n}{2,\ldots,n},$$

which implies Hadamard's inequality.

Inequality (9) can be extended by substituting in (10) the more general inequality

$$\inf_{X,Y} \det(I,X,Y)A(I,X,Y)' \leq \inf_{X} \det(I,0,X)A(I,0,X)'.$$

For another proof of Hadamard's inequality that makes use of a monotonicity property of the product of principal minors of a Hermitian matrix, see Mirsky (1957b).

J Schur or Hadamard Products of Matrices

The Hadamard or Schur product of two $n \times n$ matrices $A = (a_{ij})$ and $B = (b_{ij})$ is defined as

$$A \circ B = (a_{ij}b_{ij}).$$

There is some question as to which name is the more appropriate; a general history of this product is provided by Styan (1973). Hadamard (1903) considered $A \circ B$ as the matrix of a quadratic form. Schur (1911) proved that $A \circ B$ is positive semidefinite if A and B are positive semidefinite.

Olkin (1985) observes that an elementary proof of this result can be based on the fact that an $n \times n$ matrix A is positive semdefinite if and only if it is the variance–covariance matrix of some random vector $X = (X_1, \ldots, X_n)$. Take X to have zero mean and variance–covariance matrix A and Y to have zero mean and variance–covariance matrix

B, where X and Y are independent. Then define Z by $Z_i = X_iY_i$, $i = 1, 2, \ldots, n$, and verify that its variance–covariance matrix is $A \circ B$. This technique can also be used to verify that if A and B are positive semidefinite, then so is their Kronecker product (cf. 19.G).

Schur also obtained some inequalities that are suggestive of majorization.

J.1. Theorem (Schur, 1911). If A and B are $n \times n$ positive semidefinite matrices, then

$$\lambda_n(A) \min\{b_{11}, \ldots, b_{nn}\} \leq \lambda_j(A \circ B) \leq \lambda_1(A) \max\{b_{11}, \ldots, b_{nn}\}. \quad (1)$$

A consequence of (1) is that

$$\lambda_n(A)\lambda_n(B) \leq \lambda_n(A \circ B) \leq \lambda_1(A \circ B) \leq \lambda_1(A)\lambda_1(B). \quad (2)$$

J.1.a. (Oppenheim, 1930). If A and B are positive semidefinite Hermitian matrices, then

$$(\det A)(\det B) \leq \det(A \circ B). \quad (3)$$

Together, (2) and (3) imply

$$\prod_2^n \lambda_i(A)\lambda_i(B) \leq \prod_2^n \lambda_i(A \circ B). \quad (4)$$

J.2. Theorem (Bapat and Sunder, 1985). If A and B are $n \times n$ positive semidefinite matrices and $b = (b_{11}, \ldots, b_{nn})$ is the vector of diagonal elements of B (arranged in decreasing order), then

$$\lambda(A \circ B) \prec_w \lambda(A) \circ b \prec_w \lambda(A) \circ \lambda(B) \quad (5)$$

and

$$\prod_k^n \lambda_i(A \circ B) \geq \prod_k^n \lambda_i(A)b_i, \quad 1 \leq k \leq n. \quad (6)$$

J.2.a. Corollary. If B is a correlation matrix so that $b_{ii} = 1$ for $i = 1, \ldots, n$, then

$$\lambda(A \circ B) \prec \lambda(A). \quad (7)$$

Proof. From J.2, $\lambda(A \circ B) \prec_w \lambda(A)$. But $\operatorname{tr}(A \circ B) = \operatorname{tr} A$ implies that $\Sigma \lambda_i(A \circ B) = \Sigma \lambda_i(A)$. ‖

Alternative proof (Bapat and Raghavan, 1997). Let G and H be orthogonal matrices such that $A \circ B = G'D_\theta G$ and $A = H'D_\alpha H$, where $D_\theta = \mathrm{diag}\,(\theta_1,\ldots,\theta_n)$, $D_\alpha = \mathrm{diag}\,(\alpha_1,\ldots,\alpha_n)$, $\theta = \lambda(A \circ B)$, and $\alpha = \lambda(A)$. Then

$$\theta_i = \sum_k \sum_\ell g_{ik} a_{k\ell} b_{k\ell} g_{i\ell} = \sum_k \sum_\ell g_{ik} g_{i\ell} b_{k\ell} \sum_j h_{jk} \alpha_j h_{j\ell}$$

$$= \sum_j \alpha_j \sum_k \sum_\ell (b_{k\ell} g_{ik} g_{i\ell} h_{jk} h_{j\ell}).$$

Let $P = (p_{ij})$, where

$$p_{ij} = \sum_k \sum_\ell (b_{k\ell} g_{ik} g_{i\ell} h_{jk} h_{j\ell}).$$

But $\sum_i g_{ik} g_{i\ell} = \delta_{k\ell}$, the Kronecker delta. Consequently,

$$\sum_i p_{ij} = \sum_k \sum_\ell \delta_{k\ell} h_{jk} h_{j\ell} b_{k\ell} = \sum_i h_{jk}^2 b_{ii} = 1,$$

and similarly $\sum_j p_{ij} = 1$, so that $\theta = \alpha P$ and hence $\alpha \succ \theta$. The fact that $\mathrm{tr}\,(A \circ B) = \mathrm{tr}\,A$ completes the proof. ||

Other extensions of J.2 are given by Bapat (1987).

J.3. Theorem (James Bondar, personal communication). Let $A = (a_{ij})$ be a positive semidefinite $n \times n$ matrix, and let f be any analytic function whose Taylor series has nonnegative coefficients. Further, let $B = (b_{ij})$, where $b_{ij} = f(a_{ij})$. Then

$$\lambda(B) \prec_w \lambda(f(A)). \qquad (8)$$

As an example, if f is the exponential function, A is positive semidefinite, and $b_{ij} = \exp(a_{ij})$, then

$$\lambda(B) \prec_w \lambda(e^A).$$

There is a corresponding result for singular values.

J.4. (Ando, 1995; Visick, 1995, 1998). For $A \geq 0$, $B \geq 0$, $0 < r \leq 1$, and $k = 1,\ldots,n$,

$$\prod_k^n \lambda_i(A \circ B) \geq \prod_k^n [\lambda_i(A^r \circ B^r)]^{1/r}$$

$$\geq \prod_k^n [\lambda_i(A^r B^r)]^{1/r} \geq \prod_k^n \lambda_i(AB).$$

The case $k = n$ was obtained earlier by Oppenheim (1930).

J.4.a. Remark. The proof of J.4 contains several interesting intermediate steps, including:

(i) for $A, B > 0$,
$$\sum_k^n \lambda_i(AB) \leq \sum_k^n [\lambda_i(A^m B^m)]^{1/m} \leq \sum_k^n \lambda_i(A)\lambda_i(B),$$
where m is a positive integer and $k = 1, \ldots, n$;

(ii) for $A, B \geq 0$, $0 \leq r \leq 1$,
$$(A \circ B)^r \geq (A^r \circ B^r);$$

(iii) for $A, B > 0$, $r > 0$, and $k = 1, \ldots, n$,
$$\sum_k^n [\lambda_i(AB)]^{-r} \geq \sum_k^n [\lambda_i(A \circ B)]^{-r};$$

(iv) for $A, B > 0$ and $k = 1, \ldots, n$,
$$\prod_k^n \lambda_i(A \circ B) > \prod_k^n \lambda_i(A \# B) \geq \prod_k^n \lambda_i(AB),$$
where $A \# B = A^{1/2}(A^{-1/2}BA^{-1/2})^{1/2}A^{1/2}$. If $AB = BA$, then $A \# B = (AB)^{1/2}$ is also called the *geometric mean*. The matrix $A \# B$ arises as the unique positive definite solution of $XA^{-1}X = B$. It also arises in a statistical context as the solution of max tr X such that the matrix $\begin{pmatrix} A & X \\ X & B \end{pmatrix} \geq 0$, where $A > 0$, $B > 0$ are $n \times n$ matrices. For further discussion of the statistical origins, see Olkin and Pukelsheim (1982), or Olkin and Rachev (1993).

See also Furuta (2007) for other inequalities involving $A \# B$.

J.4.b. (Zhan, 2002). If $A \geq 0$, $B \geq 0$, then
$$(A \circ B)^r \geq (A^r \circ B^r), \quad 0 < r \leq 1;$$
the inequality is reversed for $1 \leq r \leq 2$, $-1 \leq r \leq 0$.

The following results and proofs can be found in Bernstein (2005, Section 8.16).

J.4.c.

(i) For $A \geq 0$, $\quad (I \circ A)^2 \leq \tfrac{1}{2}(I \circ A^2 + A \circ A) \leq I \circ A^2$.

(ii) For $A \geq 0$, $\quad A \circ A \leq I \circ A^2$.

(iii) For $A = \begin{pmatrix} A_{11} & A_{12} \\ A_{21} & A_{22} \end{pmatrix}$, $A > 0$,

$$A \circ A^{-1} \geq \begin{pmatrix} A_{11} \circ A_{11}^{-1} & 0 \\ 0 & A_{22 \cdot 1} \circ A_{22 \cdot 1}^{-1} \end{pmatrix},$$

where $A_{22 \cdot 1} = A_{22} - A_{21} A_{11}^{-1} A_{12}$ is the *Schur complement* of A_{11}, also denoted by $\widetilde{A}_{11}$.

(iv) For $A \geq 0$, $B \geq 0$,

$$(A^k \circ B^k)^{1/k} \leq (A^\ell \circ B^\ell)^{1/\ell}, \quad 1 \leq k \leq \ell.$$

(v) For $A > 0$, B complex,

$$A \circ B^* A^{-1} B \leq B \circ B^* \leq A \circ B^* A^{-1} B.$$

J.5. Theorem (Ando, Horn, and Johnson, 1987). If A and B are $n \times n$ matrices, then

$$\sigma(A \circ B) \prec_w \sigma(A) \circ \sigma(B). \tag{9}$$

J.5.a. Proposition (Aujla and Silva, 2003). If $U, V, A, B \geq 0$, and $\lambda(U) \prec_w \lambda(V)$, $\lambda(A) \prec_w \lambda(B)$, then

$$\lambda(U) \circ \lambda(A) \prec_w \lambda(V) \circ \lambda(B).$$

Proof. This result is an adaptation of 5.A.4.f. ∥

Another class of matrices for which Schur–Hadamard products have been considered is that of irreducible nonnegative matrices. A matrix is said to be *reducible* if there exists a permutation matrix P such that

$$P'AP = \begin{pmatrix} B & C \\ 0 & D \end{pmatrix},$$

where B and D are square matrices.

A matrix is said to be irreducible if it is not reducible.

J.6. Proposition (Lynn, 1964). If $A = (a_{ij})$, $B = (b_{ij})$ are irreducible $n \times n$ matrices with $a_{ij} \geq 0$, $b_{ij} \geq 0$, $i, j = 1, \ldots, n$, then

$$|\lambda_1(A \circ B)| \leq |\lambda_1(A)||\lambda_1(B)|. \tag{10}$$

An application of (10) to the kth compound yields

$$|\lambda_1(A^{(k)} \circ B^{(k)})| \leq |\lambda_1(A^{(k)})| \, |\lambda_1(B^{(k)})|$$
$$= \prod_1^k |\lambda_i(A)| \, |\lambda_i(B)|, \qquad k = 1, \ldots, n.$$

J.7. Proposition (Aujla and Bourin, 2007). For $A \geq 0$, $B \geq 0$, and ϕ convex and submultiplicative [i.e., $\phi(st) \leq \phi(s)\phi(t)$] on $[0, \infty)$,

$$\lambda(\phi(A \circ B)) \prec_w \lambda(\phi(A) \circ \phi(B)).$$

J.8. Proposition (Visick, 2000). For $m \times n$ complex matrices A and B, and $0 < \alpha < 1$,

$$(AA^* \circ BB^*) + (2\alpha - 1)(AB^* + BA^*) \geq 2(A \circ B)(A \circ B)^*.$$

See also Zhang (2000).

K Diagonal Elements and Eigenvalues of a Totally Positive Matrix and of an M-Matrix

Just as Hadamard's inequality B.5.a suggests a majorization between the diagonal elements and eigenvalues of a Hermitian matrix, there is a Hadamard-type inequality for totally nonnegative matrices which is suggestive of a majorization. See Chapter 18 for an exposition of totally positive matrices.

Totally Nonnegative Matrices

A real matrix A is totally nonnegative (positive) of order m (see 18.A.1) if for $k = 1, \ldots, m$,

$$A\begin{pmatrix} i_1, \ldots, i_k \\ j_1, \ldots, j_k \end{pmatrix} \geq 0 \,(> 0), \; 1 \leq i_1 < \cdots < i_k \leq n, \; 1 \leq j_1 < \cdots < j_k \leq n.$$

For such a matrix, Gantmacher and Krein (1950) show that

$$\det A \leq \det A\begin{pmatrix} 1, \ldots, k \\ 1, \ldots, k \end{pmatrix} \det A\begin{pmatrix} k+1, \ldots, n \\ k+1, \ldots, n \end{pmatrix}, \qquad k < n, \qquad (1)$$

which implies that

$$\prod_1^n \lambda_i(A) \leq \prod_1^n a_{ii} \qquad (2)$$

[see also Gantmacher (1959, Vol. II, p. 100)].

A real $n \times n$ matrix A is called *oscillatory* if A is totally nonnegative and if there exists an integer r such that A^r is totally positive. Gantmacher and Krein (1950) prove that the eigenvalues $\lambda_1, \ldots, \lambda_n$ of an oscillatory matrix are real, distinct, and positive.

A result paralleling Schur's theorem B.1 for Hermitian matrices is available for oscillating matrices.

K.1. Theorem (Garloff, 1982). If $A = (a_{ij})$ is an $n \times n$ oscillatory matrix with $a_{11} \geq \cdots \geq a_{nn}$ and eigenvalues $\lambda_1(A) > \cdots > \lambda_n(A)$, then for each $k = 1, 2, \ldots, n-1$,

$$\sum_1^k a_{ii} < \sum_1^k \lambda_i(A) \qquad (3)$$

and consequently, because $\sum_{i=1}^n a_{ii} = \sum_{i=1}^n \lambda_i(A)$,

$$(\lambda_1(A), \ldots, \lambda_n(A)) \succ (a_{11}, \ldots, a_{nn}). \qquad (4)$$

[Note that, in fact, from (3), this majorization is strict.]

Proof. The result is readily verified for $n = 2$ and an inductive proof is described in detail in Garloff (1982). ‖

K.2. Corollary. If $A = (a_{ij})$ is an $n \times n$ oscillatory matrix with $a_{11} \geq \cdots \geq a_{nn}$ and $\lambda_1(A) > \cdots > \lambda_n(A)$, then

$$a_{11} < \lambda_1(A) \qquad (5)$$

and

$$a_{nn} > \lambda_n(A). \qquad (6)$$

K.3. Corollary (Garloff, 1982). If A and B are $n \times n$ oscillatory matrices, then

$$\operatorname{tr}(AB) > \sum_1^n \lambda_i(A) \lambda_{n-i+1}(B). \qquad (7)$$

The proof parallels the proof of H.1.h using the strict majorization (3). Note that in contrast to the weak inequality provided in H.1.h for Hermitian matrices, a strict inequality is available for oscillatory matrices.

K.4. Theorem. If A is a totally positive $n \times n$ matrix, then
$$(\log \lambda_1(A), \ldots, \log \lambda_n(A)) \succ^w (\log a_{11}, \ldots, \log a_{nn}). \qquad (8)$$

Proof. If A is totally positive, then all principal minors are positive, which implies that the kth compound $A^{(k)} = (a_{ij}^{(k)})$ is oscillatory [see Gantmacher (1959, Vol. II, p. 105)]. Consequently, (6) can be used with the kth compound to yield

$$\prod_{n-k+1}^{n} \lambda_i(A) = \min_i \lambda_i(A^{(k)})$$
$$\leq \min_i a_{ii}^{(k)} = \min_{i_1,\ldots,i_k} \det A\begin{pmatrix} i_1, \ldots, i_k \\ i_1, \ldots, i_k \end{pmatrix}$$
$$\leq \min_{i_1,\ldots,i_k} \prod_{\alpha=1}^{k} a_{i_\alpha i_\alpha} = \prod_{n-k+1}^{n} a_{ii}. \qquad (9)$$

The first inequality is an application of (6); the second inequality is an application of (2). ∥

M-Matrices

An M-matrix can be defined in a number of ways (see 19.H for a listing of equivalent definitions). For example, if $A = (a_{ij})$ is a real matrix with $a_{ij} \leq 0$ ($i \neq j$) and all principal minors of A are positive, then A is an M-matrix. Ostrowski (1937) shows that if A is an M-matrix, then

$$\prod_1^n \lambda_i(A) \leq \prod_1^n a_{ii}. \qquad (10)$$

Fan (1960) obtains the stronger result

$$\det A \leq \det A\begin{pmatrix} 1, \ldots, k \\ 1, \ldots, k \end{pmatrix} \det A\begin{pmatrix} k+1, \ldots, n \\ k+1, \ldots, n \end{pmatrix}, \quad k < n, \qquad (11)$$

as well as a variety of other determinant inequalities.

Given a matrix $A = (a_{ij})$, Lynn (1964) constructs the matrix $\widetilde{A} = (\widetilde{a}_{ij})$ by

$$\widetilde{a}_{ii} = |a_{ii}|, \qquad \widetilde{a}_{ij} = -|a_{ij}|, \qquad i \neq j,$$

and then shows that if all the principal minors of $\widetilde{A}$ are positive, then (11) holds. Lynn (1964) also proves that if $C = A \circ B$, and if $\widetilde{A}$ and $\widetilde{B}$ have positive principal minors, then

$$\prod_1^n \lambda_i(\widetilde{A})\lambda_i(\widetilde{B}) \leq \prod_1^n \lambda_i(\widetilde{C}).$$

L Loewner Ordering and Majorization

The Loewner order of two Hermitian matrices $B \geq A$ arises in several different contexts. Details and discussion are given in 16.E, 16.F, and 20.A. An import of this order is that it implies a weak majorization of the eigenvalues.

L.1. Proposition. For Hermitian matrices A and B, if $B \geq A$, then $(\lambda_1(B), \ldots, \lambda_n(B)) \succ_w (\lambda_1(A), \ldots, \lambda_n(A))$.

Proof. If $B \geq A$, then $UBU^* \geq UAU^*$ for all $k \times n$ matrices U. Consequently, for $UU^* = I_k$,

$$\operatorname{tr} UAU^* \leq \operatorname{tr} UBU^* \leq \max_{UU^* = I_k} \operatorname{tr} UBU^* = \sum_1^k \beta_i$$

(see 20.A.2). Maximization of the left-hand side yields the result. ‖

L.2. Note. A stronger result is given in 16.F.1 and 20.A.1: If $B \geq A$, then $\lambda_i(B) \geq \lambda_i(A)$, $i = 1, \ldots, n$. By 1.A(15a), $\lambda(B) \succ_w \lambda(A)$; if $\lambda(B) \succ \lambda(A)$, then $(\lambda_1(B), \ldots, \lambda_n(B)) = (\lambda_1(A), \ldots, \lambda_n(A))$ by 1.A(15b).

There are now many examples of matrices ordered by the Loewner ordering. Some are stated as weak majorizations. The following are several examples that arise in that way. For further discussion, see Furuta (1987, 2001) and Fujii and Kamei (1992). See also Bernstein (2005, p. 279). The following general weak majorization includes many special cases of interest.

L.3. Proposition (Zhan, 2002). If $B \geq A \geq 0$, and for $r, s \geq 0$, $t \geq 1$, $r + 2s \leq (1 + 2s)t$, then

$$A^{(r+2s)/t} \leq (A^s B^r A^s)^{1/t}, \tag{1}$$

$$(B^s A^r B^s)^{1/t} \leq B^{(r+2s)/t}. \tag{2}$$

The special case $r = 2$, $s = 1$, $t = 2$ yields the more familiar orderings

$$A^2 \leq (AB^2 A)^{1/2},$$

$$(BA^2 B)^{1/2} \leq B^2.$$

L.3.a. Under the conditions of L.3 with $\alpha_1 \geq \cdots \geq \alpha_n$ the ordered eigenvalues of A, and $\theta_1 \geq \cdots \geq \theta_n$ the ordered eigenvalues of $A^s B^r A^s$,

$$\alpha^{(r+2s)/t} \prec_{\mathrm{w}} \theta^{1/t}.$$

L.4. Proposition (Yamazaki, 2000). If $A \geq 0$, $0 < mI \leq B \leq MI$, and $A \geq B$, then

$$A^2 + \frac{(M-m)^2}{4} I \geq B^2.$$

See Fujii and Seo (2002) for extensions. Note that, in general, $A \geq B$ does not imply $A^2 \geq B^2$.

L.4.a. Proposition (Fujii, Nakamura, Pečarić, and Seo, 2006). For $0 < mI \leq A \leq MI$, $0 < mI \leq B \leq MI$,

(i) $(A+B) - (A^{-1} + B^{-1})^{-1} \leq 2(M + m - \sqrt{mM})I$,

(ii) $\dfrac{A+B}{2} \leq \dfrac{(M+m)^2}{4mM} \left(\dfrac{A^{-1} + B^{-1}}{2} \right)^{-1}.$

See 16.E and 16.F for a discussion of the Loewner order in the context of matrix monotone functions. See also 20.A.

M Nonnegative Matrix-Valued Functions

If a $k \times k$ matrix A has nonnegative elements, then its eigenvalue of maximum modulus is real and nonnegative and is called the *spectral radius* of A, denoted by $\rho(A)$. Consider now a function $\varphi(x)$ whose domain $\mathcal{D}$ is a subset of $\mathscr{R}^n$, which takes on values in the class of all $k \times k$ matrices with nonnegative entries. Thus $\varphi : \mathcal{D} \to \mathscr{R}_+^{k^2}$. The coordinate functions, $\varphi_{ij}(x)$, of this mapping are nonnegative real-valued functions defined on $\mathcal{D}$. Because $\varphi(x)$ is a nonnegative $k \times k$ matrix, its spectral radius $\rho(\varphi(x))$ is well defined and is a mapping from $\mathcal{D}$ into $\mathscr{R}_+$. Kingman (1961) provides a useful lemma that identifies properties of the $\varphi_{ij}(x)$'s inherited by the spectral radius function $\rho(\varphi(x))$.

M.1. Lemma (based on Kingman, 1961). Let S be a class of nonnegative real-valued functions defined on a domain $\mathcal{D}$ that is closed under the operations of addition, multiplication, raising to any positive power, and the taking of positive lim sup's of countable subsequences. If $\varphi : \mathcal{D} \to \mathscr{R}_+^{k^2}$ is a matrix-valued function with coordinate functions φ_{ij} in S, then the spectral radius function $\rho(\varphi(\cdot))$ is also in S.

Proof. Let $f_r(x) = \{\text{tr}\,[\varphi(x)]^r\}^{1/r}$. Then, by hypothesis, $f_r \in S$ for every $r = 1, 2, \ldots$. But $f_r(x)$ is the ℓ_r norm of $\lambda(\varphi(x))$, so that $\rho(\varphi(x)) = \|\lambda(\varphi(x))\| = \overline{\lim}_{r \to \infty} f_r(x)$ is also in S. ||

In particular, S could be the class of all nonnegative Schur-convex functions on $\mathcal{D}$. This class satisfies the hypothesis of the lemma; consequently, if each $\varphi_{ij}(x)$ is nonnegative and Schur-convex, then so is $\rho(\varphi(x))$.

This result was brought to our attention by James Bondar.

N Zeros of Polynomials

For z real, let $p(z) = z^n + a_n z^{n-1} + \cdots + a_2 z + a_1$ be a monic polynomial of degree $n \geq 2$ with complex coefficients, and let $p'(z)$ be its derivative. The following result compares the roots of $p(z)$ and $p'(z)$, in modulus.

N.1. Proposition (Cheung and Ng, 2006; Pereira, 2007). If $z_1, \ldots, z_n$ are the roots of $p(z)$ ordered so that $|z_1| \geq \ldots \geq |z_n|$ and $w_1, \ldots, w_{n-1}$ are the roots of $p'(z)$ ordered so that $|w_1| \geq \ldots \geq |w_{n-1}|$, then

$$\prod_1^k |w_j| \leq \prod_1^k |z_j|, \quad k = 1, \ldots, n-1,$$

or equivalently, if $|w_{n-1}| > 0$, $|z_{n-1}| > 0$.

$$(\log|w_1|, \ldots, \log|w_{n-1}|) \prec_w (\log|z_1|, \ldots, \log|z_{n-1}|).$$

The proof is based on first noting that if $p(z) = \prod_1^n (z - z_j)$, then the roots of the matrix $A = D(I - (e'e)/n)$ are the roots of $zp'(z)$, where $D = \text{diag}\,(z_1, \ldots, z_n)$. The result is based on the majorization E.1.

Define the *Frobenius companion matrix of p* by

$$C(p) = \begin{bmatrix} -a_n & -a_{n-1} & \cdots & -a_2 & -a_1 \\ 1 & 0 & \cdots & 0 & 0 \\ & & \cdots & & \\ 0 & 0 & \cdots & 1 & 0 \end{bmatrix}.$$

Remark. The zeros, $z_1, z_2, \ldots, z_n$, of $p(z) = z^n + a_n z^{n-1} + \cdots + a_1$ coincide with the eigenvalues of $C(p)$, which are functions of $a_1, \ldots, a_n$. See, e.g., Horn and Johnson (1985, p. 316).

N.2. Proposition (Kittaneh, 2007). With $z_1, \ldots, z_n$ the roots of $p(z)$ and $a_1, \ldots, a_n$ the eigenvalues of $C(p)$, let $\xi_i = \mathscr{R}(z_i)$ be ordered such that $\xi_1 \geq \ldots \geq \xi_n$, $\alpha_i = \mathscr{R}(a_i)$, and $\beta_i = |a_i|$. Then

$$\sum_1^k \xi_i \leq A(a) + \sum_1^k \cos \tfrac{i\pi}{n+1}, \quad k = 1, \ldots, n-1,$$

$$\sum_1^n \xi_i = -\alpha_n,$$

where

$$A(a) = \frac{1}{2}\left\{-\alpha_n + \sqrt{\alpha_n^2 + \sum_1^{n-1} \beta_i^2}\right\}.$$

Related results are given by Kittaneh (1995).

O   Other Settings in Matrix Theory Where Majorization Has Proved Useful

Majorization appears in a variety of contexts that involve concepts that would take us too far afield. Without giving details, we mention a sample of the matrix literature in which majorization played an important role.

O.1. Eigenvalue clusters (Serra-Capizzano, Bertaccini, and Golub, 2005)

O.2. Wiener–Hopf factorizations (Amparan, Marcaida, and Zaballa, 2004)

9. Matrix Theory

O.3. Group majorization for correlation matrices (Giovagnoli and Romanazzi, 1990)

O.4. Group-invariant orderings and experimental design (Giovagnoli, Pukelsheim, and Wynn, 1987)

O.5. A majorization theorem for binary designs (Giovagnoli and Wynn, 1980)

O.6. Points of continuity of the Kronecker canonical form (de Hoyos, 1990)

O.7. Invariant factors of a polynomial matrix (Zaballa, 1987, 1991)

O.8. A majorization bound for the eigenvalues of some graph Laplacians (Stephen, 2007)

O.9. Graph algorithm for degree sequences in parallel (Arikati and Maheshwari, 1996)

O.10. Determinant of the sum of a symmetric and a skew-symmetric matrix (Bebiano, Li, and da Providência, 1997)

O.11. Linear systems with prescribed similarity structural invariants (Baragaña, Fernández, and Zaballa, 2000)

O.12. Majorization inequalities related to von Neumann algebras (Harada, 2008)

O.13. The construction of Huffman codes (Parker and Ram, 1999)

O.14. Structural perturbation of a matrix (Baragaña, Asunción Beitia and de Hoyos, 2009)

O.15. Matrix mean inequalities (Bhatia and Kittaneh, 2008)

O.16. Monotonicity of order-preserving functions (Furuta, 2008)

10
Numerical Analysis

Majorization has been used in two areas in numerical analysis: (i) finding a matrix closest to a given matrix, and (ii) obtaining bounds for the condition number and norm of a matrix. Both (i) and (ii) depend on a relation between unitarily invariant norms and symmetric gauge functions (see 3.I.1) obtained by von Neumann (1937). Majorization arises from the fact that symmetric gauge functions are Schur-convex.

For a general discussion of gauge functions, see Schatten (1950), Rockafellar (1970), Horn and Johnson (1991), Bhatia (1997), or Bernstein (2005).

A *unitarily invariant norm* $\|\cdot\|_{\mathrm{UI}}$ is a matrix norm satisfying $\|AU\|_{\mathrm{UI}} = \|VA\|_{\mathrm{UI}}$ for all unitary matrices U and V and every complex matrix A. The Euclidean norm is denoted by $\|A\|_{\mathrm{E}}$.

A   Unitarily Invariant Norms and Symmetric Gauge Functions

A.1. Theorem (von Neumann, 1937). If Φ is a symmetric gauge function, and A is an $n \times n$ complex matrix with singular values ordered $\sigma_1(A) \geq \cdots \geq \sigma_n(A)$, then the matrix function defined by $\Phi(\sigma_1(A), \ldots, \sigma_n(A))$ is a unitarily invariant norm. Conversely, every unitarily invariant norm $\|\cdot\|_{\mathrm{UI}}$ has a representation of the form $\|A\|_{\mathrm{UI}} = \Phi(\sigma_1(A), \ldots, \sigma_n(A))$, where Φ is a symmetric gauge function.

The proof of this result is omitted.

Remark. Because $\sigma(A) = \sigma(A^*)$, it immediately follows that for any unitarily invariant norm $\|\cdot\|_{\mathrm{UI}}$, $\|A\|_{\mathrm{UI}} = \|A^*\|_{\mathrm{UI}}$. If A and B are $n \times n$ matrices, then $\sigma(AB) = \sigma(BA)$, so that $\|AB\|_{\mathrm{UI}} = \|BA\|_{\mathrm{UI}}$. These facts are used frequently in the proofs below.

Because every symmetric gauge function Φ is Schur-convex and increasing on $\mathscr{R}_+^n$ (see 3.I.1), it follows that if

$$(\alpha_1, \ldots, \alpha_n) \prec_w (\beta_1, \ldots, \beta_n) \quad \text{on} \quad \mathscr{R}_+^n, \tag{1}$$

then

$$\Phi(\alpha_1, \ldots, \alpha_n) \leq \Phi(\beta_1, \ldots, \beta_n). \tag{2}$$

The implication (1) $\Rightarrow$ (2) is due to Fan (1951).

A.2. Let A and B be $n \times n$ complex matrices. Then

$$\|A\|_{\mathrm{UI}} \leq \|B\|_{\mathrm{UI}} \tag{3}$$

for every unitarily invariant norm $\|\cdot\|_{\mathrm{UI}}$ if and only if

$$(\sigma_1(A), \ldots, \sigma_n(A)) \prec_w (\sigma_1(B), \ldots, \sigma_n(B)). \tag{4}$$

Proof. If $\|A\|_{\mathrm{UI}} \leq \|B\|_{\mathrm{UI}}$ for every unitarily invariant norm $\|\cdot\|_{\mathrm{UI}}$, then by A.1,

$$\Phi(\sigma_1(A), \ldots, \sigma_n(A)) \leq \Phi(\sigma_1(B), \ldots, \Phi_n(B))$$

for all symmetric gauge functions Φ. By 4.B.6, this implies that $\sigma(A) \prec_w \sigma(B)$.

If $\sigma(A) \prec_w \sigma(B)$, then $\Phi(\sigma_1(A), \ldots, \sigma_n(A)) \leq \Phi(\sigma_1(B), \ldots, \sigma_n(B))$ for every symmetric gauge function Φ, so that by A.1, $\|A\|_{\mathrm{UI}} \leq \|B\|_{\mathrm{UI}}$ for every unitarily invariant norm. ∥

Unitarily Invariant Norm Inequalities

As noted in A.2, unitarily invariant norm inequalities can be translated to majorization inequalities. A number of new norm inequalities have now appeared and are listed by Bernstein (2005, Section 9.9). See also Ando (1994), Seo and Tominaga (2008), or Matsumoto and Fujii (2009). The following are several examples, each of which can be translated to a weak majorization on the singular values.

A. Unitarily Invariant Norms and Symmetric Gauge Functions

A.3. Proposition (Bhatia and Davis, 1993). For $A \geq 0$, $B \geq 0$, define the *Heinz mean*

$$H_\alpha(A, B) = \frac{1}{2}(A^\alpha B^{\bar{\alpha}} + A^{\bar{\alpha}} B^\alpha), \quad 0 \leq \alpha \leq 1, \quad \bar{\alpha} = 1 - \alpha;$$

then

$$\|A^{1/2} B^{1/2}\|_{\mathrm{UI}} \leq \|H_\alpha(A, B)\|_{\mathrm{UI}} \leq \|(A + B)/2\|_{\mathrm{UI}}.$$

Thus the Heinz mean lies between the geometric and arithmetic means.

A.4. Proposition (Ando and Zhan, 1999). If $A, B \geq 0$, and ϕ is a monotone nonnegative function on $[0, \infty)$, then

$$\|\phi(A) + \phi(B)\|_{\mathrm{UI}} \geq \|\phi(A + B)\|_{\mathrm{UI}}; \tag{5}$$

if ψ is a nonnegative increasing function on $[0, \infty)$, with $\psi(0) = 0$, $\psi(\infty) = \infty$, and whose inverse function is monotone, then

$$\|\psi(A) + \psi(B)\|_{\mathrm{UI}} \leq \|\psi(A + B)\|_{\mathrm{UI}}. \tag{6}$$

A.5. Examples. For $A, B \geq 0$,

$$\|A^r + B^r\|_{\mathrm{UI}} \geq \|(A + B)^r\|_{\mathrm{UI}}, \quad 0 \leq r \leq 1, \tag{7}$$
$$\|A^r + B^r\|_{\mathrm{UI}} \leq \|(A + B)^r\|_{\mathrm{UI}}, \quad 1 \leq r \leq \infty. \tag{8}$$

A.6. Examples. If A and B are $n \times n$ Hermitian matrices, then for $k \in N$,

$$\|(A - B)^{2k+1}\|_{\mathrm{UI}} \leq 2^{2k} \|A^{2k+1} - B^{2k+1}\|_{\mathrm{UI}}; \tag{9}$$

for $A \geq 0$, $B \geq 0$,

$$\|\log(A + I) + \log(B + I)\|_{\mathrm{UI}} \geq \|\log(A + B + I)\|_{\mathrm{UI}} \tag{10}$$

and

$$\|e^A + e^B\|_{\mathrm{UI}} \leq \|e^{A+B} + I\|_{\mathrm{UI}}. \tag{11}$$

A.7. Examples. For A, B complex,

$$\|A^* B\|_{\mathrm{UI}} \leq \frac{1}{2} \|AA^* + BB^*\|_{\mathrm{UI}}, \tag{12}$$

$$\|(A^* A)^{1/2} - (B^* B)^{1/2}\|_{\mathrm{UI}} \leq (2\|A + B\|_{\mathrm{UI}} \|A - B\|_{\mathrm{UI}})^{1/2}. \tag{13}$$

B Matrices Closest to a Given Matrix

It is often of interest to know how much matrices in a given class can deviate from a given matrix. More specifically, for a given class $\mathscr{X}$ of matrices and a given matrix A, what are the upper or lower bounds for $\|A - X\|$ for $X \in \mathscr{X}$?

General discussions of this topic from different points of view are given by Mirsky (1960a), Golub (1968), Halmos (1972), and Keller (1975).

Hermitian Matrix Closest to an Arbitrary Matrix

B.1. Theorem (Fan and Hoffman, 1955). Let A be an $n \times n$ complex matrix. Then for all Hermitian matrices H,

$$\left\| A - \frac{A + A^*}{2} \right\|_{\mathrm{UI}} \leq \|A - H\|_{\mathrm{UI}} \tag{1a}$$

for every unitarily invariant norm $\|\cdot\|_{\mathrm{UI}}$, or equivalently,

$$\sigma\left(A - \frac{A + A^*}{2}\right) \prec_{\mathrm{w}} \sigma(A - H). \tag{1b}$$

Proof. Because of the identity

$$A - \frac{A + A^*}{2} = \frac{A - H}{2} - \frac{A^* - H}{2} = \frac{A - H}{2} - \frac{(A - H)^*}{2},$$

it follows that

$$\left\| A - \frac{A + A^*}{2} \right\|_{\mathrm{UI}} \leq \left\| \frac{A - H}{2} \right\|_{\mathrm{UI}} + \left\| \frac{(A - H)^*}{2} \right\|_{\mathrm{UI}} = \|A - H\|_{\mathrm{UI}}$$

for every unitarily invariant norm. Equivalently, by A.2,

$$\sigma\left(A - \frac{A + A^*}{2}\right) \prec_{\mathrm{w}} \sigma(A - H). \quad \|$$

Skew-Symmetric Matrix Closest to an Arbitrary Matrix

B.2. Theorem (Causey, 1964). Let A be an $n \times n$ complex matrix. Then for all skew-symmetric matrices S,

$$\left\| A - \frac{A - A^*}{2} \right\|_{\mathrm{UI}} \leq \|A - S\|_{\mathrm{UI}} \tag{2a}$$

B. Matrices Closest to a Given Matrix

for every unitarily invariant norm $\|\cdot\|_{\mathrm{UI}}$, or equivalently,

$$\sigma\left(A - \frac{A - A^*}{2}\right) \prec_{\mathrm{w}} \sigma(A - S). \tag{2b}$$

Proof. For any skew-symmetric matrix S,

$$A - \frac{A - A^*}{2} = \frac{A - S}{2} + \frac{A^* + S}{2} = \frac{A - S}{2} + \frac{(A - S)^*}{2},$$

and hence

$$\left\|A - \frac{A - A^*}{2}\right\|_{\mathrm{UI}} \leq \left\|\frac{A - S}{2}\right\|_{\mathrm{UI}} + \left\|\frac{(A - S)^*}{2}\right\|_{\mathrm{UI}} = \|A - S\|_{\mathrm{UI}},$$

for every unitarily invariant norm $\|\cdot\|_{\mathrm{UI}}$. Equivalently, by A.2,

$$\sigma\left(A - \frac{A - A^*}{2}\right) \prec_{\mathrm{w}} \sigma(A - S). \quad \|$$

Unitary Matrix Closest to a Positive Semidefinite Hermitian Matrix

B.3. Theorem (Fan and Hoffman, 1955). Let H be an $n \times n$ positive semidefinite Hermitian matrix. Then for all unitary matrices Γ,

$$\|H - I\|_{\mathrm{UI}} \leq \|H - \Gamma\|_{\mathrm{UI}} \leq \|H + I\|_{\mathrm{UI}} \tag{3a}$$

for every unitarily invariant norm $\|\cdot\|_{\mathrm{UI}}$, or equivalently,

$$\sigma(H - I) \prec_{\mathrm{w}} \sigma(H - \Gamma) \prec_{\mathrm{w}} \sigma(H + I). \tag{3b}$$

Proof. Consider first the right-hand inequality of (3b). By 9.G.1.d, $\sigma_i(H - \Gamma) \leq \sigma_i(H) + \sigma_1(-\Gamma)$, $i = 1, \ldots, n$. Because $H \geq 0$, $\sigma_i(H) = \lambda_i(H)$, $i = 1, \ldots, n$. Also, $\sigma_1(-\Gamma) = [\lambda_1(\Gamma\Gamma^*)]^{1/2} = 1$, so that

$$\sigma_i(H - \Gamma) \leq \sigma_i(H) + \sigma_1(-\Gamma) = \lambda_i(H) + 1 = \lambda_i(H + I)$$
$$= \sigma_i(H + I), \quad i = 1, \ldots, n,$$

which is stronger than the right-hand inequality.

To prove the left-hand inequality, note that for $k = 1, \ldots, n$,

$$\sum_1^k \sigma_i(H-I) = \max_{1 \leq i_1 < \cdots < i_k \leq n} \sum_{s=1}^k |\lambda_{i_s}(H-I)|$$
$$= \max_{1 \leq i_1 < \cdots < i_k \leq n} \sum_{s=1}^k |\lambda_{i_s}(H) - 1|$$
$$= \max_{1 \leq i_1 < \cdots < i_k \leq n} \sum_{s=1}^k |\sigma_{i_s}(H) - 1|. \qquad (4)$$

We need to show that

$$\max_{1 \leq i_1 < \cdots < i_k \leq n} \sum_{s=1}^k |\sigma_{i_s}(H) - 1| \leq \sum_{s=1}^k \sigma_i(H - \Gamma), \qquad k = 1, \ldots, n. \quad (5)$$

To prove (5), define for any matrix M the symmetrized matrix

$$\widetilde{M} = \begin{bmatrix} 0 & M \\ M^* & 0 \end{bmatrix}.$$

The nonzero eigenvalues of $\widetilde{M}$ are the nonzero singular values of M and their negatives (see 9.A.2). From 9.G.1(3),

$$\max_{1 \leq i_1 < \cdots < i_k \leq n} \sum_{s=1}^k |\lambda_{i_s}(\widetilde{H}) - \lambda_{i_s}(\widetilde{\Gamma})| \leq \sum_{i=1}^k \lambda_i(\widetilde{H} - \widetilde{\Gamma}), \quad k = 1, \ldots, n. \quad (6)$$

That (6) implies (5) follows from the fact that the eigenvalues of $\widetilde{H}$, $\widetilde{\Gamma}$, and $\widetilde{H} - \widetilde{\Gamma}$ are

$$\lambda(\widetilde{H}) = (\sigma_1(H), \ldots, \sigma_n(H), -\sigma_n(H), \ldots, -\sigma_1(H)),$$
$$\lambda(\widetilde{\Gamma}) = (1, \ldots, 1, -1, \ldots, -1),$$
$$\lambda(\widetilde{H} - \widetilde{\Gamma}) = (\sigma_1(H-\Gamma), \ldots, \sigma_n(H-\Gamma), -\sigma_n(H-\Gamma), \ldots, -\sigma_1(H-\Gamma)),$$

respectively. ||

Let A be an $n \times n$ complex matrix. Then by the polar decomposition 19.C.3, there exists a unitary matrix U and a positive semidefinite Hermitian matrix H such that

$$A = UH. \qquad (7)$$

The following theorem is equivalent to B.3, although it appears to be more general.

B.4. Theorem (Fan and Hoffman, 1955). Let A be an $n \times n$ complex matrix, and let U be a unitary matrix satisfying (7). Then for all unitary matrices Γ,

$$\|A - U\|_{\text{UI}} \leq \|A - \Gamma\|_{\text{UI}} \leq \|A + U\|_{\text{UI}} \tag{8a}$$

for every unitarily invariant norm $\|\cdot\|_{\text{UI}}$, or equivalently,

$$\sigma(A - U) \prec_{\text{w}} \sigma(A - \Gamma) \prec_{\text{w}} \sigma(A + U). \tag{8b}$$

Proof. If $A = H$ is a positive semidefinite Hermitian matrix, then (8a) and (8b) follow from (3a) and (3b).

If U is a unitary matrix satisfying $A = UH \equiv U(AA^*)^{1/2}$, and Γ is a unitary matrix, then

$$\sigma(A \pm \Gamma) = \sigma(UH \pm UU^*\Gamma) = \sigma(H \pm U^*\Gamma). \tag{9}$$

In particular, if $\Gamma = U$, then

$$\sigma(A \pm U) = \sigma(H \pm I). \tag{10}$$

The relations (9) and (10) with (3a) or (3b) yield (8a) or (8b). ∥

Closest Matrix of a Given Rank

Let A be an $m \times n$ complex matrix of rank r. Then by the singular value decomposition 19.B.1, there exist unitary matrices Γ and Δ such that

$$A = \Gamma D_\alpha \Delta, \tag{11}$$

where $D_\alpha = \text{diag}(\alpha_1, \ldots, \alpha_r, 0, \ldots, 0)$ and $\alpha_1 \geq \cdots \geq \alpha_r$ are the nonzero singular values of A.

B.5. Theorem (Eckart and Young, 1936; Mirsky, 1960a; Keller, 1962). Let A be an $m \times n$ complex matrix of rank r. Then for all $m \times n$ matrices X of rank $k \leq r$,

$$\|A - B\|_{\text{UI}} \leq \|A - X\|_{\text{UI}} \text{ for every unitarily invariant norm } \|\cdot\|_{\text{UI}},$$

where

$$B = \Gamma \text{ diag}(\alpha_1, \ldots, \alpha_k, 0, \ldots, 0)\Delta;$$

Γ and Δ are unitary matrices satisfying (11), $\alpha_i = \sigma_i(A)$, $i = 1, \ldots, r$.

Remark. Note that $\|A - B\|_{\text{UI}} = \|\text{diag}(0, \ldots, 0, \alpha_{k+1}, \ldots, \alpha_r)\|_{\text{UI}}$.

Theorem B.5 was proved by Eckart and Young (1936) for the Euclidean norm $\|X\|_E = (\text{tr } XX^*)^{1/2}$, and generalized to unitarily invariant norms by Mirsky (1960a). The extension to operators is due to Keller (1962).

Comment on the proof. The proof of Mirsky (1960a) is lengthy and is omitted. An essential feature of the proof is the fact that if $A = (\dot{A}, \ddot{A})$, then

$$\sigma(A) \succ_w (\sigma(\dot{A}), 0).$$

This follows from 9.G.3.b with A replaced by $(\dot{A}, 0)$ and B replaced by $(0, \ddot{A})$.

A Bound for the Difference Between Two Hermitian Matrices

The *Cayley transform* U of an $n \times n$ Hermitian matrix G is defined by

$$U = (G - iI)(G + iI)^{-1} = I - 2i(G + iI)^{-1}.$$

B.6. Theorem (Fan and Hoffman, 1955). Let H and K be two $n \times n$ Hermitian matrices with respective Cayley transforms U and V. Then

$$\|H - K\|_{\text{UI}} \geq \left\|\frac{U - V}{2}\right\|_{\text{UI}} \tag{12a}$$

for every unitarily invariant norm $\|\cdot\|_{\text{UI}}$, or equivalently,

$$\sigma(H - K) \prec_w \sigma((U - V)/2). \tag{12b}$$

Proof. A direct computation yields the identity

$$\frac{U - V}{2i} = (K + iI)^{-1}(H - K)(H + iI)^{-1}.$$

It follows from 9.H.1 and 5.A.2.b that, for $k = 1, \ldots, n$,

$$\sum_{j=1}^{k} \sigma_j((U - V)/(2i)) \leq \sum_{j=1}^{k} [\sigma_j((K + iI)^{-1})\sigma_j(H - K)\sigma_j((H + iI)^{-1})].$$

But for any Hermitian matrix H, $(H + iI)^*(H + iI) = H^2 + I$, so that $\sigma_j(H + iI) = [\lambda_j(H^2 + I)]^{1/2} \geq 1$; hence, $\sigma_j((H + iI)^{-1}) \leq 1$, $j = 1, \ldots, n$. The proof is completed by noting that $\sigma(iA) = \sigma(-iA) = \sigma(A)$. ∥

B. Matrices Closest to a Given Matrix   375

Matrix That Minimizes the Residual

For any matrix A denote by A^+ the unique matrix that satisfies

$$AA^+A = A,\ A^+AA^+ = A^+,\ (AA^+)^* = AA^+,\ (A^+A)^* = A^+A. \quad (13)$$

The matrix A^+ is called the *pseudoinverse* of A. See Penrose (1955).

B.7. Theorem. Let A, B be $p \times n$ complex matrices. Then for all $n \times n$ matrices X,

$$\|A(A^+B) - B\|_{\mathrm{UI}} \leq \|AX - B\|_{\mathrm{UI}}$$

for every unitarily invariant norm $\|\cdot\|_{\mathrm{UI}}$.

Proof. Let $L = AX - B$, $P = AX - AA^+B$, $Q = B - AA^+B$, so that $L = P - Q$. From (13), it follows that $A^* = A^*AA^+$ and $AA^+ = AA^+AA^+ = A^{+*}A^*AA^+$; a direct computation then yields $P^*Q = 0$. Hence, $L^*L = P^*P + Q^*Q$.

By 20.A.1.b, $\lambda_i(L^*L) \geq \lambda_i(Q^*Q)$; and hence, $\sigma_i(L^*) \geq \sigma_i(Q^*)$, for $i = 1,\ldots,n$, so that $\sigma(L^*) \succ_{\mathrm{w}} \sigma(Q^*)$. This implies that $\|L^*\|_{\mathrm{UI}} \geq \|Q^*\|_{\mathrm{UI}}$, which yields the result (see Remark following A.1). ∥

Theorem B.7 was obtained by Penrose (1956) for Euclidean norms.

B.8. Theorem (Green, 1952; Keller, 1962; Schönemann, 1966). Let A and B be arbitrary real $n \times n$ matrices; let U and V be unitary matrices satisfying the singular value decomposition

$$B^*A = UD_\theta V^*,$$

where $D_\theta = \mathrm{diag}(\theta_1,\ldots,\theta_n)$ and $\theta_1,\ldots,\theta_n$ are the singular values of B^*A.

Then for all unitary matrices Γ,

$$\|A - B(UV^*)\|_{\mathrm{E}} \leq \|A - B\Gamma\|_{\mathrm{E}}.$$

A two-sided version of B.8 can be given.

B.8.a. (Kristof, 1970). Let A and B be arbitrary real $n \times n$ matrices with singular value decompositions

$$A = U_1 D_\alpha V_1, \qquad B = U_2 D_\beta V_2,$$

where U_1, V_1, U_2, V_2 are unitary, $D_\alpha = \mathrm{diag}(\alpha_1,\ldots,\alpha_n)$, $D_\beta = \mathrm{diag}(\beta_1,\ldots,\beta_n)$, and $\alpha_1 \geq \alpha_2 \ldots \geq \alpha_n$ and $\beta_1 \geq \beta_2 \ldots \geq \beta_n$ are the singular values of A and B, respectively. Then for all unitary matrices Γ and Δ,

$$\|A - (V_1^*U_2^*)B(V_2^*U_1^*)\|_{\mathrm{E}} \leq \|A - \Gamma B \Delta\|_{\mathrm{E}}.$$

Remark. Mathias (1993) and Wang, Xi, and Zhang (1999) show that B.8 is not true for arbitrary unitarily invariant norms; however, B.8.a is true for such norms.

B.9. Definition. A matrix A is *normal* if $AA^* = A^*A$.

The class of normal matrices includes symmetric, Hermitian, orthogonal, and unitary matrices. A normal matrix is unitarily diagonalizable. See 9.C.7.

B.10. Theorem (Hoffman and Wielandt, 1953). Suppose A and B are $n \times n$ normal matrices with eigenvalues $\alpha_1, \ldots, \alpha_n$ and $\beta_1, \ldots, \beta_n$, respectively. Then for some permutation matrix P,

$$\min_{VV^*=I} \|D_\alpha - VD_\beta V^*\|_E = \|D_\alpha - PD_\beta P'\|_E, \qquad (14)$$

where $D_\alpha = \mathrm{diag}(\alpha_1, \ldots, \alpha_n)$, $D_\beta = \mathrm{diag}(\beta_1, \ldots, \beta_n)$.

Remark. If A in B.10 is Hermitian with $\alpha_1 \geq \cdots \geq \alpha_n$, and $\mathscr{R}(\beta_1) \geq \cdots \geq \mathscr{R}(\beta_n)$, where $\mathscr{R}(\beta)$ denotes the real part of β, then the minimum in (14) is achieved for $P = I$.

Remark. If the matrices A and B are Hermitian, then Theorem B.10 holds for all unitarily invariant norms, but this is not true in general (Zhang, 1999).

C Condition Numbers and Linear Equations

The term "condition number" is due to Turing (1948). These quantities were introduced to measure the stability of the solution of a system of equations when the coefficients of the system are subjected to a small perturbation. When the solution is stable, the system is called *well-conditioned*; when the solution is unstable, the system is called *ill-conditioned*.

The *condition* or *condition number* of a nonsingular matrix A is usually defined as

$$c_\phi(A) = \phi(A)\phi(A^{-1}),$$

where ordinarily ϕ is a norm. Occasionally a scaling factor is included.

Turing (1948) used $\phi(A) = \max_{i,j}|a_{ij}|$ and $\phi(A) = (\mathrm{tr}\,AA^*)^{1/2}$, whereas von Neumann and Goldstine (1947) used $\phi(A) = \max_i |\lambda_i(A)|$.

General discussions of condition numbers are given in Faddeev and Faddeeva (1963), Forsythe and Moler (1967, pp. 20–26), Todd (1968),

C. Condition Numbers and Linear Equations 377

Bhatia (1997, p. 232), and Horn and Johnson (1985, p. 335). In Section E it is shown how the above definition of the condition of a matrix arises naturally from several alternative points of view.

In solving the system $xA = b$, it may be advantageous to solve instead the system $xAB = bB \equiv c$, where B is chosen to improve the condition of the system; i.e., B is chosen so that $c_\phi(AB) \leq c_\phi(A)$.

An intuitively appealing candidate for B is $B = A^*$, since AA^* is Hermitian, whereas A need not be. However, von Neumann and Goldstine (1947) show that for the norm $\phi(A) = \sigma_1(A)$, symmetrizing in this form does not improve the condition number. Taussky-Todd (1950) showed that the condition number is not improved for $\phi(A) = |\lambda_1(A)|$ and $\phi(A) = (\operatorname{tr} AA^*)^{1/2}$.

The following theorem shows that if the norm ϕ is unitarily invariant, then the condition of the matrix A is better than the condition of AA^*.

C.1. Theorem (Marshall and Olkin, 1965). Let A be an $n \times n$ nonsingular matrix; then

$$c_\phi(A) \leq c_\phi(AA^*); \tag{1}$$

that is,

$$\phi(A)\phi(A^{-1}) \leq \phi(AA^*)\phi((AA^*)^{-1}), \tag{2}$$

for every unitarily invariant norm ϕ.

If ϕ is a unitarily invariant norm, then by A.1 there exists a symmetric gauge function Φ such that

$$\phi(A) = \Phi(\sigma_1(A), \ldots, \sigma_n(A)) \equiv \Phi(\sigma(A)).$$

Note that

$$\sigma_i(A^{-1}) = [\lambda_i(A^{-1}A^{-1*})]^{1/2} = [\lambda_i((A^*A)^{-1})]^{1/2}$$

$$= 1/[\lambda_i(A^*A)]^{1/2} = 1/\sigma_i(A),$$

$$\sigma_i(AA^*) = [\lambda_i((AA^*)^2)]^{1/2} = \lambda_i(AA^*) = \sigma_i^2(A), \quad i = 1, \ldots, n.$$

Write $a_i = \sigma_i(A)$. Then inequality (2) becomes

$$\Phi(a_1, \ldots, a_n)\Phi(a_1^{-1}, \ldots, a_n^{-1}) \leq \Phi(a_1^2, \ldots, a_n^2)\Phi(a_1^{-2}, \ldots, a_n^{-2}). \tag{3}$$

The following theorem provides a stronger result than (3), and hence yields C.1.

C.1.a. Theorem (Marshall and Olkin, 1965). If Φ is a symmetric gauge function, and $a_i > 0$, $i = 1, \ldots, n$, then

$$\Phi(a_1^r, \ldots, a_n^r)\Phi(a_1^{-r}, \ldots, a_n^{-r})$$

is increasing in $r > 0$.

Proof. The following facts are needed:

(i) A symmetric gauge function Φ is Schur-convex (see 3.I.1).

(ii) $\Phi(x_1^{-1}, \ldots, x_n^{-1})$ is Schur-convex on $\mathscr{R}_+^n$ (see 3.I.1.a).

(iii) If $a_1 \geq \cdots \geq a_n > 0$ and, for $i = 1, \ldots, n$ and $0 < r < s$, $u_i = a_i^r / \sum a_j^r$, $v_i = a_i^s / \sum a_j^s$, then $u \prec v$ (see 5.B.2.b).

A consequence of (iii) together with the fact that $\Phi(x_1, \ldots, x_n)$ and $\Phi(x_1^{-1}, \ldots, x_n^{-1})$ are Schur-convex yields

$$\Phi\left(\frac{a_1^r}{\Sigma a_i^r}, \ldots, \frac{a_n^r}{\Sigma a_i^r}\right) \leq \Phi\left(\frac{a_1^s}{\Sigma a_i^s}, \ldots, \frac{a_n^s}{\Sigma a_i^s}\right), \qquad (4)$$

$$\Phi\left(\frac{\Sigma a_i^r}{a_1^r}, \ldots, \frac{\Sigma a_i^r}{a_n^r}\right) \leq \Phi\left(\frac{\Sigma a_i^s}{a_1^s}, \ldots, \frac{\Sigma a_i^s}{a_n^s}\right). \qquad (5)$$

For a scalar c, $\Phi(ca) = |c|\Phi(a)$, so that multiplication of (4) and (5) yields the result. ‖

Remark. In some instances, a lower bound on $c_\phi(A)$ can be obtained to complement (1). If ϕ is a unitarily invariant norm with $\phi(E_{ij}) = 1$, where E_{ij} is the matrix with unity in the (i,j)th place and zeros elsewhere, then

$$[c_\phi(AA^*)]^{1/2} \leq c_\phi(A).$$

This result is obtained by Marshall and Olkin (1965).

The condition $\phi(E_{ij}) = 1$ holds for norms of the form

$$\phi(A) = \left[\sum \sigma_i^p(A)\right]^{1/p}, \qquad p > 0.$$

C.2. Theorem (Marshall, Olkin, and Proschan, 1967). Let H be a positive definite Hermitian matrix, let

$$\psi(H) = u_1 H^{v_1} + \cdots + u_m H^{v_m},$$

where $u_i \geq 0$, $i = 1, \ldots, m$, $1 \leq v_1 \leq \cdots \leq v_m$, $m \leq \infty$, and let ϕ be a unitarily invariant norm. Then

$$c_\phi(H) \leq c_\phi(\psi(H)).$$

This result shows that the Hermitian matrix H is better conditioned than a power of H greater than one, a polynomial or a power series in H. For example, if H and $I - H$ are positive definite Hermitian, then

$$c_\phi(H) \leq c_\phi(H(I - H)^{-1}).$$

Condition of a Perturbed Matrix and Ridge Regression

The result C.1 shows that the condition of AA^* is larger than the condition of A. We now compare the condition of $A + B$ with the condition of A when A is positive definite and B is "small" with respect to A in the sense that its condition is smaller.

A norm ϕ is said to be *monotone* if $\phi(U) \leq \phi(V)$ whenever $V - U$ is positive semidefinite. Unitarily invariant norms are monotone [see Marshall and Olkin (1969)].

C.3. Theorem (Marshall and Olkin, 1969). Let A and B be positive definite Hermitian matrices satisfying

$$c_\phi(B) \leq c_\phi(A), \tag{6}$$

where ϕ is a monotone norm. Then

$$c_\phi(A + B) \leq c_\phi(A). \tag{7}$$

The import of C.3 is as follows. Suppose that $xA = b$ is to be solved for x, where A is positive definite but ill-conditioned. Further suppose $C = A+B$ is better conditioned than A. It is preferable to solve $\widetilde{x}C = b$ for $\widetilde{x}$, provided the solution x can be retrieved. Since $A = C - B$,

$$A^{-1} = C^{-1} + C^{-1}(B^{-1}C) + C^{-1}(B^{-1}C)^2 + C^{-1}(B^{-1}C)^3 + \cdots,$$

so that

$$\begin{aligned} x = bA^{-1} &= bC^{-1} + bC^{-1}(B^{-1}C) + bC^{-1}(B^{-1}C)^2 + \cdots \\ &= \widetilde{x} + \widetilde{x}(B^{-1}C) + \widetilde{x}(B^{-1}C)^2 + \cdots. \end{aligned}$$

Thus, we would like to choose B so that C is well-conditioned and the series for x converges rapidly.

Riley (1955) shows that $B = kI$, where k is a constant that depends on the number of decimals carried, satisfies (6) for any positive definite matrix A. Starting from the context of regression analysis, this is the result of Hoerl and Kennard (1970a, b); this procedure is called *ridge regression*.

Denote by A^+ the pseudoinverse of a matrix A. Klinger (1968) shows that if A is normal and nonsingular, then $c_\phi(A + \epsilon A^{*+}) \leq c_\phi(A)$; Tewarson and Ramnath (1969) obtain the same result without the normality assumption.

D Condition Numbers of Submatrices and Augmented Matrices

Comparisons can be made between the condition numbers of the matrices

$$H = \begin{bmatrix} H_{11} & H_{12} \\ H_{21} & H_{22} \end{bmatrix}, \quad \overline{H} = \begin{bmatrix} H_{11} & 0 \\ 0 & H_{22} \end{bmatrix}, \quad \widehat{H} = \begin{bmatrix} H_{11} & 0 \\ 0 & 0 \end{bmatrix}. \quad (1)$$

Since $\widehat{H}$ is singular, its condition number is defined by substituting the pseudoinverse $\widehat{H}^+$ for the inverse.

D.1. Let H be a positive definite Hermitian matrix partitioned as in (1), and let ϕ be a unitarily invariant norm. Then

$$c_\phi(H) \geq c_\phi(\overline{H}) \geq c_\phi(\widehat{H}). \quad (2)$$

Proof. From 9.C.1 and 9.C.1.b, $\lambda(H) \succ \lambda(\overline{H}) \succ_w \lambda(\widehat{H})$, and because $\lambda(H) \geq 0$, $\sigma(H) \succ \sigma(\overline{H}) \succ_w \sigma(\widehat{H})$. Consequently, it follows from A.1 that for any symmetric gauge function Φ,

$$\Phi(\sigma_1(H), \ldots, \sigma_n(H)) \geq \Phi(\sigma_1(\overline{H}), \ldots, \sigma_n(\overline{H})) \geq \Phi(\sigma_1(\widehat{H}), \ldots, \sigma_n(\widehat{H})).$$

By (ii) in the proof of C.1.a,

$$\Phi([\sigma_1(H)]^{-1}, \ldots, [\sigma_n(H)]^{-1}) \geq \Phi([\sigma_1(\overline{H})]^{-1}, \ldots, [\sigma_n(\overline{H})]^{-1})$$
$$\geq \Phi(\sigma_1(\widehat{H}^+), \ldots, \sigma_n(\widehat{H}^+)).$$

By combining these results, (2) follows. ||

D.2. Theorem (Marshall and Olkin, 1973b). Let A be an $m \times n$ matrix of rank k, and let ϕ be a unitarily invariant norm. Then for all $n \times q$ matrices U satisfying $U^*U = I$ and $\text{rank}(A^*, U) = \text{rank } A^*$,

$$c_\phi(AU) \leq c_\phi(A).$$

E Condition Numbers and Norms

In this section we show how the condition of a matrix arises in the context of linear equations, least squares, and eigenvalues.

E.1. Solution of linear equations. Consider a system of linear equations

$$xA = b. \quad (1)$$

If b is perturbed by an amount Δb, then the solution is also perturbed; i.e.,

$$(x + \Delta x)A = b + \Delta b. \tag{2}$$

Let $\|\cdot\|$ be a vector norm and let

$$\|A\| = \sup_x \frac{\|xA\|}{\|x\|}$$

be its subordinate matrix norm. Notice that $\|xA\| \leq \|x\|\|A\|$. [For a discussion of subordinate norms, see Householder (1964, Section 2.2).]

From (1), $\|b\| = \|xA\| \leq \|x\|\|A\|$, and from (2),

$$\|\Delta x\| = \|\Delta b\, A^{-1}\| \leq \|\Delta b\|\|A^{-1}\|,$$

so that

$$\frac{\|\Delta x\|}{\|x\|} \leq \|A\|\|A^{-1}\|\frac{\|\Delta b\|}{\|b\|} = c(A)\frac{\|\Delta b\|}{\|b\|}.$$

That is, the relative uncertainty in the solution vector x with respect to the relative uncertainty in the data vector b is bounded by the condition of A.

Suppose now that A is perturbed by an amount ΔA. Then the solution of (1) is perturbed by Δx, where

$$(x + \Delta x)(A + \Delta A) = b, \tag{3}$$

i.e., $\Delta x = -(x+\Delta x)(\Delta A)A^{-1}$, so that $\|\Delta x\| \leq \|A^{-1}\|\|\Delta A\|\|x+\Delta x\|$. Consequently,

$$\frac{\|\Delta x\|}{\|x + \Delta x\|} \leq \|A\|\|A^{-1}\|\frac{\|\Delta A\|}{\|A\|}.$$

That is, the uncertainty in x relative to $x + \Delta x$ as compared to the relative uncertainty in A is bounded by the condition of A.

E.2. A least-squares model. Consider a linear regression model of a dependent variable y on p regression variables $x_1, \ldots, x_p$. For a sample of n observations, the model is

$$y \equiv (y_1, \ldots, y_n) = (\beta_1, \ldots, \beta_p)X + (v_1, \ldots, v_n), \tag{4}$$

where X is a $p \times n$ matrix of rank $p \leq n$. The error vector v is random with mean zero and covariance matrix $\text{Cov}(v) = \Sigma$. The vector β is unknown and is to be estimated.

If Σ is known, then this information is taken into account by the renormalization

$$\widetilde{y} \equiv y\Sigma^{1/2} = \beta X \Sigma^{1/2} + v\Sigma^{-1/2} \equiv \beta \widetilde{X} + \widetilde{v}.$$

382   10. Numerical Analysis

The least-squares estimate of β obtained by minimizing $\|\widetilde{y} - \beta\widetilde{X}\|$ is given by

$$\widetilde{b} = \widetilde{y}\widetilde{X}'(\widetilde{X}\widetilde{X}')^{-1} = y\Sigma^{-1}X'(X\Sigma^{-1}X')^{-1}.$$

On the other hand, the method of least squares applied to (4) yields the estimator

$$b = yX'(XX')^{-1}.$$

The efficiency of b with respect to $\widetilde{b}$ is a function of the covariance matrices of the two estimates, namely,

$$\mathrm{Cov}(\widetilde{b}) = (X\Sigma^{-1}X')^{-1},$$
$$\mathrm{Cov}(b) = (XX')^{-1}(X\Sigma X')(XX')^{-1}.$$

Comparisons can be made in a variety of ways. One such is to consider the norm of the "ratio" of covariance matrices

$$\|(X\Sigma^{-1}X')[(XX')^{-1}X\Sigma X'(XX')^{-1}]\| = \|(U\Sigma^{-1}U')(U\Sigma U')\|, \quad (5)$$

where $U = (XX')^{-1/2}X$ is a $p \times n$ matrix satisfying $UU' = I$.

If this same model is used with various design matrices X (or, equivalently, various matrices U), then it may be of interest to compute the upper bound of (5) over all matrices X; i.e.,

$$\sup_{UU'=I_p} \|(U\Sigma^{-1}U')(U\Sigma U')\|. \quad (6)$$

The following theorem shows that for a unitarily invariant multiplicative norm, i.e., a unitarily invariant norm satisfying $\|AB\| \leq \|A\|\|B\|$, the upper bound of (6) is the condition number of Σ. This provides a measure of the loss in efficiency for not knowing Σ. [For a general discussion of the efficiency of least-squares estimates, see Watson (1955).]

E.2.a. Let Σ be a positive definite Hermitian matrix, and let $\|\cdot\|_{\mathrm{UIM}}$ be a unitarily invariant multiplicative norm. Then for all $p \times n$ $(p \leq n)$ matrices U satisfying $UU^* = I$,

$$\|(U\Sigma^{-1}U^*)(U\Sigma U^*)\|_{\mathrm{UIM}} \leq \|\Sigma\|_{\mathrm{UIM}}\|\Sigma^{-1}\|_{\mathrm{UIM}}. \quad (7)$$

Proof. A $p \times n$ matrix U satisfying $UU^* = I$ can be written as $(I_k, 0)V$, where V is an $n \times n$ unitary matrix. Let $\psi = V\Sigma V^*$, so that (7) becomes

$$\left\| [I\ 0]\, \psi^{-1} \begin{bmatrix} I \\ 0 \end{bmatrix} [I\ 0]\, \psi \begin{bmatrix} I \\ 0 \end{bmatrix} \right\|_{\mathrm{UIM}} \leq \|\psi\|_{\mathrm{UIM}}\|\psi^{-1}\|_{\mathrm{UIM}}. \quad (8)$$

E. Condition Numbers and Norms   383

Starting with the left-hand side of (8), we obtain

$$\left\| [I \ 0] \, \psi^{-1} \begin{bmatrix} I & 0 \\ 0 & 0 \end{bmatrix} \psi \begin{bmatrix} I \\ 0 \end{bmatrix} \right\|_{\mathrm{UIM}} = \left\| \psi^{-1} \begin{bmatrix} I & 0 \\ 0 & 0 \end{bmatrix} \psi \begin{bmatrix} I & 0 \\ 0 & 0 \end{bmatrix} \right\|_{\mathrm{UIM}}$$

$$\leq \|\psi^{-1}\|_{\mathrm{UIM}} \left\| \begin{bmatrix} \psi_{11} & 0 \\ 0 & 0 \end{bmatrix} \right\|_{\mathrm{UIM}}$$

$$\leq \|\psi^{-1}\|_{\mathrm{UIM}} \|\psi\|_{\mathrm{UIM}}$$

$$= \|\Sigma^{-1}\|_{\mathrm{UIM}} \|\Sigma\|_{\mathrm{UIM}}.$$

The last inequality follows from D.1 and the last equality follows from the unitary invariance of the norm. ∥

E.3. Eigenvalues. If an $n \times n$ matrix A has distinct eigenvalues, then by 19.A.2 there exists a matrix S such that

$$SAS^{-1} = \mathrm{diag}(\lambda_1(A), \ldots, \lambda_n(A)).$$

If A is perturbed by a small matrix B, then it is of interest to measure how much any eigenvalue of $A+B$ can deviate from the eigenvalues of A. Let $\|x\|$ denote the norm of a finite-dimensional vector x, and let $\|A\|$ denote any matrix norm "consistent" with the vector norm, i.e., satisfying $\|xA\| \leq \|A\|\|x\|$. Then

$$\min_{1 \leq i \leq n} |\lambda_j(A+B) - \lambda_i(A)|/\|B\| \leq c(S),$$

where $\lambda_j(A+B)$ is any eigenvalue of $A+B$ and $c(S) = \|S\|\|S^{-1}\|$ is the condition number of S. For a proof of this result, see Bauer and Fike (1960).

Part III

Stochastic Applications

11
Stochastic Majorizations

A comparison between two random vectors X and Y might be called a *stochastic majorization* if the comparison reduces to the ordinary majorization $x \prec y$ in case X and Y are degenerate at x and y; i.e.,

$$P\{X = x\} = 1, \qquad P\{Y = y\} = 1.$$

Similarly, the comparison might be called a *stochastic weak majorization* if it reduces to a weak majorization $x \prec_w y$ or $x \prec^w y$ for degenerate random vectors. A number of such concepts of stochastic majorization and stochastic weak majorization can be defined. Notable published works on this subject may be found in the papers of Nevius, Proschan, and Sethuraman (1977a, b), where one important notion of stochastic majorization and stochastic weak majorization is studied. The work of these authors appears particularly in Sections D and E.

A   Introduction

Perhaps the most obvious notion of stochastic majorization is the condition

$$P\{(X_1, \ldots, X_n) \prec (Y_1, \ldots, Y_n)\} = 1. \qquad (1)$$

This is a very strong condition which involves not only the distributions of X and Y but also the joint distribution. A modification of (1) that eliminates this possible objection is given ahead in (4).

More useful concepts of stochastic majorization are suggested by certain theorems which give conditions equivalent to majorization. In particular, suppose $\mathscr{C}$ is some class of well-behaved functions defined on $\mathscr{R}^n$ with the property that

$$x \prec y \text{ if and only if } \phi(x) \leq \phi(y) \quad \text{for all} \quad \phi \in \mathscr{C}. \quad (2)$$

For example, $\mathscr{C}$ might consist of all continuous symmetric convex functions defined on $\mathscr{R}^n$ or it might consist of functions ϕ having the form $\phi(x) = \sum \psi(x_i)$, where $\psi : \mathscr{R} \to \mathscr{R}$ is continuous and convex.

The notation $X \leq^{st} Y$ means that X is stochastically less than or equal to Y (see 17.A).

For any class $\mathscr{C}$ satisfying (2), two kinds of stochastic majorization conditions are suggested by 17.A.2:

$$P_\mathscr{C}: \quad \phi(X) \leq^{st} \phi(Y) \quad \text{for all} \quad \phi \in \mathscr{C},$$

and

$$E_\mathscr{C}: \quad E\phi(X) \leq E\phi(Y) \quad \text{for all} \quad \phi \in \mathscr{C} \text{ such that all the expectations are defined.}$$

Of course, $P_\mathscr{C} \Rightarrow E_\mathscr{C}$ because stochastically ordered random variables have ordered expectations. If $\mathscr{C}$ and $\widetilde{\mathscr{C}}$ both satisfy (2) and if $\mathscr{C} \subset \widetilde{\mathscr{C}}$, then it is immediate that

$$P_{\widetilde{\mathscr{C}}} \Rightarrow P_\mathscr{C} \quad \text{and} \quad E_{\widetilde{\mathscr{C}}} \Rightarrow E_\mathscr{C}.$$

Thus the conditions $P_\mathscr{C}$ and $E_\mathscr{C}$ are strongest when $\mathscr{C}$ is as large as possible, i.e., when $\mathscr{C}$ consists of all Schur-convex functions ϕ sufficiently well behaved that the expectations are defined. At the other extreme, one might take

$$\mathscr{C} = \left\{ \phi : \phi(x) = \sum_1^k x_{[i]} \text{ for some } k = 1, \ldots, n, \text{ or } \phi(x) = -\sum_1^n x_i \right\}.$$

There are a number of intermediate possibilities for $\mathscr{C}$, but most of the resulting stochastic majorization conditions are not well understood. In this book, more than passing attention is given to only two possibilities:

$\mathscr{C}_1 = \{\phi : \phi$ is a real-valued Borel-measurable Schur-convex function defined on $\mathscr{R}^n\}$

and

$\mathscr{C}_2 = \{\phi : \phi$ is a real-valued continuous, symmetric, and convex function defined on $\mathscr{R}^n\}$.

A. Introduction 389

These are cases for which useful methods are known for identifying interesting examples. Below, we write P_i in place of $P_{\mathscr{C}_i}$ and E_i in place of $E_{\mathscr{C}_i}$, $i = 1, 2$.

For some possible choices of $\mathscr{C}$, it is true that

$$\phi \in \mathscr{C} \Rightarrow I_{\{Z:\phi(Z)>t\}} \in \mathscr{C} \qquad \text{for all} \quad t. \tag{3}$$

For example, (3) is satisfied if $\mathscr{C} = \mathscr{C}_1$ or $\mathscr{C}$ consists of the Borel-measurable symmetric quasi-convex functions (see 3.C.3). When (3) holds, $E_{\mathscr{C}} \Rightarrow P_{\mathscr{C}}$ because $P\{\phi(X) > t\} = EI_{\{Z:\phi(Z)>t\}}(X)$. Property (3) fails for $\mathscr{C} = \mathscr{C}_2$.

The above arguments establish the following relationships:

$$\begin{array}{ccc} P_1 & \Rightarrow & P_2 \\ \Updownarrow & & \Downarrow \\ E_1 & \Rightarrow & E_2. \end{array}$$

It is shown in F.9.a and F.9.b that $E_2 \not\Rightarrow P_2$ and $P_2 \not\Rightarrow P_1$, so that implications not obtainable from the diagram are false.

Although condition (1) is stronger than E_1 (P_1), there is an interesting intimate connection between these conditions that was pointed out to us by Tom Snijders. In fact, E_1 (and P_1) are equivalent to the following modification of (1):

There exist random variables U and V such that

(i) U and X have the same distribution, as do V and Y,

(ii) U and V satisfy (1). (4)

The proof that E_1 and (4) are equivalent is an application of 17.B.6.

Observe that every condition $P_{\mathscr{C}}$ is equivalent to $E_{\widetilde{\mathscr{C}}}$ in case $\widetilde{\mathscr{C}}$ consists of all indicator functions of sets A having the form

$$A = \{z : \phi(z) > t\}$$

for some $\phi \in \mathscr{C}$ and some $t \in \mathscr{R}$. On the other hand, it appears unlikely that every $E_{\mathscr{C}}$ condition is equivalent to $P_{\mathscr{C}^*}$ for some class $\mathscr{C}^*$ of functions.

Note. Rüschendorf (1981) shows that in the definition of the ordering E_1, the class $\mathscr{C}_1$ can be replaced by the subclass of $\mathscr{C}_1$ including its nonnegative bounded continuous members.

Some Notation

When X and Y satisfy condition $P_{\mathscr{C}}$, we write

$$X \prec^{P_{\mathscr{C}}} Y;$$

similarly,

$$X \prec^{E_{\mathscr{C}}} Y$$

means that X and Y satisfy condition $E_{\mathscr{C}}$.

For certain random variables X and Y, condition E_2 is vacuous. Even with $n = 1$, it may be that $E\phi(X)$ and $E\phi(Y)$ are equal or together undefined for all continuous convex functions ϕ. This happens, for example, when X and Y have Cauchy distributions. In this case, the expectations may be $+\infty$, $-\infty$, or undefined; they exist finitely only if ϕ is a constant.

Random vectors to be compared by a stochastic majorization often have distributions belonging to the same parametric family, where the parameter space is a subset of $\mathscr{R}^n$. In these examples, random variables X and Y having corresponding distributions F_θ and $F_{\theta'}$ are ordered by stochastic majorization if and only if the parameters θ and θ' are ordered by ordinary majorization. To be more specific, let $A \subset \mathscr{R}^n$ and let $\{F_\theta, \theta \in A\}$ be a family of n-dimensional distribution functions indexed by a vector-valued parameter θ. Let

$$P_\theta\{\phi(X) > t\} = \int_{\{\phi(x)>t\}} dF_\theta(x)$$

denote the probability that $\phi(X)$ exceeds t when X has distribution F_θ, and let

$$E_\theta \phi(X) = \int_{\mathscr{R}^n} \phi(x)\, dF_\theta(x)$$

denote the expectation of $\phi(X)$ when X has distribution F_θ.

A. Introduction   391

The above approach to stochastic majorization suggests the following conditions:

$P_{\mathscr{C}}^*$: $P_\theta\{\phi(X) > t\}$ is Schur-convex in θ for all $\phi \in \mathscr{C}$ and all t,

$E_{\mathscr{C}}^*$: $E_\theta\phi(X)$ is Schur-convex in θ for all $\phi \in \mathscr{C}$ such that the expectations are defined.

If X_θ has distribution F_θ, then $P_{\mathscr{C}}^*$ means $X_\theta \prec^{P_{\mathscr{C}}} X_{\theta'}$ when $\theta \prec \theta'$ and $E_{\mathscr{C}}^*$ means $X_\theta \prec^{E_{\mathscr{C}}} X_{\theta'}$ when $\theta \prec \theta'$. Below we write E_i^* and P_i^* in place of $E_{\mathscr{C}_i}^*$ and $P_{\mathscr{C}_i}^*$.

Stronger conditions might be imposed, namely, that $P_\theta\{\phi(X) > t\}$ or $E_\theta\phi(X)$ (as functions of θ) are themselves in $\mathscr{C}$ or in some other subset of the Schur-convex functions. A particular case is of interest, namely,

E_2^{**}: $E_\theta\phi(X)$ is a continuous symmetric convex function of θ for all continuous symmetric convex functions ϕ such that the expectation exists.

Condition P_2^{**} is similarly defined. Notice that E_2^{**} and P_2^{**} are concerned with the preservation of symmetry and convexity, whereas E_1^* and P_1^* are concerned with the preservation of Schur-convexity. In this sense, these concepts are companions. Such preservation properties are more useful in compounding than are properties like E_2^* and P_2^* (see Table 1).

Compounding Families of Distribution Functions

If $\{F_\theta, \theta \in A\}$ is a family of distribution functions, then by treating θ as a random variable with distribution function G_λ, one comes (with obvious measurability conditions) to the distribution function H_λ defined by

$$H_\lambda(x) = \int F_\theta(x)\, dG_\lambda(\theta).$$

The family $\{H_\lambda, \lambda \in B\}$ of *compound distributions* is obtained from $\{F_\theta, \theta \in A\}$ by the compounding distributions $\{G_\lambda, \lambda \in B\}$.

Suppose that $\{F_\theta, \theta \in A\}$ and $\{G_\lambda, \lambda \in B\}$ both satisfy E_1^*. If ϕ is Schur-convex, then $\int \phi(x)\, dF_\theta(x)$ is a Schur-convex function of θ, so

$$\int\int \phi(x)\, dF_\theta(x)\, dG_\lambda(\theta) = \int \phi(x)\, dH_\lambda(x)$$

is a Schur-convex function of λ. Thus $\{H_\lambda, \lambda \in B\}$ satisfies E_1^*. Similar arguments lead to a variety of such results, which are tabulated in Table 1.

Table 1
Conditions inherited by H_λ in compounding F_θ and G_λ.

Assumptions on	$\{F_\theta, \theta \in A\}$ $\{G_\lambda, \lambda \in B\}$	E_1^* E_1^*	E_2^{**} E_2^{**}	E_2^* E_1^*	P_2^{**} E_2^{**}	P_2^* E_1^*
Conclusions about $\{H_\lambda, \lambda \in B\}$		E_1^*	E_2^{**}	E_2^*	P_2^{**}	P_2^*

Sometimes the easiest way to obtain one of these conditions for a family of distributions is to observe that the distributions can be represented as compound distributions.

B Convex Functions and Exchangeable Random Variables

Suppose that Φ is a function of two vector arguments; that is, $\Phi : \mathscr{R}^{2n} \to \mathscr{R}$. In this section, conditions on Φ and on the random vector $X = (X_1, \ldots, X_n)$ are obtained that ensure

$$\psi(a) = E\Phi(X; a)$$

is a symmetric convex function of $a = (a_1, \ldots, a_n)$. A result of this kind together with some of its implications was obtained by Marshall and Proschan (1965). Such results have interest beyond the topic of stochastic majorization. They are presented here because they provide indispensable tools for demonstrating the property E_2^{**}.

In all cases, it is assumed that $X_1, \ldots, X_n$ are *exchangeable* random variables, i.e., that the distribution of $X_{\pi(1)}, \ldots, X_{\pi(n)}$ does not depend upon the permutation π. This is just a way of saying that the joint distribution of $X_1, \ldots, X_n$ is invariant under permutations of its arguments. For example, independent and identically distributed random variables are exchangeable. More generally, suppose that $\{F^{(a)}, a \in \mathscr{A}\}$ is an indexed family of univariate probability distributions. With appropriate measure-theoretic requirements, suppose that F is a distribution function of the form

$$F(x) = \int_{\mathscr{A}} \prod_i F^{(a)}(x_i)\, dP(a) \qquad (1)$$

B. Convex Functions and Exchangeable Random Variables

for some probability measure P defined on subsets of $\mathscr{A}$. Then F is the distribution of exchangeable random variables, but the distribution of exchangeable random variables need not have this special form [e.g., when F places mass $\frac{1}{2}$ at each of the points $(-1, 1)$ and $(1, -1)$ in $\mathscr{R}^2$ or F is a bivariate normal distribution with equal means, equal variances, and negative correlation]. Of course, if G is any distribution function on $\mathscr{R}^n$, then

$$F(x) = \frac{1}{n!} \sum_\pi G(x_{\pi(1)}, \ldots, x_{\pi(n)})$$

is the distribution of exchangeable random variables. Distributions having the form of (1) arise in Section 12.D, where they are called *positively dependent by mixture*.

When $X_1, \ldots, X_n$ are exchangeable, there are two prime examples for which $\psi(a) = E\Phi(X; a)$ is a symmetric convex function of a. These examples are

$$\Phi(x; a) = \phi(a_1 x_1, \ldots, a_n x_n),$$

where $\phi : \mathscr{R}^n \to \mathscr{R}$ is symmetric and convex, or

$$\Phi(x; a) = \phi(x_1 - a_1, \ldots, x_n - a_n),$$

where again $\phi : \mathscr{R}^n \to \mathscr{R}$ is symmetric and convex. In these cases, the vector a can be thought of as a vector of scale parameters or as a vector of location parameters.

B.1. Proposition. Let $X_1, \ldots, X_n$ be exchangeable random variables and suppose that $\Phi : \mathscr{R}^{2n} \to \mathscr{R}$ satisfies

(i) $\Phi(x; a)$ is convex in a for each fixed x,
(ii) $\Phi(x\Pi; a\Pi) = \Phi(x; a)$ for all permutations Π,
(iii) $\Phi(x; a)$ is Borel-measurable in x for each fixed a.

Then

$$\psi(a) = E\Phi(X; a)$$

is symmetric and convex.

Proof. The convexity of ψ is immediate from (i). To show that ψ is symmetric, it is necessary to use the exchangeability of $X_1, \ldots, X_n$ and (ii);

$$\psi(a\Pi) = E\Phi(X, a\Pi) = E\Phi(X\Pi, a\Pi) = E\Phi(X, a) = \psi(a). \quad \|$$

B.2. Proposition. If $X_1, \ldots, X_n$ are exchangeable random variables and $\phi: \mathscr{R}^n \to \mathscr{R}$ is a symmetric Borel-measurable convex function, then the function ψ defined by

$$\psi(a_1, \ldots, a_n) = E\phi(a_1 X_1, \ldots, a_n X_n)$$

is symmetric and convex. Thus, ψ is Schur-convex, so that $\widetilde{a} \prec a$ implies $\psi(\widetilde{a}) \leq \psi(a)$.

Although a direct proof of this proposition is easy (by mimicking the proof of B.1), it is also easy to verify the conditions of B.1 with $\Phi(x;a) = \phi(a_1 x_1, \ldots, a_n x_n)$.

The fact that ψ, as defined in B.2, is Schur-convex is due to Marshall and Proschan (1965). This fact has a simple direct proof that is analogous to the proof of 3.C.2. By 3.A.5, it is sufficient to prove the result for $n=2$ with the other variables suppressed. In this case, $a \succ b$ means that for some α, $0 \leq \alpha \leq 1$, $\overline{\alpha} = 1 - \alpha$,

$$b_1 = \alpha a_1 + \overline{\alpha} a_2, \qquad b_2 = \overline{\alpha} a_1 + \alpha a_2.$$

Thus

$$\begin{aligned} E\phi(b_1 X_1, b_2 X_2) &= E\phi((\alpha a_1 + \overline{\alpha} a_2) X_1, (\overline{\alpha} a_1 + \alpha a_2) X_2) \\ &= E\phi(\alpha(a_1 X_1, a_2 X_2) + \overline{\alpha}(a_2 X_1, a_1 X_2)) \\ &\leq \alpha E\phi(a_1 X_1, a_2 X_2) + \overline{\alpha} E\phi(a_2 X_1, a_1 X_2) \\ &= E\phi(a_1 X_1, a_2 X_2). \end{aligned}$$

A generalization of this result is given in 15.D.3.

There are several simple consequences of B.2.

B.2.a. Proposition. Suppose that numbers $t_1, \ldots, t_n$ exist such that

$$P\{(X_1, \ldots, X_n) = (t_{\pi(1)}, \ldots, t_{\pi(n)})\} = 1/n!$$

for all permutations π. If ϕ is a symmetric Borel-measurable convex function, then according to B.1,

$$\psi(a) = \frac{1}{n!} \sum_\pi \phi(a_1 t_{\pi(1)}, \ldots, a_n t_{\pi(n)})$$

is symmetric and convex.

Proof. This conclusion also follows from 3.G.2.a; it can be used to provide an alternative proof of B.2. ||

Various consequences of 3.G.2.a can be obtained from B.2 using the above distribution. In particular, Muirhead's theorem 3.G.2.e is a consequence of B.2.

B. Convex Functions and Exchangeable Random Variables

B.2.b. Proposition (Marshall and Proschan, 1965). If $g: \mathscr{R} \to \mathscr{R}$ is continuous and convex, and if $X_1, X_2, \ldots$ is a sequence of independent, identically distributed random variables with distribution function F, then

$$Eg\left(\sum_1^n \frac{X_i}{n}\right) = \int_{-\infty}^{\infty} g\left(\frac{x}{n}\right) dF^{(n)}(x)$$

is nonincreasing in $n = 1, 2, \ldots$, where $F^{(n)}$ is the nth convolution of F.

Proof. If $a = ((n-1)^{-1}, \ldots, (n-1)^{-1}, 0)$ and $\tilde{a} = (n^{-1}, \ldots, n^{-1})$, then $a \succ \tilde{a}$, so that the result follows from B.2 with $\phi(z_1, \ldots, z_n) = \sum g(z_i)$. ∥

In case $X_1, X_2, \ldots$ are not independent but only exchangeable, then the monotonicity of $Eg(\sum_1^n X_i/n)$ is still present, although this expectation can no longer be written simply in terms of a convolution.

B.2.c. If $X_1, \ldots, X_n$ are exchangeable and g is a continuous convex function, then

$$\psi(a_1, \ldots, a_n) = Eg\left(\sum a_i X_i\right)$$

is symmetric and convex.

This generalization of B.2.b is a special case of B.2.

B.2.d. (Marshall and Proschan, 1965). If $X_1, X_2, \ldots$ is a sequence of exchangeable random variables, then

$$n^{-1} E \max[0, X_1, \ldots, X_n] \qquad (2)$$

is nonincreasing in $n = 1, 2, \ldots$.

Proof. This follows from B.2 with $\phi(z_1, \ldots, z_n) = \max(0, z_1, \ldots, z_n)$, using the same a and $\tilde{a}$ as in the proof of B.2.b. ∥

It was pointed out to us by Tom Snijders that if $P\{X_1 > 0\} > 0$, then (2) is strictly decreasing in $n = 1, 2, \ldots$.

B.3. Proposition. If $X_1, \ldots, X_n$ are exchangeable random variables and ϕ is a symmetric Borel-measurable convex function, then the function ψ defined by

$$\psi(a_1, \ldots, a_n) = E\phi(X + a)$$

is symmetric and convex.

Proof. Let $\Phi(x,a) = \phi(x+a)$. Then the conditions of B.1 are clearly satisfied. ‖

Proposition B.3 is to be compared with E.5.

B.4. Proposition. Let $X_1, \ldots, X_n$ be exchangeable random variables. Let $\Phi(x;a) = \phi(w(x_1,a_1), \ldots, w(x_n,a_n))$, where ϕ is symmetric, convex and increasing (decreasing), and $w(z,\alpha)$ is convex (concave) in α for each fixed z. With the appropriate measurability,

$$\psi(a) = E\Phi(X;a)$$

is symmetric and convex.

Proof. The result follows from B.1. Condition (i) is proved in 16.B.7 and 16.B.7.a; the permutation invariance condition (ii) is trivial. ‖

In the study of weak majorization, it is of interest to know when ψ is increasing or decreasing as well as symmetric and convex. The obvious modification required in B.1 to get this monotonicity is that $\Phi(x;a)$ must be increasing or decreasing in a for each fixed x. This leads to a result similar to B.4.

B.5. Proposition. Let $X_1, \ldots, X_n$ be exchangeable random variables. If ϕ and w satisfy any of the conditions of Table 2, then $\psi(a) = E\phi(w(X_1,a_1), \ldots, w(X_n,a_n))$ satisfies the corresponding indicated conditions (with measurability conditions required for the expectation to be defined).

Table 2
$\psi(a_1, \ldots, a_n) = E\phi(w(X_1,a_1), \ldots, w(X_n,a_n))$.

$w(x,a)$	ϕ	ψ
Convex and increasing in a	Symmetric, convex, increasing	Symmetric, convex, increasing
Convex and decreasing in a	Symmetric, convex, increasing	Symmetric, convex, decreasing
Concave and decreasing in a	Symmetric, convex, decreasing	Symmetric, convex, increasing
Concave and increasing in a	Symmetric, convex, decreasing	Symmetric, convex, decreasing

B.5.a. Proposition. If $X_1, \ldots, X_n$ are nonnegative exchangeable random variables and $\phi : \mathscr{R}^n \to \mathscr{R}$ is Borel-measurable, increasing (decreasing), symmetric, and convex, then the function ψ defined by

$$\psi(a_1, \ldots, a_n) = E\phi(a_1 X_1, \ldots, a_n X_n)$$

is Borel-measurable, increasing (decreasing), symmetric, and convex.

Proof. This is an application of B.5, where $w(x, a) = ax$ is convex and increasing in a for all $x \geq 0$. ||

A result similar to B.5.a was obtained by Chong (1976a); he concludes that ψ is increasing (decreasing) and Schur-convex.

B.5.b. Proposition. If $X_1, \ldots, X_n$ are exchangeable random variables and $\phi : \mathscr{R}^n \to \mathscr{R}$ is Borel-measurable, increasing (decreasing), symmetric, and convex, then the function ψ defined by

$$\psi(a_1, \ldots, a_n) = E\phi(X_1 + a_1, \ldots, X_n + a_n)$$

is Borel-measurable, increasing (decreasing), symmetric, and convex.

Proof. This result follows directly from B.5. ||

Comments About Extensions

It was observed by Eaton and Olshen (1972) that the Schur-convexity of ψ implied by B.2 holds when $X_1, \ldots, X_n$ are exchangeable random vectors, and the proof of Marshall and Proschan (1965) requires no change. A similar comment applies to B.1 with the domain of Φ suitably altered. By the same token, $X_1, \ldots, X_n$ can be exchangeable random matrices. Further generalizations of B.1 play an important role in multivariate versions of majorization; these are discussed in Section 15.D.

C Families of Distributions Parameterized to Preserve Symmetry and Convexity

For $A \subset \mathscr{R}^n$, let $\{F_\theta, \theta \in A\}$ be a family of distribution functions defined on $\mathscr{R}^n$, and let

$$\psi(\theta) = E_\theta \phi(X) = \int \phi(x)\, dF_\theta(x), \qquad \theta \in A.$$

Under what circumstances is it true that ψ is symmetric and convex whenever ϕ is symmetric and convex? This property depends not only on the family $\{F_\theta, \theta \in A\}$ but also upon the way the family is parameterized. Of course, it is natural to expect A to be a convex set, although this is not essential.

C.1. Definition. The family $\{F_\theta, \theta \in A \subset \mathscr{R}^n\}$ of distribution functions defined on $\mathscr{R}^n$ is said to be *parameterized to preserve symmetry and convexity* if $\psi(\theta) = E_\theta \phi(X)$ is continuous, symmetric, and convex whenever the expectations are defined and ϕ is continuous, symmetric, and convex (or in other words, the family satisfies E_2^{**}).

The purpose of this section is to give a number of examples of families parameterized to preserve symmetry and convexity.

Of course, if ψ is symmetric and convex, then ψ is Schur-convex. Families that preserve Schur-convexity (ψ is Schur-convex whenever ϕ is Schur-convex) are considered in Section E.

The following examples of families parameterized to preserve symmetry and convexity can be obtained as consequences of B.1.

C.1.a. Suppose $\theta \in \mathscr{R}_{++}^n$ is a scale parameter; i.e.,

$$F_\theta(x) = F_e(x_1/\theta_1, \ldots, x_n/\theta_n), \quad \text{where} \quad e = (1, \ldots, 1). \quad (1)$$

If F_e is the distribution of exchangeable random variables, i.e.,

$$F_e(x) = F_e(x\Pi) \quad \text{for all permutation matrices } \Pi, \quad (2)$$

then it follows from B.2 that the distributions F_θ form a family that preserves symmetry and convexity, because

$$E_\theta \phi(X) = E_{(1,\ldots,1)} \phi(\theta_1 X_1, \ldots, \theta_n X_n).$$

C.1.b. Similarly, if $\theta \in \mathscr{R}^n$ is a location parameter; i.e.,

$$F_\theta(x) = F_\mathbf{0}(x - \theta), \quad \text{where} \quad \mathbf{0} = (0, \ldots, 0), \quad (3)$$

and if $F_\mathbf{0}$ is the distribution of exchangeable random variables, i.e.,

$$F_\mathbf{0}(x) = F_\mathbf{0}(x\Pi) \quad \text{for all permutation matrices } \Pi, \quad (4)$$

then it follows from B.3 that the distributions F_θ form a family that preserves symmetry and convexity, because

$$E_\theta \phi(X) = E_{(0,\ldots,0)} \phi(X - \theta).$$

These facts are stated formally in the following proposition.

C.2. Proposition. Suppose that $\{F_\theta, \theta \in \mathscr{R}_{++}^n\}$ is a family of distribution functions satisfying (1) and (2), or alternatively suppose that $\{F_\theta, \theta \in \mathscr{R}^n\}$ is a family of distribution functions satisfying (3) and (4).

C. Parameterization to Preserve Symmetry and Convexity

Then $\psi(\theta) = E_\theta \phi(X)$ is a continuous symmetric convex function of θ whenever ϕ is continuous, symmetric, and convex.

Examples of Families That Preserve Symmetry and Convexity

In the following examples, Proposition C.2 is applied to some familiar families of distributions.

Exchangeable Normal Random Variables

C.2.a. Let $Y_1 = X_1 - \mu_1, \ldots, Y_n = X_n - \mu_n$ be exchangeable multivariate normal random variables with expectations 0, variances σ^2, and covariances $\sigma^2 \rho$. If ϕ is symmetric and convex, then

$$\psi(\mu_1, \ldots, \mu_n) = E_\mu \phi(X_1, \ldots, X_n)$$

is symmetric and convex in $\mu_1, \ldots, \mu_n$.

C.2.b. Let $Y_1 = X_1/\sigma_1, \ldots, Y_n = X_n/\sigma_n$ be exchangeable multivariate normal random variables, with expectations μ, variances 1, and covariances ρ. If ϕ is symmetric and convex, then

$$\psi(\sigma_1, \ldots, \sigma_n) = E_\sigma \phi(X_1, \ldots, X_n)$$

is symmetric and convex in $\sigma_1, \ldots, \sigma_n$.

Independent Gamma Random Variables

C.2.c. If $X_1, \ldots, X_n$ are independent random variables such that for some fixed $r > 0$, X_i has the gamma density

$$f(x; r, \theta_i) = \frac{\theta_i^{-r} x^{r-1}}{\Gamma(r)} e^{-x/\theta_i}, \qquad x \geq 0, \quad \theta_i > 0, \quad i = 1, \ldots, n,$$

and if ϕ is symmetric and convex, then

$$\psi(\theta) = E_\theta \phi(X_1, \ldots, X_n)$$

is symmetric and convex in θ.

In particular, if $X_1, \ldots, X_n$ are independent and exponentially distributed with expectations $\theta_1, \ldots, \theta_n$, then ψ is symmetric and convex.

11. Stochastic Majorizations

This result is to be compared with E.8.a, where the scale parameter θ is the same for each X_i, but the shape parameter is allowed to vary. See also E.8.b.

Here the assumption of independence can be replaced by the assumption of exchangeability. For example, the conclusion of C.2.c holds if $X_1, \ldots, X_n$ have the Dirichlet density f_2 of (9), Section E, with $r_1 = \cdots = r_n$.

Independent Uniform Random Variables

C.2.d. If $X_1, \ldots, X_n$ are independent random variables, X_i having density

$$f_{\theta_i}(x) = \frac{1}{\theta_i} I_{(0,\theta_i)}(x), \qquad i = 1, \ldots, n,$$

and if ϕ is symmetric and convex, then $\psi(\theta) = E_\theta \phi(X)$ is symmetric and convex.

C.2.e. If $X_1, \ldots, X_n$ are independent random variables, X_i having density

$$f_{\theta_i}(x) = I_{(\theta_i, \theta_i+1)}(x), \qquad i = 1, \ldots, n,$$

and if ϕ is symmetric and convex, then $\psi(\theta) = E_\theta \phi(X)$ is symmetric and convex.

Commentary on Discrete Random Variables

Examples of discrete distributions parameterized to preserve symmetry and convexity can be obtained by restricting the components of θ to be integer-valued (or to take values in some lattice) in C.2. But interesting examples are not so easily obtained. In the first edition of this book, putative examples involving Poisson, negative binomial, and multinomial distributions were presented. For example, it was proposed that if $X_1, X_2, \ldots, X_n$ were independent random variables with

$$P(X_i = x) = \frac{e^{-\lambda_i} \lambda_i^x}{x!}, \qquad x = 0, 1, 2, \ldots,$$

where $\lambda_i > 0$ for all i, and if ϕ is a symmetric convex function, then

$$\psi(\lambda) = E_\lambda(\phi(X_1, \ldots, X_n))$$

would be a symmetric convex function of λ.

D. Some Consequences of the Stochastic Majorization $E_1(P_1)$

Rolski (1985) provides a counterexample to this claim. He verifies that in the case $n = 2$, with $\phi(x_1, x_2) = \max(x_1, x_2)$, the corresponding function $\psi(\lambda)$ is not convex.

A plausible argument for the false claim of convexity of $\psi(\lambda)$ in the Poisson case was based on a claim that, in a lattice situation, the matrix of second differences of a convex function would be positive semidefinite. The Rolski example shows this to be incorrect. This flawed argument was also used to claim convexity of $E_\theta(\phi(X))$ in the negative binomial and multinomial cases. Counterexamples to the claims for the negative binomial and the multinomial cases have not been provided, but if they are correct, new proofs will be necessary.

D Some Consequences of the Stochastic Majorization $E_1(P_1)$

Condition E_1 is shown to be equivalent to P_1 in Section A and again in D.1 below. This condition is quite strong and has a number of implications, some of which are given in this section. Further implications and properties can be found in Section F.

D.1. Proposition (Nevius, Proschan, and Sethuraman, 1977a). The following conditions are equivalent:

(1) $E\phi(X) \leq E\phi(Y)$ for all Schur-convex functions ϕ on $\mathscr{R}^n$ such that the expectations are defined.

(2) $P\{\phi(X) > t\} \leq P\{\phi(Y) > t\}$ for all Borel-measurable Schur-convex functions ϕ on $\mathscr{R}^n$.

(3) $P\{X \in B\} \leq P\{Y \in B\}$ for every Borel-measurable set B such that $x \in B$, $x \prec y \Rightarrow y \in B$.

Proof. (2) implies (1) because stochastically ordered random variables have ordered expectations (see 17.A.2). (1) implies (3) because $P\{X \in B\} = EI_B(X)$, where the indicator function I_B is Schur-convex. (3) implies (2) because one can take $B = \{x : \phi(x) > t\}$. ||

D.1 is a special case of 17.B.10 and 17.B.10.a. The following results are consequences of D.1.

D.1.a. Proposition. If $X \prec_{E_1} Y$, then

$$P\{r_1 < X_i < r_2, i = 1, \ldots, n\} \geq P\{r_1 < Y_i < r_2, i = 1, \ldots, n\}$$

and

$$P\{r_1 \leq X_i \leq r_2, i = 1, \ldots, n\} \geq P\{r_1 \leq Y_i \leq r_2, i = 1, \ldots, n\},$$
$$-\infty \leq r_1 < r_2 \leq \infty.$$

Proof. In (1), take $-\phi$ to be the indicator function of the Cartesian product $(r_1, r_2)^n$ or $[r_1, r_2]^n$. ||

This proposition was noted by Cheng (1977), but various authors had previously given special cases.

D.1.b. Proposition (Nevius, Proschan, and Sethuraman, 1977a). Suppose that X and Y are nonnegative random variables such that $X \prec_{E_1} Y$. Let Z_X and Z_Y be the number of zero components of X and Y, respectively. Then $Z_X \leq^{\text{st}} Z_Y$.

Proof. This follows from the fact that $\phi(x) = \sum_{i=1}^{n} I_{\{z:z_i=0\}}(x)$ is Schur-convex on $\mathscr{R}_+^n$. ||

Of course, D.1.b is of no interest when X and Y have zero components with zero probability, but there are interesting applications to discrete distributions (see E.11.b).

D.1.c. Proposition. If $X \prec_{E_1} Y$, then

$$P\left\{X \Big/ \sum X_i \succ a\right\} \leq P\left\{Y \Big/ \sum Y_i \succ a\right\}$$

for all vectors a such that $\sum a_i = 1$.

Proof. This follows from the fact that $\phi(x) = I_{\{z:z/\Sigma z_i \succ a\}}(x)$ is Schur-convex; i.e., $x/\sum x_i \succ a$ and $y \succ x \Rightarrow y/\sum y_i \succ a$. ||

There is a variation of Proposition D.1.c due to Nevius, Proschan, and Sethuraman (1977a) which says that $P\{X \succ a\} \leq P\{Y \succ a\}$, under the hypothesis of D.1.c. This statement is more often vacuous because in many cases $P\{X \succ a\} = 0$.

D.2. Note. Nachman (2005) provides some alternative equivalent conditions for $X \prec_{E_1} Y$. For example, $X \prec_{E_1} Y$ if there exists a random vector $(\widetilde{X}, \widetilde{Y})$ with X and $\widetilde{X}$ identically distributed, Y and $\widetilde{Y}$ identically distributed, and the support of the distribution of $(\widetilde{X}, \widetilde{Y})$ contained in K, the graph of the majorization antecedent function γ defined in 1.B(7).

E Families of Distributions Parameterized to Preserve Schur-Convexity

Section C provides a discussion of families that preserve symmetry and convexity. Such families also preserve Schur-convexity. However, families that preserve Schur-convexity need not preserve symmetry and convexity. The Poisson family is an example that preserves Schur-convexity, but not symmetry and convexity. Other examples in this section are open to study as to whether they satisfy the stronger property of preserving symmetry and convexity. A more formal discussion follows.

There are a number of families of multivariate distributions parameterized by a vector θ with the property that expectations of Schur-convex functions lead to Schur-convex functions of θ. This idea is formalized in the following definition.

E.1. Definition. The family $\{F_\theta, \theta \in A \subset \mathscr{R}^n\}$ of distribution functions defined on $\mathscr{R}^n$ is said to be *parameterized to preserve Schur-convexity* if

$$\psi(\theta) = E_\theta \phi(X) = \int \phi(x) \, dF_\theta(x)$$

is Schur-convex in $\theta \in A$ for all Schur-convex functions ϕ of n arguments such that the expectations are defined (i.e., the family satisfies E_1^*).

Here, it is natural to expect the set A to have a Schur-concave indicator function (i.e., $\theta \in A$ and $\theta' \prec \theta \Rightarrow \theta' \in A$), but this is not essential. Note that this property is like that discussed in Section C except that symmetry and convexity have been replaced by Schur-convexity.

There are several conditions equivalent to the preservation of Schur-convexity as defined in E.1; these equivalences can be obtained by writing E_1 in the form (4) of Section A, and are given by the following proposition. It is interesting to note that none of these equivalences has an analog for the preservation of symmetry and convexity as defined in C.1. This negative result can be found in Section F.

E.2. Proposition (Nevius, Proschan, and Sethuraman, 1977a). The following conditions are equivalent:

$\psi(\theta) = E_\theta \phi(X)$ is Schur-convex in θ for all Schur-convex functions

ϕ on $\mathscr{R}^n$ such that the expectations are defined; (1)

$$P_\theta\{\phi(X) > t\} = \int_{\{\phi(x)>t\}} dF_\theta(x) \text{ is Schur-convex in } \theta \text{ for every Borel}$$

measurable Schur-convex function ϕ on $\mathscr{R}^n$; (2)

$$P_\theta(B) = \int_B dF_\theta(x) \text{ is Schur-convex in } \theta \text{ for every Borel-measurable}$$

set B such that $x \in B$, $x \prec y \Rightarrow y \in B$. (3)

The following results are consequences of E.2. They also have simple direct proofs and all follow from corresponding results in Section D.

E.2.a. Proposition. If $\{F_\theta, \theta \in A\}$ is a family of distributions parameterized to preserve Schur-convexity, then

$$P_\theta\{s < X_i < t, i = 1, \ldots, n\} \quad \text{and} \quad P_\theta\{s \leq X_i \leq t, i = 1, \ldots, n\}$$

are Schur-concave functions of θ, $-\infty \leq s, t \leq \infty$.

E.2.b. Proposition (Nevius, Proschan, and Sethuraman, 1977a). Let $\{F_\theta, \theta \in A\}$ be parameterized to preserve Schur-convexity and suppose the corresponding random vectors X_θ are nonnegative. Let Z_θ be the number of zero components of X_θ. Then $\theta' \prec \theta$ implies $Z_{\theta'} \leq^{st} Z_\theta$; i.e., $P\{Z_\theta > t\}$ is a Schur-convex function of θ, $t = 0, 1, 2, \ldots$.

E.2.c. Proposition. If $\{F_\theta, \theta \in A\}$ is parameterized to preserve Schur-convexity, then for all a such that $\sum a_i = 1$,

$$P_\theta\{X/\Sigma X_i \succ a\}$$

is a Schur-convex function of θ and

$$P_\theta\{X/\Sigma X_i \prec a\}$$

is a Schur-concave function of θ.

Theorem 3.J.2 is a basic tool for demonstrating that many commonly encountered multivariate families are naturally parameterized to preserve Schur-convexity. Theorem 3.J.1 also yields some examples. Some special forms of these results are particularly useful for this purpose.

E.3. Proposition (Proschan and Sethuraman, 1977). Suppose that $\{F_\theta, \theta \in \Theta^n\}$ is a family of n-dimensional distribution functions having discrete densities of the form

$$p(x_1, \ldots, x_n; \theta) = C\left(\sum x_i, \sum \theta_i\right) \prod_{i=1}^{n} \alpha(\theta_i, x_i)$$

whenever $x_1, \ldots, x_n$ are nonnegative integers, and

$$p(x_1, \ldots, x_n; \theta) = 0 \quad \text{otherwise.}$$

Here $C(\cdot, \cdot)$ is a normalizing constant.

If either

$$\alpha(\xi, z) = \frac{\xi^z}{z!}, \qquad z = 0, 1, 2, \ldots, \quad \xi \in \Theta = (0, \infty), \tag{4}$$

$$\alpha(\xi, z) = \binom{\xi}{z}, \qquad z = 0, 1, 2, \ldots, \quad \xi \in \Theta = \{0, 1, 2, \ldots\}, \tag{5}$$

or

$$\alpha(\xi, z) = \frac{\Gamma(z + \xi)}{z!\,\Gamma(\xi)}, \qquad z = 0, 1, 2, \ldots, \quad \xi \in (0, \infty), \tag{6}$$

then $\{F_\theta, \theta \in \Theta^n\}$ is parameterized to preserve Schur-convexity.

Proof. Define $\alpha(\xi, z) = 0$ if $z < 0$, so that α satisfies the conditions of 3.J.2 as demonstrated in 3.J.2.b, 3.J.2.c, and 3.J.2.d. Let ϕ be a Schur-convex function of n variables, and let

$$f^*(x) = C\left(\sum x_i, \sum \theta_i\right) \phi(x).$$

Then for each fixed $\sum \theta_i$, $f^*(x)$ is Schur-convex and by 3.J.2, $E_\theta f^*(x)$ is a Schur-convex function of θ. ∥

A companion proposition for E.3 in the continuous case is

E.4. Proposition. Let $\{F_\theta, \theta \in \mathscr{R}_{++}^n\}$ be a family of n-dimensional distribution functions having densities with respect to Lebesgue measure of the form

$$f(x_1, \ldots, x_n; \theta) = \begin{cases} C(\sum x_i, \sum \theta_i) \prod_{i=1}^{n} \dfrac{x_i^{\theta_i - 1}}{\Gamma(\theta_i)} & \text{if } x_i \geq 0 \text{ for all } i \\ 0 & \text{otherwise.} \end{cases}$$

Then the family $\{F_\theta, \theta \in \mathscr{R}_{++}^n\}$ is parameterized to preserve Schur-convexity. Here, "Lebesgue measure" may be Lebesgue measure on a subspace of $\mathscr{R}^n$.

Proof. The proof is essentially the same as the proof of E.3. ||

E.5. Proposition. If $X_1, \ldots, X_n$ are exchangeable random variables with a joint density f that is Schur-concave, then $\psi(\theta) = E\phi(X + \theta)$ is Schur-convex in θ whenever ϕ is a Schur-convex function such that the expectation exists.

Of course, this proposition says that under appropriate circumstances, families of distributions parameterized by a location parameter preserve Schur-convexity.

Proof of E.5. To show that $P\{\phi(X + \theta) > c\}$ is Schur-convex, let $A = \{u : \phi(u) \leq c\}$. Then $y \in A$ and $x \prec y$ imply $x \in A$. By 3.J.1.a,

$$\int_{A-\theta} f(x)\, dx = P\{(X_1, \ldots, X_n) \in A - \theta\}$$
$$= P\{X + \theta \in A\} = P\{\phi(X + \theta) \leq c\}$$

is Schur-concave in θ; i.e., $P\{\phi(X + \theta) > c\}$ is Schur-convex. ||

It is interesting to compare E.5 with its counterpart B.3, which holds for a much larger class of exchangeable random variables.

E.5.a. Proposition (Marshall and Olkin, 1974). Suppose that $X_1, \ldots, X_n$ are exchangeable random variables with a joint density f that is Schur-concave. If $A \subset \mathscr{R}^n$ is a Lebesgue measurable set satisfying

$$y \in A \quad \text{and} \quad x \prec y \Rightarrow x \in A,$$

then

$$\int_{A+\theta} f(x)\, dx = P\{X \in A + \theta\}$$

is a Schur-concave function of θ.

This is essentially a restatement of 3.J.1.a.

Examples of Schur-Concave Densities

E.5.b. If $X_1, \ldots, X_n$ are independent and identically distributed random variables with common density g, then by 3.E.1, their joint density is Schur-concave if and only if $\log g$ is concave. Common examples of logarithmically concave densities are given in 18.B.2.c.

E.5.c. If the density of $X_1, \ldots, X_n$ has the form

$$f(x) = \int_A \prod_i g_a(x_i)\, dP(a)$$

for some probability measure P and each density g_a is logarithmically concave, then f is Schur-concave.

A special case of interest follows.

Multivariate Chi-Square Density

Suppose that $S = (s_{ij})$ is the sample covariance matrix based on a sample of size $N \geq n$ from an n-variate normal distribution with covariance matrix $\Sigma = (\sigma_{ij})$, $\sigma_{ii} = \sigma^2$, $\sigma_{ij} = \sigma^2 \rho$, $i \neq j$. Then the joint density of $s_{11}, \ldots, s_{nn}$ has the form of a mixture of independent noncentral chi-square densities which are log concave.

E.5.d. If the joint density f has the form

$$f(x) = h(x\Lambda x'),$$

where h is a decreasing function and $\Lambda = (\lambda_{ij})$ is positive definite with $\lambda_{11} = \cdots = \lambda_{nn}$ and $\lambda_{ij} = \lambda$, $i \neq j$, then f is Schur-concave.

Proof. By 3.C.3 it is sufficient to show that f is quasi-concave; that is, sets of the form $\{x : h(x\Lambda x') \geq c\}$ are convex. But this follows from the monotonicity of h and the convexity of $x\Lambda x'$ in x. See 16.B.3.d. ||

A special case of E.5 is given below.

Exchangeable Multivariate Normal Density, and Multivariate "t" Density

If $U_1, \ldots, U_n$ are exchangeable and jointly normally distributed, and if Z^2 is a chi-square distributed ($Z \geq 0$) random variable independent of $U_1, \ldots, U_n$, then

$$X_1 = U_1/Z, \ldots, X_n = U_n/Z$$

have a joint density of the form $f(x) = h(x\Lambda x')$, where $h(w)$ is proportional to $(1+w)^{-a}$, $a > 0$.

With suitable transformations, it is possible to convert E.5 to a statement concerning scale parameter families of distributions.

E.5.e. Proposition. If $X_1, \ldots, X_n$ are exchangeable nonnegative random variables with joint density f such that

$$\widetilde{f}(z) = f(e^{z_1}, \ldots, e^{z_n})$$

defines a Schur-concave function, and if $\widetilde{\phi}(z) = \phi(e^{z_1}, \ldots, e^{z_n})$ is Schur-concave, then

$$\psi(\alpha) = E\phi(e^{-\alpha_1} X_1, \ldots, e^{-\alpha_n} X_n)$$

is Schur-concave in $\alpha_1, \ldots, \alpha_n$.

Proof. With the change of variables $x_i = e^{y_i}$,

$$\psi(\alpha) = \int \phi(e^{-\alpha_1} x_1, \ldots, e^{-\alpha_n} x_n) f(x_1, \ldots, x_n) \prod dx_i$$

$$= \int \phi(e^{y_1-\alpha_1}, \ldots, e^{y_n-\alpha_n}) f(e^{y_1}, \ldots, e^{y_n}) e^{\Sigma y_i} \prod dy_i$$

$$= \int \widetilde{\phi}(y-\alpha) \widetilde{f}(y) e^{\Sigma y_i} \prod dy_i.$$

But this is Schur-concave by E.5. ||

In case $X_1, \ldots, X_n$ are independent and each has density g, the condition that $\widetilde{f}$ is Schur-concave reduces to the condition that $u(d \log g(u)/du)$ is decreasing in u.

Notice that if ϕ is decreasing and Schur-concave, then $\widetilde{\phi}$ is Schur-concave because $u \prec v \Rightarrow (e^{u_1}, \ldots, e^{u_n}) \prec_w (e^{v_1}, \ldots, e^{v_n})$.

A special case of E.5.e is given by Mudholkar and Dalal (1977).

E.5.f. Proposition. Let $X_1, \ldots, X_n$ be exchangeable random variables satisfying $P\{0 \leq X_i \leq 1\} = 1$, with joint density f such that

$$\widetilde{f}(z) = f(\exp(-e^{-z_1}), \ldots, \exp(-e^{-z_n})) \exp\left(-\sum e^{-z_i}\right)$$

is Schur-concave. If $\widetilde{\phi}(z) = \phi(\exp(-e^{-z_1}), \ldots, \exp(-e^{-z_n}))$ is Schur-concave, then

$$\psi(\alpha) = E\phi(X_1^{\exp \alpha_1}, \ldots, X_n^{\exp \alpha_n})$$

is a Schur-concave function of $\alpha_1, \ldots, \alpha_n$.

Proof. With the change of variables $x_i = \exp(-e^{-y_i})$,

$$\psi(\alpha) = \int \phi(x_1^{\exp \alpha_1}, \ldots, x_n^{\exp \alpha_n}) f(x)\, dx$$

$$= \int \phi(\exp(-e^{-(y_1-\alpha_1)}), \ldots, \exp(-e^{-(y_n-\alpha_n)}))$$

$$\times f(\exp(-e^{-y_1}), \ldots, \exp(-e^{-y_n})) \exp(-\sum e^{-y_i}) e^{-\sum y_i} \prod dy_i$$

$$= \int \widetilde{\phi}(y - \alpha) \widetilde{f}(y) e^{-\Sigma y_i} \prod dy_i.$$

This is Schur-concave by E.5. ||

The remainder of this section is devoted to examples of families of joint distributions that preserve Schur-convexity.

Independent Poisson Random Variables

E.6. Proposition (Rinott, 1973; Nevius, Proschan, and Sethuraman, 1977a). If $X_1, \ldots, X_n$ are independent random variables such that

$$P\{X_i = x\} = e^{-\lambda_i}(\lambda_i^x/x!), \qquad x = 0, 1, \ldots, \qquad \lambda_i > 0 \text{ for all } i,$$

and if ϕ is a Schur-convex function, then

$$\psi(\lambda) = E_\lambda \phi(X_1, \ldots, X_n)$$

is a Schur-convex function of $\lambda = (\lambda_1, \ldots, \lambda_n)$.

Proof. This follows from E.3(4). ||

An alternative proof is given ahead in Remark E.11.a.

Independent Binomial Random Variables

E.7. Proposition (Nevius, Proschan, and Sethuraman, 1977a). If $X_1, \ldots, X_n$ are independent random variables such that, for some fixed $p \in (0,1)$,

$$P\{X_i = x_i\} = \binom{k_i}{x} p^x (1-p)^{k_i - x}, \qquad x = 0, 1, \ldots, k_i, \qquad k_i \in \{1, 2, \ldots,\},$$

and if ϕ is a Schur-convex function, then

$$\psi(k) = E_k \phi(X_1, \ldots, X_n)$$

is a Schur-convex function of $k = (k_1, \ldots, k_n)$.

Proof. This result follows from E.3(5). ||

Independent Gamma Random Variables

E.8. Proposition (Nevius, Proschan, and Sethuraman, 1977a). If $X_1, \ldots, X_n$ are independent random variables and if for some fixed $\theta > 0$, X_i has the gamma density

$$f(x; r_i, \theta) = \frac{\theta^{r_i} x^{r_i - 1}}{\Gamma(r_i)} e^{-\theta x}, \qquad x \geq 0, \quad r_i > 0, \quad i = 1, \ldots, n,$$

then

$$\psi(r) = E_r \phi(X_1, \ldots, X_n)$$

is a Schur-convex function of $r = (r_1, \ldots, r_n)$ whenever ϕ is a Schur-convex function such that the relevant expectations are defined.

Proof. This is a consequence of E.4. ||

E.8.a. Proposition. Let $X_1, \ldots, X_n$ be independent random variables such that for some fixed $r > 0$, X_i has the gamma density

$$f(x; r, \theta_i) = \frac{\theta_i^r x^{r-1}}{\Gamma(r)} e^{-\theta_i x}, \qquad x \geq 0, \quad \theta_i > 0, \quad i = 1, \ldots, n.$$

If $\theta_i = e^{-\alpha_i}$, $i = 1, \ldots, n$, then

$$\psi(\alpha) = E_\alpha \phi(X_1, \ldots, X_n)$$

is a Schur-convex function of $\alpha = (\alpha_1, \ldots, \alpha_n)$ whenever $\tilde{\phi}(z) = \phi(e^{z_1}, \ldots, e^{z_n})$ is a Schur-convex function such that the relevant expectations are defined.

Proof. This is a direct consequence of E.5.a. ||

The above result is to be compared with C.2.c.

The particular case $r = \frac{1}{2}$ of E.8.a arises when $Z_1, \ldots, Z_n$ are independent normal random variables (mean 0, variance 1), $Y_i = Z_i^2$, and $X_i = e^{-\alpha_i} Y_i$, $i = 1, \ldots, n$. With $-\phi$ the indicator function of the set $\{u : \sum u_i \leq c\}$, it follows that

$$P\left\{ \sum_1^n e^{-\alpha_i} Y_i \leq c \right\} \tag{7}$$

is a Schur-concave function of $\alpha = (\alpha_1, \ldots, \alpha_n)$. This in turn yields the following:

E.8.b. Proposition (Okamoto, 1960). Let $W_1, \ldots, W_k$ be independent random variables and suppose that W_i has a χ^2 distribution with

E. Parameterization to Preserve Schur-Convexity

n_i degrees of freedom, $i = 1, \ldots, k$. If $a_i > 0$, $i = 1, \ldots, k$, then

$$P\left\{\sum_1^k b_i W_i \leq c\right\} \leq P\{bW \leq c\},$$

where $b = (\prod_1^k b_i^{n_i})^{1/n}$, $n = \sum_1^k n_i$, and W has a χ^2 distribution with n degrees of freedom.

Proof. Let

$$\alpha = (\overbrace{\alpha_1, \ldots, \alpha_1}^{n_1}, \overbrace{\alpha_2, \ldots, \alpha_2}^{n_2}, \ldots, \overbrace{\alpha_k, \ldots, \alpha_k}^{n_k}),$$

and let $b_i = e^{-\alpha_i}$, $i = 1, \ldots, k$. The result follows from the Schur-concavity in (7). ||

Exchangeable Normal Random Variables

E.9. If $Y_1 = X_1 - \mu_1, \ldots, Y_n = X_n - \mu_n$ are exchangeable multivariate normal random variables with expectations 0, variances σ^2, and covariances $\sigma^2 \rho$, then

$$\psi(\mu_1, \ldots, \mu_n) = E_\mu \phi(X_1, \ldots, X_n)$$

is Schur-convex for all Schur-convex ϕ such that the relevant expectations exist.

Proof. This is an application of E.5. ||

Independent Uniform Random Variables

E.10. If $X_1, \ldots, X_n$ are independent and X_i has density

$$f_{\theta_i}(x) = I_{(\theta_i, \theta_i+1)}(x), \qquad i = 1, \ldots, n,$$

then $\psi(\theta) = E_\theta \phi(X)$ is Schur-convex whenever ϕ is a Schur-convex function such that the relevant expectations exist.

Proof. This is another application of E.5. ||

Multinomial Distributions

E.11. Proposition (Rinott, 1973). Let X be a random variable having the multinomial distribution

$$P\{X = x\} = \binom{N}{x_1, \ldots, x_n} \prod_{i=1}^{n} \theta_i^{x_i},$$

where $x = (x_1, \ldots, x_n) \in \{z : z_i \text{ are nonnegative integers}, \sum z_i = N\}$. If ϕ is a Schur-convex function, then $\psi(\theta) = E_\theta \phi(x)$ is a Schur-convex function of θ.

Proof. This result follows from (4) with

$$C(\textstyle\sum x_i, \sum \theta_i) = \begin{cases} N! & \text{if } \sum x_i = N, \\ 0 & \text{otherwise.} \end{cases}$$

Alternatively, Rinott proves this theorem by verifying the derivative conditions of 3.A.4 for Schur-convexity in a straightforward way. ||

A number of consequences of E.11 are worth stating.

E.11.a. Remark. As pointed out by Rinott (1973), Proposition E.6 concerning independent Poisson random variables is a direct consequence of E.11. To see this, observe that the conditional distribution of independent Poisson random variables $X_1, \ldots, X_n$ given $\sum_1^n X_i = N$ is a multinomial distribution. Then use the fact that Schur-convex functions form a convex cone.

Now suppose that an experiment with n possible outcomes is repeated N times. The number K of distinct outcomes is a random variable which, described in terms of a multinomial random vector X, is the number of nonzero components.

E.11.b. Proposition (Wong and Yue, 1973). With K as defined above, $\psi(\theta) = P_\theta\{K \leq k\}$ is a Schur-convex function of θ for all k.

Proof. In view of the above remarks, this is just an application of E.2.b with $Z_\theta = n - K$. ||

Because $P_\theta\{K > 1\} = 1 - P_\theta\{K = 1\}$ is Schur-concave in $\theta_1, \ldots, \theta_n$, and since $(\theta_1, \ldots, \theta_n) \succ (1/n, \ldots, 1/n)$, it follows that

$$\sum \binom{N}{x_1, \ldots, x_n} \theta_1^{x_1} \cdots \theta_n^{x_n} \leq \sum \binom{N}{x_1, \ldots, x_n} \left(\frac{1}{n}\right)^N,$$

where the summations are over the set $\{x : 0 \leq x_i \leq N-1, \Sigma x_i = N\}$.

This inequality reduces to

$$\sum \frac{\theta_1^{x_1} \cdots \theta_n^{x_n}}{x_1! \cdots x_n!} \leq \frac{N^n - n}{N!\, n^N},$$

which is a result given by Mitrinović (1970, p. 214).

Birthday Problem

Among the applications of E.11.b is a result concerning the "birthday problem" which was pointed out by Persi Diaconis and David Siegmund (private communication, 1977). In a collection of l people, what is the probability $P(l)$ that at least two people have the same birthday? This is an often-quoted representative of a large class of matching problems; it is usually discussed under the assumption that birthdays are equally likely to fall on any of the days $1, \ldots, 365$. If a birthday falls on day i with probability θ_i, $i = 1, \ldots, 365$, and the θ_i are not necessarily equal, then because

$$P(l) = P_\theta\{K \leq l - 1\},$$

it follows from E.11.b that $P(l)$ is a Schur-convex function of θ. Hence, $P(l)$ is a minimum when the θ_i are equal; this fact is obtained by Rust (1976).

Karlin and Rinott (1984) show that this result holds even when the individuals have different probabilities of having "birthdays" on particular days. Thus associated with individual j is a vector of probabilities $\theta^{(j)}$, where $\theta_i^{(j)}$ is the probability that individual j's "birthday" falls on day i. Provided that the vectors $\theta^{(j)}, j = 1, 2, \ldots, l$, are similarly ordered, it remains true that $P(l)$ is a minimum when all $\theta_i^{(j)}$'s are equal.

As a second application of E.11.b, suppose there are n cells into which balls are placed one by one, independently, with cell probabilities $\theta_1, \ldots, \theta_n$. If Z is the number of balls placed at the first time there are two balls in one cell, then for $z = 1, 2, \ldots$, $P_\theta\{Z > z\} = P_\theta\{K_z \geq z\}$, where K_z is the number of occupied cells after z balls have been placed. It follows from E.11.b that $P_\theta\{Z > z\}$ is a Schur-concave function of θ and so is a maximum when $\theta_1 = \cdots = \theta_n$.

If instead of waiting until one cell has two balls in it, the process is continued until all cells are occupied, this can be identified with the "coupon collector's problem." Let W denote the waiting time until all cells are occupied. Toshio Nakata (personal communication, 2008) showed that, for any integer w, $P_\theta\{W > w\}$ is a Schur-convex function of θ. To verify this, let K_w denote the number of occupied cells after w balls have been placed. From E.11.b, $P_\theta\{K_w \leq n-1\}$ is a Schur-convex function of θ. However, the event $\{K_w \leq n-1\}$ occurs if and only if $\{W > w\}$. So $P_\theta\{W > w\}$ is a Schur-convex function of θ, and also $E_\theta W = \sum_{w=0}^\infty P_\theta\{W > w\}$ is Schur-convex. The expected waiting time is thus minimized if the θ_i's are equal. Note that this minimization result holds even when the cell probability vectors change with each drawing, provided they are similarly ordered, as discussed in Karlin and Rinott (1984).

There is a generalization of E.11.b which was suggested by Frank Proschan (private communication, 1971).

E.11.c. If X is a multinomial random variable and $a \in \mathscr{X}_N$, then $P_\theta\{X \succ a\}$ is a Schur-convex function of θ and $P_\theta\{X \prec a\}$ is a Schur-concave function of θ.

Proof. This is a special case of E.2.c. ||

To obtain E.11.b from E.11.c, choose a to have exactly k nonzero components which are as "nearly equal" as the constraint $a \in \mathscr{X}_N$ allows. Since a direct proof of E.11.b is given, the details are omitted.

E.11.d. Proposition. If X has a multinomial distribution with parameter $\theta = (\theta_1, \ldots, \theta_n)$, then

$$P_\theta\{s \leq X_i \leq t, i = 1, \ldots, n\}$$

is a Schur-concave function of θ, $-\infty \leq s \leq t \leq \infty$.

Proof. This is another application of E.2.a, or it can be obtained from D.1.a. ||

For the case $t = \infty$, E.11.d was obtained by Olkin (1972); this generalizes a still more special case due to Alam (1970).

The above proposition can be generalized in a way that is sometimes useful.

E.11.e. Proposition. If $X = (X_1, \ldots, X_n)$ has a multinomial distribution with parameter θ and if $\theta_{m+1}, \ldots, \theta_n$ are fixed, then for any set $\mathscr{X} \subset \mathscr{R}^{n-m}$ and any s, t, $-\infty \leq s \leq t \leq \infty$,

$$P_{\theta_1,\ldots,\theta_m}\{s \leq X_1 \leq t, \ldots, s \leq X_m \leq t, (X_{m+1}, \ldots, X_n) \in \mathscr{X}\} \quad (8)$$

is a Schur-concave function of $\theta_1, \ldots, \theta_m$.

Proof. Let $\ddot{X} = (X_{m+1}, \ldots, X_n)$ and note that

$$P_{\theta_1,\ldots,\theta_m}\{s \leq X_1 \leq t, \ldots, s \leq X_m \leq t, \ddot{X} \in \mathscr{X}\}$$
$$= \sum_{\ddot{x} \in \mathscr{X}} P_{\theta_1,\ldots,\theta_m}\{s \leq X_1 \leq t, \ldots, s \leq X_m \leq t | \ddot{X} = \ddot{x}\} P\{\ddot{X} = \ddot{x}\}.$$

But $P_{\theta_1,\ldots,\theta_m}\{s \leq X_1 \leq t, \ldots, s \leq X_m \leq t | \ddot{X} = \ddot{x}\}$ is Schur-concave by E.11.d (with N replaced by $N - \sum_{m+1}^{n} \ddot{x}_i$ and $\theta_1, \ldots, \theta_m$ renormalized). Because the Schur-concave functions form a convex cone, the proof is complete. ||

With $\mathscr{X} = \mathscr{R}^{n-m}$ and $t = \infty$, (8) is due to Olkin (1972), but see also Alam (1970).

Dirichlet Distributions

There are three distinct distributions to which the name "Dirichlet" is usually attached. The first two have the following densities:

$$f_1(x_1, \ldots, x_n; r) = \Gamma\left(\beta + \sum r_i\right) \frac{(1 - \sum_1^n x_i)^{\beta-1}}{\Gamma(\beta)} \prod_1^n \frac{x_i^{r_i-1}}{\Gamma(r_i)}, \quad (9)$$

where $x_i \geq 0$, $i = 1, \ldots, n$, $\sum_1^n x_1 \leq 1$, $0 < r_i < \infty$, $i = 1, \ldots, n$, and $0 < \beta < \infty$;

$$f_2(x_1, \ldots, x_n; r) = \frac{\Gamma(\beta + \sum r_i)}{\Gamma(\beta)(1 + \sum x_i)^{\beta + \Sigma x_i}} \prod_1^n \frac{x_i^{r_i-1}}{\Gamma(r_i)}, \quad (10)$$

where $x_i \geq 0$ and $0 < r_i < \infty$, $i = 1, \ldots, n$, $0 < \beta < \infty$.

The third Dirichlet distribution is a singular version which has the density (with respect to Lebesgue measure on the hyperplane $\sum x_i = 1$) given by

$$f_3(x_1, \ldots, x_n; r) = \Gamma\left(\sum_1^n r_i\right) \prod_1^n \frac{x_i^{r_i-1}}{\Gamma(r_i)}, \quad x_i \geq 0, \quad \sum x_i = 1, \quad (11)$$

where $0 < r_i < \infty$, $i = 1, \ldots, n$.

E.12. Proposition. If $X = (X_1, \ldots, X_n)$ has the Dirichlet density (9), (10), or (11), then

$$\psi(r) = E_r \phi(X)$$

is a Schur-convex function of r whenever ϕ is a Schur-convex function such that the relevant expectations exist.

Proof. This result follows from E.4. ‖

There is a close connection between the multinomial and Dirichlet distributions (Olkin and Sobel, 1965): If $X_1, \ldots, X_n$ have a multinomial distribution with parameters N and $\theta = (\theta_1, \ldots, \theta_n)$, as in E.10, then

$$P_\theta\{X_1 \geq r_1, \ldots, X_n \geq r_n\} = \int_0^{\theta_1} \cdots \int_0^{\theta_n} f_1(x_1, \ldots, x_n; r) \prod dx_i, \quad (12)$$

where $f_1(x_1, \ldots, x_n; r)$ is the Dirichlet density given by (9) with $\beta = N + 1 - \sum_1^n r_i$. Similarly, for $m \leq \min(n-1, N)$,

$$P_\theta\{X_1 < r_1, \ldots, X_m < r_m\}$$
$$= \int_{\theta_1}^{1-\Sigma_2^m \theta_i} \int_{\theta_2}^{1-\Sigma_3^m \theta_i - x_1} \cdots \int_{\theta_m}^{1-\Sigma_1^{m-1} x_i} f_1(x; r) \prod dx_i. \quad (13)$$

The proof of E.11.d with $s = -\infty$ given by Olkin (1972) makes use of these integral representations and consists of verifying the conditions of 3.A.4. These integral representations can also be used in conjunction with E.12 to obtain yet another majorization result for the multinomial distribution.

E.12.a. Proposition. If $Y = (Y_1, \ldots, Y_n)$ has the Dirichlet distribution (9) and $X = (X_1, \ldots, X_n)$ has a multinomial distribution with parameter $(\theta, \theta, \ldots, \theta)$,

$$P_r\{Y_1 \leq \theta, \ldots, Y_n \leq \theta\} = P_{\theta,\ldots,\theta}(X_1 \geq r_1, \ldots, X_n \geq r_n)$$

is a Schur-concave function of $r = (r_1, \ldots, r_n)$.

Proof. This follows from (12) and E.12 with ϕ the indicator function of $\{z : z_1 \leq \theta, \ldots, z_n \leq \theta\}$. ‖

Liouville–Dirichlet Distributions

Liouville's extension of an integral of Dirichlet is as follows. If g is continuous on $[a, b]$ and $r_i > 0$, $i = 1, \ldots, n$, then

$$\int_{\{0 \leq x_i, a \leq \Sigma x_i \leq b\}} \prod x_i^{r_i - 1} g\left(\sum_1^n x_i\right) \prod dx_i = \frac{\prod \Gamma(r_i)}{\Gamma(\sum r_i)} \int_a^b t^{\Sigma r_i - 1} g(t)\, dt$$

in the sense that if either integral is finite, so is the other and they are equal (see Edwards, 1922, p. 160). From this, it follows that if g is continuous and nonnegative on $[a, b]$, then for $x_i \geq 0, i = 1, \ldots, n$,

$$f(x_1, \ldots, x_n; r) = \frac{\Gamma(\sum r_i) g(\sum x_i)}{\int_a^b t^{\Sigma r_i - 1} g(t)\, dt} \prod \frac{x_i^{r_i - 1}}{\Gamma(r_i)}, \quad a \leq \sum x_i \leq b, \quad (14)$$

is a probability density function.

E.13. Proposition. If $X_1, \ldots, X_n$ have a joint density of the form (14), then $\psi(r) = E_r \phi(X)$ is a Schur-convex function of r whenever ϕ is a Schur-convex function such that the relevant expectations exist.

Proof. This is just an application of E.4. ||

Special cases of (14) include the following:

(a) Dirichlet distribution (9): $a = 0$, $b = 1$, $g(t) = (1-t)^\beta$, $0 \leq t \leq 1$;

(b) Dirichlet distribution (10): $a = 0$, $b = \infty$, $g(t) = (1+t)^{-\beta}$, $t \geq 0$;

(c) independence gamma distributions: $a = 0$, $b = \infty$, $g(t) = e^{-t}$;

(d) gamma marginals with correlation: If $a = 0$, $b = \infty$, $g(t) = t^\delta e^{-t}$, then with $x_i \geq 0$, $i = 1, \ldots, n$, (14) becomes

$$f(x_1, \ldots, x_n; r) = \frac{\Gamma(\sum r_i)}{\Gamma(\sum r_i + \delta)} \left(\sum x_i\right)^\delta \prod \frac{x_i^{r_i - 1}}{\Gamma(r_i)} e^{-r_i x_i}.$$

E.13.a. Remark. If $X_1, \ldots, X_n$ have joint density (14), then $X_1, \ldots, X_{n-1}$ have density (14) with $n - 1$ in place of n.

Multivariate Hypergeometric Distribution

If N balls are drawn without replacement from an urn containing $K > N$ balls, M_i being of color i, $i = 1, \ldots, n$, and if X_i is the number drawn of color i, then

$$P_1(X_1 = x_1, \ldots, X_n = x_n) = \prod_{i=1}^n \binom{M_i}{x_i} \Big/ \binom{K}{N},$$

$$x_i = 0, 1, \ldots, M_i, \quad i = 1, \ldots, n, \quad \sum x_i = N.$$

Here all M_i, K, and N are nonnegative integers satisfying

$$\sum_{i=1}^n M_i = N \leq K = 1, 2, \ldots.$$

This distribution is called a *multivariate hypergeometric distribution* with parameters $M_1, \ldots, M_n$.

E.14. Proposition. If $X_1, \ldots, X_n$ have a multivariate hypergeometric distribution, then

$$\psi(M_1, \ldots, M_n) = E_{M_1, \ldots, M_n} \phi(X_1, \ldots, X_n)$$

is a Schur-convex function of $M_1, \ldots, M_n$ whenever ϕ is a Schur-convex function.

Proof. This follows directly from E.3(5). ||

There are several other families of distributions which can be parameterized to preserve Schur-convexity by making use of E.3 or E.4. These families have also been listed by Nevius, Proschan, and Sethuraman (1977a).

Negative Multinomial Distribution

E.15. Suppose $X_1, \ldots, X_n$ have the joint density

$$P\{X_1 = x_1, \ldots, X_n = x_n\} = \frac{\Gamma(k + \sum_1^n x_i)}{\Gamma(k)} (1 - \sum p_i)^k \prod \frac{p_i^{x_i}}{x_i!},$$

$x_i = 0, 1, \ldots$ for $i = 0, 1, \ldots, n$, $0 < k < \infty$, $p_i \geq 0$ for all i, $\sum_1^n p_i < 1$. Here k is fixed and the family preserving convexity is parameterized by $p_1, p_2, \ldots, p_n$. With a reparameterization of the form

$$p_i = \frac{\lambda_i}{1 + \sum_1^n \lambda_i},$$

where the λ_i's are positive, this distribution is also known as a *multivariate negative binomial distribution*.

Multivariate Logarithmic Series Distribution

E.16. For $\lambda_i > 0$, $x_i = 0, 1, \ldots, i = 1, \ldots, n$, $\sum x_i \geq 1$,

$$P\{X_1 = x_1, \ldots, X_n = x_n\} = \frac{(\sum_1^n x_i - 1)!}{\log(1 + \sum_1^n \lambda_i)} \prod_1^n \frac{\lambda_i^{x_i}}{x_i!} (1 + \sum_1^n \lambda_i)^{-\sum_1^n x_i}.$$

The family is parameterized by $\lambda_1, \ldots, \lambda_n$.

E. Parameterization to Preserve Schur-Convexity   419

Multivariate Modified Logarithmic Distribution

E.17. For $0 < \delta < 1$, $\lambda_i > 0$ for all i,

$$P\{X_1 = x_1, \ldots, X_n = x_n\} = \frac{(1-\delta)(\sum_1^n x_i - 1)!}{\log(1 + \sum_1^n \lambda_i)} \prod_1^n \frac{\lambda_i^{x_i}}{x_i!} (1 + \sum_1^n \lambda_i)^{-\Sigma_1^n x_i}$$

$$\text{if} \quad x_i = 0, 1, \ldots \text{ and } \sum x_i \geq 1;$$

$$P\{X_1 = 0, \ldots, X_n = 0\} = \delta.$$

The family is parameterized by $\lambda_1, \ldots, \lambda_n$ and δ.

Multivariate Inverse Hypergeometric Distribution

E.18. For $x_i = 0, 1, \ldots$ and $N_i = 0, 1, \ldots, i = 1, \ldots, n$, $\sum N_i \leq M - k$,

$$P\{X_1 = x_1, \ldots, X_n = x_n\}$$

$$= \binom{M}{k + \sum x_i - 1}^{-1} \binom{M - \sum N_i}{k - 1} \frac{M - \sum N_i - k + 1}{M - \sum x_i - k + 1} \prod_1^n \binom{N_i}{x_i}.$$

Here M and k are fixed, $k < M$. The family is parameterized by $N_1, \ldots, N_n$.

Negative Multivariate Hypergeometric Distribution

E.19. For $x_i = 0, 1, \ldots, N$, $\sum x_i = N$, $\lambda_i > 0$, $i = 1, 2, \ldots, n$,

$$P\{X_1 = x_1, \ldots, X_n = x_n\} = \frac{N! \Gamma(\sum_1^n \lambda_i)}{\Gamma(N + \sum_1^n \lambda_i)} \prod_1^n \frac{\Gamma(x_i + \lambda_i)}{x_i! \Gamma(\lambda_i)}.$$

The family is parameterized by $\lambda_1, \ldots, \lambda_n$ for fixed N.

That this family preserves Schur-convexity follows from E.3(6). Alternatively, the result follows from E.11, E.12.a, and the fact that the negative multivariate hypergeometric is obtained from the multinomial distribution by treating the parameters as random variables with a singular Dirichlet density (11). (See Section A on compounding.)

Dirichlet Compound Negative Multinomial Distribution

E.20. For $x_i = 0, 1, \ldots,\ i = 1, \ldots, n,\ \beta > 0$, and $k = 1, 2, \ldots$,

$$P\{X_1 = x_1, \ldots, X_n = x_n\}$$
$$= \frac{\Gamma(k + \sum x_i)\Gamma(\beta + \sum r_i)\Gamma(k + \beta)}{\Gamma(k)\Gamma(\beta)\Gamma(k + \beta + \sum r_i + \sum x_i)} \prod_1^n \frac{\Gamma(r_i + x_i)}{x_i!\Gamma(r_i)}.$$

When parameterized by $r_1, \ldots, r_n$ with k and β fixed, this family preserves Schur-convexity. This follows from E.3(6), or from the fact that the distribution is a compounded negative multinomial distribution E.13 with $p_1, \ldots, p_n$ having a Dirichlet distribution (9).

F Additional Stochastic Majorizations and Properties

If $\mathscr{C}$ is any "nice" class of functions defined on $\mathscr{R}^n$ with the property that $x \prec y$ if and only if $\phi(x) \leq \phi(y)$ for all $\phi \in \mathscr{C}$, then, as indicated in Section A, the two kinds of stochastic majorizations $P_\mathscr{C}$ and $E_\mathscr{C}$ can be considered. In earlier sections, both $\mathscr{C}_1$ and $\mathscr{C}_2$ (defined in Section A) have been prominent. Two additional classes are natural:

$\mathscr{C}_3 = \{\phi : \phi(x) = \sum \psi(x_i)$ for a continuous convex function ψ on $\mathscr{R}\}$

and

$$\mathscr{C}_4 = \left\{\phi : \phi(x) = \sum_1^k x_{[i]} \text{ or } \phi(x) = -\sum_k^n x_{[i]} \text{ for some } k = 1, \ldots, n\right\}.$$

Using the facts that $\mathscr{C}_1 \supset \mathscr{C}_2 \supset \mathscr{C}_3$ and $\mathscr{C}_2 \supset \mathscr{C}_4$, it follows from arguments outlined in Section A that the following implications hold:

$$P_1 \Rightarrow P_2 \Rightarrow P_3, \qquad P_2 \Rightarrow P_4, \qquad E_1 \Rightarrow E_2 \Rightarrow E_3, \qquad E_2 \Rightarrow E_4,$$
$$P_i \Rightarrow E_i, \quad i = 1, 2, 3, 4, \qquad \text{and} \qquad E_1 \Rightarrow P_1.$$

No additional implications are known, and counterexamples to most possibilities are given later in this section.

Remark. Chang (1992) studies the additional classes

$\mathscr{C}_5 = \{\phi : \phi$ is symmetric, L-subadditive, convex in each argument $x_i\}$

and for $i = 1, 2, \ldots, 5$,

$$\mathscr{C}_{i\uparrow} = \{\phi : \phi \in \mathscr{C}_i \text{ and } \phi \text{ is increasing}\},$$

F. Additional Stochastic Majorizations and Properties   421

$$\mathscr{C}_{i\downarrow} = \{\phi : \phi \in \mathscr{C}_i \text{ and } \phi \text{ is decreasing}\}.$$

(L-superadditivity is defined in 6.C.2.)

Comments About the Conditions

F.1. An alternative for P_4. Because $\mathscr{C}_4$ was motivated by the condition that $x \prec y$ if and only if $\sum_1^k x_{[i]} \leq \sum_1^k y_{[i]}$, $k = 1, \ldots, n$, and $\sum_1^n x_i = \sum_1^n y_i$, it might have been more natural to take

$$\mathscr{C}_4' = \left\{\phi : \phi(x) = \sum_1^k x_{[i]} \text{ for some } k = 1, \ldots, n, \text{ or } \phi(x) = -\sum_1^n x_i\right\}$$

in place of $\mathscr{C}_4$. This would yield a somewhat weaker version P_4' of P_4, but it would not change E_4. The set $\mathscr{C}_4'$ lacks a certain symmetry, and it is equally natural to consider

$$\mathscr{C}_4'' = \left\{\phi : \phi(x) = -\sum_k^n x_{[i]} \text{ for some } k = 1, \ldots, n, \text{ or } \phi(x) = \sum_1^n x_i\right\},$$

leading to P_4''. It turns out that P_4' and P_4'' are distinct conditions, both of which are implied by P_4.

F.2. Condition E_2 and dilations. Condition E_2 is reminiscent of the concept of a dilation. The probability measure P_Y associated with Y is called a *dilation* of the probability measure P_X associated with X if

$$E\phi(X) \leq E\phi(Y)$$

for all convex functions. This condition is often studied for X and Y taking values in a locally convex linear space. But here X and Y are required to take values in $\mathscr{R}^n$ for some n, so ϕ has n arguments and the additional condition that ϕ is symmetric makes sense. If X and Y have exchangeable components, then E_2 is equivalent to the condition that P_Y is a dilation of P_X. The reason for this is that if $X_1, \ldots, X_n$ are exchangeable and ϕ is convex, then

$$E\phi(X) = E\frac{1}{n!}\sum_{\Pi} \phi(X\Pi)$$

and $\widetilde{\phi}(x) = (1/n!)\sum_{\Pi} \phi(x\Pi)$ is a symmetric convex function.

F.3. Condition $E_1(P_1)$ and stochastic ordering. Condition E_1 is equivalent to condition P_1 (Section A). These conditions can be characterized in terms of stochastic orderings without reference to

Schur-convex functions because Schur-convex functions are related to functions with certain monotonicity properties. To see this, some notation is useful. For any vector $x \in \mathscr{R}^n$, let

$$\widetilde{x} = (x_{[1]}, x_{[1]} + x_{[2]}, \ldots, x_{[1]} + \cdots + x_{[n]}),$$

and let $C \subset \mathscr{R}^n$ be the set of all such vectors $\widetilde{x}$. The transformation $x \to \widetilde{x}$ is not invertible, but $\widetilde{x}$ does determine $x_{\downarrow} = (x_{[1]}, \ldots, x_{[n]})$. Thus, for any function g defined on C, there is a unique symmetric function f such that

$$g(\widetilde{x}) = f(x) \qquad \text{for all} \quad x \in \mathscr{R}^n.$$

Let $\mathscr{G}$ be the set of all functions $g : C \to \mathscr{R}$ which are increasing in the first $n - 1$ arguments (the nth argument being fixed). Then $g \in \mathscr{G}$ if and only if f is Schur-convex.

This proves the following result.

F.3.a. Proposition (Nevius, Proschan, and Sethuraman, 1977a).

$$X \prec_{E_1} Y \Leftrightarrow g(\widetilde{X}) \leq^{\text{st}} g(\widetilde{Y}) \qquad \text{for all} \quad g \in \mathscr{G}.$$

Of course, $\mathscr{G} \supset \mathscr{H}$ where $\mathscr{H}$ is the set of all functions defined on C increasing in each argument. Thus

$$X \prec_{E_1} Y \Rightarrow \widetilde{X} \leq^{\text{st}} \widetilde{Y}$$

in the sense that $g(\widetilde{X}) \leq^{\text{st}} g(\widetilde{Y})$ for all $g \in \mathscr{H}$.

The condition that $g(\widetilde{X}) \leq^{\text{st}} g(\widetilde{Y})$ for all $g \in \mathscr{G}$ implies that

$$P\left\{\left(\widetilde{X}, -\sum X_i\right) > t\right\} \leq P\left\{\left(\widetilde{Y}, -\sum Y_i\right) > t\right\} \qquad \text{for all } t \in \mathscr{R}^{n+1}.$$

This provides an interesting comparison between conditions P_1 and P_4; P_4 asks only that the corresponding components of the vectors $(\widetilde{X}, -\sum X_i)$ and $(\widetilde{Y}, -\sum Y_i)$ each individually be stochastically ordered.

Additional Properties and Closure Theorems for the Conditions

F.4. Distribution of the sum. Notice that the functions $\sum x_i$ and $-\sum x_i$ are both in the classes $\mathscr{C}_1, \ldots, \mathscr{C}_4$. This observation shows that if X and Y satisfy P_j for some j, then $\sum X_i$ and $\sum Y_i$ have the same distribution. Similarly, if X and Y satisfy E_j for some j, then $E \sum X_i = E \sum Y_i$.

F.5. The case of "equality." Suppose X, Y and $\tilde{Y}$, $\tilde{X}$ both satisfy the same condition. Can one conclude that $X = Y$ in some sense?

For condition E_1 (P_1), the answer to this question is at hand. In this case, it follows from F.3 that $\tilde{X} \leq^{\text{st}} \tilde{Y}$ and $\tilde{Y} \leq^{\text{st}} \tilde{X}$, so $\tilde{X}$ and $\tilde{Y}$ have the same distribution (17.A.1). Consequently, $(X_{[1]}, \ldots, X_{[n]})$ and $(Y_{[1]}, \ldots, Y_{[n]})$ have the same distribution.

If X, Y and $\tilde{Y}$, $\tilde{X}$ both satisfy P_2 (or only P_4), then one can conclude that corresponding components of $\tilde{X}$ and $\tilde{Y}$ have the same distribution. To see this, note that $\sum_1^k x_{[1]}$, $k = 1, \ldots, n$, are symmetric and convex. Thus $P\{X_{[1]} + \cdots + X_{[k]} > t\} = P\{Y_{[1]} + \cdots + Y_{[k]} > t\}$, $k = 1, \ldots, n$. But this does not mean $X_{[i]}$ and $Y_{[i]}$ have the same distribution for all i.

In Example F.9.c, X, Y and $\tilde{Y}$, $\tilde{X}$ both satisfy P_4, but X and Y have quite different distributions.

F.6. Closure under convolutions. Suppose some condition P_i or E_i holds for $X^{(1)}$, $Y^{(1)}$ and for $X^{(2)}$, $Y^{(2)}$. Under what circumstances does this imply that the same condition holds for $X^{(1)} + X^{(2)}$, $Y^{(1)} + Y^{(2)}$? This question is first considered here under the assumptions that $X^{(1)}$ and $X^{(2)}$ are independent, $Y^{(1)}$ and $Y^{(2)}$ are independent, and all four of these random vectors have exchangeable components.

F.6.a. Proposition. Suppose $X^{(1)}$ and $X^{(2)}$ are independent, $Y^{(1)}$ and $Y^{(2)}$ are independent, and these random vectors have exchangeable components. If $X^{(1)} \prec_{E_i} Y^{(1)}$ and $X^{(2)} \prec_{E_i} Y^{(2)}$, then

$$X^{(1)} + X^{(2)} \prec_{E_i} Y^{(1)} + Y^{(2)}, \quad i = 2, 3.$$

Proof. Consider the case of E_2. Note that if ϕ is symmetric and convex, then for any fixed $x \in \mathscr{R}^n$, the summation $\tilde{\phi}(u) = \sum_\Pi \phi(u + x\Pi)$ over all permutation matrices Π defines another symmetric convex function. To avoid notational complexities, suppose that the distribution function F of $X^{(2)}$ is continuous. Then

$E\phi(X^{(1)} + X^{(2)})$

$= \int_{\mathscr{R}^n} E\phi(X^{(1)} + x)\, dF(x) = \sum_\Pi \int_{\mathscr{D}} E\phi(X^{(1)} + x\Pi)\, dF(x)$

$= \int_{\mathscr{D}} E\left[\sum_\Pi \phi(X^{(1)} + x\Pi)\right] dF(x)$

$\leq \int_{\mathscr{D}} E\left[\sum_\Pi \phi(Y^{(1)} + x\Pi)\right] dF(x) = E\phi(Y^{(1)} + X^{(2)}).$

Similarly, $E\phi(Y^{(1)} + X^{(2)}) \leq E\phi(Y^{(1)} + Y^{(2)})$. The proof for E_3 is similar. ||

F.6.b. In F.6.a, neither E_1 (P_1) nor P_2 can take the place of E_2. To see this, take $n = 2$ and suppose that

$$P\{X^{(1)} = (1/2, 1/2)\} = 1,$$
$$P\{X^{(2)} = (0, 1)\} = P\{X^{(2)} = (1, 0)\} = 1/2,$$

and suppose that $Y^{(1)}$ and $Y^{(2)}$ have the same distribution as $X^{(2)}$. Then

$$P\{X^{(1)} + X^{(2)} = (1/2, 3/2)\} = P\{X^{(1)} + X^{(2)} = (3/2, 1/2)\} = 1/2,$$
$$P\{Y^{(1)} + Y^{(2)} = (0, 2)\} = P\{Y^{(1)} + Y^{(2)} = (2, 0)\} = 1/4,$$
$$P\{Y^{(1)} + Y^{(2)} = (1, 1)\} = 1/2.$$

To see that $X^{(1)} + X^{(2)}$, $Y^{(1)} + Y^{(2)}$ do not satisfy E_1 or P_2, observe that $X^{(1)} + X^{(2)}$, $Y^{(1)} + Y^{(2)}$ do not even satisfy P_4.

Next, consider the question of closure under convolution when the vectors $X^{(1)}$, $Y^{(1)}$, $X^{(2)}$, $Y^{(2)}$ take on values in $\mathscr{D}$ with probability 1. Equivalently, one might ask when $(X^{(1)}_{[1]} + X^{(2)}_{[1]}, \ldots, X^{(1)}_{[n]} + X^{(2)}_{[n]})$ and $(Y^{(1)}_{[1]} + Y^{(2)}_{[1]}, \ldots, Y^{(1)}_{[n]} + Y^{(2)}_{[n]})$ satisfy the same stochastic majorization as do $X^{(1)}$, $Y^{(1)}$ and $X^{(2)}$, $Y^{(2)}$.

F.6.c. Suppose that $X^{(1)}$ and $X^{(2)}$ are independent, $Y^{(1)}$ and $Y^{(2)}$ are independent, and all of these random vectors take values in $\mathscr{D}$. If $X^{(1)} \prec_{E_i} Y^{(1)}$ and $X^{(2)} \prec_{E_i} Y^{(2)}$, then $X^{(1)} + X^{(2)} \prec_{E_i} Y^{(1)} + Y^{(2)}$, $i = 1, 2, 3, 4$.

Proof. The proof is similar to the proof of F.6.a. For the case of E_1, this depends upon the fact that if $u \prec v$ on $\mathscr{D}$ and $x \in \mathscr{D}$, then $u + x \prec v + x$ on $\mathscr{D}$ (5.A.6). This means that if ϕ is Schur-convex on $\mathscr{D}$, then $\phi_x(u) = \phi(u + x)$ is also Schur-convex. If $X^{(2)}$ has distribution function F,

$$E\phi(X^{(1)} + X^{(2)}) = \int_{\mathscr{D}} E\phi(X^{(1)} + x)\, dF(x) \leq \int_{\mathscr{D}} E\phi(Y^{(1)} + x)\, dF(x)$$
$$= E\varphi(Y^{(1)} + X^{(2)}).$$

Similarly, $E\phi(Y^{(1)} + X^{(2)}) \leq E\phi(Y^{(1)} + Y^{(2)})$. The proof for E_2 and E_3 is virtually identical and the case of E_4 is a consequence of 5.A.6. ||

F.7. Preservation under mixtures. Suppose that for each fixed u some condition holds relating X_u and Y_u. Does that condition

F. Additional Stochastic Majorizations and Properties   425

hold when u is replaced by a random variable U? If so, the condition is said to be *preserved under mixtures*. A conditioning argument can be used to show that E_i and P_i, $i = 1, 2, 3, 4$, are all preserved under mixtures. For example, consider P_i: For $\phi \in \mathscr{C}_i$,

$$P\{\phi(X_U) > t\} = \int P\{\phi(X_u) > t | U = u\} dP\{U \leq u\}$$

$$\leq \int P\{\phi(Y_u) > t | U = u\} dP\{U \leq u\} = P\{\phi(Y_U) > t\}.$$

The inequality here follows from the definitions in Section A.

For the case of $E_1(P_1)$, preservation under mixtures was observed by Nevius, Proschan, and Sethuraman (1977a).

F.8. Closure under limits in distribution. If $X^{(j)} \prec_{P_i} Y^{(j)}$, $j = 1, 2, \ldots$, and if $\{X^{(j)}\}$ converges in distribution to X and $\{Y^{(j)}\}$ converges in distribution to Y, then $X \prec_{P_i} Y$, $i = 1, 2, 3, 4$. To see this, note first that if $\{F_n\}$ is a sequence of distributions converging to the distribution F, then $\lim_{n \to \infty} \int_A dF_n(x) = \int_A dF(x)$ for all sets A with boundary ∂A satisfying $\int_{\partial A} dF(x) = 0$ (Billingsley, 1968, Theorem 2.1). With sets A of the form $\{x: \phi(x) > t\}$, it follows that since $\{X^{(j)}\}$ converges in distribution to X, $\{\phi(X^{(j)})\}$ converges in distribution to $\phi(X)$. Thus, if $P\{\phi(X^{(j)}) > t\} \leq P\{\phi(Y^{(j)}) > t\}$, $j = 1, 2, \ldots$, and if t is a continuity point of the distributions of $\phi(X)$ and $\phi(Y)$, then

$$P\{\phi(X) > t\} = \lim_{j \to \infty} P\{\phi(X^{(j)}) > t\}$$

$$\leq \lim_{j \to \infty} P\{\phi(Y^{(j)}) > t\} = P\{\phi(Y) > t\}.$$

On the other hand, there is no guarantee that $X \prec_{E_i} Y$ even when $X^{(j)} \prec_{E_i} Y^{(j)}$ and $\{X^{(j)}\}$ converges in distribution to X and $\{Y^{(j)}\}$ converges in distribution to Y. Indeed, the relations $X^{(j)} \prec_{E_i} Y^{(j)}$ might all be satisfied vacuously, but this might be false for the limits X and Y, $i = 1, 2, 3, 4$.

F.9. Relationships among the various conditions. All of the implications in Fig. 1 are easy to prove. That $E_1 \Rightarrow P_1$ is a consequence of D.1. As already observed in Section A, $P_i \Rightarrow E_i$, $i = 1, 2, 3, 4$, because stochastically ordered random variables have ordered expectations. The remainder of the implications follow from the fact that $\mathscr{C}_1 \supset \mathscr{C}_2 \supset \mathscr{C}_3$ and $\mathscr{C}_2 \supset \mathscr{C}_4$.

426   11. Stochastic Majorizations

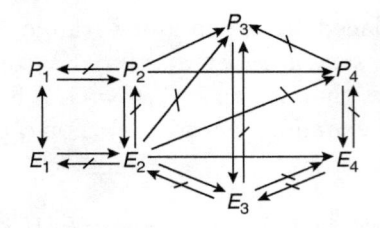

Figure 1. Relations among conditions.

The possibility of further implications is not entirely settled by the indicated counter-implications. In particular, it is not known that $P_3 \not\Rightarrow E_4$, $P_3 \not\Rightarrow P_4$, or even that $P_3 \not\Rightarrow P_2$. However, the following counterexamples show that most of the implications not given in the above diagram are false.

F.9.a. $E_2 \not\Rightarrow P_4$ (hence $E_i \not\Rightarrow P_j$ for all j, $i > 1$). Suppose that $P\{X = (\frac{1}{2}, \frac{1}{2})\} = 1$, $P\{Y = (0,0)\} = P\{Y = (1,1)\} = \frac{1}{2}$. If ϕ is symmetric and convex,

$$E\phi(Y) - E\phi(X) = \tfrac{1}{2}[\phi(0,0) + \phi(1,1) - 2\phi(\tfrac{1}{2}, \tfrac{1}{2})] \geq 0,$$

so X and Y satisfy E_2. But $X_1 + X_2$ and $Y_1 + Y_2$ do not have the same distribution, so P_2, P_3, and P_4 all fail to hold.

F.9.b. $P_2 \not\Rightarrow P_1$ (hence $E_2 \not\Rightarrow E_1$). To see this, suppose that

$$P\{X = (14, 8, 2)\} = P\{X = (8, 8, 8)\} = \tfrac{1}{2},$$
$$P\{Y = (16, 4, 4)\} = P\{Y = (12, 12, 0)\} = \tfrac{1}{2}.$$

Suppose that ϕ is symmetric and convex. If $\phi(8,8,8) > t$, then $\phi(14,8,2) > t$, $\phi(16,4,4) > t$, and $\phi(12,12,0) > t$, so in this case

$$P\{\phi(X) > t\} = P\{\phi(Y) > t\} = 1.$$

Suppose $\phi(8,8,8) < t$ and $\phi(14,8,2) > t$. Then because $(14,8,2) = \tfrac{1}{2}[(16,4,4) + (12,12,0)]$, either $\phi(16,4,4) > t$ or $\phi(12,12,0) > t$ (or both), so in this case

$$\tfrac{1}{2} = P\{\phi(X) > t\} \leq P\{\phi(Y) > t\}.$$

This shows that X, Y satisfy P_2.

To see that P_1 fails, let $S = \{u : u \prec (16,5,3) \text{ or } u \prec (13,11,0)\}$. Notice that $(16,4,4) \in S$ and $(12,12,0) \in S$ so $P\{Y \in S\} = 1$, but $(14,8,2) \notin S$ so $P\{X \in S\} = \tfrac{1}{2}$. If

$$\phi(z) = \begin{cases} 0 & \text{if } z \in S, \\ 1 & \text{otherwise,} \end{cases}$$

then ϕ is Schur-convex because $u \prec v$ and $\phi(v) = 0 \Rightarrow \phi(u) = 0$. On the other hand, $\phi(X) >^{st} \phi(Y)$, so P_1 fails.

F.9.c. $P_4 \not\Rightarrow P_3$. Suppose that X takes on the values $(9,7)$, $(9,3)$, $(11,5)$, $(11,1)$, $(13,7)$, $(13,3)$, $(15,5)$, and $(15,1)$ each with probability $\frac{1}{8}$, and Y takes on the values $(9,7)$, $(11,1)$, $(13,3)$, and $(15,5)$ each with probability $\frac{1}{4}$. Then X and Y have the same marginal distributions. Since $X_1 > X_2$, $Y_1 > Y_2$, this means $X_{[1]}$ and $Y_{[1]}$ have the same distribution, as do $X_{[2]}$ and $Y_{[2]}$. Moreover, $X_1 + X_2$ and $Y_1 + Y_2$ have the same distribution. Consequently, both X, Y and Y, X satisfy P_4. If $\psi(z) = \max(0, z - \frac{7}{8})$, then ψ is convex. In this case also, $P\{\psi(X_1) + \psi(X_2) > \frac{1}{10}\} = \frac{1}{8} > 0 = P\{\psi(Y_1) + \psi(Y_2) > \frac{1}{10}\}$. Notice that although P_3 is violated here, E_3 is in fact satisfied.

F.9.d. $E_4 \not\Rightarrow E_3$ and $E_3 \not\Rightarrow E_4$ (hence $E_3 \not\Rightarrow E_2$). To see this, let
$$P\{X = (2,2)\} = P\{X = (-2,-2)\} = \tfrac{1}{2},$$
$$P\{Y = (1,-1)\} = P\{Y = (-1,1)\} = \tfrac{1}{2}.$$
Here, $EX_{[1]} = EX_{[2]} = 0$, and $EY_{[1]} = 1$, $EY_{[2]} = -1$. Thus E_4 is satisfied. If $\psi : \mathscr{R} \to \mathscr{R}$ is convex, then
$$E[\psi(X_1) + \psi(X_2)] = \psi(2) + \psi(-2) \geq \psi(1) + \psi(-1) = E[\psi(Y_1) + \psi(Y_2)]$$
with strict inequality if ψ is strictly convex. Thus, E_3 fails. To see that $E_3 \not\Rightarrow E_4$, interchange X and Y in this example.

G Weak Stochastic Majorizations

Many of the results of the preceding sections have analogs for the two versions $\prec_w$ and $\prec^w$ of weak majorization. It is easy to see that all of the notions of stochastic majorization which have been introduced have weak versions. For consider the conditions

$$P_{\mathscr{C}}: \quad \phi(X) \leq^{st} \phi(Y) \qquad \text{for all } \phi \in \mathscr{C}$$

and

$$E_{\mathscr{C}}: \quad E\phi(X) \leq E\phi(Y) \qquad \text{for all } \phi \in \mathscr{C} \text{ such that the expectations are defined.}$$

Here, $\mathscr{C}$ has the property that

$$x \prec y \qquad \text{if and only if} \quad \phi(x) \leq \phi(y) \text{ for all } \phi \in \mathscr{C}.$$

428   11. Stochastic Majorizations

All of the classes $\mathscr{C}_1$, $\mathscr{C}_2$, $\mathscr{C}_3$ and $\mathscr{C}_4$ (see Section F) have the property that

$x \prec_w y$ if and only if $\phi(x) \leq \phi(y)$ for all increasing $\phi \in \mathscr{C}$,

$x \prec^w y$ if and only if $\phi(x) \leq \phi(y)$ for all decreasing $\phi \in \mathscr{C}$.

For any such class $\mathscr{C}$, the stochastic majorizations $P_\mathscr{C}$ and $E_\mathscr{C}$ have weak analogs. Some notation for this is convenient:

$X \prec_w P_\mathscr{C} Y$ if X and Y satisfy $P_\mathscr{C}^\uparrow$: $\phi(X) \leq^{st} \phi(Y)$
for all increasing $\phi \in \mathscr{C}$;

$X \prec_w E_\mathscr{C} Y$ if X and Y satisfy $E_\mathscr{C}^\uparrow$: $E\phi(X) \leq E\phi(Y)$
for all increasing $\phi \in \mathscr{C}$ such that the expectations are defined;

$X \prec^w P_\mathscr{C} Y$ if X and Y satisfy $P_\mathscr{C}^\downarrow$: $\phi(X) \leq^{st} \phi(Y)$
for all decreasing $\phi \in \mathscr{C}$;

$X \prec^w E_\mathscr{C} Y$ if X and Y satisfy $E_\mathscr{C}^\downarrow$: $E\phi(X) \leq E\phi(Y)$
for all decreasing $\phi \in \mathscr{C}$ such that the expectations are defined.

As for the case of strong stochastic majorization, consideration here is primarily of

$\mathscr{C}_1 = \{\phi : \phi : \mathscr{R}^n \to \mathscr{R}$ is Borel-measurable and Schur-convex$\}$

and

$\mathscr{C}_2 = \{\phi : \phi : \mathscr{R}^n \to \mathscr{R}$ is continuous, symmetric, and convex$\}$.

With the same kind of arguments that were used for strong majorization, the following implications can easily be established:

$$\begin{array}{ccc} X \prec_w P_1 Y \Rightarrow X \prec_w P_2 Y & \quad & X \prec^w P_1 Y \Rightarrow X \prec^w P_2 Y \\ \Updownarrow \qquad \qquad \Downarrow & & \Updownarrow \qquad \qquad \Downarrow \\ X \prec_w E_1 Y \Rightarrow X \prec_w E_2 Y & & X \prec^w E_1 Y \Rightarrow X \prec^w E_2 Y. \end{array}$$

It should be noted that the relationship

$$x \prec^w y \quad \text{if and only if} \quad -x \prec_w -y$$

has its counterpart for the stochastic versions considered here. To see this, observe that

$$\phi \in \mathscr{C}_i \quad \text{if and only if} \quad \widehat{\phi}(x) = \phi(-x) \in \mathscr{C}_i, \quad i = 1, 2, 3, 4.$$

Of course, $\widehat{\phi}$ is decreasing if and only if ϕ is increasing, and

$$E\widehat{\phi}(X) \le E\widehat{\phi}(Y) \quad \text{if and only if} \quad E\phi(-X) \le E\phi(-Y),$$

$$\widehat{\phi}(X) \le^{\text{st}} \widehat{\phi}(Y) \quad \text{if and only if} \quad \phi(-X) \le^{\text{st}} \phi(-Y).$$

In spite of this duality, both versions of weak majorization are discussed in most of what follows.

As in the case of strong majorization, the most interesting cases of stochastic weak majorizations are found among random vectors with distributions belonging to the same parametric family. In a number of examples, it is shown that $\psi(\theta) = E_\theta \phi(X)$ inherits as a function θ the properties required of ϕ. In such cases it is convenient to speak of the families as being parameterized to preserve the properties. On the other hand, ψ may not inherit the properties of ϕ, but rather ψ may be guaranteed to have certain other properties. For example, ψ may be decreasing when ϕ is increasing unless an unnatural parameterization of the distributions is used. Because of the multiplicity of possibly interesting conditions, we do not define weak majorization analogs of such conditions as $P^*_\mathscr{C}$, $E^*_\mathscr{C}$, or E^{**}_2.

Families of Distributions That Preserve Symmetry and Convexity with Monotonicity

Most of the examples of Section C have analogs for weak majorization. Several are based upon the following proposition.

G.1. Proposition. Suppose that $\{F_\theta, \theta \in \mathscr{R}^n_{++}\}$ is a family of distribution functions defined on $\mathscr{R}^n_+$ and satisfying

$$F_\theta(x) = F_e(x_1/\theta_1, \ldots, x_n/\theta_n), \quad \text{where} \quad e = (1, \ldots, 1), \quad (1)$$

and

$$F_e(x) = F_e(x\Pi) \quad \text{for all permutations } \Pi. \quad (2)$$

Alternatively, suppose $\{F_\theta, \theta \in \mathscr{R}^n\}$ is a family of distribution functions satisfying

$$F_\theta(x) = F_{\mathbf{0}}(x + \theta), \quad \text{where} \quad \mathbf{0} = (0, \ldots, 0), \quad (3)$$

and

$$F_{\mathbf{0}}(x) = F_{\mathbf{0}}(x\Pi) \quad \text{for all permutations } \Pi. \quad (4)$$

Then $\psi(\theta) = E_\theta \phi(X)$ is increasing (decreasing), symmetric, and convex in θ whenever ϕ is a Borel-measurable, increasing (decreasing), and convex function such that the expectations are defined.

430   11. Stochastic Majorizations

Proof. This follows directly from B.5.a and B.5.b. ||

G.2. Examples. If $X_1, \ldots, X_n$ have any of the following distributions, then

$$\psi(\theta) = E_\theta \phi(X)$$

is increasing (decreasing), symmetric, and convex in θ whenever ϕ is a function with the same properties such that the expectations are defined.

(a) *Exchangeable normal random variables.* $(X_1 - \theta_1, \ldots, X_n - \theta_n)$ are exchangeable and normally distributed. Note that the result C.2.b for normal random variables with scale parameter has no parallel here because normal random variables are not nonnegative as required by G.1.

(b) *Independent gamma random variables.* $X_1, \ldots, X_n$ are independent, and for some fixed $r > 0$, X_i has the density

$$f(x; r, \theta_i) = \frac{\theta_i^{-r} x^{r-1}}{\Gamma(r)} e^{-x/\theta_i}, \qquad x \geq 0, \quad \theta_i > 0, \quad i = 1, \ldots, n.$$

See also G.3 ahead.

(c) *Independent uniform random variables.* $X_1, \ldots, X_n$ are independent, and X_i has density

$$f_{\theta_i}(x) = \frac{1}{\theta_i} I_{(0,\theta_i)}(x), \qquad \theta_i > 0, \quad i = 1, \ldots, n,$$

or X_i has density

$$f_{\theta_i}(x) = I_{(\theta_i, \theta_i+1)}(x), \qquad \theta_i \geq 0, \quad i = 1, \ldots, n.$$

(d) *Independent Poisson random variables.* $X_1, \ldots, X_n$ are independent and

$$P\{X_i = x\} = e^{-\theta_i}(\theta_i^x / x!), \qquad x = 0, 1, \ldots, \quad \theta_i > 0, \quad i = 1, \ldots, n.$$

In this case, the preservation of monotonicity follows from G.4(5) ahead (or a direct proof is not difficult).

(e) *Multinomial (incomplete) random variables.* $X_1, \ldots, X_n$ have a distribution given by

$$P\{X = x\} = \binom{N}{x_1, \ldots, x_n} \left(1 - \sum \theta_i\right)^{N - \Sigma x_i} \prod_i^n \theta_i^{x_i},$$

$$x_i = 0, 1, 2, \ldots, \quad \sum_1^n x_i \leq N, \quad \theta_i \geq 0, \quad i = 1, \ldots, n, \quad \sum_1^n \theta_i \leq 1.$$

Again, preservation of monotonicity follows from G.4(5).

G.2.a. Proposition. If $X = (X_1, \ldots, X_n)$ has a (complete) multinomial distribution with parameter θ, then for $m < n$,

$$P_{\theta_1, \ldots, \theta_m}\{X_1 \geq s, \ldots, X_m \geq s\}$$

is an increasing Schur-convex function of $\theta_1, \ldots, \theta_m$, and

$$P_{\theta_1, \ldots, \theta_m}\{X_1 \leq t, \ldots, X_m \leq t\}$$

is a decreasing Schur-convex function of $\theta_1, \ldots, \theta_m$.

Proof. The Schur-convexity follows from E.11.e and the monotonicity follows from G.4 below. ∥

G.3. Corollary. Suppose that $\{F_\theta, \theta \in \mathscr{R}_{++}^n\}$ is a family of distribution functions defined on $\mathscr{R}_+^n$ and satisfying (1) and (2) of G.1. Let $\psi(\theta) = E_\theta \varphi(X)$, where φ is an increasing (decreasing) symmetric convex function. If $\lambda_i = 1/\theta_i$, $i = 1, \ldots, n$, and

$$\widetilde{\psi}(\lambda) = \psi(1/\lambda_1, \ldots, 1/\lambda_n),$$

then $\widetilde{\psi}$ is a decreasing (increasing) symmetric convex function.

Proof. This follows from G.1 by using B.5 with $w(x, a) = x/a$. ∥

Note the reversal of the direction of monotonicity here. From this result, it follows that $\lambda \prec^w \lambda'$ implies $\widetilde{\psi}(\lambda) \leq \widetilde{\psi}(\lambda')$ whenever ϕ is increasing, symmetric, and convex.

Families of Distributions That Preserve Schur-Convexity and Monotonicity

In Section E, various families $\{F_\theta, \theta \in A \subset \mathscr{R}^n\}$ of distributions are identified that have the property

$\psi(\theta) = E_\theta \phi(X)$ is Schur-convex in θ whenever ϕ is Schur-convex such that the expectation is defined.

These results are obtained using E.3, E.4, or E.5, which can be modified so as to guarantee the preservation of both Schur-convexity and monotonicity. The following proposition is given by Nevius, Proschan, and Sethuraman (1977b) for the case that $X_1, \ldots, X_n$ are independent.

G.4. Proposition (Cheng, 1977). Let $\{F_\theta, \theta \in \Theta^n\}$ be a family of n-dimensional discrete distributions such that

$$P_\theta\{X_1 = x_1, \ldots, X_n = x_n\} = C\left(\sum x_i, \sum \theta_i\right) \prod_{i=1}^{n} \alpha(\theta_i, x_i)$$

whenever $x_1, \ldots, x_n$ are nonnegative integers, and equals 0 otherwise. If C satisfies

$$C(u, \xi) = \sum_{v=0}^{\infty} C(u+v, \xi+\eta) \alpha(\eta, v)$$

whenever $\eta, \xi \in \Theta$, and if

$$\alpha(\xi, z) = \frac{\xi^z}{z!}, \qquad z = 0, 1, 2, \ldots, \quad \xi \in \Theta = (0, \infty), \qquad (5)$$

$$\alpha(\xi, z) = \binom{\xi}{z}, \qquad z = 0, 1, 2, \ldots, \quad \xi \in \Theta = \{0, 1, 2, \ldots\}, \qquad (6)$$

or

$$\alpha(\xi, z) = \frac{\Gamma(\xi+z)}{z!\,\Gamma(\xi)}, \qquad z = 0, 1, 2, \ldots, \quad 0 < \xi < \infty, \qquad (7)$$

then $\psi(\theta) = \int \phi(x)\, dF_\theta(x)$ is Schur-convex and increasing (decreasing) whenever ϕ has the same properties.

Proof. This follows from 3.J.3. ∥

The following proposition was also given by Nevius, Proschan, and Sethuraman (1977b) for the case that the function C is a constant.

G.5. Proposition (Cheng, 1977). Let $\{F_\theta, \theta \in \mathscr{R}^n_{++}\}$ be a family of n-dimensional distribution functions having densities of the form

$$f(x_1, \ldots, x_n; \theta) = \begin{cases} C\left(\sum x_i, \sum \theta_i\right) \prod_{i=1}^{n} \dfrac{x_i^{\theta_i - 1}}{\Gamma(\theta_i)}, & \text{if } x_i \geq 0 \text{ for all } i, \\ 0 & \text{otherwise.} \end{cases}$$

If C satisfies

$$C(u, \xi) = \int_0^\infty C(u+v, \xi+\eta) \frac{v^{\eta-1}}{\Gamma(\eta)}\, dv,$$

then $\psi(\theta) = \int \phi(x)\, dF_\theta(x)$ is Schur-convex and increasing (decreasing) whenever ϕ is a Schur-convex increasing (decreasing) function such that the expectations are defined.

Proof. This follows from 3.J.3. ∥

As pointed out by Cheng (1977), the conditions on the function C in G.4 and G.5 are natural ones here; they can be interpreted as saying that if $X_1, \ldots, X_n$ have density (with respect to counting measure or Lebesgue measure) of the form

$$f(x_1, \ldots, x_n; \theta) = C\left(\sum_1^n x_i, \sum_1^n \theta_i\right) \prod_1^n \alpha(\theta_i, x_i),$$

then $X_1, \ldots, X_{n-1}$ have density $C(\sum_1^{n-1} x_i, \sum_1^{n-1} \theta_i) \prod_1^{n-1} \alpha(\theta_i, x_i)$ of the same form.

G.6. Proposition. If $X_1, \ldots, X_n$ are exchangeable and have a Schur-concave density, then $\psi(\theta) = E\phi(X + \theta)$ is an increasing Schur-convex function of θ whenever ϕ is a function with the same properties such that the expectations are defined.

Proof. This is a trivial consequence of E.5. ∥

Propositions G.4, G.5, and G.6 can be used to show that most interesting families of distributions which preserve Schur-convexity also preserve monotonicity as well. In particular, this is true of the following examples given in Section E:

Multivariate chi-square	(E.5.d)
Exchangeable multivariate normal and multivariate t	(E.5.e, E.5.f)
Independent Poisson	(E.6)
Independent binomial	(E.7)
Independent gamma	(E.8)
Exchangeable normal	(E.9)
Independent uniform	(E.10)
Dirichlet	(E.12)
Liouville–Dirichlet	(E.13)

Multivariate hypergeometric (E.14)
Negative multinomial (E.15)
Multivariate logarithmic series (E.16)
Multivariate modified logarithmic (E.17)
Multivariate inverse hypergeometric (E.18)
Negative multivariate hypergeometric (E.19)
Dirichlet compound negative multinomial (E.20)

The cases of independent Poisson, binomial, gamma, and the multivariate negative binomial are examples due to Nevius, Proschan, and Sethuraman (1977b). Most of the remaining examples are due to Cheng (1977).

Some distributions are conspicuous by their absence from the above list. In particular, the multinomial is not listed. The reason for this is that the parameters of the distribution add to unity, and it is not meaningful to talk about monotonicity in such parameters. However, there is a nonsingular version of the distribution for which this is not the case.

G.7. Additional examples. If $X_1, \ldots, X_n$ have any of the following distributions, then $\psi(\xi) = E_\xi \phi(X)$ is increasing (decreasing) and Schur-convex whenever ϕ is a function with the same properties such that the expectations are defined. In each case, the appropriate parameter ξ is indicated.

(a) *Incomplete multinomial distribution:*

$$P\{X = x\} = \frac{N!}{(N - \sum x_i)!} \left(1 - \sum \theta_i\right)^{N - \Sigma x_i} \prod_1^n \frac{\theta_i^{x_i}}{x_i!},$$

where the x_i are nonnegative integers such that $\sum x_i \leq N$, $\theta_i \geq 0$, $i = 1, \ldots, n$, $\sum_1^n \theta_i \leq 1$. Here, $\xi = (\theta_1, \ldots, \theta_n)$. Monotone Schur-convexity follows from G.4(5).

(b) *Multivariate hypergeometric distribution:*

$$P\{X = x\} = \binom{K}{N}^{-1} \binom{K - \sum M_i}{N - \sum x_i} \prod_1^n \binom{M_i}{x_i},$$

$$x = 0, 1, \ldots, \quad \sum x_i \leq N,$$

$M_i = 1, \ldots, \sum M_i \leq K$. Here, $\xi = (M_1, \ldots, M_n)$. Monotone Schur-convexity follows from G.4(6).

(c) *Negative multivariate hypergeometric distribution:*

$$P\{X = x\} = \frac{N!\Gamma(M)}{\Gamma(N+M)} \frac{\Gamma(M+N-\sum x_i - \sum \lambda_i)}{(N-\sum x_i)!\Gamma(M-\sum \lambda_i)} \prod_1^n \frac{\Gamma(x_i + \lambda_i)}{x_i!\Gamma(\lambda_i)},$$

$x_i = 0, 1, \ldots, \sum x_i \leq N$, $\lambda_i > 0$, $\sum \lambda_i < M$. Here, $\xi = (\lambda_1, \ldots, \lambda_n)$. Monotone Schur-convexity follows from G.4(7).

H Additional Stochastic Weak Majorizations and Properties

Following the ideas and notations of Section F, the stochastic weak majorizations defined in terms of $\mathscr{C}_1$, $\mathscr{C}_2$, $\mathscr{C}_3$, and $\mathscr{C}_4$ are considered here. As before, subscripts i are used in place of $\mathscr{C}_i$ to identify the various stochastic weak majorizations defined in terms of $\mathscr{C}_i$.

Arguments given in the introduction to this chapter can be used to show that

$$P_1^\uparrow \Rightarrow P_2^\uparrow \Rightarrow P_3^\uparrow, \qquad P_2^\uparrow \Rightarrow P_4^\uparrow, \qquad E_1^\uparrow \Rightarrow E_2^\uparrow \Rightarrow E_3^\uparrow, \qquad E_2^\uparrow \Rightarrow E_4^\uparrow,$$

$$P_i^\uparrow \Rightarrow E_i^\uparrow, \qquad i = 1, 2, 3, 4, \qquad \text{and} \qquad E_1^\uparrow \Rightarrow P_1^\uparrow.$$

Similar implications hold when "↑" is replaced by "↓."

In the remainder of this section, various properties and implications are discussed.

Some Inequalities for Probabilities

H.1. Proposition (Nevius, Proschan, and Sethuraman, 1977b). If X and Y satisfy $E_1^\uparrow$ and $S \subset \mathscr{R}^n$ is a Borel-measurable set having an increasing Schur-convex indicator function, then

$$P\{X \in S\} \leq P\{Y \in S\}.$$

Similarly, if X and Y satisfy $E_1^\downarrow$ and the indicator function of S is decreasing, the same result holds.

The proofs of these results follow immediately upon taking expectations of the indicator function of S evaluated at X or Y. There is a converse to this proposition:

H.1.a. (Nevius, Proschan, and Sethuraman, 1977b). If

$$P\{X \in S\} \leq P\{Y \in S\}$$

for all Borel-measurable sets S with increasing Schur-convex indicator functions, then $X \prec_w E_1 Y$. With "decreasing" in place of "increasing," $X \prec^w E_1 Y$.

The proof of this involves the approximation of increasing Schur-convex functions by linear combinations of increasing Schur-convex indicator functions.

H.1.b. If $X \prec_w E_1 Y$, then for all $a \in \mathscr{R}^n$,
$$P\{X \succ_w a\} \leq P\{Y \succ_w a\} \qquad \text{and} \qquad P\{X \prec_w a\} \geq P\{Y \prec_w a\}.$$
Similarly, if $X \prec^w E_1 Y$,
$$P\{X \succ^w a\} \leq P\{Y \succ^w a\} \qquad \text{and} \qquad P\{X \prec^w a\} \geq P\{Y \prec^w a\}.$$

Proof. To prove the results for $E_1^\uparrow$, let
$$S = \{x : x \succ_w a\}$$
or let
$$S = \{x : x \prec_w a\}^c.$$
A similar proof holds for $E_1^\downarrow$. ||

As pointed out by Nevius, Proschan, and Sethuraman (1977b), the condition
$$P\{X \succ_w a\} \leq P\{Y \succ_w a\} \qquad \text{for all vectors } a$$
might be used as a definition of stochastic weak majorization because $y \succ_w a$ implies $x \succ_w a$ for all $a \in \mathscr{R}^n$ if and only if $x \succ_w y$. However, this definition is probably not very useful.

H.1.c. If $X \prec_w E_1 Y$, then
$$P\{\max X_i \leq r\} \geq P\{\max Y_i \leq r\},$$
or equivalently,
$$P\{\max X_i > r\} \leq P\{\max Y_i > r\}.$$
If $X \prec^w E_1 Y$, then
$$P\{\min X_i > r\} \geq P\{\min Y_i > r\},$$
or equivalently,
$$P\{\min X_i \leq r\} \leq P\{\min Y_i \leq r\}.$$

H. Additional Stochastic Weak Majorizations and Properties 437

Proof. Again the proof follows by taking expectations of the obvious indicator functions which are Schur-convex and, respectively, increasing and decreasing. ||

H.2. Suppose that both X and Y are nonnegative random vectors and let Z_U be the number of zero components of U. If $X \prec^w E_i\, Y$, then $Z_X \leq^{st} Z_Y$.

Proof. On $\mathscr{R}_+^n$, $\phi(x) = \sum_{i=1}^n I_{\{z:z_i=0\}}(x)$ is Schur-convex, symmetric, and decreasing. ||

H.3.

$$\text{If } X \prec_w P_4\, Y, \quad \text{then } \sum X_i \leq^{st} \sum Y_i;$$
$$\text{if } X \prec^w P_4\, Y, \quad \text{then } \sum X_i \geq^{st} \sum Y_i;$$
$$\text{if } X \prec_w E_4\, Y, \quad \text{then } \sum EX_i \leq \sum EY_i;$$
$$\text{if } X \prec^w E_4\, Y, \quad \text{then } \sum EX_i \geq \sum EY_i.$$

Proof. These results follow because $\phi(x) = \sum x_i$ is in $\mathscr{C}_4$ and is increasing; $\phi(x) = -\sum x_i$ is in $\mathscr{C}_4$ and is decreasing. ||

Condition $E_1^\uparrow(P_1^\uparrow)$ and Stochastic Ordering

In accordance with the discussion of F.3, let $C \subset \mathscr{R}^n$ be the set of all vectors $\widetilde{x}$ of the form

$$\widetilde{x} = (x_{[1]}, x_{[1]} + x_{[2]}, \ldots, x_{[1]} + \cdots + x_{[n]}),$$

where $x \in \mathscr{R}^n$. For any function g defined on C, there is a unique symmetric function f such that

$$g(\widetilde{x}) = f(x) \qquad \text{for all} \quad x \in \mathscr{R}^n.$$

Let $\mathscr{G}$ be the set of all functions g defined on C such that g is increasing in each argument. Then $g \in \mathscr{G}$ if and only if f is increasing and Schur-convex. This yields the following proposition.

H.4. Proposition (Nevius, Proschan, and Sethuraman, 1977b).

$$X \prec_w E_1\, Y \Leftrightarrow \widetilde{X} \leq^{st} \widetilde{Y},$$

where $\widetilde{X} \leq^{st} \widetilde{Y}$ means $g(\widetilde{X}) \leq^{st} g(\widetilde{Y})$ for all $g \in \mathscr{G}$.

The corresponding result for $\prec^w E_1$ requires some modifications: $\widetilde{x}$ is replaced by $\widetilde{x}^* = (\sum_1^n x_{[i]}, \sum_2^n x_{[i]}, \ldots, x_{[n]})$, C is replaced by the set C^* of such vectors, and $\mathscr{G}$ is replaced by the set $\mathscr{G}^*$ of all functions g decreasing in each argument. Then

$$X \prec^w E_1\, Y \Leftrightarrow \widetilde{X}^* \geq^{st} \widetilde{Y}^*.$$

Results of Combining Conditions

The weak stochastic majorization conditions can be combined in certain interesting ways that raise obvious questions.

It is easy to see that $x \prec_w y$ and $x \prec^w y$ implies $x \prec y$. Is this implication true for the various stochastic analogs? For most such analogs, the answer is not known. However, in two cases an affirmative answer is easily obtained.

H.5. If $X \prec_w P_4 Y$ and $X \prec^w P_4 Y$, then $X \prec P_4 Y$. If $X \prec_w E_4 Y$ and $X \prec^w E_4 Y$, then $X \prec E_4 Y$.

Proof. This is immediate because the functions in $\mathscr{C}_4$ are all either increasing or decreasing. ||

H.5.a. If $X \prec_w P_3 Y$ and $X \prec^w P_3 Y$, then $X \prec P_3 Y$. The same result holds with E_3 in place of P_3.

Proof. This results from the fact that convex functions $\psi : \mathscr{R} \to \mathscr{R}$ can be written as a sum $\psi = \psi_1 + \psi_2$, where ψ_1 is convex and increasing, ψ_2 is convex and decreasing. ||

Another natural way to combine conditions is to keep the same notion of stochastic weak majorization but interchange the two random vectors. If $X \prec_w E_i Y$ and $Y \prec_w E_i X$ or if P_i replaces E_i, what conclusions are possible?

As with the case of strong majorization, this question can be answered for $E_1(P_1)$. By H.4, $X \prec_w E_i Y$ and $Y \prec_w E_i X$ together imply $\widetilde{X}$ and $\widetilde{Y}$ have the same distribution, so $(X_{[1]}, \ldots, X_{[n]})$ and $(Y_{[1]}, \ldots, Y_{[n]})$ also have the same distribution. The same result holds for $\prec^w$.

If $X \prec_w P_4 Y$ and $Y \prec_w P_4 X$, then it is easily verified that $\sum_1^k X_i$ and $\sum_1^k Y_i$ both have the same distribution, $k = 1, \ldots, n$. Similarly, $X \prec^w P_4 Y$ and $Y \prec^w P_4 X$ imply that $\sum_k^n X_i$ and $\sum_k^n Y_i$ have the same distribution. But this does not mean $X_{[i]}$ and $Y_{[i]}$ have the same distribution for all i.

Closure Properties

Consider first the case of mixtures.

H.6. If, for each fixed u, F_u and G_u are distribution functions on $\mathscr{R}^n$ ordered by the same weak stochastic majorization $\prec_w E_i$, $\prec_w P_i$, $\prec^w E_i$, or $\prec^w P_i$, $i = 1, 2, 3, 4$ (in the sense that the corresponding random variables are so ordered), then mixtures $\int F_u \, dH(u)$ and $\int G_u \, dH(u)$ are ordered in the same sense.

H. Additional Stochastic Weak Majorizations and Properties   439

For the case of $\prec_w E_1$, this result was obtained by Nevius, Proschan, and Sethuraman (1977b). The proofs are all straightforward, being essentially the same as for strong majorization F.7.

Next, consider the case of convolutions. Suppose $X^{(j)} \prec_w E_i Y^{(j)}$, $j = 1, 2$; is it true that $(X^{(1)}+X^{(2)}) \prec_w E_i (Y^{(1)}+Y^{(2)})$ for $i = 1, 2, 3, 4$?

H.7. Proposition. Suppose $X^{(1)}$ and $X^{(2)}$ are independent, $Y^{(1)}$ and $Y^{(2)}$ are independent, and each of these random vectors has exchangeable components. If $X^{(1)} \prec_w E_i Y^{(1)}$ and $X^{(2)} \prec_w E_i Y^{(2)}$, then $(X^{(1)} + X^{(2)}) \prec_w E_i (Y^{(1)} + Y^{(2)})$, $i = 2, 3$. The same result is true for $\prec^w$ in place of $\prec_w$.

Proof. The proof follows that of F.6.a. For E_2, it is only necessary to observe that if ϕ is increasing (decreasing), symmetric, and convex, then $\widetilde{\phi}(u) = \sum_\Pi \phi(u + x\Pi)$ defines an increasing (decreasing), symmetric, convex function. For E_3, it is necessary to observe that if $\psi : \mathscr{R} \to \mathscr{R}$ is increasing (decreasing) and convex, then $\sum_\Pi \sum_i \psi[u_i + (x\Pi)_i]$ is increasing (decreasing) and convex. ||

For a counterexample to H.7 with P_1, P_2, or P_3 in place of E_2 or E_3, see F.6.b.

H.7.a. Proposition. Suppose that $X^{(1)}$ and $X^{(2)}$ are independent, $Y^{(1)}$ and $Y^{(2)}$ are independent, and these random variables take values in $\mathscr{D}$. If $X^{(j)} \prec_w E_i Y^{(j)}$, $j = 1, 2$, then $(X^{(1)}+X^{(2)}) \prec_w E_i (Y^{(1)}+Y^{(2)})$, $i = 1, 2, 3, 4$. The same result is true for $\prec^w$ in place of $\prec_w$.

Proof. The proof is similar to the proof of H.7. For E_1 and E_4, see F.6.b. ||

For E_1, this result is due to Nevius, Proschan, and Sethuraman (1977b).

Some Counterexamples

For stochastic versions of the weak majorization $\prec_w$, implications already established together with counterimplications demonstrated below are indicated in Fig. 2. To establish the counterimplications, note that

$$\text{F.9.b shows } P_2^\uparrow \not\Rightarrow P_1^\uparrow,$$
$$\text{F.9.d shows } E_4^\uparrow \not\Rightarrow E_3^\uparrow \text{ and } E_3^\uparrow \not\Rightarrow E_4^\uparrow.$$

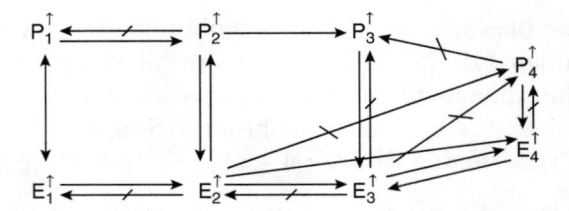

Figure 2. Relations among conditions.

The following example shows that $P_4^\uparrow \not\Rightarrow E_3^\uparrow$.

H.8. Example. Suppose that
$$P\{X = (4,0)\} = P\{X = (3,3)\} = \tfrac{1}{2},$$
$$P\{Y = (4,2)\} = P\{Y = (3,1)\} = \tfrac{1}{2}.$$

Here $X_{[1]}$ and $Y_{[1]}$ have the same distribution, as do $X_{[1]} + X_{[2]}$ and $Y_{[1]} + Y_{[2]}$. This means $X \prec_w P_4 Y$ and $Y \prec_w P_4 X$. If $\psi : \mathscr{R} \to \mathscr{R}$ is convex, then

$$E[\psi(X_1)+\psi(X_2)]-E[\psi(Y_1)+\psi(Y_2)] = \frac{1}{2}[\psi(0)+\psi(3)-\psi(1)-\psi(2)] \geq 0$$

with strict inequality if ψ is strictly convex. Thus, $X \prec_w E_3 Y$ fails.

In Fig. 2, "↑" can be replaced by "↓." Counterexamples for the other version $\prec^w$ of weak majorization can be obtained using the duality

$$X \prec^w E_i Y \Leftrightarrow (-X) \prec_w E_i (-Y), \quad X \prec^w P_i Y \Leftrightarrow (-X) \prec_w P_i (-Y).$$

I Stochastic Schur-Convexity

Liyanage and Shanthikumar (1992) introduce a spectrum of concepts of stochastic Schur-convexity. [See also Shaked, Shanthikumar, and Tong (1995).] A family $Z(\theta)$ of random variables parameterized by θ is said to be *stochastically Schur-convex* in the sense of a stochastic ordering $\leq^*$ if $\theta \prec \theta'$ implies $Z(\theta) \leq^* Z(\theta')$. Here $\leq^*$ can be any one of a variety of stochastic orderings (17.B.1). Indeed, the concept can be broadened to allow $\leq^*$ to be any preorder on the space of random variables.

12
Probabilistic, Statistical, and Other Applications

In this chapter are collected a variety of probabilistic results closely related to those of Chapter 11, but which differ in various ways.

The relationships of Chapter 11 between pairs of random vectors all reduce to ordinary majorization when the random vectors are degenerate. There are additional conditions for random vectors which do not have this qualification to be called "stochastic majorizations" but which can still be put into the general form

$$P_{\mathscr{C}}: \quad \phi(X) \leq^{\text{st}} \phi(Y) \quad \text{for all} \quad \phi \in \mathscr{C},$$

or

$$E_{\mathscr{C}}: \quad E\phi(X) \leq E\phi(Y) \quad \text{for all} \quad \phi \in \mathscr{C}$$
$$\text{such that the expectations are defined.}$$

A number of results are known for the class $\mathscr{C}$ consisting of functions ϕ having the form $\phi(x) = g(\sum x_i)$, where g is continuous and convex. For example, Hoeffding (1963) shows that if $X_1, \ldots, X_n$ are obtained by sampling without replacement from a finite population and $Y_1, \ldots, Y_n$ are obtained by sampling with replacement from the same population, then

$$Eg\left(\sum X_i\right) \leq Eg\left(\sum Y_i\right)$$

A.W. Marshall et al., *Inequalities: Theory of Majorization and Its Applications*, Springer Series in Statistics, DOI 10.1007/978-0-387-68276-1_12,
© Springer Science+Business Media, LLC 2011

for all continuous convex g. This inequality and some others of the same form can be obtained as special cases of more general results. Generalizations of Hoeffding's sampling theory inequality are given in Section A.

One of the weakest conditions discussed in Section 11.F is E_4. The stochastic majorization $X \prec_{E_4} Y$ says only that

$$(EX_{[1]}, \ldots, EX_{[n]}) \prec (EY_{[1]}, \ldots, EY_{[n]}).$$

Examples of this kind of majorization are given in Sections C, D, and E. These examples are concerned, respectively, with the probability of realizing k out of n events, with ordered random variables, and with eigenvalues of random matrices. The basic results of these sections can all be obtained using the same method, discussed in Section B, which involves an extremal representation and an application of Jensen's inequality.

Another kind of result (encountered in Section J) relates to "peakedness" of linear combinations. Birnbaum (1948) defined U to be "more peaked about a" than V if

$$P\{|U - a| > t\} \leq P\{|V - a| > t\}, \qquad t \geq 0. \qquad (1)$$

If the distributions of U and V are symmetric about a, this is equivalent to saying that

$$\begin{aligned} P\{U \leq x\} \leq P\{V \leq x\}, & \qquad x \leq a, \\ P\{U \leq x\} \geq P\{V \leq x\}, & \qquad x \geq a, \end{aligned} \qquad (2)$$

but of course (2) is stronger than (1) in general. Section J contains a peakedness result for linear combinations of certain random variables with symmetry.

There are cases when (2) fails but still one can say that

$$\begin{aligned} P\{U \leq x\} \leq P\{V \leq x\}, & \qquad x \leq a, \\ P\{U \leq x\} \geq P\{V \leq x\}, & \qquad x \geq b, \end{aligned}$$

for some fixed $a < b$. Such results are discussed in Section K.

A Sampling from a Finite Population

Suppose that $X_1, \ldots, X_n$ are obtained by sampling without replacement from a finite population, and $Y_1, \ldots, Y_n$ are obtained by sampling with replacement from the same population. According to an inequality of Hoeffding (1963),

$$E\psi\left(\sum X_i\right) \leq E\psi\left(\sum Y_i\right)$$

whenever ψ is continuous and convex.

Hoeffding's result has stimulated several authors to look for generalizations. Such generalizations might compare other sampling plans besides sampling with and without replacement, or the convex function of the sum of observations might be replaced by more general functions. These kinds of results are the subject of this section.

Suppose that members of a finite population of size N are indexed by the numbers $j = 1, \ldots, N$. To each index $j \in \{1, \ldots, N\} \equiv \Omega$ there corresponds an individual in the population with some particular numerical characteristic y_j that is of interest. A sample of size n from the population consists of a set of ordered pairs (v_i, y_{v_i}), $i = 1, \ldots, n$, where each $v_i \in \Omega$.

A sample (v_i, y_{v_i}), $i = 1, \ldots, n$, determines a vector $k = (k_1, \ldots, k_N)$, where k_j is the number of times the pair (j, y_j) occurs in the sample, $j = 1, \ldots, N$. Of course, $\sum_{j=1}^{N} k_j = n$ and each k_j is a nonnegative integer. Denote the set of all such vectors by $\mathcal{K}$. Notice that given $k \in \mathcal{K}$ and the numbers y_j for which $k_j > 0$, the original sample can be recovered apart from order.

A probability distribution P on $\mathcal{K}$ is called a *sampling plan*. The sampling plan is *symmetric* if $P\{k\} = P\{k\Pi\}$ for all permutations Π. For any symmetric sampling plan P, let

$$Q(k) = t_k P\{k\},$$

where t_k is the number of distinct permutations of k. Since P is symmetric, it is determined by Q because all permutations of k are equally likely.

The most familiar symmetric sampling plans are those of sampling with and without replacement.

For *sampling without replacement*, $N \geq n$ and

$$P\{k\} = \begin{cases} 1 / \binom{N}{n} & \text{if } k \text{ is a permutation of } (\underbrace{1, \ldots, 1}_{n}, 0, \ldots, 0), \\ 0 & \text{otherwise.} \end{cases}$$

Here,

$$Q(k) = \begin{cases} 1 & \text{if } k \text{ is a permutation of } (\underbrace{1,\ldots,1}_{n},0,\ldots,0), \\ 0 & \text{otherwise.} \end{cases}$$

For *sampling with replacement*,

$$P\{k\} = \binom{n}{k_1,\ldots,k_N}\left(\frac{1}{N}\right)^n, \qquad k \in \mathscr{K}.$$

Various symmetric generalizations of these sampling plans have been studied. One kind consists of the so-called *random replacement models*. In such a model, the ith individual to be sampled is replaced with probability π_i and is removed from the population with probability $1-\pi_i$, $i=1,\ldots,n$. At each step of the sampling, individuals remaining in the population are equally likely to be selected.

For any $a \in \mathscr{R}$, let

$$a^{\langle i \rangle} = (a,\ldots,a)$$

be a vector of length i having all components equal to a. Let $K = (K_1,\ldots,K_N)$ be a random vector taking values in $\mathscr{K}$ according to the distribution P, and let $Y = (y_1^{\langle K_1 \rangle},\ldots,y_n^{\langle K_N \rangle})$. The possible values for Y are ordinarily unknown, but it is assumed that $y_1,\ldots,y_N$ are known to be in $\mathscr{A} \subset \mathscr{R}$, so $Y \in \mathscr{A}^n$, the Cartesian product of $\mathscr{A}$ with itself n times. An observation of the random variable Y is just a reordering of the sample values $y_{v_1},\ldots,y_{v_n}$.

This section is concerned with two kinds of expected values:

$$E_P \phi(K) = \sum_{k \in \mathscr{K}} P\{k\} \phi(k)$$

and

$$E_P \xi(Y) = \sum_{k \in \mathscr{K}} P\{k\} \xi(y_1^{\langle k_1 \rangle},\ldots,y_N^{\langle k_N \rangle}),$$

for certain symmetric functions ϕ and ξ defined, respectively, on $\mathscr{K}$ and $\mathscr{A}^n$. Comparisons of such expected values are made for different symmetric sampling plans.

The sampling plans for which comparisons are made are related by a notion of "domination." Let P and P^* be symmetric sampling plans.

Say that P^* is an *elementary dominant* of P if for some $l, m \in \mathcal{K}$ such that $l \prec m$,

$$Q^*(m) > Q(m), \qquad Q^*(l) < Q(l),$$
$$Q^*(m) + Q^*(l) = Q(m) + Q(l),$$
$$Q^*(k) = Q(k) \qquad \text{if} \quad k \text{ is not a permutation of } l \text{ or } m.$$

Say that P^* *dominates* P if there exists a finite sequence $P = P_0, P_1, \ldots, P_r = P^*$ of symmetric sampling plans such that P_j is an elementary dominant of P_{j-1}, $j = 1, \ldots, r$.

A.1. Theorem. The symmetric sampling plan P^* dominates P if and only if

$$E_P \phi(K) \leq E_{P^*} \phi(K)$$

for all Schur-convex functions ϕ defined on $\mathcal{K}$.

Remark. The condition that $E_P \phi(K) \leq E_{P^*} \phi(K)$ for all Schur-convex functions ϕ defined on $\mathcal{K}$ is a stochastic ordering condition in the sense of 17.B.1. There is a close connection between A.1 and 17.B.6. See also 11.A(4). The result of A.1 has been obtained in a more general setting by Snijders (1976).

Proof. Suppose first that P^* dominates P. It is sufficient to prove the inequality for the case of elementary domination with P and P^* differing only at permutations of l and m where $l \prec m$. Then

$$E_{P^*}\phi(K) - E_P\phi(K) = [Q^*(m) - Q(m)]\phi(m) - [Q(l) - Q^*(l)]\phi(l)$$
$$= \alpha[\phi(m) - \phi(l)] \geq 0,$$

where $\alpha = Q^*(m) - Q(m) = Q(l) - Q^*(l) \geq 0$.

Next, suppose that $E_P\phi(K) \leq E_{P^*}\phi(K)$ for all Schur-convex functions ϕ. Let $D = \{k : P^*\{k\} > P\{k\}\}$ and for $k \in D$, let $d(k) = P^*\{k\} - P\{k\}$. Similarly, let $S = \{k : P^*\{k\} < P\{k\}\}$ and for $k \in S$, let $s(k) = P\{k\} - P^*\{k\}$. Consider a transportation problem in which points in S are thought of as "sources" (suppliers) and points in D are thought of as "sinks" (consumers). For $k \in S$, $s(k)$ is the supply at k, and for $k \in D$, $d(k)$ is the demand at k. The transportation problem is constrained by the requirement that shipments can be made from $k_0 \in S$ to $k_1 \in D$ if and only if $k_0 \prec k_1$. To show that P^* dominates P, it is sufficient to show that this transportation problem is feasible.

A transportation problem is feasible if for any subset $D_0 \subset D$ of sinks, the total demand at these sinks is not greater than the supply available [Gale (1957); see also Ford and Fulkerson (1962, p. 38)].

This means that with the notation $I_0 = \{k : k \prec l \text{ for some } l \in D_0\}$,

$$\sum_{k \in I_0 \cap S} s(k) \geq \sum_{k \in D_0} d(k).$$

To show that this inequality holds, consider the Schur-convex function

$$\phi(k) = \begin{cases} -1 & \text{if } k \in I_0, \\ 0 & \text{otherwise.} \end{cases}$$

Rewrite the inequality $E_P \phi(k) \leq E_{P^*} \phi(k)$ as

$$\sum_{k \in I_0} P\{k\} \geq \sum_{k \in I_0} P^*\{k\};$$

that is,

$$\sum_{k \in I_0 \cap S} P\{k\} + \sum_{k \in I_0 \cap D} P\{k\} \geq \sum_{k \in I_0 \cap S} P^*\{k\} + \sum_{k \in I_0 \cap D} P^*\{k\},$$

or

$$\sum_{k \in I_0 \cap S} [P\{k\} - P^*\{k\}] \geq \sum_{k \in I_0 \cap D} [P^*\{k\} - P\{k\}].$$

Because $D_0 \subset I_0 \cap D$, this means that

$$\sum_{k \in I_0 \cap S} s(k) \geq \sum_{k \in I_0 \cap D} d(k) \geq \sum_{k \in D_0} d(k). \quad \|$$

For certain kinds of sampling plans and in case ϕ is symmetric and convex, the inequality of Theorem A.1 is obtained by Karlin (1974) using quite different methods.

Notice that Theorem A.1 says that K under distribution P^* stochastically majorizes K under distribution P in the sense of E_1 (see Section 11.A); that is,

$$K_P \prec_{E_1} K_{P^*}.$$

This implies that $K_P \prec_{E_2} K_{P^*}$, which is equivalent to saying that the measure P^* dilates P. Particularly for the case of sampling with and without replacement, this dilation has been studied by Kemperman (1973).

A.1.a. Corollary. Let W be the number of nonzero components of K; i.e., W is the number of distinct individuals represented in the sample. If P^* dominates P, then

$$P\{W > w\} \geq P^*\{W > w\} \quad \text{for all} \quad w.$$

Proof. This follows from the fact that the set

$$\{k : k \text{ has at least } w \text{ nonzero components}\}$$

has a Schur-concave indicator function. ‖

This corollary is essentially 11.D.1.b.

For each $l \in \mathcal{K}$, let P_l be the symmetric sampling plan under which each permutation of l is equally likely and $P_l(m) = 0$ if m is not a permutation of l. That is, P_l is the symmetric sampling plan that concentrates all probability on the permutations of l. In place of E_{P_l}, write E_l.

A.1.b. Proposition. Let P and P^* be symmetric sampling plans. Then

$$E_P \phi(K) \leq E_{P^*} \phi(K) \qquad \text{whenever} \quad P^* \text{ dominates } P \qquad (1)$$

if and only if

$$\widehat{\phi}(k) = \frac{1}{N!} \sum_\pi \phi(k_{\pi(1)}, \ldots, k_{\pi(N)})$$

is Schur-convex.

Proof. Suppose first that $\widehat{\phi}$ is Schur-convex. Because the sampling plans P and P^* are symmetric,

$$E\phi(K) = E\phi(K\Pi)$$

for all permutation matrices Π. This means

$$E_P \phi(K) = \frac{1}{N!} E_P \sum_\Pi \phi(K\Pi) = E_P \widehat{\phi}(K).$$

But $E_P \widehat{\phi}(K) \leq E_{P^*} \widehat{\phi}(K)$ by A.1.

Next, suppose that (1) holds and that $l \prec m$. With the choice $P = P_l$ and $P^* = P_m$, it follows that P^* dominates P, so that by (1),

$$\widehat{\phi}(l) = \frac{1}{N!} \sum_\Pi \phi(l\Pi) = E_l \phi(K) \leq E_m \phi(K) = \frac{1}{N!} \sum_\Pi \phi(m\Pi) = \widehat{\phi}(m).$$

Hence, $\widehat{\phi}$ is Schur-convex. ‖

Although the characteristics $y_1, \ldots, y_N$ are unknown in general, they are fixed in any population to be sampled. Consequently,

$$\xi(y_1^{\langle k_1 \rangle}, \ldots, y_N^{\langle k_N \rangle}) = \phi(K_1, \ldots, K_N)$$

448   12. Probabilistic, Statistical, and Other Applications

establishes a relationship between functions ϕ defined on $\mathcal{K}$ and symmetric functions ξ defined on $\{y_1, \ldots, y_N\}^n$. This relationship is exploited in the following theorem.

A.2. Theorem. For a symmetric function ξ defined on $\{y_1, \ldots, y_N\}^n$, let
$$\phi(k_1, \ldots, k_N) = \xi(y_1^{\langle k_1 \rangle}, \ldots, y_N^{\langle k_N \rangle}),$$
$$\widehat{\phi}(k_1, \ldots, k_N) = \frac{1}{N!} \sum_{\Pi} \phi(k\Pi).$$

Then
$$E_P \xi(Y) \leq E_{P^*} \xi(Y) \qquad \text{whenever} \quad P^* \text{ dominates } P \qquad (2)$$

if and only if $\widehat{\phi}$ is Schur-convex.

Proof. Suppose first that $\widehat{\phi}$ is Schur-convex and P^* dominates P, so that by A.1,
$$\frac{1}{N!} E_P \sum_{\Pi} \phi(K\Pi) \leq \frac{1}{N!} E_{P^*} \sum_{\Pi} \phi(k\Pi).$$

But
$$\frac{1}{N!} E_P \sum_{\Pi} \phi(K\Pi) = \frac{1}{N!} E_P \sum_{\pi} \xi(y_1^{\langle k_{\pi(1)} \rangle}, \ldots, y_N^{\langle k_{\pi(N)} \rangle})$$
$$= \frac{1}{N!} \sum_{k} P\{k\} \sum_{\pi} \xi(y_1^{\langle k_{\pi(1)} \rangle}, \ldots, y_N^{\langle k_{\pi(N)} \rangle})$$
$$= \frac{1}{N!} \sum_{\pi} \sum_{k} P\{k_{\pi(1)}, \ldots, k_{\pi(N)}\} \xi(y_1^{\langle k_{\pi(1)} \rangle}, \ldots, y_n^{\langle k_{\pi(N)} \rangle})$$
$$= \frac{1}{N!} \sum_{\pi} E_P \xi(y_1^{\langle k_1 \rangle}, \ldots, y_N^{\langle k_N \rangle})$$
$$= E_P \xi(y_1^{\langle k_1 \rangle}, \ldots, y_N^{\langle k_N \rangle}) = E_P \xi(Y).$$

Similarly,
$$\frac{1}{N!} E_{P^*} \sum_{\Pi} \phi(K\Pi) = E_{P^*} \xi(Y).$$

Thus (2) holds.

Suppose next that (2) holds. Then the equality just demonstrated can be used to rewrite (2) in the form
$$E_P \widehat{\phi}(K) \leq E_{P^*} \widehat{\phi}(K) \qquad \text{whenever} \quad P^* \text{ dominates } P.$$

Consequently, $\widehat{\phi}$ is Schur-convex by A.1.b. ||

Ordinarily, the characteristics $y_1, \ldots, y_N$ are unknown. When it is known only that $y_i \in \mathscr{A}$, $i = 1, \ldots, N$, then A.2 can be appropriately modified.

A.2.a. Let ξ be a symmetric function defined on $\mathscr{A}^n$, and for each fixed $a = (a_1, \ldots, a_N) \in \mathscr{A}^N$, let

$$\phi_a(k_1, \ldots, k_N) = \xi(a_1^{\langle k_1 \rangle}, \ldots, a_N^{\langle k_N \rangle}),$$

$$\widehat{\phi}_a(k_1, \ldots, k_n) = \frac{1}{N!} \sum_{\Pi} \phi_a(k\Pi).$$

Then

$$E_P \xi(Y) \leq E_{P^*} \xi(Y)$$

whenever P^* dominates P and whatever the values $y_1, \ldots, y_N \in \mathscr{A}$ if and only if $\widehat{\phi}_a$ is Schur-convex for all $a \in \mathscr{A}^N$.

In proving a very special case of A.2, Karlin (1974) introduced a class $\mathscr{C}_{\mathscr{A}}$ of functions ξ which satisfy the conditions of A.2 as follows:

$\xi : \mathscr{A}^n \to \mathscr{R}$ is in $\mathscr{C}_{\mathscr{A}}$ if and only if

$$\xi \text{ is symmetric,} \tag{3}$$

and for all $(a_1, a_2, \dot{a}) \in \mathscr{A}^n$,

$$\xi(a_1, a_1, \dot{a}) + \xi(a_2, a_2, \dot{a}) \geq 2\xi(a_1, a_2, \dot{a}). \tag{4}$$

Usually, we write $\mathscr{C}$ in place of $\mathscr{C}_{\mathscr{A}}$.

A.2.b. Corollary. If $\xi \in \mathscr{C}$ and P^* dominates P,

$$E_P \xi(Y) \leq E_{P^*} \xi(Y).$$

Proof. Let $\phi(k_1, \ldots, k_N) = \xi(y_1^{\langle k_1 \rangle}, \ldots, y_N^{\langle k_N \rangle})$, and let $\widehat{\phi}(k) = (1/N!) \sum_{\Pi} \phi(k\Pi)$. Because of (4),

$$\phi(k_1 + 2, k_2, \ldots, k_N) + \phi(k_1, k_2 + 2, k_3, \ldots, k_N)$$
$$\geq 2\phi(k_1 + 1, k_2 + 1, k_3, \ldots, k_N);$$

that is, $\phi(k_1, s - k_1, k_3, \ldots, k_N)$ is convex in k_1 for each fixed s, $k_3, \ldots, k_N$. This means that $\widehat{\phi}$ has the same convexity property. Because $\widehat{\phi}$ is also symmetric, it follows (by 3.C.2.b) that $\widehat{\phi}$ is Schur-convex. ∥

The condition $\xi \in \mathscr{C}$ is considerably weaker than the condition that ξ is symmetric and L-superadditive (see Definition 6.C.2 and

Section 6.D). This means that examples of symmetric L-superadditive functions are examples of functions in $\mathscr{C}$.

Closure properties of $\mathscr{C}$ are also useful in identifying examples. Following Rosén (1967), Karlin (1974) also noted that

$$\xi_1, \xi_2 \in \mathscr{C} \quad \text{implies} \quad \max(\xi_1, \xi_2) \in \mathscr{C}, \tag{5}$$

$$\xi \in \mathscr{C}_{g(\mathscr{A})} \quad \text{implies} \quad \xi^*(a) = \xi(g(a_1), \ldots, g(a_n)) \in \mathscr{C}_A$$
$$\text{for any function } g : \mathscr{A} \to \mathscr{R}, \tag{6}$$

$$\xi \in \mathscr{C} \text{ and } \psi \text{ convex increasing} \quad \text{implies} \quad \psi \circ \xi \in \mathscr{C}, \tag{7}$$

$$\mathscr{C} \text{ is a convex cone.} \tag{8}$$

Some specific examples of functions $\xi \in \mathscr{C}$ are

$$\xi(x) = \psi\left(\sum x_i\right), \quad \text{where } \psi \text{ is convex,} \tag{9}$$

$$\xi(x) = \prod_{i=1}^{n} |x_i|^\alpha, \quad \alpha \in \mathscr{R}, \tag{10}$$

$$\xi(x) = \left(\sum_{1}^{n} |x_i|^\alpha\right)^{1/\gamma}, \quad \alpha \in \mathscr{R}, \ \gamma \leq 1, \tag{11}$$

$$\xi(x) = \min(x_1, \ldots, x_n), \tag{12}$$

$$\xi(x) = x_{[k]} + \cdots + x_{[n]}, \quad k = 1, \ldots, n, \tag{13}$$

$$\xi(x) = I_{\{z : a \leq z_i \leq b, i=1,\ldots,n\}}(x), \quad -\infty \leq a < b \leq \infty, \tag{14}$$

$$\xi(x) = k\text{th elementary symmetric function on } \mathscr{R}_+^n. \tag{15}$$

Example (9) was identified by Lorentz (1953) as an L-superadditive function. In the present context, it was first used by Hoeffding (1963). Examples (10), (11), and (12) are due to Rosén (1967).

Through the correspondence

$$\phi(k_1, \ldots, k_N) = \xi(x_1^{\langle k_1 \rangle}, \ldots, x_N^{\langle k_N \rangle}),$$

Schur-convex functions $\widehat{\phi}$ identify functions ξ satisfying the conditions of A.2. It is interesting to note that this idea is not very useful because often quite complex functions ϕ are required to obtain very simple functions ξ. Here are some examples:

(i) $\phi(k) = \prod_i a_i^{k_i}$, $\widehat{\phi}(k) = (1/N!)\sum_\pi a_{\pi(i)}^{k_i}$ is Schur-convex (Muirhead's theorem 3.G.2.e). Here $\xi(x) = \prod_1^n x_i \in \mathscr{C}$.

(ii) $\phi(k) = \psi(\sum_{i=1}^N k_i a_i)$, $\xi(x) = \psi(\sum x_i)$, ψ convex.

The class $\mathscr{C}$ does not exhaust the functions ξ which satisfy the inequality (2) of A.2. For example, if $N = 3$ and

$$\xi(y_1, y_2, y_3) = \begin{cases} (y_1 + y_2 + y_3)/3 & \text{when } y_1, y_2, y_3 \text{ are distinct,} \\ \text{median } (y_1, y_2, y_3) & \text{otherwise,} \end{cases}$$

then ξ satisfies (2) but $\xi \notin \mathscr{C}$. Nevertheless, the condition $\xi \in \mathscr{C}$ is an important sufficient condition for (2) since it suffices to identify so many interesting examples.

Recall that P_l is the symmetric sampling plan that concentrates all probability on the permutations of l. Note that $P_{(1,\ldots,1,0,\ldots,0)} \equiv P_W$ corresponds to sampling without replacement.

A.2.c. Corollary (Karlin, 1974). For any symmetric sampling plan P,

$$E_{(1,\ldots,1,0,\ldots,0)}\xi(Y) \leq E_P \xi(Y) \leq E_{(n,0,\ldots,0)}\xi(Y) \qquad \text{for all } \xi \in \mathscr{C}.$$

Proof. This follows from the fact that $k \in \mathscr{K}$ implies

$$(1,\ldots,1,0,\ldots,0) \prec k \prec (n,0,\ldots,0).$$

Consequently, P dominates $P_{(1,\ldots,1,0,\ldots,0)}$ and P is dominated by $P_{(n,0,\ldots,0)}$. ∥

Various special cases of Corollary A.2.c were obtained by Rosén (1967).

Let $P_W = P_{(1,\ldots,1,0,\ldots,0)}$ correspond to sampling without replacement and let P_R correspond to sampling with replacement.

A.2.d. Corollary. For any $\xi \in \mathscr{C}$,

$$E_{P_W}\xi(Y) \leq E_{P_R}\xi(Y).$$

Proof. This is an immediate consequence of A.2.c. ∥

A.2.e. Corollary (Hoeffding, 1963). If $\psi : \mathscr{R} \to \mathscr{R}$ is convex,

$$E_{P_W}\psi\left(\sum Y_i\right) \leq E_{P_R}\psi\left(\sum Y_i\right).$$

Proof. This follows from A.2.d using $\xi(x) = \psi(\sum x_i)$. ∥

A.2.f. Corollary (Karlin, 1974). If $l \prec k$, then

$$E_l\xi(Y) \leq E_k\xi(Y) \qquad \text{for all } \xi \in \mathscr{C}.$$

Proof. This is an immediate consequence of A.2. ∥

Although A.2.f follows easily from A.2, the reverse is also true: It is easy to see from A.2.f that $E_P \xi(Y) \leq E_{P^*} \xi(Y)$ when P^* is an elementary dominant of P, and from this A.2 follows.

Corollary A.2.f plays a key role in the approach taken by Karlin (1974) to the subject of this section. Because his direct proof is long and involved, an alternative direct proof is offered here. This alternative proof is divided into two parts.

A.3.a. If $\xi \in \mathscr{C}$ and $u_1, u_2 \in A$, then

$$\xi(u_1^{\langle n-1 \rangle}, u_2) + \xi(u_2^{\langle n-1 \rangle}, u_1) \leq \xi(u_1^{\langle n \rangle}) + \xi(u_2^{\langle n \rangle}).$$

Proof. Because $\xi \in \mathscr{C}$,

$$2\xi(u_1^{\langle n-1-j \rangle}, u_2^{\langle j-1 \rangle}) \leq \xi(u_1^{\langle n-j \rangle}, u_2^{\langle j \rangle}) + \xi(u_1^{\langle n-2-j \rangle}, u_2^{\langle j+2 \rangle})$$

for $j = 0, 1, \ldots, n-2$. Summation on j yields

$$\sum_{j=0}^{n-2} \xi(u_1^{\langle n-j \rangle}, u_2^{\langle j \rangle}) - \sum_{j=0}^{n-2} \xi(u_1^{\langle n-1-j \rangle}, u_2^{\langle j+1 \rangle})$$
$$+ \sum_{j=0}^{n-2} \xi(u_1^{\langle n-2-j \rangle}, u_2^{\langle j+2 \rangle}) - \sum_{j=0}^{n} \xi(u_1^{\langle n-1-j \rangle}, u_2^{\langle j+1 \rangle}) \geq 0.$$

With cancellation, this reduces to the desired inequality. ||

A.3.b. Let k and l be vectors of length N having integer components such that $\sum_1^N k_i = \sum_1^N l_i = n$. If $l \prec k$, $u_1, \ldots, u_N \in \mathscr{A}$ and $\xi \in \mathscr{C}$, then

$$\sum_\Pi \xi(u_{\Pi(1)}^{\langle l_1 \rangle}, \ldots, u_{\Pi(N)}^{\langle l_N \rangle}) \leq \sum_\Pi \xi(u_{\Pi(1)}^{\langle k_1 \rangle}, \ldots, u_{\Pi(N)}^{\langle k_N \rangle}).$$

Proof. Because of 5.D.1, it is sufficient to prove this proposition for the case that $k_1 - 1 = l_1 \geq k_2 + 1 = l_2$ and $k_j = l_j$, $j = 3, \ldots, N$. This also means that it is sufficient to take $N = 2$. Then the proposition reduces to

$$\xi(u_1^{\langle k_1-1 \rangle}, u_2^{\langle k_2+1 \rangle}) + \xi(u_2^{\langle k_1-1 \rangle}, u_1^{\langle k_2+1 \rangle}) \leq \xi(u_1^{\langle k_1 \rangle}, u_2^{\langle k_2 \rangle}) + \xi(u_2^{\langle k_1 \rangle}, u_1^{\langle k_2 \rangle}).$$

Because ξ is symmetric, this can be rewritten as

$$\xi(u_1^{\langle k_1-k_2-1 \rangle}, u_2, u_1^{\langle k_2 \rangle}, u_2^{\langle k_2 \rangle}) + \xi(u_2^{\langle k_1-k_2-1 \rangle}, u_1, u_1^{\langle k_2 \rangle}, u_2^{\langle k_2 \rangle})$$
$$\leq \xi(u_1^{\langle k_1-k_2 \rangle}, u_1^{\langle k_2 \rangle}, u_2^{\langle k_2 \rangle}) + \xi(u_2^{\langle k_1-k_2 \rangle}, u_1^{\langle k_2 \rangle}, u_2^{\langle k_2 \rangle}).$$

Suppress the common arguments here and take $n = k_1 - k_2$ in A.3.a to see that this inequality holds. ||

Alternative proof of A.2.f. Notice that upon dividing the inequality of A.3.b by $n!$, a restatement of A.2.f is obtained. ∥

Random Replacement Sampling Plans

Let $P_{\pi_1,\ldots,\pi_{n-1}}$ denote the random sampling plan in which the ith observation is replaced with probability π_i, $i = 1, \ldots, n-1$. At each step of the sampling, individuals not previously removed from the population are equally likely to be selected. In place of $E_{P_{\pi_1,\ldots,\pi_{n-1}}}$ write E_π. Karlin (1974) conjectured that

$$E_\pi \xi(Y_1, \ldots, Y_n) \geq E_{\pi'} \xi(Y_1, \ldots, Y_n) \tag{16}$$

for all $(y_1, \ldots, y_N) \in \mathscr{A}^N$ and all $\phi \in \mathscr{C}_\mathscr{A}$ if and only if

$$\pi_i \geq \pi_i', \quad i = 1, \ldots, n-1. \tag{17}$$

This conjecture remains unsettled, though some progress is reported by Karlin and Rinott (1984).

Removal of Duplicate Observations

It was pointed out by Basu (1958) that for certain purposes, repeated observations of the same individual in a sample should be ignored. Results of this kind have been obtained by Lanke (1974).

Let W be the number of nonzero components of K (number of distinct individuals sampled) and let $\widetilde{Y} = (\widetilde{Y}_1, \ldots, \widetilde{Y}_W)$ be the characteristics of these individuals. Of course, $\widetilde{Y}$ is a subvector of Y obtained by eliminating repetitions which result from the same individual being sampled more than once. The components of $\widetilde{Y}$ need not be distinct because different individuals in a population can share the same character.

A.4. Proposition. If $\psi : \mathscr{R} \to \mathscr{R}$ is continuous and convex and P is a symmetric sampling plan,

$$E_P\left[\psi\left(\sum_1^W \theta_i \widetilde{Y}_i\right)\bigg| W = w\right]$$

is a Schur-convex function of θ.

Proof. This is a consequence of 11.B.2; $\widetilde{Y}_1, \ldots, \widetilde{Y}_w$ are exchangeable because P is symmetric. ∥

A.4.a. Proposition (Lanke, 1974).   If $\psi : \mathscr{R} \to \mathscr{R}$ is continuous and convex and P is a symmetric sampling plan,

$$E_P \psi \left(\frac{\sum_1^W \tilde{Y}_i}{W} \right) \leq E_P \psi \left(\frac{\sum_1^n Y_i}{n} \right).$$

Proof.   If $\sum_1^W \theta_i = 1$, it follows from A.4 that

$$E_P \left[\psi \left(\frac{\sum_1^W \tilde{Y}_i}{W} \right) \middle| W = w \right] \leq E_P \left[\psi \left(\sum_1^W \theta_i \tilde{Y}_i \right) \middle| W = w \right].$$

Choose $\theta_i = K_i/n$ so that $\sum_1^W \theta_i \tilde{Y}_i = (1/n) \sum_1^n Y_i$, and then take expectations of both sides to get unconditional expectations. $\|$

A.4.b. Proposition.   If $\psi : \mathscr{R} \to \mathscr{R}$ is continuous and convex, and if P^* dominates P, where both P and P^* are symmetric sampling plans, then

$$E_P \psi \left(\frac{\sum_1^W \tilde{Y}_i}{W} \right) \leq E_{P^*} \psi \left(\frac{\sum_1^W \tilde{Y}_i}{W} \right).$$

Proof.   Define

$$g(w) = E_P \left[\psi \left(\frac{\sum_1^W \tilde{Y}_i}{W} \right) \middle| W = w \right]. \tag{18}$$

Observe that

$$\begin{aligned} g(w-1) &= E_P \left[\psi \left(\frac{\sum_1^W \tilde{Y}_i}{W} \right) \middle| W = w-1 \right] \\ &= E_P \left[\psi \left(\frac{\sum_1^{W-1} \tilde{Y}_i}{W-1} \right) \middle| W = w-1 \right] \\ &= E_P \left[\psi \left(\frac{\sum_1^{W-1} \tilde{Y}_i}{W-1} \right) \middle| W = w \right] \\ &\geq E_P \left[\psi \left(\frac{\sum_1^W \tilde{Y}_i}{W} \right) \middle| W = w \right] = g(w). \tag{19} \end{aligned}$$

The inequality in (19) follows from A.4 since

$$\left(\frac{1}{w-1}, \ldots, \frac{1}{w-1}, 0 \right) \succ \left(\frac{1}{w}, \ldots, \frac{1}{w} \right).$$

Moreover, note that these expectations are independent of the symmetric sampling plan P. Now recall from A.1.b that under P, W is stochastically larger than it is under P^*. Using this stochastic ordering and the fact that g of (18) is a decreasing function which does not depend upon P, it follows from 17.A.2 that $E_{P^*}g(W) \geq E_P g(W)$. ∥

For sampling without replacement, A.4.b is due to Lanke (1974).

Comparisons for Different Populations

Consider two populations of size N, both indexed by $j = 1, \ldots, N$. Suppose that the respective characteristics of the individuals in these populations are $x_1, \ldots, x_N$ and $y_1, \ldots, y_N$. Following notation already introduced, let

$$X = (x_1^{\langle K_1 \rangle}, \ldots, x_N^{\langle K_N \rangle}), \qquad Y = (y_1^{\langle K_1 \rangle}, \ldots, y_N^{\langle K_N \rangle}).$$

A.5. Proposition (Karlin, 1974). For any symmetric sampling plan P and any continuous convex function ψ,

$$x \prec y \Rightarrow E_P \psi\left(\sum X_i\right) \leq E_P \psi\left(\sum Y_i\right).$$

This proposition was obtained by Kemperman (1973) for the cases of sampling with and without replacement.

To prove A.5, first recall that for each $k \in \mathscr{K}$, t_k is the number of distinct permutations of k. For any $y \in \mathscr{R}^N$, let $y(k)$ be a vector of length t_k in which $\sum_{i=1}^N k_{\Pi(i)} y_i$ occurs exactly once as a component for each distinct permutation $k\Pi$ of k. Proposition A.5 is a consequence of the following observations.

A.5.a. $x \prec y \Rightarrow x(k) \prec y(k)$.

Proof. Let $\phi_r(x) = \sum_{r,\pi}[k_{\pi(1)}x_1 + \cdots + k_{\pi(N)}x_N]$, where $\sum_{r,\Pi}$ denotes summation over the r largest values of $k_{\pi(1)}x_1 + \cdots + k_{\pi(N)}x_N$ as π ranges over the distinct permutations of k. Since ϕ_r is symmetric and convex (see 3.G.2.b), $x(k) \prec_w y(k)$. But the sum of all components of $x(k)$ is just $c \sum x_i$, where c is the sum over distinct components of k, so $x(k) \prec y(k)$. ∥

A.5.b. $x \prec y$ and ψ convex $\Rightarrow E_k \psi(\sum X_i) \leq E_k \psi(\sum Y_i)$, where $E_k \equiv E_{P_k}$ and P_k is the sampling plan that concentrates on permutations of k.

Proof. This is immediate from A.5.a and the fact that $u \prec v \Rightarrow \sum \psi(u_i) \leq \sum \psi(v_i)$. ∥

Proof of A.5. This follows from the fact that any symmetric sampling plan is a mixture of the sampling plans P_k. ||

B Majorization Using Jensen's Inequality

A general method for demonstrating certain majorizations involving expectations is outlined here. The method makes use of Jensen's inequality in a straightforward way and yields many of the results of Sections C, D, and E.

B.1. Proposition. If $X_1, \ldots, X_n$ are random variables with finite expectations $EX_i = \mu_i$, $i = 1, \ldots, n$, then for all continuous convex functions ϕ,

$$\phi(\mu_1, \ldots, \mu_n) \leq E\phi(X_1, \ldots, X_n). \tag{1}$$

If ϕ is also symmetric, then

$$\phi(\mu_{[1]}, \ldots, \mu_{[n]}) \leq E\phi(X_{[1]}, \ldots, X_{[n]}). \tag{2}$$

Proof. (1) is a restatement of Jensen's inequality for random vectors. When ϕ is symmetric, (1) can be rewritten as (2). ||

Proposition B.1 yields the following weak majorization result.

B.2. Proposition. Let $\mathscr{A}$ be a convex subset of $\mathscr{R}^m$ and let Z be a random vector taking values in $\mathscr{A}$. Suppose that the expectation EZ exists and let $f_1, \ldots, f_n$ be continuous functions defined on $\mathscr{A}$ with the properties that

(i) $f_1(EZ) \geq \cdots \geq f_n(EZ)$,
(ii) $\sum_1^k f_i(z)$ is a convex function of $z \in \mathscr{A}$, $k = 1, \ldots, n$.

Then

$$(Ef_1(Z), \ldots, Ef_n(Z)) \succ_w (f_1(EZ), \ldots, f_n(EZ)) \tag{3}$$

whenever the expectations exist.

Proof. Since $\sum_1^k f_i(z)$ is convex, it follows from (1) that

$$\sum_1^k Ef_i(Z) = E\sum_1^k f_i(Z) \geq \sum_1^k f_i(EZ), \qquad k = 1, \ldots, n.$$

This means that the sum of the k largest of $Ef_i(Z)$, $i = 1, \ldots, n$, also exceeds $\sum_1^k f_i(EZ)$, and because of (i), (3) follows. ||

All of the applications of B.2 in the next three sections involve some kind of extremal representation, as indicated in the following proposition.

B.3. Proposition. Let $f_1, \ldots, f_n$ be defined by the equations

$$\sum_1^k f_i(z) = \sup_{u \in U_k} g(u, z), \qquad k = 1, \ldots, n, \quad z \in \mathscr{A} \subset \mathscr{R}^m,$$

where $U_1, \ldots, U_n$ are such that $f_1(z) \geq \cdots \geq f_n(z)$, $z \in \mathscr{A}$. If $g(u, z)$ is continuous and convex in z for each fixed $u \in \bigcup_{k=1}^n U_k$, then for any random vector taking values in $\mathscr{A}$,

$$(Ef_1(Z), \ldots, Ef_n(Z)) \succ_w (f_1(EZ), \ldots, f_n(EZ)).$$

Proof. This result follows from B.2 because $\sup_{u \in U_k} g(u, z)$ is a convex function of z. ||

There is a dual to B.2 and to B.3 in case $\sum_1^k f_i(z)$ is concave. For example, if

$$\sum_k^n f_i(z) = \inf_{u \in U_k} g(u, z), \qquad k = 1, \ldots, n,$$

where again $f_1(z) \geq \cdots \geq f_n(z)$ but now g is concave in z for each fixed $u \in \bigcup_1^n U_k$, then by a similar argument,

$$(Ef_1(Z), \ldots, Ef_n(Z)) \succ_w (f_1(EZ), \ldots, f_n(EZ)). \qquad (4)$$

Because $a \prec^w b$ and $a \prec_w b$ together imply $a \prec b$, (3) and (4) can sometimes be combined to give a strong majorization. Strong majorization can also be obtained if U_n contains just one element, say $\tilde{u}$, and if $g(\tilde{u}, z)$ is linear in z. Then in B.2, $\succ_w$ is replaced by $\succ$.

C   Probabilities of Realizing at Least k of n Events

Let $A_1, \ldots, A_n$ be events on some probability space, with respective probabilities $p_1, \ldots, p_n$. Let q_k be the probability that at least k of the events $A_1, \ldots, A_n$ occur. It is shown in Chapter 7, as a consequence of

458   12. Probabilistic, Statistical, and Other Applications

7.D.2, that $(p_1,\ldots,p_n) \prec (q_1,\ldots,q_n)$ when the p_i's and q_i's are multiples of $1/n$. Here the latter restriction is eliminated and a probabilistic proof is provided.

C.1. Proposition. With the above notation,
$$(p_1,\ldots,p_n) \prec (q_1,\ldots,q_n).$$

Three proofs of this result are given here that are all quite different, and may have some intrinsic interest. Yet another proof was given by Galambos (1971).

First proof. Let $B_i = \{$at least i of the events $A_1,\ldots,A_n$ occur$\}$, and observe that
$$\sum_{i=1}^{k} I_{B_i}(\omega) = \sup_{u \in U_k} \sum_{i=1}^{n} u_i I_{A_i}(\omega),$$
where U_k consists of all vectors in $\mathscr{R}_n$ with k components equal to one and with the remaining components equal to zero. By taking expectations and using Jensen's inequality, it follows that
$$\sum_{i=1}^{k} q_i \geq \sum_{i=1}^{k} p_{[i]}, \qquad k = 1,\ldots,n.$$
Equality holds for $k = n$ because $U_n = \{(1,\ldots,1)\}$ has but one member, and so $\sum_1^n I_{B_i}(\omega) = \sum_1^n I_{A_i}(\omega)$. ||

Second proof of C.1. For convenience, relabel the events $A_1,\ldots,A_n$ to achieve $p_1 \geq p_2 \geq \cdots \geq p_n$. Of course, it is always true that $q_1 \geq q_2 \geq \cdots \geq q_n$. The majorization we wish to prove follows easily once it has been shown that $\sum_1^n p_i = \sum_1^n q_i$. For suppose this equality holds and apply it to the case that $n = k$ to obtain

$$\sum_{1}^{k} p_i = \sum_{1}^{k} P\{\text{at least } i \text{ of the events } A_1, A_2,\ldots,A_k \text{ occur}\}$$
$$\leq \sum_{1}^{k} P\{\text{at least } i \text{ of the events } A_1, A_2,\ldots,A_n \text{ occur}\} = \sum_{1}^{k} q_i.$$

To show that $\sum_1^n p_i = \sum_1^n q_i$, make use of the well-known fact (Feller, 1968, p. 106) that
$$q_i = S_i - \binom{i}{i-1} S_{i+1} + \binom{i+1}{i-1} S_{i+2} - \cdots \pm \binom{n-1}{i-1} S_n,$$

C. Probabilities of Realizing at Least k of n Events

where
$$S_i = \sum_{j_1 < j_2 < \cdots < j_i} P\{A_{j_1} \cap \cdots \cap A_{j_i}\}.$$

Write this out more fully as follows:

$$q_1 = S_1 - \binom{1}{0}S_2 + \binom{2}{0}S_3 - \binom{3}{0}S_4 + \cdots \pm \binom{n-1}{0}S_n,$$

$$q_2 = \binom{1}{1}S_2 - \binom{2}{1}S_3 + \binom{3}{1}S_4 - \cdots \mp \binom{n-1}{1}S_n,$$

$$q_3 = \binom{2}{2}S_3 - \binom{3}{2}S_4 + \cdots \pm \binom{n-1}{2}S_n,$$

$$\vdots$$

$$q_n = \binom{n-1}{n-1}S_n.$$

Since
$$\sum_{j=0}^{l} \binom{l}{j}(-1)^j = 0,$$

addition yields $\sum_1^n q_i = S_1 = \sum_1^n p_i$. ∥

Third proof of C.1. As noted in the second proof, the majorization is easy to obtain once $\sum_1^n p_i = \sum_1^n q_i$ has been proved. An elementary proof of this fact was suggested by Alfred Rényi after a seminar at the Statistical Laboratory, Cambridge University, in the spring of 1968. Let

$$r_i = q_i - q_{i+1} = P\{\text{exactly } i \text{ of the events } A_1, A_2, \ldots, A_n \text{ occur}\}.$$

Let v_i be the indicator (characteristic) function of the set A_i; i.e.,

$$v_i = \begin{cases} 1 & \text{if } A_i \text{ occurs,} \\ 0 & \text{otherwise,} \end{cases} \quad i = 1, \ldots, n.$$

Then $v = \sum_{i=1}^n v_i$ is the number of the events $A_1, \ldots, A_n$ that occur and v is a random variable with expectation

$$Ev = \sum_{i=1}^n ir_i = \sum_{i=1}^n q_i.$$

But also,

$$Ev = \sum_{i=1}^n Ev_i = \sum_{i=1}^n p_i. \quad \|$$

Proposition C.1 was conjectured by Alfred Rényi; the basis for his conjecture was the inequality

$$\prod_{i=1}^{n} p_i \geq \prod_{i=1}^{n} q_i,$$

a result known to him, and which follows from C.1 using 3.F.1.a.

The following is a converse of B.1.

C.2. Proposition. If $p \prec q$ and $1 \geq q_1 \geq \cdots \geq q_n \geq 0$, then there exist a probability space $(\Omega, \mathscr{F}, P)$ and sets $A_1, \ldots, A_n$ in $\mathscr{F}$ such that $p_i = P\{A_i\}$ and $q_i = P\{$at least i of the events A_j occur$\}$, $i = 1, \ldots, n$.

This proposition has been proved by Galambos (1971) using $\Omega = [0, 1]$, $\mathscr{F}$ the Borel subsets of $[0, 1]$, and P the restriction of Lebesgue measure to $\mathscr{F}$. The following proof was obtained in 1969 in collaboration with Roger J.-B. Wets.

Proof of C.2. Let $\Omega = \{x = (x_1, \ldots, x_n) : x_i = 0 \text{ or } 1 \text{ for all } i\}$, let $\mathscr{F}$ include all subsets of Ω, and let $A_i = \{x : x \in \Omega \text{ and } x_i = 1\}$, $i = 1, \ldots, n$. Consider the set Q of all vectors r for which a probability measure P on $\mathscr{F}$ exists satisfying

$$\sum_{\{x : x_i = 1\}} P\{x\} = r_i, \qquad \sum_{\{x : \Sigma_j x_j = i\}} P\{x\} = q_i, \qquad i = 1, \ldots, n. \qquad (1)$$

To prove C.2, it is necessary to show that $p \in Q$, which can be done by showing that $\{r : r \prec q\} \subset Q$.

(a) To see that $q \in Q$, take

$$P\{(0, \ldots, 0)\} = 1 - q_1,$$
$$P\{(1, 0, \ldots, 0)\} = q_1 - q_2,$$
$$\vdots$$
$$P\{(1, 1, \ldots, 1, 0)\} = q_{n-1} - q_n,$$
$$P\{(1, \ldots, 1)\} = q_n,$$
$$P\{x\} = 0 \qquad \text{if the components of } x \text{ are not decreasing.}$$

(b) If $r = q\Pi$ for some permutation matrix Π, then $r \in Q$. This follows from (a), for the A_i can simply be relabeled to achieve $r = q$.

(c) Q is convex. To see this, suppose that $p^{(j)}$ is a probability measure which satisfies (1) when $r = r^{(j)}$, $j = 1, 2$. Then $\alpha P^{(1)} + (1-\alpha)P^{(2)}$ satisfies (1) when $r = \alpha r^{(1)} + (1-\alpha)r^{(2)}$, $0 \leq \alpha \leq 1$.

It follows from 2.B.3 that $\{r : r \prec q\} \subset Q$, and hence, $p \in Q$. ∥

D Expected Values of Ordered Random Variables

There are several ways that majorization arises in the study of ordered random variables; indeed, the results of Chapter 6 concerning rearrangements have already suggested such possibilities. Some stochastic ordering results for ordered random variables are given in Section H. Here, the emphasis is on expected values.

The term "order statistics" is not quite appropriate here because this term usually refers to random variables obtained by ordering independent, identically distributed random variables. In this section both the independence assumption and the assumption of a common distribution are sometimes dropped.

In keeping with the convention of majorization, random variables are put in decreasing order below. Order statistics with decreasing order are sometimes called *reverse order statistics*.

D.1. Proposition. If X_i, $i = 1, \ldots, n$, are random variables with $EX_i = \mu_i < \infty$, then

$$(\mu_{[1]}, \ldots, \mu_{[n]}) \prec (EX_{[1]}, \ldots, EX_{[n]}). \tag{1}$$

First proof. According to B(2), $(\mu_{[1]}, \ldots, \mu_{[n]}) \prec_{E_2} (X_{[1]}, \ldots, X_{[n]})$. Because E_2 implies E_4 (see Fig. 1 in Section 11.F), this majorization implies (1). ||

Another proof of D.1 can be obtained as an application of B.3, but the arguments leading to B.3 are repeated here.

Second proof. Let U_k be the set of all vectors in $\mathscr{R}^n$ with k components equal to one and $n - k$ components equal to zero. Since

$$x_{[1]} + \cdots + x_{[k]} = \sup_{u \in U_k} \sum u_i x_i, \quad k = 1, \ldots, n,$$

it follows from Jensen's inequality that

$$\sum_1^k EX_{[i]} \geq \sup_{u \in U_k} \sum u_i EX_i = \sum_1^k \mu_{[i]}, \quad k = 1, \ldots, n.$$

That $\sum_1^n EX_{[i]} = \sum_1^n \mu_i$ is trivial. ||

Yet another proof of D.1 can be obtained as an application of 6.A.1.a.

D.1.a. Let $Z_1, \ldots, Z_n$ be random variables and let X_i be the rank of Z_i, $i = 1, \ldots, n$. If $p_i = EX_i$, then

$$(p_1, \ldots, p_n) \prec (n, n-1, \ldots, 2, 1). \tag{2}$$

This observation is an application of D.1.

The following is a kind of converse of D.1.

D.2. Proposition. If $a \prec b$, then there exist random variables $X_1, \ldots, X_n$ such that $EX_i = a_i$ and $EX_{[i]} = b_i$, $i = 1, \ldots, n$.

Proof. Apply 6.A.1.d to write

$$a_j = \frac{1}{m} \sum_{i=1}^{m} \alpha_{ij} \quad \text{and} \quad b_j = \frac{1}{m} \sum_{i=1}^{m} \alpha_{i[j]}, \quad j = 1, \ldots, n,$$

where for each i, $\alpha_{i[j]}$ are obtained by reordering α_{ij} decreasingly. Then let the X_j be independent random variables such that

$$P\{X_j = \alpha_{ij}\} = 1/m, \quad i = 1, \ldots, m. \quad \|$$

The majorization (1) of expected values has a counterpart for probabilities. To see this, let A_i be the event $\{X_i \in E_i\}$, $i = 1, \ldots, n$, and let B_i be the event that at least i of the events $A_i, \ldots, A_n$ occur. Then by B.1,

$$(P(A_1), \ldots, P(A_n)) \prec (P(B_1), \ldots, P(B_n)).$$

If, for all i, $E_i = (t, \infty)$, then $B_i = \{X_{[i]} > t\}$ and it follows that

$$(\overline{F}_1(t), \ldots, \overline{F}_n(t)) \prec (\overline{G}_1(t), \ldots, \overline{G}_n(t)), \quad -\infty < t < \infty, \tag{3}$$

where $\overline{F}_i(t) = P\{X_i > t\}$ and $\overline{G}_i(t) = P\{X_{[i]} > t\}$, $i = 1, \ldots, n$.

It is easy to verify directly from the definition of majorization that

$$a \prec b \Rightarrow e - a \prec e - b,$$

where $e = (1, \ldots, 1)$. It follows from (3) that

$$(F_1(t), \ldots, F_n(t)) \prec (G_1(t), \ldots, G_n(t)), \quad -\infty < t < \infty, \tag{4}$$

where $F_i(t) = 1 - \overline{F}_i(t)$ and $G_i(t) = 1 - \overline{G}_i(t)$. In fact, it is also true that under some circumstances (3) implies (1).

D.3. Proposition. Let $\overline{F}_i(t) = P\{X_i > t\}$, $\overline{G}_i(t) = P\{Y_i > t\}$, $i = 1, \ldots, n$. If

$$\overline{G}_1(t) \geq \cdots \geq \overline{G}_n(t), \quad -\infty < t < \infty,$$

and if (3), i.e.,
$$(\overline{F}_1(t),\ldots,\overline{F}_n(t)) \prec (\overline{G}_1(t),\ldots,\overline{G}_n(t)), \quad -\infty < t < \infty,$$
then for all monotonic functions h such that the expectations exist,
$$(Eh(X_1),\ldots,Eh(X_n)) \prec (Eh(Y_1),\ldots,Eh(Y_n)).$$

Proof. Because of (3) and the stochastic ordering $\overline{G}_1 \geq \cdots \geq \overline{G}_n$,
$$\sum_1^k \overline{F}_i(t) \leq \sum_1^k \overline{G}_i(t), \quad k=1,2,\ldots,n,$$
with equality for $k = n$, $-\infty < t < \infty$, whatever the ordering of $\overline{F}_1,\ldots,\overline{F}_n$. Suppose that h is increasing and relabel the F_i's so that $Eh(X_i)$ is decreasing in i. Then by 17.A.2, for $k = 1,\ldots,n$,
$$\sum_1^k Eh(X_i) = \int h(t)\, d\sum_1^k \overline{F}_i(t) \leq \int h(t)\, d\sum_1^k \overline{G}_i(t) = \sum_1^k Eh(Y_i),$$
with equality for $k = n$. Because of the stochastic ordering $\overline{G}_1 \geq \cdots \geq \overline{G}_n$, $Eh(Y_i)$ is decreasing in i, so this proves the majorization for increasing h. If h is decreasing, replace h by $-h$ and use the fact that $a \prec b$ if and only if $-a \prec -b$. ||

As special cases, it follows that under the hypotheses of D.3,
$$(EX_1,\ldots,EX_n) \prec (EY_1,\ldots,EY_n)$$
and more generally,
$$(EX_1^{2k+1},\ldots,EX_n^{2k+1}) \prec (EY_1^{2k+1},\ldots,EY_n^{2k+1}), \quad k=0,1,\ldots.$$
In case the X_i and Y_i are nonnegative random variables, a similar majorization also holds for even powers or noninteger powers.

The following result is due to Sen (1970) in the special case that $F_1(x) = \cdots = F_n(x) = \frac{1}{n}\sum_{j=1}^n G_j(x)$.

D.4. Proposition. Let $\overline{F}_i(x) = P\{X_i > x\}$, $\overline{G}_i(x) = P\{Y_i > x\}$, $i = 1,\ldots,n$. If
$$(\overline{F}_1(x),\ldots,\overline{F}_n(x)) \prec (\overline{G}_1(x),\ldots,\overline{G}_n(x)), \quad -\infty < x < \infty,$$
then
$$X_{[1]} \geq^{\text{st}} Y_{[1]} \quad \text{and} \quad X_{(1)} \leq^{\text{st}} Y_{(1)}.$$

Proof. Because $\phi(z) = \prod z_i$ defines a Schur-concave function on $\mathscr{R}_+^n$,

$$P\{X_{[1]} > t\} = \prod_1^n \overline{F}_i(t) \geq \prod_1^n \overline{G}_i(t) = P\{Y_{[1]} > t\} \quad \text{for all} \quad t.$$

Similarly,

$$P\{X_{(1)} \leq t\} = \prod_1^n F_i(t) \geq \prod_1^n G_i(t) = P\{Y_{(1)} \leq t\},$$

so

$$P\{X_{(1)} > t\} \leq P\{Y_{(1)} > t\} \quad \text{for all} \quad t. \quad \|$$

F Star-Shaped with Respect to G

When F and G are distribution functions which satisfy $F(0) = G(0) = 0$, then F is said to be *star-shaped with respect to G* if $\psi(x) = G^{-1}F(x)$ is star-shaped on $[0, \infty)$ [see (11) in 16.B]. This concept, sometimes written $F \leq_* G$, yields a partial ordering on distribution functions of positive random variables which has been studied by various authors [see Barlow and Proschan (1975; reprinted 1996)]. Several equivalent conditions for $F \leq_* G$ have been given by Marshall, Olkin, and Proschan (1967). In reliability theory, the concept is of particular interest when $G(x) = 1 - e^{-x}$, $x \geq 0$ [again, see Barlow and Proschan (1975; reprinted 1996)].

D.5. Proposition. Let $X_1, \ldots, X_n$ be positive random variables, and for some positive star-shaped function ψ defined on $[0, \infty)$, let $Z_i = \psi(X_i)$, $i = 1, \ldots, n$. Then

$$P\left\{\left(X_1/\sum X_i, \ldots, X_n/\sum X_i\right) \prec \left(Z_1/\sum Z_i, \ldots, Z_n/\sum Z_i\right)\right\} = 1.$$

Proof. This is an immediate application of 5.B.2. $\|$

The above proposition illustrates condition (1) of 11.A.

If the Z_i above are replaced by random variables Y_i distributed as Z_i but not so simply dependent on $X_1, \ldots, X_n$, then D.5 may fail, whereas the somewhat weaker condition E_1 of 11.A still holds.

D.6. Proposition. Let $X_1, \ldots, X_n$ be independent random variables with distribution F, and let $Y_1, \ldots, Y_n$ be independent random variables with distribution G. If F is star-shaped with respect to G, then

$$E\phi\left(X_1/\sum X_i, \ldots, X_n/\sum X_i\right) \leq E\phi\left(Y_1/\sum Y_i, \ldots, Y_n/\sum Y_i\right)$$

for all Schur-convex functions ϕ such that the expectations are finite.

Proof. Since $Y_1, \ldots, Y_n$ have the same joint distribution as $Z_1, \ldots, Z_n$, where $Z_i = \psi(X_i)$, $i = 1, \ldots, n$, it follows that

$$E\phi\left(Y_1/\sum Y_i, \ldots, Y_n/\sum Y_i\right) = E\phi\left(Z_1/\sum Z_i, \ldots, Z_n/\sum Z_i\right)$$

for all Schur-convex functions ϕ such that the expectations are finite. But as a consequence of D.5,

$$\phi\left(X_1/\sum X_i, \ldots, X_n/\sum X_i\right) \leq \phi\left(Z_1/\sum Z_i, \ldots, Z_n/\sum Z_i\right)$$

with probability 1, so the expectations are also ordered. ∥

We remark that Marshall, Olkin, and Proschan (1967) obtain the somewhat weaker result that P_4 of Section 11.F holds rather than E_1 as in D.5.

The normalizations by total sums in D.5 and D.6 are necessary, but possibly detract some from the interest of the results. The following proposition eliminates the normalizations but substitutes the condition that F and G have equal finite means.

D.7. Proposition (Barlow and Proschan, 1966). Let $X_1, \ldots, X_n$ be independent random variables with distribution F, and let $Y_1, \ldots, Y_n$ be independent random variables with distribution G. If F is star-shaped with respect to G and if $EX_1 = EY_1$, then

$$EX_{[i]}/EY_{[i]} \text{ is increasing in } i = 1, \ldots, n,$$

and

$$(EX_{[1]}, \ldots, EX_{[n]}) \prec (EY_{[1]}, \ldots, EY_{[n]}).$$

Proof. Let $\psi(x) = G^{-1}F(x)$ for $x \geq 0$ and let $c > 0$. It is easily verified that

$$EX_{[i]} - cEY_{[i]} = \int_0^\infty [x - c\psi(x)] i \binom{n}{i} F^{n-i}(x)[1 - F(x)]^{i-1} \, dF(x).$$

Since ψ is star-shaped on $[0, \infty)$, $x - c\psi(x)$ changes sign at most once (+ to −) as x increases from 0 to ∞. It is straightforward to check that the kernel

$$\frac{n!}{(i-1)!(n-i)!} F^{n-i}(x)[1 - F(x)]^{i-1}$$

is totally positive of order 2 in $i = 1, \ldots, n$ and $-x \leq 0$. Hence, by the variation-diminishing property of totally positive kernels (18.A.5), $EX_{[i]} - cEY_{[i]}$ changes sign at most once (− to +) as i increases from 1 to n. Since $c > 0$ is arbitrary and $EY_{[i]} > 0$, this means that $EX_{[i]}/EY_{[i]}$ is increasing in i. By 5.B.1, this implies the majorization result. ||

Open problem. D.7 shows a majorization between order statistics (E_4). Is it true that E_3 or E_2 holds? (See notation of Sections 11.A and 11.F.) Clearly, P_4 will fail because $\sum X_i$ and $\sum Y_i$ have different distributions.

Positive Dependence by Mixtures

Suppose that for each $a \in \mathscr{A}$, $F^{(a)}$ is a univariate distribution function and let P be a probability measure defined on a σ-field of subsets of $\mathscr{A}$. With suitable measurability conditions on $F^{(a)}$,

$$F(x_1, \ldots, x_n) = \int_{\mathscr{A}} F^{(a)}(x_1) F^{(a)}(x_2) \cdots F^{(a)}(x_n) \, dP(a)$$

is an n-variate distribution function. Random variables $X_1, \ldots, X_n$ having such a distribution, or the distribution itself, are said to be *positively dependent by mixture*. Such distributions are studied, e.g., by Dykstra, Hewett, and Thompson (1973) and by Shaked (1977). They arise naturally from various models for dependence. Examples given by Shaked (1977) include the symmetric normal distribution with nonnegative correlation and exchangeable multivariate Poisson, geometric, logistic, gamma, t, beta, and F distributions.

There is good reason for using the term "positively dependent" here: $X_1, \ldots, X_n$ tend to be more alike than $Y_1, \ldots, Y_n$, where the Y_i's are independent and have the same common distribution as the X_i's. This translates precisely into a majorization relating the distribution functions or expected values of the ordered X_i's and Y_i's. The treatment here follows that of Shaked (1977) but differs in some respects because reverse order statistics are considered. Moreover, Shaked found directly the majorization relating expected values, whereas here use is made of D.3.

D. Expected Values of Ordered Random Variables   467

The following lemma is a useful preliminary.

D.8. Lemma. Let
$$h_{i,n}(p) = \sum_{j=i}^{n} \binom{n}{j} p^j (1-p)^{n-j},$$

and let $H_k(p) = \sum_{i=1}^{k} h_{i,n}(p)$. The function H_k is concave on $[0,1]$.

Proof. Because $H_n(p) = np$, the result is true for $k = n$. It is straightforward to verify that, for $1 \leq k \leq n-1$, the derivative
$$H'_k(p) = n[1 - h_{k,n-1}(p)]$$
decreases on $[0,1]$. ||

D.9. Proposition (Shaked, 1977). Let $X_1, \ldots, X_n$ be positively dependent by mixtures and let $Y_1, \ldots, Y_n$ be independent random variables with the same common marginal distributions as $X_1, \ldots, X_n$. Denote the distribution function of $X_{[i]}$ by F_i and the distribution function of $Y_{[i]}$ by G_i. Then
$$(\overline{F}_1(x), \ldots, \overline{F}_n(x)) \prec (\overline{G}_1(x), \ldots, \overline{G}_n(x)), \quad -\infty < x < \infty.$$

Proof. It is well known that
$$\overline{F}_i(x) = \int_{\mathscr{A}} h_{i,n}(\overline{F}^{(a)}(x)) \, dP(a).$$
Then, by using D.8 and Jensen's inequality,
$$\sum_{i=1}^{k} \overline{F}_i(x) = \int_{\mathscr{A}} \sum_{i=1}^{k} h_{i,n}(\overline{F}^{(a)}(x) \, dP(a)) = \int_{\mathscr{A}} H_k(\overline{F}^{(a)}(x)) \, dP(a)$$
$$\leq H_k\left(\int_{\mathscr{A}} \overline{F}^{(a)}(x) \, dP(a)\right) = \sum_{i=1}^{k} \overline{G}_i(x), \quad k = 1, \ldots, n-1.$$
Of course, $\sum_1^n \overline{F}_i(x) = \sum_1^n \overline{G}_i(x)$, and this completes the proof. ||

Another proof and a generalization of the above result are obtained by Shaked (1978a); see also Shaked (1978b).

D.10. Proposition (Shaked, 1977). Under the hypotheses of D.9,
$$(EX_{[1]}, \ldots, EX_{[n]}) \prec (EY_{[1]}, \ldots, EY_{[n]}).$$

Proof. This follows from D.3 and D.9. ||

Although D.10 follows easily from D.9, the reverse is also true. The reason for this is that if $X_1, \ldots, X_n$ are positively dependent by mixtures and g is monotonic on the common support of the X_i's, then $g(X_1), \ldots, g(X_n)$ are positively dependent by mixtures. Thus it follows from D.10 that

$$(Eg(X_{[1]}), \ldots, Eg(X_{[n]})) \prec (Eg(Y_{[1]}), \ldots, Eg(Y_{[n]})).$$

In particular, if $g(z) = 0$ for $z \leq x$ and $g(z) = 1$ for $z > x$, then D.9 is obtained.

Proposition D.10 says that condition E_4 of Section 11.F holds for $X_1, \ldots, X_n$ and $Y_1, \ldots, Y_n$; one can ask if the stronger results E_2 or P_4 hold. The bivariate normal distribution with common marginals and positive correlation provides a counterexample to

$$P\{X_{(1)} + X_{(2)} \leq x\} = P\{Y_{(1)} + Y_{(2)} \leq x\},$$

thereby showing that P_4 fails. Somewhat more complex counterexamples showing that E_2 fails have been given by Shaked (1977).

Dependence Ordering of Exchangeable Random Variables

The inequalities in D.9 and D.10 relate certain exchangeable random vectors with their counterparts having independent components but the same marginal distributions. Shaked and Tong (1985) propose several related dependence or dispersion orderings among exchangeable random vectors with common marginal distributions.

For two n-dimensional exchangeable random vectors X and Y with the same marginal distributions, three dispersion orders are defined as follows:

D.11. Definition.

(I) Y *is more dispersed in the sense I*, denoted $X \prec_I Y$, if $\Sigma_1^n c_i = 0$ implies

$$\left| \sum_1^n c_i X_{(i)} \right| \leq^{st} \left| \sum_1^n c_i Y_{(i)} \right|.$$

(II) X *is more dispersed in the sense II*, denoted $X \prec_{II} Y$, if

$$(F_{X_{[1]}}(t), \ldots, F_{X_{[n]}}(t)) \prec (F_{Y_{[1]}}(t), \ldots, F_{Y_{[n]}}(t)) \text{ for all } t.$$

(III) *X is more dispersed in the sense III*, denoted $X \prec_{III} Y$, if
$$(EX_{[1]}, \ldots, EX_{[n]}) \prec (EY_{[1]}, \ldots, EY_{[n]}).$$

Note that it is only assumed that X and Y are exchangeable; it is not assumed that X and Y are positively dependent by mixtures. Consequently, the arguments in the preceding section (assuming dependence by mixing) provide some motivation for the following results proved by Shaked and Tong (1985) for exchangeable vectors X and Y for which the marginal distributions of X and Y are equal:
$$X \prec_I Y \Rightarrow X \prec_{III} Y$$
and
$$X \prec_{II} Y \Rightarrow X \prec_{III} Y.$$

Among exchangeable distributions with a given marginal distribution, the distribution with independent marginals is the most dispersed in all three orderings. Shaked and Tong (1985) provide an extensive list of models in which the above orderings have interesting interpretations (many, but not all, are positively dependent by mixtures).

E Eigenvalues of a Random Matrix

In Chapter 9, a number of majorization results for eigenvalues are obtained as consequences of extremal representations. Because these representations possess convexity properties, the methods introduced in Section B apply to yield results comparing the expectation of a function of the eigenvalues of a random matrix with the same function of the eigenvalues of the expected value of the random matrix.

Eigenvalues of a Random Hermitian Matrix

If H is an $n \times n$ Hermitian matrix, then the eigenvalues $\lambda_i(H)$ are all real and can be arranged in decreasing order:
$$\lambda_1(H) \geq \cdots \geq \lambda_n(H).$$
With this convention and the notation
$$\mathscr{U}_k = \{U : U \text{ is a } k \times n \text{ complex matrix and } UU^* = I_k\},$$

it follows (see 20.A.2) that

$$\sum_1^k \lambda_i(H) = \max_{U \in \mathcal{U}_k} \operatorname{tr} UHU^*, \qquad k = 1, \ldots, n. \tag{1}$$

Of course, for $k = n$, $\operatorname{tr} UHU^* = \operatorname{tr} H$ is independent of U and $\sum_1^n \lambda_i(H) = \operatorname{tr} H$.

E.1. Theorem (Cacoullos and Olkin, 1965). If Z is a random $n \times n$ Hermitian matrix, then

$$(E\lambda_1(Z), \ldots, E\lambda_n(Z)) \succ (\lambda_1(EZ), \ldots, \lambda_n(EZ)). \tag{2}$$

Proof. Using the representation (1), weak majorization follows from Proposition B.3. Strong majorization then follows because $\sum_1^n \lambda_i(Z) = \operatorname{tr} Z$ and the trace is linear, so $\sum_1^n E\lambda_i(Z) = \operatorname{tr} EZ = \sum_1^n \lambda_i(EZ)$. ∥

The special result $E\lambda_1(Z) \geq \lambda_1(EZ)$, $E\lambda_n(Z) \leq \lambda_n(EZ)$ was noted by van der Vaart (1961), who gave a proof communicated by Theodore W. Anderson.

Notice that as a companion to (2),

$$(\lambda_1(EZ), \ldots, \lambda_n(EZ)) \succ (a_{11}, \ldots, a_{nn}), \tag{3}$$

where $a_{11}, \ldots, a_{nn}$ are the diagonal elements of EZ. This result follows from 9.B.1.

E.2. Theorem (Cacoullos and Olkin, 1965). If Z is a random $m \times m$ positive definite Hermitian matrix with expectation $EZ = A$, and if C is an $n \times m$ complex matrix, then

$$(E\lambda_1(CZ^{-1}C^*), \ldots, E\lambda_n(CZ^{-1}C^*))$$
$$\succ_w (\lambda_1(CA^{-1}C^*), \ldots, \lambda_n(CA^{-1}C^*)). \tag{4}$$

If $n \leq m$ and C is of rank n, then

$$(E\lambda_1(CZ^{-1}C^*)^{-1}, \ldots, E\lambda_n(CZ^{-1}C^*)^{-1})$$
$$\succ^w (\lambda_1(CA^{-1}C^*)^{-1}, \ldots, \lambda_n(CA^{-1}C^*)^{-1}). \tag{5}$$

Proof. Consider (4) first. The representation (1) applied to the Hermitian matrix $CH^{-1}C^*$ yields

$$\sum_1^k \lambda_i(CH^{-1}C^*) = \max_{U \in \mathcal{U}_k} \operatorname{tr} UCH^{-1}C^*U^*, \qquad k = 1, \ldots, n.$$

E. Eigenvalues of a Random Matrix   471

To apply B.3, it is only necessary to note that $g(V, H) = \text{tr}\, VH^{-1}V^*$ is convex in H for each fixed V (see 16.E.7.f).

The proof of (5) is similar but requires the fact $(CH^{-1}C^*)^{-1}$ is a concave function of H (see 16.E.7.h), so that $\text{tr}\, U(CH^{-1}C^*)^{-1}U^*$ is also a concave function of H. ||

Although the right-hand sides of (4) and (5) are related because $\lambda_i(A^{-1}) = [\lambda_{n-i+1}(A)]^{-1}$, $i = 1, \ldots, n$, the left-hand sides of (4) and (5) are not obtainable one from the other.

If W and Z are independent random $n \times n$ positive definite Hermitian matrices with $EZ = A$, $EW = B$, then the roots of $|W - \lambda Z| = 0$ are of interest in multivariate analysis. These roots are the eigenvalues of WZ^{-1} and the eigenvalues of $W^{1/2}Z^{-1}W^{1/2}$, where $W^{1/2}$ is the positive definite square root of W.

E.2.a. If W and Z are independent random $n \times n$ positive definite matrices, then

$$(E\lambda_1(WZ^{-1}), \ldots, E\lambda_n(WZ^{-1})) \succ_w (\lambda_1(BA^{-1}), \ldots, \lambda_n(BA^{-1})). \quad (6)$$

Proof. With $C = W^{1/2}$ in (4), it follows that

$$E(\lambda_1(W^{1/2}Z^{-1}W^{1/2}), \ldots, \lambda_n(W^{1/2}Z^{-1}W^{1/2}))$$
$$\succ_w (\lambda_1(W^{1/2}A^{-1}W^{1/2}), \ldots, \lambda_n(W^{1/2}A^{-1}W^{1/2}))$$
$$= (\lambda_1(A^{-1/2}WA^{-1/2}), \ldots, \lambda_n(A^{-1/2}WA^{-1/2})).$$

Taking expectations again and reapplying (4) with W in place of Z and $A^{-1/2}$ in place of C yields (6). ||

Singular Values of a Random Complex Matrix

Let A be an $n \times m$ complex matrix and with $t = \min(m, n)$, let

$$\sigma_1(A) \geq \cdots \geq \sigma_t(A)$$

denote the singular values of A arranged in decreasing order. From 20.B.1.a, it follows that

$$\sum_1^k \sigma_i(A) = \max_{(U,V) \in \mathscr{U}_k} \mathscr{R}\, \text{tr}\, UAV^*, \qquad k = 1, \ldots, t, \quad (7)$$

where $\mathscr{U}_k = \{(U,V) : U \text{ and } V \text{ are complex matrices}, U \text{ is } k \times n, V \text{ is } k \times m, \text{ and } UU^* = I_k = VV^*\}$.

E.3. Theorem. If Z is a random $n \times m$ complex matrix with finite expectation EZ, then

$$(E\sigma_1(Z), \ldots, E\sigma_t(Z)) \succ_w (\sigma_1(EZ), \ldots, \sigma_t(EZ)).$$

Proof. The proof is a direct application of B.3, making use of (7) and noting that $E\mathscr{R}\operatorname{tr} UZV^* = \mathscr{R}\operatorname{tr} U(EZ)V^*$. ||

There is an extension of E.3 to several matrices which uses the extremal representation 20.B.3: If $Z_1, \ldots, Z_l$ are independent random $n \times n$ matrices with finite expectations $A_1, \ldots, A_l$, then

$$\left(E\prod_1^l \sigma_1(Z_i), \ldots, E\prod_1^l \sigma_n(Z_i)\right) \succ_w \left(\prod_1^l \sigma_1(A_i), \ldots, \prod_1^l \sigma_n(A_i)\right).$$

Converse Theorems

E.4. Proposition. If $b \succ a$, then there exists a random $n \times n$ Hermitian matrix Z such that $E\lambda_i(Z) = b_{[i]}$, $\lambda_i(EZ) = a_{[i]}$, $i = 1, \ldots, n$.

Proof. Take Z to be diagonal and apply D.2. ||

The question whether converses can be given for the other majorizations of this section is unresolved. For (4) of E.2, one would like the following: Let C be a given $n \times m$ matrix and suppose CC^* has rank r. Given $b \succ_w a$, $a_{[i]} > 0$, $b_{[i]} > 0$, $i = 1, \ldots, r$, and $a_{[i]} = b_{[i]} = 0$, $i = r+1, \ldots, n$, find a distribution for a random positive definite $m \times m$ Hermitian matrix Z such that

$$E\lambda_i(CZ^{-1}C^*) = b_{[i]}, \qquad \lambda_i[C(EZ)^{-1}C^*] = a_{[i]}, \qquad i = 1, \ldots, n.$$

Unless $b_{[i]} \geq a_{[i]}$, $i = 1, \ldots, n$, it can be shown that no such distribution for Z exists that concentrates all mass on diagonal matrices even when $m = n$ and C is diagonal. This suggests that if a converse theorem for (4) of E.2 is true, then it is not as trivial as E.4.

Efficiency of Estimators

In many statistical problems involving a random $n \times m$ matrix Z, the expectation $EZ = A$ is a natural parameter for the distribution of Z. In choosing a procedure for making a statistical inference, the concept of invariance is often utilized. In particular, statistics invariant under the group of transformations $Z \to \Gamma Z \Delta$, where Γ and Δ are unitary, are often used. This group of transformations induces the transformation $A \to \Gamma A \Delta$ in the parameter space. Because the maximal invariants here are $(\sigma_1(Z), \ldots, \sigma_t(Z))$ and $(\sigma_1(A), \ldots, \sigma_t(A))$, where $t = \min(m, n)$, it follows that any statistic invariant under this group is a function of the singular values $\sigma_1(Z), \ldots, \sigma_t(Z)$ of Z and, moreover, the distribution of the statistics depends upon the parameter A only through the singular values $\sigma_1(A), \ldots, \sigma_t(A)$. This means, for example, that any invariant test of a hypothesis will be based upon a function of the singular values $\sigma_i(Z)$, and the rejection probability will be a function of the singular values $\sigma_i(A)$. Because $EZ = A$, Z is itself an unbiased estimator of A. But E.3 shows that $\sum_1^k \sigma_i(Z)$ is a positively biased estimator of $\sum_1^k \sigma_i(A)$.

If Z is a random positive definite matrix with $EZ = A$, then a group of transformations that often arises is $Z \to \Gamma Z \Gamma^*$, where Γ is unitary. In this case, the eigenvalues take the place of the singular values in the above comments.

With two random positive definite Hermitian matrices U and V having expectations $EU = A$ and $EV = B$, invariance under the group $(U, V) \to (LUL^*, LVL^*)$, where L is nonsingular, may be a natural requirement, say, when testing for equality of A and B. The induced group on the parameter space is $(A, B) \to (LAL^*, LBL^*)$. In this case, the maximal invariants in the sample and parameter spaces are the eigenvalues of UV^{-1} and the eigenvalues of AB^{-1}. A comparison between these is provided by E.2.a.

The matrix $(CV^{-1}C^*)^{-1}$ arises from efficiency considerations in a regression model. Suppose that Y is a p-dimensional random vector with expectation $EY = \beta X$ and covariance matrix $\text{cov}(Y) = \Sigma$, where β is $1 \times m$ and X is a known $m \times p$ matrix of rank $m \leq p$. When Σ is known, the Gauss–Markov estimate of β is

$$\widehat{\beta} = Y \Sigma^{-1} X^* (X \Sigma^{-1} X^*)^{-1};$$

$\widehat{\beta}$ has covariance matrix

$$\text{cov}(\widehat{\beta}) = (X \Sigma^{-1} X^*)^{-1}.$$

When Σ is unknown, a consistent estimate $\widehat{\Sigma}$ may be substituted to provide an estimated $\text{cov}(\beta)$:

$$\text{est cov}(\widehat{\beta}) = (X \widehat{\Sigma}^{-1} X^*)^{-1}.$$

474   12. Probabilistic, Statistical, and Other Applications

Various measures of efficiency of an *estimator* depend upon the eigenvalues of the covariance matrix $(X\Sigma^{-1}X^*)^{-1}$ of $\hat{\beta}$. When Σ is unknown, the efficiency can be estimated using the eigenvalues of $(X\hat{\Sigma}^{-1}X')^{-1}$. Comparisons between these sets of eigenvalues are given by E.2.

F   Special Results for Bernoulli and Geometric Random Variables

In Section 11.C, families of distributions are studied which preserve symmetry and convexity in the sense that $\psi(\theta) = E_\theta \phi(x)$ is symmetric and convex whenever ϕ is symmetric and convex (and the expectation is defined). Similarly, families of distributions that preserve Schur-convexity are found in Section 11.E. There are some cases not quite so neat in that properties obtained for ψ do not coincide with those imposed upon ϕ. Some such results are given here. Assume throughout the existence of all indicated expectations.

Bernoulli Random Variables

Suppose that $X_1, \ldots, X_n$ are independent random variables with Bernoulli distributions

$$P\{X_i = 1\} = p_i, \qquad P\{X_i = 0\} = 1 - p_i, \qquad i = 1, \ldots, n. \qquad (1)$$

Hoeffding (1956) showed that, for $p = (p_1, \ldots, p_n)$, and for the vector $\lambda = (\bar{p}, \ldots, \bar{p}), \bar{p} = \sum p_i/n$,

$$E_p \psi \left(\sum X_i \right) \leq E_\lambda \psi \left(\sum X_i \right),$$

where $\psi: \{0, 1, \ldots, n\} \to \mathscr{R}$ is convex. Karlin and Novikoff (1963) show that the vector λ can be replaced by any vector majorized by p. This generalization of Hoeffding's result has also been proved by Gleser (1975), Karlin and Studden (1966), and Rinott (1973).

F.1. Proposition (Karlin and Novikoff, 1963).   Let $X_1, \ldots, X_n$ be independent random variables with Bernoulli distributions (1). If $\psi: \{0, 1, \ldots, n\} \to \mathscr{R}$ is convex, then $g(p) = E_p \psi(\sum_1^n X_i)$ is a Schur-concave function of p.

Proof.   If $E_{p_1,p_2} \psi(X_1 + X_2 + z)$ is Schur-concave in p_1 and p_2, then so is $E_p \phi(X) = E_{p_3,\ldots,p_n}\{E_{p_1,p_2}[\psi(X_1+X_2+\sum_3^n X_i)|\sum_3^n X_i]\}$. Because

F. Special Results for Bernoulli and Geometric Random Variables

Schur-convexity in pairs implies Schur-convexity (2.B.1), it is sufficient to prove the result for $n = 2$, in which case

$$E_p\psi(X_1+X_2) = [\psi(2)-2\psi(1)+\psi(0)]p_1p_2+(p_1+p_2)[\psi(1)-\psi(0)]+\psi(0).$$

Because p_1p_2 is Schur-concave in p_1 and p_2, and because ψ is convex (see 16.B.10.a), $\psi(2) - 2\psi(1) + \psi(0) \geq 0$ and the desired result follows (for majorization comparison, $p_1 + p_2$ is fixed). ||

A generalization of F.1 is given in 15.E.

F.1.a. Proposition. Let $X_1, \ldots, X_n$ be independent random variables with Bernoulli distributions (1) and let $R_i = -\log p_i$ for $i = 1, \ldots, n$. If ψ is a real function defined on $\{0, 1, \ldots, n\}$ such that

$$\psi(0) \leq \cdots \leq \psi(n-1),$$

then $g(R_1, \ldots, R_n) = E_R\psi(\sum X_i)$ is a decreasing Schur-convex function of $R_1, \ldots, R_n$.

Proof. As in F.1, it is sufficient to prove that $E_{R_1,R_2}\psi(X_1+X_2+z)$ is a decreasing Schur-convex function of R_1, R_2 for $z = 0, 1, \ldots, n-2$. Note that

$$E_{R_1,R_2}\psi(X_1 + X_2 + z) = [\psi(2+z) - 2\psi(1+z) + \psi(z)]e^{-(R_1+R_2)}$$
$$+ (e^{-R_1} + e^{-R_2})[\psi(1+z) - \psi(z)] + \psi(z).$$

Because e^{-x} is a decreasing convex function, $e^{-R_1} + e^{-R_2}$ is decreasing and Schur-convex. Since $\psi(1+z) - \psi(z) \geq 0$, the proof is complete. ||

F.1.b. Proposition. Let $X_1, \ldots, X_n$ be independent random variables with binomial distributions

$$P\{X_i = x\} = \binom{m}{x}p_i^x(1-p_i)^{m-x}, \quad x = 0, 1, \ldots, m.$$

If $\psi : \{0, 1, \ldots, mn\} \to \mathcal{R}$ is convex, then $E_p\psi(\sum X_i)$ is a Schur-concave function of p.

Proof. Because each X_i is a sum of m independent random variables with a Bernoulli distribution, this result follows directly from Proposition F.1 and 5.A.1.g or 5.A.6. ||

In the above proposition, the fact that m does not depend upon i is essential.

Geometric Random Variables

Let $X_1, \ldots, X_n$ be independent random variables and suppose that X_i has a geometric distribution with parameter p_i; i.e.,

$$P\{X_i = k\} = p_i(1 - p_i)^k, \qquad k = 0, 1, \ldots, \qquad i = 1, \ldots, n. \qquad (2)$$

It is surprising that, for such random variables no results are known regarding either the preservation of symmetry and convexity (Section 16.C), or regarding the preservation of Schur-convexity (Section 16.E). However, with the notation $p_i = 1/a_i, i = 1, \ldots, n$, the following result can be given.

F.2. Proposition (Rinott, 1973). Let $X_1, \ldots, X_n$ be independent random variables with geometric distributions (2). If $\phi : \mathscr{R}^n \to \mathscr{R}$ is symmetric, convex in each variable separately, and if $g(u, v, \dot{x}) = \phi((u+v)/2, (u-v)/2, \dot{x})$ is increasing in v and L-superadditive in u and v for all fixed $\dot{x} \in \mathscr{R}^{n-2}$ (see Definition 6.C.2), then $\psi(a) = E_a\phi(X)$ is Schur-convex in a.

This result was proved by Rinott (1973) by verifying the derivative conditions of 3.A.4. The details are omitted here.

G Weighted Sums of Symmetric Random Variables

If ϕ is a continuous symmetric convex function on $\mathscr{R}^n$ and $X_1, \ldots, X_n$ are exchangeable, then according to 11.B.2, $E\phi(a_1X_1, \ldots, a_nX_n)$ is symmetric and convex, hence Schur-convex, in $a = (a_1, \ldots, a_n)$. In particular, when $X_1, \ldots, X_n$ are independent and g is convex,

$$\psi(a) = Eg\left(\sum a_iX_i\right)$$

is Schur-convex; i.e.,

$$a \prec b \Rightarrow \psi(a) \leq \psi(b). \qquad (1)$$

For certain select functions $g : \mathscr{R} \to \mathscr{R}$ including some that are convex and certain random variables $X_1, \ldots, X_n$, there is a kind of reversal of this inequality, namely,

$$(a_1^2, \ldots, a_n^2) \prec (b_1^2, \ldots, b_n^2) \Rightarrow \psi(a) \geq \psi(b). \qquad (2)$$

Notice that there is no implication relating the conditions $a \prec b$ and $(a_1^2, \ldots, a_n^2) \prec (b_1^2, \ldots, b_n^2)$, although it is true that $a \prec b$ implies $(a_1^2, \ldots, a_n^2) \prec_w (b_1^2, \ldots, b_n^2)$ (see 5.A.1.b).

There are companion theorems to (2) that give conditions under which, for independent normal (mean 0, variance 1) random variables $Z_1, \ldots, Z_n$,

$$Eg\left(\sum a_i X_i\right) \leq Eg\left(\sum a_i Z_i\right) \equiv Eg\left(c \sum Z_i\right),$$

where $c^2 = \sum a_i^2/n$.

G.1. Theorem. Suppose that $X_1, \ldots, X_n$ are independent, identically distributed random variables, with distributions symmetric about zero, and having finite moments $\mu_{2r} = EX_j^{2r}$, $r = 1, \ldots, m$. If $\lambda_r \equiv \mu_{2r}/[2^r \Gamma(r+\frac{1}{2})/\sqrt{\pi}\,]$ is logarithmically concave in $r = 0, 1, \ldots, m$, then for $m = 1, 2, \ldots$,

$(a_1^2, \ldots, a_n^2) \prec (b_1^2, \ldots, b_n^2)$ implies

$$E\left(\sum_1^n a_i X_i\right)^{2m} \geq E\left(\sum_1^n b_i X_i\right)^{2m}. \qquad (3)$$

Notice that for a normal distribution with zero expectation, λ_r is logarithmically linear, and equality holds in the conclusion of (3) because $\sum a_i^2 = \sum b_i^2$.

If U has a χ^2 distribution with one degree of freedom, that is, U has density

$$f_U(u) = u^{-1/2} e^{-u/2}/\sqrt{2\pi}, \qquad u \geq 0, \qquad (4)$$

then $EU^r = 2^r \Gamma(r+\frac{1}{2})/\sqrt{\pi}$; thus λ_r is the rth moment of X_i^2 divided by the rth moment of U. By Lyapunov's inequality 16.D.1.d, μ_{2r} and EU^r are logarithmically convex in $r \geq 0$, so λ_r is a ratio of two logarithmically convex functions.

G.1.a. Corollary (Eaton, 1970). If $X_1, \ldots, X_n$ are independent symmetric Bernoulli random variables, i.e.,

$$P\{X_i = 1\} = P\{X_i = -1\} = \tfrac{1}{2}, \qquad i = 1, \ldots, n,$$

then (3) holds.

Proof. Here, $\mu_{2r} \equiv 1$. Since EU^r is logarithmically convex, λ_r is logarithmically concave. ∥

Efron (1969) obtains (3) for the special case $a_i = 1/\sqrt{n}$, $i = 1, \ldots, n$; this result is also a special case of G.2 ahead. Efron encounters G.1.a in studying the distribution of Student's t-statistic $\sum_1^n U_i/\sqrt{U_i^2}$ when the underlying joint distribution of $\varepsilon_1 U_1 + \cdots + \varepsilon_n U_n$ is invariant for all choices $\varepsilon_i = \pm 1$, $i = 1, \ldots, n$.

478   12. Probabilistic, Statistical, and Other Applications

To indicate some additional distributions for $X_1, \ldots, X_n$ that satisfy the conditions of G.1, let V have an exponential distribution with density

$$f_V(v) = e^{-v}, \qquad v \geq 0.$$

Then EV^r/EU^r is logarithmically concave (Karlin, Proschan, and Barlow, 1961, Theorem 1). Furthermore, if T is a nonnegative random variable having an increasing hazard rate (IHR) (i.e., $\log P\{T > t\}$ is concave in $t \geq 0$), then ET^r/EV^r is logarithmically concave (Barlow, Marshall, and Proschan, 1963). This means that ET^r/EU^r is logarithmically concave because the product of logarithmically concave functions is logarithmically concave.

The class of IHR distributions is quite broad and includes the gamma distributions with shape parameter ≥ 1 and uniform distributions. As a consequence of G.1, it follows that (3) holds whenever X_i^2 has an IHR distribution, and the X_i's are independent with common distribution symmetric about 0. See Marshall and Olkin (2007, Section 4C).

Proof of G.1. Assume, without loss of generality, that $\sum_1^n a_i^2 = \sum_1^n b_i^2 = 1$ and let $\theta_i = a_i^2$, $i = 1, \ldots, n$. Then

$$E\left(\sum_1^n a_i X_i\right)^{2m} = \sum_{m_1,\ldots,m_n} \binom{2m}{m_1,\ldots,m_n} \prod_1^n a_i^{m_i} \prod_1^n EX_i^{m_i}$$

$$= \sum \binom{2m}{2k_1,\ldots,2k_n} \prod_1^n a_i^{2k_i} \prod_1^n \mu_{2k_i}$$

$$= \sum \left[\binom{2m}{2k_1,\ldots,2k_n} \bigg/ \binom{m}{k_1,\ldots,k_n}\right] \prod_1^n \mu_{2k_i} \binom{m}{k_1,\ldots,k_n} \prod_1^n \theta_i^{k_i}$$

$$= E \sum \left[\binom{2m}{2K_1,\ldots,2K_n} \bigg/ \binom{m}{K_1,\ldots,K_n}\right] \prod_1^n \mu_{2K_i},$$

where $K_1, \ldots, K_n$ have a multinomial distribution.

According to 11.E.11, this expectation is a Schur-concave function of $\theta_1, \ldots, \theta_n$ if

$$h(k_1, \ldots, k_n) = \left[\binom{2m}{2k_1,\ldots,2k_n} \bigg/ \binom{m}{k_1,\ldots,k_n}\right] \prod_1^n \mu_{2k_i}$$

is Schur-concave. By using the Gauss–Legendre duplication formula (16.B.8b)

$$\Gamma(2r+1)/\Gamma(r+1) = 2^{2r}\Gamma(r+\tfrac{1}{2})/\sqrt{\pi}, \qquad (5)$$

G. Weighted Sums of Symmetric Random Variables

h can be rewritten in the form

$$h(k_1, \ldots, k_n) = \frac{\Gamma(2m+1)}{\Gamma(m+1)} \prod_1^n \frac{\Gamma(k_i+1)}{\Gamma(2k_i+1)} \prod_1^n \mu_{2k_i}$$

$$= \frac{\Gamma(2m+1)}{2^m \Gamma(m+1)} \prod_1^n \frac{\mu_{2k_i}}{2^{k_i} \Gamma(k_i + \tfrac{1}{2})/\sqrt{\pi}} = \frac{\Gamma(2m+1)}{2^m \Gamma(m+1)} \prod_1^n \lambda_{k_i}.$$

But this is Schur-concave in $k_1, \ldots, k_n$ if and only if λ_j is a logarithmically concave function of j (see 3.E.1). ∥

According to Theorem G.1, $E(\sum_1^n a_i X_i)^{2m}$ is a Schur-concave function of $a_1^2, \ldots, a_n^2$ for certain independent random variables X_i, including those that have a symmetric Bernoulli distribution. For such random variables, Schur-concavity is known to hold for a wider class of functions.

G.2. Theorem (Eaton, 1970). Suppose that $X_1, \ldots, X_n$ are independent symmetric Bernoulli random variables; i.e.,

$$P\{X_i = 1\} = P\{X_i = -1\} = \tfrac{1}{2}, \qquad i = 1, \ldots, n.$$

If $g : \mathscr{R} \to \mathscr{R}$ is continuously differentiable and

$$t^{-1}[g'(t+\Delta) - g'(-t+\Delta) + g'(t-\Delta) - g'(-t-\Delta)] \qquad (6)$$

is increasing in $t > 0$ whenever $\Delta \geq 0$, then

$$(a_1^2, \ldots, a_n^2) \prec (b_1^2, \ldots, b_n^2) \text{ implies } Eg\left(\sum_1^n a_i X_i\right) \leq Eg\left(\sum_1^n b_i X_i\right).$$

The proof of this, which is omitted here, consists of verifying the conditions of 3.A.4; in fact, this approach leads directly to (6).

The condition (6) of G.2 is equivalent to the condition that

$$t^{-1} E[g'(t+W) - g'(-t+W)]$$

is increasing in t for all bounded symmetric random variables W. A sufficient condition for (6) is that

$$t^{-1}[g'(t+\Delta) - g'(-t+\Delta)]$$

is increasing in $t > 0$ for all real Δ. Examples of functions which satisfy (6) are

$$g(t) = t^m, \qquad m = 1, 2, \ldots, \qquad (7)$$

$$g(t) = e^{at}, \qquad a \neq 0, \qquad (8)$$

$$g(t) = e^{at} + e^{-at}, \qquad a \neq 0. \qquad (9)$$

Of course, any odd function satisfies (6), but these lead only to the inequality $0 \leq 0$ because $\sum a_i X_i$ and $\sum b_i X_i$ are symmetric random variables. Since the class of functions satisfying (6) is convex, example (9) is obtainable from (8). By the same token, (8) is obtainable from (7).

The following theorem does not involve majorization but is included because of its close relationship with G.1.

G.3. Theorem. Suppose that $X_1, \ldots, X_n$ satisfy the hypotheses of G.1 and, additionally, suppose $EX_i^2 = 1$. Let $Z_1, \ldots, Z_n$ be independent normal (mean 0, variance 1) random variables. If $\sum a_i^2 = 1$, then

$$E\left(\sum a_i X_i\right)^{2m} \leq E\left(\frac{1}{\sqrt{n}} \sum Z_i\right)^{2m} = \frac{(2m)!}{2^m m!}, \quad m = 1, 2, \ldots. \quad (10)$$

For the case that the X_i are symmetric Bernoulli random variables, G.3 is due to Khintchine (1923). An independent proof in this case was given by Efron (1969), who used the fact that it is sufficient to prove

$$E\left(\frac{1}{\sqrt{n}} \sum_1^n X_i\right)^{2m} \leq E\left(\frac{1}{\sqrt{n}} \sum_1^n Z_i\right)^{2m}, \quad m = 1, 2, \ldots. \quad (11)$$

Efron's proof is based on moment comparisons. As a consequence of (10), by treating the weights as random variables, Efron obtains the inequality

$$E \sum_1^n \left[Y_j \Big/ \sum_1^n Y_i^2\right]^{2m} \leq E\left(\frac{1}{\sqrt{n}} \sum_1^n Z_i\right)^{2m}, \quad m = 1, 2, \ldots,$$

for random variables $Y_1, \ldots, Y_n$ such that $(\varepsilon_1 Y_1, \ldots, \varepsilon_n Y_n)$ has the same distribution for every choice of $\varepsilon_1, \ldots, \varepsilon_n$, $\varepsilon_i = \pm 1$.

Proof of G.3. Let U have a χ^2 distribution with one degree of freedom; i.e., let U have the density (4). Then (11) can be rewritten as

$$\sum \binom{2m}{2k_1, \ldots, 2k_n} \prod_1^n EU^{k_i} \prod_1^n \frac{\mu_{2k_i}}{EU^{k_i}} \leq \sum \binom{2m}{2k_1, \ldots, 2k_n} \prod_1^n EU^{k_i}.$$

Since $\lambda_r = \mu_{2r}/EU^r$ is logarithmically concave, $\lambda_r^{1/r}$ is decreasing in $r = 1, 2, \ldots$. By hypothesis, $\lambda_1 = 1$. Thus, (11) is immediate, and (10) follows with the aid of G.1. ||

Theorem G.3 is a generalization of Khintchine's (1923) result to random variables that need not be symmetric Bernoulli. Eaton (1970) has given a generalization of Khintchine's result which replaces the functions $g(x) = x^{2m}$ by a more general class of functions. Newman (1975a, b, 1975/1976) generalizes Khintchine's result by allowing some dependence of the random variables (arising in ferromagnetic models) or by permitting them to be other than symmetric Bernoulli random variables.

Bounds for a Ratio of Expectations

Suppose that $T_1, \ldots, T_n$ are independent symmetric random variables with $ET_i^{2k} = \mu_{2k}$. Then

$$E\left(\sum_1^n a_i T_i\right)^{2m} = \sum \binom{2m}{2k_1, \ldots, 2k_n} \prod_1^n a_i^{2k_i} \prod_1^n \mu_{2k_i}.$$

Since $\prod_1^n \mu_{2k_i}$ is Schur-convex in $k_1, \ldots, k_n$ (Tong, 1977; see also 3.E.3),

$$\mu_{2\bar{k}}^n \leq \prod_1^n \mu_{2k_i} \leq \mu_{2m},$$

where $\bar{k} = \sum k_i/n$, $m = \sum k_i$. Hence,

$$\mu_{2\bar{k}}^n \leq \frac{E(\sum_1^n a_i T_i)^{2m}}{E(\sum_1^n a_i X_i)^{2m}} \leq \mu_{2m},$$

where $X_1, \ldots, X_n$ are independent symmetric Bernoulli random variables.

H Stochastic Ordering from Ordered Random Variables

Many results of Chapter 11 give conditions on random vectors X and Y that imply $\sum_1^n X_i \leq^{st} \sum_1^n Y_i$. For example, suppose $U \prec_{P_1} V$ or even $U \prec_{P_3} V$ and let $X_i = g(U_i)$, $Y_i = g(V_i)$, $i = 1, \ldots, n$, where g is continuous and convex. Then $\sum X_i \leq^{st} \sum Y_i$ because $U \prec_{P_3} V$ requires $\sum g(U_i) \leq^{st} \sum g(V_i)$. Another example, not quite so transparent, is given in 11.E.8.b. The purpose of this section is to give some stronger stochastic ordering results that give still other examples of stochastically ordered sums.

Exponential Random Variables

H.1. Theorem (Proschan and Sethuraman, 1976). Let $Y_1, \ldots, Y_n$ be independent random variables with the same exponential distribution

$$P\{Y_i > t\} = e^{-t}, \qquad t \geq 0, \quad i = 1, \ldots, n.$$

Let $X^{(\theta)} = (Y_1/\theta_1, \ldots, Y_n/\theta_n)$, where $\theta_i > 0$ for all i. If $\lambda \prec \nu$ on $\mathscr{R}_{++}^n$, then

$$(X_{(1)}^{(\lambda)}, \ldots, X_{(n)}^{(\lambda)}) \leq^{st} (X_{(1)}^{(\nu)}, \ldots, X_{(n)}^{(\nu)}).$$

Proof. Suppose first that $n = 2$. Then, because $\lambda_1 + \lambda_2 = \nu_1 + \nu_2$,

$$P\{X_{(1)}^{(\lambda)} > x\} = P\{X_{(1)}^{(\nu)} > x\} = e^{-(\lambda_1 + \lambda_2)x}, \qquad x \geq 0.$$

Next, observe that for $0 \leq x_1 \leq x_2$,

$$P\{X_{(2)}^{(\lambda)} > x_2 | X_{(1)}^{(\lambda)} = x_1\} = [\lambda_1 e^{-\lambda_2(x_2 - x_1)} + \lambda_2 e^{-\lambda_1(x_2 - x_1)}]/(\lambda_1 + \lambda_2)$$

$$= [\lambda_1 e^{\lambda_1(x_2 - x_1)} + \lambda_2^{\lambda_2(x_2 - x_1)}]e^{-(x_2 - x_1)(\lambda_1 + \lambda_2)}/(\lambda_1 + \lambda_2).$$

Because $g(z) = ze^{az}$ is convex in z for all $a \geq 0$, it follows from 3.C.1 that $P\{X_{(2)}^{(\lambda)} > x_2 | X_{(1)}^{(\lambda)} = x_1\}$ is Schur-convex in λ.

By 17.A.2, $U \leq^{st} V$ if and only if $h(U) \leq^{st} h(V)$ for all increasing functions h. Thus from the stochastic ordering

$$P\{X_{(2)}^{(\lambda)} > x_2 | X_{(1)}^{(\lambda)} = x_1\} \leq P\{X_{(2)}^{(\nu)} > x_2 | X_{(1)}^{(\nu)} = x_1\},$$

it follows that for any increasing function $h: \mathscr{R}^2 \to \mathscr{R}$,

$$P\{h(x_1, X_{(2)}^{(\lambda)}) > t | X_{(1)}^{(\lambda)} = x_1\} \leq P\{h(x_1, X_{(2)}^{(\nu)}) > t | X_{(1)}^{(\nu)} = x_1\}.$$

Because $X_{(1)}^{(\lambda)}$ and $X_{(1)}^{(\nu)}$ have the same distribution, unconditioning yields

$$P\{h(X_{(1)}^{(\lambda)}, X_{(2)}^{(\lambda)}) > t\} \leq P\{h(X_{(1)}^{(\nu)}, X_{(2)}^{(\nu)}) > t\}. \qquad (1)$$

This proves the theorem for $n = 2$.

Because of 3.A.5, it is sufficient to prove the theorem for the case that λ and ν differ in but two components, say $\lambda_i = \nu_i$, $i = 3, \ldots, n$. By 17.B.6, it follows from (1) that there exist random variables $V_1^{(\lambda)}$, $V_2^{(\lambda)}$, $V_1^{(\nu)}$, $V_2^{(\nu)}$ such that

(i) $(V_1^{(\lambda)}, V_2^{(\lambda)})$ and $(X_{(1)}^{(\lambda)}, X_{(2)}^{(\lambda)})$ have the same distribution,

(ii) $(V_1^{(\nu)}, V_2^{(\nu)})$ and $(X_1^{(\nu)}, X_2^{(\nu)})$ have the same distribution,
(iii) $V_1^{(\lambda)} \leq V_1^{(\nu)}$, $V_2^{(\lambda)} \leq V_2^{(\nu)}$ with probability 1,

and these random variables can be chosen so as to be independent of $Y_3, \ldots, Y_n$. Consequently,

$$V^{(\lambda)} = (V_1^{(\lambda)}, V_2^{(\lambda)}, Y_3/\lambda_3, \ldots, Y_n/\lambda_n)$$
$$\leq (V_1^{(\nu)}, V_2^{(\nu)}, Y_3/\nu_3, \ldots, Y_n/\nu_n) = V^{(\nu)}$$

with probability 1. Thus $(V_{(1)}^{(\lambda)}, \ldots, V_{(n)}^{(\lambda)}) \leq (V_{(1)}^{(\nu)}, \ldots, V_{(n)}^{(\nu)})$ with probability 1, so that for all increasing functions $h: \mathscr{R}^n \to \mathscr{R}$,

$$Eh(V^{(\lambda)}) \leq Eh(V^{(\nu)}).$$

Because

$(V_{(1)}^{(\lambda)}, \ldots, V_{(n)}^{(\lambda)})$ and $(X_{(1)}^{(\lambda)}, \ldots, X_{(n)}^{(\lambda)})$ have the same distribution,

$(V_{(1)}^{(\nu)}, \ldots, V_{(n)}^{\nu})$ and $(X_{(1)}^{(\nu)}, \ldots, X_{(n)}^{(\nu)})$ have the same distribution,

this completes the proof. ||

H.1.a. In the notation of H.1, if $\lambda \prec^w \nu$ on $\mathscr{R}_{++}^n$, then

$$(X_{(1)}^{(\lambda)}, \ldots, X_{(n)}^{(\lambda)}) \leq^{st} (X_{(1)}^{(\nu)}, \ldots, X_{(n)}^{(\nu)}).$$

Proof. If $\lambda \prec^w \nu$ on R_{++}^n, then by 5.A.9.a, there exists $\theta \in \mathscr{R}_{++}^n$ such that $\theta \geq \nu$ and $\lambda \prec \theta$. Then with θ in place of ν in H.1, it follows that $(X_{(1)}^{(\lambda)}, \ldots, X_{(n)}^{(\lambda)}) \leq^{st} (X_{(1)}^{(\theta)}, \ldots, X_{(n)}^{(\theta)})$. Because $\theta \geq \nu$, it follows that $X_{(i)}^{(\theta)} \leq^{st} X_{(i)}^{(\nu)}$, $i = 1, \ldots, n$. ||

H.1.b. Corollary (Proschan and Sethuraman, 1976). Under the conditions of H.1.a, $\sum_{i \in I} X_{(i)}^{(\lambda)} \leq^{st} \sum_{i \in I} X_i^{(\nu)}$ for all subsets I of $\{1, \ldots, n\}$. Thus

$$\sum_{i=1}^k X_{[i]}^{(\lambda)} \leq^{st} \sum_{i=1}^k X_{[i]}^{(\nu)}, \quad \sum_{i=1}^k X_{(i)}^{(\lambda)} \leq^{st} \sum_{i=1}^k X_{(i)}^{(\nu)}, \quad k = 1, \ldots, n,$$

and in particular,

$$\sum_{1}^n X_i^{(\lambda)} \leq^{st} \sum_{1}^n X_i^{(\nu)}.$$

Proof. This follows from H.1.a since $I_{\{z: \Sigma_{i \in I} z_i > t\}}(x)$ is increasing in x. ||

Boland, El-Neweihi, and Proschan (1994) prove that if $\lambda \prec \nu$, then $\sum_{i=1}^{n} X_i^{(\lambda)} \leq_{\mathrm{lr}} \sum_{i=1}^{n} X_i^{(\nu)}$, where $\leq_{\mathrm{lr}}$ denotes the likelihood ratio ordering (defined in 17.A.11). However, they show that an extension of H.1 to likelihood ratio ordering is not possible. They also provide a parallel result for sums of independent heterogeneous geometric random variables. Specifically, suppose that $X(p_1), \ldots, X(p_n)$ are independent random variables and for each i, $X(p_i)$ has a geometric distribution with parameter p_i. If $(p_1, \ldots, p_n) \prec (p'_1, \ldots, p'_n)$, or if $(\log p_1, \ldots, \log p_n) \prec (\log p'_1, \ldots, \log p'_n)$, then

$$\sum_{i=1}^{n} X(p_i) \leq^{\mathrm{lr}} \sum_{i=1}^{n} X(p'_i).$$

Families with Proportional Hazard Functions

If F is a univariate distribution function such that $F(x) = 0$ for $x < 0$, the function $R(x) = -\log[1 - F(x)]$ is called the *hazard function* of F. A family $\{F_\lambda, \lambda > 0\}$ of distribution functions is said to have *proportional* hazard functions if

$$\overline{F}_\lambda(x) \equiv 1 - F_\lambda(x) = e^{-\lambda R(x)},$$

where R is the hazard function of F_1. See Marshall and Olkin (2007, p. 232); there the parameter λ is called a *frailty parameter*. Families with proportional hazard functions are often used in survival analysis, where the random variables are nonnegative. The most familiar case is $R(x) = x$, in which case $F_\lambda(x) = 1 - e^{-\lambda x}$, $x \geq 0$, is an exponential distribution.

H.1.c. Corollary (Kochar and Rojo, 1996). In the notation of H.1, if $\lambda \prec \nu$ on $\mathscr{R}_{++}^n$, then

$$(X_{(2)}^{(\lambda)} - X_{(1)}^{(\lambda)}, \ldots, X_{(n)}^{(\lambda)} - X_{(1)}^{(\lambda)}) \leq^{\mathrm{st}} (X_{(2)}^{(\nu)} - X_{(1)}^{(\nu)}, \ldots, X_{(n)}^{(\nu)} - X_{(1)}^{(\nu)}).$$

The proof utilizes the representation of stochastic ordering described in 17.B.6. As a consequence, the ranges are stochastically ordered; that is, $X_{(n)}^{(\lambda)} - X_{(1)}^{(\lambda)} \leq^{\mathrm{st}} X_{(n)}^{(\nu)} - X_{(1)}^{(\nu)}$. This means that the range is stochastically larger if the parameters are more dispersed in the sense of majorization. In case $n = 2$, the stochastic ordering can be replaced by the stronger likelihood ratio ordering (17.A.11).

H.1.d. Corollary (Kochar and Rojo, 1996)). In the notation of H.1, for $0 \leq x_1 \leq x_2 \leq \ldots \leq x_n$, the function

$$P\{X_{(2)}^{(\theta)} > x_2, X_{(3)}^{(\theta)} > x_3, \ldots X_{(n)}^{(\theta)} > x_n | X_{(1)}^{(\theta)} = x_1\}$$

is Schur-convex in θ.

Proof. Use H.1.c and the fact that

$$P\{X_{(2)}^{(\theta)} > x_2, \ldots, X_{(n)}^{(\theta)} > x_n | X_{(1)}^{(\theta)} = x_1\}$$
$$= P\{X_{(2)}^{(\theta)} - X_{(1)}^{(\theta)} > x_2 - x_1, \ldots, X_n^{(\theta)} - X_{(1)}^{(\theta)} > x_n - x_1\}. \quad \|$$

The following theorem is essentially due to Proschan and Sethuraman (1976), who assume $\lambda \prec \nu$.

H.2. Theorem. Let $\{F_\lambda, \lambda > 0\}$ be a family of distribution functions with proportional hazard functions. Let $U_1^{(\lambda)}, \ldots, U_n^{(\lambda)}$ and $U_1^{(\nu)}, \ldots, U_n^{(\nu)}$ be independent random variables where, for $\theta > 0$, $U_i^{(\theta)}$ has distribution F_{θ_i}. If $(\lambda_1, \ldots, \lambda_n) \prec^w (\nu_1, \ldots, \nu_n)$ on $\mathscr{R}_{++}^n$, then

$$(U_{(1)}^{(\lambda)}, \ldots, U_{(n)}^{(\lambda)}) \leq^{\text{st}} (U_{(1)}^{(\nu)}, \ldots, U_{(n)}^{(\nu)}).$$

Proof. Let $R(x) = -\log \overline{F}_1(x)$, so that $\overline{F}_\lambda(x) = e^{-\lambda R(x)}$, and let $R^{-1}(y) = \inf\{x : R(x) \geq y\}$. If $Y_i = \lambda_i R(U_i^{(\lambda)})$, then

$$P\{Y_i > t\} = P\{U_i^{(\lambda)} > R^{-1}(t/\lambda_i)\} = e^{-t}, \quad t \geq 0, \quad i = 1, \ldots, n,$$

so that by H.1.a,

$$(R(U_{(1)}^{(\lambda)}), \ldots, R(U_{(n)}^{(\lambda)})) \leq^{\text{st}} (R(U_{(1)}^{(\nu)}), \ldots, R(U_{(n)}^{(\nu)})).$$

For any increasing function $h : \mathscr{R}^n \to \mathscr{R}$, let

$$\widetilde{h}(x) = h(R^{-1}(x_1), \ldots, R^{-1}(x_n)).$$

Then $\widetilde{h}$ is also increasing, so

$$h(U_{(1)}^{(\lambda)}, \ldots, U_{(n)}^{(\lambda)}) = \widetilde{h}(R(U_{(1)}^{(\lambda)}), \ldots, R(U_{(n)}^{(\lambda)}))$$
$$\leq^{\text{st}} \widetilde{h}(R(U_{(1)}^{(\nu)}), \ldots, R(U_{(n)}^{(\nu)})) = h(U_{(1)}^{(\nu)}, \ldots, U_{(n)}^{(\nu)}). \quad \|$$

Alternative proof of H.2. It is possible to prove H.2 with $\lambda \prec \nu$ by directly generalizing the proof of H.1. For any family $\{F_\lambda, \lambda > 0\}$ of absolutely continuous distribution functions, it is easy to compute that for $n = 2$,

(i) $P\{X_{(1)}^{(\lambda)} > t\} = \overline{F}_{\lambda_1}(t)\overline{F}_{\lambda_2}(t)$ for all t,

and for $x_1 \leq x_2$,

(ii) $P\{X_{(2)}^{(\lambda)} > x_2 | X_{(1)}^{(\lambda)} = x_1\} = \dfrac{f_{\lambda_1}(x_1)\overline{F}_{\lambda_2}(x_2) + f_{\lambda_2}(x_1)\overline{F}_{\lambda_1}(x_2)}{f_{\lambda_1}(x_1)\overline{F}_{\lambda_2}(x_1) + f_{\lambda_2}(x_1)\overline{F}_{\lambda_1}(x_1)}.$

From this, it is easy to see that with proportional hazard functions, $P\{X_{(1)}^{\lambda} > t\}$ is a function of $\lambda_1 + \lambda_2$. The same argument as in the proof of H.1 shows that $P\{X_{(2)}^{(\lambda)} > x_2 | X_{(1)}^{(\lambda)} = x_1\}$ is Schur-convex in λ. ||

H.2.a. Corollary (Proschan and Sethuraman, 1976). With the notation and hypotheses of H.2, $\sum_{i \in I} U_{(i)}^{(\lambda)} \leq^{\text{st}} \sum_{i \in I} U_{(i)}^{(\nu)}$ for all subsets $I \subset \{1, \ldots, n\}$.

Proof. This result follows from H.2 because the indicator function $I_{\{z : \Sigma_{i \in I} z_i > t\}}(x)$ is increasing in x. ||

H.2.b. Corollary (Pledger and Proschan, 1971). If $\lambda \prec \nu$, then with the notation of H.2, $U_{(1)}^{(\lambda)}$ and $U_{(1)}^{(\nu)}$ have the same distribution and $U_{(i)}^{(\lambda)} \leq^{\text{st}} U_{(i)}^{(\nu)}$, $i = 2, 3, \ldots, n$.

Proof. That $U_{(1)}^{(\lambda)}$ and $U_{(1)}^{(\nu)}$ have the same distribution is trivial. The stochastic ordering is a special case of H.2.a. ||

Various applications of H.2 can be found by starting with some distribution function F satisfying $F(x) = 0$ for $x < 0$, and generating the proportional hazards family $F_\lambda(x) = \exp\{\lambda \log[1 - F(x)]\}$. Sometimes this yields a family not parameterized naturally so some adjustments are required, as in the following examples.

Bernoulli Distributions

H.3. Theorem (Proschan and Sethuraman, 1976). Let $X_1, \ldots, X_n$ be independent random variables with Bernoulli distributions

$$P\{X_i = 1\} = p_i, \quad P\{X_i = 0\} = 1 - p_i, \quad i = 1, \ldots, n.$$

Similarly, let $Y_1, \ldots, Y_n$ be independent random variables with Bernoulli distributions having parameters $r_1, \ldots, r_n$. If

$$(-\log p_1, \ldots, -\log p_n) \prec (-\log r_1, \ldots, -\log r_n),$$

then $\sum X_i \leq^{\text{st}} \sum Y_i$.

Proof. Proschan and Sethuraman prove this result (in case of strong majorization) as a corollary to H.2 with the hazard function $R(x) = 1$,

$0 < x \leq 1$, and $R(x) = \infty$, $1 < x < \infty$. As an alternative proof, notice that $\phi(x) = I_{\{z:\Sigma z_i > t\}}(x)$ satisfies the conditions of F.1.a (because $\sum z_i$ is an increasing function). Thus $E\phi(x) = P\{\sum X_i > t\}$ is a decreasing Schur-convex function of $(-\log p_1, \ldots, -\log p_n)$. ||

Weibull Distributions

H.4. Corollary (Proschan and Sethuraman, 1976). Let $V_1, \ldots, V_n$ be independent, identically distributed random variables with a Weibull distribution given (for some $\alpha > 0$) by

$$P\{V_i > x\} = \exp\{-x^\alpha\}, \qquad x > 0.$$

If $(\mu_1^{-\alpha}, \ldots, \mu_n^{-\alpha}) \prec (\theta_1^{-\alpha}, \ldots, \theta_n^{-\alpha})$, then

$$\sum \mu_i V_i \leq^{\text{st}} \sum \theta_i V_i.$$

Proof. This follows from H.2 because the $\mu_i V_i$'s have proportional hazards with constants of proportionality $\mu_i^{-\alpha}, i = 1, \ldots, n$. ||

I Another Stochastic Majorization Based on Stochastic Ordering

A version of stochastic majorization not discussed in Chapter 11 is obtainable by mimicking the usual definition of majorization on $\mathscr{D}$ with stochastic ordering replacing ordinary inequalities. Suppose the random variables X_i and Y_i can be stochastically ordered so that

$$X_1 \geq^{\text{st}} \cdots \geq^{\text{st}} X_n, \qquad Y_1 \geq^{\text{st}} \cdots \geq^{\text{st}} Y_n. \tag{1}$$

If

$$\sum_1^k X_i \leq^{\text{st}} \sum_1^k Y_i, \qquad k = 1, \ldots, n, \tag{2}$$

then write

$$X \prec_w^{(\text{st})} Y.$$

If, in addition, $\sum_1^n X_i$ and $\sum_1^n Y_i$ have the same distribution, write

$$X \prec^{(\text{st})} Y.$$

Analogously, $X \prec^{w(st)} Y$ can also be defined. Various examples of these kinds of orderings can be found.

I.1. Proposition. Let $\{F_\lambda, \lambda \in \Lambda\}$ be a family of distribution functions indexed by a real parameter λ and suppose that

$$\lambda_1, \lambda_2 \in \Lambda \quad \text{implies} \quad \lambda_1 + \lambda_2 \in \Lambda, \tag{3}$$

$$F_{\lambda_1} * F_{\lambda_2} = F_{\lambda_1 + \lambda_2}, \quad \text{where } * \text{ denotes convolution,} \tag{4}$$

$$\lambda_1 < \lambda_2 \quad \text{implies} \quad 1 - F_{\lambda_1}(x) \le 1 - F_{\lambda_2}(x) \text{ for all } x. \tag{5}$$

Let $X_1, \ldots, X_n$ be independent random variables and let $Y_1, \ldots, Y_n$ be independent random variables such that X_i has distribution F_{λ_i}, Y_i has distribution F_{ν_i}, $i = 1, \ldots, n$. If $\lambda \prec \nu$, then $X \prec^{(st)} Y$.

Proof. Because $\sum_1^k \lambda_i \le \sum_1^k \nu_i$, it follows from (4) and (5) that

$$1 - F_{\sum_1^k \lambda_i}(x) = 1 - (F_{\lambda_1} * \cdots * F_{\lambda_k})(x) \le 1 - (F_{\nu_1} * \cdots * F_{\nu_k})(x)$$
$$= 1 - F_{\sum_1^k \nu_i}(x);$$

that is, $\sum_1^k X_i \le^{st} \sum_1^k Y_i$, $k = 1, \ldots, n$. By a similar argument, it follows that $\sum_1^n \lambda_i = \sum_1^n \nu_i$ implies $\sum_1^n X_i$ and $\sum_1^n Y_i$ have the same distribution. ||

By similar arguments, it can be shown that

$$\lambda \prec_w \nu \quad \text{implies} \quad X \prec_w^{(st)} Y,$$

$$\lambda \prec^w \nu \quad \text{implies} \quad X \prec^{w(st)} Y.$$

Various special cases of I.1 are apparent:

(i) $\Lambda = (0, \infty)$ and F_λ is a Poisson distribution with expectation λ.
(ii) $\Lambda = \{1, 2, 3, \ldots\}$ and F_λ is a binomial distribution with parameters λ and p; i.e., F_λ has (discrete) density function

$$f_\lambda(k) = \binom{\lambda}{k} p^k (1-p)^{\lambda - k}, \quad k = 0, 1, \ldots, \lambda.$$

(iii) $\Lambda = (0, \infty)$ and F_λ is a gamma distribution with shape parameter λ; i.e., F_λ has density

$$f_\lambda(x) = \frac{\theta^\lambda x^{\lambda - 1}}{\Gamma(\lambda)} e^{-\theta x}, \quad x \ge 0.$$

I.2. Proposition. Suppose $\{F_\lambda, \lambda > 0\}$ is a family of distribution functions with proportional hazard functions; i.e.,

$$\overline{F}_\lambda(x) \equiv 1 - F_\lambda(x) = \exp\{-\lambda R(x)\}$$

I. Another Stochastic Majorization Based on Stochastic Ordering

for some increasing function R. Let U_i have distribution F_{λ_i}, let V_i have distribution F_{ν_i}, and let $X_i = U_{[i]}$, $Y_i = V_{[i]}$, $i = 1, \ldots, n$. If $\nu \prec \lambda$ on $\mathscr{R}_{++}^n$, then $X \prec_{\mathrm{w}}^{(\mathrm{st})} Y$.

Proof. This is a direct consequence of H.2. ‖

The following result is somewhat different than the previous ones of this section, but it yields results of the same kind. The proposition is essentially due to Kadiyala (1968), who took $a_1 = \cdots = a_n = 1$ and assumed $\lambda_n > 0$. The proof given here is virtually the same as that of Kadiyala.

I.3. Proposition. Suppose $X_1, \ldots, X_n$ are positive random variables, $\lambda_1 \geq \lambda_2 \geq \cdots \geq \lambda_n$, $a_1 \geq a_2 \geq \cdots \geq a_n > 0$, and b_i/a_i is decreasing in $i = 1, \ldots, n$; then for all $t \in \mathscr{R}$,

$$P\left\{\sum_{i=1}^n \lambda_i \frac{a_i X_i}{\sum_{j=1}^n a_j X_j} \leq t\right\} \geq P\left\{\sum_{i=1}^n \lambda_i \frac{b_i X_i}{\sum_{j=1}^n b_j X_j} \leq t\right\}.$$

Proof. Let $r_i = b_i/a_i$, $i = 1, \ldots, n$. It is sufficient to prove that if $x_1 > 0, \ldots, x_n > 0$, then

$$\sum_i \lambda_i \frac{a_i x_i}{\sum_j a_j x_j} \leq \sum_i \lambda_i \frac{b_i x_i}{\sum_j b_j x_j} = \sum_i \lambda_i \frac{r_i a_i x_i}{\sum_j r_j a_j x_j}.$$

With the notation $p_i = a_i x_i / \sum_j a_j x_j$, this inequality becomes

$$\sum \lambda_i p_i \leq \sum \lambda_i r_i p_i \Big/ \sum r_i p_i.$$

But this follows from the fact that λ_i and r_i are similarly ordered. ‖

If $U_i = a_i X_i / \sum_j a_j X_j$ and $V_i = b_i X_i / \sum_j b_j X_j$, $i = 1, \ldots, n$, then with $\lambda_1 = \cdots = \lambda_k = 1$, $\lambda_{k+1} = \cdots = \lambda_n = 0$, it follows from I.1 that

$$\sum_1^k U_i \leq^{\mathrm{st}} \sum_1^k V_i, \quad k = 1, \ldots, n.$$

Similarly, with $\lambda_1 = \cdots = \lambda_{k-1} = 0$, $\lambda_k = \cdots = \lambda_n = -1$, it follows that

$$\sum_k^n U_i \geq^{\mathrm{st}} \sum_k^n V_i, \quad k = 1, \ldots, n.$$

The additional orderings
$$U_1 \geq^{\text{st}} \cdots \geq^{\text{st}} U_n \quad \text{and} \quad V_1 \geq^{\text{st}} \cdots \geq^{\text{st}} V_n$$
are automatically satisfied, e.g., if $X_1, \ldots, X_n$ are exchangeable, in which case $U \prec^{(\text{st})} V$.

According to 5.B.1, the condition b_i/a_i is decreasing in $i = 1, \ldots, n$ implies $a/\sum a_i \prec b/\sum b_i$. However, this majorization cannot replace the hypothesis of I.3 that b_i/a_i is decreasing in i even when $X_1, \ldots, X_n$ are exchangeable. To see this, take $n = 3$, $\lambda_1 = 1$, $\lambda_2 = \lambda_3 = 0$, $a = (4, 2, 2)$, $b = (4, 4, 0)$, and let (X_1, X_2, X_3) take on the values $(1, 1, 0)$, $(1, 0, 1)$, and $(0, 1, 1)$ each with probability $\frac{1}{3}$. Then with $\frac{1}{2} < t < \frac{2}{3}$, the inequality of I.3 fails.

J Peakedness of Distributions of Linear Combinations

According to a definition of Birnbaum (1948), the random variable U_1 is *more peaked* about s_1 than U_2 about s_2 if
$$P\{|U_1 - s_1| > t\} \leq P\{|U_2 - s_2| > t\} \quad \text{for all} \quad t \geq 0.$$
In case $s_1 = s_2 = 0$, U_1 is said simply to be more peaked than U_2.

If U_1 and U_2 have densities symmetric about 0, then U_1 is more peaked than U_2 if and only if
$$P\{U_1 > t\} \leq P\{U_2 > t\} \quad \text{for all} \quad t \geq 0.$$
The notion of peakedness has been generalized; see, e.g., Mudholkar (1972) and Section O.

The following proposition gives a peakedness comparison for linear combinations when the vectors of coefficients are ordered by majorization.

J.1. Theorem (Proschan, 1965). Let $X_1, \ldots, X_n$ be independent random variables with common density f which satisfies

(i) $f(t) = f(-t)$ for all real t, i.e., f is symmetric,

(ii) $\log f$ is concave, i.e., f is a Pólya frequency function of order 2, denoted PF_2.

Then for all $t \geq 0$,
$$\psi(a) = P\left\{\sum a_i X_i \leq t\right\}$$
is a Schur-concave function of a, $a_i \geq 0$ for all i.

Proof. By 3.A.5, it is sufficient to show that for fixed $\dot{a} = (a_3, \ldots, a_n)$,

$$\tilde{\psi}(a_1, a_2) = \psi(a_1, a_2, \dot{a})$$

is Schur-convex in $a_1 \geq 0$ and $a_2 \geq 0$, i.e., that $h(a_1) = \tilde{\psi}(a_1, b - a_1)$ is increasing in a_1, $0 \leq a_1 \leq b/2$. Because

$$P\left\{\sum a_i X_i \leq t\right\} = E\left[P\left\{a_1 X_1 + a_2 X_2 \leq t - \sum_3^n a_i X_i | X_3, \ldots, X_n\right\}\right]$$

and because $t \geq 0$ is arbitrary, it is sufficient to prove the result for $n = 2$ and $b = 1$.

If F is the distribution function corresponding to f, then with $\bar{a} = 1 - a$,

$$h(a) = P\{a X_1 + \bar{a} X_2 \leq t\} = \int_{-\infty}^{\infty} F\left(\frac{t - \bar{a}u}{a}\right) f(u)\, du.$$

It is possible to justify differentiation under the integral sign here, so that

$$a^2 h'(a) = \int_{-\infty}^{\infty} f\left(\frac{t - \bar{a}u}{a}\right)(u - t) f(u)\, du$$

$$= \int_{-\infty}^{t} f\left(\frac{t - \bar{a}u}{a}\right)(u - t) f(u)\, du + \int_{t}^{\infty} f\left(\frac{t - \bar{a}u}{a}\right)(u - t) f(u)\, du.$$

Now, let $v = t - u$ in the first integral and let $v = u - t$ in the second integral to obtain

$$a^2 h'(a) = \int_0^{\infty} v \left[f\left(t - \frac{\bar{a}}{a} v\right) f(v + t) - f\left(t + \frac{\bar{a}}{a} v\right) f(t - v) \right] dv.$$

Because f is symmetric, the integrand here can be rewritten as

$$v \left[f\left(\frac{\bar{a}}{a} v - t\right) f(v + t) - f\left(\frac{\bar{a}}{a} v + t\right) f(v - t) \right].$$

But this is nonnegative because $\log f$ is concave and because $t \geq 0$, $\bar{a} \geq a$. ∥

Note: Chan, Park, and Proschan (1989) show that the conditions for Theorem J.1 can be weakened. It is enough to assume that $(X_1, X_2, \ldots, X_n)$ has a sign-invariant Schur-concave joint density; that is,

$$f(x_1, \ldots, x_n) = f(|x_1|, \ldots, |x_n|).$$

Further conditions are required for $\psi(a)$ in Theorem J.1 to be strictly Schur-concave, as provided by Proschan (1965).

The condition of J.1 that $\log f$ be concave is clearly not a necessary condition. Indeed, if $X_1, \ldots, X_n$ have a Cauchy distribution symmetric about 0, then $\psi(a)$ is independent of a so long as $\sum a_i$ is fixed. The class of densities f for which the conclusion of J.1 holds has not been identified. However, Proschan has shown that it is closed under convolutions.

Ibragimov (2004) shows that J.1 also holds under any of the following conditions:

(i) the X_i's have a centered stable distribution with characteristic exponent $\alpha > 1$, i.e., if the common characteristic function of the X_i's is of the form

$$E(e^{itX}) = \exp[-\sigma^\alpha |t|^\alpha (1 - i\beta\sigma(t)\tan(\pi\alpha/2))],$$

where $\alpha > 1, \beta \in [-1, 1]$;

(ii) the common distribution of the X's is a convolution of centered symmetric stable distributions all with characteristic exponent $\alpha \leq 1$, but possibly with different characteristic exponents;

(iii) $X_1, \ldots, X_n$ are independent and identically distributed, where X_1 admits a representation of the form $X_1 = \sum_{i=1}^m Z_i$, where the Z_i's are independent symmetric random variables which either have log concave densities or have stable distributions with characteristic exponent in the interval $[1, 2]$. Note that the Z_i's are permitted to have different characteristic exponents.

Applications of (iii) are discussed in detail by Ibragimov (2005).

Note. A straightforward consequence of Theorem J.1 is that if the common density of the X_i's satisfies conditions (i) and (ii), then $\overline{X}_n = \sum_1^n X_i/n$ is more peaked than $\overline{X}_{n-1} = \sum_1^{n-1} X_i/(n-1)$. The comparison of $\overline{X}_n$ and $\overline{X}_{n-1}$ involves a comparison of two particular linear combinations with weights $(\frac{1}{n}, \ldots, \frac{1}{n})$ and $(\frac{1}{n-1}, \ldots, \frac{1}{n-1}, 0)$. This suggests a more general result given in J.3.

J.1.a. Theorem. Under the conditions of J.1,

$$\widetilde{\psi}(a) = P\left\{\left|\sum a_i X_i\right| > t\right\}$$

is a Schur-convex function of a, $a_i \geq 0$ for all i.

J. Peakedness of Distributions of Linear Combinations

Proof. According to J.1, $P\{\sum a_i X_i < -t\} = P\{\sum a_i X_i > t\}$ is Schur-convex in a, $t \geq 0$. Consequently, the sum of these probabilities is Schur-convex in a. ||

Theorem J.1.a is just a recasting of J.1 in a new form.

J.1.b. Theorem. Let $h: \mathscr{R} \to \mathscr{R}$ be increasing on $(-\infty, 0)$ and decreasing on $(0, \infty)$. Under the conditions of J.1, $Eh(\sum a_i X_i)$ is a Schur-convex function of a, $a_i \geq 0$ for all i.

Proof. Let G_a be the distribution function of $\sum a_i X_i$, so that

$$Eh\left(\sum a_i X_i\right) = \int_0^\infty [h(z) + h(-z)]\, dG_a(z).$$

Because $h(z) + h(-z)$ is increasing in $z > 0$, and since $G_a(0) = \frac{1}{2}$ for all a, this result follows from the version of stochastic ordering given by J.1 and from 17.A.2. ||

Of course, J.1.b is equivalent to J.1 and J.1.a.

A concept closely related to peakedness is formulated by Lawton (1965) as follows. A random variable U_1 is *more concentrated* about s_1 than U_2 about s_2 if

$$P\{a < U_1 - s_1 < b\} \geq P\{a < U_2 - s_2 < b\} \quad \text{whenever} \quad a < 0 < b.$$

In case $s_1 = s_2 = 0$, U_1 is said simply to be more concentrated than U_2. For random variables U_1 and U_2 with densities symmetric about 0, U_1 is more concentrated than U_2 if and only if U_1 is more peaked than U_2.

J.2. Theorem (Lawton, 1965). Let $h: \mathscr{R} \to (0, \infty)$ and let X be a random variable such that the functions

$$g_a(z) = P\{a < X/h(z) < 0\}, \qquad \bar{g}_b(z) = P\{0 \leq X/h(z) < b\}$$

are concave in $z \geq 0$. If $V_1, \ldots, V_m$ are independent, identically distributed random variables independent of X, then

$$P\left\{a < \frac{X}{h(\sum \lambda_i V_i)} < b\right\}$$

is a Schur-concave function of $\lambda_1, \ldots, \lambda_m$ whenever $a < 0 < b$.

Proof. From the concavity of g_a and $\bar{g}_b$, it follows that

$$P\left\{a < \frac{X}{h(\sum \lambda_i V_i)} < b\right\} = E\left[g_a\left(\sum \lambda_i U_i\right) + \bar{g}_b\left(\sum \lambda_i U_i\right)\right]$$

is a symmetric concave function of $\lambda_1, \ldots, \lambda_m$, and hence is Schur-concave. ||

Several statistical applications of this result are given by Lawton (1965). For extensions, see Lawton (1968).

A Multivariate Version

An extension of Theorem J.1 to cover k-dimensional random variables is provided by Olkin and Tong (1988). A k-dimensional random variable X is said to be more peaked than a k-dimensional random variable Y if

$$P\{Y \in A\} \geq P\{X \in A\}$$

for all measurable compact, convex, and symmetric (about 0) subsets A of $\mathscr{R}^k$. Paralleling Theorem J.1, we have

J.3. Theorem (Olkin and Tong, 1988). Let $X_1, X_2, \ldots, X_n$ be independent, identically distributed k-dimensional random variables with common density $f(x)$ which satisfies

(i) $f(x) = f(-x)$ for all $x \in \mathscr{R}^k$,

(ii) $\log f(x)$ is a concave function of x.

If $a \prec b$, then the random vector $\sum_1^n a_i X_i$ is more peaked than the random vector $\sum_1^n b_i X_i$. In particular, if $\overline{X}_n = \frac{1}{n} \sum_1^n X_i$, then $\overline{X}_n$ is more peaked than $\overline{X}_{n-1}$.

Olkin and Tong (1988) also discuss peakedness of linear combinations of dependent X's.

K Tail Probabilities for Linear Combinations

Because of the symmetry present in Section J, the peakedness results can be reformulated to say that if $\sum a_i X_i$ has distribution F_a and if $a \prec b$, then

$$F_a(t) \leq F_b(t), \quad t \leq 0,$$
$$F_a(t) \geq F_b(t), \quad t \geq 0.$$

This single crossing property of two distribution functions with the crossing point specified is stronger than the results of this section which assert only that for some $t_0 < t_1$,

$$F_a(t) \leq F_b(t), \quad t \leq t_0,$$
$$F_a(t) \geq F_b(t), \quad t \geq t_1.$$

K. Tail Probabilities for Linear Combinations

Results of this kind, where it is not possible to take $t_0 = t_1$, are apparently more difficult intrinsically than the cleaner results of Section J or the stochastic ordering of Section H. We are able to properly discuss only the case of sums of Bernoulli random variables and to give some partial results about exponential random variables.

Independent Bernoulli Random Variables

Let $X_1, \ldots, X_n$ be independent random variables with Bernoulli distributions

$$P\{X_i = 1\} = p_i, \qquad P\{X_i = 0\} = 1 - p_i, \qquad i = 1, 2, \ldots, n.$$

For integer values of t, let

$$h_t(p_1, \ldots, p_n) = P\left\{\sum X_i \leq t\right\} \qquad \text{and} \qquad \bar{p} = \sum p_i/n.$$

Hoeffding (1956) shows that

$$\begin{aligned} h_t(p_1, \ldots, p_n) &\leq h_t(\bar{p}, \ldots, \bar{p}) &&\text{if } 0 \leq t \leq n\bar{p} - 1, \\ h_t(p_1, \ldots, p_n) &\geq h_t(\bar{p}, \ldots, \bar{p}) &&\text{if } n\bar{p} \leq t \leq n. \end{aligned} \tag{1}$$

If $n\bar{p} - 1 < t < n\bar{p}$, the inequality might go either way. Gleser (1975) extended Hoeffding's result to make more general comparisons.

K.1. Theorem (Gleser, 1975). *The function $h_t(p_1, \ldots, p_n)$ is Schur-concave in p for $0 \leq t \leq n\bar{p} - 2$ and it is Schur-convex in p for $n\bar{p} + 1 \leq t \leq n$.*

Proof. Let $f(k; \dot{p}) = P\{\sum_3^n X_i = k\}$, where $\dot{p} = (p_3, \ldots, p_n)$. For integers k and t, let

$$g_t(k) = \begin{cases} 1 & \text{if } k \leq t, \\ 0 & \text{if } k \geq t + 1, \end{cases}$$

so that

$$h_t(p) = E g_t\left(\sum_{i=1}^n X_i\right) = \sum_{k=0}^n g_t(k) P\left\{\sum_{i=1}^n X_i = k\right\}.$$

The proof consists of checking the derivative conditions of 3.A.4 for h_t to be Schur-convex or Schur-concave. With the observation that

$$P\left\{\sum_1^n X_i = k\right\} = p_1 p_2 f(k-2; \dot{p})$$

$$+ [p_1(1-p_2) + p_2(1-p_1)] f(k-1; \dot{p})$$

$$+ (1-p_1)(1-p_2) f(k; \dot{p}),$$

and with the notation $\Delta^2 \psi(k) = \psi(k+2) - 2\psi(k+1) + \psi(k)$, it is not difficult to verify that

$$(p_1 - p_2)\left(\frac{\partial h_t}{\partial p_1} - \frac{\partial h_t}{\partial p_2}\right) = -(p_1 - p_2)^2 \sum_{k=0}^{n} g_t(k) \Delta^2 f(k-2; \dot{p})$$

$$= -(p_1 - p_2)^2 \sum_{k=0}^{n-2} \Delta^2 g_t(k) f(k; \dot{p}).$$

Because $\Delta^2 g_t(t) = 1$, $\Delta^2 g_t(t-1) = -1$, and $\Delta^2 g_t(k) = 0$ if $k \neq t$ and $k \neq t - 1$, this equation reduces to

$$(p_1 - p_2)\left(\frac{\partial h_t}{\partial p_1} - \frac{\partial h_t}{\partial p_2}\right) = -(p_1 - p_2)^2 [f(t; \dot{p}) - f(t-1; \dot{p})].$$

Let $f_m(k)$ be the probability of k successes in m not necessarily identical Bernoulli trials and let $\tau = \sum_0^m k f_m(k)$. Samuels (1965) has shown that

$$f_m(k) \quad \text{is increasing in } k \leq \tau,$$
$$f_m(k) \quad \text{is decreasing in } k \geq \tau.$$

Because $\sum_0^{n-2} k f(k; \dot{p}) = n\bar{p} - p_1 - p_2$, it follows that

$$f(k; \dot{p}) \quad \text{is increasing in } k \leq n\bar{p} - p_1 - p_2,$$
$$f(k; \dot{p}) \quad \text{is decreasing in } k \geq n\bar{p} - p_1 - p_2.$$

Furthermore, $0 \leq p_1 + p_2 \leq 2$, so that

$$f(k; \dot{p}) - f(k-1; \dot{p}) \begin{cases} \geq 0 & \text{for } k \leq n\bar{p} - 2, \\ \leq 0 & \text{for } k - 1 \geq n\bar{p} \quad (k \geq n\bar{p} + 1). \end{cases}$$

By virtue of 3.A.4, this completes the proof. ||

Notice that the inequalities (1) of Hoeffding hold for a slightly larger range of t-values than do the results of K.1. Gleser has shown by counterexamples that this is inevitable if $h_t(p)$ is to be compared with $h_t(r)$ for arbitrary $r \prec p$. However, one can see from the proof of K.1 that if the restriction $0 \leq p_i + p_j \leq 2$ ($i \neq j$) is replaced by more stringent inequalities, then some extension of the range of Schur-convexity or Schur-concavity can be made.

K.2. Corollary (Gleser, 1975). If $0 \leq s \leq n\bar{p} - 2$ and $n\bar{p} + 1 \leq t \leq n$, then

$$P\left\{s \leq \sum_1^n X_i \leq t\right\}$$

is Schur-convex in $(p_1, \ldots, p_n)$.

Gleser has also obtained from K.1 that for any continuous convex function $g: \mathscr{R} \to \mathscr{R}$, $Eg(\sum X_i)$ is Schur-concave as a function of $(p_1, \ldots, p_n)$. See F.1 for further discussion.

Consistency of the Sample Median

A statistic of a sample of size n is said to be *consistent* if it converges in probability to the true parameter value as $n \to \infty$. For example, a sample variance is consistent if it converges in probability to the variance of the underlying distribution. With independent, identically distributed random variables, consistency of the sample mean and the sample median as estimates of their population counterparts is readily verified. An extension to nonindependent, identically distributed random variables with density $f(x_1, \ldots, x_n) = f(|x_1|, \ldots, |x_n|)$ for the sample mean has been available for some time. Mizera and Wellner (1998) use majorization arguments that involve the use of Theorem K.1 to identify necessary and sufficient conditions for consistency of the sample median in the nonindependent, identically distributed case. Because the empirical distribution function of a sample is expressible as a sum of indicator random variables, a role for nonidentically distributed Bernoulli random variables is assured.

More specifically, consider a triangular array of random variables $\{X_{nj} : n = 1, 2, \ldots; j = 1, 2, \ldots, n\}$, with corresponding distribution functions denoted by F_{nj}. For each n, define the empirical distribution function $\widetilde{F}_n$ by

$$\widetilde{F}_n(x) = \frac{1}{n} \sum_{j=1}^{n} I\{X_{nj} \leq x\},$$

where I is the indicator function, and define the average distribution function $F_n^{\#}$ by

$$F_n^{\#} = \frac{1}{n} \sum_{j=1}^{n} F_{nj}.$$

The notation $F^{\#}$ to denote the average is used instead of the more customary $\overline{F}$, which in this book denotes a survival function.

For any strictly increasing distribution function F, the median is uniquely defined to be $F^{-1}(\frac{1}{2})$. The sample median is said to be consistent if $\widetilde{F}_n^{-1}(\frac{1}{2}) - F_n^{\#-1}(\frac{1}{2})$ converges in probability to 0.

Matters are simplified when the F_{ni}'s have the same median, i.e., when $F_{ni}^{-1}(\frac{1}{2}) = \xi_{\frac{1}{2}}$, say, for every $i \leq n$.

Define, for each $\epsilon > 0$,

$$a_n(\epsilon) = F_n^\#(F_n^{\#-1}(\tfrac{1}{2}) + \epsilon)$$

and

$$b_n(\epsilon) = F_n^\#(F_n^{\#-1}(\tfrac{1}{2}) - \epsilon).$$

In this common median case, Mizera and Wellner (1998) show that $\widetilde{F}_n^{-1}(\tfrac{1}{2})$ converges in probability to $\xi_{\frac{1}{2}}$ if and only if for every $\xi > 0$, $\lim \sqrt{n}(a_n(\epsilon) - \tfrac{1}{2}) = \infty$ and $\lim \sqrt{n}(\tfrac{1}{2} - b_n(\xi)) = \infty$. More complicated necessary and sufficient conditions for consistency in the absence of a common median for the X_{nj}'s are also provided by Mizera and Wellner (1998).

Independent Exponential Random Variables

K.3. Theorem (Persi Diaconis, private communication, 1976). Let X_1 and X_2 be independent and let X_i have density

$$f_i(x) = \frac{1}{\theta_i} e^{-x/\theta_i}, \qquad x \geq 0, \quad i = 1, 2.$$

Then for $\theta_1 + \theta_2$ fixed,

$$P\{X_1 + X_2 \leq t\} = (\theta_1 - \theta_2)(\theta_1 e^{-t/\theta_1} - \theta_2 e^{-t/\theta_2}), \quad \theta_1 \neq \theta_2,$$

is a Schur-convex function of (θ_1, θ_2) for $t \leq (\theta_1 + \theta_2)$ and it is a Schur-concave function of (θ_1, θ_2) for $t \geq \tfrac{3}{2}(\theta_1 + \theta_2)$.

The proof of this result, obtained by Diaconis, consists of verifying the derivative conditions of 3.A.4, just as does the proof of K.1. However, here the verification involves a detailed analysis, so it is omitted.

Diaconis has also obtained partial results for a sum of n independent, exponentially distributed random variables.

The following result, though related to those of this section, is rather different from other results of this book and the proof is unlike any other. The extent to which its methods might be applied to other problems is not clear.

K.4. Theorem (Kanter, 1976). Let $X_1, \ldots, X_n$ be independent random variables such that for $j = 1, \ldots, n$

$$P\{X_j = 1\} = P\{X_j = -1\} = \lambda_j/2,$$

$$P\{X_j = 0\} = 1 - \lambda_j, \quad 0 \leq \lambda_j \leq 1/2.$$

Then $P\{\sum X_j = 0\} + P\{\sum X_j = m\}$ is a Schur-concave function of $\lambda_1, \ldots, \lambda_n$ for any $m = \pm 1, \ldots, \pm n$.

Proof. First, note that the characteristic function of X_j is given by

$$\phi_j(t) = Ee^{itX_j} = 1 + \lambda_j[(\cos t) - 1] = 1 + \lambda_j m(t),$$

where $m(t) = (\cos t) - 1$. Thus, $\sum_1^n X_j$ has characteristic function

$$\phi(t|\lambda) = \prod_{j=1}^n [1 + \lambda_j m(t)].$$

Because $m(t) \geq -2$, this function is Schur-concave in λ, $0 \leq \lambda_j \leq 1/2$. Using the inversion formula (Feller, 1971, p. 511), it follows that

$$p_k \equiv P\left\{\sum_1^n X_j = k\right\} = \frac{1}{2\pi}\int_{-\pi}^{\pi} \phi(t|\lambda)e^{-ikt}\, dt$$
$$= \frac{1}{2\pi}\int_{-\pi}^{\pi} \prod_{j=1}^n [1 + \lambda_j m(t)]e^{-ikt}\, dt.$$

Because p_k is real, this means that the imaginary part of the integral vanishes, so

$$p_0 + p_m = \frac{1}{2\pi}\int_{-\pi}^{\pi} \prod_{j=1}^n [1 + \lambda_j m(t)](1 + \cos mt)\, dt, \quad m = \pm 1, \ldots \pm n.$$

From the Schur-concavity of $\phi(t|\lambda)$ and the fact that $1 + \cos mt \geq 0$, it follows that $p_0 + p_m$ is Schur-concave in λ, $0 \leq \lambda_j \leq 1/2$. Note that $1 + \cos mt + \cos \ell t$ can be negative, and consequently $p_0 + p_m + p_\ell$ may not be Schur-concave. Mattner and Roos (2007) note that as stated in the first edition of this book, Theorem K.4 is false because the condition $0 \leq \lambda_j \leq 1/2$ was omitted. ∥

Generalized Rayleigh Distribution

The *generalized Rayleigh distribution* is the distribution of $X = \sigma(\sum_1^k Z_i^2)^{1/2}$, where $Z_1, \ldots, Z_k$ are independent, each having a standard normal distribution. (Here $\sigma > 0$.)

Denote this distribution by $F_{k,\sigma}$.

K.5. Proposition (Hu and Lin, 2001).   Let $X_1, \ldots, X_n$ be pairwise independent random variables having a common $F_{k,\sigma}$ distribution. If $(b_1^2, \ldots, b_n^2) \prec (a_1^2, \ldots, a_n^2)$, then for all $t > 0$,

$$P\left\{\sum_1^n a_i X_i \geq t\right\} \leq P\left\{\sum_1^n b_i X_i \geq t\right\}.$$

L   Schur-Concave Distribution Functions and Survival Functions

There are a number of examples of random variables $X_1, \ldots, X_n$ with the property that the joint distribution function

$$F(x) = P\{X_1 \leq x_1, \ldots, X_n \leq x_n\}$$

or the joint survival function

$$\overline{F}(x) = P\{X_1 > x_1, \ldots, X_n > x_n\}$$

is a Schur-concave function of x. Such random variables are necessarily exchangeable.

Of course, Schur-concavity of F or $\overline{F}$ leads to various inequalities. For example, if $\bar{x} = \sum x_i/n$, then

$$F(\bar{x}, \ldots, \bar{x}) \geq F(x) \quad \text{or} \quad \overline{F}(\bar{x}, \ldots, \bar{x}) \geq \overline{F}(x).$$

If $x_i \geq 0$ for all i, it also follows that

$$F(x) \geq F\left(\sum x_i, 0, \ldots, 0\right) \quad \text{or} \quad \overline{F}(x) \geq \overline{F}\left(\sum x_i, 0, \ldots, 0\right).$$

Schur-Concave Densities

L.1. Proposition.   If $X_1, \ldots, X_n$ have a joint density that is Schur-concave, then F and $\overline{F}$ are Schur-concave.

Proof.   In Lemma 3.J.1.a, take $A = \{z : z_1 \leq 0, \ldots, z_n \leq 0\}$. Then

$$F(x) = \int_{A+x} f(u)\, du,$$

and consequently F is Schur-concave. Similarly, with

$$A = \{z : z_1 > 0, \ldots, z_n > 0\},$$

it follows from 3.J.1.a that $\overline{F}$ is Schur-concave.   ∥

L. Schur-Concave Distribution Functions and Survival Functions

When $X_1, \ldots, X_n$ have a Schur-concave density, the choice of other sets A as in the proof of L.1 leads to various other inequalities.

There are a number of cases in which F or $\overline{F}$ is Schur-concave even though the density is not Schur-concave, so L.1 does not apply.

L.2. Proposition (Tong, 1982). If $X_1, \ldots, X_n$ have a Schur-concave joint density, then

$$P\{|X_i| \leq x_i, i = 1, \ldots, n\} \tag{1}$$

is a Schur-concave function of $x_1, \ldots, x_n$, and

$$P\left\{\sum_1^n X_i^2/c_i \leq t\right\}, \quad t > 0, \tag{2}$$

is a Schur-concave function of $c_1, \ldots, c_n$.

The proofs of these results are not simple, and are not reproduced here.

L.3. Proposition (Karlin and Rinott, 1983). If $X_1, \ldots, X_n$ are nonnegative random variables with a Schur-concave density, then for $i = 1, \ldots, n$,

$$P\left\{\sum_1^n X_i^\alpha/c_i^\beta \leq t\right\}, \quad t > 0, \ \alpha \geq 1, \ 0 \leq \beta \leq \alpha - 1, \ c_i > 0, \tag{3}$$

is a Schur-concave function of $c_1, \ldots, c_n$.

L.3.a. Proposition. If $X_1, \ldots, X_n$ have a Schur-concave density, then

$$P\left\{\sum_1^n X_i^\alpha/c_i^{\alpha-1} \leq t\right\}, \quad t > 0, \ \alpha > 1, \tag{4}$$

is a Schur-concave function of $c_1, \ldots, c_n$. The case $\alpha = 2$ is (2) in L.2. Note that here, unlike in Proposition L.3, $X_1, \ldots, X_n$ are not required to be nonnegative.

Remark. Under the conditions of L.2, it follows that

$$P\left\{\sum_1^n X_i^2/c_i > t\right\}, \quad t > 0, \tag{5}$$

is a Schur-concave function of $c_1, \ldots, c_n$. A similar comment applies to L.3 and L.3.a.

L.3.b. Example. If $Y_1, \ldots, Y_n$ are independent random variables with chi-squared distributions and respective degrees of freedom $k_1, \ldots, k_n$, then as a function of $c_1, \ldots, c_n$,

$$P\left\{\sum_1^n Y_i/c_i \leq t\right\} \text{ is Schur-concave.} \tag{6}$$

To verify (6), let $\sum_1^n k_i = m$ and let $X_1, X_2, \ldots, X_m$ be independent, normally distributed random variables with means 0 and variances 1. Make use of the fact that

$$(\underbrace{c_1, \ldots, c_1}_{k_1}, \underbrace{c_2, \ldots, c_2}_{k_2}, \ldots, \underbrace{c_n, \ldots, c_n}_{k_n}) \prec (\underbrace{d_1, \ldots, d_1}_{k_1}, \ldots, \underbrace{d_n, \ldots, d_n}_{k_n})$$

if and only if $(c_1, \ldots, c_n) \prec (d_1, \ldots, d_n)$ to obtain (6) from Proposition L.2. For a related result, see Proposition 11.E.8.b.

The regions for $(X_1, \ldots, X_n)$ discussed in L.2, L.3 and L.3.a are all symmetric about the origin. Similar results for asymmetric regions can be obtained using multivariate majorization. See Section 15.E. For a version of these and related inequalities, see Tong (1988).

The following is a related result.

L.3.c. Proposition (Székely and Bakirov, 2003). Suppose that $Z_1, \ldots, Z_n$ are independent standard normal random variables. If $(\lambda_1, \ldots, \lambda_n) \prec_w (\mu_1, \ldots, \mu_n)$, $\Sigma \mu_i = 1$, then

$$P\left\{\sum_1^n \lambda_i Z_i^2 \leq x\right\} \leq P\left\{\sum_1^n \mu_i Z_i^2 \leq x\right\},$$

for all $x \geq 2$.

The condition that $x \geq 2$ is sharp in the sense that the result does not hold in the interval $1 < x < 2$.

Case of Independence

L.4. Proposition. Let G be a univariate distribution function, and let $\overline{G} = 1 - G$. If $F(x) = \prod_1^n G(x_i)$, and if $\overline{F}(x) = \prod_1^n \overline{G}(x_i)$, then

F is Schur-concave   if and only if $\log G$ is concave,

$\overline{F}$ is Schur-concave   if and only if $\log \overline{G}$ is concave.

Proof. This is a direct application of 3.E.1.

L. Schur-Concave Distribution Functions and Survival Functions

The condition that $\log G$ be concave has not received much attention in the literature. By contrast, when $\log \overline{G}$ is concave, then G is said to have an *increasing hazard* (failure) *rate*, and this condition has been extensively studied in the literature of reliability theory [see, e.g., Barlow and Proschan (1975; reprinted 1996)]. Both conditions are implied by the condition that G has a density that is logarithmically concave (see 18.B.2.c).

Exchangeable Sequences

The De Finetti representation theorem states that any infinite sequence of exchangeable random variables can be represented as a mixture of independent, identically distributed sequences. [See, for example, Spizzichino (2001).] Proposition L.2 above suggests the conjecture that if an exchangeable sequence has Schur-concave distributions for $(X_1, \ldots, X_n)$ for every n, then it may be possible to represent the sequence as a mixture of independent, identically distributed sequences with log concave (increasing hazard rate) survival functions. This conjecture remains unverified. However, Barlow and Spizzichino (1993) show that this is true if for each n, the density of $(X_1, \ldots, X_n)$ is log concave.

L.5. Theorem (Hayakawa, 1993). If, for each n, the joint survival function F_n of $(X_1, \ldots, X_n)$ is Schur-concave, and for some continuous strictly decreasing univariate survival function $\overline{G}$ it is the case that $\overline{F}_n(x_1, \ldots, x_n)$ and $\prod_{i=1}^n \overline{G}(x_i)$ have the same level sets, then the sequence $X_1, X_2, \ldots$ can be represented as a mixture of independent, identically distributed sequences with log concave survival functions.

Models for Dependence

L.6. Proposition (Marshall and Olkin, 1974). Let $\phi_z(u)$ be concave and increasing in u for all z. If $U_1, \ldots, U_n$ and Z are independent random variables and the U_i have a common distribution function G such that $\overline{G} = 1 - G$ is logarithmically concave, then

$$X_1 = \phi_Z(U_1), \ldots, X_n = \phi_Z(U_n)$$

are such that $P\{X_1 > x_1, \ldots, X_n > x_n\}$ is a Schur-concave function of x.

Proof. Assume that ϕ_z is strictly increasing and differentiable so that it has an increasing differentiable inverse. Assume also that G has a density g. Then

$$P\{X_1 > x_1, \ldots, X_n > x_n\} = P\{\phi_Z(U_1) > x_1, \ldots, \phi_Z(U_n) > x_n\}$$
$$= EP\{\phi_Z(U_1) > x_1, \ldots, \phi_Z(U_n) > x_n | Z\}$$
$$= EP\{U_1 > \phi_Z^{-1}(x_1), \ldots, U_n > \phi_Z^{-1}(x_n) | Z\}$$
$$= E\prod_1^n P\{U_i > \phi_Z^{-1}(x_k) | Z\} = E\prod_1^n \overline{G}(\phi_Z^{-1}(x_i)).$$

Now, observe that

$$-\frac{d}{dx}\log \overline{G}(\phi_Z^{-1}(x)) = \frac{g(\phi_Z^{-1}(x))}{\overline{G}(\phi_Z^{-1}(x))} \cdot \frac{1}{\phi_Z'(\phi_Z^{-1}(x))}$$

is the product of two nonnegative increasing functions: ϕ_Z^{-1} is increasing and $\log \overline{G}$ is concave so $g(\phi_Z^{-1}(x)/\overline{G}(\phi_Z^{-1}(x))$ is increasing. Also, ϕ_Z' is decreasing, so $\phi_Z'(\phi_Z^{-1}(x))$ is decreasing. By using the fact that a mixture of Schur-concave functions is Schur-concave, the result follows from L.2. ∥

L.6.a. The bivariate exponential survival function

$$\overline{F}(x_1, x_2) = \exp\{-\lambda x_1 - \lambda x_2 - \lambda_{12} \max(x_1, x_2)\}$$

is Schur-concave.

Proof. This result follows from L.6 with $\phi_z(u) = \min(u, z)$ and with U_1, U_2, Z independently distributed with exponential distributions having respective parameters λ, λ, and λ_{12}. In this case,

$$X_1 = \min(U_1, Z) \quad \text{and} \quad X_2 = \min(U_2, Z). \quad ∥$$

The bivariate exponential distribution of L.6.a is discussed by Marshall and Olkin (1967).

L.7. Proposition (Marshall and Olkin, 1974). Let $\phi_z(u)$ be convex and increasing in u for all z. If $X_1, \ldots, X_n$ are defined as in L.6 and $\log G$ is concave, then $P\{X_1 \leq x_1, \ldots, X_n \leq x_n\}$ is a Schur-concave function of x.

The proof of this result is similar to the proof of L.6 and is omitted.

M Bivariate Probability Distributions with Fixed Marginals

Let $\Gamma(F, G)$ be the class of all bivariate probability distributions with marginal distribution functions F and G. Thus, if $H \in \Gamma(F, G)$, then

$$H(x, \infty) = F(x), \qquad H(\infty, y) = G(y), \qquad -\infty \leq x, y \leq \infty.$$

M.1. Proposition (Hoeffding, 1940; Fréchet, 1951).

$$H^*(x, y) = \min[F(x), G(y)] \in \Gamma(F, G),$$
$$H_*(x, y) = \max[F(x) + G(y) - 1, 0] \in \Gamma(F, G).$$

Moreover, for all $H \in \Gamma(F, G)$,

$$H_*(x, y) \leq H(x, y) \leq H^*(x, y) \qquad \text{for all} \quad x, y \in \mathscr{R}. \tag{1}$$

The proof is quite elementary; see, e.g., Mardia (1970, pp. 30, 31). A rearrangement proof based on 6.A.3 is given by Whitt (1976).

The ordering of distribution functions implicit in (1) is of some interest.

M.2. Definition. Let $H^{(1)}$ and $H^{(2)} \in \Gamma(F, G)$. If

$$H^{(1)}(x, y) \leq H^{(2)}(x, y) \qquad \text{for all} \quad x, y \in \mathscr{R},$$

then $H^{(1)}$ is said to be *less concordant* than $H^{(2)}$.

This definition is essentially due to Tchen (1980), although the word "concordance" was already used in this context by Gini (1915/1916).

Suppose that $H^{(1)}$, $H^{(2)} \in \Gamma(F, G)$, where F and G concentrate mass on finitely many points. Suppose also that for some $\varepsilon > 0$,

$$H^{(1)}\{x_1, y_2\} \geq \varepsilon, \qquad H^{(1)}\{x_2, y_1\} \geq \varepsilon,$$

where $x_1 < x_2$, $y_1 < y_2$, and $H^{(1)}\{x, y\}$ is the probability $H^{(1)}$ gives to the point (x, y). Transform $H^{(1)}$ to obtain a new bivariate distribution by adding mass ε to the points (x_1, y_1), (x_2, y_2) and subtracting mass ε from the points (x_1, y_2), (x_2, y_1). Of course, $H^{(1)} \in \Gamma(F, G)$ implies that the transformed distribution is in $\Gamma(F, G)$. According to a theorem of Tchen (1980), $H^{(1)}$ is less concordant than $H^{(2)}$ if and only if $H^{(2)}$ can be obtained from $H^{(1)}$ by a finite sequence of such transformations.

Suppose (X_i, Y_i) is a bivariate random vector with distribution function $H^{(i)}$, $i = 1, 2$. Then intuitively, $H^{(1)}$ is less concordant than $H^{(2)}$ if large values of X_2 go with large values of Y_2 to a greater extent than for X_1 and Y_1.

M.3. Proposition (Cambanis, Simons, and Stout, 1976; Tchen, 1980). Suppose F and G have compact support and suppose $H^{(1)}$, $H^{(2)} \in \Gamma(F, G)$. Then $H^{(1)}$ is less concordant than $H^{(2)}$ if and only if

$$\int \phi \, dH^{(1)} \le \int \phi \, dH^{(2)} \tag{2}$$

for all continuous L-superadditive functions ϕ (see Definition 6.C.2) such that the expectations exist.

Indication of proof. The proof indicated here utilizes several key ideas due to Whitt (1976).

Probability measures which, for some integer $n > 0$, assign mass $1/n$ to each of n points are called *data distributions* by Whitt (1976). Suppose H_1 and H_2 are data distributions on $\mathscr{R}^2$ and that $H_1, H_2 \in \Gamma(F_n, G_n)$. Let $(x_1, y_{\pi_k(1)}), \ldots, (x_n, y_{\pi_k(n)})$ be the points to which H_k assigns mass $1/n$ and let $x = (x_1, \ldots, x_k)$, $y^{(k)} = (y_{\pi_k(1)}, \ldots, y_{\pi_k(n)})$, $k = 1, 2$. Notice that H_1 is less concordant than H_2 if and only if $(x, y^{(1)}) \le^a (x, y^{(2)})$ (notation of Section 6.F). Because $\int \phi \, dH_k = (1/n) \sum_i \phi(x_i, y_{\pi_k(i)})$, it follows from 6.F.9 that $\int \phi \, dH_1 \le \int \phi \, dH_2$ for all L-superadditive functions ϕ if and only if H_1 is less concordant than H_2. This proves the proposition for data distributions.

For any sequence $H, H_1, H_2, \ldots$ of distribution functions, write $H_n \Rightarrow H$ to mean that $\lim_{n \to \infty} H_n(z) = H(z)$ for all continuity points z of H.

Suppose that $H^{(1)}$ is less concordant than $H^{(2)}$. For $i = 1, 2$, let $\{H_n^{(i)}\}$ be sequences of data distributions such that

(a) $H_n^{(i)} \in \Gamma(F_n, G_n)$,
(b) $H_n^{(i)} \Rightarrow H^{(i)}$, and
(c) $H_n^{(1)}$ is less concordant than $H_n^{(2)}$ for all n.

(The existence of such sequences is not proved here.) Then for all continuous superadditive functions ϕ, $\int \phi \, dH_n^{(i)}$ converges to $\int \phi \, dH^{(i)}$ as $n \to \infty$ (Billingsley, 1968, p. 18). By combining this with what is proved above for data distributions, it follows that

$$\int \phi \, dH^{(1)} = \lim \int \phi \, dH_n^{(1)} \le \lim \int \phi \, dH_n^{(2)} = \int \phi \, dH^{(2)}.$$

Next, suppose that $\int \phi \, dH^{(1)} \leq \int \phi \, dH^{(2)}$ for all continuous L-superadditive functions ϕ. Fix x_0, y_0 and approximate the indicator function of the set $\{(x,y) : x \leq x_0 \text{ and } y \leq y_0\}$ with the continuous L-superadditive function ϕ_k defined by

$$\phi_k(x,y) = 1 \quad \text{if} \quad x \leq x_0 \text{ and } y \leq y_0,$$
$$\phi_k(x,y) = k\min[(1/k) + x_0 - x, (1/k) + y_0 - y]$$
$$\quad \text{if} \quad x_0 \leq x \leq x_0 + (1/k) \text{ and } y \leq y_0 + (1/k),$$
$$\quad \text{or } y_0 \leq y \leq y_0 + (1/k) \text{ and } x \leq x_0 + (1/k),$$
$$\phi_k(x,y) = 0 \quad \text{if} \quad x \geq x_0 + (1/k) \text{ or } y \geq y_0 + (1/k).$$

Because $\int \phi_k \, dH^{(1)} \leq \int \phi_k \, dH^{(2)}$, it follows that

$$H^{(1)}(x_0, y_0) = \lim_{k \to \infty} \int \phi_k \, dH^{(1)} \leq \lim_{k \to \infty} \int \phi_k \, dH^{(2)} = H^{(2)}(x_0, y_0).$$

Because x_0 and y_0 are arbitrary, this proves that $H^{(1)}$ is less concordant than $H^{(2)}$. ||

M.3.a. Corollary (Lorentz, 1953). If F and G have compact support and φ is a continuous L-superadditive function, then

$$\int \phi \, dH_* \leq \int \phi \, dH \leq \int \phi \, dH^*$$

for all $H \in \Gamma(F, G)$, where H_* and H^* are the lower and upper Hoeffding–Fréchet bounds defined in M.1.

N Combining Random Variables

Majorization from Convolutions

The concept of "more random" for discrete vectors is introduced in Definition 17.E.10. Here, more randomness is obtained through convolutions.

N.1. Proposition (Hickey, 1983). Let X and Y be independent discrete random variables. The distribution of $Z = X + Y$ is more random than the distributions of X and Y.

Proof. Suppose first that X and Y take on a finite number of values, say $x_1, \ldots, x_n$ and $y_1, \ldots, y_n$, with respective probabilities

508   12. Probabilistic, Statistical, and Other Applications

$p_i = P\{X = x_i\}, q_i = P\{Y = y_i\}, i = 1,\ldots,n$. According to the convolution formula,

$$P\{Z = z_j\} = \sum_i P\{X = x_i\}P\{Y = z_j - x_i\}, \quad j = 1,\ldots,m,$$

where $m \leq n^2$ is the number of possible values of Z. Introduce the notation $r_j = P(Z = z_j)$, $j = 1,\ldots,m$, and rewrite the convolution formula as

$$r = pD,$$

where $d_{ij} = P\{Y = z_j - x_i\}, i = 1,\ldots,n, j = 1,\ldots,m$. It can be verified that each q_i appears once and only once in every row of D, so the row sums of D are all one. However, the sum c_j of the jth column of D can be less than one.

Let E be the diagonal matrix with elements $1-c_1, 1-c_2, \ldots, 1-c_m$, and form the doubly stochastic matrix

$$P = \begin{bmatrix} E & D' \\ D & O \end{bmatrix}.$$

Let $p^* = (0,\ldots,0,p_1,\ldots,p_n)$ have m zeros and note that p^*P has the form

$$p^*P = (pD, 0, \ldots, 0) = (r, 0, \ldots, 0) = r^*,$$

where r^* has n zeros.

Because P is doubly stochastic, $p^* \succ r^*$, and consequently

$$(p_1,\ldots,p_n,0,0,\ldots) \succ (r_1,\ldots,r_m,0,0,\ldots).$$

Thus the distribution of $Z = X + Y$ is more random than the distribution of X (and, by symmetry, of Y).

Next, consider the case that X and Y can take on a countable number of values, $x_1, x_2, \ldots$ and $y_1, y_2, \ldots$, with respective probabilities $p_1, p_2, \ldots$ and $q_1, q_2, \ldots$. Denote the possible values of $Z = X + Y$ by $z_1, z_2, \ldots$ and let $r_i = P\{Z = z_i\}, i = 1, 2, \ldots$.

Truncate the distributions of X and Y to obtain X_n and Y_n, where X_n takes on the values $x_1, x_2, \ldots, x_n$ with respective probabilities

$$p_i^{(n)} = p_i \Big/ \sum_1^n p_j, \quad i = 1,\ldots,n,$$

and similarly for Y_n. Denote the possible values of $Z_n = X_n + Y_n$ by $z_1^{(n)}, \ldots, z_{m_n}^{(n)}$ and their respective probabilities by $r_1^{(n)}, \ldots, r_{m_n}^{(n)}$.

Then
$$r^{(n)} = (r_1^{(n)}, \ldots, r_{m_n}^{(n)}, 0, 0, \ldots) \prec (p_1^{(n)}, \ldots, p_n^{(n)}, 0, 0, \ldots) = p^{(n)}.$$
Because $\lim_{n \to \infty} p^{(n)} = p$, $\lim_{n \to \infty} r^{(n)} = r$, it follows that $r \prec p$. ||

N.2. Definition. Let $\{p_\theta : \theta \in \Theta\}$ be a family of discrete probability distributions, where $\Theta = (0, \infty)$ or $\Theta = 0, 1, 2, \ldots$. If the parameters add with convolutions, that is, if $p_{\theta_1} * p_{\theta_2} = p_{\theta_1 + \theta_2}$, then $\{p_\theta : \theta \in \Theta\}$ is said to be a *convolution family*.

N.3. Proposition. If $\{p_\theta, \theta \in \Theta\}$ is a convolution family of discrete probability distributions, then
$$p_{\theta_1} \prec p_{\theta_2} \text{ for all } \theta_1 > \theta_2;$$
that is, randomness increases with θ.

Proof. Because $p_{\theta_1} = p_{\theta_2} * p_{\theta_1 - \theta_2}$, this result follows from Proposition N.1. ||

N.4. Examples.

(a) Binomial distributions
$$P\{X = k\} = \binom{n}{k} p^k (1-p)^{n-k}, \quad k = 0, 1, \ldots, n,$$
$n = 1, 2, \ldots$, $0 < p < 1$, form a convolution family in the parameter n (with fixed p).

(b) Negative binomial distributions
$$P\{X = k\} = \binom{k-1}{n-1} p^r (1-p)^{k-r}, \quad k = n, n+1, \ldots,$$
$n = 1, 2, \ldots$, $0 < p < 1$, form a convolution family in the parameter n (with fixed p).

(c) Poisson distributions
$$P\{X = k\} = e^{-\lambda} \frac{\lambda^k}{k!}, \quad k = 1, 2, \ldots, \ \lambda > 0,$$
form a convolution family in the parameter λ.

Majorization from Finite Groups

Let X and Y be independent random variables taking values in a finite group G and let $Z = X \circ Y$, where $\circ$ denotes the group operation. Denote the inverse element of $g \in G$ by g^{-1}. For a particular ordering $g_1, \ldots, g_m$ of the elements of G, let
$$p_i = P\{X = g_i\}, \quad q_i = P\{Y = g_i\}, \quad s_i = P\{Z = g_i\}, \quad i = 1, \ldots, m.$$

N.5. Proposition. $s \prec p$ and $s \prec q$.

An interesting special case of N.1 is obtained by Brown and Solomon (1979). They consider the group of vectors $(x_1, \ldots, x_k)$, where each x_i takes on one of the values $0, 1, \ldots, m-1$ and the group operation adds vectors componentwise modulo m. The idea of the following proof is due to Brown and Solomon.

Proof. In this argument it will be convenient to denote q_i by $q(i)$ and p_i by $p(i)$. Moving from X to $X \circ Y$ is like taking a step in a Markov chain on G with transition matrix $Q = (Q_{jl})$ given by

$$Q_{jl} = q(j^{-1} \circ l), \qquad j, l = 1, \ldots, m.$$

Notice that $\sum_j Q_{jl} = \sum_i q_i = 1$ so that Q is doubly stochastic. Since $s = pQ$, it follows that $s \prec p$.

To see that $s \prec q$, consider the Markov chain on G which moves from Y to $X \circ Y$ according to the transition matrix $P = (p_{il})$, where

$$p_{il} = p(l \circ i^{-1}).$$

Like Q, P is doubly stochastic and $s = qP$. ∥

Proposition N.5 is related to the fact that the only limit distributions for random variables of the form $X_1 \circ \cdots \circ X_n$ are uniform on a subgroup of G [see, e.g., Heyer (1977)].

O Concentration Inequalities for Multivariate Distributions

Take as a starting point the following well-known result.

O.1. Proposition (Anderson, 1955). If X and Y have n-dimensional normal distributions with means 0 and respective covariance matrices Σ_X and Σ_Y with $\Sigma_Y - \Sigma_X$ positive definite, then X is more concentrated about 0 than is Y, in the sense that $P\{X \in C\} \geq P\{Y \in C\}$ for every convex set $C \subset \mathscr{R}^n$ with $C = -C$.

Because $\Sigma_Y - \Sigma_X$ is positive definite, Y can be represented as $X + Z$, where X and Z are independent. Proposition O.1 holds more generally for elliptically contoured distributions, that is, for distributions with densities that are functions of $x\Sigma^{-1}x'$ (Fefferman, Jodeit, and Perlman, 1972).

Applications often involve an inequality of the form $P\{X \in C\} \geq P\{Y \in C\}$ for sets C not necessarily centrally symmetric and convex.

To this end, Eaton and Perlman (1991) identify classes of subsets $\mathscr{C}$ of $\mathscr{R}^n$ such that $\Sigma_Y \geq \Sigma_X$ implies $P\{X \in C\} \geq P\{Y \in C\}$ for $C \in \mathscr{C}$, in which case they say that X is *more concentrated* than Y relative to $\mathscr{C}$.

Anderson's result corresponds to the case

$$\mathscr{C} = \{C : C \in \mathscr{R}^n \text{ is convex}, -C = C\}.$$

Eaton and Perlman (1991) replace the symmetry requirement by one of G-invariance, where G is a finite subgroup of orthogonal $n \times n$ matrices. They conclude that X is more concentrated than Y relative to the class of convex G-invariant sets, provided that Σ_X itself is G-invariant and that G acts effectively on $\mathscr{R}^n$. Counterexamples are provided to show which additional assumptions are in general needed.

The requirement of convexity can be replaced by a requirement that C be a G-decreasing set when G is a reflection group (Eaton and Perlman, 1991). See 14.C for related discussion on G-invariance and G-majorization.

Eaton (1988) shows that Proposition O.1 implies that the best linear unbiased estimator, when it exists, is more concentrated at its mean than any other linear unbiased estimator when the error vector $Y - \mu$ is normally distributed. Eaton shows this to be true also when $Y - \mu$ has an elliptically contoured distribution. He also discusses additional conditions under which the result holds when $Y - \mu$ has a log concave density.

P Miscellaneous Cameo Appearances of Majorization

Covering the Circle by Random Arcs

Suppose that n arcs of lengths $\ell_1, \ell_2, \ldots, \ell_n$ are placed independently and uniformly on the unit circle. With $\ell = (\ell_1, \ldots, \ell_n)$, let $P(\ell)$ denote the probability that the unit circle is completely covered by these arcs. Stevens (1939) gave the following explicit expression for this coverage probability when all arcs are of equal length $\bar{\ell} = \sum_1^n \ell_i/n$:

$$P(\bar{\ell}, \ldots, \bar{\ell}) = \sum_{k=0}^{n} (-1)^k \binom{n}{k} [(1 - k\bar{\ell})^+]^{n-1}. \tag{1}$$

Huffer and Shepp (1987) show that (1) represents an extremal case by verifying that $P(\ell)$ is a Schur-convex function. Thus, for a given total sum of arc lengths, increased inequality among the lengths of the arcs yields a greater coverage probability. By 3.A.2.b, it suffices to consider the effect on $P(\ell)$ of making a small change in two unequal ℓ_i's (to make them more alike), holding the other ℓ_i's fixed. The result, conjectured by Frank Proschan, turns out to be more troublesome to verify than might have been hoped. [See Huffer and Shepp (1987) for details.]

Unequal Catchability

Assume that an island community contains an unknown number ν of butterfly species. Butterflies are trapped sequentially until n have been captured. Let r denote the number of distinct species represented among the n butterflies that have been trapped. On the basis of r, we wish to estimate ν. A plausible model involves the assumption that butterflies from species j, $j = 1, 2, \ldots, \nu$, enter the trap according to a Poisson (λ_j) process and that these processes are independent. If $p_j = \lambda_j / \sum_{i=1}^{\nu} \lambda_i$, then p_j denotes the probability that a particular trapped butterfly is of species j. The p_j's reflect the relative catchability of the various species. Under the assumption of equal catchability (that is, $p_j = 1/\nu$, $j = 1, 2, \ldots, \nu$), and under the (somewhat restrictive) assumption that $\nu \leq n$, there exists a minimum variance unbiased estimate $\tilde{\nu}$ of ν based on r, namely,

$$\tilde{\nu} = S(n+1, r)/S(n, r), \qquad (2)$$

where $S(n, x)$ denotes a Stirling number of the second kind [see; e.g., Abramowitz and Stegun (1972, p. 835)]. Nayak and Christman (1992) investigate the effect of unequal catchability on the performance of the estimate (2). They observe that the random number, R, of species captured has a distribution function that is a Schur-convex function of p and conclude that the estimate (2) is negatively biased in the presence of unequal catchability.

Waiting for a Pattern

Suppose that $X_1, X_2, \ldots$ is a sequence of independent, identically distributed random variables with possible values $1, 2, \ldots, k$ and associated positive probabilities $p_1, p_2, \ldots, p_k$. Let N denote the waiting time for a run of k consecutive values of the X_i's that includes all k possible values $1, 2, \ldots, k$; that is,

$$N = \min\{n \geq k : X_{n-k+1}, X_{n-k+2}, \ldots, X_n \text{ are all distinct}\}.$$

Ross (1999) proves that for any n, $P\{N > n\}$ is a Schur-convex function of p and consequently that EN is a Schur-convex function of p.

Connected Components in a Random Graph

Following Ross (1981), consider a random graph with n nodes numbered $1, 2, \ldots, n$. Let $X_1, X_2, \ldots, X_n$ be independent, identically distributed random variables with distributions determined by the probability vector $p = (p_1, p_2, \ldots, p_n)$, where

$$P\{X_i = j\} = p_j, \quad j = 1, 2, \ldots, n.$$

The random graph is constructed by drawing n random arcs that connect i to X_i, $i = 1, 2, \ldots, n$. Thus one arc emanates from each node. Let C denote the number of connected components of this random graph. ($C = k$, if the set of nodes of the graph can be divided into k subsets with each subset being connected and no arcs joining nodes from different subsets.) In this type of random graph, the expected number of connected components is equal to the expected number of cycles (i.e., closed paths without repetitions) in the graph and thus

$$EC = \sum_S (|S| - 1)! \prod_{j \in S} p_j,$$

where the summation extends over all nonempty subsets of $\{1, 2, \ldots, n\}$ and $|S|$ denotes the cardinality of S. Using 3.A(10), Ross proves that EC is a Schur-concave function of p. Consequently, the expected number of connected components in the random graph is maximized when $p_j = 1/n$, $j = 1, 2, \ldots, n$.

Infection in a Closed Population

A simple model of potential utility in the study of disease transmission was introduced by Eisenberg (1991) and further studied by Lefèvre (1994). Subsequently, Tong (1997) identified a facet of the model involving majorization. Consider a closed population of $n+1$ individuals. One individual (number $n+1$) is susceptible to the disease but as yet is uninfected. The other n individuals are carriers of the disease. Let p_i denote the probability of escaping infection after a single contact with individual i, $i = 1, 2, \ldots, n$. Assume that individual $n+1$ makes a total of J contacts with individuals in the population governed by a preference vector $\alpha = (\alpha_1, \alpha_2, \ldots, \alpha_n)$, where $\alpha_i > 0$ and $\sum_{i=1}^n \alpha_i = 1$. Individual $n+1$ selects a "partner" among the n carriers according to the preference distribution α. He or she then makes k_1 contacts with this partner. He or she then selects a second partner (which could be the same one) independently according to the preference distribution α and has k_2 contacts with this partner. This continues until J contacts have been made.

The probability of escaping infection under this model is denoted by $H(k, \alpha, p)$, to highlight its dependence on the preference vector α, on nontransmission probabilities $p = (p_1, \ldots, p_n)$, and on the lifestyle vector $k = (k_1, \ldots, k_J)$. Two extreme lifestyles are associated with the vectors, $(J, 0, \ldots, 0)$ and $(1, 1, \ldots, 1)$. In the first case, the individual chooses one partner and stays with that partner for all J contacts. In the second case, each contact is made with a new individual chosen at random. It is not difficult to verify that the probability of escaping infection in these two cases is given by $\sum_{i=1}^{n} \alpha_i p_i^J$ and $(\sum_{i=1}^{n} \alpha_i p_i)^J$, respectively. Thus, from Jensen's inequality (16.C.1), it follows that the probability of escaping infection is larger with lifestyle $(J, 0, \ldots, 0)$ than it is with lifestyle $(1, 1, \ldots, 1)$. This result holds uniformly in α and p. Because these lifestyle vectors are extreme cases with respect to majorization, a plausible conjecture is that the probability of escaping infection is a Schur-convex function of the lifestyle vector k. Tong (1997) confirms this conjecture. An extension is also provided to cover some cases in which a random number of contacts are made (using 3.J.2).

Apportionment in Proportional Representation

Proportional representation seeks to assign to each political party a proportion of seats that closely reflects the proportion of votes obtained by that party. Because individual seats in a legislative body are potentially highly influential in subsequent decision making, and because typically exact proportionality is unobtainable, there has been considerable discussion of alternative proposals regarding which method of rounding should be used in the calculation. For more detailed general discussions of voting, see Saari (1995) or Balinski and Young (2001). Five apportionment schemes that have received considerable attention in the United States are named after their well-known supporters: John Quincy Adams, James Dean, Josef A. Hill, Daniel Webster, and Thomas Jefferson (an impressive list!). In the order given, they move from a method (Adams) kinder to small parties to the method (Jefferson) which most favors large parties.

P. Miscellaneous Cameo Appearances of Majorization

All five methods operate via a sequence of sign-posts that govern rounding decisions. The sign-posts $s(k)$ are numbers in the interval $[k, k+1]$ such that $s(k)$ is a strictly increasing function of k, and the associated rounding rule is that a number in the interval $[k, k+1]$ is rounded down if the number is less than $s(k)$ and rounded up if greater than $s(k)$. If the number equals $s(k)$, we are allowed to round up or down. A particular choice of sign-post sequence is a so-called power-mean sign-post sequence of the form

$$s_p(k) = \left(\frac{k^p + (k+1)^p}{2}\right)^{1/p}, \quad -\infty \le p \le \infty.$$

The five apportionment methods named above can all be interpreted as being based on a power-mean sign-post sequence: (Adams) $p = -\infty$, which means rounding up; (Dean) $p = -1$; (Hill) $p = 0$; (Webster) $p = 1$; (Jefferson) $p = \infty$, which means rounding down.

Marshall, Olkin, and Pukelsheim (2002) show that for two sign-post sequences $s(k)$ and $s'(k)$, a sufficient condition to ensure that the seating vector produced by the method using s is always majorized by the seating vector produced by the method using s' is that the sequence of sign-post ratios $s(k)/s'(k)$ is strictly increasing in k. It follows that the result of a power-mean rounding of order p is always majorized by the corresponding power-mean rounding of order p' if and only if $p \le p'$. Consequently, the five popular apportionment procedures moving from Adams to Jefferson move toward favoring large parties in the sense of majorization. Indeed, an inspection of the results of applying these five methods to any particular case shows that one can move from an Adams apportionment toward a Jefferson apportionment by moving assigned seats from smaller parties to larger parties [in a series of reverse Dalton transfers from "poorer" parties (with fewer votes) to "richer" parties (with more votes)].

P.1. Example. Pólya (1919) shows the allocation of 10 seats given different vote counts in three regions.

Vote counts	Adams	Dean/Hill	Webster	Jefferson
5950	5	6	6	7
2532	3	2	3	2
1518	2	2	1	1

Here $(7, 2, 1) \succ (6, 3, 1) \succ (6, 2, 2) \succ (5, 3, 2)$, and the allocations clearly show that the Jefferson method favors the larger community, and the Adams method favors the smaller communities.

Paired Comparisons

During the 1952–1953 season, the six National Hockey League teams played 70 games. Each pair of teams played 14 games. This can be viewed as a prototypical paired comparison situation. To model the situation in which n teams (or alternatives) compete (or are compared) in pairs, it is customary to consider an $n \times n$ matrix $P = (p_{ij})$ in which for $i \neq j$, p_{ij} denotes the probability that team i beats team j in a match. Assume that ties do not occur, so that $p_{ij} + p_{ji} = 1$ (Many sporting events use extra time periods to resolve ties to satisfy this rule). The diagonal elements of P are left undefined. For each i, define $p_i = \sum_{j \neq i} p_{ij}$. This row total provides a measure of the strength of team i. Let $p = (p_1, \ldots, p_n)$ and define $\mathscr{P}(p)$ to be the class of all probability matrices P(with only off-diagonal elements defined) and with row totals given by p.

Joe (1988) defines a variability ordering on the members of the class $\mathscr{P}(p)$ based on majorization. For $P, Q \in \mathscr{P}(p)$, the matrix P is majorized by the matrix Q ($P \prec Q$) if and only if $P^* \prec Q^*$ in the usual sense of majorization, where P^* (respectively Q^*) is the $n(n-1)$-dimensional vector whose entries are all the defined elements of P (respectively Q). A matrix $P \in \mathscr{P}(p)$ is said to be *minimal* if $Q \prec P$ implies $Q^* = P^*$ up to rearrangement. In applications, it is often reasonable to assume that if team i dominates team j (reflected by $p_{ij} > 0.5$) and if team j dominates team k, then team i dominates team k.

The matrix P is *weakly transitive* if $p_{ij} \geq 0.5$ and $p_{jk} \geq 0.5$ implies that $p_{ik} \geq 0.5$. The matrix P is *strongly transitive* if $p_{ij} \geq 0.5$ and $p_{jk} \geq 0.5$ implies that $p_{ik} \geq \max(p_{ij}, p_{jk})$. Joe (1988) relates the concepts of minimality and transitivity as follows:

(i) A necessary condition for P to be minimal is that $p_{ij} \geq 0.5$ whenever $p_i \geq p_j$;

(ii) A necessary condition for P to be minimal is that p be strongly transitive.

Extensions can be provided to allow the p_i's to be weighted sums of the p_{ij}'s (to reflect the differing frequencies of matches between pairs of teams). In addition, order effects (home-field advantage) and ties can be considered.

Admissibility of Tests in Multivariate Analysis of Variance

In the canonical multivariate analysis of variance problem (Anderson, 2003), the null hypothesis is accepted if certain ordered sample eigenvalues fall in a region $A \subset \mathscr{D}$. Anderson and Takemura (1982), using a result of Stein (1956), verify that such tests are admissible provided that A is closed, convex, and has the property that if $\lambda \in A, \nu \in \mathscr{D}$, and $\nu \prec_w \lambda$, then $\nu \in A$.

Gaussian Correlation

Suppose that the random vector Z has a normal distribution with mean zero and identity covariance matrix, and that A and B are symmetric convex sets in $\mathscr{R}^n$. It was conjectured that in such a case,

$$P\{Z \in A \cap B\} \geq P\{Z \in A\}P\{Z \in B\}.$$

The conjecture was verified in the case $n = 2$ by Pitt (1977). Vitale (1999) verified that, in n dimensions, the conjecture is true when A and B are *Schur cylinders*. A set C in $\mathscr{R}^n$ is a Schur cylinder if $x \in C$ implies $x + ke \in C$ for every $k \in \mathscr{R}$ [and $e = (1, 1, \ldots, 1)$] and the indicator function of C is Schur-concave.

A Stochastic Relation Between the Sum and Maximum of Two Variables

In the context of constructing confidence intervals for a difference between the means of two normal distributions with unknown unequal variances (the so-called Behrens–Fisher setting), Dalal and Fortini (1982) derive an inequality relating the distribution of the sum of two nonnegative random variables to the distribution of the maximum of the two variables.

P.2. Proposition (Dalal and Fortini, 1982). If X_1 and X_2 are nonnegative random variables with a symmetric joint density $f(x_1, x_2)$, such that $f(\sqrt{x_1}, \sqrt{x_2})$ is a Schur-convex function of x, then

$$P\{X_1 + X_2 \leq c\} \geq P\{\sqrt{2}\max(X_1, X_2) \leq c\}$$

for every $c > 0$.

An important example of a nonnegative random vector with a joint density f such that $f(\sqrt{x_1}, \sqrt{x_2})$ is Schur-convex is one of the form

$(X_1, X_2) = (|Y_1|, |Y_2|)$, where Y_1 and Y_2 are normally distributed with zero means, common variance σ^2, and correlation ρ.

Proposition P.2 is proved by conditioning on $X_1^2 + X_2^2$, using the fact that on any circle the density f at x increases as x moves away from the line $x_1 = x_2$.

The conclusion of the proposition can be restated as $X_1 + X_2 \leq_{st} \sqrt{2}\max(X_1, X_2)$.

Using the same idea of conditioning on the sum of squares but using stronger restrictions on the joint density, Dalal and Fortini (1982) provide two related n-dimensional results.

P.3. Proposition. Let $X_1, X_2, \ldots, X_n$ be independent, identically distributed nonnegative random variables whose common density f is such that $\log f(\sqrt{x})$ is concave; if $a \prec b$, then

$$\sum_{i=1}^{n} \sqrt{a_i} X_i \leq^{st} \sum_{i=1}^{n} \sqrt{b_i} X_i.$$

P.4. Proposition. Let $X_1, X_2, \ldots, X_n$ be independent, identically distributed positive random variables with common density f such that $\log f(\sqrt{x})$ is concave and $f(x)/x$ is decreasing, then

$$\sum_{i=1}^{n} X_i \leq^{st} \sqrt{n}\max(X_1, X_2, \ldots, X_n).$$

Tests for Homogeneity of Variances Under Nonstandard Conditions

Let $Y_{ij}, i = 1, 2, \ldots, k, \; j = 1, 2, \ldots, n$, be such that

$$Y_{ij} = \mu_i + \sigma_i Z_{ij},$$

where the Z_{ij}'s are independent, identically distributed standard normal variables, i.e., a standard analysis of variance setup with equal sample sizes and possibly different variances in the k populations. To test the hypothesis that $\sigma_1 = \sigma_2 = \ldots = \sigma_k$, three commonly used statistics are

$$T_{1n} = \prod_{i=1}^{k} \left(\sum_{j=1}^{k} \frac{S_j^2}{S_i^2} \right) \quad \text{(a Bartlett statistic)},$$

$$T_{2n} = \frac{(\max_i S_i^2)}{(\sum_{j=1}^{k} S_j^2)} \quad \text{(a Cochran statistic)},$$

and

$$T_{3n} = \frac{\max_i S_i^2}{\min_i S_i^2} \quad \text{(a Hartley statistic)},$$

where for each i,

$$S_i^2 = \frac{1}{n-1} \sum_{j=1}^{n}(Y_{ij} - \overline{Y}_i)^2, \quad \overline{Y}_i = \sum Y_{ij}/n.$$

In each case, the hypothesis of variance homogeneity is rejected if the corresponding test statistic is large. Rivest (1986) uses majorization arguments and 12.D.6 to investigate how these tests behave under non-standard conditions. (Rivest's notation is used in the above to facilitate reference to his paper for more details.)

Remark. The three test statistics T_{1n}, T_{2n}, and T_{3n} are comparisons of power means $(\sum a_i^r/n)^{1/r}$ and $(\sum a_i^s/n)^{1/s}$ for different values of r and s. But power means are Schur-convex or Schur-concave functions depending on r or s, which clarifies how majorization arises in these tests.

In order to determine appropriate critical values for the three statistics, it is necessary to compute $P\{T_{in} > x\}$ under the assumption that the variances are homogeneous.

Write $T_{i,n}^{(0)}$ to denote the test statistics under the assumption that the Z_{ij}'s are normally distributed and $\sigma_i = \sigma$, $i = 1, 2, \ldots, k$, for some $\sigma > 0$. Consider $T_{in}^{(F)}$ the test statistics under the assumption that the Z_{ij}'s have a common distribution F (which is not normal with mean 0). Rivest shows that if F is a scale-mixture of normal distributions, or if F is a scale-mixture of χ_1^2 distributions, then

$$T_{in}^{(F)} \leq^{\text{st}} T_{in}^{(0)} \text{ for } i = 1, 2, 3.$$

Thus in each case, the true size of the test is larger than the nominal size. An analogous result is obtained relating the true and nominal sizes of the tests under the assumption that the Z_{ij}'s are normal but are correlated within the populations.

Further discussion of the performance of tests for variance homogeneity under standard conditions (when the Z_{ij}'s are independent, identically distributed standard normal variables) may be found in 13.A.1.

Wireless Networks

The basic elements of a wireless network are a transmitting unit and its receiving unit. The transmitter communicates with the receiver by sending data with a certain power over the air to the receiver. However, this communication is disturbed by *interferers*, which themselves are part of the wireless network, and which reduce the quality of the received data. Thus, the receiver observes a superposition of the data from the transmitter, that is, the desired signal and the undesired signals from the interferers. An important performance metric is the ratio of the power of the desired signal to the power of the undesired signals originating from the interferers. This signal-to-interference ratio (SIR) is measured at the receiver and indicates whether a certain amount of data can be received reliably within a certain time period. The parameters $c_1, c_2, \ldots, c_m$ determine the level of interference.

The survival function of the SIR is given by

$$\overline{F}(x;c) = \sum_{j=1}^{m} \prod_{\substack{i=1 \\ i \neq j}}^{m} \left[\frac{c_j}{(c_j - c_i)(\frac{1}{xc_j} - 1)} \right].$$

Pereira, Sezgin, Paulraj, and Papanicolaou (2008) show that

$$\overline{F}(x;c) = 1 \bigg/ \prod_{1}^{m}(xc_j + 1)$$

and use the fact that $\overline{F}(x;c)$ is Schur-convex in $(c_1, \ldots, c_n)$ to note that if one interference geometry $(c_1, \ldots, c_m)$ majorizes another, then its SIR scaling is higher.

Server Assignment Policies in Queueing Networks

In an open queueing network with M stations, assume that all stations are single-server stations with service rate μ_i for station i. Let λ_i denote the total arrival rate from external and internal sources to station i. Let $\rho_i = \lambda_i/\mu_i$ and assume that $\rho_i < 1$ for every i. ρ_i is referred to as the loading of station i. Yao (1987) discusses optimal assignment of servers to stations in this context. Using majorization and arrangement orderings, he shows that a better loading policy is one which distributes the total work more uniformly to the stations, i.e., one that makes the ρ_i's more uniform, and that better server assignment policies are those which assign faster servers to busier stations.

A Musical Interlude

Hall and Tymoczko (2007) apply weak majorization to music theory. They are interested in changes as a vocal or instrumental line moves from one note to another. One measure of the magnitude of change that they consider is simply the number of half-steps necessary to reach one note from the other; this is analogous to the way changes in monetary values are evaluated.

Also considered is a somewhat more involved measure of change magnitude in which they regard pitches an octave apart as equivalent. In this case, the distance between two pitches is the minimum number of half-steps (up or down) necessary to reach one note from the other. Thus, to find the distance from C to G, count on a keyboard half-steps up from C to G, and count half-steps down from C to the G below; take the minimum of these counts as the distance between C and G. Because there are 12 tones in a chromatic scale, the maximum distance between two notes is 6.

Hall and Tymoczko (2007) analyze the simultaneous movements of several voices. To compare one simultaneous movement with another, they examine the vectors of voice changes. By imposing some musical criteria, they conclude that the ordering of weak majorization gives an appropriate comparison. Note that when pitches an octave apart are regarded as equivalent, the largest vector that can be encountered is the vector $(6, \ldots, 6)$ and the smallest vector is $(0, \ldots, 0)$.

A key part of their analysis is the following result:
If $a, b \in \mathscr{R}^n$, then

$$(b_{[1]} - a_{[1]}, \ldots, b_{[n]} - a_{[n]}) \prec_w (|b_1 - a_1|, \ldots, |b_n - a_n|).$$

This submajorization follows from 5.A.1.a and 6.A.2.

Occupancy Problems

Occupancy problems involve the allocation of m balls into n bins, where ordinarily m and n are large. Under one rule, each ball is placed into a bin at random with each bin equally likely, but other rules are also of interest. Rules are compared with regard to "load balance" expected, and probabilistic bounds are obtained for the maximum load.

Berenbrink, Czumaj, Steger, and Vöcking (2006, and their references) investigate allocation rules. In particular, they compare two rules for placing balls into bins and show that in terms of majorization, one rule produces a stochastically better load balancing than the other.

Occupancy models have many applications such as assigning tasks to a set of servers. For a model called the *neighboring coupling model*, a ball in the ith-fullest bin is moved into the jth-fullest bin. This operation is a Dalton transfer. The numerical question is to determine the number of balls that need to be transferred until the two allocations are almost indistinguishable.

Comparison of Gibbsian States

For a vector $x \in \mathscr{D}$, the probability vector

$$\left(\frac{e^{x_1}}{\Sigma e^{x_i}}, \ldots, \frac{e^{x_n}}{\Sigma e^{x_i}}\right)$$

is called the *Gibbsian state given by* x (Alberti and Uhlmann, 1982, p. 19). According to 5.B.1.d, if $x, y \in \mathscr{D}$ and $y_i - x_i$ is decreasing in $i = 1, \ldots, n$, then the Gibbsian state of x is majorized by the Gibbsian state of y. Alberti and Uhlmann (1982) remark on two simple situations where this applies in physics. The raising of the temperature in a Gibbsian state gives increasingly more chaotic Gibbsian states. The same is true with Gibbsian states describing an isothermic expansion of a free gas.

If A and B are Hermitian matrices with respective eigenvalues $\alpha_1 \geq \ldots \geq \alpha_n$ and $\beta_1 \geq \ldots \geq \beta_n$, satisfying $\alpha_i - \beta_i \geq \alpha_{i+1} - \beta_{i+1}$, then

$$\left(\frac{e^{\alpha_1}}{\Sigma e^{\alpha_i}}, \ldots, \frac{e^{\alpha_n}}{\Sigma e^{\alpha_i}}\right) \prec \left(\frac{e^{\beta_1}}{\Sigma e^{\beta_i}}, \ldots, \frac{e^{\beta_n}}{\Sigma e^{\beta_i}}\right).$$

This follows from 5.B.1.d.

Density Matrices in Quantum Physics

For the study of quantum systems, density matrices play an important role. In $\mathscr{R}^n$, a matrix A is a *density matrix* if it is positive semidefinite and if $\operatorname{tr} A = 1$. A density matrix A is said to be *more chaotic* or *less pure* than the density matrix B, written $A >^{\mathrm{mc}} B$, if the eigenvalues $\alpha_1, \ldots, \alpha_n$ of A and the eigenvalues $\beta_1, \ldots, \beta_n$ of B satisfy $\alpha \prec \beta$. Note the "reversal" of these inequalities.

P.5. Proposition. $A >^{\mathrm{mc}} B$ if and only if for every nonnegative continuous convex function ϕ defined on $[0, 1]$ such that $\phi(0) = 0$, $\sum_1^n \phi(\alpha_i) < \sum_1^n \phi(\beta_i)$.

For related results, see Wehrl (1973).

Statistical Mechanics

A thermodynamic system consists of n independent subsystems, each described by a Hamiltonian $H = H_0 + \alpha_i H_1$, $i = 1, \ldots, n$, where H_0 and H_1 are Hermitian. The parameter α is called a *coupling* parameter or a *perturbation* parameter. A partition function for the ith subsystem is defined by

$$\varphi(\alpha_i; \beta) = \text{tr } \exp\{-\beta(H_0 + \alpha_i H_1)\},$$

where $\beta = 1/KT$, K is the Boltzmann constant, and T is temperature. The partition function for the system is

$$\psi(\alpha_1, \ldots, \alpha_n) = \prod_1^n \varphi(\alpha_i; \beta).$$

Bogoljubov (1966) and Okubo and Isihara (1972) prove that $\log \phi(\alpha; \beta)$ is convex in α and in β. Consequently, if $(\mu_1, \ldots, \mu_n) \prec (\nu_1, \ldots, \nu_n)$, then $\psi(\mu_1, \ldots, \mu_n) \leq \psi(\nu_1, \ldots \nu_n)$.

For further discussion of applications in physics, see Zylka (1990) and Zylka and Tok (1992).

Genetic Algorithms

An *evolutionary system* consists of basic units called *replicators*, an example being an individual in a population. To the ith replicator, $i = 1, \ldots, n$, there are associated two nonnegative time-dependent functions, a *fitness* function $f_i(t)$, and a *proportion* function $p_i(t) \geq 0$, $\Sigma_1^n p_i(t) = 1$, that represents the fraction of the population that is identical to the ith replicator. A model that connects the fitness and proportion functions is called a *replicator selection model*. One such model is based on *discrete replicator selection equations*:

$$p_i(t+1) = p_i(t) f_i(t) / \overline{f}(t),$$

where $\overline{f}(t) = \Sigma_1^n p_i(t) f_i(t)$ denotes the average fitness. Here t is an integer, but in continuous models $t \in \mathscr{R}_+$.

The following propositions by Menon, Mehrotra, Mohan, and Ranka (1997) provide the connection between majorization and replicator models.

P.6. Proposition. If $x(t) \in \mathscr{R}_+^n$, $x(0) \neq 0$, is a sequence of vectors where t is an integer, such that

$$x(t) = x(t+1)M,$$

where M is a doubly stochastic matrix that is independent of t, so that $x(t) \prec x(t+1)$, then there exists a replicator system whose proportions and fitness are related by a matrix $A = (a_{ij})$ such that

$$f_i(t) = \sum_{j=1}^{n} a_{ij} \frac{p_j(t)}{p_i(t)}.$$

Here

$$p_i(t) = \frac{x_i(t)}{\Sigma_1^n x_j(t)}.$$

P.7. Proposition. If $p(t) \in \mathscr{R}_+^n$, $\Sigma p_i(t) = 1$, satisfies a replicator selection model, and if the vectors $f(t) = (f_1(t), \ldots, f_n(t))$ and $p(t) = (p_1(t), \ldots, p_n(t))$ are similarly ordered for each $t > 0$, then $p(t) \prec p(t+1)$.

A *crossover* or *random mating* model is a quadratic system consisting of a vector $\widetilde{p}(t)$ with n^2 components:

$$\widetilde{p}(t) = (p_1(t)p_1(t), p_1(t)p_2(t), \ldots, p_n(t)p_n(t)),$$

and elements $q(i,j|k,l) \geq 0$, $\Sigma_{i,j} q(i,j|k,l) = 1$, that satisfy exchangeable conditions

$$q(i,j|k,l) = q(k,l|i,j),$$

and symmetry conditions

$$q(i,j|k,l) = q(j,i|k,l) = q(i,j|l,k).$$

P.8. Proposition. If

$$p_i(t+1) = \sum_{j,k,\ell} q(i,j|k,l) p_k(t) p_\ell(t),$$

then $\widetilde{p}(t+1) \prec \widetilde{p}(t)$.

P.8.a. Example. For $R = (r_{ij})$ a symmetric doubly stochastic matrix, let $q(i,j|k,l) = r_{ij} r_{k\ell}$. This system can be described succinctly in terms of Kronecker products (see 19.G). The vector $\widetilde{p}(t)$ can be written as

$$\widetilde{p}(t) = (p(t) \otimes p(t)).$$

By 2.H.7.b, the matrix $(R \otimes R)$ is a symmetric doubly stochastic matrix, and

$$\widetilde{p}(t+1) = (p(t) \otimes p(t))(R \otimes R),$$

so that $\widetilde{p}(t+1) \prec \widetilde{p}(t)$.

P.9. Example. For $R = (r_{ij})$ a symmetric doubly stochastic matrix, let

$$q(i,j|k,l) = r_{ij} + r_{k\ell}.$$

This system can be described in terms of Kronecker sums (see 19.G). The vector $\widetilde{p}(t)$ can be written as

$$\widetilde{p}(t) = (p(t) \oplus p(t)).$$

By 2.H.7.c, the matrix $(R \oplus R)$ is a symmetric doubly stochastic matrix, and

$$\widetilde{p}(t) = (p(t) \oplus p(t))(R \oplus R),$$

so that $\widetilde{p}(t+1) \prec \widetilde{p}(t)$.

For further discussion of replicator genetic algorithms and references, see Menon, Mehrotra, Mohan, and Ranka (1997).

Q Some Other Settings in Which Majorization Plays a Role

The list of scenarios in which majorization has been profitably used is extremely long. Without giving details, we mention here a representative sampling of this literature.

Q1. Optimality properties of the first-come–first-served discipline for $G/G/s$ queues (Daley, 1987). See also Liu and Towsley (1994).

Q2. Stochastic versions of classical deterministic scheduling problems (Chang and Yao, 1993).

Q3. Discrete random variables with proportional equilibrium rates (with queueing applications) (Shanthikumar, 1987).

Q4. Stochastic allocation problems (Liyanage and Shanthikumar, 1992).

Q5. Convex optimization problems under linear constraints (Kim and Makowski, 1998).

Q6. Robust testing of several location parameters and tests for outliers (Kimura and Kakiuchi, 1989; Kakiuchi and Kimura, 1995).

Q.7. Monotone optimal multipartitions (Hwang, Rothblum, and Shepp, 1993).

Q.8. Variables of Boolean functions (Hammer, Kogan, and Rothblum, 2000).

Q.9. Extremal sets in Hamming graphs (Azizoğlu and Eğecioğlu, 2003).

13
Additional Statistical Applications

Majorization has been used as a mathematical tool in a variety of statistical contexts. To illustrate these uses, several examples from diverse areas are given. These examples have been chosen in part because the exposition of the statistical background is minimal, so that the main emphasis lies in the use of majorization. There are other examples, not given here, where the statistical material is more involved and/or the majorization does not play as critical a role.

The examples deal with unbiasedness of tests, monotonicity of power functions, linear estimation, ranking and selection methods, reliability, entropy, inequality and diversity, and design and comparison of experiments.

To see how majorization enters each of these topics, consider first tests of hypotheses. Tests are unbiased when the power function has a minimum at the null hypothesis. Consequently, if a power function is Schur-convex and the null hypothesis holds when the parameters are equal, then majorization clearly can be useful.

When the goodness of a linear estimate is measured by a Schur-convex function, then comparisons among estimators can be made by comparing, via majorization, the weights in the linear estimator.

In selection procedures, identification of the "least favorable configuration" leads to bounds for the probability of a correct selection. This least favorable configuration is often the least or largest vector in the sense of majorization.

In reliability theory, the probability that the system operates is given by a function of component reliabilities called the *reliability function*. Several Schur-convexity results concerning reliability functions are given.

A Unbiasedness of Tests and Monotonicity of Power Functions

Let X be a random variable, vector, or matrix with distribution function F_θ, where $\theta = (\theta_1, \ldots, \theta_k) \in \Omega \subset \mathscr{R}^k$. A test of a hypothesis $H : \theta \in \Omega_H$, which has the form "reject H when $\phi(X) > c$," has power function

$$\beta(\theta) \equiv P_\theta\{\phi(X) > c\} = E_\theta I_{\{\phi(X) > c\}}.$$

A test has *level* α if $\sup_{\theta \in \Omega_H} \beta(\theta) = \alpha$. A level-$\alpha$ test is *unbiased* if $\beta(\theta) \geq \alpha$ for all $\theta \notin \Omega_H$.

For the homogeneity hypothesis $H : \theta_1 = \cdots = \theta_k$ with Ω having a Schur-concave indicator function, sufficient conditions for unbiasedness are

$\beta(\theta)$ is Schur-convex on Ω, so that for fixed $\sum \theta_i$, $\beta(\theta)$ achieves a minimum when $\theta_1 = \cdots = \theta_k$, (1)

and

$\beta(\theta^*, \ldots, \theta^*)$ is independent of θ^* when $(\theta^*, \ldots, \theta^*) \in \Omega$, so that $\beta(\theta)$ is constant for $\theta \in \Omega_H$. (2)

Notice that these conditions for unbiasedness do not depend upon the alternative hypothesis.

Of course, Schur-convexity of β also yields monotonicity of the power function as θ moves away from the point $(\theta^*, \ldots, \theta^*)$ in the sense of majorization.

Suppose X is a random vector, so that the domain of the test function ϕ is a subset of $\mathscr{R}^n$. If ϕ is Schur-convex, then $g(x) \equiv I_{\{y : \phi(y) > c\}}(x)$ is Schur-convex. This observation is useful when combined with results of Section 11.E. There, a number of families $\{F_\theta, \theta \in \Omega\}$ of distributions are listed for which

$$\psi(\theta) \equiv \int g(x)\, dF_\theta(x)$$

is Schur-convex in θ whenever g is Schur-convex. In this way, sometimes with certain variations, condition (1) for unbiasedness can often be easily established. For a general discussion, see Perlman (1980a,b).

A. Unbiasedness of Tests and Monotonicity of Power Functions

A.1. Tests for equality of variances, independent normal distributions. Let $X_1, \ldots, X_k$ be independent random variables, where X_i is normally distributed with mean μ_i and variance τ_i, $i = 1, \ldots, k$. Suppose that independent samples, each of size n, are available from these k distributions. The usual tests for the hypothesis $H: \tau_1 = \cdots = \tau_k$ are based on statistics $V_1, \ldots, V_k$, where each V_i/τ_i has a chi-square distribution. The exact form of the statistics V_i and their degrees of freedom $2m$ depend upon whether the means μ_i are known $[m = n/2]$ or are unknown $[m = (n-1)/2]$.

Tests of the form "reject H if $\phi(V_1, \ldots, V_k) > c$" have power function

$$\beta(\tau_1, \ldots, \tau_k) = \text{const} \int I_{\{u:\phi(u)>c\}}(v) \prod_{i=1}^{k} h\left(v_i/\tau_i\right) \prod_{i=1}^{k} \frac{dv_i}{\tau_i},$$

where $h(z) = [\Gamma(m)2^m]^{-1} z^{m-1} \exp(-z/2)$ if $z \geq 0$ and $h(z) = 0$ otherwise. As a consequence of 11.E.5.e, $\beta(\tau_1, \ldots, \tau_k)$ is Schur-convex in $(\log \tau_1, \ldots, \log \tau_k)$ provided

(i) $\prod_1^k h(e^{v_i})$ is Schur-concave in $(v_1, \ldots, v_k)$, and

(ii) $\phi(e^{v_1}, \ldots, e^{v_k})$ is Schur-convex in $(v_1, \ldots, v_k)$.

Condition (i) is satisfied for h as defined above because it is log concave (3.E.1).

Various choices of ϕ are possible. The class

$$\phi(v_1, \ldots, v_k) = \left(\sum v_i^\lambda/k\right)^{1/\lambda} / \left(\sum v_i^\eta/k\right)^{1/\eta} \equiv R(\lambda, \eta)$$

is considered by Cohen and Strawderman (1971). Particular cases include $R(1, 0) = (\sum v_i/k) \prod v_i^{1/k}$, which is equivalent to Bartlett's test or the likelihood ratio test, and

$$R(\infty, -\infty) = \max(v_1, \ldots, v_k)/\min(v_1, \ldots, v_k),$$

which is equivalent to Hartley's test.

For $\lambda \geq 0 > \eta$, it is not difficult to show (ii) directly by means of 3.A.4. This together with (i) yields (1). Because $R(\lambda, \eta)$ is homogeneous, (2) is satisfied. Consequently, the tests are unbiased.

A.2. Multivariate normal distribution: Test for sphericity. Let S be a $p \times p$ sample covariance matrix based on n observations from a multivariate normal distribution with an unknown mean vector and an unknown covariance matrix Σ. To test the sphericity hypothesis $H: \Sigma = \tau I$ against general alternatives A: not H, the likelihood ratio test is equivalent to "reject H if $(\text{tr } S/p)/(\det S)^{1/p} > c$."

Consequently, the power function is

$$\beta(\Sigma) = P_\Sigma \left\{ \frac{\operatorname{tr} S/p}{(\det S)^{1/p}} > c \right\}.$$

Because the likelihood ratio test is invariant under transformations $S \to \Gamma S \Gamma'$, where Γ is orthogonal, and because the distribution of $\Gamma S \Gamma'$ depends only on the parameter $\Gamma \Sigma \Gamma'$, we can choose Γ so that $\Sigma = D_\tau = \operatorname{diag}(\tau_1, \ldots, \tau_p)$. Then the power function is

$$\beta(\tau) \equiv \beta(\tau_1, \ldots, \tau_p) = P_\tau \left\{ \frac{\operatorname{tr} S/p}{(\det S)^{1/p}} > c \right\}. \tag{3}$$

To show unbiasedness, write $S = D_v R D_v$, where

$$D_v = \operatorname{diag}(v_1, \ldots, v_p), \quad v_i^2 = s_{ii}, \quad R = (r_{ij}), \quad r_{ij} = s_{ij}/\sqrt{s_{ii}s_{jj}},$$

$i, j = 1, \ldots, p$. Then

$$\frac{\operatorname{tr} S/p}{(\det S)^{1/p}} = \frac{\sum v_i^2/p}{(\prod v_i^2)^{1/p}} \frac{1}{(\det R)^{1/p}},$$

and (3) becomes

$$\beta(\tau_1, \ldots, \tau_p) = P_\tau \left\{ \frac{\sum v_i^2/p}{(\prod v_i^2)^{1/p}} > c(\det R)^{1/p} \right\}$$

$$= E_R P_\tau \left\{ \frac{\sum v_i^2/p}{(\prod v_i^2)^{1/p}} > c(\det R)^{1/p} | R \right\}.$$

When $\Sigma = D_\tau$, the vector $(v_1, \ldots, v_p)$ and R are independent, and indeed $v_1, \ldots, v_p$ are mutually independent, where each v_i^2/τ_i has a chi-square distribution with $n - 1$ degrees of freedom.

It now follows from A.1 that for each fixed R,

$$P_\tau \left\{ \frac{\sum v_i^2/p}{(\prod v_i^2)^{1/p}} > c(\det R)^{1/p} \right\}$$

is Schur-convex, and hence β is Schur-convex. Thus the likelihood ratio test is unbiased.

That the likelihood ratio test is unbiased is due to Gleser (1966). The above proof that the power function is Schur-convex is due to Michael D. Perlman (private communication).

A.2.a. Multivariate normal distribution: Tests for structured covariance matrices. Two patterned structures for the covariance matrix $\Sigma = (\sigma_{ij})$ of a p-variate normal distribution with unknown mean vector are the intraclass correlation model in which $\sigma_{ii} = \tau$, $\sigma_{ij} = \tau \rho$, $i, j = 1, \ldots, p$, and the circular symmetric model in which

A. Unbiasedness of Tests and Monotonicity of Power Functions 531

$\sigma_{ii} = \tau_0$, $\sigma_{i,i+j} = \tau_0 \rho_j$, $\rho_j = \rho_{p-j}$, $i = 1, \ldots, p$, $j = 1, \ldots, p-1$, $2 \le i + j \le p$ [see, e.g., Cohen (1969), Olkin (1974), Olkin and Press (1969)]. Denote these covariance matrices by Σ_{IC} and Σ_{CS}, respectively. Further, denote the spherical covariance matrix (i.e., when $\sigma_{ii} = \tau$, $\sigma_{ij} = 0$, $i, j = 1, \ldots, p$) by Σ_{S}.

The hierarchical hypotheses of interest are

$$H_1 : \Sigma_{\mathrm{S}} \text{ versus } \Sigma_{\mathrm{IC}},$$
$$H_2 : \Sigma_{\mathrm{IC}} \text{ versus } \Sigma_{\mathrm{CS}},$$
$$H_3 : \Sigma_{\mathrm{CS}} \text{ versus general } \Sigma.$$

In some contexts, other hypotheses involving Σ_{S}, Σ_{IC}, Σ_{CS}, and Σ may be of interest.

Following the development of A.2, the likelihood ratio tests are all based on statistics that are invariant under orthogonal transformations of the form $S \to \Gamma S \Gamma'$, where Γ is a $p \times p$ orthogonal matrix. In each of the cases, Σ_{S}, Σ_{CS}, Σ_{IC}, the likelihood ratio statistics are of the form

$$\prod_{j=1}^{k} \left(\frac{\sum_{i=1}^{p_j} v_i^{(j)}/p_j}{(\prod_{i=1}^{p_j} v_i^{(j)})^{1/p_j}} \right) (\det R)^{1/p}, \tag{4}$$

where $(s_{11}, \ldots, s_{pp}) = (v_1^{(1)}, \ldots, v_{p_1}^{(1)}, v_1^{(2)}, \ldots, v_{p_2}^{(2)}, \ldots, v_1^{(k)}, \ldots, v_{p_k}^{(k)})$, for some partition $p_1 + \cdots + p_k = p$. Because of the invariance discussed above, Γ can be chosen so that Σ has the form

$$\Sigma_D = \mathrm{diag}(\tau_1 I_{p_1}, \ldots, \tau_k I_{p_k}).$$

Then the sets $\{v_1^{(j)}, \ldots, v_{p_j}^{(j)}\}$, $j = 1, \ldots, k$, are independent. Furthermore, within each set, $v_1^{(j)}, \ldots, v_{p_j}^{(j)}$, $j = 1, \ldots, k$, are independently and identically distributed with $v_i^{(j)}/\tau_j$, $i = 1, \ldots, p_j$, $j = 1, \ldots, k$, having a chi-square distribution with $n - 1$ degrees of freedom. It follows (as in A.2) by conditioning on R and invoking A.1 that the likelihood ratio tests within the class of hypotheses listed are unbiased.

Note that in (4), the statistic is based on the ratio of the arithmetic to geometric means. As noted in A.1, tests based on other ratios of means would also be unbiased.

A.3. Test for means in multivariate normal distributions. In the canonical multivariate analysis of variance model, there are r independent p-variate normal distributions all having the same covariance matrix Σ, but with different unknown mean vectors $\mu^{(1)}, \ldots, \mu^{(r)}$. Let $\Theta = (\mu_j^{(i)})$ be the $r \times p$ matrix of means.

If independent samples of size n are taken from all of the r distributions, the resulting data can be summarized by the sufficient statistic (X, S), where $X = (x_{ij})$ is the $r \times p$ matrix of sample means and $S = (s_{ij})$ is the $p \times p$ pooled sample covariance matrix. The joint density of X and S is

$$f(X, S) = \text{const}|S|^{(r-p-1)/2} \exp\{-\tfrac{1}{2} \text{tr} \, \Sigma^{-1}[S + (X + \Theta)'(X - \Theta)]\}$$

defined for S positive definite and $-\infty < x_{ij} < \infty$, $i = 1, \ldots, r$, $j = 1, \ldots, p$. The problem of testing $H: \Theta = 0$ versus the alternative $A: \Theta \neq 0$ is invariant under the transformation

$$(X, S) \to (\Gamma X A', A S A'), \qquad (5)$$

where Γ is an $r \times r$ orthogonal matrix and A is a $p \times p$ nonsingular matrix. A maximal invariant statistic is

$$(z_1, \ldots, z_t) = (\lambda_1(X S^{-1} X'), \ldots, \lambda_t(X S^{-1} X')),$$

where $t = \min(r, p)$ and $z_1 \geq \cdots \geq z_t$ are the t-largest eigenvalues of $X S^{-1} X'$. The maximal invariant in the parameter space is

$$(\zeta_1, \ldots, \zeta_t) = (\lambda_1(\Theta \Sigma^{-1} \Theta'), \ldots, \lambda_t(\Theta \Sigma^{-1} \Theta')),$$

where $\zeta_1 \geq \cdots \geq \zeta_t$ are the t-largest eigenvalues of $\Theta \Sigma^{-1} \Theta'$.

Any invariant test has a distribution that depends only on $\zeta_1, \ldots, \zeta_t$. Consequently, the power function of any invariant test is a function, $\beta(\zeta_1, \ldots, \zeta_t)$, of $\zeta_1, \ldots, \zeta_t$. In terms of the ζ_i's, the problem is to test $H: \zeta_1 = \cdots = \zeta_t = 0$ versus A: not H.

Within this framework, Eaton and Perlman (1974) prove the following.

A.3.a. Theorem (Eaton and Perlman, 1974). If K is any convex set such that $(X, S) \in K$ implies that $(\Gamma X A', A S A') \in K$ for any orthogonal matrix Γ and any nonsingular matrix A, then the power function given by

$$\beta(\zeta_1, \ldots, \zeta_t) = 1 - \text{const} \int_{(X,S) \in K} |S|^{(r-p-1)/2}$$
$$\times \exp\{-\tfrac{1}{2} \text{tr}[S + (X - D_\zeta^*)'(X - D_\zeta^*)]\} \, dX \, dS,$$

where $D_\zeta^* = \text{diag}(\zeta_1, \ldots, \zeta_t, 0, \ldots, 0)$, is Schur-convex in $(\zeta_1, \ldots, \zeta_t)$.

A consequence of this is the following more useful form:

A.3.b. Corollary. If h is any increasing symmetric convex function on $\mathscr{R}^t$, then any test of the form "reject H if $h(z_1, \ldots, z_t) \geq c$" has a Schur-convex power function.

A. Unbiasedness of Tests and Monotonicity of Power Functions   533

In particular, the Lawley–Hotelling trace test based on $h(z) = \sum_1^t z_i$ and the Roy maximum root test based on $h(z) = \max\{z_1, \ldots, z_t\}$ both satisfy the conditions of A.3.b.

Remark. The full import of the results of Eaton and Perlman (1974) requires some additional discussion which is not given here. However, some details required to prove A.3.b are provided.

First note that $f(X, S) \equiv X S^{-1} X'$ is a convex function of (X, S) (see 16.E.7.f). Consequently, for $0 \le \alpha \le 1$, $\bar{\alpha} = 1 - \alpha$, S and T positive definite,

$$G(\alpha) \equiv (\alpha X + \bar{\alpha} Y)(\alpha S + \bar{\alpha} T)^{-1}(\alpha X + \bar{\alpha} Y)'$$
$$\le \alpha(X S^{-1} X') + \bar{\alpha}(Y T^{-1} Y') \equiv \alpha G(1) + \bar{\alpha} G(0), \qquad (6)$$

where $A \le B$ means that $B - A$ is positive semidefinite. By 20.A.1.b and 9.G.1, inequality (6) implies that

$$(\lambda_1(G(\alpha)), \ldots, \lambda_t(G(\alpha)))$$
$$\prec_w (\lambda_1(\alpha G(1) + \bar{\alpha} G(0)), \ldots, \lambda_t(\alpha G(1) + \bar{\alpha} G(0)))$$
$$\prec (\alpha \lambda_1(G(1)) + \bar{\alpha} \lambda_1(G(0)), \ldots, \alpha \lambda_t(G(1)) + \bar{\alpha} \lambda_t(G(0))).$$

By 3.A.8, if h is any increasing symmetric convex function, then

$$h(\lambda(G(\alpha))) \le \alpha h(\lambda(G(1))) + \bar{\alpha} h(\lambda(G(0))).$$

Thus the region $\{(X, S) : h(z_1, \ldots, z_t) \le c\}$ is convex, which implies the conclusion of A.3.b.

A.4. Multinomial distribution. For the multinomial distribution

$$P\{X_1 = x_1, \ldots, X_k = x_k\} = \binom{N}{x_1, \ldots, x_k} \prod_1^k \theta_i^{x_i},$$

where the x_i's are nonnegative integers, $\theta_i \ge 0$, $i = 1, \ldots, k$, $\sum_1^k \theta_i = 1$ and $\sum_1^k x_i = N$, consider the hypothesis $H : \theta_1 = \cdots = \theta_k = 1/k$ versus the alternative A: not H. A key result, due to Perlman and Rinott (1977), is as follows.

A.4.a. Theorem (Perlman and Rinott, 1977). *If $\phi(x_1, \ldots, x_k)$ is Schur-convex, then the test "reject H if $\phi(x_1, \ldots, x_k) > c$" has a Schur-convex power function*

$$\beta(\theta_1, \ldots, \theta_k) = E_\theta I_{\{\phi(X) > c\}}.$$

Proof. This is a consequence of 11.E.11.   ∥

Three tests that have this property are the chi-square test based on $\phi(x_1,\ldots,x_k) = \sum x_i^2$, the likelihood ratio test based on $\phi(x_1,\ldots,x_k) = \sum x_i \log x_i$, and the divergence test based on information statistics of Kullback (1959, p. 113), $\phi(x_1,\ldots,x_k) = \sum [(x_i/N) - (1/k)] \log x_i$.

Cohen and Sackrowitz (1975) consider the class of functions $\phi(x_1,\ldots,x_k) = \sum h(x_i)$, where h is convex. They prove that the power function

$$\beta(\theta_1,\ldots,\theta_k) = P\left\{\sum h(X_i) > c \,|\, \theta(\alpha)\right\}, \tag{7}$$

where

$$\theta(\alpha) = \alpha(\theta_1,\ldots,\theta_k) + (1-\alpha)(1/k,\ldots,1/k)$$

is monotonically increasing in α. That is, the power function increases as the alternative $\theta(\alpha)$ moves away from the hypothesis $\theta(0)$. Perlman and Rinott (1977) note this result is implied by A.4.a. To see this, write

$$\theta(\alpha) = \theta(1)[\alpha I + (1-\alpha)Q],$$

where $Q = (q_{ij})$ is a $k \times k$ matrix with each element equal to $1/k$. Consequently, $\theta(1) \succ \theta(\alpha) \succ \theta(0)$. Since $\sum h(X_i)$ is Schur-convex for any convex h, it follows that $\beta(\theta(1)) \geq \beta(\theta(\alpha)) \geq \beta(\theta(0))$ (see A.4.a); that is,

$$\beta(\theta_1,\ldots,\theta_k) \geq \beta(\theta(\alpha)) \geq \beta(1/k,\ldots,1/k).$$

A.5. Unbiased tests for homogeneity. Cohen and Sackrowitz (1987) obtain unbiasedness results for tests of homogeneity in exponential families of PF_2 densities (18.A.11 and 18.B), though monotonic power functions are not guaranteed in these more general settings. Specifically, they assume that $X_1, X_2, \ldots, X_k$ are independent random variables, each having its density in a given one-parameter PF_2 exponential family. Thus, for $i = 1, 2, \ldots, k$,

$$f(x_i, \theta_i) = \beta(\theta_i) h(x_i) \exp\{x_i \theta_i\},$$

where h is log concave. This condition ensures that the density is PF_2. Cohen and Sackowitz (1987) restrict tests of the hypothesis

$$H : \theta_1 = \theta_2 = \ldots = \theta_k$$

to be permutation-invariant, and show that any test of size α with convex conditional acceptance sets (given $T = \sum_{i=1}^n X_i$) is unbiased. This is obtained as a corollary to the result that a sufficient condition for unbiasedness of the test is that the test function $\phi(x)$ be Schur-convex.

Consequently, permutation-invariant tests of homogeneity are unbiased in a broad spectrum of distributional cases: normal, gamma (with shape parameter ≥ 1), Poisson, binomial, geometric, etc.

In the following, p is the number of dimensions and $n > p$ is the sample size.

A.6. Log-eigenvalues of a Wishart matrix. Suppose that the $p \times p$ random matrix S has a Wishart distribution with mean μ and $ES = n\Sigma$. Denote the eigenvalues of Σ and S in decreasing order by $\lambda_1, \lambda_2, \ldots, \lambda_p$ and $\ell_1, \ell_2, \ldots, \ell_p$, respectively. The corresponding log-eigenvalues are denoted by $\tau_i = \log \lambda_i$, $t_i = \log \ell_i$, and $t = (t_1, t_2, \ldots, t_p)$.

The distribution of t depends on Σ. Perlman (1996) conjectured that if the set $L \subset \mathcal{D}^p$ is Schur-concave, then

$$P\{t \in L | \Sigma\}$$

is a Schur-concave function of $\tau = \tau(\Sigma)$. The conjecture was verified in the case $p = 2$ by Perlman (1984). A variety of other special cases in p dimensions ($p > 2$) are discussed by Perlman (1996), all of which lend credence to the conjecture. The conjecture, if proved true, would allow verification of unbiasedness of a variety of tests of hypotheses that can be stated in terms of the eigenvalues of covariance matrices.

B   Linear Combinations of Observations

Comparison of Linear Estimators

In the model

$$Y_i = \mu + U_i, \qquad i = 1, \ldots, n,$$

where μ is a constant and the U_i are independent, identically distributed random variables with zero means and common variance σ^2, any weighted average

$$T(w_1, \ldots, w_n) = \sum_1^n w_i Y_i, \qquad \sum_1^n w_i = 1,$$

is an unbiased estimator of μ. The variance of $T(w)$ is $\sigma^2 \sum w_i^2$, which is Schur-convex. Consequently, among unbiased estimators of the form $T(w)$, the estimator $T(1/n, \ldots, 1/n) = \sum Y_i/n$ has minimum variance.

If $(U_1, \ldots, U_n)$ are exchangeable random variables with $EU_i = 0$, $\text{Var}(U_i) = \sigma^2$, and for $i \neq j$, $\text{Cov}(U_i, U_j) = \sigma^2 \rho$, where necessarily $-1/(n-1) < \rho < 1$, then the variance $\text{Var}\, T(w) = w\Sigma w'$ is convex and symmetric and hence is Schur-convex. Thus the minimum variance unbiased estimator is again $T(1/n, \ldots, 1/n) = \sum Y_i/n$.

B.1. Two-stage nested design. In a two-stage random-effects nested design model,

$$Y_{ij} = \mu + R_i + Z_{ij}, \qquad i = 1, \ldots, m, \quad j = 1, \ldots, n_i,$$

$n_1 \geq \cdots \geq n_m$, $\sum n_i = n$. The "row effects" random variables R_i and the "error" random variables Z_{ij} are independently distributed with

$$ER_i = EZ_{ij} = 0, \qquad \text{Var}(R_i) = \sigma_R^2, \qquad \text{Var}(Z_{ij}) = \sigma_E^2,$$

for all i and j. With $w = (w_{11}, \ldots, w_{1n_1}, \ldots, w_{m1}, \ldots, w_{mn_m})$, any linear estimator

$$T(w) = \sum_{i=1}^{m} \sum_{j=1}^{n_i} Y_{ij} w_{ij}, \qquad \sum_{i,j} w_{ij} = 1,$$

is an unbiased estimator of μ. The variance of $T(w)$ is

$$\text{Var}\, T(w) = \text{Var}\left(\sum_{i,j} R_i w_{ij}\right) + \text{Var}\left(\sum_{i,j} Z_{ij} w_{ij}\right)$$

$$= \sigma_R^2 \sum_i w_{i0}^2 + \sigma_E^2 \sum_{i,j} w_{ij}^2,$$

$$\equiv \sigma_R^2 V_R(T(W)) + \sigma_E^2 V_E(T(W)),$$

where $w_{i0} = \sum_j w_{ij}$.

Because of the nested design, estimators are confined to be of the form

$$T(d) \equiv \sum_{1}^{m} \frac{(Y_{i1} + \cdots + Y_{in_i})}{n_i} d_i$$

$$= \mu + \sum_{1}^{m} R_i d_i + \sum_{1}^{m} \frac{(Z_{i1} + \cdots + Z_{in_i})}{n_i} d_i,$$

B. Linear Combinations of Observations   537

where the weights $d_1, \ldots, d_m$ satisfy $\sum d_i = 1$. Then

$$\text{Var } T(d) = \sigma_R^2 \sum_1^m d_i^2 + \sigma_E^2 \sum_1^m \frac{d_i^2}{n_i}$$

$$\equiv \sigma_R^2 V_R(T(d)) + \sigma_E^2 V_E(T(d)).$$

Koch (1967a) compares three estimators using the weights

(i) $d_i = \dfrac{1}{m}$,   (ii) $d_i = \dfrac{n_i}{n}$,   (iii) $d_i = \dfrac{n_i(n - n_i)}{n^2 - \sum n_j^2}$,

where $i = 1, \ldots, m$ and $n = \sum n_j$. Denote the estimators corresponding to these weights by T_1, T_2, T_3, respectively. Koch (1967a) proves that

$$V_R(T_1) \leq V_R(T_2), \qquad V_E(T_1) \leq V_E(T_2),$$

and conjectures that

$$V_R(T_1) \leq V_R(T_3) \leq V_R(T_2), \tag{1a}$$

$$V_E(T_2) \leq V_E(T_3) \leq V_E(T_1). \tag{1b}$$

Low (1970) proves (1a) and (1b) using 5.B.3. A more direct proof is based on the following majorization.

B.1.a. Lemma. If $n_i \geq 0$, $i = 1, \ldots, m$, and $n = \sum_1^m n_i > 0$, then

$$\left(\frac{n_1}{n}, \ldots, \frac{n_m}{n}\right) \succ \left(\frac{n_1(n - n_1)}{n^2 - \sum n_i^2}, \ldots, \frac{n_m(n - n_m)}{n^2 - \sum n_i^2}\right) \succ \left(\frac{1}{m}, \ldots, \frac{1}{m}\right).$$

Proof. The second majorization is immediate. To prove the first majorization, assume without loss of generality that $n_1 \geq \cdots \geq n_m$. Because $z_1 \geq z_2$ and $z_1 + z_2 \leq 1$ together imply $z_1(1 - z_1) \geq z_2(1 - z_2)$, it follows that $n_1(n - n_1) \geq \cdots \geq n_m(n - n_m)$. In (a′) of 5.B.1, take $x_i = [n_i(n - n_i)]/[n^2 - \sum n_j^2]$, $y_i = n_i/n$, $i = 1, \ldots, m$, to obtain the desired majorization. ||

Inequalities (1a,b) follow directly from the lemma and the Schur-convexity of $\sum d_i^2$ and $\sum (1/n_i)d_i^2$ on $\mathscr{D}$ (3.H.2.b).

B.2. Two-way classification. In a two-way classification random-effects model

$$Y_{ij} = \mu + R_i + C_j + Z_{ij}, \qquad i = 1, \ldots, r, \quad j = 1, \ldots, c,$$

where $R_i, C_j,$ and Z_{kl} are mutually independent,

$$ER_i = EC_j = EZ_{ij} = 0,$$

$$\text{Var } R_i = \sigma_R^2, \qquad \text{Var } C_j = \sigma_C^2, \qquad \text{Var } Z_{ij} = \sigma_E^2.$$

To estimate μ, consider the class of linear estimators

$$T(w) = \sum_{i,j} Y_{ij} w_{ij}$$

$$= \mu + \sum_i \frac{(w_{i1} + \cdots + w_{ic})}{c} R_i + \sum_j \frac{(w_{1j} + \cdots + w_{rj})}{r} C_j + \sum_{i,j} w_{ij} Z_{ij},$$

where $\sum_{i,j} w_{ij} = 1$ and

$$w = (w_{11}, \ldots, w_{1c}, w_{21}, \ldots, w_{2c}, \ldots, w_{r1}, \ldots, w_{rc})$$

is the vector of weights. Then

$$\operatorname{Var} T(w) = \sigma_R^2 \sum_i w_{i0}^2 + \sigma_C^2 \sum_j w_{0j}^2 + \sigma_E^2 \sum_{i,j} w_{ij}^2,$$

$$= \sigma_R^2 V_R(T(w)) + \sigma_C^2 V_C(T(w)) + \sigma_E^2 V_E(T(w)),$$

where

$$w_{i0} = \sum_j w_{ij}/c, \qquad w_{0j} = \sum_i w_{ij}/r.$$

It is of interest to compare the variances that are obtained using different weights. Let $N = (n_{ij})$, where $n_{ij} = 1$ if an observation appears in the (i,j)th cell, and $n_{ij} = 0$ otherwise; $n_{i0} = \sum_j n_{ij}$, $n_{0j} = \sum_i n_{ij}$, $n = \sum_{i,j} n_{ij}$. Consider weights

(i) $w_{ij}^{(1)} = 1/rc$,

(iia) $w_{ij}^{(2a)} = n_{i0}/nc$,

(iib) $w_{ij}^{(2b)} = n_{0j}/nr$,

(iii) $w_{ij}^{(3)} = \dfrac{(n - n_{i0} - n_{0j} + n_{ij}) n_{ij}}{n^2 - \sum_i n_{i0}^2 - \sum_j n_{0j}^2 + n}$, $i = 1, \ldots, r$, $j = 1, \ldots, c$.

For a discussion of these weights, see Koch (1967b).

Denote the respective weight vectors by $w^{(1)}, w^{(2a)}, w^{(2b)}, w^{(3)}$, and the corresponding estimators by T_1, T_{2a}, T_{2b}, T_3.

B.3. Lemma.

$$w^{(1)} \prec w^{(2a)} \prec w^{(3)}, \tag{2a}$$

$$w^{(1)} \prec w^{(2b)} \prec w^{(3)}. \tag{2b}$$

Proof. The left-hand majorizations in (2a) and (2b) are immediate. To obtain the right-hand majorization in (2a), note that

$$w^{(2a)} \equiv (\underbrace{n_{10}/nc, \ldots, n_{10}/nc}_{c}, \ldots, \underbrace{n_{r0}/nc, \ldots, n_{r0}/nc}_{c})$$
$$= (n_{11}, \ldots, n_{1c}, n_{21}, \ldots, n_{2c}, \ldots, n_{r1}, \ldots, n_{rc})\operatorname{diag}(D, \ldots, D),$$

where D is a $c \times c$ doubly stochastic matrix with each element $1/c$. The elements n_{ij} are either 0 or 1. If any $n_{ij} = 0$, then the corresponding element in $w^{(2a)}$ and in $w^{(3)}$ is zero. If any $n_{ij} = 1$, the corresponding element of $w^{(2a)}$ is 1. Consequently, $w^{(2a)}$ can be permuted to obtain $(e, 0)$ and $w^{(3)}$ can be permuted to obtain $(w^{(3)}, 0)$, where the 0 vectors are of the same length. Since the total sums in both vectors are equal, by 5.A.7, $w^{(2a)} \prec w^{(3)}$.

The proof that $w^{(3)} \succ w^{(2b)}$ is parallel to the above, with columns replacing rows. ||

As a consequence of B.3 and the Schur-convexity of $\sum_{i,j} w_{ij}^2$,

$$V_E(T_3) \geq V_E(T_{2a}) \geq V_E(T_1),$$
$$V_E(T_3) \geq V_E(T_{2b}) \geq V_E(T_1).$$

It also follows that $V_C(T_{2b}) \geq V_C(T_1)$, $V_R(T_{2a}) \geq V_R(T_1)$. However, other comparisons cannot be made in this way since the variance $\sum_j w_{0j}^2$, say, is not a symmetric function of the w_{ij}'s.

For connections between majorization and weighted linear estimators in the context of portfolio diversification and value at risk, see Ibragimov and Walden (2007).

Subsampling Quantile Estimators

In the subsampling method, estimates are generated from subsamples of a complete sample and then averaged over the subsamples. Such a procedure has been shown to provide a robust estimator of location for symmetric distributions, and also to have a smoothing effect for the sample quantile for any continuous distribution.

More specifically, let $X_1, \ldots, X_n$ be a complete sample. For fixed k, $1 \leq k \leq n$, select from the complete sample a random subsample of size k without replacement, and denote the ordered observations in the subsample by $X_{1:k}, \ldots, X_{k:k}$. A more accurate notation would be $X_{i:k:n}$ for $X_{i:k}$, but for simplicity the n is omitted.

For a single subsample, the αth quantile ($0 < \alpha < 1$) is estimated by $X_{r:k}$, where r is the greatest integer less than or equal to $(k+1)\alpha$.

540   13. Additional Statistical Applications

However, for fixed r, instead of using a single subsample, an average of $\binom{n}{k}$ estimators obtainable from distinct subsamples yields the following quantile estimator that is a linear combination of the order statistics of the complete sample:

$$u(r,k,n) = \sum_{j=r}^{r+n-k} \left[\binom{j-1}{r-1}\binom{n-j}{k-r} \bigg/ \binom{n}{k}\right] x_{j:n}.$$

This estimator and two others which differ in the weights assigned to the complete sample order statistics have been proposed as nonparametric smoothed quantile estimators:

$$u(r,k,n) = \sum_{j=1}^{n} a_j(r,k,n) x_{j:n}, \qquad (3a)$$

$$v(r,k,n) = \sum_{j=1}^{n} b_j(r,k,n) x_{j:n}, \qquad (3b)$$

$$w(r,k,n) = \sum_{j=1}^{n} c_j(r,k,n) x_{j:n}, \qquad (3c)$$

where the weights are

$$a_j(r,k,n) = \left[\binom{j-1}{r-1}\binom{n-j}{k-r} \bigg/ \binom{n}{k}\right], \quad r \leq k, \qquad (4a)$$

$$b_j(r,k,n) = \int_{(j-1)/n}^{j/n} \frac{z^{r-1}(1-z)^{n-r}}{B(r,n-r+1)} dz, \qquad (4b)$$

and for $r \leq k$,

$$c_j(r,k,n) = \left[\binom{r+j-2}{r-1}\binom{n+k+r-j}{k-r} \bigg/ \binom{n+k-1}{k}\right]. \qquad (4c)$$

Note that

$$\sum_{j=1}^{n} a_j(r,k,n) = \sum_{j=1}^{n} b_j(r,k,n) = \sum_{j=1}^{n} c_j(r,k,n) = 1.$$

For a fixed subsample size k, let

$$u_k = (u(1,k,n),\ldots,u(k,k,n)), \qquad (5a)$$

$$v_k = (v(1,k,n),\ldots,v(k,k,n)), \qquad (5b)$$

$$w_k = (w(1, k, n), \ldots, w(k, k, n)). \tag{5c}$$

Thus u_k, v_k, and w_k represent vectors of estimates of the αth quantile when $[(k+1)\alpha] = r$ for $r = 1, \ldots, k$. A key result is that these vectors are ordered by majorization.

B.4. Proposition (Kaigh and Sorto, 1993). For u_k, v_k, and w_k defined by (3a,b,c), (4a,b,c), and (5a,b,c),

$$u_k \succ v_k \succ w_k.$$

For details of the proof and for further references and discussion of quantile estimators, see Kaigh and Sorto (1993).

C Ranking and Selection

In ranking and selection problems, there is an underlying distribution $F(x; \theta_1, \ldots, \theta_k)$, with unknown parameters $\theta_1, \ldots, \theta_k$ lying in some set Ω. Various goals are considered, such as ordering the θ's, selecting the t-largest θ's, or selecting the t-smallest θ's.

The emphasis of this section is on selection problems. A decision procedure R which depends on a sample $X_1, \ldots, X_n$ is used to make the selection. To control error probabilities, the procedure is ordinarily required to satisfy

$$P_R\{\text{correct selection}|\,\theta \in \Omega^*\} \equiv P_R\{\text{CS}|\,\theta \in \Omega^*\} \geq p_0,$$

where p_0 is a preassigned probability level and Ω^* consists of points in Ω bounded away from the boundary of Ω in some sense appropriate to the problem at hand. If there exists a configuration θ_{LF} (called a *least favorable configuration*) such that

$$P_R\{\text{CS}|\,\theta\} \geq P_R\{\text{CS}|\,\theta_{\text{LF}}\} \qquad \text{for all } \theta \in \Omega^*,$$

then the right-hand side can be set equal to p_0 in the determination of a procedure R.

The utility of majorization is that sometimes $P_R\{\text{CS}|\,\theta_1, \ldots, \theta_k\}$ is Schur-concave in $(\theta_1, \ldots, \theta_k)$. If θ^* is the largest vector θ (in the sense of majorization) satisfying the constraints, then $P_R\{\text{CS}|\,\theta\} \geq P_R\{\text{CS}|\,\theta^*\}$ and θ^* is the least favorable configuration. More commonly, an additional step is required: The probability of a correct selection is Schur-concave only after some conditioning and a further argument is required to remove the conditioning.

These ideas are illustrated here for the multinomial and normal distributions. They are applicable also to various problems involving other distributions [e.g., see Alam and Thompson (1973) or Dudewicz and Tong (1976)].

Multinomial Distribution

Let $X_1, \ldots, X_k$ have a multinomial distribution

$$P\{X_1 = x_1, \ldots, X_k = x_k\} = \binom{N}{x_1, \ldots, x_k} \prod_1^k \theta_i^{x_i},$$

$$\sum_1^k x_i = N, \qquad 0 \leq \theta_i, \qquad \sum_1^k \theta_i = 1,$$

and the x_i's are nonnegative integers. Recall that the ordered X's are denoted by $X_{(1)} \leq \cdots \leq X_{(k)}$ and the ordered θ's by $\theta_{(1)} \leq \cdots \leq \theta_{(k)}$.

C.1. Selecting the most likely event. For the goal of choosing the cell with the highest cell probability, i.e., choosing the cell corresponding to $\theta_{(k)}$, Bechhofer, Elmaghraby, and Morse (1959) use the procedure: Assert that the cell corresponding to $X_{(k)}$ has the largest θ-value. (If ties occur, they are broken by randomization.) Subject to the constraints

$$\theta_{(k)} \geq a\theta_{(k-1)}, \qquad a > 1, \tag{1}$$

Kesten and Morse (1959) obtain the least favorable configuration

$$\theta_{\mathrm{LF}} = \left(\frac{a}{a+k-1}, \frac{1}{a+k-1}, \ldots, \frac{1}{a+k-1} \right). \tag{2}$$

In spite of the fact that this result is quite intuitive, it is somewhat troublesome to prove.

Let $\widetilde{X}_i$ be the random variable associated with the event having probability $\theta_{(i)}$. The probability $\phi(\theta_1, \ldots, \theta_k)$ of a correct selection is

$$\phi(\theta_1, \ldots, \theta_k) = P\{\widetilde{X}_k > \widetilde{X}_\alpha, \alpha \neq k\}$$

$$+ \frac{1}{2} \sum_{j \neq k} P\{\widetilde{X}_k = \widetilde{X}_j, \widetilde{X}_k > \widetilde{X}_\alpha, \alpha \neq j\}$$

$$+ \frac{1}{3} \sum_{j_1 \neq k, j_2 \neq k} P\{\widetilde{X}_k = \widetilde{X}_{j_1} = \widetilde{X}_{j_2}, \widetilde{X}_k > \widetilde{X}_\alpha, \alpha \neq j_1, j_2\}$$

$$+ \cdots + \frac{1}{k} P\{\widetilde{X}_k = \widetilde{X}_{k-1} = \cdots = \widetilde{X}_1\}. \tag{3}$$

The function ϕ can be written in terms of a conditional expectation for which the following lemma is useful.

C.1.a. Lemma. For each $z \in \mathscr{R}$, define the function

$$g_z : \mathscr{R}^l \to \mathscr{R} \text{ by } g_z(u_1, \ldots, u_l) = 1/(m+1)$$

if m of the $u_1, \ldots, u_l$ are equal to z, and the remaining $l - m$ of the $u_1, \ldots, u_l$ are strictly less than z; $g_z(u_1, \ldots, u_l) = 0$ otherwise. Then $g_z(u_1, \ldots, u_l)$ is Schur-concave in $u_1, \ldots, u_l$.

Proof. Because g_z is symmetric, by 3.A.5 it suffices to show that for fixed $\ddot{u} = (u_3, \ldots, u_l), 0 \leq \alpha \leq 1, \bar{\alpha} = 1 - \alpha$,

$$g_z(u_1, u_2, \ddot{u}) \leq g_z(\alpha u_1 + \bar{\alpha} u_2, \bar{\alpha} u_1 + \alpha u_2, \ddot{u}). \tag{4}$$

Let r be the number of $u_3, \ldots, u_l$ equal to z. Then

$$g_z(u_1, u_2, \ddot{u}) = \begin{cases} 1/r & \text{if } u_1 < z, u_2 < z, u_3 \leq z, \ldots, u_l \leq z, \\ 1/(r+1) & \text{if } u_1 < z, u_2 = z \text{ or } u_1 = z, \\ & u_2 < z, u_3 \leq z, \ldots, u_l \leq z, \\ 1/(r+2) & u_1 = u_2 = z, u_3 \leq z, \ldots, u_l \leq z, \\ 0 & \text{elsewhere.} \end{cases}$$

Using this, (4) can be verified directly. ∥

Rewrite (3) as

$$\phi(\theta_1, \ldots, \theta_k) = E\{E_\theta[g_z(\widetilde{X}_1, \ldots, \widetilde{X}_{k-1}) | \widetilde{X}_k = z]\}.$$

By 11.E.11, it follows that if g is Schur-concave, then

$$E_\theta[g_z(\widetilde{X}_1, \ldots, \widetilde{X}_{k-1}) | \widetilde{X}_k = z] \quad \text{is Schur-concave in the ratios}$$

$$\left(\frac{\theta_{(1)}}{1 - \theta_{(k)}}, \ldots, \frac{\theta_{(k-1)}}{1 - \theta_{(k)}} \right).$$

Because $\theta_{(k)} = 1 - \sum_1^{k-1} \theta_{(i)}$, the conditional expectation is Schur-concave in $(\theta_{(1)}, \ldots, \theta_{(k-1)})$ with $\theta_{(k)}$ fixed.

Alternatively, C.1.a can be restated as follows:

C.1.b. Proposition. Let ϕ be the function defined by (3). If $(\alpha_1, \ldots, \alpha_{k-1}) \prec (\beta_1, \ldots, \beta_{k-1})$, then

$\phi(\alpha_1, \ldots, \alpha_{k-1}, \theta_{(k)}) \geq \phi(\beta_1, \ldots, \beta_{k-1}, \theta_{(k)})$, where $\theta_{(k)} = 1 - \Sigma_1^{k-1} \alpha_i$.

For fixed $\theta_{(k)}$, $a/(a+k-1) \leq \theta_{(k)} \leq 1$, determine μ and an integer q by

$$0 \leq \mu \leq \frac{\theta_{(k)}}{a}, \qquad \theta_{(k)} + (q-2)\frac{\theta_{(k)}}{a} + \mu = 1, \tag{5}$$

and let

$$\tilde{\theta} = (\tilde{\theta}_k, \ldots, \tilde{\theta}_1) = (\theta_{(k)}, \underbrace{\theta_{(k)}/a, \ldots, \theta_{(k)}/a}_{q-2}, \mu, \underbrace{0, \ldots, 0}_{k-q}). \tag{6}$$

By 5.C.1, $\theta \prec \tilde{\theta}$ for all probability vectors with $\theta_{(k)}$ fixed that satisfy the constraints (1). It follows from C.1.b that $\phi(\tilde{\theta}) \leq \phi(\theta)$. This is Theorem 1 of Kesten and Morse (1959).

To identify the least favorable configuration, it must be shown that, for $\theta_{(k)} = a(1-\mu)/(a-q-2)$ determined by (6), $\phi(\tilde{\theta})$ is decreasing in μ (Kesten and Morse, 1959, Lemma 2). This means that

$$\phi\left(\frac{a(1-\mu)}{a+q-2}, \underbrace{\frac{1-\mu}{a+q-2}, \ldots, \frac{1-\mu}{a+q-2}}_{q-2}, \mu, \underbrace{0, \ldots, 0}_{k-q}\right)$$

$$\geq \phi\left(\frac{a}{a+q-1}, \underbrace{\frac{1}{a+q-1}, \ldots, \frac{1}{a+q-1}}_{q-1}, \underbrace{0, \ldots, 0}_{k-q}\right)$$

$$\geq \phi\left(\frac{a(1-\nu)}{a+q-1}, \underbrace{\frac{1-\nu}{a+q-1}, \ldots, \frac{1-\nu}{a+q-1}}_{q-1}, \nu, \underbrace{0, \ldots, 0}_{k-q-1}\right),$$

where ν (in place of μ) satisfies (5) with $q-1$ in place of $q-2$. Iteration of this leads to the least favorable configuration (2).

C.1.c. If the constraints (1) are replaced by

$$\theta_{(k)} \geq \theta_{(k-1)} + a, \qquad 0 < a < 1/(k-1), \tag{7}$$

then the least favorable configuration is not easily described. Arguments similar to those above can be used to show that for appropriately fixed $\theta_{(k)}$, $\phi(\widetilde{\theta}) \leq \phi(\theta)$, where $\widetilde{\theta}$ is a probability vector of the form

$$\widetilde{\theta} = (\theta_{(k)}, \theta_{(k)} - a, \ldots, \theta_{(k)} - a, \mu, 0, \ldots, 0),$$

$0 \leq \mu \leq \theta_{(k)} - a$. It would then be expected that the least favorable configuration is

$$\left(\frac{1 + (k-1)a}{k}, \frac{1-a}{k}, \ldots, \frac{1-a}{k} \right),$$

but an analog of the monotonicity result of the previous argument is not available. Indeed, Chen and Hwang (1984) provided some counterexamples to the conjecture regarding the nature of the least favorable configuration. Subsequently, Bhandari and Bose (1987) investigated the situation in which the constraint (7) is replaced by the more general constraint

$$\theta_{(k)} \geq a\theta_{(k-1)} + b.$$

They verify that if $a > 1$, $b \leq 0$, and $a + bk > 1$, then the least favorable configuration is given by

$$\left(\frac{a + b(k-1)}{a+k-1}, \frac{1-b}{a+k-1}, \ldots, \frac{1-b}{a+k-1} \right).$$

However, when $a = 1$ and $b > 0$, the monotonicity argument breaks down, and the nature of the least favorable configuration actually depends on N. If N is sufficiently large, the least favorable configuration is $\frac{1}{2}(1+b, 1-b, 0, \ldots, 0)$. Chen and Hwang (1984) also discuss the more general problem of selecting the t most likely events in this context.

C.2. Selecting the least likely event. To select the cell with the smallest probability, Alam and Thompson (1972) use the procedure: Assert that the cell corresponding to $X_{(1)}$ has the smallest θ-value.

The probability of a correct selection $\phi(\theta_1, \ldots, \theta_k)$ is

$$\phi(\theta_1, \ldots, \theta_k) = P\{\widetilde{X}_1 < \widetilde{X}_\alpha, \alpha \neq 1\}$$
$$+ \frac{1}{2} \sum_{j>1} P\{\widetilde{X}_1 = \widetilde{X}_j, \widetilde{X}_1 < \widetilde{X}_\alpha, \alpha \neq j, \alpha > 1\} \tag{8}$$
$$+ \cdots + \frac{1}{k} P\{\widetilde{X}_1 = \cdots = \widetilde{X}_k\}.$$

With the aid of the following lemma, expression (8) can be written in terms of a conditional expectation.

C.2.a. Lemma. The function $\bar{g}_z(u_1, \ldots, u_l) = 1/(m+1)$ if m of $u_1, \ldots, u_l$ are equal to z and the remaining $l - m$ of $u_1, \ldots, u_l$ are strictly greater than z; $\bar{g}_z(u_1, \ldots, u_l) = 0$ otherwise. Then $g_z(u_1, \ldots, u_l)$ is Schur-concave in $u_1, \ldots, u_l$.

This lemma follows from C.1.a by noting that

$$\bar{g}_z(u_1, \ldots, u_l) = g_{-z}(-u_1, \ldots, -u_l).$$

Conditioning on $\widetilde{X}_1$ with $l = k - 1$ yields

$$\phi(\theta_1, \ldots, \theta_k) = E\{E_\theta[\bar{g}_z(\widetilde{X}_2, \ldots, \widetilde{X}_k)|\widetilde{X}_1 = z]\}.$$

By 11.E.11, it follows that because $\bar{g}$ is Schur-concave,

$$E_\theta[\bar{g}_z(\widetilde{X}_2, \ldots, \widetilde{X}_k)|\widetilde{X}_1 = a]$$

is Schur-concave in $(\theta_{(2)}/(1 - \theta_{(1)}), \ldots, \theta_{(k)}/(1 - \theta_{(1)}))$.

Since $\theta_{(1)} = 1 - \sum_2^k \theta_{(i)}$, the conditional expectation is Schur-concave in $(\theta_{(2)}, \ldots, \theta_{(k)})$. Hence, the unconditional expectation is Schur-concave in $(\theta_{(2)}, \ldots, \theta_{(k)})$ with $\theta_{(1)}$ fixed.

Alternatively, this may be stated as

C.2.b. Proposition. If $(\alpha_2, \ldots, \alpha_k) \prec (\beta_2, \ldots, \beta_k)$, then

$$\phi(\theta_{(1)}, \alpha_2, \ldots, \alpha_k) \geq \phi(\theta_{(1)}, \beta_2, \ldots, \beta_k),$$

where ϕ is defined by (8) and $\theta_{(1)} = 1 - \Sigma_1^{k-1} \alpha_i$.

Alam and Thompson (1972) implicitly prove the above proposition by an argument similar to the one used here.

For the constraint set

$$\theta_{(1)} \leq \theta_{(2)} - a, \quad \text{where} \quad 0 < a < 1/(k-1),$$

the maximal vector for fixed $\theta_{(1)}$ is obtainable from 5.C.1:

$$(\widetilde{\theta}_1, \ldots, \widetilde{\theta}_k) = (\theta_{(1)}, \theta_{(1)} + a, \ldots, \theta_{(1)} + a, \mu),$$

where

$$\mu = 1 - (k-1)\theta_{(1)} - (k-2)a.$$

Alam and Thompson (1972) complete the derivation of the least favorable configuration with a monotonicity argument to obtain

$$\theta_{\text{LF}} = \left(\frac{1-(k-1)a}{k}, \frac{1+a}{k}, \ldots, \frac{1+a}{k}\right).$$

Remark. Alam, Rizvi, Mitra, and Saxena (1986) discuss the problem of selecting the most diverse multinomial population (i.e., the population whose corresponding probability vector θ majorizes each of the probability vectors corresponding to the other populations) based on indices of diversity (13.F) computed for samples of size n from each of the populations. In particular, they give approximate expressions for the probability of correct selection for the binomial case with n large.

Normal Distribution

C.3 Analysis of variance. Bechhofer, Santner, and Turnbull (1977) consider an analysis of variance two-way classification with 2 rows and c columns. The goal is to choose the treatment with the largest interaction that represents the departure from additivity of row and column effects. For this purpose, n observations are obtained from each cell.

Denote by Y_{ijk}, $i = 1, 2$, $j = 1, \ldots, c$, $k = 1, \ldots, n$, the kth observation on the ith row and jth column. The random variables Y_{ijk} are independently and normally distributed with means

$$EY_{ijk} = \mu + \alpha_i + \beta_j + \gamma_{ij},$$

where μ, α_i, β_j, and γ_{ij} are unknown constants which satisfy

$$\sum_i \alpha_i = \sum_j \beta_j = \sum_i \gamma_{ij} = \sum_j \gamma_{ij} = 0.$$

The Y_{ijk}'s have a common known variance σ^2.

In order to select the cell corresponding to the largest γ_{ij}, estimate γ_{ij} using

$$X_{ij} = Y_{ij\cdot} - Y_{i\cdot\cdot} - Y_{\cdot j\cdot} + Y_{\cdots},$$

where

$$Y_{ij\cdot} = \sum_k Y_{ijk}/n, \qquad Y_{i\cdot\cdot} = \sum_{j,k} Y_{ijk}/nc,$$

$$Y_{\cdot j\cdot} = \sum_{i,k} Y_{ijk}/nr, \qquad Y_{\cdots} = \sum_{i,j,k} Y_{ijk}/nrc.$$

The procedure is to assert that the cell corresponding to the largest interaction is the one with the largest X_{ij} value.

If $\gamma_{2c} > 0$ is the unique largest interaction, then $\gamma_{1c} = -\gamma_{2c}$ is the smallest interaction, and because $\gamma_{2j} = -\gamma_{1j}$, $j = 1, \ldots, c-1$, all

548   13. Additional Statistical Applications

interactions will be at least a prescribed magnitude δ^* smaller than γ_{2c} provided that

$$-(\gamma_{2c} - \delta^*) \leq \gamma_{1j} \leq \gamma_{2c} - \delta^*, \qquad j = 1, \ldots, c-1.$$

This constraint set is nonempty if $\gamma_{2c} > \delta^*$. Our object here is to show how majorization can be used to identify a least favorable configuration subject to these constraints.

To simplify notation, let $a = \gamma_{2c} - \delta^* > 0$, $\gamma_{1j} = \delta_j$, $j = 1, \ldots, c-1$, and rewrite the constraints as

$$-a \leq \delta_j \leq a, \qquad j = 1, \ldots, c-1. \tag{9}$$

The probability of a correct selection,

$$P\{X_{2c} > X_{ij} \text{ for all } (i,j) \neq (2,c)\},$$

can conveniently be written in terms of the random variables

$$W_j = \sum_{i=1}^{c-1} X_{2i} - X_{2j}, \qquad j = 1, \ldots, c-1.$$

These random variables have a multivariate normal distribution with means 0, variances $\sigma^2(c-2)/cn$, and covariances $(c-4)/[2(c-2)]$. If A is the region

$$A = \left\{ (w_1, \ldots, w_{c-1}) : -\gamma_{2c} \leq w_j \leq \gamma_{2c} + \frac{2}{c-2} \sum_{i=1}^{c-1} w_i - \frac{2}{c-2}\gamma_{2c}, \right.$$
$$\left. j = 1, \ldots, c-1 \right\},$$

then the probability of a correct selection can be written as

$$P\{(W_1, \ldots, W_{c-1}) \in A + \delta\},$$

where $\delta = (\delta_1, \ldots, \delta_{c-1})$. From this, it is easy to apply 3.J.1.a to conclude that the probability of a correct selection is a Schur-concave function of $\delta_1, \ldots, \delta_{c-1}$. To see this, note that $W_1, \ldots, W_{c-1}$ are exchangeable multivariate normal random variables; hence, they have a Schur-concave joint density (11.E.5.d). Further, if

$$(u_1, u_2) \in \{a \leq u_i \leq b + u_1 + u_2, i = 1, 2\} \equiv B,$$

then

$$(\alpha u_1 + \overline{\alpha} u_2, \overline{\alpha} u_1 + \alpha u_2) \in B.$$

Consequently, if $y \in A$, then $yT \in A$, where T is a T-transform, so the hypotheses of 3.J.1.a are satisfied.

Subject to the constraints (9), it follows from 5.C.1 that a maximal δ in the sense of majorization is

$$\widetilde{\delta} = (\underbrace{a, \ldots, a}_{c-q-2}, \underbrace{\mu}_{1}, \underbrace{-a, \ldots, -a}_{q}), \quad -a \leq \mu < a,$$

where q, determined by the condition $\sum_{1}^{c-1} \delta_j = \gamma_{2c}$, is the unique integer in the interval

$$[\tfrac{1}{2}(c - 1 - \gamma_{2c}/a) - 1, \tfrac{1}{2}(c - 1 - \gamma_{2c}/a)].$$

Because the probability of a correct selection is a Schur-concave function of the parameters $(\delta_1, \ldots, \delta_{c-1})$, and subject to certain constraints, $\widetilde{\delta}$ is the maximal vector,

$$P\{\text{correct selection}|\delta\} \geq P\{\text{correct selection}|\widetilde{\delta}\}.$$

This is the main result of Theorem 6.1 of Bechhofer, Santner, and Turnbull (1977).

Rinott and Santner (1977) use majorization to obtain a least favorable configuration in an analysis of covariance setting. Their results are not discussed here.

D Majorization in Reliability Theory

Reliability of k-out-of-n Systems

For most systems of practical interest having n independent components, the system reliability (probability that the system functions) is a function h of component reliabilities. This function $h: [0, 1]^n \to [0, 1]$ is called the *reliability function* of the system.

Systems with n components that function if and only if at least k components function are called *k-out-of-n systems*. One-out-of-n systems are commonly called *parallel systems*, and n-out-of-n systems are called *series systems*. See Marshall and Olkin (2007) for further discussion of k-out-of-n systems.

Let $p_1, \ldots, p_n$ be the reliabilities of the n independent components and let h_k be the reliability function of a k-out-of-n system. It is easy to see that $h_1(p_1, \ldots, p_n) = 1 - \prod_1^n (1 - p_i)$ and $h_n(p_1, \ldots, p_n) = \prod_1^n p_i$. Consequently, it is easy to verify that h_1 is Schur-convex and h_n is Schur-concave. For $1 < k < n$, h_k is neither Schur-convex nor Schur-concave.

Let $X_i = 1$ if the ith component functions and $X_i = 0$ otherwise. Then $p_i = P\{X_i = 1\}$ and

$$h_k(p_1,\ldots,p_n) = P\{X_1 + \cdots + X_n \geq k\}.$$

From 12.K.1, it follows that h_k is Schur-convex for $k \leq \sum_1^n p_i - 1$ and h_k is Schur-concave for $k \geq \sum_1^n p_i + 2$. For $\sum_1^n p_i = A < k$, fixed, Derman, Lieberman, and Ross (1974) show that $h_k(p_1,\ldots,p_n)$ is maximized if $(p_1,\ldots,p_n)$ has the form $(A/r,\ldots,A/r,0,\ldots,0)$ for some $r = 1,\ldots,n$.

Boland and Proschan (1983) confirm that $h_k(p)$ is a Schur-concave function in the region $[0,(k-1)/(n-1)]^n$, and is Schur-convex in the region $[(k-1)/(n-1),1]^n$.

Note. The problem of obtaining confidence bounds for $h_k(p)$ based on component data [i.e., independent binomial (n_i, p_i) samples] is of some importance but of considerable difficulty. Under certain conditions, Buehler (1957), and subsequently Soms (1989) provide bounds for the system reliability in a k-out-of-n system.

For some purposes, the *hazard transform* $\eta: [0,\infty)^n \to [0,\infty)$ defined by

$$\eta(R_1,\ldots,R_n) = -\log h(e^{-R_1},\ldots,e^{-R_n})$$

is more convenient to work with than the reliability function [see Esary, Marshall, and Proschan (1970)].

D.1. Proposition (Pledger and Proschan, 1971). The hazard transform η_k of a k-out-of-n system is increasing and Schur-concave on $[0,\infty)^n$.

Proof. Let $X_1,\ldots,X_n$ be independent Bernoulli random variables where $X_i = 0$ or 1 according to whether the ith component fails or functions, so that $p_i = P\{X_i = 1\}$. Let $R_i = -\log p_i$, $i = 1,\ldots,n$. Because the indicator function ϕ of the set

$$\mathscr{X} = \{x : \max_\pi (z_{\pi(1)} + \cdots + z_{\pi(k)}) = k\}$$

is increasing in $x \in \{z : z_i = 0 \text{ of } 1 \text{ for all } i\}$, it follows that ϕ satisfies the conditions of 12.F.1.a, so that

$$E_R\phi(X) = P_R\left\{\max_\pi X_{\pi(1)} + \cdots + X_{\pi(k)} = k\right\}$$

is decreasing and Schur-convex in the vector R. The hazard transform is $\eta_k = -\log E_R \phi(X)$, where
$$E_R\phi(X) = h_k(e^{-R_1}, \ldots, e^{-R_n}).$$
Thus η_k is increasing and Schur-concave. ‖

D.1.a. Proposition (Pledger and Proschan, 1971). If $R \succ^w R^*$, where $R_i = -\log p_i$ and $R_i^* = -\log p_i^*$, then
$$h_k(p) \geq h_k(p^*), \quad k = 1, \ldots, n-1,$$
$$h_n(p) = h_n(p^*).$$

Proof. From D.1, it follows that $\eta_k(R) \leq \eta_k(R^*)$; that is,
$$h_k(e^{-R_1}, \ldots, e^{-R_n}) \geq h_k(e^{-R_1^*}, \ldots, e^{-R_n^*}), \quad k = 1, \ldots, n.$$
That equality holds for $k = n$ is trivial because $\eta_n(R) = \sum_1^n R_i$. ‖

D.1.b. Proposition (Pledger and Proschan, 1971). Denote the "odds ratio" by $r_i = (1 - p_i)/p_i$, $i = 1, \ldots, n$. Then
$$h_k(p_1, \ldots, p_n) = h_k((r_1 + 1)^{-1}, \ldots, (r_n + 1)^{-1})$$
is a decreasing Schur-convex function of r. Hence, $r \succ^w r^*$ implies $h_k(p) \geq h_k(p^*)$, where $r_i^* = (1 - p_i^*)/p_i^*$, $i = 1, \ldots, n$.

Proof. From $r_i = (1 - p_i)/p_i$ and $p_i = e^{-R_i}$, it follows that $R_i = \log(r_i + 1)$. Because $\phi(R_1, \ldots, R_n) = h(e^{-R_1}, \ldots, e^{-R_n})$ is decreasing and Schur-convex on $[0, \infty)^n$ and because $\log(r_i + 1)$ is increasing and concave on $[0, \infty)$, it follows from (vi) of Table 2 of Section 3.B that the composition
$$\phi(\log(r_1 + 1), \ldots, \log(r_n + 1))$$
is decreasing and Schur-convex; i.e., $h_k((r_1 + 1)^{-1}, \ldots, (r_n + 1)^{-1})$ is decreasing and Schur-convex. ‖

When k Components Are Equally Reliable

Park (1988) studies the k-out-of-n system in which k of the components are equally reliable, and $n - k$ units might have different reliabilities. Thus the vector of component reliabilities is of the form
$$p = (p_0, \ldots, p_0, p_1, \ldots, p_{n-k})$$
in which the first k coordinates are equal to p_0.

Suppose that $n - k \geq 2$ and that $0 < p_0 < 1$ is fixed. Park (1988) shows that the reliability function $h(p)$ is a Schur-convex function of $(p_1, \ldots, p_{n-k})$ if $k - 1 \leq (k+1)p_0$ and is Schur-concave if $2k - n \geq (k+1)p_0$.

Optimal Component Allocation in Parallel-Series and Series-Parallel Systems

Consider a parallel-series system consisting of k subsystems connected in parallel where the ith subsystem consists of n_i components connected in series. Assume that $n_1 \leq n_2 \leq n_3 \leq \ldots \leq n_k$ and let $n = \sum_{i=1}^{k} n_i$ denote the total number of components in the system. Suppose that the reliabilities of the components are given by $p_1, p_2, \ldots, p_n$ and that the components function independently. Without loss of generality, assume that $p_1 \geq p_2 \geq \ldots \geq p_n$; i.e., the components are ordered in terms of their reliabilities, with the first component being the most reliable and the nth component, least reliable. Assume that the components are interchangeable in the sense that they can function when placed in any position in the system. The goal is to allocate the components to the subsystems in order to maximize system reliability.

D.2. Theorem (El-Neweihi, Proschan, and Sethuraman, 1986). The reliability of the parallel-series system is maximized by assigning components $1, 2, \ldots, n_1$ to subsystem 1 (i.e., the most reliable components to the smallest series subsystem), components $n_1 + 1, \ldots, n_1 + n_2$ to subsystem 2 (the next-most-reliable components to the second-smallest series subsystem), ... ,the n_k least reliable components to the largest series subsystem.

Proof. Denote the subsystems by $S_1, \ldots, S_k$. The reliability of a particular assignment of components is

$$1 - \prod_{j=1}^{k} \left(1 - \prod_{i \in S_j} p_i\right),$$

where $i \in S_j$ if component i has been assigned to subsystem j. Define $x_i = -\log p_i$ (the hazard of component i) and for each subsystem S_j define $y_j = \sum_{i \in S_j} x_i$ (the hazard of subsystem j). Let $y = (y_1, \ldots, y_k)$ denote the vector of subsystem hazards. The reliability of the system, expressed as a function of y, is $g(y) = 1 - \prod_{j=1}^{k}(1 - e^{-y_j})$. By Proposition 3.E.1, $g(y)$ is Schur-convex in y. Denote the vector of subsystem hazards corresponding to the allocation discussed in the statement of the theorem by y^*, and let y denote the corresponding vector associated with any other allocation of components to subsystems; it can be verified that $y \prec y^*$. The Schur-convexity of g, as a function of x, then guarantees that the allocation associated with y^* yields the maximal system reliability. ||

This optimal allocation might be surmised without any computation, but a rigorous proof is not as transparent. But for a series-parallel system, no obvious optimal allocation comes to mind for good reason. It is not difficult in the spirit of Theorem D.2 to identify the allocation that leads to minimal system reliability. Unfortunately, the optimal allocation to maximize the reliability depends on the individual reliabilities $p_1, p_2, \ldots, p_n$ and not just their ordering. It is possible to compare allocations using majorization, but identification of the optimal allocation can be recast as an integer linear programming problem [see El-Neweihi, Proschan, and Sethuraman (1986) for more details].

An allocation of the type described in D.2 in which the best parts are assigned to one subsystem, the next-best parts go to a second subsystem, etc. can be called a *monotone allocation*. El-Neweihi, Proschan, and Sethuraman (1987) show that such monotone allocations are optimal in more general k-out-of-n systems. Subsequently, Du and Hwang (1990) verified the optimality of monotone allocations in s-stage k-out-of-n systems. For $s \geq 2$, an s-stage k-out-of-n system is a k-out-of-n system whose ith component is itself an $(s-1)$-stage k_i-out-of-n_i system.

It is, of course, reasonable to assume that the reliability of a component in one of these systems depends not only on the component but also on its operating environment, i.e., the subsystem in which it is placed. Denote by p_{ij} the reliability of component i when it is placed in subsystem j, perhaps for simplicity assuming that a multiplicative representation such as $p_{ij} = a_i b_j$ is possible. Rajendra Prasad, Nair, and Aneja (1991) study a more general version in which the reliability of component i depends on the precise position within a subsystem to which it is allocated. They describe an algorithm to be used in the parallel-series setting and also discuss a special case of the problem in the series-parallel setting. Revyakov (1993) studies series-parallel settings in which component reliability depends on the subsystem to which the component is allocated; i.e., $p_{ij} = a_i b_j$. He discusses series-parallel systems in which $n_j = n_0$ for every j, and series-parallel systems in which $a_i = a$ for all i (i.e., an interchangeable setting in which the reliability only depends on the system to which a component is assigned).

Allocation of Standbys in Series or Parallel Systems

Suppose the life lengths $X_1, \ldots, X_n$ of n units have a symmetric joint density $f(x)$ with support in $\mathscr{R}_+^n$. The n units are to be allocated to $k(< n)$ subsystems which are to be connected in parallel or in series. Let $r = (r_1, \ldots, r_k)$, with $\sum_1^k r_i = n$, denote a typical allocation. In subsystem i, one unit is installed and the remaining $r_i - 1$ units are available as standbys. The lifetime of subsystem i is $\sum_{j=1}^{r_i} X_{n_j}$, where $n_1, \ldots, n_{r_i}$ identify the units assigned to subsystem i. Without loss of generality, units $1, 2, \ldots, r_1$ are assigned to subsystem 1, units $r_1 + 1, r_1 + 2, \ldots, r_1 + r_2$ are assigned to subsystem 2, etc. Thus the lifetimes of the subsystems are

$$Y_1^{(r)} = \sum_{i=1}^{r} X_i, \quad Y_2^{(r)} = \sum_{i=r_1+1}^{r_1+r_2} X_i, \quad \ldots, \quad Y_k^{(r)} = \sum_{i=r_1+r_2+\ldots+r_{k-1}+1}^{n} X_i.$$

Boland, Proschan, and Tong (1990) show that if $\phi(y)$ is a permutation-invariant concave function, then

$$E\phi(Y_1^{(r)}, \ldots, Y_k^{(r)})$$

is a Schur-convex function of r, provided that the expectation exists.

As an application of this, it follows that if the subsystems are connected in series, the units should be divided among the subsystems as equally as possible, i.e., with $|r_i - r_j| \leq 1$ for all i, j. If the subsystems are connected in parallel, the best allocation puts $r - k + 1$ units in subsystem 1 and one unit in every other subsystem.

Stochastic Ordering of Normalized Spacings

Suppose that $X_1, \ldots, X_n$ are exchangeable positive random variables. The normalized spacings

$$D_k = (n - k + 1)(X_{(k)} - X_{(k-1)}), \quad k = 1, 2, \ldots, n$$

play a key role in certain reliability contexts (they are intimately related to the empirical total time on test transform). Ebrahimi and Spizzichino (1997) show that if X has a Schur-concave (convex) density, then $D_k \geq^{\text{st}} (\leq^{\text{st}}) D_{k+1}$.

Operation of Repairable Machines

Suppose that for $i = 1, \ldots, n$, machine i alternates between the states "operating" and "undergoing repair." Upon entering the operating state, the machine remains there for a random length of time having distribution F_i; repair times have distribution G_i. All periods are mutually independent. Let $\{N(t), t \geq 0\}$ be the number of machines operating at time t. Similarly, let F_i^*, G_i^*, and $\{N^*(t), t \geq 0\}$ be corresponding quantities for another set of n machines.

D.3. Proposition (Pledger and Proschan, 1973). Assume that either $N(0) = N^*(0) = n$ or that $N(0) = N^*(0) = 0$.

(a) For all $t \geq 0$, suppose that

$$F_i(t) = 1 - e^{-\lambda_i t}, \qquad F_i^*(t) = 1 - e^{-\lambda_i^* t}, \qquad i = 1, \ldots, n,$$

$$G_1(t) = \cdots = G_n(t) = G_1^*(t) = \cdots = G_n^*(t) = 1 - e^{-\rho t}$$

(where λ_i, λ_i^*, ρ are positive). If $(\lambda_1, \ldots, \lambda_n) \prec (\lambda_1^*, \ldots, \lambda_n^*)$, then for all $t \geq 0$, $N(t) \leq^{\text{st}} N^*(t)$, where $\leq^{\text{st}}$ denotes stochastic order (see Section 17.A).

(b) For all $t \geq 0$, suppose that

$$F_1(t) = \cdots = F_n(t) = F_1^*(t) = \cdots = F_n^*(t) = 1 - e^{-\lambda t},$$

$$G_i(t) = 1 - e^{-\rho_i t}, \qquad G_i^*(t) = 1 - e^{-\rho_i^*(t)}, \qquad i = 1, \ldots, n$$

(again, ρ_i, ρ_i^*, λ are positive). If $(\rho_1, \ldots, \rho_n) \prec (\rho_1^*, \ldots, \rho_n^*)$, then for all $t \geq 0$, $N(t) \geq^{\text{st}} N^*(t)$.

The proof of these results is not given here.

Positive Dependence of a Class of Multivariate Exponential Distributions

As a starting point, suppose that $U_1, \ldots, U_n$, $V_1, \ldots, V_n$, and W are independent exponential random variables with respective parameters λ_1 (for the U_j's), λ_2 (for the V_j's), and λ_0 (for W). Let $k = (k_1, \ldots, k_n)$ be a vector of nonnegative integers with

$$\sum k_i = n, \qquad k_1 \geq \cdots \geq k_r \geq 1, \qquad k_{r+1} = \cdots = k_n = 0, \qquad (1)$$

for some $r \leq n$. Further, define $X = (X_1, \ldots, X_n)$ by

$$X_j = \begin{cases} \min(U_j, V_1, W), & j = 1, \ldots, k_1, \\ \min(U_j, V_2, W), & j = k_1 + 1, \ldots, k_1 + k_2, \\ \quad \vdots & \quad \vdots \\ \min(U_j, V_r, W), & j = \Sigma_1^{r-1} k_i + 1, \ldots, n. \end{cases}$$

The random vector X thus defined has a multivariate exponential distribution [see Marshall and Olkin (1967)].

D.4. Proposition (Olkin and Tong, 1994). If $k = (k_1, \ldots, k_n)$ and $k' = (k'_1, \ldots, k'_n)$ satisfy (1), and $k \succ k'$, then

$$P_k\{X_1 > t, \ldots, X_n > t\} \geq P_{k'}\{X_1 > t, \ldots, X_n > t\}.$$

D.4.a Let n and $k = (k_1, \ldots, k_n)$ be fixed, with k satisfying (1). If $(\lambda_1, \lambda_2, \lambda_0) \prec (\lambda'_1, \lambda'_2, \lambda'_0)$, then

$$P_\lambda\{X_1 \geq x_1, \ldots, X_n \geq x_n\} \geq P_{\lambda'}\{X_1 \geq x_1, \ldots, X_n \geq x_n\}.$$

In particular, these results are applicable to various parallel-series systems.

Additional Appearances of Majorization in the Context of Reliability

Use of majorization in reliability is also made by El-Neweihi, Proschan, and Sethuraman (1978), Proschan (1975), and Proschan and Sethuraman (1976). The work of Derman, Lieberman, and Ross (1972) is also suggestive of majorization. Boland and El-Neweihi (1998) present a majorization result in the context of minimal repair of two-component parallel systems with exponential components.

E Entropy

The entropy, $H(\xi_1, \ldots, \xi_r) = -\sum_{k=1}^{r} \xi_k \log \xi_k$, of a probability mass function $\xi_k \geq 0$, $k = 1, \ldots, r$, $\sum_k \xi_k = 1$, provides a measure of the degree of uniformness of the distribution. That is, the larger $H(\xi_1, \ldots, \xi_r)$ is, the more uniform the distribution is. In 3.D.1 it is shown that

$$H(1, 0, \ldots, 0) \leq H(\xi_1, \ldots, \xi_r) \leq H(1/r, \ldots, 1/r),$$

and indeed, that $H(\xi)$ is Schur-concave in ξ.

For some probability mass functions, each $\xi_k = \xi_k(\theta_1, \ldots, \theta_m)$ is a function of $\theta_1, \ldots, \theta_m$, in which case write

$$\widetilde{H}(\theta_1, \ldots, \theta_m) \equiv H(\xi_1, \ldots, \xi_r).$$

If each ξ_k is a decreasing Schur-convex function or an increasing Schur-concave function of $\theta_1, \ldots, \theta_m$, then $\widetilde{H}(\theta_1, \ldots, \theta_m)$ is Schur-concave (Table 1, Section 3.B). However, $\widetilde{H}$ can still be Schur-concave even though ξ_k is not Schur-convex or Schur-concave. This is the case in the two examples E.1 and E.2.

These results are obtained by Mateev (1978) and Shepp and Olkin (1978, 1981); the present development follows the latter paper.

Entropy of the Distribution of the Sum of Independent Bernoulli Random Variables

E.1. Proposition (Shepp and Olkin, 1978, 1981). Let $X_1, \ldots, X_n$ be independent Bernoulli random variables with

$$P\{X_i = 1\} = \theta_i, \qquad P\{X_i = 0\} = \overline{\theta}_i, \qquad i = 1, \ldots, n, \qquad (1)$$

and

$$\xi_k^n \equiv \xi_k(\theta_1, \ldots, \theta_n) = P\{X_1 + \cdots + X_n = k\}, \qquad k = 0, 1, \ldots, n. \quad (2)$$

The entropy $\widetilde{H}(\theta_1, \ldots, \theta_n)$ of the distribution of the sum $X_1 + \cdots + X_n$ is a Schur-concave function.

Proof. For $k = 0, 1, \ldots, n$, define

$$\xi_k^n \equiv \xi_k^n(\theta_1, \ldots, \theta_n) = P\{X_1 + \cdots + X_n = k \mid \theta_1, \ldots, \theta_n\},$$
$$\xi_k^{n-2} \equiv \xi_k^{n-2}(\theta_3, \ldots, \theta_n) = P\{X_3 + \cdots + X_n = k \mid \theta_3, \ldots, \theta_n\}.$$

By a conditioning argument,

$$\xi_k^n = \theta_1 \theta_2 \xi_k^{n-2} + (\theta_1 \overline{\theta}_2 + \overline{\theta}_1 \theta_2) \xi_{k-1}^{n-2} + \overline{\theta}_1 \overline{\theta}_2 \xi_{k-2}^{n-2},$$

where $\overline{\theta}_i = 1 - \theta_i$, so that

$$\frac{\partial \xi_k^n}{\partial \theta_1} - \frac{\partial \xi_k^n}{\partial \theta_2} = -(\theta_1 - \theta_2)(\xi_k^{n-2} - 2\xi_{k-1}^{n-2} + \xi_{k-2}^{n-2}), \qquad (3)$$

$$\frac{\partial \widetilde{H}}{\partial \theta_1} - \frac{\partial \widetilde{H}}{\partial \theta_2} = (\theta_1 - \theta_2) \sum_k (1 + \log \xi_k^n)(\xi_k^{n-2} - 2\xi_{k-1}^{n-2} + \xi_{k-2}^{n-2}). \qquad (4)$$

After summing (4), using a change in the index of summation, (4) becomes

$$\frac{\partial \widetilde{H}}{\partial \theta_1} - \frac{\partial \widetilde{H}}{\partial \theta_2} = (\theta_1 - \theta_2) \sum_k \xi_k^{n-2} \log \frac{\xi_k^n \xi_{k-2}^n}{(\xi_{k-1}^n)^2}, \qquad (5)$$

where the sum is over those k for which the argument of the logarithm is finite and nonzero.

558   13. Additional Statistical Applications

The proof is completed by noting that
$$\xi_k^n \, \xi_{k-2}^n \le (\xi_{k-1}^n)^2$$
is equivalent to the fact that the convolution of Bernoulli random variables is PF_2 (see 18.B). ||

Entropy of the Multinomial Distribution

E.2. Proposition (Mateev, 1978; Shepp and Olkin, 1978, 1981). Let $X_1, \ldots, X_m$ have the multinomial distribution
$$\xi_x^n \equiv \xi_x^n(\theta_1, \ldots, \theta_m) = P\{X_1 = x_1, \ldots, X_m = x_m\}$$
$$= \binom{n}{x_1, \ldots, x_m} \theta_1^{x_1} \cdots \theta_m^{x_m}, \quad \sum_1^m \theta_i = 1, \quad \sum x_i = n, \quad (6)$$
where $x = (x_1, \ldots, x_m)$. Now $H(\xi) = -\sum_x \xi_x \log \xi_x$, where the sum is over all configurations x with $\sum_1^m x_i = n$. Then the entropy $\widetilde{H}(\theta_1, \ldots, \theta_m)$ is symmetric and concave on the simplex $0 \le \theta_i$, $i = 1, \ldots, m$, $\sum_1^m \theta_i = 1$.

Proof. A direct computation yields
$$\widetilde{H}(\theta_1, \ldots, \theta_m) = -\sum \xi_x^n \log \xi_x^n$$
$$= -\log \Gamma(n+1) + \sum_1^m [-n\theta_i \log \theta_i + E \log \Gamma(X_i + 1)], \quad (7)$$
where each X_i has a binomial distribution with $EX_i = n\theta_i$, $i = 1, \ldots, m$. The essence of the proof lies in showing that each term in the sum on the right-hand side of (7) is concave. This is proved in the following lemma.

E.3. Lemma. If X has a binomial distribution with $EX = np$, then
$$g(p) = -np \log p + E \log \Gamma(X + 1)$$
is a concave function of p.

Proof. Write $q = 1 - p$ and
$$g(p) = -np \log p + \sum_{j=0}^n \binom{n}{j} p^j q^{n-j} \log \Gamma(j+1).$$
Differentiating with respect to p and collapsing terms yields
$$\frac{dg(p)}{dp} = -n - n \log p + n \sum_{\alpha=0}^{n-1} \binom{n-1}{\alpha} p^\alpha q^{n-1-\alpha} \log(\alpha + 1), \quad (8)$$

$$\frac{d^2 g(p)}{dp^2} = -\frac{n}{p} + n(n-1) \sum_{\beta=0}^{n-2} \binom{n-2}{\beta} p^\beta q^{n-2-\beta} \log\left(\frac{\beta+2}{\beta+1}\right). \quad (9)$$

From the fact that $\log(1+u) < u$ for $u > 0$ and

$$\sum_{j=0}^{m} \binom{m}{j} p^j q^{m-j} \frac{1}{j+1} = \frac{1-q^{m+1}}{(m+1)p},$$

(9) becomes

$$\frac{d^2 g(p)}{dp^2} < -\frac{n}{p} + n(n-1) \frac{1-q^{n-1}}{(n-1)p} = -\frac{nq^{n-1}}{p} < 0,$$

which completes the proof of the lemma. ||

F Measuring Inequality and Diversity

The concept of inequality arises in various contexts and there is considerable interest in its measurement. As already discussed in Section 1.A, economists have long been interested in the measurement of inequality of wealth and income. In economics, inequality measurements related to the Lorenz curve and inequality comparisons related to the Lorenz order have been particularly prominent (see Section 17.C.8). In political science and sociology, inequality of voting strength resulting from legislative malapportionment, of tax structure, and even of racial imbalance in schools has been measured using various indices [see Alker (1965)]. The measurement of species diversity in ecology is essentially a problem of measuring equality (Pielou, 1975). See also Rousseau and Van Hecke (1999) for a discussion of measures of biodiversity, and Rao (1984) for a general discussion of measures of diversity. Measurement of income inequality is discussed and surveyed by Sen (1973) and Szal and Robinson (1977). See also Blackorby and Donaldson (1978). For an axiomatic approach to income inequality, see Krämer (1998).

The term "measure of inequality" is ambiguous in the sense that it can refer to an index of inequality or to an estimated value of such an index. Here, the term is used in the former sense, and in spite of the chapter heading, statistical aspects of the problem are not discussed.

The intuitive idea that the components of x are "more nearly equal" than the components of y is translated in Section 1.A to the precise statement that $x \prec y$; indeed, this is done, starting from several points of view.

If one accepts the idea that "$x \prec y$" is the proper way of saying the components of x are "more nearly equal" than the components of y, then care must be exercised in using any measure of inequality. Indeed if ϕ is such a measure and if x and y are incomparable by majorization, then it will still be true that $\phi(x) < \phi(y)$, $\phi(x) > \phi(y)$, or $\phi(x) = \phi(y)$. Each statement can be misleading because each suggests a comparison of noncomparable quantities. For other cautionary comments, see Kondor (1975).

Criteria for Indices of Inequality

The above ideas suggest that if a function ϕ is to be used as a measure of inequality, then it should satisfy

(i) $x \prec y \Rightarrow \phi(x) \leq \phi(y)$;

i.e., ϕ should be Schur-convex. Even more, ϕ should satisfy

(i') $x \prec y$ and x is not a permutation of $y \Rightarrow \phi(x) < \phi(y)$;

i.e., ϕ should be strictly Schur-convex.

These conditions were first formulated by Dalton (1920) although they are hinted at or are implicit in the work of Lorenz (1905) and Pigou (1912). Economists usually refer to (i') as the *Dalton condition, strong Dalton condition,* or *Pigou–Dalton condition.*

If $\phi : \mathscr{R}^n \to \mathscr{R}$ is used as a measure of inequality, then the additional requirement

(ii) $\phi(x) = \phi(ax)$ for all $a > 0$

is sometimes also imposed [see, e.g., Fields and Fei (1978)] to ensure that scale factors play no role. As already noted by Dalton (1920), if ϕ is a proposed measure of inequality, then the function ψ defined for all x such that $\sum x_i \neq 0$ by

$$\psi(x) = \phi\left(x_1 / \sum x_i, \ldots, x_n / \sum x_i\right)$$

satisfies (ii). Moreover, if ϕ satisfies (i) or (i'), then so does ψ.

For measures of equality or species diversity in biology, it is desirable that a maximum be achieved when all arguments are equal, so in (i) and (i'), Schur-concavity should replace Schur-convexity.

Some additional criteria for measures of inequality have been discussed particularly in the context of economics [see, e.g., Sen (1973)],

F. Measuring Inequality and Diversity 561

but no set of criteria is available that will characterize a particular measure. Consequently, a number of measures have been proposed that remain of current interest. Some of these are listed here. Notice that many of these have the form

$$\phi(x) = \sum_1^n g(x_i) \quad \text{or} \quad \phi(x) = \sum_1^n g\left(\frac{x_i}{\sum x_j}\right).$$

In the following, $\bar{x} = (1/n)\sum_1^n x_i$, and $T = \sum_1^n x_i$.

F.1. The variance. The variance

$$\phi_1(x) = \frac{1}{n}\sum_1^n (x_i - \bar{x})^2$$

is a familiar measure of dispersion. It is strictly Schur-convex by 3.C.1.a.

The closely related measures

$$\phi_{1a}(x) = \left[\frac{1}{n}\sum_1^n (\log x_i - \log \bar{x})^2\right]^{1/2},$$

$$\phi_{1b}(x) = \left[\frac{1}{n}\sum \left(\log x_i - \frac{\sum \log x_j}{n}\right)^2\right]^{1/2}$$

have been used in economics to measure inequality [see, e.g., Sen (1973) or Szal and Robinson (1977)]. The measures ϕ_{1a} and ϕ_{1b} are not Schur-convex, as noted by Szal and Robinson (1977) and by Dasgupta, Sen, and Starrett (1973), respectively. Consequently, these are not valid measures [see also Kondor (1975)].

A normalized version of the variance (or rather of its square root) is the *coefficient of variation*

$$\phi_2(x) = [\phi_1(x)]^{1/2}/\bar{x}.$$

This measure is strictly Schur-convex and also satisfies (ii).

F.2. Sums of squares. The measure

$$\phi_3(x) = \sum x_i^2$$

is proposed by Simpson (1949). This measure is strictly Schur-convex by 3.C.1.a. Simpson also suggests the modification:

$$\phi_4(x) = \frac{\sum x_i(x_i - 1)}{T(T-1)} = \frac{\sum x_i^2 - T}{T(T-1)}.$$

Both ϕ_3 and ϕ_4 are strictly Schur-convex. To measure species diversity or equality, a Schur-concave function is desired. Modifications to this end are

$$\phi_5 = 1/\phi_4,$$

suggested by Emlen (1973), and

$$\phi_6 = 1 - \phi_4,$$

which is often called *Simpson's measure of diversity* in biological literature.

Yet another version is the measure of McIntosh (1967),

$$\phi_7(x) = \frac{T - (\sum x_i^2)^{1/2}}{T - T^{1/2}},$$

which is strictly Schur-concave.

When $(x_1, \ldots, x_n)$ denote multinomial probabilities, $0 \leq x_i, \Sigma x_i = 1$, then

$$\sum x_i(1 - x_i) = 1 - \sum x_i^2$$

has been used as a measure of diversity [see Weaver (1948)].

F.3. Entropy. A commonly used measure of equality is the entropy function

$$\phi_8(x) = -\sum_1^n x_i \log x_i, \quad x_i > 0, \quad \sum x_i = 1,$$

which is strictly Schur-concave (3.D.1). A related measure, obtained from this by substituting $e^{-x_i/T}$ for x_i, is suggested by Emlen (1973):

$$\phi_9(x) = \sum_1^n \frac{x_i}{T} e^{-x_i/T}.$$

This is also strictly Schur-concave, and so is a measure of equality.

F.3.a. Measures of diversity related to ϕ_8 are

$$\phi_{8a}(x) = \frac{1 - \Sigma x_i^\alpha}{\alpha - 1}, \quad \alpha > 0, \ \alpha \neq 1,$$

due to Havrda and Charvát (1967), and

$$\phi_{8b}(x) = \frac{\log \Sigma x_i^\alpha}{1 - \alpha}, \quad \alpha > 0, \ \alpha \neq 1,$$

due to Rényi (1961). Both ϕ_{8a} and ϕ_{8b} are Schur-concave.

F.3.b. In a discrete setting, where $x_1, \ldots, x_n$ are integers (say for the problem of measuring species diversity), the measure

$$\phi_{10}(x) = \frac{1}{T} \log \binom{T}{x_1, \ldots, x_n}$$

has been proposed by Brillouin (1962) and by Margalef (1958) [see, e.g., Pielou (1975)]. It can be shown that for large $x_1, \ldots, x_n$,

$$\phi_{10}(x) \approx \phi_8(x_1/T, \ldots, x_n/T),$$

so this measure is closely related to entropy. This measure is not Schur-concave.

Examples Related to the Lorenz Curve

F.4. The Lorenz curve. The Lorenz curve, described in Section 1.A and discussed in more detail and generality in Chapter 17, suggests several possible measures of inequality.

F.4.a. Gini coefficient. The measure of inequality proposed by Gini (1912) is twice the shaded area of Fig. 1, i.e., twice the area between the Lorenz curve and the 45° line. The Gini coefficient (also known as the *Gini index*) can be written in several ways:

$$\phi_{11}(x) = \frac{1}{2n^2\bar{x}} \sum_{i=1}^{n} \sum_{j=1}^{n} |x_i - x_j| = 1 - \frac{1}{n^2\bar{x}} \sum_{i=1}^{n} \sum_{j=1}^{n} \min(x_i, x_j)$$

$$= 1 + \frac{1}{n} - \frac{2}{n^2\bar{x}} \sum_{i=1}^{n} i x_{[i]}.$$

This measure is strictly Schur-convex, as was already proved by Dalton (1920). One way to show this is with the first or second form above using the idea of "transfers" or "T-transforms." Alternatively, Schur-convexity can be demonstrated using the third form and 3.H.2.b.

Solomon (1978) proposes a linear function of ϕ_{11} as a diversity index in a biological context.

F.4.b. Gini mean difference. The unnormalized version of the Gini coefficient

$$\phi_{11a}(x) = \frac{1}{n^2} \sum_i \sum_j |x_i - x_j|$$

is known as the *Gini mean difference*. It is a direct competitor of the variance as a strictly Schur-convex measure of dispersion. It has a long history. Prior to being "rediscovered" by Gini, it was discussed

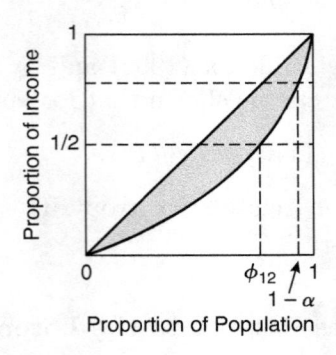

Figure 1. The Lorenz curve.

by Helmert (1876) and other German writers in the 1870s. A history of the Gini mean difference is provided by David (1968).

For an extensive general discussion of the Gini mean difference, see, e.g., Yitzhaki (2003). A survey of bounds for the Gini mean difference is given by Cerone and Dragomir (2008).

F.4.c. Minimal majority. In the context of political science [see Alker (1965, p. 39)], the minimal majority is the smallest number of individuals controlling a majority of the legislature. If $x_1, \ldots, x_n$ determine the Lorenz curve h, then the minimal majority is

$$\phi_{12}(x) = h^{-1}(\tfrac{1}{2}).$$

It is not difficult to see that this measure is Schur-convex, but it is not strictly Schur-convex.

F.4.d. Top 100α percent. If $x_1, \ldots, x_n$ determine the Lorenz curve h, then

$$\phi_{13}(x) = h(\alpha)$$

is called the *top 100α percent*. In the context of wealth distribution, this measure represents the total worth of the richest 100α percent of the population. This measure, discussed by Alker and Russett (1966), is Schur-convex but not strictly Schur-convex.

F.4.e. Fishlow poverty measure. With the usual notation $u^+ = \max(u, 0)$, the function

$$\phi_{14}(x) = \sum_{i=1}^{n}(L_p - x_i)^+$$

is the total aggregate income that must be transferred from those above the poverty level L_p to those below in order to bring everyone up to that level. This measure, proposed by Fishlow (1973), is Schur-convex but not strictly Schur-convex.

Another measure of poverty, called the *proportion of the population in relative poverty*, is the number of individuals in the population who receive less than half the median income. By considering transfers, it is not difficult to see that this measure is not Schur-convex. For a general discussion of poverty orderings that includes many references, see, e.g., Foster and Shorrocks (1988).

F.4.f. Schutz coefficient. The function

$$\phi_{15}(x) = \sum_{x_i \geq \bar{x}}\left(\frac{x_i}{\bar{x}} - 1\right) = \frac{\sum_{i=1}^{n}(x_i - \bar{x})^+}{\bar{x}}$$

was proposed by Schutz (1951) as a measure of income inequality. This measure, which represents the total relative excess above the mean, is Schur-convex (3.C.1.a), but it is not strictly Schur-convex because $g(z) \equiv z^+$ is not a strictly convex function. The Schutz coefficient has a geometrical representation in terms of the slopes of the Lorenz curve.

F.4.g. Let $\bar{x}_+$ and $\bar{x}_-$ denote, respectively, the means of all incomes more than $\bar{x}$ and less than $\bar{x}$. Éltető and Frigyes (1968) discuss three indices:

$$\phi_{16}(x) = \bar{x}/\bar{x}_+,$$
$$\phi_{17}(x) = \bar{x}_-/\bar{x}_+,$$
$$\phi_{18}(x) = \bar{x}_-/\bar{x}.$$

These measures are Schur-convex, but not strictly Schur-convex, as can be seen by considering transfers.

F.4.h. The length of the Lorenz curve can also be used as a measure of inequality (Amato, 1968; Kakwani, 1980).

Measures Based on Utility

F.5. Utility. Various arguments have led economists to consider $\sum_{1}^{n} U(x_i)$ as a measure of equality, where ordinarily U is a concave utility function. Such functions are Schur-concave and strictly Schur-concave if U is strictly concave (3.C.1, 3.C.1.a). Certain normalizing methods have been proposed.

F.5.a. Dalton's measure. This measure of equality is defined as

$$\phi_{19}(x) = \sum_1^n U(x_i)/nU(\bar{x}).$$

See Dalton (1925) and Sen (1973).

F.5.b. Atkinson's measures. A general measure of inequality is defined as

$$\phi_{20}(x) = 1 - \frac{1}{\bar{x}} \sum_1^n U(x_i).$$

See Atkinson (1970).

A family of closely related income inequality measures was introduced in Atkinson (1975, p. 48). The measures are indexed by a distributional parameter $a \in (0, \infty)$ and are of the form

$$\phi_{21}^{(a)} = 1 - \frac{1}{\bar{x}} \left[\frac{1}{n} \sum_1^n x_i^{1-a} \right]^{1/(1-a)}.$$

Atkinson observes that as a increases, more weight is attached to inequality in the lower ranges of income. The choice of a is of importance since it is possible for two vectors x and y and two choices a_1 and a_2 of the distributional parameter a to have $\phi_{21}^{(a_1)}(x) < \phi_{21}^{(a_1)}(y)$ while $\phi_{21}^{(a_2)}(x) > \phi_{21}^{(a_2)}(y)$. Atkinson provides some guidance regarding the appropriate choice of a.

G Schur-Convex Likelihood Functions

If the random vector X has a multinomial distribution with parameters N and $\theta = (\theta_1, \ldots, \theta_k)$, $\theta_i \geq 0$, $\sum \theta_i = 1$, the corresponding likelihood function is given by

$$L(x) = \sup_{\theta} \binom{N}{x_1, \ldots, x_k} \prod_{i=1}^k \theta_i^{x_i} = \binom{N}{x_1, \ldots, x_k} \prod_{i=1}^k \left(\frac{N}{N}\right)^{x_i}.$$

That this function is Schur-convex was noted by Boland and Proschan (1987) as a consequence of 3.E.8.b. They also verify the Schur-convexity of the likelihood function of the multivariate hypergeometric distribution.

H Probability Content of Geometric Regions for Schur-Concave Densities

Suppose that a p-dimensional random variable X has a Schur-concave density f. An important example is the symmetric multivariate normal distribution, for which the means satisfy $\mu_1 = \mu_2 \ldots = \mu_p$ and the variances satisfy $\sigma_{ii} = \sigma^2$ for each i and covariances $\sigma_{ij} = \rho\sigma^2$ for $i \neq j$ [where $-(p-1)^{-1} < \rho < 1$]. In many statistical applications, it is of interest to determine quantities such as $P\{X \in A\}$, where A is a given geometric region in $\mathscr{R}^p$.

For example, if $A(x) = \{y : y \leq x\}$ for $x \in \mathscr{R}^p$, then of course $P\{X \in A(x)\}$ corresponds to the joint distribution function F of X. According to 12.L.1, F inherits the property of Schur-concavity from its density f. For regions of the form

$$B_\infty(x) = \{y : -x \leq y \leq x\}, \quad x > 0,$$

Tong (1982) showed that if the density of X is Schur-concave, then $P\{X \in B_\infty(x)\}$ is a Schur-concave function of x. He also proved that $P\{X \in B_2^\lambda(x)\}$ is a Schur-concave function of $(x_1^2, \ldots, x_p^2)$ for every $\lambda > 0$, where $B_2^\lambda(x) = \{y : \sum_1^p (y_i/x_i)^2 \leq \lambda\}$ represent elliptical regions. Subsequently, Karlin and Rinott (1983) proved the more general result that if X is a nonnegative random variable with a Schur-concave density, then

$$P\left\{\sum_{i=1}^p (X_i^\alpha / y_i^\beta) \leq \lambda\right\}$$

is a Schur-concave function of y on $\mathscr{R}_{++}^p$ for every $\alpha \geq 1$, $0 \leq \beta \leq \alpha - 1$, and every $\lambda > 0$.

Tong (1982) proved that the p-dimensional cube has the highest probability content among all p-dimensional rectangles centered at the origin with fixed perimeter. The proof is a consequence of the Schur-concavity of $P\{X \in B_\infty(x)\}$.

It is possible to generate related inequalities dealing with p-dimensional rectangles that are not centered at the origin. Consider a $2 \times p$ matrix

$$A = \begin{pmatrix} a_{11} & a_{12} & \cdots & a_{1p} \\ a_{21} & a_{22} & \cdots & a_{2p} \end{pmatrix} = \begin{pmatrix} a^{(1)} \\ a^{(2)} \end{pmatrix}$$

with $a_{1j} < a_{2j}, j = 1, \ldots, p$. Define a corresponding rectangle $R(A)$ by

$$R(A) = \{x : a^{(1)} \leq x \leq a^{(2)}\}.$$

For a similarly defined rectangle $R(B)$, if B is less "variable" than A in the sense of being more like a cube, then B should have a higher probability content. The following proposition utilizes chain majorization (15.A.1) to obtain a sufficient condition for such a result.

H.1. Proposition (Karlin and Rinott, 1983; Tong, 1989). If X has a Schur-concave density and if $A \prec\prec B$ (A is chain majorized by B), then $P\{X \in R(A)\} \geq P\{X \in R(B)\}$.

Tong shows by a counterexample that rowwise majorization (15.A.6) between A and B is not sufficient to ensure the conclusion of H.1.

Shaked and Tong (1988) discuss related results when the volume rather than the perimeter of the region is held fixed.

The fact that $P\{X \in B_2^\lambda(x)\}$ as a function of $(x_1^2, \ldots, x_p^2)$ is Schur-concave when X has a Schur-concave density was used by Tong to obtain results related to those in Section 12.L.2 concerning linear combinations of independent χ^2 random variables. Without loss of generality, consider linear combinations of p independent random variables $U_1, U_2, \ldots, U_p$ with a common chi-square distribution with one degree of freedom. Define

$$\Phi_\lambda(a) = P\left\{\sum_{i=1}^p a_i U_i \leq \lambda\right\},$$

where $a_i > 0, i = 1, 2, \ldots, n$, and $\lambda > 0$. Because the joint density of the U_i's is Schur-concave, it follows that if $(\frac{1}{a_1}, \ldots, \frac{1}{a_p}) \prec (\frac{1}{b_1}, \ldots, \frac{1}{b_p})$, then $\Phi_\lambda(a) \geq \Phi_\lambda(b)$ for every $\lambda > 0$. The parallel result that if $\log a \succ \log b$, then $\Phi_\lambda(a) \geq \Phi_\lambda(b)$ for every $\lambda > 0$ is closely related to Proposition 11.E.8.b.

I Optimal Experimental Design

Under the classical linear model, it has long been recognized that certain design configurations are preferable to others when compared using a variety of information measures. A typical statistical model takes the form

$$y = X\beta + \sigma u, \tag{1}$$

where y is the n-dimensional vector of observed yields or responses, and X is an $n \times p$ "design matrix." The p-dimensional vector β is an unknown parameter vector. The error vector u is assumed to have independent components with zero mean and unit variance. The error scaling factor σ in (1) is positive and unknown. Assume further that the corresponding information matrix

$$M = X'X$$

is nonsingular. Denote the class of all designs by $\widetilde{\mathcal{D}}$ and denote by $\mathscr{X} = \{X_d : d \in \widetilde{\mathcal{D}}\}$ the corresponding indexed collection of design matrices. The corresponding class of information matrices is $\{M_d : d \in \widetilde{\mathcal{D}}\}$. For any such information matrix M_d, denote the ordered eigenvalues by

$$\lambda_1 \geq \lambda_2 \geq \ldots \geq \lambda_p$$

and the vector of ordered eigenvalues by λ. A real-valued mapping Φ whose domain is $\{M_d : d \in \widetilde{\mathcal{D}}\}$ is called an *optimality criterion*. For such a function to serve as an information functional, it should be nonnegative, positive homogeneous [i.e., satisfy $\Phi(cx) = c\Phi(x)$, for $c > 0$], and concave. The historically popular optimality criteria introduced by Kiefer (1975) are $D, A,$ and E optimality. Other criteria have been added, but as noted by Pukelsheim (1993, Chapter 6), many of these are special cases of power means of the eigenvalues of the information matrix M_d.

Let

$$\Phi(M_d|r) = \left(\frac{\Sigma \lambda_i^r}{p}\right)^{1/r} = \left(\frac{\operatorname{tr} M_d^r}{p}\right)^{1/r};$$

special cases are

determinant $\qquad \Phi(M_d|0) = |M_d| = \prod \lambda_i,$

mean $\qquad \Phi(M_d|1) = \sum \lambda_i/p,$

harmonic mean $\qquad \Phi(M_d|-1) = \left(\sum \lambda_i^{-1}/p\right)^{-1},$

minimum $\qquad \Phi(M_d|-\infty) = \lambda_p.$

A more general set of criteria is based on

$$\Phi(M_d|r,s) = \left(\frac{\Sigma \lambda_i^r}{p}\right)^{1/s} = \left(\frac{\operatorname{tr} M_d^r}{p}\right)^{1/s};$$

special cases are

$$\Phi(M_d|2,1) = \sum \lambda_i^2/p,$$

$$\Phi(M_d|-r,r) = \left(\sum \lambda_i^{-r}/p\right)^{1/r}, \quad 0 < r < \infty.$$

Of note is the fact that each of these functions is a Schur function.

It is not obvious which of these optimality criteria should be used, or indeed whether some other criterion would be even better.

This has motivated a search for a universal optimality criteria. Typically, invariance [that is, $\varphi(M) = \varphi(GMG')$ for orthogonal G] has been invoked in order to aid in the identification of a suitably universal optimality. Without invariance, the information matrices M_d can be ordered by the Loewner ordering (see Section 16.E). If orthogonal invariance is invoked, as it often is, then the appropriate ordering of information matrices is equivalent to weak supermajorization of the corresponding vector of eigenvalues.

I.1. Definition. A design $d^* \in \widetilde{\mathscr{D}}$ is *universally optimal* in $\mathscr{D}$ if d^* is Φ-optimal in $\mathscr{D}$ for every Φ which is an increasing Schur-concave function of the eigenvalues of M.

I.2. Proposition (Bondar, 1983). A design d^* is universally optimal in $\mathscr{D}$ if and only if

$$\sum_{i=k}^{p} \lambda_i(M_d) \leq \sum_{i=k}^{p} \lambda_i(M_{d^*}), \quad k = 1, 2, \ldots, p,$$

for every $d \in \mathscr{D}$.

For a general discussion of optimal design of experiments, see Pukelsheim (1993, p. 925, Chapter 14) or Pázman (1986). The term "Schur optimality" was introduced by Magda (1980) and is equivalent to universal optimality. A more detailed discussion of universal optimality is given by Druilhet (2004).

J Comparison of Experiments

As a motivating example, consider the problem of allocation of experimental units to blocks in a one-way random-effects model. The n observations are allocated to the blocks in order to compare different n-dimensional random vectors whose distributions depend on a common parameter θ. In this context, the concept of *information ordering* introduced by Blackwell (1951) becomes relevant. A link with majorization was provided by Shaked and Tong (1992a,b). Let $X = (X_1, \ldots, X_n)$ and $Y = (Y_1, \ldots, Y_n)$ be random vectors with respective distribution functions F_θ and G_θ that depend on $\theta \in \Theta \subset \mathscr{R}^k$.

J.1. Definition. The experiment associated with Y is said to be *at least as informative* as the experiment associated with X for θ, denoted $X \leq_I Y$, if for every decision problem involving θ and for every prior distribution on Θ, the expected Bayes risk from F_θ is not less than that from G_θ.

The following useful sufficient condition for information ordering was provided by Lehmann (1959).

J.2. Proposition (Lehmann, 1959). The ordering $X \leq_I Y$ occurs if there exist a function $\psi : \mathscr{R}^{n+r} \to \mathscr{R}^n$ and an r-dimensional random vector Z independent of Y that has a distribution which does not depend on θ, such that X and $\psi(Y, Z)$ have the same distribution.

For example, let X and Y be normal random vectors with mean vectors θ_X, θ_Y and covariance matrices Σ_X, Σ_Y, respectively. If $\Sigma_X > \Sigma_Y$, then X and $Y + Z$ have the same distribution, where Z has a normal distribution with zero means and covariance matrix $\Sigma_X - \Sigma_Y$. Consequently, using Proposition J.2, $X \leq_I Y$.

Another multivariate normal setting in which this ordering is encountered is provided by Shaked and Tong (1990). They consider X, an exchangeable n-dimensional normal random variable with $EX_i = \theta$, $\text{Var}\, X_i = \sigma^2 > 0$, and common correlation ρ_X. Analogously, Y is an exchangeable n-dimensional normal random vector with $EY_i = \theta$, $\text{Var}\, Y_i = \sigma^2$, and common correlation ρ_Y. It follows that if $\rho_Y \leq \rho_X$, then $X \leq_I Y$. Note that this result does not follow from the above because the difference of two correlation matrices is not positive definite.

A related result is that if $X(n) = (X_1, \ldots, X_n)$ is normally distributed with $EX_i = 0$ for all i, $\text{Var}\, X_i = \sigma^2 > 0$ for all i, and $\text{corr}(X_i, X_j) = \rho$ for all $i \neq j$, then $X(n-1) \leq_I X(n)$; that is, $X(n)$ becomes more informative as n increases.

Shaked and Tong (1992a) also study cases in which the coordinates of the normal random vector X have a common mean but are not exchangeable. Assume that the coordinate random variables of X form

r groups of sizes $k_1, k_2, \ldots, k_r$. The correlation between two variables in the same group is ρ_2, whereas the correlation between variables in different groups is the smaller quantity ρ_1. Such correlation matrices arise in certain genetic modeling settings. The corresponding correlation matrix is denoted by $R(k)$, where $k = (k_1, \ldots, k_r)$.

Denote by $X(k)$ an n-dimensional normal random vector with mean vector $(\theta, \theta, \ldots, \theta)$ and covariance matrix $\sigma^2 R(k)$. The following proposition shows how different choices of k lead to more or less informative $X(k)$'s.

J.3. Proposition (Shaked and Tong, 1992a). Suppose that $X(k)$ and $X(k^*)$ are two n-dimensional normal random vectors with mean vector $(\theta, \ldots, \theta)$ and covariance matrices $\sigma^2 R(k)$ and $\sigma^2 R(k^*)$, respectively, as described above. Assume that $\theta \in \mathscr{R}$ is unknown, $\sigma^2 > 0$ is known, and $0 \leq \rho_1 < \rho_2 < 1$ are fixed but arbitrary. If $k \prec k^*$, then $X(k) \leq_I X(k^*)$.

See also Stepniak (1989) for an alternative proof of Proposition J.3.

A related result due to Eaton (1991) deals with the case in which the vector k above is fixed but the correlations ρ_1 and ρ_2 are allowed to vary. To indicate the dependence of $R(k)$ on ρ_1 and ρ_2, write $R_{\rho_1, \rho_2}(k)$ for $R(k)$. Let $X_{\rho_1, \rho_2}(k)$ denote a p-dimensional normal random vector with mean $(\theta, \ldots, \theta)$ and covariance $\sigma^2 R_{\rho_1, \rho_2}(k)$. If θ is unknown and $\sigma^2 > 0$ is known, it can be verified that

(i) if $\rho_2 = \rho_2' \geq \rho_1 \geq \rho_1'$, then $X_{\rho_1, \rho_2}(k) \leq_I X_{\rho_1', \rho_2'}(k)$;

(ii) if $\rho_2 \geq \rho_2' \geq \rho_1 = \rho_1'$, then $X_{\rho_1, \rho_2}(k) \leq_I X_{\rho_1', \rho_2'}(k)$.

Shaked and Tong (1992a) and Eaton (1991) warn against the appealing conclusion that decreasing the correlations between normal variables with identical marginal distributions necessarily leads to more information. Some additional structural assumptions on the correlation matrices are needed for such a conclusion. Eaton (1992) provides a relevant counterexample.

More complex hierarchical structures can be considered. For example, suppose that random variables $X_1, \ldots, X_n$ have identical normal marginal distributions with mean θ and variance σ^2, and have a correlation structure as follows. There are r groups of the X_i's. The jth group consists of s_j subgroups, $j = 1, 2, \ldots, r$. The correlation between X_i's is ρ_3 if they are in the same subgroup, ρ_2 if they are in the same group but different subgroups, and ρ_1 otherwise, where $0 \leq \rho_1 \leq \rho_2 \leq \rho_3 \leq 1$. In this setting (and related more complex settings), the information in X is shown by Hauke and Markiewicz (1994) to respect a group majorization ordering (14.C).

A useful tool in such discussions is the following

J.4. Proposition (Torgersen, 1984). If X and Y are normal vectors with a common unknown mean vector $(\theta, \ldots, \theta)$ and respective covariance matrices $\Sigma_X = \sigma^2 R_X, \Sigma_Y = \sigma^2 R_Y$, where R_X and R_Y are known positive definite correlation matrices and σ^2 is unknown, then $X \leq_I Y$ if and only if $e R_X^{-1} e' \leq e R_Y^{-1} e'$.

Zhang, Fang, Li, and Sudjianto (2005) recommend the use of majorization in the selection of balanced lattice designs. Consider experiments involving s factors each having q levels. A lattice design with n runs is associated with a set of n points chosen from the lattice space $\mathcal{L}(q^s) = \{0, 1, \ldots, q-1\}^s$. Coordinates of $\mathcal{L}(q^s)$ correspond to factors. The design is balanced if every one of the q levels occurs equally often for each factor. The set of balanced lattice designs is denoted by $\mathcal{U}(n, q^s)$. Zhang, Fang, Li, and Sudjianto (2005) address the problem of selecting a design from a given subclass $\mathcal{D}(n, q^s) \subset \mathcal{U}(n, q^s)$. They argue for the use of a majorization condition based on pairwise coincidence vectors defined as follows. For $x, y \in \mathcal{L}(q^s)$, define the coincidence number $\beta(x, y) = \sum_{j=1}^{s} \delta_{x_j, y_j}$, where $\delta_{i,j}$ is the Kronecker delta function. A lattice design can be associated with a matrix X of dimension $n \times s$ with rows $x_1, x_2, \ldots, x_n$ which are members of $\mathcal{L}(q^s)$. The *pairwise coincidence* (PC) vector of a design X, denoted by $\beta(X)$, is a vector of dimension $m = n(n-1)/2$ whose coordinates are the $\beta(x_i, x_k)$'s (where $1 \leq i < k \leq n$). The jth coordinate of $\beta(X)$ is denoted by $\beta_j(X)$. A design X is said to be *inadmissible* if there exists Y with $\beta(Y) \prec \beta(X)$ and $\beta(Y)$ is not a permutation of $\beta(X)$.

A random variable X is said to be a *majorant* in the class $\mathcal{D}$ if $\beta(X) \prec \beta(Y)$ for every Y in $\mathcal{D}$. If such a majorant design exists, it can be recommended for use. If not, then a Schur-ψ-optimality condition can be used, where ψ is a convex function called a *kernel*. X is said to be *Schur-ψ-optimal* in the class $\mathcal{D}$ if $\Psi(X) \leq \Psi(Y)$ for all $Y \in \mathcal{D}$, where

$$\Psi(X) = \sum_{r=1}^{m} \psi(\beta_r(X)). \tag{1}$$

13. Additional Statistical Applications

Particular choices of the kernel ψ in (1) can be shown to yield preference orderings classically used in the comparison of designs. This justifies the argument in favor of ordering in terms of majorization of the PC-vectors, because such majorization guarantees preference with respect to all kernels. For further details, refer to Zhang, Fang, Li, and Sudjianto (2005).

Part IV

Generalizations

14
Orderings Extending Majorization

Majorization can be defined in several ways, each of which suggests generalizations as well as related orderings of $\mathscr{R}^n$. Here are three general approaches:

(i) $x \prec y$ if $x = yD$ for some doubly stochastic matrix D. This relation is a preorder because the set of $n \times n$ doubly stochastic matrices contains the identity and is closed under multiplication. A preorder is obtained if the doubly stochastic matrices are replaced by another semigroup of matrices with identity. Well-known examples are discussed in detail in Sections A and B; a more general examination is given in Section C.

(ii) On the set $\mathscr{D}$, $x \prec y$ if $y - x \in \mathscr{C}$, where $\mathscr{C} \subset \mathscr{R}^n$ is the convex cone

$$\mathscr{C} = \left\{ z : \sum_1^k z_i \geq 0,\ k = 1, \ldots, n-1,\ \sum_1^n z_i = 0 \right\}.$$

With $\mathscr{C}$ replaced by other convex cones, various preorders can be obtained, as described in Section D.

(iii) Several sets Φ of real-valued functions ϕ defined on $\mathscr{R}^n$ are known with the property that

$$x \prec y \text{ if and only if } \phi(x) \leq \phi(y) \text{ for all } \phi \in \Phi.$$

This very general approach is discussed in Section E.

Just as majorization can be defined by any of the approaches (i), (ii), and (iii), other orderings can be obtained in more than one way. Thus, the examples of Sections C, D, and E exhibit a fair amount of overlap, but each section offers a different approach.

Finally, some additional orderings are discussed in Sections F, G, and H.

A Majorization with Weights

The definition of majorization provided by Hardy, Littlewood, and Pólya (1934, 1952) involving the condition

$$\sum_1^n g(x_i) \leq \sum_1^n g(y_i)$$

for all continuous convex functions $g : \mathscr{R} \to \mathscr{R}$ permits the introduction of weights.

A rather general extension is the condition

$$\sum p_i \, g\left(\frac{x_i}{u_i}\right) \leq \sum q_i \, g\left(\frac{y_i}{v_i}\right)$$

for all continuous convex functions $g : \mathscr{R} \to \mathscr{R}$.

This equation has not been studied in its complete generality. The case $u_i = v_i = 1$ was studied already by Blackwell (1951, 1953). The case $p_i = q_i$, $u_i = v_i = 1$ leads to what is called *p-majorization*. The case $p_i = u_i, q_i = v_i$ has been studied by Ruch, Schranner, and Seligman (1978), with particular attention to the continuous version. The case $p_i = q_i, u_i = v_i$ leads to another majorization, which has not been studied to our knowledge.

p-Majorization

Majorization is defined in 4.B.1 by the condition

$$\sum_1^n g(x_i) \leq \sum_1^n g(y_i) \tag{1}$$

for all continuous convex functions $g : \mathscr{R} \to \mathscr{R}$.

A. Majorization with Weights

This raises the question: What corresponds to majorization if the sums are replaced by weighted averages? Because $x \prec y$ if and only if there exists a doubly stochastic matrix P such that $x = yP$, an answer to this question is given by the following proposition.

A.1. Proposition (Blackwell, 1951, 1953). Let $p = (p_1, \ldots, p_n)$ and $q = (q_1, \ldots, q_m)$ be fixed vectors with nonnegative components such that $\sum_1^n p_i = \sum_1^m q_j = 1$. For $x \in \mathscr{R}^n$, $y \in \mathscr{R}^m$,

$$\sum_1^n p_i g(x_i) \leq \sum_1^m q_i g(y_i) \tag{2}$$
for all continuous convex functions $g: \mathscr{R} \to \mathscr{R}$

if and only if there exists an $m \times n$ matrix $A = (a_{ij})$ with the properties

(i) $a_{ij} \geq 0$ for all i, j,

(ii) $eA = e$ [recall that $e = (1, \ldots, 1)$],

(iii) $Ap' = q'$,

such that $x = yA$.

Of course, when $m = n$ and $p_i = q_i = 1/n$, $i = 1, \ldots, n$, then conditions (i), (ii), and (iii) are just the conditions that A be doubly stochastic.

Proposition A.1 is due to Blackwell (1951, 1953) in the sense that it follows quite directly from his more general results [see, e.g., Kemperman (1975, p. 114)].

There is an intermediate specialization of some interest: $m = n$ and $p = q$. As above, regard p as fixed, with nonnegative components that sum to 1.

A.1.a. Corollary. For $x, y \in \mathscr{R}^n$ and $p_i \geq 0$, $i = 1, \ldots, n$,

$$\sum_1^n p_i g(x_i) \leq \sum_1^n p_i g(y_i) \tag{3}$$
for all continuous convex functions $g: \mathscr{R} \to \mathscr{R}$

if and only if there exists an $n \times n$ matrix $A = (a_{ij})$ with the properties

(i) $a_{ij} \geq 0$ for all i, j,

(ii) $eA = e$,

(iii) $Ap' = p'$

such that $x = yA$.

580   14. Orderings Extending Majorization

For fixed p, a natural analog of majorization is obtained by defining x to be less than or equal to y if (3) holds. Can the partial sums conditions of 1.A.1 for majorization be extended to yield an equivalent definition of this new ordering? At least under some conditions, described below, the answer to this question is "yes."

For any permutation π, write $x \in \mathscr{D}^{\pi}$ to mean $x_{\pi_1} \geq \cdots \geq x_{\pi_n}$. When π is the identity permutation, $\mathscr{D}^{\pi} = \mathscr{D}$.

A.2. Definition. For arbitrary real numbers $p_1, \ldots, p_n$, x is said to be *p-majorized* by y on $\mathscr{D}^{\pi}$, written $x \prec_p y$ on $\mathscr{D}^{\pi}$, if

$$\sum_{1}^{k} p_{\pi_i} x_{\pi_i} \leq \sum_{1}^{k} p_{\pi_i} y_{\pi_i}, \quad k = 1, \ldots, n-1, \tag{4}$$

$$\sum_{1}^{n} p_{\pi_i} x_{\pi_i} = \sum_{1}^{n} p_{\pi_i} y_{\pi_i} \quad \left(\text{i.e.,} \sum_{1}^{n} p_i x_i = \sum_{1}^{n} p_i y_i\right). \tag{5}$$

The term "p-majorized" is due to Cheng (1977). To be ordered by p-majorization, x and y must be similarly ordered.

A.3. Proposition (Fuchs, 1947). *If $p_1, \ldots, p_n$ are arbitrary real numbers and $x \prec_p y$ on $\mathscr{D}^{\pi}$ for some permutation π, then (3) holds. If g is strictly convex, then strict inequality holds in (3).*

Proof. Suppose $x, y \in \mathscr{D}$ (otherwise, relabel the components). Let $A_0 = B_0 = 0$, $A_k = \sum_1^k p_i x_i$, $B_k = \sum_1^k p_i y_i$, $k = 1, \ldots, n$. If $x_k \neq y_k$, let $Q_k = [g(x_k) - g(y_k)]/[x_k - y_k]$; if $x_k = y_k$, let Q_k be the right-hand derivative of g at x_k. Because g is convex, Q_k is decreasing in $k = 1, \ldots, n$. Thus

$$\sum_{k=1}^{n-1}(A_k - B_k)(Q_k - Q_{k+1}) + (A_n - B_n)Q_n \leq 0.$$

This inequality can be rewritten in the form

$$\sum_{k=1}^{n} p_k[g(x_k) - g(y_k)] = \sum_{k=1}^{n}[(A_k - A_{k-1}) - (B_k - B_{k-1})]Q_k \leq 0. \quad \|$$

Notice that unlike A.1.a, the p_i's here need not be of one sign. If the p_i's are of one sign (say $p_i > 0$ for all i), there is a converse to A.3.

Note. Pečarić and Abramovich (1997) discuss an analog of Proposition A.3 in which the requirement that x and y be similarly ordered is relaxed.

The following is a companion result to A.3 with the equality in (5) replaced by an inequality.

A.3.a. Proposition (Bullen, Vasić, and Stanković, 1973). If (4) holds for $k = 1, \ldots, n$, then $\Sigma p_i g(x_i) \leq \Sigma p_i g(y_i)$ for all continuous increasing convex functions $g : \mathcal{R} \to \mathcal{R}$.

A.3.b. Proposition (Cheng, 1977). If $p_i > 0$, $i = 1, \ldots, n$, and (3) holds, then for any permutation π such that $x, y \in \mathscr{D}^\pi$, $x \prec_p y$ on $\mathscr{D}^\pi$.

The proof of this result is quite similar to the proof of 4.B.1.

For fixed $p_i > 0$, $i = 1, \ldots, n$, let $\mathscr{A}_p$ denote the set of all $n \times n$ matrices with nonnegative entries such that for all $y \in \mathscr{D}$, $yA \in \mathscr{D}$, and $yA \prec_p y$ on $\mathscr{D}$.

A.4. Proposition (Cheng, 1977). Let A be an $n \times n$ matrix with nonnegative entries. Then $A \in \mathscr{A}_p$ if and only if

(i) $\sum_{i=1}^k a_{ij}$ is decreasing in j for $k = 1, \ldots, n-1$,

(ii) $eA = e$,

(iii) $Ap' = p'$.

Proof. Suppose first that $A \in \mathscr{A}_p$. Then (i) follows from 2.E.1. Because $e \in \mathscr{D}$ and $-e \in \mathscr{D}$, $eA \prec_p e$ and $-eA \prec_p -e$ on $\mathscr{D}$, so (ii) holds. Finally, let $f^{(k)} = (1, \ldots, 1, 0, \ldots, 0)$ be the vector with first k components equal to 1 and the remaining components equal to 0. Because $f^{(k)}A \prec_p f^{(k)}$ on $\mathscr{D}$, $f^{(k)}Ap' = f^{(k)}p'$, $k = 1, \ldots, n$. This set of equalities is equivalent to (iii).

Next, suppose that A is a matrix with nonnegative entries such that (i), (ii), and (iii) hold. By 2.E.1, $yA \in \mathscr{D}$ for all $y \in \mathscr{D}$; by A.1.a, (3) holds. Thus $yA \prec_p y$ on $\mathscr{D}$ (A.3.a), and so $A \in \mathscr{A}_p$. ||

The various propositions above can be combined to yield the following:

A.4.a. Proposition (Cheng, 1977). If $x, y \in \mathscr{D}$, then $x \prec_p y$ if and only if there exists $A \in \mathscr{A}_p$ such that $x = yA$.

It is not difficult to show that $\mathscr{A}_p$ has the following properties:

(i) $\mathscr{A}_p$ is closed under multiplication.

(ii) If $A \in \mathscr{A}_p$, $B \in \mathscr{A}_q$, then

$$\begin{pmatrix} A & 0 \\ 0 & B \end{pmatrix} \in \mathscr{A}_{(p,q)}.$$

(iii) $\mathscr{A}_p$ is convex (but the characterization of its extreme points is somewhat more complicated than for the doubly stochastic matrices).

In various studies of majorization, the role played by T-transforms (definition precedes 2.B.1) is quite critical. For p-majorization, a result similar to 2.B.1 holds.

A.5. Proposition (Cheng, 1977). If $x \prec_p y$ on $\mathscr{D}$, there exists a finite sequence $u^{(1)}, \ldots, u^{(h)}$ of vectors such that

(i) $x \equiv u^{(0)} \prec_p u^{(1)} \prec_p \cdots \prec_p u^{(h)} \prec_p u^{(h+1)} \equiv y$ on $\mathscr{D}$, and

(ii) for $i = 0, 1, \ldots, h$, $u^{(i)}$ and $u^{(i+1)}$ differ in but two components.

Proof. The theorem is trivially true for vectors x and y of length 2. Suppose it is true for vectors of length $2, 3, \ldots, n-1$. Two cases arise.

I. If equality holds in one of the inequalities (4), say for $k = l$, then $\dot{x} \prec_{\dot{p}} \dot{y}$ and $\ddot{x} \prec_{\ddot{p}} \ddot{y}$, where $x = (\dot{x}, \ddot{x})$, $y = (\dot{y}, \ddot{y})$, and $p = (\dot{p}, \ddot{p})$; $\dot{x}$, $\dot{y}$, and $\dot{p}$ are of dimension l. Then the result can be obtained from the induction hypotheses applied to each partition of the vectors x, y, and p.

II. If the inequalities (4) are all strict, take

$$\delta = \min_{1 \leq k \leq n-1} \sum_{i=1}^{k} p_i(y_i - x_i) > 0, \quad p_i > 0 \text{ for all } i,$$

and

$$x^{\delta} = (x_1 + \delta p_1^{-1}, x_2, \ldots, x_{n-1}, x_n - \delta p_n^{-1}).$$

Then $x \prec_p x^{\delta} \prec_p y$ on $\mathscr{D}$. For the $n-1$ component inequalities of $x^{\delta} \prec_p y$, at least one is an equality. An application of case I to x^{δ} and y completes the proof. ‖

The Order-Preserving Functions

Let $\phi: \mathscr{R}^n \times \mathscr{R}^n_{++} \to \mathscr{R}$ be a function such that

$$\phi(x;p) \le \phi(y;p) \quad \text{whenever} \quad p \in \mathscr{R}^n_{++} \text{ and } x \prec_p y \text{ on } \mathscr{D}, \tag{6}$$

$$\phi(x_{\pi_1}, \ldots, x_{\pi_n}; p_{\pi_1}, \ldots, p_{\pi_n}) = \phi(x;p) \tag{7}$$

for all permutations π, $x \in \mathscr{R}^n$, and $p \in \mathscr{R}^n_{++}$. Then ϕ has the property that for all $p \in \mathscr{R}^n_{++}$,

$$x \prec_p y \text{ on } \mathscr{D}^\pi \quad \text{implies} \quad \phi(x;p) \le \phi(y;p). \tag{8}$$

A.6. Proposition (Cheng, 1977). Let $\phi: \mathscr{R}^n \times \mathscr{R}^n_{++} \to \mathscr{R}$ be a differentiable function satisfying 7. Then (8) is satisfied if and only if for all x,

$$(x_i - x_j)\left(\frac{1}{p_i}\frac{\partial \phi(x;p)}{\partial x_i} - \frac{1}{p_j}\frac{\partial \phi(x;p)}{\partial x_j}\right) \ge 0, \quad i,j = 1, \ldots, n.$$

This result can be proved with the aid of A.5 in a manner similar to the way 3.A.4 is proved. The details are omitted.

A.7. Corollary. If g is differentiable, then $\phi(x;p) = \sum_1^n p_i g(x_i)$ satisfies (8) if and only if g is convex.

One use of Schur-convexity is in finding the minimum of a function: Because, for all $x \in \mathscr{R}^n$,

$$(\bar{x}, \ldots, \bar{x}) \prec x, \quad \text{where} \quad \bar{x} = \frac{1}{n}\sum x_i,$$

it follows that for all Schur-convex functions ϕ, $\phi(\bar{x}, \ldots, \bar{x}) \le \phi(x)$. It is possible to use p-majorization for the same purpose. Here,

$$(\bar{x}, \ldots, \bar{x}) \prec_p x, \quad \text{where} \quad \bar{x} = \sum_1^n p_i x_i \bigg/ \sum_1^n p_i.$$

Weak majorization versions of $\prec_p$ have also been studied by Cheng (1977), but these are not discussed here.

Continuous p-Majorization

Continuous majorization is briefly discussed in Section H and Section 1.D. Analogous results have been obtained for p-majorization by Pečarić (1984). See also Pečarić, Proschan, and Tong (1992, p. 328).

A.8. Proposition (Pečarić, 1984). Let x and y be decreasing continuous functions defined on $[0,1]$ and let H be a function of bounded variation defined on $[0,1]$. If

$$\int_0^z x(t)dH(t) \leq \int_0^z y(t)dH(t), \quad 0 \leq z < 1, \tag{9}$$

and

$$\int_0^1 x(t)dH(t) \leq \int_0^1 y(t)dH(t), \tag{10}$$

then

$$\int_0^1 \phi(x(t))dH(t) \leq \int_0^1 \phi(y(t))dH(t) \tag{11}$$

for all continuous convex functions ϕ for which the integrals exist.

A.8.a. Example. Let the function $y : [0,1] \to \mathscr{R}_+$ be decreasing and continuous. For $\theta \leq 1$ and for a distribution function H, let

$$x(t) = y^\theta(t) \int_0^1 y(z)dH(z) \Big/ \int_0^1 y^\theta(z)dH(z).$$

Then x and y satisfy conditions (9) and (10) of Proposition A.8, and consequently (11) holds.

Proof. Clearly, (10) is satisfied. To obtain (9), note first that because $\theta \leq 1$, $y(z)/y^\theta(z) = [y(z)]^{1-\theta}$ is decreasing in z. Thus, for $u \leq z$, $y(u)y^\theta(z) \geq y^\theta(u)y(z)$, and for $u \leq w$,

$$y(w)\int_w^1 y^\theta(z)dH(z) \geq y^\theta(u)\int_w^1 y(z)dH(z).$$

Thus

$$\int_0^w y(u)dH(u)\int_w^1 y^\theta(z)dH(z) \geq \int_0^w y^\theta(u)dH(u)\int_w^1 y(z)dH(z).$$

To obtain (9), add to both sides of this inequality the quantity

$$\int_0^w y(u)dH(u)\int_0^w y^\theta(z)dH(z). \quad \|$$

B Majorization Relative to d

Let x and y be n-dimensional vectors such that $\Sigma x_i = \Sigma y_i = ns$. A statement that $x \prec y$ can be regarded as saying that the elements of x are "more equal" than those of y. In other words, x is "closer" than y to the vector $(s, \ldots, s) = se$ with all components equal. Order-preserving functions can be regarded as measures of the distance.

A generalization of majorization can be obtained by substituting for the vector e a more general vector $d \in \mathscr{R}^{n}_{++}$. The resulting generalization, here termed "d-majorization," can be defined in several ways. The idea seems to have originated with Veinott (1971), and his approach, followed here, is to start by generalizing the notion of a doubly stochastic matrix.

B.1. Definition. An $n \times n$ matrix $A = (a_{ij})$ is said to be d-*stochastic* $(d \in \mathscr{R}^{n}_{++})$ if

(i) $a_{ij} \geq 0$ for all i, j,

(ii) $dA = d$,

(iii) $Ae' = e'$.

A d-stochastic matrix is *simple* if it has at most two nonzero off-diagonal elements.

Conditions (i), (ii), and (iii) of Definition B.1 are to be contrasted with those of A.1.a. When $d = e$, a d-stochastic matrix is doubly stochastic and a simple d-stochastic matrix is called a "T-transform" in Chapter 2.

B.2. Definition. For $x, y \in \mathscr{R}^n$, x is said to be d-*majorized* by y if $x = yA$ for some d-stochastic matrix A, and is denoted by $x \prec^{r}_{d} y$.

The notation $x \prec^{r}_{d} y$ is introduced by Joe (1990). In place of "x is d-majorized by y," he uses the terminology "x is majorized by y relative to d." Thus the letter r in the notation $\prec^{r}_{d}$ stems from the word "relative."

B.2.a. Definition. If $x = yP$ for some matrix P that is a product of finitely many simple d-stochastic matrices, then x is said to be *simply d-majorized* by y.

Because products of d-stochastic matrices are d-stochastic, x is d-majorized by y if it is simply d-majorized by y. In case $d = e$, the converse is true (2.B.1). But unpublished work of Arthur Veinott (private communication) shows that in general the converse is false.

The lack of a stepwise path lemma analogous to 2.B.1 makes the order-preserving functions difficult to identify. However, some such functions are known.

B.3. Proposition (Veinott, 1971). Functions of the form

$$\phi(x) = \sum d_i g\left(\frac{x_i}{d_i}\right), \qquad (1)$$

where g is convex, preserve the ordering of d-majorization.

Notice that if x is d-majorized by y, that is, $x = yA$, where A is d-stochastic, then

$$\Sigma x_i = xe' = yAe' = ye' = \Sigma y_i.$$

Notice also that if x is d-majorized by y, then for any positive constant c, x is cd-majorized by y.

It can be verified directly from Definition A.8 that the matrix

$$A = \frac{1}{\Sigma d_i} \begin{pmatrix} d_1 & d_2 & \cdots & d_n \\ \vdots & \vdots & & \vdots \\ d_1 & d_2 & \cdots & d_n \end{pmatrix}$$

is d-stochastic. Moreover, if $\Sigma y_i = \Sigma d_i$, then $d = yA$; that is, d is d-majorized by y. This means that in the ordering of d-majorization, the smallest vector is a multiple of d.

When $\Sigma d_i = 1$, a d-stochastic matrix can be viewed as the transition matrix of a Markov chain. Let $\{X_n\}_{n=1}^{\infty}$ be a Markov chain with transition matrix A and let $p^{(n)}$ denote the probability distribution of X_n. Because $p^{(n)} = p^{(n-1)}A$, it follows that $p^{(n)} \prec_d^r p^{(n-1)}$. If the chain is irreducible, then $p^{(n)}$ converges to d.

In spite of the fact that Proposition B.3 does not identify all of the functions preserving the ordering of d-majorization, there is a converse included in the following proposition.

B.4. Proposition (Ruch, Schranner, and Seligman, 1978; Joe, 1990). Let x and y be real vectors such that $\Sigma x_i = \Sigma y_i$, and let $d \in \mathcal{R}_{++}^n$ be fixed. The following are equivalent:

(a) $\phi(x) \leq \phi(y)$ for all functions of the form (1), where g is continuous and convex;

(b) $\Sigma|x_i - d_i t| \leq \Sigma|y_i - d_i t|$ for all $t \in \mathscr{R}$;

(c) $\Sigma(x_i - d_i t)^+ \leq \Sigma(y_i - d_i t)^+$ for all t in the set
$$\left\{\frac{x_1}{d_1}, \ldots, \frac{x_n}{d_n}, \frac{y_1}{d_1}, \ldots, \frac{y_n}{d_n}\right\};$$

(d) x is d-majorized by y.

Joe (1990) uses condition (a) to define d-majorization. In order to verify d-majorization, condition (c) is often the easiest to check.

Joe (1990) extends the ordering $\prec_d^r$ by replacing the vector d (viewed as a positive function defined on the set $\{1, 2, \ldots, n\}$) by a positive measurable function defined on a measure space $(\mathscr{X}, \mathscr{F}, \nu)$. For nonnegative measurable functions f and g defined on $(\mathscr{X}, \mathscr{F}, \nu)$ that satisfy $\int_{\mathscr{X}} f \, d\nu = \int_{\mathscr{X}} g \, d\nu$, write $f \prec_d^r g$ to mean that

$$\int_{\mathscr{X}} d(x) \, \psi\left(\frac{f(x)}{d(x)}\right) d\nu(x) \leq \int_{\mathscr{X}} d(x) \, \psi\left(\frac{g(x)}{d(x)}\right) d\nu(x) \qquad (2)$$

for all real continuous convex functions ψ satisfying $\psi(0) = 0$ such that the integrals exist. Joe (1990) discusses equivalent conditions for this extension.

Another extension of the ordering $\prec_d^r$ has been studied by Ruch, Schranner, and Seligman (1978). In place of the condition (2) of Joe (1990), they require

$$\int_0^1 d(x) \, \psi\left(\frac{f(x)}{d(x)}\right) dx \leq \int_0^1 e(x) \, \psi\left(\frac{g(x)}{e(x)}\right) dx$$

for all real continuous convex functions ψ defined on $[0, 1]$. Here the functions d and e need not be equal.

C Semigroup and Group Majorization

According to Theorem 2.B.2, $x \prec y$ if and only if $x = yP$ for some doubly stochastic matrix P. The set $\mathscr{P}$ of all $n \times n$ doubly stochastic matrices constitutes a semigroup; that is, it is closed under the formation of products. Moreover, the identity $I \in \mathscr{P}$.

Cautionary comment. A semigroup with identity is properly called a *monoid*. However, in what follows, the term "semigroup" is used in place of "monoid" to mean "semigroup with identity."

C.1. Definition. Let $\mathscr{A}$ be a subset of $\mathscr{R}^n$ and let S be a semigroup of linear transformations (matrices) mapping $\mathscr{A}$ to $\mathscr{A}$. A vector $x \in \mathscr{A}$ is said to be *semigroup majorized* by y, written $x \prec_S y$, if $x = yM$ for some $M \in S$.

The relation $\prec_S$ is a preorder; it is reflexive ($x \prec_S x$ for all $x \in \mathscr{A}$) because $I \in S$, and it is transitive ($x \prec_S y$, $y \prec_S z$ implies $x \prec_S z$) because S is closed under the formation of products.

Semigroup majorization is defined by Parker and Ram (1997) but otherwise has received very little attention in the literature. The reader can expect to notice a number of open questions in the following discussion.

C.2. Observations.

(i) Suppose that S_1 and S_2 are two semigroups of matrices mapping $\mathscr{A}$ to $\mathscr{A}$. If $S_1 \subset S_2$, then
$$\{x : x \prec_{S_1} y\} \subset \{x : x \prec_{S_2} y\} \text{ for all } y \in \mathscr{A}.$$

(ii) If S is a semigroup of matrices mapping $\mathscr{A}$ to $\mathscr{A}$, then the convex hull cS of S is a semigroup of matrices mapping $\mathscr{A}$ to $\mathscr{A}$.

(iii) If S is a convex semigroup with extreme points S_e, then $x \prec_S y$ if and only if x lies in the convex hull of the points yM, $M \in S_e$. This can be particularly useful when S_e is finite.

C.3. Example: Majorization. As mentioned at the beginning of this section, the set of $n \times n$ doubly stochastic matrices forms a convex semigroup. Thus, majorization is a semigroup order with $\mathscr{A} = \mathscr{R}^n$. The extreme points of the set of doubly stochastic matrices are the permutation matrices; these matrices constitute a finite group. The importance of this underlying group structure is discussed in a subsection on group majorization later in this section.

C.4. Example: p-majorization. The set $\mathscr{A}$ of matrices A that satisfy (i), (ii), and (iii) of Corollary A.1.a forms a convex semigroup, so that p-majorization is a semigroup majorization. When $p \in \mathscr{R}^n_{++}$ and p-majorization is restricted to $\mathscr{D}$, another semigroup ordering is obtained; here the semigroup is a subset of $\mathscr{A}$ and consists of matrices satisfying (i), (ii), and (iii) of Proposition A.4.

C.5. Example: d-majorization. The set $\mathscr{A}'$ of matrices that satisfy (i), (ii), and (iii) of Definition B.1 consists of transposes of matrices in the set $\mathscr{A}$ of Example C.4 when $p = d \in \mathscr{R}^n_{++}$.

C.6. Example: Componentwise ordering. Let S consist of all $n \times n$ diagonal matrices with diagonal elements in $[0, 1]$. This semigroup leads to the usual componentwise ordering on $\mathscr{R}_+^n$. When applied to vectors in $\mathscr{R}^n$, it leads to the ordering

$$x \prec y \text{ if } |x_i| \leq |y_i|, \quad i = 1, \ldots, n.$$

Componentwise ordering of $\mathscr{R}^n$ is not a semigroup order.

C.7. Example: Unordered majorization. Let S consist of all $n \times n$ upper triangular row-stochastic matrices (all row sums are one and all entries are nonnegative). This convex set is a semigroup but not a group. It can be verified that the extreme points of S are upper triangular matrices with a single entry of one in each row and all other entries zero. Parker and Ram (1997) show that for this example, $x \prec_S y$ if and only if x is unordered majorized by y, as defined in Example E.6.

G-Majorization

Semigroup majorization is based upon a monoid (semigroup with identity) of linear transformations. In case the monoid is actually a group or the convex hull of a group, the terms *group majorization* or *G-majorization* are often used.

The ordering of majorization is intimately tied to the group of permutations. This can be seen, for example, with the aid of 2.B.3 or 4.C.1 which states that $\{x : x \prec y\}$ is the convex hull $C(y)$ of the orbit of y under the group of permutations.

C.8. Definition. Let G be a group of linear transformations mapping $\mathscr{R}^n$ to $\mathscr{R}^n$. Then x is *G-majorized* by y, written $x \prec_G y$, if x lies in the convex hull of the orbit of y under the group G.

This section offers only a brief introduction to the theory of G-majorization. For further discussions of the general theory, see, e.g., Eaton (1987), Eaton and Perlman (1977), and Steerneman (1990).

The idea of G-majorization has not been fully exploited. Undoubtedly, many majorization results hold in this more general setting.

Applications of G-majorization have been limited. Giovagnoli and Romanazzi (1990) suggest the use of a G-majorization ordering for correlation matrices based on the sign-change group and the permutation group. Miranda and Thompson (1994) discuss G-majorization in a matrix theory context.

The idea of G-majorization seems to have been first considered by Rado (1952). Rado was concerned primarily with generalizations of

Muirhead's inequality 3.G.2.e and confined his attention primarily to subgroups of the permutation group. Further extensions of Rado's work are given by Daykin (1971).

C.9. Observation. G-majorization is equivalent to S-majorization (as defined in C.1) with S the convex hull of G.

Proof. First, recall that by a theorem of Carathéodory, a point in the convex hull of a subset of $\mathscr{R}^n$ can always be written as the convex combination of at most $n+1$ points in the subset: see, e.g., Roberts and Varberg (1973, p. 76). Thus if $x \prec_G y$, then $x = \sum_1^{n+1} a_i g_i(y)$, where $a_i \geq 0$, $i = 1, \ldots, n+1$, $\sum_1^{n+1} a_i = 1$, and $g_i(y) \in G$, $i = 1, \ldots, n+1$. But $\sum_1^{n+1} a_i g_i(y) \in S$, so $x \prec_S y$.

Next, suppose that $x \prec_S y$; i.e., $x = g(y)$ for some $g \in S$. Because S is the convex hull of G, g can be written in the form $g = \sum_1^m b_i g_i$, where $b_i \geq 0$, $\sum_1^m b_i = 1$, and $g_i \in G$, $i = 1, \ldots, m$; again by Carathéodory's theorem, m is finite. Consequently, $x \prec_S y$. ||

C.10. Example: Majorization. With Definition C.8 and the group of permutations as a starting point, the theory of majorization has been developed by various authors: See Eaton and Perlman (1977) and Eaton (1982, 1987). This development uses the following proposition.

C.10.a. Proposition. For the permutation group $\mathscr{P}$, the following are equivalent:

(i) $x \prec y$; i.e., $x \prec_{\mathscr{P}} y$;

(ii) $C(x) \subset C(y)$;

(iii) $m[u, x] \leq m[u, y]$ for all $u \in \mathscr{R}^n$, where

$$m[u, z] = \sup_{P \in \mathscr{P}} y P u'.$$

The equivalence of (i) and (ii) is easily verified; the equivalence of (i) and (iii) is given by Proposition 4.B.8. All of these equivalences remain valid if the permutation group is replaced by some other group of linear transformations.

C.11. Proposition (Eaton, 1984; Giovagnoli and Wynn, 1985). The majorization $x \prec_G y$ holds if and only if

$$\sup_{g \in G} \sum z_i [g(x)]_i \leq \sup_{g \in G} \sum z_i [g(y)]_i \quad \text{for all } z \in \mathscr{R}^n.$$

This condition, which involves an infinite set of inequalities, simplifies to a finite set of inequalities for certain groups. For example, this can be achieved for any finite group G.

For additional results related to C.11, see Steerneman (1990).

C.12. Some terminology. A real-valued function ϕ defined on $\mathscr{R}^n$ is said to be *G-invariant* if $\phi(z) = \phi(g(z))$ for all $g \in G$.

If $x \prec_G y$ implies $\phi(x) \leq \phi(y)$, ϕ is said to be *G-increasing*; that is, ϕ is order-preserving. If $x \prec_G y$ implies $\phi(x) \geq \phi(y)$, then ϕ is said to be *G-decreasing*.

In general, the convex cones of G-increasing and G-decreasing functions are not well understood. However, an important class of G-decreasing functions can be identified that involves the following definition.

C.13. Definition. A real-valued function ϕ defined on $\mathscr{R}^n$ is said to be *convex-unimodal* if for each real constant α, $\{x : f(x) \geq \alpha\}$ is convex.

C.14. Proposition. If ϕ is a real-valued function defined on $\mathscr{R}^n$ that is G-invariant and convex-unimodal, then ϕ is G-decreasing.

Proof. Fix $y \in \mathscr{R}^n$ and recall that $\{x : x \prec_G y\}$ is the smallest convex set that contains the points $g(y)$, $g \in G$. Because ϕ is convex-unimodal, $C = \{x : \phi(x) \geq \phi(y)\}$ is a convex set. Because ϕ is G-invariant, $g(y) \in C$ for all $g \in G$. Thus $\{x : x \prec_G y\} \subset C$; that is, $x \prec_G y$ implies $\phi(x) \geq \phi(y)$. ∥

Convolution Theorems

To begin a discussion of convolution theorems, consider the following example.

C.15. Example. The set $G_0 = \{I, -I\}$ of $n \times n$ matrices forms a group for which $x \prec_{G_0} y$ if for some $\alpha \in [0, 1]$,

$$x = \alpha y + (1 - \alpha)(-y) = (2\alpha - 1)y.$$

Thus a function ϕ is G_0-increasing if ϕ is G_0-invariant (symmetric about the origin) and if $\phi(x) \leq \phi(y)$ for all x lying on the line segment that joins y with $-y$, $y \in \mathscr{R}^n$. This means that ϕ is G_0-increasing if for all $y \in \mathscr{R}^n$, $\phi(y) = \phi(-y)$ and $\phi(\beta y)$ is increasing in β, $\beta \geq 0$ [equivalently, $\phi(\beta y) \leq \phi(y)$, $0 \leq \beta \leq 1$]. Such functions are sometimes said to be symmetric and *ray-increasing*. Similarly, ϕ is G_0-decreasing if it is symmetric and $\phi(\beta y) \geq \phi(y)$, $0 \leq \beta \leq 1$.

C.16. Theorem (Anderson, 1955). Let $E \subset \mathscr{R}^n$ be a convex set symmetric about the origin and let f be a nonnegative function defined on $\mathscr{R}^n$ that is both convex-unimodal and symmetric about the origin. If $\int_E f(z)\,dz < \infty$, then

$$\int_E f(x+ky)\,dx \geq \int_E f(x+y)\,dx, \quad 0 \leq k \leq 1.$$

Anderson's theorem is often stated in a more general form obtained using the fact that non-negative symmetric convex-unimodal functions can be approximated by positive combinations of symmetric convex indicator functions.

C.16.a. Theorem. If f_1 and f_2 are nonnegative symmetric convex-unimodal functions defined on $\mathscr{R}^n$, the convolution

$$f(z) = \int_{\mathscr{R}^n} f_1(z-x) f_2(x)\,dx \tag{1}$$

is G_0-decreasing.

According to Proposition C.14, the functions f_1 and f_2 of Theorem C.16.a are G_0-decreasing. But Theorem C.16.a falls short of stating that the convolution of nonnegative G_0-decreasing functions is G_0-decreasing. This is to be contrasted with known results for the group G_1 of permutation matrices; according to Theorem 3.J.1, the convolution of two G_1-decreasing (Schur-concave) functions is G_1-decreasing.

It is known that the conditions imposed on f_1 and f_2 in Theorem C.16.a can be relaxed.

C.16.b. Theorem (Sherman, 1955). Let $\mathscr{C}$ be the class of functions taking the form

$$h(z) = \sum_{i=1}^{r} \alpha_i h_i(z), \quad z \in \mathscr{R}^n, \tag{2}$$

where $\alpha_i \geq 0$, h_i is nonnegative, symmetric and convex-unimodal for all $i = 1, \ldots, r$, where r is a positive integer. If $f_1, f_2 \in \mathscr{C}$, then the convolution (1) is G_0-decreasing.

C. Semigroup and Group Majorization   593

Beyond the fact that functions in $\mathscr{C}$ are G_0-decreasing, little is known about the relation between the convex cone $\mathscr{C}$ and the convex cone of G_0-decreasing functions.

Mudholkar (1966) recognized the role that the group G_0 played in Anderson's Theorem C.16, and he introduced G-majorization to obtain the following generalization.

C.17. Theorem (Mudholkar, 1966). Let G be a finite group of Lebesgue-measure-preserving linear transformations mapping $\mathscr{R}^n$ to $\mathscr{R}^n$, and let f_1 and f_2 be nonnegative functions defined on $\mathscr{R}^n$. If f_1 and f_2 are G-invariant and convex-unimodal, then the convolution f in (1) is G-decreasing; that is, $x \prec_G y$ implies $f(x) \geq f(y)$.

The ideas that Sherman (1955) used in Theorem C.16.b to extend Anderson's theorem can be utilized to extend Mudholkar's theorem. But the results fall short of stating that the convolution of G-decreasing functions is G-decreasing. According to Theorem 3.J.1, such a convolution result holds for the group G of permutations. For what other groups does it hold?

For a vector $r \in \mathscr{R}^n$ such that $rr' = 1$, $S_r = I - 2r'r$ is an orthogonal matrix that reflects points in $\mathscr{R}^n$ through the hyperplane

$$\{x : x \in \mathscr{R}^n,\ rx' = 0\}.$$

Such a matrix S_r is called a *reflection*.

C.18. Definition. A group G is called a *reflection group* if it is the smallest closed group that contains a given set of reflections.

C.19. Proposition (Eaton and Perlman, 1977). If G is a reflection group and f_1, f_2 are G-decreasing functions defined on $\mathscr{R}^n$, then their convolution (1) is is G-decreasing.

Eaton and Perlman (1977) show that the convolution theorem is not true for all groups of linear transformations. For reflection groups, they also obtain analogs of the basic stepwise path Lemma 2.B.1 of Hardy, Littlewood, and Pólya (1934, 1952) and they obtain analogs of the Schur conditions (10) of 3.A.4 for a differentiable function to preserve the ordering $\prec_G$:

C.19.a. Proposition (Fernando, 1997). Let G be a finite linear group. If the convolution (1) of G-increasing functions defined on $\mathscr{R}^n$ is G-decreasing, then G is a reflection group.

C.20. Theorem (Eaton and Perlman, 1977). Suppose G is a finite reflection group, and let ϕ be a G-invariant differentiable function on $\mathscr{R}^n$. A necessary and sufficient condition that ϕ preserve the ordering of G-majorization (ϕ is G-increasing) is that

$$\left(\sum r_i z_i\right)\left(\sum r_i \frac{\partial \phi(z)}{\partial z_i}\right) \geq 0$$

for all $z \in \mathscr{R}^n$ and all unit vectors r such that the linear transformation $I - 2r'r$ is in G.

Of course, the group of permutations plays a fundamental role also in Chapter 6. A number of important results of that chapter, particularly those of Hollander, Proschan, and Sethuraman (1977), have been obtained for reflection groups by Conlon, León, Proschan, and Sethuraman (1977).

Stochastic G-Majorization

Exchangeable random variables arise in a number of contexts, and for such variables, the connection with the permutation group is clear. It is of interest to consider other groups of linear transformations.

C.21. Definition. A random vector X is said to be G-invariant if gX has the same distribution as X for all $g \in G$.

A version of 11.B.2 for G-majorization with G finite has been obtained by León and Proschan (1977). Using their ideas, it is as easy to obtain a G-majorization version of the more general 11.B.1.

C.22. Proposition (León and Proschan, 1977). Let G be a finite group of linear transformations acting on $\mathscr{R}^n$ and let X be a G-invariant random vector. Let $\Phi : \mathscr{R}^n \times \mathscr{R}^n \to \mathscr{R}$ be a function with the property that $\Phi(x, a)$ is convex in a for each fixed x. Suppose also that for each $g \in G$, there exists $g^* \in G$ such that $\Phi(g^*x, ga) = \Phi(x, a)$. If $a \prec_G b$ and the expectations exist, then

$$E\Phi(X, a) \leq E\Phi(X, b).$$

Proof. Let $\psi(b) = E\Phi(X, b)$ and note that for all $g \in G$,

$$\psi(gb) = E\Phi(X, gb) = E\Phi(g^*X, gb) = E\Phi(X, b) = \psi(b).$$

Because $a \prec_G b$, a can be written in the form $a = \sum_1^m \alpha_i g_i b$, where each $\alpha_i \geq 0$, $\sum_1^m \alpha_i = 1$, each $g_i \in G$, and $m \leq n+1$ by Carathéodory's theorem (Roberts and Varberg, 1973, p. 76). Thus

$$\psi(a) = E\Phi\left(X, \sum_1^m \alpha_i g_i b\right) \leq E \sum_1^m \alpha_i \Phi(X, g_i b)$$

$$= E \sum_1^m \alpha_i \Phi(X, b) = \psi(b). \quad \|$$

A number of applications and special cases of the above result are presented in detail by León and Proschan (1979).

D   Partial Orderings Induced by Convex Cones

Cone orderings are briefly described in Section 1.D.

D.1. Definition. A cone ordering on a set $\mathscr{A} \subset \mathscr{R}^n$ induced by a convex cone $\mathscr{C} \subset \mathscr{R}^n$ is the relation $\leq$ on $\mathscr{A}$ defined by

$$x \leq y \quad \text{if and only if} \quad y - x \in \mathscr{C}. \tag{1}$$

It is easy to see that cone orderings are preorderings; i.e.,

$$x \leq x \quad \text{for all} \quad x \in \mathscr{A}, \tag{2}$$

$$x \leq y \text{ and } y \leq z \text{ imply } x \leq z \quad \text{when} \quad x, y, z \in \mathscr{A}. \tag{3}$$

If $\mathscr{A}$ is itself a convex cone, then additionally such orderings satisfy

$$x \leq y \text{ implies } x + z \leq y + z \quad \text{for all} \quad z \in \mathscr{A}, \tag{4}$$

$$x \leq y \text{ implies } \lambda x \leq \lambda y \quad \text{for all} \quad \lambda \geq 0. \tag{5}$$

Conversely, relations which satisfy (2)–(5) are cone orderings induced by $\mathscr{C} = \{x : x \geq 0\}$. The cone $\mathscr{C}$ is *pointed*, i.e., $x \in \mathscr{C}$ and $-x \in \mathscr{C}$ imply $x = 0$, if and only if the ordering $\leq$ satisfies

$$x \leq y \text{ and } y \leq x \quad \text{imply} \quad x = y, \tag{6}$$

in which case $\leq$ is a partial ordering.

A most familiar example is the usual componentwise ordering $\leq$ on $\mathscr{R}^n$:

$$x \leq y \quad \text{if and only if} \quad x_i \leq y_i, \quad i = 1, \ldots, n.$$

Here the associated convex cone is the nonnegative orthant

$$\mathscr{R}_+^n = \{x : x_i \geq 0, i = 1, \ldots, n\}.$$

The ordering of majorization does not arise from a convex cone in $\mathscr{R}^n$; if $\mathscr{A} = \mathscr{R}^n$, majorization fails to satisfy (4). On the other hand, if the ordering is confined to the set $\mathscr{A} = \mathscr{D}$, then majorization is a cone order obtained from the cone

$$\mathscr{C} = \{x : \Sigma_1^k x_i \geq 0, k = 1, \ldots, n-1, \Sigma_1^n x_i = 0\}.$$

A set $\mathscr{T} \subset \mathscr{C} \subset \mathscr{R}^n$ is said to *span $\mathscr{C}$ positively* if every point in $\mathscr{C}$ can be written as a nonnegative linear combination of a finite number of points in $\mathscr{T}$. Of course, the n unit coordinate vectors e_i (ith component 1, other components 0) span $\mathscr{R}_+^n$ positively.

For the cone ordering $\leq$ on $\mathscr{A} \subset \mathscr{R}^n$ induced by the convex cone $\mathscr{C}$, a set $\mathscr{T}$ which spans $\mathscr{C}$ positively is of considerable interest for its usefulness in the identification of the order-preserving functions. If $\mathscr{A}$ is a convex set with nonempty interior, f preserves $\leq$ on $\mathscr{A}$ whenever

(i) f is continuous on the boundary of $\mathscr{A}$, and

(ii) $f(x+\lambda t) - f(x) \geq 0$ for all $t \in \mathscr{T}$ and $\lambda > 0$ such that $x + \lambda t \in \mathscr{A}$

(Marshall, Walkup, and Wets, 1967). In case f is continuous on $\mathscr{A}$ and has a gradient

$$\nabla f(x) = (\partial f/\partial x_1, \ldots, \partial f/\partial x_n)$$

at each point in the interior of $\mathscr{A}$, f preserves the ordering $\leq$ if and only if

$$\nabla f(x) \cdot t \geq 0 \qquad \text{for all} \quad t \in \mathscr{T} \text{ and } x \text{ in the interior of } \mathscr{A}. \qquad (7)$$

Often a convex cone $\mathscr{C}$ is given by m simultaneous linear inequalities

$$\mathscr{C} = \{x : xA \geq 0\},$$

where A is an $n \times m$ matrix. In case $n = m$ and A is nonsingular, it is noted by Marshall, Walkup, and Wets (1967) that the rows of A^{-1} span $\mathscr{C}$ positively. To see this, observe that

$$\mathscr{C} = \{x : xA \geq 0\} = \{x : x = yA^{-1} \text{ for some } y \geq 0\}.$$

Because $y \geq 0$, the rows of A^{-1} span $\mathscr{C}$ positively. It can also be shown that no subset of the rows of A^{-1} spans $\mathscr{C}$ positively.

As examples, consider the weak majorizations $\prec_w$ and $\prec^w$ on $\mathscr{D}$. On $\mathscr{D}$, both of these orderings satisfy (2)–(5), so both orderings are cone

D. Partial Orderings Induced by Convex Cones 597

orderings on $\mathscr{D}$. The corresponding convex cones are: For $\prec_w$,

$$\mathscr{C} = \{x : x \succ_w 0\} = \left\{x : \Sigma_1^k x_i \geq 0, k = 1, \ldots, n\right\} = \{x : xA \geq 0\};$$

$$A = \begin{bmatrix} 1 & 1 & \cdots & & 1 \\ 0 & 1 & \cdots & & 1 \\ 0 & 0 & 1 & \cdots & 1 \\ \vdots & & & \ddots & \vdots \\ 0 & \cdots & & 0 & 1 \end{bmatrix}; \quad A^{-1} = \begin{bmatrix} 1 & -1 & 0 & 0 & \cdots & 0 & 0 \\ 0 & 1 & -1 & 0 & \cdots & 0 & 0 \\ \vdots & & & & & & \vdots \\ 0 & \cdots & & & & 1 & -1 \\ 0 & \cdots & & & & 0 & 1 \end{bmatrix}.$$

For $\prec^w$,

$$\mathscr{C} = \{x : x \succ^w 0\} = \{x : \Sigma_k^n x_i \leq 0, k = 1, \ldots, n\} = \{x : xA \geq 0\};$$

$$A = \begin{bmatrix} 0 & \cdots & & 0 & -1 \\ 0 & 0 & & -1 & -1 \\ \vdots & & & & \\ -1 & \cdots & & & -1 \end{bmatrix}; \quad A^{-1} = \begin{bmatrix} 0 & \cdots & 0 & & 1 & -1 \\ 0 & \cdots & 0 & 1 & -1 & 0 \\ \vdots & & \vdots & & & \vdots \\ 1 & -1 & 0 & \cdots & & 0 \\ -1 & 0 & & \cdots & & 0 \end{bmatrix}.$$

The ordering $\prec$ on $\mathscr{D}$ is also a cone ordering. Here

$$\mathscr{C} = \{x : x \succ 0\} = \left\{x : \Sigma_1^k x_i \geq 0, k = 1, \ldots, n-1, \Sigma_1^n x_i = 0\right\}$$
$$= \{x : xA \geq 0\};$$

$$A = \begin{bmatrix} 1 & 1 & \cdots & 1 & -1 \\ 0 & 1 & \cdots & 1 & -1 \\ 0 & 0 & 1 & \cdots & 1 & -1 \\ \vdots & & & \vdots & \vdots \\ 0 & \cdots & & 0 & 1 & -1 \end{bmatrix}.$$

This matrix is not square, so a set which spans $\mathscr{C}$ positively cannot be found by inverting A. However, it can be shown that $\mathscr{C}$ is spanned positively by the vectors

$$(1, -1, \ 0, 0, \cdots, \ 0),$$
$$(0, \ 1, -1, 0, \cdots, \ 0),$$
$$\vdots$$
$$(0, \quad \cdots, 0, 1, -1).$$

In fact, $x \in \mathscr{C}$ implies
$$x = x_1(1, -1, 0, \ldots, 0) + (x_1 + x_2)(0, 1, -1, 0, \ldots, 0) + \cdots$$
$$+ (x_1 + \cdots + x_{n-1})(0, \ldots, 0, 1, -1).$$

These results can be coupled with (7) to show that if $f : \mathscr{R}^n \to \mathscr{R}$ is differentiable, and

if $\partial f/\partial x_1 \geq \cdots \geq \partial f/\partial x_n \geq 0$ on $\mathscr{D}$, then
$$x \prec_w y \text{ on } \mathscr{D} \quad \text{implies} \quad f(x) \leq f(y); \tag{8}$$
if $0 \geq \partial f/\partial x_1 \geq \cdots \geq \partial f/\partial x_n$ on $\mathscr{D}$, then
$$x \prec^w y \text{ on } \mathscr{D} \quad \text{implies} \quad f(x) \leq f(y); \tag{9}$$
if $\partial f/\partial x_1 \geq \cdots \geq \partial f/\partial x_n$ on $\mathscr{D}$, then
$$x \prec y \text{ on } \mathscr{D} \quad \text{implies} \quad f(x) \leq f(y). \tag{10}$$

In order to preserve $\prec_w$, $\succ^w$, or $\prec$ on $\mathscr{R}^n$, then in addition to the corresponding condition (8), (9), or (10), f must be invariant under permutations of its arguments. Separate proofs of these facts from first principles are given in Section 3.A.

Other examples of cone orderings are G-majorizations, where G is a finite reflection group. Steerneman (1990) shows that finite reflective groups are the only finite groups for which $\prec_G$ is a cone ordering.

Niezgoda (1998a,b) discusses the problem of reducing a group majorization induced by an infinite group to a finite group majorization. In general, this is shown to be possible only in a somewhat restricted sense, and when it is possible, the resulting finite group is a reflection group.

E Orderings Derived from Function Sets

Let Φ be a set of real-valued functions ϕ defined on a subset $\mathscr{A}$ of $\mathscr{R}^n$. For $x, y \in \mathscr{A}$, write $x \prec_\Phi y$ to mean that
$$\phi(x) \leq \phi(y) \text{ for all } \phi \in \Phi. \tag{1}$$

If (1) holds, then it holds for all linear combinations of functions in Φ with positive coefficients. These linear combinations form a convex cone $\mathscr{C}$ and $\mathscr{C}$ is said to be *generated* by Φ. This leads to the following definition.

E. Orderings Derived from Function Sets

E.1. Definition. Let $\mathscr{A}$ be a subset of $\mathscr{R}^n$ and let $\mathscr{C}$ be a convex cone of real-valued functions defined on $\mathscr{A}$. For $x, y \in \mathscr{A}$, write $x \leq_\mathscr{C} y$ to mean that $\phi(x) \leq \phi(y)$ for all $\phi \in \mathscr{C}$. The ordering $\leq_\mathscr{C}$ is said to be *generated* by the cone $\mathscr{C}$.

The ordering $\leq_\mathscr{C}$ is a preordering of $\mathscr{A}$. In fact, all preorderings of $\mathscr{A}$ arise from a convex cone of functions in the manner of Definition E.1. To see this, let $\leq$ be an arbitrary preordering of $\mathscr{A}$ and for each $x \in \mathscr{A}$ let I_x denote the indicator function of $H_x = \{y : x \leq y\}$. If $\mathscr{C}$ is the smallest convex cone containing these indicator functions, then $\leq_\mathscr{C}$ is just the ordering $\leq$. This means that generating orderings via Definition E.1 is a more general procedure than generating them via D.1; not all preorders are cone orders, in the sense of Definition D.1.

E.2. Definition. Let $\mathscr{C}^*$ denote the set of all real-valued functions ϕ defined on $\mathscr{A}$ with the property that $x \leq_\mathscr{C} y$ implies $\phi(x) \leq \phi(y)$. The set $\mathscr{C}^*$ is called the *completion* of $\mathscr{C}$. If $\mathscr{C} = \mathscr{C}^*$, then $\mathscr{C}$ is said to be *complete*.

The order-preserving functions defined initially in this chapter for a given cone ordering are clearly complete.

E.3. Proposition. *If a convex cone is complete, then it contains the constant functions and is closed under pointwise convergence and under the formation of maxima and minima.*

E.4. Proposition. *If $\{\phi(\cdot, t), t \in T\}$ is a family of functions belonging to the convex cone $\mathscr{C}$, then the mixture*

$$\int_T \phi(\cdot, t) d\mu(t)$$

belongs to $\mathscr{C}$ whenever the integral exists.

Proposition 3.C.5 is an important special case of Proposition E.4.

Note that the orderings $\prec_\Phi$, $\prec_\mathscr{C}$, and $\prec_{\mathscr{C}^*}$ are equivalent.

Given a set Φ of functions, two basic problems arise:

(i) Identify the completion $\mathscr{C}^*$ of the convex cone $\mathscr{C}$ generated by Φ. This cone is of interest because it consists of all functions that preserve the order $\prec_\mathscr{C}$.

(ii) Find a subset of $\mathscr{C}^*$ that

    (a) generates a convex cone, the completion of which is $\mathscr{C}^*$,

and
>   (b) is small enough to be useful in determining the validity of the relation $x \prec_{\mathscr{C}} y$.

For further details about convex cones of functions, see Marshall (1991).

E.5. Example: Majorization. For majorization, one starting point is the convex cone $\mathscr{C}$ of functions ϕ having the form $\phi(x) = \Sigma_1^n g(x_i)$ for some real-valued convex function g defined on $\mathscr{R}$. Through Definition E.1, this provides a possible definition of majorization (Proposition 3.C.1), but such a definition leaves both problems (i) and (ii) to be solved.

As an alternative, consider starting with the set $\Phi = \{\phi_1, \ldots, \phi_{n+1}\}$, where

$$\phi_k(x) = \sum_{i=1}^k x_{[i]}, \quad k = 1, \ldots, n, \quad \phi_{n+1}(x) = -\sum_{i=1}^n x_{[i]}. \qquad (2)$$

According to Definition 1.A.1, $x \prec y$ if

$$\phi_k(x) \leq \phi_k(y), \quad k = 1, \ldots, n+1. \qquad (3)$$

The smallest convex cone $\mathscr{C}$ containing the functions (2) consists of functions having the form

$$\phi(x|a) = \sum_1^n a_i x_{[i]}, \quad \text{where} \quad a \in \mathscr{D}. \qquad (4)$$

To verify this, note that

$$\phi(x|a) = \sum_{k=1}^{n+1} b_k \phi_k(x), \qquad (5)$$

where $b_i = a_i - a_{i+1}$, $i = 1, \ldots, n-1$, $b_n = a_n + b_{n+1}$, and $b_{n+1} > 0$ is arbitrary but sufficiently large that $b_n > 0$.

The $n+1$ functions (2) constitute a *frame* for the convex cone $\mathscr{C}$; that is, these functions are a minimal set with the property that all functions in $\mathscr{C}$ take the form (5).

The completion $\mathscr{C}^*$ of $\mathscr{C}$ consists of all functions that preserve the order of majorization, i.e., the Schur-convex functions. This convex cone is the completion of several convex cones in addition to the one that introduced this example; it is the completion of the cone of permutation-symmetric quasi-convex functions (3.C.3) and of the cone of permutation-symmetric convex functions (3.C.2).

E.6. Example: Unordered majorization (Parker and Ram, 1997). Let

$$\phi_k(x) = \sum_1^k x_i, \quad k = 1, \ldots, n, \quad \phi_{n+1}(x) = -\phi_n(x), \quad x \in \mathscr{R}^n. \qquad (6)$$

A vector x is *unordered majorized* by y (written $x \stackrel{\mathrm{uo}}{\prec} y$) if

$$\phi_k(x) \le \phi_k(y), \quad k = 1, \ldots, n+1. \qquad (7)$$

Note that (6) is similar to (3), but here x_i has replaced $x_{[i]}$.

In many applications of majorization, the components of x are arbitrarily ordered; e.g., the numbering of individuals is arbitrary when x_i represents the income of the ith individual. Unordered majorization is appropriate only if the components of x are not arbitrarily ordered; they might, e.g., represent variables measured sequentially in time.

In a manner similar to the derivation of (5), it can be shown that functions of the form (6) constitute a frame for the convex cone $\mathscr{C}$ of functions taking the form

$$\phi(x|a) = \sum_1^n a_i x_i, \quad a \in \mathscr{D}, \quad x \in \mathscr{R}^n.$$

E.7. Example: Variance majorization (Neubauer and Watkins, 2006). Consider a preorder of $\mathscr{R}^n$ in which the functions (2) of Example E.5 are replaced by the functions

$$v(x|k) = \sum_1^k \frac{(x_{(i)} - m_k)^2}{k}, \quad k = 1, \ldots, n, \quad v(x|n+1) = -v(x|n), \qquad (8)$$

where $m_k = \sum_1^k x_{(i)}/k$, $k = 1, \ldots, n$. The vector x is *variance majorized* by y (written $x \stackrel{\mathrm{var}}{\prec} y$) if

$$v(x|k) \le v(y|k), \quad k = 1, \ldots, n+1.$$

Neither the convex cone $\mathscr{C}$ of functions generated by those of the form (8) nor its completion has been characterized. However, a differentiable function $\phi : \mathscr{R}^n \to \mathscr{R}$ preserves the order of variance majorization if its gradient $\nabla \phi(x) = (\phi_1(x), \ldots, \phi_n(x))$ satisfies

$$\frac{\phi_{i+1}(z) - \phi_i(z)}{z_{i+1} - z_i} \text{ is decreasing in } i = 1, 2, \ldots, n-1$$

whenever $z_1 < z_2 < \cdots < z_n$.

Let $m(x) = \sum_1^n x_i/n$, $v(x) = \sum(x_i - m)^2/n$. Neubauer and Watkins (2006) show that for any vector x with $m(x) = m$ and $v(x) = v$,

$$x_{\min} \stackrel{\text{var}}{\prec} x \stackrel{\text{var}}{\prec} x_{\max},$$

where

$$x_{\min} = (a, \ldots, a, b), \qquad x_{\max} = (c, d, \ldots, d),$$
$$a = m - \sqrt{v/(n-1)}, \quad d = m + \sqrt{v/(n-1)},$$
$$b = m + \sqrt{v(n-1)}, \quad c = m - \sqrt{v(n-1)}.$$

E.8. Example: Entropy majorization. For $x \in \mathscr{R}_{++}^n$, let

$$\phi_k(x) = -\sum_1^k x_{[i]} \log x_{[i]}, \quad k = 1, \ldots, n, \quad \phi_{n+1}(x) = -\phi_n(x).$$

If $\phi_k(x) \leq \phi_k(y)$, $k = 1, \ldots, n+1$, then x is said to be *entropy majorized* by y. Little is known about entropy majorization. However, if $x \prec y$ or $x \stackrel{\text{var}}{\prec} y$, then $\phi_n(x) \leq \phi_n(y)$.

E.9. Example: Componentwise Majorization. The functions

$$\phi_k(x) = x_k, \quad k = 1, \ldots, n,$$

generate a convex cone Φ, the completion of which consists of all functions increasing in each argument.

Transformations

Suppose that $\prec_\Phi$ is the ordering of Definition E.1 defined on the set I^n for some interval $I \subset \mathscr{R}$. Let u be a strictly increasing function mapping I to the interval J, and let

$$\psi(x|\phi) = \phi(u(x_1), \ldots, u(x_n)), \quad \phi \in \Phi, \quad x \in I^n.$$

Write $x \prec_\Phi^u y$ to mean that $\psi(x|\phi) \leq \psi(y|\phi)$ for all $\phi \in \Phi$. It can be verified that ψ preserves the order $\prec_\Phi^u$ if $\phi(x) = \psi(u^{-1}(x_1), \ldots, u^{-1}(x_n))$ preserves the order $\prec_\Phi$.

As an example, suppose that the functions constituting Φ are given by (2), so that $\prec_\Phi$ is the ordering of majorization. Restrict majorization to the set $\mathscr{R}_{++}^n$; i.e., take I to be $(0,\infty)$ and let $u(z) = \log z$, $z \in I$. It follows that $J = \mathscr{R}$. Let

$$\psi_i(x) = \phi_i(u(x_1), \ldots, u(x_n)), \quad i = 1, \ldots, n+1,$$

where the ϕ_i's are given by (2). These functions constitute a new family Φ^* of functions that determine the order $\prec_\Phi^*$ via Definition E.1. It follows that a function ψ that maps $\mathscr{R}^n$ to $\mathscr{R}$ preserves the order $\prec_\Phi^*$ if $\phi(x) = \psi(\exp(x_1), \ldots, \exp(x_n))$ is Schur-convex.

F Other Relatives of Majorization

Relatives of majorization have arisen in diverse contexts. Two such orderings, defined in terms of partial sums, are mentioned here. In addition, a measure of diversity difference, that is intimately related to majorization, is described.

Weak Bimajorization

F.1. Definition (Sanderson, 1974). A real vector x is said to be *weakly bimajorized* by a real vector y if $x_1 \geq \cdots \geq x_n$, $y_1 \geq \cdots \geq y_n$, and

(i) $\sum_{i=1}^k x_i \leq \sum_{i=1}^k y_i$, $k = 1, \ldots, n-1$,

(ii) $\sum_{i=k}^n x_i \leq \sum_{i=k}^n y_i$, $k = 2, \ldots, n$,

(iii) $\sum_1^n x_i \leq \sum_1^n y_i$.

Equivalent conditions are $x \prec_w y$ and $x \succ^w y$. Sanderson encountered this ordering in a study of the role of constraints in the economic theory of demand. Here, x_i is the production of household i under one set of constraints, and y_i is the corresponding production under relaxed constraints. In this application, Sanderson requires strict inequality in (iii).

The motivation for this ordering was a need to provide conditions under which

$$\sum_1^n \phi(x_i) \leq \sum_1^n \phi(y_i) \tag{1}$$

for all increasing functions ϕ that are convex, concave, or positive linear combinations of such functions. According to 4.B.2, (1) holds for all increasing convex functions and all increasing concave functions if and only if $x \prec_w y$ and $x \succ^w y$, so that weak bimajorization is exactly the required ordering.

Ordering for Complex Vectors

Let x and y be complex vectors such that $|x_1| \geq \cdots \geq |x_n|$, and $|y_1| \geq \cdots \geq |y_n|$. Under what conditions on x and y does there exist a matrix $Q = (q_{ij})$ of the form

$$q_{ij} = |u_{ij}|^2, \quad \text{where} \quad U = (u_{ij}) \text{ is a unitary matrix}$$

such that $x = yQ$?

F.2. Proposition (Thompson, 1978). Necessary and sufficient conditions for the existence of a matrix $Q = (q_{ij})$, where $q_{ij} = |u_{ij}|^2$, and $U = (u_{ij})$ is unitary, such that $x = yQ$ are

$$\sum_{i=1}^{k} |x_i| \leq \sum_{i=1}^{k} |y_i|, \quad k = 1, \ldots, n,$$

$$\sum_{i=1}^{k-1} |x_i| - \sum_{i=k}^{n} |x_i| \leq \sum_{i=1}^{n} |y_i| - 2|y_k|, \quad k = 1, \ldots, n,$$

$$\sum_{i=1}^{n-3} |x_i| - |x_{n-2}| - |x_{n-1}| - |x_n| \leq \sum_{i=1}^{n-2} |y_i| - |y_{n-1}| - |y_n|.$$

For applications in matrix analysis, see Chapter 9.

Relative Difference in Diversity

Let $\mathscr{P}$ denote the set of all n-dimensional probability vectors with elements arranged in increasing order; that is, $p \in \mathscr{P}$ if and only if $0 \leq p_1 \leq p_2 \leq \cdots \leq p_n$ and $\sum_{i=1}^{n} p_i = 1$. Alam and Williams (1993) propose a measure of dissimilarity in diversity between members of $\mathscr{P}$ that is intimately related to majorization. For $p = (p_1, \ldots, p_n) \in \mathscr{P}$, and $p' = (p'_1, \ldots, p'_n) \in \mathscr{P}$, define

$$\rho(p, p') = \inf ||p - p'Q||, \qquad (2)$$

where the infimum is over the class of all $n \times n$ doubly stochastic matrices Q and $||\cdot||$ is a norm on $\mathscr{R}^n$. Note that $\rho(p, p') = 0$ if and only if $p \prec p'$ and consequently $\rho(p, p')$ measures the departure from the majorization $p \prec p'$. Thus, if $\rho(p, p') \leq \rho(p, p'')$, then p is closer to being majorized by p' than it is to being majorized by p''.

If

$$d(p, p') = \rho(p, p') + \rho(p', p), \text{ for } p, p' \in \mathscr{P}, \tag{3}$$

then d is a metric on $\mathscr{P}$. Note that $d(p, p') = 0$ if and only if $p \prec p'$ and $p' \prec p$, i.e., if $p = p'$.

F.3. Proposition. If $p \prec p' \prec p''$, then $d(p', p'') \leq d(p, p'')$ and $d(p, p') \leq d(p, p'')$.

F.4. Proposition. If $p' = \sum_{i=1}^{m} \lambda_i q^{(i)}$, where $\lambda = (\lambda_1, \ldots, \lambda_n) \in \mathscr{P}$, and $q^{(i)} = (q_{(1)}^{(i)}, \ldots, q_{(n)}^{(i)}) \in \mathscr{P}$, then $d(p, p') \leq \sum_{i=1}^{n} \lambda_i d(p, q^{(i)})$.

Alam and Williams (1993) also suggest a diversity measure H defined on $\mathscr{P}$ using the metric (3):

$$H(p) = d(p, e_n); \tag{4}$$

here e_n is the vector $(0, 0, \ldots, 0, 1)$.

Computation of the metric $d(\cdot, \cdot)$ and the related diversity measure H depends on the norm selected for use in (2). For the L_1 or L_2 norm, the required values can be obtained by linear or quadratic programming.

G Majorization with Respect to a Partial Order

In the context of identifying optimal multipartitions, Hwang, Rothblum, and Shepp (1993) introduce the concept of majorization with respect to a given partial order, $\Rightarrow$, on the integers $\{1, 2, \ldots, n\}$. If $i \Rightarrow j$, then i is said to *dominate* j. Attention is restricted to partial orders consistent with the usual ordering of the integers. Thus it is assumed that if $i \Rightarrow j$, then $i > j$. A subset I of $\{1, 2, \ldots, n\}$ is said *to be closed with respect to* $\Rightarrow$, denoted by $\Rightarrow$closed, if I contains all integers that are dominated by any integer in I. A vector a is majorized by a vector b with respect to $\Rightarrow$, written $a \prec^{\Rightarrow} b$, if

$$\sum_{i \in I} a_i \leq \sum_{i \in I} b_i \text{ for every } \Rightarrow\text{closed subset } I,$$

and
$$\sum_{i=1}^{n} a_i = \sum_{i=1}^{n} b_i.$$

A function g is said to be $\Rightarrow$*Schur-convex* if $g(a) \leq g(b)$ whenever $a \prec^{\Rightarrow} b$.

Hwang (1979) provides an analog of the Schur–Ostrowski theorem (3.A.4) in this context. See also Hwang and Rothblum (1993), where several alternative characterizations of $\Rightarrow$Schur-convexity are discussed.

Hwang, Rothblum, and Shepp (1993) use these concepts to identify monotone optimal multipartitions with applications to optimal assembly problems, more general than those discussed in 13.D.

H Rearrangements and Majorizations for Functions

An n-dimensional vector can be regarded as defining a real-valued function with domain the integers $\{1, 2, \ldots, n\}$. Hardy, Littlewood, and Pólya (1929) develop an analogous partial order for real-valued functions with domain $[0, 1]$ and introduce the concept of a decreasing rearrangement. Two key elements here are the domain and the measure space. Generalizations are obtained by other versions of these two elements.

Joe (1987b) [who refers to Day (1973) and Chong (1974c)] observes that a parallel discussion can be provided for functions whose domain is a quite arbitrary measure space. Applications frequently involve a space that is a subset of $\mathscr{R}^n$, and use either Lebesgue or counting measure, but the abstract formulation provides a unifying framework for discussion of these ideas.

Let $(\mathscr{X}, \mathscr{F}, \nu)$ be a measure space and let f be a nonnegative ν-integrable function defined on $\mathscr{X}$. With the notation

$$m_f(t) = \nu(\{x : f(x) > t\}), \quad t \geq 0, \qquad (1)$$

define

$$f_\downarrow(u) = \sup\{t : m_f(t) > u\}, \quad 0 \leq u \leq \nu(\mathscr{X}). \qquad (2)$$

The function $f_\downarrow$ is called the *decreasing rearrangement* of f. This definition agrees with Hardy, Littlewood, and Pólya's definition of $f_\downarrow$

when $\mathscr{X}$ is the unit interval with Lebesgue measure. Observe that the domain of $f_\downarrow$ is $[0, \nu(\mathscr{X})]$, which usually differs from the domain $\mathscr{X}$ of f.

Note. A close relationship exists between the generalized ordering introduced here and the Lorenz ordering discussed in some detail in Chapter 17. In the Lorenz order context, ν is a probability measure and increasing rather than decreasing rearrangements are utilized.

H.1. Definition (Joe, 1987b). Let f and g be nonnegative integrable functions on $(\mathscr{X}, \mathscr{F}, \nu)$ such that $\int f \, d\nu = \int g \, d\nu$. The function f is *majorized by* g, denoted $f \prec g$, if

$$\int_0^t f_\downarrow(u) \, d\nu(u) \leq \int_0^t g_\downarrow(u) \, d\nu(u) \quad \text{for all } t \in [0, \nu(\mathscr{X})). \tag{3}$$

H.1.a. Proposition. The following conditions are equivalent to (3):

(a) $\int \phi(f) \, d\nu \leq \int \phi(g) \, d\nu$ for all continuous convex functions ϕ with $\phi(0) = 0$, for which the integrals exist;

(b) $\int_t^\infty m_f(s) \, ds \leq \int_t^\infty m_g(s) \, ds$ for all $t \geq 0$;

(c) $\int [f - t]^+ d\nu \leq \int [g - t]^+ d\nu$ for all $t \geq 0$.

Ruch, Schranner, and Seligman (1978) prove the equivalence of (a), (b), and (c) for ν a probability measure uniform on $[0, 1]$. The general case is due to Joe (1987b).

Condition (c) is the extension to the continuous case of one of the definitions of majorization in 1.A. The restriction to nonnegative functions in H.1 can be relaxed if $\nu(\mathscr{X})$ is finite.

A concept of a Schur-convex function can be introduced in the present context. A real-valued function ϕ defined on a subset $\mathscr{A}$ of the class of all nonnegative integrable functions on $\mathscr{X}$ is said to be Schur-convex on $\mathscr{A}$, if $f_1, f_2 \in \mathscr{A}$ and $f_1 \prec f_2$ imply that $\phi(f_1) \leq \phi(f_2)$. In the case that $\mathscr{X}$ is the unit interval, Chan, Proschan, and Sethuraman (1987) provide an analog of the Schur–Ostrowski characterization of

Schur-convex functions (3.A.4) involving *Gateaux differentials*. [For an exposition of Gateaux differentials, see Nashed (1966).]

Remark. The functions f and g appearing in Definition G.1 can be naturally associated with measures on $(\mathscr{X}, \mathscr{F})$ that are absolutely continuous with respect to ν [by defining $\nu_f(A) = \int_A f d\nu$, etc.]. Consequently, the majorization order (3) can be viewed as a partial order on such measures absolutely continuous with respect to ν. Kadane and Wasserman (1996) provide an extension of this partial order to deal with measures on $(\mathscr{X}, \mathscr{F})$ not necessarily absolutely continuous with respect to ν.

Hickey (1983, 1984) discusses an ordering of probability densities in terms of randomness. For this he assumes that the functions f and g in Definition H.1 integrate to 1, and are thus densities (usually in this context, $\mathscr{X}$ is a countable set or a subset of $\mathscr{R}^m$, where m denotes the dimension of the random vector associated with the given density). Hickey's randomness ordering is majorization, as defined in H.1, restricted to functions that integrate to 1, and ν taken to be either Lebesgue or counting measure. Here f is said to be *more random* than g if $f \prec g$.

If $\mathscr{X}$ is finite, Hickey's randomness ordering is equivalent to the classical majorization ordering applied to the corresponding discrete probability density functions. Consequently, the most random distribution over the n points in $\mathscr{X}$ is the uniform distribution over those n points.

In parallel fashion, in the general measure space $(\mathscr{X}, \mathscr{F}, \nu)$, the most random density with support in a given subset A of $\mathscr{X}$ of finite measure is the uniform density over A.

As a parallel to doubly stochastic matrices (which play a pivotal role in classical majorization), define a *doubly stochastic function* to be a function $k : \mathscr{X} \times \mathscr{X} \to [0, \infty)$ such that $\int k(x,y) \, d\nu(x) = 1$ for all $x \in \mathscr{X}$ and $\int k(x,y) \, d\nu(y) = 1$ for all $y \in \mathscr{X}$. It is readily verified using Jensen's inequality that if $f(x) = \int k(x,y)g(y) \, d\nu(y)$, then $f \prec g$. Hickey (1984) uses this to verify that if Z_1, Z_2 are independent m-dimensional random vectors with densities f_{Z_1} and f_{Z_2}, then the density of $Z_1 + Z_2$ is majorized by that of Z_1; that is, $f_{Z_1+Z_2} \prec f_{Z_1}$. In Hickey's words, the density of $Z_1 + Z_2$ is more random than that of Z_1 or Z_2. The result can be viewed as an extension of 12.N.5 by Brown and Solomon (1979) to deal with an infinite group.

Joe (1987b) advocates the use of density majorization as an ordering of dependence among k-dimensional densities with given marginals. For this, he considers densities on a product space $\mathscr{X}_1 \times \mathscr{X}_2 \times \cdots \times \mathscr{X}_k$ with given marginal densities $f_1, f_2, \ldots, f_k$ on $\mathscr{X}_1, \mathscr{X}_2, \ldots, \mathscr{X}_k$, respectively. Denote the set of all such densities by $\mathscr{S}(f_1, f_2, \ldots, f_k)$. If the members of $\mathscr{S}(f_1, f_2, \ldots, f_k)$ are partially ordered in the sense of Definition H.1, then the joint density $f(x) = \Pi_{i=1}^k f_i(x_i)$ (with independent marginals) is minimal (though not the unique minimal density), and thus the ordering can be viewed as one reflecting the dependence of members of $\mathscr{S}(f_1, f_2, \ldots, f_k)$.

Density majorization permits comparisons between diverse categories. Condition (3) of Definition H.1 involves decreasing rearrangement functions corresponding to f and g with domain a subset of $\mathscr{R}$, usually distinct from the original domains of f and g. Definition H.1 can be extended to allow f and g to be defined on very different measurable spaces. Thus consider f defined on $(\mathscr{X}_1, \mathscr{F}_1, \nu_1)$ and g defined on $(\mathscr{X}_2, \mathscr{F}_2, \nu_2)$ to be non-negative integrable functions normalized to have $\int f \, d\nu_1 = \int g \, d\nu_2$ and define $f \prec g$ if condition (3) of Definition H.1 holds. This allows a comparison of the variability in the geographic topography of Illinois and the variability in the income distribution in Kansas. Further discussion of this ordering, including the role of doubly stochastic functions in it, is given by Arnold and Joe (2000).

15
Multivariate Majorization

The definition of the majorization $x \prec y$ is motivated in Section 1.A as a way of making precise the idea that the components of x are "less spread out" than the components of y. This basic idea makes sense whether the components of x and y are points on the real line or points in a more general linear space.

Univariate majorization arises, e.g., in comparisons of income allocations. When allocations of more than one attribute are to be compared simultaneously, then some notion of multivariate majorization is required. In this case, the linear space to be considered is the space of real $m \times n$ matrices.

In this book, row vectors are used instead of column vectors, so that $x \prec y$ means $x = yP$ for some doubly stochastic matrix P. The reader is cautioned to be aware that in the multivariate case, some authors use row vectors and some use column vectors, so this can be confusing at times.

A Some Basic Orders

In the following, each row of a matrix represents allocations of a particular attribute, and each column represents allocations to one of the n receivers. In making a comparison, the univariate row vectors x and y are replaced by $m \times n$ matrices

A.W. Marshall et al., *Inequalities: Theory of Majorization and Its Applications*,
Springer Series in Statistics, DOI 10.1007/978-0-387-68276-1_15,
© Springer Science+Business Media, LLC 2011

$$X = (x_1^C, \ldots, x_n^C), \qquad Y = (y_1^C, \ldots, y_n^C),$$

where x_i^C and y_i^C are all column vectors of length m.

There are several ways now to make precise the idea that $x_1^C, \ldots, x_n^C$ are "less spread out" than $y_1^C, \ldots, y_n^C$.

Chain and Matrix Majorization

Consider first the concept of ordinary majorization ($m = 1$). The idea of a transfer, introduced by Muirhead (1903) and Dalton (1920) and discussed in Section 1.A, can be phrased as follows: If y_i and y_j are replaced by $\widetilde{y}_i$ and $\widetilde{y}_j$ to obtain a new vector $\widetilde{y}$ from y, then with the constraints that

(i) $\widetilde{y}_i$ and $\widetilde{y}_j$ lie in the convex hull of y_i and y_j,
(ii) $\widetilde{y}_i + \widetilde{y}_j = y_i + y_j$,

inequality among the components of $\widetilde{y}$ is certainly not greater than inequality among the components of y. Notice that $\widetilde{y} = yT$, where T is a T-transform; i.e., T is doubly stochastic and has exactly two nonzero off-diagonal entries.

When phrased in the above manner, the idea of a transfer also applies if the components of y are vectors. This leads to the following definition.

A.1. Definition. Let X and Y be $m \times n$ matrices. Then X is said to be *chain majorized* by Y, written $X \lll Y$, if $X = YP$, where P is a product of finitely many $n \times n$ T-transforms.

Suppose again that x and y are vectors of real numbers. Think of the components of y as incomes and think of the components of x as representing a redistribution of the total income $\sum_1^n y_i$. If each x_j is an average of $y_1, \ldots, y_n$, i.e.,

$$x_j = \sum_{i=1}^{n} y_i p_{ij},$$

where each $p_{ij} \geq 0$ and $\sum_{i=1}^{n} p_{ij} = 1$ for all j, then the components of x are surely "less spread out" than the components of y. Because $x_1, \ldots, x_n$ represents a redistribution of incomes $y_1, \ldots, y_n$, it must be that $\sum_{j=1}^{n} p_{ij} = 1$. Thus, $P = (p_{ij})$ is doubly stochastic.

These ideas carry over to the case that the components of x and y are vectors.

A. Some Basic Orders

A.2. Definition. Let X and Y be $m \times n$ real matrices. Then X is said to be *majorized* by Y, written $X \prec Y$, if $X = YP$, where the $n \times n$ matrix P is doubly stochastic.

Because a product of T-transforms is doubly stochastic,

$$X \prec\!\prec Y \quad \text{implies} \quad X \prec Y.$$

When $m = 1$, the converse is true by 2.B.1; it is also true for $n = 2$ because all 2×2 doubly stochastic matrices are T-transforms. When $m \geq 2$ and $n \geq 3$, majorization does not imply chain majorization, as the following example shows. See also Berg, Christensen, and Ressel (1984, p. 25).

A.3. Example. If $(1, \frac{1}{2}, \frac{1}{2}) = (1, 1, 0)P$, where P is doubly stochastic, it can be verified that P has the form

$$P = \frac{1}{2} \begin{bmatrix} \alpha & \beta & 2 - \alpha - \beta \\ 2 - \alpha & 1 - \beta & \alpha + \beta - 1 \\ 0 & 1 & 1 \end{bmatrix}, \tag{1}$$

where $0 \leq \alpha \leq 2$, $0 \leq \beta \leq 1$, $1 \leq \alpha + \beta \leq 2$. Similarly, $(3, 4, 5) = (2, 4, 6)P$, where P has the form (1) if and only if $\alpha = \beta = 1$. This means that if

$$X = \begin{bmatrix} 1 & \frac{1}{2} & \frac{1}{2} \\ 3 & 4 & 5 \end{bmatrix} \quad \text{and} \quad Y = \begin{bmatrix} 1 & 1 & 0 \\ 2 & 4 & 6 \end{bmatrix}$$

and $X = YP$, where P is doubly stochastic, then

$$P = \frac{1}{2} \begin{bmatrix} 1 & 1 & 0 \\ 1 & 0 & 1 \\ 0 & 1 & 1 \end{bmatrix}.$$

This doubly stochastic matrix is not a product of T-transforms (see Example 2.G.1). Consequently, X is majorized by Y, but X is not chain majorized by Y.

A well-known equivalent condition for the majorization $x \prec y$ is that $\Sigma_1^n \phi(x_i) \leq \Sigma_1^n \phi(y_i)$ for all convex functions $\phi : \mathscr{R} \to \mathscr{R}$ (see 4.B.1). A parallel result exists for multivariate majorization.

A.4. Proposition (Karlin and Rinott, 1983). $X \prec Y$ if and only if

$$\sum_{i=1}^{n} \phi(x_i^C) \leq \sum_{i=1}^{n} \phi(y_i^C) \qquad (2)$$

for all continuous convex functions $\phi : \mathscr{R}^m \to \mathscr{R}$; here x_i^C and y_i^C are column vectors.

Proof. If $X \prec Y$, then there exists $P = (p_{ij})$, doubly stochastic, with $X = YP$.
Then

$$\sum_{j=1}^{n} \phi(x_j^C) = \sum_{j=1}^{n} \phi\left(\sum_{i=1}^{n} p_{ij} y_i^C\right) \leq \sum_{j=1}^{n} \sum_{i=1}^{n} p_{ij} \phi(y_i^C)$$
$$= \sum_{i=1}^{n} \phi(y_i^C).$$

The converse can be justified by an appeal to a result of Meyer (1966) which relates balayages and dilations in a more abstract setting [see Karlin and Rinott (1983) for details]. ||

Note. In addition to Meyer's (1966) abstract treatment of Proposition A.4, several precursors can be identified. Somewhat earlier, Sherman (1951) provides a slightly more general version of A.4. See also Blackwell (1953), who refers to Charles Stein.

Fischer and Holbrook (1980) discuss several variants of Proposition A.4. For example, they observe that it is sufficient to restrict to continuous, convex, and coordinatewise increasing functions ϕ. In addition, they permit X and Y to be of different dimensions (i.e., X of dimension $m \times r$ and Y of dimension $m \times n$). A good survey of related results is given by Dahl (1999a).

Recall the notation $\langle A, B \rangle = \Sigma_i \Sigma_j a_{ij} b_{ij} = \text{tr} AB'$.

A.5. Proposition (Komiya, 1983). $X \prec Y$ if and only if

$$\max\{\langle U, XP \rangle : P \in \mathscr{P}_n\} \leq \max\{\langle U, YP \rangle : P \in \mathscr{P}_n\}$$

for every $m \times n$ matrix U, where $\mathscr{P}_n$ denotes the class of all $n \times n$ permutation matrices.

Borobia (1996) describes an algorithm to determine whether $X \prec Y$ in which he recasts the problem as a linear programming problem.

A.6. Example. As defined in Section 1.D, for complex vectors x, y, $x \prec y$ if $x = yP$ for some doubly stochastic matrix P. To see that this majorization can be regarded as multivariate majorization, write $x = a + ib$, $y = u + iv$, where a, b, u, v are real. Then $x = yP$ can be written in the form

$$\begin{pmatrix} a \\ b \end{pmatrix} = \begin{pmatrix} u \\ v \end{pmatrix} P.$$

In this context, Goldberg and Straus (1977/1978) noted that chain majorization implies majorization, but not conversely.

A.7. Example. The following statements are equivalent:

(i) $x \prec y$, (ii) $\begin{pmatrix} x \\ e-x \end{pmatrix} \prec\prec \begin{pmatrix} y \\ e-y \end{pmatrix}$, (iii) $\begin{pmatrix} x \\ e-x \end{pmatrix} \prec \begin{pmatrix} y \\ e-y \end{pmatrix}$,

where $e = (1, \ldots, 1)$. To see this, suppose first that $x \prec y$. Then $x = yP$, where P is a product of T-transforms (2.B.1). Because P is doubly stochastic, it follows that $(e-x) = (e-y)P$ and thus (ii) holds. Trivially, (ii) $\Rightarrow$ (iii) $\Rightarrow$ (i).

More generally, it can be shown that if $X \prec Y$, then

$$\begin{pmatrix} X \\ a_0 e + \sum_1^m a_i x_i^R \end{pmatrix} \prec \begin{pmatrix} Y \\ a_0 e + \sum_1^m a_i y_i^R \end{pmatrix},$$

where the x_i^R and y_i^R are row vectors of X and Y and the $a_i \in \mathscr{R}$. A similar statement can be made for chain majorization.

A.8. Example. For $l = 1, \ldots, m$, let $A^{(l)} = (a_{ij}^{(l)})$ be Hermitian matrices that commute with each other so that they can be simultaneously diagonalized:

$$A^{(l)} = UD^{(l)}U^* \quad \text{for some unitary matrix } U, \quad l = 1, \ldots, m,$$

where $D^{(l)} = (d_{ij}^{(l)})$ is a diagonal matrix. Then, for $l = 1, \ldots, m$,

$$(a_{11}^{(l)}, \ldots, a_{nn}^{(l)}) = (d_{11}^{(l)}, \ldots, d_{nn}^{(l)})P,$$

where $P = (p_{ij})$, $p_{ij} = u_{ij}\bar{u}_{ij}$. Since P is doubly stochastic (in fact, P is orthostochastic—see 2.B.5),

$$\begin{bmatrix} a_{11}^{(1)} & \cdots & a_{nn}^{(1)} \\ \vdots & & \vdots \\ a_{11}^{(m)} & \cdots & a_{nn}^{(m)} \end{bmatrix} \prec \begin{bmatrix} d_{11}^{(1)} & \cdots & d_{nn}^{(1)} \\ \vdots & & \vdots \\ d_{11}^{(m)} & \cdots & d_{nn}^{(m)} \end{bmatrix}.$$

This example generalizes 9.B.1.

A.9. Proposition. If $X \prec Y$, then for all $r \times m$ matrices A,

$$AX \prec AY.$$

Similarly, $X \prec\prec Y$ implies $AX \prec\prec AY$.

Proposition A.9 follows immediately from the observation that if $X = YP$, then $AX = AYP$. In particular, $X \prec Y$ implies $AX \prec AY$ for all idempotent matrices A. With $r = m - 1$, or $r = 1, \ldots, m - 1$, one might expect a converse to A.8. However, Elton and Hill (1992) provide an example in which $AX \prec AY$ for every 1×2 matrix A, but $X \not\prec Y$.

Row Majorization

Let $x_1^R, \ldots, x_m^R$ and $y_1^R, \ldots, y_m^R$ be the rows of X and Y, so that these quantities are row vectors of length n. Notice that $X \prec Y$ if and only if there exists a doubly stochastic matrix P such that

$$x_i^R = y_i^R P, \qquad i = 1, \ldots, m. \tag{3}$$

A similar remark applies to chain majorization, with P a product of T-transforms. The equalities (3) can be written alternatively in the form

$$(x_1^R, \ldots, x_m^R) = (y_1^R, \ldots, y_m^R) \begin{bmatrix} P & 0 & 0 & \cdots & 0 & 0 \\ 0 & P & 0 & \cdots & 0 & 0 \\ \vdots & \vdots & \vdots & & \vdots & \vdots \\ 0 & 0 & 0 & \cdots & 0 & P \end{bmatrix}. \tag{4}$$

This implies that

$$x_i^R \prec y_i^R, \qquad i = 1, \ldots, m, \tag{5}$$

in the sense of ordinary majorization. But, of course, (5) does not imply (4); (5) implies only that there exist doubly stochastic matrices $P_1, \ldots, P_m$ such that

$$x_i^R = y_i^R P_i, \qquad i = 1, \ldots, m,$$

but there is no guarantee that one can take $P_1 = \cdots = P_m$.

A.10. Definition. Let X and Y be $m \times n$ matrices. Then X is said to be *rowwise majorized* by Y, written $X \prec^{\text{row}} Y$, if (5) holds.

Notice that if $X \prec^{\text{row}} Y$, then there exist doubly stochastic matrices $P_1, \ldots, P_m$ such that

$$(x_1^{\text{R}}, \ldots, x_m^{\text{R}}) = (y_1^{\text{R}}, \ldots, y_m^{\text{R}}) \begin{bmatrix} P_1 & 0 & \cdots & 0 \\ 0 & P_2 & \cdots & 0 \\ \vdots & \vdots & \cdots & \vdots \\ 0 & 0 & \cdots & P_m \end{bmatrix}.$$

This shows that if $X \prec^{\text{row}} Y$, then

$$(x_1^{\text{R}}, \ldots, x_m^{\text{R}}) \prec (y_1^{\text{R}}, \ldots, y_m^{\text{R}})$$

because the matrix $\text{diag}(P_1, \ldots, P_m)$ is doubly stochastic. Various other special doubly stochastic matrices can be used to define other concepts of multivariate majorization.

Note that in contrast to Proposition A.9, if $X \prec^{\text{row}} Y$, it does not necessarily follow that $AX \prec^{\text{row}} AY$. To see this, consider

$$X = \begin{pmatrix} 1 & 2 \\ 3 & 4 \end{pmatrix}, \quad Y = \begin{pmatrix} 1 & 2 \\ 4 & 3 \end{pmatrix}, \quad A = \begin{pmatrix} 1 & 1 \\ 1 & 1 \end{pmatrix}.$$

Here, $X \prec^{\text{row}} Y$ trivially, but $AX \not\prec^{\text{row}} AY$.

A.11. Proposition (Das Gupta and Bhandari, 1989). For $m \times n$ matrices X and Y, $X \prec^{\text{row}} Y$ if and only if

$$\sum_{i=1}^{m}\sum_{j=1}^{n} \varphi_i(x_{ij}) \leq \sum_{i=1}^{m}\sum_{j=1}^{n} \varphi_i(y_{ij})$$

for all convex functions $\varphi_1, \ldots, \varphi_m$.

Proof. This result follows directly from Proposition 3.C.1. ||

Note. Alternative approaches to the definitions of multivariate majorization are discussed by Tsui (1999).

Linear-Combinations Majorization

Recall from Proposition A.9 that if X and Y are $m \times n$ matrices such that $X \prec Y$, then for all $r \times m$ matrices A, $AX \prec AY$. Here the focus is on the case that $r = 1$, so that A is a row vector a. With $r = 1$, the order $aX \prec aY$ reduces to ordinary majorization. Two versions of this type of multivariate majorization have received considerable attention [the names of the orderings used here are the same as those suggested by Joe and Verducci (1992)].

A.12. Definition. For $m \times n$ real matrices X and Y, X is said to be *linear-combinations majorized* by Y, written $X \prec^{LC} Y$, if for all $a \in \mathscr{R}^m$, $aX \prec aY$.

A.13. Definition. For $m \times n$ real matrices X and Y, X is said to be *positive-combinations majorized* by Y, written $X \prec^{PC} Y$, if for all $a \in \mathscr{R}_+^m$, $aX \prec aY$.

Other names for these orderings exist in the literature. Linear-combinations majorization is sometimes called *directional majorization*. Positive-combinations majorization or positive directional majorization is sometimes called *price majorization* [see e.g., Mosler (2002)]. In an economic context discussed further in Section 17.C, it is a more appealing concept than is linear-combinations majorization. However, as explained in Section 17.C, linear-combinations majorization admits an attractive interpretation involving the natural extension of the Lorenz curves to higher dimensions. Mosler (2002) provides a link between positive-combinations majorization and a construct known as an *inverse Lorenz function*, so in a sense both Definitions B.6 and B.7 have attractive economic interpretations. Joe and Verducci (1992) discuss algorithms useful to identify cases in which positive-combinations Lorenz ordering can occur. The fact that the two orderings are different is illustrated by the following simple example.

A.14. Example (Joe and Verducci, 1992). If

$$X = \begin{pmatrix} 1 & 3 \\ 4 & 2 \end{pmatrix}, \quad Y = \begin{pmatrix} 1 & 3 \\ 2 & 4 \end{pmatrix},$$

then $X \prec^{PC} Y$ but $X \not\prec^{LC} Y$ [shown by letting $a = (1, -1)$].

A.15. Example (Malamud, 2003, 2005). If

$$X = \begin{pmatrix} 12 & 12 & 5 & 3 \\ 12 & 12 & 3 & 5 \end{pmatrix} \quad \text{and} \quad Y = \begin{pmatrix} 8 & 16 & 0 & 8 \\ 16 & 8 & 0 & 8 \end{pmatrix},$$

then $X \prec^{LC} Y$ but $X \prec Y$ fails. That $X \prec^{LC} Y$ can be verified by a direct but tedious argument. Malamud (2003, 2005) shows that if $X = YP$, where P is doubly stochastic, then necessarily P must have the form

$$P = \begin{pmatrix} \frac{1}{2} & \frac{1}{2} & 0 & 0 \\ \frac{1}{2} & \frac{1}{2} & 0 & 0 \\ 0 & 0 & p & \bar{p} \\ 0 & 0 & \bar{p} & p \end{pmatrix}, \quad \text{where } \bar{p} = 1 - p;$$

but this is not possible, so that $X \prec Y$ fails.

A.15.a. Example (Martinez Pería, Massey, and Silvestre, 2005). If

$$X = \begin{pmatrix} 2 & -2 & 0 & 0 \\ 0 & 0 & -2 & 2 \end{pmatrix} \quad \text{and} \quad Y = \begin{pmatrix} 0 & 3 & -3 & 0 \\ 0 & -2 & -2 & 4 \end{pmatrix},$$

then $X \prec^{LC} Y$ but $X \prec Y$ fails.

Bhandari (1995) describes a technique to identify situations in which linear-combinations majorization does not imply majorization.

A.16. Observation. If $X \prec^{PC} Y$, then $X \prec^{\text{row}} Y$. This follows from the fact that $X \prec^{PC} Y$ implies that $e^{(i)}X \prec e^{(i)}Y, i = 1, \ldots, n$, where $e^{(i)}$ is the vector with 1 in the ith place and 0 elsewhere.

A.17. Example (Martinez Pería, Massey, and Silvestre, 2005). If

$$X = \begin{pmatrix} 1 & 0 \\ 1/2 & 1/2 \end{pmatrix} \quad \text{and} \quad Y = \begin{pmatrix} 1 & 0 \\ 0 & 1 \end{pmatrix},$$

then $X \prec^{\text{row}} Y$ but $X \prec^{PC} Y$ fails.

Column-Stochastic Majorization

Yet another version of matrix majorization is proposed by Martinez Pería, Massey, and Silvestre (2005).

A.18. Definition. For $m \times n$ real matrices X and Y, X is said to be *column-stochastic majorized* by Y, written $X \prec^{CS} Y$, if $X = YR$, where the $n \times n$ matrix R is column stochastic.

Martinez Pería, Massey and Silvestre (2005) use the term "weak majorization" in place of "column-stochastic majorization" and write $X \prec_w Y$ in place of $X \prec^{CS} Y$. Alternative terminology and notation are introduced here to avoid potential confusion; the ordering of Definition A.18 does not reduce to standard weak majorization (Definition 1.A.2) when $m = 1$. The natural multivariate extension of that notion would define $X \prec^{CS} Y$ to mean $X = YP$ for some doubly substochastic matrix P. See Theorem 2.C.4.

A parallel to Proposition A.4 is

A.19. Proposition (Martinez Pería, Massey, and Silvestre, 2005). For $m \times n$ real matrices X and Y, $X \prec^{CS} Y$ if and only if

$$\max_{1 \leq i \leq n} \phi(x_i^C) \leq \max_{1 \leq i \leq n} \phi(y_i^C)$$

for every convex function $\phi : \mathscr{R}^m \to \mathscr{R}$.

For a real $m \times n$ matrix X, let $\widetilde{X}(k)$ be an $m \times \binom{n}{k}$ matrix in which each column is the average of k different columns of X, arranged in lexicographic order. Using this notation, an insight into the relationship between linear combinations majorization and column stochastic majorization is provided in the following result.

A.20. Proposition (Martinez Pería, Massey, and Silvestre, 2005). Suppose X and Y are real $m \times n$ matrices. Then $X \prec^{LC} Y$ if and only if $\widetilde{X}(k) \prec^{CS} \widetilde{Y}(k)$ for $k = 1, 2, \ldots, [\frac{n}{2}]$ and $k = n$, where $[\frac{n}{2}]$ is the greatest integer less than $n/2$.

A.21. Example. Take $m = 1$, $n = 4$ and let
$$X = (12, 3, 3, 1), \quad Y = (8, 8, 2, 1).$$
Clearly, $X \prec Y$ fails; that is, $X \prec^{\text{row}} Y$ fails. However, $X = YR$, where
$$R = \begin{pmatrix} \frac{5}{9} & \frac{5}{9} & 0 & 0 \\ \frac{4}{9} & \frac{4}{9} & 0 & 0 \\ 0 & 0 & \frac{1}{2} & 0 \\ 0 & 0 & \frac{1}{2} & 1 \end{pmatrix}$$
is column-stochastic, so that $X \prec^{CS} Y$.

Additional Orderings

Boland and Proschan (1988) suggest a version of multivariate majorization that is defined in terms of *correlation increasing transfers*. Joe (1985) discusses a constrained multivariate majorization ordering in which only matrices with identical row and column totals are compared. Subject to that constraint, the ordering is defined in terms of ordinary majorization of the matrices viewed as vectors of dimension mn. He proposes such an ordering as a suitable dependence ordering in contingency tables. An extension to k-tuples is discussed in Joe (1987a).

Summary of Relationships

The various notions of multivariate majorizations introduced in this section relate as follows:
$$X \prec\!\prec Y \Longrightarrow X \prec Y \Longrightarrow X \prec^{LC} Y \Longrightarrow X \prec^{PC} Y$$
$$\Longrightarrow X \prec^{\text{row}} Y \Longrightarrow X \prec^{CS} Y. \qquad (6)$$

None of the above implications can be reversed, as has been shown by counterexamples:

$$X \prec Y \not\Longrightarrow X \prec\!\!\prec Y \quad \text{(Example A.3)},$$
$$X \prec^{LC} Y \not\Longrightarrow X \prec Y \quad \text{(Examples A.15 and A.15.a)},$$
$$X \prec^{PC} Y \not\Longrightarrow X \prec^{LC} Y \quad \text{(Example A.14)},$$
$$X \prec^{\text{row}} Y \not\Longrightarrow X \prec^{PC} Y \quad \text{(Example A.16)},$$
$$X \prec^{CS} Y \not\Longrightarrow X \prec^{\text{row}} Y \quad \text{(Example A.21)}.$$

Additional relationships between the various notions of multivariate majorization have been obtained under special conditions by Joe and Verducci (1992).

B The Order-Preserving Functions

For the case that $X \prec Y$, classes of order-preserving functions are identified in Propositions A.4 and A.5. Similarly, Proposition A.11 identifies a class of functions that preserve the order of row majorization, and Proposition A.19 identifies some functions that preserve column-stochastic majorization. None of these convex cones of order-preserving functions is complete. In this section, some convex cones of order-preserving functions are complete apart from differentiability requirements.

For any order $\prec^*$, denote the complete convex cone of order-preserving functions by $\mathscr{C}(\prec^*)$. If $X \prec_1 Y$ implies $X \prec_2 Y$, then clearly $\mathscr{C}(\prec_1) \supset \mathscr{C}(\prec_2)$. This observation together with A(6) leads to a chain of such inclusions.

The families $\mathscr{C}(\prec\!\!\prec)$ and $\mathscr{C}(\prec^{\text{row}})$ have been characterized by Rinott (1973), with some confusion due to the fact that the orderings $\prec\!\!\prec$ and $\prec$ are not distinguished.

B.1. Proposition (Rinott, 1973). A function $\phi : \mathscr{R}^{mn} \to \mathscr{R}$ that is differentiable satisfies

$$\phi(X) \leq \phi(Y) \qquad \text{for all} \quad X \prec\!\!\prec Y$$

if and only if

(i) $\phi(X) = \phi(X\Pi)$ for all permutation matrices Π,

(ii) $\sum_{i=1}^{m}(x_{ik} - x_{ij})[\phi_{(ik)}(X) - \phi_{(ij)}(X)] \geq 0$ for all $j, k = 1, \ldots, n$. Here $\phi_{(ij)}(X) = \partial \phi(U)/\partial u_{ij}|_{U=X}$.

Proof. Suppose first that $\phi(X) \leq \phi(Y)$ for all $X \prec\prec Y$. Because $X \prec\prec X\Pi$ for all permutation matrices Π, (i) follows. To obtain (ii), let

$$T = \begin{bmatrix} \alpha & 1-\alpha & 0 \\ 1-\alpha & \alpha & 0 \\ 0 & 0 & I_{n-2} \end{bmatrix}, \qquad 0 \leq \alpha \leq 1,$$

where I_{n-2} is the identity matrix of order $n-2$. Then T is a T-transform, so

$$[\phi(Y) - \phi(YT)]/(1-\alpha) \geq 0, \qquad 0 \leq \alpha \leq 1.$$

Thus

$$0 \leq \lim_{\alpha \to 1} \frac{\phi(Y) - \phi(YT)}{1-\alpha} = \sum_{i=1}^{m}(y_{i1} - y_{i2})[\phi_{(i1)}(Y) - \phi_{(i2)}(Y)].$$

By permuting the rows and corresponding columns of T and repeating the above argument, or by using the symmetry of ϕ, (ii) follows.

Next suppose that (i) and (ii) hold. Let $g(\alpha) = \phi(YT)$ and observe that with $\overline{\alpha} = 1 - \alpha$, $u_1^C = \alpha y_1^C + \overline{\alpha} y_2^C$, $u_2^C = \overline{\alpha} y_1^C + \alpha y_2^C$,

$$g'(\alpha) =$$
$$\sum_{i=1}^{m}(y_{i1} - y_{i2})[\phi_{(i1)}(u_1^C, u_2^C, y_3^C, \ldots, y_n^C) - \phi_{(i2)}(u_1^C, u_2^C, y_3^C, \ldots, y_n^C)]$$

$$= \sum_{i=1}^{m} \frac{u_{i1} - u_{i2}}{2\alpha - 1}[\phi_{(i1)}(u_1^C, u_2^C, y_3^C, \ldots, y_n^C) - \phi_{(i2)}(u_1^C, u_2^C, y_3^C, \ldots, y_n^C)]$$

$$\geq 0 \quad \text{for} \quad \alpha > \tfrac{1}{2}.$$

Because g is symmetric about $\tfrac{1}{2}$, this means $g(\alpha) \leq g(1)$, $0 < \alpha < 1$, and so $\phi(YT) \leq \phi(Y)$. By iteration, this means $\phi(YP) \leq \phi(Y)$ when P is a product of T-transforms. ||

B.2. Proposition (Rinott, 1973). Let $\phi: \mathscr{R}^{mn} \to \mathscr{R}$ be a differentiable function. It satisfies

$$\phi(X) \leq \phi(Y) \qquad \text{for all} \quad X \prec^{\text{row}} Y$$

if and only if it satisfies the conditions of 3.A.4 in each row, whatever the fixed values of the other rows.

The proof of B.2 follows from the fact that $X \prec^{\text{row}} Y$ means that $x_i^R \prec y_i^R$ for each i.

Little is known about functions that preserve the $\prec$ ordering. The difficulty here is that there is no stepwise path lemma like 2.B.1. Of course, any function that satisfies the conditions of B.2 preserves the ordering because $\mathscr{C}(\prec^{\text{row}}) \subset \mathscr{C}(\prec)$. Some additional examples are obtainable from the following theorem, which is a generalization of B.1.

B.3. Proposition. Let X and Y be $m \times n$ matrices. If $X \prec Y$, then $\phi(X) \leq \phi(Y)$ for all functions $\phi: \mathscr{R}^{mn} \to \mathscr{R}$ which are symmetric and convex in the sense that

(i) $\phi(X) = \phi(X\Pi)$ for all $n \times n$ permutation matrices Π,

(ii) $\phi(\alpha U + (1-\alpha)V) \leq \alpha\phi(U) + (1-\alpha)\phi(V)$,

$0 \leq \alpha \leq 1$, and U and V are $m \times n$ matrices.

Proof. Let $\Pi_1, \ldots, \Pi_{n!}$ be the $n \times n$ permutation matrices. Suppose that $X = YP$, where P is doubly stochastic. Then by Birkhoff's theorem 2.A.2, there exist nonnegative numbers $\alpha_1, \ldots, \alpha_{n!}$ such that $\sum_1^{n!} \alpha_i = 1$ and $P = \sum \alpha_i \Pi_i$. Then

$$\phi(X) = \phi(YP) = \phi\left(\sum_{i=1}^{n!} \alpha_i Y\Pi_i\right)$$

$$\leq \sum_{i=1}^{n!} \alpha_i \phi(Y\Pi_i) = \sum_{i=1}^{n!} \alpha_i \phi(Y) = \phi(Y). \quad \|$$

Note. Beasley and Lee (2000) provide a characterization of linear operators on the space of $m \times n$ matrices that preserve multivariate majorization.

C Majorization for Matrices of Differing Dimensions

In this section, three methods of comparing matrices having different dimensions are discussed. In the first two methods, the matrices differ in the number of rows, and in the third they differ in the number of columns.

In the following two definitions, X is an $\ell \times n$ matrix and Y is an $m \times n$ matrix where $\ell \leq m$.

C.1. Definition (Fischer and Holbrook, 1980). If there exists an $(m-\ell) \times n$ matrix Z such that $\begin{pmatrix} X \\ Z \end{pmatrix} \prec Y$ in the sense of Definition A.2, i.e., $\begin{pmatrix} X \\ Z \end{pmatrix} = YP$ for some doubly stochastic matrix P, then write $X \prec_{\mathrm{ds}} Y$.

Of course, when $\ell = m$, the ordering $\prec_{\mathrm{ds}}$ is just the ordering $\prec$ of Definition A.2.

The following definition is motivated by Remark 1.A.1.c, which offers a characterization of ordinary majorization.

C.2. Definition (Malamud, 2003, 2005). Denote the rows of X and Y by $x_1^R, \ldots, x_\ell^R$ and $y_1^R, \ldots, y_m^R$. If for $j = 1, \ldots, \ell$,

$$\operatorname{conv} \{x_{i_1}^R + \cdots + x_{i_j}^R,\ 1 \leq i_1 < \cdots < i_j \leq \ell\}$$

$$\subset \operatorname{conv} \{y_{i_1}^R + \cdots + y_{i_j}^R,\ 1 \leq i_1 < \cdots < i_j \leq m\},$$

then X is said to be *Malamud majorized* by Y, written $X \prec_{\mathrm{M}} Y$.

The following is a brief sketch of some results regarding the orderings of Definitions C.1 and C.2.

C.3. Proposition (Malamud, 2003). If $X \prec_{\mathrm{ds}} Y$, then $X \prec_{\mathrm{M}} Y$.

Example A.15 shows that the converse is false.

C.4. Proposition (Malamud, 2005). Suppose that $\ell = m$. If $\operatorname{conv} \{y_1^R, \ldots, y_m^R\}$ is affine isometric to the simplex

$$\{(t_1, \ldots, t_m) \in \mathscr{R}^m : t_j \geq 0 \text{ for all } j \text{ and } \Sigma_1^m t_j = 1\},$$

then $X \prec_{\mathrm{M}} Y$ is equivalent to $X \prec Y$. As already noted, $\prec$ and $\prec_{\mathrm{ds}}$ are identical when $\ell = m$.

C.5. Proposition (Fischer and Sendov, 2010). If

$$\begin{pmatrix} x_{j_1}^R \\ x_{j_2}^R \end{pmatrix} \prec_{\mathrm{M}} Y \quad \text{implies} \quad \begin{pmatrix} x_{j_1}^R \\ x_{j_2}^R \end{pmatrix} \prec_{\mathrm{ds}} Y$$

whenever $1 \leq j_1 < j_2 \leq \ell$, then $X \prec_{\mathrm{M}} Y$ implies $X \prec_{\mathrm{ds}} Y$.

C.6. Proposition (Fischer and Holbrook, 1980). $X \prec_{\text{ds}} Y$ if and only if

$$\sum_{i=1}^{\ell} f(x_i^R) \leq \sum_{i=1}^{m} f(y_i^R) \qquad (1)$$

for all continuous convex functions defined on

$$\text{conv}\,\{x_1^R, \ldots, x_\ell^R, y_1^R, \ldots, y_m^R\}.$$

C.7. Proposition (Malamud, 2005). $X \prec_{\text{M}} Y$ if and only if (1) holds for all functions of the form $f(x) = g(xz')$ for some $z \in \mathscr{R}^n_{;,}$ where g is a nonnegative convex function defined on $\mathscr{R}$.

Recall that a matrix $Q = (q_{ij})$ is row stochastic if $q_{ij} \geq 0$ for all i, j and all rows of Q sum to 1.

C.8. Definition (Dahl, 1999a). Let X be an $m \times r$ matrix and let Y be $m \times n$. Write $X \prec_{\text{S}} Y$ to mean that

$$X = YQ \qquad (2)$$

for some $n \times r$ row stochastic matrix Q.

The subscript S on the symbol $\prec_{\text{S}}$ serves as a reminder that Q is only required to be stochastic. Observe also that X has n columns, whereas Y has r columns. When $n = r$ and Q is doubly stochastic, then $\prec_{\text{S}}$ agrees with Definition A.2 of matrix majorization.

However, when $n = r$ and $m = 1$, the ordering $\prec_{\text{S}}$ does not reduce to the usual notion of majorization because Q is required only to be stochastic, not doubly stochastic. Nevertheless, the ordering possesses a number of desirable properties.

C.9. Proposition (Dahl, 1999a). If X is $m \times r$, Y is $m \times n$, and Z is $m \times s$, then the following properties hold:

(i) $X \prec_{\text{S}} X$;

(ii) if $X \prec_{\text{S}} Y$ and $Y \prec_{\text{S}} Z$, then $X \prec_{\text{S}} Z$;

(iii) if $X \prec_{\text{S}} Y$ and A is $m \times m$, then $AX \prec_{\text{S}} AY$.

Dahl (1999a) lists several other useful properties of the order $\prec_{\text{S}}$.

A characterization of $\prec_{\text{S}}$ is provided in terms of two classes of functions defined on $\mathscr{R}^m$: the positive homogeneous subadditive functions

$$\Psi = \{\phi : \phi(\lambda x) = \lambda \phi(x),\ \phi(x+y) \leq \phi(x) + \phi(y)$$

$$\text{for all } x, y \in \mathscr{R}^n,\ \text{and for all } \lambda \geq 0\},$$

and

$$\Psi^* = \{\phi : \text{ for some integer } k, \ \phi = \max_{1 \leq i \leq k} \phi_i,$$

where the ϕ_i are linear functions$\}$.

C.10. Proposition (Dahl, 1999a).   The following are equivalent:

(i) $X \prec_S Y$;

(ii) $\sum_{i=1}^{r} \phi(x_i^C) \leq \sum_{i=1}^{n} \phi(y_i^C)$ for all $\phi \in \Psi$;

(iii) $\sum_{i=1}^{r} \phi(x_i^C) \leq \sum_{i=1}^{n} \phi(y_i^C)$ for all $\phi \in \Psi^*$.

When $r = n$, the orders $\prec_S$ and $\prec$ are related by the condition

$$X \prec Y \text{ if and only if } \begin{pmatrix} e \\ X \end{pmatrix} \prec_S \begin{pmatrix} e \\ Y \end{pmatrix}, \quad e = (1, \ldots, 1).$$

This relationship can be used to derive Proposition A.4 as a corollary of Proposition C.10.

Dahl (1999b) discusses properties of multivariate majorization polytopes. For X and Y of dimensions $m \times n$ and $m \times r$, respectively, consider the polytope

$$\mathscr{P}(X \prec_S Y) = \{Q : Q \text{ is row stochastic and } X = YQ\}$$

of row stochastic matrices associated with $X \prec_S Y$. Dahl (1999b) shows that $\mathscr{P}(X \prec_S Y)$ can be identified as the intersection of m scaled "transportation polytopes."

Application to Thermodynamics

It is interesting that the concept of "d-majorization" (14.B.2) has arisen in a thermodynamics setting and is related to the partial order $\prec_S$. In this context, a state is an n-dimensional probability vector p. The following discussion of this and related concepts is based on information kindly provided by Zylka (2004), now available in Alberti, Crell, Uhlmann, and Zylka (2008). They consider the partial order $\prec_S$ restricted to the space of $m \times n$ stochastic matrices. For two $m \times n$ stochastic matrices P and Q, $P \prec_S Q$ if there exists an $n \times n$ *stochastic* matrix A such that $P = QA$.

Note. In a thermodynamic context, the row vectors of P, denoted by $\{p_{(1)}, \ldots, p_{(m)}\}$, and of Q, denoted by $\{q_{(1)}, \ldots, q_{(m)}\}$ are viewed

C. Majorization for Matrices of Differing Dimensions   627

as m-tuples of states. The majorization $P \prec_S Q$ is denoted by $\{p_{(1)}, \ldots, p_{(m)}\} \prec^{(m)} \{q_{(1)}, \ldots, q_{(m)}\}$ and is called *(m)-majorization*.

A characterization of (m)-majorization in terms of homogeneous convex functions is possible, paralleling the Hardy, Littlewood, and Pólya characterization of majorization using convex functions (Proposition 4.B.1).

C.11. Lemma. The majorization $P \prec_S Q$, or equivalently, the (m)-majorization

$$(p_{(1)}, \ldots, p_{(m)}) \prec^{(m)} (q_{(1)}, \ldots, q_{(m)}),$$

holds if and only if

$$\sum_{j=1}^n g(p_{1j}, p_{2j}, \ldots, p_{mj}) \leq \sum_{j=1}^n g(q_{1j}, q_{2j}, \ldots, q_{mj}) \qquad (3)$$

for all functions $g : \mathscr{R}^m \to \mathscr{R}$ that are convex and homogeneous in their arguments. [In (3) the coordinates of $p_{(i)}$ are denoted by p_{ij}.]

In the case $m = 2$, Lemma C.11 can be rewritten in the following form:

$$\{p_{(1)}, p_{(2)}\} \prec^{(2)} \{q_{(1)}, q_{(2)}\}$$

if and only if

$$\sum_{j=1}^n p_{2j} h\left(\frac{p_{1j}}{p_{2j}}\right) \leq \sum_{j=1}^n q_{2j} h\left(\frac{q_{1j}}{q_{2j}}\right) \qquad (4)$$

for any convex function h, where it is assumed that the components p_{2j} and q_{2j} are positive. The expressions appearing in (4) are called *generalized relative entropies* because the special choice $h(x) = x \log x$ corresponds to the relative entropy (of $p_{(1)}$ with respect to $p_{(2)}$).

Suppose $m = 2$. If one state, say q, is fixed as a reference state, then (2)-majorization is defined as a partial order on the state space relative to, or with respect to, q as follows.

C.12. Definition. $p_{(1)} \prec_q^r p_{(2)}$ if and only if $\{p_{(1)}, q\} \prec^{(2)} \{p_{(2)}, q\}$.

The notation used in C.12 is not meant to confuse. It is the same notation as was used in Definition 14.B.2 for q-majorization or majorization relative to q [as introduced by Veinott (1971)]. Comparison of 14.B(1) and (4), or reference to Proposition 14.B.4.(c) and

Definition C.8, confirms that indeed the ordering defined in C.12 is a reincarnation of majorization relative to q, with classical majorization as the special case corresponding to $q = e$.

A stochastic process $\{X(t) : t \geq 0\}$ with state space $1, 2, \ldots, n$ is said to respect relative majorization with respect to q if the set $\{p(t) : t \geq 0\}$, where $p(t)$ corresponds to the probability distribution of $X(t)$, satisfies

$$p(t_1) \prec_q^r p(t_2) \quad \text{for all } t_1 \leq t_2. \tag{5}$$

The study of such processes with $q = e$ dates back to Lassner and Lassner (1973). The extension to a general state q was introduced by Ruch and Mead (1976), who described the ordering using the term *mixing distance relative to q*.

Zylka (1985, 1990) discusses the nature of the class of all states accessible from a fixed initial state in a process satisfying (5). Inter alia he discusses extensions of several classes of stochastic matrices related to the doubly stochastic matrices discussed in 2.B.5, replacing e in the definitions by a general state q.

D Additional Extensions

In Section A, the ordinary majorization $x \prec y$ is generalized by replacing each component of x and y by a vector. Here the idea is carried one step further; each component of x and y is replaced by a matrix.

Let $X_1, \ldots, X_n$ and $Y_1, \ldots, Y_n$ be $k \times l$ matrices. The idea of a majorization between $X = (X_1, \ldots, X_n)$ and $Y = (Y_1, \ldots, Y_n)$ can be obtained directly from the definitions of Section A because, after all, X and Y are matrices. This approach is not really appropriate because it does not treat the matrices $X_1, \ldots, X_n$ and $Y_1, \ldots, Y_n$ as entities in themselves. For example, the appropriate analog of a T-transform applied to $(Y_1, \ldots, Y_n)$ would yield an image of the form

$$(Y_1, \ldots, Y_{i-1}, \alpha Y_i + \overline{\alpha} Y_j, Y_{i+1}, \ldots, Y_{j-1}, \overline{\alpha} Y_i + \alpha Y_j, Y_{j+1}, \ldots, Y_n),$$

where $0 \leq \alpha \leq 1$ and $\overline{\alpha} = 1 - \alpha$.

In stating the definition below, the notion of the Kronecker product (Section 19.G) is useful.

Note that if P is doubly stochastic, then the Kronecker product $P \otimes I$ is doubly stochastic. If T is a T-transform, then $T \otimes I$ is not a T-transform, but it is a product of l T-transforms if I is $l \times l$.

D. Additional Extensions

D.1. Definition. Let $X_1, \ldots, X_n$ and $Y_1, \ldots, Y_n$ be $k \times l$ matrices. Then $(X_1, \ldots, X_n)$ is *chain majorized* by $(Y_1, \ldots, Y_n)$, written

$$(X_1, \ldots, X_n) \lll (Y_1, \ldots, Y_n),$$

if

$$(X_1, \ldots, X_n) = (Y_1, \ldots, Y_n)(P \otimes I), \tag{1}$$

where P is a product of finitely many $n \times n$ T-transforms and I is $l \times l$. Similarly, $(X_1, \ldots, X_n)$ is *majorized* by $(Y_1, \ldots, Y_n)$, written

$$(X_1, \ldots, X_n) \prec (Y_1, \ldots, Y_n),$$

if (1) holds for some $n \times n$ doubly stochastic matrix P.

These concepts of majorization are virtually unexplored. Use is made of them in the following two propositions.

D.2. Proposition. If $(X_1, \ldots, X_n) \prec (Y_1, \ldots, Y_n)$, then

$$\phi(X_1, \ldots, X_n) \leq \phi(Y_1, \ldots, Y_n)$$

for all functions $\phi : \mathcal{R}^{kln} \to \mathcal{R}$ such that

(i) $\phi(U) = \phi[U(\Pi \otimes I)]$ for all $n \times n$ permutation matrices Π and all $k \times ln$ matrices U,

(ii) $\phi(\alpha U + (1-\alpha)V) \leq \alpha \phi(U) + (1-\alpha)\phi(V)$ for all $0 \leq \alpha \leq 1$ and all $k \times ln$ matrices U and V.

Proof. As in the proof of C.3, write $P = \sum_1^{n!} \alpha_i \Pi_i$, where P is a doubly stochastic matrix satisfying $(X_1, \ldots, X_n) = (Y_1, \ldots, Y_n)(P \otimes I)$. Then

$$\begin{aligned}
\phi[(X_1, \ldots, X_n)] &= \phi[(Y_1, \ldots, Y_n)(P \otimes I)] \\
&= \phi\{(Y_1, \ldots, Y_n)[(\sum \alpha_i \Pi_i) \otimes I]\} \\
&= \phi\{(Y_1, \ldots, Y_n)[\sum \alpha_i (\Pi_i \otimes I)]\} \\
&\leq \sum \alpha_i \phi[(Y_1, \ldots, Y_n)(\Pi \otimes I)] \\
&= \phi[(Y_1, \ldots, Y_n)]. \quad \|
\end{aligned}$$

The following proposition generalizes 11.B.2.

D.3. Proposition. Let $\phi : \mathcal{R}^{kpn} \to \mathcal{R}$ satisfy conditions (i) and (ii) of D.2 and let $Z_1, \ldots, Z_n$ be exchangeable random $l \times p$ matrices. If $(A_1, \ldots, A_n) \lll (B_1, \ldots, B_n)$, where the A_i's and B_i's are $k \times l$, then

$$E\phi(A_1 Z_1, \ldots, A_n Z_n) \leq E\phi(B_1 Z_1, \ldots, B_n Z_n).$$

630   15. Multivariate Majorization

Proof. It is sufficient to prove the theorem for the case that $(A_1,\ldots,A_n) = (B_1,\ldots,B_n)(T \otimes I)$, where T is an $n \times n$ T-transform, say

$$T = \begin{bmatrix} \alpha & \overline{\alpha} & 0 \\ \overline{\alpha} & \alpha & 0 \\ 0 & 0 & I \end{bmatrix}, \quad \overline{\alpha} = 1-\alpha, \quad 0 \leq \alpha \leq 1.$$

In this case, $(A_1,\ldots,A_n) = (\alpha B_1 + \overline{\alpha} B_2, \overline{\alpha} B_1 + \alpha B_2, B_3, \ldots, B_n)$, so that

$$\begin{aligned} E\phi(A_1 Z_1, &\ldots, A_n Z_n) \\ &= E\phi[(\alpha B_1 + \overline{\alpha} B_2)Z_1, (\overline{\alpha} B_1 + \alpha B_2)Z_2, B_3 Z_3, \ldots, B_n Z_n] \\ &= E\phi[\alpha(B_1 Z_1, B_2 Z_2) + \overline{\alpha}(B_2 Z_1, B_1 Z_2), B_3 Z_3, \ldots, B_n Z_n] \\ &\leq \alpha E\phi(B_1 Z_1, B_2 Z_2, B_3 Z_3, \ldots, B_n Z_n) \\ &\quad + \overline{\alpha} E\phi(B_2 Z_1, B_1 Z_2, B_3 Z_3, \ldots, B_n Z_n) \\ &= E\phi(B_1 Z_1, \ldots, B_n Z_n). \end{aligned}$$

The last equality uses the symmetry of ϕ and exchangeability of Z_1 and Z_2. ||

E   Probability Inequalities

Inequalities Involving Mixtures

To introduce the results of this section, a special case is given where ordinary majorization suffices.

Let W and Z be random variables such that $W \leq^{st} Z$. For $i = 1,\ldots,n$, let X_{p_i} be a "mixture" of W_i and Z_i, where $W_1,\ldots,W_n$ are independent random variables distributed as W and $Z_1,\ldots,Z_n$ are independent random variables distributed as Z. That is,

$$X_{p_i} = \begin{cases} W_i & \text{with probability } 1 - p_i, \\ Z_i & \text{with probability } p_i. \end{cases}$$

Then $X_p = (X_{p_1},\ldots,X_{p_n})$ is a random vector with independent components.

E.1. Proposition.   If ϕ is a symmetric L-superadditive function on $\mathscr{R}^n$ and $p = (p_1,\ldots,p_n) \prec (q_1,\ldots,q_n) = q$, then $E\phi(X_p) \geq E\phi(X_q)$.

E. Probability Inequalities   631

Notice that if $W \equiv 0$ and $Z \equiv 1$, then the components of X_p and X_q have Bernoulli distributions. In this case, E.1 reduces to 12.F.1.

Recall from Example A.5 that $p \prec q$ if and only if
$$\begin{pmatrix} p \\ e-p \end{pmatrix} \prec\prec \begin{pmatrix} q \\ e-q \end{pmatrix}.$$

In order to analyze mixtures of more than two random variables, multivariate majorization is required.

Let $U_1, \ldots, U_m$ be random variables such that $U_1 \leq^{\mathrm{st}} \cdots \leq^{\mathrm{st}} U_m$. For any $m \times n$ matrix $P = (p_{ij})$ of probabilities with column vectors p_j^{C} and column sums one, let $X_{p_j^{\mathrm{C}}}$ be "mixture" random variables such that, for $i = 1, \ldots, m$ and $j = 1, \ldots, n$, $X_{p_j^{\mathrm{C}}}$ has the same distribution as U_i with probability p_{ij}. Assume that $X_{p_1^{\mathrm{C}}}, \ldots, X_{p_n^{\mathrm{C}}}$ are independent and let $X_P = (X_{p_1^{\mathrm{C}}}, \ldots, X_{p_n^{\mathrm{C}}})$. Conditions are obtained on functions $\phi : \mathscr{R}^n \to \mathscr{R}$ and on the random variables $U_1, \ldots, U_m$ so that

$$P \prec\prec Q \quad \text{implies} \quad E\phi(X_P) \geq E\phi(X_Q). \tag{1}$$

It is sufficient to find these conditions under the assumption that $P = QT$, where T is a T-transform. Because of this, it is enough to consider the case $n = 2$. Of course, it is essential that ϕ be symmetric.

Because $U_1 \leq^{\mathrm{st}} \cdots \leq^{\mathrm{st}} U_m$, by 17.B.6 there exist random variables $V_1, \ldots, V_m$ such that

(i) $P\{V_1 \leq \cdots \leq V_m\} = 1$,

(ii) U_i and V_i have the same distribution, $i = 1, \ldots, m$.

Let $\widetilde{V} = (\widetilde{V}_1, \ldots, \widetilde{V}_n)$ be a random vector independent of, and having the same distribution as, $V = (V_1, \ldots, V_n)$. Then

$$\psi(P) \equiv E\phi(X_P) = \sum_{i,j} p_{1i} p_{2j} \phi(V_i, \widetilde{V}_j) = (p_1^{\mathrm{C}})' A p_2^{\mathrm{C}},$$

where $A = (a_{ij})$ and $a_{ij} = E\phi(V_i, \widetilde{V}_j)$. Because V and $\widetilde{V}$ have the same distribution and ϕ is symmetric, $a_{ij} = a_{ji}$. To apply the conditions of C.1, let e_j be the row vector with jth component one and all other components zero, and compute

$$\psi_{(i1)}(P) = e_i A p_2^{\mathrm{C}} - e_m A p_2^{\mathrm{C}},$$
$$\psi_{(i1)}(P) = (p_1^{\mathrm{C}})' A(e_i - e_m)' = e_i A p_1^{\mathrm{C}} - e_m A p_1^{\mathrm{C}}.$$

Thus

$$\psi_{(i1)}(P) - \psi_{(i2)}(P) = (e_i - e_m) A (p_2^{\mathrm{C}} - p_1^{\mathrm{C}}),$$

and the condition

$$\sum_{i=1}^{m}(p_{i1} - p_{i2})(e_i - e_m)A(p_2^C - p_1^C) \leq 0$$

can be written, with $p_{i2} - p_{i1} = z_i$, in the form

$$zAz' \geq 0 \quad \text{whenever} \quad \sum_{i=1}^{m} z_i = 0. \tag{2}$$

Sufficient conditions to apply C.1 are that

(i) ϕ is symmetric in its n arguments;

(ii) for fixed $x_3, \ldots, x_n$, $\tilde{\phi}(x_1, x_2) = \phi(x_1, x_2, x_3, \ldots, x_n)$ satisfies

$$\sum_{i,j=1}^{m} z_i z_j \, \tilde{\phi}(u_i, v_j) \geq 0 \text{ for all } u_1 \leq \cdots \leq u_m, v_1 \leq \cdots \leq v_m,$$

and all $z_1, \ldots, z_m$ such that $\sum_{i=1}^{m} z_i = 0$.

Conditions (i) and (ii) reduce to the conditions of C.1 in case $m = 2$. However, they are too strong to identify examples where (2) is satisfied. For example, if $\phi(x_1, \ldots, x_m) = \prod_{i=1}^{m} x_i$, then (2) holds but (ii) fails to hold.

Probability Content of Rectangular Regions

Let A and B be $2 \times n$ matrices

$$A = \begin{pmatrix} a_{11}, \cdots, a_{1n} \\ a_{21}, \cdots, a_{2n} \end{pmatrix}, \quad B = \begin{pmatrix} b_{11}, \cdots, b_{1n} \\ b_{21}, \cdots, b_{2n} \end{pmatrix}$$

such that $a_{1j} < a_{2j}$, $b_{1j} < b_{2j}$, $j = 1, \ldots, n$.

E.2. Proposition (Karlin and Rinott, 1983; Tong, 1988, 1989). If $X_1, \ldots, X_n$ have a Schur-concave joint density and $B \prec\!\prec A$, then

$$P\{a_{1j} \leq X_j \leq a_{2j}, j = 1, .., n\} \leq P\{b_{1j} \leq X_j \leq b_{2j}, j = 1, .., n\}. \tag{3}$$

Note that $B \prec\!\prec A$ implies the existence of a doubly stochastic matrix P such that $B = AP$. Thus $(-1, 1)B = (-1, 1)AP$; that is,

$$(a_{21} - a_{11}, \ldots, a_{2n} - a_{1n}) \succ (b_{21} - b_{11}, \ldots, b_{2n} - b_{1n}).$$

Thus the rectangle $b_{1j} \leq x_j \leq b_{2j}$, $j = 1, \ldots, n$, has edge lengths closer to being equal (in the sense of majorization) than those of the rectangle $a_{1j} \leq x_j \leq a_{2j}$, $j = 1, \ldots, n$. As could be expected from the exchangeability of $X_1, \ldots, X_n$, among all rectangles with fixed edge-length sum, the cube contains the highest probability.

E.2.a. Proposition (Karlin and Rinott, 1983; Tong, 1983, 1988). If $X_1, \ldots, X_n$ have a permutation symmetric log concave density and $B \prec\!\prec A$, then (3) holds.

As compared to Proposition E.2, Proposition E.2.a has stronger conditions on the density of $X_1, \ldots, X_n$, and weaker conditions on A and B.

Part V
Complementary Topics

16
Convex Functions and Some Classical Inequalities

Convex functions arise in a variety of contexts and are basic to a number of results. For more extensive discussions of convexity, see Roberts and Varberg (1973), Rockafellar (1970), Stoer and Witzgall (1970), van Tiel (1984), Pečarić, Proschan, and Tong (1992), Webster (1994), or Niculescu and Persson (2006). The book by Pachpatte (2005, Chapter 1) provides a compendium of inequalities involving convex functions.

A Monotone Functions

For any $x, y \in \mathscr{R}^n$, write $x \leq y$ if $x_i \leq y_i$, $i = 1, \ldots, n$. In this book, a function $\phi : \mathscr{R}^n \to \mathscr{R}$ is said to be *increasing* if

$$x \leq y \Rightarrow \phi(x) \leq \phi(y),$$

and the term "nondecreasing" is not used. If

$$x \leq y \text{ and } x \neq y \Rightarrow \phi(x) < \phi(y),$$

then ϕ is said to be *strictly increasing*. If $-\phi$ is increasing (strictly increasing), then ϕ is said to be *decreasing* (*strictly decreasing*).

A.1. Proposition. Let $I \subset \mathscr{R}$ be an open interval and let $\phi: I \to \mathscr{R}$ be differentiable. Then

(i) ϕ is increasing on I if and only if $\phi'(x) \geq 0$ for all $x \in I$,

(ii) ϕ is strictly increasing on I if and only if $\phi'(x) \geq 0$ for all $x \in I$ and the set where $\phi'(x) = 0$ contains no intervals.

Proof of (ii). Suppose that ϕ is strictly increasing on I. If $\phi'(x) = 0$ for x in some interval, say (a, b), then $\phi(x)$ is constant for $x \in (a, b)$, so ϕ is not strictly increasing. This contradiction means that there is no interval on which $\phi'(x) = 0$.

Next, suppose the set where $\phi'(x) = 0$ contains no intervals. If ϕ is not strictly increasing, a contradiction is again easily arrived at. ||

For functions ϕ defined on $\mathscr{R}^n$, denote by $\phi_{(i)}$ the partial derivative (if it exists) of ϕ with respect to its ith argument, $i = 1, \ldots, n$. If the *gradient*

$$\nabla \phi(x) = (\phi_{(1)}(x), \ldots, \phi_{(n)}(x))$$

exists for all x in the open set $\mathscr{A} \subset \mathscr{R}^n$, then ϕ is said to be differentiable on $\mathscr{A}$.

A.1.a. Let $\mathscr{A} \subset \mathscr{R}^n$ be a convex set with nonempty interior and let $\phi: \mathscr{A} \to \mathscr{R}$ be differentiable on the interior of $\mathscr{A}$ and continuous on the boundary of $\mathscr{A}$. Then

(i) ϕ is increasing on $\mathscr{A}$ if and only if $\nabla \phi(x) \geq 0$ for all x in the interior of $\mathscr{A}$,

(ii) ϕ is strictly increasing on $\mathscr{A}$ if and only if $\nabla \phi(x) \geq 0$ for all x in the interior of $\mathscr{A}$ and for fixed $x_1, \ldots, x_{i-1}, x_{i+1}, \ldots, x_n$, the set of all x_i such that $\phi_{(i)}(x_1, \ldots, x_i, \ldots, x_n) = 0$ contains no intervals, $i = 1, \ldots, n$.

A.1.a follows from A.1 and the fact that a function ϕ defined on a convex set with interior is increasing (strictly increasing) if and only if it is increasing (strictly increasing) in each argument, the other arguments being fixed.

The convexity of $\mathscr{A}$ is not essential here; it is sufficient that

(iii) $\mathscr{A}$ is contained in the closure of its interior, and

(iv) for each fixed $x, y \in \mathscr{A}$ such that $x \leq y$, there exists a polygonal path joining x to y that moves alternately parallel to one or another coordinate axis and lies entirely within $\mathscr{A}$.

A.2. Proposition. Let μ be a signed measure (difference of two nonnegative measures) defined on the Borel subsets of $\mathscr{R}$. Then

(i) $\int \phi \, d\mu \geq 0$ for all nonnegative increasing functions $\phi : \mathscr{R} \to \mathscr{R}$ if and only if
$$\mu(t, \infty) \geq 0 \qquad \text{for all} \quad t \in \mathscr{R},$$

(ii) $\int \phi \, d\mu \geq 0$ for all nonnegative decreasing functions $\phi : \mathscr{R} \to \mathscr{R}$ if and only if
$$\mu(-\infty, t] \geq 0 \qquad \text{for all} \quad t \in \mathscr{R},$$

(iii) $\int \phi \, d\mu \geq 0$ for all increasing functions $\phi : \mathscr{R} \to \mathscr{R}$ if and only if
$$\mu(t, \infty) \geq 0 \qquad \text{for all} \quad t \in \mathscr{R} \qquad \text{and} \qquad \mu(-\infty, \infty) = 0.$$

The above proposition has certainly been known for a long time, but we do not know to whom it should be attributed. It was given in the above form by Marshall and Proschan (1970). In the absolutely continuous case, A.2 was given by Steffensen (1925) [see Mitrinović (1970, p. 114)].

Proposition A.2 for discrete measures is particularly useful in this book and is here stated explicitly.

A.2.a. The inequality
$$\sum a_i x_i \leq \sum b_i x_i \tag{1}$$
holds whenever $x_1 \leq \cdots \leq x_n$ if and only if
$$\sum_{i=1}^{k} a_i \geq \sum_{i=1}^{k} b_i, \qquad k = 1, \ldots, n-1, \tag{2}$$
$$\sum_{i=1}^{n} a_i = \sum_{i=1}^{n} b_i. \tag{3}$$

Proof. If (1) holds whenever $x_1 \leq \cdots \leq x_n$, then the choices $x = (1, \ldots, 1)$ and $x = (-1, \ldots, -1)$ yield (3). The choices $x = (0, \ldots, 0, 1, \ldots, 1)$, where the length of the 0 subvector is $1, \ldots, n-1$, together with 3 yield (2). Next, suppose (2) and (3), and let $y_1 = x_1$, $y_j = x_j - x_{j-1}$, $j = 2, \ldots, n$. Then $x_i = \sum_{j=1}^{i} y_j$, $i = 1, \ldots, n$, and

$$\sum_{i=1}^{n} a_i x_i = \sum_{i=1}^{n} a_i \sum_{j=1}^{i} y_j = \sum_{j=1}^{n} y_j \sum_{i=j}^{n} a_i \le \sum_{j=1}^{n} y_j \sum_{i=j}^{n} b_i = \sum_{i=1}^{n} b_i x_i. \quad \|$$

The Discrete Steffensen Inequality

The following case of A.2.a involving nonnegative x's is often referred to as the discrete Steffensen inequality.

A.3. Theorem (Evard and Gauchman, 1997). Suppose that $x \in \mathscr{D}_+$ and $y \in \mathscr{R}^n$ has coordinates satisfying $0 \le y_i \le 1$ for every i. Let $k_1 \in \{0, 1, 2, \ldots, n\}$ and $k_2 \in \{1, 2, \ldots, n\}$ be such that

$$k_2 \le \sum_{i=1}^{n} y_i \le k_1.$$

Then

$$\sum_{i=n-k_2+1}^{n} x_i \le \sum_{i=1}^{n} x_i y_i \le \sum_{i=1}^{k_1} x_i. \tag{4}$$

Inequality (4) is a consequence of the following refined version of A.3 which does not require that the decreasing sequence of x_i's contain only nonnegative terms.

A.4. Theorem (Shi and Wu, 2007). If $x \in \mathscr{D}$ and y, k_1 and k_2 satisfy the conditions in A.3, then

$$\sum_{i=n-k_2+1}^{n} x_i + \left(\sum_{i=1}^{n} y_i - k_2 \right) x_n \le \sum_{i=1}^{n} x_i y_i \le \sum_{i=1}^{k_1} x_i - \left(k_1 - \sum_{i=1}^{n} y_i \right) x_n. \tag{5}$$

Proof. Here only the right-hand inequality in (5) is proved; the left-hand inequality is proved in an analogous manner. Define $z_i = -x_i$ for $i = 1, 2, \ldots, n$ and let $z_{n+1} = -x_n$. The z_i's are increasing, so that A.2.a can be applied. Define the $(n+1)$-dimensional vectors a and b by

$$a = (\underbrace{1, 1, \ldots, 1}_{k_1}, 0, 0, \ldots, 0),$$

$$b = (y_1, y_2, \ldots, y_n, k_1 - \Sigma_{i=1}^{n} y_i).$$

It can be verified that Equations (1) and (2) are satisfied by this choice of a and b (with $n+1$ instead of n). Consequently,

$$\sum_{i=1}^{n} x_i y_i = -\sum_{i=1}^{n} z_i y_i = -\sum_{i=1}^{n+1} z_i b_i + \left(k_1 - \sum_{i+1}^{n} y_i\right) z_{n+1}$$

$$\leq -\sum_{i=1}^{n+1} z_i a_i + \left(k_1 - \sum_{i=1}^{n} y_i\right) z_{n+1} \text{ [by (1)]}$$

$$= -\sum_{i=1}^{n} z_i a_i + \left(k_1 - \sum_{i=1}^{n} y_i\right) z_{n+1}$$

$$= \sum_{i=1}^{k_1} x_i - \left(k_1 - \sum_{i=1}^{n} y_i\right) x_n. \quad \|$$

Shi and Wu (2007) provide an alternative proof that relies on the observations that if y, k_1, and k_2 are as defined in A.3, then

$$y \prec^w (\underbrace{0, \ldots, 0}_{n-k_2}, \underbrace{1, \ldots, 1}_{k_2}),$$

and

$$y \prec_w (\underbrace{1, \ldots, 1}_{k_1}, \underbrace{0, \ldots, 0}_{n-k_1}).$$

B Convex Functions

This section is intended to be only a brief outline concerning some selected aspects of convex functions. More complete discussions have been given, for example, by Rockafellar (1970), Stoer and Witzgall (1970), Roberts and Varberg (1973), Webster (1995), and Niculescu and Persson (2006).

In the following, ϕ denotes a function defined on $\mathscr{A} \subset \mathscr{R}^n$, taking on values in $\mathscr{R} \cup \{-\infty\}$ or in $\mathscr{R} \cup \{+\infty\}$.

Because ϕ can take on the values $\pm\infty$, some conventions are necessary:

$$\infty a = a\infty = \begin{cases} \infty & \text{if } a > 0, \\ 0 & \text{if } a = 0, \\ -\infty & \text{if } a < 0; \end{cases}$$

$$a + \infty = \infty + a = \infty \qquad \text{if } -\infty < a \leq \infty;$$

$$a - \infty = -\infty + a = -\infty \qquad \text{if } -\infty \leq a < \infty.$$

The expression $\infty - \infty$ is avoided by assuming that ϕ does not take on both of the values $\pm\infty$. Recall that $\overline{\alpha} = 1 - \alpha$, where α is a real number.

B.1. Definition. Let $\mathscr{A} \in \mathscr{R}^n$ be convex. A function $\phi: \mathscr{A} \to \mathscr{R}$ is *convex* on $\mathscr{A}$ if

$$\phi(\alpha x + \overline{\alpha} y) \leq \alpha \phi(x) + \overline{\alpha} \phi(y) \tag{1}$$

for all $x, y \in \mathscr{A}$, and all $\alpha \in [0, 1]$. If strict inequality holds in (1) whenever $x \neq y$ and $\alpha \in (0, 1)$, ϕ is said to be *strictly convex*. If $-\phi$ is convex, ϕ is said to be *concave*, and if $-\phi$ is strictly convex, ϕ is said to be *strictly concave*. If ϕ is both convex and concave, ϕ is said to be *affine*.

Notice that if ϕ is defined and convex on $\mathscr{A}$ and ϕ does not take on the value $-\infty$, then ϕ can be extended to $\mathscr{R}^n$ while preserving convexity. In fact,

$$\widehat{\phi}(x) = \begin{cases} \phi(x) & \text{if } x \in \mathscr{A}, \\ +\infty & \text{if } x \notin \mathscr{A} \end{cases}$$

is such an extension.

If ϕ is convex, the restriction of ϕ to the set $\operatorname{dom}\phi = \{x : \phi(x) < \infty\}$ is also convex. The set $\operatorname{dom}\phi$ is called the *effective domain* of ϕ and can be considered as the proper domain of definition of ϕ, although we do not adopt this point of view.

For $n > 1$, ϕ is convex on $\mathscr{A} \subset \mathscr{R}^n$ if and only if $\mathscr{A}$ is convex and the restriction of ϕ to any line segment in $\mathscr{A}$ is convex. Thus the notion of a convex function is essentially a concept in one dimension, and to check convexity of functions on arbitrary convex domains it is enough to check convexity on $[0, 1]$. This is the content of the following proposition [cf. Berge (1963, p. 190)].

B.2. Proposition. If $\phi: \mathscr{A} \to \mathscr{R}$ is defined and convex on the convex set $\mathscr{A} \subset \mathscr{R}^n$, then for each $x, y \in \mathscr{A}$, the function

$$g(\alpha) \equiv \phi(\alpha x + \overline{\alpha} y) \tag{2}$$

is convex in $\alpha \in A \equiv \{\alpha : \alpha x + \overline{\alpha} y \in \mathscr{A}\}$. In particular, g is convex on $[0, 1]$. Conversely, if g is convex on $[0, 1]$ for all $x, y \in \mathscr{A}$, then ϕ is convex on $\mathscr{A}$.

Proof. Fix x and $y \in \mathscr{A}$ and let $\alpha, \beta \in A$, $\eta \in [0, 1]$, $u = \alpha x + \overline{\alpha} y$, $v = \beta x + \overline{\beta} y$. Then

$$g(\eta\alpha + \overline{\eta}\beta) = \phi((\eta\alpha + \overline{\eta}\beta)x + (\eta\overline{\alpha} + \overline{\eta}\overline{\beta})y) = \phi(\eta u + \overline{\eta} v).$$

If ϕ is convex, then
$$g(\eta\alpha + \overline{\eta}\beta) = \phi(\eta u + \overline{\eta}v) \leq \eta\phi(u) + \overline{\eta}\phi(v) = \eta g(\alpha) + \overline{\eta}g(\beta),$$
so g is convex on A. If g is convex on $[0,1]$ and $x, y \in [0,1]$, then
$$\phi(\eta x + \overline{\eta}y) = g(\eta) \leq \eta g(1) + \overline{\eta}g(0) = \eta\phi(x) + \overline{\eta}\phi(y). \quad \|$$

B.2.a. If $\mathscr{A}$ is open and g is convex on $(0,1)$ for all $x, y \in \mathscr{A}$, then ϕ is convex on $\mathscr{A}$.

B.2.b. The function ϕ defined on the convex set $\mathscr{A}$ is strictly convex if and only if for each $x, y \in \mathscr{A}$, the function g defined by (2) is strictly convex in $\alpha \in [0,1]$.

B.3. Proposition. ϕ is convex on the convex set $\mathscr{A} \subset \mathscr{R}^n$ if and only if for each $x, y \in \mathscr{A}$ and $\alpha, \beta \in (0,1]$,
$$\frac{\phi(\overline{\alpha}x + \alpha y) - \phi(x)}{\alpha} \leq \frac{\phi(y) - \phi(\beta x + \overline{\beta}y)}{\beta}. \tag{3}$$

ϕ is strictly convex on $\mathscr{A}$ if and only if (3) holds with strict inequality unless $x = y$ or $\alpha = \beta = 1$.

Proof. Suppose first that ϕ is convex. Then
$$\frac{\phi(\overline{\alpha}x + \alpha y) - \phi(x)}{\alpha} \leq \phi(y) - \phi(x) \leq \frac{\phi(y) - \phi(\beta x + \overline{\beta}y)}{\beta}.$$

Conversely, if (3) holds, then take α or $\beta = 1$ to see that ϕ is convex. The case of strict convexity is proved similarly. $\quad \|$

B.3.a. Let ϕ be defined on an interval $I \subset \mathscr{R}$. If ϕ is convex on I, then whenever $x_1 < y_1 \leq y_2$, $x_1 \leq x_2 < y_2$,
$$\frac{\phi(y_1) - \phi(x_1)}{y_1 - x_1} \leq \frac{\phi(y_2) - \phi(x_2)}{y_2 - x_2}. \tag{4}$$

Conversely, if (4) holds in the special case that $x_1 < y_1 = x_2 < y_2$ and $y_1 - x_1 = y_2 - x_2$, then ϕ is convex on I. This special case of (4) is exactly the condition that ϕ has nonnegative second differences.

With the notation $r = y_2$, $s = x_2 = y_1$, and $t = x_1$, the special case of (4) takes the form
$$(r - t)\phi(s) \leq (s - t)\phi(r) + (r - s)\phi(t), \tag{4a}$$
for all $r \geq s \geq t$.

B.3.b. Let ϕ be a function defined and differentiable on the interval $I = (a, b)$. ϕ is convex on (a, b) if and only if

$$\phi'(x) \leq \phi'(y), \qquad a < x \leq y < b. \tag{5}$$

ϕ is strictly convex on (a, b) if and only if (4) holds with strict inequality when $a < x < y < b$.

Proof. If ϕ is convex, then (5) follows from (4). If (5) and $x < y$, then by the mean-value theorem, there exist $\xi_1 \in (x, \alpha x + \overline{\alpha} y)$ and $\xi_2 \in (\alpha x + \overline{\alpha} y, y)$ such that

$$l \equiv \frac{\phi(\alpha x + \overline{\alpha} y) - \phi(x)}{(\alpha x + \overline{\alpha} y) - x} = \phi'(\xi_1), \quad u \equiv \frac{\phi(y) - \phi(\alpha x + \overline{\alpha} y)}{y - (\alpha x + \overline{\alpha} y)} = \phi'(\xi_2).$$

Because $\xi_1 < \xi_2$, it follows from (5) that $l \leq u$ and this inequality reduces to (1). The case of strict convexity is proved similarly. ||

B.3.c. Let ϕ be a real function twice differentiable on (a, b). Then ϕ is convex on (a, b) if and only if

$$\phi''(x) \geq 0 \qquad \text{for all} \quad x \in (a, b). \tag{6}$$

ϕ is strictly convex on (a, b) if and only if $\phi''(x) \geq 0$ for all $x \in (a, b)$ and the set where $\phi''(x) = 0$ contains no intervals.

Proof. Because ϕ is convex if and only if ϕ' is increasing on (a, b), the result follows from A.1. ||

B.3.d. Let ϕ be a real function defined and twice differentiable on the open convex set $\mathscr{A} \subset \mathscr{R}^n$. Denote the *Hessian matrix* of ϕ by

$$H(x) = \left(\frac{\partial^2 \phi(x)}{\partial x_i \, \partial x_j} \right).$$

(i) ϕ is convex on $\mathscr{A}$ if and only if $H(x)$ is positive semidefinite on $\mathscr{A}$;

(ii) ϕ is strictly convex on $\mathscr{A}$ if and only if H is positive definite on $\mathscr{A}$.

Proof. By B.2, B.2.a, and B.2.b, ϕ is convex (strictly convex) on $\mathscr{A}$ if and only if $g(\alpha) = \phi(\alpha x + \overline{\alpha} y)$ is convex (strictly convex) in $\alpha \in (0, 1)$ for all $x, y \in \mathscr{A}$. Thus, ϕ is convex on $\mathscr{A}$ if and only if $g''(\alpha) \geq 0$ for all $\alpha \in (0, 1)$, and ϕ is strictly convex on $\mathscr{A}$ if $g''(\alpha) > 0$ for all $\alpha \in (0, 1)$.

Because

$$g''(\alpha) = (x - y) H(\alpha x + \overline{\alpha} y)(x - y)',$$

it follows that if H is positive semidefinite (positive definite), then ϕ is convex (strictly convex).

Next, suppose that ϕ is convex on $\mathscr{A}$ and let $z \in \mathscr{A}$. Because $\mathscr{A}$ is open, there exists $\varepsilon > 0$ such that $u \in B = \{w : \|w\| < \varepsilon\}$ implies $z + u \in \mathscr{A}$. Let $u \in B$, $x = z + (u/2)$, and $y = z - (u/2)$ so that $x - y = u$, $z = (x+y)/2$, and

$$g''(\tfrac{1}{2}) = uH(z)u'.$$

But $g''(\tfrac{1}{2}) \geq 0$ since ϕ is convex. Because $u \in B$ and $z \in \mathscr{A}$ are arbitrary, this shows that H is positive semidefinite on $\mathscr{A}$. ‖

B.4. Proposition (Hardy, Littlewood, and Pólya, 1929). If ϕ is a convex function defined on a finite interval (a, b), then ϕ can be approximated uniformly by positive linear combinations of finite numbers of these convex functions:

(i) linear functions;
(ii) functions of the form $(x - c)^+ \equiv \max(x - c, 0)$.

The functions $(x - c)^+$ are termed "angles" by Hardy, Littlewood, and Pólya. In their words, the above proposition "is intuitive, and easy to prove." In this proposition, the angles $(x - c)^+$ can as well be replaced by functions of the form $(c - x)^+$ because they differ from angles only by a linear function.

Proposition B.4 is of great utility in certain applications. It is used by Karamata (1932) (who discovered it independently) to give a simple proof of the following important result.

B.4.a. Proposition (Karamata, 1932). Let μ be a signed measure defined on the Borel subsets of (a, b). Then

$$\int \phi \, d\mu \geq 0 \qquad \text{for all convex functions } \phi : (a, b) \to \mathscr{R}$$

if and only if

$$\int_a^b d\mu = \int_a^b x \, d\mu = 0 \quad \text{and} \quad \int_a^t \mu(a, x] \, dx \geq 0, \qquad a \leq t \leq b.$$

This result was also obtained by Levin and Stečkin (1948) and by Brunk (1956).

Special cases of B.4.a were given by Hardy, Littlewood, and Pólya (1929). Some consequences and generalizations of B.4.a are given by Karlin and Novikoff (1963) and by Karlin and Ziegler (1965).

B.5. Definition. The set

$$\operatorname{epi}\phi = \{(x,y) : x \in \mathscr{A}, y \in \mathscr{R} \text{ and } \phi(x) \leq y\} \qquad (7)$$

is called the *epigraph* of ϕ.

B.5.a. Proposition. Let $\mathscr{A} \subset \mathscr{R}^n$ be convex. Then ϕ is convex on $\mathscr{A}$ if and only if $\operatorname{epi}\phi$ is a convex set.

Proof. If $\mathscr{A}$ is empty or $\phi \equiv \infty$ on $\mathscr{A}$, then $\operatorname{epi}\phi$ is empty (hence convex) and ϕ is trivially convex. So suppose that $\mathscr{A}$ is nonempty and that ϕ is not identically ∞.

If ϕ is convex on $\mathscr{A}$, then for any $x, y \in \mathscr{A}$ and $(x, u), (y, v) \in \operatorname{epi}\phi$,

$$\phi(\alpha x + \overline{\alpha}y) \leq \alpha\phi(x) + \overline{\alpha}\phi(y) \leq \alpha u + \overline{\alpha}v,$$

so that $\alpha(x, u) + \overline{\alpha}(y, v) \in \operatorname{epi}\phi$.

Conversely, suppose that $\operatorname{epi}\phi$ is convex. Because $(x, \phi(x)) \in \operatorname{epi}\phi$ and $(y, \phi(y)) \in \operatorname{epi}\phi$ for all $x, y \in \mathscr{A}$, it follows from convexity that $(\alpha x + \overline{\alpha}y, \alpha\phi(x) + \overline{\alpha}\phi(y)) \in \operatorname{epi}\phi$ for all $\alpha \in [0,1]$. Thus

$$\phi(\alpha x + \overline{\alpha}y) \leq \alpha\phi(x) + \overline{\alpha}\phi(y),$$

so that ϕ is convex. ||

A function ϕ defined on $\mathscr{A} \subset \mathscr{R}^n$ is said to be *closed* if $\operatorname{epi}\phi$ is a closed subset of $\mathscr{R}^{n+1}$. The function

$$\operatorname{cl}\phi(x) = \lim_{\varepsilon \to 0} \inf\{\phi(z) : z \in \mathscr{A}, \|z - x\| < \varepsilon\}$$

is defined on the closure of $\mathscr{A}$ and is called the *closure* of ϕ. The function ϕ is said to be *closed* if $\phi \equiv \operatorname{cl}\phi$. The closure of a convex function is convex.

Continuity of Convex Functions

The convex function ϕ defined on $[-1, 1]$ by

$$\phi(x) = \begin{cases} x^2 & \text{if } -1 < x < 1, \\ 17 & \text{if } |x| = 1 \end{cases}$$

is not continuous, but $\operatorname{cl}\phi(x) = x^2$, $|x| \leq 1$, is continuous. In general, a closed convex function defined and finite-valued on an interval $[a, b] \subset \mathscr{R}$ is continuous. On the other hand, a closed convex function defined on a closed convex subset of $\mathscr{R}^n$, $n > 1$, need not be continuous [for an example, see Stoer and Witzgall (1970, p. 137)]. A convex function defined and finite on an open set must be continuous, so that difficulties occur only on the boundary.

Gradients

Let $\phi: \mathscr{A} \to \mathscr{R}$. A vector $a \in \mathscr{R}^n$ is called a *subgradient* of ϕ at $z \in \mathscr{A}$ if

$$\phi(x) \geq \phi(z) + a(x-z)' \qquad \text{for all} \quad x \in \mathscr{A}. \tag{8}$$

If $\mathscr{A}$ is an open convex set and ϕ is a convex function finite on $\mathscr{A}$, then ϕ has a subgradient at each $z \in \mathscr{A}$. On the other hand, if ϕ is the closed convex function defined on the closed interval $[-1, 1]$ by

$$\phi(x) = 1 - \sqrt{1-x^2},$$

then ϕ has no subgradient at $x = \pm 1$.

The following are useful basic facts:

B.6.a. If the convex function ϕ is finite and differentiable at a point z in the interior of the set $\mathscr{A}$, then the gradient $\nabla \phi(z)$ is the unique subgradient of ϕ at z.

For a proof of this, see Rockafellar (1970, p. 242), Stoer and Witzgall (1970, p. 149), or Roberts and Varberg (1973, p. 102).

B.6.b. If $\mathscr{A}$ is open and the convex function ϕ is differentiable on $\mathscr{A}$, then the gradient $\nabla \phi$ is continuous on $\mathscr{A}$.

A proof of this fact is given by Rockafellar (1970, p. 246), and by Stoer and Witzgall (1970, p. 151).

B.6.c. If $\mathscr{A}$ is open and ϕ is convex, then a Borel-measurable version of the subgradient of ϕ exists. In fact, if e_i is the vector with ith component 1 and other components 0, if

$$\phi_{(i)}^+(x) = \lim_{\delta \downarrow 0} \frac{\phi(x + \delta e_i) - \phi(x)}{\delta},$$

and

$$\nabla^+ \phi(x) = (\phi_{(1)}^+(x), \ldots, \phi_{(n)}^+(x)), \qquad x \in \mathscr{A},$$

then $\nabla^+ \phi$ is the limit of continuous functions, and hence is measurable. Of course, $\nabla^+ \phi$ is a subgradient; that is,

$$\phi(x) \geq \phi(z) + [\nabla^+ \phi(z)](x-z)' \qquad \text{for all} \quad x, z \in \mathscr{A}. \tag{9}$$

Notice that $l(x) \equiv \phi(z) + [\nabla^+ \phi(z)](x-z)'$ is an affine function such that

$$\phi(x) \geq l(x) \quad \text{for all} \quad x \in \mathscr{A}, \quad \phi(z) = l(z). \tag{10}$$

Functions l satisfying (10) are called *support functions* of ϕ at z.

Compositions of Convex Functions

B.7. Proposition. If $\phi_1, \ldots, \phi_k$ are convex functions defined on the convex set $\mathscr{A} \subset \mathscr{R}^n$ and if $h : \mathscr{R}^k \to \mathscr{R}$ is an increasing convex function, then the function $\psi : \mathscr{R}^n \to \mathscr{R}$ defined by $\psi(x) = h(\phi_1(x), \ldots, \phi_k(x))$ is convex on $\mathscr{A}$.

Proof. If $x, y \in \mathscr{A}$, then for all $\alpha \in [0, 1]$,

$$\begin{aligned}
\psi(\alpha x + \overline{\alpha} y) &= h(\phi_1(\alpha x + \overline{\alpha} y), \ldots, \phi_k(\alpha x + \overline{\alpha} y)) \\
&\leq h(\alpha \phi_1(x) + \overline{\alpha} \phi_1(y), \ldots, \alpha \phi_k(x) + \overline{\alpha} \phi_k(y)) \\
&= h(\alpha [\phi_1(x), \ldots, \phi_k(x)] + \overline{\alpha} [\phi_1(y), \ldots, \phi_k(y)]) \\
&\leq \alpha h(\phi_1(x), \ldots, \phi_k(x)) + \overline{\alpha} h(\phi_1(y), \ldots, \phi_k(y)) \\
&= \alpha \psi(x) + \overline{\alpha} \psi(y).
\end{aligned}$$

Here the first inequality uses the monotonicity of h together with the convexity of $\phi_1, \ldots, \phi_k$; the second inequality uses the convexity of h. ||

B.7.a. If $h : \mathscr{R}^k \to \mathscr{R}$ is a convex function monotone in each argument, and if ϕ_i is convex or concave on the convex set $\mathscr{A} \subset \mathscr{R}^n$ according to whether h is increasing or decreasing in its ith argument, $i = 1, \ldots, k$, then $\psi(x) = h(\phi_1(x), \ldots, \phi_k(x))$ is convex on $\mathscr{A}$.

B.7.b. Let $\mathscr{A} \subset \mathscr{R}^n$ and let $\phi : \mathscr{A} \to \mathscr{R}_+$. If $\log \phi$ is convex, then ϕ is convex; if ϕ is concave, then $\log \phi$ is concave.

Proof. If $\log \phi$ is convex, then by B.7, $\exp(\log \phi)$ is convex because $h(x) = e^x$ is increasing and convex. If ϕ is nonnegative and concave, then by B.7.a, $-\log \phi$ is convex because $h(x) = -\log x$ is convex and decreasing. ||

Of course, convexity does not imply log convexity and log concavity does not imply concavity. In fact, $\phi(x) = e^x - 1$ is convex and log concave.

Preservation of Log Convexity Under Mixtures

B.8. Theorem (Artin, 1931). Let $\mathscr{A}$ be an open convex subset of $\mathscr{R}^n$ and let $\phi : \mathscr{A} \times (a,b) \to [0,\infty)$ satisfy

(i) $\phi(x,z)$ is Borel-measurable in z for each fixed x,

(ii) $\log \phi(x,z)$ is convex in x for each fixed z.

If μ is a measure on the Borel subsets of (a,b) such that $\phi(x,\cdot)$ is μ-integrable for each $x \in \mathscr{A}$, then

$$\psi(x) \equiv \int_a^b \phi(x,z)\, d\mu(z)$$

is log convex on $\mathscr{A}$.

Proof. By B.2, $\log \phi(x,z)$ is convex in $x \in \mathscr{A}$ if and only if $\log \xi(\alpha, z) \equiv \log \phi(\alpha x + \overline{\alpha} y, z)$ is convex in $\alpha \in [0,1]$ for each $x, y \in \mathscr{A}$. By B.3.a, $\log \xi(\alpha, z)$ is convex in α if and only if it has nonnegative second differences, i.e., if and only if for $\Delta > 0$ and $0 \leq \alpha$,

$$\log \xi(\alpha + 2\Delta, z) - 2 \log \xi(\alpha + \Delta, z) + \log(\alpha, z) \geq 0.$$

But this is equivalent to the inequality $\det A(z) \geq 0$, where

$$A(z) = \begin{bmatrix} \xi(\alpha, z) & \xi(\alpha + \Delta, z) \\ \xi(\alpha + \Delta, z) & \xi(\alpha + 2\Delta, z) \end{bmatrix}.$$

Because $\xi(\alpha, z) \geq 0$, this is equivalent to the condition that $A(z)$ is positive semidefinite for all z. If $A(z)$ is positive semidefinite, then so is $\int A(z)\, d\mu(z)$, and this is equivalent to the convexity of $\log \psi$. ||

For finitely discrete measures μ, B.8 can be proved with the aid of B.7 from the fact that $h(x) = \sum a_i e^{x_i}$ is increasing and convex whenever each $a_i \geq 0$. An alternative proof of B.8 is given in D.4.

B.8.a. Example The gamma function

$$\Gamma(x) = \int_0^\infty t^{x-1} e^{-t} dt$$

is a mixture of log convex functions and hence is log convex.

B.8.b. Example The Gauss–Legendre multiplication formula [see Erdélyi, Magnus, Oberhettinger, and Tricomi (1953, p. 4)]

$$\Gamma(m(z+b)) = c \prod_{j=0}^{m-1} \Gamma(z+b+j/m), \quad m = 2, 3, 4, \ldots,$$

where

$$c = m^{m(z+b)-1/2}/(2\pi)^{(m-1)/2},$$

is log convex.

Star-Shaped and Superadditive Functions

The properties of pseudo-convexity and quasi-convexity, discussed in Section 3.C, are strictly weaker than the property of convexity. Here two additional properties are mentioned which, in some circumstances, are also implied by convexity.

A function $\phi\colon [0,\infty) \to \mathscr{R}$ is said to be *star-shaped* if

$$\phi(\alpha x) \leq \alpha \phi(x) \quad \text{for all} \quad \alpha \in [0,1] \text{ and all } x \geq 0. \tag{11}$$

B.9. Proposition. If ϕ is a real function defined on $[0,\infty)$, then the following conditions are equivalent:

(i) ϕ is star-shaped;

(ii) $\phi(0) \leq 0$ and $\phi(x)/x$ is increasing in $x > 0$;

(iii) $z \in \operatorname{epi} \phi$ implies $\alpha z \in \operatorname{epi} \phi$ for all $\alpha \in [0,1]$.

If $\phi(0) \leq 0$ and ϕ is convex, then ϕ is star-shaped, but convexity is not a property of all star-shaped functions.

A real function ϕ defined on a set $\mathscr{A} \subset \mathscr{R}^n$ is said to be *superadditive* if $x, y \in \mathscr{A}$ implies $x + y \in \mathscr{A}$ and

$$\phi(x+y) \geq \phi(x) + \phi(y).$$

If $-\phi$ is superadditive, then ϕ is said to be *subadditive*.

B.9.a. If $\phi\colon [0,\infty) \to \mathscr{R}$ is star-shaped, then ϕ is superadditive.

Proof. Because ϕ is star-shaped,

$$\phi(x) \leq \frac{x}{x+y}\phi(x+y), \quad \phi(y) \leq \frac{y}{x+y}\phi(x+y).$$

Addition of these inequalities completes the proof. ‖

B. Convex Functions

B.9.b. If $\mathscr{A} \subset \mathscr{R}^n$ is a convex cone and if $\phi : \mathscr{A} \to \mathscr{R}$ is subadditive and homogeneous, then ϕ is convex.

Proof. $\phi(\alpha x + \overline{\alpha} y) \leq \phi(\alpha x) + \phi(\overline{\alpha} y) = \alpha \phi(x) + \overline{\alpha} \phi(y).$ ||

Star-shaped functions and related families have been discussed by Bruckner and Ostrow (1962). Subadditive functions are studied by Rosenbaum (1950).

Convexity of Functions on Integers

For functions defined on the integers $Z = \{\ldots, -1, 0, 1, 2, \ldots\}$, or on intervals of integers, the following is a version of convexity:

B.10. Definition. Let $I = (a, b)$, $-\infty \leq a < b \leq \infty$, and let ϕ be a real-valued function defined on $I \cap Z$. The function ϕ is said to be *convex* if

$$\phi(\alpha x + \overline{\alpha} y) \leq \alpha \phi(x) + \overline{\alpha} \phi(y)$$

for all $x, y \in I \cap Z$ and all $\alpha \in [0, 1]$ such that $\alpha x + \overline{\alpha} y \in I \cap Z$.

B.10.a. It is not difficult to see that ϕ is convex if and only if ϕ has nonnegative second differences; i.e.,

$$\phi(x) - 2\phi(x+1) + \phi(x+2) \geq 0$$

for all $x \in Z$ such that $a < x$, $x + 2 < b$.

Hadamard-Type Inequalities

The following inequality was first obtained by Charles Hermite in 1881 and independently obtained by Jacques Hadamard in 1893. For a history of this inequality and its variations, see Pečarić, Proschan, and Tong (1992, Chapter 5).

B.11. Proposition. If ϕ is a convex function defined on an interval $I \subset \mathscr{R}$, and $a, b, \in I$ with $a < b$, then

$$\phi\left(\frac{a+b}{2}\right) \leq \frac{1}{b-a} \int_a^b \phi(x) dx \leq \frac{\phi(a) + \phi(b)}{2}. \qquad (12)$$

Note that (12) can be rewritten in terms of a random variable U which has a uniform distribution on the interval (a, b). Thus, for ϕ convex,

$$\phi\left(\frac{a+b}{2}\right) \leq E\phi(U) \leq \frac{\phi(a) + \phi(b)}{2}. \quad (12\text{a})$$

Proof. The first inequality in (12a) is a direct consequence of Jensen's inequality (C.1). The second inequality is verified as follows. Let $g(x) = \phi(x) - \ell(x)$, where $\ell(x)$ is a linear function chosen such that $\ell(a) = \phi(a)$ and $\ell(b) = \phi(b)$. Because ϕ is convex, g is nonpositive on (a, b) and the right-hand inequality in (12) [or (12a)] is equivalent to the statement that the integral of g is over (a, b) is nonpositive. ∥

The following proposition provides a refinement of the left-hand inequality of (12).

B.12.a. Proposition (Dragomir, 1992). If ϕ is a convex function defined on $[a, b]$, and $g : [0, 1] \to \mathscr{R}$ is defined by

$$g(\alpha) = \frac{1}{b-a} \int_a^b \phi\left(\alpha x + (1-\alpha)\frac{(a+b)}{2}\right) dx,$$

then g is convex and increasing on $[0, 1]$. Thus, for every $\alpha \in [0, 1]$,

$$\phi\left(\frac{a+b}{2}\right) = g(0) \leq g(\alpha) \leq g(1) = \frac{1}{b-a} \int_a^b \phi(x) dx.$$

B.12.b. Proposition (Dragomir, 1992). If ϕ is a convex function defined on $[a, b]$, and h on $[0, 1]$ is defined by

$$h(\alpha) = \frac{1}{(b-a)^2} \int_a^b \int_a^b \phi(\alpha x + (1-\alpha)y) dx dy,$$

then

(i) $h(x)$ is convex on $[0, 1]$ and symmetric about $\frac{1}{2}$,

(ii) h is increasing on $[0, \frac{1}{2}]$ and decreasing on $[\frac{1}{2}, 1]$,

(iii) for every $\alpha \in [0, 1]$,

$$h(\alpha) \leq h(1) = \frac{1}{b-a} \int_a^b \phi(x) dx,$$

and
$$h(\alpha) \geq h\left(\frac{1}{2}\right) = \frac{1}{(b-a)^2} \int_a^b \int_a^b \phi\left(\frac{x+y}{2}\right) dx dy \geq \phi\left(\frac{a+b}{2}\right),$$
(iv) for every $\alpha \in [0, 1]$,
$$h(\alpha) \geq \max\{g(\alpha), g(1-\alpha)\},$$
where $g(\alpha)$ is as defined in B.12.a.

The expression $\frac{1}{b-a}\int_a^b \phi(x)dx$ and the function h defined in B.12.b can be viewed as defining functions of (a, b). By this route Schur-convexity enters the discussion.

B.13. Proposition (Elezović and Pečarić, 2000). If I is an interval in $\mathscr{R}$, and ϕ is a continuous function on I, then
$$\Phi(a, b) = \frac{1}{b-a}\int_a^b \phi(t)dt, \quad a, b \in I, a \neq b,$$
$$= \phi(a) \text{ if } a = b$$
is Schur-convex on I^2 if and only if ϕ is convex on I.

B.14. Proposition (Shi, 2007). If I is an interval in $\mathscr{R}$, and ϕ is a continuous convex function on I, then for any $t \in [0, 1]$,
$$Q(a, b) = h(t), \quad a, b \in I, \ a \neq b,$$
$$= \phi(a), \quad a = b,$$
is Schur-convex on I^2, where h is defined in B.12.b.

Schur's condition, Equation (10) in 3.A, can be used to verify Schur-convexity in these two theorems. For further details, together with additional related applications, see Shi (2007).

The following basic theorem has a variety of applications.

B.15. Theorem (Prékopa, 1971). Suppose that ϕ is a nonnegative function defined and log concave on $\mathscr{R}^m \times \mathscr{R}^n$. If the function
$$h(x) = \int_{\mathscr{R}^n} \phi(x, z)\, dz$$
is finite for all x, then h is log concave on $\mathscr{R}^m$. When $m = 1$ and mild regularity conditions are satisfied, this can be written in the form
$$\int_{\mathscr{R}^n} \phi(x, z)\, dz \int_{\mathscr{R}^n} \frac{\partial^2 \phi(x, z)}{\partial x^2} dz \leq \left[\int_{\mathscr{R}^n} \frac{\partial \phi(x, z)}{\partial x} dz\right]^2.$$

For a proof of Prékopa's theorem, see Brascamp and Lieb (1976).

B.15.a. Example. If f and g are log concave densities, then Prékopa's theorem can be used to verify that their convolution is log concave. Since f and g are log concave, it follows that $\phi(x,z) = f(x-z)g(z)$ is log concave and consequently, using Theorem B.15, it follows that the convolution $h(x) = \int f(x-z)g(z)\,dz$ is log concave.

C Jensen's Inequality

The following inequalities are versions of what is called *Jensen's inequality* and is perhaps the most widely cited inequality in mathematics, in part because the class of convex functions is a rich class.

For any convex function ϕ defined on (a,b), for all $x_1,\ldots,x_n \in (a,b)$, and for all nonnegative numbers $\alpha_1,\ldots,\alpha_n$ such that $\sum_1^n \alpha_i = 1$, it is easy to see that

$$\phi\left(\sum \alpha_i x_i\right) \leq \sum \alpha_i \phi(x_i).$$

An integral analog of this inequality using Lebesgue measure was obtained by Jensen (1906).

C.1. Proposition. Let $(\Omega, \mathscr{B}, P)$ be a probability space and let X be a random vector taking values in the open convex set $\mathscr{A} \subset \mathscr{R}^n$ with finite expectation $EX = \int X\,dP$. If $\phi\colon \mathscr{A} \to \mathscr{R}$ is convex, then

$$E\phi(X) \geq \phi(EX), \tag{1}$$

with equality if and only if ϕ is affine on the convex hull of the support of X. Conversely, if (1) holds for all random variables X taking values in $\mathscr{A}$ such that the expectations exist, then ϕ is convex.

Proof. Since $\mathscr{A}$ is an open set, and EX is finite, $EX \in \mathscr{A}$. Thus there exists an affine function l (see B.6.c) such that

$$\phi(x) \geq l(x) \quad \text{for all} \quad x \in \mathscr{A}, \quad \phi(EX) = l(EX).$$

Because $\phi(X) \geq l(X)$, it follows that $E\phi(X) \geq El(X) = l(EX) = \phi(EX)$. Moreover, equality holds if and only if $\phi(X) = l(X)$ with probability 1; i.e., ϕ is affine on the convex hull of the support of X. The converse is immediate. ∥

C.1.a. Arithmetic–Geometric mean inequality. If X is a nonnegative random variable, then

$$EX \geq \exp E \log X. \tag{2}$$

Equality holds if and only if X is degenerate or $E \log X = \infty$.

Proof. If $EX = \infty$, the result is trivial. If $EX < \infty$, in C.1 take $n = 1$ and $\phi(x) = -\log x$ if $x > 0$, $\phi(x) = \infty$ if $x \leq 0$. Note that X need not be nonnegative, provided $EX > 0$. ‖

Note. There are many proofs of the arithmetic–geometric mean inequality. For a discussion of inequalities involving these and other means, see Bullen, Mitrinovič, and Vasić (1988) and Bullen (2003).

In case X is a discrete random variable, $P\{X = a_i\} = q_i \geq 0$, $i = 1, \ldots, n$, where $\sum q_i = 1$ and $a_i \geq 0$, then inequality (2) can be written as

$$\sum_1^n a_i q_i \geq \prod_1^n a_i^{q_i}. \tag{3}$$

Here, X is degenerate (equality holds) if and only if $a_1 = \cdots = a_n$ or all but one $q_i = 0$.

C.1.b. If X is a nonnegative random variable, then

$$(EX^r)^{1/r} \geq \exp E \log X, \quad r > 0,$$
$$(EX^r)^{1/r} \leq \exp E \log X, \quad r < 0.$$

Equality holds if and only if X is degenerate, or $E \log X = \infty$.

Proof. Replace X by X^r in C.1.a. ‖

C.1.c. If X is a nonnegative random variable and $r < s$, then

$$(EX^r)^{1/r} \leq (EX^s)^{1/s}.$$

Equality holds if and only if X is degenerate, or $r \geq 0$ and $EX^r = \infty$, or $s \leq 0$ and $EX^s = \infty$.

Indication of proof. If $t > 1$ and $\phi(x) = x^t$, then $EX^t \geq (EX)^t$ by C.1, with equality if and only if X is degenerate or $EX = \infty$. If $X = Y^r$ and $s = rt$, it follows that $EY^s \geq (EY^r)^{s/r}$. The cases $r > 0$ and $s < 0$ now must be treated separately; the case $r \leq 0 \leq s$ follows from C.1.b and the fact that $\lim_{r \to 0} (EX^r)^{1/r} = \exp E \log X$ [see Hardy, Littlewood, and Pólya (1934, 1952, p. 139)].

C.2. Proposition. Let ϕ be a convex function defined on the open convex set $\mathscr{A} \subset \mathscr{R}^n$ and let X be a random variable defined on the probability space $(\Omega, \mathscr{B}, P)$ taking values in $\mathscr{A}$. Let $\mathscr{F} \subset \mathscr{B}$ be a σ-algebra such that $E(X|\mathscr{F})$ exists finitely almost everywhere (P). Then

$$E[\phi(X)|\mathscr{F}] \geq \phi(E[X|\mathscr{F}]) \quad \text{a.e. } (P). \tag{4}$$

Proof. According to B.6.c, for any fixed $z \in \mathscr{A}$,
$$\phi(x) \geq \phi(z) + [\nabla^+\phi(z)](x-z)' \qquad \text{for all} \quad x \in \mathscr{A}.$$
Because $E(X|\mathscr{F}) \in \mathscr{A}$ almost surely,
$$\phi(X) \geq \phi(E(X|\mathscr{F})) + [\nabla^+\phi(E(X|\mathscr{F}))][X - E(X|\mathscr{F})]'. \tag{5}$$
Because $\nabla^+\phi$ is Borel-measurable, $\nabla^+\phi(E(X|\mathscr{F}))$ is $\mathscr{F}$-measurable. Thus, (4) follows upon taking conditional expectations given $\mathscr{F}$ in (5). ||

For an alternative proof of C.2, notice that because ϕ is convex and $\mathscr{A}$ is open, ϕ has at least one support function at each $z \in \mathscr{A}$. Thus, if L is the set of all support functions of ϕ,
$$\phi(x) = \sup_{l \in L} l(x).$$
For any $l \in L$, $\phi(x) \geq l(x)$ for all x, so
$$E[\phi(X)|\mathscr{F}] \geq E[l(X)|\mathscr{F}] = l(E(X|\mathscr{F})).$$
Thus,
$$E[\phi(X)|\mathscr{F}] \geq \sup_{l \in L} l(E(X|\mathscr{F})) = \phi(E(X|\mathscr{F})).$$

C.2.a. Under the conditions of C.2,
$$E\phi(X) \geq E\phi(E(X|\mathscr{F})).$$

Proof. This follows from (4) upon taking expectations. ||

C.2.b. As a first application of Jensen's inequality for conditional expectations, an alternative proof is given for 3.C.1, which says that if $x \prec y$ and $\phi : \mathscr{R} \to \mathscr{R}$ is convex, then $\sum \phi(x_i) \leq \sum \phi(y_i)$. If $x \prec y$, then there exists a doubly stochastic matrix P such that $x = yP$. Let $Q = (q_{ij}) = (1/n)P$, and let X and Y be random variables such that $P\{X = x_i, Y = y_j\} = q_{ij}$, $i, j = 1, \ldots, n$. Then $P\{X = x_i\} = \sum_{j=1}^n q_{ij} = 1/n = \sum_{i=1}^n q_{ij} = P\{Y = y_j\}$ and
$$E(Y|X = x_i) = \sum_{j=1}^n y_j[q_{ij}/(1/n)] = \sum_{j=1}^n y_j p_{ij} = x_i.$$
As a consequence of C.2.a, it follows that $E\phi(Y) \geq E\phi(E(Y|X))$; that is,
$$\frac{1}{n}\sum \phi(y_i) \geq \frac{1}{n}\sum \phi(x_i).$$

C.2.c. Let Z be a random vector defined on the probability space $(\Omega, \mathscr{B}, P)$ and let $\mathscr{F}_1$ and $\mathscr{F}_2$ be sub-σ-fields of $\mathscr{B}$. If $\mathscr{F}_1 \subset \mathscr{F}_2$ and

$$X = E(Z|\mathscr{F}_1), \qquad Y = E(Z|\mathscr{F}_2), \tag{6}$$

then

$$E\phi(X) \leq E\phi(Y) \tag{7}$$

for all convex functions ϕ defined on $\mathscr{R}^n$ for which the expectations are defined.

Equation (7) says that if X and Y have a representation like (6), then $X \prec^{E_2} Y$, a relationship discussed in Section 11.A.

D Some Additional Fundamental Inequalities

The arithmetic–geometric mean inequality is obtained in C.1.a as a consequence of Jensen's inequality. In a sense, the arithmetic–geometric mean (AM–GM) inequality and the familiar inequalities of Hölder, Cauchy–Bunyakovskii–Schwarz (C–B–S), Lyapunov, and Artin's Theorem B.8 are all equivalent: Each of these results can be used to derive any of the others. The following derivations are given in this section:

$$\begin{array}{c} \text{AM–GM} \\ \text{C.1.a} \end{array} \Rightarrow \begin{array}{c} \text{Hölder} \\ \text{D.1} \end{array} \begin{array}{c} \nearrow \text{Artin B.8} \\ \searrow \text{C–B–S D.1.e} \end{array} \begin{array}{c} \searrow \text{Lyapunov} \\ \nearrow \text{D.1.d} \end{array} \Rightarrow \begin{array}{c} \text{AM–GM} \\ \text{C.1.a} \end{array}$$

In addition, the inequality of Minkowski is given as a consequence of Hölder's inequality.

D.1. Hölder's inequality. Let $(\Omega, \mathscr{B}, \mu)$ be a measure space, let $f_i : \Omega \to [0, \infty)$ be finitely μ-integrable, $i = 1, \ldots, n$, and let $q_i \geq 0$, $\sum_1^n q_i = 1$. Then $\prod_1^n f_i^{q_i}$ is finitely integrable and

$$\int \prod_1^n f_i^{q_i} \, d\mu \leq \prod_1^n \left(\int f_i \, d\mu \right)^{q_i}. \tag{1}$$

Equality holds in (1) if and only if

(i) all but one $q_i = 0$,

or

(ii) the f_i's are proportional a.e. (μ),

or

(iii) $f_i = 0$ a.e. (μ) for some i.

Proof. By the arithmetic–geometric mean inequality C.1.a,

$$a_i \geq 0, \quad q_i \geq 0, \quad \sum q_i = 1 \quad \text{implies} \quad \prod_1^n a_i^{q_i} \leq \sum_1^n a_i q_i$$

with strict inequality unless $a_1 = \cdots = a_n$ or all but one $q_i = 0$. Suppose that $\int f_i \, d\mu \neq 0$ (otherwise, the inequality is trivial), and let $a_i = f_i(\omega) / \int f_i \, d\mu$, so that

$$\prod_1^n \left(\frac{f_i(\omega)}{\int f_i \, d\mu} \right)^{q_i} \leq \sum_1^n q_i \frac{f_i(\omega)}{\int f_i \, d\mu}.$$

Integration of both sides yields (1). ∥

A number of variations of Hölder's inequality can be given.

D.1.a. Let $p_1, \ldots, p_n$ be numbers in $[1, \infty]$ such that $\sum_1^n 1/p_i = 1$. If f_i is a complex-valued function defined on the measure space $(\Omega, \mathscr{B}, \mu)$ such that $\int |f_i|^{p_i} \, d\mu < \infty$, $i = 1, \ldots, n$, then

$$\int \left| \prod_1^n f_i \right| d\mu \leq \prod_1^n \left(\int |f_i|^{p_i} \, d\mu \right)^{1/p_i}, \quad (2)$$

with equality if and only if (i) all but one $p_i = \infty$, or (ii) the $|f_i|^{p_i}$ are proportional a.e., or (iii) for some i, $f_i = 0$ a.e.

Proof. Replace f_i in D.1 by $|f_i|^{p_i}$, where $p_i = 1/q_i$. ∥

D.1.b. Let $q_i > 0$, $i = 1, \ldots, n$, $\sum_1^n q_i = 1$, and $r \in \mathscr{R}$. If $f_i : \Omega \to [0, \infty)$ and f_i^{r/q_i} is μ-integrable, $i = 1, \ldots, n$, then $(\prod f_i)^r$ is μ-integrable and

$$\left[\int \left(\prod f_i \right)^r d\mu \right]^{1/r} \leq \prod \left(\int f_i^{r/q_i} \, d\mu \right)^{q_i/r} \quad \text{if} \quad r > 0. \quad (3)$$

Unless $\prod f_i = 0$ a.e.,

$$\left[\int \left(\prod f_i \right)^r d\mu \right]^{1/r} \geq \prod \left(\int f_i^{r/q_i} \, d\mu \right)^{q_i/r} \quad \text{if} \quad r < 0. \quad (4)$$

Equality holds if and only if (i) $f_1^{1/q_1}, \ldots, f_n^{1/q_n}$ are proportional a.e., or (ii) $f_i = 0$ a.e. for some i.

Proof. In D.1, replace f_i by f_i^{r/q_i}. ∥

Numbers p and q are said to be *conjugate* if (i) $(1/p) + (1/q) = 1$, or (ii) $p = 1$, $q = \infty$, or $p = \infty$, $q = 1$, or (iii) $p = q = 0$.

D.1.c. Let p and q be conjugate and let $f, g: \Omega \to [0, \infty)$.

(i) If $p > 1$ and $\int f^p \, d\mu < \infty$, $\int g^q \, d\mu < \infty$, then $\int fg \, d\mu < \infty$ and

$$\int fg \, d\mu \leq \left(\int f^p \, d\mu \right)^{1/p} \left(\int g^q \, d\mu \right)^{1/q}. \tag{5}$$

(ii) If $0 < p < 1$ ($q < 0$) and $\int fg \, d\mu < \infty$, $\int g^q \, d\mu < \infty$, then $\int f^p \, d\mu < \infty$ and

$$\int fg \, d\mu \geq \left(\int f^p \, d\mu \right)^{1/p} \left(\int g^q \, d\mu \right)^{1/q}. \tag{6}$$

(iii) If $p < 0$ ($0 \leq q \leq 1$) and $\int fg \, d\mu < \infty$, $\int f^p \, d\mu < \infty$, then $\int g^q \, d\mu < \infty$ and

$$\int fg \, d\mu \geq \left(\int f^p \, d\mu \right)^{1/p} \left(\int g^q \, d\mu \right)^{1/q}.$$

Proof. (5) is an obvious special case of (1). To obtain (6) from (1) with $n = 2$, take $q_1 = p$, $q_2 = -p/q$, $f_1 = fg$, $f_2 = g^q$. Case (iii) is the same as (ii) but with p and q, f and g interchanged. ∥

D.1.d. Lyapunov's inequality. If $a \geq b \geq c$ and $f: \Omega \to \mathscr{R}$ is μ-integrable, then

$$\left(\int |f|^b \, d\mu \right)^{a-c} \leq \left(\int |f|^c \, d\mu \right)^{a-b} \left(\int |f|^a \, d\mu \right)^{b-c}, \tag{7}$$

with equality if and only if (i) f is a constant on some subset of Ω and 0 elsewhere, or (ii) $a = b$, or (iii) $b = c$, or (iv) $c(2a - b) = ab$.

Proof. If $a = b$ or $b = c$, the result is trivial. Otherwise, in D.1 take $n = 2$, $f_1 = |f|^c$, $f_2 = |f|^a$, $q_1 = (a - b)/(a - c)$, $q_2 = (b - c)/(a - c)$. If $f_1 = kf_2$ a.e., then either f is constant on some subset of Ω and 0 elsewhere or $c(a-b)/(a-c) = a(b-c)/(a-c)$; that is, $c(2a-b) = ab$. ∥

In the more familiar form of Lyapunov's inequality, $\mu \equiv P$ is a probability measure and $f \equiv X$ is a random variable with absolute moment $\nu_r = \int |X|^r \, dP$. Then (7) takes the form

$$\nu_b^{a-c} \leq \nu_c^{a-b} \nu_a^{b-c}. \tag{8}$$

Inequality (8) implies an inequality for quadratic forms: If A is a symmetric positive definite matrix, and z is a unit vector, i.e., $||z|| = 1$, then for $a \geq b \geq c$,

$$(zA^b z')^{a-c} \leq (zA^c z')^{a-b} (zA^a z')^{b-c}.$$

This follows from the fact that $zA^r z'$ can be expressed as the rth moment of a distribution on the eigenvalues of A.

The Lyapunov inequality is also discussed in 3.E.2 and in D.5,6,7.

D.1.e. Cauchy–Bunyakovskiĭ–Schwarz inequality. Let f_1, f_2 be real (or complex-valued) functions defined on Ω. If $|f_i|^2$ are finitely μ-integrable, $i = 1, 2$, then $f_1 f_2$ is finitely μ-integrable and

$$\left| \int f_1 f_2 \, d\mu \right|^2 \leq \int |f_1|^2 \, d\mu \int |f_2|^2 \, d\mu. \tag{9}$$

Proof. In D.1, take $n = 2$, $q_1 = q_2 = \frac{1}{2}$ and replace f_i there by $|f_i|^2$. ∥

For historical comments concerning this inequality, see Dunford and Schwartz (1958, p. 372). Steele (2004) provides a discussion of the Cauchy–Bunyakovskiĭ–Schwarz inequality and its relation to other inequalities.

D.1.f. Minkowski inequality. Let $p \geq 1$ and let $f_i : \Omega \to \mathscr{R}$ be such that $\int |f_i|^p \, d\mu < \infty$, $i = 1, \ldots, n$. Then $\int |\sum f_i|^p \, d\mu < \infty$ and

$$\left(\int \left| \sum f_i \right|^p d\mu \right)^{1/p} \leq \sum \left(\int |f_i|^p \, d\mu \right)^{1/p}. \tag{10}$$

Equality holds if and only if the $f_i(\omega)$'s are of the same sign for almost all $\omega \in \Omega$ and

(i) $p = 1$

or

(ii) the f_i's are proportional a.e. (μ).

Proof. Let q satisfy $(1/p)+(1/q) = 1$. By first applying the triangle inequality and then Hölder's inequality, it follows that

$$\int \left|\sum f_i\right|^p d\mu = \int \left|\sum f_j\right| \left|\sum f_i\right|^{p-1} d\mu \leq \sum_j \int |f_j| \left|\sum f_i\right|^{p-1} d\mu$$

$$\leq \sum_j \left(\int |f_j|^p d\mu\right)^{1/p} \left(\int \left|\sum f_i\right|^{(p-1)q} d\mu\right)^{1/q}$$

$$= \sum_j \left(\int |f_j|^p d\mu\right)^{1/p} \left(\int \left|\sum f_i\right|^p d\mu\right)^{1/q}.$$

This yields (10). The conditions for equality yield equality in both inequalities of this proof. ||

D.1.g. If $0 < p < 1$, $f_i \geq 0$, $\int |f_i|^p d\mu < \infty$, and $\int |\sum f_i|^p d\mu < \infty$, then

$$\left(\int \left|\sum f_i\right|^p d\mu\right)^{1/p} \geq \sum \left(\int |f_i|^p d\mu\right)^{1/p}.$$

The proof of this is essentially the same as the proof of D.1.f but makes use of (6) rather than (1).

The following is a generalization of Hölder's inequality which eliminates the restriction that only a finite number of functions be involved.

D.2. A generalized Hölder's inequality. Let $(\Omega, \mathscr{B}, P)$ be a probability space and let $(\mathscr{X}, \mathscr{F}, \mu)$ be a σ-finite measure space. Let $f: \mathscr{X} \times \Omega \to [0, \infty)$ be an $\mathscr{F} \times \mathscr{B}$-measurable function such that $\int_{\mathscr{X}} f(x, \omega) d\mu(x) < \infty$ for almost all $\omega(P)$.
If $\int_\Omega \log \int_{\mathscr{X}} f(x, \omega) d\mu(x) dP(\omega) < \infty$, then

$$\int_{\mathscr{X}} \exp\left(\int_\Omega \log f(x, \omega) dP(\omega)\right) d\mu(x) < \infty$$

and

$$\int_{\mathscr{X}} \exp \int_\Omega \log f(x, \omega) dP(\omega) d\mu(x)$$

$$\leq \exp \int_\Omega \log \int_{\mathscr{X}} f(x, \omega) d\mu(x) dP(\omega). \qquad (11)$$

Equality holds in (11) if and only if (i) $f(x,\omega) = g(x)h(\omega)$ except for x in a set A of μ-measure 0, or $x \notin A$ and ω in a set B_x of P-measure 0, or (ii) for each fixed ω in a set of positive P-measure, $f(x,\omega) = 0$ a.e. (μ) (the exceptional set possibly depending on ω).

Proof. Let $\widehat{f}(x,\omega) = f(x,\omega)/\int_{\mathcal{X}} f(y,\omega)\, d\mu(y)$. By the arithmetic–geometric mean inequality C.1.a,

$$\exp \int_\Omega \log \widehat{f}(x,\omega)\, dP(\omega) \leq \int_\Omega \widehat{f}(x,\omega)\, dP(\omega) \quad \text{for all} \quad x.$$

Thus,

$$\int_{\mathcal{X}} \exp \int_\Omega \log \widehat{f}(x,\omega)\, dP(\omega)\, d\mu(x) \leq \int_{\mathcal{X}} \int_\Omega \widehat{f}(x,\omega)\, dP(\omega)\, d\mu(x)$$

$$= \int_\Omega \int_{\mathcal{X}} \widehat{f}(x,\omega)\, d\mu(x)\, dP(\omega) = \int_\Omega dP(\omega) = 1,$$

which can be rewritten as

$$\int_{\mathcal{X}} \exp \left[\int_\Omega \log f(x,\omega) dP(\omega) - \int_\Omega \log \int_{\mathcal{X}} f(y,\omega) d\mu(y) \right] dP(\omega) d\mu(x) \leq 1;$$

that is, (11).

To determine conditions for equality, it is necessary to determine conditions under which for almost all x, $\widehat{f}(x,\omega)$ is degenerate (as a random variable) or conditions under which both sides of (11) are 0. This part of the proof is omitted. ∥

The above development has established the implications

Jensen's inequality C.1 $\Rightarrow$ Hölder's inequality D.1

$\Rightarrow$ Lyapunov's inequality D.1.d

There is also a close connection with Artin's theorem B.8 which establishes the fact that "mixtures" of log convex functions are log convex. In fact, B.8 can be used to establish Hölder's inequality and conversely.

D.3. Hölder's inequality from Artin's theorem. Since $\sum q_i \log f_i$ is linear (hence convex) in $(q_1, \ldots, q_n)$, the function

$$\xi(q_1, \ldots, q_n) = \log \int \prod f_i^{q_i}\, d\mu$$

is convex in $(q_1, \ldots, q_n) = \sum_1^n q_i e_i$, where e_i is the vector with ith component 1 and other components 0. Thus

$$\xi(q_1, \ldots, q_n) \leq \sum q_i \xi(e_i),$$

and this is just Hölder's inequality (1) of D.1. ∥

D.4. Artin's theorem from Hölder's inequality. Because $\phi(x, z)$ is log convex in x for each fixed z, $\phi(\alpha x + \overline{\alpha} y, z) \leq [\phi(x, z)]^\alpha [\phi(y, z)]^{\overline{\alpha}}$. Thus, by Hölder's inequality,

$$\psi(\alpha x + \overline{\alpha} y) = \int \phi(\alpha x + \overline{\alpha} y, z) \, d\mu(z) \leq \int [\phi(x, z)]^\alpha [\phi(y, z)]^{\overline{\alpha}} \, d\mu(z)$$

$$\leq \left[\int \phi(x, z) \, d\mu(z) \right]^\alpha \left[\int \phi(y, z) \, d\mu(z) \right]^{\overline{\alpha}} = [\psi(x)]^\alpha [\psi(y)]^{\overline{\alpha}}. \quad \|$$

D.5. Lyapunov's inequality from Artin's theorem. Because $\log |f|^r$ is linear (hence convex) as a function of r, the mixture $\int |f|^r \, d\mu$ is logarithmically convex, and this is equivalent to Lyapunov's inequality. ∥

D.6. Lyapunov's inequality from the Cauchy–Bunyakovskiĭ–Schwarz inequality. In (9), set $f_1 = |f|^{(r-r')/2}, f_2 = |f|^{(r+r')/2}$, $r' \leq r$, to obtain

$$\left| \int |f|^r \, d\mu \right|^2 \leq \int |f|^{r-r'} \, d\mu \int |f|^{r+r'} \, d\mu.$$

Upon taking logarithms, it follows that $\log \int |f|^r$ is "midpoint convex"; i.e.,

$$\log \int |f|^{(u+v)/2} \, d\mu \leq \tfrac{1}{2} \log \int |f|^u \, d\mu + \tfrac{1}{2} \log \int |f|^v \, d\mu.$$

Convexity follows from the continuity in r of $\log \int |f|^r$. ∥

Logarithmic Convex (Concave) Functions

A number of important inequalities arise from the logarithmic convexity or concavity of some functions. Logarithmic convexity (concavity) also leads to Schur-convexity (concavity).

Log convexity (concavity) plays an important role in fields of application such as reliability and survival analysis [see Marshall and Olkin (2007)] and in economics [see An (1998) or Bagnoli and

Bergstrom (2005)]. For applications in applied mathematics, see Borell (1975) and Brascamp and Lieb (1976).

For a discussion of the convolution of log concave functions see 18.B.1.

Recall that a function $\phi : \mathscr{R} \to \mathscr{R}$ is *log convex* if

$$\log \phi(\alpha x + \overline{\alpha} y) \leq \alpha \log \phi(x) + \overline{\alpha} \log \phi(y), \quad 0 \leq \alpha \leq 1, \quad x, y \in \mathscr{R}, \quad (12)$$

where $\overline{\alpha} = 1 - \alpha$. With $x = a > c = y$ and $\alpha a + \overline{\alpha} c = b$, inequality (12) can be written in the form

$$[\phi(b)]^{a-c} \leq [\phi(c)]^{a-b}[\phi(a)]^{b-c}, \quad a > b > c. \quad (13)$$

Another inequality for log convex functions follows from 16.B.3.a:

If $a \geq d > c$, $a > b \geq c$, then

$$\frac{\log \phi(d) - \log \phi(c)}{d - c} \leq \frac{\log \phi(a) - \log \phi(b)}{a - b};$$

that is,

$$\left[\frac{\phi(d)}{\phi(c)}\right]^{\frac{1}{d-c}} \leq \left[\frac{\phi(a)}{\phi(b)}\right]^{\frac{1}{a-b}}, \quad (14a)$$

or

$$[\phi(b)]^{d-c}[\phi(d)]^{a-b} \leq [\phi(a)]^{d-c}[\phi(c)]^{a-b}. \quad (14b)$$

With $d = b$, (14b) reduces to (13).

Inequalities (12), (13), (14a) and (14b) are reversed if ϕ is log concave.

D.7. Example. According to 3.E.2, the function

$$\phi(x) = \nu_x = \int |z|^x d\mu(z)$$

is log convex. For this example, the application of (13) yields Lyapunov's inequality (8), and (14a) yields

$$\left(\frac{\nu_b}{\nu_a}\right)^{d-c} \leq \left(\frac{\nu_c}{\nu_d}\right)^{a-b}, \quad a \geq d > c, \ a > b \geq c.$$

If $x \prec y$, then from 3.E.1 it follows that

$$\prod_1^n \nu_{x_i} \leq \prod_1^n \nu_{y_i}.$$

D. Some Additional Fundamental Inequalities   665

Specific functions are identified as moments in 3.E.5-3.E.8. In particular,

$$\mu_r = \Gamma(r+u), \quad r > -u, \tag{15}$$

$$\mu_r = \Gamma(r+u)/\Gamma(r+u+v), \quad u, v > 0, \ r > -u, \tag{16}$$

$$\mu_r = \Gamma(r+1)/r^{r+1}, \quad r > 0, \tag{17}$$

are all moments of some measure. Consequently, these functions are all log convex and hence admit a Lyapunov-type inequality by applying (13). For example, (16) yields, for $a \geq b \geq c > -u$, $v > 0$,

$$\left[\frac{\Gamma(b+u)}{\Gamma(b+u+v)}\right]^{a-c} \leq \left[\frac{\Gamma(c+u)}{\Gamma(c+u+v)}\right]^{a-b} \left[\frac{\Gamma(a+u)}{\Gamma(a+u+v)}\right]^{b-c}, \tag{18a}$$

and (17) yields, for $a \geq b \geq c > -1$,

$$\left[\frac{\Gamma(b+1)}{b^{b+1}}\right]^{a-c} \leq \left[\frac{\Gamma(c+1)}{c^{c+1}}\right]^{a-b} \left[\frac{\Gamma(a+1)}{a^{a+1}}\right]^{b-c}. \tag{18b}$$

For a probability density f with corresponding distribution function F satisfying $F(0) = 0$, the normalized moments

$$\lambda_r = \mu_r/\Gamma(r+1)$$

possess log concavity (convexity) properties summarized in 3.E.4. According to (8) or (13), log convexity of λ_r can be expressed in the form

$$\lambda_b^{a-c} \leq \lambda_c^{a-b} \lambda_a^{b-c}. \tag{19}$$

D.8. Proposition.

(i) If f is completely monotone, then $\log \lambda_r$ is convex in $r > -1$, and thus (19) holds for $a > b > c > -1$;

(ii) if $\log f$ is concave, then $\log \lambda_r$ is concave in $r \geq 0$, so that the reversal of (19) holds for $a > b > c \geq 0$;

iii if $\log f$ is convex, then $\log \lambda_r$ is convex in $r \geq 0$, so that (19) holds for $a > b > c \geq 0$;

(iv) if $\overline{F} = 1 - F$ is log concave, then $\log \lambda_r$ is concave in $r \geq 1$, so that the reversal of (19) holds for $a > b > c \geq 1$;

(v) if $\overline{F} = 1 - F$ is log convex, then $\log \lambda_r$ is convex in $r \geq 1$, and (19) holds for $a > b > c \geq 1$.

D.8.a. Example. The gamma density

$$f(x|\lambda,\nu) = \frac{\lambda^\nu x^{\nu-1} e^{-\lambda x}}{\Gamma(\nu)}, \quad x \geq 0, \ \lambda, \nu > 0,$$

is log concave for $\nu \geq 1$ and log convex for $0 < \nu \leq 1$. For this density, $\mu_r = \Gamma(r+\nu)/\lambda^r \Gamma(\nu)$. Take $\lambda = 1$ and conclude from D.8 that, as a function of r,

$$\lambda_r = \frac{\Gamma(r+\nu)}{\Gamma(r+1)\Gamma(\nu)} = \frac{\Gamma(r+\nu)}{r\Gamma(r)\Gamma(\nu)} = \frac{1}{rB(r,\nu)}$$

is log concave in $r > -\nu$, $r > 0$, $\nu > 0$ and log convex in $r \geq 0$, $0 < \nu \leq 1$.

More Moment Inequalities from Log Convexity

Following Simić (2007), for $x > 0$, let

$$\psi_s(x) = \frac{x^s}{s(s-1)}, \quad s \neq 0, 1,$$
$$= -\log x, \quad s = 0,$$
$$= x \log x, \quad s = 1.$$

For each s, ψ_s has the second derivative $\psi_s'' = x^{s-2}$, $x > 0$, and consequently, ψ_s is convex. If $p_i \geq 0$, $i = 1, \ldots, n$, $\Sigma_1^n p_i = 1$, then from Jensen's inequality C.1, it follows that

$$\psi_s\left(\sum p_i x_i\right) \leq \sum_1^n p_i \psi_s(x_i).$$

More generally, suppose that $p_1, \ldots, p_n \in \mathscr{R}$ and that $x \prec_p y$. By 14.A.3,

$$\sum_1^n p_i \psi_s(x_i) \leq \sum_1^n p_i \psi_s(y_i).$$

With the goal of refining this inequality, the following proposition considers the difference:

$$\phi_s(x,y;p) = \sum_1^n p_i \psi_s(y_i) - \sum_1^n p_i \psi_s(x_i). \tag{20}$$

D.9. Proposition (Latif, Anwar, and Pečarić, 2009, private communication). If $p \in \mathscr{R}^n$, $x, y \in \mathscr{D}$, and $x \prec_p y$ on $\mathscr{D}$, then $\phi_s(x,y;p)$ is log convex as a function of s, with x, y, and p fixed.

D. Some Additional Fundamental Inequalities 667

Proof. Suppose that $r = (s+t)/2$ and $u, v \in \mathscr{R}$. Because the function

$$f(z) = u^2 \psi_s(z) + 2uw\psi_r(z) + w^2 \psi_t(z), \quad z > 0,$$

has a positive second derivative, it follows that f is convex on $(0, \infty)$. With the aid of 14.A.3 and the assumption that $x \prec_p y$, this ensures that

$$\sum_1^n p_i f(y_i) - \sum_1^n p_i f(x_i) \geq 0.$$

More explicitly,

$$u^2 \phi_s(x, y; p) + 2uw\phi_r(x, y; p) + w^2 \phi_t(x, y; p) \geq 0,$$

so that by 18.A.10.a, ϕ_s is a log convex function of s. ∥

D.10. Corollary (Simić, 2007). The function

$$\phi_s(y; p) = \sum_1^n p_i \psi_s(y_i) - \psi_s(\overline{y}) \sum_1^n p_i \qquad (21)$$

is log convex as a function of s, where $\overline{y} = \sum_1^n p_i y_i / \sum_1^n p_i$.

This follows from D.9 and the fact that $(\overline{y}, \ldots, \overline{y}) \prec_p y$.

For the functions ϕ_s of D.9 and D.10, various inequalities can be obtained from (13), (14a), and (14b).

Continuous versions of D.9 and D.10 can be obtained either by a limiting argument or from 14.A.8.

D.11. Proposition (Latif, Anwar, and Pečarić, 2009, private communication). If x and y are decreasing continuous functions defined on $[0, 1]$, H is a function of bounded variation defined on $[0, 1]$, and

$$\int_0^u x(z) dH(z) \leq \int_0^u y(z) dH(z), \quad 0 \leq u \leq 1,$$

with equality when $u = 1$, then

$$\phi_s(x, y; H) = \int_0^1 \psi_s(y(z)) dH(z) - \int_0^1 \psi_s(x(z)) dH(z) \qquad (22)$$

is log convex in s.

The proof of D.11 is nearly identical to the proof of D.9, but makes use of 14.A.8 rather than 14.A.3.

668   16. Convex Functions and Some Classical Inequalities

D.12. Corollary. If W is a positive random variable for which the expectations exist and $\alpha \geq \beta$, then the function

$$g(t) = \frac{EW^{\alpha t} - (EW^{\beta t})(EW^{\alpha}/EW^{\beta})^t}{t(t-1)}, \quad t \neq 0, 1, \quad (23)$$

$$g(t) = (\log EW^{\alpha} - E\log W^{\alpha}) - (\log EW^{\beta} - E\log W^{\beta}), \quad t = 0,$$

$$g(t) = E(W^{\alpha}\log W^{\alpha}) - (EW^{\alpha})(\log EW^{\alpha})$$
$$\quad - E(W^{\beta}\log W^{\beta}) - (EW^{\beta})(\log EW^{\beta})(EW^{\alpha}/EW^{\beta}), \quad t = 1,$$

is log convex.

Proof. Assume first that the distribution F of W is strictly increasing on its support, and continuous. In (22), take $H(z) = z$ for $0 \leq z \leq 1$ and let $y(z) = [F^{-1}(1-z)]^{\alpha}$, $x(z) = K[F^{-1}(1-z)]^{\beta}$, where $K = EW^{\alpha}/EW^{\beta}$, $\alpha \geq \beta$. Because W is positive, x and y are nonnegative. It follows from 14.A.8.a that x and y satisfy the conditions of Proposition D.11. To apply this proposition, take $t \neq 0, 1$ and compute

$$\int_0^1 \psi_t(y(z))dH(z) = \int_0^1 \psi_t([F^{-1}(1-z)]^{\alpha})dz = \int_{-\infty}^{\infty} \psi_t(w^{\alpha})dF(w)$$

$$= \int_{-\infty}^{\infty} \frac{w^{\alpha t}}{t(t-1)}dF(w) = \frac{EW^{\alpha t}}{t(t-1)},$$

$$\int_0^1 \psi_t(x(z))dH(z) = \int_0^1 \psi_t(K[F^{-1}(1-z)]^{\beta})dz = \int_{-\infty}^{\infty} \psi_t(Kw^{\beta})dF(w)$$

$$= \int_{-\infty}^{\infty} \frac{K^t w^{\beta t}}{t(t-1)}dF(w) = \frac{K^t EW^{\beta t}}{t(t-1)}.$$

By substituting these quantities in (22), it follows that $d(t)$ is log convex, $t \neq 0, 1$. For $t = 0$ or 1, the result follows by taking limits.

If F is not strictly increasing or continuous, the limiting arguments can be used. One way to do this is to note that the convolution of F with an exponential distribution $G(z) = 1 - e^{-\lambda z}$, $z \geq 0$, is strictly increasing and continuous. Apply the above result to this convolution, and then let $\lambda \to 0$. ∥

D. Some Additional Fundamental Inequalities 669

With $\alpha = 1$, $\beta = 0$, $g(t)$ takes the particularly simple form

$$g(t) = \frac{EW^t - (EW)^t}{t(t-1)}, \quad t \neq 0, 1, \tag{24}$$

$$g(t) = \log EW - E \log W, \quad t = 0,$$

$$g(t) = EW \log W - EW \log EW, \quad t = 1.$$

The log convexity of this special case is due to Simić (2007).

The application of (13) to the log convex function $d(t)$ as defined in (23) yields (for $a > b > c$, $a, b, c \neq 0, 1$, $\alpha > \beta$) the inequality

$$\left(\frac{EW^{\alpha b} - EW^{\beta b}(EW^{\alpha}/EW^{\beta})^b}{b(b-1)}\right)^{a-c} \tag{25}$$

$$\leq \left(\frac{EW^{\alpha c} - EW^{\beta c}(EW^{\alpha}/EW^{\beta})^c}{c(c-1)}\right)^{a-b}$$

$$\times \left(\frac{EW^{\alpha a} - EW^{\beta a}(EW^{\alpha}/EW^{\beta})^a}{a(a-1)}\right)^{b-c}.$$

Various special cases of this complex inequality may be of interest. In particular, if $\alpha = 1$, and $\beta = 0$ as for (24), it follows that for $a > b > c$, $a, b, c \neq 0, 1$,

$$\left(\frac{EW^b - (EW)^b}{b(b-1)}\right)^{a-c} \tag{26}$$

$$\leq \left(\frac{EW^c - (EW)^c}{c(c-1)}\right)^{a-b} \left(\frac{EW^a - (EW)^a}{a(a-1)}\right)^{b-c}.$$

With $c = 0$, (26) becomes, for $a > b > 0$, $a, b \neq 1$,

$$\left(\frac{EW^b - (EW)^b}{b(b-1)}\right)^a \tag{27}$$

$$\leq (\log EW - E \log W)^{a-b} \left(\frac{EW^a - (EW)^a}{a(a-1)}\right)^b.$$

Assume that the distribution function F of W is not degenerate, so that $\log EW - E \log W \neq 0$. With $b = 1$, (27) becomes

$$EW^a - (EW)^a \geq \frac{a(a-1)(EW \log W - EW E \log W)}{\log EW - E \log W}, \quad a > 1.$$

Here the lower bound is positive; Jensen's inequality gives the lower bound of 0, but does not require W to be positive. The case of equality in Jensen's inequality has been ruled out by the assumption that F is not degenerate.

Various other special cases of (25) may be of interest. More specific inequalities can be obtained by specifying the distribution F of W.

E Matrix-Monotone and Matrix-Convex Functions

Let $\mathscr{H}_n$ be the set of all $n \times n$ Hermitian matrices. For each n, a function $\phi : \mathscr{R} \to \mathscr{R}$ can be extended to a function on $\mathscr{H}_n$ to $\mathscr{H}_n$ in the following way: Write $A \in \mathscr{H}_n$ in the form $A = \Gamma D \Gamma^*$, where $D = \mathrm{diag}(\lambda_1, \ldots, \lambda_n)$ is the diagonal matrix of eigenvalues of A and Γ is unitary (see 19.A.4). Then define

$$\phi(A) = \Gamma D_\phi \Gamma^*,$$

where $D_\phi = \mathrm{diag}(\phi(\lambda_1), \ldots, \phi(\lambda_n))$. Thus the eigenvalues of $\phi(A)$ are obtained by applying the function ϕ to each eigenvalue of A, and the eigenvectors of $\phi(A)$ are the same as the eigenvectors of A. Such extensions of ϕ satisfy, for any unitary matrix Γ,

$$\phi(\Gamma A \Gamma^*) = \Gamma \phi(A) \Gamma^*.$$

Matrix-valued functions of matrices also arise naturally by way of standard matrix operations, as some of the examples below show.

To define monotonicity for matrix-valued functions of matrices, a partial ordering of $\mathscr{H}_n$ is required. One standard ordering, often called the *Loewner ordering*, makes use of the convex cone of positive semidefinite matrices in $\mathscr{H}_n$:

$A \leq B$ means $B - A$ is positive semidefinite;

$A < B$ means $B - A$ is positive definite.

If $\mathscr{A} \subset \mathscr{H}_n$, a function $\phi : \mathscr{A} \to \mathscr{H}_n$ is said to be *matrix-increasing* or *matrix monotone* on $\mathscr{A}$ if for $A, B \in \mathscr{A}$,

$$A \leq B \text{ implies } \phi(A) \leq \phi(B); \tag{1}$$

ϕ is *strictly matrix-increasing* if for $A, B \in \mathscr{A}$ (1) holds and

$$A < B \text{ implies } \phi(A) < \phi(B) \quad \text{whenever} \quad A, B \in \mathscr{A}. \tag{2}$$

Matrix-monotone functions have been studied, e.g., by Loewner (1934, 1950), Bendat and Sherman (1955), and Davis (1963). A general

E. Matrix-Monotone and Matrix-Convex Functions

discussion of matrix-monotone functions is provided by Bhatia (1997, Chapter V), Horn and Johnson (1991, Section 6.6), and Zhan (2002, Chapter 1). See also Kwong (1989) for an exposition of matrix-monotone and matrix-convex functions.

Loewner (1934) shows that in case $\mathscr{A}$ is the set of $n \times n$ Hermitian matrices with eigenvalues in (a, b), then ϕ as a function on (a, b) generates, for all n, a matrix-monotone function on $\mathscr{A}$ if and only if ϕ is analytic on (a, b), can be analytically continued into the whole upper half-plane, and there represents an analytic function whose imaginary part is nonnegative.

Notice that the class of matrix-increasing functions on a set $\mathscr{A}$ forms a convex cone. Moreover, there is an obvious closure under compositions: If $\phi_1 : \mathscr{A}_n \to \mathscr{B}_n$ and $\phi_2 : \mathscr{B}_n \to \mathscr{C}_n$ are matrix-monotone, then $\phi_1 \circ \phi_2 : \mathscr{A}_n \to \mathscr{C}_n$ is matrix-monotone.

In some proofs of matrix-monotonicity and matrix-convexity (defined below), the following lemma is a useful tool.

E.1. Lemma. Let A and $G \in \mathscr{H}_n$. If $A > 0$ and $GA + AG \geq 0$, then $G \geq 0$; if $A > 0$ and $GA + AG > 0$, then $G > 0$.

Proof. Let $G = \Gamma D_\theta \Gamma^*$, where Γ is unitary and $D_\theta = \mathrm{diag}(\theta_1, \ldots, \theta_n)$ [see 19.A.4], and let $B = \Gamma^* A \Gamma$. Because $GA + AG \geq 0$ (>0),

$$\Gamma^* GA\Gamma + \Gamma^* AG\Gamma = D_\theta B + BD_\theta \geq 0 \ (>0).$$

But $b_{ii} > 0$ because $B > 0$, so that the diagonal elements $2\theta_i b_{ii}$ of $D_\theta B + BD_\theta$ are nonnegative (positive). Consequently, $\theta_i \geq 0$ (>0), $i = 1, \ldots, n$. ‖

E.2. Proposition (Loewner, 1934). On the set of $n \times n$ positive definite Hermitian matrices, the function $\phi(A) = \log A$ is matrix-increasing.

Loewner's proof of this result involves analytic continuation of ϕ and is omitted here.

Monotonicity of Powers of a Matrix

Rather surprising conditions under which A^r is or is not monotone are given here in a series of propositions. Some limited results about strict monotonicity are also given.

E.3. Proposition (Loewner, 1934). On the set of $n \times n$ positive semidefinite Hermitian matrices, the functions $\phi(A) = A^r$, $0 < r \leq 1$, are increasing.

Loewner's proof of this result also involves analytic continuation of ϕ and is not given here. Another proof using an integral representation of A^r is given by Bhagwat and Subramanian (1978). The special case $r = \frac{1}{2}$ has simple proofs.

E.3.a. The function $\phi(A) = A^{1/2}$ is strictly matrix-increasing on the set of $n \times n$ positive semidefinite Hermitian matrices.

First proof. Let $B > A \geq 0$ and let $g(\alpha) = (\alpha B + \overline{\alpha} A)^{1/2} \equiv Q^{1/2}$. It suffices to prove that g is strictly increasing in $\alpha \in [0, 1]$; that is, $0 \leq \alpha < \beta \leq 1$ implies $g(\beta) - g(\alpha) > 0$. A continuity argument shows that it is sufficient to prove this in case $0 < \alpha < \beta < 1$. We prove the slightly stronger result that $dg/d\alpha$ is positive definite. Since $Q^{1/2} Q^{1/2} = Q$, it follows that

$$\frac{dQ^{1/2}}{d\alpha} Q^{1/2} + Q^{1/2} \frac{dQ^{1/2}}{d\alpha} = \frac{dQ}{d\alpha} = B - A > 0.$$

Since $Q^{1/2} > 0$ for $0 < \alpha < 1$, $dQ^{1/2}/d\alpha > 0$, $0 < \alpha < 1$, by E.1. ‖

Second proof. With continuity, it is sufficient to show that $B > A > 0$ implies $B^{1/2} > A^{1/2}$. Denote the eigenvalues of a matrix $M \in \mathscr{H}_n$ by $\lambda_1(M) \geq \cdots \geq \lambda_n(M)$. Because $B > A > 0$, it follows that $A^{-1/2} B A^{-1/2} > I$, or equivalently, $\lambda_n(A^{-1/2} B A^{-1/2}) > 1$. It is well known [see, e.g., Marcus and Minc (1964, p. 144)] that for any $n \times n$ complex matrix U with absolute eigenvalues $|\lambda_1(U)| \geq \cdots \geq |\lambda_n(U)|$, $\lambda_n(UU') \leq |\lambda_n(U)|^2$, so that

$$1 < \lambda_n(A^{-1/2} B A^{-1/2}) \leq [\lambda_n(A^{-1/2} B^{1/2})]^2 = [\lambda_n(A^{-1/4} B^{1/2} A^{-1/4})]^2.$$

But the above arguments show that $\lambda_n(A^{-1/4} B^{1/2} A^{-1/4}) > 1$, which is equivalent to $A^{-1/4} B^{1/2} A^{-1/4} > I$; i.e., $B^{1/2} > A^{1/2}$. ‖

Yet another proof of E.3.a is given by Davis (1963).

E.3.b. On the set of positive definite Hermitian matrices, the function $\phi(A) = A^{-1}$ is strictly matrix-decreasing.

Proof. Let $B > A > 0$ and let $g(\alpha) = (\alpha B + \overline{\alpha} A)^{-1} \equiv Q^{-1}$. As in the first proof of E.3.a, it is sufficient to show that $dg/d\alpha$ is negative definite. Since $QQ^{-1} = I$, $(dQ/d\alpha)Q + Q(dQ^{-1}/d\alpha) = 0$, so that $dQ^{-1}/d\alpha = -Q^{-1}(dQ/d\alpha)Q^{-1} = -Q^{-1}(B - A)Q^{-1} < 0$. ‖

E. Matrix-Monotone and Matrix-Convex Functions

Extensions of E.3 to the set of positive semidefinite Hermitian matrices using the Moore–Penrose inverse have been obtained by Milliken and Akdeniz (1977).

E.3.c. On the set of positive definite matrices, the function $\phi(A) = A^r$ is matrix-decreasing, $-1 \leq r < 0$.

This result follows from E.3 and E.3.b because a matrix-decreasing function of a matrix-increasing function is matrix-decreasing.

The monotonicity of A^r is established above for $-1 \leq r \leq 1$. The following counterexample shows that corresponding results for $|r| > 1$ are false.

E.4. Counterexample.

$$A = \begin{bmatrix} 1 & 1 \\ 1 & 1 \end{bmatrix} = \begin{bmatrix} \frac{1}{\sqrt{2}} & \frac{1}{\sqrt{2}} \\ \frac{1}{\sqrt{2}} & -\frac{1}{\sqrt{2}} \end{bmatrix} \begin{bmatrix} 2 & 0 \\ 0 & 0 \end{bmatrix} \begin{bmatrix} \frac{1}{\sqrt{2}} & \frac{1}{\sqrt{2}} \\ \frac{1}{\sqrt{2}} & -\frac{1}{\sqrt{2}} \end{bmatrix} \text{ and } B = \begin{bmatrix} b_1 & 0 \\ 0 & b_2 \end{bmatrix},$$

so that

$$A^r = 2^{r-1} \begin{bmatrix} 1 & 1 \\ 1 & 1 \end{bmatrix} \quad \text{and} \quad B^r = \begin{bmatrix} b_1^r & 0 \\ 0 & b_2^r \end{bmatrix}.$$

Then

$$B - A = \begin{bmatrix} b_1 - 1 & -1 \\ -1 & b_2 - 1 \end{bmatrix} > 0$$

whenever $b_1 > 1$ and $(b_1 - 1)(b_2 - 1) > 1$. If $r > 1$, then $B^r - A^r$ is not positive semidefinite when $b_1^r < 2^{r-1}$. It follows that $B - A > 0$, but $B^r - A^r$ is not positive semidefinite when $1 < b_1 < 2^{1-1/r}$ and $b_2 - 1 > 1/(b_1 - 1)$. The same choice shows that if $r < -1$, then $A^r - B^r$ is not positive semidefinite even though $B - A > 0$.

It is possible to show, by differentiating $(\alpha A + \overline{\alpha} B)^r (\alpha A + \overline{\alpha} B)^{-r} = I$ with respect to α, that $(d/d\alpha)(\alpha A + \overline{\alpha} B)^r$ is not positive semidefinite when $(d/d\alpha)(\alpha A + \overline{\alpha} B)^{-r}$ is not negative semidefinite. So $\phi(A) = A^r$ is not matrix-decreasing when $r < -1$ if it is not increasing when $r > 1$. This observation shows that counterexamples for $r > 1$ are all that are needed.

In summary, the function $\phi(A) = A^r$ is matrix-decreasing in $A > 0$, $-1 \leq r \leq 0$, and is matrix-increasing in $A \geq 0$, $0 \leq r \leq 1$. It is not matrix-monotone if $r < -1$ or $r > 1$.

Several additional examples of nonmonotone matrix functions are known. These include the extensions of step functions and of e^x (Bendat and Sherman, 1955). Counterexamples can be obtained from E.4. If

$$\phi(x) = \begin{cases} 0, & x < 1.6, \\ 1, & x \geq 1.6, \end{cases}$$

then with $b_1 = \frac{3}{2}$ and $b_2 > \frac{5}{3}$, it is seen that the matrix extension of ϕ is not increasing. With $b_1 = 6$, $b_2 = 1.2$, it is seen that $\phi(A) = e^A$ is not matrix-increasing. As was noted by Davis (1963), the extension of $\max(x, 0)$ is not matrix-increasing.

There are a number of matrix-valued functions of matrices that do not arise as extensions of functions on $\mathscr{R}$ to $\mathscr{R}$ in the manner described at the beginning of this section. The monotonicity of such functions is a neglected subject, but some examples follow.

E.5. Additional Examples of Matrix-Monotone Functions

E.5.a. Let

$$A = \begin{bmatrix} A_{11} & A_{12} \\ A_{21} & A_{22} \end{bmatrix}$$

denote a partitioned matrix. On the set of Hermitian matrices, the function

$$\phi(A) = A_{11}$$

is strictly matrix-increasing.

Proof. This result is trivial, because $B > A$ implies

$$(I, 0)B(I, 0)^* > (I, 0)A(I, 0)^*. \quad \|$$

E.5.b. Denote the conformably partitioned inverse of

$$A = \begin{bmatrix} A_{11} & A_{12} \\ A_{21} & A_{22} \end{bmatrix}$$

by

$$A^{-1} = \begin{bmatrix} A^{11} & A^{12} \\ A^{21} & A^{22} \end{bmatrix}.$$

On the set of positive definite Hermitian matrices, the function
$$\phi(A) = A^{11}$$
is strictly matrix-decreasing.

Proof. If $B > A > 0$, then $0 < B^{-1} < A^{-1}$, so that $(I,0)B^{-1}(I,0)^* < (I,0)A^{-1}(I,0)^*$; that is, $B^{11} < A^{11}$. ||

E.5.c. On the set of positive semidefinite $n \times n$ Hermitian matrices, the kth compound function (see 19.F.1)
$$\phi(A) = A^{(k)}$$
is strictly matrix-increasing, $k = 1, \ldots, n$.

Proof. If $B > A > 0$, then $A^{-1/2}BA^{-1/2} > I$. This means that all of the eigenvalues of $A^{-1/2}BA^{-1/2}$ exceed 1 (see 20.A.1.b), so that products of eigenvalues of $A^{-1/2}BA^{-1/2}$, k at a time, also exceed 1. This means that $(A^{-1/2}BA^{-1/2})^{(k)} = (A^{-1/2})^{(k)}B^{(k)}(A^{-1/2})^{(k)} > I$, that is, $B^{(k)} > A^{(k)}$, after noting that $[(A^{-1/2})^{(k)}(A^{-1/2})^{(k)}]^{-1} = A^{(k)}$. ||

E.5.d. For a fixed $m \times m$ matrix M, let
$$\phi_1(A) = A \otimes M,$$
$$\phi_2(A) = M \otimes A$$
be *Kronecker products* of A and M (see Section 19.G). If M is positive semidefinite Hermitian, ϕ_1 and ϕ_2 are matrix-increasing on the set of $n \times n$ Hermitian matrices. The monotonicity is strict if M is positive definite.

Proof. If $M \geq 0$ and $B - A \geq 0$, then by 19.G.2.a, $(B-A) \otimes M \geq 0$. This shows that ϕ_1 is matrix-increasing. A similar argument applies to ϕ_2 and a similar argument shows strict monotonicity when $M > 0$. ||

E.5.e. From E.5.d, it follows that if $0 \leq B_1 \leq A_1$ and $0 \leq B_2 \leq A_2$, then
$$A_1 \otimes A_2 \geq B_1 \otimes B_2$$
because $A_1 \otimes A_2 \geq B_1 \otimes A_2 \geq B_1 \otimes B_2$. Generalizations of this have been obtained by Marcus and Nikolai (1969).

E.5.f. (Furuta, 1987). If $A \geq B \geq 0$, then for all $r \geq 0$ and $s \geq 1$,
$$(B^r A^s B^r)^{(1+2r)/(s+2r)} \geq B^{(1+2r)},$$
$$A^{(1+2r)} \geq (A^r B^s A^r)^{(1+2r)/(s+2r)}.$$

For extensions, see Fujii and Kamei (1992).

Matrix-Convex Functions

The concept of a matrix-convex function was first studied by Krauss (1936). Matrix-convex functions have also been studied by Bendat and Sherman (1955) and by Davis (1963); see also Roberts and Varberg (1973, pp. 259–261). Bhatia (1997, Chapter V) provides a detailed discussion of matrix-monotone and matrix-convex functions.

A function ϕ defined on a convex set $\mathscr{A}$ of matrices and taking values in $\mathscr{H}_n$ is said to be *matrix-convex* if

$$\phi(\alpha A + \overline{\alpha} B) \leq \alpha \phi(A) + \overline{\alpha} \phi(B) \text{ for all } \alpha \in [0,1] \text{ and } A, B \in \mathscr{A}, \quad (3)$$

where the inequality denotes the Loewner ordering. The function ϕ is *strictly matrix-convex* if (3) and

$$\phi(\alpha A + \overline{\alpha} B) < \alpha \phi(A) + \overline{\alpha} \phi(B) \quad (4)$$

for all $\alpha \in (0,1)$ and all $A, B \in \mathscr{A}$ such that $B - A$ has full rank.

E.6. Proposition. Let ϕ be a function defined on a convex set $\mathscr{A}$ of $m \times k$ matrices, taking values in $\mathscr{H}_n$ for some n. The following are equivalent:

(i) ϕ is matrix-convex on $\mathscr{A}$.

(ii) For all fixed A and B in $\mathscr{A}$, the function $g(\alpha) = \phi(\alpha A + \overline{\alpha} B)$ is convex in $\alpha \in [0,1]$ in the sense that $\eta g(\alpha) + \overline{\eta} g(\beta) - g(\eta \alpha + \overline{\eta} \beta)$ is positive semidefinite for all $\alpha, \beta, \eta \in [0,1]$.

In case $\mathscr{A}$ is open, another equivalent condition is

(iii) for all random matrices X taking values in $\mathscr{A}$ and having finite expectation EX,

$$\phi(EX) \leq E\phi(X).$$

If $\mathscr{A}$ is open and g is twice differentiable for all $A, B \in \mathscr{A}$, yet another equivalent condition is

(iv) for all fixed A and B in $\mathscr{A}$, $d^2 g(\alpha)/d\alpha^2$ is positive semidefinite, $0 < \alpha < 1$.

There is also a version of E.6 for strict matrix-convexity:

E.6.a. Proposition. With the notation E.6, the following are equivalent:

(i) ϕ is strictly matrix-convex on $\mathscr{A}$.

(ii) For all matrices A and B in $\mathscr{A}$ such that $B - A$ has full rank, $g(\alpha) = \phi(\alpha A + \overline{\alpha} B)$ is strictly convex in $\alpha \in [0, 1]$ in the sense that $\eta g(\alpha) + \overline{\eta} g(\beta) - g(\eta \alpha + \overline{\eta} \beta)$ is positive definite for all $\alpha, \beta \in [0, 1]$, $\alpha \neq \beta$, and $\eta \in (0, 1)$.

If

(iii) for all A and B in $\mathscr{A}$ such that $B - A$ has full rank, g is twice differentiable and $d^2 g(\alpha)/d\alpha^2$ is positive definite, $0 < \alpha < 1$, then (i) holds.

Proof of E.6 and E.6.a. The function ϕ is matrix-convex (strictly matrix-convex) on $\mathscr{A}$ if and only if, for all $x \in \mathscr{R}^k$, $\psi(A) = x\phi(A)x'$ is convex (strictly convex). Consequently, E.6 and E.6.a follow from B.2, B.2.b, B.3.c, and C.1. ||

As noted by Roberts and Varberg (1973), remarkably few explicit examples of matrix-convex functions have been found. However, E.6 provides some useful tools for identifying a few such examples, and other methods are also illustrated below.

E.7. Matrix-convex functions: Examples. The proofs of E.7.a–E.7.h are collected after E.7.h. Several methods of proof are illustrated.

E.7.a. Let L be a fixed $n \times n$ positive semidefinite Hermitian matrix. The function ϕ defined on the space of all $m \times n$ complex matrices by

$$\phi(A) = ALA^*$$

is matrix-convex. The convexity is strict if L is positive definite and $m \leq n$.

The special case $L = I$ and A Hermitian was obtained by Davis (1968).

E.7.b. (Ando, 1979). On the set of $n \times n$ positive definite Hermitian matrices, the function

$$\phi(A) = A^r$$

is matrix-convex for $1 \leq r \leq 2$ or $-1 \leq r \leq 0$, and matrix-concave for $0 \leq r \leq 1$.

The following three special cases are singled out because they have elementary proofs. See also Kwong (1989).

E.7.c. (Olkin and Pratt, 1958; Whittle, 1958). On the set of $n \times n$ positive definite Hermitian matrices, the function

$$\phi(A) = A^{-1}$$

is strictly matrix-convex.

E.7.d. On the set of $n \times n$ positive definite Hermitian matrices, the function

$$\phi(A) = A^{1/2}$$

is strictly matrix-concave.

E.7.e. On the set of $n \times n$ positive definite Hermitian matrices, the function

$$\phi(A) = A^{-1/2}$$

is strictly matrix-convex.

E.7.f. (Kiefer, 1959; Haynsworth, 1970; Olkin, 1973; Lieb and Ruskai, 1974). On the set where M is an $m \times n$ complex matrix and A is an $n \times n$ positive definite Hermitian matrix, the function

$$\phi(A, M) = MA^{-1}M^*$$

is matrix-convex.

E.7.g. For any partitioned nonsingular matrix

$$A = \begin{bmatrix} A_{11} & A_{12} \\ A_{21} & A_{22} \end{bmatrix},$$

denote the conformably partitioned inverse by

$$A^{-1} = \begin{bmatrix} A^{11} & A^{12} \\ A^{21} & A^{22} \end{bmatrix}.$$

On the set of positive definite Hermitian matrices, the function

$$\phi(A) = (A^{11})^{-1} = A_{11} - A_{12}A_{22}^{-1}A_{21}$$

is matrix-concave.

E.7.h. (Ingram Olkin; see Ylvisaker, 1964). If $\mathbf{M}$ is a fixed $m \times n$ complex matrix of rank $m \leq n$, then on the set of positive definite Hermitian matrices, the function

$$\phi(A) = (MA^{-1}M^*)^{-1}$$

is matrix-concave.

E. Matrix-Monotone and Matrix-Convex Functions 679

An extension of this to the set of positive semidefinite matrices is given by Pukelsheim (1977).

All of the above examples are strictly matrix-convex or matrix-concave except the last three. In E.7.f, even with $n = m = 1$, the function is not strictly convex because $\phi(a, m) = m^2/a$ is linear on the line $a = m$. However, ϕ is strictly matrix-convex in A for fixed M of rank $m \leq n$ (as follows from E.7.c) and ϕ is strictly matrix-convex in M for fixed A when $m \leq n$ (as follows from E.7.a). For similar reasons, Example E.7.g is not strictly matrix-concave even in the case that A is a 2×2 matrix, and E.7.h is not strictly convex when $m = n = 1$.

E.7.i. Proposition (Zhan, 2002). If $A \geq 0$, $B \geq 0$, then for all $0 \leq r \leq 1$, the Hadamard–Schur product

$$\phi(A, B) = A^r \circ B^{1-r}$$

is matrix-convex.

Proofs of E.7.a–E.7.h

The results E.7.a–E.7.h can be proved by showing that the second derivative of $g(\alpha) \equiv \phi(\alpha A + \overline{\alpha} B)$ is positive definite or positive semidefinite, $\alpha \in (0, 1)$. This method is illustrated ahead for E.7.c, d, f, and h. Other kinds of proofs are given for E.7.a, c, e, f, and h in order to illustrate other methods which are also of independent interest.

Except possibly for the question of strict convexity, several of the above examples follow from others as special cases. These implications are easy to find but are not fully exploited here. Our purpose is not to give a collection of concise proofs, but rather to illustrate possible methods of proof.

Proof of E.7.a. Notice that the inequality

$$(\alpha A + \overline{\alpha} B) L (\alpha A + \overline{\alpha} B)^* \leq \alpha A L A^* + \overline{\alpha} B L B^*$$

is equivalent to $0 \leq \alpha \overline{\alpha} (A - B) L (A - B)^*$. ||

First proof of E.7.c. Let $g(\alpha) = (\alpha A + \overline{\alpha} B)^{-1} \equiv Q^{-1}$, where A and B are positive definite and $B - A$ has full rank. Then

$$\frac{dg(\alpha)}{d\alpha} = -Q^{-1} \frac{dQ}{d\alpha} Q^{-1} \quad \text{and} \quad \frac{d^2 g(\alpha)}{d\alpha^2} = 2 Q^{-1} \frac{dQ}{d\alpha} Q^{-1} \frac{dQ}{d\alpha} Q^{-1} > 0$$

because $dQ/d\alpha = A - B$ has full rank, as does Q^{-1}. ||

Second proof of E.7.c. Let A and B be positive definite Hermitian matrices such that $B - A$ has full rank. According to 19.E.1, there exist a matrix W and a diagonal matrix D such that $A = WW^*$, $B = WDW^*$. Then the inequality $(\alpha A + \overline{\alpha} B)^{-1} < \alpha A^{-1} + \overline{\alpha} B^{-1}$ becomes $[W(\alpha I + \overline{\alpha} D)W^*]^{-1} < \alpha(WW^*)^{-1} + \overline{\alpha}(WDW^*)^{-1}$, which is equivalent to $(\alpha I + \overline{\alpha} D)^{-1} < \alpha I + \overline{\alpha} D^{-1}$. Here, all matrices are diagonal. Thus the result follows from the strict convexity of the function x^{-1} on $(0, \infty)$. ||

Another proof of E.7.c that $\phi(A) = A^{-1}$ is matrix-convex is obtained by Whittle (1958) by showing that

$$\alpha A^{-1} + \overline{\alpha} B^{-1} - (\alpha A + \overline{\alpha} B)^{-1}$$
$$= \alpha \overline{\alpha}(A^{-1} - B^{-1})(\alpha B^{-1} + \overline{\alpha} A^{-1})^{-1}(A^{-1} - B^{-1}) \geq 0.$$

Olkin and Pratt (1958) and Whittle (1958) prove that $\operatorname{tr} A^{-1}C$ is convex in A for all positive semidefinite matrices C. This fact is equivalent to the convexity of A^{-1}: It is easy to see that A^{-1} is convex implies $\operatorname{tr} A^{-1}C$ is convex when C is positive semidefinite, and conversely with $C = x'x$, the convexity of $\operatorname{tr} A^{-1}C = xA^{-1}x'$ implies that A^{-1} is convex. A proof of E.7.c similar to the first proof above is given by Groves and Rothenberg (1969). A proof similar to the second above proof is given by Moore (1973).

Proof of E.7.d. Let $Q = \alpha A + \overline{\alpha} B$, where A and B are positive definite Hermitian matrices such that $B - A$ has full rank. Since $Q^{1/2}Q^{1/2} = Q$, it follows that

$$\frac{dQ^{1/2}}{d\alpha} Q^{1/2} + Q^{1/2} \frac{dQ^{1/2}}{d\alpha} = \frac{dQ}{d\alpha} = B - A$$

has full rank. Since $Q^{1/2}$ has full rank, this means that $dQ^{1/2}/d\alpha$ has full rank. Differentiating a second time yields the fact that

$$\frac{d^2 Q^{1/2}}{d\alpha^2} Q^{1/2} + Q^{1/2} \frac{d^2 Q^{1/2}}{d\alpha^2} = -2 \left(\frac{dQ^{1/2}}{d\alpha} \right)^2$$

is negative definite. Since $Q^{1/2}$ is positive definite, this means that $d^2 Q^{1/2}/d\alpha^2$ is negative definite (E.1). ||

Proof of E.7.e. By E.3 and E.7.c, $\psi(A) = A^{-1}$ is strictly matrix-decreasing and strictly matrix-convex. Since $\phi(A) = A^{1/2}$ is strictly matrix-concave, the composition $\psi \circ \phi$ is strictly matrix-convex. ||

E. Matrix-Monotone and Matrix-Convex Functions   681

First proof of E.7.f. Let M and N be $m \times n$ complex matrices, and let A and B be $n \times n$ positive definite matrices. Let $g(\alpha) = WS^{-1}W^*$, where $W = \alpha M + \overline{\alpha} N$, $S = \alpha A + \overline{\alpha} B$. Then

$$\frac{dg}{d\alpha} = \frac{dW}{d\alpha} S^{-1} W^* + WS^{-1} \frac{dW^*}{d\alpha} - WS^{-1} \frac{dS}{d\alpha} S^{-1} W^*,$$

$$\frac{d^2 g}{d\alpha} = 2 \left(WS^{-1} \frac{dS}{d\alpha} - \frac{dW}{d\alpha} \right) S^{-1} \left(WS^{-1} \frac{dS}{d\alpha} - \frac{dW}{d\alpha} \right)^* \geq 0. \quad \|$$

Second proof of E.7.f (Rizvi and Shorrock, 1979). Here it is convenient to use (iii) of E.6. So regard A as a random positive definite Hermitian matrix with finite expectation $\Sigma > 0$, and regard M as a random complex matrix with expectation μ. Then $(M - \mu\Sigma^{-1}A)A^{-1}(M - \mu\Sigma^{-1}A)' \geq 0$, so

$$E(M - \mu\Sigma^{-1}A)A^{-1}(M - \mu\Sigma^{-1}A)' \geq 0,$$

which is equivalent to $E(MA^{-1}M') \geq \mu\Sigma^{-1}\mu'$. $\quad \|$

Proof of E.7.g. Because A_{11} is a linear function of A, this follows from E.7.f with the choices $M = A_{12}$ and $A = A_{22}$. $\quad \|$

First proof of E.7.h. Let $W = \alpha A + \overline{\alpha} B$, where A and B are positive definite, let $Q = MW^{-1}M^*$, and let $g(\alpha) = Q^{-1}$. Compute

$$\frac{d^2 g(\alpha)}{d\alpha^2} = 2Q^{-1} \frac{dQ}{d\alpha} Q^{-1} \frac{dQ}{d\alpha} Q^{-1} - Q^{-1} \frac{d^2 Q}{d\alpha^2} Q^{-1},$$

where

$$\frac{dQ}{d\alpha} = -MW^{-1} \frac{dW}{d\alpha} W^{-1} M^*,$$

$$\frac{d^2 Q}{d\alpha^2} = 2MW^{-1} \frac{dW}{d\alpha} W^{-1} \frac{dW}{d\alpha} W^{-1} M^*.$$

This shows that

$$d^2 g(\alpha)/d\alpha^2 = 2XSX^*,$$

where $X = Q^{-1}MW^{-1}(dW/d\alpha)W^{-\frac{1}{2}}$ and

$$S = W^{-\frac{1}{2}} M' Q^{-1} MW^{-\frac{1}{2}} - I.$$

With $R = MW^{-\frac{1}{2}}$, it is easy to see that $S + I = R'(RR')^{-1}R$ is idempotent and hence $S = -S^2 \leq 0$. Thus $d^2 g(\alpha)/d\alpha^2 \leq 0$. $\quad \|$

Second proof of E.7.h. By 19.C.2, there exist a nonsingular $m \times m$ matrix T and an $n \times n$ unitary matrix Γ such that $M = T(I, 0)\Gamma$.

Let $\Gamma A \Gamma^* = \widetilde{A}$ and observe that it is sufficient to show that $\phi(A) = T^{*-1}[(I,0)\widetilde{A}^{-1}\binom{I}{0}]^{-1}T^{-1}$ is concave in $\widetilde{A}$. This follows from the concavity of $(\widetilde{A}^{11})^{-1} = [(I,0)\widetilde{A}^{-1}\binom{I}{0}]^{-1}$ given by E.7.g. ∥

Here, E.7.h is obtained from E.7.g. Notice that it is also easy to obtain E.7.g from E.7.h as a special case by choosing $M = (I,0)$.

There is an interesting combination of E.7.c and E.7.h. To see this, regard A as a random matrix and write E.7.h in the form $E(MA^{-1}M^*)^{-1} \leq (M(EA)^{-1}M^*)^{-1}$; similarly, with A replaced by $MA^{-1}M^*$ in E.7.c, it follows that $(EMA^{-1}M^*)^{-1} \leq E(MA^{-1}M^*)^{-1}$. Together, these inequalities yield

$$(ME(A^{-1})M^*)^{-1} \leq E(MA^{-1}M^*)^{-1} \leq (M(EA)^{-1}M^*)^{-1};$$

that is,

$$ME(A^{-1})M^* \geq [E(MA^{-1}M^*)^{-1}]^{-1} \geq M(EA)^{-1}M^*.$$

Notice that the comparison of the two extremes here, $ME(A^{-1})M^* \geq M(EA)^{-1}M^*$, follows directly from E.7.c.

E.7.j. A convexity-like result related to E.5.e has been obtained by Watkins (1974): If A_1, A_2, B_1, B_2 are Hermitian matrices such that $0 \leq B_1 \leq A_1$ and $0 \leq B_2 \leq A_2$, then for all $\alpha \in [0,1]$,

$$(\alpha A_1 + \overline{\alpha} B_1) \otimes (\alpha A_2 + \overline{\alpha} B_2) \leq \alpha(A_1 \otimes A_2) + \overline{\alpha}(B_1 \otimes B_2).$$

Proof. Let

$$g(\alpha) = (\alpha A_1 + \overline{\alpha} B_1) \otimes (\alpha A_2 + \overline{\alpha} B_2),$$

and notice that

$$\frac{d^2}{d\alpha^2} g(\alpha) = 2(A_1 - B_1) \otimes (A_2 - B_2). \tag{3}$$

But the eigenvalues of this Kronecker product are just products of roots of $A_1 - B_1$ and of $A_2 - B_2$, hence nonnegative. Thus the matrix (3) is positive semidefinite. ∥

Watkins (1974) also obtains a generalization of the above result.

E.8. Nonconvex matrix functions: Examples

E.8.a. (Rizvi and Shorrock, 1979). On the set of positive definite matrices, let

$$\phi(A) = A^r.$$

For $r \notin [-1, 2]$, ϕ is not matrix-convex.

E. Matrix-Monotone and Matrix-Convex Functions 683

Proof. According to Theorems 2 and 4 of Davis (1963), a function ψ is matrix-convex on $(-1,1)$ [i.e., the domain of ψ is restricted to matrices with roots in $(-1,1)$] if and only if $\psi''(0) \geq 0$ and for some random variable Z such that $P\{|Z| \leq 1\} = 1$,

$$\psi(x) = \psi(0) + \psi'(0)x + \frac{\psi''(0)}{2} E\left(\frac{x^2}{1+Zx}\right). \qquad (4)$$

For the particular choice of the function ψ, $\psi(x) = (1+x)^r$, (4) yields

$$(1+x)^r = 1 + rx + \frac{r(r-1)}{2} E \frac{x^2}{1+Zx}.$$

By expanding the last term and equating coefficients, it is not difficult to compute that for such a random variable Z, $\operatorname{Var} Z = (2-r)(r+1)/36$, which is negative if $r \notin [-1, 2]$. ||

Remark. Ando (1979) unifies and extends the results on matrix convexity of powers using an integral representation of functions that are matrix-monotone of order n for every n, due to Loewner. Ando verifies that the function $\phi(A) = A^r$ defined on the class of positive definite Hermitian matrices is matrix-convex if $1 \leq r \leq 2$ or if $-1 \leq r \leq 0$, and concave if $0 \leq r \leq 1$. For other values of r, ϕ is neither matrix-concave nor matrix-convex (Ando, 1979, p. 215).

E.8.b. (Davis, 1963). The matrix extension of $\phi(x) = |x|$ is not matrix-convex even on $(-1, 1)$. Davis shows this by exhibiting a counterexample.

E.8.c. The function $\phi(A) = e^A$ is not matrix-convex. To see this, let

$$A = \begin{bmatrix} 1 & 1 \\ 1 & 1 \end{bmatrix} = \frac{1}{2}\begin{bmatrix} 1 & 1 \\ 1 & -1 \end{bmatrix}\begin{bmatrix} 2 & 0 \\ 0 & 0 \end{bmatrix}\begin{bmatrix} 1 & 1 \\ 1 & -1 \end{bmatrix}, \qquad B = \begin{bmatrix} 10 & 0 \\ 0 & 0 \end{bmatrix},$$

so that

$$e^A \approx 3.69 A, \qquad e^B = \begin{bmatrix} e^{10} & 0 \\ 0 & 1 \end{bmatrix}.$$

Then

$$\frac{A+B}{2} \approx \begin{bmatrix} 0.995 & 0.1 \\ 0.1 & -0.995 \end{bmatrix}\begin{bmatrix} 5.55 & 0 \\ 0 & 0.45 \end{bmatrix}\begin{bmatrix} 0.995 & 0.1 \\ 0.1 & -0.995 \end{bmatrix}$$

and
$$e^{(A+B)/2} \approx \begin{bmatrix} 254.65 & 25.44 \\ 25.44 & 4.13 \end{bmatrix}.$$

Here,
$$e^{(A+B)/2} \not\leq \frac{1}{2}e^A + \frac{1}{2}e^B = \begin{bmatrix} 11015.10 & -1.85 \\ -1.85 & 2.35 \end{bmatrix}.$$

F Real-Valued Functions of Matrices

Section E is concerned with matrix-valued functions of matrices. Here, some real-valued functions of matrices are discussed which are monotone or convex. A real-valued function ϕ defined on some set $\mathcal{H}$ of $n \times n$ Hermitian matrices is *increasing* on $\mathcal{H}$ if, for $A, B \in \mathcal{H}$, $A \leq B$ implies

$$\phi(A) \leq \phi(B);$$

ϕ is *strictly increasing* on $\mathcal{H}$ if, for $A, B \in \mathcal{H}$, $A < B$ implies

$$\phi(A) < \phi(B).$$

A real-valued function φ defined on some set $\mathcal{H}$ of $n \times n$ Hermitian matrices is *convex* on $\mathcal{H}$ if, for $A, B \in \mathcal{H}$,

$$\varphi(\alpha A + \overline{\alpha} B) \leq \alpha \varphi(A) + \overline{\alpha} \varphi(B).$$

For any $n \times n$ Hermitian matrix M, let $\lambda_1(M) \geq \cdots \geq \lambda_n(M)$ denote the eigenvalues of M in decreasing order.

F.1. Theorem (Loewner, 1934). *If $A \leq B$, then $\lambda_i(A) \leq \lambda_i(B)$; if $A < B$, then $\lambda_i(A) < \lambda_i(B)$, $i = 1, \ldots, n$.*

As noted by Beckenbach and Bellman (1961, p. 72), this is an immediate consequence of the Fischer minmax theorem (see 20.A.1).

Remark. As a consequence of F.1, if $A \leq B$, then

$$(\lambda_1(A), \ldots, \lambda_n(A)) \prec_w (\lambda_1(B), \ldots, \lambda_n(B)).$$

Theorem F.1 is a basic result because it can be used to show that various increasing functions of eigenvalues are also increasing.

Determinant Examples

F.2. Theorem (Oppenheim, 1954). On the set of positive semidefinite $n \times n$ Hermitian matrices, the function

$$\phi(A) = \left[\prod_{i=1}^{k} \lambda_{n-i+1}(A)\right]^{\frac{1}{k}}$$

is concave and strictly increasing, $k = 1, \ldots, n$. Thus if A and B are positive semidefinite, then

$$\left[\prod_{1}^{k} \lambda_{n-i+1}(A+B)\right]^{\frac{1}{k}} \geq \left[\prod_{1}^{k} \lambda_{n-i+1}(A)\right]^{\frac{1}{k}} + \left[\prod_{1}^{k} \lambda_{n-i+1}(B)\right]^{\frac{1}{k}}. \quad (1)$$

Proof. According to 20.A.5,

$$\min \frac{\operatorname{tr} AM}{k} = \left[\prod_{1}^{k} \lambda_{n-i+1}(A)\right]^{1/k},$$

where the minimum is over all matrices $M = X^*X$, X is $k \times n$, and $\det XX^* = 1$. Because

$$\min \frac{\operatorname{tr}(\alpha A + \overline{\alpha} B)M}{k} \geq \alpha \min \frac{\operatorname{tr} AM}{k} + \overline{\alpha} \min \frac{\operatorname{tr} BM}{k}, \quad 0 \leq \alpha \leq 1,$$

the concavity of ϕ is immediate. That ϕ is strictly increasing follows from F.1. Inequality (1) follows from the concavity with $\alpha = \frac{1}{2}$. ||

F.2.a. On the set of $n \times n$ positive semidefinite Hermitian matrices, the function

$$\phi(A) = (\det A)^{1/n}$$

is concave and increasing. Consequently, if A and B are positive semidefinite,

$$[\det(A+B)]^{1/n} \geq (\det A)^{1/n} + (\det B)^{1/n}. \quad (2)$$

Proof. In F.2, take $k = n$. ||

As an alternative proof when A and B are positive definite, use 19.E.1 to write $A = WW^*$, $B = WD_\beta W^*$, where D_β is a diagonal matrix with the eigenvalues β_i of BA^{-1} as diagonal elements. Then (2) reduces to

$$\left[\prod_1^n (1+\beta_i)\right]^{1/n} \geq 1 + \left(\prod_1^n \beta_i\right)^{1/n}.$$

This inequality follows from 3.F.2. It is also possible to prove F.2.a by differentiating $g(\alpha) = (\det Q)^{1/n}$, $Q = \alpha A + \overline{\alpha} B$. Here,

$$\frac{d^2 g(\alpha)}{d\alpha^2} = -\frac{(\det Q)^{1/n}}{n}\left[\operatorname{tr} W^2 - \frac{(\operatorname{tr} W)^2}{n}\right] \leq 0,$$

where $W = Q^{-1/2}(A-B)Q^{-1/2}$. The proof is completed by a continuity argument when A and B are positive semidefinite. ||

F.2.b. (Fan, 1950). On the set of positive definite Hermitian matrices, the functions

$$\phi_k(A) = \log\left[\prod_{i=1}^k \lambda_{n-i+1}(A)\right], \qquad k = 1, \ldots, n,$$

are concave and strictly increasing. Consequently, if A and B are positive definite and $1 \leq k \leq n$, $0 \leq \alpha \leq 1$, $\overline{\alpha} = 1 - \alpha$,

$$\prod_{i=1}^k \lambda_{n-i+1}(\alpha A + \overline{\alpha} B) \leq \left[\prod_{i=1}^k \lambda_{n-i+1}(A)\right]^{\alpha} \left[\prod_{i=1}^k \lambda_{n-i+1}(B)\right]^{\overline{\alpha}}. \quad (3)$$

Proof. If $\psi(x) = \log x$, $x > 0$, and $f(A) = [\prod_{i=1}^k \lambda_{n-i+1}(A)]^{1/k}$, then because f is concave and ψ is concave and increasing, the composition $\psi \circ f = (1/k)\phi$ is concave. The monotonicity of ϕ follows from F.1. ||

F.2.c. (Fan, 1950). On the set of positive definite Hermitian matrices, the function

$$\phi(A) = \log \det A$$

is concave and strictly increasing. Consequently, if A and B are positive definite Hermitian,

$$\det(\alpha A + \overline{\alpha} B) \geq (\det A)^{\alpha} (\det B)^{\overline{\alpha}}, \qquad 0 \leq \alpha \leq 1. \quad (4)$$

Proof. This is the special case $k = n$ of F.2.b. ‖

Various other proofs of F.2.c can be given [for example, see Beckenbach and Bellman (1961, p. 63)]. See Mirsky (1955b) for a proof by induction.

Partitioned Matrices

Let
$$A = \begin{bmatrix} A_{11} & A_{12} \\ A_{21} & A_{22} \end{bmatrix}$$
be an $n \times n$ nonsingular matrix and let
$$A^{-1} = \begin{bmatrix} A^{11} & A^{12} \\ A^{21} & A^{22} \end{bmatrix},$$
where A_{11} and A^{11} are $k \times k$ submatrices. If A_{11} is nonsingular, then it is easy to verify that
$$A^{22} = (A_{22} - A_{21} A_{11}^{-1} A_{12})^{-1}.$$
Because
$$\begin{bmatrix} A_{11} & A_{12} \\ A_{21} & A_{22} \end{bmatrix} \begin{bmatrix} I & -A_{11}^{-1} A_{12} \\ 0 & I \end{bmatrix} = \begin{bmatrix} A_{11} & 0 \\ A_{21} & A_{22} - A_{21} A_{11}^{-1} A_{12} \end{bmatrix},$$
it follows that
$$\det A = \det A_{11} (\det A^{22})^{-1}. \tag{5}$$
Similarly, if A^{22} is nonsingular, $A^{11} = (A_{11} - A_{12} A_{22}^{-1} A_{21})^{-1}$ and
$$\det A = (\det A_{22})(\det A^{11})^{-1}. \tag{6}$$

F.2.d. (Fan, 1955b). On the set of positive definite Hermitian matrices, the functions
$$\phi_1(A) = (\det A^{11})^{-1/k}, \qquad \phi_2(A) = (\det A^{22})^{-1/(n-k)}$$
are decreasing and concave. Consequently, if A and B are positive definite Hermitian,
$$\left(\frac{\det(A+B)}{\det(A_{11} + B_{11})} \right)^{1/(n-k)} \geq \left(\frac{\det A}{\det A_{11}} \right)^{1/(n-k)} + \left(\frac{\det B}{\det B_{11}} \right)^{1/(n-k)}. \tag{7}$$

Proof. Because $(A^{11})^{-1}$ is matrix-concave (E.7.g) and because the function $(\det M)^m$ is concave and increasing on the $m \times m$ positive definite Hermitian matrices, it follows that the composition ϕ_1 of these functions is concave. The proof for ϕ_2 is analogous.

To obtain (7), use the concavity of ϕ_2 together with (5). ||

F.2.e. (Bergström, 1952). If A and B are positive definite Hermitian matrices and A_i, B_i are obtained by deleting the ith row and column from A and B, then

$$\frac{\det(A+B)}{\det(A_i+B_i)} \geq \frac{\det A}{\det A_i} + \frac{\det B}{\det B_i}. \tag{8}$$

This inequality is essentially (7) with $k = n-1$.

F.3. (Fan, 1949). On the set of $n \times n$ Hermitian matrices, the functions

$$\phi_k(A) = \sum_1^k \lambda_i(A), \qquad k = 1, \ldots, n,$$

are increasing and convex; the functions

$$\widetilde{\phi}_k(A) = \sum_{n-k+1}^n \lambda_i(A), \qquad k = 1, \ldots, n,$$

are increasing and concave.

Proof. These results are immediate from the representations (20.A.2):

$$\phi_k(A) = \max \operatorname{tr} XAX^*, \qquad \widetilde{\phi}_k(A) = \min \operatorname{tr} XAX^*,$$

where the extrema are over $k \times n$ matrices X such that $XX^* = I_k$. ||

Notice that it is sufficient to prove F.3 for $k = 1$ because the result can then be applied to the kth compound of A.

F.4. (Muir, 1974/1975). Let X be a $k \times n$ complex matrix of rank k. On the set of $n \times n$ positive definite Hermitian matrices, the function

$$\phi(A) = \log \det X A^{-1} X^*$$

is decreasing and convex.

Proof. Write ϕ in the form

$$\phi(A) = -n \log[\det(XA^{-1}X^*)^{-1}]^{1/n}.$$

By E.7.h, $(XA^{-1}X^*)^{-1}$ is concave in A and by F.2.a, $(\det B)^{1/n}$ is an increasing concave function of B. Because $-\log$ is strictly convex and decreasing, it follows that ϕ is strictly convex. ‖

This proof was suggested to us by Friedrich Pukelsheim.

F.4.a. On the set of positive definite Hermitian matrices, the function

$$\phi(A) = \log \det A^{11} = \log \frac{\det A_{22}}{\det A}$$

is decreasing and strictly convex.

Proof. This is the special case $X = (I, 0)$ in F.4. The two forms of ϕ follow from (6). ‖

The special case that A^{11} is 1×1 is due to Bergström (1952).

F.4.b. (Muir, 1974/1975). Let S_k be the kth elementary symmetric function. On the set of positive definite Hermitian matrices, the function

$$\phi(A) = \log S_k(\lambda_1(A^{-1}), \dots, \lambda_n(A^{-1}))$$

is strictly convex.

Proof. For a complex matrix Z, the kth elementary symmetric function $S_k(\lambda_1, (Z), \dots, \lambda_n(Z)) = \operatorname{tr} Z^{(k)}$, where $Z^{(k)}$ is the kth compound of Z (see 19.F.1 and 19.F.2.d). It is thus necessary to prove that if $0 < \alpha < 1$, and $A \ne B$ are positive definite Hermitian matrices, then

$$\operatorname{tr}[(\alpha A + \overline{\alpha} B)^{(k)}]^{-1} > [\operatorname{tr}(A^{(k)})^{-1}]^\alpha [\operatorname{tr}(B^{(k)})^{-1}]^{\overline{\alpha}}.$$

From 19.E.1, there exists a nonsingular $n \times n$ matrix M such that

$$A = M D_\theta M^* \text{ and } B = M M^*,$$

where $D_\theta = \operatorname{diag}(\theta_1, \theta_2, \dots, \theta_n)$ and $\theta_1 \ge \dots \ge \theta_n \ge 0$ are the eigenvalues of AB^{-1}. From this it follows, using Theorem 19.F.2, that

$$\begin{aligned}\operatorname{tr}[(\alpha A + \overline{\alpha} B)^{(k)}]^{-1} &= \operatorname{tr}[(\alpha M D_\theta M^* + \overline{\alpha} M M^*)^{(k)}]^{-1} \\ &= \operatorname{tr}[(M(\alpha D_\theta + \overline{\alpha} I) M^*)^{(k)}]^{-1} \\ &= \operatorname{tr}[M^{(k)} (\alpha D_\theta + \overline{\alpha} I)^{(k)} M^{*(k)}]^{-1} \\ &= \operatorname{tr}[M^{(k)}]^{-1} [(\alpha D_\theta + \overline{\alpha} I)^{(k)}]^{-1} [M^{*(k)}]^{-1} \\ &= \operatorname{tr}[M^{(k)} M^{*(k)}]^{-1} [D(\psi)]^{(k)},\end{aligned}$$

where $\psi_i = (\alpha\theta_i + \overline{\alpha})^{-1}$. The desired result then follows since the function $1/(\alpha x + \overline{\alpha})$ is strictly log convex. ||

Convex Trace Functions

Motivated by problems in quantum physics, Lieb (1973) obtained a number of convexity results for the trace. See also Bhatia (1997, p. 271) for proofs.

F.5.a. Suppose A, $B \geq 0$ are $m \times m$ and $n \times n$ Hermitian matrices, respectively, and X is a complex matrix. If

$$\phi_1(A, B, X) = (\operatorname{tr} A^r X B^s X^*)^q, \quad 0 \leq r, s, \ r + s \leq 1,$$

$$\phi_2(A, X) = \operatorname{tr} A^r X A^s X^*, \quad 0 \leq r, s, \ r + s \leq 1,$$

then

(i) $\phi_1(A, B, X)$ is concave in (A, B) for $0 < q \leq 1/(r+1)$ and convex for $q < 0$,

(ii) $\phi_1(A, B, X)$ is convex in X for $q \geq 1/2$,

(iii) $\phi_2(A, X)$ is concave in A and convex in X.

F.5.b. With $A > 0$, $B > 0$, if

$$\phi_3(A, B, X) = (\operatorname{tr} A^{-r} X B^{-s} X^*)^q, \quad 0 \leq r, s, \ r + s \leq 1,$$

$$\phi_4(A, X) = \operatorname{tr} A^{-r} X A^{-s} X^*, \quad 0 \leq r, s, \ r + s \leq 1,$$

then

(i) $\phi_3(A, B, X)$ is convex in (A, B, X) for $q \geq 1/(2-r-s)$,

(ii) $\phi_4(A, X)$ is convex in (A, X).

Two special cases are that $\phi(A) = \operatorname{tr} A^{-r}$ is convex for $r > 0$, and $\phi(A) = (\operatorname{tr} A^{-r})^{-s}$ is concave for $s \leq 1$.

F.5.c. If $A \geq 0$, then

$$\phi_1(A, X) = \operatorname{tr} \int_0^\infty d\mu \, (A + \mu I) X (A + \mu I) X^*$$

is convex in (A, X).

If $A > 0$, then

$$\phi_2(A, X) = \text{tr} \int_0^\infty d\mu \, (A + \mu I)^{-1} X (A + \mu I)^{-1} X^*$$

is convex in (A, X).

F.5.d. If $A \geq 0$, then

$$\phi(A, B, X) = \left[\text{tr} \int_0^\infty d\mu \, (A + \mu I)^{-1} X (B + \mu I)^{-1} X^* \right]^q$$

is convex in (A, B, X) for $q \geq 1$; convex in X for $q \geq 1/2$; convex in (A, B) for $q > 0$; concave in (A, B) for $-1 \leq q < 0$, $X \neq 0$.

Ordering Arbitrary Square Matrices

The partial ordering of Loewner that $A \leq B$ when $B - A$ is positive semidefinite is defined for Hermitian matrices. It is of some interest to extend the ordering so as to order arbitrary complex square matrices. One way to do this is to define $A \leq B$ when $x(B - A)x^* \geq 0$ for all x. It is not difficult to show that this achieves very little because $x(B - A)x^*$ is real for all x only when $B - A$ is Hermitian.

An alternative extension of the Loewner ordering has been studied by Lax (1958). Lax's ordering, written here as $\leq^{\text{r}}$, is as follows:

$A \leq^{\text{r}} B$ means $B - A$ has nonnegative eigenvalues;

$A <^{\text{r}} B$ means $B - A$ has positive eigenvalues.

F.6. Theorem (Lax, 1958). If $aA + bB$ has real eigenvalues for all a, $b \in \mathscr{R}$ and if $A \leq^{\text{r}} B$, then $\lambda_i(A) \leq \lambda_i(B)$, $i = 1, \ldots, n$. This theorem is a generalization of F.1.

F.7. Theorem (Lax, 1958). If $aA + bB$ has real eigenvalues for all $a, b \in \mathscr{R}$, then for all α, $0 \leq \alpha \leq 1$,

$$\lambda_1(\alpha A + \overline{\alpha} B) \leq \alpha \lambda_1(A) + \overline{\alpha} \lambda_1(B),$$
$$\lambda_n(\alpha A + \overline{\alpha} B) \geq \alpha \lambda_n(A) + \overline{\alpha} \lambda_n(B).$$

Theorems F.6 and F.7 are proved by Lax using differential equations. Alternative matrix-theoretic proofs are given by Weinberger (1958).

F.8. Theorem. If $aA+bB$ has real eigenvalues for all $a, b \in \mathscr{R}$, then for all α, $0 \leq \alpha \leq 1$, and $k = 1, \ldots, n$,

$$\sum_1^k \lambda_i(\alpha A + \overline{\alpha} B) \leq \alpha \sum_1^k \lambda_i(A) + \overline{\alpha} \sum_1^k \lambda_i(B),$$

$$\sum_1^k \lambda_{n-i+1}(\alpha A + \overline{\alpha} B) \geq \alpha \sum_1^k \lambda_{n-i+1}(A) + \overline{\alpha} \sum_1^k \lambda_{n-i+1}(B).$$

These generalizations of F.3 were proved by Davis (1963) making use of F.7. A proof similar to that of Davis can be accomplished by using the kth additive compound (see 19.F.4 and 19.F.5) in F.6.

17
Stochastic Ordering

The notion of stochastic ordering for random variables is a familiar and useful concept. A basic reference is Lehmann (1955). More recent work, with many results in stochastic ordering and further references, is in Stoyan (1977, 1983). However, the most comprehensive discussion of stochastic and related orders is given by Shaked and Shanthikumar (2007), to which frequent reference is made in this chapter. Other useful references are Szekli (1995) and Müller and Stoyan (2002).

Section A of this chapter reviews key properties and concepts associated with some basic stochastic orders. Stochastic orders derived from convex cones of functions are discussed in Section B.

The second part of chapter, Sections C and D, is concerned with the Lorenz order and certain related variability orders. The concept of majorization is perhaps most easily motivated by reference to the familiar income distribution curve of Lorenz (1905). The natural extension of this concept to deal with random variables and eventually multivariate random variables is the central theme of the presentation. In many cases, parallel results are available for variability orders related to, but distinct from, the Lorenz order. For details, reference to Shaked and Shanthikumar (2007) will be rewarding. The Lorenz curve and Lorenz order scenario has the advantage that simple motivation and insights are often available in terms of income distributions.

A Some Basic Stochastic Orders

The usual stochastic order, the hazard rate order, and the likelihood ratio order are perhaps the best-known orders of distribution functions. The most basic of these orders, the "usual stochastic order," was first known simply as "stochastic order" and has never been given a distinguishing name.

A.1. Definition. A random variable X is said to be *stochastically less than* (or equal to) Y, written $X \leq^{\text{st}} Y$, if the upper tail probabilities satisfy

$$P\{X > t\} \leq P\{Y > t\}, \qquad -\infty < t < \infty.$$

In the economics literature, this ordering is called *first-order stochastic dominance*. See B.19.

To see how this ordering can be extended to random vectors, some equivalent conditions are useful.

A.2. Proposition. The following conditions are equivalent:

$$X \leq^{\text{st}} Y; \tag{1}$$

$$E\phi(X) \leq E\phi(Y) \quad \text{for all increasing functions such that the expectations exist;} \tag{2}$$

$$\phi(X) \leq^{\text{st}} \phi(Y) \quad \text{for all increasing functions } \phi; \tag{3}$$

$$P\{X \in A\} \leq P\{Y \in A\} \quad \text{for all sets } A \text{ with increasing indicator functions.} \tag{4}$$

Proof. Suppose that (1) holds. If ϕ is an increasing function and $\phi^{-1}(t) = \inf\{z : \phi(z) > t\}$, then

$$P\{\phi(X) > t\} = P\{X > \phi^{-1}(t)\} \leq P\{Y > \phi^{-1}(t)\} = P\{\phi(Y) > t\},$$

and this proves (3). To see that (3) implies (2), use (iii) of 16.A.2 with $\mu(t, \infty) = P\{Y > t\} - P\{X > t\}$. If ϕ is the indicator function of the set A, then (2) reduces to (4). Finally, (4) clearly implies (1). ∥

Notice that the equivalence of (1) and (2) is also given by (iii) of 16.A.2.

Some possible multivariate conditions suggested by A.1 that the upper right orthant probabilities satisfy are

$$P\{X_1 > t_1, \ldots, X_n > t_n\} \leq P\{Y_1 > t_1, \ldots, Y_n > t_n\}$$
$$\text{for all } t = (t_1, \ldots, t_n) \in \mathscr{R}^n, \quad (1')$$

$$P\{X_1 \leq t_1, \ldots, X_n \leq t_n\} \geq P\{Y_1 \leq t_1, \ldots, Y_n \leq t_n\}$$
$$\text{for all } t = (t_1, \ldots, t_n) \in \mathscr{R}^n, \quad (1'')$$

$$E\phi(X_1, \ldots, X_n) \leq E\phi(Y_1, \ldots, Y_n) \text{ for all increasing functions}$$
$$\phi: \mathscr{R}^n \to \mathscr{R} \text{ such that the expectations exist,} \quad (2')$$

$$\phi(X_1, \ldots, X_n) \leq^{\text{st}} \phi(Y_1, \ldots, Y_n) \text{ for all increasing functions}$$
$$\phi: \mathscr{R}^n \to \mathscr{R}, \quad (3')$$

$$P\{X \in A\} \leq P\{Y \in A\} \text{ for all measurable sets } A \subset \mathscr{R}^n \text{ with}$$
$$\text{increasing indicator functions.} \quad (4')$$

In conditions (2′) and (3′), "ϕ is increasing" ordinarily means that ϕ is increasing in each argument separately, the other arguments being fixed. These functions are just the order-preserving functions for the ordering $x \leq y$, which means $x_i \leq y_i$, $i = 1, \ldots, n$. As discussed in Section B, other partial orderings or preorderings (see Section 1.B) can be used here. In fact, if the ordering is majorization, then "ϕ is increasing" means ϕ is Schur-convex. Then, (2′) and (3′) are just the conditions E_1 and P_1 of Section 11.A.

With componentwise ordering $\leq$, it can be shown that

$$(4') \iff (3') \iff (2') \begin{array}{c} \nearrow (1') \\ \searrow (1'') \end{array}.$$

But for $n > 1$ no further implications can be added to this diagram.

A.3. Definition. If (2′), or equivalently, if (3′) or (4′) holds, then the random vector X is said to be *stochastically less than* (or equal to) Y, written $X \leq^{\text{st}} Y$.

A.4. Examples. If X has the bivariate distribution $P\{X = (0,0)\} = P\{X = (0,1)\} = P\{X = (1,0)\} = P\{X = (1,1)\} = 1/4$ and also if $P\{Y = (0,0)\} = P\{Y = (1,1)\} = 1/2$, then (1′) is satisfied, but (1″)

and (2′) fail. If X has the same distribution but $P\{Y = (1,0)\} = P\{Y = (0,1)\} = 1/2$, then (1″) is satisfied but (1′) and (2′) fail.

Because (1′) and (1″) are distinct conditions not implying (2′), condition (2′) or (3′) is probably the most interesting multivariate extension of stochastic ordering.

The following result is essentially due to Veinott (1965); some simplifications of the hypotheses are due to Kamae, Krengel, and O'Brien (1977), who also state a much more general version involving general preorders.

A.5. Proposition (Veinott, 1965; Kamae, Krengel, and O'Brien, 1977). Let $X = (X_1, \ldots, X_n)$ and $Y = (Y_1, \ldots, Y_n)$ be random vectors such that for all $t \in \mathscr{R}$ and all $u \leq v$ $(u, v \in \mathscr{R}^{j-1})$, $j = 2, \ldots, n$,

$$P\{X_1 > t\} \leq P\{Y_1 > t\}$$

and

$$P\{X_j > t|\ X_1 = u_1, \ldots, X_{j-1} = u_{j-1}\}$$

$$\leq P\{Y_j > t|\ Y_1 = v_1, \ldots, Y_{j-1} = v_{j-1}\}.$$

Then $X \leq^{\text{st}} Y$.

A simple proof of this result is given by Franken and Kirstein (1977) and by Arjas and Lehtonen (1978).

Conditions Weaker Than Stochastic Ordering

As already noted, conditions (1′) and (1″) are strictly weaker than the condition of stochastic ordering. The following result shows that at least for some monotone functions, inequalities (1′) and (1″) imply $E\phi(X) \leq E\phi(Y)$.

A.6. The survival functions satisfy

$$\overline{F}(t) \equiv P\{X_1 > t_1, \ldots, X_n > t_n\}$$
$$\leq P\{Y_1 > t_1, \ldots, Y_n > t_n\} \equiv \overline{G}(t) \qquad \text{for all}\quad t \in \mathscr{R}^n \qquad (1')$$

if and only if

$$E\phi(X) \leq E\phi(Y)$$

whenever ϕ is the distribution function of some n-dimensional random vector Z. The lower left orthant probabilities satisfy

$$F(t) \equiv P\{X_1 \leq t_1, \ldots, X_n \leq t_n\}$$
$$\geq P\{Y_1 \leq t_1, \ldots, Y_n \leq t_n\} \equiv G(t) \qquad \text{for all}\quad t \in \mathscr{R}^n \qquad (1'')$$

if and only if
$$E\phi(X) \geq E\phi(Y)$$
whenever ϕ is the survival function of some random vector Z, that is, $\phi(t) = P\{Z_1 > t_1, \ldots, Z_n > t_n\}$ for all $t \in \mathscr{R}^n$.

Proof. Suppose that $E\phi(X) \leq E\phi(Y)$ for all distribution functions ϕ. In particular, for the choice
$$\phi_t(z) = \begin{cases} 1 & \text{if } z_i \geq t_i, \quad i = 1, \ldots, n, \\ 0 & \text{otherwise}, \end{cases}$$
it follows that
$$\overline{F}(t) = E\phi_t(X) \leq E\phi_t(Y) = \overline{G}(t),$$
which is (1').

Next, suppose that (1') holds. If Z takes on only finitely many values, say $t^{(1)}, \ldots, t^{(k)}$ with respective probabilities $p_1, \ldots, p_k$, then
$$E\phi(X) = \sum_i p_i \phi_{t^{(i)}}(X) \leq \sum p_i \phi_{t^{(i)}}(Y) = E\phi(Y),$$
and limiting arguments will complete the proof. Alternatively, $E\phi(X) \leq E\phi(Y)$ can be obtained directly using conditional expectations.

The case of (1'') is proved similarly. ‖

The Hazard Rate Ordering

A.7. Definition. Let X and Y be random variables with corresponding distribution functions F and G; then X is said to be *smaller in the hazard rate ordering* than Y, denoted by $X \leq_{\text{hr}} Y$ (or $F \leq_{\text{hr}} G$), if
$$\overline{F}_t(x) = P\{X > x + t | X > t\} \leq P\{Y > x + t | Y > t\} = \overline{G}_t(x) \quad (5)$$
for every $x \geq 0$ and every t such that $\overline{F}(t) > 0$ and $\overline{G}(t) > 0$.

Note. $\overline{F}_t(x)$ is called the *residual life survival function* of F at time t.

A condition equivalent to (5) is that
$$\overline{F}(z)/\overline{G}(z) \text{ is decreasing in } z \text{ such that } \overline{G}(z) > 0. \quad (6)$$
If F and G are absolutely continuous with corresponding densities f and g, then condition (6) reduces to the condition
$$r_X(t) \geq r_Y(t) \text{ for every } t, \quad (7)$$

where for a univariate random variable Z with density function f_Z, distribution function F_Z, and survival function $\overline{F}_Z = 1 - F_Z$,

$$r_Z(t) = f_Z(t)/[\overline{F}_Z(t)], \qquad -\infty < t < \infty.$$

This function is called the *hazard rate* of Z.

The name "hazard rate ordering" is actually motivated by condition (7), though Definition A.7 is more general.

A.8. If $X \leq_{\text{hr}} Y$, then $X \leq^{\text{st}} Y$.

Proof. This result is immediate from the definitions. ∥

An alternative condition equivalent to (5) and (6) [and (7) in the absolutely continuous case] is obtained by substituting $u = \overline{G}(z)$ in (6). The condition then becomes

$$\frac{\overline{F}(\overline{G}^{-1}(u))}{u} \text{ is increasing in } u, \quad 0 < u < 1. \tag{8}$$

Note. Replacement of $\overline{F}$ and $\overline{G}$ by F and G in (5), (6), and (8) results in what is called the *reverse hazard rate order*.

Multivariate extensions of the hazard rate order have not been extensively studied, and there are a number of possible definitions. A most obvious multivariate version is to use componentwise ordering and allow all quantities in (5) to be vectors:

Condition (i). For random vectors X, Y, and for every $t \in \mathcal{R}^n$ such that $P\{X > t\} > 0$ and $P\{Y > t\} > 0$, the inequality

$$P\{X > x + t \mid X > t\} \leq P\{Y > x + t \mid Y > t\}$$

holds for all $x \in \mathcal{R}_+^n$.

Of course, with componentwise ordering of $\mathcal{R}^n$, $x > t$ and $x \not\leq t$ are the same conditions only when $n = 1$. This fact suggests

Condition (ii). For random vectors X, Y,

$$P\{X \not\leq x + t \mid X \not\leq t\} \leq P\{Y \not\leq x + t \mid Y \not\leq t\}.$$

The following proposition offers multivariate versions of (7).

A.9. Proposition. If Condition (i) is satisfied and the partial derivatives exist, then

$$\frac{\partial \overline{F}(t)}{\partial t_i} \bigg/ \overline{F}(t) \leq \frac{\partial \overline{G}(t)}{\partial t_i} \bigg/ \overline{G}(t), \quad i = 1, \ldots, n. \tag{9}$$

A. Some Basic Stochastic Orders   699

If Condition (ii) is satisfied and the partial derivatives exist, then
$$\frac{\partial F(t)}{\partial t_i}/[1-F(t)] \le \frac{\partial G(t)}{\partial t_i}/[1-G(t)], \quad i=1,\ldots,n. \quad (10)$$

Of course, $\overline{F}$ and $1-F$ are the same only when $n=1$, in which case (9) and (10) both reduce to (7).

Proof. If Condition (i) holds, then
$$1 - P\{X > x+t\} \le 1 - P\{Y > x+t | Y > t\}$$
for all $x \ge 0$ and all $t \in \mathscr{R}^n$; that is,
$$\frac{P\{X > t\} - P\{X > t+x\}}{P\{X > t\}} \le \frac{P\{Y > t\} - P\{Y > t+x\}}{P\{Y > t\}}.$$

Set $x = \Delta e_i$, where e_i is the vector with 1 in the ith place and other components 0. Divide by Δ and let $\Delta \to 0$ to obtain (9).

If Condition (ii) holds, then it similarly follows that
$$\frac{P\{X \not\le t\} - P\{X \not\le t+\Delta e_i\}}{P\{X \not\le t\}} \le \frac{P\{Y \not\le t\} - P\{Y \not\le t+\Delta e_i\}}{P\{Y \not\le t\}},$$
which can be rewritten in the form
$$\frac{1-P\{X \le t\} - 1 + P\{X \le t+\Delta e_i\}}{1 - P\{X \le t\}} \le \frac{P\{Y \le t+\Delta e_i\} - P\{Y \le t\}}{1 - P\{Y \le t\}}.$$
From this, (10) follows by taking limits. ||

The quantity $-\frac{\partial \overline{F}(t)}{\partial t_i}/\overline{F}(t)$ can be written as $r_i(t) = \partial R(t)/\partial t_i$, where $R = -\log \overline{F}$. The quantity $r = (r_1, \ldots, r_n) = \nabla R$ is known as the *hazard gradient* of F. Condition (9) is the condition that the hazard gradient of F dominates that of G (in the sense of componentwise ordering). Hazard gradients are discussed by Marshall (1975).

A.10. Example. If a multivariate survival function $\overline{F}$ can be parameterized to take the form $\overline{F}(x|a) = \exp\{-aR(x)\}$, then the hazard gradient is increasing in a.

The Likelihood Ratio Ordering

A.11. Definition. Let X and Y be random variables with distribution functions F and G. X is said to be *smaller in the likelihood ratio ordering* than Y, written $X \le_{\text{lr}} Y$ or $F \le_{\text{lr}} G$, if, for every u,
$$P\{X > u \mid a < X \le b\} \le P\{Y > u \mid a < Y \le b\} \quad (11)$$
whenever $a < b$ and the conditional probabilities are defined.

The explanation for the name of this ordering comes from a possible reinterpretation in the absolutely continuous case, i.e., when densities f and g exist. In that case, f and g are likelihoods and (11) is equivalent to

$$\frac{f(u)}{g(u)} \text{ is decreasing in } u. \tag{12}$$

This is a statement involving likelihood ratios.

A.12. Proposition (Lehmann and Rojo, 1992). $F \leq_{lr} G$ if and only if $\overline{F}\,\overline{G}^{-1}(u)$ is convex in u, $0 \leq u \leq 1$.

Proof. In the absolutely continuous case, it is possible to verify that the derivative of $\overline{F}\,\overline{G}^{-1}$ is increasing because of (12). In general, a differencing argument can be used. ||

It is clear from the definitions that $X \leq_{lr} Y$ implies $X \leq_{hr} \leq Y$ and also that X is less than Y in the reverse hazard rate ordering.

Because of the monotonicity of the likelihood ratio noted in (12), it becomes clear that if $F \leq_{lr} G$, the corresponding densities cross exactly once (unless $F = G$) and the sign of $f - g$ changes from $+$ to $-$ at the crossing point.

B Stochastic Orders from Convex Cones

Starting with a convex cone of real-valued functions defined on a set $\mathscr{A} \subset \mathscr{R}^n$, the generation of a preorder $\leq_\mathscr{C}$ of $\mathscr{A}$ is discussed in Section 14.D. In particular, for $x, y \in \mathscr{A}$, write $x \leq_\mathscr{C} y$ to mean that

$$\phi(x) \leq \phi(y) \tag{1}$$

for all $\phi \in \mathscr{C}$. As in Example 14.E.5, it can happen that $x \leq_\mathscr{C} y$ implies that (1) holds for some functions not in $\mathscr{C}$. The set $\mathscr{C}^*$ of all functions such that $x \leq_\mathscr{C} y$ implies (1) is called the *completion* of $\mathscr{C}$. Clearly, $\mathscr{C}^*$ is a convex cone.

Example. Let $\leq^p$ be a preorder of $\mathscr{A}$ contained in $\mathscr{R}^n$, and let $\mathscr{C}$ consist of all real-valued functions defined on $\mathscr{A}$ that preserve the ordering $\leq^p$. Then $\mathscr{C}$ is a complete convex cone, and $\leq_\mathscr{C}$ is the order $\leq^p$.

B.1. Definition. Let $\mathscr{C}$ be a convex cone of real-valued measurable functions ϕ defined on a measurable subset $\mathscr{A}$ of $\mathscr{R}^n$. Write $X \leq^{st}_\mathscr{C} Y$ to mean that

B. Stochastic Orders from Convex Cones   701

$$E\phi(X) \leq E\phi(Y) \qquad (2)$$

for all $\phi \in \mathscr{C}$ such that the expectations exist. When $X \leq_{\mathscr{C}}^{\text{st}} Y$, then X is said to be *stochastically less than* Y (with respect to $\mathscr{C}$).

B.2. Definition. The *stochastic completion* of $\mathscr{C}$ is the convex cone $\mathscr{C}^+$ of all measurable functions $\phi : \mathscr{A} \to \mathscr{R}$ for which $X \leq_{\mathscr{C}}^{\text{st}} Y$ implies (2) (whenever the expectations exist).

B.3. Proposition. For all convex cones of real-valued measurable functions defined on $\mathscr{A}$, the completion $\mathscr{C}^*$ of $\mathscr{C}$ and the stochastic completion $\mathscr{C}^+$ of $\mathscr{C}$ satisfy the relationship

$$\mathscr{C} \subset \mathscr{C}^+ \subset \mathscr{C}^*.$$

Moreover, $\mathscr{C}^+$ is closed in the sense of uniform convergence, $\mathscr{C}^+$ contains the constant functions, and every monotone pointwise limit of functions in $\mathscr{C}$ is in $\mathscr{C}^+$.

B.4. Example. Let $\mathscr{C}$ be the convex cone of (componentwise) increasing functions defined on $\mathscr{R}^n$. This cone is complete and the resulting stochastic order is that of Definition A.3. More generally, let $\leq^p$ be a preordering of $\mathscr{A} \subset \mathscr{R}^n$ and let $\mathscr{C}$ consist of all functions defined on $\mathscr{A}$ that preserve the order $\leq^p$. Then $\mathscr{C}$ is complete.

B.5. Example. Let $\mathscr{A} = \mathscr{R}$ and let $\mathscr{C}$ be the convex cone of functions ϕ having the form $\phi(x) = ax + b$, $x \in \mathscr{R}$, for some $a \geq 0$ and some $b \in \mathscr{R}$. In this case, $X \leq_{\mathscr{C}}^{\text{st}} Y$ if and only if $EX \leq EY$. Clearly, $\mathscr{C}$ is stochastically complete. However, the ordering $x \leq_{\mathscr{C}} y$ of $\mathscr{R}$ generated by $\mathscr{C}$ (in the manner of Definition 14.E.2) is just $x \leq y$ in the usual sense. Consequently, $\mathscr{C}^*$ consists of all increasing functions. In this example, $\mathscr{C}^+$ and $\mathscr{C}^*$ differ markedly.

The following fundamental theorem is essentially due to Strassen (1965), but see also Marshall (1991).

B.6. Theorem. Suppose that $\mathscr{A} \subset \mathscr{R}^n$ is closed and that $\leq_{\mathscr{C}}$ is the preorder of $\mathscr{A}$ generated by the convex cone $\mathscr{C}$ of real-valued functions defined on $\mathscr{A}$. Suppose further that $\{(x, y) : x \leq_{\mathscr{C}} y\}$ is a closed set. Then the conditions

(i) $X \leq_{\mathscr{C}}^{\text{st}} Y$,

(ii) there exists a pair $\tilde{X}, \tilde{Y}$ of random variables such that

 (a) X and $\tilde{X}$ are identically distributed, Y and $\tilde{Y}$ are identically distributed,

 (b) $P\{\tilde{X} \leq_{\mathscr{C}} \tilde{Y}\} = 1$

are equivalent if and only if $\mathscr{C}^+ = \mathscr{C}^*$; i.e., the stochastic completion $\mathscr{C}^+$ of $\mathscr{C}$ is complete.

Proof. Suppose first that $\mathscr{C}^+$ is complete. The fact that (i) and (ii) then hold is given by Strassen (1965) as an application of his Theorem 11. On the other hand, if (i) and (ii) hold, then for all $\phi \in \mathscr{C}^*, P\{\phi(\tilde{X}) \leq \phi(\tilde{Y})\} = 1$, and hence $E\phi(X) = E\phi(\tilde{X}) \leq E\phi(\tilde{Y}) = E\phi(Y)$ for all $\phi \in \mathscr{C}^*$. Thus $\mathscr{C}^+ = \mathscr{C}^*$. ||

Mixtures and Convolutions

B.7. Proposition. Suppose that $X_\theta \leq_{\mathscr{C}}^{\text{st}} Y_\theta$ for all θ in an index set B, and suppose that the respective distributions F_θ and G_θ are measurable in $\theta \in B$. If X and Y have respective distributions F and G, where

$$F(x) = \int F_\theta(x) dH(\theta), \quad G(x) = \int G_\theta(x) dH(\theta),$$

then $X \leq_{\mathscr{C}}^{\text{st}} Y$.

Proof. For any $\phi \in \mathscr{C}$,

$$E\phi(X) = E\{E[\phi(X)|\Theta]\} \leq E\{E[\phi(Y)|\Theta]\} = E\phi(Y),$$

where Θ has the distribution H. ||

B.8. Proposition. Suppose that $\phi \in \mathscr{C}$ implies $\phi_u \in \mathscr{C}$, where

$$\phi_u(x) = \phi(x + u), \quad u, x \in \mathscr{R}^n.$$

If $X \leq_{\mathscr{C}}^{\text{st}} Y$ and $U \leq_{\mathscr{C}}^{\text{st}} V$, where X and U, Y and V are independent, then $X + U \leq_{\mathscr{C}}^{\text{st}} Y + V$. If $\phi \in \mathscr{C}$ implies $\phi_{(a)} \in \mathscr{C}$, where

$$\phi_{(a)}(x) = \phi(ax), \quad x \in \mathscr{R}^n, \ a > 0,$$

then $X \leq_{\mathscr{C}}^{\text{st}} Y$ implies $aX \leq_{\mathscr{C}}^{\text{st}} aY$.

B.9. Proposition. Let $\mathscr{C}_i$ be a convex cone of measurable functions defined on the measurable subset $\mathscr{A}_i$ of $\mathscr{R}^i$, $i = m, n$. Let $\mathscr{C}$ be the convex cone of all functions ϕ on $\mathscr{A}_m \times \mathscr{A}_n$ with the property that for each fixed $y \in \mathscr{A}_n$, $\phi(\cdot, y) \in \mathscr{C}_m$ and for each fixed $x \in \mathscr{A}_m$, $\phi(x, \cdot) \in \mathscr{C}_n$. If $X \leq^{\text{st}}_{\mathscr{C}_m} Y$ and $U \leq^{\text{st}}_{\mathscr{C}_n} V$, where X and U, Y and V are independent, then $(X, U) \leq^{\text{st}}_{\mathscr{C}} (Y, V)$.

B.10. Proposition. Let $\mathscr{S}$ be a set of real-valued measurable functions defined on the measurable set $\mathscr{A} \subset \mathscr{R}^n$, and let $\mathscr{C}$ be the smallest convex cone containing $\mathscr{S}$. Then $X \leq^{\text{st}}_{\mathscr{C}} Y$ if and only if $E\phi(X) \leq E\phi(Y)$ for all $\phi \in \mathscr{S}$.

B.10.a. Proposition. The ordering $X \leq^{\text{st}}_{\mathscr{C}} Y$ holds if and only if $P(X \in A\} \leq P\{Y \in A\}$ for all sets A with the property that

$$x \in A \text{ and } x \leq_{\mathscr{C}} y \quad \text{imply } y \in A. \tag{3a}$$

To show that ordered probabilities of the above kind imply $X \leq^{\text{st}} Y$, it is necessary to approximate increasing functions ϕ using positive linear combinations of indicator functions.

B.10.b. Let $\leq^p$ be a preordering of $\mathscr{R}^n$ such that probability measures on $\mathscr{R}^n$ are determined by their values on sets satisfying

$$x \in \mathscr{A} \text{ and } x \leq^p y \text{ imply } y \in \mathscr{A}. \tag{3b}$$

If $X \leq^{\text{st}} Y$ and $Y \leq^{\text{st}} X$, then X and Y have the same distribution.

Proposition A.2 includes, for the cone of increasing functions, a condition A(3) alternative to (2) for the order $\leq^{\text{st}}$. For a general convex cone $\mathscr{C}$, this alternative takes the form

$$\phi(X) \leq^{\text{st}}_{\mathscr{C}} \phi(Y) \quad \text{for all } \phi \in \mathscr{C}. \tag{4}$$

If X and Y satisfy this condition, the notation $X \leq^p_{\mathscr{C}} Y$ has been used.

Because (4) means that $Eh\phi(X) \leq Eh\phi(Y)$ for all increasing functions $h : \mathscr{R} \to \mathscr{R}$ and all $\phi \in \mathscr{C}$,

$$X \leq^p_{\mathscr{C}} Y \quad \text{implies } X \leq^{\text{st}}_{\mathscr{C}} Y.$$

To compare the orders $\leq^{\text{st}}_{\mathscr{C}}$ and $\leq^p_{\mathscr{C}}$, yet another extension of $\mathscr{C}$ enters the picture.

B.11. Notation. For a convex cone $\mathscr{C}$ of functions $\phi : \mathscr{A} \to \mathscr{R}$, let

$$\widetilde{\mathscr{C}} = \{f : \text{for some } \phi \in \mathscr{C} \text{ and some increasing function}$$

$$\psi : \mathscr{R} \to \mathscr{R}, \ f = \psi \circ \phi\}.$$

B.12. Example. In Section 11.A, two convex cones are considered to obtain stochastic versions of majorization:

$$\mathscr{C}_1 = \{\phi : \phi \text{ is a real-valued measurable Schur-convex function defined on } \mathscr{R}^n\},$$

$$\mathscr{C}_2 = \{\phi : \phi \text{ is a real-valued function, continuous, permutation-symmetric, and convex on } \mathscr{R}^n\}.$$

As noted in Section 11.A, $\leq^{\text{st}}_{\mathscr{C}_1}$ and $\leq^{p}_{\mathscr{C}_1}$ are equivalent, but the equivalence fails for $\mathscr{C}_2$. Of course, $\mathscr{C}_1$ is complete and $\widetilde{\mathscr{C}_1} = \mathscr{C}_1$. But $\mathscr{C}_2$ is not complete. Functions in $\widetilde{\mathscr{C}_2}$ are quasi-convex but need not be convex.

B.13. Proposition. The orders $\leq^{p}_{\mathscr{C}}$ and $\leq^{\text{st}}_{\widetilde{\mathscr{C}}}$ are equivalent. Thus the orderings $\leq^{p}_{\mathscr{C}}$ and $\leq^{\text{st}}_{\mathscr{C}}$ are equivalent if and only if $\widetilde{\mathscr{C}} \subset \mathscr{C}^+$.

Convex Order

The convex order is a prime example of a stochastic order derived from a convex cone.

B.14. Definition. Suppose that $\mathscr{A} \subset \mathscr{R}^n$ is convex and that $\mathscr{C}$ consists of all continuous convex functions defined on $\mathscr{A}$. If $X \leq^{\text{st}}_{\mathscr{C}} Y$, then X is said to be *smaller in the convex order* than Y. In this case, the notation $X \leq_{\text{cx}} Y$ is often used.

This order was studied by Karamata (1932); see Proposition 16.B.4.a. The convex order was encountered by Blackwell (1953) in his studies regarding comparisons of experiments. In more general settings, this order arises in probabilistic potential theory and it provides the setting for Choquet's theorem [see, e.g., Phelps (1966)]. Particularly in this context, the convex order is sometimes called *balayage order* [see e.g., Meyer (1966, p. 239)]. See also Shaked and Shanthikumar (2007, Chapter 3) or Marshall and Olkin (2007, p. 62).

The case that the random variables X and Y are real-valued is of particular importance.

B.15. Definition. For real-valued random variables X, Y, write $X \leq_{\text{cx}} Y$ if $E\phi(X) \leq E\phi(Y)$ for all convex functions $\phi : \mathscr{R} \to \mathscr{R}$ such that the expectations exist.

Generalizations of Hadamard Inequalities

For definitions and introduction to Hadamard inequalities, see 16.B.

Let ϕ be a convex function defined on the interval $[a,b]$. According to Proposition 16.B.11,

$$\phi\left(\frac{a+b}{2}\right) \leq \frac{1}{b-a}\int_a^b \phi(x)dx \leq \frac{\phi(a)+\phi(b)}{2}. \tag{5}$$

If X has a distribution degenerate at $(a+b)/2$, Y is uniformly distributed on $[a,b]$, and Z takes on the values a,b each with probability $1/2$, then (5) can be restated as

$$X \leq_{\mathrm{cx}} Y \leq_{\mathrm{cx}} Z.$$

The following proposition leads to a variety of generalizations of Hadamard's inequalities (5).

B.16. Proposition. If ϕ is a convex function defined on the convex set $\mathscr{A} \subset \mathscr{R}^n$ and if X, Y are random vectors taking values in $\mathscr{A}$, then

$$g(\alpha) = E\phi(\alpha X + \overline{\alpha}Y), \quad 0 \leq \alpha \leq 1, \tag{6}$$

is a convex function of α, provided that the expectation exists.

Proof. This is a direct consequence of Proposition 16.B.2. ∥

B.17. Proposition. If $X \geq_{\mathrm{cx}} Y$, then $g(\alpha)$ as defined in (6) is an increasing function of α, $0 \leq \alpha \leq 1$.

Proof. Because $X \geq_{\mathrm{cx}} Y$, $E\phi(\alpha X + \overline{\alpha}z) \geq E\phi(\alpha Y + \overline{\alpha}z)$, $z \in \mathscr{A}$. Consequently, for all $\alpha \in [0,1]$,

$$E\phi(\alpha X + \overline{\alpha}Y) = E\{E[\phi(\alpha X + \overline{\alpha}Y)|Y]\}$$
$$\geq E\{E[\phi(\alpha Y + \overline{\alpha}Y)|Y]\} = E\phi(Y),$$

and similarly

$$E\phi(X) = E\{E[\phi(\alpha X + \overline{\alpha}X)|X]\}$$
$$\geq E\{E[\phi(\alpha Y + \overline{\alpha}X)|X]\} = E\phi(\overline{\alpha}X + \alpha Y).$$

By interchanging α and $\overline{\alpha}$ in the last inequality, it follows that

$$E\phi(X) \geq E\phi(\alpha X + \overline{\alpha}Y) \geq E\phi(Y). \tag{7}$$

The first inequality of (7) indicates that $X \geq_{\mathrm{cx}} \alpha X + \overline{\alpha}Y$, $0 \leq \alpha \leq 1$. Because (7) is based only on the assumption that $X \geq_{\mathrm{cx}} Y$, (7) remains valid if Y is replaced by $\beta X + \overline{\beta} Y$, $0 \leq \beta \leq \alpha$, and α is replaced by $\gamma = (\alpha - \beta)/(1 - \beta)$. With this replacement, the second inequality of (7) becomes

$$g(\alpha) = E\phi(\alpha X + \overline{\alpha} Y) \geq E\phi(\beta X + \overline{\beta} Y) = g(\beta), \ 0 \leq \beta \leq \alpha \leq 1. \ \ ||$$

Note. If X is uniformly distributed on $[a, b]$ and Y is degenerate at $(a+b)/2$, then B.17 yields 16.B.12.a.

B.17.a. Corollary. If X has a finite expectation

$$EX = (EX_1, \ldots, EX_n)$$

and $P\{Y = EX\} = 1$, then $X \geq_{\mathrm{cx}} Y$ and g as defined in (6) becomes

$$g(\alpha) = E\phi(\alpha X + \overline{\alpha} EX).$$

This function is convex and increasing in α, $0 \leq \alpha \leq 1$.

Proof. It follows directly from Jensen's inequality that $X \geq_{\mathrm{cx}} Y$, so this result is an application of Proposition B.17. $||$

With the assumption that ϕ is differentiable, Corollary B.17.a can be proved by writing the derivative g' of g in terms of the inner product

$$g'(\alpha) = E\langle \nabla \phi(\alpha X + \overline{\alpha} EX), X - EX \rangle$$

$$= E\sum_1^n \phi_i(\alpha X + \overline{\alpha} EX)(X_i - EX_i),$$

where ϕ_i is the partial derivative of ϕ with respect to its ith component. Thus $g'(0) = E\sum_1^n \phi_i(EX)(X_i - EX_i) = 0$. Because g is convex, its derivative is increasing, so that $g'(\alpha) \geq 0$.

From the monotonicity of g in Corollary B.17.a, it follows that $g(0) \leq g(\alpha) \leq g(1)$, $0 \leq \alpha \leq 1$; that is,

$$\phi(EX) \leq g(\alpha) \leq E\phi(X).$$

The fact that $\phi(EX) \leq E\phi(X)$ is Jensen's inequality, but here $g(\alpha)$ is inserted between these extremes.

B.17.b. Corollary. If $X^{(1)}, X^{(2)}, \ldots$ is a sequence of independent, identically distributed random vectors with finite expectation, then

$$\frac{1}{k}\sum_{1}^{k} X^{(i)} \geq_{\text{cx}} \frac{1}{k+1}\sum_{1}^{k+1} X^{(i)}, \quad k = 1, 2, \ldots. \tag{8}$$

Proof. In the left-hand inequality of (7), take $X = \frac{1}{k}\sum_{1}^{k} X^{(i)}$, with $\alpha = n/(n+1)$ and $Y = X^{(n+1)}$. This yields (8). ||

B.17.c. Example (Dragomir, 1992). In B.17.a, take $n = 1$, $\mathscr{A} = [a,b]$; and assume that X is uniformly distributed on $[a,b]$, then 16.B.12.a is obtained.

B.18. Proposition. If in Proposition B.16, X and Y are exchangeable random vectors, then g is symmetric about $1/2$; that is, $g(\alpha) = g(1-\alpha)$, $0 \leq \alpha \leq 1$.

Proof. In (6), exchanging X and Y is equivalent to interchanging α and $\overline{\alpha}$. ||

B.18.a. Example (Dragomir, 1992). In B.18, take $n = 1$, $\mathscr{A} = [a,b]$, and suppose that X and Y are independent with distributions uniform on $[a,b]$; then 16.B.12.b is obtained.

Much more could be said about the convex order. Example 1.D.3 relates it to continuous majorization, and Proposition C.8 relates it to the Lorenz order. Through these relationships, several results in the the following Section C apply to the convex order.

Additional Orderings

B.19. Stochastic dominance in economics. Economists ordinarily use the term "stochastic dominance" in place of "stochastic order". Stochastic dominance underlies decision making under uncertainty; it is a central theme, for example, in comparison of investment policies, risk analyses, and portfolio analyses. For a detailed exposition and extensive lists of references, see Hadar and Russell (1978) and Levy (2006).

For each of the three kinds of stochastic dominance that are introduced here, two alternative definitions are available. Both of the definitions are given here together with proofs of equivalence.

The following classes of utility functions are of interest. Let

$\mathscr{C}_1$ be the class of increasing functions $\phi : \mathscr{R} \to \mathscr{R}$,

$\mathscr{C}_2$ be the class of increasing concave functions $\phi : \mathscr{R} \to \mathscr{R}$,

$\mathscr{C}_3$ be the class of increasing concave functions $\phi : \mathscr{R} \to \mathscr{R}$ that have convex derivatives.

The assumption that a utility function is in $\mathscr{C}_1$ says only that more money has a higher utility than less money.

The additional assumption that a utility function is concave (and so is in $\mathscr{C}_2$) corresponds to the assumption that the decision-maker is *risk-averse*. For example, if the investor has a choice between receiving the quantity μ or receiving a random quantity X such that $EX = \mu$, the risk-averse investor will select the quantity μ. That is, the utility function ϕ satisfies $E\phi(X) \leq \phi(EX)$; according to Jensen's inequality 16.C.1, this holds for all random variables with finite expectations if and only if ϕ is concave.

A decision-maker's *local risk aversion* is often measured by the quantity $r(x) = -\phi''(x)/\phi'(x)$. In order that this be a decreasing function, it is necessary (though not sufficient) that $\phi \in \mathscr{C}_3$.

In the following, F and G are, respectively, the distributions of the random variables X and Y.

B.19.a. Definitions. For $i = 1, 2, 3$, G is said to *ith-order dominate* F (alternatively, Y *ith-order dominates* X) if

$$E\phi(X) = \int \phi(x)\, dF(x) \leq \int \phi(x)\, dG(x) = E\phi(Y) \qquad (9)$$

for all $\phi \in \mathscr{C}_i$ such that the integrals converge.

Note that first-, second- and third-order stochastic dominance are all cone orderings in the sense of Definition B.1.

Although B.19.a offers good conceptual definitions based upon properties of utility functions, the conditions are not easily checked directly. The following definitions remedy this fault, but require proofs of equivalence.

B.19.b. Definitions.
(i) The distribution G is said to *first-order stochastically dominate F* (alternatively, Y *first-order stochastically dominates X*) if

$$F(x) \geq G(x) \text{ for all } x; \tag{10}$$

that is, $X \leq^{\text{st}} Y$.

(ii) The distribution G is said to *second-order stochastically dominate F* (alternatively, Y *second-order stochastically dominates X*) if

$$\int_{-\infty}^{x} G(t)\,dt \leq \int_{-\infty}^{x} F(t)\,dt < \infty \text{ for all } x < \infty. \tag{11}$$

(iii) The distribution G is said to *third-order stochastically dominate F* (alternatively, Y *third-order stochastically dominates X*) if

$$\int_{-\infty}^{x}\int_{-\infty}^{z} G(t)\,dt\,dz \leq \int_{-\infty}^{x}\int_{-\infty}^{z} F(t)\,dt\,dz \text{ for all } x < \infty. \tag{12}$$

It is often convenient to abbreviate first-, second- and third-order stochastic dominance by

$$FSD, \quad SSD, \quad TSD,$$

respectively. Note that

$$FSD \Rightarrow SSD \Rightarrow TSD;$$

this follows from Definition B.19.a because

$$\mathscr{C}_3 \subset \mathscr{C}_2 \subset \mathscr{C}_1,$$

and it also follows directly from Definition B.19.b.

Remarks. Some authors add the requirement that strict inequality holds for some x in (10), (11), and (12), but this does not play a role in what follows.

The condition in (11) and (12) that the integrals be finite avoids some meaningless comparisons. The integrals are always finite if $F(\ell) = G(\ell)$ for some $\ell > -\infty$. It is often assumed that $\ell = 0$, in which case the lower limits of integration in (10) and (11) can be replaced by 0.

Condition (10) is sometimes written in the form $\overline{F}(x) \leq \overline{G}(x)$ for all x, where $\overline{F}(x) = 1 - F(x)$, $\overline{G}(x) = 1 - G(x)$. If $F(\ell) = G(\ell) = 0$

for some $\ell > -\infty$, then (11) can be rewritten in the form

$$\int_\ell^x \overline{F}(t)\,dt \le \int_\ell^x \overline{G}(t)\,dt, \quad x \ge \ell;$$

similarly, (12) can be rewritten in terms of $\overline{F}$ and $\overline{G}$.

B.19.c. Proposition. For first-, second- and third-order stochastic dominance, the conditions of Definitions B.19.a and B.19.b are equivalent.

Proof. For FSD, the proof is given in Proposition A.2. To prove the equivalence for SSD, suppose first that (11) holds. With the aid of Fubini's theorem, it follows that

$$\int_{-\infty}^x F(t)\,dt = \int_{-\infty}^x \int_{-\infty}^t dF(z)\,dt = \int_{-\infty}^x \int_z^x dt\,dF(z) \quad (13)$$

$$= \int_{-\infty}^x (x-z)\,dF(z) = \int_{-\infty}^\infty (x-z)^+\,dF(z).$$

It follows from (13) and (11) that for all constants c and x,

$$\int_{-\infty}^\infty [c - (x-z)^+]\,dF(z) \le \int_{-\infty}^\infty [c - (x-z)^+]\,dG(z).$$

Because concave increasing functions can be approximated by positive linear combinations of functions having the form

$$\phi(x) = c - (x - z)^+, \quad -\infty < x < z \quad (14)$$

(this fact is a variant of Proposition 16.B.4), it follows that (9) holds for all $\phi \in \mathscr{C}_2$.

Conversely, if (9) holds for all $\phi \in \mathscr{C}_2$, then in particular it holds for functions of the form (14); this is equivalent to (11).

It remains to prove the proposition for third-order dominance. Again with the aid of Fubini's theorem, it follows that

$$\int_{-\infty}^x \int_{-\infty}^z F(t)\,dt = \int_{-\infty}^x \int_{-\infty}^z (z-w)^+\,dF(w)\,dz \quad (15)$$

$$= \int_{-\infty}^x \int_w^x (z-w)^+\,dz\,dF(w) = \int_{-\infty}^\infty \frac{1}{2}[(x-w)^+]^2\,dF(w).$$

If (12) holds, it follows from (15) that

$$\int_{-\infty}^\infty \left\{c - \frac{1}{2}[(x-w)^+]^2\right\} dF(w) \ge \int_{-\infty}^\infty \left\{c - \frac{1}{2}[(x-w)^+]^2\right\} dG(w)$$

for all $c, x \in \mathscr{R}$.

B. Stochastic Orders from Convex Cones 711

Let
$$\phi(w|x,c) = c - \frac{1}{2}[(x-w)^+]^2,$$

and note that
$$\phi'(w|x,c) = x - w, \quad w \leq x, \tag{16}$$
$$= 0, \quad w \geq x.$$

Suppose that $u \in \mathscr{C}_3$; that is, u is an increasing concave function with convex derivative u'. Then

$$u' \geq 0, \quad u' \text{ is decreasing and } u'' \text{ is increasing.}$$

In a manner similar to that used in Proposition 16.B.4, it can be verified that u' can be approximated by a positive linear combination of functions of the form (16). Consequently, u can be approximated by a linear combination of functions of the form $\phi(\cdot|x,c)$. Thus (12) implies (9) for all $\phi \in \mathscr{C}_3$.

Conversely, if (9) holds for all $\phi \in \mathscr{C}_3$, it holds in particular for functions of the form $\phi(\cdot|x,c)$; i.e., (12) holds. ∥

Remarks.

1. If Y first-, second-, or third-order stochastically dominates X, then $EX \leq EY$ because the function $\phi(x) = x$ is in $\mathscr{C}_i$, $i = 1,2,3$.

2. If $EX = EY$, then the stochastic completion of $\mathscr{C}_2$ includes all concave functions, increasing or not; and the stochastic completion of $\mathscr{C}_3$ includes all concave functions with convex derivatives, increasing or not. It follows that if $EX = EY$ and Y second-order stochastically dominates X, then $\operatorname{Var} X \geq \operatorname{Var} Y$. To see this, take $\phi(x) = -x^2$ in (9).

B.20. Peakedness. Let $\mathscr{C}$ consist of all centrally symmetric nonnegative quasi-concave functions defined on $\mathscr{R}^n$. If X and Y are random variables with centrally symmetric distributions and if $X \leq_{\mathscr{C}}^{\text{st}} Y$, then X is said to be *less peaked than* Y. This definition, due to Birnbaum (1948) in the univariate case, has been studied by various authors [see Dharmadhikari and Joag-Dev (1988, p. 160) and Bergmann (1991)]; see Section 12.J for an extended discussion of peakedness.

The cone of this example is not complete, and in fact its completion consists of all reflection-symmetric functions ϕ such that $\phi(\alpha x) \leq \phi(x)$ for all x and α in $[0, 1]$. Of course, the cone $\mathscr{C}$ does not even include all constant functions. On the other hand, it is clear that $\mathscr{C} = \widetilde{\mathscr{C}}$, where $\widetilde{\mathscr{C}}$ is defined in B.11. This means that $X \leq_{\mathscr{C}}^{\text{st}} Y$ if and only if $\phi(X) \leq^{\text{st}} \phi(Y)$ for all ϕ in $\mathscr{C}$.

B.21. Concordance. Suppose that $\mathscr{C}$ consists of the L-superadditive functions defined on $\mathscr{R}^2$, i.e., functions ϕ for which

$$\phi(\alpha_1 + \delta_1, \alpha_2 + \delta_2) + \phi(\alpha_1 - \delta_1, \alpha_2 - \delta_2)$$
$$\geq \phi(\alpha_1 + \delta_1, \alpha_2 - \delta_2) + \phi(\alpha_1 - \delta_1, \alpha_2 + \delta_2)$$

whenever $\delta_1, \delta_2 \geq 0$. Then $X \leq_{\mathscr{C}}^{\text{st}} Y$ if and only if X is *less concordant* than Y in the sense of Cambanis, Simons, and Stout (1976) or Tchen (1980). Because of its connection with the notion of *positive quadrant dependence* (Lehmann, 1966), this ordering was introduced and studied by Yanagimoto and Okamoto (1969). See also Section 12.M and Rüschendorf (1981). It is easily shown that in this case, X and Y necessarily have the same marginal distributions.

The convex cone of L-superadditive functions is stochastically complete but not complete; in fact, its completion consists of all real functions defined in $\mathscr{R}^2$.

B.22. Scaled order statistics. For $a_i > 0$, $i = 1, \ldots, n$, the ordered values of $a_1 X_1, \ldots, a_n X_n$ are called *scaled order statistics;* these reduce to the usual order statistics when $a_i = 1$, $i = 1, \ldots, n$. See 12.D.

Scarsini and Shaked (1987) define a preordering $\leq$ of nonnegative random vectors by the condition that the kth order statistic of $a_1 X_1, \ldots, a_n X_n$ be stochastically smaller than the kth order statistic of $a_1 Y_1, \ldots, a_n Y_n$ for all $a_i > 0, i = 1, 2, \ldots, n$. They identify a rather complicated set of functions ϕ for which $E\phi(X) \leq E\phi(Y)$ implies $X \leq Y$ in their ordering. It would be of interest to characterize the convex cone generated by their set of functions.

C The Lorenz Order

Motivation

The original motivation for studying the Lorenz curve was given in terms of income or wealth distributions. It was introduced at a time when there was considerable debate regarding the merits of several competing summary measures of inequality that were currently in use. Indeed, the Lorenz curve was regarded as an excellent alternative to single-number summaries of the inequality in economic populations.

This is a parallel to the fact that, though a mean (or median) gives a useful summary or typical value of a density, the density itself is surely more informative. Nevertheless, the attraction of simple summary inequality measures remained. What was generally conceded was that such measures should "preserve" the Lorenz order based on nested Lorenz curves introduced in this section.

The Lorenz curve introduced in 1.A for comparing income or wealth distributions among finite populations with n individuals in the population admits a straightforward extension to allow comparisons between populations of different sizes, and also admits an extension to allow variability comparison of nonnegative random variables with finite positive expectations. To this end, a more general definition of the Lorenz curve is required that subsumes the original definition provided by Lorenz (and described in detail in 1.A). Along the way extensions of the inequality measures described in 13.F for finite populations are introduced. The Lorenz order is compared with several other "variability" orderings available in the literature. Much of the motivation given is still in terms of inequalities of wealth and income, though it must be recalled that diversity or inequality measurement is of interest in a broad spectrum of fields outside economics.

It is observed in Chapter 15 that a number of candidate multivariate extensions of majorization exist. Likewise, several multivariate extensions of the Lorenz curve have been proposed. One particular extension involving zonoids that might lay claim to being "the" natural extension of the Lorenz curve is described in this section.

The Lorenz Curve

Denote the class of univariate distribution functions with positive finite expectations by $\mathscr{L}$ and denote by $\mathscr{L}_+$ the class of all distributions in $\mathscr{L}$ with $F(0) = 0$, i.e., those corresponding to nonnegative random variables.

C.1. Definition (Gastwirth, 1971). The *Lorenz curve* L of a random variable X with distribution $F \in \mathscr{L}$ is

$$L(u) = \frac{\int_0^u F^{-1}(y)dy}{\int_0^1 F^{-1}(y)dy} = \frac{\int_0^u F^{-1}(y)dy}{EX}, \quad 0 \leq u \leq 1, \qquad (1)$$

where

$$F^{-1}(y) = \sup\{x : F(x) \leq y\}, \quad 0 \leq y < 1,$$
$$= \sup\{x : F(x) < 1\}, \quad y = 1,$$

is the *right continuous inverse distribution function* or *quantile function* corresponding to F. [See Marshall and Olkin (2007, p. 639) for a detailed discussion of alternative definitions of inverse distribution functions.]

It is readily verified that this definition of a Lorenz curve agrees with the definition in 1.A, in which the Lorenz curve corresponding to n ordered numbers $x_{(1)} \leq x_{(2)} \leq \ldots \leq x_{(n)}$ is obtained by linear interpolation of the points

$$\left(\frac{i}{n}, \frac{\sum_1^i x_{(j)}}{\sum_1^n x_{(j)}} \right), \quad i = 1, 2, \ldots, n. \tag{2}$$

The interpretation of the Lorenz curve, "as the bow is bent, inequality increases," continues to be valid with the more general definition (1).

Figure 1 provides illustrations of empirical Lorenz curves based on data provided by Atkinson (1975). It shows the Lorenz curves for income distributions in the United Kingdom (1964), the Netherlands (1962), and West Germany (1964). The figure confirms the observation that Lorenz curves are in some cases nested, but that they can cross (in fact, multiple crossing points can be encountered).

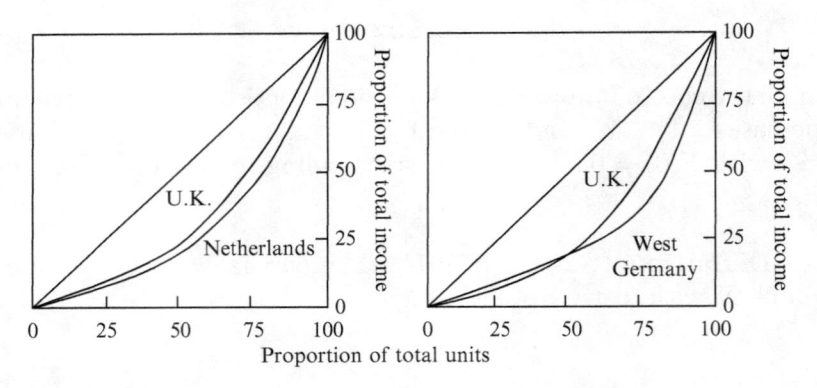

Figure 1. Lorenz curve comparisons.

Because every distribution function can be expressed as a limit in distribution (as $n \to \infty$) of a sequence of discrete distributions with n support points, it is verified by taking limits that the definition presented in (1) is inevitable in the sense that it is the only definition that is consistent with Lorenz's original definition for distributions with n support points.

Several properties of Lorenz curves corresponding to distributions in $\mathscr{L}_+$ are self-evident from (1). Such a Lorenz curve is a nondecreasing convex function that is differentiable almost everywhere in $[0,1]$ and satisfies $L(0) = 0, L(1) = 1$. The Lorenz curve always lies below the line joining $(0,0)$ and $(1,1)$ and coincides with this diagonal line if and only if F is degenerate. Observe also that the Lorenz curve determines the distribution F up to a scale change. If F is an absolutely continuous distribution, then the Lorenz curve is twice differentiable.

C.2. Example: The Pareto distribution. The classical Pareto distribution function with finite mean is defined by

$$F(x) = 1 - (x/\sigma)^{-\xi}, \quad x > \sigma, \quad \xi > 1. \tag{3}$$

The corresponding quantile function is

$$F^{-1}(u) = \sigma(1-u)^{-1/\xi}, \quad 0 < u < 1,$$

and the Lorenz curve is thus given by

$$L(u) = 1 - (1-u)^{(\xi-1)/\xi}, \quad 0 \leq u \leq 1. \tag{4}$$

C.3. Example: The Uniform distribution. For the uniform distribution on the interval $(a, a+b)$, where $a, b > 0$, the distribution function is

$$F(x) = \begin{cases} 0, & x \leq a, \\ (x-a)/b, & a < x \leq a+b, \\ 1, & x > a+b. \end{cases}$$

The quantile function is

$$F^{-1}(u) = a + bu, \quad 0 \leq u \leq 1,$$

and the Lorenz curve is

$$L(u) = \frac{2au + bu^2}{2a + b}, \quad 0 \leq u \leq 1.$$

Lorenz Curves for Nonnegative Random Variables

In many areas, such as engineering, economics, reliability theory, or medical survival analysis, the random variables involved are necessarily nonnegative. Write $X \in \mathscr{L}_+$ if X is nonnegative with positive finite expectation. Note that the notation $\mathscr{L}_+$ is used to denote the class of random variables and the class of corresponding distribution functions. The restriction of random variables under consideration to those which are nonnegative has the advantage that their Lorenz curves, as defined in C.1, are closer in form to those described in the original vision of Lorenz.

If $X \in \mathscr{L}_+$, the Lorenz curve, L_X, is always contained in the area below the diagonal in the unit square. It is a continuous convex function joining $(0,0)$ to $(1,1)$. If the Lorenz curve is twice differentiable in an interval (u_1, u_2), then the corresponding distribution of X has a finite positive density on the interval

$$((EX)L'(u_{1+}), (EX)L'(u_{2-})),$$

and in that interval its density is given by

$$f(x) = [(EX)L''(F(x))]^{-1}. \qquad (5)$$

If a continuous convex function $L(u)$ defined on $[0,1]$ is the Lorenz curve of some random variable in $\mathscr{L}_+$, then

$$L(0) = 0, \quad L(1) = 1, \quad L'(0) \geq 0, \quad L'(1) \geq 1.$$

Much of the early discussion of Lorenz curves was presented with reference to a somewhat different (but equivalent) parametric definition of the Lorenz curve. For any random variable $X \in \mathscr{L}_+$ with distribution function F, define its *first moment distribution function*, $F_{(1)}$, to be

$$F_{(1)}(x) = \frac{\int_0^x y\, dF(y)}{\int_0^\infty y\, dF(y)}. \qquad (6a)$$

The set of points comprising the Lorenz curve of X can be identified as the set of points

$$\{(F(x), F_{(1)}(x)) : 0 \leq x \leq \infty\}, \qquad (6b)$$

completed if necessary by linear interpolation. Make a natural change of variables in (6a) to obtain the expression for the Lorenz curve:

$$L(u) = F_{(1)}(F^{-1}(u)), \quad 0 \leq u \leq 1. \qquad (7)$$

The advantage of the representation (6b) is that it avoids the necessity of computing the quantile function of X.

There are, in fact, relatively few families of distributions for which analytic expressions for the corresponding Lorenz curves are available. The classical Pareto family and the uniform distribution (Examples C.2, C.3) are, of course, such families. Other examples are the exponential distribution and the arcsin distribution.

It is possible to begin with parametric families of Lorenz curves with simple analytic forms, and then identify analytic expressions for the corresponding densities or distribution functions. For example, Villaseñor and Arnold (1989) begin with general quadratic forms for Lorenz curves and identify the corresponding density functions. Because much income distribution data is presented in terms of Lorenz curves, it is desirable to identify parametric families of Lorenz curves that can be used to "fit" such data. For more details, refer to Section D.

The exponential distribution is a favored building block for many reliability and survival models, so it is indeed fortunate that it has an available analytic expression for its Lorenz curve; see, e.g., Marshall and Olkin (2007, p. 293). In the income distribution literature, the Pareto distribution (and its variants) holds a place of honor. There is, and has been for a long time, a challenger for "supremacy" in the income distribution area. The lognormal distribution has frequently been proposed as an alternative to the classical Pareto model.

C.4. Example: The lognormal distribution. A nonnegative random variable X is said to have a *lognormal distribution* with parameters μ and σ if its density is

$$f(x) = \frac{1}{\sigma x \sqrt{\pi}} \exp\left\{-\frac{1}{2}\left(\frac{\log x - \mu}{\sigma}\right)^2\right\}, \quad x > 0. \tag{8}$$

Such a random variable can be represented in the form

$$X = \exp(\mu + \sigma Z),$$

where Z has a standard normal distribution. Consequently, e^μ is a scale parameter for X, and σ is a parameter which determines the shape of the distribution. Detailed discussion of the lognormal distribution is provided by Marshall and Olkin (2007, pp. 431–441). A simple analytic form for the lognormal Lorenz curve is not available, but there is a very useful expression for this Lorenz curve that takes advantage of readily available tables of the standard normal distribution and its corresponding quantiles.

In computation of the Lorenz curve of X, the assumption that $e^\mu = 1$ (i.e., $\mu = 0$) can be made without loss of generality.

It can be verified that if X has the lognormal density (8), then

$$L(u) = \Phi(\Phi^{-1}(u) - \sigma), \quad 0 \le u \le 1, \tag{9}$$

where Φ denotes the standard normal distribution function.

Will an expression such as

$$L(u) = F(F^{-1}(u) - \sigma), \quad 0 \le u \le 1, \qquad (10)$$

for some distribution function F other than Φ yield a family of Lorenz curves? A sufficient condition can be identified.

C.5. Proposition (Arnold, Robertson, Brockett and Shu, 1984). A sufficient condition for (10) to represent a family of Lorenz curves indexed by $\sigma > 0$ is that F has a log concave (also called strongly unimodal) density (18.B).

The Lorenz Order

Lorenz originally proposed an ordering of income distributions in terms of nested Lorenz curves, or in his phraseology, in terms of the degree to which "the bow is bent." By using the more general Definition C.1, the ordering that he proposed can be extended to provide a partial order in the class $\mathscr{L}$ (of univariate distributions with positive finite expectations).

C.6. Definition: Lorenz order. Let $F_X, F_Y \in \mathscr{L}$, with corresponding Lorenz curves L_X and L_Y. Then X is less than Y in the *Lorenz order*, denoted $X \le_L Y$, or equivalently, $F_X \le_L F_Y$ if $L_X(u) \ge L_Y(u)$ for all $u \in [0, 1]$.

C.7. Example. A family of distributions with Lorenz curves of the form (10) is, in the Lorenz order, increasing in σ. In particular, if X has the lognormal density (8) with parameters μ_X and σ_X, and Y has the density (8) with parameter μ_Y and σ_Y, then $\sigma_X \le \sigma_Y$ implies $X \le_L Y$.

The interpretation of the Lorenz partial order defined in C.6 is that if $L_X(u) \ge L_Y(u)$ for all $u \in [0, 1]$, then X exhibits less (or equal) inequality in the Lorenz sense than does Y [or equivalently that the distribution function F_X exhibits less (or equal) inequality than the distribution function F_Y].

The reader is cautioned that the reverse ordering is sometimes called the Lorenz ordering.

The Lorenz order is a natural extension of classical majorization in the following sense. Suppose that $x, y \in \mathscr{R}^n$. Let X denote a random variable corresponding to a random selection of a coordinate of x, i.e., $P\{X = x_i\} = 1/n$, $i = 1, \ldots, n$. Similarly, associate a random variable Y with y. It can be verified that $x \prec y$ if and only if $X \le_L Y$.

As a consequence, it is not surprising that several of the characterizations of majorization included in Chapter 1 extend readily to the Lorenz order setting. The proofs can be obtained using limiting arguments, though in fact Hardy, Littlewood, and Pólya (1929) discuss more general settings also.

The Lorenz order is intimately related to the convex order (Definition B.14), which is defined on a larger class of random variables.

C.8. Theorem. Suppose that $X, Y \in \mathscr{L}$ and $EX = EY$. Then $X \leq_L Y$ if and only if $Eh(X) \leq Eh(Y)$ for every continuous convex function h, that is, if and only if $X \leq_{\text{cx}} Y$.

C.9. Corollary. For $X, Y \in \mathscr{L}$, $X \leq_L Y$ if and only if $Eg(X/EX) \leq Eg(Y/EY)$ for every continuous convex g, such that expectations exist.

C.10. Corollary C.9 can be restated follows: For $X, Y \in \mathscr{L}_+$,

$$X \leq_L Y \text{ if and only if } X/EX \leq_{\text{cx}} Y/EY.$$

C.11. Theorem. If $X, Y \in \mathscr{L}$ and $EX = EY$, then $X \leq_L Y$ if and only if $E(X - c)^+ \leq E(Y - c)^+$ for every $c \in \mathscr{R}$.

The relation between C.8 and C.11 is illuminated by considering 16.B.4, which relates convex functions (in C.8) with "angle" functions (in C.11).

There is an analog to Theorem 2.B.2 that is best understood as a consequence of the fact that when $x = yP$ for some doubly stochastic matrix P (and so $x \prec y$), then the coordinates of x are averages of the coordinates of y. Identify x and y with discrete random variables X and Y with n equally likely possible values given by the coordinates of x and y, respectively; then it follows that $x \prec y$ implies that X and $E(Y|Z)$ have the same distribution, where Z has a discrete uniform distribution. This remains true in more general settings.

C.12. Theorem (Strassen, 1965). Let $X, Y \in \mathscr{L}$ with $EX = EY$. The following are equivalent:

(i) $X \leq_L Y$;

(ii) there exist jointly distributed random variables Y', Z' such that Y and Y' have the same distribution, and X and $E(Y'|Z')$ have the same distribution.

That (ii) implies (i) is a direct consequence of Jensen's inequality and Theorem C.8. The proof of the converse is given by Strassen (1965).

Theorem C.12 makes precise the statement that averaging decreases inequality in the Lorenz ordering sense.

C.13. Example. Suppose that X has a Weibull distribution with $P\{X > x\} = \exp\{-(\lambda x)^\alpha\}, x > 0; \lambda, \alpha > 0$, and Y has a Pareto (IV) distribution with $P\{Y > y\} = (1+(\delta y)^\alpha)^{-\xi}, y > 0$ and $\lambda, \delta > 0$, where $\alpha\xi > 1$. Then $X \leq_L Y$.

To see that $X \leq_L Y$, begin by noting that because the Lorenz order is unaffected by changes of scale, assume with no loss in generality that $\lambda = \delta = 1$, so that $P\{X > x\} = \exp\{-x^\alpha\}$, $x > 0$, and $P\{Y > y\} = (1 + y^\alpha)^{-\xi}$, $y > 0$. Let Z be a random variable that is independent of X, and having a gamma density $f(z) = z^{\xi-1}e^{-z}/\Gamma(\xi), z > 0, \xi > 0$. If $Y' = X/Z^{1/\alpha}$, then Y and Y' have the same distribution with $E(Y'|X) = XEZ^{-1/\alpha}$. By Theorem C.12, $XEZ^{-1/\alpha} \leq_L Y$ and by the scale invariance of the Lorenz order, $X \leq_L Y$.

Other examples involving distributions that are expressible as scale mixtures can be similarly treated.

Inequality Measures

In 13.F a spectrum of candidate summary inequality measures is introduced in the discrete setting. In economic terms, the measures in 13.F are suitable for comparing finite populations with the same number, n, of individuals in the populations being compared. The extended Definition C.1 of the Lorenz curve allows comparison of infinite populations and populations of different sizes.

In a general context, a reasonable measure of inequality is a realvalued quantity $h(X)$ whose value is determined by the distribution of X that satisfies

$$X \leq_L Y \Rightarrow h(X) \leq h(Y).$$

The notation used here might cause confusion. The expression $h(X)$ does not refer to a random variable that is a function of X. It refers to a typically positive quantity that is associated with the random variable X. Usage of this form is familiar, for example, when we denote the standard deviation of X by $\sigma(X)$, implying that $\sigma(X)$ is a positive quantity and not a random variable.

According to Proposition C.8,

$$h(X) = E(g(X/EX)) \tag{11}$$

is a suitable choice for such a measure, where g is any continuous convex function. For example, the choice $g(x) = x \log x$ leads to a measure related to the entropy measures of inequality in 13.F.3.

A fairly common inequality measure for random variables in $\mathscr{L}_+$ that preserves the Lorenz order is the *coefficient of variation* defined by

$$h(X) = \sqrt{E\left[\frac{X - EX}{EX}\right]^2}, \tag{12}$$

which is location- and scale-invariant. It is recognizable as the square root of a function of the form (11).

Observe that measures of the form (11) essentially compare the value of X with a typical value EX. There are, however, several attractive measures of inequality that respect the Lorenz order and are not of this form. These measures are defined in terms of geometric features of the graph of the Lorenz curve, though they often admit alternative interpretations.

The Gini Index

The best-known inequality measure associated with the Lorenz curve is the *Gini index* [proposed by Gini (1912)]. For an extensive bibliography of the Gini index, see Giorgi (1990). The description of this measure (or index) provided in 13.F.4.a remains valid in the more general context. The Gini index is geometrically described as twice the area between the Lorenz curve and the egalitarian line [the line joining $(0,0)$ to $(1,1)$]. By construction, it preserves the Lorenz order. Denote the Gini index of a random variable $X \in \mathscr{L}_+$ by $G(X)$.

The Gini index can be defined without reference to the Lorenz curve. Instead of determining how far X is from a typical value on the average, the variability or inequality can be assessed in terms of how far apart two independent and identically distributed copies X_1 and X_2 of X are on the average. To determine the Gini index of X, evaluate

$$G(X) = E\frac{|X_1 - X_2|}{2EX}. \tag{13a}$$

It is customary to divide by twice the mean rather than the more natural division by the mean in order to have a measure ranging in value between 0 and 1 (for $X \geq 0$).

When the variables X_1 and X_2 are regarded as representing a sample of size 2, (13a) can be rewritten in terms of order statistics. Denote by $X_{i:m}$ the ith order statistic from a sample of size m. The Gini index $G(X)$ can then be expressed as follows:

$$G(X) = \frac{E|X_1 - X_2|}{2EX} = \frac{EX_{2:2} - EX_{1:2}}{EX_{2:2} + EX_{1:2}}$$

$$= 1 - \frac{EX_{1:2}}{EX_{2:2}}. \tag{13b}$$

An alternative measure based on the Lorenz curve is the *Pietra index* $\pi(X)$ introduced by Pietra (1915). It is the maximum vertical deviation between the Lorenz curve and the egalitarian line joining $(0,0)$ to $(1,1)$. By construction, it preserves the Lorenz order. An alternative expression for $\pi(X)$ is given by

$$\pi(X) = \frac{E|X - EX|}{2EX}. \tag{14}$$

Amato (1968) suggested measuring inequality by the length of the Lorenz curve [see also Kakwani (1980)]. Such a measure clearly preserves the Lorenz order, but is somewhat troublesome with regard to its evaluation in specific cases. Kakwani actually suggested that, instead of the length, a standardized version of the length (ranging in value between 0 and 1) be used. For simplicity, standardization is foregone and the length of the Lorenz curve, denoted by $K(X)$, is used as an inequality measure. The three inequality orderings, in terms of $G(X), \pi(X)$, and $K(X)$, all preserve the Lorenz order, but they provide intrinsically different orderings of random variables in $\mathscr{L}$.

It is not difficult to construct examples of pairs of random variables in $\mathscr{L}$ such that any two of the three orders disagree, i.e., such that

(i) $G(X) < G(Y)$ and $\pi(X) > \pi(Y)$,

(ii) $G(X) < G(Y)$ and $K(X) > K(Y)$,

(iii) $\pi(X) < \pi(Y)$ and $K(X) > K(Y)$.

Reference to Fig. 1 in Chapter 1 provides a visual confirmation of the fact that the three indices $G(X)$ (area between the Lorenz curve and the egalitarian line), $\pi(X)$ (maximal vertical deviation between the Lorenz curve and the egalitarian line), and $K(X)$ (length of the Lorenz curve) preserve the Lorenz order.

Rather trivial one-point summaries of the Lorenz curve can be also used as inequality measures. For example, the "top 100α percent" $L_X(\alpha)$ defined in 13.F.4.d could be used. Generalizing the minimal majority measure in 13.F.4.c, inequality can be measured by evaluating $L_X^{-1}(\beta)$ for some fixed value of β (not necessarily $1/2$).

One clear advantage of the use of summary measures of inequality rather than the full Lorenz ordering is that a summary measure provides a total ordering on $\mathscr{L}$, whereas the Lorenz order is only a partial order because Lorenz curves can cross.

Orderings Related to the Lorenz Order

Determining whether $X \leq_L Y$ in a particular case can be a non-trivial exercise, because analytic expressions are frequently not available for the Lorenz curves of the random variables. However, there are orderings stronger than the Lorenz order that are on occasion easier to check. For simplicity, focus on orderings on $\mathscr{L}_+$ (the class of nonnegative integrable random variables).

C.14. Definition. Let F, G be the distributions of $X, Y \in \mathscr{L}_+$. Then X is said to be *star-shaped* with respect to Y, denoted $X \leq_* Y$, if $F^{-1}(u)/G^{-1}(u)$ is increasing on $(0, 1)$.

This is equivalent to the definition in Section 12.D.

The star-shaped ordering is obviously scale-invariant; i.e., if $X \leq_* Y$, then $aX \leq_* bY$ for any $a, b > 0$.

C.15. Proposition. If $X, Y \in \mathscr{L}_+$ and $X \leq_* Y$, then $X \leq_L Y$.

Proof. Without loss of generality, assume $EX = EY = 1$. Then

$$L_X(u) - L_Y(u) = \int_0^u [F^{-1}(v) - G^{-1}(v)] dv. \tag{15}$$

Because $F^{-1}(u)/G^{-1}(u)$ is increasing, the integrand is first positive and then negative as v ranges over $(0, 1)$. So the integral in (15) is smallest when $u = 1$ and so $L_X(u) - L_Y(u) \leq L_X(1) - L_Y(1) = 1 - 1 = 0$, for every $u \in (0, 1)$. ||

An essential ingredient in the proof is that $F^{-1}(v) - G^{-1}(v)$ has only one sign change from + to −. This motivates the following:

C.16. Definition. If $X, Y \in \mathscr{L}_+$ and if
$$\frac{F^{-1}(v)}{EX} - \frac{G^{-1}(v)}{EY}$$
has at most one sign change (from + to −) as v varies over $(0,1)$, then say that X is *sign-change ordered* with respect to Y denoted $X \leq_{sc} Y$.

C.17. Proposition. The sign-change order, $X \leq_{sc} Y$, implies the Lorenz order, $X \leq_L Y$.

Proof. The argument used in Proposition C.15 applies. ||

If X and Y have densities $f(x)$ and $g(y)$, then the following density crossing condition provides a convenient sufficient condition for sign-change ordering and hence Lorenz ordering.

C.18. Proposition. If $X, Y \in \mathscr{L}_+$ have corresponding densities f and g on $\mathscr{R}_+$ and expectations μ and ν and if the function
$$\mu f(\mu x) - \nu g(\nu x) \tag{16}$$
has either two sign changes (from − to + to −) or one sign change (from + to −) as x varies from 0 to ∞, then $X \leq_{sc} Y$.

Proof. The expression (16) is just the density of X/μ minus the density of Y/ν. The fact that (16) exhibits at most two sign changes is sufficient to guarantee a single sign change for the difference between the respective distribution functions $F(\mu x) - G(\nu x)$, and because inverse functions cross only once if the original functions cross only once, it follows that $[F^{-1}(v)/\mu] - G^{-1}(v)/\nu]$ has at most one sign change from + to −; i.e., $X \leq_{sc} Y$. ||

Proposition C.18 has the potential advantage of allowing the verification of sign-change ordering, and hence Lorenz ordering, without the need to compute the inverse distribution functions F^{-1} and G^{-1}.

Observe that a condition equivalent to the sufficient condition of Proposition C.18 is that the ratio of the densities in (16) crosses the level 1 at most twice, and if twice, then from − to + to −.

C.19.a. Example. A random variable X is said to have a *gamma distribution* with parameters λ and ν if its density is of the form
$$f(x) = \frac{\lambda^\nu x^{\nu-1} e^{-\lambda x}}{\Gamma(\nu)}, \quad x > 0, \; \lambda; \; \nu > 0.$$
Suppose that, with $\lambda = 1$, X and Y have gamma distributions with parameters ν_1 and ν_2, respectively, where $\nu_1 < \nu_2$. The condition of Proposition C.18 can be verified so that $X \leq_{sc} Y$, and thus $X \leq_L Y$.

An alternative derivation of this fact is given by Marshall and Olkin (2007, p. 318).

C.19.b. Example. Let $U_{i:n}$ denote the ith order statistic corresponding to a sample of size n from a uniform distribution on $(0, 1)$. The corresponding density of $U_{i:n}$ is

$$f_{U_{i:n}}(u) = n \binom{n-1}{i-1} u^{i-1}(1-u)^{n-i}, \quad 0 < u < 1.$$

Using the density crossing criterion of Proposition C.18 and the fact that $EU_{i:n} = i/(n+1)$, it can be verified that $U_{i-1:n} \geq_* U_{i:n}$ and hence $U_{i-1:n} \geq_L U_{i:n}$.

There is another variability ordering called *dispersion ordering* that is intimately related to star ordering.

C.20. Definition (Doksum, 1969). Suppose that X and Y are random variables with respective distributions F and G. Then X is said to be *smaller than Y in the dispersion order*, written $X \leq_{\text{disp}} Y$ or $F \leq_{\text{disp}} G$, if for every $0 < \alpha < \beta < 1$

$$F^{-1}(\beta) - F^{-1}(\alpha) \leq G^{-1}(\beta) - G^{-1}(\alpha).$$

To see the relationship between dispersion ordering and star ordering, it is convenient to observe that $X \leq_* Y$ if and only if for every $c > 0$, X and cY have distribution functions that cross at most once, and if there is a sign change, then the distribution of X crosses that of Y from $-$ to $+$. Analogously, $X \leq_{\text{disp}} Y$ if and only if, for every real c, X and $c + Y$ have distribution functions that cross at most once and if there is a crossing, then the distribution of X crosses that of $c + Y$ from $-$ to $+$ (Shaked, 1982). So another sufficient condition for Lorenz ordering $X \leq_L Y$ is that $\log X \leq_{\text{disp}} \log Y$.

A more detailed discussion of these relationships is given by Marshall and Olkin (2007) and by Shaked and Shantikumar (2007). Shaked and Shantikumar (2007, Chapter 3) provide an exhaustive coverage of variability ordering and several other related orderings. Examples not considered here are the total time on test ordering, the excess wealth ordering, and the new better than used in expectation ordering. Further discussion of these orderings is provided in Section D.

C.21. Example (Korwar, 2002). Let $X_1, X_2, \ldots, X_n$ be independent random variables uniformly distributed on $(0, 1)$. For $\lambda, \mu \in \mathscr{R}_{++}^n$, a sufficient condition for

$$\sum_{i=1}^{n} \frac{X_i}{\lambda_i} \leq_{\text{disp}} \sum_{i=1}^{n} \frac{X_i}{\mu_i}$$

is that $\lambda \prec \mu$. Subsequently, Khaledi and Kochar (2002) show that the condition $\lambda \prec \mu$ can be replaced by the weaker condition $\log \lambda \prec_w \log \mu$ [called *p-ordering* by Bon and Pălțănea (1999)]. A parallel result holds if the X_i's have a gamma distribution with a common parameter $\nu \geq 1$ (Korwar, 2002, and Khaledi and Kochar, 2004).

Transformations

Within the context of income distributions there is considerable interest in the effects of transformations on the Lorenz order. A frequent interpretation is that the random variable $X \geq 0$ represents the initial income distribution, and $g(X)$ represents a modified distribution after some intervention in the economic process, such as the imposition of an income taxation policy. Two classes of functions are of particular interest here.

C.22. Definition. A function g is said to be *inequality-preserving* if $X \leq_L Y$ implies $g(X) \leq_L g(Y)$ for $X, Y \in \mathscr{L}_+$.

C.23. Definition. A function g is said to be *inequality-attenuating* if $g(X) \leq_L X$ for every $X \in \mathscr{L}_+$.

A trivial example of an inequality-preserving function is one of the form $g(x) = cx$ for some $c > 0$. There are, in fact, only three types of inequality-preserving functions:

$$g_{1c}(x) = cx \quad \text{for some} \quad c > 0; \tag{17}$$

$$g_{2c}(x) = c \quad \text{for some} \quad c > 0; \tag{18}$$

$$g_{3c}(x) = \begin{cases} 0, & x = 0, \\ c, & x > 0 \end{cases} \quad \text{for some} \quad c > 0. \tag{19}$$

This conclusion can be compared with the result in 5.A.1.e in which measurable functions that preserve majorization are linear. In the context of preservation of the Lorenz order, it can be verified that preservation of inequality implies monotonicity, and hence measurability. Moreover, a function of the form $cx + b$ with $b \neq 0$ preserves majorization but not the Lorenz order. For details, see Arnold and Villaseñor (1985) or Arnold (1991).

Note. In contrast, the class of transformations that preserve the star order is broader; for example, it includes $g(x) = x^p$ for any $p \neq 0$ (Shaked and Shanthikumar, 2007, p. 212, Theorem 4.B.6).

Inequality-attenuating functions can be readily characterized as follows (compare with Proposition 5.B.2, which involves the parallel result for majorization in one direction).

C.24. Proposition (Fellman, 1976; Arnold and Villaseñor, 1985). Let $g : \mathscr{R}_+ \to \mathscr{R}_+$. The following are equivalent:

(i) $g(X) \leq_L X$ for all $X \in \mathscr{L}_+$;

(ii) $g(x) > 0$ for all $x > 0$, $g(x)$ is increasing on $[0, \infty)$, and $g(x)/x$ is decreasing on $(0, \infty)$.

Proof. (ii) implies (i). If $X \in \mathscr{L}_+$ and g satisfies (ii), then it can be verified that $g(X) \in \mathscr{L}_+$. Without loss of generality, assume that $X = F^{-1}(U)$, where U has a uniform distribution on $(0, 1)$ and that $Y = g(F^{-1}(U))$. For $u \in (0, 1)$,

$$L_Y(u) - L_X(u) = \int_0^u \frac{g(F^{-1}(v))dv}{EY} - \int_0^u \frac{F^{-1}(v)dv}{EX}$$
$$= \int_0^u \left[g(F^{-1}(v)) - \frac{EY}{EX} F^{-1}(v) \right] \frac{dv}{EY}.$$

But (compare the proof of Proposition C.15) because $g(x)/x$ is decreasing on $(0, \infty)$, the above integrand is first positive and then negative as v ranges from 0 to 1. The integral is thus smallest when $u = 1$, but $L_Y(1) - L_X(1) = 1 - 1 = 0$. So $L_Y(u) - L_X(u) \geq 0$ for all $u \in [0, 1]$, and consequently $Y = g(X) \leq_L X$.

To prove the converse, verify that if any one of the conditions in (ii) is violated, a random variable X with just two possible values can be constructed to violate (i). ∥

C.25. Example. Suppose that X is a random variable in $\mathscr{L}_+$ with $EX^\alpha < \infty$ and $EX^\beta < \infty$ for some $\alpha, \beta > 0$. By Proposition C.24, it follows that $X^\alpha \leq_L X^\beta$ if and only if $\alpha \leq \beta$.

Transformations that include a random component are more difficult to deal with. Suppose that $X \in \mathscr{L}_+$ and $Y = \psi(X, Z) \geq 0$, where Z is random. What conditions must be placed on ψ and on the joint distribution of X and Z to ensure inequality attenuation, that is, that $Y \leq_L X$? And what conditions are needed to ensure increased inequality, that is, $X \leq_L Y$?

Because the introduction of additional randomness typically increases variability, it is to be expected that increased inequality will be more frequently encountered than inequality attenuation. A representative sufficient condition is provided in the following:

C.26. Theorem (Arnold and Villaseñor, 1985). *Suppose that the function $g : \mathscr{R}_+^2 \to \mathscr{R}_+$ is such that $g(z,x)/x$ is increasing in x for every z, and $g(z,x)$ is increasing in x for every z. If X and Z are independent nonnegative random variables with $X \in \mathscr{L}_+$ and $g(Z,X) \in \mathscr{L}_+$, then $X \leq_L g(Z,X)$.*

Multivariate Extensions

Extension of the Lorenz curve concept to higher dimensions was long frustrated by the fact that the usual definition of the Lorenz curve involved either order statistics or the quantile function of the corresponding distribution, neither of which has a simple multivariate analog.

There is one readily available representation of the univariate Lorenz curve that does not explicitly involve the quantile function, namely, the Lorenz curve given in (6b). Analogously, Taguchi (1972) and Lunetta (1972) define, for a bivariate distribution F with density f, a Lorenz surface parameterized by (x,y) to be the set of points in $\mathscr{R}^3$ with coordinates

$$\left\{ F(x,y), \int_{-\infty}^{x} \int_{-\infty}^{y} u f(u,v) du dv, \int_{-\infty}^{x} \int_{-\infty}^{y} v f(u,v) du dv \right\}.$$

Arnold (1987) proposed an alternative parametric definition of a Lorenz surface for bivariate distributions, again indexed by (x,y) with marginal distributions F_1 and F_2. The points on this surface are

$$\left\{ F_1(x), F_2(y), \int_{-\infty}^{x} \int_{-\infty}^{y} uv f(u,v) du dv \right\}.$$

Both of these proposals are difficult to interpret, and neither has received much subsequent attention.

To move smoothly from one dimension to higher dimensions, a new definition of the Lorenz curve is required. A seminal paper for the identification of a suitable definition is that of Koshevoy (1995). Subsequent results obtained by Koshevoy and Mosler (1996, 1997b) are summarized by Mosler (2002). The following presentation introduces the topic, but reference to Mosler is recommended for an in-depth discussion in which zonoids not only are discussed with relation to multivariate dispersion ordering but also are shown to play a fundamental role in the study of central regions and data depth (as indicated by the title of Mosler's monograph).

Begin by again considering the Lorenz curve associated with n ordered numbers $x_1 \leq x_2 \leq \ldots \leq x_n$ as a linear interpolation of the points

$$\left(\frac{i}{n}, \sum_{j=1}^{i} x_j \bigg/ \left(\sum_{j=1}^{n} x_j\right)\right). \tag{20}$$

For each i, an income interpretation is available for the point (20). Its first coordinate represents the fraction of the total population (i.e., i/n) accounted for by the poorest i individuals in the population. The second coordinate corresponds to the fraction of the total income of the population accruing to the poorest i individuals in the population. An alternative to considering such extreme subsets of the population is to plot, for every subset of j of the individuals in the population, the point whose coordinates are (a) the proportion of the population accounted for by the j individuals (i.e., j/n), and (b) the proportion of the total income accounted for by the j individuals. No ordering of the x_i's is required to plot these points. In this setting it is convenient to define also a "reverse" Lorenz curve in which are plotted the income share of the richest i individuals against i/n, $i = 1, 2, \ldots, n$.

See Fig. 2, in which the Lorenz curve and the reverse Lorenz curve for the 5 numbers $(3, 5, 9, 2, 1)$ are plotted. The lower curve in the figure is the Lorenz curve. The upper curve is the reverse Lorenz curve. The points that are graphed in the figure correspond to the "income shares" for the various subsets of the population (there are 2^5 subsets of the set of $n = 5$ numbers in the population). It is evident from the figure that the region between the Lorenz curve and the reverse Lorenz curve is the convex hull of these 2^5 points. If one Lorenz curve is uniformly below a second Lorenz curve, their corresponding reverse Lorenz curves are ordered in the reverse order. It then becomes evident that Lorenz ordering can be defined in terms of the nesting of the convex hulls of the income shares of all subsets of the populations. This avoids ordering and happily permits a straightforward extension to higher dimensions.

The set of points between the Lorenz curve and the reverse Lorenz curve is called the *Lorenz zonoid*. Before attempting an extension of this concept to higher dimensions, an extension of the definition to associate a Lorenz zonoid with every $X \in \mathscr{L}_+$ is required. To this

730   17. Stochastic Ordering

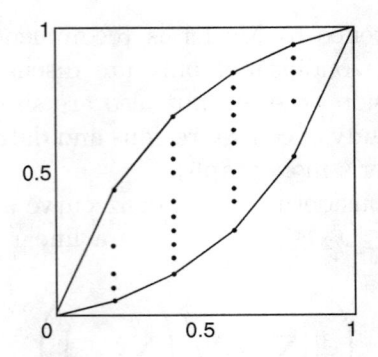

Figure 2. The Lorenz curve, the reverse Lorenz curve, and the corresponding Lorenz zonoid.

end, envision computing income shares for subsets of the population that include fractional individuals. Thus, for a given vector $\alpha \in [0,1]^n$, consider the income share comprising α_1 times the income of individual 1, plus α_2 times the income of individual 2, etc. The size of this subset is $\Sigma_1^n \alpha_i/n$ and its corresponding income share is $\Sigma_{i=1}^n \alpha_i x_i / \Sigma_{i=1}^n x_i$. It is then evident that the Lorenz zonoid corresponding to the population can be envisioned as the set of all points $(\frac{1}{n}\Sigma\alpha_i, \Sigma_{i=1}^n \alpha_i x_i / \Sigma_{i=1}^n x_i)$ in which α ranges over $[0,1]^n$.

The extension to $\mathscr{L}_+$ is then straightforward.

C.27. Definition. Let Ψ denote the class of all measurable mappings from $\mathscr{R}_+$ to $[0,1]$. The *Lorenz zonoid* $L(X)$ of the random variable X with distribution function F is defined to be the set of points

$$L(X) = \left\{ \left(\int_0^\infty \psi(x) dF(x), \frac{\int_0^\infty x\psi(x) dF(x)}{EX} \right) : \psi \in \Psi \right\}$$
$$= \left\{ \left(E\psi(X), \frac{EX\psi(X)}{EX} \right) : \psi \in \Psi \right\}. \qquad (21)$$

It can be verified that the set of points defined in (21) does indeed, in the finite population setting, coincide with the set of points between the Lorenz curve and the reverse Lorenz curve as illustrated in Fig. 2. Again, it is important to emphasize the fact that in Definition C.27, no ordering of the x_i's and no reference to a quantile function are required. Thus the definition has potential for extension to higher dimensions without requiring a suitable definition for higher-dimensional quantiles. Note also that the definition of the Lorenz order on $\mathscr{L}_+$ is expressible as

$$X \leq_L Y \iff L(X) \subseteq L(Y) \quad \text{for} \quad X, Y \in \mathscr{L}_+, \qquad (22)$$

C. The Lorenz Order 731

where the Lorenz zonoid is defined in (21). Nesting of Lorenz zonoids describes the ordering precisely.

An extension to k dimensions can now be developed. Denote by $\mathscr{L}_+^k$ the set of all k-dimensional nonnegative (though this can be relaxed) random vectors X with finite positive marginal expectations (i.e., such that $EX_1, \ldots, EX_k \in \mathscr{R}_{++}$). In addition, let $\Psi^{(k)}$ denote the class of all measurable functions from $\mathscr{R}_+^k$ to $[0, 1]$.

C.28. Definition. Let $X \in \mathscr{L}_+^k$. The *Lorenz zonoid* $L(X)$ of the random vector $X = (X_1, \ldots, X_k)$ with distribution F is

$$L(X) = \left\{ \left(\int \psi(x) dF(x), \int x_1 \frac{\psi(x)}{EX_1} dF(x), \int x_2 \frac{\psi(x)}{EX_2} dF(x), \ldots \right. \right.$$

$$\left. \left. \ldots, \int \frac{x_k \psi(x) dF(x)}{EX_k} \right) : \psi \in \Psi^{(k)} \right\} \qquad (23)$$

$$= \left\{ \left(E\psi(X), \frac{E(X_1 \psi(X))}{EX_1}, \ldots, \frac{E(X_k \psi(X))}{EX_k} \right) : \psi \in \Psi^{(k)} \right\}.$$

The Lorenz zonoid is thus a convex "football"-shaped (American football) subset of the $(k+1)$-dimensional unit cube that includes the points $(0, 0, \ldots, 0)$ and $(1, \ldots, 1)$.

The Lorenz order is defined in terms of nested Lorenz zonoids as in the one-dimensional case. Thus for, $X, Y \in \mathscr{L}_+^k$,

$$X \leq_L Y \iff L(X) \subseteq L(Y), \qquad (24)$$

where $L(X)$ is as defined in (23).

Recall that a definition of Lorenz order in one dimension was possible in terms of expectations of convex functions. Thus in one dimension, $X \leq_L Y$ if and only if $E(g(X/EX)) \leq E(g(Y/EY))$ for every continuous convex function g. This suggests several obvious extensions to k dimensions, using subscripts to identify Lorenz-like orderings on $\mathscr{L}_+^k$ that are not necessarily equivalent to the Lorenz order $\leq_L$ based on nested Lorenz zonoids.

C.29. Definition. Let $X, Y \in \mathscr{L}_+^k$ and define the orders

(i) $X \leq_L Y$ if $L(X) \subseteq L(Y)$,

(ii) $X \leq_{L_1} Y$ if

$$Eg\left(\frac{X_1}{EX_1}, \ldots, \frac{X_k}{EX_k}\right) \leq Eg\left(\frac{Y_1}{EY_1}, \ldots, \frac{Y_k}{EY_k}\right)$$

for every continuous convex function $g : \mathscr{R}^k \to \mathscr{R}$ for which expectations exist,

(iii) $X \leq_{L_2} Y$ if $\sum a_i X_i \leq_L \sum a_i Y_i$ for every $a \in \mathscr{R}^k$,

(iv) $X \leq_{L_3} Y$ if $\sum c_i X_i \leq_L \sum c_i Y_i$ for every $c \in \mathscr{R}_+^k$,

(v) $X \leq_{L_4} Y$ if $X_i \leq_L Y_i$, $i = 1, 2, \ldots, k$.

It can be verified that

$$\leq_{L_1} \implies \leq_{L_2} \iff \leq_L \implies \leq_{L_3} \implies \leq_{L_4}.$$

It is evident that the marginal Lorenz ordering $\leq_{L_4}$ is weaker than $\leq_L$ or $\leq_{L_3}$, because it corresponds to particular choices for c in $\Sigma c_i X_i$. It is evident that the convex ordering $\leq_{L_1}$ implies all of the other orderings $\leq_L, \leq_{L_2}, \leq_{L_3}$, and $\leq_{L_4}$. The convex order is stronger than the Lorenz order $\leq_L$. Examples of simple two-dimensional cases in which $X \leq_L Y$ but $X \not\leq_{L_1} Y$ are provided by Elton and Hill (1992).

In an economic context, $\leq_{L_3}$ seems to be the most natural version of multivariate Lorenz ordering and has been called the *price Lorenz order*. Joe and Verducci (1992) call it the *positive-combinations Lorenz order*. Alternatively, it might be called the *exchange rate Lorenz ordering* using the following interpretation. Imagine that the coordinates of X and Y represent financial holdings in k different currencies. Now suppose that all k currencies are to be exchanged for, say, euros according to k exchange rates $c_1, \ldots, c_k$. The corresponding random variables $\Sigma c_i X_i$ and $\Sigma c_i Y_i$ can now be compared in terms of inequality. The exchange rate Lorenz ordering postulates that X exhibits less inequality than Y if $\Sigma c_i X_i \leq_L \Sigma c_i Y_i$ for every exchange rate vector $c \in \mathscr{R}_+^k$. In this context it is reasonable to restrict the c's to be positive because a negative exchange rate is difficult to interpret. Nevertheless, because $\leq_L$ and $\leq_{L_2}$ are equivalent, the definition of Lorenz ordering does require Lorenz ordering of $\Sigma a_i X_i$ with respect to $\Sigma a_i Y_i$ for $a \in \mathscr{R}^k$, i.e., even allowing some negative exchange rates.

A variety of summary measures of inequality have been suggested for k-dimensional distributions. We mention but a few. For the convex order $\leq_{L_1}$, any specific choice of a continuous convex function g could be used to measure inequality by the quantity

$$Eg\left(\frac{X_1}{EX_1}, \ldots, \frac{X_k}{EX_k}\right).$$

If the Lorenz ordering via nested Lorenz zonoids [as in (22)] is used, then attractive analogs to univariate measures are available: (i) the $(k+1)$-dimensional volume of the Lorenz zonoid, (ii) the k-dimensional volume of the boundary of the Lorenz zonoid, (iii) the maximal distance between two points in the Lorenz zonoid. When $k = 1$, relatively simple expressions for these indices are available. In higher dimensions, this is not true. Koshevoy and Mosler (1997a) do provide an analytic expression for the volume of the Lorenz zonoid, though it is not easy to evaluate. For $X \in \mathscr{L}_+^k$, define a normalized version of X, denoted by $\widetilde{X}$, in which $\widetilde{X}_i = X_i/EX_i$. Consider $k+1$ independent, identically distributed k-dimensional random vectors $\widetilde{X}_1, \ldots, \widetilde{X}_{k+1}$ each with the same distribution as $\widetilde{X}$. Let Q be a $(k+1) \times (k+1)$ matrix whose ith row is $(1, \widetilde{X}_i)$, $i = 1, 2, \ldots, k+1$. It follows that

$$\text{volume}(L(X)) = \frac{1}{(k+1)!} E|\det Q|. \tag{25}$$

A drawback associated with the use of the volume of the Lorenz zonoid as a measure of inequality is that it can assume the value of 0 for certain nondegenerate distributions. See Mosler (2002) for discussion of a variant definition avoiding this pitfall.

When $k = 1$,

$$Q = \begin{pmatrix} 1 & \widetilde{X}_1 \\ 1 & \widetilde{X}_2 \end{pmatrix},$$

so that (25) reduces to an expression for the Gini index of X in the one-dimensional case that is equivalent to (13a), namely,

$$G(X) = \frac{1}{2} E \left| \frac{X^{(1)}}{EX^{(1)}} - \frac{X^{(2)}}{EX^{(2)}} \right|, \tag{26}$$

where $X^{(1)}$ and $X^{(2)}$ are independent and identically distributed copies of X; i.e., it is one half of the expected distance between independent normalized copies of X.

The expression (26) leads to the following extension to k dimensions. For $X \in \mathscr{L}^k$, define

$$G(X) = \frac{1}{2^k} E||\widetilde{X}^{(1)} - \widetilde{X}^{(2)}||, \qquad (27)$$

where $\widetilde{X}^{(1)}$ and $\widetilde{X}^{(2)}$ are independent, identically distributed normalized copies of X (i.e., rescaled so that the marginal means are all equal to 1) and where $||\cdot||$ denotes the k-dimensional Euclidean norm. A proof that if $X \leq_L Y$, then $G(X) \leq G(Y)$ [where G is defined by (27)] is given by Mosler (2002). Other norms or other measures of distance (instead of Euclidean distance) can be used in (27), perhaps with an advantage of computational simplicity.

D Lorenz Order: Applications and Related Results

The Lorenz order has, since its introduction in 1905, been a focal point of discussion regarding inequality measurement in socioeconomic settings. A truly enormous literature has been developed to deal with extensions, variations, and properties of the ordering. This section makes no attempt to navigate all of this ocean of research. However, the topics and examples included inevitably lead the interested reader more deeply into that literature. In the following discussion, the focus is on the mathematical features of the results; in many cases the supplied references lead directly or indirectly to discussion of related theoretical and applied economic concepts. Without such motivational material, the results may seem to be, in some cases, mathematical curiosities. Nevertheless, challenging mathematical problems arise that are of interest even without subject area motivation.

Parametric Families of Lorenz Curves

For a nonnegative random variable with distribution function F and finite expectation, the corresponding Lorenz curve is defined by

$$L(u) = \int_0^u F^{-1}(v)dv \Big/ \int_0^1 F^{-1}(v)dv, \quad 0 \leq u \leq 1. \qquad (1)$$

Properties of Lorenz curves are discussed in Section C. The following result provides sufficient conditions for a given curve to be a Lorenz curve.

D.1. Proposition. Sufficient conditions for a twice-differentiable function $L(u)$ defined on $[0,1]$ to be the Lorenz curve of some nonnegative integrable random variable are

$$L(0) = 0, \quad L(1) = 1, \qquad (2)$$

$$L'(u) \geq 0 \quad \text{for all } u \in (0,1), \qquad (3)$$

$$L''(u) \geq 0 \quad \text{for all } u \in (0,1). \qquad (4)$$

Pakes (1981) shows that it is sufficient to replace condition (3) by the condition that $L'(0) \geq 0$. Rather than consider parametric families of distributions, it is often reasonable to consider parametric families of Lorenz curves satisfying only (2), (3), and (4), and to select from such families a representative member that closely resembles or "fits" a given data-based empirical Lorenz curve.

To find familiar examples of Lorenz curves, note that conditions (2), (3), and (4) are satisfied when L is a distribution on $[0,1]$ with increasing density.

D.1.a. Example. Rasche, Gaffney, Koo, and Obst (1980) study the family of curves

$$L(u) = [1 - (1-u)^a]^{1/b}, \quad 0 \leq u \leq 1, \ 0 < a \leq 1, \ 0 < b \leq 1. \qquad (5)$$

This family includes classical Pareto Lorenz curves (when $b = 1$).

D.1.b. Example. A more general family of the form

$$L(u) = u^c[1 - (1-u)^a]^{1/b}, \quad 0 \leq u, a, b \leq 1, \ c \geq 0, \qquad (6)$$

was proposed by Sarabia, Castillo, and Slottje (1999). Flexible families of Lorenz curves such as (6) can be used to identify better-fitting alternatives to the classical Pareto model in many settings.

Other parametric families of Lorenz curves have been proposed. Villaseñor and Arnold (1989) propose a general quadratic family of curves [with coefficients selected to ensure that (2), (3), and (4) hold] that provides a convenient flexible family for modeling purposes. Particular cases in which the curves are elliptical or hyperbolic in form have received special attention.

D.1.c. Example. Hyperbolic curves take the form

$$L(u) = \frac{u(1+au)}{1+au+b(1-u)}, \quad 0 \le u \le 1, \quad a > 1, \quad b > 0 \qquad (7)$$

(Arnold, 1986). Explicit expressions for the distribution and density corresponding to (7) are available. Villaseñor and Arnold (1989) identify the density and distribution function corresponding to an elliptical Lorenz curve.

D.1.d. Example. Gupta (1984) proposes the family

$$L(u) = uc^{u-1}, \quad 0 \le u \le 1, \quad c \ge 1. \qquad (8)$$

D.1.e. Example. Sarabia (1997) analyzes a popular family of distributions that are defined in terms of their quantile functions, namely the Tukey-lambda family, which leads to the candidate Lorenz curves

$$L(u) = a + bu + c_1 u^{d_1} + c_2 (1-u)^{d_2}, \quad 0 \le u \le 1. \qquad (9)$$

Constraints on the parameters in (9) are identified to ensure that $L(u)$ is a Lorenz curve [i.e., that equations (2), (3), and (4) hold].

D.1.f. Example. Sarabia, Castillo, and Slottje (1999) describe a useful procedure for constructing more flexible families of Lorenz curves beginning with a given family. Let $L_0(u;\theta)$ be a family of Lorenz curves parameterized by θ, $\theta \in \Theta \subseteq \mathscr{R}^p$, and define

$$L_1(u;\theta,\alpha,\beta) = u^\alpha [L_0(u;\theta)]^\beta, \qquad (10)$$

where α and β are chosen to ensure that (3) and (4) are satisfied. For example, $\alpha > 1$ and $\beta \ge 1$ suffice.

Lorenz Order Within Parametric Families

It is observed in Example C.4 that the lognormal family of distributions is parametrically ordered by the Lorenz order. A similar statement can be made for the classical Pareto family of distributions [see C(4)]. Several other parametric families have been studied to determine whether similar orderings can be identified. The family of generalized gamma distributions was studied initially by Taillie (1981) and subsequently by Wilfling (1996a).

D.2. Definition. The random variable X has a *generalized gamma distribution* if its density is of the form

$$f(x) = \frac{\alpha x^{\nu\alpha - 1} \exp(-x^\alpha)}{\Gamma(\nu)}, \quad x > 0, \quad \alpha, \nu > 0. \qquad (11)$$

This density arises from the representation $X = U^{1/\alpha}$, where U has a gamma distribution with shape parameter ν and scale parameter 1. Marshall and Olkin (2007, p. 348) provide further details on the origin and properties of the generalized gamma distribution. The Lorenz order within the classical gamma family was discussed in C.19.a, and the extension to the generalized gamma family is contained in the following:

D.2.a. Proposition (Wilfling, 1996a). Let X and Y have generalized gamma distributions with respective parameters (ν_1, α_1) and (ν_2, α_2). The following are equivalent:

(i) $X \leq_L Y$;

(ii) $\alpha_1 \geq \alpha_2$ and $\alpha_1 \nu_1 \geq \alpha_2 \nu_2$.

Wilfling proves this result using a variation of the density crossing argument. Taillie (1981) also studies the case in which the α's are negative.

D.3. Definition. A distribution with density of the form

$$f(x) = \frac{\alpha x^{\alpha\theta-1}}{B(\xi,\theta)[1+x^\alpha]^{\xi+\theta}}, \quad x = 0, \ \alpha, \xi, \theta \geq 0, \tag{12}$$

is variously called a *generalized F distribution*, a *generalized beta distribution of the second kind*, or a *Feller–Pareto distribution*. For a detailed discussion of these distributions, see Marshall and Olkin (2007, Section 11.C).

D.3.a. Proposition (Wilfling, 1996b). Suppose that X and Y have the density (12) with respective parameters $\alpha_1, \xi_1, \theta_1$ and $\alpha_2, \xi_2, \theta_2$. If $\alpha_1 \geq \alpha_2, \theta_1 > \theta_2$, and $\xi_1 > \xi_2$, then $X \leq_L Y$.

Wilfing (1996b) obtains these sufficient conditions for Lorenz ordering, again by using a density crossing argument.

D.4. Example. A distribution with density of the form

$$f(x|a,b,\alpha) = \frac{\alpha x^{a\alpha-1}(1-x^\alpha)^{b-1}}{B(a,b)}, \quad 0 \leq x \leq 1, \ a,b,\alpha > 0, \tag{13}$$

is called a *generalized beta distribution of the first kind*, or a *beta distribution with power parameter*. For a discussion of this and other generalized beta distributions, see Marshall and Olkin (2007, Section 14.C.i).

D.4.a. Proposition (Wilfling, 1996c). Suppose that X and Y have the density (13) with respective parameters a_1, b_1, α_1 and a_2, b_2, α_2. Any one of the following conditions is sufficient to ensure that $X \leq_L Y$:

(i) $\alpha_1 = \alpha_2 \geq 1$, $a_1 = a_2$, $b_1 = b_2 = a_1 - 1$;

(ii) $\alpha_1 = \alpha_2$, $a_1 > a_2$, $b_1 = b_2 \geq 1$;

(iii) $\alpha_1 = \alpha_2$, $a_1 > a_2$, $b_1 > \xi > 0$, where ξ is the solution of the equation $EX = EZ$, where Z has the density (13) with parameters a_2, ξ and α_1.

(iv) $\alpha_1 \geq \alpha_2$, $a_1 = a_2$, $b_1 = b_2$.

Note. The term "generalized beta distribution" is applied by Marshall and Olkin (2007, p. 488) to a four-parameter distribution with density different from (13).

Lorenz Ordering of Sample Statistics

Suppose that $X_1, X_2, \ldots$ is a sequence of independent, identically distributed nonnegative random variables with common distribution function F with finite mean. Because the Lorenz order, in a sense, reflects variability, it is to be expected that certain sample statistics are ordered by the Lorenz order in a decreasing fashion as sample size increases. Some results in this direction are available. Denote the sample mean by $\overline{X}_n = \Sigma_{i=1}^n X_i / n$.

D.5. Proposition (Arnold and Villaseñor, 1986). If $n \geq 2$, then $\overline{X}_n \leq_L \overline{X}_{n-1}$.

Proof. Observe that $E(\overline{X}_{n-1} | \overline{X}_n) = \overline{X}_n$ and apply Theorem C.12.

D.5.a. A finite population version of D.5 is also true. Consider a finite population of N units with attributes $x_1, x_2, \ldots, x_N$. Let $\overline{X}_n$ denote the mean of a random sample of size n drawn without replacement from this population. It follows that for $n \geq 2$, $\overline{X}_n \leq_L \overline{X}_{n-1}$. This is just a restatement of the set of inequalities found in 3.C.1.f. Alternatively, the result can be obtained by verifying that in the finite population sampling setting, $E(\overline{X}_{n-1} | \overline{X}_n) = \overline{X}_n$, just as in the case of independent, identically distributed X_i's.

The results of Pečarić and Svrtan (2002) can alternatively be used to argue that $\overline{X}_n \leq_L X_{n+1}$ in the context of finite population sampling without and with replacement.

In fact, only exchangeability, not independence, of the X_i's is required in D.5. An analogous result is possible for more general U-statistics provided expectations exist.

Sample medians, however, are not generally Lorenz ordered by sample size. Restricting attention to odd sample sizes (to ensure a unique unambiguous definition of the median), Arnold and Villaseñor (1986) prove that if F has a symmetric density on some interval $[0, c]$, then the medians satisfy

$$X_{n+2:2n+3} \leq_L X_{n+1:2n+1} \tag{14}$$

for any n.

The sample mean typically has a smaller variance than the corresponding sample median, which leads to the speculation that

$$\overline{X}_{2n+1} \leq_L X_{n+1:2n+1}, \quad n = 1, 2, \ldots . \tag{15}$$

This result is known to hold if the common distribution of the X_i's is exponential (proved by a density crossing argument). However, it is not universally true. An example is available in which the Lorenz curves of the random variables in (15) cross. Sufficient conditions for (15) are not known. For further discussion, see Arnold and Villaseñor (1986).

It was remarked in C.19.b that certain uniform order statistics are Lorenz ordered. More generally, what are the conditions on i_1, n_1 and i_2, n_2 and the common distribution of the X_i's, to ensure that

$$X_{i_1:n_1} \leq_L X_{i_2:n_2}? \tag{16}$$

D.5.b. Example (Arnold and Nagaraja, 1991). Suppose that the common distribution is exponential. Then for $i_1 \geq i_2$, (16) holds if and only if $(n_2 - i_2 + 1)EX_{i_2:n_2} \leq (n_1 - i_1 + 1)EX_{i_1:n_1}$. Because $EX_{i:n} = \Sigma_{j=n-i+1}^{n} 1/j$, a complete characterization of values of (i_1, n_1, i_2, n_2) for which (16) holds is obtained.

D.5.c. Example (Arnold and Villaseñor, 1991). If the distribution is uniform on the interval $(0, 1)$, then only partial results are available for (16) to hold. Denote the ith order statistic in a sample of size n from a uniform distribution by $U_{i:n}$. Then

$$U_{i+1:n} \leq_L U_{i:n} \quad \text{for all } i, n, \tag{17}$$

$$U_{i:n} \leq_L U_{i:n+1} \quad \text{for all } i, n, \tag{18}$$

$$U_{n-j+1:n+1} \leq_L U_{n-j:n} \quad \text{for all } j, n, \tag{19}$$

$$U_{n+2:2n+3} \leq_L U_{n+1:2n+1} \quad \text{for all } n. \tag{20}$$

The proofs of (17), (18), and (19) follow from Theorem C.12. Equation (20) [which is a special case of (14)] is verified by a density crossing argument. It can be verified that (17), (18), and (19) hold for random variables having a uniform distribution with a power parameter [$F(x) = x^\lambda, 0 \leq x \leq 1, \lambda > 0$] and are reversed if the X_i's have a common classical Pareto distribution [as defined in C(3)].

Wilfling (1996c) describes Lorenz ordering relationships between order statistics from uniform distributions with different power parameters.

Some analogous results have been obtained for Lorenz ordering of record values [see, for example, Arnold and Villaseñor (1998)].

Total Time on Test Curves

In the study of lifetime data, an important statistic is the *total time on test*. For a sample $X_1, X_2, \ldots, X_n$ from a common distribution F [with $F(0) = 0$ and finite mean μ], the total time on test at the time of the ith failure is defined to be

$$T_{n,i} = \sum_{j=1}^{i} (n - j + 1)(X_{j:n} - X_{j-1:n}). \tag{21}$$

A scaled version of the total time on test is provided by

$$\widetilde{T}_{n,i} = T_{n,i} \bigg/ \sum_{j=1}^{n} X_{j:n}. \tag{22}$$

Population analogs of these statistics are

$$T(u) = \int_0^{F^{-1}(u)} [1 - F(v)] dv, \quad 0 \leq u \leq 1, \tag{23}$$

the *total time on test transform of F*, and

$$\widetilde{T}(u) = \frac{1}{\mu} T(u), \quad 0 \leq u \leq 1, \tag{24}$$

the *scaled total time on test transform of* F. There is an intimate relationship between $T(u)$ [or $\tilde{T}(u)$] and the Lorenz curve corresponding to the distribution F. As pointed out by Chandra and Singpurwalla (1981), this suggests an interrelationship between results in the reliability literature using total time on test concepts and results in the economics literature involving the Lorenz order. Marshall and Olkin (2007, p. 35) provide details on this topic.

In addition, Shaked and Shantikumar (1998) introduce what they call the *excess wealth transform* of the distribution function F, defined by

$$W(u) = \int_{F^{-1}(u)}^{\infty} [1 - F(v)] dv. \qquad (25)$$

The excess wealth function is intimately related to the unscaled Lorenz curve $(\mu L(u))$ and the (unscaled) total time of test transform. By a direct verification,

$$W(u) = \mu - T(u), \quad 0 \leq u \leq 1, \qquad (26)$$

and

$$T(u) = \mu L(u) + (1-u) F^{-1}(u), \quad 0 \leq u \leq 1. \qquad (27)$$

D.6. Definition. The *excess wealth order* is defined by

$$X \leq_{\text{ew}} Y \iff W_X(u) \leq W_Y(u), \quad 0 \leq u \leq 1. \qquad (28)$$

The excess wealth order differs from the Lorenz order in that it is location-invariant, i.e.,

$$X \leq_{\text{ew}} Y \implies X + a \leq_{\text{ew}} Y \quad \text{for all } a \in \mathscr{R}. \qquad (29)$$

[The location parameter a can be negative because the definition of the excess wealth transform continues to be meaningful even if $F(0) < 0$.]

D.6.a. Definition. If $Eg(X) \leq Eg(Y)$ for all increasing convex functions g for which the expectations exist, then X is said to be less than Y in the *increasing convex order*, denoted by $X \leq_{\text{icx}} Y$.

D.6.b. Proposition (Shaked and Shantikumar, 2007, p. 196). If $X \leq_{\text{ew}} Y$ and if $F_X^{-1}(0) \leq F_Y^{-1}(0)$, then $X \leq_{\text{icx}} Y$.

Reference to Section 1.A confirms that the increasing convex ordering is a natural extension of the concept of weak submajorization defined on $\mathscr{R}^n$ (or if you wish, associated with uniform distributions with n points in their support sets).

The relationship between increasing convex order and ordering by unscaled Lorenz curves [$\mu L(u)$), also called *generalized Lorenz curves*] is discussed by Ramos, Ollero, and Sordo (2000). See also Shorrocks (1983). Meilijson and Nádas (1979) discuss a closely related ordering in which the increasing convex functions are also required to be nonnegative.

Aging concepts introduced in reliability analysis such as "new better than used," "new better than used in expectation," and so on can be used to define partial orders among distributions of nonnegative random variables. Such orderings sometimes can be interpreted as variability orderings. See Kochar (1989) for details, and for verification that the Lorenz order can be identified with a "harmonic new better than used in expectation" order.

The difference between the total time on test transform $T(u)$ and the Lorenz curve $L(u)$ is highlighted by the observation of Barlow and Campo (1975) that a lifetime distribution F has increasing hazard rate if and only if $T(u)$ is concave. If $T(u)$ is convex, then F has a decreasing hazard rate on the interval $(F^{-1}(0), F^{-1}(1))$. However, it was observed that the related Lorenz curve is always convex. The second term on the right in (27) is responsible for any concavity in $T(u)$.

Note. Empirical total time on test transforms based on exchangeable (rather than independent) lifetimes are discussed by Nappo and Spizzichino (1998).

Finally, note that there is a relationship between the scaled total time on test transform $\widetilde{T}(u)$ and the "equilibrium distribution" F_e of F (arising in renewal process contexts) defined by

$$F_e(x) = \frac{1}{\mu} \int_0^x [1 - F(v)] dv. \qquad (30)$$

Evidently,

$$F_e(x) = \widetilde{T}(F(x)), \qquad (31)$$

thus permitting a comparison of equilibrium distributions in terms of total time on test transforms and indirectly in terms of the Lorenz order.

Hitting Times in Continuous-Time Markov Chains and Lorenz Order

Consider a continuous-time Markov chain with $n+1$ states, in which states $1, 2, \ldots, n$ are transient and state $n+1$ is absorbing. The time, T, until absorption in state $(n+1)$ is said to have a *phase-type distribution* (Neuts, 1975). This distribution is determined by an initial distribution over the transient states denoted by $\alpha = (\alpha_1, \alpha_2, \ldots, \alpha_n)$ (assume that the chain has probability 0 of being initially in the absorbing state). The intensity matrix Q for transitions among the transient states has elements satisfying $q_{ii} < 0$ and $q_{ij} \geq 0$ for $j \neq i$. In this setting, the time, T, to absorption in state $(n+1)$ is said to have a phase-type distribution with parameters α and Q. A particularly simple case is one in which $\alpha = \alpha^* = (1, 0, \ldots, 0)$ and $Q = Q^*$, where $q_{ii}^* = -\delta$ for each i and $q_{ij}^* = \delta$ for $j = i+1$, $q_{ij}^* = 0$ otherwise. In this case, the Markov chain begins in state 1 with probability 1, and spends an exponential time with mean $1/\delta$ in each state before moving to the next state. The corresponding time to absorption, T^*, is thus a sum of n independent and identically distributed random variables having an exponential distribution with parameter δ; and T^* has a gamma distribution with scale parameter δ and shape (convolution) parameter n. (See C.19.a.)

There are multiple possible representations of phase-type distributions. The same distribution of time to absorption can be associated with more than one choice of n, α, and Q.

A phase-type distribution is said to be of order n if n is the smallest integer such that the distribution can be identified as an absorption time for a chain with n transient states and one absorbing state. In some sense the variable T^* clearly exhibits the least variability among phase-type distributions of order n. Aldous and Shepp (1987) show that the T^* having a gamma distribution with parameters δ and n has the smallest coefficient of variation among phase-type distributions of order n. In fact, O'Cinneide (1991) shows that T^* exhibits the least variability in a more fundamental sense. For any phase-type variable T of order n, $T^* \leq_L T$.

Dependence Orderings via Lorenz Curves

Scarsini (1990) introduces an ordering of dependence on the class of probability measures on a finite probability space with given marginals. In two dimensions, such a probability measure can be viewed as an $I \times J$ matrix $P = (p_{ij})$ with nonnegative elements that sum to one with given row and column sums by prescribed vectors p_R^* and p_C^*. Thus $\Sigma_{j=1}^{J} p_{ij} = p_{Ri}^*$ for each i, and $\Sigma_{i=1}^{I} p_{ij} = p_{Cj}^*$ for each j. For simplicity of discussion, assume that row and column sums are positive. Denote the class of such matrices by $\mathscr{P}^*$. Among such matrices there is one, denoted by Q, which has independent marginals, i.e., $q_{ij} = p_{Ri}^* p_{Cj}^*$, for each pair (i,j).

Any matrix in $\mathscr{P}^*$ distinct from Q exhibits more dependence than does Q which exhibits no dependence. For any matrix $P \in \mathscr{P}^*$, define a measure on the space $(1, 2, \ldots, I) \times (1, 2, \ldots, J)$ by

$$P\{A\} = \sum_{(i,j) \in A} p_{ij}. \tag{32}$$

In (32), a convenient abuse of notation is introduced. P denotes the matrix in $\mathscr{P}^*$, and also P denotes the associated measure defined on subsets of $(1, 2, \ldots, I) \times (1, 2, \ldots, J)$. The *likelihood ratio of P with respect to Q* is defined by

$$LR_P(i,j) = p_{ij}/q_{ij}. \tag{33}$$

A random variable X_P can be associated with this likelihood ratio as follows. For each $(i,j) \in (1, \ldots, I) \times (1, \ldots, J)$, let

$$P\left\{X_P = \frac{p_{ij}}{q_{ij}}\right\} = q_{ij}.$$

Each such random variable X_P has mean 1 and a corresponding Lorenz curve $L_P(u)$. If $P = Q$, the random variable is degenerate and thus $L_Q(u) = u$. Increased dependence between the rows and columns of P is reflected by a lowered Lorenz curve, L_P, and it is thus natural for $P_1, P_2 \in \mathscr{P}^*$ to rank P_1 more dependent than P_2 if $X_{P_1} \geq_L X_{P_2}$ or equivalently if $L_{P_1}(u) \leq L_{P_2}(u)$.

Interestingly, L_P admits an interpretation as the size versus power curve of most powerful tests of the independence hypothesis, i.e., of Q vs. P.

These concepts readily extend to the case of m-fold product spaces ($m > 2$). As Scarsini (1990) points out, the rationale for this dependence ordering breaks down if attention is not restricted to finite spaces.

Partial Sums of Vector-Valued Random Variables

Let $X_1, X_2, \ldots, X_n$ be independent k-dimensional random variables. Define $S_n = \sum_{i=1}^n X_i$. Berger (1991) describes techniques that lead to theorems for such sums S_n from parallel or related results for sums of independent real-valued random variables (for example, laws of large numbers). A key tool in this endeavor involves the Lorenz order.

Denote the k-dimensional Euclidean norm by $||\cdot||$. Berger (1991) shows that the following results are valid for X_i's taking on values in an abstract vector space.

Assume that $E||X_j|| < \infty$, $j = 1, 2, \ldots, n$, and define the vector $V = (V_1, V_2, \ldots, V_n)$, where

$$V_j = ||X_j|| + E||X_j||. \tag{34}$$

In addition, let V' denote an independent copy of V, and let $R_1, R_2, \ldots, R_n$ be independent Bernoulli random variables (i.e., with $P\{R_i = -1\} = P\{R_i = 1\} = 1/2$) that are independent of V and V'. Then define

$$T_n = \sum_{j=1}^n R_j(V_j + V_j'), \tag{35}$$

$$T_n^* = \sum_{j=1}^n R_j||X_j||. \tag{36}$$

It can be verified that

$$||S_n|| - E||S_n|| \leq_{\text{cx}} T_n \leq_{\text{cx}} 4T_n^*, \tag{37}$$

where $X \leq_{\text{cx}} Y$ means $Eg(X) \leq Eg(Y)$ for all convex functions g provided the expectations exist. Note that the random variables in (37) all have mean 0 so that convex ordering is appropriate but Lorenz ordering is not well-defined.

Two elementary results regarding the convex order (and consequently the Lorenz order) used in the proof of (37) are:

D.7. Lemma (Berger, 1991). If X and X' are identically distributed and not necessarily independent with $E|X| < \infty$, then

$$X + X' \leq_{\mathrm{cx}} 2X.$$

Proof. For g convex such that all expectations exist,

$$Eg(X + X') \leq \frac{1}{2}[Eg(2X) + Eg(2X')] = Eg(2X). \quad \|$$

D.7.a. If $X, X' \in \mathscr{L}_+$ (see p. 713) are identically distributed and not necessarily independent, then $X + X' \leq_L 2X$ and so $X + X' \leq_L X$.

D.8. Lemma (Berger, 1991). If X is a real-valued random variable with finite expectation, then

$$X + EX \leq_{\mathrm{cx}} 2X.$$

Proof. Let X' be an independent copy of X. For g convex such that all expectations exist,

$$Eg(X + EX) = Eg(E(X + X'|X))$$
$$\leq Eg(X + X') \leq Eg(2X).$$

The first inequality is a consequence of Jensen's inequality (16.C.1), and the second inequality follows from D.7. $\|$

D.8.a. If $X \in \mathscr{L}_+$, then $X + EX \leq_L 2X$ and $X + EX \leq_L X$.

By using (37) and C.12, Berger (1991) deduces several results for vector-valued X_j's from corresponding results for real-valued variables.

Probability Forecasting

A weather forecaster each day announces his subjective probability of rain on that day. His announced subjective probability x is assumed to be a realization of a random variable X. Let Y be an indicator random variable with $Y = 1$ if it rains, and 0 otherwise. The performance of the forecaster can be summarized by the density $\nu(x)$ of X, and for each x the conditional probability $\rho(x)$ of rain given that the forecaster's prediction was x. If $\rho(x) = x$, the forecaster is said to be *well-calibrated*. If the probability of rain in the forecaster's city is 0.25, then a forecaster who every day predicts 0.25 is well-calibrated, but not very helpful. In contrast, if the forecaster predicts rain with

D. Lorenz Order: Applications and Related Results   747

probability 1 on days when it actually rains and 0 on other days, then the forecaster is also well-calibrated and amazingly skillful. Well-calibrated forecasters are discussed by DeGroot and Fienberg (1983). They order such forecasters using a concept called *refinement*. However, it turns out that this refinement ordering on random variables with support $[0,1]$ and mean μ is identifiable with the Lorenz order. The better forecasters (in terms of refinement) are those who predictions are most variable, subject to being well-calibrated. A definition of proper scoring rules is provided (rules that encourage forecasters to announce their true subjective probability of rain), and DeGroot and Fienberg (1983) show that more refined forecasters receive higher expected scores using such rules.

See DeGroot and Eriksson (1985) for more detailed discussion of the relationship between refinement and the Lorenz order.

A Rational Fraction Inequality

The Lorenz curve definition can prove useful in unexpected situations. In the following a property of the Lorenz curve is used to justify a polynomial inequality. For $x \geq 0$, consider the polynomial $P_n(x) = \sum_{k=0}^{n} x^k$, and for $m > n$ let $f(x) = P_m(x)/P_n(x)$ and $g(x) = f(x)x^{n-m}$.

D.9. Theorem (Jichang, 2002). If $x > 1$, then

$$1 < g(x) < \frac{m+1}{n+1} < f(x),$$

whereas if $x < 1$,

$$\max\left\{1, \, x^{m-n}\frac{m+1}{n+1}\right\} < f(x) < \frac{m+1}{n+1} < g(x).$$

Proof. First, note that $g(x) = f(x^{-1})$. It is thus only necessary to consider $x > 1$ because the results for $x < 1$ follow readily. To verify that for $x > 1$, $f(x) > (m+1)/(n+1)$ observe that this is equivalent to the statement that

$$\frac{n+1}{m+1} > \frac{P_n(x)}{P_m(x)} = \frac{\sum_{k=0}^{n} x^k}{\sum_{k=0}^{m} x^k}.$$

However, this follows by considering the Lorenz curve corresponding to the set of numbers $\{1, x, x^2, \ldots, x^m\}$ at the point $(n+1)/(m+1)$, since the Lorenz curve, L_X for any nondegenerate random variable X satisfies $L_X(u) < u$ for $0 < u < 1$. The other inequalities in the

748   17. Stochastic Ordering

theorem follow from this fact [and the fact that $g(x) = f(x^{-1})$]. An alternative argument, not involving the Lorenz curve, uses the fact that $P_m(x)/(m+1)$ is a power mean, so that $h(n) = \Sigma_0^n x^k/(n+1)$ is increasing in n. ∥

Shi (2006) obtains refinements of the inequalities in D.9 using majorization arguments. For example, for $x > 1$, he proves that

$$g(x) < \frac{m+1}{n+1} - \frac{x^{n-m}(1 - x^{-\frac{1}{2}(m+1)(n+1)(m-n)})}{(n+1)P_n(x)} < \frac{m+1}{n+1}.$$

E An Uncertainty Order

There have been a number of attempts to measure the "uncertainty" associated with a random variable X. In statistical contexts, the variance of X is often used. In economics the Gini index may replace the variance, and in the physical sciences uncertainty is ordinarily measured using entropy. These approaches attempt to measure "uncertainty" without defining it. When measures such as variance and entropy are used to order two random variables in terms of uncertainty, these measures can give opposite orderings. To avoid this problem, an uncertainty ordering of random variables is defined here. This uncertainty ordering is a preorder; random variables may or may not be comparable.

A random variable X might be thought of as exhibiting "more uncertainty" than Y if the value of X can be predicted "less precisely" (with confidence p) than can the value of Y. The following definition serves to make this idea precise.

Let λ be a measure defined on the Borel subsets $\mathscr{B}$ of $\mathscr{R}^n$, and for a random variable X taking values in $\mathscr{R}^n$, let

$$\mathscr{A}(X;p) = \{A \in \mathscr{B} : P\{X \in A\} \geq p\},$$

and

$$\mu(X,p) = \inf_{A \in \mathscr{A}(X;p)} \lambda(A).$$

E.1. Definition. A random variable X is said to be *more level-p uncertain* than Y if $\mu(X;p) \geq \mu(Y;p)$. If X is more level-p uncertain than Y at all levels $p \in (0,1)$, then X is said to be *more uncertain* than Y, written $X \geq_U Y$.

E. An Uncertainty Order   749

In this book, λ is usually Lebesgue measure or counting measure and the random variables usually take values in $\mathscr{R}^n$.

Uncertainty Parameters in Absolutely Continuous Distributions

In this subsection, the measure λ in Definition E.1 is taken to be Lebesgue measure. With this provision, Definition E.1 can profitably be connected to continuous majorization, briefly introduced in Section 1.D. But first, a reexamination of the notion of a decreasing rearrangement of a function f is required. In the following, it is assumed that f is a nonnegative integrable function defined on $(-\infty, \infty)$ such that $\int_{-\infty}^{\infty} f(x)\,dx < \infty$.

To make clear the definition of a decreasing rearrangement of a nonnegative function f, imagine the area between the horizontal axis and the graph of f to be cut into very narrow vertical strips. Now start at the origin (an arbitrary choice) to reassemble the strips starting with the tallest strip, then the next tallest, etc. By continuing in this way, the profile of a new function, decreasing on $[0, \infty)$, will emerge; call this function the *decreasing rearrangement* of f. Because the strips are merely rearranged, the total area is the same before and after the rearrangement.

Note that the above procedure places points on $(-\infty, \infty)$ into a one-to-one correspondence with points on $[0, \infty)$; the original location of a strip is identified with its new location.

The essential feature of this construction is that whereas the sets $\{u : f(u) > y\}$ and $\{u : f_\downarrow(u) > y\}$ may be quite different, they have the same Lebesgue measure:

$$m(y) = \lambda\{u : f(u) > y\} = \lambda\{u : f_\downarrow(u) > y\}, \quad y > 0.$$

Moreover, the profile of $f_\downarrow$ as constructed above has the property that

$$f_\downarrow(m(y)) = y.$$

The function m is finite because f is assumed to be nonnegative and integrable. If f is defined on a bounded closed interval, say $[0, 1]$, then $m(y)$ cannot exceed the measure of the interval, whether or not f is nonnegative.

E.2. Definition. Let $m^{-1}(x) = \sup\{y : m(y) > x\}$ be the right-continuous inverse of the decreasing function m. The function $f_\downarrow$ defined by

$$f_\downarrow(x) = \begin{cases} 0, & x < 0, \\ m^{-1}(x), & x \geq 0 \end{cases}$$

is called the *decreasing rearrangement* of f.

E.3. Lemma. Let f be a nonnegative integrable function defined on $(-\infty, \infty)$ and let ϕ be a real-valued function defined on the range of f such that $\int_{-\infty}^{\infty} \phi(f(x))\, dx < \infty$. Then

$$\int_{-\infty}^{\infty} \phi(f(x))\, dx = \int_{-\infty}^{\infty} \phi(f_\downarrow(x))\, dx.$$

Proof. Let $B_{ni} = \{x : (i-1)/2^n \leq f(x) < i/2^n\}$, $i = 1, 2, \ldots$, and let

$$f_n^-(x) = \sum_1^\infty \frac{i-1}{2^n} I_{B_{ni}}(x), \qquad f_n^+(x) = \sum_1^\infty \frac{i}{2^n} I_{B_{ni}}(x),$$

where I_S is the characteristic (indicator) function of S. Note that f_n^- is increasing in n, f_n^+ is decreasing in n, and

$$\lim_{n\to\infty} f_n^-(x) = \lim_{n\to\infty} f_n^+(x) = f(x) \quad \text{almost everywhere.}$$

Let $A = \{u : \phi(u) \text{ is increasing at } u\}$, $A^* = \{x : f(x) \in A\}$, and let

$$f_n(x) = \begin{cases} f_n^-(x), & x \in A^*, \\ f_n^+(x), & x \notin A^*. \end{cases}$$

With this construction, the function $\phi(f_n(x))$ is increasing in n and $\lim_{n\to\infty} \phi(f_n(x)) = \phi(f(x))$ almost everywhere. It follows from the Lebesgue monotone convergence theorem that

$$\lim_{n\to\infty} \int_{-\infty}^{\infty} \phi(f_n(x))\, dx = \int_{-\infty}^{\infty} \phi(f(x))\, dx.$$

Now repeat the above construction with $f_\downarrow$ in place of f, and define $f_{\downarrow n}$ analogously to the definition of f_n. Because

$$\lambda\left\{x : \frac{i-1}{2^n} \leq f(x) < \frac{i}{2^n}\right\} = \lambda\left\{x : \frac{i-1}{2^n} \leq f_\downarrow(x) < \frac{i}{2^n}\right\}, \quad i = 1, 2, \ldots,$$

where λ is Lebesgue measure, it follows that

$$\int_{-\infty}^{\infty} \phi(f_n(x))\, dx = \int_{-\infty}^{\infty} \phi(f_{\downarrow n}(x))\, dx.$$

The proof is completed by taking limits. ∥

The following proposition is a modification of Theorem 1.D.2 of Hardy, Littlewood, and Pólya (1929). This modification allows the functions f and g to be defined on $(-\infty, \infty)$ rather than on the bounded interval $[0, 1]$, but it requires that f and g be nonnegative.

E.4. Proposition. Let f and g be nonnegative integrable functions defined on $(-\infty, \infty)$. Then

$$\int_{-\infty}^{\infty} \phi(f(x))\, dx \leq \int_{-\infty}^{\infty} \phi(g(x))\, dx \tag{1}$$

for all continuous convex functions such that the integrals exist if and only if

$$\int_0^x f_\downarrow(u)\, du \leq \int_0^x g_\downarrow(u)\, du, \quad x \geq 0, \tag{2}$$

and

$$\int_0^\infty f_\downarrow(u)\, du \leq \int_0^\infty g_\downarrow(u)\, du. \tag{3}$$

Proof. Because $\int_{-\infty}^{\infty} \phi(f(u))\, du = \int_0^\infty \phi(f_\downarrow(u))\, du$ (Lemma E.3), it is sufficient to prove the result with f and g replaced by $f_\downarrow$ and $g_\downarrow$.

Suppose first that (1) holds. Denote $\max(x, 0)$ by x^+ and note that $\phi(x) = x^+$ is convex. Because $g_\downarrow$ is decreasing, it follows that $g_\downarrow(u) \geq g_\downarrow(x)$, $u \leq x$. From (1) with $\phi(x) = x^+$, it follows that

$$\int_0^x [g_\downarrow(u) - g_\downarrow(x)]\, du = \int_0^x [g_\downarrow(u) - g_\downarrow(x)]^+ du$$
$$\geq \int_0^x [f_\downarrow(u) - g_\downarrow(x)]^+ du \geq \int_0^x [f_\downarrow(u) - g_\downarrow(x)]\, du. \tag{4}$$

But (4) is equivalent to (2). With the choices $\phi(x) = x$ and $\phi(x) = -x$, (1) yields (3).

Next suppose that (2) and (3) hold. Because all values of $f_\downarrow$ and $g_\downarrow$ fall between 0 and $g_\downarrow(0)$, it is sufficient to prove that (1) holds for all continuous convex functions defined on $[0, g_\downarrow(0)]$. As already noted, (2) is equivalent to (4), and (5) is a statement that (1) holds for all functions ϕ of the form $\phi(x) = (x - z)^+$, $0 \leq z \leq g_\downarrow(0)$. It follows from (3) that (1) holds when ϕ is linear.

It is well known that any continuous convex function defined on an interval J can be approximated from below by a sum of a linear function and a linear combination of a finite number of functions of the form $\phi(x) = (x-z)^+$, $x \in J$. The proof is completed by taking limits. ||

E.5. Proposition. Let X and Y be random variables with respective densities f and g. Then $X \geq_U Y$ (with λ Lebesgue measure) if and only if

$$\int_{-\infty}^{\infty} \phi(f(x))dx \leq \int_{-\infty}^{\infty} \phi(g(x))dx$$

for all continuous convex functions ϕ such that the integrals exist.

Proof. Let $f_\downarrow$ and $g_\downarrow$ be the decreasing rearrangements of f and g. Then $X \geq_U Y$ if and only if

$$\int_0^z f_\downarrow(x)\,dx = p = \int_0^w g_\downarrow(x)\,dx \iff w \leq z.$$

Because

$$\int_0^\infty f_\downarrow(x)\,dx = \int_0^\infty g_\downarrow(x)\,dx = 1,$$

the proposition follows from Proposition E.4. ||

E.6.a. Example. The function $\int_{-\infty}^{\infty} -f(x)\log f(x)\,dx$ is called the *entropy* of X (or f). Because $\phi(z) = -z \log z$ is concave, it follows from Proposition E.5 that if $X \geq_U Y$, then the entropy of X is greater than the entropy of Y. Note that entropy provides a measure of disorder or randomness.

E.6.b. Example. Let X_α have the density

$$f_\downarrow(x) = \begin{cases} \frac{1}{2}(\alpha+1)|x-1|^\alpha, & 0 \leq x \leq 2, \quad \alpha \geq 0, \\ 0, & \text{elsewhere.} \end{cases}$$

In the order $\geq_U$, X_α is decreasing in α and consequently the entropy of X_α is decreasing in α. But the variance of X_α is increasing in α.

E.7. Notation. Let ψ be an increasing right-continuous function defined on $\mathscr{R}$ and let ψ^{-1} be its right-continuous inverse. If

$$\psi^{-1}(v) - \psi^{-1}(u) \geq v - u \quad \text{for all} \quad u \leq v$$

and if $X = \psi^{-1}(Y)$, write $X \geq_T Y$. Here ψ^{-1} is a transformation that "stretches" the axis.

E.8. Proposition. If $X \geq_T Y$, then $X \geq_U Y$ (in the sense of Lebesgue measure).

Proof. Let $A = (u, v]$ be a finite interval in $\mathscr{A}(X;p)$, for which $P\{X \in A\} \geq p$. Also, $u < X \leq v$ if and only if $\psi(u) < Y \leq \psi(v)$. Thus, for all finite intervals in $\mathscr{A}(X;p)$, there exists an interval $(\psi(u), \psi(v)]$ in $\mathscr{A}(Y;p)$ such that $\lambda(u, v] \geq \lambda(\psi(u), \psi(v)]$.

To complete the proof, this must be extended to sets A that are not intervals. Note that $\lambda(\psi(u), \psi(v)] = \lambda_\psi(u, v]$, where λ_ψ is the Lebesgue–Stieltjes measure determined by ψ. Because $\lambda_\psi(I) \leq \lambda(I)$ for all half-open intervals I, the extension of these set functions retains this order. Thus, with $A^* = \{z : z = \psi(x), x \in A\}$, $\lambda(A) \geq \lambda(A^*)$. Consequently for every set $A \in \mathscr{A}(X;p)$, there exists a set $A^* \in \mathscr{A}(Y;p)$ such that $\lambda(A^*) \leq \lambda(A)$. ∥

E.9. Proposition. If $X \geq_T Y$ and the expectations of X and Y are finite, then

$$E\phi(X - EX) \geq E\phi(Y - EY) \tag{5}$$

for all continuous convex functions such that the expectations are finite.

Proof. First note that $X \geq_T Y$ implies $X \geq_T Y + c$ for all $c \in \mathscr{R}$. Consequently, no generality is lost by assuming $EX = EY = 0$.

Denote the distributions of X and Y by F and G, respectively. As a consequence of the fact that $X = \psi^{-1}(Y)$, $F(x) = G(\psi(x))$ and $F^{-1}(u) = \psi^{-1}(G^{-1}(u))$, $0 \leq u \leq 1$. Because $\psi^{-1}(v) - \psi^{-1}(u) \geq v - u$, it follows that $\psi^{-1}(z) - z$ is increasing in z. Thus

$$h(z) = \int_0^z [F^{-1}(1 - u) - G^{-1}(1 - u)]\, du$$

$$= \int_0^z [\psi^{-1}(G^{-1}(1-u)) - G^{-1}(1 - u)]\, du$$

is decreasing in z. Because $EX = EY$, it follows that $h(1) = 0$, and consequently $h(z) \geq 0$. This means that

$$\int_0^z F^{-1}(1-u)\, du \geq \int_0^z G^{-1}(1-u)\, du, \quad 0 \leq z \leq 1.$$

Observe that $E\phi(X) = \int_{-\infty}^\infty \phi(x)\, dF(x) = \int_0^1 \phi(F^{-1}(u))\, du$ and $E\phi(Y) = \int_0^1 \phi(G^{-1}(u))\, du$ to obtain (5) from either Theorem 1.D.2 or Proposition E.4. ∥

Note that according to Proposition E.9, $X \geq_T Y$ implies that the variance of X, var(X), is greater than or equal to the variance of Y, var(Y). This is in contrast to the order $\geq_U$; Example 6.b shows that it is possible for $X \geq_U Y$ but var(X) $\leq$ var(Y).

Uncertainty Parameters in Discrete Distributions

In this subsection, the notion of majorization for infinite sequences is utilized (see Section 1.D).

Let $p = (p_1, p_2, \ldots)$ and $q = (q_1, q_2, \ldots)$ be discrete probability vectors; i.e., $p_i, q_i \geq 0, i = 1, 2, \ldots$ and $\sum_1^\infty p_i = \sum_1^\infty q_i = 1$.

E.10. Definition. The probability vector p is said to be *more random* than q if $p \prec q$.

Cautionary note: In terms of randomness, the ordering of majorization is reversed from what might be natural. In fact, physicists often write "$\prec$" in place of "$\succ$," a source of possible confusion.

E.11. Proposition. Let X and Y be discrete random variables taking on values in the countable set $\Omega = \{\omega_1, \omega_2, \ldots\}$ such that

$$P\{X = \omega_i\} = p_i, \quad P\{Y = \omega_i\} = q_i, \quad i = 1, 2, \ldots.$$

Then $X \geq_U Y$ if and only if p is more random than q; that is, $p \prec q$.

Proof. Without loss of generality, assume that $p_1 \geq p_2 \geq \cdots$ and $q_1 \geq q_2 \geq \cdots$. In Definition E.1, replace the letter "p" by "r" to avoid dual use of "p," and suppose that $p \prec q$. By definition, $\mu(X; r) = k$ if $\sum_1^{k-1} p_i < r$ and $\sum_1^k p_i \geq r$. Because $r \leq \sum_1^k p_i \leq \sum_1^k q_i$, it follows that $\mu(Y; r) \leq k$. Thus $\mu(X; r) \geq \mu(Y; r)$ for all $r \in (0, 1)$; that is, $X \geq_U Y$.

Conversely, if $X \geq_U Y$, then $\mu(X; r) \geq \mu(Y; r)$ for all $r \in (0, 1)$. Let $r = \sum_1^k q_i$. For this choice of r, $\sum_1^k q_i = \mu(Y; r) \leq \mu(X; r)$; that is, $\sum_1^k p_i \leq r = \sum_1^k q_i$. ||

Note that Proposition E.11, when restricted so that only finitely many of the p_i and q_i are positive, is essentially a recasting of Proposition 4.D.1.

For a parametric family of discrete distributions, denote the density (probability mass function) by

$$p_\theta(x) = P\{X = x | \theta\}.$$

Write $p_\theta = (p_\theta(x_1), p_\theta(x_2), \ldots)$, where $x_1, x_2, \ldots$ are the possible values of X.

E.12. Definition (Hickey, 1983). Let $\{p_\theta : \theta \in \Theta \subset \mathscr{R}\}$ be a parametric family of discrete probability vectors. The parameter θ is called an *uncertainty parameter* if, when $\theta > \theta'$, p_θ majorizes $p_{\theta'}$ and $p_\theta, p_{\theta'}$ differ by more than a permutation of elements.

E.13. Example. For the geometric distribution on $1, 2, \ldots$,

$$p_\theta(x) = (1-\theta)^{x-1}\theta, \quad x = 1, 2, \ldots, \quad 0 < \theta \leq 1.$$

Set $p_\theta = (p_\theta(1), p_\theta(2), \ldots)$ and note that $p_\theta(i)$ is a decreasing function of i. Moreover,

$$\sum_1^k p_\theta(i) = 1 - (1-\theta)^k, \quad k = 1, 2, \ldots.$$

Because these partial sums are increasing in θ, $p_\theta \prec p_{\theta'}$, when $\theta < \theta'$. Thus, θ is an uncertainty parameter.

E.14. Example. For θ a positive integer, let

$$p_\theta(x) = \frac{1}{\theta + 1}, \quad x = 0, 1, \ldots, \theta.$$

Clearly, θ is an uncertainty parameter with uncertainty increasing in θ.

Remark. Examples E.13 and E.14 are easily verified using the partial sums definition of majorization because in both cases $p_\theta(x)$ is decreasing in x for all θ. In such cases, the concepts of more randomness and stochastic order coincide. In Section 12.N.4, examples are given in which $p_\theta(x)$ is not monotone, and the concepts of more randomness and stochastic order are distinct.

E.15. Example. Let $\theta \in (0, 1)$ and let

$$p_\theta(x) = \frac{\theta^x}{x\, a(\theta)},$$

where $a(\theta) = -\log(1-\theta)$. Then $p_\theta(x)$ is decreasing in x, and $q_k(\theta) = \Sigma_1^k p_\theta(x)$ is decreasing in θ, $k = 1, 2, \ldots$. Thus θ is an uncertainty parameter.

Proof. Because $\theta < 1$, the monotonicity in x of $p_\theta(x)$ is clear. To prove that $q_k(\theta)$ is decreasing, note that $p_\theta(x)$ is TP_∞ in θ and x (18.A.2 and 18.A.6.a). Let $I(x) = 1$ if $x \leq k$, and $I(x) = 0$ if $x > k$. Then $I(x) - c$ changes sign at most once, from $+$ to $-$ if there is a sign change. By the variation-diminishing property of totally positive functions (18.A.5), it follows that

$$q_k(\theta) - c = \sum_{x=1}^{\infty} [I(x) - c]\, p_\theta(x)$$

has at most one sign change, from $+$ to $-$ if one occurs. Because c is arbitrary, it follows that $q_k(\theta)$ is decreasing in θ.

The monotonicity of $q_k(\theta)$ can also be verified by showing that its derivative is negative. ||

18
Total Positivity

The theory of totally positive matrices and functions has its origins in work of Pólya (1913, 1915). Such matrices and functions were investigated by I. Schoenberg in a series of beautiful papers starting in 1930. Much early history of the subject can be found in later papers of Schoenberg (1951, 1953).

In more recent years, the theory of total positivity has found applications in a variety of fields. Important books devoted to the subject have been written by Gantmacher and Krein (1961) and by Karlin (1968). In addition, totally positive matrices are treated by Gantmacher (1959). A more recent collection of papers on the subject has been edited by Gasca and Micchelli (1996). A survey of the subject is offered by Barlow and Proschan (1975; reprinted 1996) and by Ando (1987). Interesting historical details not well known are given by Pinkus (1996).

A Totally Positive Functions

A.1. Definition. Let A and B be subsets of the real line. A function K defined on $A \times B$ is said to be *totally positive of order k*, denoted TP_k, if for all m, $1 \leq m \leq k$, and all $x_1 < \cdots < x_m$, $y_1 < \cdots < y_m$ ($x_i \in A$, $y_j \in B$),

$$K\begin{pmatrix} x_1, \ldots, x_m \\ y_1, \ldots, y_m \end{pmatrix} \equiv \det \begin{bmatrix} K(x_1, y_1) & \cdots & K(x_1, y_m) \\ \vdots & & \vdots \\ K(x_m, y_1) & \cdots & K(x_m, y_m) \end{bmatrix} \geq 0. \quad (1)$$

When the inequalities (1) are strict for $m = 1, \ldots, k$, K is called *strictly totally positive of order k* (STP_k).

If K is TP_k (STP_k) for $k = 1, 2, \ldots$, then K is said to be *totally positive (strictly totally positive) of order ∞*, written TP_∞ (STP_∞).

When A and B are finite sets, K can be regarded as a matrix and the same terminology applies.

There are several obvious consequences of the definition:

A.2. If a and b are nonnegative functions defined, respectively, on A and B and if K is TP_k, then $a(x)b(y)K(x,y)$ is TP_k.

A.3. If g and h are defined on A and B, respectively, and monotone in the same direction, and if K is TP_k on $g(A) \times h(B)$, then $K(g(x), h(y))$ is TP_k on $A \times B$.

The following fundamental identity is an indispensable tool in the study of total positivity, and is often called the *basic composition formula*:

A.4. Lemma (Andréief, 1883; Pólya and Szegö, 1972, p. 61, Problem 68). If σ is a σ-finite measure and the integral $M(x,y) \equiv \int K(x,z)L(z,y)\,d\sigma(z)$ converges absolutely, then

$$M\begin{pmatrix} x_1, \ldots, x_m \\ y_1, \ldots, y_m \end{pmatrix}$$
$$= \int \cdots \int_{z_1 < \cdots < z_m} K\begin{pmatrix} x_1, \ldots, x_m \\ z_1, \ldots, z_m \end{pmatrix} L\begin{pmatrix} z_1, \ldots, z_m \\ y_1, \ldots, y_m \end{pmatrix} d\sigma(z_1) \cdots d\sigma(z_m).$$

A proof of this result is outlined by Karlin (1968, p. 17).

A.4.a. Theorem. If K is TP_m, L is TP_n, and σ is a σ-finite measure, then the convolution

$$M(x,y) = \int K(x,z)L(z,y)\,d\sigma(z)$$

is $\text{TP}_{\min(m,n)}$.

The Variation Diminishing Property

The interest in totally positive functions is due in large part to their *variation-diminishing* property. If $f: B \to \mathscr{R}$, where $B \subset \mathscr{R}$, then the *number of sign changes* of f on B is the supremum of the numbers of sign changes in sequences of the form $f(x_1), \ldots, f(x_m)$, where m is finite, $x_1, \ldots, x_m \in B$, $x_1 < \cdots < x_m$, and zero values in the sequences are discarded.

A.5. Theorem. For $A, B \subset \mathscr{R}$, let $K: A \times B \to \mathscr{R}$ be Borel-measurable and TP_k. Let σ be a regular σ-finite measure on B, and let $f: B \to \mathscr{R}$ be a bounded measurable function such that the integral

$$g(x) = \int_B K(x, y) f(y) \, d\sigma(y)$$

converges absolutely. If f changes sign at most $j \leq k-1$ times on B, then g changes sign at most j times on A. Moreover, if g changes sign j times, then it must have the same arrangement of signs as does f.

The above theorem was put in its present form by Karlin, following earlier work of Schoenberg, Motzkin, and Gantmacher and Krein. For this history, see Karlin (1968, pp. 21 and 22; for a more general result, see p. 233).

With the aid of A.2, A.3, and A.4a, many examples of totally positive functions are obtainable from a few relatively basic examples.

A.6. Example. The function

$$K(x, y) = e^{xy}, \quad -\infty < x, y < \infty, \quad \text{is } \text{STP}_\infty. \tag{2}$$

In this case, the positivity of the relevant determinants is well known because they are generalized Vandermonde determinants [see, e.g., Pólya and Szegö (1976, Problem 76, p. 46)].

A.6.a. The function

$$K(x, y) = x^y, \quad 0 < x < \infty, \quad -\infty < y < \infty, \quad \text{is } \text{STP}_\infty. \tag{3}$$

For $0 \leq x < \infty$ and $-\infty < y < \infty$, K is TP_∞. Here e^x of A.6 has been replaced by x.

A.6.b. The function

$$K(x, y) = e^{-(x-y)^2}, \quad -\infty < x, y < \infty, \quad \text{is } \text{STP}_\infty. \tag{4}$$

The result follows from A.6 and A.2 because $e^{-(x-y)^2} = e^{-x^2 - y^2} \cdot e^{2xy}$.

A.7. Example. The function
$$K(x,y) = \begin{cases} 1 & \text{if } x \leq y, \\ 0 & \text{if } x > y, \end{cases} \quad -\infty < x, y < \infty, \qquad \text{is TP}_\infty. \qquad (5)$$

A.7.a. The function
$$K(x,y) = \begin{cases} 0 & \text{if } x < y, \\ 1 & \text{if } x \geq y, \end{cases} \quad -\infty < x, y < \infty, \qquad \text{is TP}_\infty. \qquad (6)$$

The fact that (5) and (6) define TP_∞ functions is easily verified directly. Of course, these functions are not strictly totally positive of any order.

A.8. Example. The function
$$K(x,y) = \frac{1}{x+y}, \qquad 0 < x, y < \infty, \qquad (7)$$
is STP_∞.

To verify this, it is sufficient to note that if $C = (c_{ij})$, where $c_{ij} = 1/(x_i + y_j)$, then
$$\det C = \prod_{i<j}(x_i - x_j)(y_i - y_j) \bigg/ \prod_{i,j}(x_i + y_j)$$
[see, e.g., Noble (1969, p. 223), where this result is given as an exercise; see also Karlin (1968, p. 149) and Bernstein (2005, p. 119)]. The evaluation of $\det C$ is due to Cauchy, so C is sometimes called *Cauchy's matrix*. When $x_i = i$, $y_j = j + \gamma$, where $\gamma > 0$ is a constant, C is also called *Hilbert's matrix*.

A.9. Example. The functions
$$K_1(x,y) = \binom{x}{y}, \quad K_2(x,y) = \binom{x+y-1}{y}, \qquad x, y = 0, 1, \ldots, \qquad (8)$$
are TP_∞. These results can be found in Karlin (1968, p. 137).

The class of log concave functions occurs in many contexts, and the following is a fundamental result.

A.10. Example: Log concave functions (Schoenberg, 1951). The function
$$K(x,y) = f(y-x), \qquad -\infty < x, y < \infty,$$
is TP_2 if and only if f is nonnegative and $\log f$ is concave on $\mathscr{R}$.

A. Totally Positive Functions

Here the required positivity of relevant 2×2 determinants is essentially the definition of log concavity, so a direct verification is not difficult.

A.10.a. A positive function f is *log convex* on $\mathscr{R}$ if and only if

$$\Lambda = \begin{bmatrix} f(x_1 + y_1) & f(x_1 + y_2) \\ f(x_2 + y_1) & f(x_2 + y_2) \end{bmatrix} \qquad (9)$$

has a nonnegative determinant for all $x_1 \leq x_2$, $y_1 \leq y_2$.

A positive function is *log convex in the sense of Jensen*, i.e.,

$$\log f\left(\frac{x+y}{2}\right) \leq \frac{1}{2}\log f(x) + \frac{1}{2}\log f(y),$$

if and only if $\det \Lambda \geq 0$ holds under the additional restriction that $x_1 + y_2 = x_2 + y_1$. In this case Λ is symmetric and the condition that f is log convex in the sense of Jensen reduces to the condition that Λ is positive definite. This is sometimes useful because convexity in the sense of Jensen together with continuity implies convexity. See 16.C.

Statistical Examples

A.11. Example: Exponential families. A family of probability density functions that have the form

$$f(x, \theta) = a(x)b(\theta)e^{x\theta}, \qquad \theta \in B \subset \mathscr{R},$$

is called an *exponential family*. From A.6, it follows that such densities are TP_∞ in x and θ. Particular examples (with appropriate parameterization) include (i) normal distributions with mean θ and variance 1, (ii) exponential distributions with mean $-1/\theta$, $\theta < 0$, (iii) binomial distributions, and (iv) Poisson distributions [see, e.g., Karlin (1968, p. 19)].

A.12. Example: Noncentral distributions. A number of families of probability density functions have total positivity properties by virtue of representations of the form

$$f(x, \theta) = \int g(x, t) h(t, \theta) \, d\sigma(t),$$

where g and h are totally positive of some order. To verify the following special cases, use is made of A.2, A.3, and A.6, and the density (with respect to counting measure on $\{0, 1, 2, \ldots\}$) given by

$$h(j, \theta) = e^{-\theta}\theta^j/j!.$$

A.12.a. Noncentral χ^2 distribution with noncentrality parameter θ:
$$f(x,\theta) = \sum_{j=0}^{\infty} e^{-\theta} \frac{\theta^j}{j!} \frac{x^{[(n+2j)/2]-1} e^{-x/2}}{\Gamma((n+2j)/2) 2^{(n+2j)/2}}, \qquad x \geq 0.$$

A.12.b. Noncentral F distribution with n, m degrees of freedom and noncentrality parameter θ:
$$f(x,\theta) = \sum_{j=0}^{\infty} e^{-\theta} \frac{\theta^j}{j!} \left(\frac{x}{1+x}\right)^{(n+2j)/2} \left[x(1+x)^{m/2} B\left(\frac{n+2j}{2}, \frac{m}{2}\right)\right]^{-1},$$

where $x \geq 0$ and B is the beta function.

A.12.c. Squared multiple correlation based on k "independent" variables:
$$f(r^2, \rho^2)$$
$$= \sum_{j=0}^{\infty} a(j) \rho^{2j} (1-\rho^2)^{(n-1)/2} (r^2)^{(k/2)+j-1} (1-r^2)^{[(n-k-1)/2]-1},$$

where $r^2 > 0$ and
$$a(j) = \frac{\Gamma((n-1+2j)/2)}{j! \Gamma((n-1)/2)} \left[B\left(\frac{k}{2}+j, \frac{n-k-1}{2}\right)\right]^{-1}.$$

A.12.d. Noncentral t distribution:
$$f(x,\theta) = c \int_0^{\infty} \exp\left[-\frac{1}{2}\left(x\sqrt{\frac{t}{(2\alpha)^{1/2}}} - \theta\right)^2\right] t^{\alpha-1} e^{-t/2} \, dt,$$

where $-\infty < x, \theta < \infty$, c is a normalizing constant, and $\alpha > 0$ is fixed.

The total positivity in this case is apparently more difficult to verify than the preceding examples, but see Karlin (1968, p. 118).

B Pólya Frequency Functions

An important class of totally positive functions is those which have the form
$$K(x,y) = L(y-x), \qquad -\infty < x, y < \infty. \tag{1}$$

Examples include A.6.b, A.7, A.7.a, and A.10. If such a function K is TP$_k$ for some $k \geq 2$, then it follows from A.10 that L is either monotone or unimodal. In case L is unimodal, then Schoenberg (1951) showed that $\int_{-\infty}^{\infty} L(z)\,dz < \infty$, and he called such a function a *Pólya frequency function of order k* (PF_k). This term has come to be used even when L is monotone.

B.1. Proposition. If f and g are PF_k, then the convolution

$$h(x) = \int_{-\infty}^{\infty} g(x-y)f(y)\,dy$$

is PF_k.

This proposition is a special case of A.4.a.

From Example A.10 and Proposition B.1, it follows that the convolution of log concave functions is log concave.

A more general result, obtained by Davidovič, Korenbljum, and Hacet (1969), is that if $x, y \in \mathscr{R}^n$, and f, g are log concave, then

$$\phi(x) = \int_{\mathscr{R}^n} f(x-y)g(y)\,dy$$

is log concave.

B.1.a. If the probability density function f is PF_k, then the corresponding distribution function F and survival function $\overline{F} = 1 - F$ are PF_k.

Proof. This follows from B.1 by successively taking $g(x-y) = K(x,y)$ as defined in A.7 and A.7.a. ∥

B.2. The following conditions are equivalent:

  (i) the hazard rate $r(x) = f(x)/\overline{F}(x)$ is increasing in x on $\{x : F(x) < 1\}$;

  (ii) $\overline{F} = 1 - F$ is PF_2;

  (iii) $\log \overline{F}$ is concave.

Proof. That (ii) and (iii) are equivalent follows from A.10. Since $r(x) = -(d/dx)\log \overline{F}(x)$, it follows that (i) and (iii) are equivalent. ∥

In a similar way, a companion result can be proved:

B.2.a. If $F(x) = 0$ for all $x < 0$, the following conditions are equivalent:

  (i) $r(x)$ is decreasing in $x > 0$;

(ii) $\overline{F}(x+y)$ is TP$_2$ in x and y, $x+y \geq 0$;

(iii) $\log \overline{F}$ is convex on $(0, \infty)$.

Distributions with increasing or decreasing hazard rate have been extensively studied in the context of reliability theory [see, e.g., Barlow and Proschan (1975; reprinted 1996)]. The usual examples are obtained with the aid of the following theorem.

B.2.b. If f is a logarithmically concave probability density, then the distribution function F has an increasing hazard rate; if $\log f$ is convex on $(0, \infty)$, then F has a decreasing hazard rate.

Proof. The first part of this result is a consequence of A.10, B.1.a with $k = 2$, and B.2. The second part can be proved similarly. ||

B.2.c. Examples of logarithmically concave or convex densities. A logarithmically concave (convex) density can be written in the form

$$f(x) = e^{-\phi(x)},$$

where ϕ is convex (concave). This observation is useful for verifying the indicated properties of the following examples.

(i) *Normal density:*

$$f(x) = \frac{1}{\sqrt{2\pi}\sigma} e^{-(x-\mu)^2/2\sigma^2}, \quad -\infty < x < \infty, \quad -\infty < \mu < \infty, \quad \sigma^2 > 0.$$

This density is logarithmically concave, and hence has an increasing hazard rate.

(ii) *Gamma density:* For $\lambda, r > 0$,

$$f(x) = \begin{cases} \dfrac{\lambda^r x^{r-1}}{\Gamma(r)} e^{-\lambda x}, & x \geq 0, \\ 0, & x < 0. \end{cases}$$

This density is logarithmically concave on $(-\infty, \infty)$ if $r \geq 1$ and logarithmically convex on $[0, \infty)$ if $0 < r \leq 1$.

(iii) *Beta density:* For $a, b > 0$,

$$f(x) = \begin{cases} [B(a,b)]^{-1} x^{a-1}(1-x)^{b-1}, & 0 \leq x \leq 1, \\ 0 & \text{elsewhere,} \end{cases}$$

where B is the beta function. This density is logarithmically concave if $a \geq 1$ and $b \geq 1$. In particular, the uniform density ($a = b = 1$) is logarithmically concave.

(iv) *Weibull density:* For $\lambda, \alpha > 0$,

$$f(x) = \begin{cases} \lambda \alpha x^{\alpha-1} e^{-\lambda x}, & x \geq 0, \\ 0, & x < 0. \end{cases}$$

This density is logarithmically concave on $[0, \infty)$ if $\alpha \geq 1$ and logarithmically convex on $[0, \infty)$ if $\alpha \leq 1$.

(v) *Gompertz density:* For $\lambda, \xi > 0$,

$$f(x) = \begin{cases} \lambda \xi \exp\{\lambda x + \xi - \xi e^{\lambda x}\}, & x \geq 0, \\ 0, & x < 0. \end{cases}$$

This density is logarithmically concave on $[0, \infty)$.

Other examples of logarithmically concave densities are contained in Marshall and Olkin (2007).

Inequalities for Normalized Moments

Suppose f is a probability density with distribution F such that $F(0) = 0$. Let $\mu_r = \int_0^\infty x^r \, dF(x)$ and let $\lambda_r = \mu_r / \Gamma(r+1)$. Several logarithmic convexity and concavity results for λ_r are summarized in 3.E.4. These results are proved here.

B.3. If $f(x) = 0$ for $x < 0$ and $\log f$ is concave (convex) on $[0, \infty)$, then $\log \lambda_r$ is concave (convex) in $r \geq 0$.

Proof. Suppose that $\log f$ is concave on $[0, \infty)$. If $0 \leq \alpha \leq 1$, $\overline{\alpha} = 1 - \alpha$, $s + \alpha > 0$, and $t + \overline{\alpha} > 0$, then

$$\lambda_{s+t-1} = \int_0^\infty \frac{z^{s+t-1}}{\Gamma(s+t)} f(z) \, dz$$

$$= \int_0^\infty \int_0^z \frac{(z-x)^{s+\alpha-1}}{\Gamma(s+\alpha)} \frac{x^{t+\overline{\alpha}-1}}{\Gamma(t+\overline{\alpha})} \, dx \, f(z) \, dz$$

$$= \int_0^\infty \frac{y^{s+\alpha-1}}{\Gamma(s+\alpha)} \int_0^\infty \frac{x^{t+\overline{\alpha}-1}}{\Gamma(t+\overline{\alpha})} f(x+y) \, dx \, dy.$$

Because $f(x+y)$ is TP$_2$ in x and $-y$, and since x^t is TP$_\infty$ (by A.6.a), it follows from A.4.a that the inner integral is TP$_2$ in t and $-y$. Again by A.6.a, y^s is TP$_\infty$ in $-s$ and $-y$, so it follows from A.4.a that λ_{s+t-1} is TP$_2$ in $-s$ and t for $s+\alpha > 0$ and $t+\overline{\alpha} > 0$; i.e., $s+t > -1$. Thus $\log \lambda_r$ is concave in $r > 0$, so it is concave in $r \geq 0$ by continuity.

If $\log f$ is convex, the proof is similar. ||

The above result is essentially due to Karlin, Proschan, and Barlow (1961).

B.4. If $F(0) = 0$ and $\log(1 - F)$ is concave (convex) on $[0, \infty)$, then $\log \lambda_r$ is concave (convex) in $r \geq 1$.

Proof. It follows from an integration by parts that

$$\int_0^\infty \frac{z^{r+1}}{\Gamma(r+2)} dF(z) = \int_0^\infty \frac{z^r}{\Gamma(r+1)}[1 - F(z)] dz.$$

Thus the proof is essentially the same as the proof of B.3, but with $1 - F$ in place of f. ||

The above result was obtained by Barlow, Marshall, and Proschan (1963).

B.5. Definition. A probability density f on $[0, \infty)$ is *completely monotone* if it has the form

$$f(z) = \int_0^\infty \frac{1}{\mu} e^{-z/\mu} dH(\mu), \qquad z \geq 0, \tag{2}$$

for some distribution function H.

By virtue of 16.B.8, completely monotone densities are logarithmically convex. Thus by B.3, their normalized moments are logarithmically convex on $[0, \infty)$. A slightly stronger result is obtainable.

B.6. If f is a probability density function such that $f(x) = 0$, $x < 0$, and f is completely monotone on $[0, \infty)$, it follows that for $r > -1$, λ_r is logarithmically convex.

Proof.

$$\lambda_r = \int_0^\infty \frac{z^r}{\Gamma(r+1)} f(z) dz$$

$$= \int_0^\infty \frac{\mu^r}{\Gamma(r+1)} \left[\int_0^\infty \left(\frac{z}{\mu}\right)^r e^{-z/\mu} d\left(\frac{z}{\mu}\right) \right] dH(\mu) = \int_0^\infty \mu^r dH(\mu).$$

But this is logarithmically convex by 16.D.1.d. ||

The Lyapunov inequality is also based on logarithmic convexity and concavity; see 3.E.2 and 16.D.1.d.

For further discussion of completely monotone functions, see Feller (1971, p. 439).

C Pólya Frequency Sequences

If $K(x,y) = f(y-x)$ where x and y are integers, and if for some $k \geq 2$, K is TP_k (with A and B of Definition A.1 taken to consist of the integers), then

$$\ldots, f(-1), f(0), f(1), \ldots$$

is called a *Pólya frequency sequence* of order k. Alternatively, f is said to be PF_k *on the integers*.

Of course, the convolution theorem A.4.a applies to Pólya frequency sequences, as do other results of Section A. In a manner similar to A.10, f is PF_2 on the integers if and only if $f \geq 0$ and $\log f$ is concave in the sense of 16.B.10.

Examples of Pólya frequency sequences are provided by certain discrete probability mass functions. For example, Poisson probability mass functions yield PF_∞ sequences (see A.9), and binomial probability mass functions yield PF_2 sequences. In addition, convolutions of Bernoulli probability mass functions with possibly different parameters yield PF_2 sequences, as can be seen using A.4.a.

D Total Positivity of Matrices

In the Definition A.1, let the sets A and B be $\{1, \ldots, n\}$; then a matrix $X = (x_{ij})$ can be regarded as a function defined on $\{1, \ldots, n\}^2$. This function (matrix) is TP_k (STP_k) if the mth compound $X^{(m)}$ has nonnegative (positive) elements for $m = 1, \ldots, k$.

D.1. Proposition (Salinelli and Sgarra, 2006). If R is an STP_2 correlation matrix, then

(i) $\rho_{ij} < \rho_{sj}$, $1 \leq j < s < i \leq n$,

(ii) $\rho_{sj} < \rho_{ij}$, $1 \leq s < i < j \leq n$.

Condition (i) means that the subdiagonal column elements are strictly decreasing, and condition (ii) means that the superdiagonal column elements are strictly increasing.

D.1.a. Examples. The matrices $R = (\rho_{ij})$ with
  (i) $\rho_{ij} = \exp\{-\beta|\tau_i - \tau_j|\}$, $\quad \beta > 0$, $\quad \tau_1 < \cdots < \tau_n$,
  (ii) $\rho_{ij} = \exp\{-\beta|i - j|^q\}$, $\quad \beta > 0$, $\quad q \geq 1$,
satisfy D.1.

19
Matrix Factorizations, Compounds, Direct Products, and M-Matrices

It is often convenient to represent a matrix in terms of other matrices that have special properties. Of the many such known representations, a few are listed here that relate to the development of this book. General references for some of the material are Bellman (1960), Householder (1964), and Mirsky (1955a). An exposition of exponential and polar representations of matrices is given by de Bruijn and Szekeres (1955). For a compendium on matrix factorizations, see Bernstein (2005, Chapter 5).

The eigenvalues of an $n \times n$ matrix A are denoted by $\lambda_1(A), \ldots, \lambda_n(A)$. When the eigenvalues are real, they are ordered $\lambda_1(A) \geq \cdots \geq \lambda_n(A)$.

A Eigenvalue Decompositions

In this section, some representations in terms of triangular and diagonal matrices are given for $n \times n$ complex matrices.

A.1. Definition. When two $n \times n$ complex matrices A and B satisfy the relation $S^{-1}AS = B$ for some nonsingular complex matrix S, then A and B are said to be *similar*. If the matrix S is unitary, then A and B are said to be *unitarily similar*.

Of particular interest is the case when B is a diagonal or triangular matrix, for then the eigenvalues of A are equal to the diagonal elements of B.

When the eigenvalues of A are distinct, then A is similar to a diagonal matrix, but not in general. However, it is similar, and in fact, unitarily similar, to a triangular matrix.

A.2. Theorem. If A is an $n \times n$ complex matrix with distinct eigenvalues, then there exists a nonsingular complex matrix S such that

$$A = S^{-1} D_\alpha S, \qquad (1)$$

where $D_\alpha = \operatorname{diag}(\alpha_1, \ldots, \alpha_n), \alpha_i = \lambda_i(A), i = 1, \ldots, n$.

If $|\alpha_1| > \cdots > |\alpha_n|$, the representation is unique up to a scale factor. That is, if $A = S^{-1} D_\alpha S = U^{-1} D_\alpha U$, then $U = SD_c$, where $D_c = \operatorname{diag}(c_1, \ldots, c_n)$.

A.3. Theorem (Schur, 1909). If A is an $n \times n$ complex matrix, then there exists a unitary matrix Γ such that

$$A = \Gamma T \Gamma^*, \qquad (2)$$

where T is lower triangular (i.e., $t_{ij} = 0, i < j$), and where $t_{ii} = \lambda_i(A), i = 1, \ldots, n$.

If the eigenvalues of A are distinct and there are two representations of the form (2), say, $A = \Gamma_1 T_1 \Gamma_1^* = \Gamma_2 T_2 \Gamma_2^*$, with Γ_1, Γ_2 $n \times n$ unitary matrices, T_1 and T_2 lower triangular, then $T_2 = D_\epsilon T_1 D_\epsilon$ and $\Gamma_2 = \Gamma_1 D_\epsilon$, where $D_\epsilon = \operatorname{diag}(\epsilon_1, \ldots, \epsilon_n), \epsilon_i = \pm 1, i = 1, \ldots, n$.

A representation analogous to (2) for upper triangular matrices follows from A.3 by applying the theorem to A^*.

A.3.a. Theorem. Let A be a real $n \times n$ matrix. Then there exists a real orthogonal matrix Γ such that $A = \Gamma T \Gamma'$, where T is lower triangular and $t_{ii} = \lambda_i(A), i = 1, \ldots, n$, if and only if the eigenvalues of A are real.

If A is Hermitian, that is, $A = A^*$, it follows from A.3 that $\Gamma T \Gamma^* = \Gamma T^* \Gamma^*$, where Γ is unitary and T is lower triangular. Consequently, $T = T^*$, which implies that T is diagonal and that the diagonal elements $\lambda_1(A), \ldots, \lambda_n(A)$ are real.

A.3.b. If S is a real $n \times n$ symmetric matrix, then there exists a real orthogonal matrix Γ such that

$$S = \Gamma D_\alpha \Gamma',$$

where $D_\alpha = \mathrm{diag}(\alpha_1, \ldots, \alpha_n)$ and $\alpha_1 \geq \cdots \geq \alpha_n$ are the ordered eigenvalues of S.

This follows from A.3.a since $S = \Gamma T\Gamma' = \Gamma T'\Gamma'$, where T is lower triangular, implies that T is diagonal. The ordering of the eigenvalues is achieved by a permutation matrix.

A.4. Theorem. If H is an $n \times n$ Hermitian matrix, then there exists a unitary matrix Γ such that

$$H = \Gamma D_\alpha \Gamma^*, \tag{3}$$

where $D_\alpha = \mathrm{diag}(\alpha_1, \ldots, \alpha_n)$ and $\alpha_1, \ldots, \alpha_n$ are the real eigenvalues of H ordered $\alpha_1 \geq \cdots \geq \alpha_n$.

If the eigenvalues are distinct and there are two representations

$$H = \Gamma_1 D_\alpha \Gamma_1^* = \Gamma_2 D_\alpha \Gamma_2^*,$$

where Γ_1, Γ_2 are unitary, then $\Gamma_2 = \Gamma_1 D_\epsilon$, where $D_\epsilon = \mathrm{diag}(\epsilon_1, \ldots, \epsilon_n)$ and $\epsilon_i = \pm 1, i = 1, \ldots, n$.

B Singular Value Decomposition

The *singular values* $\sigma_1(A), \ldots, \sigma_m(A)$ of an $m \times n$ complex matrix, A, are defined as $\sigma_i(A) = [\lambda_i(AA^*)]^{1/2}, i = 1, \ldots, m$. Note that AA^* is Hermitian and positive semidefinite so that its eigenvalues are real and nonnegative.

The decomposition in B.1 below has had a long history. Special cases were obtained by Beltrami (1873) and by Jordan (1874). The case for square matrices with real elements was obtained by Sylvester (1889), and for complex square matrices by Autonne (1915) and Browne (1930b). The rectangular case B.1.a for complex matrices is due to Eckart and Young (1936, 1939).

B.1. Theorem. If A is an $n \times n$ complex matrix, then there exist unitary matrices Γ and Δ such that

$$A = \Gamma D_\sigma \Delta, \tag{1}$$

where $D_\sigma = \mathrm{diag}(\sigma_1, \ldots, \sigma_n)$ and $\sigma_1 \geq \cdots \geq \sigma_n \geq 0$ are the singular values of A.

If there are two representations $A = \Gamma_1 D_\sigma \Delta_1 = \Gamma_2 D_\sigma \Delta_2$, where $\Gamma_1, \Gamma_2, \Delta_1, \Delta_2$ are unitary, and if $\sigma_1 > \cdots > \sigma_n > 0$, then $\Gamma_2 = \Gamma_1 D_\epsilon$, $\Delta_2 = D_\epsilon \Delta_1$, where $D_\epsilon = \mathrm{diag}(\epsilon_1, \ldots, \epsilon_n)$, $\epsilon_i = \pm 1, i = 1, \ldots, n$.

The singular value decomposition can be stated for rectangular matrices by applying (1) to

$$\begin{bmatrix} B \\ 0 \end{bmatrix} = \Gamma \begin{bmatrix} D_\sigma & 0 \\ 0 & 0 \end{bmatrix} \Delta$$

$$\equiv \begin{bmatrix} \Gamma_{11} & \Gamma_{12} \\ \Gamma_{21} & \Gamma_{22} \end{bmatrix} \begin{bmatrix} D_\sigma & 0 \\ 0 & 0 \end{bmatrix} \begin{bmatrix} \Delta_{11} & \Delta_{12} \\ \Delta_{21} & \Delta_{22} \end{bmatrix} = \begin{bmatrix} \Gamma_{11} D_\sigma(\Delta_{11}, \Delta_{12}) \\ \Gamma_{21} D_\sigma(\Delta_{11}, \Delta_{12}) \end{bmatrix}, \quad (2)$$

where B is an $m \times n, m \leq n$, complex matrix. In (2) the n singular values of $\binom{B}{0}$ consist of the m singular values of B and $(n-m)$ zeros. From (2),

$$\begin{bmatrix} BB^* & 0 \\ 0 & 0 \end{bmatrix} = \begin{bmatrix} \Gamma_{11} & \Gamma_{12} \\ \Gamma_{21} & \Gamma_{22} \end{bmatrix} \begin{bmatrix} D_\sigma^2 & 0 \\ 0 & 0 \end{bmatrix} \begin{bmatrix} \Gamma_{11}^* & \Gamma_{21}^* \\ \Gamma_{12}^* & \Gamma_{22}^* \end{bmatrix}. \quad (3)$$

Assume that BB^* is positive definite. Then $\Gamma\Gamma^* = \Gamma^*\Gamma = I$, and (3) implies that $\Gamma_{21} = 0$, and hence that $\Gamma_{12} = 0$. This argument yields the following theorem.

B.1.a. Theorem. If B is an $m \times n$ complex matrix, $m \leq n$, then there exist an $m \times n$ complex matrix Ψ, with $\Psi\Psi^* = I_m$, and an $n \times n$ unitary matrix Δ such that

$$B = \Psi(D_\sigma, 0)\Delta,$$

where $D_\sigma = \text{diag}(\sigma_1, \ldots, \sigma_m)$ and $\sigma_1, \ldots, \sigma_m$ are the singular values of B.

If B is an $m \times n$ complex matrix with $m \geq n$, then an application of B.1.a to B^* yields a parallel representation.

C Square Roots and the Polar Decomposition

If H is an $n \times n$ Hermitian matrix, then the square roots of H are defined according to the first paragraph of 16.E as

$$H^{1/2} = \Gamma D_\alpha^{1/2} \Gamma^*,$$

where $H = \Gamma D_\alpha \Gamma^*$ is a representation of A.4. If any eigenvalue of H is negative, some square roots $H^{1/2}$ are not Hermitian, but when H is positive semidefinite, any matrix of the form $B = \Gamma \,\text{diag}(\epsilon_1 \alpha_1^{1/2}, \ldots, \epsilon_n \alpha_n^{1/2})\Gamma^*$, where $\epsilon_i = \pm 1, i = 1, \ldots, n$, is a Hermitian square root of H in the sense that $B^2 = H$. However, the positive semidefinite square root of H is unique.

Indeed, if H is an $n \times n$ positive semidefinite Hermitian matrix, and m is any positive integer, there is a unique positive semidefinite

Hermitian matrix $\widetilde{H}$ such that $\widetilde{H}^m = H$. This result is due to Autonne (1902, 1903). Asymmetric square roots can also be defined:

C.1. Definition. If H is a positive semidefinite $n \times n$ Hermitian matrix, then any $n \times m$ matrix X satisfying

$$H = XX^*$$

is called an *asymmetric square root* of H.

If X is an asymmetric square root of H, then for any $m \times m$ unitary matrix Δ, $X\Delta$ is also a square root. Two classes of square roots of interest are the positive semidefinite Hermitian and triangular square roots. These can be obtained from the following representations.

C.2. Theorem (Schmidt, 1907). If X is an $m \times n$ complex matrix, $m \leq n$, then there exists an $m \times m$ upper triangular matrix U with $u_{ii} \geq 0, i = 1, \ldots, m$, and an $m \times m$ lower triangular matrix L with $l_{ii} \geq 0, i = 1, \ldots, m$, such that

(i) $X = L\Gamma_1 = (L \quad 0)\Gamma = L(I \quad 0)\Gamma$,

(ii) $X = U\Delta_1 = (U \quad 0)\Delta = U(I \quad 0)\Delta$,

where

$$\Gamma = \begin{pmatrix} \Gamma_1 \\ \Gamma_2 \end{pmatrix} \text{ and } \Delta = \begin{pmatrix} \Delta_1 \\ \Delta_2 \end{pmatrix}$$

are $n \times n$ unitary matrices, and Γ_1 and Δ_1 are $m \times n$ complex matrices satisfying $\Gamma_1\Gamma_1^* = \Delta_1\Delta_1^* = I_m$.

If X is of rank m, then there exists a representation with $l_{ii} > 0, u_{ii} > 0, i = 1, \ldots, m$, and the matrices L, Γ_1, U, and Δ_1 are unique. Notice that $L\Gamma_1 = (LD_\epsilon)(D_\epsilon\Gamma_1)$, where $D_\epsilon = \text{diag}(\epsilon_1, \ldots, \epsilon_n)$, $\epsilon_i = \pm 1, i = 1, \ldots, n$. Consequently, it is possible to assign arbitrary signs to the diagonal elements of L. A similar discussion holds for the diagonal elements of U in (ii).

C.3. Polar decomposition theorem (Autonne, 1902, 1913; Browne, 1928; Wintner and Murnaghan, 1931; von Neumann, 1932). If X is an $m \times n$ complex matrix, $m \leq n$, then there exists a positive semidefinite $m \times n$ Hermitian matrix G such that

$$X = G\Psi,$$

where Ψ is an $m \times n$ complex matrix satisfying $\Psi\Psi^* = I_m$.

The matrix G is the positive semidefinite Hermitian square root of XX^*. When X is $n \times n$ and nonsingular, then Ψ is unique.

Theorem C.3 can be stated equivalently as a representation for a positive semidefinite Hermitian matrix. This equivalence is stated more precisely in D.1 ahead.

C.4. Theorem (Toeplitz, 1907). If H is a positive semidefinite $n \times n$ Hermitian matrix, then there exist a lower triangular matrix L with nonnegative diagonal elements and an upper triangular matrix U with nonnegative diagonal elements, such that

$$H = LL^* = UU^*.$$

If H is positive definite, then $l_{ii} > 0, u_{ii} > 0, i = 1, \ldots, n$, and the matrices L and U are unique.

D A Duality Between Positive Semidefinite Hermitian Matrices and Complex Matrices

The following result shows how some representations for positive semidefinite Hermitian matrices can be obtained from representations for arbitrary complex matrices, and vice versa.

D.1. Theorem (Parker, 1945; Vinograde, 1950). If A is a complex $p \times m$ matrix and B is a complex $p \times n$ matrix, $m \leq n$, then $AA^* = BB^*$ if and only if $B = A\Omega$, where Ω is an $m \times n$ complex matrix satisfying $\Omega\Omega^* = I_m$.

To illustrate the duality between positive semidefinite Hermitian matrices and complex matrices, suppose that X is a complex $n \times r$ matrix, $n \leq r$. Then $XX^* \equiv H$ is a positive semidefinite Hermitian matrix. From A.3.b, there exists a unitary matrix Γ and a nonnegative diagonal matrix D_θ such that

$$XX^* = H = \Gamma D_\theta \Gamma^* = (\Gamma D_\theta^{1/2})(D_\theta^{1/2}\Gamma^*). \tag{1}$$

Applying D.1 to (1) yields the singular value decomposition B.1:

$$X = \Gamma D_\sigma^{1/2}\Delta_1 = \Gamma(D_\sigma^{1/2}\ 0)\Delta,$$

where $\Delta = \binom{\Delta_1}{\Delta_2}$ is an $r \times r$ unitary matrix, and Δ_1 is $n \times r$. The diagonal elements $\theta_i^{1/2} = [\lambda_i(XX^*)]^{1/2} \equiv \sigma_i(X), i = 1, \ldots, n$, are the singular values of X.

There is a parallel duality between C.2 and C.4 which is also a consequence of D.1. Further details relating to D.1 are given by Horn and Olkin (1996).

E Simultaneous Reduction of Two Hermitian Matrices

In general, two Hermitian matrices V and W cannot be simultaneously diagonalized by a unitary matrix. However, if V and W are positive definite Hermitian matrices, then a simultaneous reduction is possible, though not necessarily by a unitary matrix.

E.1. Theorem. If V and W are $n \times n$ positive definite Hermitian matrices, then there exists a nonsingular $n \times n$ matrix M such that
$$V = MM^*, \qquad W = MD_\theta M^*,$$
where $D_\theta = \mathrm{diag}(\theta_1, \ldots, \theta_n)$, in which $\theta_1 \geq \cdots \geq \theta_n \geq 0$ are the eigenvalues of WV^{-1}.

If $\theta_1 > \cdots > \theta_n > 0$ and there are two representations
$$V = M_1 M_1^* = M_2 M_2^*, \qquad W = M_1 D_\theta M_1^* = M_2 D_\theta M_2^*,$$
then $M_2 = M_1 D_\epsilon$, where $D_\epsilon = \mathrm{diag}(\epsilon_1, \ldots, \epsilon_n), \epsilon_i = \pm 1, i = 1, \ldots, n$. Consequently, the representations are unique up to the signs of the first row of M.

The hypothesis that both V and W be positive definite can be weakened somewhat to the case where W is positive semidefinite.

F Compound Matrices

The kth compound of a matrix A is important partly because its eigenvalues are products (k at a time) of the eigenvalues of A. Consequently, results involving the largest or smallest eigenvalue of a matrix can often be extended to products of the k largest or smallest eigenvalues of A by applying the results to compounds.

For a general discussion of compounds, see Aitken (1939, 1956, Chapter V) or Wedderburn (1934, Chapter V).

F.1. Definition. If A is an $m \times n$ complex matrix and $1 \leq k \leq \min(m, n)$, then the kth compound, denoted $A^{(k)}$, is the $\binom{m}{k} \times \binom{n}{k}$ matrix whose elements are determinants
$$A\begin{pmatrix} i_1, \ldots, i_k \\ j_1, \ldots, j_k \end{pmatrix}$$
arranged lexicographically. (For a definition of this notation, see 9.A.4.) The kth compound is sometimes referred to as a skew-symmetric tensor power and denoted by $\Lambda^k(A)$ [see, e.g., Bhatia (1997)].

In lexicographic ordering, the subscript $i_1 i_2 \cdots i_m j \cdots$ appears before $i_1 i_2 \cdots i_m l \cdots$ if $j < l$.

For example, if A is a 4×4 matrix, then

$$A^{(3)} = \begin{bmatrix} A\binom{123}{123} & A\binom{123}{124} & A\binom{123}{134} & A\binom{123}{234} \\ A\binom{124}{123} & A\binom{124}{124} & A\binom{124}{134} & A\binom{124}{234} \\ A\binom{134}{123} & A\binom{134}{124} & A\binom{134}{134} & A\binom{134}{234} \\ A\binom{234}{123} & A\binom{234}{124} & A\binom{234}{134} & A\binom{234}{234} \end{bmatrix}.$$

Clearly, $A^{(1)} \equiv A$. If A is an $n \times n$ matrix, then $A^{(n)} = \det A$.

Some basic facts about compounds follow directly from the definition:

(i) $(A^{(k)})^* = A^{*(k)}$, $(A^{(k)})' = A'^{(k)}$.

(ii) If $D_a = \text{diag}(a_1, \ldots, a_n)$, then $D_a^{(k)}$ is an $\binom{n}{k} \times \binom{n}{k}$ diagonal matrix with elements $a_{i_1} \cdots a_{i_k}, 1 \leq i_1 < \cdots < i_k \leq n$. In particular, $I_n^{(k)} = I_{\binom{n}{k}}$.

(iii) If A is Hermitian, then $A^{(k)}$ is Hermitian.

(iv) If A is lower (upper) triangular, then $A^{(k)}$ is lower (upper) triangular.

Binet–Cauchy Theorem and Eigenvalues of a Compound Matrix

A result of central importance from which many properties of a compound are derived is the Binet–Cauchy theorem, proved in special cases by Binet (1812) and Cauchy (1812). A detailed description of the contents of these papers is given in Muir (1906), who notes that both memoirs were read at a meeting on the same day.

F.2. Theorem (Binet, 1812; Cauchy, 1812). If A is a $p \times m$ complex matrix, B is an $m \times n$ complex matrix, and $1 \leq k \leq \min(p, m, n)$, then $(AB)^{(k)} = A^{(k)} B^{(k)}$.

The following are some important consequences of F.2:

F.2.a. If A is a nonsingular $n \times n$ matrix, then $(A^{-1})^{(k)} = (A^{(k)})^{-1}$.

Proof. An application of F.2 to $AA^{-1} = I$ yields $A^{(k)}(A^{-1})^{(k)} = I^{(k)} = I$. ∥

F.2.b. If Γ is an $n \times n$ unitary matrix, then $\Gamma^{(k)}$ is an $\binom{n}{k} \times \binom{n}{k}$ unitary matrix.

Proof. This is a consequence of F.2.a and the fact that $\Gamma^* = \Gamma^{-1}$. ‖

F.2.c. If A is an $n \times n$ complex matrix with eigenvalues $\lambda_1, \ldots, \lambda_n$, then $A^{(k)}$ has eigenvalues $\lambda_{i_1} \cdots \lambda_{i_k}, 1 \leq i_1 < \cdots < i_k \leq n$.

Proof. By A.3 there exists an $n \times n$ unitary matrix Γ and a lower triangular matrix T such that $A = \Gamma T \Gamma^*$. Further, the diagonal elements of T are the eigenvalues of A. By applying F.2, it follows that

$$A^{(k)} = (\Gamma T \Gamma^*)^{(k)} = \Gamma^{(k)} T^{(k)} \Gamma^{*(k)} = \Gamma^{(k)} T^{(k)} \Gamma^{(k)*}.$$

Since $T^{(k)}$ is lower triangular with diagonal elements $\lambda_{i_1} \cdots \lambda_{i_k}, 1 \leq i_1 < \cdots < i_k \leq n$, and $\Gamma^{(k)}$ is unitary (F.2.b), the eigenvalues of $A^{(k)}$ are the diagonal elements of $T^{(k)}$. ‖

As a consequence of F.2.c, if H is a positive semidefinite Hermitian matrix, the largest and smallest eigenvalues of $H^{(k)}$ are $\prod_1^k \lambda_i(H)$ and $\prod_1^k \lambda_{n-i+1}(H)$, respectively. Since $H^{(k)}$ is Hermitian, it is positive semidefinite. Similarly, if H is a positive definite Hermitian matrix, then $H^{(k)}$ is a positive definite Hermitian matrix.

F.2.d. If A is an $n \times n$ complex matrix with eigenvalues $\lambda_1, \ldots, \lambda_n$, then

$$\operatorname{tr} A^{(k)} = S_k(\lambda_1, \ldots, \lambda_n) = \sum_{1 \leq i_1 < \cdots < i_k \leq n} A\binom{i_1, \ldots, i_k}{i_1, \ldots, i_k},$$

where $S_k(\lambda_1, \ldots, \lambda_n)$ is the kth elementary symmetric function of the eigenvalues.

The first expression for $\operatorname{tr} A^{(k)}$ follows from F.2.c, and the second proceeds directly from the definition. The notation $\operatorname{tr}_k A$ is frequently used for $\operatorname{tr} A^{(k)}$.

F.2.e.

$$\det A^{(k)} = \sum_{1 \leq i_1 < \cdots < i_k \leq n} (\lambda_{i_1} \cdots \lambda_{i_k}) = \left(\prod_1^n \lambda_i\right)^{\binom{n-1}{k-1}} = (\det A)^{\binom{n-1}{k-1}}.$$

This is another consequence of F.2.c.

Additive Compound Matrix

The usefulness of the kth compound $A^{(k)}$ of a matrix A stems in part from the fact that the eigenvalues of $A^{(k)}$ are products of the eigenvalues of A k at a time, without repetitions. There is an additive version of this result that can be stated in several different ways; here we follow the development of Wielandt (1967).

A matrix, called the *kth additive compound* of A, is defined. This matrix has two important properties: (a) the mapping from A to its kth additive compound is linear (F.4); and (b) the eigenvalues of the kth additive compound are sums of k of the eigenvalues, without repetition, of A (F.5).

In a private communication from Helmut Wielandt of January 27, 1979, he stated that he developed the concept of additive compound and believed that it was original after checking his notes from Issai Schur's class in matrix theory.

F.3. Definition. If A is an $n \times n$ complex matrix, the *kth additive compound (of order 1)* $\Delta_k(A)$ is the $\binom{n}{k} \times \binom{n}{k}$ matrix

$$(i) \qquad \Delta_k(A) = \frac{d}{dt}(I + tA)^{(k)}\bigg|_{t=0}.$$

Alternatively, $\Delta_k(A)$ is the coefficient matrix of t in the expansion

$$(ii) \qquad (I + tA)^{(k)} = I + t\Delta_k(A) + t^2 \Delta_k^{(2)}(A) + \cdots.$$

The kth additive compound can be viewed as a sum of tensor products [see e.g., Bhatia (1997, p. 19)].

F.4. Theorem. If A and B are $n \times n$ complex matrices, then

$$\Delta_k(\alpha A + \beta B) = \alpha \Delta_k(A) + \beta \Delta_k(B),$$

for all α, β.

Proof. Elements of $\Delta_k(A + B)$ are obtained upon differentiation from matrices of the form

$$\det(E + t(\widetilde{A} + \widetilde{B})),$$

where $\widetilde{A}$ and $\widetilde{B}$ are $k \times k$ submatrices of A and B, and E is a matrix obtainable from the $k \times k$ matrix

$$\begin{bmatrix} I_l & 0 \\ 0 & 0 \end{bmatrix}$$

by permuting rows and columns. Denote the cofactor of a_{ij} by $(\operatorname{cof} A)_{ij}$ and compute

$$\frac{d}{dt}\det(E+t(\alpha\widetilde{A}+\beta\widetilde{B}))\bigg|_{t=0}$$

$$=\sum_{i,j}(\operatorname{cof} E+t(\alpha\widetilde{A}+\beta\widetilde{B}))_{ij}(\alpha a_{ij}+\beta b_{ij})\bigg|_{t=0}$$

$$=\alpha\sum_{i,j}(\operatorname{cof} E)_{ij}\widetilde{a}_{ij}+\beta\sum_{i,j}(\operatorname{cof} E)_{ij}\widetilde{b}_{ij}$$

$$=\alpha\frac{d}{dt}\det(E+t\widetilde{A})\bigg|_{t=0}+\beta\frac{d}{dt}\det(E+t\widetilde{B})\bigg|_{t=0}.$$

Consequently,

$$(\Delta_k(\alpha A+\beta B))_{ij}=\alpha(\Delta_k(A))_{ij}+\beta(\Delta_k(B))_{ij},$$

for all i,j, which completes the proof. ∥

F.5. Theorem. If A is an $n\times n$ complex matrix with eigenvalues $\lambda_1,\ldots,\lambda_n$, then the eigenvalues of the additive compound $\Delta_k(A)$ are $\lambda_{i_1}+\cdots+\lambda_{i_k}, 1\leq i_1<\cdots<i_k\leq n$.

Proof. Using the representation A.3, write $A=\Gamma T\Gamma^*$, where Γ is unitary and T is lower triangular, with $t_{ii}=\lambda_i(A), i=1,\ldots,n$. Then by the Binet–Cauchy theorem F.2,

$$(I+tA)^{(k)}=(I+t\Gamma T\Gamma^*)^{(k)}=\Gamma^{(k)}(I+tT)^{(k)}\Gamma^{(k)*}$$
$$=\Gamma^{(k)}\widetilde{T}^{(k)}\Gamma^{(k)*},$$

where $\widetilde{T}=I+tT$ is a lower triangular matrix with diagonal elements $(1+t\lambda_i), i=1,\ldots,n$. Then $\widetilde{T}^{(k)}$ is lower triangular with diagonal elements $\prod_{j=1}^k(1+t\lambda_{i_j}), 1\leq i_1<\cdots<i_k\leq n$. The eigenvalues of $\Delta_k(A)$ are the eigenvalues of

$$\frac{d}{dt}\Gamma^{(k)}\widetilde{T}^{(k)}\Gamma^{(k)*}\bigg|_{t=0}=\Gamma^{(k)}\left(\frac{d}{dt}\widetilde{T}^{(k)}\right)\Gamma^{(k)*}\bigg|_{t=0}.$$

These eigenvalues are the diagonal elements of the triangular matrix $(d/dt)\widetilde{T}^{(k)}$ and have the form

$$\frac{d}{dt}\prod_1^k(1+t\lambda_{i_j})\bigg|_{t=0}=\lambda_{i_1}+\cdots+\lambda_{i_k}. \quad \|$$

Recall from F.2.e that the kth compound $A^{(k)}$ has determinant

$$\det A^{(k)}=(\det A)^{\binom{n-1}{k-1}}.$$

A counterpart for the kth additive compound is

F.5.a.
$$\operatorname{tr} \Delta_k(A) = \binom{n-1}{k-1} \operatorname{tr} A.$$

Proof. This follows from the fact that $\operatorname{tr}\Delta_k(A)$ is the sum of its eigenvalues; i.e.,
$$\sum_{1 \leq i_1 < \cdots < i_k \leq n} (\lambda_{i_1} + \cdots + \lambda_{i_k}) = \binom{n-1}{k-1} \sum_1^n \lambda_i. \quad \|$$

F.6. To prove F.4 and F.5, it is not necessary to evaluate the elements in the kth additive compound. However, it may be of interest to give an example. The following are all the additive compounds for $n = 3$:

$$\Delta_1(A) = A,$$

$$\Delta_2(A) = \begin{bmatrix} a_{11} + a_{22} & a_{23} & -a_{13} \\ a_{32} & a_{11} + a_{33} & a_{12} \\ -a_{31} & a_{21} & a_{22} + a_{33} \end{bmatrix},$$

$$\Delta_3(A) = a_{11} + a_{22} + a_{33}.$$

G Kronecker Product and Sum

If A is an $m \times n$ matrix and B is a $p \times q$ matrix, the *Kronecker product* (also called *direct product*) $A \otimes B$ is the $mp \times nq$ matrix

$$A \otimes B = \begin{bmatrix} a_{11}B & \cdots & a_{1n}B \\ \vdots & & \vdots \\ a_{m1}B & \cdots & a_{mn}B \end{bmatrix}.$$

The *Kronecker sum*, $A \oplus B$, is the $mp \times nq$ matrix

$$A \oplus B = \begin{bmatrix} a_{11}J + B & \cdots & a_{1n}J + B \\ \vdots & & \vdots \\ a_{m1}J + B & \cdots & a_{mn}J + B \end{bmatrix},$$

where J is a $p \times q$ matrix with elements 1.

Alternatively,
$$A \oplus B = (A \otimes I_m) + (I_n \otimes B).$$

In particular, if $x = (x_1, \ldots, x_n)$, $y = (y_1, \ldots, y_n)$, then

$$x \oplus y = (x_1 + y_1, x_1 + y_2, \ldots, x_1 + y_n, \ldots, x_n + y_n).$$

There is an extensive matrix calculus for Kronecker products, and we list here only those results that are used in this book. For more details see Bernstein (2005, Chapter 7).

G.1. Whenever the matrices are conformable for multiplication,

$$(A \otimes B)(U \otimes V) = AU \otimes BV.$$

Proof. For a proof, see, e.g., Lancaster (1969, p. 257). ∥

G.2. Let A be an $n \times n$ matrix with eigenvalues $\alpha_1, \ldots, \alpha_n$ and let B be an $l \times l$ matrix with eigenvalues $\beta_1, \ldots, \beta_l$. The nl eigenvalues of $A \otimes B$ are given by $\alpha_i \beta_j, i = 1, \ldots, n, j = 1, \ldots, l$.

Proof. The result follows by applying G.1 to the representation A.3: $A = \Gamma T \Gamma^*, B = \Delta U \Delta^*$, where Γ and Δ are unitary, and T and U are lower triangular with diagonal elements $t_{ii} = \alpha_i, i = 1, \ldots, n$, and $u_{jj} = \beta_j, j = 1, \ldots, l$. Then

$$A \otimes B = (\Gamma T \Gamma^*) \otimes (\Delta U \Delta^*) = (\Gamma \otimes \Delta)(T \otimes U)(\Gamma^* \otimes \Delta^*).$$

But $\Gamma \otimes \Delta$ is unitary and $T \otimes U$ is lower triangular with diagonal elements $\alpha_i \beta_j$, which are the eigenvalues of $A \otimes B$. ∥

G.2.a. If A is a positive definite Hermitian matrix and B is a positive definite (semidefinite) Hermitian matrix, then $A \otimes B$ is a positive definite (semidefinite) Hermitian matrix.

Proof. This is a direct consequence of G.2. ∥

As a consequence of G.2, it follows that the eigenvalues of the product $A \otimes A \otimes \cdots \otimes A$ (k times) are $\alpha_{i_1} \alpha_{i_2} \cdots \alpha_{i_k}$, where the indices include repetitions. This is in contrast to the kth compound, where the indices do not include repetitions.

G.3. If A is an $n \times n$ matrix, B is an $m \times m$ matrix, and C is an $r \times r$ matrix, then

$$A \oplus (B \oplus C) = (A \oplus B) \oplus C.$$

H M-Matrices

The class of M-matrices introduced by Ostrowski (1937) can be defined in a number of ways.

H.1. Definition. A real $n \times n$ matrix A is called an *M-matrix* if $A = cI - B$, where $b_{ij} \geq 0$ for all i,j and $c > |\lambda_i(B)|, i = 1,\ldots,n$.

Fan (1964) shows that each of the following conditions (i), (ii), and (iii) are necessary and sufficient for a real $n \times n$ matrix $A = (a_{ij})$ with $a_{ij} \leq 0, i \neq j$, to be an M-matrix:

(i) A is nonsingular and $A^{-1} = (a^{ij})$ has $a^{ij} \geq 0$, for all i,j;
(ii) all principal minors of A are positive;
(iii) $\mathscr{R}\lambda_i(A) > 0, i = 1,\ldots,n$.

An exposition of M-matrices is given by Keilson and Styan (1973).

20
Extremal Representations of Matrix Functions

A number of real-valued functions of the eigenvalues of a matrix have variational or extremal representations. These representations are frequently useful in that they yield comparisons between the extreme and other values of the function. In addition, the extremal representation may yield in a simple manner properties about the function of the eigenvalues.

A Eigenvalues of a Hermitian Matrix

If H is an $n \times n$ Hermitian matrix, with ordered eigenvalues $\lambda_1(H) \geq \cdots \geq \lambda_n(H)$, then

$$\max_{xx^*=1} xHx^* = \lambda_1(H), \qquad \min_{xx^*=1} xHx^* = \lambda_n(H). \tag{1}$$

These classical examples of representations can be extended in a variety of ways: (i) to the ith eigenvalue, (ii) to the sum of the k largest (smallest) eigenvalues, and (iii) to the jth elementary symmetric function of the k largest (smallest) eigenvalues, $j \leq k$.

A.1. Minmax theorem (Fischer, 1905; Courant, see Courant and Hilbert, 1953). If H is an $n \times n$ Hermitian matrix with eigenvalues $\lambda_1 \geq \cdots \geq \lambda_n$, then

$$\max_{xx^*=1} xHx^* = \lambda_1,$$

$$\min_{y^{(1)},\ldots,y^{(j)}} \max_{\substack{xx^*=1 \\ y^{(1)}x^*=\cdots=y^{(j)}x^*=0}} xHx^* = \lambda_{j+1}, \qquad j=1,\ldots,n-1,$$

$$\min_{xx^*=1} xHx^* = \lambda_n,$$

$$\max_{y^{(1)},\ldots,y^{(j)}} \min_{\substack{xx^*=1 \\ y^{(1)}x^*=\cdots=y^{(j)}x^*=0}} xHx^* = \lambda_{n-j+1}, \qquad j=2,\ldots,n.$$

Equivalently,

$$\lambda_k = \min_U \max_x xUHU^*x^*,$$
$$\lambda_{n-k+1} = \max_U \min_x xUHU^*x^*, \qquad 1 \leq k \leq n,$$

where U runs over all $r \times n$ complex matrices satisfying $UU^* = I_r$, with $r = 1,\ldots,n-k+1$, and x runs over all r-dimensional complex vectors satisfying $xx^* = 1$.

Proofs are given by Bellman (1960, p. 113) and by Courant and Hilbert (1953, pp. 31 and 405).

A.1.a. If A is an $n \times n$ positive semidefinite Hermitian matrix and H is an $n \times n$ positive definite Hermitian matrix, then

$$\lambda_j(HA)\lambda_1(H^{-1}) \geq \lambda_j(A) \geq \lambda_n(H^{-1})\lambda_j(HA), \qquad j=1,\ldots,n.$$

A.1.b. If A and B are $n \times n$ Hermitian matrices and $A-B$ is positive semidefinite, then

$$\lambda_j(A) \geq \lambda_j(B), \qquad j=1,\ldots,n.$$

If $A - B$ is positive definite, the inequalities are strict. This result is due to Loewner (1934).

A.1.c. Let

$$H = \begin{bmatrix} H_{11} & H_{12} \\ H_{21} & H_{22} \end{bmatrix}$$

be an $n \times n$ positive semidefinite matrix partitioned with H_{11} an $l \times l$ submatrix. Then

$$\lambda_i(H) \geq \lambda_i(H_{11}),$$
$$\lambda_{n-i+1}(H) \leq \lambda_{l-i+1}(H_{11}), \qquad i=1,\ldots,l.$$

The next result, due to Fan (1950), extends (1) to the sum of the k largest (smallest) eigenvalues and is of fundamental importance as a tool for obtaining other results. The proof given here makes use of majorization.

A.2. Theorem (Fan, 1950). If H is an $n \times n$ Hermitian matrix with eigenvalues $\lambda_1(H) \geq \cdots \geq \lambda_n(H)$, then

$$\max_{UU^*=I_k} \operatorname{tr} UHU^* = \sum_1^k \lambda_i(H), \qquad \min_{UU^*=I_k} \operatorname{tr} UHU^* = \sum_1^k \lambda_{n-i+1}, \quad (2)$$

$k = 1, \ldots, n$, where the extrema are over $k \times n$ complex matrices U satisfying $UU^* = I_k$.

Proof. By 19.A.4, there exists a unitary matrix Γ such that $H = \Gamma D_\lambda \Gamma^*$, where $D_\lambda = \operatorname{diag}(\lambda_1(H), \ldots, \lambda_n(H))$. Consequently, there is no loss in generality if H is assumed to be diagonal. Then with $\lambda_i \equiv \lambda_i(H), i = 1, \ldots, n,$

$$\operatorname{tr} UD_\lambda U^* = \sum_{i=1}^k \sum_{j=1}^n u_{ij}\overline{u}_{ij}\lambda_j \equiv \sum_{i=1}^k \sum_{j=1}^n p_{ij}\lambda_j = eP\lambda', \quad (3)$$

where $e = (1, \ldots, 1)$, $\lambda = (\lambda_1, \ldots, \lambda_n)$, and $P = (p_{ij})$ is a $k \times n$, $k \leq n$, stochastic matrix. By 2.C.1(4) it follows that there exists an $(n-k) \times n$ matrix Q such that $\binom{P}{Q}$ is doubly stochastic. Thus (3) can be written as

$$\operatorname{tr} UD_\lambda U^* = (1, \ldots, 1, 0, \ldots, 0)\binom{P}{Q}\begin{bmatrix}\lambda_1\\ \vdots \\ \lambda_n\end{bmatrix}.$$

But $(\lambda_1, \ldots, \lambda_n)(P', Q') \prec (\lambda_1, \ldots, \lambda_n)$, so that with the aid of 3.H.2.b (or directly from the definition of majorization), it follows that

$$\operatorname{tr} UD_\lambda U^* \leq \sum_1^k \lambda_i, \quad \operatorname{tr} UD_\lambda U^* \geq \sum_1^k \lambda_{n-i+1}, \quad k = 1, \ldots, n. \quad (4)$$

The proof is completed by noting that equality in (4) is achieved for $U\Gamma = (I_k, 0)$ and $(0, I_k)$, respectively. ||

Remark. Essentially the same argument as in A.2 was used by Ostrowski (1952) to prove the following more general result. If ϕ is a Schur-convex function on $\mathscr{R}^n$ and if H is an $n \times n$ Hermitian matrix, then

$$\max_{UU^*=I_n} \phi(\lambda(UHU^*)) = \phi(\lambda(H)).$$

A.2.a. Proposition. If G is an $n \times n$ Hermitian matrix with eigenvalues $\mu_1 \geq \cdots \geq \mu_n$, and H is an $m \times m$ Hermitian matrix with eigenvalues $\lambda_1 \geq \cdots \geq \lambda_m$, $m \leq n$, then

$$\max_{\Psi\Psi^* = I_m} \operatorname{tr} \Psi G \Psi^* H = \sum_{1}^{m} \lambda_i \mu_i,$$

where the extremum is over $m \times n$ complex matrices Ψ satisfying $\Psi\Psi^* = I_m$.

Proof. As in the proof of A.2, let $G = \Gamma D_\mu \Gamma^*$, $H = \Delta D_\lambda \Delta^*$, where Γ and Δ are unitary, $D_\mu = \operatorname{diag}(\mu_1, \ldots, \mu_n)$, and $D_\lambda = \operatorname{diag}(\lambda_1, \ldots, \lambda_m)$. Then

$$\operatorname{tr} \Psi G \Psi^* H = \operatorname{tr} \Psi \Gamma D_\mu \Gamma^* \Psi^* \Delta D_\lambda \Delta^*$$
$$= \operatorname{tr} U D_\mu U^* D_\lambda,$$

where $U = \Delta^* \Psi \Gamma$ satisfies $UU^* = I_m$. Consequently,

$$\operatorname{tr} U D_\mu U^* D_\lambda = \sum_{i=1}^{m} \sum_{j=1}^{n} u_{ij} \overline{u}_{ij} \mu_i \lambda_j = \sum_{i=1}^{m} \sum_{j=1}^{n} p_{ij} \mu_i \lambda_j,$$

where $P = (p_{ij})$ is an $m \times n$ stochastic matrix. The remainder of the proof follows that of A.2. ||

The result in Theorem A.2 corresponds to the case in which $\phi(x) = \sum_{i=1}^{k} x_{[i]}$. The parallel result when ϕ is Schur-concave includes results A.3 and A.3.a below as special cases.

Multiplicative Versions

An application of A.2 to the kth compound yields a set of multiplicative versions in terms of the elementary symmetric functions of the kth largest (smallest) eigenvalues.

A.3. If H is an $n \times n$ Hermitian matrix with eigenvalues $\lambda_i \equiv \lambda_i(H)$, $i = 1, \ldots, n$, ordered so that $\lambda_1(H) \geq \cdots \geq \lambda_n(H)$, and if U is a $k \times n$ complex matrix, $k \leq n$, then for $j \leq k$,

$$\max_{UU^* = I_k} \operatorname{tr}_j UHU^* = \max_{UU^* = I_k} S_j(\lambda_1(UHU^*), \ldots, \lambda_k(UHU^*))$$
$$= S_j(\lambda_1, \ldots, \lambda_k),$$

and
$$\min_{UU^*=I_k} \mathrm{tr}_j UHU^* = \min_{UU^*=I_k} S_j(\lambda_1(UHU^*), \ldots, \lambda_k(UHU^*))$$
$$= S_j(\lambda_n, \ldots, \lambda_{n-k+1}),$$

where $\mathrm{tr}_j A = \mathrm{tr}\, A^{(j)}$ (see 19.F.2.d), and S_j is the jth elementary symmetric function.

Proof. Using the Binet–Cauchy theorem 19.F.2,
$$\mathrm{tr}_j UHU^* = \mathrm{tr}(UHU^*)^{(j)} = \mathrm{tr}\, U^{(j)} H^{(j)} U^{*(j)}.$$
An application of A.2 then yields
$$\max_{UU^*=I_k} \mathrm{tr}\, U^{(j)} H^{(j)} U^{*(j)} \leq \max_{U^{(j)} U^{*(j)}=1} \mathrm{tr}\, U^{(j)} H^{(j)} U^{*(j)}$$
$$= \sum_{i=1}^{\binom{k}{j}} \lambda_{[i]}(H^{(j)}) = S_j(\lambda_1, \ldots, \lambda_k),$$
$$\min_{UU^*=I_k} \mathrm{tr}\, U^{(j)} H^{(j)} U^{*(j)} \geq \min_{U^{(j)} U^{*(j)}=1} \mathrm{tr}\, U^{(j)} H^{(j)} U^{*(j)}$$
$$= \sum_{i=1}^{\binom{k}{j}} \lambda_{(i)}(H^{(j)}) = S_j(\lambda_n, \ldots, \lambda_{n-k+1}).$$

The proof is completed by noting that equality is achieved in the two cases by $U\Gamma = (I_k, 0)$ and $(0, I_k)$, where $H = \Gamma D_\lambda \Gamma^*$, and Γ is unitary. ‖

A.3.a. A case of special interest is $j = k$:
$$\max_{UU^*=I_k} \det UHU^* = \prod_1^k \lambda_i(H), \quad \min_{UU^*=I_k} \det UHU^* = \prod_1^k \lambda_{n-i+1}(H).$$

This result is due to Fan (1949, 1950).

The additive version (A.2) and multiplicative version (A.3.a) are contained in a number of books, e.g., Bellman (1960, p. 132), Householder (1964, pp. 76 and 77), and Beckenbach and Bellman (1961, p. 77). Householder obtains the multiplicative version A.3.a by using compounds as above. The idea of a hierarchical structure in a related context is used by Marcus and Moyls (1957) and by Mirsky (1958b).

Bounds for the function $\mathrm{tr}\, UHU^*$ can be obtained by applying a rearrangement theorem and majorization.

A.4. Theorem. If H is an $n \times n$ Hermitian matrix with eigenvalues $\lambda_1 \geq \cdots \geq \lambda_n$, U is a $k \times n$ complex matrix, $k \leq n$, and $\beta_i = \lambda_i(UU^*), i = 1, \ldots, k$, ordered $\beta_1 \geq \cdots \geq \beta_k \geq 0$, then

$$\sum_1^k \lambda_i \beta_i \geq \operatorname{tr} UHU^* \geq \sum_1^k \lambda_{n-i+1} \beta_i, \qquad k = 1, \ldots, n. \qquad (5)$$

Proof. Let $H = \Gamma D_\lambda \Gamma^*$ be the eigenvalue decomposition (19.A.4) of H and let $V = U\Gamma$. Because $\lambda(UU^*) = \lambda(VV^*)$, we assume, with no loss in generality, that H is diagonal.

Let $B = U^*U$. Then

$$\operatorname{tr} UD_\lambda U^* = \operatorname{tr} D_\lambda B = \sum \lambda_i b_{ii}.$$

By the rearrangement theorem 6.A.3,

$$\sum_1^n \lambda_{[i]} b_{[ii]} \geq \sum \lambda_i b_{ii} \geq \sum_1^n \lambda_{(i)} b_{[ii]}.$$

Further, $(\lambda_1, \ldots, \lambda_n) \succ (b_{11}, \ldots, b_{nn})$, so that

$$\sum_1^n \lambda_{(i)} b_{[ii]} \geq \sum_1^n \lambda_{(i)} \beta_{[i]} = \sum_1^n \lambda_{n-i+1} \beta_i,$$

$$\sum_1^n \lambda_{[i]} b_{[ii]} \leq \sum_1^n \lambda_{[i]} \beta_{[i]} = \sum \lambda_i \beta_i. \quad \|$$

As a consequence of A.4, A.2 can easily be obtained:

A.4.a. Alternative proof of A.2. If $UU^* = I$, then (5) with $\beta_1 = \cdots = \beta_k = 1$ yields

$$\sum_1^k \lambda_i \geq \operatorname{tr} UHU^* \geq \sum_1^k \lambda_{n-i+1}, \qquad k \leq n.$$

Equality in the left- and right-hand inequalities are achieved for $U = (I_k, 0)\Gamma$ and $U = (0, I_k)\Gamma$, respectively, where $H = \Gamma D_\lambda \Gamma^*$ is the eigenvalue decomposition. $\|$

The right-hand inequality of (5) yields another extremal representation.

A.5. If H is an $n \times n$ positive definite Hermitian matrix with eigenvalues $\lambda_1 \geq \cdots \geq \lambda_n > 0$, and U is a $k \times n$ complex matrix, $k \leq n$, then

$$\min_{\det UU^*=1} \frac{\operatorname{tr} UHU^*}{k} = \left(\prod_1^k \lambda_{n-i+1}\right)^{1/k}.$$

Proof. From (5) and the arithmetic–geometric mean inequality,

$$\frac{\operatorname{tr} UHU^*}{k} \geq \sum_1^k \frac{\lambda_{n-i+1}\beta_i}{k} \geq \left(\prod_1^k \lambda_{n-i+1}\right)^{1/k} \left(\prod_1^k \beta_i\right)^{1/k}.$$

But $\det UU^* = 1$ is equivalent to $\prod_1^k \beta_i = 1$, so that

$$\min_{\det UU^*=1} \frac{\operatorname{tr} UHU^*}{k} \geq \left(\prod_1^k \lambda_{n-i+1}\right)^{1/k}.$$

The proof is completed by noting that equality can be achieved for

$$\beta_j = \left(\prod_1^k \lambda_{n-i+1}\right)^{1/k} \bigg/ \lambda_{n-j+1},$$

and $\quad B = U^*U = \operatorname{diag}(\beta_1,\ldots,\beta_k,0,\ldots,0). \quad \|$

B Singular Values

One of the earliest results for the sum of the k largest (smallest) singular values of a matrix is due to von Neumann (1937) and later to Fan (1951). The proof given below uses majorization. An extension to several matrices is discussed.

The real part of a complex number z is denoted $\mathscr{R}z$.

B.1. Theorem (von Neumann, 1937; Fan, 1951). If A and B are $n \times n$ complex matrices, U and V are $n \times n$ unitary matrices, and $\sigma_1 \geq \cdots \geq \sigma_n \geq 0$ denote ordered singular values, then

$$\mathscr{R}\operatorname{tr} UAVB \leq |\operatorname{tr} UAVB| \leq \sum_1^n \sigma_i(A)\sigma_i(B), \qquad (1a)$$

$$\sup_{U,V} \mathscr{R}\operatorname{tr} UAVB = \sup_{U,V} |\operatorname{tr} UAVB| = \sum_1^n \sigma_i(A)\sigma_i(B). \qquad (1b)$$

Denote the singular value decompositions (19.B.1) of A and B by

$$A = \Gamma_1 D_\alpha \Delta_1, \qquad B = \Gamma_2 D_\beta \Delta_2,$$

where $\alpha_i = \sigma_i(A), \beta_i = \sigma_i(B), i = 1, \ldots, n$, and $\Gamma_1, \Delta_1, \Gamma_2, \Delta_2$ are unitary; then equality is achieved in (1a) for $U = \Delta_2^* \Gamma_1^*, V = \Delta_1^* \Gamma_2^*$.

Proof. For any complex number z, $\mathscr{R}(z) \leq |z|$, so the left-hand inequality is immediate. To prove the right-hand inequality, using the singular value decompositions for A and B, let $\widetilde{U} = \Delta_2 U \Gamma_1, \widetilde{V} = \Delta_1 V \Gamma_2$, so that, in effect, we can assume A and B to be diagonal. Then

$$|\operatorname{tr} \widetilde{U} D_\alpha \widetilde{V} D_\beta| = \left|\sum_{j,l} u_{jl} \alpha_l v_{lj} \beta_j\right| \leq \sum_{j,l} \alpha_l |u_{jl} v_{lj}| \beta_j$$
$$= \sum_{j,l} \alpha_l p_{jl} \beta_j \equiv (\alpha_1, \ldots, \alpha_n) P (\beta_1, \ldots, \beta_n)', \quad (2)$$

where $p_{jl} = |u_{jl} v_{lj}|, P = (p_{ij})$. From 2.H.7.a, the matrix P is doubly substochastic, so that with the aid of 3.H.2.b, it follows that

$$(\alpha_1, \ldots, \alpha_n) P (\beta_1, \ldots, \beta_n)' \leq (\alpha_1, \ldots, \alpha_n)(\beta_1, \ldots, \beta_n)' = \sum_{1}^{n} \alpha_i \beta_i.$$

That equality in (2) is achieved for $\widetilde{U} = \widetilde{V} = I$ is immediate. $\|$

The result of von Neumann (1937) is

$$\max_{UU^* = VV^* = I} \mathscr{R} \operatorname{tr} UAVB = \sum_{1}^{n} \sigma_i(A) \sigma_i(B), \quad (3)$$

whereas the result of Fan (1951) is

$$\max_{UU^* = VV^* = I} |\operatorname{tr} UAVB| = \sum_{1}^{n} \sigma_i(A) \sigma_i(B). \quad (4)$$

In view of the left-hand inequality in (1a), (3) implies (4). Since (3) achieves equality for a matrix for which $\mathscr{R} \operatorname{tr} UVAB = |\operatorname{tr} UVAB|$, (4) implies (3).

An important case is obtained by the choice

$$B = \begin{bmatrix} I_k & 0 \\ 0 & 0 \end{bmatrix}, \quad A = \begin{bmatrix} A_{11} & 0 \\ 0 & 0 \end{bmatrix},$$

where A_{11} is $m \times p$. Partition U and V:

$$U = \begin{bmatrix} U_{11} & U_{12} \\ U_{21} & U_{22} \end{bmatrix}, \quad V = \begin{bmatrix} V_{11} & V_{12} \\ V_{21} & V_{22} \end{bmatrix}.$$

where U_{11} is $k \times m$, and V_1 is $p \times k$. Then

$$\operatorname{tr} UAVB = \operatorname{tr} U_{11} A_{11} V_{11}.$$

Thus, the following corollary is obtained.

B.1.a. Corollary. If A is an $m \times p$ complex matrix, U and V are complex $k \times m$ and $k \times p$ matrices, respectively, $k \leq m, k \leq p$, then

$$\max_{UU^*=VV^*=I_k} \mathscr{R}\operatorname{tr} UAV^* = \max_{UU^*=VV^*=I_k} |\operatorname{tr} UAV^*| = \sum_1^k \sigma_i(A).$$

An Extension to an Arbitrary Number of Matrices

The extension of B.1 to an arbitrary number of matrices is clear. The proof, however, is not obvious. We give an inductive proof that is elementary, though still somewhat lengthy.

B.2. Theorem (Fan, 1951). Let $A_1, \ldots, A_m$ be $n \times n$ complex matrices with singular values $\sigma_1(A_j) \geq \cdots \geq \sigma_n(A_j) \geq 0, j = 1, \ldots, m$, and let $U_1, \ldots, U_m$ be $n \times n$ unitary matrices. Then

$$\mathscr{R}\operatorname{tr}(U_1 A_1 U_2 A_2 \cdots U_m A_m) \leq |\operatorname{tr}(U_1 A_1 U_2 A_2 \cdots U_m A_m)|$$

$$\leq \sum_1^n \sigma_i(A_1) \cdots \sigma_i(A_m), \qquad (5a)$$

$$\sup_{U_1, \ldots, U_m} \mathscr{R}\operatorname{tr}(U_1 A_1 U_2 A_2 \cdots U_m A_m) = \sup_{U_1, \ldots, U_m} |\operatorname{tr}(U_1 A_1 U_2 A_2 \cdots U_m A_m)|$$

$$= \sum_1^n \sigma_i(A_1) \cdots \sigma_i(A_m). \qquad (5b)$$

Equality in (5a) is achieved for $U_1 = \Delta_m^* \Gamma_1^*, U_2 = \Delta_1^* \Gamma_2^*, \ldots, U_m = \Delta_{m-1}^* \Gamma_m^*$, where the Γ_j and Δ_j are obtained from the singular value decompositions $A_j = \Gamma_j D_j \Delta_j, i = 1, \ldots, m$, of 19.B.1.

Proof. The case $m = 2$ was proved as B.1. Assume that (5a) holds for $m - 1$, and assume, with no loss in generality, that each $A_j = D_j = \operatorname{diag}(a_1^{(j)}, \ldots, a_n^{(j)})$, with ordered $a_1^{(j)} \geq \cdots \geq a_n^{(j)} \geq 0, j = 1, \ldots, m-1$. That is, the singular values are ordered.

In the following, the maxima are always over the set of $n \times n$ unitary matrices. Using B.1 and writing $R = D_1 U_2 D_2 \cdots D_{m-2}, S = D_{m-1} U_m D_m$,

$$|\operatorname{tr} U_1 (D_1 U_2 D_2 \cdots D_{m-2}) U_{m-1} (D_{m-1} U_m D_m)| \equiv |\operatorname{tr} U_1 R U_{m-1} S|$$

$$\leq \sum_1^n \sigma_i(R) \sigma_i(S). \quad (6)$$

792   20. Extremal Representations of Matrix Functions

Suppose the following two weak majorizations can be established:

$$\sum_1^k \sigma_i(S) \le \sum_1^k \sigma_i(D_{m-1})\sigma_i(D_m), \qquad k=1,\ldots,n; \qquad (7)$$

$$\sum_1^k \sigma_i(R) \le \sum_1^k \sigma_i(D_1)\cdots\sigma_i(D_{m-2}), \qquad k=1,\ldots,n. \qquad (8)$$

It would then follow from 3.H.2.c that

$$\sum_1^k \sigma_i(R)\sigma_i(S) \le \sum_1^k \sigma_i(D_1)\cdots\sigma_i(D_m),$$

in which case it follows from (6) that

$$|\operatorname{tr} U_1 D_1 U_2 D_2 \cdots U_m D_m| \le \sum_1^n \sigma_i(D_1)\cdots\sigma_i(D_m).$$

Equality is achieved for $U_i = I, i = 1,\ldots,m$, as claimed.

It remains to prove (7) and (8).

The weak majorization (8) is a direct consequence of the induction hypothesis with the choices

$$D_{m-1} = \begin{bmatrix} I_k & 0 \\ 0 & 0 \end{bmatrix}, \qquad k=1,\ldots,n.$$

To prove (7), write D_a, D_b in place of D_{m-1} and D_m. Let $U_3 : n \times n$ be unitary. Then by B.1.a,

$$\sum_1^l \sigma_i\left[D_b U_3 \begin{bmatrix} I_k & 0 \\ 0 & 0 \end{bmatrix}\right] = \max_{\substack{VV^*=I_l \\ WW^*=I_l}} \left|\operatorname{tr} W D_b U_3 \begin{bmatrix} I_k & 0 \\ 0 & 0 \end{bmatrix} V^*\right| \qquad (9)$$

$$\le \max_{\substack{VV^*=I_l \\ WW^*=I_l}} |\operatorname{tr} W D_b \widetilde{V}| = \sum_1^l b_i, \qquad l=1,\ldots,n,$$

where

$$\widetilde{V} = U_3 \begin{bmatrix} I & 0 \\ 0 & 0 \end{bmatrix} V^*.$$

Next let $U_1 : n \times n$ be unitary and apply B.1 to obtain

$$\left|\operatorname{tr} U_1 D_a U_{m-1} D_b U_3 \begin{bmatrix} I_k & 0 \\ 0 & 0 \end{bmatrix}\right| \le \sum_1^n a_i \sigma_i\left[D_b U_3 \begin{bmatrix} I_k & 0 \\ 0 & 0 \end{bmatrix}\right]$$

$$= \sum_1^k a_i \sigma_i\left[D_b U_3 \begin{bmatrix} I_k & 0 \\ 0 & 0 \end{bmatrix}\right]. \qquad (10)$$

From the weak majorization (9), it follows with the aid of 3.H.2.c that

$$\left| \operatorname{tr} U_1 D_a U_{m-1} D_b U_3 \begin{bmatrix} I_k & 0 \\ 0 & 0 \end{bmatrix} \right| \leq \sum_1^k a_i b_i. \tag{11}$$

Finally, by B.1.a and (11),

$$\sum_1^k \sigma_i(S) = \max_{U_1, U_3} \left| \operatorname{tr} \begin{bmatrix} I_k & 0 \\ 0 & 0 \end{bmatrix} U_1 D_a U_{m-1} D_b U_3 \begin{bmatrix} I_k & 0 \\ 0 & 0 \end{bmatrix} \right|$$

$$= \max_{U_1, U_3} \left| \operatorname{tr} U_1 D_a U_{m-1} D_b U_3 \begin{bmatrix} I_k & 0 \\ 0 & 0 \end{bmatrix} \right| \leq \max_{U_1, U_3} \sum_1^k a_i b_i = \sum_1^k a_i b_i. \quad \|$$

A proof using compounds is given by Marcus and Moyls (1957), and an inductive proof is given by Kristof (1970).

Multiplicative Versions

Multiplicative versions of (5a, b) for the determinant have been obtained by Fan (1951) and subsequently generalized to symmetric functions by Marcus and Moyls (1957) and by Mirsky (1958b). Closely related results are contained in de Bruijn (1956) and Visser and Zaanen (1952).

B.3. Theorem. Let $A_1, \ldots, A_m$ be $n \times n$ complex matrices and let

$$A = U_1 A_1 U_2 A_2 \cdots U_m A_m,$$

where $U_1, \ldots, U_m$ are $n \times n$ unitary matrices. Then

$$\mathscr{R} S_j(\lambda_1(A), \ldots, \lambda_n(A)) \leq |S_j(\lambda_1(A), \ldots, \lambda_n(A))|$$
$$\leq S_j \left(\prod_1^m \sigma_1(A_i), \ldots, \prod_1^m \sigma_n(A_i) \right), \qquad j = 1, \ldots, n, \tag{12a}$$

and

$$\sup_{U_1, \ldots, U_m} \mathscr{R} S_j(\lambda_1(A), \ldots, \lambda_n(A))$$
$$= \sup_{U_1, \ldots, U_m} |S_j(\lambda_1(A), \ldots, \lambda_n(A))| \tag{12b}$$
$$= S_j \left(\prod_1^m \sigma_1(A_i), \ldots, \prod_1^m \sigma_n(A_i) \right).$$

Equality in (12a) is achieved for $U_1, \ldots, U_m$ as in B.2.

In (12a) the choice of one matrix, say

$$A_m = \begin{bmatrix} I_k & 0 \\ 0 & 0 \end{bmatrix},$$

yields the apparently more general form:

B.3.a. Corollary. If $A_1, \ldots, A_m$ and $n \times n$ complex matrices V_1 and V_2 are $k \times n, k \leq n$ matrices satisfying $V_1 V_1^* = V_2 V_2^* = I_k, U_2, \ldots, U_m$ are $n \times n$ unitary matrices, and

$$A = V_1 A_1 U_2 A_2 \cdots U_m A_m V_2^*,$$

then

$$\mathscr{R} S_j(\lambda_1(A), \ldots, \lambda_k(A)) \leq |S_j(\lambda_1(A), \ldots, \lambda_k(A))|$$

$$\leq S_j \left(\prod_1^m \sigma_1(A_i), \ldots, \prod_1^m \sigma_k(A_i) \right), \quad j \leq k = 1, \ldots, n, \quad (13a)$$

and

$$\sup_{V_1, V_2, U_2, \ldots, U_m} \mathscr{R} S_j(\lambda_1(A), \ldots, \lambda_k(A))$$

$$= \sup_{V_1, V_2, U_2, \ldots, U_m} |S_j(\lambda_1(A), \ldots, \lambda_k(A))| \quad (13b)$$

$$= S_j \left(\prod_1^m \sigma_1(A_i), \ldots, \prod_1^m \sigma_k(A_i) \right).$$

Equality in (13a) is achieved for $U_1 = V_2^* V_1, U_2, \ldots, U_m$ as in B.2. An application of B.2 using the polar decomposition 19.C.3 yields

B.3.b. Corollary. If H is Hermitian, U is $n \times n$, and V is $k \times n$, then for $j \leq k = 1, \ldots, n$,

$$\max_{\substack{UU^* = I_n \\ VV^* = I_k}} S_j(\lambda(V(HU)^r(U^*H^*)^r V^*)) = S_j(|\lambda_1(H)|^{2r}, \ldots, |\lambda_k(H)|^{2r}).$$

C Other Extremal Representations

The following provides a representation for the determinant of a principal submatrix of a positive definite Hermitian matrix.

Let

$$H = \begin{bmatrix} H_{11} & H_{12} \\ H_{21} & H_{22} \end{bmatrix}, \quad G = H^{-1} = \begin{bmatrix} G_{11} & G_{12} \\ G_{21} & G_{22} \end{bmatrix}$$

be $n \times n$ Hermitian matrices with $p \times p$ submatrices H_{11}, G_{11}.

C. Other Extremal Representations

C.1. Theorem (Fan, 1955b). If H is positive definite, then
$$\min_X \det[(X + H_{12}H_{22}^{-1})H_{22}(X^* + H_{22}^{-1}H_{21}) + G_{11}^{-1}] = \det G_{11}^{-1}$$
$$= \det(H_{11} - H_{12}H_{22}^{-1}H_{21}) = \det H / \det H_{22},$$
where the minimum is over all $p \times (n-p)$ matrices X. The minimum is achieved if and only if $X = -H_{12}H_{22}^{-1}$.

An equivalent formulation of C.1 is

C.1.a. Theorem. $\min_X \det(I, X)H(I, X)^* = \det G_{11}^{-1}$, where the minimum is over all $p \times (n-p)$ matrices X.

Proof. The result follows from C.1 after noting that
$$(I, X)H(I, X)^* = H_{11} + XH_{12} + H_{21}X^* + XH_{22}X^*$$
$$= (X + H_{12}H_{22}^{-1})H_{22}(X^* + H_{22}^{-1}H_{21}) + (H_{11} - H_{12}H_{22}^{-1}H_{21}),$$
and $H_{11} - H_{12}H_{22}^{-1}H_{21} = G_{11}^{-1}$. ||

Theorem C.1.a for $p = 1$ is given by Olkin and Pratt (1958) and by Mirsky (1963), who then obtained determinant inequalities as a consequence.

Biographies

BARON EDWARD HUGH JOHN NEAL DALTON
1887–1962

Hugh Dalton was born in 1887 at Neath, Glamorgan County, Wales. He was educated at Eton and King's College, Cambridge, where he won the Winchester Reading Prize in 1909 and received his M.A. From 1911 to 1913, he studied at the London School of Economics on a Hutchinson Research Studentship, leading to a D.Sc. In 1914 he became a Lecturer at the London School of Economics and also passed legal examinations.

During the First World War, Dalton served in the Army Service Corps and Royal Garrison Artillery, and in 1919 set up his law practice. From 1920 to 1925, he was the Sir Ernest Cassel Reader in Commerce and from 1925 to 1936 was Reader of Economics at the University of London. From 1929 to 1935, he was a Lecturer at the London School of Economics. He served on the Council of the Royal Statistical Society.

In 1924 Dalton won a seat in Parliament. When Ramsay MacDonald, the Labor Party leader, became Prime Minister in 1929, he was chosen as Parliamentary Undersecretary at the Foreign Office (1929–1931).

During the Second World War, he was a member of the Cabinet as Minister of Economic Warfare (1940–1942). In 1942 he became President of the Board of Trade and in 1945 again joined the Cabinet as Chancellor of the Exchequer under Prime Minister Clement Attlee.

Hugh Dalton died on February 13, 1962.

References

Current Biography, p. 132, H. W. Wilson, New York (1945).
H. Dalton, *Call Back Yesterday*; *Memoirs 1887–1960*, 3 vols. Miller, London (1953/1962).
Obituary, February 14, p. 17, *The Times*, London, England (1962).

Figure 1. Hugh Dalton

GODREY HAROLD HARDY, 1877–1947

Godfrey Harold Hardy was born on February 7, 1877, at Cranleigh, Surrey. He began his university studies at Trinity College, Cambridge, in 1896, where he was elected to a Prize Fellowship and was awarded a Smith's Prize. From 1906 to 1919, he was Lecturer in Mathematics at Trinity and was given the honorary title of Cayley Lecturer at the University of Cambridge in 1914. In 1919 he was elected to the Savilian Chair of Geometry at New College, Oxford.

In 1928–1929 he was a Visiting Professor at Princeton University and at the California Institute of Technology. In 1931 he returned to Cambridge in the Sadleirian Chair of Pure Mathematics, and again became a Fellow of Trinity. He retired from the Chair in 1945.

Hardy was a Fellow of the Royal Society and the Royal Astronomical Society. He served on the Council of the London Mathematical Society from 1905 to 1908 and subsequently almost continuously from 1914 until 1945; he was a secretary 1917–1926, 1941–1945, and president 1926–1928, 1939–1941.

He won the Royal Medal in 1920, the Sylvester Medal in 1940, the Copley Medal in 1947 from the Royal Society, the De Morgan Medal in 1929 from the London Mathematical Society, and the Chauvenet Prize in 1933 from the American Mathematical Association, and received numerous fellowships and honorary degrees throughout the world.

Hardy died on December 1, 1947.

References

List of papers by G. H. Hardy, *J. London Math. Soc.* **25**, 89–101, (1950).
Some aspects of Hardy's mathematical work, *J. London Math. Soc.* **25**, 102–138 (1950).
Collected papers of G. H. Hardy, Vols. I–VI. Oxford Univ. Press, London (1966–1974).
Obituary, December 2, p. 7, *The Times*, London, England (1947).
E. C. Titchmarsh, Godfrey Harold Hardy, *J. London Math. Soc.* **25**, 81–88 (1950).

Figure 2. Godfrey Harold Hardy

JOHAN LUDWIG WILLIAM VALDEMAR JENSEN, 1859–1925

Johan L.W.V. Jensen was born on May 8, 1859, in Nakskov, Denmark, the son of a bookseller. Shortly after he began school, the family moved to the north of Sweden, where his father was a farmer. He later returned to Denmark to attend the Polytechnical Institute in 1876, and subsequently worked as a mathematics teacher. In 1881 he became an assistant at the International Bell Telephone Company, which later became the Copenhagen Telephone Company. Incidentally, his father also worked at the telephone company as an accountant. While working at the telephone company, he exhibited his mathematical ability as well as an unusual technical ability in a variety of tasks, and was promoted rapidly. In 1890, at the young age of 31, he became senior engineer and head of the technical department. He continued working with the telephone company until 1924. Although Jensen never had an academic position, he reached as high a level as a mathematician as he did as an engineer. His contributions were on the Riemann hypothesis, infinite series, gamma functions, and inequalities for convex functions in 1906, for which he is best remembered. He was elected to the Royal Danish Academy of Sciences and Letters and in 1918 received an honorary doctorate from Lund University in Sweden. He suffered from angina pectoris attacks and died on March 6, 1925, in Copenhagen.

Figure 3. Johan Ludwig William Valdemar Jensen

JOVAN KARAMATA, 1902–1967

Jovan Karamata was born in Zagreb, Croatia, on February 1, 1902. Shortly thereafter the family moved to Zemun in Serbia, where he was educated until high school. Because of the First World War, his father sent him, together with his brothers and sister, to Lausanne, Switzerland, where he finished high school in 1920. He then enrolled in Belgrade University, and graduated in 1925 with a major in mathematics.

He spent the years 1927–1928 in Paris, as a fellow of the Rockefeller Foundation, and in 1928 he became Assistant for Mathematics at the Faculty of Philosophy of Belgrade University. In 1930 he became Assistant Professor, and in 1937 Associate Professor; after the end of the Second World War, in 1950 he became Full Professor. In 1951 he was elected Full Professor at the University of Geneva. He also taught at the University of Novi Sad.

In 1933 he became a member of Yugoslav Academy of Sciences and Arts, Czech Royal Society in 1936, and Serbian Royal Academy in 1939 as well as a fellow of Serbian Academy of Sciences in 1948. He was one of the founders of the Mathematical Institute of the Serbian Academy of Sciences and Arts in 1946.

Karamata was a member of the Swiss, French, and German mathematical societies, the French Association for the Development of Science, and the primary editor of the journal *l'Enseignement Mathematique* in Geneva.

After a long illness, Jovan Karamata died on August 14, 1967, in Geneva, but his ashes rest in his native town of Zemun.

References

S. Janković and T. Ostrogorski. Two Serbian Mathematicians. *The Mathematical Intelligencer*, 80 (2002).

M Tomić. Jovan Karamata, 1902-1967. *Bulletin T. CXXII de l'Acadmie Serbe des Sciences et des Arts.*, **26**, 1–29 (2001).

M. Tomić and S. Aljančić. Remembering Jovan Karamata. *Publications de l'Institute Mathematique*, **48** (62), 1–6 (1990).

Jovan Karamata biography and analysis of work (http://www.emis.de/journals/NSJOM/$32_1/r_1$.pdf).

Jovan Karamata biography and achievements (http://www.emis.de/journals/BSANU/26/$r2001_1$.pdf)

Figure 4. Jovan Karamata

JOHN EDENSOR LITTLEWOOD, 1885–1977

John Edensor Littlewood was born in Rochester, England, on June 9, 1885. From 1892 to 1900 he lived in South Africa and returned to England in 1900. In 1903 he began his university studies as a scholar of Trinity College, Cambridge. He won a Smith's Prize in 1908 and was elected a Fellow of Trinity. From 1908 to 1911, he was a Richardson Lecturer, Victoria University, Manchester, and returned to Trinity in 1910 as a College Lecturer. At the University of Cambridge, he was Cayley Lecturer from 1920 to 1928, and then was elected to the Rouse Ball Chair of Mathematics, a position he held until he retired in 1950.

Littlewood obtained an M.A. from Cambridge in 1950, an Honorary D.Sci. from Liverpool, an Honorary L.L.D. from St. Andrews, and an Honorary Sc.D. from Cambridge. He won the Royal Medal in 1929, the Sylvester Medal in 1944, the Copley Medal in 1948 from the Royal Society, the De Morgan Medal from the London Mathematical Society in 1939, and the Senior Berwick Prize in 1960. He was a Fellow of the Royal Society and the Cambridge Philosophical Society, a Corresponding Member of the French and Göttingen Academics, and a Foreign Member of the Royal Dutch, Royal Danish, and Royal Swedish Academies.

Littlewood died on September 7, 1977.

References

Notices Amer. Math. Soc. **25**, 68 (1977).
Obituary, September 8, p. 14, *The Times*, London, England (1977).
Who Was Who. A. and C. Black, London (1975).

Figure 5. John Edensor Littlewood

MAX OTTO LORENZ, 1876–1959

Max Otto Lorenz was born in Burlington, Iowa, on September 19, 1876. He received a B.A. degree from the University of Iowa in 1899 and a Ph.D. in economics from the University of Wisconsin in 1906.

He started his career in government agencies as Deputy Commissioner of Labor and Industrial Statistics for the State of Wisconsin, and subsequently worked as Statistician and Economist for the U.S. Bureau of the Census, the Bureau of Railway Economics, and the Interstate Commerce Commission. From 1920 until his retirement in 1944, he was Director of the Bureau of Statistics and the later Bureau of Transport Economics and Statistics. Lorenz died in Sunnyvale, California, on July 1, 1959.

While working for the Bureau of the Census in 1910, he applied the Lorenz curve which he had developed in 1905; the curve continues to be used extensively by economists.

References

National Cyclopedia of American Biography, Vol. 47, p. 490, J. T. White, Clifton, NJ (1965).

Figure 6. Max Otto Lorenz

ROBERT FRANKLIN MUIRHEAD, 1860–1941

Robert Franklin Muirhead was born on January 22, 1860, near Glasgow, Scotland. He attended Glasgow University, 1876–1881, and received his M.A. and B.Sc. degrees with highest honors in mathematics and natural philosophy. With a scholarship, he attended St. Catherine's College, Cambridge, where he was awarded a Smith's Prize in 1886. After another year's study at Göttingen, Muirhead returned to Britain and held a series of teaching positions. He unsuccessfully applied for several professorships, and finally settled in Glasgow about 1893 as a "Coach" in mathematics, physics, and engineering. About 1900 he founded the Glasgow Tutorial College and continued as Principal until his death in 1941.

Muirhead was elected a member of the Edinburgh Mathematical Society in its second session, in 1884, and was president of the Society in 1899 and 1909. He was also active in promoting socialism, was for a number of years a Member of Council of the Scottish National Party, and was for a time editor of the party publication, *Scots Independent*.

References

J. Dougall, Robert Franklin Muirhead, B.A., D.Sc, *Proc. Edinburgh, Math. Soc.* [2] **6**, 259–260 (1941).

Figure 7. Robert Franklin Muirhead

Figure 8. Muirhead

GEORGE PÓLYA, 1887–1985

George Pólya was born in Budapest, Hungary, on December 13, 1887, and studied at the Eötvös Lorand University, Budapest, and the University of Vienna. He received the Ph.D. degree at Budapest in 1912.

He spent the academic years 1912–1913 and 1913–1914 in Göttingen and Paris and then joined the Federal Polytechnical School in Zürich, Switzerland, as "Privatdozent" from 1914 to 1919, "Titular Professor" from 1920 to 1928, and Professor from 1928 to 1940.

Pólya taught at Brown University from 1940 to 1942, at Smith College in 1942, and then joined the faculty of Stanford University. His official "retirement" was in 1953, but he was still teaching in 1977.

Pólya was a Rockefeller Traveling Fellow at Oxford and Cambridge in 1924–1925, a visiting lecturer in Princeton in 1933, and at various times a Visiting Professor at Princeton, University of Geneva, University of Paris, University of Göttingen, University of Cambridge, University of British Columbia, and University of Toronto.

He received an Honorary D.Sci. from the Federal Polytechnical Institute in Zürich in 1947, and from the University of Wisconsin–

Milwaukee in 1969, an Honorary L.L.D. from the University of Alberta in 1961, and a D. Math. from the University of Waterloo in 1971.

He was awarded the Distinguished Service Award of the American Mathematical Association in 1963. Memberships include the National Academy of Sciences U.S.A., the American Academy of Arts and Sciences, the Hungarian Academy of Sciences, and the French Academy of Sciences.

The book *Studies in Mathematical Analysis and Related Topics, Essays in Honor of George Pólya,* published in 1962 on his 75th birthday, contains articles by some of his many friends, students, and colleagues. Pólya continued to give occasional talks, even at age 90. He died in Palo Alto, California, on September 7, 1985.

References

G. Pólya, *Collected Papers* (R. P. Boas, ed.), Vols. 1 and 2. MIT Press, Cambridge, MA (1974).

G. Szegö, C. Loewner, S. Bergman, M.M. Schiffer, J. Neyman, D. Gilbarg, and H. Solomon, eds. *Studies in Mathematical Analysis and Related Topics, Essays in Honor of George Pólya,* Stanford Univ. Press, Stanford, CA (1962).

Figure 9. George Pólya

ISSAI SCHUR, 1875–1941

Issai Schur was born on January 10, 1875, in Mogilev, Russia. He attended the Gymnasium in Libau (now Liepaja, Latvian SSR) and began his studies at the University of Berlin in 1894, where he was awarded a doctorate summa cum laude in 1901.

Schur taught in Berlin from 1903 to 1913, was an "assistant" professor at Bonn from 1913 to 1916, and returned to the University of Berlin in 1916 where he became a full professor in 1919. From 1933 to 1935 his position became precarious and in 1935 he was forced to retire by the Nazi authorities. In 1936 he visited the Eidgenössische Technische Hochschule in Zürich.

He became a member of the Prussian Academy of Science in 1922, and was also a member of the Academies at Leningrad, Leipzig, Halle, and Göttingen.

In 1939 Schur managed in ill health to emigrate to Israel (then Palestine). His health did not improve, and he died there two years later on his 66th birthday, January 10, 1941.

References

Special issue to commemorate Schur's eightieth birthday, *Math. Z.* **63** (1955/1956).

H. Boerner, Issai Schur, *Dictionary of Scientific Biography*, Vol. 12, p. 237. Scribner's, NY (1975).

A. Brauer, Gedenkrede auf Issai Schur. In *Issai Schur Gesammelte Abhandlungen* (A. Brauer and H. Rohrbach, eds.), pp. v–xiv. Springer-Verlag, Berlin and New York (1973).

A. Brauer, Eine Bemerkung zum Vornaman Schurs, *Jber. Deutsch. Math.-Verein.* **77**, 165, 166 (1976).

810 Biographies

Figure 10. Issai Schur

Figure 11. Hardy and Pólya

Biographies 811

Figure 12. Hardy and Littlewood

Figure 13. Pólya and Littlewood

References

Abramowitz, M., and I. A. Stegun (1972). *Handbook of Mathematical Functions with Formulas, Graphs and Mathematical Tables* (10th printing). National Bureau of Standards Applied Mathematics Series. U.S. Government Printing Office, Washington, DC. **55**.

Abramowitz, S., J. Barić, M. Matić and J. Pečarić (2007). On van de Lune-Alzer's inequality. *J. Math. Inequal.* **1**, 563–587. [*MR* **2009b:26018**]

Achilles, E., and R. Sinkhorn (1995). Doubly stochastic matrices whose squares are idempotent. *Linear Multilinear Algebra* **38**, 343–349. [*MR* **96h:15023**]

Aczél, J. (1966). *Lectures on Functional Equations and Their Applications*. Academic Press, New York. [*MR* **34**(1967)8020; *Zbl.* **139**(1968)93]

Aitken, A. C. (1939, 1956). *Determinants and Matrices*. 1st ed., 9th ed. Oliver & Boyd, Edinburgh. [*MR* **1**(1940)35; *Zbl.* **22**(1940)100]

Alam, K. (1970). Monotonicity properties of the multinomial distribution. *Ann. Math. Statist.* **41**, 315–317. [*MR* **41**(1971)2811; *Zbl.* **188**(1970)509]

Alam, K., M. H. Rizvi, A. Mitra, and K. M. L. Saxena (1986). Selection of the most diverse multinomial population. *Amer. J. Math. Management Sci.* **6**, 65–86. [*MR* **88c:62038**]

Alam, K., and J. R. Thompson (1972). On selecting the least probable multinomial event. *Ann. Math. Statist.* **43**, 1981–1990. [*MR* **50**(1975)3422; *Zbl.* **249**(1973)62062]

Alam, K., and J. R. Thompson (1973). A problem of ranking and estimation with Poisson processes. *Technometrics* **15**, 801–808. [*MR* **49**(1975)10012; *Zbl.* **269**(1975)62080]

Alam, K., and C. L. Williams (1993). Relative difference in diversity between populations. *Ann. Inst. Statist. Math.* **45**, 383–399. [*MR* **94k:62003**]

Alberti, P. M., B. Crell, A. Uhlmann, and C. Zylka (2008). Order structure (majorization) and irreversible processes. In *Vernetzte Wissenschaften: Crosslinks in Natural and Social Sciences* (P. J. Plath and E. C. Hass, eds.), pp. 281-290. Logos-Verlag, Berlin.

Alberti, P. M., and A. Uhlmann (1982). *Stochasticity and Partial Order. Doubly Stochastic Maps and Unitary Mixing*. Mathematics and its Applications. Reidel Publishing Co., Dordrecht–Boston. **9**. [*MR* **84i:46057b**]

Aldous, D., and L. Shepp (1987). The least variable phase type distribution is Erlang. *Comm. Statist. Stochastic Models* **3**, 467–473. [*MR* **89h:60115**]

Alker, H. R. (1965). *Mathematics and Politics*. Macmillan, New York.

Alker, H. R., and B. M. Russet (1966). Indices for comparing inequality. In *Comparing Nations: The Use of Quantitative Data in Cross-National Research* (R. L. Merritt and S. Rokkan, eds.), pp. 349–372. Yale University Press, New Haven, CT.

Alpargu, G., and G. P. H. Styan (1996). Some remarks and a bibliography on the Kantorovich inequality. In *Multidimensional Statistical Analysis and Theory of Random Matrices*, (A. K. Gupta and V. L. Girko, eds.), 1–13, VSP, Utrecht. [*MR* **98h:15033**]

Alpargu, G. and G. P. H. Styan (2000). Some comments and a bibliography on the Frucht-Kantorovich and Wielandt inequalities. In *Innovations in Multivariate Statistical Analysis: A Festschrift for Heinz Neudecker*. (R. D. H. Heijmans, D. S. G. Pollock, and A. Satorra, eds), Kluwer, London.

Alzer, H. (1993). On an inequality of H. Minc and L. Sathre. *J. Math. Anal. Appl.* **179**, 396–402. [*MR* **94k:26021**]

Amato, V. (1968). *Metodologia Statistica Strutturale*, Vol. 1. Cacucci, Bari.

Amir-Moéz, A. R. (1956). Extreme properties of eigenvalues of a Hermitian transformation and singular values of the sum and product of linear transformations. *Duke Math. J.* **23**, 463–476. [*MR* **18**(1957)105; *Zbl.* **71**(1957/1958)16]

Amir-Moéz, A. R., and A. Horn (1958). Singular values of a matrix. *Amer. Math. Monthly* **65**, 741–748. [*MR* **20**(1959)7037]

Amparan, A., S. Marcaida, and I. Zaballa (2004). Wiener–Hopf factorization indices and infinite structure of rational matrices. *SIAM J. Control Optim.* **42**, 2130–2144. [*MR* **2005g:15022**]

An, M. Y. (1998). Logconcavity versus logconvexity: a complete characterization. *J. Econ. Theory* **80**, 350–369.

Anderson, T. W. (1955). The integral of a symmetric unimodal function over a symmetric convex set and some probability inequalities. *Proc. Amer. Math. Soc.* **6**, 170–176. [*MR* **16**(1955)1005; *Zbl.* **66**(1956)374]

Anderson, T. W. (2003). *An Introduction to Multivariate Statistical Analysis*, 3rd ed. Wiley-Interscience [John Wiley & Sons], Hoboken, NJ. [*MR* **2004c:62001**]

Anderson, T. W., and A. Takemura (1982). A new proof of admissibility of tests in the multivariate analysis of variance. *J. Multivariate Anal.* **12**, 457–468. [*MR* **84g:62094**]

Andersson, S. A., and M. D. Perlman (1988). Group-invariant analogues of Hadamard's inequality. *Linear Algebra Appl.* **110**, 91–116. [*MR* **89i:15028**]

Ando, T. (1979). Concavity of certain maps on positive definite matrices and applications to Hadamard products. *Linear Algebra Appl.* **26**, 203–241. [*MR* **80f:15023**]

Ando, T. (1987). Totally positive matrices. *Linear Algebra Appl.* **90**, 165–219. [*MR* **88b:15023**]

Ando, T. (1989). Majorization, doubly stochastic matrices, and comparison of eigenvalues. *Linear Algebra Appl.* **118**, 163–248. [*MR* **90g:15034**]

Ando, T. (1994). Majorizations and inequalities in matrix theory. *Linear Algebra Appl.* **199**, 17–67. [*MR* **95d:15008**]

Ando, T. (1995). Majorization relations for Hadamard products. *Linear Algebra Appl.* **223/224**, 57–64. [*MR* **96e:15026**]

Ando, T. (2001). Bloomfield–Watson–Knott type inequalities for eigenvalues. *Taiwanese J. Math.* **5**, 443–469. [*MR* **2002f:15022**]

Ando, T., and F. Hiai (1994). Log majorization and complementary Golden–Thompson type inequalities. *Linear Algebra Appl.* **197/198**, 113–131. [*MR* **95d:15006**]

Ando, T., F. Hiai, and K. Okubo (2000). Trace inequalities for multiple products of two matrices. *Math. Inequal. Appl.* **3**, 307–318. [*MR* **2001d:15020**]

Ando, T., R. A. Horn, and C. R. Johnson (1987). The singular values of a Hadamard product: a basic inequality. *Linear Multilinear Algebra* **21**, 345–365. [*MR* **89g:15018**]

Ando, T., and X. Zhan (1999). Norm inequalities related to operator monotone functions. *Math. Ann.* **315**, 771–780. [*MR* **2000m:47008**]

Andréief, C. (1883). Note sur une rélation entre les intégrales définies des produits des fonctions. *Mem. Soc. Sci. Bordeaux* [3] **2**, 1–14.

Anwar, M., N. Latif, and J. E. Pečarić (2009). On logarithmic convexity and majorization. Private communication.

Araki, H. (1990). On an inequality of Lieb and Thirring. *Lett. Math. Phys.*. **19**, 167–170. [*MR* **91d:47020**]

Arikati, S. R., and A. Maheshwari (1996). Realizing degree sequences in parallel. *SIAM J. Discrete Math.* **9**, 317–338. [*MR* **97b:68074**]

Arikati, S. R., and U. N. Peled (1999). The realization graph of a degree sequence with majorization gap 1 is Hamiltonian. *Linear Algebra Appl.* **290**, 213–235. [*MR* **99m:05097**]

Arjas, E., and T. Lehtonen (1978). Approximating many server queues by means of single server queues. *Math. Oper. Res.* **3**, 205–223. [*MR* **80c:60105**]

Arnold, B. C. (1986). A class of hyperbolic Lorenz curves. *Sankhyā Ser. B.* **48**, 427–436. [*MR* **88k:62194**]

Arnold, B. C. (1987). *Majorization and the Lorenz Order: A Brief Introduction. Lecture Notes in Statistics*, **43**. Springer-Verlag, Berlin. [*MR* **89a:60046**]

Arnold, B. C. (1991). Preservation and attenuation of inequality as measured by the Lorenz order. *Stochastic Orders and Decision Under Risk*. (K. Mosler and M. Scarsini, eds.), IMS Lec. Notes – Monograph Ser. **19**, 26–37. [*MR* **94b:60018**]

Arnold, B. C., and H. Joe (2000). Variability ordering of functions. *Int. J. Math. Stat. Sci.* **9**, 179–189. [*MR* **2001m:60030**]

Arnold, B. C., and H. N. Nagaraja (1991). Lorenz ordering of exponential order statistics. *Statist. Probab. Lett.* **11**, 485–490. [*MR* **92k:62097**]

Arnold, B. C., C. A. Robertson, P. L. Brockett, and B. Shu (1987). Generating ordered families of Lorenz curves by strongly unimodal distributions. *J. Business Econ. Stat.* **5**, 305–308.

Arnold, B. C., and J. A. Villaseñor (1985). Inequality preserving and inequality attenuating transformations. Technical Report, Colegio de Postgraduados, Chapingo, Mexico.

Arnold, B. C., and J. A. Villaseñor (1986). Lorenz ordering of means and medians. *Statist. Probab. Lett.* **4**, 47–49. [*MR* **87d:62035**]

Arnold, B. C., and J. A. Villaseñor (1991). Lorenz ordering of order statistics. In *Stochastic Orders and Decision Under Risk* (K. Mosler and M. Scarsini, eds.), *IMS Lec. Notes – Monograph Ser.* **19**, 38–47. [*MR* **94b:60019**]

Arnold, B. C., and J. A. Villaseñor (1998). Lorenz ordering of order statistics and record values. In *Order Statistics: Theory and Methods. Handbook of Statistics* (N. Balakrishnan, and C. R. Rao, eds.), **16**, 75–87. North-Holland, Amsterdam. [*MR* **1668743**]

Artin, E. (1931). *Einführung in die Theorie der Gammafunktion*, Hamburger Mathematische Einzelschriften, Heft II. (Transl. by M. Butler, *The Gamma Function*. Holt, Rinehart & Winston, New York, 1964.) [*MR* **29**(1965)2437; *Zbl.* **1**(1931)286]

Atkinson, A. B. (1970). On the measurement of inequality. *J. Econ. Theory* **5**, 244–263

Atkinson, A. B. (1975). *The Economics of Inequality*. Clarendon Press, Oxford.

Audenaert, K. M. R. (2009). A Lieb–Thirring inequality for singular values. *Linear Algebra Appl.* **430**, 3053–3057.

Aujla, J. S., and J-C. Bourin (2007). Eigenvalue inequalities for convex and log-convex functions. *Linear Algebra Appl.* **424**, 25–35. [*MR* **2008j:47013**]

Aujla, J. S., and F. C. Silva (2003). Weak majorization inequalities and convex functions. *Linear Algebra Appl.* **369**, 217–233. [*MR* **2004g:47021**]

Ault, J. C. (1967). An inequality for traces. *J. London Math. Soc.* **42**, 497–500. [*MR* **35**(1958)5458; *Zbl.* **147**(1968)277]

Autonne, L. (1902). On linear, real and orthogonal groups. *Bull. Soc. Math. France* **30**, 121–134.

Autonne, L. (1903). Sur l'hypohermitien. *Bull. Soc. Math. France* **31**, 140–155.

Autonne, L. (1913). Sur les matrices hypohermitiennes et les unitaires. *C. R. Acad. Sci., Paris* **156**, 858–860.

Autonne, L. (1915). Sur les matrices hypohermitiennes et sur les matrices unitaires. *Ann. Univ. Lyon II* **38**, 1–77.

Azizoğlu, M. C., and O. Eğecioğlu (2003). Extremal sets minimizing dimension-normalized boundary in Hamming graphs. *SIAM J. Discrete Math.* **17**, 219–236. [*MR* **2005c:05114**]

Bacharach, M. (1970) *Biproportional Matrices and Input-Output Change. University of Cambridge, Department of Applied Economics, Monographs*, **16**. Cambridge University Press, London. [*MR* **41:8014**]

Bagdasar, O. (2008). A productive inequality. *Amer. Math. Monthly.* **115**, 268–269.

Bagnoli, M., and T. Bergstrom (2005). Log-concave probability and its applications. *J. Econ. Theory* **26**, 445–469. [*MR* **2213177**]

Balinski, M. L., and H. P. Young (2001). *Fair Representation - Meeting the Ideal of One Man One Vote,* 2nd Edition. Brookings Institute Press, Washington, DC.

Bapat, R. B. (1987). Majorization and singular values. *Linear and Multilinear Algebra* **21**, 211–214. [*MR* **89j:15015**]

Bapat, R. B. (1991). Majorization and singular values. III. *Linear Algebra Appl.* **145**, 59–70. [*MR* **91k:15018**]

Bapat, R. B., and T. E. S. Raghavan (1997). *Nonnegative Matrices and Applications. Encyclopedia of Mathematics and Its Applications*, **64**. Cambridge University Press, Cambridge. [*MR* **98h:15038**]

Bapat, R. B., and V. S. Sunder (1985). On majorization and Schur products. *Linear Algebra Appl.* **72**, 107–117. [*MR* **87c:15018**]

Baragaña, I., M. Asunción Beitia, and I. de Hoyos (2009). Structured perturbation of the Brunovsky form: A particular case. *Linear Algebra Appl.* **430**, 1613–1625. [*MR* **2490702**]

Baragaña, I., V. Fernández, and I. Zaballa (2000). Linear systems with prescribed similarity structural invariants. *SIAM J. Control Optim.* **38**, 1033–1049. [*MR* **2001d:93047**]

Barlow, R. E., D. J. Bartholomew, J. M. Bremner, and H. D. Brunk (1972). *Statistical Inference Under Order Restrictions. The Theory and Application of Isotonic Regression.* Wiley, New York. [*MR* 48(1974)5229; *Zbl.* **246**(1973)62038]

Barlow, R. E. and R. Campo (1975). Total time on test processes and applications to failure data analysis. In *Reliability and Fault Tree analysis.* (R. E. Barlow, J. B. Fussell and N. D. Singpurwalla, eds.) pp. 451–481, SIAM, Philadelphia. [*MR* **56:7076**]

Barlow, R. E., A. W. Marshall, and F. Proschan (1963). Properties of probability distributions with monotone hazard rate. *Ann. Math. Statist.* **34**, 375–389. [*MR* **30**(1965)1559]

Barlow, R. E., A. W. Marshall, and F. Proschan (1969). Some inequalities for starshaped and convex functions. *Pacific J. Math.* **29**, 19–42. [*MR* 41(1971)8788; *Zbl.* **176**(1969)12]

Barlow, R. E., and F. Proschan (1966). Inequalities for linear combinations of order statistics from restricted families. *Ann. Math. Statist.* **37**, 1574–1592. [*MR* 34(1967)898; *Zbl.* **149**(1968)154]

Barlow, R. E., and F. Proschan (1975). *Statistical Theory of Reliability and Life Testing: Probability Models.* Holt, Rinehart & Winston, New York. [*MR* **55**(1978)11534]

Barlow, R. E., and F. Proschan (1996). *Mathematical Theory of Reliability. With Contributions by Larry C. Hunter.* Reprint of the 1965 original. *Classics in Applied Mathematics*, **17**. Society for Industrial and Applied Mathematics (SIAM), Philadelphia. [*MR* **97c:62235**]

Barlow, R. E., and F. Spizzichino. (1993). Schur-concave survival functions and survival analysis. *J. Comput. Appl. Math.* **46**, 437–447. [*MR* **94d:62232**]

Baston, V. J. (1976/1977). Some inequalities involving the symmetric functions. *Proc. Edinburgh Math. Soc.* **20**, 199–204. [*MR* **56:5312**]

Baston, V. J. (1978). Inequalities for the generalized symmetric functions. *J. Math. Anal. Appl.* **63**, 50–53. [*MR* **58:270**]

Basu, D. (1958). On sampling with and without replacement. *Sankhyā* **20**, 287–294. [*MR* **21**(1960)4517; *Zbl.* **88**(1961)126]

Bauer, F. L., and C. T. Fike (1960). Norms and exclusions theorems. *Numer. Math.* **2** 137–141. [*MR* **22**(1961)9500]

Beasley, L. B., and S.-G. Lee (2000). Linear operators preserving multivariate majorization. *Linear Algebra Appl.* **304**, 141–159. [*MR* **2000i:15005**]

Bebiano, N., C.-K. Li, and J. da Providência (1997). Determinant of the sum of a symmetric and a skew-symmetric matrix. *SIAM J. Matrix Anal. Appl.* **18**, 74–82. [*MR* **98c:15023**]

Bechhofer, R. E., S. Elmaghraby, and N. Morse (1959). A single-sample multiple-decision procedure for selecting the multinomial event which has the highest probability. *Ann. Math. Statist.* **30**, 102–119. [*MR* **21**(1960)4515]

Bechhofer, R. E., T. J. Santner, and B. W. Turnbull (1977). Selecting the largest interaction in a two-factor experiment. In *Statistical Decision Theory and Related Topics II* (S. S. Gupta and D. S. Moore, eds.), pp. 1–18. Academic Press, New York.

Beckenbach, E. F., and R. Bellman (1961, 1965). *Inequalities*, 1st ed., 2nd ed. Springer-Verlag, Berlin and New York. [*MR* **31**(1966)5937; *Zbl.* **126**(1966)280]

Beineke, L. W., and F. Harary (1965). The thickness of the complete graph. *Canad. J. Math.* **17**, 850–859. [*MR* **32**(1966)4032]

Bellman, R. (1953a). Notes on matrix theory II. *Amer. Math. Monthly* **60**, 173–175. [*MR* **14**(1953)731; *Zbl.* **50**(1954)10]

Bellman, R. (1953b). On an inequality due to Weinberger. *Amer. Math. Monthly* **60**, 402. [*MR* **14**(1953)957]

Bellman, R. (1960, 1972). *Introduction to Matrix Analysis*, 1st ed., 2nd ed. McGraw-Hill, New York. [*MR* **32A**(1962)153; *Zbl.* **124**(1966)10]

Beltrami, E. (1873). On bilinear functions. *Giorn. Mat. Battagline* **11**, 98–106.

Bendat, J., and S. Sherman (1955). Monotone and convex operator functions. *Trans. Amer. Math. Soc.* **79**, 58–71. [*MR* **18**(1957)588; *Zbl.* **64**(1956)369]

Bendixson, I. (1902). Sur les racines d'une équation fondamentale. *Acta Math.* **25**, 359–365.

Berenbrink, P., A. Czumaj, A. Steger, and B. Vöcking (2006). Balanced allocations: The heavily loaded case. *SIAM J. Comput.* **35**, 1350–1385. [*MR* **2007g:68174**]

Berg, C., J. P. R. Christensen, and P. Ressel (1984). *Harmonic Analysis on Semi-Groups: Theory of Positive Definite and Related Functions*. Springer-Verlag, New York. [*MR* **86b:43001**]

Berge, C. (1955). Sur une propriété des matrices doublement stochastiques. *C. R. Acad. Sci. Paris* **241**, 269–271. [*MR* **17**(1956)228; *Zbl.* **65**(1965)246]

Berge, C. (1958). *Theorie des Graphes et Ses Applications*. Dunod, Paris. [*MR* **21**(1960)1608; *Zbl.* **101**(1963)166]

Berge, C. (1959). *Espaces Topologiques; Fonctions Multivoques*. Dunod, Paris. [*MR* **21**(1960)4401; *Zbl.* **88**(1961)147]

Berge, C. (1962). *The Theory of Graphs and Its Applications* (transl. by A. Doig). Methuen, London; Wiley, New York. [*MR* **24**(1962)A238; *Zbl.* **101**(1965)166]

Berge, C. (1963). *Topological Spaces, Including a Treatment of Multi-Valued Functions, Vector Spaces and Convexity* (transl. by E. M. Patterson), 1st Engl. ed. Oliver & Boyd, Edinburgh. [*Zbl.* **114**(1965)386]

Berge, C. (1971). Sur une extension de la théorie des matrices bistochastiques, pp. 1–8. In *Studi di Probabilità, Statistica e Ricerca Operativa in Onera de Giuseppe Pompilj*, Oderisi, Gubbio. [*MR* **51**(1976)5321; *Zbl.* **287**(1975)60083]

Berger, E. (1991). Majorization, exponential inequalities and almost sure behavior of vector-valued random variables. *Ann. Probab.* **19**, 1206–1226. [*MR* **92j:60006**]

Bergmann, R. (1991). Stochastic orders and their application to a unified approach to various concepts of dependence and association. In *Stochastic Orders and Decision Under Risk* (K. Mosler and M. Scarsini, eds.), *IMS Lecture Notes Monogr. Ser.* **19**, pp. 48–73, Inst. Math. Statist., Hayward, CA. [*MR* **93k:60045**]

Bergström, H. (1952). A triangle inequality for matrices. *Den Elfte Skandinaviskie Matematiker-Kongress, Trondheim*, pp. 264–267. Johan Grundt Tanums Forlag, Oslo. [*MR* **14**(1953)716; *Zbl.* **49**(1949)295]

Bernstein, D. S. (2005). *Matrix Mathematics. Theory, Facts, and Formulas with Application to Linear Systems Theory*. Princeton University Press, Princeton, NJ. [*MR* **2005i:93001**]

Bhagwat, K. V., and R. Subramanian (1978). Inequalities between means of positive operations. *Math. Proc. Cambridge Philos. Soc.* **83**, 393–401.

Bhandari, S. K. (1995). Multivariate majorization and directional majorization: Negative results. *Calcutta Statist. Assoc. Bull.* **45**, 149–159. [*MR* **97h:62042**]

Bhandari, S. K., and A. Bose (1987). On selecting the most likely event. *J. Statist. Plann. Inference* **17**, 227–240. [*MR* **89h:62040**]

Bhandari, S. K., and S. Das Gupta (1985). Two characterizations of doubly super-stochastic matrices. *Sankhyā Ser. A.* **47**, 357–365. [*MR* **87j:15041**]

Bhatia, R. (1997). *Matrix Analysis*. Springer-Verlag, New York. [*MR* **98i:15003**

Bhatia, R. (2001). Linear algebra to quantum cohomology: The story of Alfred Horn's inequalities. *Amer. Math. Monthly* **108**, 289–318. [*MR* **2002m:15002**]

Bhatia, R., and C. Davis (1993). More matrix forms of the arithmetic-geometric mean inequality. *SIAM J. Matrix Anal. Appl.* **14**, 132–136. [*MR* **94b:15017**]

Bhatia, R., and F. Kittaneh (2008). The matrix arithmetic-geometric mean inequality revisited. *Linear Algebra Appl.* **428**, 2177–2191. [*MR* **2009f:15041**]

Bhatia, R., and F. Kittaneh (2009). The singular values of $A+B$ and $A+iB$. *Linear Algebra Appl.* **431**, 1502–1508.

Billingsley, P. (1968). *Convergence of Probability Measures*. Wiley, New York. [*MR* **38**(1969)1718; *Zbl.* **172**(1969)212]

Binet, J. P. M. (1812). Mémoire sur un systéme de formules analytiques, et leur application à des considérations géometriques. *J. École Polytech.* **9**, Cahier 16, 280–302.

Birkhoff, G. (1946). Tres observaciones sobre el algebra lineal. *Univ. Nac. Tucumán Rev. Ser. A*, **5**, 147–151. [*MR* **8**(1947)561; *Zbl.* **60**(1957)79]

Birnbaum, Z. W. (1948). On random variables with comparable peakedness. *Ann. Math. Statist.* **19**, 76–81. [*MR* **9**(1948)452; *Zbl.* **31** (1949)368]

Blackorby, C., and D. Donaldson (1978). Measures of relative equality and their meaning in terms of social welfare. *J. Econom. Theory* **18**, 59–79.

Blackwell, D. (1951). Comparison of experiments. *Proc. Second Berkeley Symp. Math. Statist. Prob.*, pp. 93–102. University of California Press, Berkeley. [*MR* **13**(1952)667; *Zbl.* **44**(1952)142]

Blackwell, D. (1953). Equivalent comparisons of experiments. *Ann. Math. Statist.* **24**, 265–272. [*MR* **15**(1954)47; *Zbl.* **50**(1954)360]

Bloom, D. M. (1966). Problem E 1929. *Amer. Math. Monthly* **73**, 1017; see also *Amer. Math. Monthly* **75**(1968), 298.

Bogoljubov, N.N. (1966). On model dynamical systems in statistical mechanics. *Physica* **32**, 933–944.

Boland, P. J., and E. El-Neweihi (1998). Statistical and information based (physical) minimal repair for k out of n systems. *J. Appl. Probab.* **35**, 731–740. [*MR* **2000a:62263**]

Boland, P. J., E. El-Neweihi, and F. Proschan (1994). Schur properties of convolutions of exponential and geometric random variables. *J. Multivariate Anal.* **48**, 157–167. [*MR* **95d:60034**]

Boland, P. J., and F. Proschan (1983). The reliability of k out of n systems. *Ann. Probab.* **11**, 760–764. [*MR* **85b:62091**]

Boland, P. J., and F. Proschan (1987). Schur convexity of the maximum likelihood function for the multivariate hypergeometric and multinomial distributions. *Statist. Probab. Lett.* **5**, 317–322. [*MR* **88h:62014**]

Boland, P. J., and F. Proschan (1988). Multivariate arrangement increasing functions with applications in probability and statistics. *J. Multivariate Anal.* **25**, 286–298. [*MR* **89d:62042**]

Boland, P. J., F. Proschan, and Y. L. Tong (1990). Some majorization inequalities for functions of exchangeable random variables. In *Topics in Statistical Dependence* (H. W. Block, A. R. Sampson, and T. H. Savits, eds.), *IMS Lec. Notes – Monograph Ser.* **16**, 85–91. [*MR* **93i:60033**]

Bon, J.-L., and E. Păltănea (1999). Ordering properties of convolutions of exponential random variables. *Lifetime Data Anal.* **5**, 185–192. [*MR* **2000k:62193**]

Bondar, J. V. (1983). Universal optimality of experimental designs: definitions and a criterion. *Canad. J. Statist.* **11**, 325–331. [*MR* **85k:62164**]

Bondar, J. V. (1994). Comments on and complements to: *Inequalities: Theory of Majorization and Its Applications* by A. W. Marshall and I. Olkin. *Linear Algebra Appl.* **199**, 115–130. [*MR* **95c:00001**]

Borell, C. (1973). A note on an inequality for rearrangements. *Pacific J. Math.* **47**, 39–41. [*MR* **48**(1974)1942; *Zbl.* **273**(1975)26009]

Borell, C. (1975). Convex set functions in d-space. *Period. Math. Hungar.* **6**, 111–136. [*MR* **53:8359**]

Borobia, A. (1996). A practical criterion for multivariate majorization. *Rev. Acad. Canar. Cienc.* **8**, 93–100. [*MR* **98h:15041**]

Borobia, A., and R. Cantó (1998). Matrix scaling: A geometric proof of Sinkhorn's theorem. *Linear Algebra Appl.* **268**, 1–8. [*MR* **98k:15030**]

Bottema, O., R. Ž. Djordjević, R. R. Janić, D. S. Mitrinović, and P. M. Vasić (1969). *Geometric Inequalities.* Wolters-Noordhoff, Groningen, the Netherlands. [*MR* **41**(1971)7537; *Zbl.* **174**(1969)524]

Brascamp, H. J., and E. H. Lieb (1976). On extensions of the Brunn–Minkowski and Prékopa–Leindler theorems, including inequalities for log concave functions, and with an application to the diffusion equation. *J. Funct. Anal.* **22**, 366–389. [*MR* **56:8774**]

Brauer, A. (1946). Limits for the characteristic roots of a matrix. *Duke Math. J.* **13**, 387–395. [*MR* **10**(1949)231]

Brauer, A., I. C. Gentry, and K. Shaw (1968). A new proof of a theorem by H. G. Landau on tournament matrices. *J. Combin. Theory* **5**, 289–292. [*MR* **38**(1969)66; *Zbl.* **165**(1969)327]

Brillouin, L. (1962). *Science and Information Theory*, 2nd ed. Academic Press, New York. [*MR* **30**(1965)3; *Zbl.* **98**(1963)322]

Bromwich, J. T. I'A. (1906). On the roots of the characteristic equation of a linear substitution. *Acta Math.* **30**, 295–304.

Brown, M., and H. Solomon (1979). On combining pseudorandom number generators. *Ann. Statist.* **7**, 691–695. [*MR* **80f:65009**]

Browne, E. T. (1928). The characteristic equation of a matrix. *Bull. Amer. Math. Soc.* **34**, 363–368.

Browne, E. T. (1930a). On the separation property of the roots of the secular equation. *Amer. J. Math.* **52**, 843–850.

Browne, E. T. (1930b). The characteristic roots of a matrix. *Bull. Amer. Math. Soc.* **36**, 705–710.

Brualdi, R. A. (1984). The doubly stochastic matrices of a vector majorization. *Linear Algebra Appl.* **61**, 141–154. [*MR* **85i:15035**]

Brualdi, R. A. (2006). *Combinatorial Matrix Classes. Encyclopedia of Mathematics and Its Applications*, **108** Cambridge University Press, Cambridge. [*MR* **2007k:05038**]

Brualdi, R. A., and S.-G. Hwang (1996). Vector majorization via Hessenberg matrices. *J. London Math. Soc.* **53**, 28–38. [*MR* **96j:15016**]

Brualdi, R. A., S. V. Parter, and H. Schneider (1966). The diagonal equivalence of a nonnegative matrix to a stochastic matrix. *J. Math. Anal. Appl.* **16**, 31–50. [*MR* **34**(1967)5844; *Zbl.* **231**(1972)15017]

Brualdi, R. A., and H. Ryser (1991). *Combinatorial Matrix Theory. Encyclopedia of Mathematics and Its Applications*, **39**, Cambridge University Press. Cambridge, England. [*MR* **93a:05087**]

de Bruijn, N. G. (1956). Inequalities concerning minors and eigenvalues. *Nieuw. Arch. Wisk.* [3] **4**, 18–35. [*MR* **18**(1957)183; *Zbl.* **74** (1960–62)252]

de Bruijn, N. G., and G. Szekeres (1955). On some exponential and polar representations of matrices. *Nieuw. Arch. Wisk.* [3] **3**, 20–32. [*MR* **16**(1955)785]

Bruckner, A. M., and E. Ostrow (1962). Some function classes related to the class of convex functions. *Pacific J. Math.* **12**, 1203–1215. [*MR* **26**(1963)6326; *Zbl.* **121**(1966)295]

Brunk, H. D. (1956). On an inequality for convex functions. *Proc. Amer. Math. Soc.* **7**, 817–824. [*MR* **18**(1957)391; *Zbl.* **71**(1957/58)279]

Buehler, R. J. (1957). Confidence intervals for the product of two binomial parameters. *J. Amer. Statist. Assoc.* **52**, 482–493. [*MR* **19:1204j**]

Bullen, P. S. (1998). *A Dictionary of Inequalities. Pitman Monographs and Surveys in Pure and Applied Mathematics*, **97**. Longman, Harlow. [*MR* **2000e:26001**]

Bullen, P. S. (2003). *Handbook of Means and Their Inequalities.* Kluwer, Dordrecht. [*MR* **2005a:26001**]

Bullen, P., and M. Marcus (1961). Symmetric means and matrix inequalities. *Proc. Amer. Math. Soc.* **12**, 285–290. [*MR* **22**(1961)12113; *Zbl.* **96**(1962)246]

Bullen, P. S., D. S. Mitrinović, and P. M. Vasić (1988). *Means and Their Inequalities.* Reidel, Dordrecht. [*MR* **89d:26003**]

Bullen, P. S., P. M. Vasić, and Lj. Stanković (1973). A problem of A. Oppenheim. *Univ. Beograd Publications. Elek. Fak. Ser. Mat. Fiz.* **412–460**, 21–30. [*MR* **48:6338**]

Burkill, H. (1964). A note on rearrangements of functions. *Amer. Math. Monthly* **71**, 887–888. [*MR* **29**(1965)5965; *Zbl.* **129**(1967)38]

Cacoullos, T., and I. Olkin (1965). On the bias of functions of characteristic roots of a random matrix. *Biometrika* **52**, 87–94. [*MR* **34**(1967)6932; *Zbl.* **132**(1967)132]

Cambanis S., G. Simons, and W. Stout (1976). Inequalities for $EK(X,Y)$ when the marginals are fixed. *Z. Wahrsch. Verw. Gebiete* **36**, 285–294. [*MR* **54:8790**]

Carlson, B. C. (1972). The logarithmic mean. *Amer. Math. Monthly* **79**, 615–618. [*MR* **46:1985**]

Caron, R. M., X. Li, P. Mikusiński, H. Sherwood, and M. D. Taylor (1996). Nonsquare "doubly stochastic" matrices. In *Distributions with Fixed Marginals and Related Topics* (L. Rüschendorf, B. Schweizer, and M. D. Taylor, eds.), *IMS Lec. Notes – Monograph Ser.* **28**, 65–75. [*MR* **99b:15025**]

Castillo, E. and M. R. Ruiz-Cobo (1992). *Functional Equations and Modelling in Science and Engineering. Monographs and Textbooks in Pure and Applied Mathematics*, **161**. Marcel Dekker, New York. [*MR* **93k:39006**]

Cauchy, A. L. (1812). Mémoire sur les fonctions qui ne peuvent obtenir que deux valeurs égales et de signes contraires par suite des transpositions opérées entre les variables qu'elles renferment. *J. École Polytech.* **10**, Cahier 17, 29–112; *Oeuvres Complétes* (2) **1**, 91–169.

Causey, R. L. (1964). *On closest normal matrices*, Tech. Rep. CS 10. Computer Science Division, Stanford University, Stanford, CA.

Cerone, P., and S. S. Dragomir (2008). A survey on bounds for the Gini mean difference. In *Advances in Inequalities from Probability Theory and Statistics* (N. S. Barnett and S. S. Dragomir, eds), pp. 81–111, Nova Science Publishers, New York. [*MR* **2459970**]

Chan, W., D. H. Park, and F. Proschan (1989). Peakedness of weighted averages of jointly distributed random variables. In *Contributions to Probability and Statistics. Essays in Honor of Ingram Olkin* (L. J. Gleser, M. D. Perlman, S. J. Press, and A. R. Sampson, eds.), pp. 58–62, Springer, New York. [*MR* **91d:60040**]

Chan, W., F. Proschan and J. Sethuraman (1987). Schur–Ostrowski theorems for functionals on $L_1(0,1)$. *SIAM J. Math. Anal.* **18**, 566–578. [*MR* **88h: 26009**]

Chandra, M., and N. D. Singpurwalla (1981). Relationships between some notions which are common to reliability theory and economics. *Math. Oper. Res.* **6**, 113–121. [*MR* **82m:90059**]

Chang, C.-S. (1992). A new ordering for stochastic majorization: Theory and applications. *Adv. Appl. Probab.* **24**, 604–634. [*MR* **93g:60039**]

Chang, C.-S. and D. D. Yao (1993). Rearrangement, majorization and stochastic scheduling. *Math. Oper. Res.* **18**, 658–684. [*MR* **95i:90027**]

Chao, K.-M. and C. S. Wong (1992). Applications of M-matrices to majorization. *Linear Algebra Appl.* **169**, 31–40. [*MR* **93d:15033**]

Chen, C.-P. (2005). Complete monotonicity properties for a ratio of gamma functions. *Univ. Beograd. Publ. Elektrotehn. Fak. Ser. Mat.* **16**, 26–28. [*MR* **2164272**]

Chen, R. W., and F. K. Hwang (1984). Some theorems, counterexamples, and conjectures in multinomial selection theory. *Comm. Statist. A — Theory Methods* **13**, 1289–1298. [*MR* **85h:62023**]

Chen, W.-K. (1971). *Applied Graph Theory*. North-Holland, Amsterdam. [*MR* **48**(1974)3620; *Zbl.* **229**(1973)05107]

Cheng, K. W. (1977). *Majorization: Its Extensions and Preservation Theorems*, Tech. Rep. No. 121. Department of Statistics, Stanford University, Stanford, CA.

Cheung, W. S., and T. W. Ng (2006). A companion matrix approach to the study of zeros and critical points of a polynomial. *J. Math. Anal. Appl.* **319**, 690–707. [*MR* **2007b:30005**]

Chong, K.-M. (1974a). Spectral orders, uniform integrability and Legesgue's dominated convergence theorem. *Trans. Amer. Math. Soc.* **191**, 395–404. [*MR* **51**(1976)8357; *Zbl.* **261**(1975)28009]

Chong, K.-M. (1974b). An induction principle for spectral and rearrangement inequalities. *Trans. Amer. Math. Soc.* **196**, 371–383. [*MR* **49**(1974)9135; *Zbl.* **261**(1975)28008]

Chong, K.-M. (1974c). Some extensions of a theorem of Hardy, Littlewood and Pólya and their applications. *Canad. J. Math.* **26**, 1321–1340. [*MR* **50**(1975)4864; *Zbl.* **295**(1975)28006]

Chong, K.-M. (1974d). Spectral order preserving matrices and Muirhead's theorem. *Trans. Amer. Math. Soc.* **200**, 437–444. [*MR* **52**(1976)685]

Chong, K.-M. (1975). Variation reducing properties of decreasing rearrangements. *Canad. J. Math.* **27**, 330–336. [*MR* **51**(1976)10553; *Zbl.* **319**(1976)28013]

Chong, K.-M. (1976a). An induction theorem for rearrangements. *Canad. J. Math.* **28**, 154–160. [*MR* **52**(1976)14200; *Zbl.* **318**(1977)26017]

Chong, K.-M. (1976b). A general induction theorem for rearrangements of n-tuples. *J. Math. Anal. Appl.* **53**, 426–437. [*MR* **53**(1977)8360; **323**(1977)60002]

Chong, K.-M. (1976c). The invariance properties of spectral inequalities under convex transformations. *Nanta Math.* **9**, 125–130. [*MR* **56**(1978)12201]

Chu, M. T. (1995). Constructing a Hermitian matrix from its diagonal entries and eigenvalues. *SIAM J. Matrix Anal. Appl.* **16**, 207–217. [*MR* **95j:65027**]

Clausing, A. (1983). Type t entropy and majorization. *SIAM J. Math. Anal.* **14**, 203–208. [*MR* **84f:94005**]

Cleveland, W. S. (1979). Robust locally weighted regression and smoothing scatterplots. *J. Amer. Statist. Assoc.* **74**, 829–836. [*MR* **81i:62127**]

Cohen, A. (1969). A note on the unbiasedness of the likelihood ratio tests for some normal covariance matrices. *Sankhyā* **A.31**, 209–216.

Cohen, A., and H. B. Sackrowitz (1975). Unbiasedness of the chi-square, likelihood ratio, and other goodness of fit tests for the equal cell case. *Ann. Statist.* **3**, 959–964. [*MR* **52**(1976)1984; **311**(1976)62021]

Cohen A. and H. B. Sackrowitz (1987). Unbiasedness of tests for homogeneity. *Ann. Statist.* **15**, 805–816. [*MR* **88g:62057**]

Cohen, A., and W. Strawderman (1971). Unbiasedness of tests for homogeneity of variances. *Ann. Math. Statist.* **42**, 355–360. [*MR* **43**(1972)1316; *Zbl.* **218**(1972)456]

Cohen, J. E., Y. Derriennic, and Gh. Zbăganu (1993). Majorization, monotonicity of relative entropy, and stochastic matrices. *Contemp. Math.* **149**, 251–259. [*MR* **94i:15017**]

Conlon, J. C., R. León, F. Proschan, and J. Sethuraman (1977). *G-Ordered Functions, with Applications in Statistics*, I, *Theory*. Technical Report No. M432, Department of Statistics, Florida State University, Tallahassee.

Constantine, G. M. (1983). Schur convex functions on the spectra of graphs. *Discrete Math.* **45**, 181–188. [*MR* **84h:05087**]

Courant, R. (1936). *Differential and Integral Calculus* (transl. by E. J. McShane), Vol. II. Blackie, Glasgow and London. [*Zbl.* **11**(1935)058]

Courant, R., and D. Hilbert (1953). *Methods of Mathematical Physics*, Vol. I. Wiley (Interscience), New York. [*MR* **16**(1955)426; *Zbl.* **51**(1954)288]

Dahl, G. (1999a). Matrix majorization. *Linear Algebra Appl.* **288**, 53–73. [*MR* **99m:15024**]

Dahl, G. (1999b). Majorization polytopes. *Linear Algebra Appl.* **297**, 157–175. [*MR* **2001a:15027**]

Dahl, G. (2004). Tridiagonal doubly stochastic matrices. *Linear Algebra Appl.* **390**, 197–208. [*MR* **2006b:15032**]

Dalal, S. R., and P. Fortini (1982). An inequality comparing sums and maxima with application to Behrens–Fisher type problem. *Ann. Statist.* **10**, 297–301. [*MR* **83b:62059**]

Daley, D. J. (1987). Certain optimality properties of the first-come first-served discipline for $G/G/s$ queues. *Stochastic Process. Appl.* **25**, 301–308. [*MR* **89a:60214**]

Dalton, H. (1920). The measurement of the inequality of incomes. *Econ. J.* **30**, 348–361.

Dalton, H. (1925). *The Inequality of Incomes. Some Aspects of the Inequality of Incomes in Modern Communities*, 2nd ed. Routledge & Kegan Paul, London.

Dantzig, G. B. (1951). Application of the simplex method to a transportation problem. In *Activity Analysis of Production and Allocation* (T. C. Koopmans, ed.), Chapter XXIII. Wiley, New York. [*MR* **15**(1954)48; *Zbl.* **45**(1953)99]

Das Gupta, S. and S. K. Bhandari (1989). Multivariate majorization. In *Contributions to Probability and Statistics. Essays in Honor of Ingram Olkin* (L. J. Gleser, M. D. Perlman, S. J. Press, and A. R. Sampson, eds.), pp. 63–74. Springer, New York. [*MR* **91f:60035**]

Dasgupta, P., A. Sen, and D. Starrett (1973). Notes on the measurement of inequality. *J. Econ. Theory* **6**, 180–187.

David, H. A. (1968). Gini's mean difference rediscovered. *Biometrika* **55**, 573–575.

Davidovič, Ju. S., B. I. Korenbljum, and B. I. Hacet (1969). A certain property of logarithmically concave functions. *Soviet Math. Dokl.* **10**, 477–480. [*MR* **39:2924**]

Davis, C. (1963). Notions generalizing convexity for functions defined on spaces of matrices. In *Convexity* (V. Klee, ed.), pp. 187–201. American Mathematical Society, Providence, RI. [*MR* **27**(1964)5771]

Davis, P. J. (1959). Leonhard Euler's integral: A historical profile of the gamma function. *Amer. Math. Monthly* **66**, 849–869. [*MR* **21:5540**]

Davis, P. J. (1979). *Circulant Matrices.* John Wiley and Sons, New York. [*MR* **81a:15003**]

Day, P. W. (1972). Rearrangement inequalities. *Canad. J. Math.* **24**, 930–943. [*MR* **46**(1973) 9258; *Zbl.* **229**(1973)26018]

Day, P. W. (1973). Decreasing rearrangements and doubly stochastic operators. *Trans. Amer. Math. Soc.* **178**, 383–392. [*MR* **47**(1974)7508; *Zbl.* **267**(1974)47022]

Daykin, D. E. (1969). Problem 5685. *Amer. Math. Monthly* **76**, 835; see also *Amer. Math. Monthly* **77**(1970), 782.

Daykin, D. E. (1971). Inequalities for functions of a cyclic nature. *J. London Math. Soc.* **3**, 453–462. [*MR* **44**(1970)1622a; *Zbl.* **211**(1971)86]

Dean, A. M., and J. S. Verducci (1990). Linear transformations that preserve majorization, Schur concavity, and exchangeability. *Linear Algebra Appl.* **127**, 121–138. [*MR* **91d:15002**]

Dedić, Lj, M. Matić, and J. Pečarić (2000). On some inequalities for generalized beta function. *Math. Inequal. Appl.* **3**, 473–483. [*MR* **2003b:33001**]

DeGroot, M. H., and E. A. Eriksson (1985). Probability forecasting, stochastic dominance, and the Lorenz curve. In *Bayesian Statist., 2* (J. M. Bernardo, M. H. DeGroot, D. V. Lindley, and A. F. M. Smith, eds.), pp.99–118. North-Holland, Amsterdam. [*MR* **88a:62013**]

DeGroot, M. H., and S. E. Fienberg (1983). The comparison and evaluation of forecasters. *The Statistician* **32**, 12–22.

Deming, W. E., and F. F. Stephan (1940). On a least squares adjustment of a sampled frequency table when the expected marginal totals are known. *Ann. Math. Statist.* **11**, 427–444. [*MR* **2**(1941)232; *Zbl.* **24**(1941)55]

Demir, H. (1965). Problem E1779. *Amer. Math. Monthly* **72**, 420; see also *Amer. Math. Monthly* **73**(1966), 668.

Derman, C., G. J. Lieberman, and S. M. Ross (1972). On optimal assembly of systems. *Naval Res. Logist. Quart.* **19**, 569–574. [*MR* **47**(1974)8089; *Zbl.* **251**(1974)90019]

Derman, C., G. J. Lieberman, and S. M. Ross (1974). Assembly of systems having maximum reliability. *Naval Res. Logist. Quart.* **21**, 1–12. [*MR* **50**(1975)6463; *Zbl.* **286**(1975)90033]

Dharmadhikari, S., and K. Joag-Dev (1988). *Unimodality, Convexity and Applications.* Academic Press, Boston. [*MR* **89k:60020**]

Dhillon, I. S., R. W. Heath, Jr., M. A. Sustik, and J. A. Tropp (2005). Generalized finite algorithms for constructing Hermitian matrices with prescribed diagonal and spectrum. *SIAM J. Matrix Anal. Appl.* **27**, 61–71. [*MR* **2006i:15019**]

Diaconis, P. (1988). *Group Representations in Probability and Statistics. Inst. Math. Stat. Lecture Notes*, **11**. Institute of Mathematical Statistics, Hayward, CA. [*MR* **90a:60001**]

Doksum, K. (1969). Starshaped transformations and the power of rank tests. *Ann. Math. Statist.* **40**, 1167–1176. [*MR* **39:5020**]

Doob, J. L. (1942). Topics in the theory of Markov chains. *Trans. Amer. Math. Soc.* **52**, 37–64. [*MR* **4**(1943)17]

Dragomir, S. S. (1992). Two mappings in connection to Hadamard's inequalities. *J. Math. Anal. Appl.* **167**, 49–56. [*MR* **93m:26038**]

Druilhet, P. (2004). Conditions for optimality in experimental designs. *Linear Algebra Appl.* **388**, 147–157. [*MR* **2005h:62194**]

Du, D. Z., and Hwang, F .K. (1990). Optimal assembly of an s-stage k-out-of-n system. *SIAM J. Discrete. Math.* **3**, 349–354. [*MR* **91f:90056**]

Dudewicz, E. J., and Y. L. Tong (1976). Optimal confidence intervals for the largest location parameter. Unpublished manuscript.

Duff, G. F. D. (1967). Differences, derivatives and decreasing rearrangements. *Canad. J. Math.* **19**, 1153–1178, [*MR* **37**(1969)357; *Zbl.* **169**(1969)386]

Dulmage, L., and I. Halperin (1955). On a theorem of Frobenius-König and J. von Neumann's game of hide and seek. *Trans. Roy. Soc. Canada, Sect. III*(3) **49**, 23–29. [*MR* **17**(1956)1222; *Zbl.* **68**(1961/1970)335]

Dunford, N., and J. T. Schwartz (1958). *Linear Operators*, Vol. I. Wiley (Interscience), New York. [*MR* **22**(1961)8302; *Zbl.* **84**(1960)104]

Dykstra, R. L., J. E. Hewett, and W. A. Thompson, Jr. (1973). Events which are almost independent. *Ann. Statist.* **1**, 674–681. [*MR* **53**(1977)1671; *Zbl.* **264**(1974)62004]

Eaton, M. L. (1970). A note on symmetric Bernoulli random variables. *Ann. Math. Statist.* **41**, 1223–1226. [*MR* **42**(1971)3827; *Zbl.* **203**(1971)518]

Eaton, M. L. (1982). A review of selected topics in multivariate probability inequalities. *Ann. Statist.* **10**, 11–43. [*MR* **83e:62063**]

Eaton, M. L. (1984). On group induced orderings, monotone functions, and convolution theorems. In *Inequalities in Statistics and Probability — IMS Lec. Notes — Monograph Ser.* **5**, 13–25. [*MR* **87d:52018**]

Eaton, M. L. (1987). *Lectures on Topics in Probability Inequalities* CWI Tract, 35. Stichting Mathematisch Centrum, Centrum voor Wiskunde en Informatica, Amsterdam. [*MR* **88m:60041**]

Eaton, M. L. (1988). Concentration inequalities for Gauss–Markov estimators. *J. Multivariate Anal.* **25**, 119–138. [*MR* **89d:62056**]

Eaton, M. L. (1992). A group action on covariances with applications to the comparison of linear normal experiments. In *Stochastic Inequalities* (M. Shaked, and Y. L. Tong, eds.), *IMS Lecture Notes — Monograph Ser.* **22**,76–90. [*MR* **94j:62014**]

Eaton, M. L., and R. A. Olshen (1972). Random quotients and the Behrens–Fisher problem. *Ann. Math. Statist.* **43**, 1852–1860. [*MR* **50**(1975)6048; *Zbl.* **255**(1974)62024]

Eaton, M. L., and M. D. Perlman (1974). A monotonicity property of the power function of some invariant tests for MANOVA. *Ann. Statist.* **2**, 1022–1028. [*MR* **52:12215**]

Eaton, M. L., and M. D. Perlman (1977). Reflection groups, generalized Schur functions and the geometry of majorization. *Ann. Probab.* **5**, 829–860. [*MR* **56:3211**]

Eaton, M. L., and M. D. Perlman (1991). Concentration inequalities for multivariate distributions, I. Multivariate normal distributions. *Statist. Probab. Lett.* **12**, 487–504. [*MR* **93d:62098**]

Ebrahimi, N., and F. Spizzichino (1997). Some results on normalized total time on test and spacings. *Statist. Probab. Lett.* **36**, 231–243. [*MR* **98m:62281**]

Eckart, C., and G. Young (1936). The approximation of one matrix by another of lower rank. *Psychometrika* **1**, 211–218.

Eckart, C., and G. Young (1939). A principal axis transformation for non-Hermitian matrices. *Bull. Amer. Math. Soc.* **45**, 118–121 [*Zbl.* **20**(1939)198].

Edwards, J. (1922). *A Treatise on the Integral Calculus*, Vol. II. Macmillan, New York.

Efron, B. (1969). Student's t-test under symmetry conditions. *J. Amer. Statist. Assoc.* **64**, 1278–1302. [*MR* **40**(1970)5053; *Zbl.* **188**(1970)503]

Egorychev, G. P. (1980). Reshenie problemy van der-Vardena dlya permanentov. (Russian). Solution of the van der Waerden problem for permanents. *M. Akad Nauk SSSR Sibirsk. Otdel., Inst. Fiz., Krasnoyarsk.* Preprint IFSO-13M, 12 pp. [*MR* **82e:15006**]

Egorychev, G. P. (1981). The solution of van der Waerden's problem for permanents. *Adv. in Math.* **42**, 299–305. [*MR* **83b:15002b**]

Egorychev, G. P. (1996). Van der Waerden conjecture and applications. In *Handbook of Algebra* (M. Hazewinkel, ed.), **1**, pp. 3–26. North-Holland, Amsterdam. [*MR* **98i:15012**]

Eisenberg, B. (1991). The effect of variable infectivity on the risk of HIV infection. *Stat. Med.* **10**, 131–139.

Elezović, N., and J. Pečarić (2000). A note on Schur-convex functions. *Rocky Mountain J. Math.* **30**, 853–856. [*MR* **2001k:26026**]

Eliezer, C. J. (1971). Problem 5798. *Amer. Math. Monthly* **78**, 549; see also *Amer. Math. Monthly* **79**(1972), 917–918.

El-Neweihi, E., F. Proschan, and J. Sethuraman (1978). A simple model with applications in structural reliability, extinction of species, inventory depletion and urn sampling. *Adv. Appl. Prob.* **10**, 232–254. [*MR* **57:1602**]

El-Neweihi, E., F. Proschan, and J. Sethuraman (1986). Optimal allocation of components in parallel-series and series-parallel systems. *J. Appl. Probab.* **23**, 770–777. [*MR* **88a:90096**]

El-Neweihi, E., F. Proschan, and J. Sethuraman (1987). Optimal assembly of systems using Schur functions and majorization. *Naval Res. Logist.* **34**, 705–712. [*MR* **88k:90084**]

Éltető, O., and E. Frigyes (1968). New income inequality measures as efficient tools for causal analysis and planning. *Econometrica* **36**, 383–396.

Elton, J., and T. P. Hill (1992). Fusions of a probability distribution. *Ann. Probab.* **20**, 421–454. [*MR* **93a:60007**]

Emlen, J. M. (1973). *Ecology: An Evolutionary Approach*. Addison-Wesley, Reading, MA.

Erdélyi, A., W. Magnus, F. Oberhettinger, and F. G. Tricomi (1953). *Higher Transcendental Functions*, Vol. I. McGraw-Hill, New York. [*MR* **15**(1954)419; *Zbl.* **51**(1954)303]

Erdős, P., and T. Gallai (1960). Graphs with prescribed degrees of vertices (Hungarian). *Math. Lapok.* **11**, 264–274.

Esary, J. D., A. W. Marshall, and F. Proschan (1970). Some reliability applications of the hazard transform. *SIAM J. Appl. Math.* **18**, 849–860. [*MR* **41**(1971)6379; *Zbl.* **198**(1971)249]

Evard, J. C., and H. Gauchman (1997). Steffensen type inequalities over general measure spaces. *Analysis* **17**, 301–322. [*MR* **99c:26016**]

Faddeev, D. K., and V. N. Faddeeva (1963). *Computational Methods of Linear Algebra*, 2nd ed. Fizmatgiz, Moscow (Engl. transl. of 1st ed., Freeman, San Francisco). [*MR* **28**(1964)1742; (review of Russian version) *Zbl.* **94**(1962)110–111]

Falikman, D. I. (1981). Proof of the van der Waerden conjecture on the permanent of a doubly stochastic matrix. *Mat. Zametki.* **29**, 931–938. [*MR* **82k:15007**]

Fan, K. (1949). On a theorem of Weyl concerning eigenvalues of linear transformations I. *Proc. Nat. Acad. Sci. U.S.A.* **35**, 652–655. [*MR* **11**(1950)600; *Zbl.* **41**(1952)6]

Fan, K. (1950). On a theorem of Weyl concerning eigenvalues of linear transformations II. *Proc. Nat. Acad. Sci. U.S.A.* **36**, 31–35. [*MR* **11**(1950)526; *Zbl.* **41**(1952)6]

Fan, K. (1951). Maximum properties and inequalities for the eigenvalues of completely continuous operators. *Proc. Nat. Acad. Sci. U.S.A.* **37**, 760–766. [*MR* **13**(1952)661; *Zbl.* **44**(1952)115; correction **54**(1956)105]

Fan, K. (1954). Inequalities for eigenvalues of Hermitian matrices. *Nat. Bur. Standards Appl. Math. Ser.* **39**, 131–139. [*MR* **16**(1955)327; *Zbl.* **58**(1957/58)11]

Fan, K. (1955a). A comparison theorem for eigenvalues of normal matrices. *Pacific J. Math.* **5**, 911–913. [*MR* **18**(1957)183; *Zbl.* **67**(1957/58)7]

Fan, K. (1955b). Some inequalities concerning positive-definite Hermitian matrices. *Proc. Cambridge Philos. Soc.* **51**, 414–421. [*MR* **17**(1956)935; *Zbl.* **67**(1957)255]

Fan, K. (1957). Existence theorems and extreme solutions for inequalities concerning convex functions on linear transformations. *Math. Z.* **68**, 205–216. [*MR* **19**(1958)1183; *Zbl.* **78**(1958/1959)102]

Fan, K. (1960). Note on M-matrices. *Quart. J. Math. Oxford Ser.* [2] **11**, 43–49. [*MR* **22**(1961)8024]

Fan, K. (1964). Inequalities for M-matrices. *Nederl. Akad. Wetensch. Proc. Ser. A* **67** (=*Indag. Math.* **26**), 602–610. [*MR* **30**(1965)1133]

Fan, K. (1966). Applications of a theorem concerning sets with convex sections. *Math. Ann.* **163**, 189–203. [*MR* **32**(1966)8101; *Zbl.* **138**(1967)374]

Fan, K. (1967). Subadditive functions on a distributive lattice and an extension of Szász's inequality. *J. Math. Anal. Appl.* **18**, 262–268. [*MR* **35**(1968)1615; *Zbl.* **204**(1971)27]

Fan, K. (1974). On strictly dissipative matrices. *Linear Algebra Appl.* **9**, 223–241. [*MR* **51:5626**]

Fan, K. (1975). Two applications of a consistency theorem for systems of linear inequalities. *Linear Algebra Appl.* **11**, 171–180. [*MR* **52**(1976)5710; *Zbl.* **307**(1976)15005]

Fan, K., and A. Hoffman (1955). Some metric inequalities in the space of matrices. *Proc. Amer. Math. Soc.* **6**, 111–116. [*MR* **16**(1955)784; *Zbl.* **64**(1956)14]

Fan, K., and G. G. Lorenz (1954). An integral inequality. *Amer. Math. Monthly* **61**, 626–631. [*MR* **16**(1955)342; *Zbl.* **57**(1956)47]

Fan, K., and G. Pall (1957). Imbedding conditions for Hermitian and normal matrices. *Canad. J. Math.* **9**, 298–304. [*MR* **19**(1958)6; *Zbl.* **77**(1958)245]

Farahat, H. K. (1965/1966). The semigroup of doubly-stochastic matrices. *Glasgow Math. Assoc. Proc.* **7**, 178–183. [*MR* **34**(1967)2590; *Zbl.* **156**(1969)260–261]

Farahat, H. K., and L. Mirsky (1960). Permutation endomorphisms and refinement of a theorem of Birkhoff. *Proc. Cambridge Philos. Soc.* **56**, 322–328. [*MR* **23**(1962)A1659; *Zbl.* **98**(1963)12]

Farnell, A. B. (1944). Limits for the characteristic roots of a matrix. *Bull. Amer. Math. Soc.* **50**, 789–794. [*MR* **6**(1943)113]

Fefferman, C., M. Jodeit, Jr. and M. D. Perlman. (1972). A spherical surface measure inequality for convex sets. *Proc. Amer. Math. Soc.* **33**, 114–119. [*MR* **45:2577**]

Feller, W. (1950). *An Introduction to Probability Theory and Its Applications*, 1st ed., Vol. 1. Wiley, New York. [*MR* **12**(1951)424; *Zbl.* **39**(1951)132]

Feller, W. (1968). *An Introduction to Probability Theory and Its Applications*, 3rd ed., Vol. 1. Wiley, New York. [*MR* **37**(1969)3604; *Zbl.* **155**(1968)231]

Feller, W. (1971). *An Introduction to Probability Theory and Its Applications*, 2nd ed., Vol. 2. Wiley, New York. [*MR* **42**(1971)5292; *Zbl.* **158**(1969)349 (Russian)]

Fellman, J. (1976). The effect of transformations on Lorenz curves. *Econometrica* **44**, 823–824. [*MR* **57:8999**]

Fernando, S. L. (1997) Reflection groups and a convolution theorem. *Pacific J. Math.* **180**, 229–249. [*MR* **98k:20065**]

Fiedler, M. (1971). Bounds for the determinant of the sum of Hermitian matrices. *Proc. Amer. Math. Soc.* **30**, 27–31. [*MR* **44**(1972)4021]

Fields, G. S., and J. C. H. Fei (1978). On inequality comparisons. *Econometrica* **46**, 303–316.

Fienberg, S. E. (1970). An iterative procedure for estimation in contingency tables. *Ann. Math. Statist.* **41**, 907–917. [*MR* **42**(1971)1300; *Zbl.* **198**(1971)234]

Fink, A. M. (1994). Majorization for functions with monotone n-th derivatives. In *Inequalities and Applications* (R. P. Agarwal, ed.), pp. 241–254. World Scientific, Singapore. [*MR* **95j:26022**]

Fink, A. M., and M. Jodeit (1990). Jensen inequalities for functions with higher monotonicities. *Aequationes Math.* **40**, 26–43. [*MR* **91i:26020**]

Fischer, E. (1905). Über quadratische formen mit reelen Koeffizienten. *Monatsh. Math. Phys.* **16**, 234–248.

Fischer, E. (1908). Über den Hadamardschen Determinantensatz. *Arch. Math.* (*Basel*) **13**, 32–40.

Fischer, P., and J. A. R. Holbrook (1980). Balayage defined by the nonnegative convex functions. *Proc. Amer. Math. Soc.* **79**, 445–448. [*MR* **81f:46012**]

Fischer, P., and H. Sendov (2010). On Malamud majorization and the extreme points of its level sets. *J. Convex Anal.* To appear.

Fishlow, A. (1973). Brazilian income size distribution. Unpublished paper, University of California, Berkeley.

Folkman, J. H., and D. R. Fulkerson (1969). Edge colorings in bipartite graphs. In *Combinatorial Mathematics and Its Applications* (R. C. Bose and T. A. Dowling, eds.), Chapter 31, pp. 561–577. University of North Carolina Press, Chapel Hill. [*MR* **41**(1971)6722; *Zbl.* **204**(1971)570]

Ford, L. R., Jr., and D. R. Fulkerson (1962). *Flows in Networks*. Princeton University Press, Princeton, NJ. [*MR* **28**(1964)2917; *Zbl.* **106**(1964)348]

Forsythe, F., and C. Moler (1967). *Computer Solution of Linear Algebraic Systems*. Prentice-Hall, Englewood Cliffs, NJ. [*MR* **36**(1968)2306; *Zbl.* **182**(1970)227]

Foster, J. E., and A. F. Shorrocks (1988). Poverty orderings and welfare dominance. *Soc. Choice Welf.* **5**, 179–198. [*MR* **89g:90040**]

Franken, P., and B. M. Kirstein (1977). Zur Vergleichbarkeit Zufälliger Prozesse. *Math. Nachr.* **78**, 197–205. [*MR* **57:1679**]

Fréchet, M. (1951). Sur les tableaux de corrélation dont les marges sont données. *Ann. Univ. Lyon, Sect. A* **14**, 53–77. [*MR* **14**(1953)189; *Zbl.* **45**(1953)229]

Frobenius, G. (1908). Über Matrizen aus positiven Elements. *Sitzungsberi, Kgl. Preussischen Akad. Wiss.*, pp. 471–476.

Fuchs, L. (1947). A new proof of an inequality of Hardy–Littlewood–Pólya. *Mat. Tidsskr. B*, pp. 53–54. [*MR* **9**(1948)501; *Zbl.* **30**(1949)27]

Fujii, J. I., M. Nakamura, J. Pečarić, and Y. Seo (2006). Bounds for the ratio and difference between parallel sum and series via Mond-Pečarić method. *Math. Inequal. Appl.* **9**, 749–759. [*MR* **2007i:47021**]

Fujii, J. I., and Y. Seo (2002) Characterizations of chaotic order associated with the Mond–Shisha difference. *Math. Inequal. Appl.* **5**, 725–734. [*MR* **2003h:47031**]

Fujii, M., and E. Kamei (1992). Furuta's inequality and a generalization of Ando's theorem. *Proc. Amer. Math. Soc.* **115**, 409–413. [*MR* **92i:47018**]

Fulkerson, D. R. (1959). A network-flow feasibility theorem and combinatorial applications. *Canad. J. Math.* **11**, 440–451. [*MR* **22**(1961)2494; *Zbl.* **98**(1963)336–337]

Fulkerson, D. R. (1960). Zero-one matrices with zero trace. *Pacific J. Math.* **10**, 831–836. [*MR* **22**(1961)10923; *Zbl.* **96**(1962)7]

Fulkerson, D. R., and H. J. Ryser (1962). Multiplicities and minimal widths for (0–1) matrices. *Canad. J. Math.* **14**, 498–508. [*MR* **26**(1963)4935; *Zbl.* **104**(1964)8]

Furuta, T. (1987). $A \geq B \geq 0$ assures $(B^r A^p B^r)^{1/q} \geq B^{(p+2r)/q}$ for $r \geq 0$, $p \geq 0$, $q \geq 1$ with $(1 + 2r)q \geq p + 2r$. *Proc. Amer. Math. Soc.* **101**, 85–88. [*MR* **89b:47028**]

Furuta, T. (2001). *Invitation to Linear Operators. From Matrices to Bounded Linear Operators on a Hilbert Space.* Taylor and Francis, London. [*MR* **2004b:47001**]

Furuta, T. (2007). Operator inequality implying generalized Bebiano–Lemos–Providencia one. *Linear Algebra Appl.* **426**, 342–348. [*MR* **2008k:47038**]

Furuta, T. (2008). Monotonicity of order preserving operator functions. *Linear Algebra Appl.* **428**, 1072–1082. [*MR* **2008k:47039**]

Gaines, F. (1967). On the arithmetic mean–geometric mean inequality. *Amer. Math. Monthly* **74**, 305–306. [*MR* **35**(1968)5564; *Zbl.* **187**(1970)12]

Galambos, J. (1971). Some probabilistic aspects of majorization. *Ann. Univ. Sci. Budapest. Eötvös Sect. Math.* **14**, 11–17. [*MR* **47**(1974) 5914; *Zbl.* **228**(1973)5009]

Gale, D. (1957). A theorem on flows in networks. *Pacific J. Math.* **7**, 1073–1082. [*MR* **19**(1958)1024; *Zbl.* **87**(1961)163]

Gantmacher, F. R. (1959). *Theory of Matrices*, Vols. I, II. Chelsea, Bronx, NY. [*MR* **21**(1960)6372c]

Gantmacher, F. R., and M. Krein (1950). *Oscillation Matrices and Kernels and Small Variations of Mechanical Systems*, 2nd Russ. ed., Izdat. Tekh.-Teor. Lit., Moscow–Leningrad. (German transl. by A. Stöhr, Akademie-Verlag, Berlin, 1960.) Translated by the U.S. Joint Publications Research Service, New York, 1961. Available from the Office of Technical Services, Department of Commerce, Washington, DC. [*MR* **14**(1953)178; *MR* **22**(1961)5161; *Zbl.* **41**(1952)355]

Garloff, J. (1982). Majorization between the diagonal elements and the eigenvalues of an oscillating matrix. *Linear Algebra Appl.* **47**, 181–184. [*MR* **83m:15012**]

Gasca, M., and C. A. Micchelli, eds. (1996). *Total Positivity and Its Applications.* Dordrecht, Boston.

Gastwirth, J. L. (1971). A general definition of the Lorenz curve. *Econometrica* **39**, 1037–1039.

Gel'fand, I. M., and M. A. Naimark (1950). The relation between the unitary representations of the complex unimodular group and its unitary subgroup (Russian). *Izv. Akad. Nauk SSSR Ser. Mat.* **14**, 239–260. [*MR* **12**(1951)9]

Gini, C. (1912). *Variabilitàe Mutabilità*, Anno. 3, Part 2, p. 80. Studi Economico-Giuridici della R. Università de Cagliari.

Gini, C. (1915/1916). Sul criterio di concordonza tra due caratter. *Atti Reale Ist. Veneto Sci. Lett. Arti. Ser. 8*, **75**(2), 309–331.

Gini, C. (1938). Di una formula compresiva delle medie. *Metron*. **13**, 3–22.

Giorgi, G. M. (1990). Bibliographic portrait of the Gini concentration ratio. *Metron*. **48**, 183–221. [*MR* **1159665**]

Giovagnoli, A., F. Pukelsheim, and H. P. Wynn (1987). Group invariant orderings and experimental designs. *J. Statist. Plann. Infer.* **17**, 159–171. [*MR* **89a:62174**]

Giovagnoli, A., and M. Romanazzi (1990). A group majorization ordering for correlation matrices. *Linear Algebra Appl.* **127**, 139–155. [*MR* **91e:62152**]

Giovagnoli, A., and H. P. Wynn (1980). A majorization theorem for the C-matrices of binary designs. *J. Statist. Plann. Infer.* **4**, 145–154. [*MR* **82e:62116**]

Giovagnoli, A., and H. P. Wynn (1985). G-majorization with applications to matrix orderings. *Linear Algebra Appl.* **67**, 111–135. [*MR* **86m:15017**]

Gleser, L. J. (1966). A note on the sphericity test. *Ann. Math. Statist.* **37**, 464–467. [*MR* **32**(1966)4781(E); *Zbl.* **138**(1967)139]

Gleser, L. J. (1975). On the distribution of the number of successes in independent trials. *Ann. Probab.* **3**, 182–188. [*MR* **51**(1976)1903; *Zbl.* **301**(1976)60010]

Goldberg, M., and E.G. Straus (1977/1978). On a theorem by Mirman. *Linear Multilinear Algebra* **5**, 77–78. [*MR* **57:3880**]

Golden, S. (1965). Lower bounds for the Helmholtz function. *Phys. Rev.* **137**, B1127–B1128.

Golub, G. H. (1968). Least squares, singular values, and matrix approximations. *Appl. Mat.* **13**, 44–51. [*MR* **37**(1969)4944; *Zbl.* **179**(1970)214]

Green, B. (1952). The orthogonal approximation of an oblique structure in factor analysis. *Psychometrika* **17**, 429–440. [*MR* **14**(1953)715; *Zbl.* **49**(1954/1959)376]

Grone, R., C. Johnson, E. Marques de Sa, and H Wolkowicz (1984). Improving Hadamard's inequality. *Linear Multilinear Algebra* **16**, 305–322. [*MR* **87b:15024**]

Grone, R., and R. Merris (1990). Coalescence, majorization, edge valuations and the Laplacian spectra of graphs. *Linear Multilinear Algebra* **27**, 139–146. [*MR* **91c:05129**]

Grone, R., and R. Merris (1994). The Laplacian spectrum of a graph. II. *SIAM J. Discrete Math.* **7**, 221–229. [*MR* **95d:05085**]

Grone, R., R. Merris, and V. S. Sunder (1990). The Laplacian spectrum of a graph. *SIAM J. Matrix Anal. Appl.* **11**, 218–238. [*MR* **91c:05130**]

Groves, T., and T. Rothenberg (1969). A note on the expected value of an inverse matrix. *Biometrika* **56**, 690–691. [*Zbl.* **183**(1970)487]

Grünbaum, B. (1967). *Convex Polytopes*. Wiley (Interscience), New York. [*MR* **37**(1969)2085; *Zbl.* **163**(1969)166]

Guan, K. (2006). Schur-convexity of the complete symmetric function. *Math. Inequal. Appl.* **9**, 567–576. [*MR* **2007f:26034**]

Guan, K., and J. Shen (2006). Schur-convexity for a class of symmetric function and its applications. *Math. Inequal. Appl.* **9**, 199–210. [*MR* **2007a:26048**]

Guggenheimer, H. (1966). Solution to Problem E1779. *Amer. Math. Monthly* **73**, 668.

Guggenheimer, H. (1967) *Plane Geometry and Its Groups*. Holden-Day, San Francisco. [*MR* **35:4796**]

Gupta, M. R. (1984). Functional form for estimating the Lorenz curve. *Econometrica* **52**, 1313–1314. [*MR* **0763075**]

Gyires, B. (1980). The common source of several inequalities concerning doubly stochastic matrices. *Publ. Math. Debrecen.* **27**, 291–304. [*MR* **82d:15002**]

Gyires, B. (1996). Elementary proof for a van der Waerden's conjecture and related theorems. *Comput. Math. Appl.* **31**, 7–21. [*MR* **98b:15005**]

Gyires, B. (2001). Contribution to van der Waerden's conjecture. *Comput. Math. Appl.* **42**, 1431–1437. [*MR* **2003d:15010**]

Hadamard, J. (1903). *Leçons sur la Propagation des Ondes et les Équations de l'Hydrodynamique*. Hermann, Paris; reprinted by Chelsea, New York, 1949.

Hadar, J. and W. Russell (1969). Rules for ordering uncertain prospects. *Amer. Econ. Rev.* **59**, 25–34.

Hadar, J. and W. Russell (1978). Applications in economic theory analysis. In *Stochastic Dominance: An Approach to Decision-making Under Risk* (G. A. Whitmore, and M. C. Findlay, eds.), pp. 39–114. D. C. Heath, Lexington, MA. 39–114.

Hall, M. (1967). *Combinatorial Theory*. Ginn (Blaisdell), Boston. [*MR* **37**(1969)80; *Zbl.* **196**(1970)24]

Hall, R. W. and D. Tymoczko (2007). Poverty and polyphony: A connection between economics and music. In *Bridges: Mathematical Connections in Art, Music, and Science* (R. Sarhanghi, ed.), pp. 259–268. Donostia, Spain.

Halmos, P. R. (1972). Positive approximants of operators. *Indiana Univ. Math. J.* **21**, 951–960. [*MR* **45**(1973)919; *Zbl.* **263**(1974)47018]

Hammer, P. L., A. Kogan, and U. G. Rothblum (2000). Evaluation, strength, and relevance of variables of Boolean functions. *SIAM J. Discrete Math.* **13**, 302–312. [*MR* **2001k:94025**]

Hammersley, J. M. (1961). A short proof of the Farahat–Mirsky refinement of Birkhoff's theorem on doubly stochastic matrices. *Proc. Cambridge Philos. Soc.* **57**, 681. [*MR* **23**(1962)A1391; *Zbl.* **104**(1964)12]

Hammersley, J. M., and J. G. Mauldon (1956). General principles of antithetic variates. *Proc. Cambridge Philos. Soc.* **52**, 476–481. [*MR* **18**(1957)344; *Zbl.* **71**(1956)355]

Harada, T. (2008). Majorization inequalities related to increasing convex functions in a semifinite von Neumann algebra. *Math. Inequal. Appl.* **11**, 449–455. [*MR* **2431209**]

Harary, F., and L. Moser (1966). Theory of round robin tournaments. *Amer. Math. Monthly* **73**, 231–246. [*MR* **33**(1967)5512; *Zbl.* **142**(1968)416]

Hardy, G. H., J. E. Littlewood, and G. Pólya (1929). Some simple inequalities satisfied by convex function. *Messenger Math.* **58**, 145–152.

Hardy, G. H., J. E. Littlewood, and G. Pólya (1934, 1952). *Inequalities*, 1st ed., 2nd ed. Cambridge University Press, London and New York. [*MR* **13**(1952)727; *Zbl.* **47**(1953)53]

Hauke, J., and A. Markiewicz (1994). Comparison of experiments via a group majorization ordering. *Metrika* **41**, 201–209. [*MR* **95i:60017**]

Havrda, J., and F. Charvát (1967). Quantification method of classification processes. Concept of structural a-entropy. *Kybernetika (Prague)* **3**, 30–35. [*MR* **34:8875**]

Hayakawa, Y. (1993). Interrelationships between l_p-isotropic densities and l_p-isotropic survival functions, and de Finetti representations of Schur-concave survival functions. *Austral. J. Statist.* **35**, 327–332. [*MR* **94j:60019**]

Haynsworth, E. V. (1970). Applications of an inequality for the Schur complement. *Proc. Amer. Math. Soc.* **24**, 512–516. [*MR* **41:241**]

Hazewinkel, M., and C. F. Martin (1983). Representations of the symmetric group, the specialization order, systems and Grassmann manifolds. *Enseign. Math.* **29**, 53–87. [*MR* **85b:14068**]

Helmert, F. R. (1876). Die Genauigkeit der Formel von Peters zur Berechnung des wahrscheinlichen Fehlers directer Beobachtungen gleicher Genauigkeit. *Astronom. Nachr.* **88**, 113–132.

Heyer, H. (1977). *Probability Measures on Locally Compact Groups.* Springer-Verlag, Berlin and New York. [*MR* **58:18648**]

Hickey, R. J. (1982). A note on the measurement of randomness. *J. Appl. Probab.* **19**, 229–232. [*MR* **83c:62031**]

Hickey, R. J. (1983). Majorisation, randomness and some discrete distributions. *J. Appl. Probab.* **20**, 897–902. [*MR* **85a:60021**]

Hickey, R. J. (1984). Continuous majorisation and randomness. *J. Appl. Probab.* **21**, 924–929. [*MR* **86h:60041**]

Hirsch, A. (1902). Sur les racines d'une équation fondamentale. *Acta Math.* **25**, 367–370.

Hobby, C., and R. Pyke (1965). Doubly stochastic operators obtained from positive operators. *Pacific J. Math.* **15**, 153–157. [*MR* **31**(1966)4062]

Hochstadt, H. (1974). On the construction of a Jacobi matrix from spectral data. *Linear Algebra Appl.* **8**, 435–446. [*MR* **52:3199**]

Hoeffding, W. (1940). Maszstabinvariante Korrelationstheorie. *Schr. Math. Inst. u. Inst. Angew. Math. Univ. Berlin* **5**, 181–233. [*MR* **3**(1942)5; *Zbl.* **24**(1941)056]

Hoeffding, W. (1956). On the distribution of the number of successes in independent trials. *Ann. Math. Statist.* **27**, 713–721. [*MR* **18**(1957)240; *Zbl.* **72**(1959/1960)139]

Hoeffding, W. (1963). Probability inequalities for sums of bounded random variables. *J. Amer. Statist. Assoc.* **58**, 13–30. [*MR* **26**(1963)
1908; *Zbl.* **127**(1967)106]

Hoerl, A. E., and R. W. Kennard (1970a). Ridge regression: Biased estimations for nonorthogonal problems. *Technometrics* **12**, 55–67. [*Zbl.* **202**(1971)172]

Hoerl, A. E., and R. W. Kennard (1970b). Ridge regression: Applications to nonorthogonal problems. *Technometrics* **12**, 69–82. [*Zbl.* **202**(1971)172]

Hoffman, A. J. (1960). Some recent applications of the theory of linear inequalities to extremal combinatorial analysis. *Proc. Sympos.*

Appl. Math. bfseries 10, 113–127. American Mathematical Society, Providence, RI. [*MR* **22**(1961)5578; *Zbl.* **96**(1962)6–7]

Hoffman, A. J. (1969). A special class of doubly stochastic matrices. *Aequationes Math.* **2**, 319–326. [*MR* **41:8447**]

Hoffman, A. J., and H. W. Wielandt (1953). The variation of the spectrum of a normal matrix. *Duke Math. J.* **20**, 37–39. [*MR* **14**(1953)611; *Zbl.* **51**(1954)9]

Hollander, M., F. Proschan, and J. Sethuraman (1977). Functions decreasing in transposition and their applications in ranking problems. *Ann. Statist.* **5**, 722–733. [*MR* **58:7965**]

Horn, A. (1950). On the singular values of a product of completely continuous operators. *Proc. Nat. Acad. Sci. U.S.A.* **36**, 374–375. [*MR* **13**(1952)565; *Zbl.* **38**(1951)72]

Horn, A. (1954a). Doubly stochastic matrices and the diagonal of a rotation matrix. *Amer. J. Math.* **76**, 620–630. [*MR* **16**(1955)105; *Zbl.* **55**(1955)246]

Horn, A. (1954b). On the eigenvalues of a matrix with prescribed singular values. *Proc. Amer. Math. Soc.* **5**, 4–7. [*MR* **15**(1954)847; *Zbl.* **55**(1955)9]

Horn, A. (1962). Eigenvalues of sums of Hermitian matrices. *Pacific J. Math.* **12**, 225–241. [*MR* **25**(1963)3941; *Zbl.* **112**(1965)15]

Horn, R. A., and C. R. Johnson (1985). *Matrix Analysis.* Cambridge University Press, Cambridge. [*MR* **87e:15001**]

Horn, R. A., and C. R. Johnson (1991). *Topics in Matrix Analysis.* Cambridge University Press, Cambridge. [*MR* **95c:15001**]

Horn, R. A., and I. Olkin (1996). When does $AA^* = BB^*$ and why does one want to know? *Amer. Math. Monthly* **103**, 470–482. [*MR* **97f:15030**]

Horn, A., and R. Steinberg (1959). Eigenvalues of the unitary part of a matrix. *Pacific J. Math.* **9**, 541–550. [*MR* **24**(1962)A129; *Zbl.* **87**(1961)17]

Householder, A. S. (1953). *Principles of Numerical Analysis.* McGraw-Hill, New York.

Householder, A. S. (1964). *The Theory of Matrices in Numerical Analysis.* Ginn (Blaisdell), Boston. [*MR* **30**(1965)5475; *Zbl.* **161**(1969)121]

de Hoyos, I. (1990). Points of continuity of the Kronecker canonical form. *SIAM J. Matrix Anal. Appl.* **11**, 278–300. [*MR* **91d:15053**]

Hu, C.-Y., and G. D. Lin (2001). An inequality for the weighted sums of pairwise i.i.d. generalized Rayleigh random variables. *J. Statist. Plann. Infer.* **92**, 1–5. [*MR* **2001k:60025**]

Hua, L. K. (1955). Inequalities involving determinants (in Chinese). *Acta Math. Sinica* **5**, 463–470. [*MR* **17**(1956)703; *Zbl.* **66**(1956/1957)266]

Huffer, F. W., and Shepp, L. A. (1987). On the probability of covering the circle by random arcs. *J. Appl. Probab.* **24**, 422–429. [*MR* **88g:60031**]

Hwang, F. K. (1979). Majorization on a partially ordered set. *Proc. Amer. Math. Soc.* **76**, 199–203. [*MR* **80j:06004**]

Hwang, F. K., and U. G. Rothblum (1993). Majorization and Schur convexity with respect to partial orders. *Math. Oper. Res.* **18**, 928–944. [*MR* **94k:06003**]

Hwang, F. K., U. G. Rothblum, and L. Shepp (1993). Monotone optimal multipartitions using Schur convexity with respect to partial orders. *SIAM J. Discrete Math.* **6**, 533–547. [*MR* **95e:90042**]

Hwang, S.-G. (1999). Majorization via generalized Hessenberg matrices. *Linear Algebra Appl.* **292**, 127–138. [*MR* **2000c:15031**]

Ibragimov, R. (2004). Shifting paradigms: On the robustness of economic models to heavy-tailedness assumptions. Working Paper, Department of Economics, Yale University, New Haven, CT.

Ibragimov, R. (2005). Thou shall not diversify: Why "Two of every sort"? Working Paper, Department of Economics, Harvard University, Cambridge, MA.

Ibragimov, R., and J. Walden (2007). Value at risk under dependence and heavy-tailedness: Models with common shocks. *Discussion Paper Number 2139.* Harvard Institute of Economic Research.

Ikramov, K. D. (1994). A simple proof of the generalized Schur inequality. *Linear Algebra Appl.* **199**, 143–149. [*MR* **95i:15024**]

Ireland, C. T., and S. Kullback (1968). Contingency tables with given marginals. *Biometrika* **55**, 179–188. [*MR* **37**(1969)4903; *Zbl.* **155**(1968)267]

James, G. D. (1978). *The Representation Theory of the Symmetric Groups.* Lecture Notes in Mathematics, **682**. Springer-Verlag, Berlin. [*MR* **80g:20019**]

Jensen, J. L. W. V. (1906). Sur les fonctions convexes et les inégalités entre les valeurs moyennnes. *Acta Math.* **30**, 175–193.

Jichang, K. (2002). *Applied Inequalities: Changyong Budengshi*, 3rd ed. Shandong Press of Science and Technology,Jinan.

Joe, H. (1985). An ordering of dependence for contingency tables. *Linear Algebra Appl.* **70**, 89–103. [*MR* **87a:62074**]

Joe, H. (1987a). Majorization, randomness and dependence for multivariate distributions. *Ann. Probab.* **15**, 1217–1225. [*MR* **89b:62101**]

Joe, H. (1987b). An ordering of dependence for distribution of k-tuples, with applications to lotto games. *Canad. J. Statist.* **15**, 227–238. [*MR* **89c:62191**]

Joe, H. (1988). Majorization, entropy and paired comparisons. *Ann. Statist.* **16**, 915–925. [*MR* **90b:62105**]

Joe, H. (1990). Majorization and divergence. *J. Math. Anal. Appl.* **148**, 287–305. [*MR* **91b:60018**]

Joe, H. (1992). Generalized majorization orderings and applications. In *Stochastic inequalities* (M. Shaked and Y. L. Tong, eds.), *IMS Lecture Notes — Monograph Ser.* **22**,145–158. [*MR* **94i:60028**]

Joe, H. and J. Verducci (1992). Multivariate majorization by positive combinations. In *Stochastic Inequalities* (M. Shaked and Y. L. Tong, eds.), *IMS Lecture Notes — Monograph Ser.* **22**, 159–181. [*MR* **94i:60029**]

Johnson, D. M., A. L. Dulmage, and N. S. Mendelsohn (1960). On an algorithm of G. Birkhoff concerning doubly stochastic matrices. *Canad. Math. Bull.* **3**, 237–242. [*MR* **24**(1962)A133; *Zbl.* **93**(1962)378]

Jordan, C. (1874). Mémoire sur les formes bilinéares. *J. Math. Pures Appl.* [2] **19**, 35–54.

Just, E., and N. Schaumberger (1964). Problem E1732. *Amer. Math. Monthly* **71**, 1041; see also *Amer. Math. Monthly* **72**(1965)909–910.

Kadane, J. B. and L. Wasserman (1996). Symmetric, coherent, Choquet capacities. *Ann. Statist.* **24**, 1250–1264. [*MR* **97j:60003**]

Kadiyala, K. R. (1968). An inequality for the ratio of quadratic forms in normal variates. *Ann. Math. Statist.* **39**, 1762–1763. [*MR* **39**(1970)1033; *Zbl.* **197**(1971)162]

Kaigh, W. D., and M. A. Sorto (1993). Subsampling quantile estimator majorization inequalities. *Statist. Probab. Lett.* **18**, 373–379. [*MR* **94m:60020**]

Kakiuchi, I., and M. Kimura (1995). Majorization methods on hyperplanes and their applications. *J. Statist. Plann. Infer.* **47**, 217–235. [*MR* **96j:60017**]

Kakwani, N.C. (1980). *Income Inequality and Poverty: Methods of Estimation and Policy Applications.* Oxford University Press, New York.

Kamae, T., U. Krengel, and G. L. O'Brien (1977). Stochastic inequalities on partially ordered spaces. *Ann. Probab.* **5**, 899–912. [*MR* **58-13308**]

Kanter, M. (1976). Probability inequalities for convex sets and multidimensional concentration functions. *J. Multivariate Anal.* **6**, 222–236. [*MR* **57:17812**;[*Zbl.* **347**(1977)60043]

Kapur, J. N. (1967). On some properties of generalised entropies. *Indian J. Math.* **9**, 427–442.

Karamata, J. (1932). Sur une inégalité rélative aux fonctions convexes. *Publ. Math. Univ. Belgrade* **1**, 145–148. [*Zbl.* **5**(1933)201]

Karlin, S. (1968). *Total Positivity*, Vol. I. Stanford University Press, Stanford, CA. [*MR* **37**(1969)5667]

Karlin, S. (1974). Inequalities for symmetric sampling plans. I. *Ann. Statist.* **2**, 1065–1094. [*MR* **51**(1976)9287; *Zbl.* **306**(1976)62004]

Karlin, S., and A. Novikoff (1963). Generalized convex inequalities. *Pacific J. Math.* **13**, 1251–1279. [*MR* **28**(1964)170; *Zbl.* **126**(1964)281]

Karlin, S., F. Proschan, and R. E. Barlow (1961). Moment inequalities of Pólya frequency functions. *Pacific J. Math.* **11**, 1023–1033. [*MR* **24**A(1962)3729; *Zbl.* **141**(1968)166–167]

Karlin, S., and Y. Rinott (1983). Comparison of measures, multivariate majorization, and applications to statistics. In *Studies in Econometrics, Time Series, and Multivariate Statistics* (S. Karlin, T. Amemiya, and L. A. Goodman, eds.), pp. 465–489, Academic Press, New York. [*MR* **87a:62072**]

Karlin, S., and Y. Rinott (1984). Random replacement schemes and multivariate majorization. In *Inequalities in Statistics and Probability*, (Y. L. Tong, ed.), *IMS Lecture Notes — Monograph Ser.* **5**, 35–40. [*MR* **86g:62017**]

Karlin, S., and Y. Rinott (1988). A generalized Cauchy–Binet formula and applications to total positivity and majorization. *J. Multivariate Anal.* **27**, 284–299. [*MR* **90m:62117**]

Karlin, S., and W. Studden (1966). *Tchebycheff Systems: With Applications in Analysis and Statistics*, Pure Appl. Math. Vol XV. Wiley (Interscience), New York. [*MR* **34**(1967)4757; *Zbl.* **153**(1968)389]

Karlin, S., and Z. Ziegler (1965). Generalized absolutely monotone functions. *Israel J. Math.* **3**, 173–180. [*MR* **34**(1967)2805; *Zbl.* **148**(1968)285]

Kästner, J., and C. Zylka (1993). On generalized uniformly tapered matrices. *Linear Algebra Appl.* **181**, 221–232. [*MR* **93k:15037**]

Kazarinoff, N. D. (1961). *Geometric Inequalities*. Random House, New Mathematical Library, 4, New York. [*MR* **24**(1962)A1]

Keilson, J., and G. P. H. Styan (1973). Markov chains and M-matrices; Inequalities and equalities. *J. Math. Anal. Appl.* **41**, 439–459. [*MR* **47**(1974)3422]

Keller, J. B. (1962). Factorization of matrices by least squares. *Biometrika* **49**, 239–242. [*MR* **25**(1963)3944; *Zbl.* **106**(1964)344]

Keller, J. B. (1975). Closest, unitary, orthogonal and Hermitian operators to a given operator. *Math. Mag.* **48**, 192–197. [*MR* **53**(1977)8103; *Zbl.* **357**(1978)47019]

Kellerer, H. G. (1961). Funktionen auf Produkträumen mit vorgegebenen Marginal-Funktionen. *Math. Ann.* **144**, 323–344. [*MR* **26**(1963) 5116; *Zbl.* **129**(1967)34]

Kellerer, H. G. (1964). Allgemeine Systeme von Repräsentanten. *Z. Wahrscheinlichkeitstheorie und Verw. Gebiete* **2**, 306–309. [*MR* **29** (1965)5264; *Zbl.* **132**(1967)5–6]

Kemperman, J. H. B. (1973). Moment problems for sampling without replacement. I, II, III. *Nederl. Akad. Wetensch. Prac. Ser. A* **76** (=*Indag. Math.* **35**), 149–164, 165–180, and 181–188. [*MR* **49**(1975)9997a,b,c; *Zbl.* **266**(1974)62006, 62007, 62008]

Kemperman, J. H. B. (1975). The dual of the cone of all convex functions on a vector space. *Aequationes Math.* **13**, 103–119. [*MR* **53**(1977)8860; *Zbl.* **328**(1977)46010]

Kendall, D. G. (1960). On infinite doubly-stochastic matrices and Birkhoff's Problem 111. *J. London Math. Soc.* **35**, 81–84. [*MR* **22**(1961)1815; *Zbl.* **94**(1962)119]

Kesten, H., and N. Morse (1959). A property of the multinomial distribution. *Ann. Math. Statist.* **30**, 120–127. [*MR* **21**(1960)4516; *Zbl.* **218**(1972)62017]

Khaledi, B.-E., and S. Kochar (2002). Dispersive ordering among linear combinations of uniform random variables. *J. Statist. Plann. Infer.* **100**, 13–21. [*MR* **2002j:60029**].

Khaledi, B.-E., and S. Kochar (2004). Ordering convolutions of gamma random variables. *Sankhyā* **66**, 466–473. [*MR* **2005i:60033**]

Khintchine, A. (1923). Überdyadische Brüche. *Math. Z.* **18**, 109–116.

Kiefer, J. (1959). Optimum experimental designs. *J. Roy. Statist. Soc. Ser. B* **21**, 272–319. [*MR* **22:4101**]

Kiefer, J. (1975). Construction and optimality of generalized Youden designs. In *A Survey of Statistical Design and Linear Models* (J. N. Srivastava, ed.), pp. 333–353. North-Holland, Amsterdam. [*MR* **52:15877**]

Kim, Y. B., and A. M. Makowski (1998). Simple optimization problems via majorization ordering. *IEEE Trans. Auto. Control* **43**, 438–442. [*MR* **1614852**]

Kimura, M., and I. Kakiuchi (1989). A majorization inequality for distributions on hyperplanes and its applications to tests for outliers. *J. Statist. Plann. Infer.* **21**, 19–26. [*MR* **90m:62115**]

Kingman, J. F. C. (1961). A convexity property of positive matrices. *Quart. J. Math. Oxford, Ser. (2)* **12**, 283–284. [*MR* **0138632**]

Kittaneh, F. (1995). Singular values of companion matrices and bounds on zeros of polynomials. *SIAM J. Matrix Anal. Appl.* **16**, 333–340. [*MR* **95m:15015**]

Kittaneh, F. (2007). Bounds and a majorization for the real parts of the zeros of polynomials. *Proc. Amer. Math. Soc.* **135**, 659–664. [*MR* **2262860**]

Klamkin, M. S. (1970). A physical application of a rearrangement inequality. *Amer. Math. Monthly* **77**, 68–69. [*Zbl.* **187**(1970)316]

Klamkin, M. S. (1975). Extensions of the Weierstrass product inequalities. II. *Amer. Math. Monthly* **82**, 741–742. [*Zbl.* **316**(1976)26014]

Klamkin, M. S. (1976). Problem E2603. *Amer. Math. Monthly* **83**, 843; see also *Amer. Math. Monthly* **84**(1977)743.

Klamkin, M. S. (1980). Inequalities for inscribed and circumscribed polygons. *Amer. Math. Monthly* **87**, 469–473. [*MR* **82e:52008**]

Klamkin, M. S., and D. J. Newman (1970). Extensions of the Weierstrass product inequalities. *Math. Mag.* **43**, 137–141. [*MR* **42**(1971)445; *Zbl.* **193**(1970)16]

Klinger, A. (1968). Approximate pseudoinverse solutions to ill-conditioned linear systems. *J. Optim. Theory Appl.* **2**, 117–124. [*MR* **39**(1970)6501; *Zbl.* **187**(1970)96]

Klyachko, A. A. (1998). Stable bundles, representation theory and Hermitian operators. *Selecta Math. (N.S.)* **4**, 419–445. [*MR* **2000b:14054**]

Knuth, D. (2010, forthcoming). *The Art of Computer Programming. Vol. 4A. Enumeration and Backtracking.* Addison-Wesley, Reading, MA.

Knutson, A., and T. Tao (1999). The honeycomb model of $GL_n(C)$ tensor products. I. Proof of the saturation conjecture. *J. Amer. Math. Soc.* **12**, 1055–1090. [*MR* **2000c:20066**]

Koch, G. G. (1967a). A general approach to the estimation of variance components. *Technometrics* **9**, 93–118. [*MR* **36**(1968)4686; *Zbl.* **147**(1968)181]

Koch, G. G. (1967b). A procedure to estimate the population mean in random effects models. *Technometrics* **9**, 577–585. [*MR* **36**(1968)4728]

Kochar, S. (1989). On extensions of DMRL and related partial orderings of life distributions. *Comm. Statist. Stochastic Models* **5**, 235–245. [*MR* **90g:62240**]

Kochar, S., and J. Rojo (1996). Some new results on stochastic comparisons of spacings from heterogeneous exponential distributions. *J. Multivariate Anal.*. **59**, 272–281. [*MR* **98e:62084**]

Kolm, S. (1969). The optimal production of social justice. In *Public Economics* (H. Guitton and J. Margolis, eds.), Macmillan, London.

Kolm, S. (1996). *Modern Theories of Justice*. MIT Press, Cambridge, MA.

Komiya, H. (1983). Necessary and sufficient conditions for multivariate majorization. *Linear Algebra Appl.* **55**, 147–154. [*MR* **84k:15015**]

Kondor, Y. (1975). Value judgements implied by the use of various measures of income equality. *Rev. Income Wealth* **21**, 309–321.

Korwar, R. M. (2002). On stochastic orders for sums of independent random variables. *J. Multivariate Anal.* **80**, 344–357. [*MR* **2003c:60035**]

Koshevoy, G. (1995). Multivariate Lorenz majorization. *Soc. Choice Welf.* **12**, 93–102. [*MR* **96c:90010**]

Koshevoy, G., and K. Mosler (1996). The Lorenz zonoid of a multivariate distribution. *J. Amer. Statist. Assoc.* **91**, 873–882. [*MR* **97b:62085**

Koshevoy, G., and K. Mosler (1997a). Multivariate Gini indices. *J. Multivariate Anal.* **60**, 252–276. [*MR* **98e:62093**]

Koshevoy, G., and K. Mosler (1997b). Zonoid trimming for multivariate distributions. *Ann. Statist.* **25**, 1998–2017. [*MR* **99c:62151**]

Krämer, W. (1998) Measurement of inequality. In *Handbook of Applied Economic Statistics* (A. Ullah and D. E. A. Giles, eds.), pp. 39–61. Marcel Dekker, New York.

Krause, M. (1996). A simple proof of the Gale–Ryser theorem. *Amer. Math. Monthly* **103**, 335–337. [*MR* **1383671**]

Krauss, F. (1936). Über konvexe Matrix funktionen. *Math. Z.* **41**, 18–42.

Kristof, W. (1970). A theorem on the trace of certain matrix products and some applications. *J. Math. Psych.* **7**, 515–530. [*MR* **42**(1971)6008; *Zbl.* **205**(1981)492.]

Krull, W. (1958). Über eine Verallgemeinerung der Hadamardschen Ungleichung. *Arch. Math.* (*Basel*) **9**, 42–45. [*MR* **21**(1960)1979]

Kullback, S. (1959). *Information Theory and Statistics*. Wiley, New York. [*MR* **21**(1960)2325; *Zbl.* **88**(1961)104–106]

Kwong, H. (2007). Problem 11280. *Amer. Math. Monthly* **114**, 259; see also *Amer. Math. Monthly* **115** (2008), 760.

Kwong, M. K. (1989). Some results on matrix monotone functions. *Linear Algebra Appl.* **118**, 129–153. [*MR* **90e:47016**]

Lancaster, P. (1969). *Theory of Matrices.* Academic Press, New York. [*MR* **39**(1970)6885; *Zbl.* **186**(1970)53]

Landau, H. G. (1953). On dominance relations and the structure of animal societies. III. The condition for a score structure. *Bull. Math. Biophys.* **15**, 143–148. [*MR* **14**(1953)1000]

Lanke, J. (1974). On an inequality of Hoeffding and Rosén. *Scand. J. Statist.* **1**, 84–86. [*MR* **52**(1976)1963; *Zbl.* **283**(1975)62012]

Lassner, G., and G. A. Lassner (1973). On the time evolution of physical systems. *Publ. JINR Dubna.* **E2-7537**.

Lawton, W. H. (1965). Some inequalities for central and non-central distributions. *Ann. Math. Statist.* **36**, 1521–1525. [*MR* **32**(1966)3175]

Lawton, W. H. (1968). Concentration of random quotients. *Ann. Math. Statist.* **39**, 466–480. [*MR* **37**(1969)1002]

Lax, P. D. (1958). Differential equations, difference equations and matrix theory. *Comm. Pure Appl. Math.* **11**, 175–194. [*MR* **20**(1959)4572; *Zbl.* **86**(1961)16]

Lefèvre, C. (1994). Stochastic ordering of epidemics. In *Stochastic Orders and Their Applications* (M. Shaked and G. J. Shanthikumar, eds.), pp. 323–348. Academic Press, Boston.

Lehmann, E. L. (1955). Ordered families of distributions. *Ann. Math. Statist.* **26**, 399–419. [*MR* **17**(1956)169; *Zbl.* **65**(1956)119–120]

Lehmann, E. L. (1959). *Testing Statistical Hypotheses.* John Wiley and Sons, New York; Chapman and Hall, London. [*MR* **21:6654**]

Lehmann, E. L. (1966). Some concepts of dependence. *Ann. Math. Statist.* **37**, 1137–1153. [*MR* **34**(1967)2101; *Zbl.* **146**(1968)406]

Lehmann, E. L., and J. Rojo (1992). Invariant directional orderings. *Ann. Statist.* **20**, 2100–2110. [*MR* **93m:62010**]

Lenard, A. (1971). Generalization of the Golden–Thompson inequality. $\text{Tr}(e^A e^B) \geq \text{Tr } e^{A+B}$. *Indiana Univ. Math. J.* **21**, 457–467. [*MR* **44**(1977)6724]

León, R. V., and F. Proschan (1979). An inequality for convex functions involving G-majorization. *J. Math. Anal. Appl.* **69**, 603–606. [*MR* **80k:26014**]

Leuenberger, F. (1961). Gejensätzliches Verhalten der arithmeischen und geometrischen Mittel. *Elem. Math.* **16**, 127–129.

Levin, V. I. and S. B. Stečkin (1948). *Inequalities* [A translation of selected material from the appendices to the Russian edition of *Inequalities*, by G. H. Hardy, J. E. Littlewood, and G. Pólya (1934), Cambridge University Press, London and New York]. *Amer. Math. Soc. Transl., Ser. 2* **14**, 1–29.

Levow, R. B. (1972). A problem of Mirsky concerning nonsingular doubly stochastic matrices. *Linear Algebra Appl.* **5**, 197–206. [*MR* **47**(1974)252; *Zbl.* **264**(1974)15005]

Levy, H. (2006). *Stochastic Dominance: Investment Decision Making under Uncertainty.* 2nd ed. Springer, New York. [*MR* **2007d:91003**]

Li, A.-J., W.-Z. Zhao and C.-P. Chen (2006). Logarithmically complete monotonicity and Shur-convexity for some ratios of gamma functions. *Univ. Beograd. Publ. Elektrotehn. Fak. Ser. Mat.* **17**, 88–92. [*MR* **2241548**]

Li, X., P. Mikusiński, H. Sherwood, and M. D. Taylor (1996). In quest of Birkhoff's theorem in higher dimensions. Distributions with fixed marginals and related topics. *IMS Lecture Notes Monogr. Ser.* **28**, 187–197. [*MR* **1485531**]

Lidskiĭ, V. (1950). The proper values of the sum and product of symmetric matrices. *Dokl. Akad. Nauk SSSR* [N.S.] **75**, 769–772 (in Russian) (transl. by C. D. Benster, U.S. Department of Commerce, National Bureau of Standards, Washington, DC. N.B.S. Rep. 2248, 1953). [*MR* **12**(1951)581; *MR* **14**(1953)528; *Zbl.* **39**(1951)10; *Zbl.* **42**(1952)13 (in Russian)]

Lieb, E. H. (1973). Convex trace functions and the Wigner–Yanase–Dyson conjecture. *Adv. Math.* **11**, 267–288. [*MR* **48:10407**]

Lieb, E. H., and M. B. Ruskai (1974). Some operator inequalities of the Schwarz type. *Adv. Math.* **12**, 269–273. [*MR* **49**(1975)1181; *Zbl.* **274**(1975)46045]

Lieb, E. H., and W. Thirring (1976). Inequalities for the moments of the eigenvalues of the Schrödinger Hamiltonian and their relation to Sobolev inequalities. In *Essays in Honor of Valentine Borgmann* (E. Lieb, B. Simon and A. Wightman, eds.), pp.269–303. Princeton University Press, Princeton, NJ.

Liu, S., and H. Neudecker (1996). Several matrix Kantorovich-type inequalities. *J. Math. Anal. Appl.* **197**, 23–26. [*MR* **97d:26023**]

Liu, Z., and D. Towsley (1994). Stochastic scheduling in in-forest networks. *Adv. Appl. Probab.* **26**, 222–241. [*MR* **94i:90058**]

Liyanage, L., and J. G. Shanthikumar (1992). Allocation through stochastic Schur convexity and stochastic transposition increasingness. In *Stochastic Inequalities* (M. Shaked and Y. L. Tong, eds.), *IMS Lecture Notes — Monograph Ser.* **22**, 253–273. [*MR* **95a:60020**]

Loewner, C. (K. Löwner) (1934). Über monotone Matrixfunktionen. *Math. Z.* **38**, 177–216. [*Zbl.* **8**(1934)113]

Loewner, C. (1950). Some classes of functions defined by difference or differential inequalities. *Bull. Amer. Math. Soc.* **56**, 308–319. [*MR* **12**(1951)396]

London, D. (1970). Rearrangement inequalities involving convex functions. *Pacific J. Math.* **34**, 749–753. [*MR* **42**(1971)4687; *Zbl.* **199**(1971)387]

Lorentz, G. G. (1953). An inequality for rearrangements. *Amer. Math. Monthly* **60**, 176–179. [*MR* **14**(1953)626; *Zbl.* **50**(1954)282]

Lorenz, M. O. (1905). Methods of measuring concentration of wealth. *J. Amer. Statist. Assoc.* **9**, 209–219.

Low, L. (1970). An application of majorization to comparison of variances. *Technometrics* **12**, 141–145.

Lunetta, G. (1972). Sulla concentrazione delle distribuzioni doppie. In *Atti della XXVII Riunione Scientifica della Societ'a Italiana di Statistica*, **2**, 127–150.

Lynn, M. S. (1964). On the Schur product of M-matrices and nonnegative matrices, and related inequalities. *Proc. Camb. Philos. Soc.* **60**, 425–431. [*MR* **29**(1965)3481]

Magda, C. G. (1980). Circular balanced repeated measurements designs. *Comm. Statist. A—Theory Methods* **9**, 1901–1918. [*MR* **82c:62101**]

Mahmoodian, E. S. (1975). A critical case method of proof in combinatorial mathematics. Doctoral dissertation, University of Pennsylvania, Philadelphia.

Makowski, A. (1964). Problem E1675. *Amer. Math. Monthly* **71**, 317; see also *Amer. Math. Monthly* **72** (1965) 187.

Malamud, S. M. (2003). An analogue of the Poincaré separation theorem for normal matrices, and the Gauss–Lucas theorem. *Funct. Anal. Appl.* **37**, 232–235. [*MR* **2021139**]

Malamud, S. M. (2005). Inverse spectral problem for normal matrices and the Gauss–Lucas theorem. *Trans. Amer. Math. Soc.* **357**, 4043–4064. [*MR* **2006e:15018**]

Marcus, M. (1956). An eigenvalue inequality for the product of normal matrices. *Amer. Math. Monthly* **63**, 173–174. [*MR* **17**(1965)820]

Marcus, M. (1958). On determinantal inequality. *Amer. Math. Monthly* **65**, 266–268. [*MR* **22**(1961)6820; *Zbl.* **83**(1960)8]

Marcus, M. (1965). Harnack's and Weyl's inequalities. *Proc. Amer. Math. Soc.* **16**, 864–866. [*MR* **31**(1966)5873; *Zbl.* **145**(1968)250]

Marcus, M. (1969). Singular value inequalities. *J. London Math. Soc.* **44**, 118–120. [*MR* **38**(1969)4500; *Zbl.* **174**(1969)63]

Marcus, M., K. Kidman, and M. Sandy (1984). Products of elementary doubly stochastic matrices. *Linear Multilinear Algebra* **15**, 331–340. [*MR* **85g:15025**]

Marcus, M., and L. Lopes (1957). Inequalities for symmetric functions and Hermitian matrices. *Canad. J. Math.* **9**, 305–312. [*MR* **18**(1957)877; *Zbl.* **79**(1959)21]

Marcus, M., and H. Minc (1962). Some results on doubly stochastic matrices. *Proc. Amer. Math. Ser.* **13**, 571–579. [*MR* **25**(1963)3057; *Zbl.* **107**(1964)14]

Marcus, M., and H. Minc (1964). *A Survey of Matrix Theory and Matrix Inequalities*. Allyn & Bacon, Boston. [*MR* **29**(1965)112; *Zbl.* **126**(1966)24]

Marcus, M., and B. N. Moyls (1957). On the maximum principle of Ky Fan. *Canad. J. Math.* **9**, 313–320. [*MR* **19**(1958)114; *Zbl.* **79**(1959)21]

Marcus, M., and P. J. Nikolai (1969). Inequalities for some monotone matrix functions. *Canad. J. Math.* **21**, 485–494. [*MR* **38**(1969)5815; *Zbl.* **196**(1970)57]

Marcus, M., and R. Ree (1959). Diagonals of doubly stochastic matrices. *Quart. J. Math. Oxford Ser.* [2] **10**, 296–302. [*MR* **22**(1961)8025; *Zbl.* **138**(1967)15]

Mardia, K. V. (1970). *Families of Bivariate Distributions*, Griffin's Statistical Monographs and Courses, No. 27. Hafner, New York. [*MR* **47**(1974)7862; *Zbl.* **223**(1972)62062]

Margalef, D. R. (1958). Information theory in ecology. *General Systems* **3**, 36–71.

Markus, A. S. (1964). Eigenvalues and singular values of the sum and product of linear operators. *Uspehi Mat. Nauk* **19**, No. 4, 93–123 [*Russian Math. Surveys* **19**, 91–120 (1964)]. [*MR* **29**(1965)6318; *Zbl.* **133**(1967)72–73]

Marshall, A. W. (1975). Some comments on the hazard gradient. *Stochastic Process. Appl.* **3**, 293–300. [*MR* **53:4431**]

Marshall, A. W. (1991). Multivariate stochastic orderings and generating cones of functions. In *Stochastic Orders and Decision Under Risk* (K. Mosler and M. Scarsini, eds.). *IMS Lecture Notes Monogr. Ser.* **19**. Inst. Math. Statist., Hayward, CA. [*MR* **94a:60023**]

Marshall, A. W., and I. Olkin (1965). Norms and inequalities for condition numbers. *Pacific J. Math.* **15**, 241–247. [*MR* **31**(1966)191; *Zbl.* **166**(1969)300]

Marshall, A. W., and I. Olkin (1967). A multivariate exponential distribution. *J. Amer. Statist. Assoc.* **62**, 30–44. [*MR* **35**(1968)6241; *Zbl.* **147**(1968)381]

Marshall, A. W., and I. Olkin (1968). Scaling of matrices to achieve specified row and column sums. *Numer. Math.* **12**, 83–90. [*MR* **39**(1970)235; *Zbl.* **165**(1969)174]

Marshall, A. W., and I. Olkin (1969). Norms and inequalities for condition numbers. II. *Linear Algebra Appl.* **2**, 167–172. [*MR* **39**(1970)4195; *Zbl.* **182**(1970)52]

Marshall, A. W., and I. Olkin (1973a). *Combinatorial analysis*, Tech. Rep. No. 70. Department of Statistics, Stanford University, Stanford, CA.

Marshall, A. W., and I. Olkin (1973b). Norms and inequalities for condition numbers. III. *Linear Algebra Appl.* **7**, 291–300. [*MR* **48**(1974)6142; *Zbl.* **351**(1978)15015]

Marshall, A. W., and I. Olkin (1974). Majorization in multivariate distributions. *Ann. Statist.* **2**, 1189–1200. [*MR* **50**(1975)15145; *Zbl.* **292**(1975)62037]

Marshall, A. W. and I. Olkin (1982). A convexity proof of Hadamard's inequality. *Amer. Math. Monthly* **89**, 687–688. [*MR* **84f:15023**]

Marshall, A. W., and I. Olkin (1983). Inequalities via majorization — An introduction. *General Inequalities, 3, Internat. Schriftenreihe Numer. Math.* **64**, 165–187. [*MR* **86e:26024**]

Marshall, A.W. and I. Olkin (2007). *Life Distributions*. Springer, New York. [*MR* **2344835**]

Marshall, A. W., I. Olkin, and F. Proschan (1967). Monotonicity of ratios of means and other applications of majorization. In *Inequalities* (O. Shisha, ed.), pp. 177–190. Academic Press, New York. [*MR* **38**(1969)6008]

Marshall, A. W., I. Olkin, and F. Pukelsheim (2002). A majorization comparison of apportionment methods in proportional representation. *Soc. Choice Welf.* **19**, 885–900. [*MR* **1935010**]

Marshall, A. W., and F. Proschan (1965). An inequality for convex functions involving majorization. *J. Math. Anal. Appl.* **12**, 87–90. [*MR* **32**(1966)2532; *Zbl.* **145**(1968)286]

Marshall, A. W., and F. Proschan (1970). Mean life of series and parallel systems. *J. Appl. Probab.* **7**, 165–174. [*MR* **41**(1971)2860; *Zbl.* **193**(1970)198]

Marshall, A. W., D. W. Walkup, and R. J.-B. Wets (1967). Order-preserving functions; applications to majorization and order statistics. *Pacific J. Math.* **23**, 569–584. [*MR* **36**(1968)2756; *Zbl.* **153**(1968)385]

Martignon, L. F. (1984). Doubly stochastic matrices with prescribed positive spectrum. *Linear Algebra Appl.* **61**, 11–13. [*MR* **85i:15036**]

Martinez Pería, F. D., P. G. Massey, and L. E. Silvestre (2005). Weak matrix majorization. *Linear Algebra Appl.* **403**, 343–368. [*MR* **2006b:15034**]

Mateev, P. (1978). On the entropy of the multinomial distribution. *Theory Probab. Appl.* **23**, 188–190. [*MR* **58:9796**]

Mathias, R. (1993). Perturbation bounds for the polar decomposition. *SIAM J. Matrix Anal. Appl.* **14**, 588–597. [*MR* **94e:15018**]

Matsumoto, A., and M. Fujii (2009). Generalizations of reverse Bebiano–Lemos–Providência inequality. *Linear Algebra Appl.* **430**, 1544–1549. [*MR* **2490696**]

Mattner, L., and B. Roos (2007). A shorter proof of Kanter's Bessel function concentration bound. *Probab. Theory Related Fields* **139**, 191–205. [*MR* **2008e:60044**]

Mauldon, J. G. (1969). Extreme points of convex sets of doubly stochastic matrices (I). *Z. Wahrscheinlichkeitstheorie und Verw. Gebiete* **13**, 333–337. [*MR* **41**(1971)4663, see also review erratum **42**(1971)1824; *Zbl.* **177**(1970)50]

McIntosh, R. P. (1967). An index of diversity and the relation of certain concepts to diversity. *Ecology* **48**, 392–404.

Meilijson, I., and A. Nádas (1979). Convex majorization with an application to the length of critical paths. *J. Appl. Probab.* **16**, 671–677. [*MR* **81c:60019**]

Melman, A. (2009). Overshooting properties of Newton-like and Ostrowski-like methods. *Amer. Math. Monthly* **116**, 238–250. [*MR* **2491980**]

Menon, A, K. Mehrotra, C. Mohan, and S. Ranka (1997). Replicators, majorization and genetic algorithms: New models, connections and analytic tools. In *Foundations of Genetic Algorithms, Vol. 4* (R. Belew and M. Vose, eds.), pp. 155–180. Morgan Kaufmann, San Francisco.

Merkle, M. (1997). On log-convexity of a ratio of gamma functions. *Univ. Beograd. Publ. Elektrotehn. Fak. Ser. Mat.* **8**, 114–119. [*MR* **1480408**]

Merkle, M. (1998). Convexity, Schur-convexity and bounds for the gamma function involving the digamma function. *Rocky Mountain J. Math.* **28**, 1053–1066. [*MR* **99m:33001**]

Meyer, P. A. (1966). *Probability and Potentials.* Ginn (Blaisdell), Boston. [*MR* **34**(1967)5119; *Zbl.* **138**(1967)104]

Milliken, G. A., and F. Akdeniz (1977). A theorem on the difference of the generalized inverses of two nonnegative matrices. *Comm. Statist.* **A6**, 73–79. [*MR* **56:390**]

Minc, H. (1970). Rearrangement theorems (abstract). *Notices Amer. Math. Soc.* **17**, 400.

Minc, H. (1971). Rearrangements. *Trans. Amer. Math. Soc.* **159**, 497–504. [*MR* **44**(1972)236; *Zbl.* **225**(1973)26020]

Minc, H. (1978). *Permanents. Encyclopedia of Mathematics and Its Applications* **6**. Addison-Wesley, Reading, MA. [*MR* **80d:15009**]

Minc, H. (1982). A note on Egoryčev's proof of the van der Waerden conjecture. *Linear Multilinear Algebra* **11**, 367–371. [*MR* **83g:15006**]

Miranda, H. F. and R. C. Thompson (1994). Group majorization, the convex hulls of sets of matrices, and the diagonal element-singular value inequalities. *Linear Algebra Appl.* **199**, 131–141. [*MR* **95a:15007**]

Mirsky, L. (1955a). *An Introduction to Linear Algebra.* Oxford University Press, London and New York. [*MR* **17**(1956)573; *Zbl.* **66**(1965)263]

Mirsky, L. (1955b). An inequality for positive-definite matrices. *Amer. Math. Monthly* **62**, 428–430. [*MR* **17**(1956)338; *Zbl.* **64**(1956)14]

Mirsky, L. (1957a). Inequalities for normal and Hermitian matrices. *Duke J. Math.* **24**, 591–599. [*MR* **19**(1958)832; *Zbl.* **81**(1959)251]

Mirsky, L. (1957b). On a generalization of Hadamard's determinantal inequality due to Szász. *Arch. Math.* **8**, 274–275. [*MR* **19**(1958)936; *Zbl.* **84**(1960)16]

Mirsky, L. (1958a). Matrices with prescribed characteristic roots and diagonal elements. *J. London Math. Soc.* **33**, 14–21. [*MR* **19**(1958)1034; *Zbl.* **101**(1963)253]

Mirsky, L. (1958b). Maximum principles in matrix theory. *Proc. Glasgow Math. Assoc.* **4**, 34–37. [*MR* **22**(1961)12112; *Zbl.* **99**(1963)247–248]

Mirsky, L. (1958c). Proofs of two theorems on doubly-stochastic matrices. *Proc. Amer. Math. Soc.* **9**, 371–374. [*MR* **20**(1959)1686]

Mirsky, L. (1959a). On a convex set of matrices. *Arch. Math.* **10**, 88–92. [*MR* **21**(1960)5643; *Zbl.* **88**(1961)251]

Mirsky, L. (1959b). On the trace of matrix products. *Math. Nachr.* **20**, 171–174. [*MR* **23**(1962)A3148]

Mirsky, L. (1959c). Remarks on an existence theorem in matrix theory due to A. Horn. *Monatsh. Math.* **63**, 241–243. [*MR* **21**(1960)2662; *Zbl.* **90**(1961)15]

Mirsky, L. (1960a). Symmetric gauge functions and unitarily invariant norms. *Quart. J. Math. Oxford Ser.* [2] **11**, 50–59. [*MR* **22**(1961)5639; *Zbl.* **105**(1964)11]

Mirsky, L. (1960b). An algorithm relating to symmetric matrices. *Monatsh. Math.* **64**, 35–38.

Mirsky, L. (1962/1963). Results and problems in the theory of doubly-stochastic matrices. *Z. Wahrscheinlichkeitstheorie und Verw. Gebiete* **1**, 319–334. [*MR* **27**(1964)3007; *Zbl.* **109**(1964)361]

Mirsky, L. (1963). Some applications of a minimum principle in linear algebra. *Monatsh. Math.* **67**, 104–112. [*MR* **27**(1964)4816]

Mirsky, L. (1964). Inequalities and existence theorems in the theory of matrices. *J. Math. Anal. Appl.* **9**, 99–118; *erratum* **10**(1965) 264. [*MR* **29**(1965)1217]

Mirsky, L. (1971). *Transversal Theory.* Academic Press, New York. [*MR* **44**(1972)87; *Zbl.* **282**(1975)05001]

Mitjagin, B. S. (1964). Normed ideals of intermediate type. *Izv. Akad. Nauk SSSR Ser. Mat.* **28**, 819–832 (*Amer. Math. Soc. Transl., Ser 2* **63**, 180–194). [*MR* **30**(1965)4142; *Zbl.* **124**(1966)68]

Mitrinović, D. S. (1964). *Elementary Inequalities.* P. Noordhoff, Groningen.

Mitrinović, D. S. (1968). Problem 5555. *Amer. Math. Monthly* **75**, 84; see also *Amer. Math. Monthly* **75**(1968), 1129–1130.

Mitrinović, D. S. (1970). *Analytic Inequalities.* Springer-Verlag, Berlin and New York. [*MR* **43**(1972)448; *Zbl.* **199**(1971)381]

Mitrinović, D. S., J. E. Pečarić, and V. Volenec (1989). *Recent Advances in Geometric Inequalities. Math. Appl. (East European Ser.* **28**. Kluwer, Dordrecht. [*MR* **91k:52014**]

Mitrinović, D. S., and P. M. Vasić (1974). History, variations and generalizations of the Čebvšev inequality and the question of some priorities. *Univ. Beograd. Publ. Elektrotehn. Fak. Ser. Mat. Fix.* No. 461, pp. 1–30. [*Zbl.* **295**(1975)26018]

Mizera, I., and J. A. Wellner (1998). Necessary and sufficient conditions for weak consistency of the median of independent but not identically distributed random variables. *Ann. Statist.* **26**, 672–691. [*MR* **99d:62020**]

Montague, J. S., and R. J. Plemmons (1973). Doubly stochastic matrix equations. *Israel J. Math.* **15**, 216–229. [*MR* **48**(1974)317; *Zbl.* **273**(1975)15014]

Moon, J. W. (1968). *Topics on Tournaments.* Holt, Rinehart & Winston, New York. [*MR* **41**(1971)1574; *Zbl.* **191**(1970)227]

Moore, M. H. (1973). A convex matrix function. *Amer. Math. Monthly* **80**, 408–409. [*MR* **47**(1974)3424; *Zbl.* **268**(1974)15006]

Mosler, K. (2002). *Multivariate Dispersion, Central Regions and Depth. The Lift Zonoid Approach*. Lecture Notes in Statistics, **165**. Springer-Verlag, Berlin. [*MR* **2003k:60038**]

Mudholkar, G. S. (1966). The integral of an invariant unimodal function over an invariant convex set—An inequality and applications. *Proc. Amer. Math. Soc.* **17**, 1327–1333. [*MR* **34**(1967)7741; *Zbl.* **163**(1969)69]

Mudholkar, G.S. (1972). G-peakedness comparisons for random vectors. *Ann. Inst. Statist. Math.* **24**, 127–135. [*MR* **48:9801**]

Mudholkar, G. S., and S. R. Dalal (1977). Some bounds on the distribution functions of linear combinations and applications. *Ann. Inst. Statist. Math.* **29**, 89–100. [*MR* **56:6963**]

Muir, T. (1906). *The Theory of Determinants in the Historical Order of Development*. Macmillan, New York.

Muir, W. W. (1974/1975). Inequalities concerning the inverses of positive definite matrices. *Proc. Edinburgh Math. Soc.* [2] **19**, 109–113. [*MR* **53**(1977)797; *Zbl.* **304**(1976)15005]

Muirhead, R. F. (1903). Some methods applicable to identities and inequalities of symmetric algebraic functions of n letters. *Proc. Edinburgh Math. Soc.* **21**, 144–157.

Müller, A., and D. Stoyan (2002). *Comparison Methods for Stochastic Models and Risks*. John Wiley and Sons, Chichester. [*MR* **2003d:60003**]

Nachman, D. C. (2005). Stochastic majorization: A characterization. Unpublished manuscript. Georgia State University, Atlanta, GA.

Nappo, G., and F. Spizzichino (1998). Ordering properties of the TTT-plot of lifetimes with Schur joint densities. *Statist. Probab. Lett.* **39**, 195–203. [*MR* **99i:62238**]

Nashed, M. Z. (1966). Some remarks on variations and differentials. *Amer. Math. Monthly* **73**, 63–76. [*MR* **33:6347**]

Nasser, J. I. (1966). Problem E1847. *Amer. Math. Monthly* **73**, 82; see also *Amer. Math. Monthly* **77**(1970), 524.

Nayak, T. K., and M. C. Christman (1992). Effect of unequal catchability on estimates of the number of classes in a population. *Scand. J. Statist.* **19**, 281–287. [*MR* **1183202**]

Neubauer, M. G., and W. Watkins (2006). A variance analog of majorization and some associated inequalities. *J. Inequal. Pure Appl. Math.* **7**, Issue 3, Article 79. [*MR* **2007h:26019**]

von Neumann, J. (1932). Über adjungierte Funktionaloperatoren. *Ann. Math.* **33**, 294–310 [(*John von Neumann, Collected Works* (A. H. Taub, ed.), Vol. II, pp. 242–258. Pergamon, Oxford, 1961)]. [*Zbl.* **4**(1932)216]

von Neumann, J. (1937). Some matrix-inequalities and metrization of matrix-space. *Tomsk. Univ. Rev.* **1**, 286–300. [*John von Neumann Collected Works* (A. H. Taub, ed.), Vol. IV, pp. 205–218. Pergamon, Oxford, 1962]. [*Zbl.* **17**(1938)098]

von Neumann, J. (1953). A certain zero-sum two-person game equivalent to the optimal assignment problem. *Contributions to the Theory of Games*, Vol. 2, pp. 5–12. Princeton University Press, Princeton, NJ. [*MR* **14**(1953)998; *Zbl.* **50**(1954)141]

von Neumann, J., and H. H. Goldstine (1947). Numerical inverting of matrices of high order. *Bull. Amer. Math. Soc.* **53**, 1021–1099. [*MR* **9**(1948)471; *Zbl.* **31**(1949)314]

Neuts, M. F. (1975). Computational uses of the method of phases in the theory of queues. *Comput. Math. Appl.* **1**, 151–166. [*MR* **52:6914**]

Nevius, S. E., F. Proschan, and J. Sethuraman (1977a). Schur functions in statistics. II. Stochastic majorization. *Ann. Statist.* **5**, 263–273. [*MR* **56:1595**]

Nevius, S. E., F. Proschan, and J. Sethuraman (1977b). A stochastic version of weak majorization, with applications. In *Statistical Decision Theory and Related Topics*, II (S. S. Gupta and D. S. Moore, eds.), pp. 281–296. Academic Press, New York. [*MR* **56:1596**]

Newman, C. M. (1975a). An extension of Khintchine's inequality. *Bull. Amer. Math. Soc.* **81**, 913–915. [*MR* **51**(1976)11651; *Zbl.* **315**(1976)42007]

Newman, C. M. (1975b). Inequalities for Ising models and field theories which obey the Lee–Yang theorem. *Comm. Math. Phys.* **41**, 1–9. [*MR* **51**(1976)12247]

Newman, C. M. (1975/1976). Gaussian correlation inequalities for ferro-magnets. *Z. Wahrscheinlichkeitstheorie und Verw. Gebiete* **33**, 75–93. [*MR* **53**(1977)2252; *Zbl.* **297**(1975)60053; *Zbl.* **308**(1976)60067]

Ng, C. T. (1987). Functions generating Schur-convex sums. *General Inequalities* 5 (W. Walter, ed.), pp. 433–438. Birkhäuser, Basel. [*MR* **91b:26018**]

Niculescu, C. P. (2000). A new look at Newton's inequalities. *J. Inequal. Pure Appl. Math.* **1**, No.2, Article 17, 1–14. [*MR* **2001h:26020**]

Niculescu, C. P. and L.-E. Persson (2006). *Convex Functions and Their Applications. A Contemporary Approach.* CMS Books in Mathematics/Ouvrages de Mathématiques de la SMC. **23**. [*MR* **2006m:26001**]

Niezgoda, M. (1998a). Group majorization and Schur type inequalities. *Linear Algebra Appl.* **268**, 9–30. [*MR* **99f:15027**]

Niezgoda, M. (1998b). An analytical characterization of effective and of irreducible groups inducing cone orderings. *Linear Algebra Appl.* **269**, 105–114. [*MR* **99d:15019**]

Noble, B. (1969). *Applied Linear Algebra.* Prentice-Hall, Englewood Cliffs, NJ. [*MR* **40**(1970)153; *Zbl.* **203**(1971)332]

O'Cinneide, C. A. (1991). Phase-type distributions and majorization. *Ann. Appl. Probab.* **1**, 219–227. [*MR* **92h:60143**]

Okamoto, M. (1960). An inequality for the weighted sum of χ^2 variates. *Bull. Math. Statist.* **9**, 69–70. [*MR* **22**(1961)10041; *Zbl.* **112**(1965)111]

Okubo, S., and A. Ishihara (1972). Inequality for convex functions in quantum-statistical mechanics. *Physica* **59**, 228–240.

Olkin, I. (1959). On inequalities of Szegö and Bellman. *Proc. Nat. Acad. Sci. U.S.A.* **45**, 230–231. [*MR* **21**(1960)3528; *Zbl.* **86**(1961)42]

Olkin, I. (1972). Monotonicity properties of Dirichlet integrals with applications to the multinomial distribution and the analysis of variance. *Biometrika* **59**, 303–307. [*MR* **49**(1975)1651; *Zbl.* **241**(1973)62037]

Olkin, I. (1973). Unpublished class notes, Stanford University, Stanford, CA.

Olkin, I. (1974). Inference for a normal population when the parameters exhibit some structure. In *Reliability and Biometry, Statistical Analysis of Lifelength* (F. Proschan and R. J. Serfling, eds.) pp. 759–773. SIAM, Philadelphia.

Olkin, I. (1985). A probabilistic proof of a theorem of Schur. *Amer. Math. Monthly* **92**, 50–51. [*MR* **86h:15017**]

Olkin, I., and J. Pratt (1958). A multivariate Tchebycheff inequality. *Ann. Math. Statist.* **29**, 226–234. [*MR* **20**(1959)385; *Zbl.* **85**(1961)352]

Olkin, I., and S. J. Press (1969). Testing and estimation for a circular stationary model. *Ann. Math. Statist.* **40**, 1358–1373. [*MR* **39**(1970)6451; *Zbl.* **186**(1970)518]

Olkin, I., and F. Pukelsheim (1982). The distance between two random vectors with given dispersion matrices. *Linear Algebra Appl.* **48**, 257–263. [*MR* **84f:62062**]

Olkin, I., and S. T. Rachev (1993). Maximum submatrix traces for positive definite matrices. *SIAM J. Matrix Anal. Appl.* **14**, 390–397. [*MR* **94f:15018**]

Olkin, I., and L. Shepp (2006). Several colorful inequalities. *Amer. Math. Monthly* **113**, 817–822. [*MR* **2007m:60046**]

Olkin, I., and M. Sobel (1965). Integral expressions for tail probabilities of the multinomial and the negative multinomial distributions. *Biometrika* **52**, 167–179. [*MR* **34**(1967)6895; *Zbl.* **129**(1967)117]

Olkin, I., and Y. L. Tong (1988). Peakedness in multivariate distributions. In *Statistical Decision Theory and Related Topics*, IV, Vol. 2. (S. S. Gupta and J. O. Berger, eds.), pp.373–383. Springer, New York. [*MR* **89c:62086**]

Olkin, I., and Y. L. Tong (1994). Positive dependence of a class of multivariate exponential distributions. *SIAM J. Control Optim.* **32**, 965–974. [*MR* **95g:60030**]

Oppenheim, A. (1930). Inequalities connected with definite Hermitian forms. *J. London Math. Soc.* **5**, 114–119.

Oppenheim, A. (1954). Inequalities connected with definite Hermitian forms, II. *Amer. Math. Monthly* **61**, 463–466. [*MR* **16**(1955)328; *Zbl.* **56**(1955)16]

Oppenheim, A. (1965a). On inequalities connecting arithmetic means and geometric means of two sets of three positive numbers. *Math. Gaz.* **49**, 160–162. [*MR* **32**(1966)2533; *Zbl.* **137**(1967)31]

Oppenheim, A. (1965b). Solution to Problem E1675. *Amer. Math. Monthly* **72**, 187.

Oppenheim, A. (1968). On inequalities connecting arithmetic means and geometric means of two sets of three positive numbers, II. *Univ. Beograd. Publ. Elektrotehn. Fak. Ser. Mat. Fiz.* No. 213, pp. 21–24. [*MR* **38**(1969)286; *Zbl.* **155**(1969)383]

Oppenheim, A. (1971). Some inequalities for triangles. *Univ. Beograd. Publ. Elektrotehn. Fak. Ser. Mat. Fiz.* No. 363, pp. 21–28. [*Zbl.* **238**(1972)50008]

Ostle, B., and H. L. Terwilliger (1957). A comparison of two means. *Proc. Montana Acad. Sci..* **17**, 69–70.

Ostrowski, A. M. (1937). Über die Determinanten mit überwiegender Hauptdiagonale. *Comment. Math. Helv.* **10**, 69–96.

Ostrowski, A. M. (1951). Über das Nichtverschwinden einer Klasse von Determinanten und die Lokalisierung der charakterischen Wurzeln von Matrizen. *Compos. Math.* **9**, 209–226. [*MR* **13**(1952)524; *Zbl.* **43**(1952)17]

Ostrowski, A. M. (1952). Sur quelques applications des fonctions convexes et concaves au sens de I. Schur. *J. Math. Pures Appl.* [9] **31**, 253–292. [*MR* **14**(1953)625; *Zbl.* **47**(1953)296]

Pachpatte, B. G. (2005). *Mathematical Inequalities.* North-Holland Mathematical Library, 67. Elsevier B.V., Amsterdam. [*MR* **2006f: 26044**]

Pakes, A. G. (1981). On income distributions and their Lorenz curves. Tech. Report, Department of Mathematics, University of Western Australia, Nedlands, W.A.

Palomar, D. P., J. M. Cioffi, and M. A. Lagunas (2003). Joint Tx-Rx beamforming design for multicarrier MIMO channels: A unified framework for convex optimization. *IEEE Trans. Signal Process.* **51**, 2381–2401.

Paris, J. B., and A. Venkovská (2008). A generalization of Muirhead's inequality. Tech. Report, School of Mathematics, University of Manchester, Manchester, UK.

Park, D. H. (1988). The reliability of k out of n systems when k components are equally reliable. *Statist. Probab. Lett.* **7**, 175–178. [*MR* **90d:90040**]

Parker, D. S., and P. Ram (1997). Greed and majorization. Tech. Report, Department of Computer Science, University of California, Los Angeles.

Parker, D. S., and P. Ram (1999). The construction of Huffman codes is a submodular ("convex") optimization problem over a lattice of binary trees. *SIAM J. Comput.* **28**, 1875–1905. [*MR* **2000k:94019**]

Parker, W. V. (1945). The characteristic roots of matrices. *Duke Math. J.* **12**, 519–526. [*MR* **7**(1946)107]

Pázman, A. (1986). *Foundations of Optimum Experimental Design.* Reidel, Dordrecht. [*MR* **88d:62128**]

Pečarić, J. E. (1984). On some inequalities for functions with nondecreasing increments. *J. Math. Anal. Appl.* **98**, 188–197. [*MR* **85c:26012**]

Pečarić, J. E., and S. Abramovich (1997). On new majorization theorems. *Rocky Mountain J. Math.* **27**, 903–911. [*MR* **99b:26041**]

Pečarić, J. E., F. Proschan, and Y. L. Tong (1992). *Convex Functions, Partial Orderings, and Statistical Applications. Mathematics in Science and Engineering*, **187**. Academic Press, Boston. **187**. [*MR* **94e:26002**]

Pečarić, J., and D. Svrtan (1998). New refinements of the Jensen inequalities based on samples with repetitions. *J. Math. Anal. Appl.* **222**, 365–373. [*MR* **99f:26020**]

Pečarić, J., and D. Svrtan (2002). Unified approach to refinements of Jensen's inequalities. *Math. Inequal. Appl.* **5**, 45–47. [*MR* **2002j:90054**]

Pečarić, J. E., and D. Zwick (1989). n-convexity and majorization. *Rocky Mountain J. Math.* **19**, 303–311. [*MR* **90i:26027**]

Penrose, R. (1955). A generalized inverse for matrices. *Proc. Cambridge Philos. Soc.* **51**, 406–413. [*MR* **16**(1955)1082; *Zbl.* **65**(1956)246]

Penrose, R. (1956). On best approximate solutions of linear matrix equations. *Proc. Cambridge Philos. Soc.* **52**, 17–19. [*MR* **17**(1956)536; *Zbl.* **70**(1957)125]

Pereira, R. (2007). Weak log-majorization, Mahler measure and polynomial inequalities. *Linear Algebra Appl.* **421**, 117–121. [*MR* **2007k: 26030**]

Pereira, S., A. Sezgin, A. Paulraj, and G. Papanicolaou (2008). Interference limited broadcast role of interferer geometry (private communication).

Perlman, M. D. (1980a). Unbiasedness of the likelihood ratio tests for equality of several covariance matrices and equality of several multivariate normal populations. *Ann. Statist.* **8**, 247–263. [*MR* **81i:62092**]

Perlman, M. D. (1980b). Unbiasedness of multivariate tests: Recent results. In *Multivariate analysis, V, (Proc. Fifth Internat. Sympos., Univ. Pittsburgh, Pittsburgh, 1978)* (P.R. Krishnaiah, ed.), pp. 413–432, North-Holland, Amsterdam-New York. [*MR* **81c:62061**]

Perlman, M. D. (1984). Stochastic majorization of the log-eigenvalues of a bivariate Wishart matrix. In *Inequalities in Statistics and Probability* (Y. L. Tong, ed.), *IMS Lecture Notes — Monograph Ser.* **5**, 173–177. [*MR* **86j:62128**]

Perlman, M. D. (1996). On stochastic majorization of the eigenvalues of a Wishart matrix. *Linear Algebra Appl.* **237/238**, 405–428. [*MR* **97j:62090**]

Perlman, M. D., and Y. Rinott (1977). On the unbiasedness of goodness-of-fit tests. Unpublished manuscript.

Phelps, R. R. (1966). *Lectures on Choquet's Theorem.* Van Nostrand-Reinhold, Princeton, NJ. [*MR* **33**(1967)1690; *Zbl.* **135**(1967) 362]

Pielou, E. C. (1975). *Ecological Diversity.* Wiley (Interscience), New York.

Pietra, G. (1915). Delle relazioni fra indici di variabilita, Note I e II. *Atti del Reale Instituto Veneto di Scienze, Lettere ed Arti* **74**, 775–804.

Pigou, A. C. (1912). *Wealth and Welfare.* Macmillan, New York.

Pinkus, A. (1996). Spectral properties of totally positive kernels and matrices. In *Total Positivity and Its Applications.* (M. Gasca and C. A. Micchelli, eds.), *Math. Appl.* **359**, 477–511. Kluwer, Dordrecht. [*MR* **97k:47003**]

Pitt, L. D. (1977). A Gaussian correlation inequality for symmetric convex sets. *Ann. Probab.* **5**, 470–474. [*MR* **56:7010**]

Pledger, G., and F. Proschan (1971). Comparisons of order statistics and of spacings from heterogeneous distributions. In *Optimizing Methods in Statistics* (J. S. Rustagi, ed.), pp. 89–113. Academic Press, New York. [*MR* **49**(1975)6484; *Zbl.* **263**(1975)62062]

Pledger, G., and F. Proschan (1973). Stochastic comparisons of random processes, with applications in reliability. *J. Appl. Probab.* **10**, 572–585. [*MR* **52**(1976)2110; *Zbl.* **271**(1975)60097]

Plemmons, R. J., and R. E. Cline (1972). The generalized inverse of a non-negative matrix. *Proc. Amer. Math. Soc.* **31**, 46–50. [*MR* **44**(1972)2759; *Zbl.* **241**(1973)15001]

Pólya, G. (1913). Über Annäherung durch Polynome mit lauter reellen Wurzeln. *Rend. Circ. Mat. Palermo* **36**, 1–17.

Pólya, G. (1915). Algebraische Unterschungen über ganze Funktionen vom Geschlechte Null und Eins. *J. für Mathematik* **145**, 224–249.

Pólya, G. (1919). Proportionalwahl und Wahrscheinlichkeitsrechnung. *Zeitschrift für die gesamte Staatswissenschaft* **74**, 297–322.

Pólya, G. (1950). Remark on Weyl's note "Inequalities between the two kinds of eigenvalues of a linear transformation." *Proc. Nat. Acad. Sci. U.S.A.* **36**, 49–51. [*MR* **11**(1950)526; *Zbl.* **41**(1952)154]

Pólya, G. (1967). Inequalities and the principle of nonsufficient reason. In *Inequalities* (O. Shisha, ed.), pp. 1–15. Academic Press, New York. [*MR* **36**(1968)3940]

Pólya, G., and G. Szegö (1951). *Isoperimetric Inequalities in Mathematical Physics.* Ann. Math. Studies, No. 27. Princeton University Press, Princeton, NJ, [*MR* **13**(1952)270]

Pólya, G., and G. Szegö (1972). *Problems and Theorems in Analysis*, Vol. I (transl. by D. Aeppli), Springer-Verlag, Berlin and New York (1st ed. in German, 1925). [*MR* **49**(1975)8782; *Zbl.* **236**(1973)00003]

Pólya, G., and G. Szegö (1976). *Problems and Theorems in Analysis*, Vol. II (transl. by C. E. Billigheimer), Springer-Verlag, Berlin and New York (1st ed. in German, 1925). [*MR* **53**(1977)2; *Zbl.* **311**(1976)00002]

Prékopa, A. (1971). Logarithmic concave measures with application to stochastic programming. *Acta Sci. Math. (Szeged)* **32**, 301–316. [*MR* **47:3628**]

Proschan, F. (1965). Peakedness of distributions of convex combinations. *Ann. Math. Statist.* **36**, 1703–1706. [*MR* **32**(1966)4722; *Zbl.* **139**(1967)411]

Proschan, F. (1975). Applications of majorization and Schur functions in reliability and life testing. In *Reliability and Fault Tree Analysis* (R. E. Barlow, J. B. Fussell, and N. D. Singpurwalla, eds.), pp. 237–258. SIAM, Philadelphia. [*MR* **56:7082**]

Proschan, F., and J. Sethuraman (1973). *Two generalizations of Muirhead's theorem.* Technical Report No. M283, Department of Statistics, Florida State University, Tallahassee.

Proschan, F., and J. Sethuraman (1976). Stochastic comparisons of order statistics from heterogeneous populations, with applications in reality. *J. Multivariate Anal.* **6**, 608–616. [*MR* **55**(1978)4511; *Zbl.* **346**(1977)60059]

Proschan, F., and J. Sethuraman (1977). Schur functions in statistics I: The preservation theorem. *Ann. Statist.* **5**, 256–262. [*MR* **56:1594**]

Proschan, F., and M. Shaked (1984). Random averaging of vector elements. *SIAM J. Appl. Math.* **44**, 587–590. [*MR* **85h:60103**]

Pukelsheim, F. (1977). On Hsu's model in regression analysis. *Math. Operationsforsch. Statist. Ser. Statist.* **8**, 323–331. [*MR* **58:18927**]

Pukelsheim, F. (1993). *Optimal Design of Experiments.* Wiley, New York. [*MR* **94k:62124**]

Rado, R. (1952). An inequality. *J. London Math. Soc.* **27**, 1–6. [*MR* **13**(1953)539; *Zbl.* **47**(1953)297]

Rajendra Prasad, V., K. P. K. Nair, and Y. P. Aneja. (1991). Optimal assignment of components to parallel-series and series-parallel systems. *Oper. Res.* **39**, 407–414. [*MR* **92b:90102**]

Ramos, H. M., J. Ollero, and M. A. Sordo. (2000). A sufficient condition for generalized Lorenz order. *J. Econ. Theory* **90**, 286–292. [*MR* **2001b:91037**]

Rao, C. R. (1984). Convexity properties of entropy functions and analysis of diversity. In *Inequalities in Statistics and Probability, IMS Lecture Notes Monogr. Ser.* **5**, 68–77. Inst. Math. Statist., Hayward, CA. [*MR* **86f:94021**]

Rasche, R. H., J. Gaffney, A. Koo, and N. Obst (1980). Functional forms for estimating the Lorenz curve. *Econometrica* **48**, 1061–1062.

Redheffer, R. M. (1964). Problem 5233. *Amer. Math. Monthly* **71**, 923; see also *Amer. Math. Monthly* **72**(1965)1031]

Rényi, A. (1961). On measures of entropy and information. *Proc. 4th Berkeley Sympos. Math. Statist. Prob., Vol. I*, pp. 547–561, University of California Press, Berkeley. [*MR* **24:A2410**]

Révész, P. (1962). A probabilistic solution of problem 111 of G. Birkhoff. *Acta Math. Acad. Sci. Hungar.* **13**, 197–198. [*MR* **25**(1963)3044; *Zbl.* **107**(1965)122]

Revyakov, M. (1993). Component allocation for a distributed system: Reliability maximization. *J. Appl. Probab.* **30**, 471–477. [*MR* **93m:90040**]

Richter, H. (1958). Zur Abschätzung von Matrizen norman. *Math. Nachr.* **18**, 178–187. [*MR* **22**(1961)2619]

Riley, J. D. (1955). Solving systems of linear equations with a positive definite, symmetric, but possibly ill-conditioned matrix. *Math. Tables Aids Comput.* **9**, 96–101. [*MR* **17**(1956)666; *Zbl.* **66**(1956)101]

Rinott, Y. (1973). Multivariate majorization and rearrangement inequalities with some applications to probability and statistics. *Israel J. Math.* **15**, 60–77. [*MR* **51**(1976)4549; *Zbl.* **262**(1974)26016]

Rinott, Y., and T. J. Santner. (1977). An inequality for multivariate normal probabilities with application to a design problem. *Ann. Statist.* **5**, 1228–1234. [*MR* **56:7014**]

Rivest, L.-P. (1986). Bartlett's, Cochran's, and Hartley's tests on variances are liberal when the underlying distribution is long-tailed. *J. Amer. Statist. Assoc.* **81**, 124–128. [*MR* **87d:62037**]

Rizvi, M. H., and R. Shorrock (1979). A note on matrix-convexity. *Canad. J. Statist.* **7**, 39–41.[*MR* **81b:15024**]

Roberts, A. W., and D. E. Varberg (1973). *Convex Functions*. Academic Press, New York. [*MR* **56:1201**; *Zbl.* **271**(1975)26009]

Rockafellar, R. T. (1970). *Convex Analysis*, Princeton Math. Ser., No. 28. Princeton University Press, Princeton, NJ. [*MR* **43**(1972)445; *Zbl.* **193**(1970)184]

Rolski, T. (1985). On non-convexity of some functions of probabilistic interest. *Bull. Polish Acad.* **33**, 441–445.

Romanovsky, V. (1931). Sur les zéros des matrices stocastiques. *C. R. Acad. Sci. Paris* **192**, 266–269. [*Zbl.* **1**(1932)055]

Romanovsky, V. (1935). Recherches sur les chaîes de Markoff. *Premier Mém., Acta Math.* **66**, 147–251. [*Zbl.* **14**(1936)028]

Rooin, J. (2008). An approach to Ky Fan type inequalities from binomial expansions. *Math. Inequal. Appl.* **11**, 679–688. [*MR* **2458161**]

Rosén, B. (1967). On an inequality of Hoeffding. *Ann. Math. Statist.* **38**, 382–392. [*MR* **34**(1967)8593; *Zbl.* **161**(1969)386]

Rosenbaum, R. A. (1950). Sub-additive functions. *Duke Math. J.* **17**, 227–247. [*MR* **12**(1951)164; *Zbl.* **38**(1951)66]

Ross, S. M. (1981). A random graph. *J. Appl. Probab.* **18**, 309–315. [*MR* **81m:05124**]

Ross, S. M. (1999). The mean waiting time for a pattern. *Probab. Engrg. Inform. Sci.* **13**, 1–9. [*MR* **200i:60097**]

Rotfel'd, S. Ju. (1967). Remarks on the singular values of a sum of completely continuous operators. *Funkcional. Anal. i Priložen* **1**, 95–96 (in Russian); *Functional Anal. Appl.* **1**, 252–253 (Engl. transl.).

Rotfel'd, S. Ju. (1969). The singular values of the sum of completely continuous operators. Problems of mathematical physics, No. 3: *Spectral Theory* (Russian), pp. 81–87. Izdat. Leningrad University, Leningrad, 1968. In *Spectral Theory* (M. S. Berman, ed.), Top. Math. Phys., Vol. 3, pp. 73–78 (Engl. version). Consultants Bureau, New York. [*MR* **50**(1975)5513]

Rothblum, U. G. (1989). Generalized scalings satisfying linear equations. *Linear Algebra Appl.* **114/115**, 765–783. [*MR* **90e:15043**]

Rousseau, R., and P. Van Hecke (1999). Measuring biodiversity. *Acta Biotheoretica* **47**, 1–5.

Ruch, E. (1975). The diagram lattice as structural principle. *Theoret. Chim. Acta (Berl.)* **38**, 167–183.

Ruch, E., and A. Mead (1976). The principle of increasing mixing character and some of its consequences. *Theoret. Chim. Acta* **41**, 95–117.

Ruch, E., R. Schranner, and T. H. Seligman (1978). The mixing distance. *J. Chem. Phys.* **69**, 386–392.

Ruch, E., R. Schranner, and T.H. Seligman (1980). Generalization of a theorem by Hardy, Littlewood and Pólya. *J. Math. Anal. Appl.* **76**, 222–229. [*MR* **81m:26015**]

Ruderman, H. D. (1952). Two new inequalities. *Amer. Math. Monthly* **59**, 29–32. [*MR* **13**(1952)539; *Zbl.* **46**(1953)51]

Ruhe, A. (1970). Perturbation bounds for means of eigenvalues and invariant subspaces. *Nordisk Tidskr. Informationsbehandling (BIT)* **10**, 343–354. [*MR* **42**(1971)8678]

Rüschendorf, L. (1981). Ordering of distributions and rearrangement of functions. *Ann. Probab.* **9**, 276–283. [*MR* **82e:60017**]

Rust, P. F. (1976). The effect of leap years and seasonal trends on the birthday problem. *Amer. Statist.* **30**, 197–198.

Ryff, J. V. (1963). On the representation of doubly stochastic operators. *Pacific J. Math.* **13**, 1379–1386. [*MR* **29**(1965)474; *Zbl.* **125**(1964)84]

Ryff, J. V. (1965). Orbits of L^1-functions under doubly stochastic transformations. *Trans. Amer. Math. Soc.* **117**, 92–100. [*MR* **35**(1968)762; *Zbl.* **135**(1967)188]

Ryff, J. V. (1967). On Muirhead's theorem. *Pacific J. Math.* **21**, 567–576. [*MR* **35**(1968)2023; *Zbl.* **163**(1969)57]

Ryser, H. J. (1957). Combinatorial properties of matrices of zeros and ones. *Canad. J. Math.* **9**, 371–377. [*MR* **19**(1958)379; *RZMat* (1958)1827; *Zbl.* **79**(1959)11]

Ryser, H. J. (1963). *Combinatorial Mathematics*, Carus Math. Monogr. No. 14. Math. Assoc. America; distributed by Wiley, New York. [*MR* **27**(1964)51; *Zbl.* **112**(1969)248]

Ryser, H. J. (1964). Matrices of zeros and ones in combinatorial mathematics. In *Recent Advances in Matrix Theory* (H. Schneider, ed.), pp. 103–124. University of Wisconsin Press, Madison. [*MR* **29**(1965)2196; *Zbl.* **129**(1967)8]

Saari, D. G. (1995). *Basic Geometry of Voting*. Springer-Verlag, Berlin. [*MR* **98d:90040**]

Salinelli, E., and C. Sgarra (2006). Correlation matrices of yields and total positivity. *Linear Algebra Appl.* **418**, 682–692. [*MR* **2007g:91072**]

Samuels, S. M. (1965). On the number of successes in independent trials. *Ann. Math. Statist.* **36**, 1272–1278. [*MR* **31**(1966)4066; *Zbl.* **156**(1969)405]

Sanderson, W. C. (1974). Does the theory of demand need the maximum principle? In *Nations and Households in Economic Growth, Essays in Honor of Moses Abramovitz* (P. David, ed.), pp. 173–221. Academic Press, New York.

Sarabia, J.-M. (1997). A hierarchy of Lorenz curves based on the generalized Tukey's lambda distribution. *Econometric Rev.* **16**, 305–320. [*MR* **98c:62203**]

Sarabia, J.-M., E. Castillo, and D. J. Slottje. (1999). An ordered family of Lorenz curves. *J. Econometrics* **91**, 43–60. [*MR* **2000h:62126**]

Satnoianu, R., and L. Zhou (2005) A majorization consequence: 11080. *Amer. Math. Monthly* **112**, 934–935.

Savage, I. R. (1957). Contributions to the theory of rank order statistics—The "trend" case. *Ann. Math. Statist.* **28**, 968–977. [*MR* **20**(1959)396; *Zbl.* **86**(1961)350]

Scarsini, M. (1990). An ordering of dependence. In *Topics in Statistical Dependence* (H. W. Block, A. R. Sampson, and T. H. Savits, eds.), *IMS Lecture Notes — Monograph Ser.* **16**, 403–414. [*MR* **93i:62053**]

Scarsini, M., and M. Shaked (1987). Ordering distributions by scaled order statistics. *Z. Oper. Res. Ser. A-B* **31**, A1–A13. [*MR* **89a:62039**]

Schatten, R. (1950). *A Theory of Cross-Spaces*. Ann. Math. Stud. No. 26. Princeton University Press, Princeton, NJ. [*MR* **12**(1951)186; *Zbl.* **41**(1952)435]

Schmidt, E. (1907). Zur Theorie der linearen und nichtlinearen Integralgleichungen, I. Teil. Entwicklung Willkürlicher Funktionen noch Systemen Vorgeschriebener. *Math. Ann.* **63**, 433–476.

Schneider, H. (1953). An inequality for latent roots applied to determinants with dominant principal diagonal. *J. London Math. Soc.* **28**, 8–20. [*MR* **14**(1953)1055; *Zbl.* **50**(1954)11]

Schoenberg, I. J. (1951). On Pólya frequency functions, I. The totally positive functions and their Laplace transforms. *J. Analyse Math.* **1**, 331–374. [*MR* **13**(1952)923; *Zbl.* **45**(1953)376]

Schoenberg, I. J. (1953). On smoothing operations and their generating functions. *Bull. Amer. Math. Soc.* **59**, 199–230. [*MR* **15**(1954)16; *Zbl.* **49**(1954/1959)361]

Schönemann, P. (1966). A generalized solution of the orthogonal procrustes problem. *Psychometrika* **31**, 1–10. [*MR* **35**(1968)6705; *Zbl.* **147**(1968)194]

Schreiber, S. (1958). On a result of S. Sherman concerning doubly stochastic matrices. *Proc. Amer. Math. Soc.* **9**, 350–353. [*MR* **20**(1959)1687; *Zbl.* **99**(1963)248]

Schur, I. (1909). Über die charakteristischen Wurzeln einer linearen Substitution mit einer Anwendung aug die Theorie der Integralgleichungen. *Math. Ann.* **66**, 488–510.

Schur, I. (1911). Bemerkungen zur Theorie der beschränken Bilinearformen mit unendlich vielen Veränderlichen. *J. Reine Angew. Math.* **140**, 1–28.

Schur, I. (1923). Über eine Klasse von Mittelbildungen mit Anwendungen die Determinanten-*Theorie Sitzungsber. Berlin. Math. Gesellschaft* **22**, 9–20 [*Issai Schur Collected Works* (A. Brauer and H. Rohrbach, eds.), Vol. II. pp. 416–427. Springer-Verlag, Berlin, 1973].

Schutz, R. R. (1951). On the measurement of income inequality. *Amer. Econ. Rev.* **41**, 107–122.

Schwarz, Š. (1967). A note on the structure of the semigroup of doubly-stochastic matrices. *Mat. Časopis Sloven. Akad. Vied.* **17**, 308–316. [*MR* **39**(1970)2791; *Zbl.* **157**(1969)49]

Schweitzer, O. (1914). An inequality concerning the arithmetic mean (in Hungarian). *Math.-Phys. Lapok* **23**, 257–261.

Sen, A. (1973). *On Economic Inequality.* Oxford University Press (Clarendon), London and New York.

Sen, P. K. (1970). A note on order statistics from heterogeneous distributions. *Ann. Math. Statist.* **41**, 2137–2139. [*MR* **42**(1971)2613; *Zbl.* **216**(1971)220]

Seneta, E. (2006). *Non-negative Matrices and Markov Chains.* Springer, New York. [*MR* **2209438**]

Seo, Y., and M. Tominaga (2008). A complement of the Ando–Hiai inequality. *Linear Algebra Appl.* **429**, 1546–1554. [*MR* **2444341**]

Serra-Capizzano, S., D. Bertaccini, and G. H. Golub (2005). How to deduce a proper eigenvalue cluster from a proper singular value cluster in the nonnormal case. *SIAM J. Matrix Anal. Appl.* **27**, 82–86. [*MR* **2006i:15032**]

Shaked, M. (1977). A concept of positive dependence for exchangeable random variables. *Ann. Math. Statist.* **5**, 505–515. [*MR* **55**(1978)9361]

Shaked, M. (1978a). A Property of Positively Dependent Exchangeable Random Variables with an Application. Tech. Rep. No. 348. Department of Mathematics and Statistics, University of New Mexico, Albuquerque.

Shaked, M. (1978b). On Mixtures of Two-Parameters-Exponential Families with Applications. Tech. Rep. No. 355. Department of Mathematics and Statistics, University of New Mexico, Albuquerque.

Shaked, M., and J. G. Shanthikumar (1998). Two variability orders. *Probab. Engrg. Inform. Sci.* **12**, 1–23. [*MR* **98j:60028**]

Shaked, M., and J. G. Shanthikumar (2007). *Stochastic Orders.* Springer, New York. [*MR* **2008g:60005**]

Shaked, M., J. G. Shanthikumar, and Y. L. Tong (1995). Parametric Schur convexity and arrangement monotonicity properties of partial sums. *J. Multivariate Anal.* **53**, 293–310. [*MR* **96e:60032**]

Shaked, M., and Y. L. Tong (1985). Some partial orderings of exchangeable random variables by positive dependence. *J. Multivariate Anal.* **17**, 333–349. [*MR* **87c:60018**]

Shaked, M., and Y. L. Tong (1988). Inequalities for probability contents of convex sets via geometric average. *J. Multivariate Anal.* **24**, 330–340. [*MR* **89h:60033**]

Shaked, M., and Y. L. Tong (1990). Positive dependence of random variables with a common marginal distribution. *Comm. Statist. Theory Methods* **19**, 4299–4313. [*MR* **92f:62067**]

Shaked, M., and Y. L. Tong (1992a). Comparison of experiments via dependence of normal variables with a common marginal distribution. *Ann. Statist.* **20**, 614–618. [*MR* **93e:62021**]

Shaked, M., and Y. L. Tong (1992b). Comparison of experiments of some multivariate distributions with a common marginal. In *Stochastic Inequalities* (M. Shaked and Y. L. Tong, eds), *IMS Lecture Notes — Monograph Ser.* **22**, 388–398. [*MR* **94h:62009**]

Shanthikumar, J. G. (1987). Stochastic majorization of random variables with proportional equilibrium rates. *Adv. Appl. Probab.* **19**, 854–872. [*MR* **89b:60040**]

Shepp, L. A., and I. Olkin (1978). Entropy of the sum of independent Bernoulli random variables and of the multinomial distribution. Tech. Rep. No. 131, Department of Statistics, Stanford University, Stanford, CA.

Shepp, L. A., and I. Olkin (1981). Entropy of the sum of independent Bernoulli random variables and of the multinomial distribution. In *Contributions to Probability* (J. Gani and V. K. Rohatgi, eds.), pp. 201–206. Academic Press, New York. [*MR* **82g:60031**]

Sherman, S. (1951). On a theorem of Hardy, Littlewood, Pólya and Blackwell. *Proc. Nat. Acad. Sci. U.S.A.* **37**, 826–831. [*MR* **0045787**]

Sherman, S. (1952). On a conjecture concerning doubly stochastic matrices. *Proc. Amer. Math. Soc.* **3**, 511–513. [*MR* **14**(1953)346; *Zbl.* **48**(1953)250]

Sherman, S. (1954). A correction to "On a conjecture concerning doubly stochastic matrices." *Proc. Amer. Math. Soc.* **5**, 998–999. [*MR* **16**(1955)326; *Zbl.* **58**(1957/1958)11]

Sherman, S. (1955). A theorem on convex sets with applications. *Ann. Math. Statist.* **26**, 763–767. [*MR* **17**(1965)655; *Zbl.* **66**(1956)374–375]

Sherman, S., and C. J. Thompson (1972). Equivalences on eigenvalues. *Indiana Univ. Math. J.* **21**, 807–814. [*MR* **45**(1978)5146]

Shi, H.-N. (2006). Refinements of an inequality for the rational fraction. *Pure Appl. Math. (Xi'an)* **22**, 256–262. [*MR* **2268686**]

Shi, H.-N. (2007). Schur-convex functions related to Hadamard-type inequalities. *J. Math. Inequal.* **1**, 127–136. [*MR* **2347711**]

Shi, H.-N., Y.-M. Jiang, and W.-D. Jiang (2009). Schur-convexity and Schur-geometrically concavity of Gini means. *Comput. Math. Appl.* **57**, 266–274. [*MR* **2488381**]

Shi, H.-N., and S.-H. Wu (2007). Majorized proof and improvement of the discrete Steffensen's inequality. *Taiwanese J. Math.* **11**, 1203–1208. [*MR* **2348562**]

Shi, H.-N., S.-H. Wu, and F. Qi (2006). An alternative note on the Schur-convexity of the extended mean values. *Math. Inequal. Appl.* **9**, 219–224. [*MR* **2225008**]

Shi, Z.-C. (Shih, C.-T.), and Wang, B.-Y. (Wang, P.-Y.) (1965). Bounds for the determinant, characteristic roots and condition number of certain types of matrices. *Acta Math. Sinica* **15**(3), 326–341, translated in *Chinese Mathematics* **7**, 21–40 (1965). [*MR* **32**(1960)4137; *Zbl.* **166**(1969)33]

Shorrocks, A. F. (1983). Ranking income distributions. *Economica* **50**, 3–17.

Simić, S. (2007). On logarithmic convexity for differences of power means. *J. Inequal. Appl.* Art. ID 37359 [*MR* **2008i:26011**]

Simpson, E. H. (1949). Measurement of diversity. *Nature* **163**, 688.

Sinkhorn, R. (1964). A relationship between arbitrary positive matrices and doubly stochastic matrices. *Ann. Math. Statist.* **35**, 876–879. [*MR* **28**(1964)5072; *Zbl.* **134**(1967)253]

Sinkhorn, R. (1967). Diagonal equivalence to matrices with prescribed row and column sums. *Amer. Math. Monthly* **74**, 402–405. [*MR* **35**(1968)1616; *Zbl.* **166**(1969)37]

Sinkhorn, R., and P. Knopp (1967). Concerning nonnegative matrices and doubly stochastic matrices. *Pacific J. Math.* **21**, 343–348. [*MR* **35**(1968)1617; *Zbl.* **152**(1968)14]

Smiley, M. F. (1966). An algorithmic proof of Muirhead's theorem. *J. Math. Sci.* **1**, 85–86. [*MR* **34**(1967)5163; *Zbl.* **156**(1969)34]

Snijders, T. (1976). *An Ordering of Probability Distributions on a Partially Ordered Outcome Space.* Report No. TW-171, Department of Mathematics, University of Groningen, the Netherlands.

Sobel, M. (1954). On a generalization of an inequality of Hardy, Littlewood and Pólya. *Proc. Amer. Math. Soc.* **5**, 596–602. [*MR* **16**(1955)118; *Zbl.* **57**(1956)9–10]

Solomon, D. L. (1978). *A Mathematical Foundation for Species Diversity.* Paper No. BU-573-M, Department of Plant Breeding and Biometry, Cornell University, Ithaca, NY.

Soms, A. P. (1989). Applications of Schur theory to reliability inference for k of n systems. *Comm. Statist. Theory Methods* **18**, 4459–4469. [*MR* **91b:62210**]

Spizzichino, F. (2001). *Subjective Probability Models for Lifetimes.* Monographs on Statistics and Applied Probability, **91**. Chapman and Hall/CRC, Boca Raton, FL. [*MR* **2004c:62003**]

Srinivasan, G.K. (2007). The gamma function: An eclectic tour. *Amer. Math. Monthly* **114**, 297–315. [*MR* **2008d:33001**]

Steele, J. M. (2004). *The Cauchy–Schwarz Master Class. An Introduction to the Art of Inequalities.* Cambridge University Press, Cambridge. [*MR* **2005a:26035**]

Steerneman, A. G. M. (1990). G-majorization, group-induced cone orderings, and reflection groups. *Linear Algebra Appl.* **127**, 107–119. [*MR* **91d:20057**]

Steffensen, J. F. (1925). On a generalization of certain inequalities by Tchebycheff and Jensen. *Skand. Aktuarietidskr.* pp. 137–147.

Stein, C. (1956). The admissibility of Hotelling's T^2 test. *Ann. Math. Statist.* **27**, 616–623. [*MR* **18:243c**]

Steinig, J. (1965). Sur quelques applications géométriques d'une inégalité relative aux fonctions convexes. *Enseignement Math.* [2] **11**, 281–285. [*MR* **33**(1967)4788; *Zbl.* **142**(1968)23]

Stephen, T. (2007). A majorization bound for the eigenvalues of some graph Laplacians. *SIAM J. Discrete Math.* **21**, 303–312. [*MR* **2008c:05117**]

Stepniak, C. (1989). Stochastic ordering and Schur-convex functions in comparison of linear experiments. *Metrika* **36**, 291–298. [*MR* **91e:62013**]

Stevens, W. L. (1939). Solution to a geometrical problem in probability. *Ann. Eugenics* **9**, 315–320. [*MR* **1:245f**]

Stewart, G. W. and Sun, J. (1990). *Matrix Perturbation Theory.* Academic Press, Boston. [*MR* **92a:65017**]

Stoer, J., and C. Witzgall (1970). *Convexity and Optimization in Finite Dimensions,* Vol. I. Springer-Verlag, Berlin and New York. [*MR* **44**(1972)683; *Zbl.* **203**(1971)522]

Stolarsky, K. B. (1975). Generalizations of the logarithmic mean. *Math. Mag.* **48**, 87–92. [*MR* **50:10186**]

Stolarsky, K. B. (1980). A stronger logarithmic inequality suggested by the entropy inequality. *SIAM J. Math. Anal.* **11**, 242–247. [*MR* **81c:94014**]

Stoyan, D. (1977). *Qualitative Eigenschaften und Abschätzungen stochastischer Modelle.* Akademie-Verlag, Berlin.

Stoyan, D. (1983). *Comparison Methods for Queues and Other Stochastic Models.* John Wiley and Sons, Chicester. [*MR* **85f:60147**]

Strassen, V. (1965). The existence of probability measures with given marginals. *Ann. Math. Statist.* **36**, 423–439. [*MR* **31**(1966)1693; *Zbl.* **135**(1967)187]

Styan, G. P. H. (1973). Hadamard products and multivariate statistical analysis. *Linear Algebra Appl.* **6**, 217–240. [*MR* **47:6724**]

Sylvester, J. J. (1889). Sur la réduction biorthogonale d'une forme linéolinéaire à sa forme canonique. *C. R. Acad. Sci. Paris* **108**, 651–653. (*The Collected Mathematical Papers of James Joseph Sylvester, 1882–1897*, Vol. IV, pp. 638–640. Cambridge University Press, Cambridge.)

Szal, R., and S. Robinson (1977). Measuring income inequality. In *Income Distribution and Growth in the Less-Developed Countries* (C. R. Frank, Jr., and R. C. Webb, eds.), pp. 491–533. Brookings Institute, Washington, DC.

Szegö, G. (1950). Über eine Verallgemeinerung des Dirichlestschen Integrals. *Math. Z.* **52**, 676–685. [*MR* **12**(1951)703; *Zbl.* **36**(1951)200]

Székely, G., and N. K. Bakirov (2003). Extremal probabilities for Gaussian quadratic forms. *Probab. Theory Related Fields* **126**, 184–202. [*MR* **2004c:60051**]

Szekli, R. (1995). *Stochastic Ordering and Dependence in Applied Probability*. Lecture Notes in Statistics, **97**. Springer-Verlag, New York. [*MR* **96f:60030**]

Taguchi, T. (1972). On the two-dimensional concentration surface and extensions of concentration coefficient and Pareto distribution to the two dimensional case (on an application of differential geometric methods to statistical analysis). I. *Ann. Inst. Statist. Math.* **24**, 355–381. [*MR* **49:10116**]

Taillie, C. (1981). Lorenz ordering within the generalized gamma family of income distributions. *Statistical Distributions in Scientific Work, Vol. 6* (C.Taillie, G. P. Patil and B. A. Baldessari, eds.), *NATO Adv. Study Inst. Ser. C: Math. Phys. Sci.* **79**, 181–192. [*MR* **83i:62175**]

Tam, T.-Y. (2000). Group majorization, Eaton triples and numerical range. *Linear Multilinear Algebra* **47**, 11–28. [*MR* **2001a:15031**]

Taussky-Todd, O. (1950). Notes on numerical analysis. II. Note on the condition of matrices. *Math. Tables Aids Comput.* **4**, 111–112. [*MR* **12**(1951)36]

Tchakaloff, L. (Čakalov, Ljubomir) (1963). Sur quelques inégalités entre la moyenne arithmétique et la moyenne géométrique. *Publ. Inst. Math. (Beograd)* [N.S.] **3**(17), 43–46. [*MR* **30**(1965)4878; *Zbl.* **132**(1967)286]

Tchen, A. H.-T. (1975). Exact inequalities for $\int \phi(x,y)dH(x,y)$ when H has given marginals. Unpublished manuscript.

Tchen, A. H. (1980). Inequalities for distributions with given marginals. *Ann. Probab.* **8**, 814–827. [*MR* **82f:60052**]

Tewarson, R. P., and B. Ramnath (1969). Some comments on the solution of linear equations. *Nordisk Tidskr. Informationsbehandling (BIT)* **9**, 167–173. [*MR* **40**(1970)189; *Zbl.* **184**(1970)196]

Theobald, C. M. (1975). An inequality for the trace of the product of two symmetric matrices. *Proc. Cambridge Philos. Soc.* **77**, 265–267. [*MR* **54**(1977)2694]

Thompson, C. J. (1965). Inequality with applications in statistical mechanics. *J. Math. Phys.* **6**, 1812–1813. [*MR* **32**(1966)7110]

Thompson, C. J. (1971). Inequalities and partial orders on matrix spaces. *Indiana Univ. Math. J.* **21**, 469–480. [*MR* **45**(1973)3442]

Thompson, R. C. (1971). On the real and absolute singular values of a matrix product. *Linear Algebra Appl.* **4**, 243–254. [*MR* **43**(1972)7444; *Zbl.* **218**(1972)110]

Thompson, R. C. (1974). Eigenvalues of matrix sums, products, minors. Paper delivered at Matrix Theory Conference, Santa Barbara, CA, 1973.

Thompson, R. C. (1975). Dissipative matrices and related results. *Linear Algebra Appl.* **11**, 155–169. [*MR* **52**(1976)444]

Thompson, R. C. (1976). Convex and concave functions of singular values of matrix sums. *Pacific J. Math.* **62**, 285–290. [*MR* **55**(1979)8066]

Thompson, R. C. (1977). Singular values, diagonal elements, and convexity. *SIAM J. Appl. Math.* **32**, 39–63. [*MR* **54**(1977)12805]

Thompson, R. C. (1978). Singular values and diagonal elements of complex symmetric matrices. Unpublished manuscript.

Thompson, R. C., and L. J. Freede (1970) On the eigenvalues of sums of Hermitian matrices, II. *Aequationes Math.* **5**, 103–115. [*MR* **45:1948**]

Thompson, R. C., and M. Ishaq (1977/1978). The convex hull of signed rearrangements with prescribed sign parity. *Linear Multilinear Algebra* **5**, 235–241. [*MR* **57:4004**]

Thompson, R. C., and S. Therianos (1972). Inequalities connecting the eigenvalues of a Hermitian matrix with the eigenvalues of complementary principal submatrices. *Bull. Austral. Math.* **6**, 117–132. [*MR* **48**(1974)6137]

Thon, D., and S. W. Wallace (2004). Dalton transfers, inequality and altrusim. *Soc. Choice Welf.* **22**, 447–465. [*MR* **2004m:91078**]

Todd, J. (1968). On condition numbers. *Programation en mathématiques numériques*. Actes Colloq. Int. C.N.R.S. No. 165. C.N.R.S., Paris. [*MR* **37**(1969)6024; *Zbl.* **207**(1971)155]

Toeplitz, O. (1907). Die Jacobische Transformation der quadratischen Formen von unendlich vielen Veränderlichen. *Nach. Kgl. Gesellschaft* Wiss. Göttingen Math.-Phys. Kl., pp. 101–109.

Tomić, M. (1949). Théorème de Gauss relatif au centre de gravité et son application (Serbian, Russian and French summaries). *Bull. Soc. Math. Phys. Serbie* **1**, 31–40. [*MR* **11**(1950)86; *Zbl.* **41**(1952)473]

Tong, Y. L. (1977). An ordering theorem for conditionally independent and identically distributed random variables. *Ann. Statist.* **5**, 274–277. [*MR* **55**(1978)6636]

Tong, Y. L. (1982). Rectangular and elliptical probability inequalities for Schur-concave random variables. *Ann. Statist.* **10**, 637–642. [*MR* **83f:60035**]

Tong, Y. L. (1988). Some majorization inequalities in multivariate statistical analysis. *SIAM Rev.* **30**, 602–622. [*MR* **89m:62050**]

Tong, Y. L. (1989). Probability inequalities for n-dimensional rectangles via multivariate majorization. In *Contributions to Probability and Statistics. Essays in Honor of Ingram Olkin* (L. J. Gleser, M. D. Perlman, S. J. Press, and A. R. Sampson, eds.), pp. 146–159. Springer-Verlag, New York. [*MR* **91c:60022**]

Tong, Y. L. (1997). Some majorization orderings of heterogeneity in a class of epidemics. *J. Appl. Probab.* **34**, 84–93. [*MR* **98d:60040**]

Topkis, D. M. (1968). Ordered optimal solutions. Doctoral dissertation. Stanford University, Stanford, CA.

Torgersen, E. (1984). Orderings of linear models. *J. Statist. Plann. Infer.* **9**, 1–17. [*MR* **85f:62009**]

Tsui, K.-Y. (1999). Multidimensional inequality and multidimensional generalized entropy measures: An axiomatic derivation. *Soc. Choice Welf.* **16**, 145–157. [*MR* **99i:90008**]

Tung, S.-H. (1964). Harnack's inequality and theorems on matrix spaces. *Proc. Amer. Math. Soc.* **15**, 375–381. [*MR* **28**(1964)4135; *Zbl.* **124**(1966)54]

Turing, A. M. (1948). Rounding-off errors in matrix processes. *Quart. J. Mech. Appl. Math.* **1**, 287–308. [*MR* **10**(1949)405]

Uspensky, J. V. (1927) A curious case of the use of mathematical induction in geometry. *Amer. Math. Monthly* **34**, 247–250. [*MR* **1521170**]

van der Vaart, R. H. (1961). On certain characteristics of the distribution of the latent roots of a symmetric random matrix under general conditions. *Ann. Math. Statist.* **32**, 864–873. [*MR* **24**(1962)A608; *Zbl.* **121**(1966)141] van der Waerden, B. L. (1926). Aufgube 45, *Jahresber. Deutsch. Math.-Verein.* **35**, 117.

van Tiel, J. (1984). *Convex Analysis. An Introductory Text.* John Wiley and Sons, New York. [MR **85m:49001**]

Veinott, A. F., Jr. (1965). Optimal policy in a dynamic, single product, non-stationary inventory model with several demand classes. *Oper. Res.* **13**, 761–778. [MR **32**(1966)3874; Zbl. **143**(1968)217]

Veinott, A. F., Jr. (1971). Least d-majorized network flows with inventory and statistical applications. *Management Sci.* **17**, 547–567. [MR **45**(1973)6405; Zbl. **239**(1973)90014]

Villaseñor, J. A., and B. C. Arnold (1989). Elliptical Lorenz curves. *J. Econometrics* **40**, 327–338. [MR **90g:62261**]

Vinograde, B. (1950). Canonical positive definite matrices under internal linear transformations. *Proc. Amer. Math. Soc.* **1**, 159–161. [MR **11**(1950)637; Zbl. **37**(1951)300]

Visick, G. (1995). A weak majorization involving the matrices $A \circ B$ and AB. *Linear Algebra Appl.* **223/224**, 731–744. [MR **97c:15031**]

Visick, G. (1998). Majorizations of Hadamard products of matrix powers. *Linear Algebra Appl.* **269**, 233–240. [MR **98m:15033**]

Visick, G. (2000). A quantitative version of the observation that the Hadamard product is a principal submatrix of the Kronecker product. *Linear Algebra Appl.* **304**, 45–68. [MR **2000m:15028**]

Visser, C., and A. C. Zaanen (1952). On the eigenvalues of compact linear transformations. *Nederl. Akad. Wetensch. Proc. Ser. A* **55** (=*Indag. Math.* **14**), 71–78. [MR **13**(1952)755; Zbl. **46**(1953)123]

Vitale, R. A. (1999). Majorization and Gaussian correlation. *Statist. Probab. Lett.* **45**, 247–251. [MR **2000k:60029**]

Vogel, W. (1963). Bemerkungen zur Theorie der Matrizen aus Nullen und Eisen. *Arch. Math.* **14**, 139–144. [MR **30**(1965)4693; Zbl. **114**(1965)362]

Walker, A. W. (1971). Problem E2284. *Amer. Math. Monthly* **78**, 297; see also *Amer. Math. Monthly* **79**(1972), 183.

Wan, H. (1984). Structure and cardinality of the class $A(R, S)$ of $(0, 1)$-matrices. *J. Math. Res. Exposition* **4**, 87–93. [MR **86h:05033**]

Wan, H. (1986). *Combinatorial and Computing Theory of Nonnegative Integral Matrices.* Dalian University Press, Dalian, China.

Wan, H., and J. Wootton (2000). A global compositional complexity measure for biological sequences: AT-rich and GC-rich genomes encode less complex proteins. *Computers and Chemistry* **24**, 71–94.

Wang, B.-Y., B.-Y. Xi, and F. Zhang. (1999). Some inequalities for sum and product of positive semidefinite matrices. *Linear Algebra Appl.* **293**, 39–49. [MR **2000d:15017**]

Wang, B.-Y., and F.-Z. Zhang. (1995). Trace and eigenvalue inequalities for ordinary and Hadamard products of positive semidefinite Hermitian matrices. *SIAM J. Matrix Anal. Appl.* **16**, 1173–1183. [*MR* **96j:15014**]

Watkins, W. (1974). Convex matrix functions. *Proc. Amer. Math. Soc.* **44**, 31–34. [*MR* **49**(1975)5046; *Zbl.* **257**(1973)15004]

Watson, G. S. (1955). Serial correlation in regression analysis I. *Biometrika* **42**, 327–341. [*MR* **17**(1956)382; *Zbl.* **68**(1961)332]

Weaver, W. (1948). Probability, rarity, interest, and surprise. *Sci. Monthly* **67**, 390–392.

Webster, R. (1994). *Convexity*. Oxford Science Publications, Oxford University Press, New York. [*MR* **98h:52001**]

Wedderburn, J. H. M. (1934). *Lectures on Matrices*, Amer. Math. Soc. Colloq. Publ., Vol. XVII. American Mathematical Society, Providence, RI.

Wehrl, A. (1973) Convex and concave traces. *Acta Phys Austriaca* **37**, 361–380.

Weinberger, H. F. (1958). Remarks on the preceding paper of Lax. *Comm. Pure Appl. Math.* **11**, 195–196. [*MR* **20**(1959)4573; *Zbl.* **86**(1961)16]

Weyl, H. (1949). Inequalities between two kinds of eigenvalues of a linear transformation. *Proc. Nat. Acad. Sci. U.S.A.* **35**, 408–411. [*MR* **11**(1950)37; *Zbl.* **32**(1949)387]

Whiteley, J. N. (1958). Some inequalities concerning symmetric forms. *Mathematika* **5**, 49–57. [*MR* **20**(1959)1739; *Zbl.* **85**(1961)11]

Whitt, W. (1976). Bivariate distributions with given marginals. *Ann. Statist.* **4**, 1280–1289. [*MR* **54**(1977)4045; *Zbl.* **367**(1978)62022]

Whittle, P. (1958). A multivariate generalization of Tchebychev's inequality. *Quart. J. Math. Oxford Ser.* [2] **9**, 232–240. [*MR* **20**(1959)6754; *Zbl.* **85**(1961)352]

Wielandt, H. (1955). An extremum property of sums of eigenvalues. *Proc. Amer. Math. Soc.* **6**, 106–110. [*MR* **16**(1955)785; *Zbl.* **64**(1956)247]

Wielandt, H. (1967). *Topics in the Analytic Theory of Matrices*. Lecture notes prepared by R. R. Meyer, Department of Mathematics, University of Wisconsin, Madison.

Wilfling, B. (1996a). Lorenz ordering of generalized beta-II income distributions. *J. Econometrics* **71**, 381–388. [*MR* **1381088**]

Wilfling, B. (1996b). A sufficient condition for Lorenz ordering. *Sankhyā Ser. B* **58**, 62–69. [*MR* **1732922**]

Wilfling, B. (1996c). Lorenz ordering of power-function order statistics. *Statist. Probab. Lett.* **30**, 313–319. [*MR* **97k:62124**]

Wintner, A., and F. D. Murnaghan (1931). On a polar representation of nonsingular square matrices. *Proc. Nat. Acad. Sci. U.S.A.* **17**, 676–678. [*Zbl.* **3**(1932)193]

Wittmeyer, H. (1936). Einfluss der Änderung einer Matrix auf die Lösung des zugehörigen Gleichungssystemes, sowie auf die charakteristischen Zahlen und die Eigenvektoren. *Z. Angew Math. Mech.* **16**, 287–300. [*Zbl.* **15**(1937)74; *Zbl.* **12**(1936)389]

Wong, C. K., and P. C. Yue (1973). A majorization theorem for the number of distinct outcomes in N independent trials. *Discrete Math.* **6**, 391–398. [*MR* **49**(1975)6303; *Zbl.* **269**(1974)60006]

Wright, E. M. (1954). An inequality for convex functions. *Amer. Math. Monthly* **61**, 620–622. [*MR* **16**(1955)341]

Wynn, H. (1977). An inequality for certain bivariate probability integrals. *Biometrika* **64**, 411–414.

Xu, C., Z. Xu, and F. Zhang (2009). Revisiting Hua–Marcus–Bellman–Ando inequalities on contractive matrices. *Linear Algebra Appl.* **430**, 1499–1508. [*MR* **2490692**]

Yamazaki, T. (2000). An extension of Specht's theorem via Kantorovich inequality and related results. *Math. Inequal. Appl.* **3**, 89–96. [*MR* **2000i:47038**]

Yanagimoto, T., and M. Okamoto (1969). Partial orderings of permutations and monotonicity of a rank correlation statistic. *Ann. Inst. Statist. Math.* **21**, 489–506. [*MR* **41**(1971)2856; *Zbl.* **208**(1971)447]

Yao, D. D. (1987). Majorization and arrangement orderings in open queueing networks. *Ann. Oper. Res.* **9**, 531–543.

Yitzhaki, S. (2003). Gini's mean difference: A superior measure of variability for non-normal distributions. *Metron* **61**, 285–316. [*MR* **2004j:60036**]

Ylvisaker, N. D. (1964). Lower bounds for minimum covariance matrices in time series regression problems. *Ann. Math. Statist.* **35**, 362–368. [*MR* **28**(1964)4636; *Zbl.* **126**(1966/1976)351]

Young, A. (1901). On quantitative substitutional analysis I. *Proc. London Math. Soc.* **33**, 97-146.

Zaballa, I. (1987). Matrices with prescribed rows and invariant factors. *Linear Algebra Appl.* **87**, 113–146. [*MR* **88d:15015**]

Zaballa, I. (1991). Pole assignment and additive perturbations of fixed rank. *SIAM J. Matrix Anal. Appl.* **12**, 16–23. [*MR* **92d:93068**]

Zhan, X. (2000). Singular values of differences of positive semidefinite matrices. *SIAM J. Matrix Anal. Appl.* **22**, 819–823. [*MR* **2001m:15028**]

Zhan, X. (2002). *Matrix Inequalities.* Springer-Verlag, Berlin. [*MR* **2003h:15030**]

Zhan, X. (2003). The sharp Rado theorem for majorizations. *Amer. Math. Monthly* **110**, 152–153. [*MR* **2003k:26029**]

Zhang, A., K.-T. Fang, R. Li, and A. Sudjianto (2005). Majorization framework for balanced lattice designs. *Ann. Statist.* **33**, 2837–2853. [*MR* **2007i:62099**]

Zhang, F. (1999). *Matrix Theory. Basic Results and Techniques.* Springer-Verlag, New York. [*MR* **1691203**]

Zhang, F. (2000). Schur complements and matrix inequalities in the Loewner ordering. *Linear Algebra Appl.* **321**, 399–410. [*MR* **2001k:15028**]

Zhang, X.-M. (1998). Schur-convex functions and isoperimetric inequalities. *Proc. Amer. Math. Soc.* **126**, 461–470. [*MR* **98d:26005**]

Zheng, B. (2007). Utility-gap dominances and inequality orderings. *Soc. Choice Welf.* **28**, 255–280. [*MR* **2008c:91102**]

Zheng, N.-G., Z.-H. Zhang, and X.-M. Zhang (2007). Schur-convexity of two types of one-parameter mean values in n variables. *J. Inequal. Appl.* Art. ID 78175 [*MR* **2008k:26020**]

Zhu, Q. J. (2004). A variational proof of Birkhoff's theorem on doubly stochastic matrices. *Math. Inequal. Appl.* **7**, 309–313. [*MR* **2005k:15048**]

Zylka, C. (1985). A note on the attainability of states by equalizing processes. *Theoret. Chim. Acta* **68**, 363–377.

Zylka, C. (1990). *Beitrage zur Thermodynamik und Statistik mittels Majorisierungs - und Wignertechniken.* Habilitation thesis, Leipzig.

Zylka, C. (2004). Majorization and irreversible processes. Unpublished manuscript.

Zylka, C., and T. Tok (1992). An application of majorization in thermodynamics: An analogue to the adiabatic demagnetization. *Physica A.* **188**, 687–691.

Zylka, C., and G. Vojta (1991). Thermodynamic proofs of algebraic inequalities. *Phys. Lett. A* **152**, 163–164. [*MR* **91k:26022**]

Author Index

Abramovich, S., 191, 581, *809*, *856*
Abramowitz, M., 512, *809*
Achilles, E., 69, *809*
Aczél, J., 166, *809*
Aitken, A. C., 775, *809*
Akdeniz, F., 673, *850*
Alam, K., 415, 542, 545–547, 604, *809*, *810*
Alberti, P. M., 188, 522, 626, *810*
Aldous, D., 743, *810*
Alker, H. R., 559, 564, *810*
Alpargu, G., 103, *810*
Alzer, H., 190, *810*
Amato, V., 563, 722, *810*
Amemiya, T., *840*
Amir-Moéz, A. R., 325, 326, 336, *810*, *811*
Amparan, A., 363, *811*
An, M. Y., 663, *811*
Anderson, T. W., 147, 470, 510, 517, 593, *810*

Andersson, S., 333, *811*
Ando, T., 3, 16, 29, 30, 44, 45, 48, 50, 159, 184, 312, 317, 331, 332, 347, 354, 356, 368, 369, 677, 683, 757, *811*, *812*
Andréief, C., 758, *812*
Aneja, Y. P., 553, *859*
Anwar, M., 666, 667, *812*
Araki, H., 346, *812*
Arikati, S. R., 265, 364, *812*
Arjas, E., 696, *812*
Arnold, B. C., 7, 609, 717, 718, 727, 728, 735, 736, 738–740, *812*, *813*, *871*
Artin, E., 108, 649, *813*
Asunción Beitia, M., 365, *814*
Atkinson, A. B., 566, 714, *813*
Audenaert, K. M. R., 342, *813*
Ault, J. C., 342, *813*
Autonne, L., 771, *813*
Azizoğlu, M. C., 526, *813*

Bacharach, M., 77, *813*
Bagdasar, O., 105, *814*
Bagnoli, M., 663, *814*
Bakirov, N. K., 502, *868*
Balakrishnan, N., *813*
Baldessari, B. A., *868*
Balinski, M. L., 514, *814*
Bapat, R. B., 19, 30, 77, 353, 354, *814*
Baragaña, I., 364, 365, *814*
Barić, J., 191, *809*
Barlow, R. E., 140, 181, 465, 478, 503, 742, 757, 766, *814*, *815*, *840*, *859*
Barnett, N. S., *821*
Bartholomew, D. J., 181, *814*
Baston, V. J., 119, *815*
Basu, D., 453, *815*
Bauer, F. L., 383, *815*
Beasley, L. B., 623, *815*
Bebiano, N., 364, *815*
Bechhofer, R. E., 542, 547, 549, *815*
Beckenbach, E. F., 30, 116, 117, 137, 140, 687, 787, *815*
Beineke, L. W., 61, *815*
Bellman, R., 30, 116, 117, 137, 140, 687, 769, 784, 787, *815*
Beltrami, E., 771, *816*
Bendat, J., 670, 674, 676, *816*
Bendixson, I., 325, *816*
Benster, C. D., *845*
Berenbrink, P., 521, *816*
Berg, C., 613, *816*
Berge, C., 30, 47, 49, 50, 67, 88, 97, 245, 260, 642, *816*
Berger, E., 745, 746, *816*
Berger, J. O., *855*
Bergmann, R., 711, *816*
Bergström, H., 664, *816*
Bergstrom, T., 649, 688, *814*
Berman, M. S., *861*

Bernado, J. M., *825*
Bernstein, D. S., 297, 355, 360, 367, 368, 760, 769, 781, *817*
Bertaccini, D., 363, *864*
Bhagwat, K. V., *817*
Bhandari, S. K., 44, 545, 617, *817*, *824*
Bhatia, R., 29, 138, 297, 301, 328, 336, 365, 367, 369, 377, 671, 676, 690, 775, 777, *817*
Billingsley, P., 425, 506, *817*
Binet, J. P. M., 776, *817*
Birkhoff, G., 10, 30, 49, *817*
Birnbaum, Z. W., 442, 490, 711, *817*
Blackorby, C., 559, *818*
Blackwell, D., 571, 578, 579, 614, 704, *818*
Block, H., *818*, *862*
Bloom, D. M., 264, *818*
Bogoljubov, N. N., 523, *818*
Bohnenblust, H. F., 116
Boland, P. J., 484, 550, 556, 566, 620, *818*
Bon, J.-L., 726, *818*
Bondar, J. V., 131, 354, 362, 570, *818*
Borell, C., 222, 226, *819*
Borobia, A., 47, 614, *819*
Bose, A., 545, *813*
Bose, R. C., *831*
Bottema, O., 269, 271, *817*
Brascamp, H. J., 653, *819*
Brauer, A., 261, 348, *819*, *863*
Bremner, J. M., 181, *814*
Brillouin, L., 563, *819*
Brockett, P. L., 718, *812*
Bromwich, J. T. I'A., 326, *819*
Brown, M., 510, 608, *819*
Browne, E. T., 301, 317, 325, 339, 773, *819*

Brualdi, R. A., 49, 50, 59–61, 76, 77, 243, 245, 249, 253, 254, 260, *819*
de Bruijn, N. G., 338, 339, 769, 793, *820*
Bruckner, A. M., 651, *820*
Brunk, H. D., 181, 645, *820*
Buehler, R. J., 550, *820*
Bullen, P. S., 117, 140, 141, 581, 655, *820*
Burkill, H., 22, *820*

Cacoullos, T., 470, *820*
Cambanis, S., 218, 506, 712, *821*
Campo, R., 742, *814*
Cantó, R., 77, *819*
Carlson, B. C., 141, *821*
Caron, R. M., 52, *821*
Castillo, E., 166, 736, *821*, *862*
Cauchy, A. L., 301, 776, *821*
Causey, R. L., 370, *821*
Cerone, P., 564, *821*
Chan, W., 23, 491, 525, 607, *821*
Chandra, M., 741, *821*
Chang, C.-S., 420, *821*
Chao, K.-M., 61, *822*
Charvát, F., 562, *835*
Chen, C.-P., 113, *822*
Chen, R. W., 545, *822*
Chen, W.-K., 260, *822*
Cheng, K. W., 151, 402, 432–434, 580–583, *822*
Cheung, W. S., 362, *822*
Chong, K.-M., 41, 87, 127, 147, 177, 179, 182–184, 203, 218, 221, 397, 606, *822*
Christensen, J. P. R., 613, *816*
Christman, M. C., 512, *852*
Chu, M. T., 304, *823*
Cioffi, J. M., 145, *856*
Clausing, A., 101, *823*
Cleveland, W. S., 190, *823*

Cline, R. E., 67, *858*
Crell, B., 626, *810*
Cohen, A., 529, 531, 534, *823*
Cohen, J. E., 175, *823*
Conlon, J. C., 594, *823*
Constantine, G. M., 267, *823*
Courant, R., 127, 783, *823*
Czumaj, A., 521, *816*

Dahl, G., 59, 614, 625, 626, *823*
Dalal, S. R., 408, 517, 518, *824*, *852*
Daley, D. J., 525, *824*
Dalton, H., 3, 5–7, 17, 20, 101, 194, 560, 563, 566, 612, 797, *824*
Dantzig, G. B., 48, *824*
Da Providência, J., 364, *815*
Dasgupta, P., 561, *824*
Das Gupta, S., 44, 617, *817*, *824*
David, H. A., 564, *824*
David, P., *862*
Davidovič, Ju. S., 763, *824*
Davis, C., 369, 670, 673, 674, 676, 683, 692, *817*, *824*
Davis, P. J., 62, 108, *824*
Day, P. W., 203, 204, 206, 208, 210, 213, 214, 216, 218, 219, 226, 606, *824*
Daykin, D. E., 115, 119, 540, *824*, *825*
Dean, A. M., 202, *825*
Dedić, Lj., 109, *825*
DeGroot, M. H., 747, *825*
Deming, W. E., 76, *825*
Derman, C., 226, 550, 556, *825*
Demir, H., 284, *825*
Derriennic, Y., 175, *823*
Dharmadhikari, S., 711, *825*
Dhillon, I. S., 308, *825*
Diaconis, P., 201, 413, 498, *825*

Djoković, D., 57
Djordjović, R. Ž., 269, *819*
Doig, A., *816*
Doksum, K., 725, *825*
Donaldson, D., 559, *818*
Doob, J. L., 68, *825*
Dowling, T. A., *831*
Dragomir, S. S., 57, 564, 652, 707, *821, 826*
Druilhet, P., 570, *826*
Du, D. Z., 233, 553, *826*
Dudewicz, E. J., 542, *826*
Duff, G. F. D., 221, *826*
Dulmage, A. L., 47, 49–52, *826, 839*
Dunford, N., 660, *826*
Dykstra, R. L., 466, *826*

Eaton, M. L., 397, 477, 479, 481, 511, 532, 572, 589, 590, 593, 594, *826, 827*
Ebrahimi, N., 551, *827*
Eckart, C., 373, 374, 771, *827*
Edwards, J., 416, *827*
Efron, B., 480, *827*
Eğecioğlu, O., 526, *813*
Egorychev, G. P., 50, *827*
Eisenberg, B., 513, *827*
Elezović, N., 114, 653, *827*
Eliezer, C. J., 111, 112, *827*
Elmaghrabi, S., 542, *815*
El-Neweihi, E., 484, 552, 553, 556, *818, 827, 828*
Éltető, O., 565, *828*
Elton, J., 732, *828*
Emlen, J. M., 562, *828*
Erdélyi, A., 650, *828*
Erdös, P., 254, *828*
Eriksson, E. A., 747, *825*
Esary, J. D., 550, *828*
Evard, J. C., 640, *828*

Faddeev, D. K., 376, *828*
Faddeeva, V. N., 376, *828*
Falikman, D. I., 50, *828*
Fan, K., 35, 79, 138–140, 160, 170, 177, 204, 218, 299, 300, 301, 308, 310, 314, 319, 324, 326, 327, 329, 331, 343, 351, 368, 371, 373, 374, 626, 686–689, 785, 787, 789–791, 793, *828, 829*
Fang, K.-T., 573, 574, *874*
Farahat, H. K., 51, 67, 69, *829*
Farnell, A. B., 348, *830*
Fefferman, C., 510, *830*
Fei, J. C. H., 560, *830*
Feller, W., 30, 150, 458, 499, 767, *830*
Fellman, J., 727, *830*
Fernández, V., 364, *814*
Fernando, S. L., 594, *830*
Fiedler, M., 333, 334, *830*
Fields, G. S., 560, *830*
Fike, C. T., 383, *815*
Fienberg, S. E., 76, 747, *825, 830*
Findlay, M. C., *834*
Fink, A. M., 126, 157, *830*
Fischer, E., 310, 783, *830*
Fischer, P., 614, 624, 625, *830*
Fishlow, A., 565, *831*
Folkman, J. H., 194, 195, 265, 266, *831*
Ford, Jr., L. R., 245, 445, *831*
Fortini, P., 517, 518, *824*
Foster, J. E., 565, *831*
Forsythe, F., 376, *831*
Frank, Jr., C. R., *868*
Franken, P., 696, *831*
Fréchet, M., 505, *831*
Freede, L. J., 336, *869*
Frigyes, E., 565, *828*
Frobenius, G., 348, *831*
Fuchs, L., 580, *831*

Fujii, M., 360, 361, 368, *831*, *849*
Fulkerson, D. R., 190, 194–196, 245, 249, 251–253, 265, 266, 445, *831*, *832*
Furuta, T., 347, 355, 360, 365, 675, *832*
Fussell, J. B., *859*

Gaffney, J., 735, *859*
Gaines, F., 319, *832*
Galambos, J., 458, 460, *832*
Gale, D., 197, 246, 249, 251, 252, 254, 258, 445, *832*
Gallai, T., 254, *828*
Gani, J., *865*
Gantmacher, F. R., 310, 351, 358, 359, 757, 759, *832*
Garloff, J., 358, *832*
Gasca, M., 757, *832*
Gastwirth, J. L., 713, *832*
Gauchman, H., 640, *828*
Gelfand, I. M., 340, *832*
Gentry, I. C., 261, *819*
Giles, D. E. A., *843*
Gini, C., 143, 505, 563, 721, *833*
Giorgi, G. M., 721, *833*
Giovagnoli, A., 364, 589, 590, *833*
Girko, V. L., *810*
Gleser, L. J., 474, 495, 496, 530, *821*, *824*, *833*, *870*
Goldberg, M., 27, 28, 615, *833*
Golden, S., 345, *833*
Goldstine, H. H., 376, 377, *853*
Golub, G. H., 363, 370, *833*, *864*
Goodman, L. A., *840*
Green, B., 375, *833*
Grone, R., 267, 305, *833*, *834*
Groves, T., 680, *834*
Grünbaum, B., 48, 52, *834*
Guan, K., 96, 119, 124, *834*

Guggenheimer, H., 275, 284, 287, *834*
Guitton, H., *843*
Gupta, A. K., *810*
Gupta, M. R., *834*
Gupta, S. S., *815*, *855*
Gyires, B., 50, *834*

Hacet, B. I., 763, *824*
Hadamard, J., 352, 651, *834*
Hadar, J., 708, *834*
Hall, M., 49, 256, *835*
Hall, P., 49
Hall, R. W., 521, *835*
Halmos, P. R., 370, *835*
Halperin, I., 47, 49–51, *826*
Hammer, P. L., 526, *835*
Hammersley, J. M., 47, 52, *835*
Harada, T., 364, *835*
Harary, F., 61, 260, *815*, *835*
Hardy, G. H., 3, 4, 8, 9, 22, 29, 32, 33, 35, 92, 93, 125, 134, 135, 155, 156, 159, 173, 203, 207, 578, 593, 627, 645, 655, 719, 751, *835*, *844*
Hass, E. C., *810*
Hauke, J., 573, *835*
Havrda, J., 562, *835*
Hayakawa, Y., 503, *835*
Haynsworth, E. V., *836*
Hazewinkel, M., 18, 201, *836*
Heath, Jr., R. W., 308, *825*
Helmert, F. R., 564, *836*
Hermite, C., 651
Hewett, J. E., 466, *826*
Heyer, H., 510, *836*
Hiai, F., 16, 317, 347, *811*
Hickey, R. J., 507, 608, 755, *836*
Higgins, P., 256
Hilbert, D., 784, *823*
Hill, T. P., 514, 515, 732, *828*
Hirsch, A., 325, *836*

Hobby, C., 77, *836*
Hochstadt, H., 313, *836*
Hoeffding, W., 441, 443, 451, 475, 496, 505, *836*
Hoerl, A. E., 379, *836*
Hoffman, A. J., 17, 35, 47, 54, 57, 58, 252, 299, 327, 371, 373, 374, 376, *836*, *837*
Holbrook, J. A. R., 614, 624, 625, *830*
Hollander, M., 203, 228, 234, 237–239, 594, *837*
Horn, A., 4, 34, 35, 54, 70, 162, 302, 305, 317, 322–326, 335, 337, 338, 343, *837*
Horn, R. A., 138, 297, 301, 356, 363, 367, 377, 671, 774, *812*, *837*
Householder, A. S., 77, 301, 303, 311, 316, 769, 787, *837*
de Hoyos, I., 364, 365, *814*, *837*
Hu, C.-Y., 500, *837*
Hua, L. K., 320, *838*
Huffer, F. W., 511, *838*
Hwang, F. K., 81, 233, 526, 553, 605, *819*, *822*, *826*, *838*
Hwang, S.-G., 60, *838*

Ibragimov, R., 492, 539, *838*
Ikramov, K. D., 319, *838*
Ireland, C. T., 76, *838*
Ishaq, M., 41, *869*
Ishihara, A., 523, *854*

James, G. D., 18, *838*
Janić, R. R., *819*
Jensen, J. L. W. V., 654, *838*
Jiang, W.-D., 143, *865*
Jiang, Y.-M., 143, *865*
Jichang, K., 747, *838*
Joag-Dev, K., 711, *825*
Jodeit, M., 126, 510, *830*

Joe, H., 23, 26, 516, 585–587, 606, 607, 609, 618, 620, 732, *812*, *838*, *839*
Johnson, C. R., 138, 297, 301, 305, 356, 363, 367, 377, 671, *812*, *833*, *837*
Johnson, D. M., 52, *839*
Jordan, C., 771, *839*
Just, E., 103, *839*

Kadane, J. B., 608, *839*
Kadiyala, K. R., 489, *839*
Kagan, A., *835*
Kaigh, W. D., 541, *839*
Kakiuchi, I., 526, *839*, *841*
Kakutani, S., 70
Kakwani, N. C., 565, 722, *839*
Kamae, T., 696, *839*
Kamei, E., 360, *831*
Kanter, M., 498, *840*
Kapur, J. N., 101, *840*
Karamata, J., 93, 157, 276, 645, 704, *840*
Karlin, S., 133, 135, 147, 150, 233, 239, 413, 446, 449–453, 455, 474, 478, 561, 567, 568, 614, 632, 645, 757–762, 766, *840*
Kästner, J., 58, *840*
Kazarinoff, N. D., 287, 288, 295, *840*
Keilson, J., 782, *840*
Keller, J. B., 370, 373–375, *841*
Kellerer, H. G., 252, *841*
Kemperman, J. H. B., 192, 579, *841*
Kendall, D. G., 25, *841*
Kennard, R. W., 379, *836*
Kesten, H., 544, *841*
Khaledi, B.-E., 726, *841*
Khintchine, A., 113, 480, 481, *841*

Kidman, K., 35, *847*
Kiefer, J., 25, 569, 678, *841*
Kim, Y. B., 525, *841*
Kimura, M., 526, *839*, *841*
Kingman, J. F. C., 362, *842*
Kirstein, B. M., 696, *831*
Kittaneh, F., 319, 328, 363, 365, *817*, *842*
Klamkin, M. S., 106, 130, 207, *842*
Klee, V., *824*
Klinger, A., 379, *842*
Klyachko, A. A., 336, *842*
Knopp, P., 77, *866*
Knuth, D., 198, 199, *842*
Knutson, A., 336, *842*
Koch, G. G., 538, *842*
Kochar, S., 484, 485, 742, 726, *841*–*843*
Kogan, A., 526, *835*
Kolm, S., 17, *843*
Komiya, H., 614, *843*
Kondor, Y., 560, 561, *843*
Konig, D., 49
Koo, A., 735, *859*
Koopmans, T. C., *824*
Korenbljum, B. I., 763, *824*
Korwar, R. M., 725, *843*
Koshevoy, G., 728, 733, *843*
Krämer, W., 559, *843*
Krause, M., 249, *843*
Krauss, F., 676, *843*
Krein, M., 358, 757, 759, *832*
Krengel, U., 696, *839*
Kristof, W., 375, 793, *843*
Krull, W., 310, *843*
Kullback, S., 76, 534, *843*
Kwong, H., 114, *843*
Kwong, M. K., 671, 677, *843*

Lagunas, M. A., 145, *856*
Lancaster, P., 781, *844*

Landau, H. G., 261, *844*
Lanke, J., 453, 454, *844*
Lassner, G., 628, *844*
Lassner, G. A., 628, *844*
Latif, N., 666, 667, *812*
Lawton, W. H., 493, 494, *844*
Lax, P. D., 691, *844*
Lee, S.-G., 623, *815*
Lefèvre, C., 513, *844*
Lehmann, E. L., 229, 571, 693, 700, 712, *844*
Lehtonen, T., 696, *812*
Lenard, A., 345, *844*
León, R. V., 594, 595, *823*, *844*
Leuenberger, F., 285, 286, *844*
Levin, V. I., 645, *844*
Levow, R. B., 35, 59, *845*
Levy, H., 708, *845*
Li, A.-J., 113, *845*
Li, C.-K., 364, *815*
Li, R., 573, 574, *845*, *874*
Li, X., 52, *821*, *845*
Lidskiĭ, V., 336, *845*
Lieb, E. H., 341, 653, 664, 678, 690, *819*, *845*
Lieberman, G. J., 226, 550, 556, *823*, *844*
Lin, G. D., 500, *837*
Lindley, D. V., *825*
Littlewood, J. E., 3, 4, 8, 9, 22, 29, 32, 33, 35, 92, 93, 125, 134, 135, 155, 156, 159, 173, 203, 207, 578, 693, 606, 627, 645, 655, 719, 751, *835*, *844*
Liu, S., 103, *845*
Liu, Z., 525, *845*
Liyanage, L., 440, 525, *845*
Loewner, C. (K. Löwner), 670–672, 684, 784, *845*, *846*
London, D., 208, 222, *846*
Lopes, L., 116, *847*

Lorentz, G. G., 170, 203, 218, 220, 225, 226, 450, 507, *829*, *846*
Lorenz, M. O., 3, 5, 7, 560, 693, *846*
Low, L., 537, *846*
Lunetta, G., 728, *846*
Lynn, M. S., 356, 360, *846*

MacDonald, R., 797
Magda, C. G., 570, *846*
Magnus, W., *828*
Maheshwari, A., 364, *812*
Mahmoodian, E. S., 259, *846*
Makowski, A., 281, 283, *846*
Makowski, A. M., 525, *841*
Malamud, S. M., 9, 313, 618, 624, 625, *846*
Marcaida, S., 363, *811*
Marcus, M., 35, 51, 69, 116, 117, 317, 320, 340, 342, 787, 793, *820*, *846*, *847*
Mardia, K. V., 505, *847*
Margalef, D. R., 563, *847*
Margolis, J., *843*
Markiewicz, A., 573, *835*
Markus, A. S., 25, 34, 40, 185, *847*
Marques de Sa, E., 305, *833*
Marshall, A. W., 3, 23, 77, 79, 106, 108, 110, 112, 125, 138, 140, 146, 148, 186, 188, 189, 259, 332, 377, 379, 380, 394, 397, 406, 464, 465, 484, 503, 504, 515, 530, 549, 556, 596, 600, 639, 663, 699, 701, 704, 714, 717, 725, 737, 738, 741, 765, 766, *828*, *847*, *848*
Martignon, L. F., 66, *849*
Martin, C. F., 18, 201, *836*
Martinez Pería, F. D., 619, 620, *849*

Massey, P. G., 619, 620, *849*
Mateev, P., 557, *849*
Mathias, R., 335, 376, *849*
Matić, M., 109, 191, *809*, *825*
Matsumoto, A., 368, *849*
Mattner, L., 499, *849*
Mauldon, J. G., 25, 47, *835*, *849*
McIntosh, R. P., 562, *849*
McShane, E. J., *823*
Mead, A., 628, *861*
Mehrota, K., 523, 525, *849*
Meilijson, I., 742, *849*
Melman, A., 139, *849*
Mendelsohn, N. S., 52, *839*
Menon, A., 523, 525, *849*
Merkle, M., 113, 114, *849*
Merris, R., 267, *834*
Merritt, R. L., *810*
Meyer, P. A., 27, 218, 614, 704, *849*
Micchelli, C. A., 757, *832*, *858*
Mikusiński, P., 52, *821*, *845*
Milliken, G. A., 673, *850*
Minc, H., 50, 69, 208, 223, 317, *847*, *850*
Miranda, H. F., 589, *850*
Mirsky, L., 29, 34, 35, 38, 40, 41, 48–51, 121, 160, 177, 179, 185, 228, 248, 249, 251, 252, 256, 298–303, 305, 315, 323, 325, 340, 351, 352, 370, 373, 374, 687, 787, 793, 795, *829*, *850*, *851*
Mitjagin, B. S., 41, *851*
Mitra, A., 547, *809*
Mitrinović, D. S., 103–105, 109, 113, 116, 124, 129–131, 135, 139, 140, 269, 270, 282, 294, 639, 655, *819*, *820*, *851*
Mizera, I., 497, 498, *851*
Mohan, C., 523, 525, *849*
Moler, C., 376, *831*

Montague, J. S., *851*
Moon, J. W., 260, 261, *851*
Moore, D., *815*
Moore, M. H., 680, *851*
Morse, N., 542, 544, *815*, *841*
Moser, L., 260, 299, *835*
Mosler, K., 618, 728, 729, 733, 734, *812*, *816*, *843*, *847*, *852*
Motzkin, T. S., 759
Moyls, B. N., 787, 793, *847*
Mudholkar, G. S., 408, 490, 593, *852*
Muir, T., 688, 689, *852*
Muir, W. W., 776, *852*
Muirhead, R. F., 3, 7, 19, 32, 33, 120, 125, 156, 159, 194, 195, 590, 612, *852*
Müller, A., 693, *852*
Murnaghan, F. D., 773, *873*

Nachman, D. C., 19, 402, *852*
Nádas, A., 742, *849*
Nagaraja, H. N., 739, *812*
Naimark, M. A., 340, *832*
Nair, K. P. K., 553, *859*
Nakamura, M., 361, *831*
Nakata, T., 413
Nappo, G., 742, *852*
Nashed, M. Z., 608, *852*
Nasser, J. I., 283, *852*
Nayak, T. K., 512, *852*
Neubauer, M. G., 601, 602, *852*
Neudecker, H., 103, *845*
von Neumann, J., 37, 48, 367, 376, 397, 773, 789, 790, *852*, *853*
Neuts, M. F., 743, *853*
Nevius, S. E., 387, 401–404, 409, 410, 418, 422, 425, 432, 434–437, 439, *853*
Newman, C. M., 481, *853*
Newman, D. J., 106, *842*

Newton, I., 134
Ng, C. T., 95, *853*
Ng, T. W., 362, *812*, *822*
Niculescu, C. P., 134, 637, 641, *853*
Niezgoda, M., 598, *854*
Nikolai, P. J., *847*
Noble, B., 760, *854*
Novikoff, A., 133, 479, 645, *840*

Oberhettinger, F., *828*
O'Brien, G. L., 696, *839*
Obst, N., 735, *859*
O'Cinneide, C. A., 743, *854*
Okamoto, M., 229, 410, 712, *854*, *873*
Okubo, S, 347, 523, *811*, *854*
Olkin, I., 23, 106, 108, 110, 112, 138, 140, 146, 148, 186, 188, 189, 259, 332, 351, 352, 355, 377–380, 406, 414–416, 464, 465, 470, 494, 503, 504, 516, 531, 556–558, 663, 680, 704, 714, 717, 725, 741, 765, 774, 795, *820*, *837*, *847*, *848*, *854*, *855*, *865*
Ollero, J., 742, *859*
Olshen, R. A., 397, *826*
Oppenheim, A., 116, 208, 270, 272, 283, 353, 354, 685, *855*
Ostle, B., 141, *855*
Ostrow, E., 651, *820*
Ostrowski, A. M., 20, 31, 79, 84, 86, 88, 348, 359, 782, 785, *855*

Pachpatte, B. G., 637, *856*
Pakes, A. G., 735, *856*
Pall, G., 343, *829*
Palomar, D. P., 145, *856*
Păltănea, E., 726, *818*

Papanicolaou, G., 520, *857*
Paris, J. B., 125, *856*
Park, D. H., 491, *821*, *856*
Parker, D. S., 193, 364, 588, 589, 601, *856*
Parker, W. V., 774, *856*
Parter, S. V., 77, *820*
Patil, G. P., *868*
Paulraj, A., 520, *851*
Pázman, A., 570, *856*
Pečarić, J. E., 16, 97, 109, 114, 191, 269, 270, 294, 361, 581, 583, 584, 637, 651, 653, 666, 667, 738, *809*, *812*, *825*, *827*, *831*, *851*, *856*, *857*
Peled, U. N., 265, *812*
Penrose, R., 305, *857*
Pereira, R., 362, *857*
Pereira, S., 520, *857*
Perlman, M. D., 333, 510, 511, 528, 530, 532–535, 589, 590, 593, 594, *811*, *821*, *824*, *827*, *830*, *857*, *870*
Persson, L.-E., 637, 641, *853*
Phelps, R. R., 27, 704, *857*
Pielou, E. C., 559, 563, *857*
Pietra, G., 722, *857*
Pigou, A. C., 6, 560, *857*
Pinkus, A., 757, *857*
Pitt, L. D., *858*
Plath, P. J., *810*
Pledger, G., 136, 172, 486, 551, 555, *858*
Plemmons, R. J., 67, *851*, *858*
Pollock, D. S. G., *810*
Pólya, G., 3, 4, 8, 9, 21, 22, 29, 32, 33, 35, 92, 93, 95, 125, 134, 135, 155–157, 159, 173, 176, 191, 203, 207, 287, 515, 578, 593, 606, 627, 645, 655, 719, 751, 757–759
Pratt, J., 351, 678, 795, *854*

Prékopa, A., 653, *858*
Press, S. J., 531, *821*, *824*, *854*, *870*
Proschan, F., 23, 74, 112, 122, 125, 126, 136, 140, 147, 148, 172, 186, 188, 189, 203, 228, 230, 233–237, 239, 378, 392, 394, 395, 397, 401–405, 409, 410, 418, 422, 425, 432–437, 439, 464, 465, 478, 482–487, 490–492, 503, 512, 550–556, 583, 594, 595, 607, 620, 637, 639, 651, 757, 764
Pukelsheim, F., 355, 364, 515, 569, 570, 679, 689, *833*, *848*, *854*, *859*
Pyke, R., 77, *836*

Qi, F., 143, *866*

Rachev. S. T., *854*
Rado, R., 10, 34, 162, 173, 589, 590, *859*
Raghavan, T. E. S., 30, 77, 353, *814*
Rajendra Prasad, V., 553, *859*
Ram, P., 193, 588, 589, 601, *856*
Ramnath, B., 379, *869*
Ramos, H. M., 742, *859*
Ranka, S., 523, 525, *849*
Rao, C. R., 559, *859*
Rasche, R. H., 735, *859*
Redheffer, R. M., 321, *859*
Ree, R., *847*
Rényi, A., 459, 460, 562, *859*
Ressel, P., 613, *816*
Révész, P., 48, *860*
Revyakov, M., 553, *860*
Richter, H., 340, *860*
Riley, J. D., 379, *861*
Rinott, Y., 147, 227, 228, 233, 239, 409, 412–414, 453, 474,

476, 501, 533, 534, 549, 567, 568, 614, 621, 622, 632, 633, *840, 857, 861*
Rivest, L.-P., 519, *860*
Rizvi, M. H., 547, 681, *809, 860*
Roberts, A. W., 38, 595, 637, 641, 647, 673, 676, 677, *860*
Robertson, C. A., 718, *812*
Robinson, S., 559, 561, *868*
Rockafellar, R. T., 38, 43, 49, 58, 138, 367, 637, 641, 647, *860*
Rohatgi, V. K., *865*
Rohrbach, H., *863*
Rojo, J., 484, 485, 700, *844*
Rokkan, S., *810*
Rolski, T., 401, *860*
Romanazzi, M., 364, 589, *833*
Romanovsky, V., 30, *860*
Rooin, J., 140, *860*
Roos, B., 499, *849*
Rosén, B., 450, 451, *860*
Rosenbaum, R. A., 651, *860*
Ross, S. M., 226, 513, 550, 556, *825, 861*
Rotfel'd, S. Ju., 329, 331, *861*
Rothblum, U. G., 77, 81, 526, 605, 606, *835, 838, 861*
Rothenberg, T., 680, *834*
Rousseau, R., 559, *861*
Ruch, E., 22, 23, 201, 578, 586, 587, 607, 628, *861*
Ruderman, H. D., 209, 222, *861*
Ruhe, A., 341, *861*
Ruiz-Cobo, M. R., 166, *821*
Rüschendorf, L., 390, 712, *821, 861*
Ruskai, M. B., 678, *845*
Russell, W., 708, *834*
Russet, B. M., 561, *810*
Rust, P. F., *861*
Rustagi, J., *858*
Ryff, J. V., 22, 23, 35, 203, *862*

Ryser, H. J., 48–50, 61, 76, 196, 197, 245, 249, 251, 253, 254, 258, 260, 261, *820, 832, 862*

Saari, D. G., 514, *862*
Sackrowitz, H. B., 534, *823*
Salinelli, E., 767, *862*
Sampson, A., *818, 821, 824, 862, 870*
Samuels, S. M., 496, *862*
Sanderson, W. C., 603, *862*
Sandy, M., 35, *847*
Santner, T. J., 547, 549, *815, 860*
Sarabia, J.-M., 735, 736, *862*
Satnoianu, R., *862*
Satorra, A., *810*
Savage, I. R., 229, 236, 237, *862*
Savits, T., *818, 862*
Saxena, K. M. L., 547, *809*
Scarsini, M., 712, 744, 745, *812, 816, 847, 862, 863*
Schatten, R., 138, *863*
Schaumberger, N., 103, *839*
Schmidt, E., 773, *863*
Schneider, H., 77, 300, 301, 348, 349, *820, 863*
Schoenberg, I. J., 757, 759, 760, *863*
Schönemann, P., 375, *863*
Schranner, R., 22, 23, 578, 586, 587, 607, *861*
Schreiber, S., 71, *863*
Schur, I., 3, 4, 10, 20, 29, 79, 80, 83–85, 92, 97, 115–118, 297, 300, 306, 307, 318, 352, 353, 770, *863*
Schutz, R. R., 565, *863*
Schwartz, J. T., 660, *826*
Schwarz, Š., 30, 69, *863*
Schweitzer, O., 102, *821, 863*
Seligman, T. H., 22, 23, 578, 586, 587, 607, *861*

Sen, A., 559, 560, 561, 566, *829*, *864*
Sen, P. K., 463, *864*
Sendov, H., 624, 625, *830*
Seneta, E., 29, 48, 77, *864*
Seo, Y., 361, 368, *831*, *864*
Serra-Capizzano, S., 363, *864*
Sethuraman, J., 23, 122, 148, 203, 228, 230, 233–237, 239, 387, 401–405, 409, 410, 418, 422, 425, 432, 434–437, 439, 482, 483, 485–487, 552, 553, 556, 594, 607, *821*, *823*, *827*, *828*, *837*, *853*, *859*
Sezgin, A., 520, *857*
Sgarra, C., 767, *862*
Shaked, M., 74, 440, 466–469, 568, 571, 572, 693, 704, 712, 725, 727, 742, *826*, *839*, *845*, *859*, *863–865*
Shanthikumar, J. G., 440, 525, 693, 704, 725, 727, 742, *845*, *864*, *865*
Shaw, K., 261, *819*
Shen, J., 96, 124, *834*
Shepp, L. A., 140, 511, 512, 526, 557, 558, 605, 606, 743, *810*, *838*, *855*, *865*
Sherman, S., 70, 328, 338, 346, 593, 614, *816*, *865*
Sherwood, H., 52, *821*, *845*
Shi, H.-N., 143, 197, 640, 641, *865*, *866*
Shi, Zhong-Ci (Shih, Chung-Tz'u) 348, 350, *866*
Shisha, O., *858*
Shorrock, R., 681, 682, *860*
Shorrocks, A. F., 565, 742, *831*, *866*
Shu, B., 653, 718, *812*
Siegmund, D., 413
Silva, F. C., 331, 356, *813*

Silvestre, L. E., 619, 620, *849*
Simić, S., 108, 667, *866*
Simons, G., 218, 506, 712, *821*
Simpson, E. H., 561, *866*
Singpurwalla, N. D., 741, *821*, *859*
Sinkhorn, R., 69, 76, 77, *809*, *866*
Slottje, D. J., 735, 736, *862*
Smiley, M. F., 35, *866*
Smith, A. F. M., *825*
Snijders, T., 67, 389, 445, *866*
Sobel, M., 229, 416, *855*, *866*
Solomon, D. L., 563, *866*
Solomon, H., 510, 608, *819*
Soms, A. P., 550, *866*
Sordo, M. A., 541, 742, *839*, *859*
Spizzichino, F., 503, 554, 742, *815*, *827*, *852*, *866*
Srinivasan, G. K., 108, *866*
Stanković, Lj., 581, *820*
Starrett, D., 561, *824*
Stečkin, S. B., 645, *844*
Steele, J. M., *867*
Steerneman, A. G. M., 589, 591, 593, *867*
Steffensen, J. F., 639, *867*
Steger, A., 521, *816*
Stegun, I. A., 512, *809*
Stein, C. M., 517, 614, *867*
Steinberg, R., 324, *837*
Steinig, J., 269, 284, *867*
Stephan, F. F., 76, *825*
Stephen, T., 364, *867*
Stepniak, C., *867*
Stevens, W. L., *867*
Stewart, G. W., 138, *867*
Stoer, J., 637, 641, 646, 647, *867*
Stolarsky, K. B., 101, 142, *867*
Stout, W., 218, 506, 712, *821*
Stoyan, D., 693, *852*, *867*
Strassen, V., 701, 702, 719, *867*
Straus, E. G., 27, 28, 615, *833*

Strawderman, W., 529, *823*
Studden, W., 474, *840*
Styan, G. P. H., 103, 352, 782, *810*, *840*, *867*
Subramanian, R., *817*
Sudjianto, A., 573, 574, *874*
Sun, J., 138, *867*
Sunder, V. S., 267, 353, *814*, *834*
Sustik, M. A., 308, *825*
Svrtan, D., 97, 738, *856*
Sylvester, J. J., 771, *868*
Szal, R., 559, 561, *868*
Szegö, G., 140, 287, 758, 759, *858*, *868*
Szekely, G., 502, *868*
Szekeres, G., 769, *820*
Szekli, R., 693, *868*

Taguchi, T., 728, *868*
Taillie, C., 736, 737, *868*
Takemura, A., 517, *811*
Tam, T.-Y., *868*
Tao, T., 336, *842*
Taussky-Todd, O., *868*
Taylor, M. D., 52, *821*, *845*
Tchakaloff, L. (Čakalov, Ljubomir), 137, *868*
Tchen, A. H.-T., 203, 218, 505, 506, *868*
Terwilliger, H. L., 141, *855*
Tewarson, R. P., *869*
Theobald, C. M., 340, *869*
Therianos, S., 311, *869*
Thirring, W., 341, *845*
Thompson, C. J., 328, 338, 344–346, *865*, *869*
Thompson, J. R., 542, 545, 546, *810*
Thompson, R. C., 41, 42, 185, 311, 315, 316, 327–329, 345, 509, 604, *850*, *869*
Thompson, Jr., W. A., 466, *826*

Thon, D., 17, *869*
Todd, J., *869*
Toeplitz, O., 774, *870*
Tok, T., 523, *879*
Tomić, M., 92, 94, 157, 179, *870*
Tominaga, M., 368, *864*
Tong, Y. L., 107, 126, 319, 440, 468, 469, 513, 514, 542, 554, 567, 568, 571, 572, 583, 632, 633, 651, *818*, *826*, *839*, *840*, *845*, *855–857*, *864*, *870*
Topkis, D. M., 218, 219, *870*
Torgerson, E., *870*
Towsley, D., 525, *845*
Tricomi, F. G., *828*
Tropp, J. A., 308, *825*
Tsui, K.-Y., 617, *870*
Tung, S.-H.. *870*
Turing, A. M., 376, *870*
Turnbull, B. W., 547, 549, *815*
Tymoczko, D., 521, *835*

Uhlmann, A., 188, 522, 626, *810*
Ullah, A., *843*
Uspensky, J. V., 289, *870*

van der Waerden, B. L., *871*
Van Heck, P., 559, *861*
Van Tiel, J., 637, *871*
Varberg, D. E., 38, 595, 647, 673, 676, 677, *860*
Vasić, P. M., 269, 581, 655, *820*
Veinott, Jr., A. F., 218, 585, 586, 627, 696, *871*
Venkovska, A., 125, *856*
Verducci, J. S., 202, 618, 732, *825*, *839*
Villaseñor, J. A., 717, 727, 728, 735, 736, 738–740, *812*, *871*
Vinograde, B., 774, *871*
Visick, G., 354, 357, *871*
Visser, C., 317, 338, 793, *871*

Author Index

Vitale, R. A., 517, *871*
Vöcking, B., 521, *816*
Vogel, W., 48, 248, *871*
Vojta, G., 153, *874*
Volenec, V., 269, 270, 294, *851*

Walden, J., 539, *838*
Walker, A. W., 103, 280, *871*
Walkup, D. W., 79, 596, *848*
Wallace, S. W., 17, *869*
Wan, H., 195, 196, 201, *871*
Wang, Bo-Ying (Wang, Po-Ying), 343, 348, 350, *866*, *871*, *872*
Wasserman, L., 608, *839*
Watkins, W., 601, 602, 682, *852*, *872*
Watson, G. S., 312, 382, *872*
Weaver, W., 562, *872*
Webb, R. C., *868*
Webster, R., 637, 641, *872*
Wedderburn, J. H. M., 775, *872*
Wehrl, A., 522, *872*
Weinberger, H. F., 691, *872*
Wellner, J. A., 497, 498, *851*
Wets, R. J.-B., 79, 460, 596, *848*
Weyl, H., 16, 97, 157, 168, 317, 319, 336, *872*
Whiteley, J. N., 119, *872*
Whitmore, G. A., *834*
Whitt, W., 218, 505, 506, *872*
Whittle, P., 678, 680, *872*
Wielandt, H. W., 47, 299, 329, 336, 376, 777, *837*, *872*
Wilfling, B., 736–738, 740, *872*
Williams, C. L., 604, 605, *810*
Wintner, A., 773, *873*
Wittmeyer, H., 331, *873*
Witzgall, C., 637, 641, 646, 647, *867*
Wolkowicz, H., 305, *833*
Wong, C. K., 376, 412, *873*
Wong, C. S., 61, *822*

Wootton, J., 196, 201, *871*
Wright, E. M., 140, *873*
Wu, S.-H., 143, 640, 641, *865*, *866*
Wynn, H. P., 292, 364, 590, *833*, *873*

Xi, B.-Y., 376, *871*
Xu, C., 321, *873*
Xu, Z., 321, *873*

Yamazaki, T., 361, *873*
Yanagimoto, T., 229, 712, *873*
Yao, D. D., 520, 525, *821*
Yitzhaki, S., 564, *873*
Ylvisaker, N. D., 678, *873*
Young, A., 201, *873*
Young, G., 371, 373, 374, *826*, *827*
Young, H. P., 514, *814*
Yue, P. C., 412, *873*

Zaanen, A. C., 317, 338, 793, *871*
Zaballa, I., 363, 364, *811*, *873*
Zbăganu, Gh., 175, *823*
Zhan, X., 331, 332, 335, 347, 355, 361, 369, 671, 679, *812*, *873*, *874*
Zhang, A., 573, 574, *874*
Zhang, F., 297, 321, 357, 376, *871*, *873*, *874*
Zhang, F.-Z., 343, *872*
Zhang, X.-M., 143, 291, *874*
Zhang, Z.-H., 143, *874*
Zhao, W.-Z., 113, *845*
Zheng, B., 187, *874*
Zheng, N.-G., 143, *874*
Zhou, L., 130, *862*
Zhu, Q. J., *874*
Ziegler, Z., 645, *840*
Zwick, D., 16, *857*
Zylka, C., 58, 153, 523, 626, 628, *810*, *840*, *874*

Subject Index

Absolute singular values, 299
Additive compound, 778
Admissibilty of Tests, 517
Affine function, 642
Altruistic transfer, 17
Analysis of variance
   ranking and selection for, 547
   two-way classification, 537
Angle function, 645
Antecedent mapping, 19
Apportionment in proportional
   representation, 514
Arc of a graph, 243
Arithmetic geometric mean
   inequality, 125
   proof of, 478, 654
Arrangement increasing function,
   230
   convex cone of, 232
   identification of, 232

Artin's theorem, 649
   and Holder's inequality, 662,
     663
   and Lyapunov's inequality, 663
Associated roots of a matrix, 299
Asymmetric square root of a
   matrix, 773
Atkinson's measure of inequality,
   566

Bartlett's test, 529
Basic composition formula, 752
Bernoulli distribution
   entropy of convolutions of, 557
   inequality for convolutions of,
     474
   stochastic majorization for,
     486
   tail probabilities of linear
     combinations, 495

Subject Index

Bernoulli random variables, symmetric
  moments of, 477
  Schur-convexity for, 479
  sum of, 498
Beta distribution
  generalized, 737
  log concavity of density, 864
Beta function, generalized, 109
Bimajorization, weak, 603
Binet–Cauchy theorem, 776
Binomial distribution
  mean, 141
  preservation of
    Schur-convexity for, 409, 433
  stochastic majorization for, 488
Birkhoff's theorem, 30, 38, 42, 47
Birthday problem, 413
Bistochastic matrix, 30
Bivariate distributions with fixed marginals, 505
Bivariate exponential distribution, 504

Capacity of network, 244
Carathéodory's theorem, 38, 52
Cauchy–Binet theorem, 776
Cauchy–Bunyakovskiĭ–Schwarz inequality, 660
Cauchy distribution, 492
Cauchy's matrix, total positivity of, 760
Cayley transform, 374
Chain in a graph, 266
Chain majorization
  for matrices, 612
  order preserving functions for, 621
  for vectors of matrices, 629
Chaotic order, 18

Chi-square distribution
  moment inequality for, 477
  multivariate, Schur-concavity of density, 407
  noncentral, total positivity of, 762
  preservation of
    Schur-convexity for, 410
Circuit in a graph, 266
Circular matrix (circulant), 62
Circular moving average, 62
Circular symmetric multivariate normal distribution, 531
Closed function, 646
Closure of a function, 646
  properties, 438
  under convolution, 423
  under limits, 438
Coefficient of ergodicity, 176
Coefficient of variation, as measure of diversity, 561, 721
Coincidence, 50
Color-feasibility in a graph, 265
Comparison of experiments, 570
Complementary inequalities, 102
Complete monotonicity, 766
Complete symmetric function, 119
Completely monotone function, 108, 766
Complex vectors, weak majorization and, 41
Composition
  of convex functions, 648
  of totally positive functions, 758
  and Schur-convexity, 88
Compound distributions, 391
Compound matrix, 502, 775
  Binet–Cauchy theorem for, 776
  eigenvalues of, 777

Subject Index 895

Compound, additive, of a matrix, 778
Concave function, 642
  majorization for, 95, 97, 165
Concavity of determinant, 685
Concentration of distributions, 493, 511
Concordance of distributions, 505, 712
Condition number, 376
  and norms, 376
  for submatrix, 380
Cone
  convex, 21
  ordering, 21, 595
  pointed, 595
Configuration
  least likely, 545
  most likely, 545
Conjugate numbers, 659
Conjugate sequence, 197, 245
  generalization of, 258
Continuity of convex functions, 646
Continuous majorization, 22
  generalized, 23
Convergence of ordered sequences, 71
Converse theorems
  for diagonal elements, 305
  for eigenvalues, 322
  for singular values, 322
  for sums of matrices, 335
Convex cone, 21
  of arrangement increasing functions, 232
Convex function, 453, 641, 651
  composition of, 648
  continuity of, 646
  Jensen sense, 20
  majorization for, 95, 97, 165
  and weak majorization, 12

Convex hull of permutation matrices, 30
Convex matrix function, 676
Convex polytope, 48
Convex trace functions, 690
Convexity
  log, preservation under mixtures, 649
  of matrix inverse, 768
Convolution
  notation for, 395
  of Schur-concave functions, 48, 235
Correct selection, probability of, 541
Correlation
  Gaussian, 517
  intraclass, 530
Covariance matrix, structured, 530

d-majorization, 585
d-stochastic matrix, 585
Dalton condition, 560
Dalton's measure of inequality, 566
Dalton transfer, 17
Data distributions, 506
Decreasing function, 637
Decreasing hazard rate, 106
Decreasing in transposition, 230
Decreasing rearrangement of functions, 22
Demidegree of a graph, 254
Density function, totally positive, 236
Density matrices, 522
Derivatives, fractional, 127
Design of experiments, 568
Design, random effects, 536
Determinant
  concavity of, 685

extremal representation for, 795
Hadamard's inequality for, 306
inequalities for, 685
Diagonal elements and singular values, majorization for, 313
Dilation (or dilatation), 26, 421
  in sampling plans, 446
Direct product of matrices, 780
Directed graph, 243
Dirichlet compound negative multinomial distribution, preservation of Schur-convexity for, 420, 434
Dirichlet distribution, 144, 415
  preservation of symmetry and convexity for 400
  Schur-convexity for, 415
Disordered, more, 18
Distinct representatives, system of, 256
Distribution, see also Compound distributions; Multivariate; and specific distributions: Bernoulli; Beta; Binomial; Bivariate exponential; Chi-square; Circular symmetric multivariate normal; Dirichlet; Exponential; Gamma; Geometric; Hypergeometric, multivariate; Inverse hypogeometric, multivariate; Liouville–Dirichlet; Logarithmetic series; Multinomial; Negative binomial, multivariate; Negative multinomial; Negative multivariate hypergeometric; Noncentral chi-square; Noncentral F;
Noncentral t; Normal; Poisson; t; Uniform; Weibull
mixtures of 393, 466
with proportional hazard function, 484, 488
Diversity
  measurement of, 559
  relative differences in, 604
DNA sequences, 201
Dominance
  and weak majorization, 18
  stochastic, 709
  utility gap, 187
Domination, for sampling plans, 445
Doubly stochastic matrix, 10, 29
  and majorization, 29, 33, 35, 155
  regular, 68
Doubly substochastic matrix, 12, 36
  augmentation of, 37
  and weak majorization, 14, 36, 39, 40
Doubly superstochastic matrix, 12, 43
  and weak majorization, 42, 43
Duality for triangle inequalities, 294
Duplication formula, Gauss–Legendre, 478, 650

Edge in a graph, 243
Edge coloring of a graph, 265
Effective domain of convex function, 642
Eigenvalue
  of compound matrix, 796
  decomposition, 771
  elementary symmetric functions of, 777

extremal property for sum of, 785
  interlacing property of, 301, 303, 311
  notations for, 298
  of random matrix, 469
  and singular values, majorization for, 317
Elementary dominant, 445
Elementary symmetric functions, 114
  of characteristic roots, 777
  and Hermitian matrices, 306
  majorization for, 172
  normalized, 137
  ratio of, 117
  for sides of triangle, 230
Elementary T-transform, 82
Entropy, 101
  of Bernoulli distributions, 557
  as measure of diversity, 562
  generalized relative, 627
  Kapur's, 101
  of multinomial distribution, 558
  Schur-concavity of, 556
Epigraph, 646
Ergodicity, coefficient of, 176
Estimation, linear, 535
Estimators
  efficiency of, 472
  minimum variance unbiased, 536
Exchangeable normal random variables
  preservation of Schur-convexity for, 411
  Schur-convexity of density, 408
Exchangeable random matrices, 397
Exchangeable random variables, 126, 392

preservation of Schur-convexity for, 406
  preservation of symmetry and convexity for, 396, 397
  Schur-concavity for, 407
  translation of, 406
Exponential distribution, 482
  bivariate, 504
  mixture of, 108
  order statistics from, 482
  preservation of symmetry and convexity for, 399
  tail probabilities of linear combinations, 498
Exponential family of distributions, total positivity of, 761
Extended logarithmic mean, 143
Extremal representations, 794
Extreme points of
  complex matrices, 42
  doubly stochastic matrices, 30
  infinite doubly stochastic matrices, 25
  uniformly tapered matrices, 58

F distribution
  generalized, 737
  noncentral, total positivity of, 762
Failure rate, 503
Feller-Pareto distribution, 737
Ferreri-Sylvester diagrams, 246
Finite graph, 243
Fischer minmax theorem, 783
Fishlow poverty measure of inequality, 565
Flow in network, 244
Fractional derivatives, 127

Function
  closure of, 646
  completion of, 599
  doubly stochastic, 608
  inequality attenuating, 726
  inequality preserving, 726
  matrix valued, 361
  ray-increasing, 592

G-increasing (decreasing), 591
G-invariant, 591
G-majorization, 589
  order preserving functions for, 594
Gale–Ryser theorem, 249
Gamma distribution
  generalized, 736
  logarithmic concavity of density, 764
  moments of, 110
  preservation of
    Schur-convexity for, 410, 433
  preservation of symmetry and convexity for, 399, 430
  stochastic majorization for, 488
Gamma function, majorization for, 109
Gateaux differentials, 608
Gauge function symmetric, *see* Symmetric gauge function
Gauss–Legendre duplication formula, 478, 650
Gauss–Markov estimate, 473
Generalized averaging operation, 23
Generalized inverse of matrix, 375
Genetic algorithms, 523
Geometric distribution,
  Schur-convexity for, 476

Gibbsian states, comparison of, 522
Gini coefficient, as measure of inequality, 563, 721
Gradient, 647
Graph
  arc of, 243
  chain in, 266
  circuit in, 266
  color-feasibility in, 265
  demidegree of, 254
  directed, 243
  edge of, 243
  edge coloring of, 265
  finite, 243
  incidence matrix of, 243
  loop of, 244
  network, 244
  node of, 243
  nondirected, 264
  random, 513
  s-, 258
  tournament, 260, 264
  vertex of, 243

Hadamard product, 352
Hadamard-type inequality
  for M-matrix, 369
  for totally positive matrix, 357
Hadamard's determinant
  inequality, 4, 300
  proof of, 306
  variations of, 347
  via extremal representation, 350
Hartley's test, 529
Hazard function, 484
Hazard rate, 763
  decreasing, 106
  increasing, 106, 478, 503
Hazard transform, 550

Heinz mean, 144
Helmert matrix, 65
Hermitian matrices
  and elementary symmetric
    functions, 306
  diagonal elements of, 300
  differences of, 374
  eigenvalue decomposition, 771
  simultaneous decomposition,
    775
  singular part, 328
  submatrices of, 308
  submatrix inequalities, 311
  sum of, 329
  with prescribed diagonal
    elements, 308
Heronian mean, 144
Hessenberg matrix, 35, 60
Hessian matrix, 644
Hilbert's matrix, total positivity
  of, 760
Hoeffding's inequality, 443
Hölder's inequality
  and Artin's theorem, 662,
    663
  generalized, 661
  proof of, 657
Hypergeometric distribution,
  multivariate, 417
  preservation of
    Schur-convexity for, 418,
    434

Idempotent matrix, 68
Imaginary singular values, 299
Incidence matrix of a graph, 243
Income inequality, measurement
  of, 5, 20
Increasing function, 637
Increasing hazard rate, 106, 478,
  503

Inequality,
  arithmetic–geometric mean,
    125
  proof of, 478, 684
  Cauchy–Bunyakovskiĭ–
    Schwarz,
    660
  complementary, 102
  for polygons and simplexes,
    295
  Hadamard's 4, 300, 306, 350
  Hoeffding's 443
  Hölder's, 657
    generalized, 661
  isoperimetric, 270
    for plane figures, 287
  Jensen's, 109, 456, 654
    for conditional expectations,
      655
  Kantorovich, 102
  Lyapunov's, 107, 659
  measurement of, 559
  Minkowski, 660
  Steffensen, 640
  for triangle, 271, 276, 281,
    287
Infinite sequences, majorization
  of, 25
Information statistics, test for
  multinomial distribution,
  534
Interlaced numbers, 177
Interlacing property of
  eigenvalues, 301, 303, 310
Interpolation formula of
  Lagrange, 303
Intraclass correlation,
  multivariate normal
  distribution, 530
Inverse matrix
  convexity of, 678
  Moore-Penrose, 67

Inverse hypergeometric
    distribution, multivariate,
    preservation of
    Schur-convexity for, 419
Isoperimetric figures, 270
Isoperimetric inequalities, 270
    for plane figures, 287
Isotonic function, 19

Jensen's inequality, 109, 654
    for conditional expectations, 655
    and majorization, 456

k-out-of-n system
    probabilities for, 457
    reliability of, 549
Kronecker matrices, 780
    monotonicity, 675
    product of, 780
    sum of, 780

L-superadditive
    (lattice-superadditive)
    function, 218
    examples, 219
Lagrange's interpolation formula, 303
Laplace transform, 107
Latin square, 61
Lawley–Hotelling trace test, 533
Least concave majorant, 181
Least favorable configuration, 542
Least-squares estimators for
    regression model, 381
Leibniz's principle of
    nonsufficient reason, 21
Likelihood ratio order, 699
Linear combinations
    peakedness of, 490
    tail probabilities, 494

Linear estimation, 535
Linear regression, least-squares
    estimators for, 381
Liouville–Dirichlet
    distribution, 416
    preservation of
        Schur-convexity, 417, 433
Loewner order, 670
    and majorization, 360
Log convexity, preservation
    under mixtures, 649
Logarithmic concave density
    beta density, 764
    gamma density, 764
    Gompertz density, 765
    normal density, 764
    Weibull density, 765
Logarithmic concave function, 105, 663
Logarithmic series distribution
    multivariate, preservation of
        Schur-convexity for, 418
    modified multivariate,
        preservation of
        Schur-convexity for, 419
Loop in a graph, 244
Lorenz curve, 5, 503, 563
    generalized, 742
    length of, 722
    lognormal distribution, 717
    parametric families of, 734
    Pareto distribution, 715
    Pietra index, 722
    positive random variables, 715
Lower weak majorization, 12, 36
Lyapunov's inequality, 107, 108, 659
    and Artin's theorem, 663

M-matrix, 782
    Hadamard-type inequality for, 359

Majorization
  chain
    for matrices, 612
    for vectors of matrices, 629
  characterization by linear transformations, 155
  characterization by order-preserving functions, 156
  column-stochastic, 619
  componentwise, 602
  continuous, 22, 583
  from convolutions, 507
  for diagonal elements and singular values, 313
  and doubly stochastic matrices, 29, 33, 35, 155
  for eigenvalues and singular values, 317
  entropy, 602
  equivalent conditions for, 155
  from finite groups, 509
  G-, 589
  generation of, 185
  geometric characterization of, 162
  group, 587
  of infinite sequences, 25
  in integers, 194
  using Jensen's inequality, 456
  linear combinations, 617
  for matrices, 612
  matrix, 623
  p-, 58
  relative to d, 585
  row, for matrices, 616
  semigroup, 588
  for sides of polygon, 281
  stochastic, 387
  and T-transforms, 32
  unordered, 589, 601
  upper weak, 42
  variance, 601
  for vectors of matrices, 629
  weak, 12
    and convex functions, 12
    and doubly substochastic matrices, 12, 36, 37, 156
    and doubly superstochastic matrix, 12, 42
    and T-transforms, 41
    stochastic, 427
  with weights, 578
Matrix, *see also* Norm; Singular Values; and specific matrices; Bistochastic; Cauchy's; Circular (circulant); Compound; d-stochastic; Doubly stochastic; Doubly substochastic; Doubly superstochastic; Helmert; Hermitian; Hessian; Hilbert's idempotent; Incidence; Inverse; M; Maximal; Orthostochastic; Oscillatory; Permutation; Random; Regular doubly stochastic; Stochastic; Sub-Markovian; Symmetric; T-transform; Totally nonnegative; Totally positive; Uniformly tapered; Unitarily similar; Unitary stochastic
  absolute singular values of, 299
  additive compound of, 778
  associated roots of, 299
  asymmetric square root of, 773
  average of, 332
  condition number of, 376
  -convex function, 676
  direct product of, 780

Hadamard product, 352
  imaginary singular values of, 299
  -increasing function, 670
  Kronecker product of, 780
  Loewner ordering of, 670
  maximal, 246
  monotonicity of powers of, 671
  normal, 313
  ordering of, 691
  pinching, 17
  products, 338
  pseudoinverse of, 375
  real roots of, 333
  real singular values of, 299
  real-valued function of, 684
  residual, 375
  Schur product, 356
  similar, 769
  skew-symmetric, 370
  totally positive, 357
  triangular representation of, 770, 773
  unitary part of, 324
  with given rank, 373
Maximal invariant, 473
  in test for means, 531
Matrix-convex functions, 676
Maximal matrix, 246
Maximal vector under constraints, 192
Means, 141
  binomial, 141
  bounds for, 141
  Heinz, 144
  Heronian, 144
  logarithmic, 141
  power, 141
Measure of diversity, Simpson's, 562

Measure of inequality
  Atkinson's, 566
  based on utility, 565
  Dalton's, 566
  Fishlow poverty, 565
  minimal majority, 564
  Schultz coefficient, 565
  top 100α percent, 564
Median, consistency of, 497
Minimal majority measure of inequality, 564
Minimal vector under constraints, 192
Minimum variance unbiased estimator, 536
Minkowski inequality, 660
Minmax theorem, 783
Mixing distance, 628
Mixture of distribution, 391, 393, 466
  convolutions of, 702
  inequalities for, 630
  and Schur-convex functions, 100
  preservation under, 425
Moments,
  normalized logarithmic concavity of, 766
  product of, 107, 480
  ratios of, 189
Monotone matrix norm, 379
Monotonicity
  of power functions, 528
  of powers of a matrix, 671
Moore–Penrose inverse, 67
Moving average, circular, 62
Muirhead's theorem, 125, 126, 159, 394, 450
Multinomial coefficients, 113
Multinomial distribution
  divergence test for, 534
  entropy of, 762

preservation of
    Schur-convexity for, 412
  preservation of symmetry and
    convexity for, 400
  ranking and selection for, 542
  Schur-convexity for, 412, 414,
    416, 434
  test for equality of parameters,
    533
Multiplicative norm, unitarily
  invariant, 382
Multivariate chi-square density,
  Schur-concavity of, 407
Multivariate exponential
  distributions, positive
  dependence of, 555
Multivariate hypergeometric
  distribution, 417
  preservation of
    Schur-concavity for, 418,
    434
Multivariate inverse
  hypergeometric distribution,
  preservation of
  Schur-convexity for, 419
Multivariate logarithmic series
  distribution, preservation of
  Schur-convexity for, 418
Multivariate modified
  logarithmic distribution,
  preservation of
  Schur-convexity for, 419
Multivariate negative binomial
  distribution, preservation of
  Schur-convexity for, 418
Multivariate normal distribution
  with circular symmetry, 531
  with intraclass correlation,
    530
  preservation of
    Schur-convexity for, 411,
    433

preservation of symmetry and
  convexity for, 430
Schur-concavity of density,
  407
test for means for, 531
test for sphericity in, 529
tests for structured covariance
  matrices in, 530
Multivariate regression, 473
Multivariate "t" distribution,
  Schur-concavity of density,
  407, 433
Musical theory, majorization in,
  521

Negative binomial distribution
  multivariate, preservation of
    Schur-convexity for, 418,
    434
  preservation of symmetry and
    convexity for, 400
Negative multinomial
  distribution, preservation of
  Schur-convexity for, 418
Negative multivariate
  hypergeometric distribution,
  preservation of
  Schur-convexity for, 419,
    435
Network, capacity of, 244
Network flow, 244
Network graph, 244
New better than used, 742
Node of a graph, 243
Noncentral chi-square
  distribution, total positivity
  of, 762
Noncentral F distribution, total
  positivity of, 762
Noncentral t distribution, total
  positivity of, 762

Norm
  matrix, consistent with vector norm, 383
  monotone matrix, 379
  multiplicative, unitarily invariant, 382
  subordinate matrix, 381
  unitarily invariant, 367
Normal distribution, see also Multivariate normal distribution
  logarithmic concavity of density, 764
  moments of, 480
  ranking and selection for, 547
  test for equality of variances, 529
Normal matrix, 313
Number of sign changes of function, 759

Ocupancy problems, 521
Odds ratio and reliability functions, 557
Order-preserving function, 819
  for chain majorization, 621
  for G-majorization, 594
  for p-majorization, 583
  for row majorization, 622
Order statistics, 461
  from exponential distribution, 482
Ordered random variables, expected values of, 461
Ordering
  cone, 21, 595
  convex, 704
  dispersion, 725
  excess wealth, 741
  exchange rate, Lorenz, 732
  for complex vectors, 604
  hazard rate, 697
  increasing convex, 741
  information, 571
  likelihood ratio, 699
  Lorenz, 718
  partial, 19
  price, Lorenz, 732
  positive combinations, Lorenz, 732
  sign change, 724
  star-shaped, 723
  stochastic, 694
  uncertainty, 748
  vector, 21
Orthostochastic matrix, 34
  examples of, 53, 65
  and majorization, 35
Oscillatory matrix, 353

p-majorization, 580
  order-preserving function for, 583
  continuous, 583
Paired comparisons, 516
Parallel system, 549, 552
Parameterization to preserve Schur-convexity, 403
Parameterization to preserve symmetry and convexity, 398
Partial ordering, 19, 595
Partial transversal, 256
Partitioned matrices, 687
Partitions, 199
Patterned matrix, 63
Peakedness
  of distributions, 490, 711
  of linear combination, 442, 490
Permanent, 50
Permutation
  notation for, 229
  ordering of, 229
Permutation invariance, 230

Permutation matrix, 30
    convex hull of, 10, 30
Permutation symmetric function, 20
Phase-type distribution, 743
Pietra index, 722
Pigou–Dalton condition, 560
Pinch, 7, 17
Pinching matrix, 17
Poisson distribution
    preservation of symmetry and convexity for, 400, 430
    preservation of Schur-convexity for, 409, 433
    stochastic majorization for, 488
Polar decomposition of Hermitian matrix, 772
Pólya frequency function, 763
    of order 2, 762
Pólya frequency sequence, 767
Polygon
    circumscribing circle, Schur-concavity for, 292
    inequalities for, 295
    inscribed in circle, Schur-concavity for, 291
    majorization for sides of, 281
Polynomial, zeros of, 362
Polytope, convex, 48
Positive dependence by mixture, 393, 466
Positive dependence for multivariate exponential distributions, 555
Positive quadrant dependence, 712
Positive set function, definition of, 219
Power functions, monotonicity of, 528

Power mean, 141, 273
Preordering, 18, 577
Preservation of Schur-convexity and monotonicity, 431
Preservation of symmetry and convexity, 431
Probability content for rectangular regions, 632
Probability density function, totally positive, 236
Proportional fitting procedure, 76
Proportional hazard functions, distributions with, 484, 488
Pseudo-convex function, 98
Pseudoinverse of matrix, 375

Quadratic form, Schur-convexity of, 136
Quantile estimator, 539
Quantile function, 714
Quasi-convex function, 98, 159
Queueing networks, 520

Random effects design, 536
Random matrix
    eigenvalues of, 469
    exchangeable, 397
    singular values of, 471
Random replacement sampling plans, 444
Random variables
    exchangeable, 126, 392
    preservation of Schur-convexity for, 403
    preservation of symmetry and convexity for, 397
    Schur concavity for, 407
    translation of, 406
    stochastic ordering of, 694

symmetric Bernoulli,
   Schur-convexity for, 479
symmetric Bernoulli, moments
   of, 480
Rank order statistics, 236
Ranking and selection, 541
   for analysis of variance, 547
   for multinomial distribution,
      542
   for the normal distribution,
      547
Rational fraction inequality, 747
Ratios, bounds for, 481
Real singular values, 299
Real-valued function of matrices,
   684
Rearrangement of functions,
   decreasing, 22, 606, 749
Reducible matrix, 72
Reflection group, 593
Reliability function, 549
   and odds ratios, 551
Regular doubly stochastic
   matrix, 68
Regression, 473, see also Linear
   regression, Multivariate
   regression
   efficiency of, 473
   ridge, 379
Repair of machines, 554
Residual life survival function,
   697
Residual matrix, 375
Reverse-order statistics, 461
Ridge regression, 379
Risk averse, local, 707
Robin Hood transfer, 7, 17
Row majorization for matrices,
   616
   order-preserving functions for,
      622
Roy maximum root test, 533

s-graph, 258
Sample statistics, Lorenz order
   of, 738
Sampling plan, 443
   domination for, 444
   random replacement, 444
   symmetric, 443
Sampling
   with replacement, 444
   without replacement, 443
Scaling of matrices, 76
Schur-concave densities, 406, 500
Schur-concave function, 80
   convolution of, 146, 235
Schur-concavity for polygon, 291
Schur's condition, 84
Schur-convex function, 80
   mixture of, 100
   terminology, 20
Schur-Hadamard product, 70
Schur product, 352
Schur transformation, 30
Schutz coefficient, measure of
   inequality, 565
Score vector of tournament
   graph, 261
Selection, probability of correct,
   541
Selection and ranking, 541
   for multinomial distribution,
      542
   for normal distribution, 547
Semigroup property, 148, 239
Sequence, conjugate, 197, 245
   generalization of, 258
Sequence of DNA, 201
Sequence of 0's and 1's, 198
Sequence, Pólya frequency,
   767
Series system, 549, 552
Shannon information entropy,
   101

Subject Index

Sign changes of function, number of, 759
Similar matrices, 769
Similarly ordered vectors, 205
Simpson's measure of diversity, 561
Singular value decomposition, 771
Singular values
  and diagonal elements, majorization for, 314
  and eigenvalues, majorization for, 317
  extremal representation for, 789
  of matrix, 298
  notation for, 298
  of random matrix, 471
Skew-symmetric matrix, 370
Snapper order, 18
Spacings, normalized, 554
Spanned positively, 45
Sphericity test for multivariate normal distributions, 530
Square root of a matrix
  asymmetric, 771
  symmetric, 770
Standard deviation, 101
Standby's, allocation of, 554
Star-shaped function, 650
  majorization for, 188
Star-shaped with respect to, 464
Statistical mechanics, 523
Statistics
  order, 461
  rank order, 236
  reverse-order, 461
Stochastic completion, 701
Stochastic dominance, 709
Stochastic G-majorization, 594
Stochastic majorization, 387
  weak, 427

Stochastic matrix, 29
Stochastic ordering
  of random variables, 694
  of random vectors, 695
Strictly concave function, 642
Strictly convex function, 642
Strictly decreasing function, 637
Strictly increasing function, 637
Strictly matrix-convex function, 676
Strictly matrix-increasing function, 670
Strictly totally positive function, 758
Student's t-statistic, moment inequality for, 477
Subadditive function, 218, 650
Subgradient, 647
Submajorization, weak, 12
Sub-Markovian matrix, 36
Submatrix, notation for, 299
Subordinate matrix norm, 381
Substochastic matrix, doubly, 12
Superadditive function, 650
Supermajorization, weak, 12
Superstochastic matrix, doubly, 12
Support function, 648
Survival functions, Schur-concave, 500
Symmetric Bernoulli random variables
  moments of, 477
  Schur-convexity for, 478, 479
  sum of, 498
Symmetric function
  complete, 119
  of eigenvalues, 777
  elementary, 114
    majorization for, 172
    normalized, 134

ratio of, 170
  permutation, 20
Symmetric gauge function, 138
  and majorization, 160
  of singular values, 377
  and unitarily invariant norms, 367
Symmetric matrix, eigenvalue decomposition of, 769
Symmetric random variables, sums of, 476
System
  of distinct representative, 256
  k-out-of-n, 549
  parallel, 549
  series, 549

t distribution
  multivariate, Schur-concavity of density, 407
  noncentral, total positivity of, 762
t-statistic, Student's, moment inequality for, 477
T-transform, 32
  elementary, 82
  and majorization, 33
  and weak majorization, 41, 43, 156
  examples of, 53
Test of significance, unbiased, 528
Thermodynamics, majorization in, 626
Top 100α percent, measure of inequality, 564
Total positivity
  of exponential densities, 761
  of noncentral chi-square densities, 762
  of noncentral F densities, 762
  of noncentral t densities, 762

Total time on test transform, 740
Totally nonnegative matrix, Hadamard-type inequality for, 357
Totally positive density functions, 236
Totally positive function, 756
  and log concave functions, 760
  composition of, 758
  examples of, 759
  generalized, 147
  variation-diminishing property of, 759
Totally positive matrix, Hadamard-type inequality for, 357
Tournament graph, 260
  score vector of, 261
Trace functions, convex, 690
Transfer, 194
  correlation increasing, 620
  Dalton, 17
  principle of, 6
  Robin Hood, 7
Transversal, 256
  partial, 256
Triangle
  elementary symmetric function for, 280
  inequalities for angles of, 271
  inequalities for exradii and altitudes of, 282
  inequalities for sides of, 276
  inequalities for sides, exradii, and medians of, 284

Unbiased test of significance, 528, 534
Uniform distribution
  preservation of
    Schur-convexity for, 411, 433

preservation of symmetry and convexity for, 430
Uniformly tapered matrix, 34
　examples of, 53
Unitarily invariant norm, 367
　inequalities for, 370
　and symmetric gauge function, 367
Unitarily similar matrices, 769
Unitary part of a matrix, 324
Unitary-stochastic matrix, 34
Upper weak majorization, 10, 36
Utility gap dominance, 187

Vandermonde determinants, and totally positive functions, 759
Variance, 101
　as measure of diversity, 561
　test for equality of, 529, 578
Vector ordering, 21
Vectors, similarly ordered, 205
Vertex of a graph, 243

van der Waerden, conjecture of, 50
Weak bimajorization, definition of, 603

Weak log majorization, 16
Weak majorization, 12
　and complex vectors, 41
　and convex functions, 13
　and doubly substochastic matrices, 14, 40, 41
　and doubly superstochastic matrices, 15, 42
　lower, 12, 36
　and T-transforms, 41, 43, 156
　upper, 12, 42
Weak stochastic majorization, 427
Weak submajorization, 12
Weak supermajorization, 12
Weibull distribution
　logarithmic concavity of density, 765
　stochastic majorization for, 487
Wireless networks, 520
Wishart distribution, eigenvalues of, 535

Young diagrams, 535

Zonoid, Lorenz, 731